THE COMPLETE ENCYCLOPEDIA OF

# BIRDS

## AND BIRD MIGRATION

# THE COMPLETE ENCYCLOPEDIA OF
# BIRDS
# AND BIRD MIGRATION

CHARTWELL
BOOKS, INC.

A MARSHALL EDITION

Published by Chartwell Books
A Division of Book Sales, Inc.
114 Northfield Avenue
Edison, New Jersey 08837

ISBN 0-7858-1667-4

This book was conceived, edited
and designed by Marshall Editions
The Old Brewery
6 Blundell Street
London N7 9BH

Printed in China

# Contents

# Using this book

The world is inhabited by more than 9,000 species of birds, and no group of animals – even the mammals such as ourselves – arouses our interest so much. Their colors, songs and conspicuousness combine to make birds the ideal objects for aesthetic appreciation. But their attractive nature does not merely make them fun to watch. The ways in which they have been observed have meant that professional zoologists have also turned to them for study, and this study has in turn led the way to our understanding of many aspects of the natural world, including taxonomy, behavior and ecology.

This book contains a wealth of information about every aspect of birds: their habits, behavior and their environment, as well as a comprehensive reference section that includes information about over 1,000 bird species from around the world.

## Birds on the move

The book opens with an essential overview of a key aspect of bird behavior, migration. Within each chapter, species are arranged according to the systematic order, which is approximately the order in which they evolved. Species have been chosen for inclusion on one of two major criteria: their migrations are typical of one or more patterns of movement and/or there are interesting stories associated with their migrations.

## The maps

One color is used for each individual bird's breeding and wintering areas, as well as for the relevant migration arrows, dotted along dispersal limit lines, and any staging posts that it may use on migration.

❶ Arrows on the map show the broad direction of travel. A broken arrow indicates that the route is suspected but not proven. If a route is not known, the broken arrow is marked "Route not known." Unless indicated otherwise, birds travel out from and back to their breeding grounds by the same route.

Where movements are more dispersive than truly migratory, such as with some sea birds that breed in clearly defined areas, then drift the oceans until the next breeding season, the maximum limits of the bird's dispersal are indicated by a dotted line.

❷ The patterned areas of the maps show the breeding and wintering ranges of one or more birds from a group. If the ranges of two birds overlap, different colored dots have been used. An equal number of dots of two colors in an area indicates that the two birds are equally widespread there.

❸ Where a bird's breeding and wintering ranges overlap, black dotted lines indicate the northern and southern limits of the ranges.

❹ For each land bird included on a map, a calendar indicates the months of migration (outward and return) and the months that the birds spend on the breeding grounds and months away from them (non-breeding).

The color used for a bird on the map is repeated in the central part of the calendar and the arrows in the concentric breeding and migration (or non-breeding) circles.

Months are indicated around the outside calendar. The points on the edge of the calendar wheel mark the ends of the months.

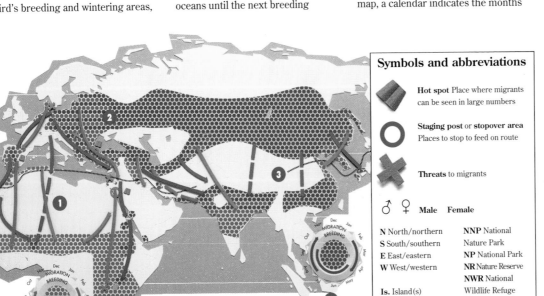

## Symbols and abbreviations

**Hot spot** Place where migrants can be seen in large numbers

**Staging post** or **stopover area** Places to stop to feed on route

**Threats** to migrants

♂ ♀ **Male Female**

| | |
|---|---|
| **N** North/northern | **NNP** National Nature Park |
| **S** South/southern | **NP** National Park |
| **E** East/eastern | **NR** Nature Reserve |
| **W** West/western | **NWR** National Wildlife Refuge |
| **Is.** Island(s) | **WR** Wildlife Refuge |
| **L.** Lake | |
| **U.S.** United States | Throughout the book, the word billion refers to one thousand million |
| **max.** maximum | |
| **pop./pops.** population(s) | |
| **sp./spp.** species | |

4 inches/10 cm

8 inches/20 cm

16 inches/40 cm

32 inches/80 cm

5 feet 4 inches/1.6 m

## The fact files

Basic facts are given for birds that feature prominently on a spread. Alongside the bird's common and Latin names, weight, wingspan, and the length of its journey is a silhouette of the bird inside a grid, to give a broad indication of its length from beak to tail. Five grids have been used, but in each case one square of every grid represents 4 inches (10 cm), so that larger birds sit on grids containing more squares than smaller ones.

## Catalog of migrants

This reference section contains essential facts about many other birds mentioned in the text, along with those of many more migratory species, including their breeding and wintering ranges and length of journey.

# Catalog of species

This section contains full-color illustrations of some 1,200 species of bird. Selected species are arranged on a series of double-page plates each of which is followed overleaf by descriptions of the birds, numerically keyed to a miniature of the illustration.

## The color plates

To give an idea of the variation that can exist between birds of the same species, illustrations may show significant differences between male (♂) and female (♀), juvenile (juv) and immature (imm) birds, and between breeding and non-breeding plumage. Except where otherwise indicated, adult breeding plumage is assumed.
A selection of distinctive races (subspecies) has also been illustrated. The birds are not drawn exactly to scale, but the biggest and smallest birds in each plate are usually depicted as such.

## Ordering of information

Except in a few cases, where the arrangement of birds on the color plate necessitated a departure from this sequence, the birds are arranged taxonomically by order and family.

## Conservation status

Where appropriate, the conservation status given to birds by the ICBP according to the *Bird Red Data Book* is designated in species accounts by a key letter:

**E**   Endangered. Known to be in danger of extinction and unlikely to survive if factors causing the threat continue to operate.

**V**   Vulnerable. Less threatened than birds Endangered, but likely to become Endangered.

**I**   Indeterminate. Thought to be Endangered, Vulnerable or Rare, but insufficiently known.

**K**   Insufficiently known, but suspected to be at risk.

**R**   Rare. Small but stable population which may be at risk and requires careful monitoring.

**S**   Of special concern. Safe at present, but of conservation interest.

**?**   Candidate *Bird Red Data Book*. Under consideration for inclusion in *Bird Red Data Book*.

**X**   Probably extinct.

# BIRDS ON THE MOVE

Migration is probably the most awe-inspiring natural phenomenon. What it lacks compared with the enormous power of the weather, an earthquake, or a volcano, it makes up for in romance – a small bird pits its wits against the elements and accomplishes, as routine, a journey that is truly superhuman. Outlandish theories have been proposed to explain the seasonal ebb and flow of bird populations, including that the birds went to the moon, were transformed into other species, or spent the winter in the mud of lakes or ponds. The knowledge of what really happens is, in many ways, no less fantastic.

Over the centuries, people have struggled to understand birds' migrations and how they manage them year after year. How can they fly such tremendous distances without becoming lost or so exhausted that they die? How have today's complex migration patterns evolved from what were once, presumably, simple movements? And what particular problems are they facing now and are they coping? Although many parts of the mystery have been unraveled, there is still much that remains to be discovered about this fascinating phenomenon.

*Enormous numbers of Dovekies mill around their breeding colonies on Svalbard. All must migrate to winter on the open ocean.*

# How migration evolved

*Shifting continents and the ebb and flow of ice sheets affect migration patterns and pathways.*

The initial evolution of migration is easy to imagine, driven by the changing seasons. Northern summers are warm and winters cold, so a bird that thrives in warmer areas will benefit by moving south in winter. If it stays in the northern hemisphere, the weather will be less severe; if it crosses the equator, it can enjoy the southern summer. There is likely to be an area to the south where the species could live year-round, but northern breeders may be forced onward by competition from residents of the same species. This results in a long migration to an area where the summers may be too hot to breed, but where winter conditions are ideal.

Many other, less immediately obvious, factors have, over geological time, caused birds to alter their movements and influenced the evolution of new species. In the long term, continental drift affects distribution and migration patterns. Some 50 million years ago, there were many bird species that would be identifiable today, at least to group level. Then, the pattern of the continents was different. South America was some 600 miles (1,000 km) from North America, and India was 1,200 miles (2,000 km) away from the rest of Asia, but Africa was close to Eurasia on a front 3,000 miles (5,000 km) long. It is no coincidence that the most complex migration systems are those that have developed between Eurasia and Africa, while those between North and South America, and between Asia and India, are simpler.

The long-term factor that has influenced migration most, however, has been the succession of ice ages that have affected the world. There have been about half a dozen very cold periods over the last two million years – two of which occurred in the last 150,000 years. In times of remission, temperatures fluctuated widely in cycles lasting between 50,000 and 100,000 years. Research suggests that some of these changes have been rapid – over tens of years, rather than hundreds – and this must have put a premium on flexibility in migratory strategy.

The cycle of ice ages has pushed the habitat that suits a particular bird species backward and forward. This may affect both its summer and winter quarters, but for a long-distance migrant, the effects are more noticeable in the northern, summer, breeding area. Birds can cope with gradual change because individuals, from year to year, have to modify their journeys only on the edges of the range. Over 1,000 years or so, ranges of birds may shift over the globe. But since the change is slow, the birds keep to their general movements over thousands, even millions, of years.

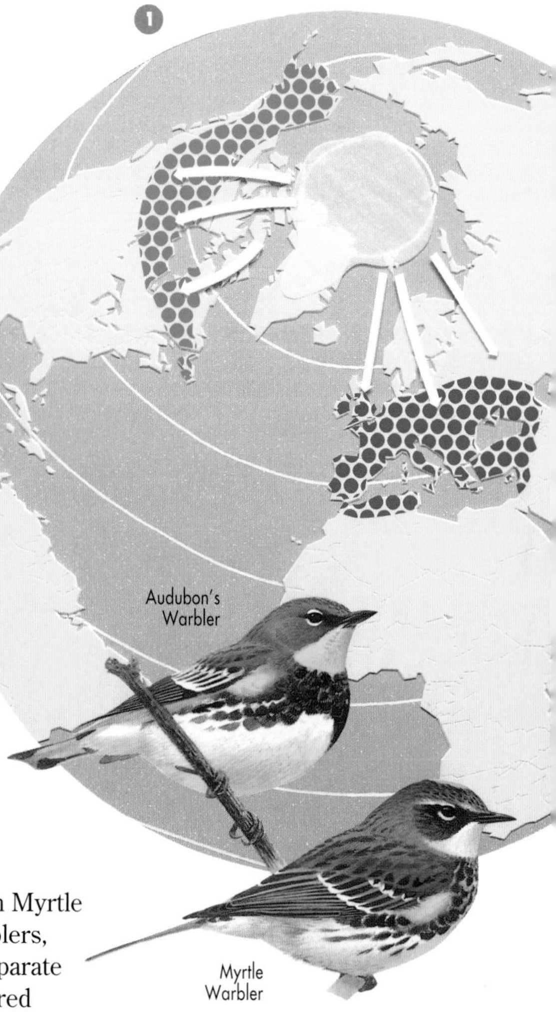

**1** *More than 100,000 years ago,* the world was warmer and the polar ice cap smaller than today. This had a significant effect on ancestral bird species in both the Old and New worlds: they extended into the far north. In North America, an ancestral warbler species also extended across the continent from Alaska in the west to Newfoundland; in Europe, the west–east range was from the Atlantic coast to the Urals.

Audubon's Warbler

Myrtle Warbler

Common Whitethroat

Lesser Whitethroat

The North American Myrtle and Audubon's warblers, once regarded as separate species, are considered forms of the same species, the Yellow-rumped Warbler. There are different races of both forms from various parts of their range, and these can be directly related to the way in which glaciations have affected North America.

The Eurasian Common and Lesser whitethroats are two distinct, though obviously related, species. Speciation occurred two glaciations ago, and at the last glaciation, Lessers were found only in the east, while Commons remained in both the east and the west.

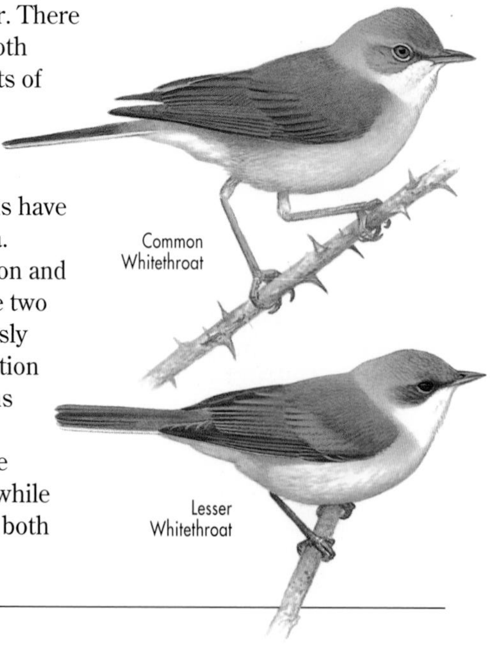

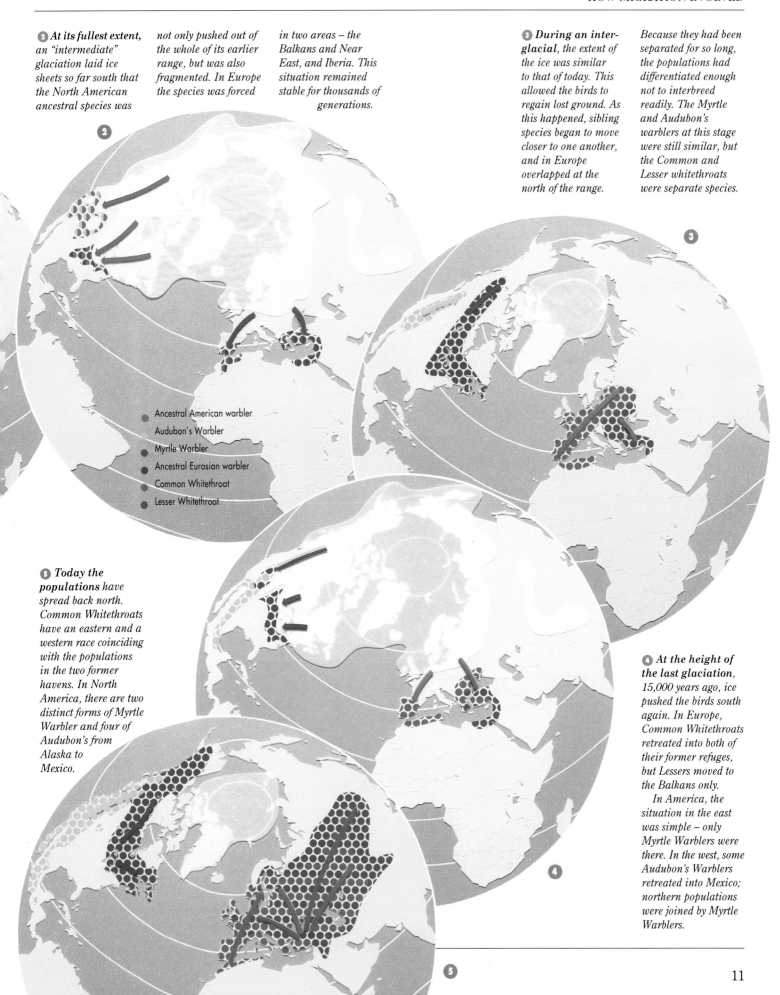

**2 At its fullest extent,** an "intermediate" glaciation laid ice sheets so far south that the North American ancestral species was not only pushed out of the whole of its earlier range, but was also fragmented. In Europe the species was forced in two areas – the Balkans and Near East, and Iberia. This situation remained stable for thousands of generations.

**3 During an inter-glacial,** the extent of the ice was similar to that of today. This allowed the birds to regain lost ground. As this happened, sibling species began to move closer to one another, and in Europe overlapped at the north of the range. Because they had been separated for so long, the populations had differentiated enough not to interbreed readily. The Myrtle and Audubon's warblers at this stage were still similar, but the Common and Lesser whitethroats were separate species.

Ancestral American warbler
Audubon's Warbler
Myrtle Warbler
Ancestral Eurasian warbler
Common Whitethroat
Lesser Whitethroat

**5 Today the populations** have spread back north. Common Whitethroats have an eastern and a western race coinciding with the populations in the two former havens. In North America, there are two distinct forms of Myrtle Warbler and four of Audubon's from Alaska to Mexico.

**4 At the height of the last glaciation,** 15,000 years ago, ice pushed the birds south again. In Europe, Common Whitethroats retreated into both of their former refuges, but Lessers moved to the Balkans only.

In America, the situation in the east was simple – only Myrtle Warblers were there. In the west, some Audubon's Warblers retreated into Mexico; northern populations were joined by Myrtle Warblers.

# Patterns of migration/1

*Half the world's bird species migrate, yet each journey is unique.*

From movements of a few hundred yards to flights that circumnavigate the globe, from north to south and east to west, birds' migratory journeys are as varied as the species that undertake them. Defining types or patterns of migration is not easy. Nonetheless, some trends can be discerned in these unique journeys, although none of these patterns is exclusive, and one species may fall into more than one of the categories.

### North to south and staying behind

Probably the easiest migratory pattern to understand is long-distance north–south migration. Barn Swallows, for example, can live in most of North America and Eurasia in summer, feeding on the seasonal crop of flying insects. Over most of their breeding range, the winter weather is so severe that there is little chance of the birds surviving, so they simply move south to areas where they can continue to find food.

This is not as clear-cut as it sounds, however. Birds have no reason to move if the climate is equable year-round and has no effect on the availability of food. Where a species is widespread, breeding over a broad band of latitudes, individuals from the northern parts of the range may have to fly far to the south. Those from the southern parts of the range – where winter conditions are less severe – by contrast, may not need to move at all. Barn Swallows in southern Spain are resident in their breeding range all year round, as are the Killdeer of the Gulf States of North America.

In many species in which this pattern occurs, another migratory phenomenon may be overlaid: that of partial migration, in which some birds of the population in an area migrate and others do not.

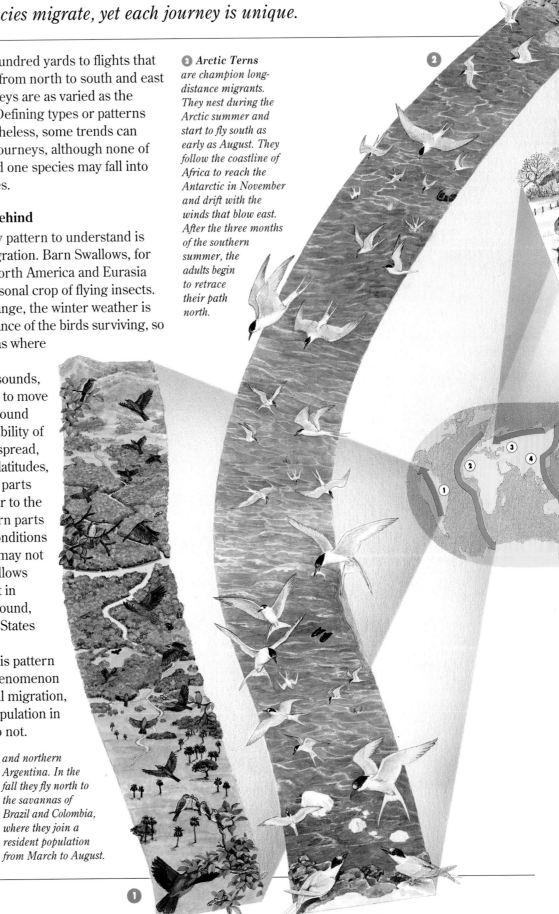

**2** *Arctic Terns are champion long-distance migrants. They nest during the Arctic summer and start to fly south as early as August. They follow the coastline of Africa to reach the Antarctic in November and drift with the winds that blow east. After the three months of the southern summer, the adults begin to retrace their path north.*

**1** *In South America, Vermilion Flycatchers are south–north migrants. They breed in the southern summer, between September and February, on the pampas of Uruguay and northern Argentina. In the fall they fly north to the savannas of Brazil and Colombia, where they join a resident population from March to August.*

**3** **Redwings** are east–west migrants, breeding across Russia and northern Europe. As the northern summer draws to a close they start to move west and south, flying by night to reach the wintering grounds of western and southern Europe in October. Birds may winter in different areas each year: those banded in Britain one winter have been found in Greece, Turkey, and the country of Georgia the next.

**4** **Red Knots** are long-distance north–south migrants, breeding in the short Arctic summer. Young birds' first flight may be over the forests of Asia to traditional shorebird staging posts in Southeast Asia. Many fly over the Pacific Ocean and South China Sea to the Australian coast, then cross the continent to winter on its southern and western coasts.

**5** **Blue Grouse** of the Rocky Mountains are altitudinal migrants, moving vertically about 1,000 feet (300 m). They breed at low altitudes in deciduous woodland clearings, feeding on berries and insects. In winter they move up the mountains to coniferous woodland. Here they feed on pine needles which, though abundant, are not nutritious enough for the birds to be able to breed and rear their young on them.

**6** **Snow Geese** breed in Arctic Canada and Alaska, and as far west as northeastern Siberia and as far east as western Greenland. Their migration is punctuated by periods spent at traditional wetland staging posts.

In winter they feed intensively on coastal marshes and farmland: reserves are vital to sustain them for the first week or two back in the Arctic.

# Patterns of migration/2

Where partial migration occurs, the juveniles often migrate while the adults stay put. The adults can always move on if winter conditions become exceptionally severe. This strategy may remain stable for generations, with short-term advantages for one of the two groups outweighed overall in the long term. If there are distinct advantages for one group for several consecutive years the other dies out and the pattern of the survivors becomes the "standard."

## Coasts and mountains

Many species have developed migrations that are more east–west than north–south. Usually these are birds that are taking advantage of the better winter climate provided by the sea at the edge of a continent. In Europe chaffinches move east from Scandinavia to Britain (they are also partial migrants with the males staying behind). In North America most White-winged Scoters breeding in western Canada and Alaska winter on the eastern seaboard. Shorebird migration is also dominated by the need to stay close to water, with routes hugging coastlines and major stopovers on estuaries.

Chaffinches in some parts of their range also typify another strategy: altitudinal migration. Birds breeding in the Alps may move horizontally, but they also move vertically to escape the winter weather on the upper slopes.

For many species, potential wintering habitats are vast. Those with special needs, by contrast, have often evolved specific migrations, with routes and places to stop and feed en route passed on from parent to young. Families of geese and swans travel and winter together, and the entire population of Whooping Cranes travels from Canada to a restricted winter site in Aransas, Texas.

## Southern hemisphere migrants

The predominant migratory pattern in the southern hemisphere might be supposed to be south–north. To a certain extent this is true: many birds breeding in the temperate latitudes of Australasia, South America, and Africa migrate to the tropics and subtropics in winter. Since there is so much less land in the southern hemisphere than in the northern, and so much more ocean, many of the birds that breed in the south are sea birds. While their migratory patterns are also dominated by the need to find food, winds and ocean currents play a more vital role than temperature in determining the direction and extent of migrations.

*Fox Sparrows are leapfrog migrants. This migratory pattern occurs when a species that is resident in an area develops migratory populations that have to overfly the area inhabited by the residents. They are unable to share the area since the competition for resources would almost certainly favor the residents with their additional local knowledge.*

*There are advantages for both populations: the residents are able to breed early; the migrants can stay on the wintering grounds until conditions are right for them to nest in their own breeding area.*

*This pattern develops as a species extends its range poleward. The different Fox Sparrows have spread along the Pacific coast from wintering areas as far south as Mexico to breeding populations on the Aleutian Islands. These populations are far enough apart to have developed into recognizable races. The race* townsendi *breeds on the coast of Canada and winters over the border in the northern U.S.; the Alaskan breeders of the race* unalaschcensis *leapfrog these birds to winter in California, Nevada, and Idaho. (Other populations are not shown.)*

Fox Sparrow
race unalaschcensis

race townsendi

● race unalaschcensis
◐ race townsendi

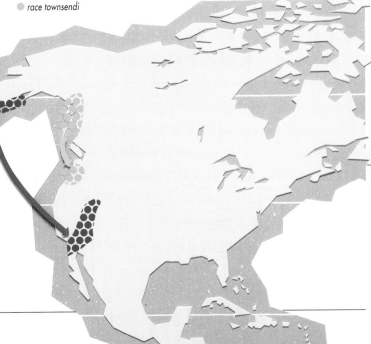

**Evening Grosbeaks** *are becoming partial migrants. On the northern fringes of their range the extent of movement away from the breeding areas is determined by food supplies. In years when food was plentiful they were able to stay; in other years they may have had to travel south. Winter feeding at bird feeders – they are partial to black sunflower seeds – has altered this situation in many areas. Today, male Evening Grosbeaks often stay, even in the northernmost areas, while females move southward.*

*The range of these birds has expanded rapidly eastward since 1920, when they first bred in Ontario. Now they breed on the eastern seaboard in Nova Scotia, 1,250 miles (2,000 km) away. There are also records of these birds having reached Europe.*

♀

Evening Grosbeak

♂

**Manx Shearwaters** *(above), in common with other sea birds, often undertake lengthy migrations because ocean resources are seasonal. In many areas the annual pattern of availability of fish and plankton is as complex as that of terrestrial plants and animals.*

*These birds spend the summer on the remote islands off the coasts of western Europe, where they breed in burrows. In the fall they leave the colonies to winter off the eastern coast of South America, from Brazil to Uruguay. Several recoveries of banded birds show that even young birds can complete this 6,000-mile (10,000-km) journey in less than three weeks. The return journey is more leisurely, with birds heading north to the Caribbean, then using the currents of the Gulf Stream to help them across the Atlantic.*

# When to travel

*Flying by day and by night both bring their own rewards.*

Although many birds show a preference for day or night flight, for most species migration regularly involves travel at both times. The major differences between day and night travel are the methods the birds use to navigate (see pp. 32–35) and the temperatures they experience en route.

## Migrating by day

There are some species whose main flights are wholly confined to daytime because they rely on the rising air from thermals (see pp. 18–19). Migrants that depend on this means of travel rarely stir until some three hours after dawn and often stop the day's flight in the early to mid-afternoon. Soaring flight is so energy-efficient that these birds do not need to feed much, if at all, and can spend the rest of the day and night roosting.

Many species of relatively short-distance migrants are perceived to migrate only in the early morning, although whether this is the case is still open to debate. Some birds appear regularly on radar screens at dawn. Radar devices have also, however, picked up echoes of birds descending and continuing to fly at low level. Whether these are the same birds is not certain. If some birds do indeed confine their migrations to the hours immediately after dawn, then the most likely candidates are such birds as Meadow Pipits, Skylarks, and finches. A four- or five-hour flight would allow them to cover a distance of up to 95–125 miles (150 to 200 km). At this rate, many birds could achieve their full migration in four or five stages. They would also not need well-developed nocturnal navigation skills.

Barn and Bank swallows roost in reedbeds at night and migrate only during the day. Their close relatives the House Martins, on the other hand, do not roost in vegetation and may continue to fly through the night unless they are able to find and occupy a spare nest in a colony.

## Nocturnal migrations

Birds rarely fly only at night, although nighttime migrants are common. Land birds are unable to come down on the sea, and since many nocturnal migrants make ocean crossings, they are forced to continue to fly by day. Shorebirds crossing the Pacific Ocean to winter on its islands, or those continuing on to Australasia, may fly long distances by day and night to avoid touching down.

Scandinavian and Russian breeding birds often move westward to winter in France, Spain, or Britain. Those that cross from Holland or Belgium to southern Britain have had a 160-mile (250-km) North Sea crossing; those arriving in Scotland from Denmark and Norway have flown 500 miles (800 km) over the sea. Birds that are usually considered nocturnal migrants, such as thrushes, Goldcrests, and starlings, may continue to arrive until the early afternoon in the south or throughout the day into the evening in the north. Often they settle on the first land that they reach, but in less than an hour or two, have dispersed inland to find a suitable place to feed.

## Flying nonstop

There are various categories of nonstop migrants. Some birds simply choose to migrate in only one or two long stages, despite the existence of suitable habitat below them. These are often small species that have put on high fat reserves for the journey at special feeding areas. The Sedge Warbler, for example, averages an additional fat load equal to 100 percent of its normal weight, with which it can probably cover more than 1,900 miles (3,000 km) in one nonstop flight of three or, perhaps, four days.

The tiny Blackpoll Warblers of the United States are also remarkable nonstop migrants. In the fall, these birds put on fat along the Massachusetts coast; some then fly out to sea to the southeast. About 36 hours later, they reach the influence of the northwest trade winds, which give them a free ride back toward the West Indies and perhaps even as far as the north coast of South America in only four days (see Wood warblers, pp. 78–79).

Many migrants were once thought to cross the Sahara nonstop. Recent research, however, suggests that some, even many, of the birds which have to cross the desert and were thought to do so without stopping may in fact land and rest during the day. Certainly large numbers of fat migrants have been found sheltering in the shade provided by shrubs, rocks, and oil drums. It may be that as the desert heats during the day, the air above it becomes too hot for the birds' metabolism to rid the body of excess water (see Wagtails and pipits, pp. 110–11).

Finally, there are those birds that are pure flying machines, living in the air and able to fly by day or night, or both, at will. Swifts are among the champions in this respect – those that leave northern Europe in the fall are likely to remain on the wing until they return to their nest sites in northern Europe nine months later. And, at sea, terns rarely stop flying since, if they settle on the water for any length of time, they become waterlogged.

**Birds flying** across the face of the moon are living proof that some species, including the Eider Duck (above), are nocturnal migrants. Their apparent size is also a measure of the height at which birds can fly.

Many moon-watchers are attracted by the romance of looking at birds seeming to float across a silver globe, but the practice also yields interesting results. The records of passes across the moon may exceed 200 per hour. For species of small birds, which are probably traveling on a front 60 miles (100 km) wide, this might mean that three million migrants an hour are passing by. The other proof of nocturnal migration comes from the birds' calls. With thrushes and other small and medium-sized birds, these often allow flocks to keep together.

# Flight techniques/1

*Moving on the wing means making the maximum use of energy.*

Although other creatures can fly using wings of skin or skinlike membrane, bird flight depends on one unique adaptation: feathers. It is easy to overlook their special properties. As well as being excellent insulators, feathers are light, flexible, strong, and resilient. They are also highly maneuverable: birds are able to use them to control airflow in far more complex ways than aircraft use aerofoils.

It is a common misconception that a bird's wing supports the bird's weight in flight by pressing down on the air and that the upbeat simply returns the wing to a position in which it can support the bird again. In fact, the wingbeat is not nearly so simple. High pressure under the wing and low pressure above it work together to keep the bird aloft. The wing first moves down and backward, pushing the air in the same directions. It then moves up and forward, speeding the movement of air over the top of the wing, thereby reducing pressure and sucking the bird upward.

*Thermal soaring (below) is one of the most cost-effective ways of migrating. By using the rising air of a thermal to gain some 1,650 feet (500 m) in height, it is possible to convert the height advantage into distance by gliding, wings outstretched, to the base of another thermal and repeating the process. Birds that use thermal* soaring – birds of prey, cranes, and storks, for example – usually have long, broad wings with separated primary feathers (the major flight feathers often referred to as fingers) for delicate directional control.

*Their preferred migration time is determined by the thermals and is usually around mid-morning, when they tend to be strongest.*

*As the ground warms up in the morning sun, more energy is absorbed by some features than others. This causes the air locally to heat up, forming an invisible, rising bubble. As it rises, more air is sucked in and heats up, and it too rises.*

Cloud forms at condensation level

As it does so, more air is sucked in

Air above roads and open spaces warms and rises

*Thermals often become visible as tufts of cloud when they reach a certain height, allowing birds to pinpoint where the next one may be found.*

Thermal soaring

Continuous
flapping

Flapping and
gliding

Bounding

**Birds not specially adapted to soaring** move forward in one of three ways: continuous flapping (right, top); bouts of flapping interspersed with periods of gliding with wings outstretched (right, center); or flapping and ballistic flight, with wings closed, known as bounding flight (right, bottom).

Continuous flapping is primarily practiced by birds with a relatively high weight compared with their wing area. They are often birds that use their wings to assist them in swimming under water. Water is denser than air so only birds with relatively small, strong wings can use them for swimming.

The best strategy for most birds with a body weight of 5 ounces (140 g) or more is to flap and glide, alternating periods of continuous flapping flight, in which the bird gains both height and speed, with periods of gliding. Gliding uses perhaps less than one-twentieth of the energy needed for flapping. The length of the glide depends on the direction and speed of the wind.

Small to medium-size birds, such as warblers, finches, and thrushes, use bounding flight. The drag created as the air passes over an outstretched small, broad wing cancels out any lift the bird would obtain from gliding. These smaller birds, therefore, fold their wings and drop between periods of flapping. Surprisingly, the bird's bodies, with wings closed, generate significant lift and reduce drag.

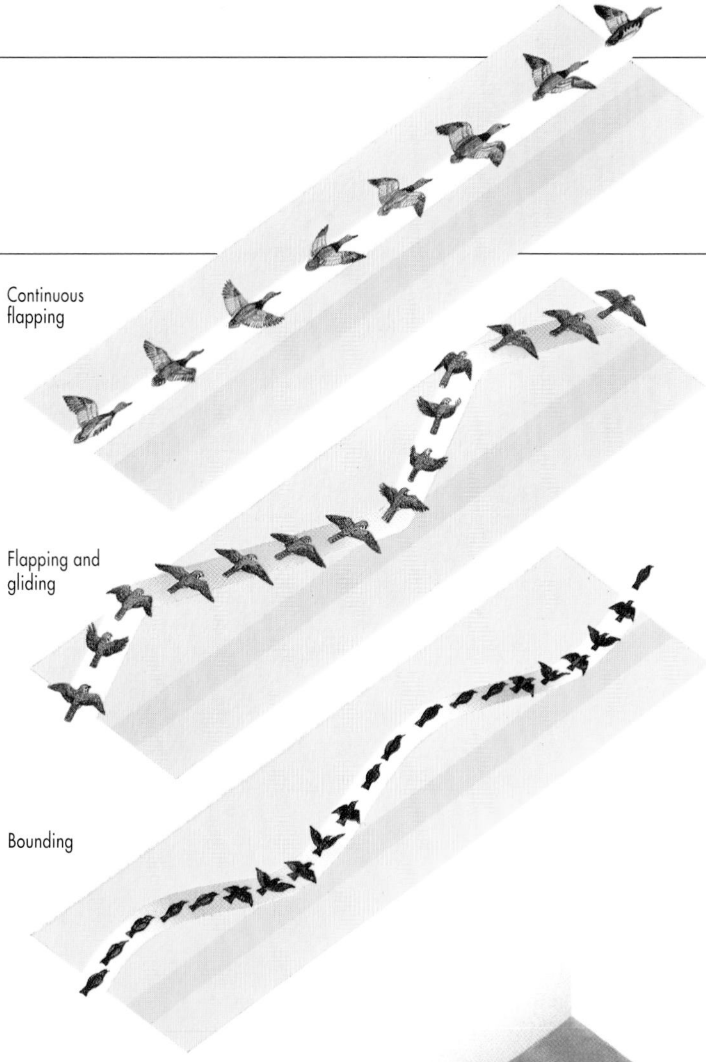

**Species that are adept** at dynamic soaring (left) make use of the friction created by the wind over water, which causes air to slow down. The bird climbs into the wind to gain height; then, when it can generate no more lift, it turns and glides with the wind, losing height but gaining ground. To enable it to make use

Wind strength
usually increases
with altitude

of this technique, a dynamic soarer has long, thin wings which it keeps rigidly outstretched, seemingly for hours on end. Its downwind glide in the rising air over the waves may move the bird forward 330 feet (100 m) or more before it starts to lose height.

The disadvantage of dynamic soaring is that larger birds, such as albatrosses, are becalmed when the wind is not blowing – not a common occurrence in the southern oceans these birds frequent, but a problem for any bird that drifts into the doldrums by mistake.

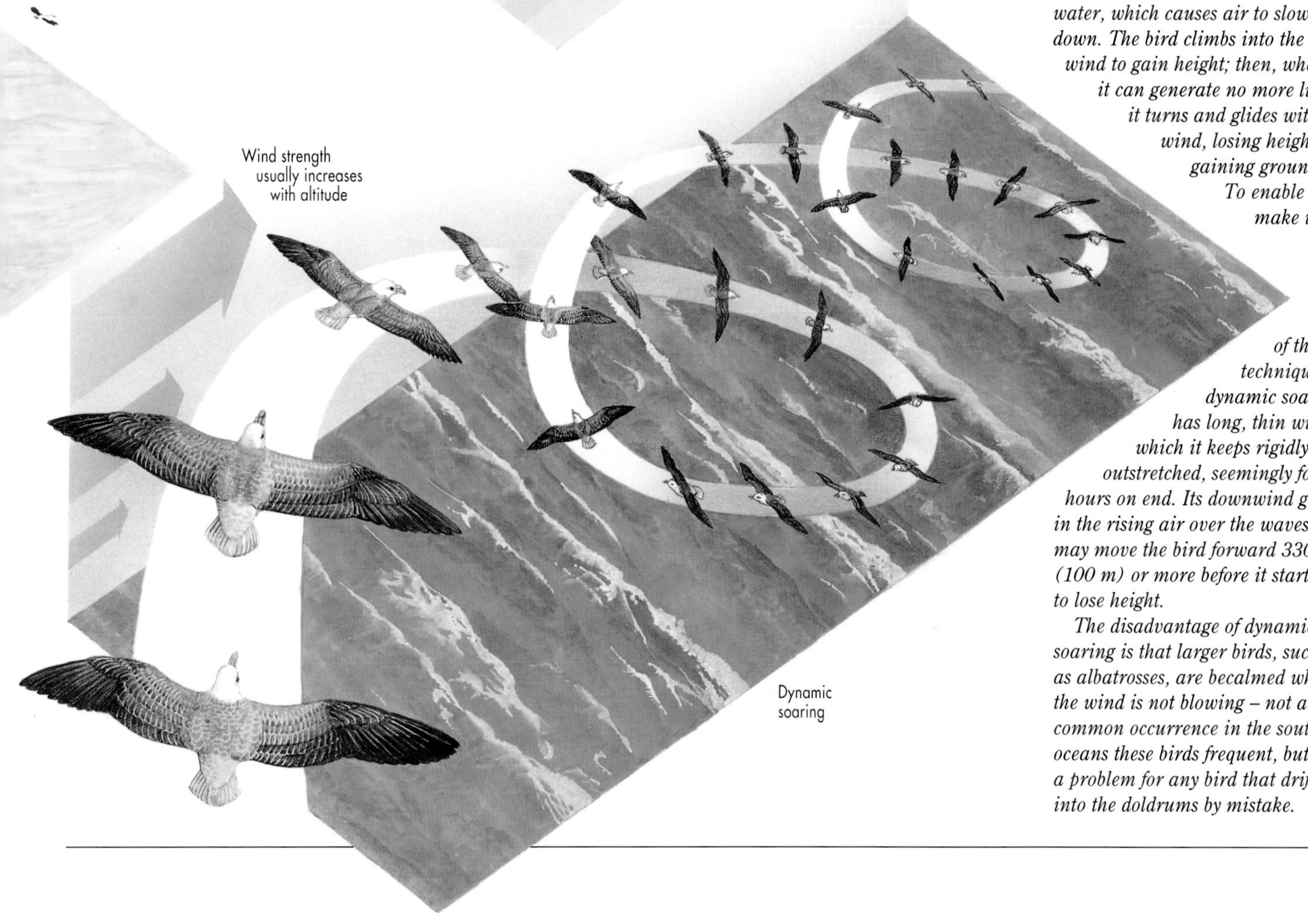

Dynamic
soaring

# Flight techniques/2

The smallest wings are capable of the most complicated maneuvers, allowing a bird to fly forward, hover, and fly backward. The wings of hummingbirds beat at least 25 (and sometimes up to 50) times a second. Problems of scale mean that a large bird, like a swan, has no chance of beating its huge wings at anything approaching that rate or being able to maneuver so precisely. A hummingbird may weigh less than ¼₄ ounce (2 g), a swan a little less than 45 pounds (20 kg) – about the same as 10,000 hummingbirds.

### Size, weight, and power

Swans and the smaller condors, storks, bustards, cranes, and albatross, at around 20–30 pounds (10–15 kg), are among the largest birds that can use flapping flight. The weight limit is determined by the efficiency with which the flight muscles provide power, which in turn is determined by the size of the muscle.

Bird weight, muscle size, and power are intrinsically linked. As a muscle doubles in width it quadruples in area, which is what gives the bird lift, but its weight increases eightfold. A bird that is twice as long as another may be carrying eight times its weight in muscle but can only generate four times as much power. Birds could not be bigger and still use powered flight unless they evolved a new type of muscle. Gliding is different, since the birds' flight muscles have only to hold the wings outstretched, so their upper weight limit is considerably higher.

Flight techniques are varied and depend to a large extent on the weight of the bird and its wing size and shape. These in turn are linked to the way in which the bird's lifestyle has evolved: it is obviously counterproductive to have long, thin wings for efficient soaring flight and live in the tree canopy chasing insects for food. Most migrant birds spend only a small proportion of their lives making migratory flights: specific adaptations for those flights, therefore, are not crucial in the species' evolution. The longer and more taxing the migration, however, the more likely it is that the bird will possess many of the features for efficient flight.

Birds can also exploit the air to the full. Takeoff, for example, is energy-inefficient, so the bird faces into the wind to become airborne and increase its speed as quickly as possible after takeoff, since flight is more efficient at a reasonable speed. Soaring birds clearly make use of the lift provided by thermals, but other birds also use the free ride they provide to reduce their energy consumption.

## WALKING MIGRANTS

The need to migrate is not confined to birds that can fly. On the African plains, the pattern of rainy and dry seasons causes some Ostriches to undertake regular movements, just as, in the cold wastes of the Antarctic, Emperor Penguins trek over the ice to their remote breeding grounds.

Emus are among the most mobile of flightless birds: banded individuals have been recorded 300 miles (500 km) from the site of banding. Once the rainy season begins, they usually move to more arid areas for breeding, then return to places with a reliable water supply when the breeding season is over. Often the only land with a regular water supply has been cleared for agricultural use, with long, Emu-proof fences erected to frustrate the birds.

Emu

The different strategies that birds use for movement are, to a large extent, determined by the bird's size and shape. Most birds are able to fly using continuous wingbeats for at least a short period, to escape predators or in another emergency. The ability to glide or soar, on the other hand, is limited to birds with the appropriate adaptations. Some of these are connected with scale: flapping and gliding is clearly not an option for birds as small as starlings, sparrows, and swallows. The aerodynamic flow over the wings of small birds cannot be smooth enough for them to function properly: the drag produced at the wingtips always outweighs the lift that can be generated by the main part of the wing.

## SWIMMING MIGRANTS

Penguins and auks regularly migrate long distances by swimming. Many auks fledge before they can fly and, accompanied by a parent, set off for new waters. Migrating male Razorbills and their chicks, for example, swim – the chick while it grows and the adult still flightless from its molt.

First-year Razorbill

*The characteristic formation for many flapping and gliding large birds is a V. This is an efficient way for birds to keep together. It allows each bird to see the one in front, without being impeded by the air it disturbs – particularly when the bird in front flaps and huge swirls of air are shed off the tips of its wings.*

*The leading bird in a V is usually an adult, unless the flock is on a routine flight, to a nighttime roost for example, when the young may take a turn.*

# Flight power and speed

*Calculating the optimum speed to cover the maximum distance requires expert tuning.*

The power of flight depends on a number of complex factors which birds must integrate for maximum effect. Obviously, they do not consciously work out a series of mathematical equations, any more than a baseball catcher or fielder uses spherical trigonometry to reach and catch a ball. Nonetheless, migrants must be aware of these factors, since mistakes can be a matter of life and death. A bird that sets off too fast on its journey may use its energy too quickly and run out of fuel before it reaches its destination. If it is crossing a desert, this may be fatal.

For a bird in flapping flight, two main activities consume power, each of which varies with the speed of the bird. The first – the power needed to keep the bird aloft – decreases the faster the bird is flying. Some birds are able to hover for a short length of time, and hummingbirds and sunbirds can even fly backward, but for most birds energy consumption is so high at low speeds that they are unable to fly slowly for any length of time. The second factor – the drag induced by the airflow over the bird's wings – increases power consumption the faster the bird flies.

Although the combined effect of these two forces differs according to the bird's size and shape, for many it means that there is both a speed below which they cannot maintain flight and one above which they cannot go. In between is a fairly wide range of maintainable speeds, one of which can be sustained with a minimum power input. This speed is the one that will provide the maximum time that the bird can fly without stopping to "refuel."

The speed that requires the minimum power input and produces the maximum time in the air is not necessarily the bird's maximum range speed, the speed at which it achieves its maximum range (in theory, the greatest distance it can cover without refueling and at minimum power). This is because maximum range also depends partly on the power the bird needs to stay alive – in other words, its metabolic energy – and on circumstances. If an extra 5 percent of speed needs only 3 percent more energy, the bird will achieve its maximum range in a shorter time and at a higher speed.

Such parameters are under the bird's control; the wind, by contrast, is not, yet it may have a huge effect on the bird's speed, energy consumption, and range. At worst, if the wind speed against the bird is greater than its maximum speed, it can make no headway. If the wind is in the bird's favor, the distance traveled over the ground at its maximum range speed may be greatly enhanced.

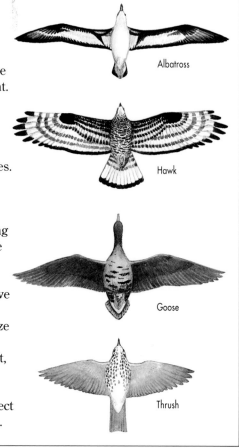

**FLIGHT AND WING SHAPE**

A migrant's wing shape and size are related to its flight. Large sea birds (top) have long thin wings for dynamic soaring low over the waves. Broad, fingered hawk wings are best for soaring over land, allowing fine control of the airflow at their tips. Large birds such as geese have wings that are heavy for their size for flapping and gliding. The short, rounded wings of small birds (bottom) are perfect for flapping flight.

Albatross

Hawk

Goose

Thrush

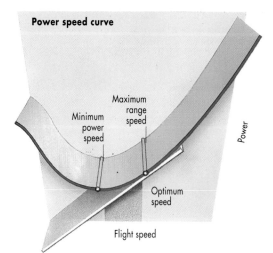

**Power speed curve**

Minimum power speed

Maximum range speed

Power

Optimum speed

Flight speed

*The graph (above) shows the relationship between power consumption and speed of flight. Power consumption is high until the bird reaches its speed of minimum power input and high again once it has passed its maximum range speed. For this reason, although actual speeds vary from bird to bird, most flapping birds fly at a speed that falls between these two points (pink shading).*

The wing of a Cetti's Warbler is short and broad with short primary flight feathers

Cetti's Warbler
Asian race *albiventris*

Reed Warbler

The wing of a Reed Warbler is long and narrow with long primary flight feathers

*Cetti's and Reed warblers* frequent similar habitats: in fact, in places their ranges overlap and they share territories. Their wings, however, are completely different: Cetti's Warblers' are short and broad, Reed Warblers' are long and rather narrow. Their migratory habits also differ. Reed Warblers are long-distance migrants while Cetti's Warblers are resident. The constraints that are imposed by this difference determine their wing shapes.

Short, broad wings are ideal for a life spent in thick, tangled vegetation foraging for small, agile insects. For efficient long-distance migration, wings must be long and thin to ensure energy-efficient flight.

Soaring birds are affected by different constraints from birds that flap to fly. Relatively little power is used to keep wings outstretched and to make any necessary small adjustments to the control surfaces. Measurements suggest that the power saving over flapping flight may be as great as 95 to 97 percent. This means that many soaring birds of prey are able to make their journeys relatively slowly and without feeding, an important factor for birds that are funneled through highly specific areas. The hundreds of thousands of hawks and buzzards that use the Isthmus of Panama or the Strait of Gibraltar on migration have little chance of competing with each other or with native birds for local food stocks. Instead, they fly when the thermals are working well and at other times roost to conserve energy.

At sea, the situation is similar. Species using dynamic soaring to travel show power savings of the same order of magnitude as land-based soaring birds. A newly fledged Manx Shearwater – which weighs about the same as a healthy adult – sets out immediately from the island of its birth to the wintering grounds of Brazil. Since the intervening 6,000 miles (10,000 km) of ocean offer little chance for surface-feeding birds to find food, the young shearwater probably does not feed en route. The fastest passage time so far recorded is 17 days, but birds' reliance on the wind can cause problems: satellite-tracked Wandering Albatross have been "grounded" when the winds are not strong enough for dynamic soaring (see p. 47).

Large amounts of fuel have an effect on the aerodynamics of a bird's flight. The way that the fat is laid down alters the bird's profile (see p. 26), and it must expend more energy to carry the extra weight. Calculation of maximum range, therefore, may be different at the beginning of the migration when a bird is heavy with fat, than at the end, when it has consumed up to half its start weight.

Air density also affects range calculations. Density is reduced at greater heights, which makes it harder for a bird to find lift at a given speed, but for the same speed, drag is reduced.

# How high do birds fly?

*Flying high brings death to migrants in collisions with airplanes.*

Birds reach their height limit when the reduced amount of oxygen in the air, and its lower density, prevents them from functioning normally. For some species this is at a great height: Bar-headed Geese have been recorded above the summit of Everest. Individual migrant birds, however, fly at the height that makes most sense on the journey they are undertaking at the time.

The most important determining factor is the height above sea level of the ground below the migrant. Birds negotiating the Alps via Col de Bretolet must fly at an altitude of some 6,600 feet (2,000 m) to get over the pass. If they are flying against the wind, they may be only 10–13 feet (3–4 m) above the ground along the pass.

Another constraint on height is the presence of cloud. Birds prefer not to fly in cloud, and heavy cloud greatly impairs their performance. This is because birds in flight produce so much water when they burn fat in their muscles as fuel that getting rid of it in cool, damp air is difficult.

## Wind speed and direction

The wind is a vital consideration for most migrants. Close to the ground, the wind is less strong than it is higher up – certainly above 1,600 feet (500 m) from the ground. Higher

### HEAD AND TAIL WINDS

For the migrating bird, the wind is the environmental factor that has the greatest effect. Many small birds have a flight speed that gives them a maximum range for each unit of energy consumed of some 25 mph (40 km/h), so that even a relatively light direct head wind of 12 mph (20 km/h) reduces their range by 50 percent and a gale of 30 mph (50 km/h) would blow them backward.

Birds have no problem in deciding the strategy for a moderately light head wind – stay low, hug the ground and make use of whatever shelter it affords. In a tail wind, the best option is to get up high and fly with it.

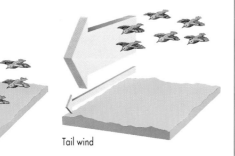

Head wind

Tail wind

*Several methods are used to measure the height at which birds fly. Radar gives accurate height readings and allows a degree of species identification by measuring size, speed, and wingbeat from the returning echo. The remains of birds hit by aircraft are logged, particularly if the birds are large enough to put aircraft at risk.*

*The heights shown in the illustration (right) are the maximum recorded. Since the altitude of flight depends to a large extent on wind, cloud, and height above sea level, these heights may or may not be regularly attained.*

feet

Whooper Swan

25,000

Bar-tailed Godwit

20,000

15,000

Fieldfare

10,000

Swift

5,000

Chaffinch

0

Bar-headed Goose

Mallard

White Stork

Lapwing

Whistling Swan

Snow Goose

Black-bellied Plover

Black-and-white Warbler

***High fliers*** *include Bar-headed Geese which cross the Himalayas at heights of up to 29,500 feet (9,000 m) as they travel between the mountain lakes of central Asia and their winter homes along the Indus valley, India. A flock of 30 Whooper Swans en route from Iceland to western Europe was logged by a pilot at 27,000 feet (8,230 m). Mallards have reached 21,000 feet (6,400 m), Bar-tailed Godwits 19,685 feet (6,000 m) and White Storks 15,750 feet (4,800 m) on migration.*

*Flocks of Lapwings often travel at modest altitudes, but have been sighted at 12,800 feet (3,900 m) while Fieldfares may reach 10,800 feet (3,300 m). Whistling Swans may fly at 8,850 feet (2,700 m) across North America. Swifts, among the most aerial of all birds, attain heights of 6,600 feet (2,000 m); Snow Geese have been noted at 4,900 feet (1,500 m); and Black-bellied Plovers at no more than 2,600 feet (800 m).*

*Many small birds keep relatively close to the ground. Among them, Chaffinches are usually well below their maximum of 3,300 feet (1,000 m) while the Black-and-white Warbler and other wood warblers reach a maximum altitude of around 1,600 feet (500 m).*

still, wind speeds and directions may be completely different from those near the ground – the wind an observer feels on the ground is often blowing in a different direction from the wind that is sending clouds racing across the sky. For this reason, if birds have to fly against the wind, they are likely to be low and clearly visible, an excellent spectacle for birdwatchers. On another day, there may be more migrants, but if the wind is behind them, they are almost certain to be flying so high that they are out of sight.

In a cross wind, the birds must take advantage of the wind speed and strength without being blown off course. The way to do this is to aim to the right (if the wind is blowing across them from the right) or the left of the ultimate target. By deliberately allowing for the effects of the wind in this way, the birds use it efficiently and reach their destination with no need for corrections at the end of the journey.

Radar observations often show migrants shifting their altitude to try to find the best height with the greatest amount of wind in their favor. It is assumed that they are able to gauge how the wind is affecting them by measuring their drift against the distant horizon.

# Preparing for the journey

*Fat, fit, and with new feathers, birds are ready to undertake their migratory journeys.*

All sorts of preparations are necessary before a migrant bird can set out on its journey. For most migratory species the late summer is the time for laying down fat reserves to use as fuel on the journey, changing their feathers, and improving the power of their flight muscles to make sure that flight is swift and efficient.

The most obvious preparation for migration is to put on subcutaneous fat, just beneath the skin. All species have to do this, unless they are able to feed while migrating – and even then, a bird may need substantial reserves if its journey involves desert or sea crossings. British Garden Warblers, for example, which usually weigh about ⅖ ounce (12 g), put on around ⅐ ounce (4 g) of fat to take them across the Bay of Biscay to northwestern Iberia. There, they feed intensively again, increasing their weight by about ⅓ ounce (10 g) so that they can fly over the rest of Iberia, northern Africa, and the Sahara in an epic three-day journey. Immediately south of the Sahara, a further small increase in fat provides fuel to take them to their wooded savanna wintering areas.

Spring weight increases in Africa are even more impressive as the journey across the desert is likely to be against head winds. Increases of 100 percent on "normal" weight have been recorded, which would allow a flight of 2,500 miles (4,000 km) with no wind, over up to five days.

Such weight increases are accomplished through changes in behavior which are triggered by hormonal activity. These have other effects on the bird, again setting in motion changes that are necessary before the journey can start. Like an athlete training for a marathon, a bird needs to tone up its whole physique, so its major flight muscles increase in size. In an average bird, these muscles account for some 15 percent of its total weight, perhaps ¹⁄₁₄–¹⁄₁₂ ounce (2–2.5 g)

**White-fronted Goose (migratory)**
Molt takes approx. 3½ weeks

**Chaffinch (resident)**
Molt takes approx. 10–11 weeks

**Chaffinch (migratory)**
Molt takes approx. 8 weeks

**Snow Bunting (migratory)**
Molt takes approx. 4 weeks

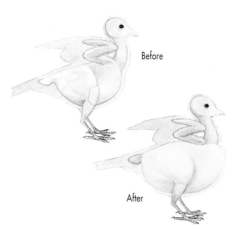

*Prior to migration a bird lays down fat both within its body cavity and underneath its skin. This is easy to see on a bird in the hand. Blowing the feathers upward reveals the transparent skin: the pale fat contrasts with the pink or red flesh. The best place to look for fat on small birds is the furculum, the pit above the breastbone.*

Before

After

*The annual molt of the main flight feathers in most species takes place gradually, so that the birds can continue to fly. The primary feathers (those nearest the wingtips) molt from the inside outward. Then, when the inner ones have regrown, the bird starts to shed its secondaries from the outside inward.*

*The speed of the molt (above) depends on circumstances. Resident Chaffinches, for example, may take 10 to 11 weeks to complete their feather change; migratory Chaffinches, on the other hand, take less than eight weeks. The fastest perching birds – at four weeks – are probably Greenland-nesting Snow Buntings.*

*These birds are flightless for a time.*
*Waterfowl and other groups become totally flightless during the molt and replace all their flight feathers at once – White-fronted Geese cannot fly for some 25 days. (Timing of the molt differs between populations, but is of the duration specified during the months indicated.)*

## MOLT MIGRATION

Some species, particularly waterfowl, undertake special migrations for the purpose of molting. These seem to be governed by the presence of food stocks which cannot be exploited by breeding birds: often they are available only late in the breeding season.

Sometimes the birds that leave the breeding area are failed breeders and nonbreeders which go, perhaps, to avoid competition for resources with growing families. Often, however, molt migrants are successful parents which leave their young in the care of "aunts," surrogates which look after "nurseries" of young from several broods.

This may be the case with the Goosanders, that molt in Finnmark, Norway, and is the strategy used by Eiders (left) and Shelducks. Shelducks have several molting grounds in Europe, the best known of which is the Knechtsand, Germany, where up to 100,000 birds gather each fall.

in a medium-sized species. When that bird is fully fat prior to migration, the amount of its body weight taken up by the flight muscles may be reduced to 12 percent, but the weight of the muscles themselves has probably risen to 1/10 ounce (3 g).

In some circumstances – if a bird is held up by contrary winds, for example, and runs out of fuel on migration – it can convert some of this extra muscle tissue into fuel to enable it to continue its journey. It is still not certain whether this happens as a matter of course (as the additional muscle was to enable the bird to cope with the extra weight of fat, it is not strictly necessary) or whether it is something that occurs only in emergencies.

Finally, many birds prepare for one or another of their seasonal migrations by molting their flight feathers. The molt is also hormonally controlled and essential for the birds because their feathers suffer wear and tear. Since the efficiency of flight depends on the quality of a bird's wing feathers, their renewal immediately before migration is sensible. And, at this time of the year, food is plentiful so the birds are sure to have the energy necessary to complete a successful feather replacement. Young birds do not need to renew their feathers prior to their first fall migration, but may do so on the wintering grounds before the return flight in spring.

# Timing

*Deciding when to leave on migration can be a tricky business.*

Migration is essentially about being in the right place at the right time, so in the broadest sense timing is crucial. The means by which migrant birds navigate (see pp. 32–35) also make precise timing, on a daily basis, necessary. For these reasons, birds have two "body clocks" built into their physiology, to give them good circannual (yearly) and circadian (daily) rhythms. Birds are not alone in having these two clocks – many organisms, including bacteria and humans, share them – but they are obviously of paramount importance for migrants.

The presence of circannual rhythms has been proved by keeping caged birds under a constant light/dark cycle, usually 12 hours of each. In these conditions, birds of several different species breed, molt, show migratory restlessness (*Zugunruhe*), and put on weight in a normal yearly cycle. If the year is compressed by accelerating the natural changes in day length, the birds speed up their functions: the record is held by a starling that was tricked into undergoing eight annual molt cycles in one year.

The change in the light/dark cycle is most striking at the equinoxes in temperate latitudes, when the rate of change from dark to light is particularly apparent. It is not so obvious in the tropics at any time, or in the Arctic in high summer, so while this environmental stimulus is important to the circannual rhythm, it is not the only factor involved. Circannual rhythms are probably not changed by periods of rain, abnormal temperatures, or the growth of vegetation, but the birds' behavior is modified by such factors. In a warm spring, they may breed a week or ten days earlier than in a year when temperatures are "normal."

Shortening days and a bird's internal clock act on its hormonal system, stimulating the physiological changes associated with fattening (see pp. 26–27) and the molt. Later, the bird's hormonal balance, and probably also its weight, stimulate migratory restlessness. In the wild, a bird at this stage would migrate; in a cage, it makes restless movements oriented toward the direction in which, if uncaged, it would be moving.

Birds are aware of the weather and its effect on the success or failure of a migratory journey. They do not generally migrate when the sky is heavily overcast, in strong contrary winds, or in rain. They are often, however, able to predict favorable winds from prevailing air conditions. The result is that birds migrate in waves – held up by bad weather, many birds move on together as soon as conditions improve. Such considerations determine the precise day or night the birds begin to migrate, so that while the week of their movement is generally preordained, the date is determined by environmental factors.

The circadian rhythm is a different matter. Under continuous dim light, caged birds are as likely to settle down to a day length of 23 or 25 hours as 24. In real life, environmental clues, or *Zeitgebers*, keep the bird on a strict 24-hour cycle. The most important factor by far is the daily light/dark cycle, but in constant dim light, a 24-hour temperature cycle that mimics the external world keeps caged birds on a 24-hour cycle. In many species, but possibly not all, the action of this clock is governed by the pineal gland, situated in the front of the brain.

For use in true navigation, the circadian rhythm would have to be staggeringly accurate. The sun is at its highest in the sky at noon: an error of 10 minutes in judgment of time would put a migrant 125 miles (200 km) off target at the latitude of New York or Paris. It is more likely that birds use the sun as a directional aid: navigating with a time-compensated sun compass gives rise to an error of 12 miles (20 km) after a journey of 300 miles (500 km).

The pressures on birds to migrate particularly early are strongest for the males of most species returning to the breeding grounds in spring. An early return gives them the opportunity to occupy the best territory and thereby mate with the best females. If they arrive too early, they may find poor weather and risk their survival, although all is not necessarily lost. Early birds, so long as they still have sufficient fat reserves, may be able to retrace their steps and try again later. In some of the larger species, these early migrants seem to act as scouts. If they set out and encounter poor conditions, such as the ice not having broken, they return to where they had started. The birds left behind then assume there is no point in their trying yet. If the scouts do not come back, they realize that they should perhaps try the journey for themselves.

*A migrant Northern Wheatear (right) experiences a variety of stimuli. Its internal clock may be telling it to go, but it is also sensing what the weather is doing. Migrating into a storm is not a good idea, but the storm may be part of a weather system that will leave favorable tail winds in its wake. The Wheatear cannot take advantage of this opportunity if it has not put enough fat into its internal stores for the next leg of its journey. In this case, the need to provision itself is paramount, and the bird must look for the best place to find food.*

*Wheatears on migration almost always leave at dusk since this is when they can see the setting sun and establish where west is. After that, they rely on the stars for an accurate directional compass.*

# Genetics and migration

*Most young birds know instinctively which way to go and find the way back.*

The true wonder of migration is that it is instinctive – generation after generation, birds are able to undertake these often complicated patterns of movement. It is obvious that young cuckoos, left by their parents which migrate early, must be able to find the way alone. It has been shown that many other birds' genetic makeup is also imprinted with enough information to enable naive juveniles to accomplish their regular migrations without the benefit of any help from their parents.

Indeed, in the majority of species, there is little chance of the young remaining in touch with their parents. In preparation for their first return flight the following spring, many juveniles spend some time exploring their home area before they depart on their first migration. This period coincides in many species with the time that their parents are raising a second brood, inevitably a full-time occupation, or undergoing their full molt.

The juveniles' exploration includes local features such as the adjacent territories, but also takes several species some 30–60 miles (50–100 km) from their nest sites. The regular appearances in the fall in western Europe of eastern European birds which migrate southeastward, such as Barred Warblers and Red-backed Shrikes, may be part of this familiarization process. It is clear that other species which would normally be found in western Europe at this time – but are absent – also venture away from their birthplaces in this way. Blackcaps from the Scandinavian population, which migrate southeastward, have been found in Britain and then picked up again in Turkey.

As if the "program" for accomplishment of the journey were not enough, birds also inherit the annual rhythm that triggers the necessary physiological changes, so that they are ready to migrate at the right time. Equally important, the rhythm stops the cycle when they reach their winter quarters (see pp. 26–29).

The genetic basis of migration causes birds to be conservative in their choice of wintering area. It is no accident that Willow Warblers from all over Eurasia, for example, still winter in Africa (see also Chats and thrushes, pp. 112–13). The location was "encoded" in their ancestral genetic material, and no mutation has happened to provide a population with a viable alternative. Even during the warmest interglacial of the last cycle of ice ages, which ended 10,000 years ago, the wintering area did not shift far

*An experiment with starlings (below) proved the roles of experience and genetics in migration. Birds caught on the fall journey in the Netherlands were taken to Switzerland and released. The juveniles, which had not migrated before, continued in their "programmed" flight direction and reached Spain. The more experienced adults corrected course to reach their winter homes in France, Britain, and Ireland.*

*Whooper Swans (right) migrate in family groups so that the young benefit from the adults' knowledge of previous migrations. The young could almost certainly manage alone, but they would be at a disadvantage, lacking site-specific details of the wintering areas which are subject to short-term change.*

Adult

Juvenile

Adult

Normal direction of migration

The Netherlands

Birds moved by plane

Normal wintering area

Adults

Switzerland

Juveniles

*As with many migrants,* Blackcaps *(below) are divided in their migratory paths. Birds breeding in western Europe fly to the southwest, while those from eastern Europe move southeastward.*

*An experiment at Radolfzell in southern Germany crossed birds from both populations. As expected, the hybrids tried to fly south – and would have failed to survive on a path that took them over the Alps and the widest part of the Mediterranean. Hybrids that occur in the wild also die; survival lies in keeping to the migratory divide.*

enough north to prompt a spread to Asia when the ice returned. Gradual change is always possible – sudden and radical change is not.

The changing nature of Blackcap migration illustrates this gradual process, as does the manner in which Evening Grosbeak migration has altered in this century (see p. 15). British Blackcaps are migratory, heading southward to winter from southern France south to the Sahel. There are, however, records of increasing numbers of Blackcaps wintering in Britain, in locations as far north as Inverness, Scotland, and in Ireland. These are German and Austrian migrants. During the winter, up to January, they feed on berries, but during the first three months of the year, they more frequently take the offerings from bird feeders.

Blackcaps are not strong migrants, but they normally travel southwestward. Since their direction of travel is not exact, a few almost certainly reached Scotland and Ireland naturally. Conditions, helped by the numbers of well-stocked bird feeders, favored their survival, and natural selection has increased the numbers taking this course.

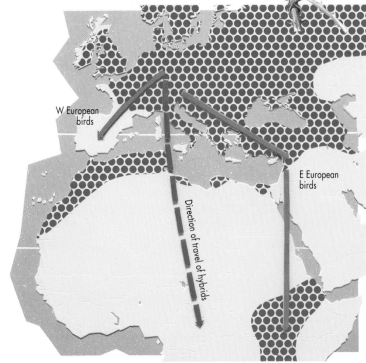

W European birds

E European birds

Direction of travel of hybrids

# Orientation and navigation/1

*Getting there involves flying in the right direction for the correct length of time.*

Navigation is the art of getting there. This generally means that a migrating bird has to know the direction in which it must fly – it must be able to orient itself – and to know when it has arrived, both of which are easier if the migrant has done it all before. For many years it seemed that bird navigation would never be understood, since observers were looking for a single answer to the question "How do birds find their way?". It is now known that there is no one answer but that birds use a host of clues. It is akin to a walker being lost: he or she might use a watch and the sun to find south, locate the moss beside a tree to detect the damper west side, walk down a river bank to reach the sea, or wait until dark when the North Star appears. A bird, similarly, cannot afford to ignore any clues.

For many birds, simply flying in the right direction for the correct length of time should be good enough to get from one place to another. Certainly, the duration of migratory activity in caged Blackcaps is related to the distance that the different populations to which they belong are moving

in the wild. This, together with the recognition of suitable habitat, is enough for a small bird with a fairly extensive wintering area to accomplish its "outward" migration.

The return journey is more crucial, but here, too, birds are looking for a large area with which they are familiar and, after they have bred, they almost certainly have a real target to aim for. Most birds have the ability to navigate to within about 6 to 12 miles (10 to 20 km) of their goal, after which they use landmarks to reach their precise destination. "Bird's-eye view" also helps – landscape features that are invisible to ground-based observers can be seen from above.

## Sun, stars, and magnets

There are three main means – all compasses – by which birds detect absolute north, south, east, and west, namely the magnetic, star, and sun compasses. The most difficult of these to understand is probably the magnetic compass, but it is likely that the ability to locate magnetic north depends on small crystals of magnetite situated above the

*The eyes of a migrant bird receive major navigational clues from the stars at night and the sun by day. They also allow it to note landmarks so that the bird can orient itself and recognize specific features once it has returned to a familiar area.*

*A bird uses its sense of balance, together with what it can see of the land surface, to assess the effect of the wind. This may be through drift from its preferred direction, or from lift. Its ears may hear infrasound from the wind on distant mountains or the soft contact calls of birds nearby. Smell or taste may be used to locate the pungent colonies of sea birds – or the sweet scent of meadows.*

*Within the bird's head, its innate sense*

*of direction also has an effect on its brain. And all these stimuli are modified by the bird's internal clock.*

Stars

Magnetic north

Polarized light

Sunrise

Moon

Winds

To destination

Weather fronts

Landscape features

UV light

Sound waves

Smells

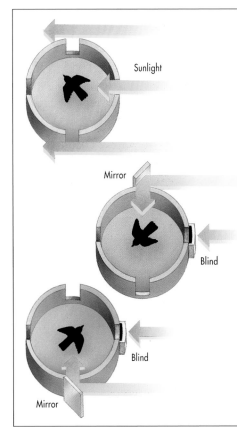

## SUN COMPASS

Experiments to prove the existence of a sun compass and its importance for daytime migrants involved caged birds and mirrors. At migration time, in natural conditions, these birds clearly showed a preferred flight direction (top).

When mirrors bent the sun's rays through 90°, the birds turned their preferred direction of movement through a right angle (middle). When the sun's rays were modified by the same amount in the opposite direction, this became the focus of the birds' interest (bottom).

nostrils. An experiment using students demonstrated that humans have a similar sense of direction. All the students wore coils on their heads, some of which canceled out the earth's magnetic field, while the rest left it unaffected. At the end of a tortuous bus ride, only those wearing the "dummy" coils could point toward home.

Robins tested for a sense of direction under changed magnetic fields show that they are able to orient well – but they have to be able to move around, crossing the lines of the magnetic field, to do so. Magnetic north itself moves around, and although it may provide a good reference point for a bird in its lifetime, over a few thousand years it may shift by up to 30°. Birds are able to cope with the regular reversals of polarity which happen every few hundred thousand years. It is believed that this change takes several years to stabilize; during this time, any species relying solely on its magnetic sense would be unable to complete its migrations. Birds, therefore, must be able to make use of other means of navigation.

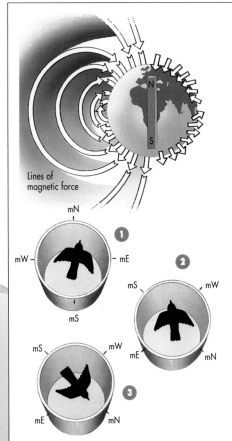

## MAGNETIC COMPASS

Robins were placed in cages surrounded by magnetic coils that mimicked the earth's magnetic field (visualized, top). Previous work had shown that these birds register the angle made by the field and the surface of the earth – which points south in the northern hemisphere and north in the southern.

Here, they detected north, the direction of their spring migration (1). When the field was twisted so that north was in the east-southeast, the birds kept to their original path for the first two nights (2). By the third night, they had detected and taken account of the change (3).

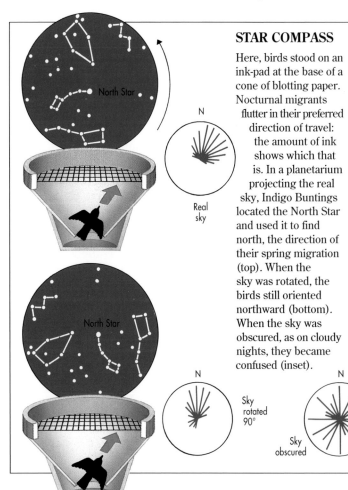

## STAR COMPASS

Here, birds stood on an ink-pad at the base of a cone of blotting paper. Nocturnal migrants flutter in their preferred direction of travel: the amount of ink shows which that is. In a planetarium projecting the real sky, Indigo Buntings located the North Star and used it to find north, the direction of their spring migration (top). When the sky was rotated, the birds still oriented northward (bottom). When the sky was obscured, as on cloudy nights, they became confused (inset).

# Orientation and navigation/2

Tests suggest that birds take some time to perfect their ability to use the magnetic compass effectively, and in some cases, they appear to use it to calibrate their star maps. Birds' use of the star map itself is now well understood as a result of a series of experiments in planetaria. Birds are not hatched with an in-built star map in their memory, but they do have the ability to detect the center of rotation of the stars. At the moment, this is near the North Star, but because the earth's axis precesses, it does not stay there: in 13,000 years' time, it will have moved by 47°. Clearly this is enough to make a huge difference for a migrating bird, and the star map would not work effectively; detecting the center of rotation, on the other hand, is perfectly safe.

The sun compass relies on the bird's internal clock (see also pp. 28–29). At 10 a.m. local time (which a bird detects with its "body clock"), the sun is always 30°E of south. Several species make use of the position of the sun, relative to the time of day, as a directional guide. Others may use the fact that it rises in the east and sets in the west to aid navigation. It has also been suggested that an internal feature of the eye – the *pecten oculi* – may, like the gnomon of a sundial, throw a shadow on the back of the eye to provide special clues on direction. A sight of the sun is not necessary for its use in navigation – light from the sun coming through the clouds is polarized, which the birds can detect.

### Sensing the way

It has become clear that the sense of smell may be used by some birds during movements – this has been proved in experiments with homing pigeons and is suspected for many petrels which have strong and characteristic scents.

Birds may use sounds in various ways. The calls of frogs and other amphibians in marshy areas, and of other birds, waves on shores, and infrasound caused by the wind on mountain ranges have all been thought to offer positional clues. It is even possible that birds can use the echoes of their own calls from the land surface in this way.

Migrants crossing the oceans can probably detect the presence of land – even patterns of islands, bays, and headlands – by looking at the overall pattern of the waves. Barometric pressure may provide useful clues – but more probably to help in making the journey efficiently rather than in navigation. Recent remarkable results also show that birds may even be conscious of small changes in gravity and are possibly able to detect the Coriolis force – the force produced by the spinning earth.

*Migration generally takes place on a broad front although many natural features funnel or concentrate migrants. Such features – known as leading lines – may, in addition, provide them with clues to navigation. Many leading lines are also excellent places to observe migrants.*

*Mountain ranges (right) can be huge obstacles, so migrants tend to be funneled through passes. Small islands and headlands are also points where migrants congregate.*

*Low mountains and hills can provide ideal soaring conditions for specialist migrants, and coastal areas may concentrate birds relying on thermals for lift. Such birds also make use of the narrow joins – such as Panama in Central America – or narrow seaways – such as the Bosporus in Turkey – between landmasses. Land birds also use valleys and sea or lake coastlines pointing in roughly the right direction as leading lines.*

# Routes and barriers

*No barrier seems insurmountable when the migration route is generations old.*

Migration routes, built up over generations, cannot change overnight. The genetic basis of migratory control (see pp. 30–31) makes change possible only through gradual evolution. This process may take place over a long period and cover huge distances – Northern Wheatear migrations change by about ⅝ mile (1 km) a year, but have been doing so for almost 10,000 years. Routes, of course, are only sustained if birds are able to use them efficiently and if enough birds survive to maintain the population.

A good route between summer and winter quarters need not be the most direct. There is often a barrier to migration which it is prudent for the birds to skirt. This may be sea for land birds, or land for sea birds, or inhospitable ground such as desert or a mountain range. Such obstacles do not necessarily hinder the birds, which may decide to overfly the barrier even if there is no chance of landing to refuel.

Birds that rely on special flight techniques have no choice in such matters. Thermal soarers cannot fly at night, over the sea, or in any area where they cannot achieve lift. And parts of the ocean are no-go areas for sea birds – when the winds are unreliable, dynamic soaring is not an option.

All sorts of barriers have shaped and influenced migration routes. The watery expanse of the Caribbean and Gulf of Mexico in the Americas, the vast Sahara desert in Africa, and the high peaks of the Himalayas in Asia are all effective barriers to migration. But none is absolute – many species have evolved routes across them.

## GREAT CIRCLE ROUTES

The shortest distance between two points is rarely apparent from conventional maps which flatten the earth's sphere. Birds, like jet airliners, take routes that follow the circumference of the earth, so-called Great Circle routes (below, left). These result in considerable distance savings, particularly for long-distance migrants.

*American Golden Plovers find that the Atlantic Ocean is no barrier to their migrations.*

*Swainson's Hawks must stay over land to soar, so they migrate through the narrow Isthmus of Panama.*

*Long-tailed Jaegers wander the oceans in winter, feeding at sea by chasing other birds, forcing them to relinquish food they are carrying.*

*Ruby-throated Hummingbirds survive the flight over the Gulf of Mexico by doubling body weight.*

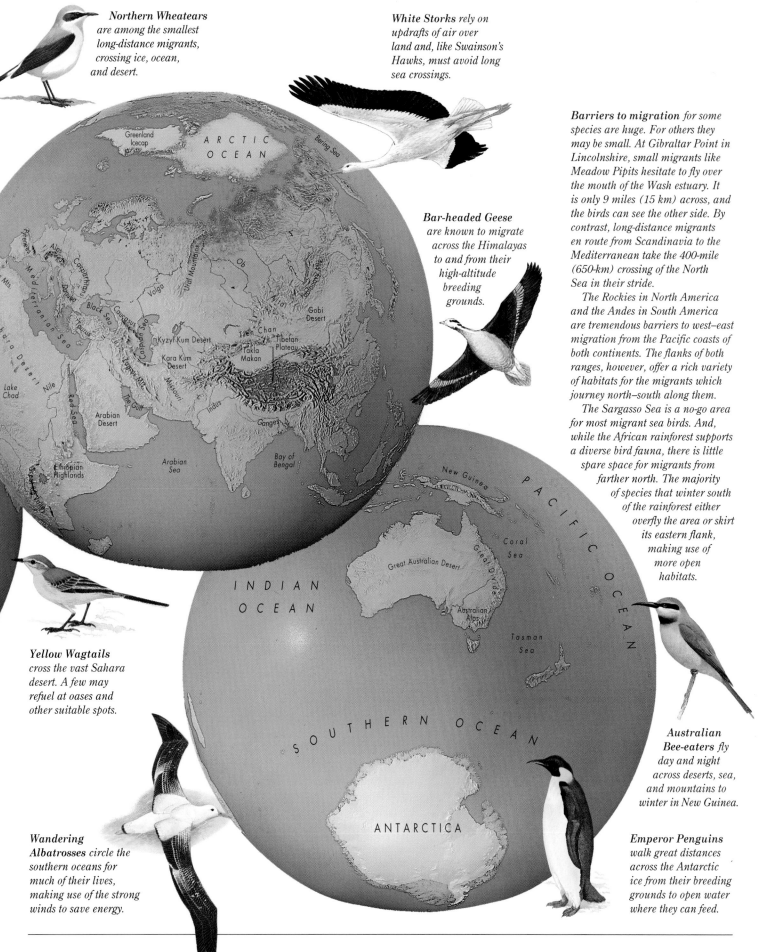

**Northern Wheatears** are among the smallest long-distance migrants, crossing ice, ocean, and desert.

**White Storks** rely on updrafts of air over land and, like Swainson's Hawks, must avoid long sea crossings.

**Bar-headed Geese** are known to migrate across the Himalayas to and from their high-altitude breeding grounds.

**Barriers to migration** for some species are huge. For others they may be small. At Gibraltar Point in Lincolnshire, small migrants like Meadow Pipits hesitate to fly over the mouth of the Wash estuary. It is only 9 miles (15 km) across, and the birds can see the other side. By contrast, long-distance migrants en route from Scandinavia to the Mediterranean take the 400-mile (650-km) crossing of the North Sea in their stride.

The Rockies in North America and the Andes in South America are tremendous barriers to west–east migration from the Pacific coasts of both continents. The flanks of both ranges, however, offer a rich variety of habitats for the migrants which journey north–south along them.

The Sargasso Sea is a no-go area for most migrant sea birds. And, while the African rainforest supports a diverse bird fauna, there is little spare space for migrants from farther north. The majority of species that winter south of the rainforest either overfly the area or skirt its eastern flank, making use of more open habitats.

**Yellow Wagtails** cross the vast Sahara desert. A few may refuel at oases and other suitable spots.

**Australian Bee-eaters** fly day and night across deserts, sea, and mountains to winter in New Guinea.

**Wandering Albatrosses** circle the southern oceans for much of their lives, making use of the strong winds to save energy.

**Emperor Penguins** walk great distances across the Antarctic ice from their breeding grounds to open water where they can feed.

# Staging posts

*Ensuring a successful migration often means stopping off en route.*

Birds that complete their migratory journeys nonstop are the exception rather than the rule. Most migrants have to stop over somewhere to rest and replenish their fuel reserves. For many small birds, these stopping places are extensive and the birds not particularly concentrated or apparent to observers, but some of the larger species gather in spectacular numbers in clearly defined areas.

The main function of a staging post is to provide a place where food is plentiful so that birds can fatten up for the next stage of their journey in safety. The location of a migration stopover for a species may, therefore, differ in spring and in fall. Similarly, the length of time a bird spends at a staging post varies from species to species. Depending on the availability of food and the speed with which a bird can put on fat, it can be as little as a few days or as much as a few weeks.

Staging areas where large numbers of migrants become concentrated are indicated on the map below. Among the smaller migrants using more diffuse and less easily defined stopovers are Reed Warblers from western Europe, which become concentrated down the Portuguese coast in August and September; Blackpoll Warblers from much of eastern Canada, which spend time in Massachusetts in the fall; and Pied Flycatchers from across western Europe into Asia, which are found in northwestern Iberia in the fall.

○ *The staging post symbol can be found on many of the maps in the chapters that follow to indicate a traditional area where migrants concentrate to feed and rest in spring or fall.*

1 *Aleutian Islands*
2 *Copper River delta*
3 *Gray's Harbor*
4 *Tule Lake*
5 *San Francisco*
6 *Freezeout Lake*
7 *Devil's Lake*
8 *James Bay*
9 *Platte River*
10 *Cheyenne Bottoms*
11 *Galveston/Live Oak/Aransas NWR*
12 *Cameron*
13 *Dauphin Island*
14 *Lake Erie*
15 *Delaware Bay*
16 *Bay of Fundy*
17 *Cuba, and other Caribbean islands*
18 *Panama*
19 *Paracas*
20 *Surinam coast*
21 *La Serena, Chile*
22 *Tierra del Fuego*
23 *Lagoa do Peixe*
24 *Bear Island*
25 *Ammassalik*
26 *Iceland*
27 *Bals fjord*
28 *L. Hornborgasjön*
29 *Gulf of Matsalu*
30 *Morecambe Bay/ The Wash*
31 *Waddenzee/ Ijsselmeer*
32 *Rugen*
33 *Caspian Sea*
34 *Banc d'Arguin*
35 *Lake Chad*
36 *Benguela Current*
37 *Islands of South China Sea*
38 *Coasts of Western Australia*
39 *Port Philip Bay/ Corner inlet*

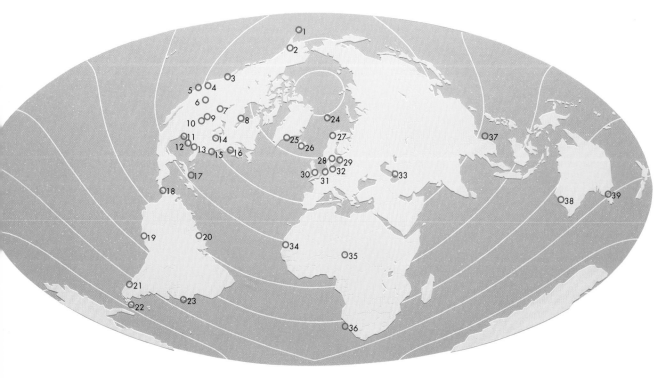

*Some estuaries are used both by birds on passage and as wintering grounds, with the result that they are important year-round. Delaware Bay (left), on the east coast of the U.S., is a special case. At the end of May, vast numbers of horseshoe crabs lay their eggs here, and every year Red Knots of the race* rufa *come to feast on this predictable food stock. At least 60,000, and perhaps as many as 95,000, birds gather here, more than half the world population of this race. Other shorebirds, such as Ruddy Turnstones, also make use of this rich resource.*

*The birds pack close together, unconcerned that a neighbor might be in competition – there is plenty for all.*

## WATCHING THE BIRDS

Some staging posts are superb places to see large numbers of migrant birds; others less so. Other good sites for birdwatchers are places such as Hawk Mountain, Pennsylvania, where soaring birds are concentrated by geographical features. Similarly, at Point Reyes, California, and Fair Isle, Scotland, migrants concentrate due to quirks of geography.

The binoculars symbol recurs throughout the book at sites where migrant birds, for whatever reason, are particularly visible. These may or may not also be staging posts. (See Watching the shorebirds, pp. 130–31.)

# Weather and climate/1

*Correctly assessing weather is vital, but mistakes may be rectified.*

On a day-to-day basis, the weather can be of overriding importance for a migrant. For individual populations and for individual birds, all aspects of the weather – warmth, cold, dryness, rain, snow, sleet, fog, wind – may play a part in migration. Some of the most obvious factors include the direction from which the wind is blowing, which may help the bird to reach its destination or hinder it; extensive cloud, which obscures the stars, making finding the way more difficult; and the temperature of the destination in spring – if it is still cold and frozen, rather than warm, insect food may not be readily available.

For a species as a whole, however, climate and the changing weather patterns from year to year are the major influences that shape migratory routes and destinations. Weather requires tactical decisions by individual birds; climate involves strategic considerations that may affect the behavior of whole populations over many years.

## The changing seasons

Birds are forced to migrate by the effects of the changing seasons. Areas where the habitat and weather afford a good living in the summer for the breeding birds may be untenable outside the breeding season. Many species respond to winter and summer, but others, particularly in the tropics, are governed by wet and dry seasons. The time to breed is determined by the flush of productivity that characterizes the rainy season. This burgeoning of plant and animal food may occur regularly, at a set time of the year, as in eastern Africa, or at long and irregular intervals, as in much of the interior of Australia.

Seasonality is also important for birds using traditional staging posts. In northern Portugal and northwestern Spain, many millions of small migrants from farther north and farther east in Europe find ideal conditions for putting on weight in the fall. Insect populations are high, and there is also plenty of fruit which can be exploited.

These same areas in spring, by contrast, are cold and inhospitable and able to sustain only relatively small populations of resident birds and breeding migrants. The insect-eating migrants heading for more northerly areas shun this part of Europe in spring and return to their breeding grounds via more easterly routes.

It is interesting to speculate what would happen if these areas could support large numbers of both residents and breeding migrants. Would the passage birds in the fall be able to compete with an enhanced local population for

*Atrocious spring weather in the Volga delta (right), although seemingly inhospitable to migrant waterfowl, does not force them to land and wait for conditions to improve. Despite the overcast sky and strong head wind, the birds can see that there is ample vegetation on which to feed remaining from the good fall many months before.*

*The survival of the species, and the continuance of its genes, means that individual birds are prepared to probe the country farther to the north to ascertain whether the next staging post is free of ice and snow and if the breeding area is clear.*

*For species that breed in the high Arctic, winters are long and summers short. There is therefore tremendous pressure to get back early to be able to exploit just a few extra days of possible fair weather. If winter comes early, latecomers among the breeding birds may find themselves unable to complete their nesting attempt successfully and will waste a whole year without producing any offspring. And the first pairs back have the advantage of choosing the best areas in which to breed, which are also easy to defend against those that arrive later.*

available food resources? Or would the rest of Europe suffer from a depleted population of migrants because a vital link in the migration chain had been broken?

## The human element

All birds are at the mercy of inclement weather, and terrible disasters do happen to migrants on occasion. Many of these are natural, but others are the direct or indirect result of human activities. Humans have engineered enormous changes to the world's climate and environments which surpass modern concerns over global warming and damage to the ozone layer. Huge shifts have come about

through the destruction of forest and ground cover. Many tracts of the Sahara desert, for example, were productive farmland and pasture as recently as 1,600 years ago.

Perhaps the most distressing immediate losses result from the attraction of migrants to bright lights in fog, which causes death by collision. The rotating beams of lighthouses were once a hazard, but modern flashing lights are not dangerous. In many cities, the lighted windows of skyscrapers have proved fatally attractive to birds: owners of some buildings in North America employ people to gather the bodies in the morning. One scientific paper in the 1970s documented the deaths of 140,000 warblers from 135 sites.

**Getting it right and getting it wrong**

Although migration is usually timed to take advantage of the weather, mistakes can happen. Some Blackpoll Warblers of North America are experts at getting it right (see pp. 16 and 78–79), waiting – already laden with enough fat for their travels – until a succession of low-pressure systems passes over the Massachusetts coast at four- or five-day intervals. When, by the change in local weather, they detect one approaching, they take off and use the winds around it to help them fly out to sea where, hundreds of miles off the coast, they come under the influence of the northeast trade winds which speed them on their journey south.

# Weather and climate/2

Many birds wait for settled conditions before migrating. These often occur during extensive high-pressure systems. If the weather is overcast and wet, migration may be held up for a few days. Some strong fliers, such as shorebirds and waterfowl, are not discouraged by local difficulties and may migrate even in seemingly inclement conditions. But they often migrate in small steps (compared with the distances they are capable of traveling in one flight and the total distance they have to cover), so are not taking great risks. A bird about to set out on a long, nonstop flight, on the other hand, cannot afford to take any additional risks and is more likely to wait until the local conditions look perfect.

Migrants that misjudge conditions may die. There are, however, several steps a bird can take to increase its chances of survival if it realizes that something is going wrong. The first thing to do is to settle and wait for conditions to improve. Many birds of different species have been found in unlikely places for this reason, but for a land bird flying over the ocean, places to touch down are at a premium. This is why headlands and islands have become such prime sites to witness migration, albeit migration going wrong. It also explains the attraction of ships and oil platforms for birds in bad weather.

If a place to settle is not immediately available, birds can drift with the wind, waiting for an opportunity of salvation. They may be able to fly for many hours at a slow speed and, with strong winds to help them, cover huge distances, albeit in the wrong direction. The number of birds of many species, representing many different groups of land birds, regularly wandering across the Atlantic Ocean in both directions shows how effective this strategy can be.

These falls – sudden appearances of large numbers of migrants in the wrong place at the wrong time – are regular, if not frequent, occurrences. Scandinavian breeders are some of the birds most often affected. Autumn migrants in their millions take off from Scandinavia in apparently excellent conditions to travel southwest across the North Sea, en route for Spain and Portugal via Britain and France. But weather fronts build up in their path. Often, overcast conditions combine with a southeasterly wind that causes the birds to drift downwind too far west and onto the nearest shore. On September 3, 1965, a fall brought the Suffolk town of Lowestoft, in England, to a standstill for more than an hour as up to half a million exhausted birds of many species settled on roads and paths.

**4** When the birds do go, most travel with others and set off soon after dawn. Sea breezes may cause problems, and although the crossing is short, may take their toll.

**5** The journey through France involves a stay of three to five days at two or three roosts: earlier arrivals show the best places to feed. Torrential rain and hailstorms in August and September often cause local damage to the grapevines – and the death of any Barn Swallows unable to find shelter.

**6** The Pyrenees represent a major hurdle. Many birds skirt the edge of this huge range, but others cross it using the major passes. This may be the birds' first experience of mountains – and their fickle weather. Some are lost to thunderstorms.
  Here, and around the Mediterranean, human hunters take a huge toll of small birds, but not usually of Barn Swallows.

**7** Birds crossing Spain to reach Gibraltar have a short over-sea flight – only 8 miles (13 km) if they choose the narrowest crossing point – into Africa. Others are not so fortunate. Birds crossing the Mediterranean may have to fly as much as 300–370 miles (500–600 km), and if not properly prepared they may perish. Those taking a route too far to the west may be swept out into the wide expanses of the Atlantic and collapse exhausted into the sea or onto a ship.

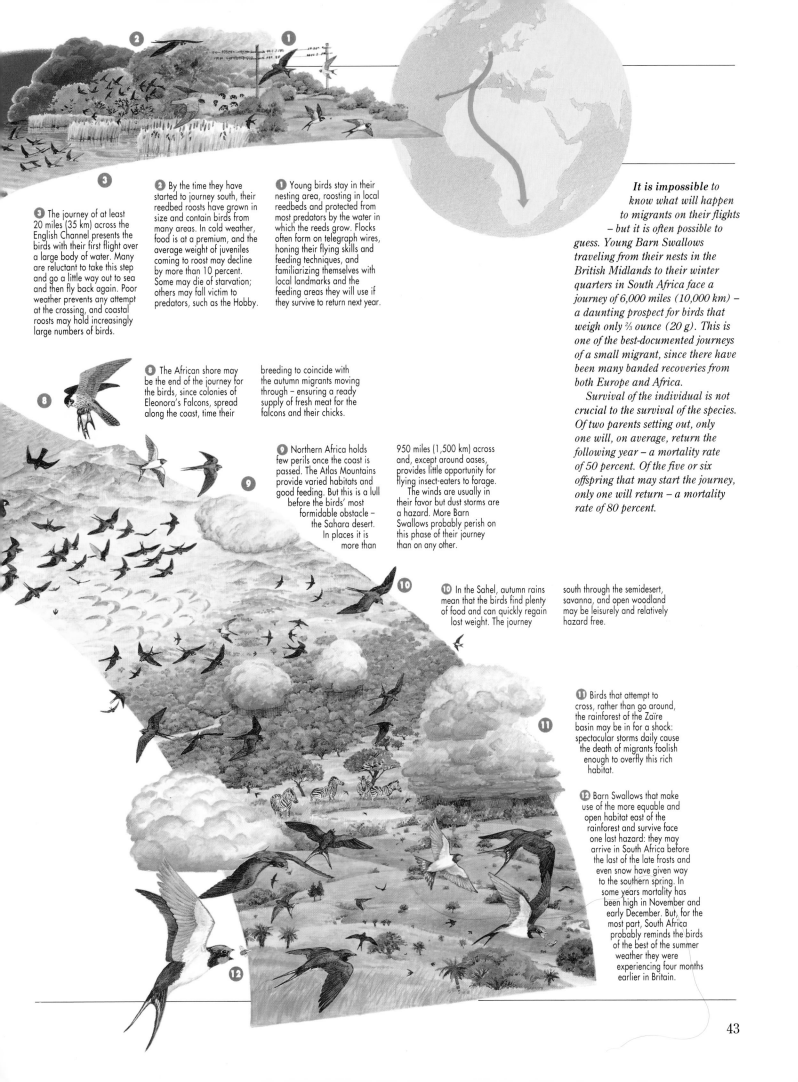

**3** The journey of at least 20 miles (35 km) across the English Channel presents the birds with their first flight over a large body of water. Many are reluctant to take this step and go a little way out to sea and then fly back again. Poor weather prevents any attempt at the crossing, and coastal roosts may hold increasingly large numbers of birds.

**2** By the time they have started to journey south, their reedbed roosts have grown in size and contain birds from many areas. In cold weather, food is at a premium, and the average weight of juveniles coming to roost may decline by more than 10 percent. Some may die of starvation; others may fall victim to predators, such as the Hobby.

**1** Young birds stay in their nesting area, roosting in local reedbeds and protected from most predators by the water in which the reeds grow. Flocks often form on telegraph wires, honing their flying skills and feeding techniques, and familiarizing themselves with local landmarks and the feeding areas they will use if they survive to return next year.

*It is impossible to know what will happen to migrants on their flights – but it is often possible to guess. Young Barn Swallows traveling from their nests in the British Midlands to their winter quarters in South Africa face a journey of 6,000 miles (10,000 km) – a daunting prospect for birds that weigh only ⅔ ounce (20 g). This is one of the best-documented journeys of a small migrant, since there have been many banded recoveries from both Europe and Africa.*

*Survival of the individual is not crucial to the survival of the species. Of two parents setting out, only one will, on average, return the following year – a mortality rate of 50 percent. Of the five or six offspring that may start the journey, only one will return – a mortality rate of 80 percent.*

**8** The African shore may be the end of the journey for the birds, since colonies of Eleonora's Falcons, spread along the coast, time their breeding to coincide with the autumn migrants moving through – ensuring a ready supply of fresh meat for the falcons and their chicks.

**9** Northern Africa holds few perils once the coast is passed. The Atlas Mountains provide varied habitats and good feeding. But this is a lull before the birds' most formidable obstacle – the Sahara desert. In places it is more than 950 miles (1,500 km) across and, except around oases, provides little opportunity for flying insect-eaters to forage. The winds are usually in their favor but dust storms are a hazard. More Barn Swallows probably perish on this phase of their journey than on any other.

**10** In the Sahel, autumn rains mean that the birds find plenty of food and can quickly regain lost weight. The journey south through the semidesert, savanna, and open woodland may be leisurely and relatively hazard free.

**11** Birds that attempt to cross, rather than go around, the rainforest of the Zaïre basin may be in for a shock: spectacular storms daily cause the death of migrants foolish enough to overfly this rich habitat.

**12** Barn Swallows that make use of the more equable and open habitat east of the rainforest and survive face one last hazard: they may arrive in South Africa before the last of the late frosts and even snow have given way to the southern spring. In some years mortality has been high in November and early December. But, for the most part, South Africa probably reminds the birds of the best of the summer weather they were experiencing four months earlier in Britain.

# How migration is studied/1

*Direct observation and skillful interpretation reveal many of the secrets of bird migration.*

The fact of bird migration was gradually discovered over many centuries through a variety of observations. Some 5,000 years ago, the seasonal movement of numbers of large birds over the Mediterranean island of Cyprus was taken as a signal to plant the crops. The Greek philosopher Aristotle wrote that the summer Redstarts, which are now known to leave Greece for sub-Saharan Africa, were transformed into Robins, which breed farther north and winter in Greece. Likewise, he thought that summer Garden Warblers became winter Blackcaps. Both are incorrect interpretations of accurate observations, but understandable given that the two pairs of species are similar in shape and size.

## From Aristotle to Gatke

Despite these errors, Aristotle believed in migration and correctly labeled a variety of birds as migrants. It was his mythic theory of transmutation, however, that was slavishly reiterated for almost 2,000 years in the writings of other observers. Among the species he classified as migratory was the Barn Swallow, coincidentally the subject of the first successful marking experiment. The prior of a Cistercian Abbey in Germany, writing in about A.D. 1250, reported that a man had tied a parchment to the leg of an adult Barn Swallow with the message "Oh, Swallow, where do you live in winter?" He must have been delighted to get the message back in spring "In Asia, in the home of Petrus."

When Swedish biologist Carl Linnaeus devised an effective system for naming species 250 years ago, he opened the way for a systematic study of bird populations and movements. Even then, there were hiccups: the letters of British naturalist Gilbert White, echoing the writings of Olaus Magnus, refer to swallows, swifts, and martins hibernating in mud at the bottom of ponds. (White may not have believed this himself, but he was not inclined to contradict his patron who did.)

Interest in collecting bird specimens and the development of taxonomy made it easier to identify patterns in the occurrence of birds all over the world and to log major patterns of migration. In an age when the gun rather than binoculars aided bird investigation, the adage "What's hit is history, what's missed is mystery" prevailed. The skills of field identification were not well developed, and sightings were more likely to be discussed over dinner and the skin than over photographs and field notes.

Collectors came to realize that rare and interesting birds could be obtained at times of migration on remote islands and headlands and, until the 1920s, dispatched crack shots to augment their collections. One of the first places explored was Heligoland at the northeastern extreme of the North Sea. Over a period of 50 years, German ornithologist Heinrich Gatke recorded 398 species; his magnum opus, *Heligoland as an Ornithological Observatory*, was published in English in 1895.

## HAULING IN THE CATCH

One of the many fanciful theories put forward to account for the seasonal changes in bird populations was that species hibernated in winter.

Olaus Magnus, Bishop of Uppsala, Sweden, although acknowledging the writings of others who claimed that Barn Swallows migrated to warmer regions for the winter, insisted that northern birds went to roost in reedbeds in the fall, allowed themselves gradually to sink into the mud, and spent the winter asleep there.

A woodcut from Magnus's *A History of the Northern Nations*, published in 1555, illustrates this notion as fishermen haul in both fish and Barn Swallows.

**Mist nets, invented in Japan,** *provide an efficient and safe means of catching small birds in flight. Birds caught in this way are banded and may also be weighed. They are weighed again if recaptured.*

*This process has demonstrated that Sedge Warblers (left) double their normal weight in the fall – from ⅖ ounce (11 g) to ⅘ ounce (22 g). This is accounted for by a store of fat sufficient for a four-day-long flight of 2,500 miles (4,000 km) from Europe to Africa.*

**The simplest way to trace a bird** *on migration is to place on its leg a metal band (above) which includes a return address and a unique serial number. In this way, anyone finding the bird can send details of place, circumstances, date, and the serial number to the address on the band. Two dates and places are then logged.*

*For small birds, the chances of recovery are remote, possibly 1 in 300 or so. For larger birds such as geese and ducks, the "recovery rate" is higher: 1 in 10 of banded birds are eventually reported.*

# How migration is studied/2

Heligoland and other headlands, as well as islands, were such prime sites for bird collectors because of their lighthouses. Many night migrants were attracted to, then disorientated by, the rotating beams and perished (modern lights, constructed differently, pose no threat). From 1880 to 1914, lighthouse keepers on the islands and headlands of northern Europe logged the birds observed and specimens killed at their lights, with counts collated in Britain.

## Migration study today

Islands, headlands, and similar sites worldwide are now bird observatories. Not all are on the fringes of the continents: Long Point on the shores of Lake Erie, Canada, has long been a well-known observatory. Often they are manned by dedicated bands of local birders, but many have developed into field stations where students of migration and birdwatchers interested in the subject – and in seeing rare birds – can stay. Most observatories have a census area where the daily totals of birds of each species are recorded and regular counts of visible migration, that is birds that can be seen actively migrating, are logged. Coastal observatories mount regular sea watches to count sea birds passing by. Banding is also usually carried out.

Most professional studies of migration are now conducted under the auspices of universities or similar institutions and tend to be more experimental than observational. Projects may involve altering birds' sensory perceptions – equipping racing pigeons with magnetic coils or frosted

*A number of studies of the behavior of migrants have been made by glider, light aircraft, and microlite. This technique is particularly successful for studying migrants soaring over land, since it allows individual birds to be followed over considerable distances, and their height, speed, position, and the amount of flapping they do to be logged.*

*Storks, pelicans, cranes, eagles, vultures, and several other species have been studied in this way. There are even instances of pilots going up at night to find out whether swifts were asleep while flying: they were, but only for very short periods.*

*One of the best studies concerned Common Cranes over southern Sweden, where individuals were continuously tracked for up to three hours at a time (see pp. 100–101).*

contact lenses, for example – but usually experiments are carried out on birds under special conditions in captivity. Pioneering work in North America involved birds in planetaria exposed to different star patterns. Others have been placed in rooms with controlled magnetic fields or in cages with mirrors to alter the apparent direction of the sun (see pp. 32–35). More time-consuming are the experiments on birds kept for years in aviaries. In such studies, the skills of the keepers in maintaining fit and healthy subjects for experiment are vital: the Max-Planck Institute at Radolfzell, southern Germany, is preeminent in this field (see p. 31).

Over the past three or four decades, two types of observational research have become common. The first, hi-tech, approach is to use radar to track the birds. Birds showed up on radar screens from the first (although they were initially not recognized as such and were labeled "angels"). Radar sets were later adapted for bird study, and modern antiaircraft detection equipment, suitably modified, can now track an individual bird over a range of more than 6 miles (10 km). The signal accurately pinpoints a bird's position, height, speed, wing- and heartbeats.

The other approach, more popular in North America than in Europe, is moon-watching. This is a means of tracking the level of nocturnal migration by watching birds flying across the moon. For best results, the moon should be full and high in the sky: September and October are good months in the northern hemisphere. A pass every one or two minutes may occur at peak times (see p. 17).

*Few techniques* for studying migration have yielded such exciting results as radio tracking. When a transmitter is fitted to a bird, its position can be plotted through a receiver tuned in to the pulses radiated back. Transmitters are becoming smaller (above): many can now be glued to the tail feathers of the bird, with the antenna down the shaft. And, as battery technology improves, the range of the signal increases.

Ongoing research since the late 1980s uses satellite tracking to log a bird's position a couple of dozen times a day. Among the species tracked so far are Bewick's Swans, on their way north from the Baltic, and Wandering Albatrosses in the Southern Ocean. It has been found that the swans appear to send out scouts (see p. 28) and that the albatrosses were frequently becalmed for up to 36 hours by the weather.

# Threats and conservation/1

*Human activities are the greatest threat to migrants, and the only solution to their problems.*

Without a doubt, the major global threat to all birds, migrant and resident, is habitat destruction. Birds have evolved over millions of years to exploit the world's rich variety of habitats. Migrant birds are particularly at risk, since they are not only likely to rely on different habitats in winter and summer, but may also use several more sites on route between them. Habitat destruction may be gross, but it can also be subtle: the replacement of a mature, natural forest by a single-species plantation can be as damaging as complete felling, altering the numbers and composition of both insect species and other forest dwellers. Most of the problems caused by habitat destruction are due – directly or indirectly – to human activities.

## The importance of water

Bird populations have been devastated by wetland modification. Often the characteristics of the wetland that are most important for birds are those that are most inconvenient for people. Seasonal waters with large areas of marsh are often vital for birds. Yet in the tropics, these areas may be turned over to rice paddies; in temperate regions, they might be ponded and banked to concentrate the water into smaller tracts for fish farming, for example, with the reclaimed area turned over to agriculture.

Estuaries have been used for centuries for trade and industry. It is difficult today to think of the Hudson River in New York or the port at Rotterdam as important places for shorebirds, but they once were. Not only are the physical characteristics of such sites – the buildings, wharves, and docks – unsuitable for birds; industrial effluent may also render the estuary sterile. Ongoing estuary development means the loss of staging posts and wintering grounds. Land-reclamation schemes, by contrast, can encourage birds. The polders in the Netherlands, for example, have provided marvelous habitats for a wide variety of water birds in the sump areas which are not destined for agricultural use.

Water may be extracted for industrial, domestic, and leisure use. Marinas destroy wetland sites; hotels and golf courses eliminate primary habitats; and the sheer weight of tourist numbers can be an overwhelming disturbance.

## Field and forest

When large tracts of the northern hemisphere were forested following the retreat of the glaciers at the end of the last ice age, woodland birds reigned supreme. Deforestation has had a devastating effect on birds in the

*Oil on the surface of the sea has left huge numbers of birds dead (below). The 1993 wreck of the* Braer*, off the Shetland Islands, killed fewer birds than usual in such disasters since storms dispersed the oil. Smaller spills have accounted for much larger losses.*

*Spills tend to have most effect on wintering sea birds, and because they are traditional in their choice of wintering area, it may take a decade or more for populations to recover.*

*Tropical rainforest is rapidly disappearing (right). Many migrants winter in secondary forest and woodland, which are also being modified or destroyed.*

*Secondary forest used to result regularly from slash-and-burn operations: after two or three years of cropping, the land returned naturally to forest that generalist migrants could exploit. Today, rainforest destruction is often total, with soil erosion or permanent grazing rendering vast tracts useless for birds.*

last few thousand years. Some of these species may have benefited from more open habitats, but most have suffered considerable declines. Recent changes in temperate regions have included replacing native forest with plantations of exotic monocultures. This inevitably results in a restricted range of bird species and a lower biomass (see p. 77). The planting of Australian eucalyptus trees in Mediterranean areas has affected birds in summer and on migration.

*Hunters in the U.S. fund conservation by buying Duck Stamps (see pp. 56–57). The stamps fund research into threatened populations and enable the planting of special fields for the ducks, to limit damage to crops.*

Northern
Pintail

Every new road, factory, office, and house is likely to displace breeding birds. Each improvement to agriculture is designed to increase yields of crops, thereby leaving less room within the crop for the weeds and pests which the birds would otherwise exploit. In Britain alone, 10 species which fed largely on seeds in the agricultural environment have declined over the last 15 years – several by more than two-thirds.

# Threats and conservation/2

Pesticides cause serious problems. Direct kills of birds tend to occur in developing countries where safety rules may be lax and where chemicals no longer approved in the developed world may be dumped. There is also an indirect, and probably more serious, aspect of pesticide contamination – the global build-up of persistent chemicals, such as DDT. Chemicals have also affected the ozone layer, which in turn affects the food supply. The greenhouse effect may prove damaging: if sea levels rise, estuaries and other prime sites will be lost.

## Hunting and caging

Migrants, including traditional quarry birds such as ducks and many other species, are often the targets of hunting. Small migrants like Blackcaps are at risk in the Mediterranean, and illegal trophy hunters shoot Honey Buzzards in southern Italy. In Senegal it is thought that as many as 25 million birds may be taken and caged each year – more than the total number of birds banded worldwide in a year. Caging is rife, too, in Southeast Asia but here birds are also eaten and used in traditional medicine.

## Redressing the balance

National and international conservation bodies are acting on their own, as well as together and with governments on behalf of migratory birds. Their projects are often locally based, but their effects may be far-reaching. (Schemes for specific species are mentioned where appropriate.) Designation of estuaries as reserves is vital, but other wetlands are crucial to other species – there are networks of reserves in North America, Europe, and Japan to protect wild swans. Similar networks exist for White Storks and cranes, and also allow teams of scientists to study the birds.

BirdLife International is the umbrella organization which coordinates and provides a focus for much of this work. Its hundreds of projects include providing identification guides to Portuguese children to try to change the culture from one of bird hunting to birdwatching; the foundation of DHKF – the Society for the Protection of Nature – in Turkey, where there are 80 important bird areas, 50 unprotected; and the protection of the Hadejia-Nguru wetlands in Nigeria from damming and irrigation, which would destroy the wintering area of huge numbers of migrants.

*Educating children may be the most effective way to get the conservation message across. When banding returns demonstrated that local children were taking Roseate Terns, which winter along the coast of Ghana, for food and as playthings, the action taken was aimed at the children. Save the Shorebirds (left), wholly run by the Ghanaian government, is increasing the awareness of the whole coastal population toward wildlife. Not only the Roseate but also other terns, and shorebirds, are benefiting from this initiative.*

*Many hunters harvest only surplus birds from well-studied populations; others kill millions of migrants each year with no thought for the local ecology (right). In some areas, birds are an important part of the local diet. More often, the slaughter is a macho occupation designed to increase status. On Malta, conservationists are winning over the children to reduce the importance of hunting in the culture. It is a long, slow task, but attitudes do appear to be changing.*

# NORTH AMERICAN MIGRANTS

The Americas, and North America in particular, are crisscrossed by the paths of enormous numbers of migrant birds. Long before Europeans reached the continent, the Inuit peoples of the north relied on migrant waterfowl and sea birds for food at certain times of the year. Today, the movements of these birds are equally important to hunters, and ways to allow sport without detriment to bird populations have been researched and developed. Indeed, the American model of treaties to protect birds, introduced in the 1920s, has paved the way for international conservation agreements.

North America stretches from the high Arctic to the tropics and provides the breeding grounds for millions of migrants – some also found elsewhere, others unique to the New World. The continent is home to some of the world's largest flying birds, such as swans and cranes, and its smallest – members of the hummingbird family. Its native birds range from those that travel only a few miles, if at all, to long-distance migrants that may journey from the far north across the equator and beyond.

*Sandhill Cranes* *breed in isolated pockets across northern North America and, with stopovers en route, winter in the southern states and Mexico.*

# Patterns of migration

*The geography of North America exerts the greatest influence on the continent's migrants.*

North America is made for migrants. Its broad expanses of tundra and boreal forest and myriad wetland habitats lie within latitudes where summer days are long and food abundant, but winter nights are also long and suitable food is minimal. To exploit the exceptionally hospitable environment, birds must retreat from the inhospitable. About 80 percent of the species and 94 percent of the individuals that breed in the northern coniferous forests migrate to the tropics. In the deciduous forests of eastern North America, 62 percent of the breeding species and 75 percent of the individuals migrate. In the central grasslands, 76 percent of breeding species and 73 percent of individuals are migrants. Among more western and southern breeding populations, the percentage of migrants declines greatly.

No more than about 130 of the nearly 650 species that nest in the United States or Canada are nonmigratory, and many of these undergo local seasonal movements – from higher to lower elevations in mountains or dispersing from nesting to non-nesting areas, for example. They include many woodpeckers, grouse, and quails, and a few owls. Others such as the Phainopepla, Wrentit, and Limpkin are limited to warmer areas and have no need to migrate.

The migrations of many species – including most of the continent's waterfowl and many sparrows and finches – are completed entirely within temperate North America. But some 330 temperate species (more than half the total) winter in the New World, or Neo-, tropics. Among them are most North American swallows, flycatchers, thrushes, vireos, wood warblers, and tanagers, and many raptors and shorebirds.

The continent's geography makes a vital contribution to North America's migratory pathways. Waterfowl biologist Frederick Lincoln, recognizing this fact, in 1952 formulated a generalization referred to as the "flyway concept." His Pacific, Central, Mississippi, and Atlantic flyways became the focus of study of hunted waterfowl populations. As with many generalizations, the flyway concept is not so simple. Through studies of banded individuals, it is now known that birds nesting in one flyway may move east to west or diagonally to migrate down another. It is also clear that some species – or even some populations – do have narrow migration pathways, but many follow broad routes that do not conform to any flyway.

For some birds, the Florida peninsula is a guiding finger to launch southbound migrants along the stepping stones of the Greater and Lesser Antilles to the rich wintering areas of South America. To others, subtropical Florida, the Bahamas, and the islands of the Caribbean provide winter retreats. For northbound migrants, Florida is a beckoning finger and its Atlantic and Gulf coasts dispersing arteries.

The broad east–west expanse of the northern coast of the Gulf of Mexico is a barrier to some southbound migrants, deflecting them to the east or west for safe passage to the south. For others, it is merely a gathering place where migrants build up reserves of fat and wait for favorable winds before striking out across 500 miles (800 km) of open water for the coast of Yucatán and beyond.

Hawaiian Islands

## HOT SPOTS

1. Point Reyes Bird Observatory, California
2. Bear River NWR, Utah
3. Hawk Ridge, Minnesota
4. Whitefish Point, Michigan
5. Cedar Grove, Wisconsin
6. Point Pelee NP, Ontario
7. Derby Hill, New York
8. Plum Island/Parker River NWR, Massachusetts
9. Martha's Vineyard, Massachusetts
10. Cape May, New Jersey/Delaware Bay, Delaware/ Hawk Mountain, Pennsylvania
11. Chesapeake Bay, Maryland
12. Cheyenne Bottoms, Kansas
13. Mazatlán to San Blas, Mexico
14. Live Oak/Aransas NWR, Texas
15. Galveston Is., Texas/ Cameron, Louisiana
16. Dauphin Island, Alabama
17. Key West, Florida
18. Dominica, Lesser Antilles
19. Panama Canal Zone

Coastlines, mountains, and rivers are attractive to migrants, both for the energy savings that can be achieved by following their course and for the abundant food supplies. For these reasons, many North American hot spots are along or close to such sites.

Cheyenne Bottoms is important for shorebirds while Cape May, Whitefish Point, Hawk Mountain, and Panama are prime sites for watching migrant hawks. Dauphin Island and Cameron are good sites in spring. For a week around April 21 each year, vast numbers of trans-Gulf migrants, exhausted by their flight, replenish energy reserves at Dauphin Island.

Some five billion land birds from 500 species annually leave their North American breeding grounds for winter quarters farther south. Most reach Central America; a few travel as far as southern South America.

Bobolinks make one of the longest migrations of any North American land bird – those breeding in Canada fly more than 5,000 miles (8,000 km) to the grasslands of southern Brazil, Uruguay, and northern Argentina.

The Sora Rail has one of the longest migration routes of any member of the rail family – some birds travel almost 3,000 miles (4,800 km) from their North American breeding marshes to the Caribbean islands.

**Nowhere else in the world** do the avenues of migratory access and retreat appear as clearly laid out as in North America. The landscape of the continent funnels southbound migrants to areas of winter concentration and disperses northbound migrants to the broad expanse of suitable breeding habitat.

The Atlantic and Pacific coasts are attractive to migrants. The abundant food resources concentrated along the shorelines support itinerant shorebirds. The difference in temperature between land and sea results in constant breezes to buoy up migrants. And the coastlines themselves provide continuous north–south leading lines (see pp. 36–37) to aid navigation.

The continent's major mountain ranges – the Sierras, Rockies, and Appalachians – extending more or less north–south, and the updrafts generated as winds are deflected by their steep slopes, both direct and facilitate the passage of migrants. And the Mississippi River and its tributaries provide yet another north–south conduit rich in food resources and potential stopover sites.

Major route

# Ducks

*People who hunt waterfowl in North America also raise funds for conservation.*

The migrations of ducks have probably been the subject of more study over a longer period than those of any other North American birds. Their annual arrivals and departures, and the habitats they favor, have been well known to hunters along the Atlantic coast for more than 300 years. Many North American waterfowl winter in protected Atlantic, Pacific, and Gulf coastal areas; others are concentrated in the wetlands of the lower Mississippi. Substantial numbers of some species winter in Mexico.

Declining populations of Wood Ducks and other waterfowl, and recognition of the potential to learn about populations and their movements, prompted the U.S. Biological Survey to initiate a formal bird-banding program in the 1920s. Knowledge of duck movements led to the development of the "flyway concept" (see pp. 54–55) and to hunting limits and seasons based both on these flyways and on population changes along them.

At the same time, natural habitats were (and still are) being lost to wetland drainage, human developments in coastal areas, and contamination of wetlands with agricultural and industrial chemicals. The damming and channelizing of rivers and streams, and diversion of whole rivers (such as the Kern River in central California) for irrigation are also having serious effects. Loss and degradation of habitats are the major problems facing ducks and other migrant waterfowl.

The Duck Stamp (see p. 49) was introduced in an effort to compensate for these habitat losses. Over $450 million has been raised from the stamps, and more than 4.1 million acres (1.7 million ha) of waterfowl nesting, migration, and wintering habitat have been bought for conservation. These lands include some 367 National Wildlife Refuges and 175 additional areas administered by the U.S. Fish and Wildlife Service, in 49 of the 50 states.

Nonhunters, too, are encouraged to purchase the stamps because of their value to conservation. An annual competition to provide the stamp artwork generates further interest, and several states also sell their own stamps to raise funds for conservation. These efforts are supplemented by the acquisition and management of habitats by Ducks Unlimited, a conservation organization funded largely by contributions from sports people.

Ecologists are still debating the long-term effects on duck populations of one aspect of human interference in the landscape: the construction of reservoirs, which has had a tremendous impact on the distribution and seasonal

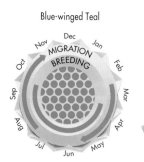

Blue-winged Teal

MIGRATION
BREEDING

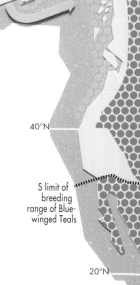

60°N

40°N

S limit of breeding range of Blue-winged Teals

20°N

***About 100 million*** *North American ducks migrate each fall, although as a result of winter losses, spring migrations are smaller. Some 62 million ducks breed each year.*

*Male Blue-winged Teals (below) are among the earliest southbound migrants, arriving in the southern states in late August and September.*

*Females and young, however, leave the breeding areas later, at times pushed south as their feeding grounds ice over.*

*In the fall, flocks of Blue-winged Teals often contain 100 or more birds. By contrast, pairs form in the wintering areas and gather into flocks of fewer than 30 for the northward journey.*

**Blue-winged Teal**
*Anas discors*
**Wingspan** 24–31 in/61–80 cm
**Weight** 13–15 oz/370–425 g
**Journey length** 0–7,000 miles/
0–11,200 km

**Oldsquaw**
*Clangula hyemalis*
**Wingspan** 26–31 in/66–80 cm
**Weight** 29–33 oz/815–930 g
**Journey length** 300–3,000 miles/
500–5,000 km

80°N

0°

Most
common in
Galápagos
Oct–Mar

20°S

Route not known

*Estimating numbers and understanding the distribution of migrating sea ducks can be difficult because these birds often feed well away from land. Range maps of the Oldsquaw, for example, rarely indicate that the species winters in the northern Gulf of Mexico. Yet it is a regular winter visitor near barrier islands about 10 miles (16 km) off the coast of Mississippi. Use of open-water marine habitats makes birds vulnerable to oil spills, and there is mounting evidence that populations are in decline.*

*These birds are unusual in that their summer and winter plumages are strikingly different. Although they nest on the tundra of northern Alaska and Canada, nonbreeding birds, those that fail to nest, and some who leave their young before they fledge make a molt migration (see p. 27) to areas north of the breeding grounds before migrating south for the winter.*

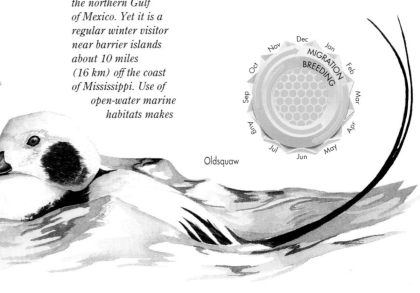

Oldsquaw

abundance of waterfowl in North America. In Kansas, for example, midwinter duck populations increased eightfold between 1949 and 1973. Reservoirs are attractive to waterfowl because they are usually both sufficiently large and deep to remain at least partially ice free well into winter. As a result, migrants winter farther north or at least take longer over the journey to more southerly wintering areas. Such shifts in wintering populations have been called "short-stopping," since the birds stop short of their traditional destination.

Most North American ducks migrate north–south, but the White-winged Scoter has an east–west migration. This species breeds in the northwestern quarter of North America, from central Canada to Alaska, yet 60 percent of these sea ducks migrate east to winter on the Atlantic and only 40 percent migrate to the Pacific coast. This pattern may reflect a past geographical separation of populations on opposite sides of North America by the mid-continent glaciers during the Pleistocene ice ages (see pp. 10–11).

# Birds of prey

*Half a million migrating raptors are funneled through the Isthmus of Panama each year.*

Earlier this century, hunters located areas where migrant soaring birds of prey were concentrated along ridges, such as the Kittatinny Ridge in Pennsylvania, and points of land in coastal areas, such as Cape May, New Jersey. They then lined the roadsides to shoot the birds that flew past. Today, binoculars have replaced the guns as thousands of human visitors are drawn each year to Hawk Mountain on the Kittatinny Ridge and to Cape May to study or simply enjoy the migrants in flight.

Migrant hawks, falcons, and vultures take advantage of rising air currents pushed up along ridges and of constant breezes in coastal areas. Concentrations of shorebird prey, and the leading lines created at the interface between land and water or mountain and valley, also contribute to the value of these unique, narrow migratory routes.

To appreciate fully the significance of such routes, it is important to visualize eastern North America before the Europeans arrived: dominated by forests from the Atlantic to west of the Mississippi. Since stands of trees absorb the sun's heat, there are no thermals over forests. Today, fields and roads can create thermal highways for the birds, but when the land was forested, soaring birds found energy savings only along ridges and shorelines.

The attraction of rising air over the land, coupled with the dramatic narrowing of the land bridge between North and South America at the Isthmus of Panama, concentrates thousands of migrating hawks and vultures as they are funneled to and from their wintering areas each year. Other points at which large numbers of migrating raptors can be seen include Whitefish Point in Michigan, where a narrow corridor separates Lakes Superior, Michigan, and Huron; Hawk Ridge, Minnesota, where raptors skirt the western end of Lake Superior; and coastal areas such as Rio Grande Valley National Wildlife Refuge in Texas.

Two further factors affect raptor migrations: diet and habitat change. Red-tailed and Broad-winged hawks must move south in cold weather, when there are no thermals to use while hunting, and when snow covers their hunting grounds, making mammal prey less common. By contrast, Sharp-shinned and Cooper's hawks, which prey on birds and frequent sheltered forest areas, may remain farther north. Prior to the 1950s, Swainson's and Broad-winged hawks rarely wintered in North America; today they are found with increasing regularity in the southern states. Swainson's Hawks wintering in Florida take advantage of the insects disturbed when fields are plowed.

### DIFFERENTIAL MIGRANTS

Not all raptors migrate, and those breeding nearer the equator are less likely to be migrants than those farther north or south. This holds true even within a species.

The American Kestrel is found throughout most of North and South America and in the West Indies. Northernmost populations – breeding into Canada and Alaska – are migratory, traveling as far as Central America. Populations in the southern United States are often resident, augmented in winter by migrants from the north. The unique Cuban race (above) is also resident. Migrant visitors to Cuba tend to winter along the flyways, a habitat not favored by the residents.

There are also gender differences in this species' movements. Some males winter in the colder parts of the range, subsisting on House Sparrows and mice captured near human habitations. Migrant males return to the breeding grounds earlier than females to establish themselves in the best territories.

**American Kestrel**
*Falco sparverius*
**Wingspan** 21–23 in/53–58 cm
**Weight** 4–4¼ oz/110–120 g
**Journey length** 0–3,700 miles/
0–6,000 km

**Swainson's Hawk**
*Buteo swainsonii*
**Wingspan** 4 ft 2 in/1.28 m
**Weight** 2 lb–2 lb 6 oz/910–1,070 g
**Journey length** 3,750–7,500 miles/
6,000–12,000 km

**Turkey Vulture**
*Cathartes aura*
**Wingspan** 5 ft 7 in/1.7 m
**Weight** 3 lb 5 oz/1.5 kg
**Journey length** 0–3,750 miles/
0–6,000 km

60°N

40°N

S limit of
breeding range of
Swainson's Hawks

20°N

Rio Grande
Valley NWR

Veracruz

N limit of
wintering range of
Turkey Vultures

A few
Swainson's Hawks
winter S Florida

Turkey Vulture

Balboa

A few Swainson's
Hawks winter in
southern U.S. and
Central America

0°

20°S

N Argentina
is major
wintering area of
Swainson's Hawks

40°S

Turkey Vultures
are resident in
S America; a few
migrants in extreme S

60°S

*The Turkey Vulture's* relatively heavy wings, and its habit of nesting later than its southern cousin, the Black Vulture, may be adaptations that allow it to migrate farther. Thousands of Turkey Vultures are funneled through Central America, at times in the company of Swainson's and Broad-winged hawks.

Turkey Vultures are strong fliers, passing through Middle America on the northbound journey in late February to early March and reaching the breeding grounds in the northern U.S. in mid to late March. So punctual are they that the citizens of Hinckley, Ohio, hold a festival to celebrate the return of the "buzzards" each March 15.

**Swainson's Hawks** typically migrate in huge flocks and travel farther than any other North American hawk. These birds of the plains spend their summers in the North American grasslands and winters in the pampas of Argentina.

This hawk was once intimately associated with the swarms of locusts on the pampas. A decline in locust populations may be responsible for its recent altered migration patterns and reduced wintering concentrations here.

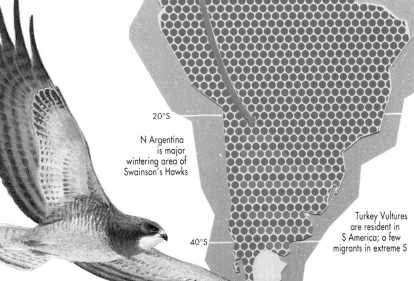

Swainson's Hawk

59

# Cranes

*Habitat loss and shooting take their toll, but migrant cranes suffer most from power lines.*

Only two of the world's fifteen species of cranes occur in the New World: the Sandhill and Whooping cranes. Although both are limited in their migrations to North and Central America, some of those migrations are truly spectacular in terms of distance traveled, precision of return to the same areas, and magnitude of congregations at some stopover and wintering areas. In active flight during migration, cranes may "cruise" at up to 45 mph (70 km/h); they also regularly take advantage of thermals and air currents by gliding (see pp. 18–19) over considerable distances.

Both North American crane species are birds of open, grassy, wetland areas that frequent prairies for feeding. They require open ground partly because of their size but also due to their characteristic behavior of running a few steps with outstretched wings as they take flight. As with many wetland birds, North American cranes have suffered from habitat losses, and like many large birds they have been the victims of hunting and indiscriminate shooting – they are big, easy targets. Close monitoring of migrant Whooping Cranes, bans on hunting in areas where they stop to rest, and the birds' adherence to traditional migration routes

60°N

S limit of breeding range, N races of Sandhill Cranes

Wood Buffalo NP

40°N

Monte Vista NWR

Platte River/ Cheyenne Bottoms

Aransas NWR

20°N

Whooping Crane

*Whooping Cranes ride the thermals to migrate by day, but at times may begin their travels before dawn or continue them after dark.*

*These birds are opportunists, feeding on a wide variety of plant and animal food taken from open land and shallow waters.*

## FROM CANADA TO TEXAS

The known population of Whooping Cranes had declined from 1,500 birds in 1850 to 15 by 1941. By 1946, it had risen to 25, only to slip back to 21 in 1952. By 1958, the population wintering at Aransas National Wildlife Refuge on the Texas coast had grown to 32; by 1965, 44. With conservation efforts, the population reached 75 in 1983 and 138 in 1988.

In 1954, after years of effort, the nesting area of these birds was found, by chance, in Wood Buffalo National Park, Canada. Thus their annual migration to Aransas is about 2,500 miles (4,000 km), flown in segments of 185–300 miles (300–500 km), with several days en route at staging areas in Saskatchewan and Nebraska.

Since 1975, Whooping Crane eggs have been placed in Sandhill nests at Grays Lake National Wildlife Refuge, Idaho, in the hope that any young Whooping Cranes would follow the Sandhills on migration and ultimately breed at Grays Lake. Both species do now migrate together to Bosque del Apache National Wildlife Refuge, New Mexico, but Whooping Cranes do not yet breed at Grays Lake.

**Whooping Crane**
*Grus americana*
**Wingspan** 6 ft 7 in–7 ft 7 in/2–2.3 m
**Weight** 14 lb 2 oz–16 lb 1 oz/6.4–7.3 kg
**Journey length** 2,500 miles/
4,000 km

**Sandhill Crane**
*Grus canadensis*
**Wingspan** 5 ft 11 in–6 ft 11 in/1.8–2.1 m
**Weight** 6 lb 6 oz–12 lb 13 oz/2.9–5.8 kg
**Journey length** 0–2,500 miles/
0–4,000 km

Sandhill Crane

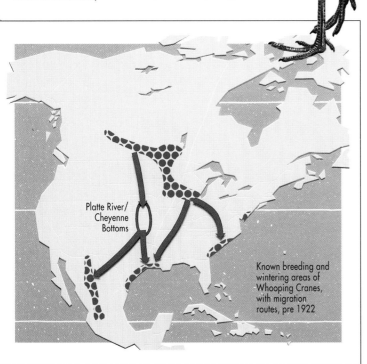

*Although their scattered populations* at prairie potholes and marshes across Canada and the northern U.S. seem small and isolated, on migration Sandhill Cranes flock together at staging areas in incredible numbers.

Along the Platte River in Nebraska, upward of half a million of these birds may congregate on migration each spring before dispersing to their breeding grounds. The din produced by this number of birds, with their grating, rattling calls, can be deafening.

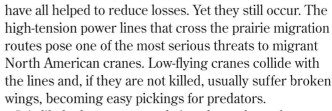

Platte River/
Cheyenne
Bottoms

Known breeding and wintering areas of Whooping Cranes, with migration routes, pre 1922

have all helped to reduce losses. Yet they still occur. The high-tension power lines that cross the prairie migration routes pose one of the most serious threats to migrant North American cranes. Low-flying cranes collide with the lines and, if they are not killed, usually suffer broken wings, becoming easy pickings for predators.

It is likely that crane populations have always been somewhat fragmented as a result of the natural distribution of suitable habitats. Today they are much more so. Sandhill Cranes migrating through the prairie provinces and grain belt of the Midwest once fed on the seeds of prairie grasses and on grasshoppers. Today they fatten on wheat, corn, and barley. Often the cranes' food is waste grain from already harvested fields, but they do also take food from, and cause damage to, unharvested fields near their roosts.

By far the largest wintering concentrations of Sandhill Cranes are found in the high plains of western Texas and eastern New Mexico. These are Lesser Sandhill Cranes, the smallest of the races and those that nest farthest north. Winter flocks of more than 100,000 individuals are not uncommon.

In addition to those visiting the southern high plains, some Sandhill Cranes migrate to similar habitats in central Mexico. Many Lesser Sandhill Cranes come from the Hudson Bay region of Canada, others from as far west and north as western Alaska or eastern Siberia.

The larger Greater Sandhill Cranes nest in the northern United States and southern British Columbia. Greater Sandhill Cranes from western areas join Lesser Sandhill Cranes to winter on the western high plains. Those from the Great Lakes states migrate through the center of the continent east of the Mississippi to the Gulf States, particularly Georgia and Florida, where they are sometimes seen with the resident cranes of that area.

In contrast to northern breeders, these southern cranes winter in their breeding areas. They include the endangered Mississippi Sandhill Crane, which now numbers about 50 birds sandwiched into a pocket of suitable habitat in Jackson County in otherwise urban coastal Mississippi. The Florida Sandhill Crane seems to have fared better on the wet prairies in the center of the state and also feeds regularly on lawns and golf courses. Little is known today of the status of the resident Sandhill Cranes of western Cuba and the Isle of Pines.

# Plovers, gulls, and terns

*Some archetypal sea birds migrate over a sea of grass, not water.*

Contrary to popular belief, there is no such creature as a "seagull." Although many gulls and terns are birds of inshore waters and some rarely leave the open ocean, others, such as Franklin's Gull, nest far from any ocean and during migration cross the "sea" of prairie grasses and farmland that characterizes the American Great Plains – the antithesis of "seagull" habitat.

The power of flight and the ability to migrate give a species freedom to exploit the best habitats for its needs at the optimum times. Given the mid-continent nesting area of Franklin's Gulls, it is reasonable to suppose that they would migrate south to the Gulf of Mexico. In fact, they cross Mexico to winter along the Pacific coast of Central and South America since that is where the best conditions are to be found. The cold waters of the Pacific offer a greater source of food than the warmer waters of the Caribbean and western Atlantic.

Bonaparte's Gulls, too, nest in a seemingly surprising habitat: northern coniferous forests. Like Franklin's Gulls, these birds migrate south through the middle of the continent, but they winter in more "traditional" gull habitats along the Mississippi and other rivers, where they stay until forced south by the rivers' freezing.

Herring Gulls, which nest along the northern Atlantic coast, find acceptable winter quarters closer to home, but illustrate a pattern common to many other birds: young and adults have different migration strategies. Young birds often migrate to the southern states or the West Indies but, as they mature, they winter closer and closer to their nesting

areas. For this reason, birders along the Gulf coast may only get to know the Herring Gull in its immature plumage.

American Golden Plovers, nesting in the northern tundra and wintering in the grasslands of Argentina, typify yet another migratory strategy. Adults leave the nesting area before the juveniles and migrate southeast to the Atlantic coast, then south over the ocean to South America. The later-departing young migrate south through the Mississippi valley, the route taken by all birds on the spring flight north.

Like gulls, terns are opportunists. Not much larger than a swallow, the Interior Least Tern follows major rivers on migration in North America and takes advantage of sandbars for nesting. Other populations use similar habitats along the shores of the Pacific, Atlantic, and Gulf of Mexico.

In part as a result of channelization and damming of rivers, Interior Least Terns have declined to the extent that they are now considered endangered. Habitat destruction has similarly limited California Least Terns. The extent to which these populations are separate, however, is not known. Banding has shown that there is some exchange of Gulf coast and inland birds. More detailed studies of migration routes, wintering areas, and movements between populations are urgently needed.

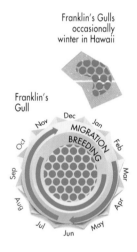

60°N

Franklin's Gulls occasionally winter in Hawaii

Franklin's Gull

MIGRATION
BREEDING

Jan Feb Mar Apr May Jun Jul Aug Sep Oct Nov Dec

---

## MIGRATORY VAGRANTS

Killdeers in the north of the range are migrants; at middle latitudes they may remain through mild winters. In the Gulf States, breeding birds are often resident, some maintaining pair bonds and territories year-round.

These birds often stray from their usual migration routes and have been seen in western Europe, Greenland, and Hawaii. Such vagrancy is no doubt a result of their normal long migrations and association with coastal habitats on migration and in winter. Killdeer nests, by contrast, are usually not near water.

*Its chosen nesting area, together with its pale gray and white plumage, have earned Franklin's Gull (right) the popular name of "Prairie Dove."*

*These birds nest beside marshes and small lakes and feed on surrounding farmland, eating agricultural pests such as wireworms and cutworms. Although their breeding range is restricted, they are numerous – nesting colonies may contain thousands of pairs.*

**Killdeer**
*Charadrius vociferus*
**Wingspan** 18–22 in/46–56 cm
**Weight** 3–3½ oz/90–100 g
**Journey length** 0–6,000 miles/
0–10,000 km

**Franklin's Gull**
*Larus pipixcan*
**Wingspan** 35–37 in/89–94 cm
**Weight** 8–12 oz/230–340 g
**Journey length** 1,900–5,000 miles/
3,000–8,000 km

**Royal Tern**
*Sterna maxima*
**Wingspan** 3 ft 7 in–3 ft 9 in/1.08–1.14 m
**Weight** 1 lb/450 g
**Journey length** 0–5,000 miles/
0–8,000 km

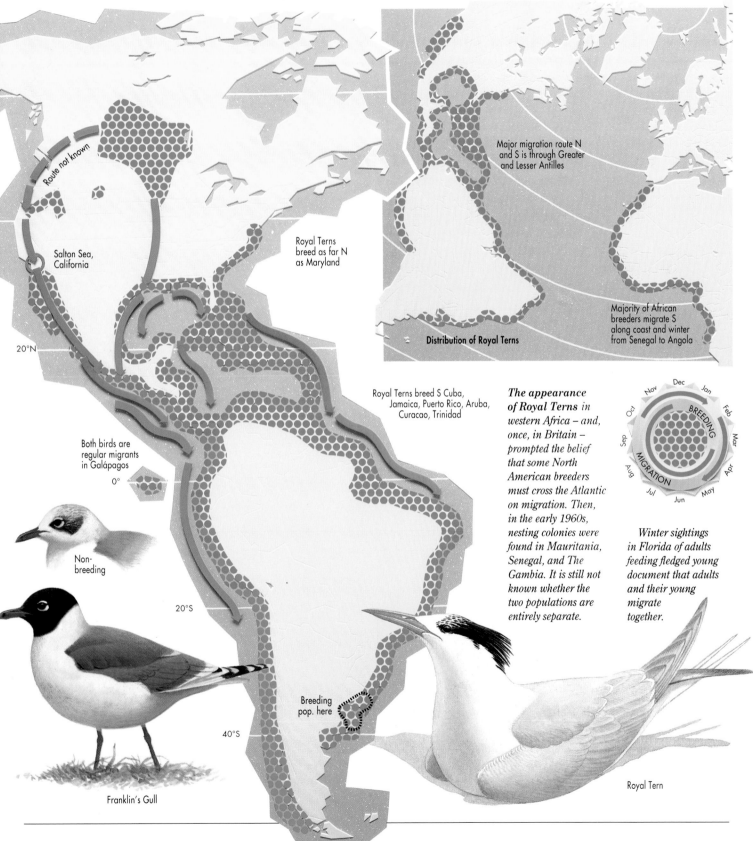

Route not known

Salton Sea,
California

Royal Terns
breed as far N
as Maryland

Major migration route N
and S is through Greater
and Lesser Antilles

Majority of African
breeders migrate S
along coast and winter
from Senegal to Angola

**Distribution of Royal Terns**

20°N

Royal Terns breed S Cuba,
Jamaica, Puerto Rico, Aruba,
Curacao, Trinidad

Both birds are
regular migrants
in Galápagos

0°

Non-
breeding

20°S

Breeding
pop. here

40°S

Franklin's Gull

*The appearance
of Royal Terns* in
western Africa – and,
once, in Britain –
prompted the belief
that some North
American breeders
must cross the Atlantic
on migration. Then,
in the early 1960s,
nesting colonies were
found in Mauritania,
Senegal, and The
Gambia. It is still not
known whether the
two populations are
entirely separate.

*Winter sightings
in Florida of adults
feeding fledged young
document that adults
and their young
migrate
together.*

BREEDING
MIGRATION
Jan Feb Mar Apr May Jun Jul Aug Sep Oct Nov Dec

Royal Tern

# Owls

*The world's smallest owl is also one of the family's only migrants.*

It is doubtful whether all populations of any North American owl are truly migratory: the vast majority of owls are either nonmigratory or nomadic. The Barred and Great Horned owls and Eastern and Western screech-owls are among the most sedentary of birds, with no evidence of seasonal movement and little of any wandering. Others are both migratory and nomadic. Nomadism is linked to a species' dependence on specific prey: Northern Saw-whet Owls, for example, depend on vole populations to the extent that adults show little faithfulness to past nesting sites and select instead an area where vole populations are high. These owls also regularly migrate south in winter.

Most owls are nocturnal in both their habitual activities and the timing of their seasonal movements. Some, such as the Snowy Owl, migrate alone; others, including the Elf Owl, travel in small groups. Several species – among them the Boreal, Snowy, Great Gray and Northern Hawk owls – are irruptive (see pp. 168–69), with some southward movement every year and larger numbers of birds moving farther south in years of low prey populations. A few banded individuals of these species have returned to the same southern locations in subsequent winters, so can be classed as true migrants.

The truest migrants among North American owls include the northern populations of the Burrowing, Short-eared, Long-eared and Northern Saw-whet owls. Long-eared Owls are often long-distance migrants, with individuals from Minnesota, Montana, and Saskatchewan recorded wintering in Mexico. The Elf Owl is also migratory in the north of its range although its migration is not well documented: in the southwestern United States, small groups have been seen in late summer, prior to the fall migration, and they are generally not seen again from late September to March (Arizona) or early May (New Mexico).

It is likely that there are age and gender differences in the seasonal movements of some species, but it can be difficult both to get reliable information about these secretive, nocturnal birds and also to interpret it effectively. One source of data derives from birds killed on highways. Of 68 Northern Saw-whet Owls killed one winter near Cape May, New Jersey, 54 were less than a year old. Is this real evidence of partial migration, the juveniles having left the adults behind, or is it simply that juveniles are less adept at avoiding traffic than adults? The sex ratio of these birds was almost 1:1, suggesting that both males and females migrate.

*One of the most cosmopolitan birds in the world, the Short-eared Owl (above) is found in appropriate habitat on every continent except Australia and Antarctica. Although it is resident in middle latitudes, the northern-nesting populations migrate to the wet grassy meadows of the south. These birds are more active during the day than most owls, hunting both day and night when food is scarce. They defer hunting until dusk where competition is rife, waiting until wintering Northern Harriers have completed their day of hunting in the same habitat.*

*With the Barn Owl, the Short-eared Owl illustrates well the* nomadic nature of owl migration. *Although northern Short-eared Owls regularly migrate, the species' success at establishing populations in places as far flung as Hawaii, on Ponape in the Caroline Islands, in the Galápagos, and in the Falkland Islands – in addition to its appearance on Bermuda, Grand Turk, and many other islands in the Caribbean – suggests considerable wandering from traditional migration routes.*

*Barn Owls do not usually migrate, although banded individuals have been found hundreds of miles from the site of banding. These may be young birds, in search of a territory in which to establish themselves.*

**Short-eared Owl**
*Asio flammeus*
**Wingspan** 3 ft 2 in–3 ft 8 in/96–112 cm
**Weight** 11–13 oz/310–370 g
**Journey length** 0–3,000 miles/
0–5,000 km

**Elf Owl**
*Micrathene whitneyi*
**Wingspan** 15 in/38 cm
**Weight** 1–1½ oz/25–41 g
**Journey length** 0–300 miles/
0–500 km

**The Elf Owl** *is the world's smallest owl – at 6 inches (15 cm) long, it is shorter than some sparrows. It nests and roosts in holes abandoned by woodpeckers in saguaro cactus (below), cottonwood, mesquite and even – occasionally – in telegraph poles in the arid southwestern U.S. and northern Mexico.*

*Elf Owls feed on large moths, crickets, beetles, and other insects, which they may take in their feet while in flight. This dependence on insect prey forces the owls nesting in colder parts of the range to migrate.*

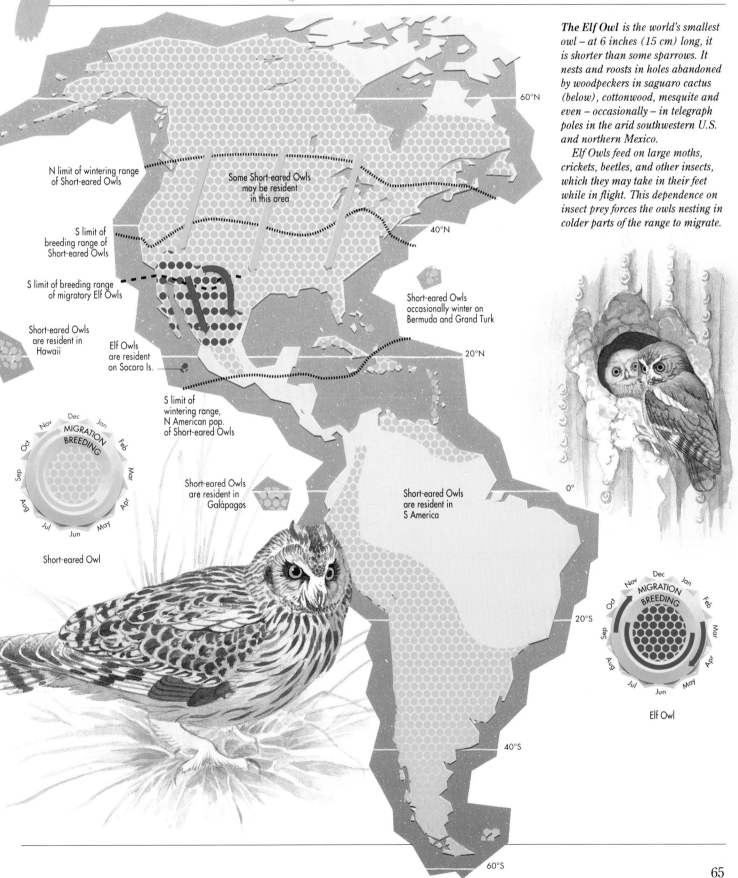

N limit of wintering range
of Short-eared Owls

Some Short-eared Owls
may be resident
in this area

S limit of
breeding range of
Short-eared Owls

S limit of breeding range
of migratory Elf Owls

Short-eared Owls
are resident in
Hawaii

Elf Owls
are resident
on Socoro Is.

Short-eared Owls
occasionally winter on
Bermuda and Grand Turk

S limit of
wintering range,
N American pop.
of Short-eared Owls

Short-eared Owls
are resident in
Galápagos

Short-eared Owls
are resident in
S America

60°N
40°N
20°N
0°
20°S
40°S
60°S

MIGRATION
BREEDING

Short-eared Owl

MIGRATION
BREEDING

Elf Owl

# Nightjars

*Hibernation is a viable alternative to migration for one bird.*

The nightjars of North America are varied in their migratory and wintering strategies. Chuck Will's Widows and Whippoorwills of eastern North America are often solitary nocturnal migrants, but may travel in loose flocks. Common Nighthawks migrate by day or night in loose flocks. The Common Poorwill comes as close as any bird to hibernation, with northern populations migrating and southern populations going into torpor during periods of inclement weather. The Pauraque, limited to the warmer areas of northern South America and north into Central America and Texas, has no need to migrate.

As aerial insect-eaters, all migrant nightjars are capable of feeding en route. Chuck Will's Widows also consume warblers, small swallows, hummingbirds, and sparrows, presumably captured during nocturnal migration. This ability to eat small birds, along with their larger size, probably allows a few Chuck Will's Widows to spend the winter in the southern United States.

The spring migrations of Chuck Will's Widows and Whippoorwills in the eastern United States are punctuated by their characteristic calls during stops of one to a few days as they progress northward. The impression of "migratory flocks" results from the sudden appearance of many calling birds in an area; it may be that the birds' flights are simply timed to occur simultaneously.

A second factor that contributes to the impression of flocking is the response of birds when they encounter a barrier, such as one of the Great Lakes. They follow the land as far as they can and, if they reach the tip of a peninsula – Point Pelee, Ontario, for example – they may pause for a few hours to a few days to wait for favorable winds before attempting to cross the lake. This allows many individuals to congregate, although whether the "flocks" departing from such areas are cohesive is not known.

*The Common Nighthawk is known colloquially as the "bull-bat" because of an imagined batlike quality to its flight and the "bull-like" roar made by its wings when it pulls out of a dive.*

*The migrations of these birds take them to and through the West Indies, en route* *to their wintering grounds in Central and South America. They regularly migrate in large numbers, often in flocks of thousands. Their diurnal hawking for insects, migration in flocks, and the common name "hawk" worked against these birds in the late 19th and early 20th centuries, when they* *were shot for sport and food, and as predators.*

*Three factors have contributed to their recovery: a ban on shooting; recognition of their value in the control of populations of insects classed as pests; and the species' ability to make use of gravel rooftops as nest sites.*

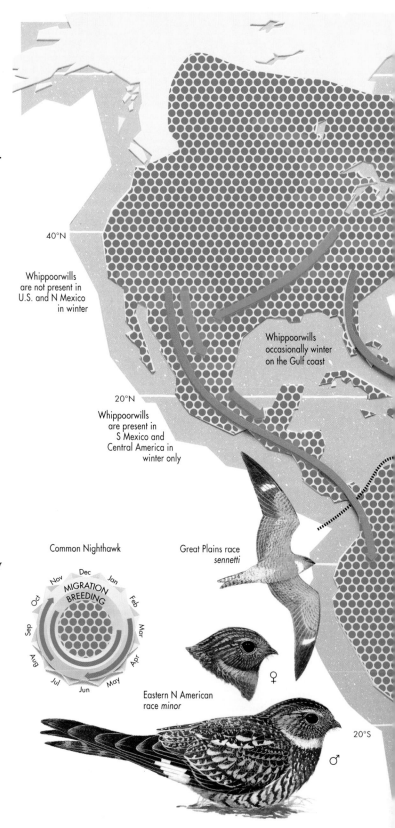

40°N

Whippoorwills are not present in U.S. and N Mexico in winter

Whippoorwills occasionally winter on the Gulf coast

20°N

Whippoorwills are present in S Mexico and Central America in winter only

Common Nighthawk

MIGRATION
BREEDING

Dec Jan Feb Mar Apr May Jun Jul Aug Sep Oct Nov

Great Plains race *sennetti*

Eastern N American race *minor*

20°S

**Common Nighthawk**
*Chordeiles minor*
**Wingspan** 21–24 in/54–61 cm
**Weight** 2¼ oz/62 g
**Journey length** 2,500–6,800 miles/
4,000–11,000 km

**Whippoorwill**
*Caprimulgus vociferus*
**Wingspan** 18–19½ in/46–50 cm
**Weight** 1¾–2 oz/51–55 g
**Journey length** 300–3,750 miles/
500–6,000 km

**Common Poorwill**
*Phalaenoptilus nuttallii*
**Wingspan** 14–16 in/36–40 cm
**Weight** 1¾ oz/52 g
**Journey length** 0–2,500 miles/
0–4,000 km

## THE SLEEPING ONE

Northern Common Poorwills migrate to southern California, New Mexico, Arizona, and into Mexico to avoid cold weather and food shortages. Poorwills from the southwestern United States, by contrast, overwinter by hibernating, hence the Hopi Indians' name for the bird, *Hölchko*, meaning "the sleeping one." A hibernating Poorwill with a ⅓ ounce (10 g) fat reserve can sustain itself for 100 days, whereas the same reserve sustains a non-torpid Poorwill for only 10 days. The hibernating Poorwill is capable of spontaneous arousal at temperatures near freezing but requires seven or more hours to wake up fully. This inability to respond quickly to danger is one of the major disadvantages of torpidity; their camouflage coloration and choice of sheltered recesses in which to hibernate help Poorwills survive (below).

Migratory Poorwills, too, may spend spells of cold weather in a torpid state.

*S limit of breeding range of Common Nighthawks*

*Until early in the 19th century, the Whippoorwill (below) and Common Nighthawk were thought to be one and the same bird. The characteristic call of the Whippoorwill was explained as simply the nocturnal call of the Common Nighthawk.*

*"Father of American ornithology," Alexander Wilson, differentiated the two species and first described the gradual northward migration of the Whippoorwill from its wintering areas in Central America to the breeding grounds of the eastern U.S. and southern Canada.*

Whippoorwill

♂

♀

MIGRATION
BREEDING
Jan Feb Mar Apr May Jun Jul Aug Sep Oct Nov Dec

# Swifts, swallows, and martins

*Migrant martins owe their survival to the prompt action of the citizens of New Orleans.*

As aerial insect-eaters, swallows and martins, together with swifts, are able to feed on the wing; both groups therefore migrate by day and roost at night. Small flocks of swallows characteristically travel together; swifts are more likely to congregate in flocks of thousands of birds. At times, mixed flocks of migrating swallows and swifts are clearly visible. Most swallows nest, winter, and stop over on migration near water which provides a steady source of insects and a buffer against extremes of temperature. Swifts also feed near water, but often roost in hollow trees or, since the arrival of Europeans in the New World, in chimneys well away from water.

Most North American swifts are long-distance migrants, with only the White-throated Swift wintering as far north as central California, southern Arizona, and New Mexico. The winter home of Chimney Swifts was a mystery well into this century. Each fall, Chimney Swifts gathered in flocks of several thousand and then disappeared. In an effort to learn more of their movements, more than 375,000 were banded at several stations in the late 1930s and early 1940s. The effort paid off in 1944 when 13 bands from Chimney Swifts were handed into the American embassy in Lima, Peru, as having come from some

*Purple Martins are long-distance migrants. In the 1980s large winter roosts were discovered in Brazil, and through a cooperative effort, the birds were sprayed at night with long-lasting fluorescent dye.*

*Banders in North America captured martins as they reached nesting areas and examined the birds under ultraviolet light to search for dye-marked individuals. Several were found, proving that birds from many areas of the eastern U.S. used the same roosts in winter.*

Purple Martin

*With its exceptionally long wings and tiny legs, the Chimney Swift cannot take off in still air from horizontal ground, since it hits the surface with its wings and cannot achieve lift. It roosts clinging to a vertical surface and, to take flight, drops from its perch. Once airborne, its flight is agile and strong.*

*Swifts are highly gregarious and migrate in large flocks to wintering areas in South America. In recent years, a few individuals have begun to winter in southern California.*

Chimney Swift

**Chimney Swift**
*Chaetura pelagica*
**Wingspan** 12–12½ in/31–32 cm
**Weight** ⅞ oz/24 g
**Journey length** 1,900–6,000 miles/
3,000–10,000 km

**Tree Swallow**
*Tachycineta bicolor*
**Wingspan** 12–13½ in/31–34 cm
**Weight** ⅔ oz/20 g
**Journey length** 600–3,400 miles/
1,000–5,500 km

**Barn Swallow**
*Hirundo rustica*
**Wingspan** 12½–13½ in/32–34 cm
**Weight** ⅔ oz/19 g
**Journey length** 1,550–6,800 miles/
2,500–11,000 km

## EXPANSIONIST TENDENCIES

The Barn Swallow is one of the world's most widespread bird species, nesting across Eurasia and North America, where it has expanded its range in recent decades. Unlike many species adversely affected by deforestation, Barn Swallows have proven capable of taking advantage of the clearing of southern forests and the construction of interstate highways, and find good nest sites under bridges and in culverts.

This increased availability of suitable nest sites has resulted in the expansion of the birds' North American breeding range southward as far as the Gulf coast and

Barn
Swallow

northern Florida. A few Barn Swallows are now wintering in southern Florida, but most must migrate farther south to the West Indies, Central and – in particular – South America.

Evidence suggests that a few migrants from North America are staying in the southern hemisphere year-round: there appears to be a nesting colony in Buenos Aires province, Argentina.

A few Tree Swallows winter as far S as Trinidad, Colombia, Venezuela, and Guyana

MIGRATION
BREEDING

Dec
Nov
Jan
Oct
Feb
Sep
Mar
Aug
Apr
Jul
May
Jun

Tree Swallow

*Nesting as far north as the tree line in Alaska and Canada, and wintering as far south as northern South America, Tree Swallows are long-distance migrants among swallows. Many, however, regularly winter closer to home, only moving as far as the Gulf States, Bahamas, and Greater Antilles.*

*These birds typically migrate by day in small flocks, feeding en route and often stopping to roost in wetland areas where they may spend the night clinging to the stems of marsh grasses.*

"swallows killed by Indians on the Yanayaco River," a tributary of the Amazon in northeastern Peru. Five of those 13 birds had been banded by Ben B. Coffey and boy scouts working with him in Memphis, Tennessee.

As the northernmost nesting swallows in North America, Tree Swallows are well adapted to coping with the sudden arrival of cold weather. By nesting and roosting in old woodpecker holes and housing provided by humans, they are insulated against cold nights. And, unlike most swallows, they will eat fruit when insects are scarce. Tree Swallows also regularly winter farther north than other swallows, many remaining in the southern United States. A few have survived winters as far north as coastal Massachusetts.

Tree Swallows generally migrate south by the most direct route, following the leading lines (see pp. 34–35) offered by major rivers, coastlines, and mountain ranges. East Coast and Great Lakes birds, for example, usually migrate along the East Coast and through the West Indies as far as Central America. Those from the Canadian prairie provinces and the north-central United States migrate through the Mississippi valley to the northern Gulf coast, with some continuing across the Gulf of Mexico to Central America. Those nesting in the Rockies often winter in Mexico. Populations in coastal California may be resident.

The spring arrivals of Purple Martins have been well chronicled. "Scouts" – typically adult males – arrive first from wintering areas in Amazonia, often appearing in nesting areas in February when freezing weather and snow can still be anticipated. Most females and second-year birds arrive a few weeks later. Early arrival gives the males an advantage in obtaining the best nest site and best mate, but mortality can be high if the weather takes a turn for the worse.

Late-summer departure from the breeding areas is less well documented. Those unsuccessful at nesting gather first, roosting near rivers and lakes where food is plentiful. They are later joined by early fledglings and their parents, and finally by those that have re-nested after failure or have attempted or completed a second nesting. Gradually, these flocks move south through river basins, coalescing into flocks of thousands. Near the Gulf coast, enormous flocks often roost at night on bridge supports where, at dusk, returning birds may be victims of rush-hour traffic. At one such roost near New Orleans, citizens successfully lobbied to have fences erected to prevent the birds from flying into the path of oncoming cars.

# Hummingbirds

*Nectar-sipping for food forces many of these colorful birds south in winter.*

The hummingbirds are an extremely diverse and generally highly colored New World group of at least 341 species. They will eat small insects, but feed primarily on nectar, which they take by hovering seemingly motionless at flowers and sipping with their somewhat tubular tongues through needlelike, often curved bills.

Many species are tropical and, since flowers abound all year round at these latitudes, have no need to migrate. They include the Ruby-topaz Hummingbird and the smallest bird in the world, the 2-inch (6-cm) long Bee Hummingbird, which is restricted to Cuba and the Isle of Pines. Some 21 species, however, breed in North America, and because of their diet, most must migrate in winter. A few avoid it by going into a state of torpor to survive short periods of exceptionally cold or wet weather, in the manner of Common Poorwills (see pp. 66–67).

Male hummingbirds tend to be highly territorial and often migrate north in spring a week or more in advance

**Ruby-throated Hummingbirds** are the only species to breed in eastern North America and also one of the most widespread hummingbirds, nesting as far north as New Brunswick and Nova Scotia and wintering from Mexico to Panama.

Males (which do in fact have brilliant red throats; those of females are usually white in color) leave the breeding areas first, often as early as July. Females and young, by contrast, may linger within the breeding range into October. These birds take a variety of routes to the Central American wintering areas. These include traveling through Florida and Cuba, through Mexico, or incredibly, across the Gulf of Mexico from the northern Gulf coast to the Yucatán peninsula and beyond. For this nonstop flight of some 500 miles (800 km) the Ruby-throats put on substantial quantities of fat and may be aided by tail winds.

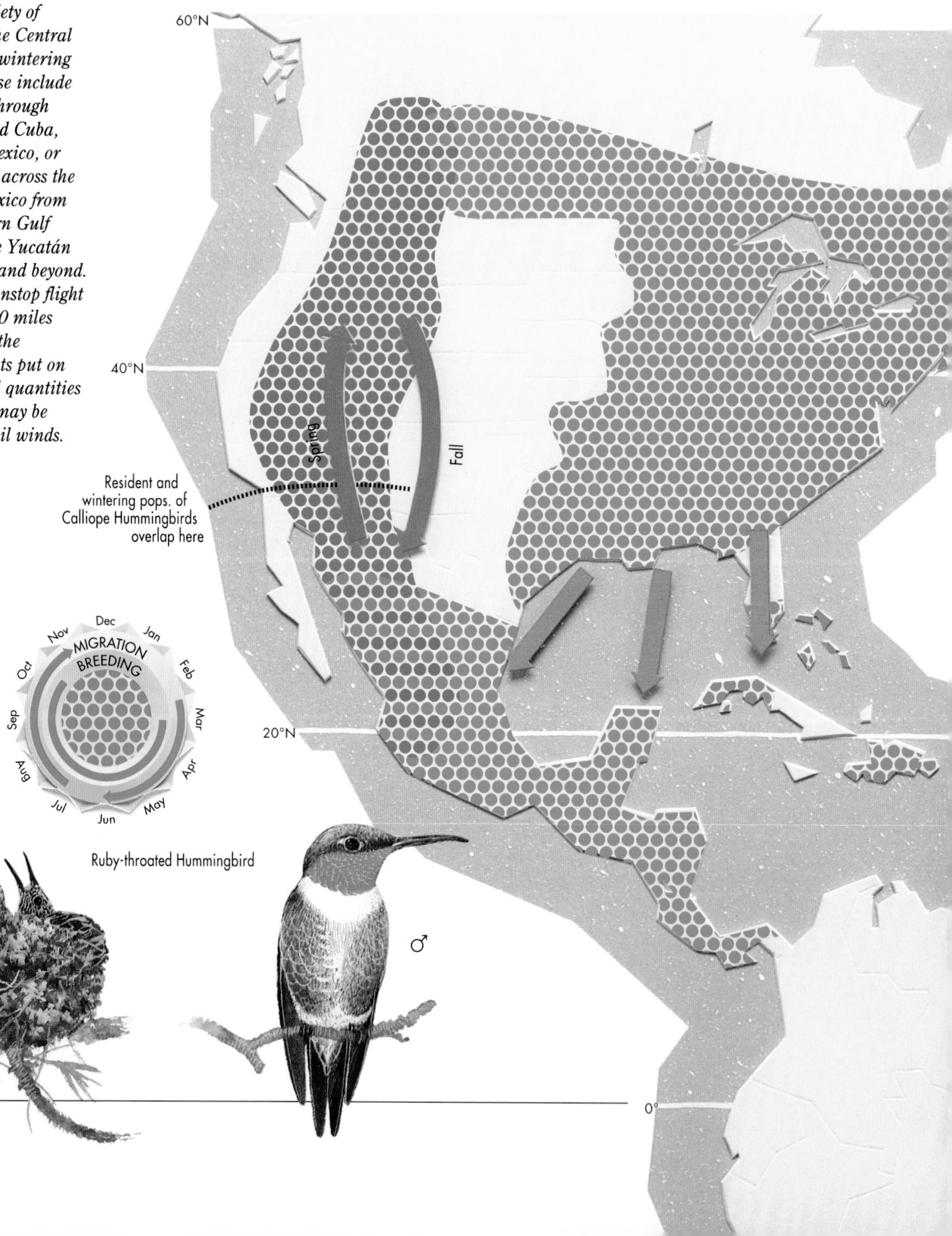

60°N

40°N

Spring

Fall

Resident and wintering pops. of Calliope Hummingbirds overlap here

20°N

Nov  Dec  Jan

Oct  MIGRATION  Feb
  BREEDING

Sep  Mar

Aug  Apr

Jul  Jun  May

♀

Ruby-throated Hummingbird

♂

0°

**Ruby-throated Hummingbird**
*Archilochus colubris*
**Wingspan** 4–4¾ in/10–12 cm
**Weight** ¹⁄₁₀–⅛ oz/3–3.5 g
**Journey length** 0–3,500 miles/
0–6,000 km

**Calliope Hummingbird**
*Stellula calliope*
**Wingspan** 4½ in/11 cm
**Weight** ¹⁄₁₁–¹⁄₁₀ oz/2.5–3 g
**Journey length** 1,250–3,000 miles/
2,000–5,000 km

of females to establish their territories for the season. Males also leave incubation of the eggs and rearing of the young to the females and begin moving south on the fall migration at least two weeks before the females and young. The flight south must take place well in advance of cold weather, not because these tiny birds cannot tolerate cold, but because of rapidly diminishing food supplies at this time of year. The return migrations of hummingbirds in spring seem perfectly timed with the blooming of hummingbird-pollinated food plants. In the southeastern United States, for example, Ruby-throated males arrive just as cross vine and red buckeye are blooming in late March.

Although many North American hummingbirds migrate to Mexico or Central America, some, such as Anna's and Costa's hummingbirds – both of which are restricted to the West Coast – remain in the breeding areas of southern California year-round. Other species show seasonal movements other than spring and fall migration. The Broad-tailed Hummingbirds of the southern Rocky Mountains, for example, arrive in spring and breed at low elevations. Once the snow has melted at higher elevations, the birds often move up the mountain slopes to areas where there is a fresh abundance of flowers, build a new nest and attempt to rear a second brood.

Nonbreeding Anna's Hummingbirds often wander north into British Columbia and, more rarely, to southern Alaska. Following nesting, other species too may stray far from their breeding grounds, taking advantage of food supplies wherever they can be found. In October 1984, a Green Violetear, a species which rarely occurs north of Mexico, made its way as far as an Arkansas backyard.

An amazing number and diversity of western hummingbird species now regularly winter along the Gulf coast and occasionally farther inland in the southeastern states. They seem to be most prominent in New Orleans, where yards are often planted to include varieties that bloom year-round. In some cases Rufous Hummingbirds have appeared at bird feeders – for these tiny birds, a bottle or dropper containing sugar water is the best food that humans can provide – in late summer before the summer-resident Ruby-throated Hummingbirds have departed.

Once these "foreigners" have been sighted, observers maintain their hummingbird-friendly yards, and as a consequence, keep their exotic visitors through the winter. Which route these errant birds take from their breeding areas is not known, but at least some that have been banded have returned to the southeastern states in subsequent winters, although often to quite distant sites. Among the most common of these birds are Rufous Hummingbirds, which breed in forests and on the edges of woodlands and thickets in the northwestern United States through British Columbia and as far north as southern Alaska. It may be that their adaptation to Alaska's cool and variable climate has made them particularly suited to the mild winter weather of the southeastern states.

Calliope Hummingbird

*Tiny even for a hummingbird,* at some 3 inches (7.5 cm) from beak to tail, the Calliope is North America's smallest hummingbird and the smallest bird of any species breeding north of the Mexican border.

It nests at a broad range of elevations from south-central British Columbia and southwestern Alberta, south through the Pacific northwest to northern Baja California, and east to western Colorado; all populations winter in central Mexico.

On migration, these birds are most common in mountain meadows, but occur in a variety of habitats, including (often in spring though rarely in fall) the streamside vegetation of the tall mesas of western Texas.

Spring migration tends to be slow as these birds keep pace with the blooming of nectar-producing flowers.

MIGRATION
BREEDING
Jan Feb Mar Apr May Jun Jul Aug Sep Oct Nov Dec

# Woodpeckers

*The search for sweet sap forces sapsuckers south in winter.*

Most of the world's woodpeckers are more or less sedentary. In North America, however, there are some strongly migratory species, a few that seasonally leave northern or high-elevation areas of their nesting range, and others that are somewhat irruptive (see pp. 166–69). Woodpeckers' seasonal movements can usually be related directly to food supplies.

The Yellow-bellied and Red-naped sapsuckers and northern populations of the Northern Flicker and Red-headed Woodpecker are long-distance migrants. In late summer, Northern Flickers gather in loose flocks and leave their breeding areas, migrating by day to the southern states. These migrations are no doubt a consequence of their ground-feeding habits and their inability to find food in snow-covered areas. Southern populations are resident.

Red-naped Sapsuckers breed from southwestern Canada to southern New Mexico in the Rocky Mountains and eastern Cascades. In late summer these sapsuckers leave northern and higher-elevation breeding areas to winter in the same latitudes as southern breeders, in Baja California and central Mexico.

Red-headed Woodpeckers also regularly leave northern parts of their breeding range, again largely due to food shortages. In summer these birds feed extensively on fruit and insects, but they undergo a significant seasonal shift in diet, eating more acorns in winter. This change may mean that movements of southern breeders are simply irruptive.

Short-distance migrants include the mountain-breeding Lewis' Woodpecker, which moves in loose groups to lower elevations in winter, and Downy and Hairy woodpeckers. The status of the movements of these two woodpeckers is uncertain: they may be true migration, irruption, or simply a dispersal of young birds from the breeding areas. Banding records reveal that some individuals move as much as 800 miles (1,300 km) from their site of banding in the fall. Return movements, however, are less well documented.

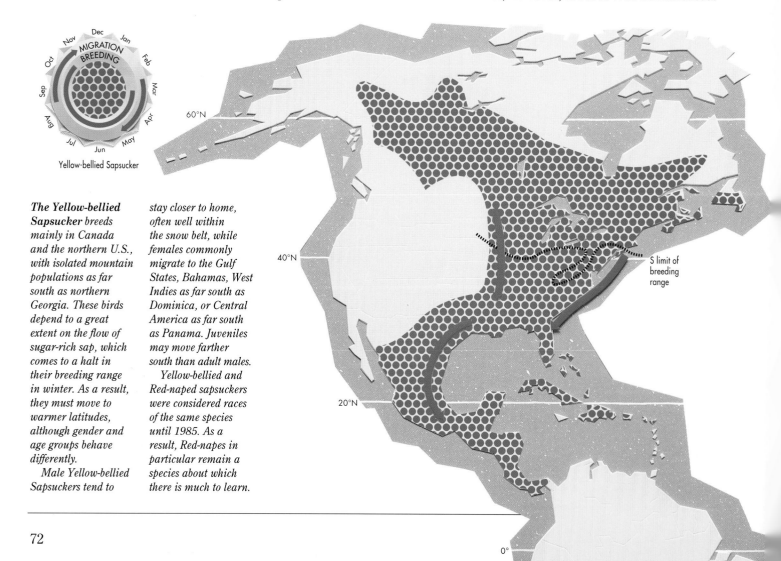

Yellow-bellied Sapsucker

*The Yellow-bellied Sapsucker breeds mainly in Canada and the northern U.S., with isolated mountain populations as far south as northern Georgia. These birds depend to a great extent on the flow of sugar-rich sap, which comes to a halt in their breeding range in winter. As a result, they must move to warmer latitudes, although gender and age groups behave differently.*

*Male Yellow-bellied Sapsuckers tend to* *stay closer to home, often well within the snow belt, while females commonly migrate to the Gulf States, Bahamas, West Indies as far south as Dominica, or Central America as far south as Panama. Juveniles may move farther south than adult males.*

*Yellow-bellied and Red-naped sapsuckers were considered races of the same species until 1985. As a result, Red-napes in particular remain a species about which there is much to learn.*

S limit of breeding range

**Yellow-bellied Sapsucker**
*Sphyrapicus varius*
**Wingspan**  14–16 in/35–40 cm
**Weight**  1¾ oz/50 g
**Journey length**  0–2,200 miles/
0–3,500 km

*Although sapsuckers are solitary, nocturnal migrants, and are rarely heard on migration and in their wintering areas, their passage, stopover and wintering areas are well marked by characteristic sap wells. These are horizontal or vertical rows of tiny holes that sapsuckers excavate in the living tissues below the surface layers of bark. A horizontal row of sap wells indicates that a sapsucker has been there looking for sap. Once a sweet vein is found, the sapsucker begins excavating sap wells in a vertical row the better to exploit the flow. Injured or diseased trees release more sugars into their sap to combat infection, thus are more apt to attract the continued attention of sapsuckers, whose extensive sap wells can give the tree a wafflelike appearance (below).*

# Tyrant flycatchers

*Wanderers return to the breeding grounds already paired.*

**Vermilion Flycatcher**
*Pyrocephalus rubinus*
**Wingspan** 10–11 in/25–27 cm
**Weight** ½ oz/14 g
**Journey length** 0–2,500 miles/
0–4,000 km

Many tyrant flycatchers – a strictly New World group of perching birds – are unremarkable in plumage color and some are undistinguished in voice. They are often, however, champions at long-distance migration. Of the 390 or so species, 31 breed in North America and most are migratory, with some, including the Eastern Kingbird, breeding as far north as Canada and migrating as far as South America.

The Eastern and Western kingbirds and Scissor-tailed Flycatcher are open-country birds that typically migrate by day, often in flocks of 100 or more individuals. By contrast, the tiny Traill's, Least, and Yellow-bellied flycatchers, which characteristically forage from perches within the cover of vegetation, migrate under cover of darkness.

Eastern Kingbirds are common breeding birds in open areas of eastern North America. In southern Canada their nesting populations span the continent, from British Columbia to Newfoundland. In spite of this broad breeding range, on migration all populations funnel into the northern Gulf coast. From the Gulf States, the migration route continues to narrow, as most birds cross the Gulf of Mexico to Yucatán and low-lying areas of Central America en route to the wintering grounds of northern South America. Some may move south along the coast of eastern Mexico, a few stray to the east and appear in eastern Cuba and other islands of the Greater Antilles, and occasionally, even in the Bahamas.

Western Kingbirds breed across most of North America west of the Mississippi, from the southern provinces of Canada in the north to northern Mexico in the south. They winter in Central America from Mexico to Nicaragua and occasionally in Costa Rica. They also wander along the Atlantic coast from South Carolina to Florida and, more commonly, in southern Florida including the Keys.

Eastern Phoebes move much shorter distances than most other flycatchers, rarely reaching the Bahamas or Cuba. Most winter in the southern United States, and in mild winters many remain farther north, ready to move back into their breeding areas as soon as possible in spring. Three factors probably contribute to this tolerance of colder climates: the temperature-buffering effect of the wetland habitats that they frequent; their opportunist nesting tendencies, which have enabled them to choose sheltered nest and roost sites close to human habitations, in farm buildings, bridge supports, and porches; and their ability to consume some fruit when insect food is scarce.

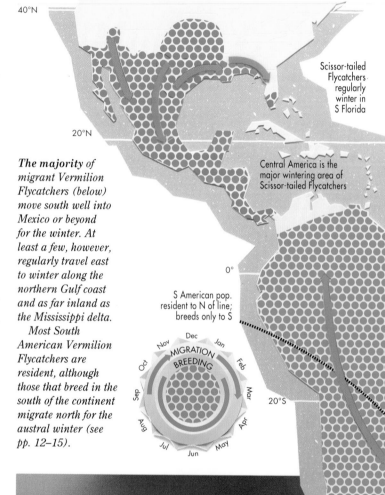

*The majority of migrant Vermilion Flycatchers (below) move south well into Mexico or beyond for the winter. At least a few, however, regularly travel east to winter along the northern Gulf coast and as far inland as the Mississippi delta.*

*Most South American Vermilion Flycatchers are resident, although those that breed in the south of the continent migrate north for the austral winter (see pp. 12–15).*

Scissor-tailed Flycatchers regularly winter in S Florida

Central America is the major wintering area of Scissor-tailed Flycatchers

S American pop. resident to N of line; breeds only to S

**Scissor-tailed Flycatcher**
*Tyrannus forficata*
**Wingspan** 14–15½ in/36–39 cm
**Weight** 1½ oz/43 g
**Journey length** 1,250–2,500 miles/
2,000–4,000 km

# Thrushes

*Robins arrive right on time.*

**American Robin**
*Turdus migratorius*
**Wingspan** 14½–16½ in/37–42 cm
**Weight** 2¾ oz/77 g
**Journey length** 0–4,000 miles/
0–6,400 km

More than any other North American bird, the American Robin symbolizes the arrival of spring, largely perhaps because of the predictable timing of its spring migration. On its northward journey, this thrush is a relatively slow migrant, following the 37°F (2°C) isotherm to appear in northern regions immediately after the spring thaw, when average temperatures rise to this level. It may take the birds 11 weeks to travel the 3,000 miles (4,800 km) from Iowa to Alaska. Males migrate earlier than females and arrive in northern states by March, but do not begin singing until the females arrive in April.

Most North American thrushes, including the Veery, and the Swainson's, Hermit, and Gray-cheeked thrushes – as well as the American Robin – are nocturnal migrants. In contrast to the American Robin, the Gray-cheeked Thrush is a relatively fast traveler, only reaching the southern United States in late April and arriving back at the Alaskan breeding grounds within a month.

Varied Thrushes nest from Alaska to northern California and typically winter in western states to the south of their nesting areas. They have also been seen at bird feeders in many eastern states in winter. Most thrushes forage on the ground for insects, snails, and earthworms. The Hermit Thrush, however, includes more fruit in its diet than other species and commonly winters in the southeastern states.

*American Robins breed over most of North America south of the tree line. They are especially common in the urban centers of the east, although they do not breed in coastal areas from Louisiana to New York, including most of peninsular Florida. (There is an isolated resident population in Tampa.) American Robins winter from southern Canada to Guatemala, Cuba, and the Bahamas.*

*They are nocturnal migrants, traveling in small groups of well-spaced birds. Feeding stops on the fall migration are often at hackberry, sugarberry, or other fall-fruiting trees. In spring the birds halt to replenish reserves in grassy areas.*

Scissor-tailed
Flycatcher

Juvenile

*Usually breeding in the southern Great Plains and wintering in Mexico and Central America, the Scissor-tailed Flycatcher (above) also regularly winters in southern Florida. On migration it wanders widely, even to southern Canada.*

*Empty nests outside the Great Plains, in eastern Mississippi for example, are common and suggest that birds are paired when they begin the spring migration. The return of birds to areas outside their normal range may indicate fidelity to routes and sites of successful nesting.*

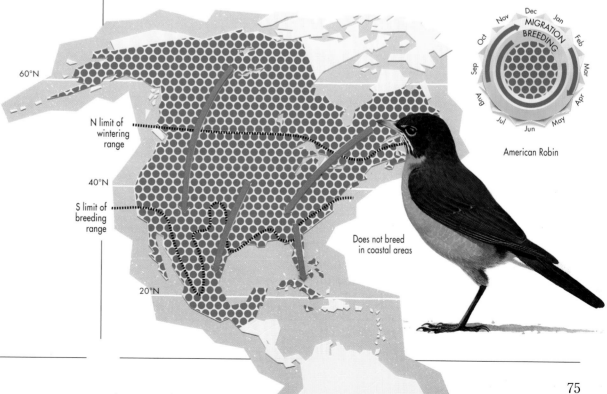

60°N

N limit of
wintering
range

40°N

S limit of
breeding
range

20°N

Does not breed
in coastal areas

American Robin

# Vireos

*Cross-continent routes betray ancient distributions.*

**Red-eyed Vireo**
*Vireo olivaceus*
**Wingspan** 9½–10½ in/24–27 cm
**Weight** ½–¾ oz/14–24 g
**Journey length** 2,500–6,000 miles/
4,000–10,000 km

Uniquely American, the vireos are a group of some 46 foliage-gleaning forest birds with uncertain family connections. Vireo species are about equally divided between North and South America, with one, the Black-whiskered Vireo, largely restricted to the West Indies. Several vireos make long migratory journeys; all are nocturnal migrants.

North American vireos can be divided into species that breed in either eastern or western North America and have similarly divided eastern and western wintering areas. Black-capped, Bell's, and Gray vireos, for example, are generally western breeders that winter in northwestern Mexico. The White-eyed, Yellow-throated, and Philadelphia vireos are eastern species with migration routes through the Greater Antilles, along the east coast of Mexico or across the Gulf to Yucatán.

Some species' migrations, however, seem to betray the manner in which ranges have changed and expanded over the generations. All populations of the Red-eyed Vireo, which is an eastern species that has spread as far as the Pacific Northwest, migrate to South America via the Gulf States. By contrast, all breeding populations of the Warbling Vireo, a western species that has extended east, winter from western Mexico into southwestern South America. A complex east–west breeding and wintering distribution is shown by the Solitary Vireo, eastern populations of which sometimes winter in the Gulf States, while western populations more frequently winter in Mexico and Central America.

The dynamic nature of species' breeding ranges and the role of migration in range expansion may be indicated by recent northward expansion of the breeding range of White-eyed Vireos. Strong favorable spring winds over the Gulf of Mexico during migration may have caused such migrants to "overshoot" their usual destinations.

Two factors contribute to the permanent expansion of a breeding range: the movement of large numbers of birds and either an improvement in climate or the adaptation by birds to the prevailing climatic conditions. Vagrant Black-whiskered Vireos from the West Indies are occasionally found in Alabama and Mississippi in spring, when there are strong southerly winds. But, since the numbers of this species reaching the Gulf Coast are very small, there is no evidence of Black-whiskered Vireos breeding, by contrast to their White-eyed relatives.

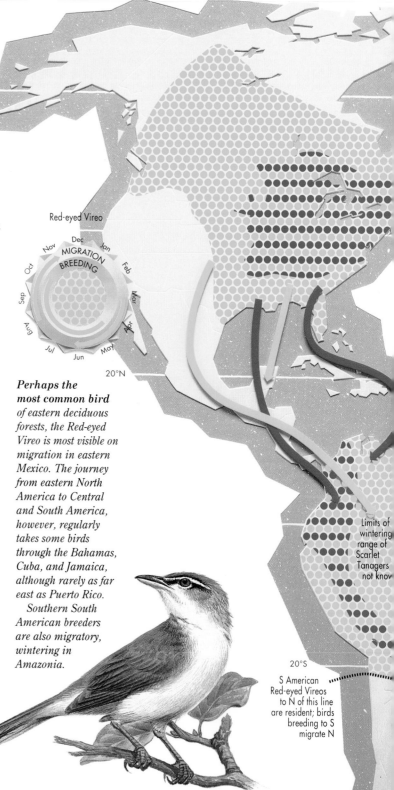

60°N

Red-eyed Vireo

Nov Dec Jan
Oct MIGRATION Feb
Sep BREEDING Mar
Aug Apr
Jul Jun May

20°N

*Perhaps the most common bird of eastern deciduous forests, the Red-eyed Vireo is most visible on migration in eastern Mexico. The journey from eastern North America to Central and South America, however, regularly takes some birds through the Bahamas, Cuba, and Jamaica, although rarely as far east as Puerto Rico.*

*Southern South American breeders are also migratory, wintering in Amazonia.*

Limits of wintering range of Scarlet Tanagers not know

20°S

S American Red-eyed Vireos to N of this line are resident; birds breeding to S migrate N

40°S

# Tanagers

*Tree felling puts pressure on forest nesters.*

**Scarlet Tanager**
*Piranga olivacea*
**Wingspan** 11–12 in/28–30 cm
**Weight** 1 oz/29 g
**Journey length** 600–4,350 miles/
1,000–7,000 km

Confined to the New World, the tanagers breed in South and Central America and the West Indies. Because they are largely fruit-eaters, most are limited to the tropics, and North American breeders usually migrate to winter in warmer latitudes. However, some tropical species and populations also migrate. These movements, such as those of the Black-and-white Tanager of northwestern Peru, are a response to seasonal rainfall cycles and consequent limited availability of food.

The Scarlet and Summer tanagers of eastern North America are birds that favor extensive forest and have no doubt declined as the forests have been altered and fragmented. Summer Tanagers are long-distance migrants, breeding almost into southern Canada and wintering as far south as Brazil and Bolivia. Western Tanagers are also forest birds, traditionally nesting in the open coniferous and mixed woodlands of western North America and wintering from Mexico south as far as Costa Rica.

*Scarlet Tanagers nest in the northern U.S. and southern Canada and migrate to South America, wintering from Colombia to Bolivia.*

*This species is a trans-Gulf/trans-Caribbean migrant. Some individuals leave from the northern Gulf coast and fly to the Yucatán peninsula; some fly directly to Honduras and Costa Rica on route to wintering areas in northwestern South America. Others reach the wintering areas via the Greater and Lesser Antilles, although they rarely reach as far east as Puerto Rico on migration. Unlike*

## DEFORESTATION

More than 80 percent of the forest present in the lower Mississippi valley 250 years ago has been cleared; what remains has been dramatically altered in age and composition, with old, mixed-species forests replaced by young, single-species plantations. There have been similar losses throughout eastern North America as a result of cutting, wetland drainage, and the construction of dams. At the same time, Dutch elm disease and chestnut blight reduced tree numbers as efficiently as the chainsaws.

All species that breed in mature forests have been affected to a greater or lesser extent. Not only have nest sites been destroyed, but the numbers of insects on which these birds feed themselves and their young have also declined. Once numerous Ivory-billed Woodpeckers, for example, may have been extinct since the 1940s in most of North America. A few may survive in Florida, Mississippi, and Alabama and there is a protected population in Cuba.

Diminution of the eastern forest and the ravaging of neotropical forests have more far-reaching effects than these losses to breeding birds. Ecologists are still pondering several questions. To what extent has forest loss changed migration routes for species that used the forests as winter homes? How many species now lack suitable winter habitat? How have the clearing of coastal forests for cities and the deforestation of West Indian islands affected transient migrants? And how many neotropical migrants are limited in their migrations by a lack of suitable habitat along the route?

Foresters argue that the continent has more forest than at any time this century, but for many species that may not be enough.

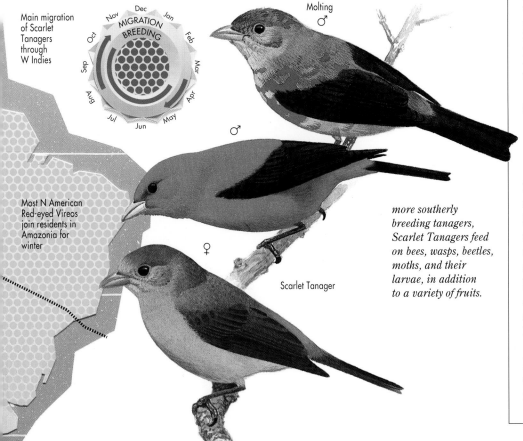

Main migration of Scarlet Tanagers through W Indies

Most N American Red-eyed Vireos join residents in Amazonia for winter

Molting ♂

♂

♀

Scarlet Tanager

*more southerly breeding tanagers, Scarlet Tanagers feed on bees, wasps, beetles, moths, and their larvae, in addition to a variety of fruits.*

# Wood warblers

*Brood parasitism has severely affected one of North America's rarest migrants.*

The wood warblers are one of the most significant groups of New World migrants, with 57 species breeding in North America. These birds are primarily insect-eaters, and although many may fly by day over continental North America, most are nocturnal migrants as they cross the Gulf of Mexico. On their northbound journey, the warblers often move only a short distance in the morning and spend much of the day foraging to replenish their energy reserves.

Since they are so dependent on insects, many warblers do not arrive in southeastern states until the leaves on which insects and their larvae feed are well developed on the trees. For this reason it is difficult for southern birders

to spot them. As they move northward, they reach the Midwest and northern areas at an earlier stage of leaf development, making them much easier to study.

A few warblers supplement their diet with berries and seeds and are thus capable of wintering at more northern latitudes. The Pine Warbler, for example, breeds in eastern North America from southern Canada to southern Florida and the Gulf coast and regularly winters as far north as Arkansas, Tennessee, and Virginia. Similarly, the eastern race of the Yellow-rumped Warbler – the Myrtle Warbler – breeds in the northern coniferous forests of eastern North

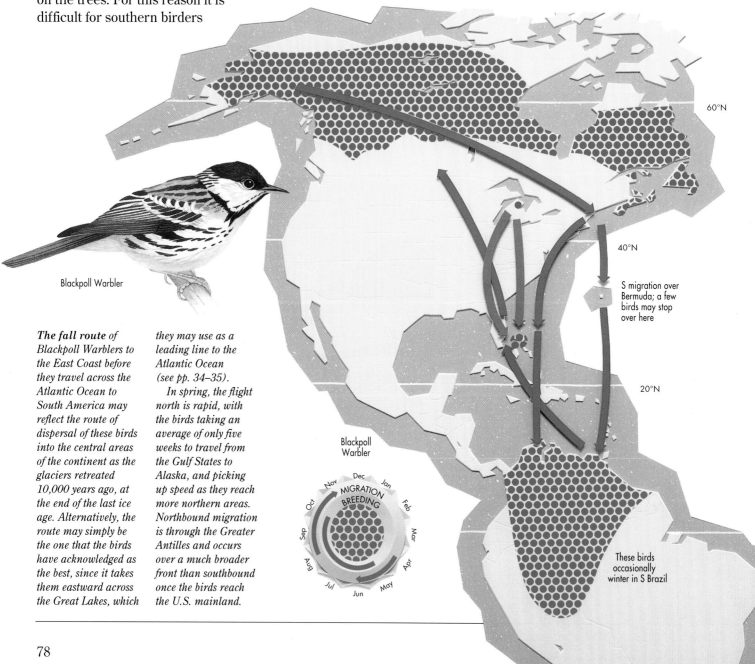

Blackpoll Warbler

Blackpoll Warbler

60°N

40°N

S migration over Bermuda; a few birds may stop over here

20°N

MIGRATION
BREEDING

Nov Dec Jan
Oct Feb
Sep Mar
Aug Apr
Jul Jun May

These birds occasionally winter in S Brazil

**The fall route** of Blackpoll Warblers to the East Coast before they travel across the Atlantic Ocean to South America may reflect the route of dispersal of these birds into the central areas of the continent as the glaciers retreated 10,000 years ago, at the end of the last ice age. Alternatively, the route may simply be the one that the birds have acknowledged as the best, since it takes them eastward across the Great Lakes, which

they may use as a leading line to the Atlantic Ocean (see pp. 34–35).

In spring, the flight north is rapid, with the birds taking an average of only five weeks to travel from the Gulf States to Alaska, and picking up speed as they reach more northern areas. Northbound migration is through the Greater Antilles and occurs over a much broader front than southbound once the birds reach the U.S. mainland.

**Blackpoll Warbler**
*Dendroica striata*
**Wingspan** 8–9¾ in/20–24 cm
**Weight** ⅓ oz/11 g
**Journey length** 2,500–5,000 miles/
4,000–8,000 km

**Kirtland's Warbler**
*Dendroica kirtlandii*
**Wingspan** 8½ in/21 cm
**Weight** ½ oz/14 g
**Journey length** 1,200 miles/
1,900 km

America and winters regularly through much of the eastern and southeastern United States.

Cape May Warblers are medium-distance migrants, leaving their breeding areas of central and eastern Canada, New York, Maine, and Vermont to winter in the Bahamas and Greater Antilles. Few of these birds reach Central or South America. Blackpoll Warblers, by contrast, are remarkable long-distance migrants. These common breeding birds of the spruce-fir forests across North America from Alaska to Nova Scotia migrate to northern South America. They follow different routes in spring and the fall, and the fall route in particular has intrigued ornithologists for decades.

Most Blackpolls migrate southeast to the Canadian maritime provinces and the New England coast. From there it was believed that the birds made a trans-Atlantic flight of more than 2,500 miles (4,000 km) to the coast of South America. To make such a flight, these birds are known to take on energy reserves as fat, increasing in weight from a norm of about ⅓ ounce (11 g) to as much as ⅔ ounce (20 g). While some may make the long flight over the Atlantic, enough records have accumulated to demonstrate that some do fly down the East Coast as far as Cape Hatteras, North Carolina, before striking out for the Bahamas and points farther south. A few seem to continue down the East Coast all the way to Florida.

## ON THE CRITICAL LIST

Kirtland's Warblers have only been known for around 150 years and have always been rare. Their status today is critical. The problems facing them are overwhelming: a small nesting area, cowbird parasitism, a small wintering area, and the hazards of migration.

The invasion of the Brown-headed Cowbird as the forests were fragmented and livestock introduced was nearly fatal. By the 1960s, more than 70 percent of Kirtland's Warbler nests were being parasitized. Today trapping of cowbirds is helping, and warbler decline has been halted, but the species has not responded with population increases.

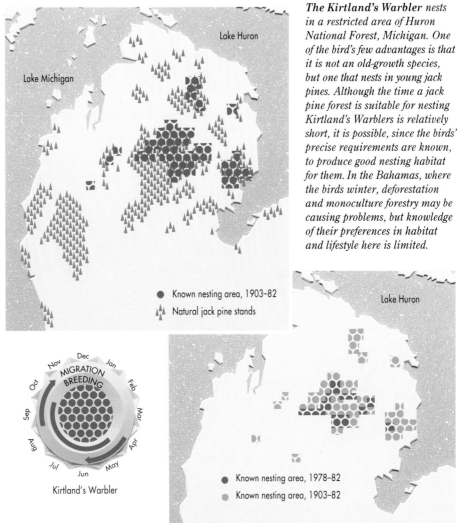

Lake Huron

Lake Michigan

● Known nesting area, 1903–82
▲▲ Natural jack pine stands

*The Kirtland's Warbler nests in a restricted area of Huron National Forest, Michigan. One of the bird's few advantages is that it is not an old-growth species, but one that nests in young jack pines. Although the time a jack pine forest is suitable for nesting Kirtland's Warblers is relatively short, it is possible, since the birds' precise requirements are known, to produce good nesting habitat for them. In the Bahamas, where the birds winter, deforestation and monoculture forestry may be causing problems, but knowledge of their preferences in habitat and lifestyle here is limited.*

Lake Huron

● Known nesting area, 1978–82
● Known nesting area, 1903–82

Kirtland's Warbler

# Buntings, grosbeaks, and starlings

*Finches move south when snow blankets food stocks.*

As seed-eaters, the buntings, grosbeaks, and other New World finches are capable of wintering much farther north than insect-eating birds. Some of these are regular winter visitors to bird feeders well into Canada. Indeed, evidence is mounting that the growing popularity of putting out seed for birds is even beginning to influence their seasonal movements. Evening Grosbeaks, for example, were once considered to be east–west migrants, nesting in the region of the Great Lakes and wintering along the northern Atlantic coast. In recent decades, however, they have appeared, admittedly in irruptive rather than truly migratory fashion, in large numbers throughout the eastern United States.

Although most bird migration typically takes place in fall and spring, in some species it can be renewed in midwinter in response to poor weather or failing food supplies. In periods of excessive snow and cold, American Tree Sparrows may be observed flying near streetlights at night and are often found dead as a result of collisions with radio antenna guy wires, phenomena that normally occur during the birds' nocturnal migration in fall and spring. And the Dark-eyed Junco is commonly known as the "snow bird," since its

**The Slate-colored Junco** nests from Alaska to Labrador and in the mountains of eastern North America as far south as northern Georgia; it is the most common wintering junco in the eastern states.

Oregon Juncos breed from British Columbia south to northern Baja California and winter chiefly in the western states and provinces, although individuals regularly appear in eastern Canada and many eastern states.

Migrant and winter flocks often contain 10 to 30 individuals, with distinctive social ranking within a flock.

Oregon Junco

Dark-eyed Junco

MIGRATION
BREEDING

Nov Dec Jan
Oct Feb
Sep Mar
Aug Apr
Jul May
Jun

Slate-colored Junco

60°N

N limit of wintering range of Dark-eyed Juncos

Gray-headed Junco

40°N

S limit of breeding range of Dark-eyed Juncos

20°N

**Dark-eyed Junco**
*Junco hyemalis*
**Wingspan** 9½–10 in/24–25 cm
**Weight** ⅗–⁹⁄₁₀ oz/18–26 g
**Journey length** 0–2,500 miles/
0–4,000 km

**White-throated Sparrow**
*Zonotrichia albicollis*
**Wingspan** 9–10 in/23–25 cm
**Weight** ⁹⁄₁₀ oz/26 g
**Journey length** 0–2,800 miles/
0–4,500 km

**European Starling**
*Sturnus vulgaris*
**Wingspan** 15½ in/39 cm
**Weight** 2⅘–3 oz/80–85 g
**Journey length** 0–600 miles/
0–1,000 km

## A SIMILAR PATH

The European Starling was released in New York's Central Park in 1890 simply because Shakespeare-lover Eugene Scheifflin wanted to introduce to North America all the birds mentioned in Shakespeare's works. Starlings began life in the New World by nesting on the American Museum of Natural History. In less than a century, they had dispersed and were successfully established – often to the detriment of native cavity-nesting birds – from the Atlantic to the Pacific and from Alaska to Mexico.

Migrants in Europe travel from northeast to southwest, and a similar path has been established in eastern North America.

European Starling

Juvenile

appearance regularly seems to coincide with the first snowfalls at middle latitudes.

There are gender and age differences in the migrations of some finches, including the Dark-eyed Junco. Until 1983 the five races of this species were considered as separate species: the Slate-colored, Oregon, White-winged, Gray-headed, and Guadalupe juncos. The fact that there is some interbreeding among the races has led them to be regarded now as one species. Female Dark-eyed Juncos of all races regularly migrate an average of 300 miles (500 km) farther south than males. Adults also seem to migrate greater distances than juveniles. Juncos are strongly area-faithful, returning each year to the area of their birth to breed.

The behavior of the House Finch clearly demonstrates how ranges expand and migratory behavior changes. These birds were once considered sedentary and, indeed, most populations still do not migrate. In the early 1940s, House Finches from the southern Californian race were introduced to the New York City region. They quickly became established and, in cold winters, shifted their range south and west. One House Finch banded in New York was recovered in North Carolina. And at least some banded birds returned to their northern breeding areas in spring, so they can be considered true migrants. Others that dispersed established new populations so that the species has now expanded throughout eastern North America. Meanwhile, populations in the west have also expanded eastward, taking advantage of bird feeders and other human changes to the landscape such as buildings and reservoirs.

*Two color types,* or morphs, of the White-throated Sparrow have been recently identified and studied: those with distinct white striping on the head and those with buff-colored striping. The differences are not fully understood, but it has been suggested that individuals select opposite color morphs as mates.

These birds tend to migrate by the easiest north–south route and do not travel great distances. As seed-eaters and frequent bird-feeder visitors, they can remain as far north as southern Canada throughout the winter. White-throated Sparrows are strongly area-faithful, returning to nest and to winter in the same locations every year.

Although it is not certain whether winter flock members migrate together, once they are all on the wintering grounds, definite dominance hierarchies are established.

White-throated Sparrow

# American blackbirds and orioles

*Death and disease give huge flocks of these birds a bad name.*

It may be the association of the color black with death, or the birds' winter numbers and flocking behavior in open country, or public health warnings of disease associated with large blackbird roosts that give North American "blackbirds" a negative image. Whatever the reason, enormous fall migrant and wintering flocks annually perpetuate the problem.

In North America the name "blackbird" is often misused and misunderstood. Among the "true" blackbirds are the orioles and meadowlarks with which few people find fault; the cowbirds, which as brood parasites are universally unpopular; and such typical blackbirds as the Common, Boat-tailed, and Great-tailed grackles, and the Red-winged, Yellow-headed, Brewer's, and Rusty blackbirds. Certainly, not all black birds are blackbirds: the crows, European Starlings, Lark Buntings, Pileated Woodpeckers, and others belong to several different families.

Loss of and damage to grain in harvest fields and threats to human health are the major causes of concern with migrant blackbirds. Accusations against the birds, which begin when premigratory flocks congregate, build as migrants become more evident, and reach a peak in winter, prior to the birds' dispersal back to the breeding grounds.

These problems may have been exacerbated by changing patterns of agriculture and irrigation, which have led to population increases and new migration patterns. Now that irrigation has meant crops can be grown in areas of former desert, Yellow-headed Blackbirds, for example, winter farther north than they did 50 years ago. Against the grain losses, which can be serious for the farmers affected, must be balanced the flocks' destruction of enormous quantities of harmful insects and weed seeds.

The threat to human health derives from the fungal disease histoplasmosis, which is potentially lethal. The fungus causing the disease grows in nitrogen-rich soil, such as that found beneath blackbird roosts. It is, however, dispersed by the wind only when the soil is disturbed, not "carried" by the birds to humans.

Millions of blackbirds have been killed and acres of trees leveled to discourage blackbirds from roosting in specific areas, in the name of histoplasmosis prevention. In fact, clearing vegetation from a roost may create a more serious threat by exposing the nitrogen-rich soils to the wind. The major reasons for concern over blackbird roosts are often the smell and noise, in combination with ignorance of the role these birds play in natural ecosystems.

## NEST PIRACY

The Brown-headed Cowbird lays its eggs in the nests of other species, causing their chicks to fail and their populations to decline (see p. 79). Now found in most of North America, this cowbird moves south in winter, flocking by midsummer for migration and often joining flocks of other blackbird species in their winter roosts.

Brown-headed Cowbird

**Brown-headed Cowbird**
*Molothrus ater*
**Wingspan** 11½–14 in/29–35 cm
**Weight** 1½–1¾ oz/39–49 g
**Journey length** 0–1,250 miles/
0–2,000 km

**Red-winged Blackbird**
*Agelaius phoeniceus*
**Wingspan** 12–14½ in/30–37 cm
**Weight** 1½–2¼ oz/41–64 g
**Journey length** 0–1,550 miles/
0–2,500 km

**Bobolink**
*Dolichonyx oryzivorus*
**Wingspan** 10–12½ in/25–32 cm
**Weight** 1¼–1⅔ oz/37–47 g
**Journey length** 5,000–6,800 miles/
8,000–11,000 km

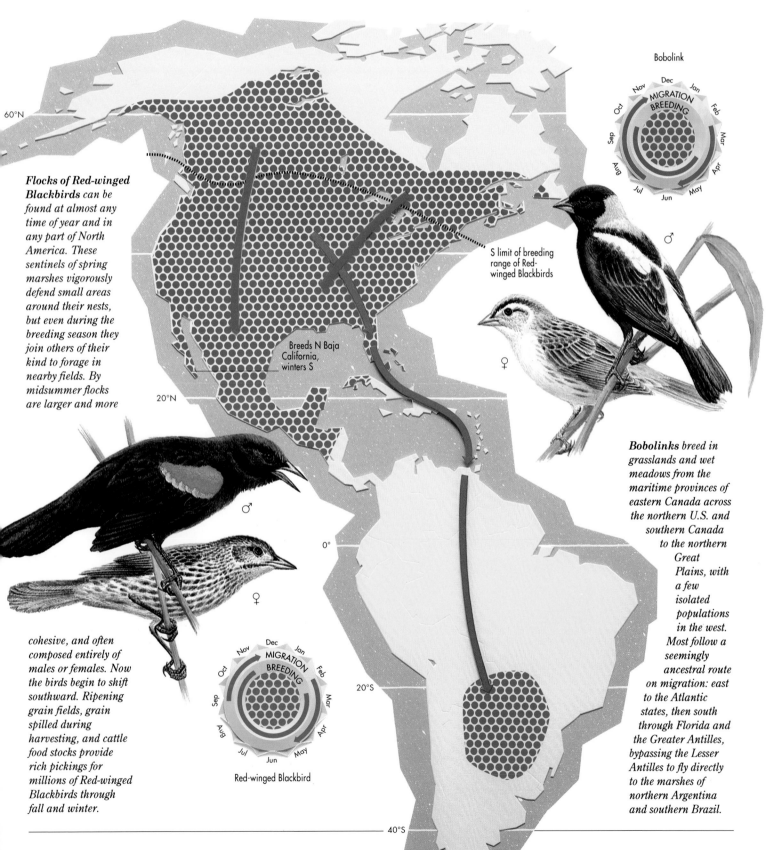

*Flocks of Red-winged Blackbirds can be found at almost any time of year and in any part of North America. These sentinels of spring marshes vigorously defend small areas around their nests, but even during the breeding season they join others of their kind to forage in nearby fields. By midsummer flocks are larger and more cohesive, and often composed entirely of males or females. Now the birds begin to shift southward. Ripening grain fields, grain spilled during harvesting, and cattle food stocks provide rich pickings for millions of Red-winged Blackbirds through fall and winter.*

Breeds N Baja California, winters S

S limit of breeding range of Red-winged Blackbirds

*Bobolinks breed in grasslands and wet meadows from the maritime provinces of eastern Canada across the northern U.S. and southern Canada to the northern Great Plains, with a few isolated populations in the west. Most follow a seemingly ancestral route on migration: east to the Atlantic states, then south through Florida and the Greater Antilles, bypassing the Lesser Antilles to fly directly to the marshes of northern Argentina and southern Brazil.*

Bobolink

Red-winged Blackbird

# EURASIAN MIGRANTS

Long before written records were kept, people in Europe were aware of bird migration. The birds were important as a source of food, and their comings and goings were the practical prompts for agricultural operations such as plowing and sowing. Although they were aware of the birds, those ancient watchers can have had little idea of the extent and complexity of their movements over the Old World and beyond.

In this chapter, the importance of Africa as a reception area for birds summering in Eurasia recurs time after time. A huge number and variety of species, involving an immense total of individuals, leave Europe and Asia for Africa every fall. Best estimates suggest that five billion individuals from more than 200 species regularly migrate to sub-Saharan Africa. But Africa is vast, and the migrant populations are spread over some 7¾ million sq miles (20 million km²) – perhaps one migrant per acre, taking into account the birds lost on the journey south. And Africa is not the only destination. The pages that follow detail a complex web of movement within Eurasia, involving both the oceans and other continents.

*Cranes fly across France* on their migratory journey between the breeding grounds of northern Europe and their Spanish winter quarters.

# Patterns of migration

*The vast landmass of the continent of Africa dominates Eurasian migration patterns.*

**M**ovements of Old World birds are primarily north to south – and are dominated, to the south, by Africa. Fewer species use the Indian subcontinent, but many others regularly migrate to the Far East – and a few reach as far as Australia. A major determinant in these patterns has been the way in which the continents have drifted over the last few million years. Africa has always been close to southern Europe and western Asia; India collided with the Asian landmass only 30 million years ago; and Australia has been isolated for some 45 million years.

In Africa and in other southern areas, the prime habitat afforded by the rainforest is not the target area of long-

## HOT SPOTS

These hot spots include islands or headlands where lost small migrants may be seen. Such birds are also funneled through mountain passes, which – with narrow stretches of water – are good sites for soaring migrants. Wetlands are excellent places to watch waterfowl and shorebirds.

| | |
|---|---|
| ① | Fair Isle Observatory, Shetland |
| ② | Cape Clear Observatory, Eire |
| ③ | Spurn Observatory, England |
| ④ | W Jutland peninsula, Denmark |
| ⑤ | Falsterbo/Ottenby, Sweden |
| ⑥ | Hanko, Finland |
| ⑦ | Rybachiy, Lithuania |
| ⑧ | Texel, the Netherlands/Heligoland, Germany |

*The Old World migration systems* cover half the globe. They have been molded by the history of the birds involved and modified by their physical environment.

Barriers to migration that are insignificant for one species are insuperable for another. The relatively short crossing of the middle of the Mediterranean holds no terrors for warblers, chats, and other long-distance small migrants, but it is testing for soarers such as storks or broad-winged birds of prey. (In fact, some White Storks and Honey Buzzards do use a middle route made possible by the short distance between Cap Bon in Tunisia and Sicily.)

Mountain ranges are physical barriers that may split routes used by migrants or channel them. Foothills often ensure reliable thermals for soaring birds. Mountainous areas often furnish a variety of habitats

which migrants may find similar to their summer homes. Dotterels from northern Europe, for example, winter in the Atlas Mountains of the Maghreb.

Deserts are not so hospitable. Here, the chances of generalist foragers, such as many long-distance migrants, surviving for any long period of time are remote. Deserts must be skirted, or overflown, as quickly as possible.

The physical problems that birds have to conquer on a route are seldom apparent from a map. A distance of 600 miles (1,000 km) may be a different prospect in the spring, when the habitat is productive and welcoming, from the fall when the land is dry and barren. And the northerly winds that helped in the fall may effectively double the distance to be covered in spring. Knowing where you are going may be half the battle, but finishing the journey is far from assured.

*Around five billion land birds of nearly 200 species breeding in Europe and Asia migrate every year. Some 50,000 birds cross each mile (1.6 km) of Mediterranean coastline every night during the peak fall migration.*

*The Wryneck, an ant-eater, is unusual among woodpeckers in that it is a long-distance migrant, breeding as far north as northern Scandinavia and traveling to central Africa and southern Asia for the winter.*

*Birds of the Siberian race of Willow Warbler make an annual migration of up to 7,000 miles (11,300 km) to their winter homes in eastern Africa – a remarkable journey for a bird weighing ⅓ ounce (10 g) or less.*

| | | | |
|---|---|---|---|
| **9** Blakeney Point/Cley Marshes/ Minsmere/Dungeness, England | **16** Camargue, France/Col de Bretolet, Switzerland | **25** Cap Bon, Tunisia | **35** Royal Chitwan NP, Nepal |
| **10** Isles of Scilly, England/ Ile d'Ouessant, France | **17** Po marshes, Italy | **26** Straits of Messina, Italy | **36** L. Ozero Khanka, China/Russia |
| **11** Lac de Grand Lieu, France | **18** Lake Neusiedler, Austria | **27** Azraq, Jordan | **37** Shiretoko NP, Japan |
| **12** Col de l'Organbidexka, France/Spain | **19** Hortabagy, Hungary | **28** Suez, Egypt | **38** Shinhama Waterfowl Preserve, Japan |
| **13** Tagus estuary, Portugal | **20** Danube delta, Romania | **29** Eilat, Israel | **39** Yangtze estuary, China |
| **14** Coto Doñana, Spain/Strait of Gibraltar | **21** Strait of Bosporus, Turkey | **30** Banc d'Arguin, Mauritania | **40** Taiwan |
| **15** Cap Formentor, Majorca | **22** Black Sea coasts, Turkey/Russia | **31** Senegal delta, Senegal | **41** Mai Po marshes, Hong Kong |
| | **23** Volga delta/Caspian Sea, Russia | **32** Lake Chad, Nigeria/Chad | **42** Dalton Pass, Philippines |
| | **24** Capri, Italy | **33** Ngulia Lodge, Kenya | **43** Fraser's Hill, Malaysia |
| | | **34** Lahore, Pakistan | |

distance migrants. The rainforest lacks seasonality, and many species have evolved to fill every available ecological niche. Long-distance migrants cannot be sufficiently specialist to compete with the residents and are therefore more likely to be found on the fringes. Here, there are seasonal differences – not winter and summer, but rainy and dry – and the local birds are more generalist and less specialist. Migrants are opportunists, able to exploit such resources as locust swarms or the insects that lose their homes when tracts of land are burned. They are also common in areas where habitats have been modified by human agricultural practices.

Long-distance migrations are by no means confined to direct north–south routes, and birds wintering in southern Africa, for example, may have traveled from the far east of Asia. The routes of enormous numbers of birds take them across the continent from east to west (and sometimes from west to east). This is because the climate in the center of the larger landmasses such as Eurasia is more extreme than on the fringes. This is particularly so for the western part of Europe, which is warmed by the Gulf Stream. Many shorebird and waterfowl species simply move to areas where the winters are ice-free, which may be to the west of their breeding ranges, but not far, if at all, to the south. Thrushes and some finches are among the birds that undertake such movements.

Migration is not confined to land birds. There are, in addition, long-distance movements by sea birds across and around the oceans that fringe Eurasia (see pp. 154–55).

⇨ Major route

# Ducks

*"First come, first served" means that female Pochards make longer migrations than males.*

Large numbers of ducks of many species breed in the northern parts of Europe and Asia and migrate south to warmer areas for the winter. They include representatives of the three major types of ducks: dabbling ducks, such as the Green-winged Teal, Wigeon, and Pintail; diving ducks, including the Tufted Duck, Pochard, and Greater Scaup; and sea ducks, among them Goldeneye, Smew, and Common Merganser.

The migratory pattern of the Green-winged Teal can vary from season to season, depending on the weather and habitat conditions which the birds find. Areas such as the Netherlands, Britain, and northern France – the major wintering areas for Scandinavian and western Russian breeders – are generally mild enough for these birds to stay throughout the winter.

Every few years, however, when ice and snow hit, Green-winged Teals are among the first to leave, heading south and west in large numbers to southern France, Spain, and Portugal. A few even cross the Mediterranean to northern Africa. (The North American race of Green-winged Teals behaves in a similar manner, in mild weather spending the winter on the prairies; if temperatures fall, continuing their southbound migration, sometimes as far as Mexico.)

Springtime drought on the breeding grounds, drying the pools and marshes, also severely affects water birds such as teals. If they arrive back in western Russia to a spring drought, they move on to look for wetter areas, even though these may be outside their normal breeding range. Equally, drought in late summer forces them off the breeding grounds early, so that migrants appear back in western Europe well before their usual time.

In common with other diving ducks, Pochards obtain almost all their food underwater, diving to depths of 7–13 feet (2–4 m) to reach submerged water plants. In both summer and winter, therefore, they frequent freshwater lakes and reservoirs with extensive shallows where vegetation grows. There has been a considerable increase in Pochard numbers in the western half of the range over the last 100 years, much of which has been attributed to the proliferation of artificial waters. Reservoirs, gravel pits, and ponds all provide Pochards with ideal conditions.

Male Pochards begin their fall flight south with a molt migration (see pp. 26–27), after which they continue their journey, reaching the wintering grounds some weeks before the females and young. The latter arrive to find the first suitable areas completely occupied and must fly on farther

*The Green-winged Teal, at some 14 inches (36 cm) from beak to tail, is one of the smallest dabbling ducks, feeding from the surface of shallow lakes and marshes on seeds, insects, and small invertebrates.*

*It is at risk during both winter and summer: when waters freeze or marshes dry out, teals face serious problems if they do not respond quickly by moving in search of more favorable conditions. Larger species and those with more varied diets, by contrast, can often wait for conditions to improve.*

North American race
*carolinensis*

Eurasian
race *crecca*

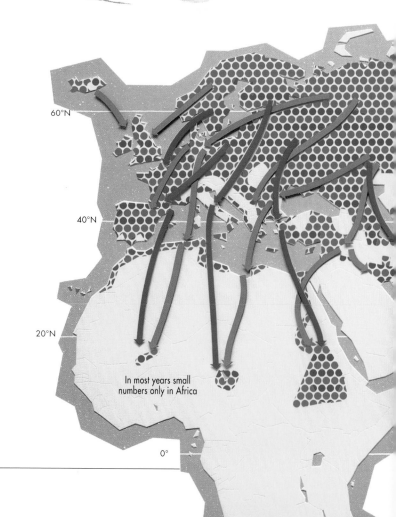

60°N

40°N

20°N

In most years small
numbers only in Africa

0°

**Green-winged Teal**
*Anas crecca*
**Wingspan** 23–25 in/58–64 cm
**Weight** 9–16 oz/250–450 g
**Journey length** 300–3,000 miles/
500–5,000 km

**Common Pochard**
*Aythya ferina*
**Wingspan** 28–32 in/72–82 cm
**Weight** 1 lb 9 oz–2 lb 7 oz/700–1,100 g
**Journey length** 190–4,600 miles/
300–7,500 km

**Smew**
*Mergus albellus*
**Wingspan** 22–27 in/55–69 cm
**Weight** 1 lb 3 oz–1 lb 12 oz/550–800 g
**Journey length** 600–2,800 miles/
1,000–4,500 km

*As soon as their part* in the breeding cycle is complete and the females have started to incubate a clutch of eggs, male Pochards leave the breeding grounds. Substantial flocks gather on a few large lakes – 50,000 on the IJsselmeer in the Netherlands, and 20,000 on the

Ismaninger reservoir, Bavaria – to undergo their annual molt before proceeding to the winter quarters.

Common Pochard

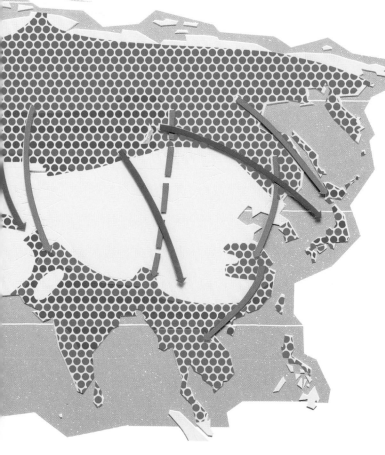

*In winter*, Smews are widespread on fresh and brackish water. In the breeding season, however, they are more restricted by the need to find holes in trees in which to nest, not too far from water. Areas of mature forests dotted with lakes and river banks where old woodland reaches the water are favorite haunts. Many pairs nest in close proximity, perhaps making use of a stand of dead trees containing plenty of holes.

south. There is, therefore, a pronounced segregation of the genders during the winter, with males predominating in the north of the range and females in the south. This widespread phenomenon is also known to occur in other species of ducks, including the Goldeneye, Wigeon, and Common Scoter.

Smews breed in a broad swathe across northern Europe and Asia from Sweden almost to the Pacific Ocean. Some 15,000 winter in northwestern Europe, with more farther east: at least 25,000 have been counted in the Sea of Azov, in the northeastern corner of the Black Sea, and nearly as many around the Volga delta in the north Caspian.

The majority of Smews migrating to northwestern Europe spend the fall in the Baltic Sea, moving on only when forced to do so by freezing conditions. They may not reach the Netherlands, their ultimate destination, until December or even January, and must then start back northeast again in March.

# Shorebirds

*Farming and freak weather conditions can bring death to many shorebirds.*

Lapwings and Redshanks are among the most familiar Eurasian shorebirds. Both are widespread, breeding in lowland areas from western Europe eastward through Russia to the Pacific. Both species have declined in the last 50 years, primarily due to summer habitat loss, but also as a result of their susceptibility to harsh winter weather.

Lapwings favor mild, often maritime, areas in winter. Britain, Ireland, and northern France are near the north of the winter range, with Russian and Scandinavian breeders flying south and west to join residents that may only move as far as the nearest coasts from breeding grounds inland. However, cold winters in these areas may force the migrants onto the major wintering sites in the Iberian Peninsula and the western Mediterranean.

Redshanks find food in the mud of coastal estuaries in winter and may starve if a sudden drop in temperature coats the mud flats with ice. A single spell of freezing weather in February 1992 killed almost 50 percent of the 4,000 Redshanks wintering on the Wash in eastern England. Counts of dead birds after sudden cold spells always include a high percentage of Redshanks.

The major contributing factor to the loss of breeding habitats for shorebirds is change in agricultural practices. In western Europe in particular, wet meadows have been drained, and grasslands rich in insect life have been plowed and reseeded or turned over to growing crops.

Lapwings nest on the ground in open fields and have always been vulnerable to trampling by cattle and sheep. Farmers who roll their pastures in late March and April to firm up the soil pose a still greater threat, destroying many nests. Lapwings are, however, resilient: they can lay a new clutch one to two weeks after losing the first and may go on to have a third or fourth clutch if previous broods fail. They have also proved capable of recolonizing former breeding grounds, nesting on reflooded previously drained wet meadows, for example.

The Redshank has suffered most as a breeding species from the drainage of low-lying wet fields. Patches of standing water and shallow ditches are essential feeding places for both adults and, especially, young, but are of no use to farmers who want to grow grass and crops. Redshanks can find suitable breeding grounds in coastal areas, but even here they are not secure: an unusually high tide can sweep nests away, and reclamation schemes are destroying this habitat.

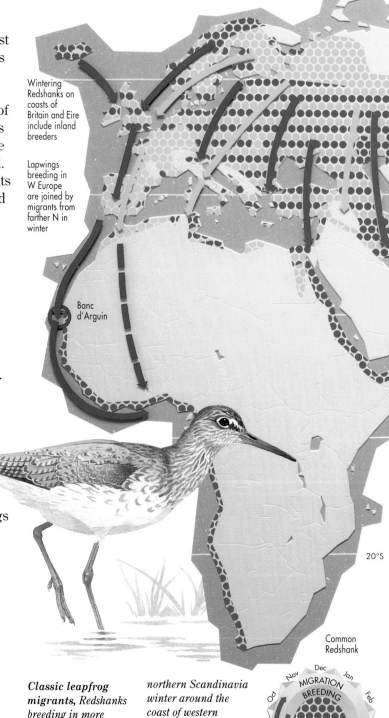

Wintering Redshanks on coasts of Britain and Eire include inland breeders

Lapwings breeding in W Europe are joined by migrants from farther N in winter

Banc d'Arguin

20°S

Common Redshank

*Classic leapfrog migrants, Redshanks breeding in more northern areas travel greater distances in winter than those that nest farther south. Redshanks breeding in* northern Scandinavia *winter around the coast of western Africa; those breeding in western Europe venture no farther south than the Mediterranean.*

MIGRATION BREEDING

**Common Redshank**
*Tringa totanus*
**Wingspan** 23–26 in/59–66 cm
**Weight** 3–5 oz/90–150 g
**Journey length** 300–4,000 miles/
500–6,500 km

**Northern Lapwing**
*Vanellus vanellus*
**Wingspan** 32–34 in/82–87 cm
**Weight** 7–10½ oz/185–300 g
**Journey length** 300–2,800 miles/
500–4,500 km

**Slender-billed Curlew**
*Numenius tenuirostris*
**Wingspan** 31–36 in/80–92 cm
**Weight** 10½–21 oz/300–600 g
**Journey length** 2,500–3,700 miles/
4,000–6,000 km

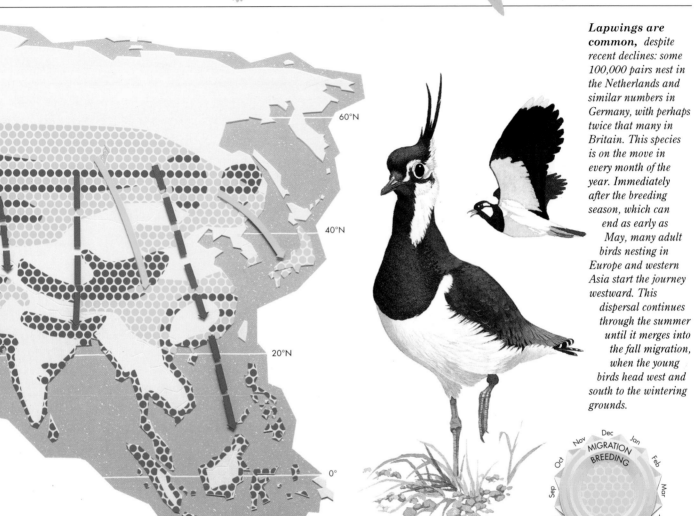

*Lapwings are common,* despite recent declines: some 100,000 pairs nest in the Netherlands and similar numbers in Germany, with perhaps twice that many in Britain. This species is on the move in every month of the year. Immediately after the breeding season, which can end as early as May, many adult birds nesting in Europe and western Asia start the journey westward. This dispersal continues through the summer until it merges into the fall migration, when the young birds head west and south to the wintering grounds.

Northern Lapwing

MIGRATION
BREEDING

Dec Jan Feb Mar Apr May Jun Jul Aug Sep Oct Nov

Slender-billed Curlew

## WITNESSES TO A GRADUAL EXTINCTION?

In the last 100 years, Slender-billed Curlew numbers have fallen dramatically. Whether this is due to loss of breeding or wintering habitat or to being shot on migration is uncertain. In addition, its similarity to the Curlew may have distorted knowledge of its former range and numbers.

These birds are thought still to breed only in the valleys of the Pechora River and one of its tributaries in Russia. The sole known migration route is across Hungary, Greece, Romania, and Turkey; winter reports come from Tunisia, Algeria, and Morocco. Some 600 to 900 were seen in Morocco in 1964, but few counts since 1980 total more than 100. It may now be so scarce that the knowledge necessary to save it is impossible to obtain.

# Storks

*The traditional bringer of babies is threatened at each stage of its migratory journey.*

Living alongside human beings has taken its toll of the White Stork. Changing fashions in architecture have dramatically reduced the number of suitable nesting places, and – in the course of the last 50 years – the increased use of agrochemicals has severely affected the populations of insects, worms, and frogs on which these birds rely for food. It is estimated that the European population of White Storks is declining at the rate of around 10 percent a year. In Spain alone, of the 26,000 pairs counted in a 1948 survey, only 40 percent remain today. And, as if these threats were not enough, migrating birds are frequently shot by hunters, particularly on the Mediterranean coasts and in the Middle East.

The White Stork is a soaring bird, relying on thermals in order to gain height, then gliding (and sometimes slowly flapping) to the next thermal (see pp. 18–19). Like other thermal soarers, White Storks avoid long sea crossings where possible. This restricts those migrating to Africa to one of two routes over the Mediterranean Sea: across the Strait of Gibraltar in the west or the Bosporus, Turkey, in the east. Broadly speaking, birds breeding west of a line running from Switzerland to the eastern Netherlands

*The European Black Stork* population is small: most countries shelter only a few hundred pairs. Numbers have declined over the last century as the wetlands on which they feed have been drained.

Black Storks are capable of sustained flight and often choose the long sea crossings that true soarers avoid. Some cross into Africa over the Tunisian coast; others have been seen "island hopping" in Sicily, Crete, and Cyprus.

German and Danish breeders are thought to favor crossing the Mediterranean at Gibraltar, although of a brood of four banded in Denmark, two were picked up on course in northern France and the Netherlands, while two had headed southeast and were found in Hungary and Romania.

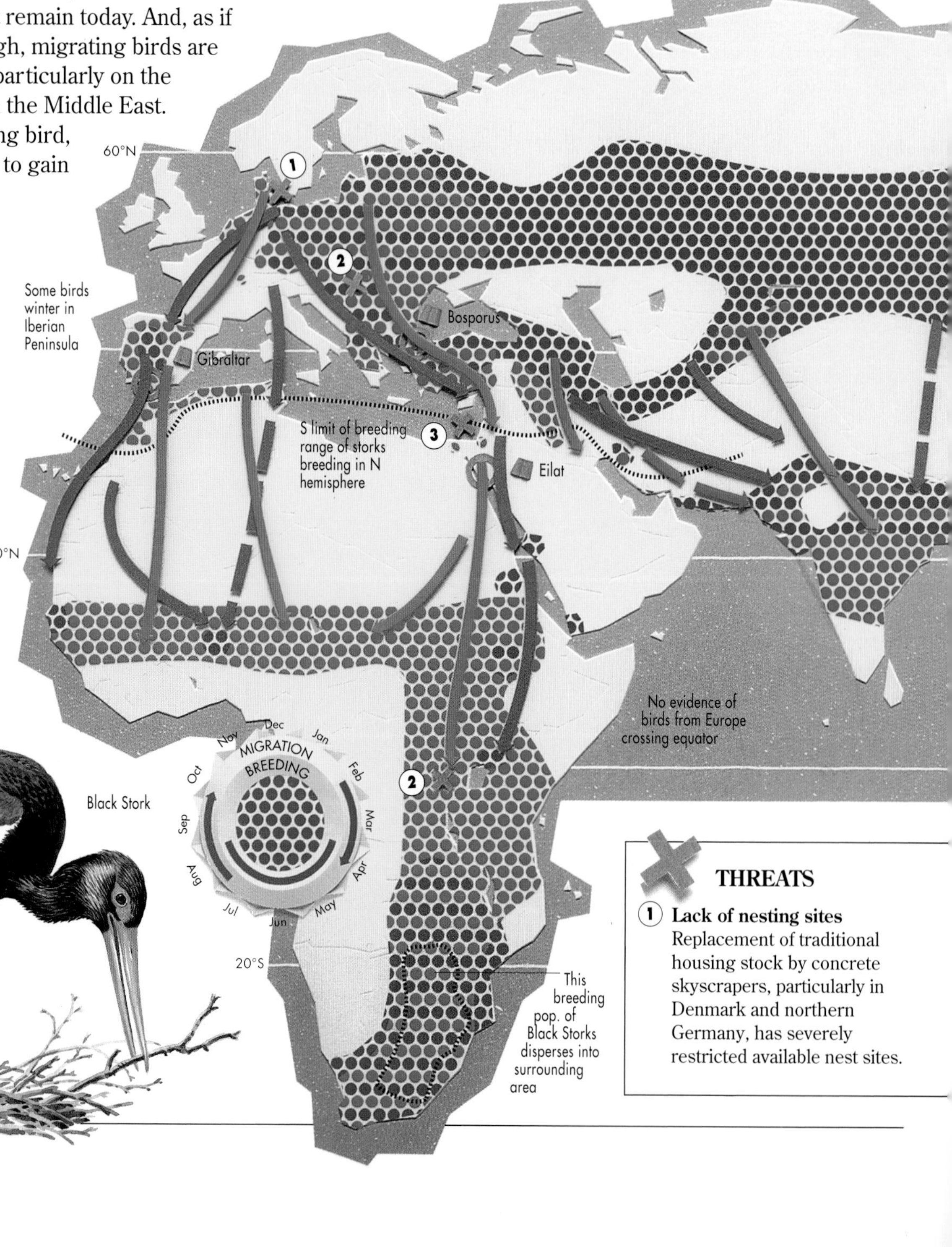

60°N

Some birds winter in Iberian Peninsula

Gibraltar

Bosporus

S limit of breeding range of storks breeding in N hemisphere

Eilat

20°N

No evidence of birds from Europe crossing equator

① ② ③ ②

Black Stork

MIGRATION
BREEDING

Oct Nov Dec Jan Feb Mar Apr May Jun Jul Aug Sep

20°S

This breeding pop. of Black Storks disperses into surrounding area

## THREATS

**① Lack of nesting sites**
Replacement of traditional housing stock by concrete skyscrapers, particularly in Denmark and northern Germany, has severely restricted available nest sites.

**Black Stork**
*Ciconia nigra*
**Wingspan** 4 ft 9 in–5 ft 1 in/1.45–1.55 m
**Weight** 5 lb 8 oz–7 lb 11 oz/2.5–3.5 kg
**Journey length** 1,250–4,000 miles/
2,000–6,500 km

**White Stork**
*Ciconia ciconia*
**Wingspan** 5 ft 1 in–5 ft 5 in/1.55–1.65 m
**Weight** 5 lb 1 oz–9 lb 11 oz/2.3–4.4 kg
**Journey length** 1,250–6,500 miles/
2,000–10,500 km

head for Gibraltar, those to the east of the line (by far the majority) fly over Turkey.

The reliance on warm-air thermals restricts White Storks to daytime migrations, and they consequently become concentrated at these narrow crossing places. These large, highly visible flocks spiral round and round, gradually climbing until they have gained enough height to glide across the sea. Flocks of 10,000 are not unusual at the Bosporus in the fall. Some 340,000 have been counted during the two-month fall migration period. A further 35,000 White Storks each year cross the Mediterranean at Gibraltar.

Once they are safely in Africa, the birds may face a journey of several thousand miles before they reach their winter homes south of the Sahara. The warmer weather as they move farther south, however, means that thermals become increasingly common and they can make good progress. Flying between 3,300 and 8,200 feet (1,000 and 2,500 m) above the ground, they can attain speeds of around 28 mph (45 km/h).

Although more common, the thermals on this leg of the journey still have to be located. White Storks maximize their chances by flying in large, widely spread flocks, typically up to 500 birds across a front some 1,600 feet (500 m) wide. As soon as some of the birds in the flock find the thermal, they cease their forward movement and start to spiral. The rest of the flock soon follows suit.

*Centuries ago White Storks discovered that chimneys, roofs, towers, and haystacks offered safe and secure nesting places. In many parts of central and northern Europe (the nest, right, is in Austria), these man-made structures came to be preferred to the more common nest site in the branches of a tree. This proximity to people has given storks a special place in human affections: in many countries, the myth exists of the White Stork as the bringer of babies, a tradition that equates the return of migrant birds in spring with fecundity.*

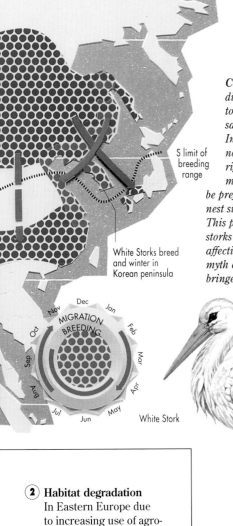

S limit of breeding range

White Storks breed and winter in Korean peninsula

MIGRATION
BREEDING
White Stork

**2 Habitat degradation**
In Eastern Europe due to increasing use of agro-chemicals; in Africa due to drainage and use of DDT.
**3 Hunting**
Middle East.

# Birds of prey/1

*Finding the shortest possible sea crossing is the prime requirement of soaring birds of prey.*

The migrations of Honey Buzzards are typical of Eurasian soaring birds of prey. The majority head for one of three routes: via Gibraltar, through the Bosporus, or over eastern Turkey. These three routes are used both in the fall and in spring. Birds have also been sighted using a fourth, over Eilat, Israel, at the head of the Red Sea, where the Dead Sea valley forms a perfect leading line (see pp. 34–35), on the spring migration north only.

Honey Buzzards breed in forests and open woodland right across Europe and into western Russia. Populations increase from west to east: there are, for example, only a handful of pairs in Britain. Regardless of breeding area, however, all Honey Buzzards winter in sub-Saharan Africa. Generally, birds breeding west of a line from Sweden to central Europe take the Gibraltar route, while those breeding to the east head for the Bosporus. Russian breeders hug the Black Sea coast before turning toward Africa. A small number make the long Mediterranean crossing, passing into Africa over the coasts of Algeria and Tunisia and probably heading straight over the Sahara. There is also a significant return in spring via this route: 8,000 individuals were counted in Tunisia in the first half of May 1975.

These migrations are spectacular affairs. More than 110,000 Honey Buzzards have been counted over Gibraltar during the fall migration, with daily peaks exceeding

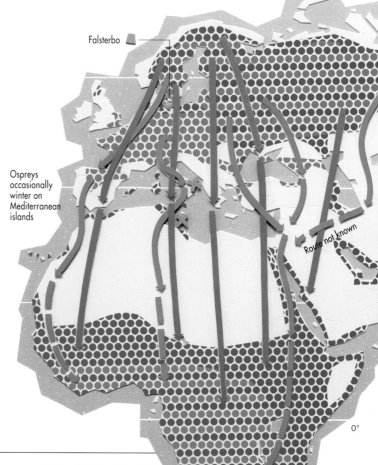

Falsterbo

Ospreys occasionally winter on Mediterranean islands

Route not known

0°

20°S

## FUNNELS AND FLYWAYS

Broad-winged birds of prey, such as eagles, buzzards, and harriers, migrate by soaring in thermals. Since thermals occur only over land, these birds avoid crossing water where possible.

Birds migrating from Europe to Africa must cross the Mediterranean and are funneled into places that give them the shortest route over water: via the Strait of Gibraltar in the west; over the Dardanelles and the Bosporus, then the Red Sea in the east; or through Italy, Sicily, and Tunisia.

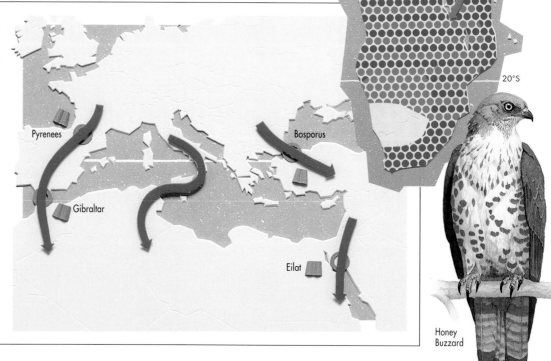

Pyrenees

Gibraltar

Bosporus

Eilat

Honey Buzzard

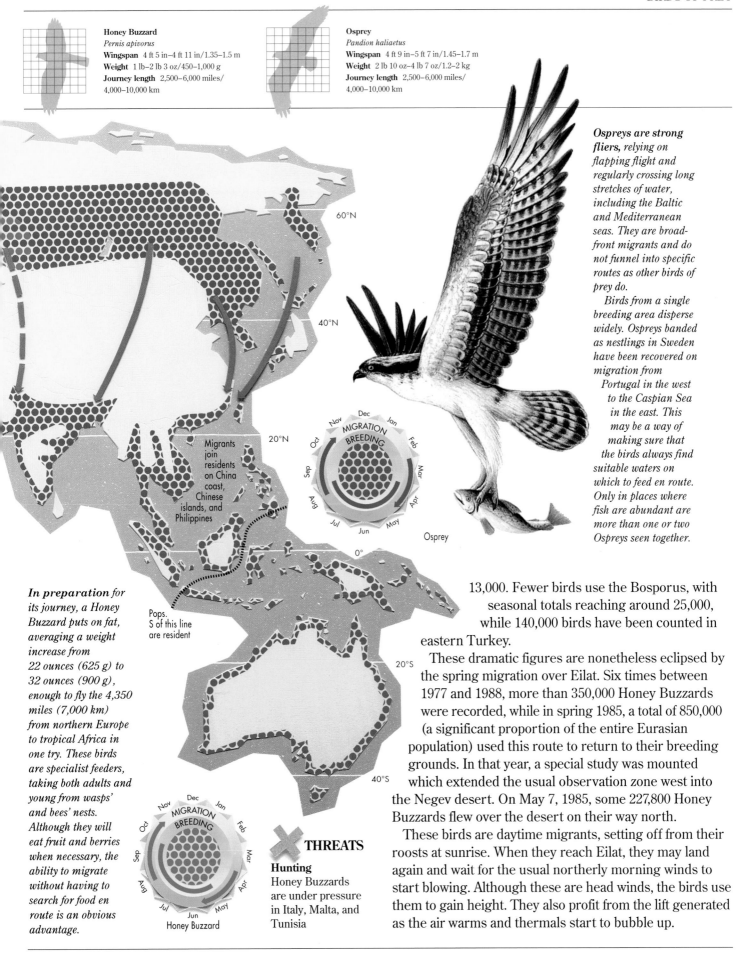

**Honey Buzzard**
*Pernis apivorus*
**Wingspan** 4 ft 5 in–4 ft 11 in/1.35–1.5 m
**Weight** 1 lb–2 lb 3 oz/450–1,000 g
**Journey length** 2,500–6,000 miles/
4,000–10,000 km

**Osprey**
*Pandion haliaetus*
**Wingspan** 4 ft 9 in–5 ft 7 in/1.45–1.7 m
**Weight** 2 lb 10 oz–4 lb 7 oz/1.2–2 kg
**Journey length** 2,500–6,000 miles/
4,000–10,000 km

60°N

40°N

Migrants
join
residents
on China
coast,
Chinese
islands, and
Philippines

20°N

MIGRATION
BREEDING

Dec
Nov · Jan
Oct · Feb
Sep · Mar
Aug · Apr
Jul · May
Jun

Osprey

*Ospreys are strong fliers, relying on flapping flight and regularly crossing long stretches of water, including the Baltic and Mediterranean seas. They are broad-front migrants and do not funnel into specific routes as other birds of prey do.*

*Birds from a single breeding area disperse widely. Ospreys banded as nestlings in Sweden have been recovered on migration from Portugal in the west to the Caspian Sea in the east. This may be a way of making sure that the birds always find suitable waters on which to feed en route. Only in places where fish are abundant are more than one or two Ospreys seen together.*

0°

Pops.
S of this line
are resident

20°S

40°S

*In preparation for its journey, a Honey Buzzard puts on fat, averaging a weight increase from 22 ounces (625 g) to 32 ounces (900 g), enough to fly the 4,350 miles (7,000 km) from northern Europe to tropical Africa in one try. These birds are specialist feeders, taking both adults and young from wasps' and bees' nests. Although they will eat fruit and berries when necessary, the ability to migrate without having to search for food en route is an obvious advantage.*

MIGRATION
BREEDING

Dec
Nov · Jan
Oct · Feb
Sep · Mar
Aug · Apr
Jul · May
Jun

Honey Buzzard

✖ **THREATS**

**Hunting**
Honey Buzzards
are under pressure
in Italy, Malta, and
Tunisia

13,000. Fewer birds use the Bosporus, with seasonal totals reaching around 25,000, while 140,000 birds have been counted in eastern Turkey.

These dramatic figures are nonetheless eclipsed by the spring migration over Eilat. Six times between 1977 and 1988, more than 350,000 Honey Buzzards were recorded, while in spring 1985, a total of 850,000 (a significant proportion of the entire Eurasian population) used this route to return to their breeding grounds. In that year, a special study was mounted which extended the usual observation zone west into the Negev desert. On May 7, 1985, some 227,800 Honey Buzzards flew over the desert on their way north.

These birds are daytime migrants, setting off from their roosts at sunrise. When they reach Eilat, they may land again and wait for the usual northerly morning winds to start blowing. Although these are head winds, the birds use them to gain height. They also profit from the lift generated as the air warms and thermals start to bubble up.

# Birds of prey/2

*Breeding late allows Eleonora's Falcons to prey on migrating songbirds.*

Eleonora's Falcons are highly specialized birds of prey which nest on the cliff faces of Mediterranean islands in colonies varying in size from a few to 200 pairs. The total population is 4,000 to 5,000 pairs. In the late fall, the birds head eastward through the Mediterranean to Egypt, where they turn south and make for Madagascar. Recently, small numbers have also wintered in Tanzania.

Most Mediterranean birds nest between March and May, but Eleonora's Falcons delay breeding until late summer, laying their first eggs at the end of July and hatching the first young about a month later. The chicks are in the nest from late August to early October, a period that coincides with the migration of songbirds south from Europe across the Mediterranean and into Africa. It is on these songbirds that the falcons mainly feed.

Each pair of Eleonora's Falcons rears an average of two young a year so that by the end of the breeding season there are, perhaps, 20,000 individuals. As many as 10 million songbirds could be taken by this number of falcons. (The total number of songbirds leaving Europe every fall runs into thousands of millions.)

These falcons, like other birds of prey, pluck their victims' feathers before eating them or feeding them to their young. An examination of these feathers, collected after the young have fledged, shows which species the falcons are taking, and in what proportions. More than 90 different species have been identified, with warblers, shrikes, swifts, small thrushes, larks, and flycatchers all common.

Prey remains also reveal a great deal about songbird migration with some species common compared with direct observations. Grasshopper Warblers, for example, are rarely seen on migration, yet regularly fall prey to Eleonora's Falcons nesting off the coast of Morocco, suggesting that this is a major route out of Europe for these birds.

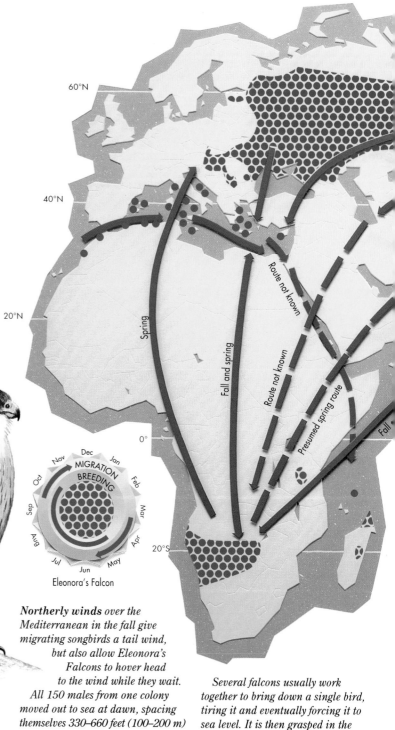

Eleonora's Falcon

**Northerly winds** *over the Mediterranean in the fall give migrating songbirds a tail wind, but also allow Eleonora's Falcons to hover head to the wind while they wait. All 150 males from one colony moved out to sea at dawn, spacing themselves 330–660 feet (100–200 m) apart and at varying heights, up to 3,300 feet (1,000 m) above the water. This "barrier" of waiting falcons formed a giant trap into which the songbirds inevitably flew.*

*Several falcons usually work together to bring down a single bird, tiring it and eventually forcing it to sea level. It is then grasped in the talons of one falcon and taken back to the nest. The success rate can be high: one male delivered five songbirds to its mate and young within 35 minutes.*

**Eleonora's Falcon**
*Falco eleonorae*
**Wingspan** 3 ft 7 in–4 ft 3 in/1.1–1.3 m
**Weight** 12–18 oz/340–500 g
**Journey length** 3,700–6,000 miles/
6,000–9,500 km

**Red-footed Falcon**
*Falco vespertinus*
**Wingspan** 27–31 in/66–78 cm
**Weight** 5–7 oz/130–200 g
**Journey length** 4,500–7,500 miles/
7,200–12,000 km

**Lesser Kestrel**
*Falco naumanni*
**Wingspan** 23–29 in/58–72 cm
**Weight** 3–7 oz/90–200 g
**Journey length** 1,900–6,000 miles/
3,000–9,500 km

Red-footed Falcon

N India

*Red-footed Falcons* breed from eastern Europe across central Siberia; a separate race breeds in eastern China, southeastern Russia, Mongolia, and Korea. All winter in the savannas of southeastern Africa.

Most Siberian breeders move west into southern Europe to join the European birds on their journey over the eastern Mediterranean and eastern Sahara. A few take the more direct route south of the Caspian and over Arabia.

Red-footed Falcons breeding in China face an extraordinary migratory journey. In the fall, they fly south of the Himalayas to India. They arrive in November and stay for some weeks, feeding on the abundance of insects to lay down fat and awaiting the northeast monsoon. This provides them with a tail wind for the 1,900-mile (3,000-km) flight across the Indian Ocean to Africa.

*Lesser Kestrels* (left) are colonial nesters, with groups of 15 to 25, and occasionally as many as 100, pairs breeding in holes in buildings and cliffs. They are also tolerant of humans and often use buildings for their communal winter roosts in South Africa.

These birds are primarily insect-eaters, feeding particularly on grasshoppers, crickets, locusts, and beetles. The increasing use of pesticides on crops has affected Lesser Kestrel populations in many countries of southern Europe, with massive declines in numbers noted.

# Gamebirds

*These reluctant fliers may make lengthy migrations.*

**Common Quail**
*Coturnix coturnix*
**Wingspan** 13–14 in/32–35 cm
**Weight** 2½–5 oz/75–140 g
**Journey length** 600–3,400 miles/
1,000–5,500 km

It is difficult to believe, seeing a gamebird in flight, that these skulking birds which take to the air only reluctantly, when flushed, can achieve lengthy migrations, often crossing large expanses of sea or desert.

Gray Partridge migrations are typical of those of many gamebirds, with birds breeding in the milder areas of western Europe being sedentary and more easterly breeding populations moving south to avoid the winter snows. The Common Quail, however, is not only one of the smallest gamebirds but also the most traveled, breeding widely in Europe and into central Asia and wintering in sub-Saharan Africa and in India.

One of the most striking features of Quail migration is that the numbers breeding in the north of the range in Europe vary enormously from year to year. Normally, only a few hundred pairs nest in the Netherlands and Britain, but at relatively rare intervals, there are major influxes, multiplying the usual population up to tenfold. This has occurred on six occasions this century, the latest being in 1989 when some 2,500 pairs were estimated to be breeding at the northern extremes of the range instead of the more usual 100 to 300 pairs.

The reasons for these influxes are still unclear. They seem to occur when a warm, dry spring in northern Europe coincides with a period of southeasterly winds. This combination might cause the Quails to overshoot their more southerly, traditional nesting areas and arrive farther north than they intended. Then, since they find the habitat suitable, they stay to breed.

*Despite references to Quail migration in the Old Testament, many aspects of it are still poorly understood. It is known, however, that these birds are subject to intense pressure from hunters when on migration through countries on both sides of the Mediterranean Sea. Many tens, perhaps even hundreds, of thousands are trapped and shot in southern Europe and northern Africa each year.*

*The extent to which this is affecting the total population is uncertain: Quails have, after all, been hunted for centuries. Yet with so much suitable breeding habitat also being destroyed, the high mortality from hunting is more likely to be having a negative effect.*

60°N

Occasionally winter in W Europe, N Africa

S limit of breeding range

Broad-front migration over Mediterranean and Sahara

S limit of wintering range of N breeders; birds to S of this line are resident

0°

20°S

Common Quail

**THREATS**

**Hunting and trapping**
Quails suffer enormous losses in N Africa, particularly Egypt and Libya.

MIGRATION BREEDING
Jan Feb Mar Apr May Jun Jul Aug Sep Oct Nov Dec

# Crakes and rails

*The Corncrake's tale is one of inexorable decline.*

**Corncrake**
*Crex crex*
**Wingspan** 19–21 in/46–53 cm
**Weight** 4½–7½ oz/125–210 g
**Journey length** 2,700–6,000 miles/
4,300–10,000 km

One of the most threatened birds breeding in Europe, the Corncrake has declined drastically in almost every part of its range in the last 30 to 40 years. Figures for Britain are typical: in 1970, the population was estimated at 2,640 pairs; in 1978–79, no more than 750; by 1988, 550 to 600. By 1993 the number had fallen to 475 individuals.

Incubating females, and their eggs and young, are killed when the long grass in which they nest is mown for hay or silage. Traditional haymaking involved scything the grass in July or August, a process which rarely harmed the birds. Mechanization, and the change to growing grass for silage instead of for hay, means that the cutting is now done as early as June. In addition, a tractor driver is less likely than a person scything to see a nest, and the practice of mowing in circles from the edges of the field gradually herds any

Corncrake families into the steadily shrinking island in the middle. These birds are extremely reluctant to break cover, so they eventually get caught by the mower blades. If they do run into the open, they are easy prey for crows and gulls.

In an attempt to save this species, British conservation agencies are now sponsoring "Corncrake-friendly" methods of farming. Since a return to traditional methods might mean financial loss to farmers, payments are made to those who delay mowing specified fields, known to be favored by Corncrakes, until August when the young have fledged. In addition, mowing is done from the middle of the field outward to give the birds more time to move. It may nonetheless prove to be too little, too late.

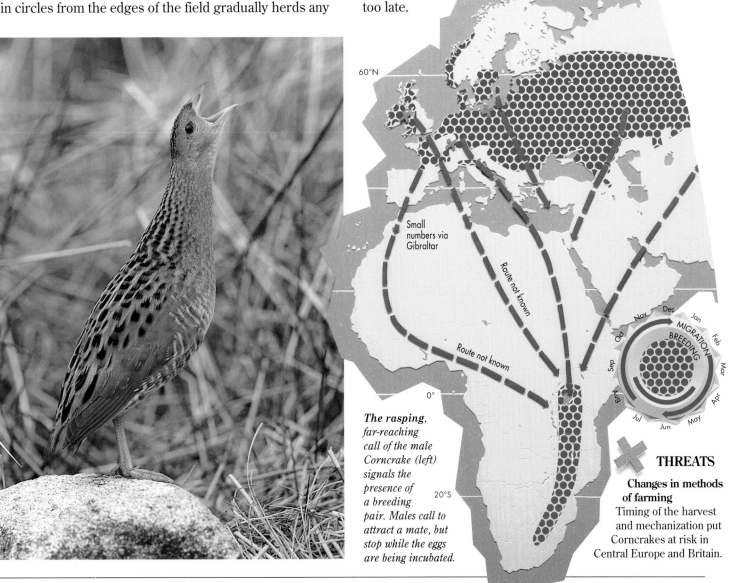

60°N

Small
numbers via
Gibraltar

Route not known

Route not known

0°

20°S

Nov Dec Jan
Oct MIGRATION Feb
Sep BREEDING Mar
Aug Apr
Jul Jun May

*The rasping, far-reaching call of the male Corncrake (left) signals the presence of a breeding pair. Males call to attract a mate, but stop while the eggs are being incubated.*

**THREATS**

**Changes in methods of farming**
Timing of the harvest and mechanization put Corncrakes at risk in Central Europe and Britain.

# Cranes

*Observations from a light airplane have revealed many of the wonders of crane migration.*

There are references to crane migration in the Old Testament, and it is small wonder that these birds have been part of human consciousness for so long. Huge but graceful, they are noted for their distinctive V-formation flight, their elaborate "dances," and their loud, echoing calls.

Common Cranes breed in marshland across northern Europe and Asia. Most of those breeding in the west of the range, in Sweden and the Baltic countries, migrate southwest to Spain and southern Portugal. Some of these birds, however, together with those from northern Scandinavia and western Russia, migrate southeastward to Turkey, where many stop; others continue either southeast to Iraq and Iran or due south to Egypt, Sudan, and Ethiopia.

Much of what is known about Common Crane migration derives from a study conducted in Sweden one spring using radar to locate the birds, combined with observations from a light airplane. Radar pinpointed the cranes heading north as they crossed the southern coast of Sweden. The aircraft then followed the flocks, with the observers noting what the birds were doing at each stage of the journey.

*Common Cranes keep to a largely vegetarian diet, taking some animal and insect food, but deriving most of their nourishment from the roots, tubers, leaves, and stems of marsh plants and from crops, including grass and clover.*

*Migrating flocks must feed en route, and many of their traditional resting places have been used for centuries. Several are now designated refuges so that the cranes are not disturbed as they refuel for the next stage of their journey.*

## HUMAN INTERVENTION: THE ONLY HOPE?

The Siberian White Crane is seriously endangered. The majority of those remaining, some 3,000 individuals, winter in China where their haunts are at risk from drainage and pollution. Two groups that breed farther west and winter in Iran and India are on the point of extinction; indeed, it is not known whether the Iranian birds still exist. Those that reach India face habitat loss and illegal hunting. In addition, Siberian White Cranes rear few young each summer.

In an attempt to save this species, a captive breeding program has been introduced. Eggs are taken to the United States where the chicks are reared. When they breed, their eggs are returned to Siberia to Common Crane nests. The hope is that the Siberian Crane young will follow the Common Cranes to safer wintering areas farther west.

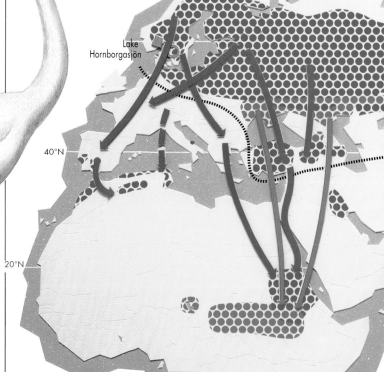

Common Crane

Siberian White Crane

Lake Hornborgasjön

80°N

40°N

20°N

0°

MIGRATION
BREEDING

Jan Feb Mar Apr May Jun Jul Aug Sep Oct Nov Dec

**Siberian White Crane**
*Grus leucogeranus*
**Wingspan** 7 ft 7 in–8 ft 6 in/2.3–2.6 m
**Weight** 11 lb–18 lb 12 oz/5–8.5 kg
**Journey length** 2,500–3,000 miles/
4,000–5,000 km

**Common Crane**
*Grus grus*
**Wingspan** 7 ft 3 in–8 ft/2.2–2.45 m
**Weight** 8 lb 13 oz–15 lb 7 oz/4–7 kg
**Journey length** 1,250–3,750 miles/
2,000–6,000 km

**Demoiselle Crane**
*Anthropoides virgo*
**Wingspan** 5 ft 5 in–6 ft 1 in/1.65–1.85 m
**Weight** 4 lb 14 oz–6 lb 10 oz/2.2–3 kg
**Journey length** 950–2,800 miles/
1,500–4,500 km

*Migrants that follow regular routes often risk attack by birds of prey. Six resident pairs of Golden Eagles preyed on many tens of thousands of Demoiselle Cranes, migrating through a 12-mile (20-km) long valley in Nepal. The eagles attacked the lowest-flying cranes, which were up to 3,300 feet (1,000 m) above the valley floor. They were not very successful: only four cranes were killed out of 67 observed attacks.*

*During the dancing display of a pair of Manchurian Cranes, the birds leap into the air with raised wings, pirouetting, bobbing, and bowing. The dance reinforces the bond between male and female.*

MIGRATION
BREEDING

Demoiselle
Crane

Common Cranes are thermal soarers, but the tracked birds needed to use flapping flight to cross the Baltic Sea from Germany. When they reached the Swedish coast, they switched back to soaring and gliding. Within a thermal, the flock kept close together, spiraling up to heights of 1,600–6,600 feet (500–2,000 m). At the top of the thermal, the birds peeled off, heading north in a V-formation.

On days when the thermals were weak, the cranes used flapping flight for extended periods, but where possible, they rode the thermals. Because of the time spent soaring in circles to gain height, they averaged 30 mph (50 km/h), less than the 42 mph (67 km/h) they achieved when gliding with occasional flaps between thermals. The energy saved amply compensates for the slower progress.

A similar study of Demoiselle Cranes could yield fascinating results, since most Siberian breeders cross the Himalayas to winter in India. This entails flying at heights of at least 13,000 feet (4,000 m) to clear even the lowest passes. Observations suggest that the birds fly much higher on occasions, perhaps to find favorable tail winds.

S limit of
breeding
range,
both spp.

Routes
across
Himalayas
not
known

# Gulls and terns

*Young gulls do not share their parents' more limited horizons on migration.*

The migratory habits of Eurasian gulls are diverse. Some species are entirely sedentary, others wholly migratory. In addition, there are species that are resident in some areas but leave others for more southerly winter quarters. Almost all the terns are long-distance migrants, traveling great distances every spring and fall.

The closely related Herring and Lesser Black-backed gulls, which often nest together in mixed colonies, behave differently. Herring Gulls are often sedentary, although those that breed in the extreme north of Scandinavia may move south to avoid the most severe winter weather. Lesser Black-backed Gulls, on the other hand, are largely migratory, with the young birds moving much farther in their first fall than the adults, some of which stay at or close to their breeding site throughout the winter.

Young Lesser Black-backs begin to disperse from their nesting areas in Scandinavia and Britain in late July. They are in western France in August, Spain and Portugal in September, and Morocco by October. Some move farther, reaching Mauritania and Senegal. Many adults also move south, but only as far as France and northern Iberia, before heading north again. Some are back in Britain in December and perhaps should be classed as wintering there.

Farther east in the breeding range, fewer birds have been banded, and migration patterns are less clear, although juveniles from northern Scandinavia and northwestern Russia seem to travel farther in winter than the adults.

Many stay in the south throughout their first summer, not returning north until they are two years old, although they probably do not breed for another two years.

Black Terns regularly cross the equator on migration. Their journeys begin early, with some dispersal from the breeding grounds in June. The adults move in advance of their young, which often go on random movements (see pp. 30–31), even northward, before they, too, head south. Huge numbers of birds – up to 80,000 have been counted in the IJsselmeer in the Netherlands – assemble in August to feed on concentrations of fish fry. They then head south and west to Iberia, and follow the coastline of Africa all the way to its southern tip. Birds from farther east use the Nile and East African Rift valleys on their southward journeys.

The spring migration of Black Terns is rapid. It does not begin until late March, but birds arrive in western Europe during April and May. Most one-year-olds remain in the winter quarters throughout their first and often second summers, moving north only at the age of three, when they may make their first breeding attempt. First-time breeders rarely nest in the colonies in which they were reared.

The European breeding range of Black Terns has contracted in the last 50 years, probably due to drainage of the low-lying wetlands in which they nest. Outside the breeding season, however, they have taken advantage of some changes in the landscape, finding plenty of food at sewage plants, reservoirs, and fishponds.

## CONSERVATION IN ACTION

The Roseate Tern, threatened both winter and summer, is the focus of a two-pronged conservation attempt. There are now some 1,600 pairs of this species in Europe (1,000 on the Azores, 500 in Britain and Ireland, and 100 in France). This compares with 2,500 pairs in Britain and Ireland, and 600 pairs in France as recently as 1969.

In spring and summer, rats, mink, and gulls prey on Roseate Tern nests on small sand or pebble islands, taking the eggs and chicks. Control of populations of rat and mink has been possible in some areas, and more tall plants are being grown and nest boxes provided to prevent gulls finding the nests.

The winter threat – trapping by children along the coast of western Africa – is being addressed in two ways. Hunting and trapping have been outlawed and the *Save the Shorebirds* education campaign (see also pp. 50–51) has been introduced.

**Roseate Tern**
*Sterna dougallii*
**Wingspan** 29–31 in/72–80 cm
**Weight** 3–4½ oz/90–130 g
**Journey length** 3,000–3,750 miles/
5,000–6,000 km

**Lesser Black-backed Gull**
*Larus fuscus*
**Wingspan** 4 ft 1 in–5 ft 1 in/1.25–1.55 m
**Weight** 1 lb 5 oz–2 lb 3 oz/600–1,000 g
**Journey length** 600–4,000 miles/
1,000–6,500 km

**Black Tern**
*Chlidonias nigra*
**Wingspan** 25–27 in/64–68 cm
**Weight** 2–3 oz/55–85 g
**Journey length** 1,850–6,500 miles/
3,000–10,500 km

*Between 1965 and 1975,* the northern limit of the wintering range of Lesser Black-backed Gulls moved north by an average 95 miles (150 km) a year, pushing them into Britain in winter.

An absence of severe winters in those years almost certainly contributed to this shift, but during this period the gulls were also becoming better adapted to living close to humans, nesting successfully on buildings and feeding on garbage dumps. Both habits reduced the incidences of mortality from predation and starvation.

Small numbers winter E coast of N America

MIGRATION
BREEDING

Lesser Black-backed Gull

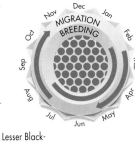

Elbe estuary

IJsselmeer

40°N

20°N

Banc d'Arguin

Some this way in spring

A few this way in fall

Some winter as far E as Gulf of Khambhat

**Black Terns** *frequent different habitats when breeding, migrating, and wintering. Their diets also differ.*

In the breeding season, they are birds of fresh water, nesting beside small pools, shallow lakes, marshes, and swampy meadows. They feed on aquatic insects and their larvae, and on insects caught by hunting low over pastures and rough vegetation.

On the way to their winter homes, they eat freshwater fish, even taking them from backyard ponds.

*Throughout the winter, they live in coastal waters and feed exclusively on small marine fish.*

Black Tern

MIGRATION
BREEDING

20°S

Note: Gulls and terns roost on land, but feed at sea, ranging up to 100 miles (160 km) from shore.

# Pigeons

*These scattered breeders often winter in flocks a million strong.*

**Turtle Dove**
*Streptopelia turtur*
**Wingspan** 19–21 in/47–53 cm
**Weight** 3½–7 oz/100–200 g
**Journey length** 600–3,750 miles/
1,000–6,000 km

Most Eurasian pigeons and doves are either sedentary or only partial migrants. They include the homing pigeon which, although renowned for its navigational skills and used to test theories on how birds migrate long distances with such accuracy, is descended from the sedentary Rock Dove.

Stock Doves and Woodpigeons breeding in the west of the range, in the countries bordering the North Sea and the Mediterranean, are also sedentary, while those nesting farther east journey south and west to avoid the ice and snow of the Eurasian continental winter. The Turtle Dove is an exception, however. These birds breed throughout Europe and in southwestern Asia. All populations are migratory, traveling to sub-Saharan Africa for the winter.

The birds return late in the spring, rarely building their widely scattered nests across woodland, farmland, orchards, and gardens until May. Fall migration may begin in late July, but peaks in August and September. Then, huge flocks of European Turtle Doves take one of three major routes over the Mediterranean: across the Strait of Gibraltar (the most popular); via Italy and Sicily; or over the eastern Mediterranean into Egypt. As many as three million Asian breeders have been observed moving southwest over Iraq on a front 60 miles (100 km) wide.

Migrating Turtle Doves are severely threatened by hunting in Mediterranean areas; an estimated minimum of 100,000 are shot annually on the island of Malta, where peak daily passage can reach 20,000 birds.

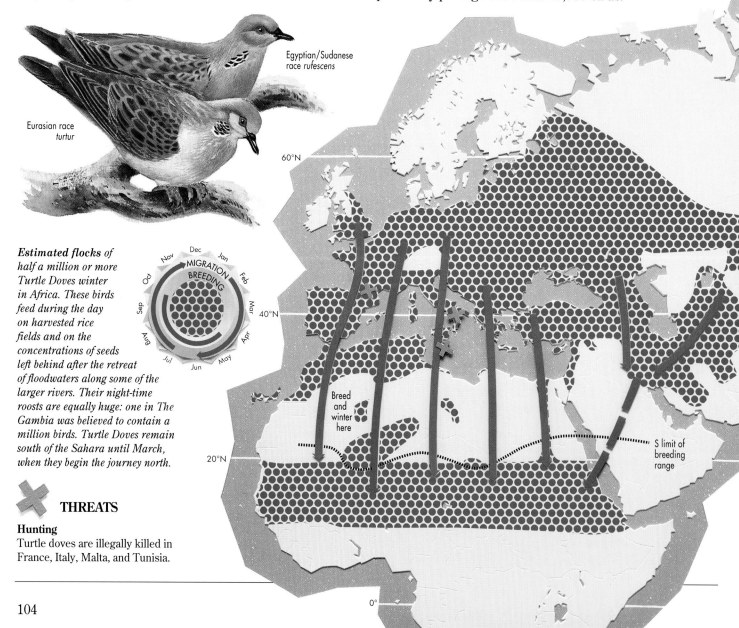

Egyptian/Sudanese
race *rufescens*

Eurasian race
*turtur*

*Estimated flocks of half a million or more Turtle Doves winter in Africa. These birds feed during the day on harvested rice fields and on the concentrations of seeds left behind after the retreat of floodwaters along some of the larger rivers. Their night-time roosts are equally huge: one in The Gambia was believed to contain a million birds. Turtle Doves remain south of the Sahara until March, when they begin the journey north.*

**THREATS**

**Hunting**
Turtle doves are illegally killed in France, Italy, Malta, and Tunisia.

# Cuckoos

*The call of these parasites heralds the beginning of spring.*

**Eurasian Cuckoo**
*Cuculus canorus*
**Wingspan** 22–24 in/55–60 cm
**Weight** 3–4½ oz/90–135 g
**Journey length** 2,800–7,500 miles/
4,500–12,000 km

Few birds capture the imagination more than cuckoos. They have a highly distinctive call, often taken to be a harbinger of spring. They lay their eggs in the nests of other birds, forcing surrogates to rear their chicks which nonetheless inherit their true parents' migration patterns.

Adult Eurasian Cuckoos tend to return to the same breeding area year after year. The female generally defends her territory against other females, but may mate with several males in the course of a season. She searches for suitable foster parents' nests in which to deposit her eggs and usually lays all of them – up to 25 laid at one- or two-day intervals – singly in the nests of the same host species. This has recently been proved to be the same species that reared her. Regardless of species, the foster parents are invariably much smaller than the Eurasian Cuckoo chick which they are obliged to rear.

Once the egg-laying period is over, by the end of July at the latest, the adults are free to migrate and set off southward immediately. There are records of migrants arriving in Africa as early as mid-August. Back on the breeding grounds the young Cuckoo ensures that it gets an adequate food supply by not sharing the nest with any other eggs or nestlings, but evicting them over the side.

About a month after their true parents have left for Africa or Southeast Asia, the young begin their migration. They do not, as might be expected, follow their foster parents. With no knowledge of the route and no parental help, young Cuckoos join the adults on the wintering grounds.

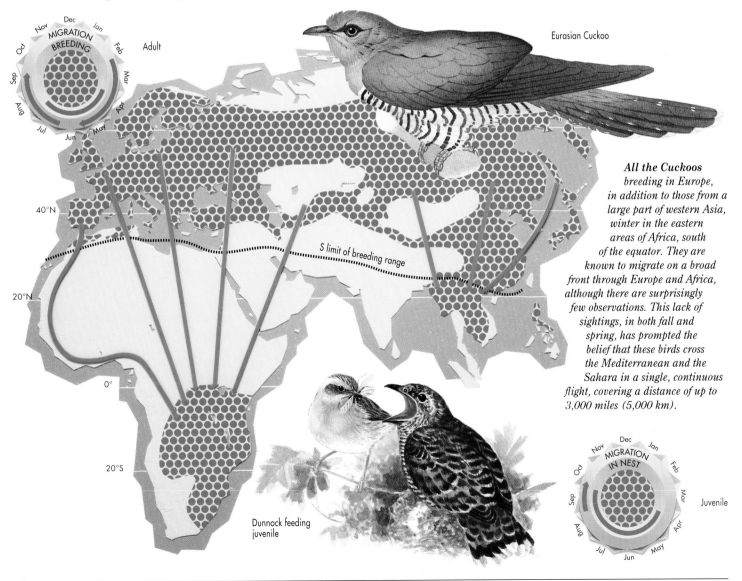

*All the Cuckoos breeding in Europe, in addition to those from a large part of western Asia, winter in the eastern areas of Africa, south of the equator. They are known to migrate on a broad front through Europe and Africa, although there are surprisingly few observations. This lack of sightings, in both fall and spring, has prompted the belief that these birds cross the Mediterranean and the Sahara in a single, continuous flight, covering a distance of up to 3,000 miles (5,000 km).*

Eurasian Cuckoo

Adult

40°N

20°N

0°

20°S

S limit of breeding range

Dunnock feeding juvenile

Juvenile

MIGRATION
BREEDING
Nov Dec Jan Feb Mar Apr May Jun Jul Aug Sep Oct

MIGRATION
IN NEST
Nov Dec Jan Feb Mar Apr May Jun Jul Aug Sep Oct

# Bee-eaters, rollers, and hoopoes

*This exotic trio from southern Europe finds that the Mediterranean is too cold in winter.*

Specialist insect-eaters, such as bee-eaters, rollers, and the Hoopoe, are restricted to the southern areas of western Europe. Their ranges extend farther north only in eastern Europe and Asia where the continental climate produces hot enough summers to support the necessary abundance of large insects on which they feed. Most birds with such limited diets must migrate south for the winter to areas where insects are still numerous enough.

In common with many birds that fly north to breed in southern Europe, these three species overshoot their breeding areas on occasion and are seen farther north, although they rarely stay to breed. In the last 150 years, the Hoopoe has bred in Britain 30 times, the European Bee-eater twice, and the European Roller not at all.

Although they are restricted to daytime migrations when their food is easy to find, insect-eaters are more fortunate than many migrants in being able to feed on the wing. They have no need to make special, traditional stops, but merely pause on their journey when they come across concentrations of insects. They cope with areas of potentially inhospitable terrain, such as the Sahara and Arabian deserts, by flying non-stop.

All the rollers breeding in Europe and Asia migrate to the eastern half of Africa for the winter. Although they are only thinly distributed, both on the breeding grounds and in winter, total numbers are thought to run into millions. Occasional large flocks occur around good food sources, such as locusts or termites, or when birds are concentrated by storms: on April 13, 1979, some 40,000 to 50,000 European Rollers were seen on migration through Somalia.

With the slow flaps of its broad, striped wings, the Hoopoe in flight looks remarkably like a large butterfly. On the ground, it runs and walks easily in its search for the large insects and occasional small lizards on which it feeds. When it gets excited, it raises its remarkable crest which completely transforms its shape.

The full extent of Hoopoe migration is confused by the presence in its main wintering quarters, in sub-Saharan Africa and in India, of year-round residents. Although these belong to separate races, they are too similar to the European Hoopoe for observers to separate them readily in the field. Thus, observations of movements of feeding flocks in these regions may be of resident or migrant birds (or a combination of the two), and the timing of the migrants' arrivals and departures is difficult to gauge.

*Hoopoes (above) bred as far north as southern Sweden a century ago. Since then, the breeding range has retreated south and numbers have fallen, though with some recovery, subsequently reversed, about 40 years ago. Although climate change may well have been involved, changes in habitat and, especially, the increased use of pesticides are the more likely causes of recent decline.*

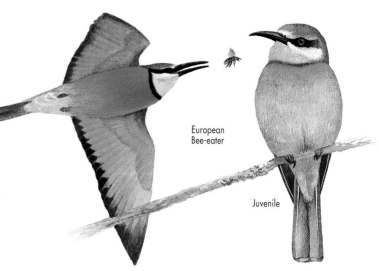

European Bee-eater

Juvenile

*Bee-eaters are specialist feeders, although not as restricted in diet as their name implies. They can be a nuisance to beekeepers, as flocks may gather around groups of hives; a pair can feed its brood of young up to 50 times an hour. However, they also take wild bees and wasps as well as other flying insects and invertebrates.*

*To avoid being stung, bee-eaters have a special technique for dealing with bees and wasps. They always take the prey back to a perch, holding it, head forward, in the bill with the insect's head protruding slightly from the bill tip. The bird then bangs the wasp's or bee's head once or twice on the perch before reversing the insect in its bill and rubbing its abdomen repeatedly back and forth against the perch. This tears the sting from the body, or at least discharges its venom.*

*The bird bangs the bee's head a few more times before swallowing it, head first. The whole procedure takes about 12 seconds.*

**Hoopoe**
*Upupa epops*
**Wingspan** 16–18 in/42–46 cm
**Weight** 2–3 oz/60–80 g
**Journey length** 300–3,000 miles/
500–5,000 km

**European Bee-eater**
*Merops apiaster*
**Wingspan** 17–19 in/44–49 cm
**Weight** 1½–2½ oz/40–65 g
**Journey length** 1,500–6,500 miles/
2,500–10,500 km

**European Roller**
*Coracias garrulus*
**Wingspan** 26–29 in/66–73 cm
**Weight** 4–6 oz/120–176 g
**Journey length** 1,500–6,000 miles/
2,500–10,000 km

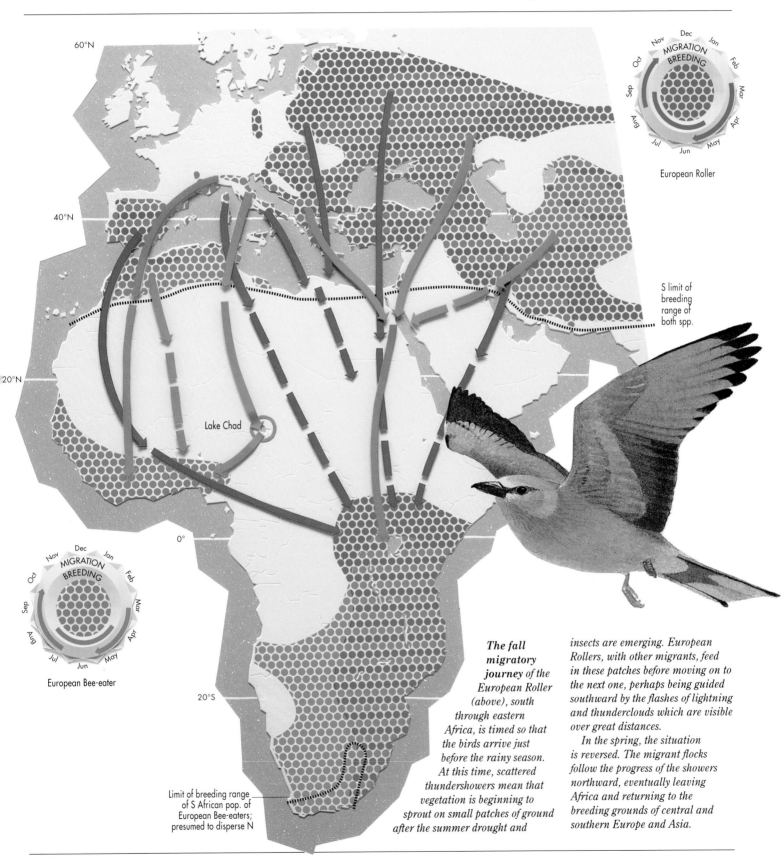

60°N

40°N

20°N

0°

20°S

Lake Chad

S limit of
breeding
range of
both spp.

European Roller

European Bee-eater

Limit of breeding range
of S African pop. of
European Bee-eaters;
presumed to disperse N

*The fall migratory journey of the European Roller (above), south through eastern Africa, is timed so that the birds arrive just before the rainy season. At this time, scattered thundershowers mean that vegetation is beginning to sprout on small patches of ground after the summer drought and* insects are emerging. European Rollers, with other migrants, feed in these patches before moving on to the next one, perhaps being guided southward by the flashes of lightning and thunderclouds which are visible over great distances.

In the spring, the situation is reversed. The migrant flocks follow the progress of the showers northward, eventually leaving Africa and returning to the breeding grounds of central and southern Europe and Asia.

# Swifts, swallows, and martins

*Slowly but surely is the most effective strategy for migratory young swallows.*

Of all northern birds, those that feed exclusively on aerial insects are obvious migrants – forced to leave by the complete lack of food during winter. The Eurasian Swift is the most spectacular of these birds since it is often present in Eurasia for only a quarter of the year, from early May to the first week of August. Others, such as the Bank Swallow, may be on the breeding grounds for up to six months, from the end of March to early October.

These birds are completely at home in the air. They move largely by day and, since they feed in flight, could be supposed to migrate in a leisurely fashion. This is indeed the case with swallows and martins, but swifts are remarkably fast migrants. One juvenile found in Madrid, Spain, had been banded only three days earlier in Oxford, England, 780 miles (1,250 km) away. This speed is probably related to their ability to roost on the wing at night.

Since they are such slow migrants, Bank and Barn swallows build up tremendous roosts on their southward passage. Over a period of many weeks, between a few hundred and several hundred thousand birds gather in reedbeds near water. Young birds on migration in the fall may spend up to two weeks in an area before moving on, traveling mainly southward, between 60 and 190 miles (100 and 300 km) at a time, thus taking a leisurely couple of months through northern and central Europe to the Mediterranean. Since experienced adult birds know where they are going, they move more briskly, staying in each roost for only a few days.

The northbound flight in spring is faster, at around five weeks, but again the adult birds lead the way. In the wintering area, whether it is in the Senegal River delta for Bank Swallows or the gold-mining areas of the Transvaal for Barn Swallows, night-time roosts may be huge. Again, these are generally in wet reedbeds since they are safe havens against ground-based predators.

Swift and House Martin roosts have not been found, although House Martins often roost in colonies in unoccupied nests. In bad weather, on migration, they have on rare occasions roosted in trees and, if it is exceptionally cold, they may roost on buildings. But it is a fact that both species normally spend their time away from the breeding

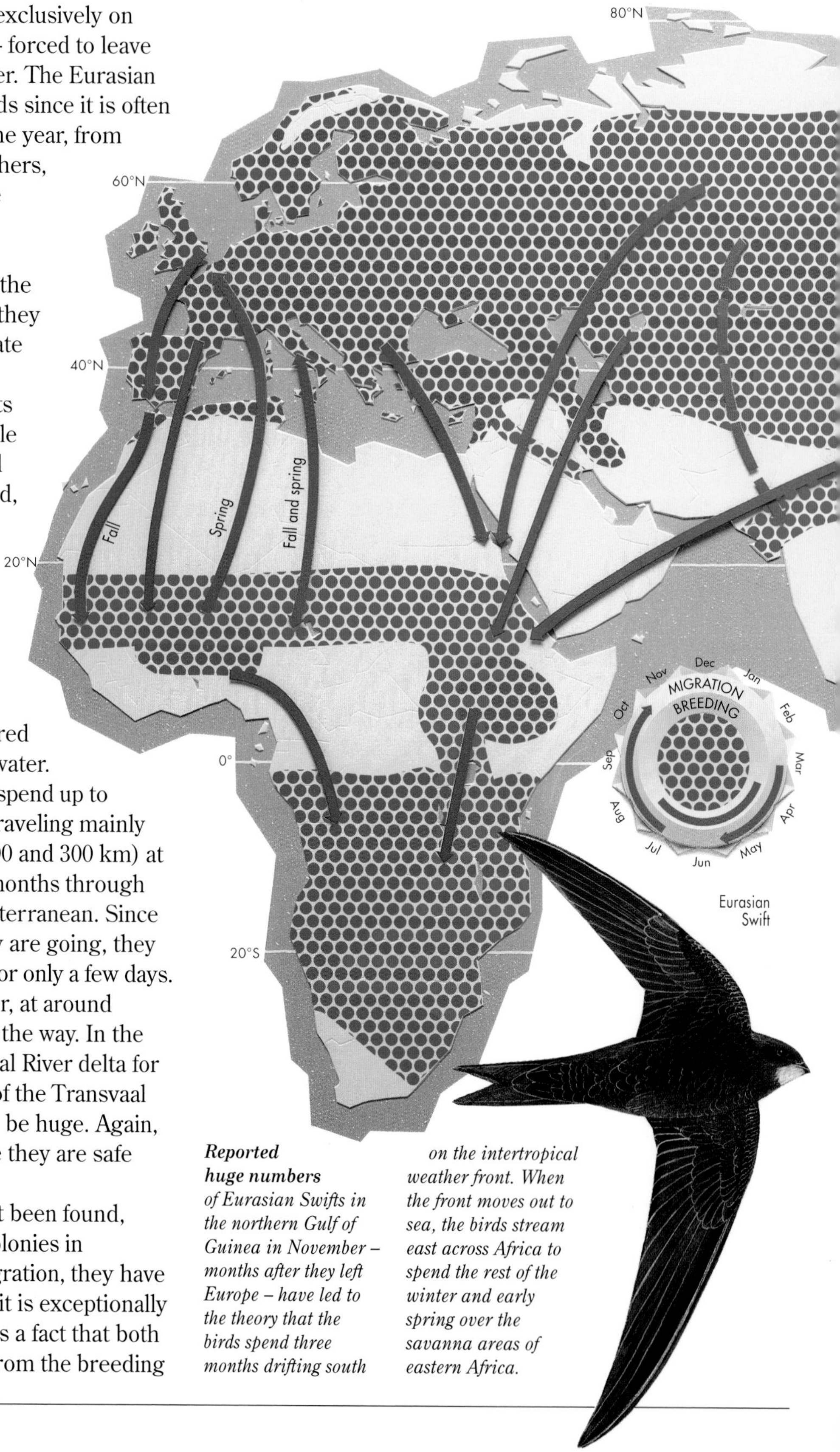

*Reported huge numbers* of Eurasian Swifts in the northern Gulf of Guinea in November – months after they left Europe – have led to the theory that the birds spend three months drifting south on the intertropical weather front. When the front moves out to sea, the birds stream east across Africa to spend the rest of the winter and early spring over the savanna areas of eastern Africa.

**Eurasian Swift**
*Apus apus*
**Wingspan** 18 in/46 cm
**Weight** 1¼–1½ oz/40–45 g
**Journey length** 1,850–7,500 miles/
3,000–12,000 km

**Bank Swallow**
*Riparia riparia*
**Wingspan** 11 in/28 cm
**Weight** ⅖ oz/12.5 g
**Journey length** 950–6,000 miles/
1,500–10,000 km

**Barn Swallow**
*Hirundo rustica*
**Wingspan** 13 in/32 cm
**Weight** ⅔ oz/19 g
**Journey length** 0–7,500 miles/
0–12,000 km

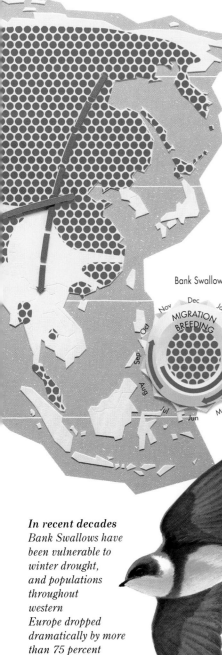

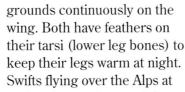
Barn Swallow

Bank Swallow

grounds continuously on the wing. Both have feathers on their tarsi (lower leg bones) to keep their legs warm at night. Swifts flying over the Alps at night, observed from gliders, drift in circular movements, beating their wings for a few seconds then gliding. On radar they can be traced rising gradually in the evening sky over towns and cities, and may drift with the wind until they have moved 20–30 miles (30–50 km).

Although Barn Swallows have been known migrants for generations, they are so widespread that it was only with the advent of banding that their winter homes could be pinpointed. Birds from central Russia join British breeders in South Africa; those from Germany winter in Zaïre; other areas are favored by birds from elsewhere in Europe. Migrant Barn Swallows winter in areas where there may be more than a dozen species of local, resident swallows and martins, and confusion between them has led to regular reports of European Barn Swallows breeding in Africa. This has not been proved, although House Martins have occasionally stayed in Africa to breed.

For all these species, winter is the time of a slow molt, when the flight feathers are gradually renewed without impairing the birds' powers of flight. Like life on migration, life in winter is not always easy, although the birds are not attached to a nest and can wander around to find the best food and conditions. The most frequent problem in winter is unseasonal cold as they arrive in Africa.

*The return of swallows to Europe in April marks the successful completion of a round-trip some 12,500 miles (20,000 km) long. If feeding trips are included, from the time they left in August or early September, the birds may have flown up to 190,000 miles (300,000 km).*

*Successful breeding birds return to the same area, perhaps even the same nest; young birds, also, tend to return to the area of their birth.*

***In recent decades** Bank Swallows have been vulnerable to winter drought, and populations throughout western Europe dropped dramatically by more than 75 percent during the winter of 1968/9. Although the species has partially recovered several times, there have been further falls, and numbers have never returned to the peak years of the mid-1960s.*

***Bank Swallows** breed in sandy banks (left). In developed areas, these natural sites are rare since the banks of streams and rivers are no longer left to erode unchecked. Quarries have now become regular nest sites, as have piles of sand already cleaned and ready for building use.*

# Wagtails and pipits

*Yellow Wagtails shelter from the desert sun behind discarded oil drums.*

The wagtails and pipits are a diverse family in terms of migratory strategy and include long- and short-distance migrants, those that simply move up and down mountains, and birds that are totally resident in one place.

The Gray Wagtail is a bird of mountain streams which often winters in the lowland areas around the Mediterranean. The White Wagtails of Scandinavia and other parts of northern Europe are migratory. Many of those in France and Britain, however, stay for the winter; others go to southern Europe or northern Africa. Some of the distinctive Icelandic White Wagtails winter in Britain; others simply pass through on their way south, some even reaching Senegal.

Yellow Wagtails are trans-Saharan migrants, traveling through western Europe and northern Africa to the Sahel – the region south of the Sahara desert that stretches eastward across the continent from Senegal. They are among the best-studied long-distance nocturnal migrants. As they move south through France and Spain using reedbed roosts, they gain weight, averaging an increase from their breeding weight of around ⅔ ounce (17 g) to ⁹⁄₁₀ ounce (25 g) or more by the time they reach Spain. At this weight they could theoretically make a

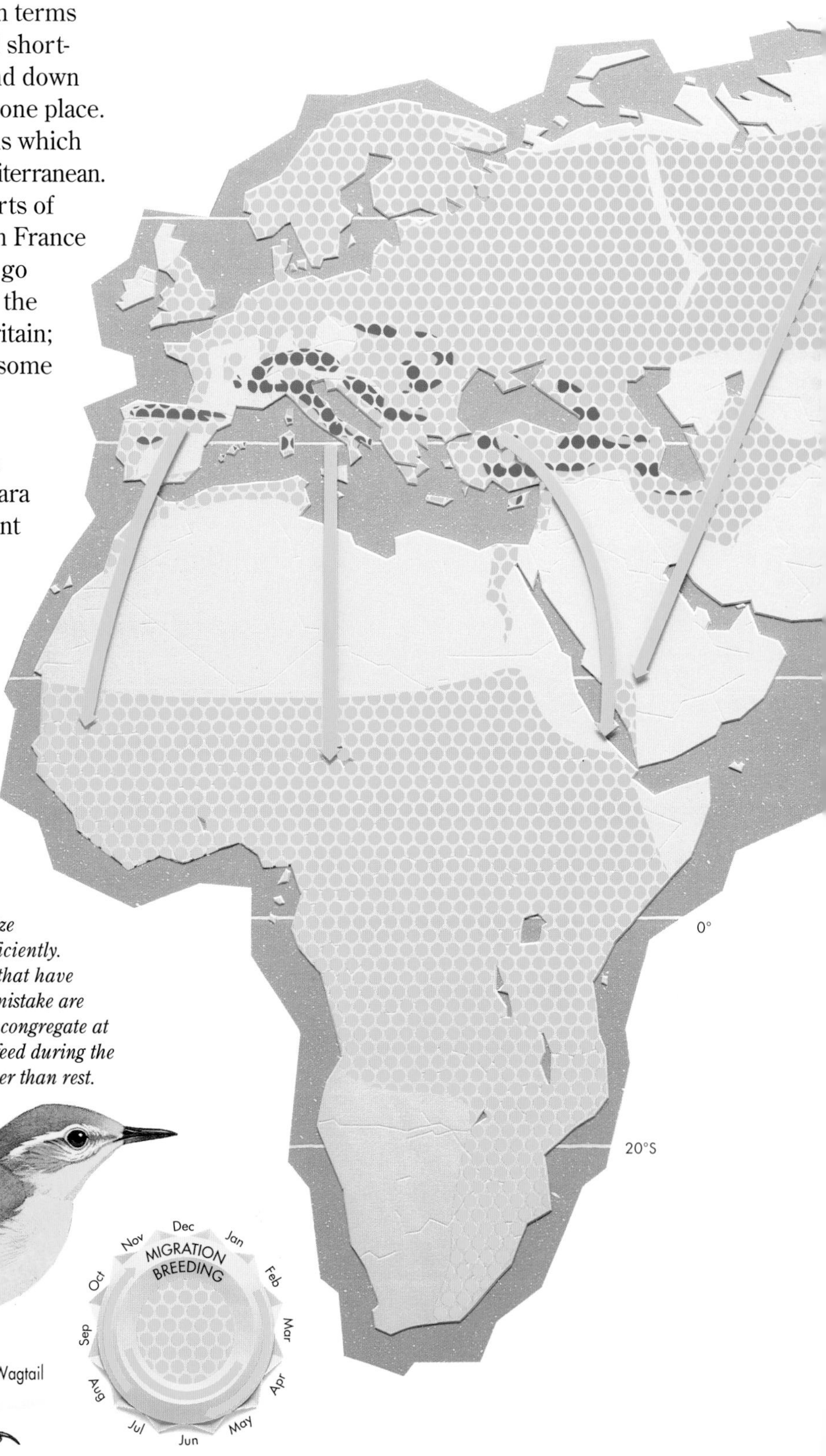

*There are many records* over the last 100 years of birds resting in shade during the day in the desert. Work in the 1980s and 1990s on such birds as Yellow Wagtails showed that they may be fit and fat and resting deliberately – not, as had been supposed, because they were exhausted, having made a navigational error or misjudged how far they had traveled.

Birds probably rest by day because temperatures are too high to allow them to metabolize water efficiently.

Birds that have made a mistake are thin and congregate at oases to feed during the day, rather than rest.

Yellow Wagtail

MIGRATION
BREEDING

Jan Feb Mar Apr May Jun Jul Aug Sep Oct Nov Dec

0°

20°S

**Yellow Wagtail**
*Motacilla flava*
**Wingspan** 10 in/26 cm
**Weight** ⅔–1 oz/17–28 g
**Journey length** 600–5,000 miles/
1,000–8,000 km

**Water Pipit**
*Anthus spinoletta*
**Wingspan** 10 in/26 cm
**Weight** ¾ oz/24 g
**Journey length** 0–950 miles/
0–1,500 km

journey lasting about 60 hours – taking them across Iberia, northern Africa, and the Sahara. Whether they do this is still a matter of debate.

It may seem strange that birds should put on such comparatively huge quantities of fat before they migrate. Surely, the argument goes, it would be better to carry no surplus weight and be as lean and fit as possible. In fact, the extra weight is not a great burden for the birds, since calculating how far they will get on a full fat load is an instinctive skill (see pp. 22–23). It is a problem if they have to escape from predators, but this is rare: they would have to be flying close to the ground and encounter an Eleonora's Falcon (see pp. 96–97). A migrant at several thousand feet is safe.

There are several races of Yellow Wagtails, with males differing in head pattern and color over their range. The British race *flavissima* (yellowest) is the only one that is predominantly yellow, although birds of the central Russian race have yellow heads. Birds belonging to the most usual European race, known as blue-headed, have pale blue-gray heads and a white stripe above the eye. Other European birds have completely dark heads. Birds from all populations winter in Africa.

Among the pipits, Tree Pipits are long-distance migrants, leaving the woodland glades of Europe for the savannas of western Africa. Meadow Pipits are a common sight to birdwatchers and one of the migrant species most likely to be seen flying from northern Europe to the Mediterranean. Since they are coastal birds, many Rock Pipits, by contrast, are able to stay at home in winter, although birds breeding in Norway and Sweden must migrate to slightly warmer climates farther south. Many of the alpine Water Pipits are altitudinal migrants; others winter in southern Britain, often on watercress beds.

Water Pipits
breed at high
altitudes and
winter lower down

60°N

40°N

20°N

0°

Water Pipit

*Many Water Pipits spend their lives in a limited area close to the nest in which they were born. Like other species, they may find their breeding sites untenable in winter, with thick snow and ice from as early as August in some years, through to May or early June. A short flight away, and downward, however, are ideal feeding grounds for the whole winter. These areas can often support many birds, albeit in well-defended individual feeding territories. At night they may come together in large roosts in protected locations, such as stands of thick evergreen shrubs.*

*Such short-distance movements are not oriented in a single direction, and birds may go north or south. Long-distance flights are not oriented either. About 100 birds from the Alps winter in Britain each year. Presumably having survived one winter there, they return to familiar territory.*

MIGRATION
BREEDING
Jan Feb Mar Apr May Jun Jul Aug Sep Oct Nov Dec

# Chats and thrushes

*These birds epitomize the advantages of migration over staying at home.*

This group includes a wide variety of birds ranging in size from the Eurasian Robin, Redstart, and Nightingale to the large and bold Fieldfare (see pp. 132–33) and Mistle Thrush. Within Europe there are species that are long-distance migrants, birds that move relatively short distances within the continent, and many millions of birds that are resident. Often the residents are members of a species living in an area where they can survive year-round, while a different population of the same species, farther to the north and east, regularly moves great distances – forced to migrate by winter weather that would make survival at best improbable, at worst impossible.

The closely related Stonechat and Whinchat provide an interesting insight into the relative effects of long- and short-distance migration on the life history of birds. The Stonechats often remain in northern Europe for the winter – or move south only as far as western Europe or the Mediterranean

*Nightingales have a reputation as specialist songsters of the night, but most also sing during the day. They are seldom heard by day since they have so many rivals then, but at night, without competition, their song is audible over great distances. These nocturnal habits also mean that many people familiar with nightingale song have never seen the bird.*

*Although many of their close relatives, including Bluethroats, (see p.132), are brightly colored, Nightingales are warm rufous brown with a brighter tail. They are larger than Eurasian Robins, skulk in bushes and undergrowth, and do not share the Robin's upright stance.*

Nightingale

Common Redstart

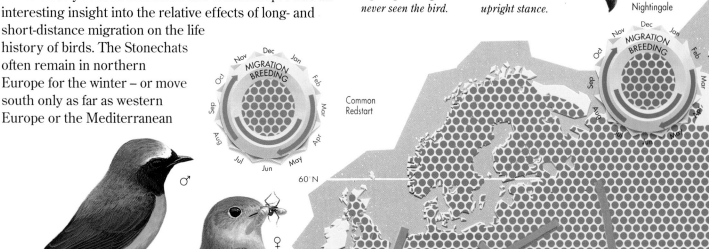

60° N

40°N

20°N

0°

*Redstarts nest in cavities or nest boxes in many areas; in others they breed in tunnels under vegetation. Nesting is carefully timed – they lay their bright blue eggs so that their young can take advantage of the high-summer*

*glut of insects in deciduous woodland.*

*Male Redstarts are among the most handsome Eurasian small birds, with a dazzling white forehead and black on the face, chin, and upper breast.*

**Common Redstart**
*Phoenicurus phoenicurus*
**Wingspan** 9 in/23 cm
**Weight** ½–⅞ oz/15–24 g
**Journey length** 1,300–3,750 miles/
2,000–6,000 km

**Nightingale**
*Luscinia megarhynchos*
**Wingspan** 10 in/25 cm
**Weight** ⅔–1¼ oz/19–36 g
**Journey length** 1,600–3,400 miles/
2,500–5,500 km

**Northern Wheatear**
*Oenanthe oenanthe*
**Wingspan** 11½–12½ in/29–32 cm
**Weight** ⅞–1½ oz/24–41 g
**Journey length** 950–10,000 miles/
1,500–16,000 km

basin. Whinchats, on the other hand, are trans-Saharan migrants, leaving Europe to spend the winter on the open savannas of Africa.

One immediate effect is that Stonechats are able to start breeding much earlier than Whinchats. Mid-March may see them laying a first clutch, while their second coincides with the first Whinchat brood. Stonechats have more third broods than Whinchats have second. This means that the potential for breeding, during a season, is much higher for a pair of Stonechats, and this is even further enhanced by the birds' choice of nest site. Stonechats often nest in gorse or other scrub; Whinchats by contrast choose to nest in grass and may have their nests in hay destroyed in the harvest.

Both species are in decline, but their current problems are due to loss of habitat and not to differences in lifestyle. Stonechats must have a high breeding potential, since in a cold winter, populations will suffer gravely. This ability to produce more young allows them to make up these losses over three or four years. Whinchats have an easier time,

since they are efficient migrants, and are able to maintain their populations at a steady level.

Long-distance migrants in this group include some birds, like the Redstart, that migrate mainly southwest through Europe, but others which migrate on a broad front. These include the Whinchat and Black-eared Wheatear. Eastern species, including the Thrush Nightingale and Isabelline Wheatear, migrate in an easterly direction around the Mediterranean. They are classic nocturnal migrants, and some seem to have specific weight-gaining areas. Most Redstarts stop off in Iberia for this purpose.

Robins, too, move by night, although many European populations are resident. Their autumn passage is sometimes spectacular, with huge numbers of birds appearing together in Belgium, the Netherlands, or Britain when the weather forces them to make an emergency landfall. Most winter in France, Spain, Portugal, and northern Africa. The return passage along the North Sea coast to the Scandinavian breeding grounds is usually concentrated in a short period in the first half of April.

## EVOLUTION IN ACTION

At the height of the last glaciation, an ancestral wheatear was breeding farther south than now, in the same habitats used today, and nesting anywhere that was free from ice for long enough to rear a brood. As the ice retreated, possible breeding sites also moved north, east, and west, at a rate of some ½–1¼ miles (1–2 km) a year.

Since the original birds had migrated to sub-Saharan Africa, their descendants continued to return from their more distant breeding areas to their ancestral winter home. Had the ancestral species also wintered in Asia, both areas might have been used, or two species might have evolved.

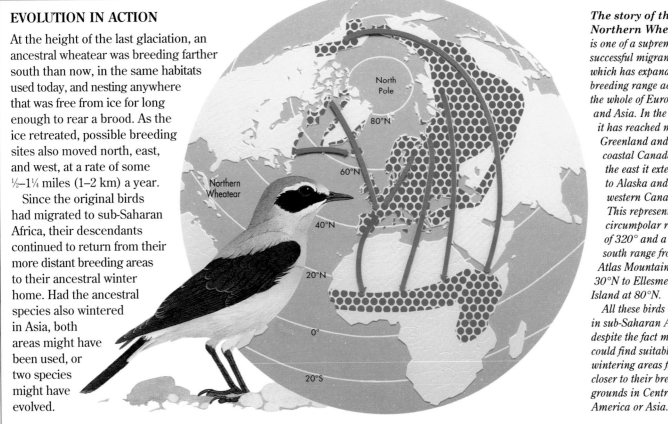

*The story of the Northern Wheatear is one of a supremely successful migrant which has expanded its breeding range across the whole of Europe and Asia. In the west, it has reached much of Greenland and coastal Canada; to the east it extends to Alaska and western Canada. This represents a circumpolar range of 320° and a north–south range from the Atlas Mountains at 30°N to Ellesmere Island at 80°N.*
*All these birds winter in sub-Saharan Africa, despite the fact many could find suitable wintering areas far closer to their breeding grounds in Central America or Asia.*

# Warblers

*The long-term survival of many warbler populations is in doubt.*

More warblers than birds of any other group leave Europe for Africa every fall. While swallows and martins dominate the wide open spaces of the air, warblers are birds of dense vegetation – sedge fields, reedbeds, scrubland, or woodland. Within this broad characterization, however, are individual warbler genera, each with its own habits and habitats.

Warblers of the *Acrocephalus* and *Locustella* genera, for example, frequent short, tangled, and often wet vegetation. The Grasshopper Warbler is a champion skulker, with a streaked coloration for easy concealment. Sedge Warblers are similar, but they are more adventurous in their habits. This species has been particularly badly affected by the winter weather in the Sahel: mid-1980s populations were around one-third of those of the mid-1960s.

The *Sylvia* warblers favor scrubland and, to a lesser extent, woodland in summer. The Common Whitethroat is equally at home in scrub and hedges. These long-tailed, relatively short-winged birds were once as numerous as Willow Warblers, but the entire Common Whitethroat population was reduced by 75 percent at a stroke in the winter of 1968/9.

Lesser Whitethroats, too, prefer scrub and hedges. All populations of this gray bird with a piratical black eyepatch winter in eastern Africa, the majority in Ethiopia, and all seem to follow the same route north in spring through the Near East and over the eastern Mediterranean. In the fall, however, British birds and perhaps others from western Europe take a more westerly route through Italy and across the Mediterranean into Egypt. Since they winter in a different area, Lesser Whitethroats have not declined in the same way as their Common cousins. Populations have fluctuated but remain within broad limits.

The two larger *Sylvia* warblers are similar in shape and size – but different in color. The Garden Warbler, a trans-Saharan migrant, is brown-olive with no distinguishing features. Blackcaps are brown-capped as juveniles, but when they molt, the males acquire glossy black caps. Southern European Blackcap populations are almost entirely resident, while Scandinavian breeders are long-distance migrants, wintering south of the Sahara. Birds from southern Germany winter in Britain and Ireland; those from Britain fly south to winter around the Mediterranean Sea.

Blackcaps are the only warblers whose populations have increased since the 1960s: numbers of birds frequenting woodland (their preferred habitat) have risen by 50 percent; those of birds on farmland by around one-third.

## WARBLERS IN DECLINE

The major problem facing migrant warblers is the weather in the Sahel region, where several species (and other migrants) spend the winter. Here disastrous droughts have severely affected the local plant, animal, and human ecology.

The Common Whitethroat winters in scrub and wooded savanna. After some years of drought, the scrub, which is resistant to arid conditions in the short term, was affected. Over the winter of 1968/9, conditions became critical, with the result that 75 percent of Common Whitethroats perished.

*In spring 1969, three-quarters of the Common Whitethroats due back in Europe failed to make it. Since then, numbers have fluctuated, but only in the late 1980s did they match those of 1969. European populations remain at risk.*

1965   '70   '75   '80   '85   '90

**Common Whitethroat**
*Sylvia communis*
**Wingspan** 8¼ in/21 cm
**Weight** ½–¾ oz/14–21 g
**Journey length** 1,250–5,600 miles/
2,000–9,000 km

**Reed Warbler**
*Acrocephalus scirpaceus*
**Wingspan** 8 in/20 cm
**Weight** ½ oz/11 g
**Journey length** 950–3,750 miles/
1,500–6,000 km

**Willow Warbler**
*Phylloscopus trochilus*
**Wingspan** 8 in/20 cm
**Weight** ³⁄₁₀–²⁄₅ oz/8–12 g
**Journey length** 2,500–8,700 miles/
4,000–14,000 km

Reed Warbler

*Eastern
Reed Warbler
populations are
grayer in color
than the
more rufous
western birds and
migrate in an easterly
direction, skirting the
Mediterranean.*

*When the migrants
reach Europe in the
spring, these birds are
looking for marshy
reedbeds in which to
nest. The males join
forces in rhythmic song
at dawn to attract
the later-returning
females. It is to every
male's advantage*
*to have more females
in the locality – the
next female may be
its mate for the year,
may stop a neighbor
from enticing a chosen
mate away, or even
provide a second
hen for a bigamist.*

*About one-fifth of all
migrants leaving
Europe and Asia to
winter south of the
Sahara are Willow
Warblers – almost a
billion birds. This
amazing number is,
however, put into
perspective by their
small size – one billion
warblers weigh the
equivalent of, perhaps,
4,000 swans.*

*Their light weight
enables these birds,
and others of the
Phylloscopus
(leafpeckers) genus, to
feed on the fringes of
stands of vegetation and
pick their food from the
leaves. Their sweet,
descending song can be
heard everywhere that
is not totally open*
*habitat or closed-
canopy woodland.*

*Unusually, most
Willow Warblers
undergo one molt in
late summer, before
they leave the breeding
grounds and another
in Africa in winter.*

*For reasons that are
unclear, after 30 years
of relative stability, the
recorded number of
Willow Warblers
returning to Europe
has declined each year
since 1990.*

Willow Warbler

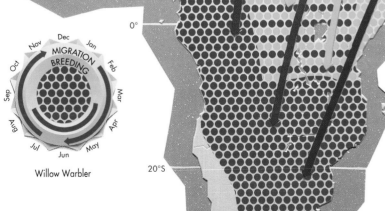

# Shrikes

*Conditions in the Great Rift Valley are ideal for migrant shrikes.*

**Red-backed Shrike**
*Lanius collurio*
**Wingspan**  10¼ in/26 cm
**Weight**  ⅓ oz/10 g
**Journey length**  2,500–6,800 miles/
4,000–11,000 km

The shrikes are predatory songbirds which feed on small birds, mammals, reptiles, and large insects. The colorful Red-backed Shrike is a southeasterly migrant, with all breeding populations heading over the eastern Mediterranean and down through the savanna areas of the Great Rift Valley. These birds winter in all but the southernmost parts of South Africa.

Today, the western limit of the breeding range of Red-backed Shrikes is in northwestern Spain; 100 years ago they were common summer residents in parts of Britain, but habitat loss and a general depletion in the numbers of large insects have pushed them south and east. They share this northwestern corner of Spain with the similarly sized and closely related Woodchat Shrikes, but elsewhere in Iberia only the latter breed.

Woodchat Shrikes are also long-distance migrants. Eastern races migrate to the south, and some may spend the winter in the extreme southwest of the Arabian peninsula. Western populations cross the Sahara to winter south of the desert in the Sahel. Their fall route takes them southwestward over the Iberian Peninsula, but like many other species, their return journey is more easterly – avoiding the generally wet weather on the fringe of the continent in late winter and early spring.

Every few years, when an anticyclone becomes established over southwestern Europe at the right time, prompting better than average spring conditions in northern Europe, Woodchat Shrikes overshoot their breeding grounds in southern France and Spain to reach northern France and Britain.

*Red-backed Shrikes are well adapted to the migratory way of life; since they are able to prey on their fellow migrants, they therefore move with them. These birds were once known as "butcher birds," because of their habit of storing surplus food – birds, mammals, and insects – on thorn bushes or barbed-wire fences.*

*Although they are common in France and Germany, reports of these birds in Britain are rare: this area is outside their usual range. Barred, brown young from the Scandinavian breeding populations may travel as far west as Britain on their fall explorations (see pp. 30–31).*

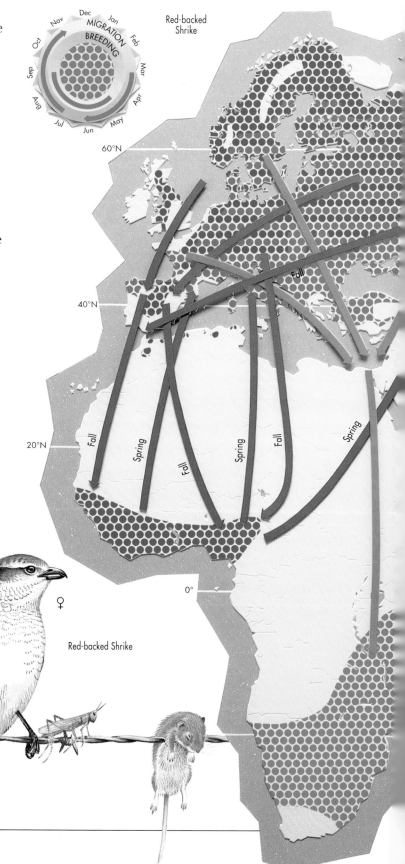

Red-backed
Shrike

Red-backed Shrike

# Flycatchers

*Cool, wet springs force birds east.*

**Pied Flycatcher**
*Ficedula hypoleuca*
**Wingspan** 9 in/23 cm
**Weight** ½–⅔ oz/12.5–19 g
**Journey length** 1,250–4,350 miles/
2,000–7,000 km

**Spotted Flycatcher**
*Muscicapa striata*
**Wingspan** 9½ in/24.5 cm
**Weight** ½–1 oz/15–28 g
**Journey length** 2,200–8,000 miles/
3,500–13,000 km

There are only two species of flycatcher widely distributed in western Europe: the Spotted, a bird of open woodland and gardens, and the Pied, a truly woodland species. Both have broad bills with well-developed bristles around them which literally extend the size of the mouth, making it easier for them to catch insects in flight. These bristles look like stiff hairs, but they are in fact modified feathers. Both species forage by sitting on a perch and keeping watch for flying insects – a quick dash and grab and back to the perch. This strategy presumes that there are plenty of large flying insects, which cannot be guaranteed until summer is well advanced.

In fact, Pied Flycatchers can also feed successfully on the ground, rather like Robins. This means that they can return to the oak woods of northern Europe as early as mid-April, at least three weeks in advance of the Spotted Flycatchers. This is essential for successful breeding and is timed to coincide with the super-abundant caterpillar crop of the woodland spring. Pied Flycatchers breed in holes, for which they are in direct competition with resident tits. It may be that this keeps them away from lowland areas in some parts of Europe and confined to higher ground, where tits are not easily able to survive the winter.

Migrating Pied Flycatchers have been studied in detail at their staging post in northwestern Portugal. Each bird has its own feeding territory, which it defends assiduously. Migrants unable to find a territory are excluded from the best feeding areas until the initial holder has put on enough weight to allow it to migrate southward.

These birds have a carefully arranged circuit of their home range because the large insects on which they feed can lie motionless for 15–20 minutes if they detect the presence of a flycatcher. The territory owner comes back every half hour or so to take the insects that are, by this time, flying around again. A flycatcher interloper would disturb this precisely timed routine.

Spotted Flycatchers are long-distance migrants, with birds from Finland and Wales discovered wintering in South Africa and an Irish breeder spending the winter in Angola. The species is one which shows a migratory divide at about 12°E, with birds breeding to the west migrating westward through Spain and those to the east traveling through the eastern Mediterranean. Although this means that birds from western Europe almost all travel to western Africa, once they have crossed the Sahara, they may continue to move east and south. To date, 35 birds banded in Europe have been found in the Zaïre River basin.

*The dappled light and shade of summer woodland tends to make male Pied Flycatchers appear pure black and white to observers. The birds do, however, have a good deal of brown coloration, although males are darker than females.*

*Most Pied Flycatchers pass through a staging post in northern Portugal in the fall where, for a couple of months, they may be the most common birds of the cork oak forests. The return route in spring is different, with birds taking a more easterly course. At this time of year, the climate in northern Portugal is cold and wet, and completely unsuitable for a flycatcher.*

Spotted
Flycatcher

*The molt of Spotted Flycatchers is unusual in that, unlike almost all other perching birds, the first of the primary feathers (the main flight feathers) to be replaced is the outermost and not the innermost. No logical reason has been found for this, but the Spotted Flycatcher is a species which relies on its powers of flight for feeding. Unlike the swallows and martins, these birds tend to hug cover, and therefore their wing feathers are susceptible to wear.*

*The molt is undertaken on the wintering grounds of Africa, Arabia, or northwestern India in the middle of the season, usually between November and February.*

Pied Flycatcher

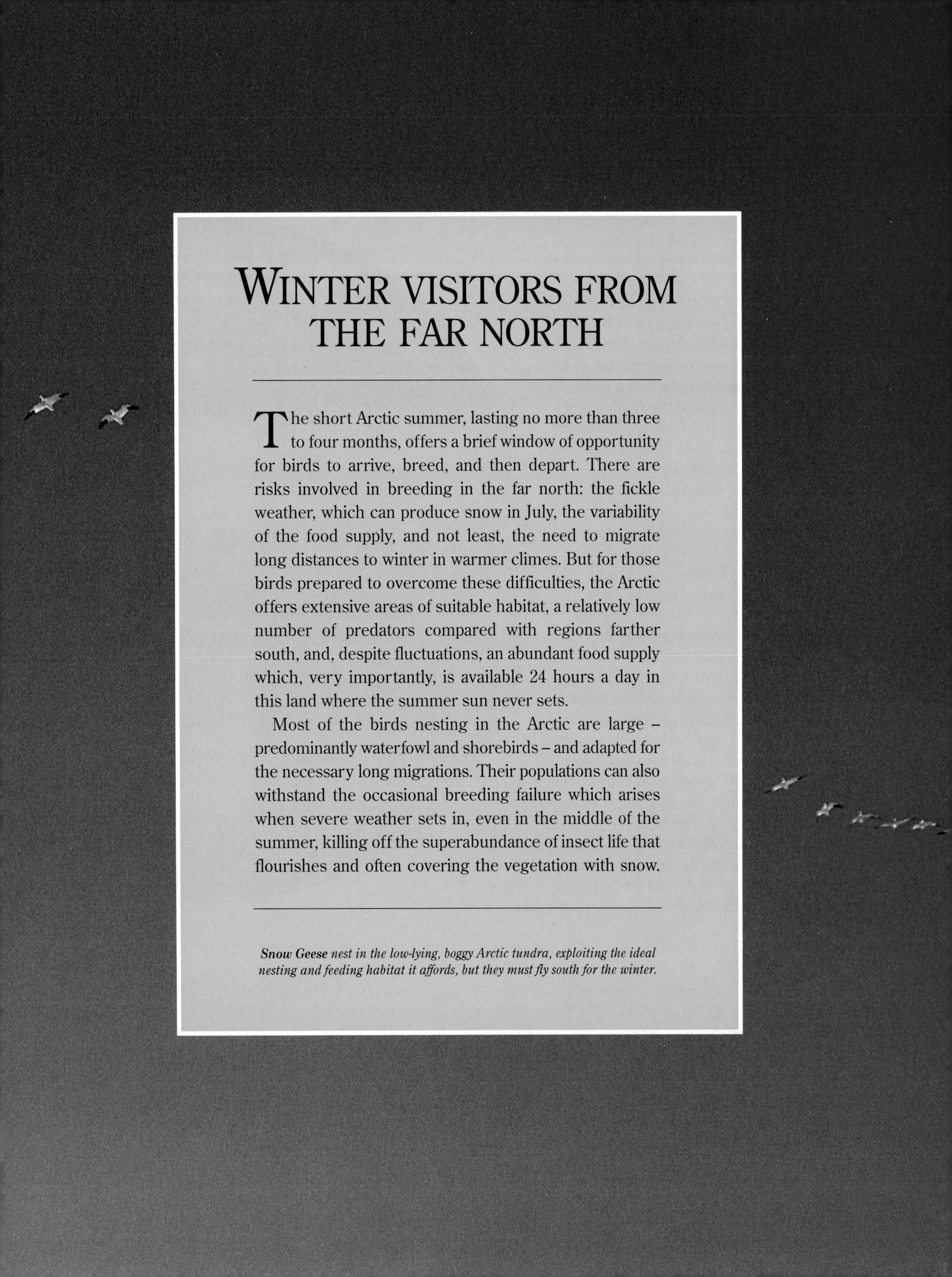

# WINTER VISITORS FROM THE FAR NORTH

The short Arctic summer, lasting no more than three to four months, offers a brief window of opportunity for birds to arrive, breed, and then depart. There are risks involved in breeding in the far north: the fickle weather, which can produce snow in July, the variability of the food supply, and not least, the need to migrate long distances to winter in warmer climes. But for those birds prepared to overcome these difficulties, the Arctic offers extensive areas of suitable habitat, a relatively low number of predators compared with regions farther south, and, despite fluctuations, an abundant food supply which, very importantly, is available 24 hours a day in this land where the summer sun never sets.

Most of the birds nesting in the Arctic are large – predominantly waterfowl and shorebirds – and adapted for the necessary long migrations. Their populations can also withstand the occasional breeding failure which arises when severe weather sets in, even in the middle of the summer, killing off the superabundance of insect life that flourishes and often covering the vegetation with snow.

*Snow Geese nest in the low-lying, boggy Arctic tundra, exploiting the ideal nesting and feeding habitat it affords, but they must fly south for the winter.*

# Patterns of migration

*Birds that breed during the brief Arctic summer must head south for the winter.*

The need to escape the Arctic winter forces almost all the birds breeding in that region to leave – some as early as August, the rest throughout September and October – and make for somewhere warmer with an assured food supply. The obvious direction is south, but that is, in fact, only a general course. Many birds more specifically move southwest or southeast in order to reach the wintering area of their choice. In some cases this direction can reveal how a particular species may have colonized the Arctic.

Many birds breeding in the Arctic make the shortest possible journey to the nearest suitable habitat each fall. Some Snowy Owls, for example, winter within the southern parts of their breeding range or move only a few hundred miles to the south, while Purple Sandpipers stay as far north as they can, in Iceland and northern Norway, and move no farther than the nearest ice-free coast.

Other Arctic breeders, however, migrate thousands of miles, several crossing the equator and reaching the southern shores of South America, South Africa, and Australia. It is difficult to be certain of the driving factor in every case of long-distance migration. Certainly the need to find the right habitat with an adequate food supply may cause birds to overfly potentially suitable areas which already hold large numbers of species that might provide unacceptable competition.

Some journeys are almost certainly governed by historical factors. Instead of taking what would seem to be the obvious route south through North America, several birds breeding in Greenland and on the numerous islands of the Canadian Arctic head southeast to western Europe.

## HOT SPOTS

Arctic breeders are often long-distance migrants; as a result every continent affords at least one prime site where these birds can be seen.

1. St. Paul Island, Alaska
2. Copper River delta, Alaska
3. Churchill, Manitoba
4. San Francisco Bay, California
5. Salt Lake, Utah
6. Cheyenne Bottoms, Kansas
7. James Bay, Ontario
8. Bay of Fundy, New Brunswick/Shapody Bay, Nova Scotia
9. Delaware Bay, Delaware
10. Panama
11. Los Olivitos, Venezuela
12. Coast of Surinam
13. Lake Myvatn, Iceland
14. Ny Alesund, Svalbard
15. Varangerfjord, Norway/Lake Inari, Finland
16. Solway Firth, Scotland
17. The Wash, England
18. Waddenzee, the Netherlands
19. Ile de la Camargue, France
20. Coast of Morocco
21. Banc d'Arguin, Mauritania
22. Danube delta, Romania
23. Volga delta, Russia
24. Kyzylagach NR, Azerbaijan
25. Bharatpur, India
26. Kamchatka peninsula, Russia
27. Mai Po marshes, Hong Kong

*About 100 bird species* breed on the Arctic tundra in the brief northern summer and all but perhaps half a dozen exceptionally hardy species migrate. About 30 of these species are waterfowl, another 30 or so shorebirds.

*The Wandering Tattler's migration* takes it from the mountain streams of Alaska and eastern Siberia to the Pacific coasts of South America, Australia, New Zealand, or Japan – a journey of up to 9,300 miles (15,000 km).

*The world's 2,000–2,600 Spoon-billed Sandpipers* breed in northeastern Siberia and Kamchatka and migrate along the Pacific coast of Asia to winter in Southeast Asia, from eastern India to southern China.

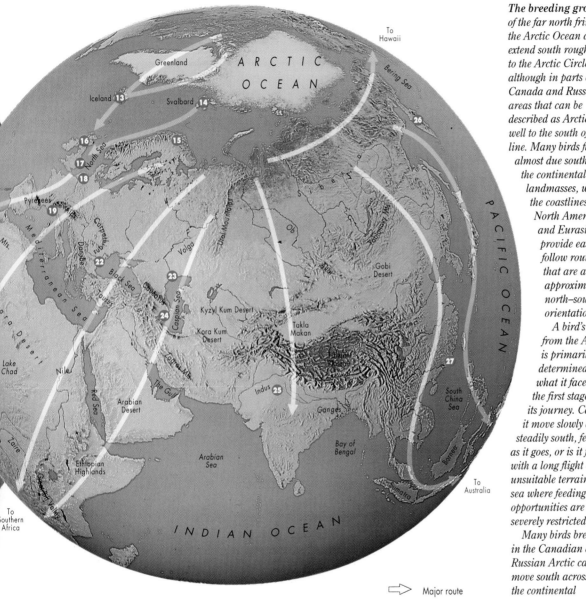

Major route

**The breeding grounds** of the far north fringe the Arctic Ocean and extend south roughly to the Arctic Circle, although in parts of Canada and Russia areas that can be described as Arctic exist well to the south of this line. Many birds fly almost due south over the continental landmasses, while the coastlines of North America and Eurasia provide easy-to-follow routes that are also approximately north–south in orientation.

A bird's route from the Arctic is primarily determined by what it faces on the first stage of its journey. Can it move slowly and steadily south, feeding as it goes, or is it faced with a long flight over unsuitable terrain or the sea where feeding opportunities are severely restricted?

Many birds breeding in the Canadian and Russian Arctic can move south across the continental landmasses, making comparatively short flights between resting places. But not all the land is favorable for birds, particularly in the eastern half of Russia, where the Gobi and other extensive deserts and high mountain ranges such as the Himalayas straddle the routes. Birds must cross such areas nonstop.

Species nesting in the far east of Siberia or in Alaska have the choice of a long journey over land, in which case they must head almost due west or east respectively before they can turn to the south, or they must commit themselves to a flight over the sea before making a landfall. The distance involved – from Alaska to California, for example – may be up to one-third shorter but there is no food to be found on the way.

Birds nesting in Greenland, Iceland, and Svalbard have no such choice – the first leg of their migration has to involve an over-sea flight of hundreds of miles.

At the end of the last ice age, 10,000 years ago, the Knot, Northern Wheatear, and the light-bellied race of the Brant, among others, were breeding in what is now western Europe. As the ice retreated, most birds nesting in this area moved steadily north and northeast to colonize Scandinavia and Russia. But a few species successfully island-hopped northwestward, via the Faroes and Iceland to Greenland, and then on to Canada. Throughout the thousands of years of this gradual expansion, the birds maintained their traditional pattern of migration to the southeast. And, although the distances involved may seem great on a map – and such a journey involves overflying or skirting the Greenland ice cap – on a globe they do not seem so daunting.

The majority of Arctic-breeding species are waterfowl and shorebirds, and their need for watery habitats, both as migration stopovers and as winter homes, dictates the directions they take and destinations they target. Many of these birds are channeled to the coasts of North America and Eurasia, or follow one of two major flyways: via the Great Lakes and down the Mississippi valley; or from the White Sea to the Baltic and into the North Sea before heading down the coasts of France and Iberia toward western Africa.

# Swans

*Keeping the family together brings rewards on the wintering grounds.*

One species of small swans and two species of large ones breed in the far north. The small Tundra Swan occurs widely in North America, where there is a race called the Whistling Swan, and across Europe and Asia, where the race is known as the Bewick's Swan. The two larger species, up to 70 percent bigger, are the Trumpeter Swan, which has a restricted range in Alaska, northwestern Canada and the U.S., and the Whooper Swan, which breeds from Iceland through northern Europe and Asia to eastern Siberia.

All these swans travel long distances from their tundra breeding grounds to the coastal and fresh waters of temperate latitudes to the south. Many of their winter haunts are traditional and have been used for almost as long as reliable records exist. Moreover, the same swans return year after year to the same site and use the same stopping places on migration.

This habituation makes sense for the birds: if they are familiar with an area, it is easy for them to find food and to learn where danger threatens. The pattern of returning year after year is passed on from one generation to the next. Since young swans take time to reach maturity, both in terms of size and in their ability to look after themselves, they are still dependent on their parents at the onset of their first Arctic winter. As a result, and contrary to the practice adopted by many species, the family migrates together so that the young learn the route, the places to stop on the way, and the ultimate wintering site. The following fall, after they have separated from their parents, the juvenile swans are able to follow the same route to the same destination and so the tradition continues.

It is not unusual for the young of the previous year to meet up with and

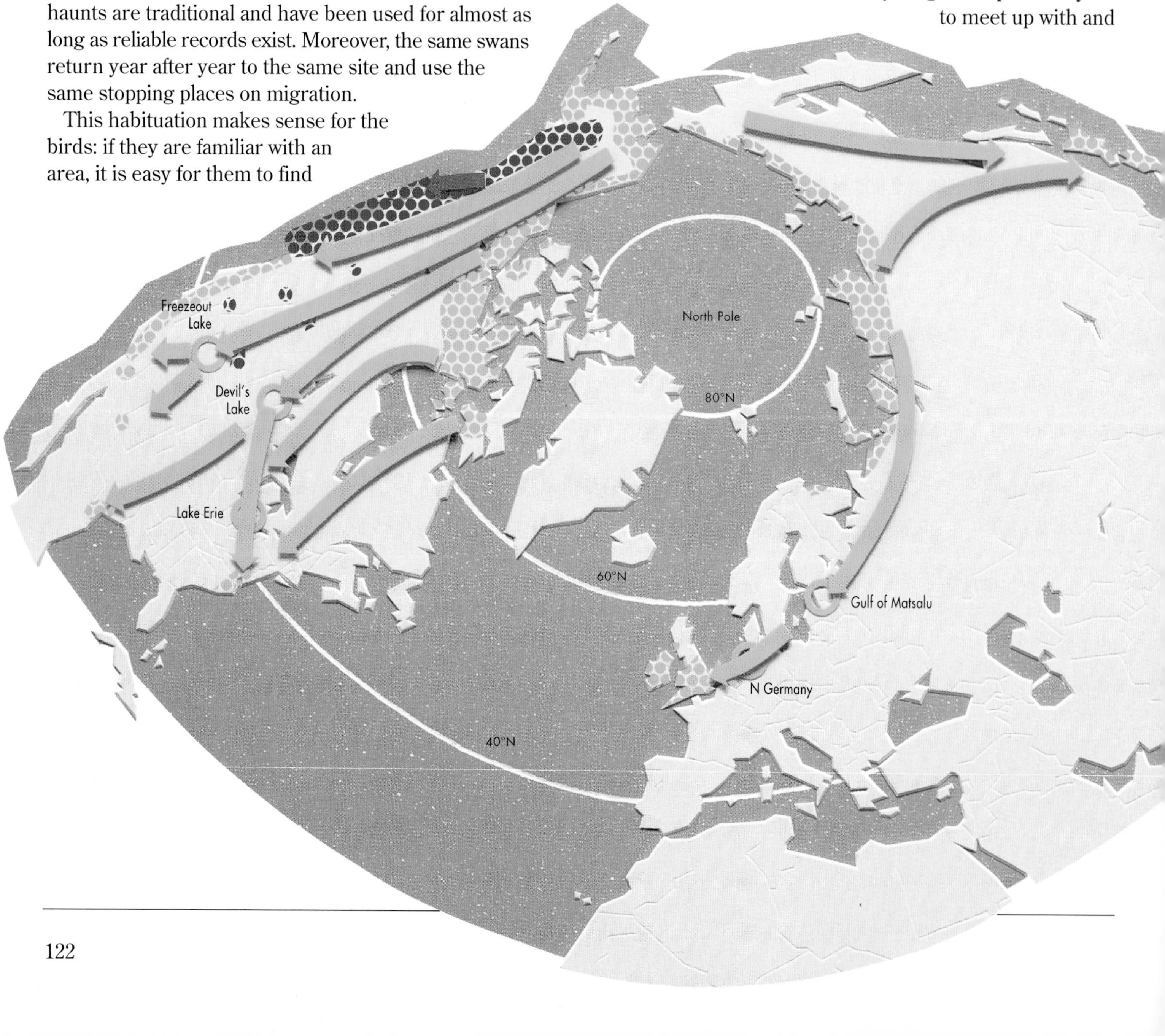

Freezeout
Lake

Devil's
Lake

Lake Erie

North Pole

80°N

60°N

40°N

Gulf of Matsalu

N Germany

**Tundra Swan**
*Cygnus columbianus*
**Wingspan** 6 ft–6 ft 11 in/1.8–2.1 m
**Weight** 7 lb 4 oz–16 lb 8oz/3.3–7.5 kg
**Journey length** 1,600–3,000 miles/
2,500–5,000 km

**Trumpeter Swan**
*Olor buccinator*
**Wingspan** 7 ft 3 in–8 ft 2 in/2.2–2.5 m
**Weight** 15 lb 7 oz–27 lb 9 oz/7–12.5 kg
**Journey length** 0–1,600 miles/
0–2,500 km

race *columbianus*
Whistling Swan

race *bewickii*
Bewick's Swan

Tundra Swan

*Whistling and Bewick's swans, once considered separate species, are now regarded as one, the Tundra Swan.*

*Much of what is known about swans derives from a study by the British Wildfowl and Wetlands Trust, using Bewick's Swans. The black and yellow bill patterns of this species are unique and can be used as identification guides by researchers studying the birds' interrelationships, behavior, and ability to return to the same wintering site.*

become reattached to their parents, even though the adult birds may have a new brood of young with them. A "super-family" then develops, which may even contain the young of two or three previous years. There are definite advantages in belonging to a super-family: larger families reign supreme, dominating both smaller ones and pairs without any young, and keeping them away from the best feeding places.

Whooper and Trumpeter swans, which can measure up to 6 feet (1.8 m) from beak to tail, are around the maximum size for long-distance movement. Large birds cannot lay down as much fat to use on migration as smaller ones, since they are already close to the heaviest weight their wings can lift off the ground (see pp. 26–27). A non-stop over-sea flight from Iceland to Britain of 550–750 miles (900–1,200 km) is approaching the limit for Whooper Swans, which often migrate in a strong tail wind to reduce the time they must spend in the air. These birds have also been recorded migrating at high altitudes, on occasion reaching 28,000 feet (8,500 m), where the winds are usually strongest.

*The Trumpeter Swan (left), hunted throughout the 19th century for its meat, skin, and feathers, was on the verge of extinction earlier this century. Conservation began in 1918 when hunting was outlawed. More recent measures include establishing birds raised in captivity in former breeding haunts and feeding flocks in winter. There has clearly been a good recovery, from some 2,000 birds in the early 1960s to perhaps 10,000 birds today.*

# Geese/1

*Barnacle Geese find lush winter pastures – but at the expense of farmers.*

There are three populations of Barnacle Geese, each with discrete breeding and wintering ranges. The largest, numbering some 100,000, breeds mainly in Arctic Russia and winters in the Netherlands and Germany. The smallest, a mere 12,000 birds, breeds on the Svalbard archipelago and winters on the Solway Firth, Scotland. The third population numbers around 35,000 and breeds in eastern Greenland, wintering on islands off Scotland and Ireland scattered between the Orkneys and County Kerry.

The separate populations use traditional migration stopovers. These sites are always in areas where there is an abundance of good grass so that the birds can lay down sufficient fat reserves to complete the fall and spring migrations and, in spring above all, to cope with the physical stresses of the nesting period.

Many of the birds wintering in the Netherlands stop off on Gotland, off the east coast of Sweden, in spring. During the 1960s, small numbers began to stay there through the summer, eventually nesting. This habit grew rapidly during the 1970s and 1980s, and today more than 1,500 pairs of Barnacle Geese nest on Gotland and join the Russian birds as they pass through in the fall en route to the Netherlands.

Those Barnacle Geese that winter on the Solway Firth stop over in spring on the hundreds of small grassy offshore islands of northern Norway. They spend about three weeks in May feeding intensively in the long hours of daylight, before crossing the Barents Sea to Svalbard. The fall stopover is different: Bear Island, midway between Svalbard and northern Norway. From there, they undertake a single flight of more than 1,250 miles (2,000 km) to reach the Solway Firth.

Iceland is an ideal stopover for the Greenland-nesting geese, the lush pastures of its northern valleys providing good feeding in both spring and the fall. The winter distribution of these birds is unusual in that one location, the island of Islay in the Inner Hebrides, supports 60 percent of the total population; the remainder is scattered over a further 50 or 60 haunts. Numbers on Islay can reach 25,000

*Barnacle Geese, migrating over the sea, fly nonstop. When they finally make landfall, they first bathe and drink, then preen briefly before tucking their heads under their wings and going to sleep. Those that fly from Iceland to Islay in the fall, a journey lasting perhaps 20 hours, sleep for three or four hours before flying to the nearest pastures to feed (right).*

**Barnacle Goose**
*Branta leucopsis*
**Wingspan** 4 ft 4 in–4 ft 9 in/1.32–1.45 m
**Weight** 3 lb 11 oz–4 lb 13 oz/1.4–2.2 kg
**Journey length** 1,100–2,000 miles/
1,800–3,200 km

**Brant**
*Branta bernicla*
**Wingspan** 3 ft 7 in–3 ft 11 in/1.1–1.2 m
**Weight** 2 lb 10 oz–3 lb 5 oz/1.2–1.5 kg
**Journey length** 1,900–4,000 miles/
3,000–6,500 km

Brant

*Parts of the breeding range of the Brant are farther north than those of any other goose – on the Arctic islands of Canada and Russia. Many populations fly more than 2,500 miles (4,000 km) to reach their winter homes. Birds nesting on Wrangel Island in northeastern Siberia fly 4,000 miles (6,500 km) to western Mexico and may cover some 3,000 miles (4,800 km) of that in a single over-sea flight from Alaska.*

birds; the next largest flock is some 2,500, on the Inishkea Islands, Ireland. Many haunts hold only 100 to 200 birds. This uneven distribution requires careful management, not only because whatever happens to the birds on Islay dramatically affects the overall population but also because this concentration in one place can create problems.

Barnacle Geese feed on the best grass they can find, which on Islay is the same grass that the farmers are growing for their sheep and cattle. After many years of conflict, when shooting was the only way of reducing the damage the geese were doing to the grass, a scheme was introduced in October 1992 whereby the farmers are paid by the government conservation agency to tolerate the geese, whose numbers, though high on Islay, are internationally vulnerable.

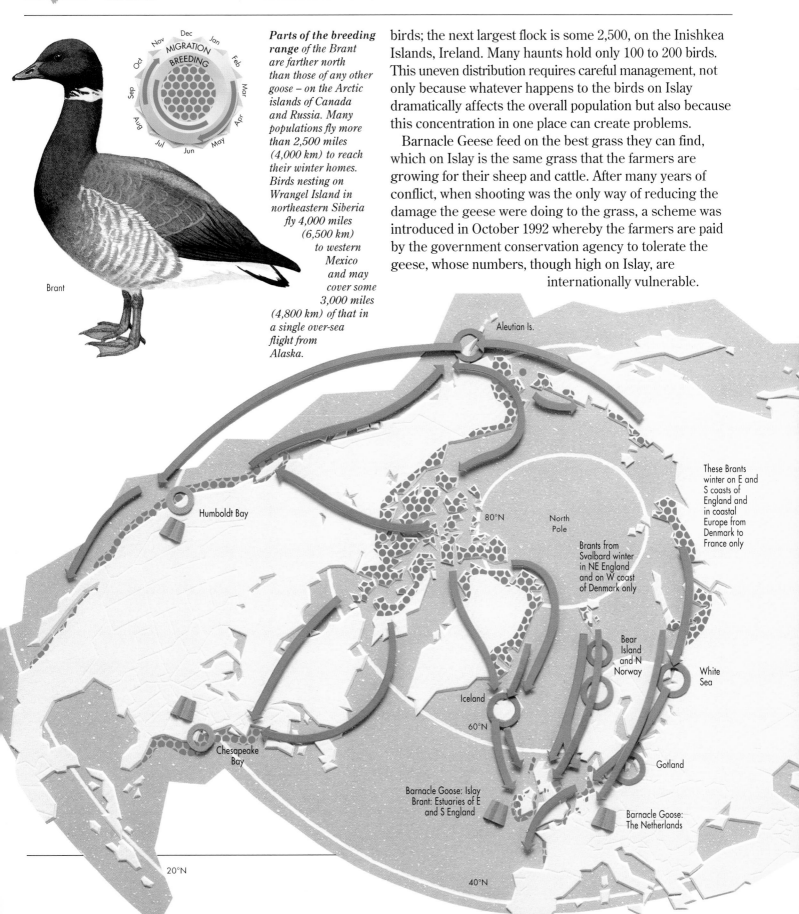

Aleutian Is.

Humboldt Bay

80°N

North Pole

These Brants winter on E and S coasts of England and in coastal Europe from Denmark to France only

Brants from Svalbard winter in NE England and on W coast of Denmark only

Bear Island and N Norway

White Sea

Iceland

60°N

Gotland

Chesapeake Bay

Barnacle Goose: Islay
Brant: Estuaries of E and S England

Barnacle Goose: The Netherlands

20°N

40°N

# Geese/2

*More than three million Snow Geese leave the far north for the winter.*

Arctic Canada is the breeding ground for between two and a half and three million Lesser Snow Geese, half a million Greater Snow Geese, and more than 30,000 of the smaller Ross's Snow Geese. There is also a single colony of Lesser Snow Geese in eastern Siberia. All migrate in winter.

Snow Geese breed in colonies of between 1,000 and 150,000 pairs. Their white plumage, relieved only by black wing tips, means that they cannot rely on camouflage to avoid detection by predators when nesting on the open tundra. Instead, they depend on the sheer number of individuals in the colony to intimidate would-be attackers. Only birds at the edges of the group are at risk; these are likely to be the immature or less fit members of the colony.

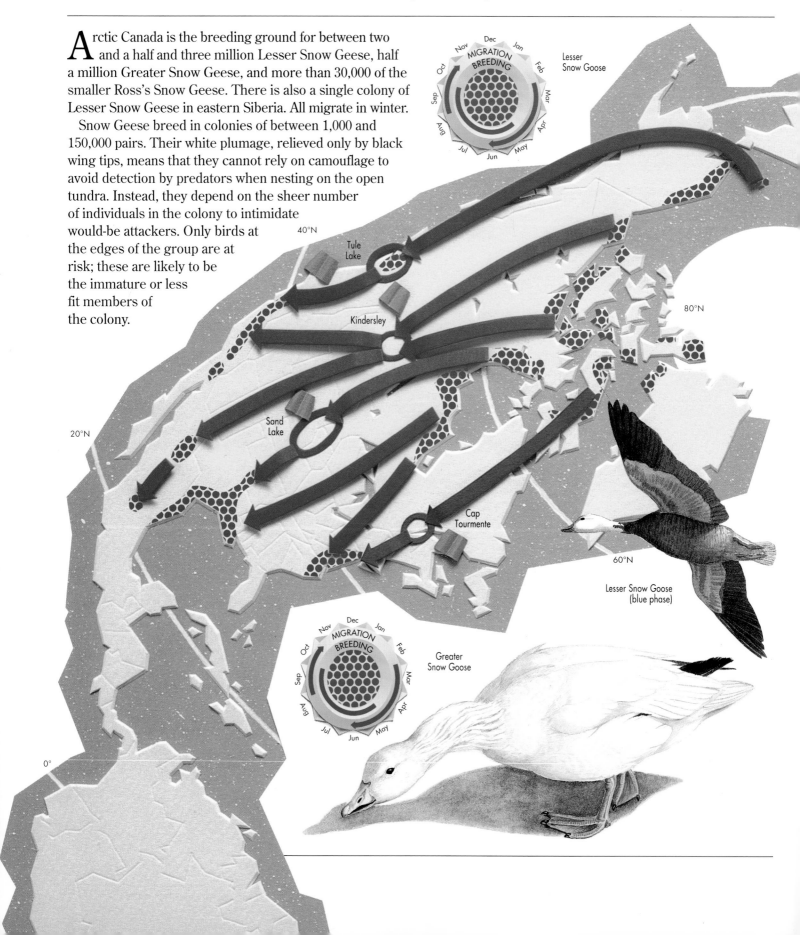

Lesser Snow Goose

MIGRATION BREEDING
Jan Feb Mar Apr May Jun Jul Aug Sep Oct Nov Dec

40°N

Tule Lake

80°N

Kindersley

20°N

Sand Lake

Cap Tourmente

60°N

Lesser Snow Goose (blue phase)

MIGRATION BREEDING
Jan Feb Mar Apr May Jun Jul Aug Sep Oct Nov Dec

Greater Snow Goose

0°

**Lesser Snow Goose**
*Anser caerulescens*
**Wingspan** 4 ft 4 in–5 ft 3 in/1.32–1.6 m
**Weight** 4 lb 7 oz–6 lb 10 oz/2–3 kg
**Journey length** 1,250–3,000 miles/
2,000–5,000 km

**Greater Snow Goose**
*Anser caerulescens atlanticus*
**Wingspan** 4 ft 9 in–5 ft 9 in/1.45–1.75 m
**Weight** 6 lb 3 oz–9 lb 4 oz/2.8–4.2 kg
**Journey length** 2,200–3,000 miles/
3,500–5,000 km

*The impact of even a single goose on a jet airliner can be disastrous. For this reason, observers south of Canada's Winnipeg airport monitor the northward progress of Lesser Snow Geese and warn air-traffic controllers of their approach. If necessary, the airport can be closed down for hours, or occasionally days, during the peak of migration.*

*Winnipeg lies on one of North America's major migration routes for northern breeders. The migratory patterns of Snow Geese and many other species are influenced by the continent's geography (see also pp. 54–55). In general, birds breeding in the eastern Canadian Arctic migrate to the Atlantic seaboard; those*

*breeding in central Canada use the Mississippi flyway to reach the Gulf of Mexico; the more westerly breeders, particularly those in Alaska, migrate along, and winter close to, the Pacific coast.*

*Lesser Snow Geese breeding around Hudson Bay follow this pattern, migrating south across the Great Lakes and down the Mississippi valley to winter on the extensive coastal marshlands and low-lying farmland bordering the Gulf of Mexico. In winter, and particularly as spring approaches, the birds must obtain enough food to lay down fat both for the return migration and for at least the first week or two back at the breeding grounds, when it is often still too cold for vegetation to grow.*

A feeding flock of geese might appear to be without structure, but the family parties and pairs stay together, moving through the flock as distinct units. Each group keeps an area around it clear of other geese so that competition for food is reduced. The adult male of a family is especially active in making sure that other geese do not come too close.

All geese pair for life during their second winter, when they are between one and two years old and still immature. The males display to the females, each of which selects a mate larger than she is. It is an obvious advantage to a female to have a mate able to defend her and the nest against both predators and the interference of other geese.

Color, too, plays a part in the process of selecting a mate. Lesser Snow Geese occur in two distinct, genetically controlled color types, or phases – white and blue (in fact, more a gray color). The female's choice is thought to be influenced by the color of her parents.

# Shorebirds/1

*Estuary stopovers are vital for most of these long-distance migrants.*

There are about 215 different species of shorebirds spread throughout the world, more than half of which migrate. While some of their journeys are comparatively short – the Wrybill, for example, breeds on South Island, New Zealand, and winters on North Island – there are at least 65 species that breed in the northern hemisphere and winter wholly or partly within the southern hemisphere.

The Arctic tundras of Europe, Asia, and Canada offer a safe breeding habitat for the vast majority of shorebirds that cross the equator from their winter homes in Africa, South America, and Australasia. These include the Curlew Sandpiper, which breeds in northern Siberia on the shores of the Arctic Ocean and winters in southern Africa, India, and Australia, and the White-rumped Sandpiper, which nests on islands in the Canadian Arctic and migrates some 8,700 miles (14,000 km) to winter in Chile and Argentina.

Several species, including the Sanderling and Black-bellied Plover, breed right around the North Pole in the North American and Eurasian Arctic. Both are equally far-flung in winter, when there are populations wintering on the coasts of South America, South Africa, and Australasia.

Although shorebirds are associated with water, feeding on tidal mud flats and in shallow fresh waters, most do not swim, making them as vulnerable on sea crossings as land birds. That they are able to cope with long ocean journeys stems from their flying ability, which is greater than that of many small land birds. The long, narrow wings of most migrant shorebirds enable them to fly quickly and efficiently, and so travel farther than a less efficient bird of equal size for each calorie of energy used.

Some species fly directly, over land and sea, between their breeding and wintering grounds; others must stop to refuel on the way. Shorebirds cannot feed at sea and have to make a landfall to find food. For many species, migration routes are dictated by the location of estuaries and coastal wetlands, where they find the invertebrates on which they feed.

The importance of these areas to migrating shorebirds is becoming increasingly clear. An estuary staging post is as vital to a migrant for the few days to few weeks that it spends refueling there as it is to a bird that stays for the whole winter. If a migrant cannot find enough food to enable it to complete the next leg of its journey, it will not survive.

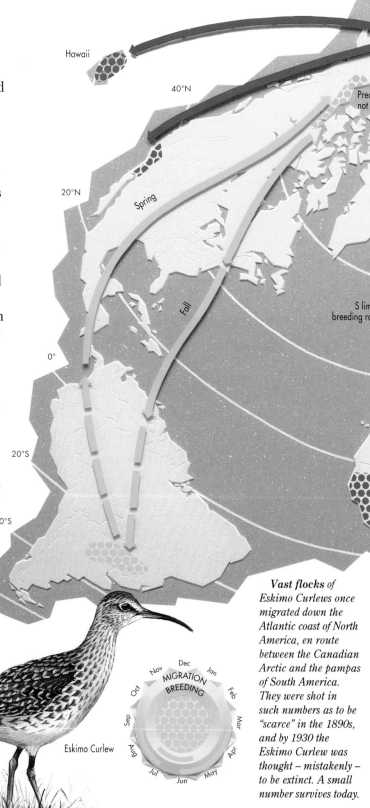

*Vast flocks of Eskimo Curlews once migrated down the Atlantic coast of North America, en route between the Canadian Arctic and the pampas of South America. They were shot in such numbers as to be "scarce" in the 1890s, and by 1930 the Eskimo Curlew was thought – mistakenly – to be extinct. A small number survives today.*

Eskimo Curlew

MIGRATION
BREEDING

Jan · Feb · Mar · Apr · May · Jun · Jul · Aug · Sep · Oct · Nov · Dec

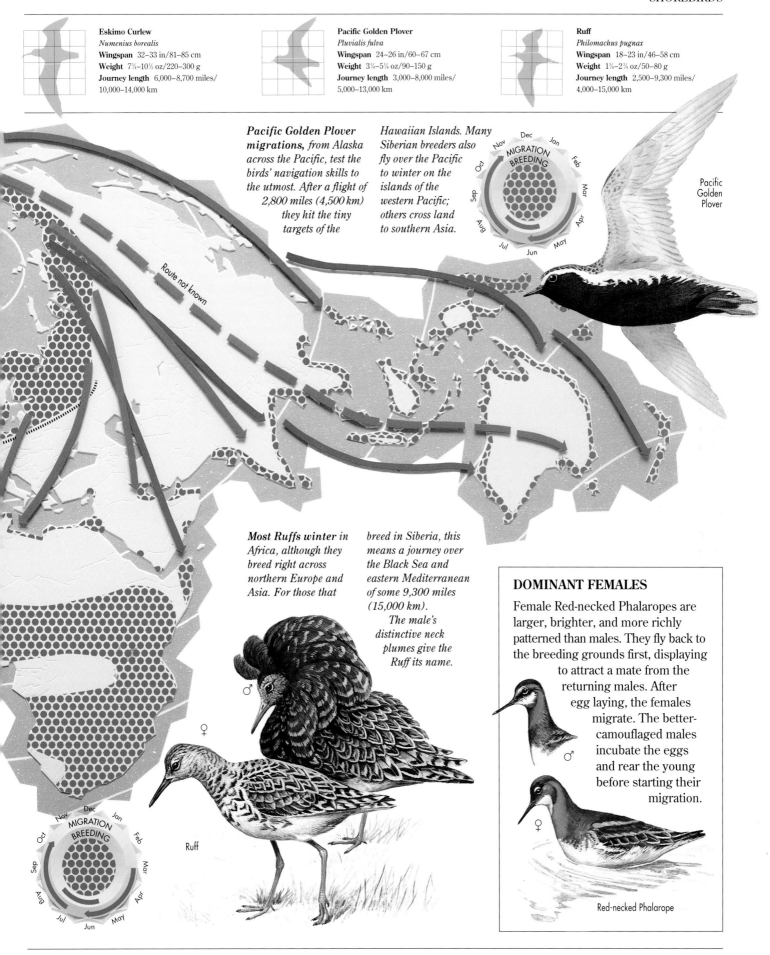

**Eskimo Curlew**
*Numenius borealis*
**Wingspan** 32–33 in/81–85 cm
**Weight** 7¾–10½ oz/220–300 g
**Journey length** 6,000–8,700 miles/ 10,000–14,000 km

**Pacific Golden Plover**
*Pluvialis fulva*
**Wingspan** 24–26 in/60–67 cm
**Weight** 3¼–5¼ oz/90–150 g
**Journey length** 3,000–8,000 miles/ 5,000–13,000 km

**Ruff**
*Philomachus pugnax*
**Wingspan** 18–23 in/46–58 cm
**Weight** 1¾–2¾ oz/50–80 g
**Journey length** 2,500–9,300 miles/ 4,000–15,000 km

*Pacific Golden Plover migrations, from Alaska across the Pacific, test the birds' navigation skills to the utmost. After a flight of 2,800 miles (4,500 km) they hit the tiny targets of the* Hawaiian Islands. Many Siberian breeders also fly over the Pacific to winter on the islands of the western Pacific; others cross land to southern Asia.

Route not known

Pacific Golden Plover

*Most Ruffs winter in Africa, although they breed right across northern Europe and Asia. For those that* breed in Siberia, this means a journey over the Black Sea and eastern Mediterranean of some 9,300 miles (15,000 km).
*The male's distinctive neck plumes give the Ruff its name.*

Ruff

## DOMINANT FEMALES

Female Red-necked Phalaropes are larger, brighter, and more richly patterned than males. They fly back to the breeding grounds first, displaying to attract a mate from the returning males. After egg laying, the females migrate. The better-camouflaged males incubate the eggs and rear the young before starting their migration.

Red-necked Phalarope

# Shorebirds/2

*Widely traveled Red Knots are on the move for up to seven months each year.*

Red Knots are among the most northerly breeding shorebirds, nesting on the Arctic islands of Canada and Siberia closest to the North Pole, and on the extreme north coast of Greenland. This far north the summer is short and the birds may be on the breeding grounds for only two months: June and July. Although they add plant shoots to their usual diet of invertebrates at this time, there is not enough food to allow them to arrive earlier or stay longer.

The advantages of breeding so far north are the lack of competition from other species for nest sites and food, and the low density of predators. Red Knots further reduce the risks of competition and predation by nesting scattered over the tundra, with families rarely less than ⅝ mile (1 km) apart. This behavior changes on migration and in winter, however, when they form flocks tens of thousands strong.

In addition to nesting farther north than other shorebirds, many Red Knots winter far south of the equator, reaching the southern tips of the Americas and Africa and the coasts of Australia and New Zealand. But not all journey so far; many stay north of the equator, congregating on the coasts of northwestern Europe and around the Gulf of Mexico.

Many Red Knots do not take the most obvious route from their breeding grounds, but head in winter for sites that are, perhaps, more distant than those used by birds from other nesting areas. Eastern Canadian breeders, for example, do not head south to the Gulf coast of the United States – the northern limit of the wintering range of central Canadian birds, and obviously suitable winter habitat. Instead, they fly southeastward, across Greenland and the North Atlantic to wintering areas in northwestern Europe.

This and other "longer-than-necessary" journeys are usually the result of birds spreading and colonizing new areas while retaining traditional migration routes. Eastern Canada, for example, was colonized by birds from Greenland which had established this southeasterly migration route.

There is a similar migratory divide in eastern Siberia. Birds breeding in the far east fly south to Australia, while those breeding in central Siberia head southwest to western Europe before journeying on down the Atlantic coast to western and southern Africa.

Red Knots frequently journey up to 1,900 miles (3,000 km) nonstop, often across open sea. Thus it is vital for them to put on enough fat for fuel. Birds leaving Britain in spring increase their weight by 50 percent before crossing to Iceland, and lose most of that en route. They feed again in Iceland, putting on more fat before the flight on to Canada.

*In the course of a year, Red Knots spend time in several locations in addition to their breeding and wintering areas. Birds that breed in the eastern Canadian Arctic leave in July and fly to Iceland, where they spend August. By September they are in southern Norway, where they stay for a few weeks before flying across the North Sea to winter on the Wash in England or the Waddenzee. They head north again in March, stopping in Iceland during April and in western Greenland in May, arriving back in their Arctic breeding grounds in early June.*

40°N

20°N

Bay of Fundy

Delaware Bay

0°

Surinam coast

20°S

Routes across or around S America not known

40°S

60°S

## WATCHING THE SHOREBIRDS

Red Knots, in common with other shorebirds, winter on estuaries and in coastal lagoons where small mollusks and crustaceans – the main elements of their diet at this time of year – abound. The largest winter concentration of these birds is on the Waddenzee in the Netherlands, followed by the Wash in Britain. Most British estuaries – the Thames, Severn, Dee, Solway Firth, and Morecambe Bay – are shorebird sites.

At peak passage times, almost any estuary or stretch of inland mud may attract migrant shorebirds to rest and

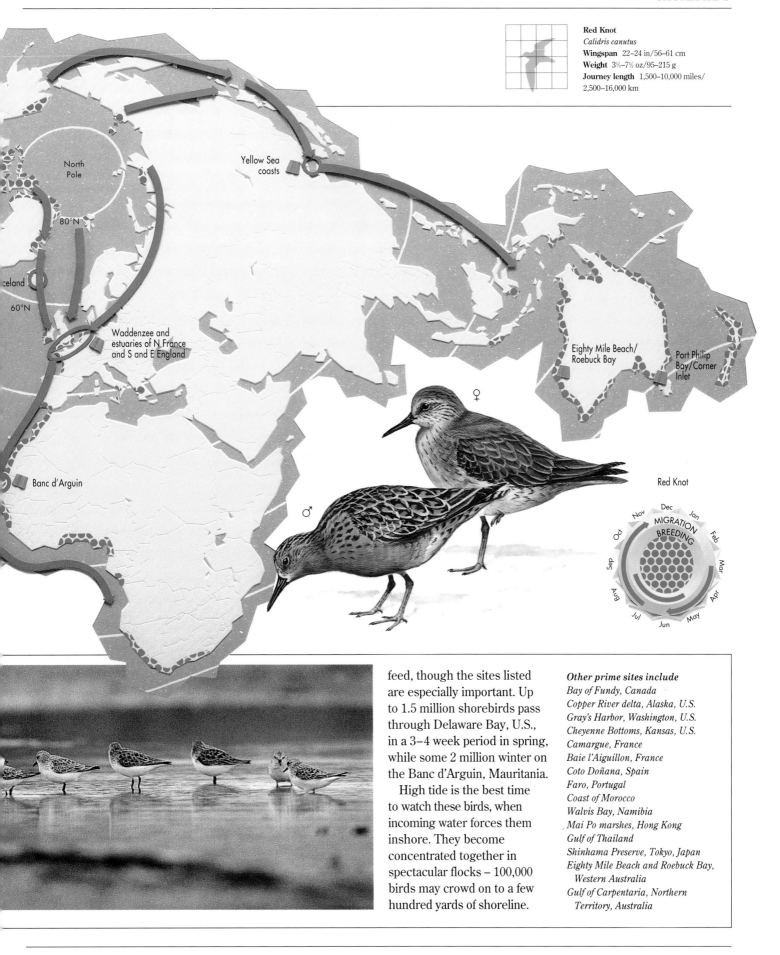

**Red Knot**
*Calidris canutus*
**Wingspan** 22–24 in/56–61 cm
**Weight** 3½–7½ oz/95–215 g
**Journey length** 1,500–10,000 miles/
2,500–16,000 km

North Pole

80°N

Yellow Sea coasts

60°N

Iceland

Waddenzee and estuaries of N France and S and E England

Eighty Mile Beach/ Roebuck Bay

Port Philip Bay/Corner Inlet

Banc d'Arguin

♀

♂

Red Knot

MIGRATION
BREEDING

Nov Dec Jan Feb Mar Apr May Jun Jul Aug Sep Oct

feed, though the sites listed are especially important. Up to 1.5 million shorebirds pass through Delaware Bay, U.S., in a 3–4 week period in spring, while some 2 million winter on the Banc d'Arguin, Mauritania.

High tide is the best time to watch these birds, when incoming water forces them inshore. They become concentrated together in spectacular flocks – 100,000 birds may crowd on to a few hundred yards of shoreline.

*Other prime sites include*
*Bay of Fundy, Canada*
*Copper River delta, Alaska, U.S.*
*Gray's Harbor, Washington, U.S.*
*Cheyenne Bottoms, Kansas, U.S.*
*Camargue, France*
*Baie l'Aiguillon, France*
*Coto Doñana, Spain*
*Faro, Portugal*
*Coast of Morocco*
*Walvis Bay, Namibia*
*Mai Po marshes, Hong Kong*
*Gulf of Thailand*
*Shinhama Preserve, Tokyo, Japan*
*Eighty Mile Beach and Roebuck Bay,*
*  Western Australia*
*Gulf of Carpentaria, Northern*
*  Territory, Australia*

# Thrushes

*Migrants blown off course have founded a new, sedentary colony.*

Wheatears, redstarts, chats, the European Robin, and the Bluethroat, as well as the larger "true" thrushes, all belong to the thrush family. Several species in the northern hemisphere are migratory, with a few breeding as far north as conditions permit and moving south for the winter. They include, among the larger thrushes, Redwings, Fieldfares, Dusky, Gray-cheeked, Siberian, and Varied thrushes, plus the smaller Northern Wheatear, Common Redstart, and Bluethroat.

Since the larger northern-breeding thrushes need cover for nesting and feeding, most do not occur in the true Arctic, where low-growing tundra plants predominate, but in the area to the south, a zone known in Eurasia as the "taiga" and in North America as "muskeg." Here scrub and scattered trees, often dotted with lakes, form a rich habitat where the insects and berries on which they feed abound.

Redwings breed throughout northern Europe and across northern Siberia almost to the Pacific coast. No population winters on the Pacific, all move south and west to reach a broad region running from the Atlantic, including western Europe and the Mediterranean, east to the Black and Caspian seas. The exception to this pattern of movement is the Icelandic population of Redwings. These birds, a different race, darker in color and with more heavily marked underparts, move south and east. Those breeding in eastern Iceland winter mainly in Britain and northern France; those from the western half of the island go farther south to southwestern France, Spain, and Portugal.

Both Redwings and Fieldfares are successful colonizers. Fieldfares have bred in small numbers in Iceland since the 1950s, and in Greenland, where their presence dates from a single influx in January 1937. A flock migrating south across the North Sea from Norway to Britain was blown westward. Individuals were seen in several parts of Greenland and those that found the milder areas in the island's southwest, where there are extensive stands of willow and birch scrub, survived the winter. Then, instead of migrating back to Europe, they stayed and bred, thereby founding a small colony of entirely sedentary birds, which is still there.

The most traveled North American thrush is the Gray-cheeked, which breeds in Arctic Canada, Alaska, and eastern Siberia north of the tree line, particularly along the banks of streams and lakes. Its migration takes it southeast through the eastern half of the U.S. and across the Caribbean to wintering grounds in northern South America.

*Bluethroats* (left) are beautifully marked small thrushes that breed widely in Europe and Asia, from the Arctic in the north to the Mediterranean. Most do not, however, breed in the tundra since they need vegetation at least 3 feet (1 m) high for nesting and feeding. They also avoid areas of dense trees.

Most Bluethroats are migratory, many making long journeys, either to sub-Saharan Africa or across the Himalayas to India and Southeast Asia.

*Redwings eat berries and fruit,* as well as invertebrates. Flocks of these large migrants, which need more food than smaller birds, can strip a hedge or tree of berries in a few days.

When the weather is severe in the wintering areas, the search for enough to eat can lead to conflict with large, aggressive residents, such as Mistle Thrushes. While stocks last, a single Mistle Thrush (or, often, a pair) sits on a well-berried tree and defends it against all comers.

At such times, windfall apples (above) and bird-feeder offerings can mean the difference between life and death for the migrants.

**Bluethroat**
*Luscinia svecica*
**Wingspan** 8–9 in/20–23 cm
**Weight** ½–1 oz/15–25 g
**Journey length** 1,600–3,750 miles/
2,500–6,000 km

**Redwing**
*Turdus iliacus*
**Wingspan** 13–14 in/33–35 cm
**Weight** 1¼–2½ oz/35–75 g
**Journey length** 600–4,000 miles/
1,000–6,500 km

**Fieldfare**
*Turdus pilaris*
**Wingspan** 16–17 in/39–42 cm
**Weight** 2½–4½ oz/70–125 g
**Journey length** 600–3,000 miles/
1,000–5,000 km

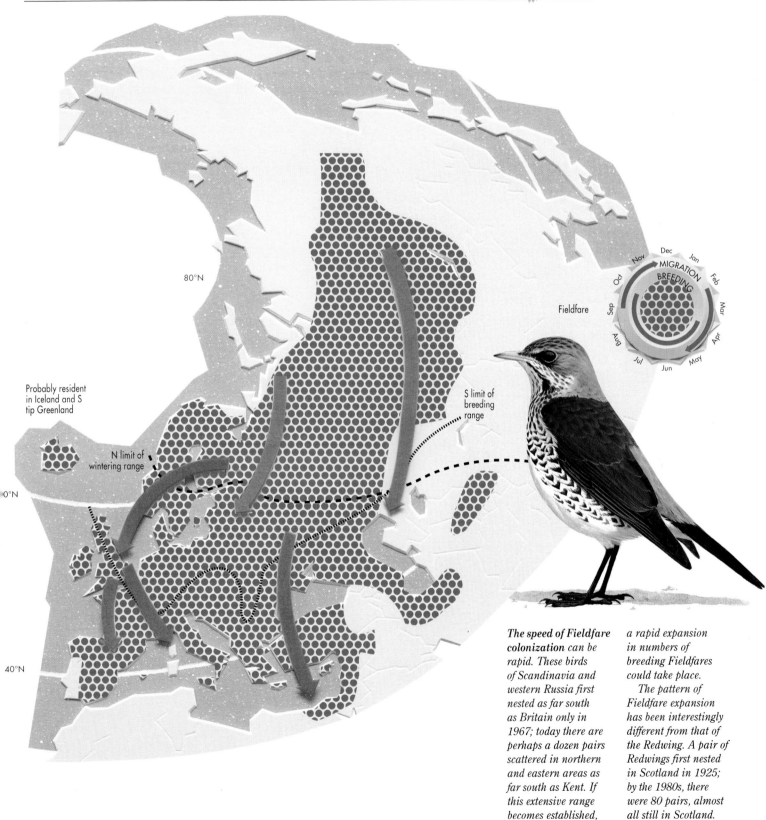

80°N

Fieldfare

S limit of
breeding
range

Probably resident
in Iceland and S
tip Greenland

N limit of
wintering range

0°N

40°N

**The speed of Fieldfare colonization** can be rapid. These birds of Scandinavia and western Russia first nested as far south as Britain only in 1967; today there are perhaps a dozen pairs scattered in northern and eastern areas as far south as Kent. If this extensive range becomes established, a rapid expansion in numbers of breeding Fieldfares could take place.

The pattern of Fieldfare expansion has been interestingly different from that of the Redwing. A pair of Redwings first nested in Scotland in 1925; by the 1980s, there were 80 pairs, almost all still in Scotland.

# Buntings and finches

*A quick change of feathers helps a speedy retreat from the Arctic winter's onset.*

Few small birds breed in the Arctic. Because most small birds lose more heat than large ones, due to their proportionately greater body surface for their size, cold climates pose greater survival problems for them. In addition, most birds that breed in the brief Arctic summer must migrate south for the winter, often crossing large expanses of water on the way. Larger, longer-winged birds are better able to do this than smaller ones.

The most successful small birds breeding in the Arctic are three buntings – the Snow Bunting and Lapland and Smith's longspurs – and a number of finches, including the Redpoll and the Chaffinch. All but the Chaffinch, which is restricted to Europe and western Asia, breed right around the North Pole in the Arctic regions of North America, Europe, and Asia.

Northern Chaffinch populations breed beyond the Arctic Circle in Scandinavia and Russia. Their range in northern Russia has expanded enormously during this century as they have steadily colonized regions farther and farther north through the vast areas of spruce forest. They do not normally breed north of the tree line.

The Snow Bunting's breeding range extends northward to all the land and islands closest to the North Pole. Although migratory, Snow Buntings do not move to "traditional" winter homes and often stay as far north as winter conditions allow. When they do move farther south, to the eastern U.S. or Britain, for example, they haunt habitats that resemble the Arctic breeding grounds, such as bleak shores and open fields.

A unique adaptation of Snow Buntings to the rigors of life so far north is their rapid molt after breeding (see p. 26). They must complete their annual change of feathers quickly so that they have a new set, particularly of wing feathers, before the onset of winter and the need to migrate. Most small birds drop one or two wing feathers at a time and wait until the new ones are nearly grown before shedding the next. In this way, although flight is affected, it remains possible. Snow Buntings are in such a hurry

*Chaffinches (right) breeding in temperate latitudes are sedentary. In fact, there are records of birds that have moved only a few miles in a 10-year lifespan. Those breeding in northern latitudes are, of necessity, migratory, reaching Britain and Ireland in winter and frequently moving on south as far as France and Iberia.*

*Males and females migrate separately, so wintering flocks comprising birds of one gender are common. Females tend to move farther than males, with the result that males are more numerous in Sweden, the factor that prompted biologist Carl Linnaeus to give them the Latin name* coelebs, *meaning "bachelor."*

Snow Bunting

♀

♂

♂ Winter

*The Snow Bunting's white or pale plumage helps it to survive cold conditions. Less heat is lost from a white surface than from a dark one but, more importantly, white feathers are hollow and filled with air, which is an excellent insulator. In colored feathers, the internal* spaces are filled with pigment cells: the more pigment, the darker the feather. Pigment cells conduct heat. Snow Buntings living in eastern Siberia, the coldest part of the Arctic, are whiter than those in relatively warmer areas, such as Iceland.*

Nov Dec Jan

Oct MIGRATION BREEDING Feb

Sep Mar

Aug Apr

Jul Jun May

Snow Bunting

**Chaffinch**
*Fringilla coelebs*
**Wingspan** 10–11½ in/25–29 cm
**Weight** ⅔–1 oz/22–30 g
**Journey length** 0–3,200 miles/
0–5,000 km

**Snow Bunting**
*Plectrophenax nivalis*
**Wingspan** 11½–13 in/29–33 cm
**Weight** 1–2 oz/30–65 g
**Journey length** 0–3,800 miles/
0–6,000 km

**Lapland Longspur**
*Calcarius lapponicus*
**Wingspan** 9½–11½ in/24–29 cm
**Weight** 1–1½ oz/30–40 g
**Journey length** 650–4,600 miles/
1,000–6,500 km

*Birds on migration* are vulnerable to sudden changes in the weather. In March 1906, an estimated 1.5 million Lapland Longspurs, migrating north over Minnesota, were caught in a sudden heavy snowfall. In what became known as the "great bird shower," birds fell out of the sky and became hopelessly disorientated by streetlights. Some crashed into buildings and died; others froze to death.

Lapland Longspurs, in common with Redpolls and Snow Buntings, burrow into snowdrifts in spells of bad weather. Snow holes offer birds excellent protection from the wind which, by reducing the air temperature and disrupting the insulation provided by the feathers, can kill.

that they lose as many as four or five (about half) of their main wing feathers at once. This means that they cannot fly for a week or two while the new ones grow. For a ground-feeding bird like the Snow Bunting that lives mainly on seeds in late summer, in an area where predators are few and far between, this loss is a small price to pay.

All these small Arctic birds lay an average of six eggs, one or two more than equivalent species farther south. They are able to rear more young because the continuous daylight and abundance of insects at high latitudes allow them to feed their chicks almost around the clock. In fact, they do take a rest period of two or three hours in every 24 hours, and this is always in the hours around midnight, even though the sun may be shining.

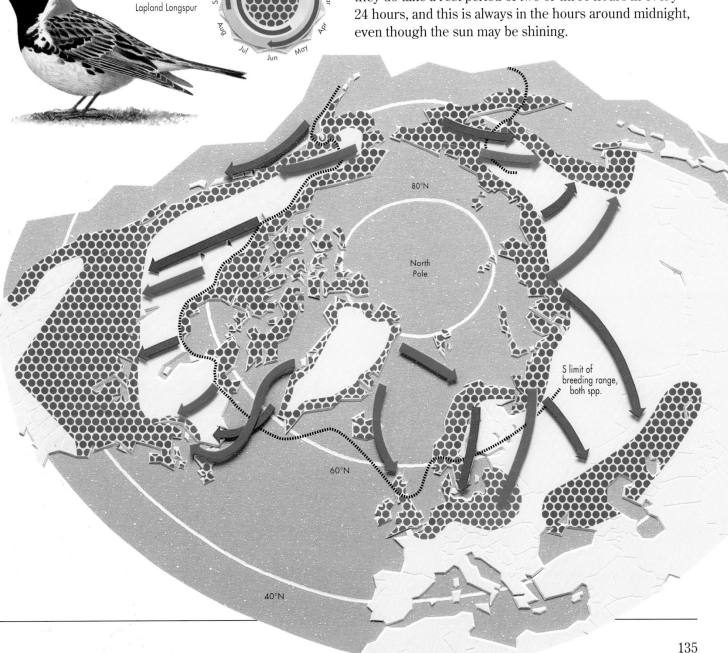

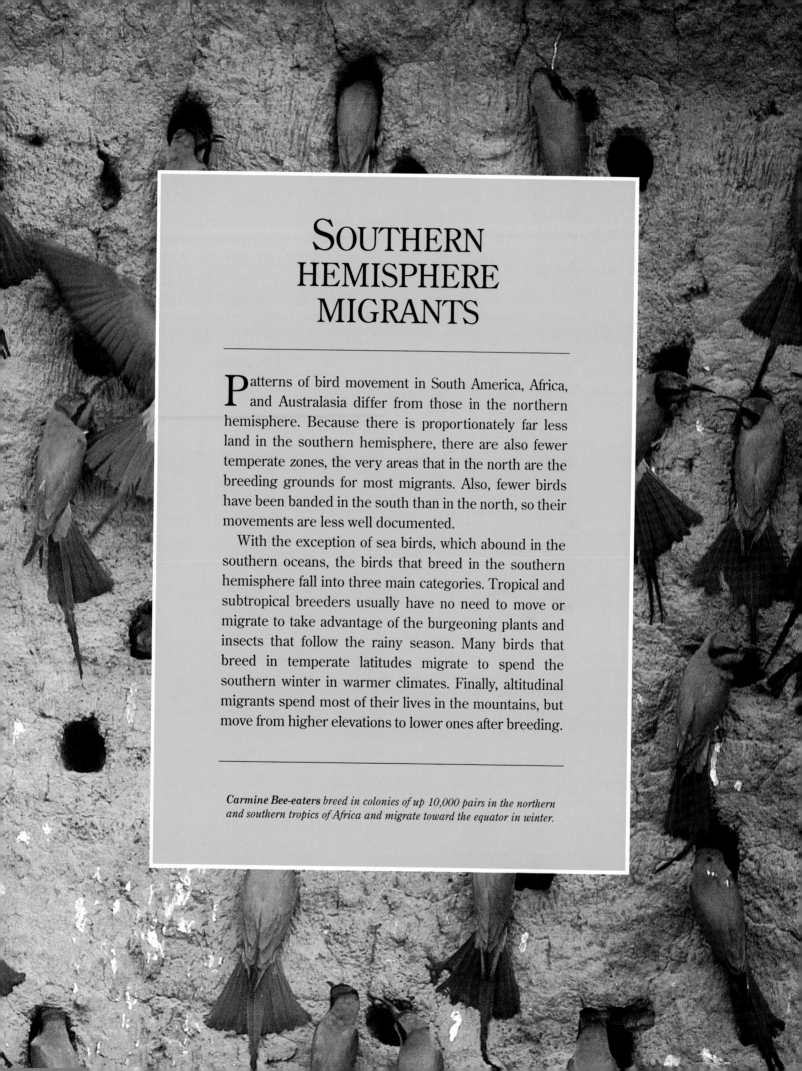

# SOUTHERN HEMISPHERE MIGRANTS

Patterns of bird movement in South America, Africa, and Australasia differ from those in the northern hemisphere. Because there is proportionately far less land in the southern hemisphere, there are also fewer temperate zones, the very areas that in the north are the breeding grounds for most migrants. Also, fewer birds have been banded in the south than in the north, so their movements are less well documented.

With the exception of sea birds, which abound in the southern oceans, the birds that breed in the southern hemisphere fall into three main categories. Tropical and subtropical breeders usually have no need to move or migrate to take advantage of the burgeoning plants and insects that follow the rainy season. Many birds that breed in temperate latitudes migrate to spend the southern winter in warmer climates. Finally, altitudinal migrants spend most of their lives in the mountains, but move from higher elevations to lower ones after breeding.

*Carmine Bee-eaters breed in colonies of up 10,000 pairs in the northern and southern tropics of Africa and migrate toward the equator in winter.*

# South American migrants

*The Andes Mountains and Amazon River basin dominate migratory patterns in South America.*

The composition of the bird life of South America is dominated by the abundance of species occupying the vast expanses of rainforest that cover almost all of the northern, broadest part of the continent. The equator crosses the continent at the Amazon delta. A wide variety of tropical and subtropical habitats extends across the huge Amazon basin and the extensive equatorial mountains of the northern Andes. An enormous diversity of bird species inhabits these high-rainfall regions. Many of the millions of migrants from North America that winter on the continent do so in this northern area.

The great length of the Andes, which stretch through 80° of latitude, means that there is a wide variety of plant and animal life associated with the mountains. A small proportion of the continent is arid, with true desert limited to the Pacific coasts of Chile, Peru, and southern Ecuador, and across the Andes into Argentina. These deserts include some of the driest places on earth – rainfall has never been recorded at Calama, Chile, in the Atacama desert. The southern tip of the continent is narrow, with the result that an extensive temperate fauna has not developed.

Migration is not a prominent feature of South America's land birds. The Amazon rainforest and northern tropics provide essentially stable conditions in which most birds are resident. The narrowness of the southern portion of the continent greatly limits the high-latitude land which, in the northern hemisphere, is extensive and provides the breeding habitat for most of the continents' migrants.

South American birds of temperate and high-altitude environments occur mainly along the Andes Mountains. For many of these species, some altitudinal migration is strongly suspected, but not well documented. It is thought that birds nesting in the high mountains move to lowland regions after breeding.

Some South American land birds leave the continent in winter. Others breed in the south and then move north to the extensive equatorial regions. A few species are restricted in distribution to the temperate southern latitudes, with some migrating north in winter. There are no migrants among the breeding land birds of the Falkland and Galápagos islands.

*South America is the fourth largest continent and has two outstanding natural features that dominate its character. The first is the Amazon, the world's greatest river, which extends 4,000 miles (6,500 km) and has a volume of flow exceeding any other. The Amazon basin contains the largest single area of rainforest on earth.*

*A second superlative is provided by the Andes. These mountains hug the full length of the west coast and constitute the longest mountain chain in the world, with some of the highest peaks and many active volcanoes. The mountains form a barrier that divides the continent's drainage between a generally narrow region to the west and a much broader area to the east. Several major rivers, including the Orinoco and Paraguay–Paraná, drain this eastern region.*

*Many birds breed and winter in the savanna of the upper Orinoco basin from southwestern Venezuela to Colombia, and in the more extensive savanna of the central south from Brazil to Patagonia.*

## HOT SPOTS

This list includes places where wintering birds from North America, in addition to native Central and South American birds, both migratory and nonmigratory, may be seen.

1. Mazatlan/San Blas, Mexico
2. Rio Lagartos, Mexico
3. Belize City
4. Panama
5. Los Olivitos, Venezuela
6. Surinam coast
7. Paracas, Peru
8. Lagoa do Peixe, Brazil
9. La Serena, Chile
10. San Clemente del Tuju/Cabo San Antonio, Argentina
11. Punta Rasa, Argentina
12. Tierra del Fuego

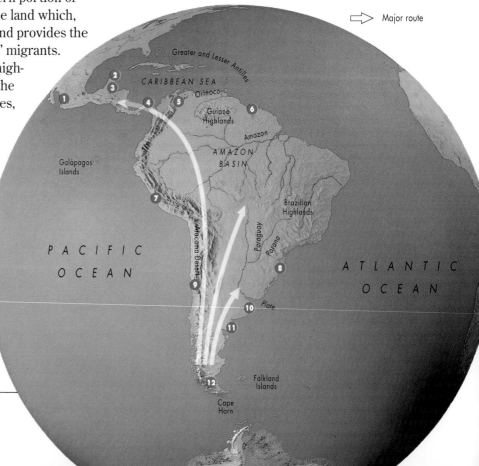

⇨ Major route

**Blue and White Swallow**
*Notiochelidon cyanoleuca*
**Wingspan** 8½–10 in/22–25 cm
**Weight** ⅓–½ oz/10–15 g
**Journey length** 0–5,000 miles/
0–8,000 km

**Dark-faced Ground Tyrant**
*Muscisaxicola macloviana*
**Wingspan** 9–10½ in/23–27 cm
**Weight** ⅔–⅞ oz/18–25 g
**Journey length** 0–3,000 miles/
0–5,000 km

**Giant Hummingbird**
*Patagona gigas*
**Wingspan** 19½–21½ in/50–55 cm
**Weight** ⅗–¾ oz/17–20 g
**Journey length** 0–500 miles/
0–800 km

## South to north migrations

Most of the well-understood migrations of land birds in South America fall into this category, with birds breeding in the temperate areas of the south and moving north for the southern winter.

Some of these birds undertake spectacular migratory journeys from the extreme south as far as, and sometimes even across, the equator. They include the Blue and White Swallow and the Brown-chested Martin, which breeds as far south as southern Chile and Argentina and occasionally reaches as far north as Mexico on migration.

Others, however, travel less far, breeding in the temperate regions of central Argentina and Chile and migrating

*In the northern parts*
*of its range, the Blue and White Swallow is resident, occupying land at high altitudes. Although widespread elsewhere, it is most common in the lowland regions of the south. Between January and March, when the breeding season is over, these birds fly north, many following the line of the Andes. The return flight in spring takes place in August.*

*Dark-faced Ground Tyrants (left) are resident in the Falkland Islands, but elsewhere, from the southern parts of Chile and Argentina south to Tierra del Fuego and Cape Horn, these birds are south–north migrants.*

*Ground tyrants are long-legged birds and essentially ground-feeding insect-eaters. There are nine other species of this group in South America, all of which occur along the Andes chain and all of which are highly migratory.*

*The "tyrant" part of the family name derives from the birds' aggressive behavior toward other species, including birds of prey, especially during the breeding season.*

Blue and White Swallow

Blue and White Swallows are believed not to winter in Amazonia

Migrants breed only to S of this line; birds to N are resident

0°

20°S

40°S

no farther than northern South America. Such birds include a number of tyrant flycatchers, members of one of the world's largest bird families, found only in the New World. It is South America's dominant family of land birds in terms of number of species, constituting about 23 percent of all perching birds in some regions. More than 70 species have been counted in some areas of western Amazonia alone. Most of the species breeding in temperate areas are migratory, including the Dark-faced Ground Tyrant and the Fork-tailed Flycatcher.

*The largest of all the hummingbirds, the Giant Hummingbird is 10 times larger than the smallest member of this New World family of specialized nectar-sipping birds. Giant Hummingbirds are mountain birds, occurring in the Andes from Ecuador in the north to Chile and Argentina in the south. Populations from the south of the range are migratory.*

Giant Hummingbird

# South American migrants/2

**Kelp Goose**
*Chloephaga hybrida*
**Wingspan** 3 ft 11 in–4ft 7 in/1.2–1.4 m
**Weight** 4 lb 7 oz–5 lb 12 oz/2–2.6 kg
**Journey length** 0–500 miles/
0–800 km

## Migrations within temperate latitudes

Few birds of the temperate southern forests and coastal lowlands of South America have clearly defined northward migrations in winter. Of those that do, the Kelp Goose and Two-banded Plover are typical, migrating short distances to join resident populations farther north.

The Black-faced Ibis also falls into this group, breeding in southern Chile and Argentina and wintering on the pampas of northern coastal Argentina. There are also sedentary populations of this species in the highlands of Ecuador, Peru, Bolivia, and northern areas of Chile.

*There are five species of gooselike birds in South America, all of which are grazers.*

*The Kelp Goose (right) is unusual among them in that it is confined to maritime areas, haunting rocky coasts and feeding on seaweed. Birds that breed in the south of the range, in Tierra del Fuego, fly north in winter but stay along the shorelines. Kelp Geese in the Falkland Islands are resident.*

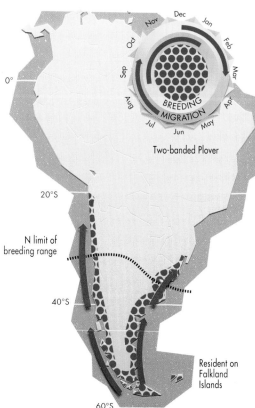

0°

20°S

N limit of
breeding range

40°S

60°S

Two-banded Plover

Resident on
Falkland
Islands

BREEDING
MIGRATION

Dec
Nov Jan
Oct Feb
Sep Mar
Aug Apr
Jul May
Jun

*The Two-banded Plover (above) occurs along most shores and coasts of the continent south of the Tropic of Capricorn. Its favorite haunts are beaches, estuaries, and river banks near the sea.*

*Falklands Islands birds are resident, but elsewhere populations are migratory, moving northward for the southern winter to reach southern Chile in the west and Uruguay in the east.*

**Two-banded Plover**
*Charadrius falklandicus*
**Wingspan** 18–22 in/45–55 cm
**Weight** 1⅜–2 oz/40–60 g
**Journey length** 0–2,250 miles/
0–3,600 km

**Andean Goose**
*Chloephaga melanoptera*
**Wingspan** 4 ft 7 in–5 ft 3 in/1.4–1.6 m
**Weight** 5 lb 8 oz–7 lb 11 oz/2.5–3.5 kg
**Journey length** 0–3 miles/
0–5 km

**Gray Gull**
*Larus modestus*
**Wingspan** 3 ft 3 in–3 ft 7 in/1–1.1 m
**Weight** 5 lb 8 oz–7 lb 11 oz/2.5–3.5 kg
**Journey length** 20–1,600 miles/
30–2,500 km

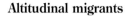

Andean Goose

Andean Geese
breed at high
altitudes and
winter lower
down

20°S

40°S

## Altitudinal migrants

The Andes provide a corridor of suitable habitat for temperate species colonizing the northern tropics. The mountains are also the route along which some long-distance migrants travel. And there are species that spend the summer at high altitudes in the Andes, then travel only short distances to reach the surrounding lowlands in winter.

There are few well-documented examples of altitudinal migration among South American birds, but the migration of the Andean Goose is believed to be typical of these altitudinal movements.

*Andean Geese (left) breed high in the mountains, often along the shores of the Andean lakes,* *at altitudes from 10,000 feet (3,300 m) up to the snow line. Many remain at high altitudes year-round; others are migratory.*
*Although they breed in isolated pairs, flocks usually come together* *outside the breeding season, as the birds graze the marshy plains of the Andean foothills and valley bottoms.*
*While males and females are similar in appearance, males are substantially larger.*

## Desert breeders

Few birds breed in the harsh conditions of the South American deserts. The Gray Gull is an exception, not only migrating to coastal regions at the end of the breeding season but also, even while nesting, "commuting" daily from its high-altitude nest to the coastal lowlands to feed.

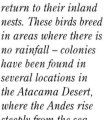

Non-breeding

Gray Gull

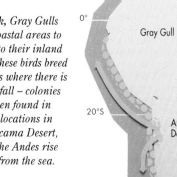

*At dusk, Gray Gulls leave coastal areas to return to their inland nests. These birds breed in areas where there is no rainfall – colonies have been found in several locations in the Atacama Desert, where the Andes rise steeply from the sea.*

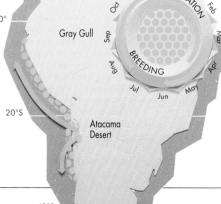

0°

Gray Gull

20°S

Atacama
Desert

40°S

141

# African migrants

*Migration patterns in the largest southern continent are governed by complex climatic variables.*

When the glaciers that covered much of Europe began to retreat at the end of the last ice age, new tracts of land became available for habitation and colonization by plants and animals. Most of the species that spread into Europe were from Africa, the largest southern continent. The kinds of birds that inhabit Europe today are the result of the continent's proximity to the African landmass.

When the ice age ended 10,000 years ago, the Sahara was not desert but woodland. Today this broad, arid wasteland is treated as part of the Palearctic faunal zone, along with the temperate and Arctic areas of Eurasia. All of Africa south of the Sahara desert is called the Afrotropical zone.

Many bird families occur in both Europe and Africa, but those that contain but a single species in Europe – such as the cuckoos, kingfishers, nightjars, and bee-eaters – can boast 10 or more species in Africa. In addition to providing a wintering area for hundreds of millions of migrant birds from Eurasia, the Afrotropical zone supports a large body of intra-African migrants. Many of these have extensive breeding ranges throughout the region, but those that extend to the southern portion of the continent breed in the southern summer (October to March) and fly northward to winter at lower latitudes, some crossing the equator. Species breeding north of the equator breed in the northern summer, then also move to lower latitudes. They are fewer in number because the belt of savanna woodland is narrower in the north than in the south.

In the equatorial region between 10°N and 10°S, the terms "summer" and "winter" become meaningless – the day length of some 12 hours varies little between the summer and winter solstices and there are no prolonged periods of twilight at dawn and dusk. The seasons are instead determined by intervals of wet and dry weather. Close to the equator, there are two rainy periods, a short one and a long one, interspersed with "dry" periods when rainfall is greatly reduced or rare.

With increasing distance north and south of the equator, the year becomes progressively more evenly divided between a warm rainy period (during which most birds breed) and a cool dry period, when the most northerly and southerly breeders may migrate.

*The landscape of Africa is dominated by rift valleys and high mountains. The continent's highest mountains – Kilimanjaro and Kenya – are, however, isolated peaks with the result that they are rarely barriers to migration. Indeed, some birds seem to use them as stepping stones on their travels. The Sahara desert, which covers an area of 3.3 million sq miles (8.6 million km²), is by contrast a formidable barrier for many migrants journeying to and from Africa.*

*The continent's major rivers – the Nile, Zaïre, and Niger – are important pathways for migrants, since their flanking vegetation affords food and somewhere to roost, particularly in the dry savanna regions. The chains of lakes and rift valleys, dominated by the Great Rift Valley in the east, provide attractive routes and destinations for many shorebirds, while their large reedbeds offer areas in which swallows and martins find plentiful roosts.*

## HOT SPOTS

Native African birds or Eurasian visitors to the continent, or both, may be seen at these sites.

1. Gulf of Suez/Nile delta, Egypt
2. Oued Massa, Morocco
3. Banc d'Arguin NP, Mauritania
4. Senegal and Gambia rivers, Senegal/Gambia
5. Niger delta, Mali
6. Air and Ténéré NNP, Niger
7. Lake Chad, Chad/Niger
8. Mount Ngulia, Kenya
9. Luangwa Valley NP, Zambia
10. Victoria Falls NP, Zambia/Zimbabwe
11. Moremi WR, Botswana
12. Nylsvley NR, South Africa
13. Langebaan Lagoon, South Africa

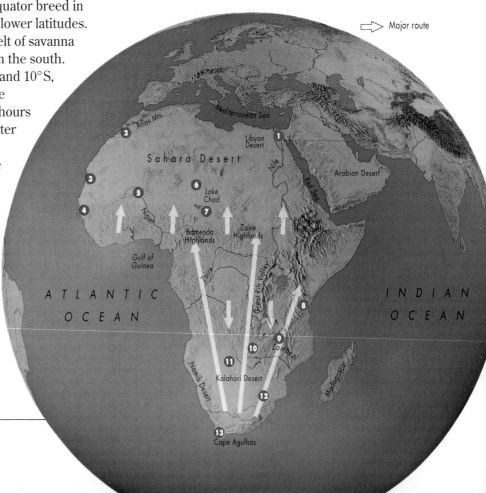

⇨ Major route

**African Pygmy Kingfisher**
*Ceyx picta*
**Wingspan** 6¼ in/16 cm
**Weight** ½ oz/15 g
**Journey length** 600–1,250 miles/
1,000–2,000 km

**Comb Duck**
*Sarkidiornis melanotos*
**Wingspan** 3 ft 8 in–5 ft 2 in/1.1–1.4 m
**Weight** 4 lb 6 oz/2 kg
**Journey length** 2,200–2,400 miles/
3,500–3,900 km

## Migrating north of the equator

The migratory journeys of many African populations take them across the equator to the continent's northern belt of savanna woodland. These include representatives of many families, such as the Comb Duck, Carmine Bee-eater, Pennant-winged Nightjar, and Wahlberg's Eagle.

In March and April, around 100,000 Wahlberg's Eagles leave their breeding grounds in the southern woods and head north. Some stay south of the equator in southern Zaïre; others reach Ethiopia. The champion is a nestling banded in the Transvaal, South Africa, and recovered 2,600 miles (4,200 km) away in Sudan.

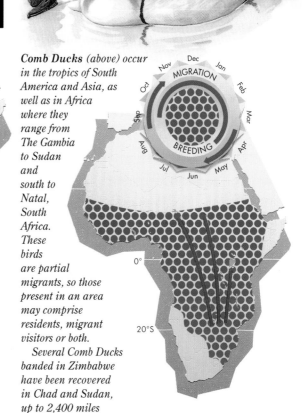

## Mid-continent migrations

The areas north and south of the equator may shelter many migrant species. It seems likely that the most northerly and southerly breeders in this area may migrate to lower latitudes. However, because many of these species appear to be "resident" breeders over very large areas of central Africa, it is seldom possible to delineate the breeding and nonbreeding ranges of the different populations. Outside the breeding season birds in any area may be residents, migrants, or a combination of the two. Pygmy Kingfishers are an exception to this generalization, since they are known migrants.

*Pygmy Kingfishers breed in southern Africa and winter as far north as Zaïre and Mozambique. Similar movements appear to occur north of the equator. These birds are faithful to their breeding areas; one individual banded in the Mkume Reserve, Zululand, was recovered there five years later.*

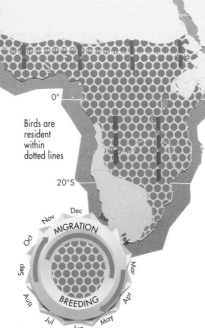

Birds are resident within dotted lines

African Pygmy Kingfisher

*Comb Ducks (above) occur in the tropics of South America and Asia, as well as in Africa where they range from The Gambia to Sudan and south to Natal, South Africa. These birds are partial migrants, so those present in an area may comprise residents, migrant visitors or both.*

*Several Comb Ducks banded in Zimbabwe have been recovered in Chad and Sudan, up to 2,400 miles (3,900 km) away.*

# African migrants/2

*The Carmine Bee-eater (right) is the largest African bee-eater. These birds breed in colonies numbering several thousand individuals, crowding high river banks with their nest tunnel entrances.*

*There are two separate populations, one in the north, of blue-throated birds, and one in the south with a breeding nucleus in the Luangwa River valley in Zambia. These southern birds usually fly south at the end of the breeding season to southern Mozambique and the Transvaal. There they may be seen from December to March, before they move north again, some as far as the equator.*

*Carmine Bee-eaters are often nomadic between breeding seasons and are strongly attracted by grass fires (an ever-present feature of the African dry season). The birds wheel through the smoke to prey on the flying insects fleeing the flames.*

**Carmine Bee-eater**
*Merops nubicus*
**Wingspan** 18–20 in/45–50 cm
**Weight** 2 oz/60 g
**Journey length** 300–750 miles/
500–1,200 km

**African Paradise Flycatcher**
*Terpsiphone viridis*
**Wingspan** 9½–11 in/24–28 cm
**Weight** ½ oz/15 g
**Journey length** 300–1,100 miles/
500–1,800 km

**South African Cliff Swallow**
*Hirundo spilodera*
**Wingspan** 10¼–11½ in/26–29 cm
**Weight** ¾ oz/21 g
**Journey length** 1,250–1,550 miles/
2,000–2,500 km

African Paradise
Flycatcher

♂

♀

*Between September
and March, Cliff
Swallows (below)
breed in large colonies
under bridges and in
culverts in the South
African highveld. Nets
dropped over both ends
of a culvert make it
easy to capture and
band an entire colony.*

*Banding has shown
that some of these
birds are remarkable
survivors, living
to be eight or nine
years
old.*

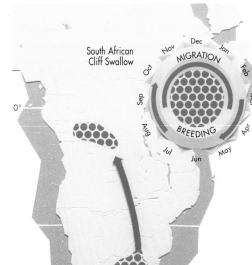

South African
Cliff Swallow

MIGRATION

BREEDING

0°

## Migrations to the tropics

Few species in Africa have discrete
southern breeding and equatorial
wintering ranges. Among those that do
are the African Paradise Flycatcher and
Amethyst Starling. These birds – which
winter in Zambia and Angola and on
occasion cross the equator into Sudan –
return year after year to the same breeding
sites. Recoveries of Cliff Swallows,
which breed in South Africa, have
demonstrated that they winter in
western Zaïre, a journey of some
1,500 miles (2,400 km) which they
accomplish in around two weeks.

Other African birds whose
migrations fall into this category
include the Red-breasted Swallow
and the African Reed Warbler.

MIGRATION

BREEDING

African Paradise Flycatcher

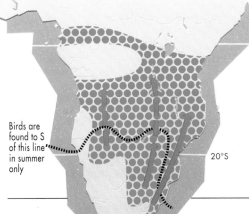

Birds are
found to S
of this line
in summer
only

20°S

*Banding
recovery rates
of small birds
are low, rarely
exceeding 1 in 300
(see pp. 44–45).
This makes more
remarkable the
recovery of two
Paradise Flycatchers
banded in South
Africa. One, banded
near Pietermaritzburg*

*in Natal
province was
next noted in
the Nambuli
Mountains of
Mozambique. The
other, banded near
Rustenburg in the
Transvaal, was
recovered in
Zimbabwe during
October, evidently
on its way back to the*

*breeding grounds
and still some 350
miles (550 km)
north of its
target.*

145

# Africa/3

**Starred Robin**
*Pogonocichla stellata*
**Wingspan** 9–11 in/23–27 cm
**Weight** ¾ oz/21 g
**Journey length** 6–120 miles/
10–200 km

**Greater Crested Tern**
*Thalasseus bergii*
**Wingspan** 3 ft 10 in–4 ft 1 in/1.18–1.25 m
**Weight** 11 oz/300 g
**Journey length** 600–1,000 miles/
1,000–1,600 km

## Altitudinal migrants

Mountains and escarpments characterize the eastern and southern parts of Africa and provide a unique and important habitat for many species of flora and fauna. Among the birds that inhabit these mountains are many that leave the cloudy forests and rocky heights at the end of the rainy season to move to lower elevations. Altitudinal migration frequently occurs over short distances with many species reaching only the surrounding foothills.

**Starred Robins** (*right*) *are altitudinal migrants, but unusual in that they also make migrations of 60 miles (100 km) or more in* *the dry season into hot river valleys where they move through the narrow strips of evergreen growth along the dry riverbeds.*

## Littoral migrants

The coastlines and inshore waters of Africa shelter many native marine birds. Some, such as the Greater Crested Tern, are littoral migrants, breeding and wintering on discrete stretches of shoreline. The Damara Tern is alone in breeding on the inhospitable Skeleton Coast of Namibia. At the end of the breeding season, these birds fly north to "winter" in the Gulf of Guinea. There, they avoid competition for resources with migrant terns from Eurasia by feeding well out to sea.

**In the south,** *Greater Crested Terns* (*right*) *nest on small rocky islands from Namibia down to Dyer Island, northwest of Cape Agulhas, the most southerly point of Africa. Once the young birds can fly, they move southward and eastward along the coast as far as southern Mozambique.*

○ Breeding areas

# Australasian migrants

*The smallest and most remote continent has a wealth of bird species but few migrants.*

Until the Torres Strait was flooded some 10,000 years ago, Australia had a broad land connection north to New Guinea. As a consequence, although many Australian plant and animal species share close affinities with species found in New Guinea and the islands of the Indonesian archipelago, the distinctive flora and fauna of Australia evolved in isolation from all other parts of the world.

The New Zealand island group has long been remote from other centers of evolution. Its flora and fauna reflect this fact in the relatively small number of different life forms and the presence of some unique species, including the existence there of forms that have long since died out elsewhere. The isolation of these islands meant that many species evolved in a forested environment free from predatory mammals. Several of the land birds became highly specialized and many lost their powers of flight.

Fewer than 15 percent of the indigenous land birds of Australia and New Zealand are judged to be truly migratory. Over much of the Australian mainland the survival of birds depends on their ability to cope with arid environments. In these areas conditions are rarely consistent from season to season, and a flexibility in movement patterns of bird populations is often the preferred strategy for survival.

Such movements cannot be classed as migratory because they are neither regular in annual occurrence nor predictable in direction of dispersal. Birds simply assemble and breed in a favorable region and depart when conditions deteriorate. There are many essentially sedentary species in both the temperate and tropical forests of Australia and even a few species that remain within some of the arid and semi-arid regions year-round.

Nor is migration common among New Zealand's land birds, although there is some internal migration, with species breeding in South Island and wintering in North Island. Altitudinal movements occur irregularly, in response to severe weather in the mountains. The country's sea and coastal birds, some 40 percent of the total, may by contrast wander considerable distances from their breeding areas outside the breeding season.

*There are three broad climatic zones in Australia. Parts of Western Australia, Northern Territory, and Queensland are tropical. Tasmania and the higher areas of the continent's southeast are temperate. Most of the remainder of Australia is arid and semi-arid. In addition, the coastal southeast and southwest are "Mediterranean," with cool wet winters and hot dry summers. The mountains of the Great Divide separate the narrow coastal plains to the east from the dry interior. New Zealand is mountainous, with high rainfall.*

*These two major landmasses are surrounded by many offshore groups of smaller islands, ranging northward to the subtropics and southward to the subantarctic.*

## HOT SPOTS

1. Gulf of Carpentaria, Northern Territory
2. Arnhem Land, N Territory
3. Eighty Mile Beach/Roebuck Bay, Western Australia
4. Port Hedland, W Australia
5. Shark Bay/Lake Macleod, W Australia
6. Lake Eyre, South Australia
7. St. Vincent Gulf/The Coorong, S Australia
8. Port Philip Bay/Corner Inlet, Victoria
9. Miranda, North Island, New Zealand

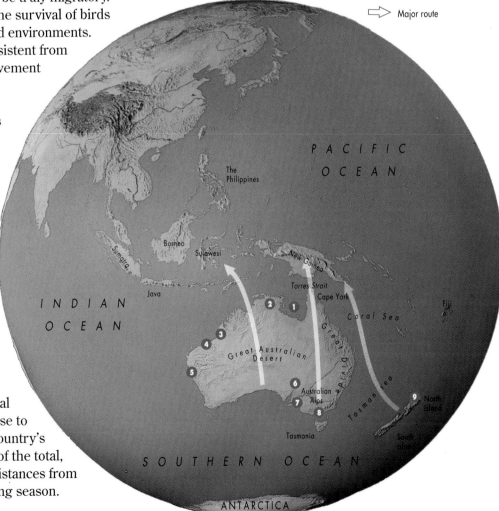

Major route

# Australasian migrants/2

**Swift Parrot**
*Lathamus discolor*
**Wingspan** 13–14½ in/33–36 cm
**Weight** 1¾–2⅝ oz/50–74 g
**Journey length** 200–1,550 miles/
350–2,500 km

## Migrants from Tasmania to Australia

Several birds breed in Tasmania and winter in Australia. They include the Orange-bellied Parrot – which travels from the island's southwestern coast to the dunes and foreshores between The Coorong and Corner Inlet – and the Swift Parrot.

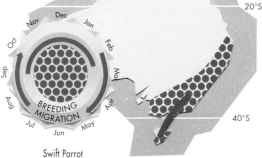

Swift Parrot

**Known to breed** only on the island of Tasmania, the Swift Parrot (above) regularly migrates to the eastern Australian mainland in winter.

The birds occur widely, but in scattered locations, in the forested areas of the east coast as far north as southern Queensland. But their chattering, flutelike calls are most commonly heard in the wooded regions of southern Victoria as flocks forage on the blossom-laden eucalyptus trees.

148

**Golden-bronze Cuckoo**
*Chalcites lucidus*
**Wingspan** 12–14 in/30–34 cm
**Weight** 1–1½ oz/28–45 g
**Journey length** 200–3,400 miles/
350–5,500 km

**Sacred Kingfisher**
*Halcyon sancta*
**Wingspan** 11½–13½ in/29–33 cm
**Weight** 1–2 oz/28–58 g
**Journey length** 0–2,400 miles/
0–3,900 km

**Australian Bee-eater**
*Merops ornatus*
**Wingspan** 16–18 in/40–45 cm
**Weight** ⅔–1⅛ oz/20–33 g
**Journey length** 0–3,000 miles/
0–4,800 km

## Migrations north from New Zealand

The Double-banded Plover is one of the few land birds migrating between New Zealand and Australia, with some populations regularly crossing the Tasman Sea. This group also includes the Long-tailed Cuckoo, which breeds in New Zealand and winters on the tropical islands of the Pacific, and the Shining-bronze Cuckoo.

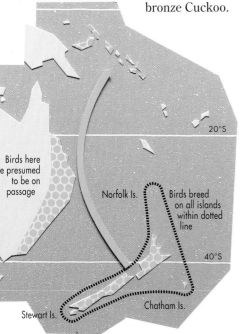

Birds here are presumed to be on passage

Norfolk Is.   Birds breed on all islands within dotted line

20°S
40°S

Stewart Is.   Chatham Is.

*Australian Golden-bronze Cuckoos (left) migrate north as far as New Guinea, the Lesser Sunda Islands, and the Bismarck Archipelago.*

*The New Zealand Shining-bronze Cuckoo, once regarded as a separate species from these Australian birds, is now classed as the same species. New Zealand birds breed throughout the island group, south to Stewart Island, east to the Chatham Islands, and as far north as Norfolk Island.*

*Their migratory route in the fall is not well understood and may involve a direct flight north, at least for the adults. Or, as is believed to be the case in spring, birds may hug – or even stop over for some time on – the east coast of Australia.*

*Sacred Kingfishers (left) are widely distributed throughout Australia. Northern populations are resident, but southern birds, which breed in all but the driest areas, join the residents or fly on to Sumatra, Borneo, Sulawesi, New Guinea, and the surrounding islands in winter.*

*New Zealand populations are also resident, but some are altitudinal migrants, moving in winter from the mountains to nearby lowlands.*

Sacred Kingfisher

## Migrants from Australia to the tropics

Several land birds migrate regularly between the continent of Australia and the tropical islands to the north, in particular to New Guinea and the surrounding area. Among the better known of these migrants are the Channel-billed Cuckoo, Sacred Kingfisher, and Australian Bee-eater.

Populations that breed in the north of the continent are often resident or only locally dispersive. Those that breed in the southern areas, however, must move north to avoid the less favorable conditions of the southern winter.

S limit of residents' range

20°S
Pops. within dotted line are resident
40°S

Australian Bee-eater

*Australian Bee-eaters breed in all parts of Australia except Tasmania, with southern populations migrating northward to winter in northern Australia, eastern Indonesia, and New Guinea.*

149

# Australasian migrants/3

**Scarlet Honeyeater**
*Myzomela sanguinolenta*
**Wingspan** 9–10 in/22–25 cm
**Weight** ⅓–½ oz/12–15 g
**Journey length** 30–1,550 miles/
50–2,500 km

**Spectacular male
Scarlet Honeyeaters**
*(left) can often be
detected in spring by
their tinkling song
as they forage on
eucalyptus and
melaleuca blossom.
Although they occur
along Australia's
eastern seaboard, these
birds are also known
on islands to the north
from Sulawesi to New
Caledonia. On the
islands, however,
they are sedentary,
and the existence of
separate races here
suggests that there is
little dispersal, and
indeed considerable
isolation, of the
different populations.
  In Australia, Scarlet
Honeyeaters breed in
the southern forests
and generally move
north to the coastal
forests in winter.*

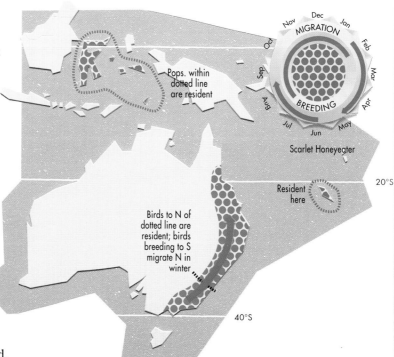

## Migrations within Australasia

Species that migrate altitudinally or
from southern regions northward each
fall and return in spring include the
majority of the true migrants in
Australasia. Among this group are
several of the honeyeaters, such as
the Little and Noisy friarbirds and the
Scarlet and Yellow-faced honeyeaters.
The fall migration of the Yellow-faced
Honeyeater is most apparent in the
Canberra area as mixed flocks
begin to leave the high-altitude
forests. Despite this conspicuous
start, details of the whole migration
are unclear and at least some birds
stay in the south for the winter.
  Migrants within New
Zealand include the South Island
Pied Oystercatcher, which breeds
in the river valleys of the south and
winters on the estuaries of North Island.

Pops. within
dotted line
are resident

Scarlet Honeyeater

MIGRATION

BREEDING

Nov Dec Jan Feb Mar Apr May Jun Jul Aug Sep Oct

20°S

Resident
here

Birds to N of
dotted line are
resident; birds
breeding to S
migrate N in
winter

40°S

**Little Friarbird**
*Philemon citreogularis*
**Wingspan** 15–19 in/38–48 cm
**Weight** 2⅔–8 oz/75–220 g
**Journey length** 30–1,500 miles/
50–2,400 km

**Noisy Friarbird**
*Philemon corniculatus*
**Wingspan** 19–22 in/48–55 cm
**Weight** 5¼–8 oz/150–220 g
**Journey length** 30–1,000 miles/
50–1,600 km

**Gray-backed White-eye**
*Zosterops lateralis*
**Wingspan** 13–14½ in/33–36 cm
**Weight** ½–⅔ oz/15–20 g
**Journey length** 30–1,250 miles/
50–2,000 km

**Southern breeding Little Friarbirds** *(left) are migratory; farther north birds are more nomadic, often staying in an area while the blossom lasts, then moving on.*

*This species also occurs in New Guinea, although there is no evidence of movement between populations.*

**Classed as true migrants** *in the south of their eastern Australian range, Noisy Friarbirds are more nomadic in the north. They also occur in New Guinea.*

*These honeyeaters are large, conspicuous, and somewhat ugly-looking birds, best known for their distinctive, raucous calls as they forage in the upper canopy of tall eucalyptus groves.*

Noisy Friarbird

**The Gray-backed White-eye** *(left) is widely distributed in Australia and is a recent colonist in New Zealand. It has also spread to many islands in the Pacific as far north as Fiji. In Australia it occurs around the coasts from the Tropic of Capricorn to Tasmania and north to Cape York.*

*The populations of southeastern Australia are spectacular migrants, moving north in winter, either toward South Australia or up the east coast as far as Queensland. Banded Tasmanian breeders have been recovered in northern Queensland.*

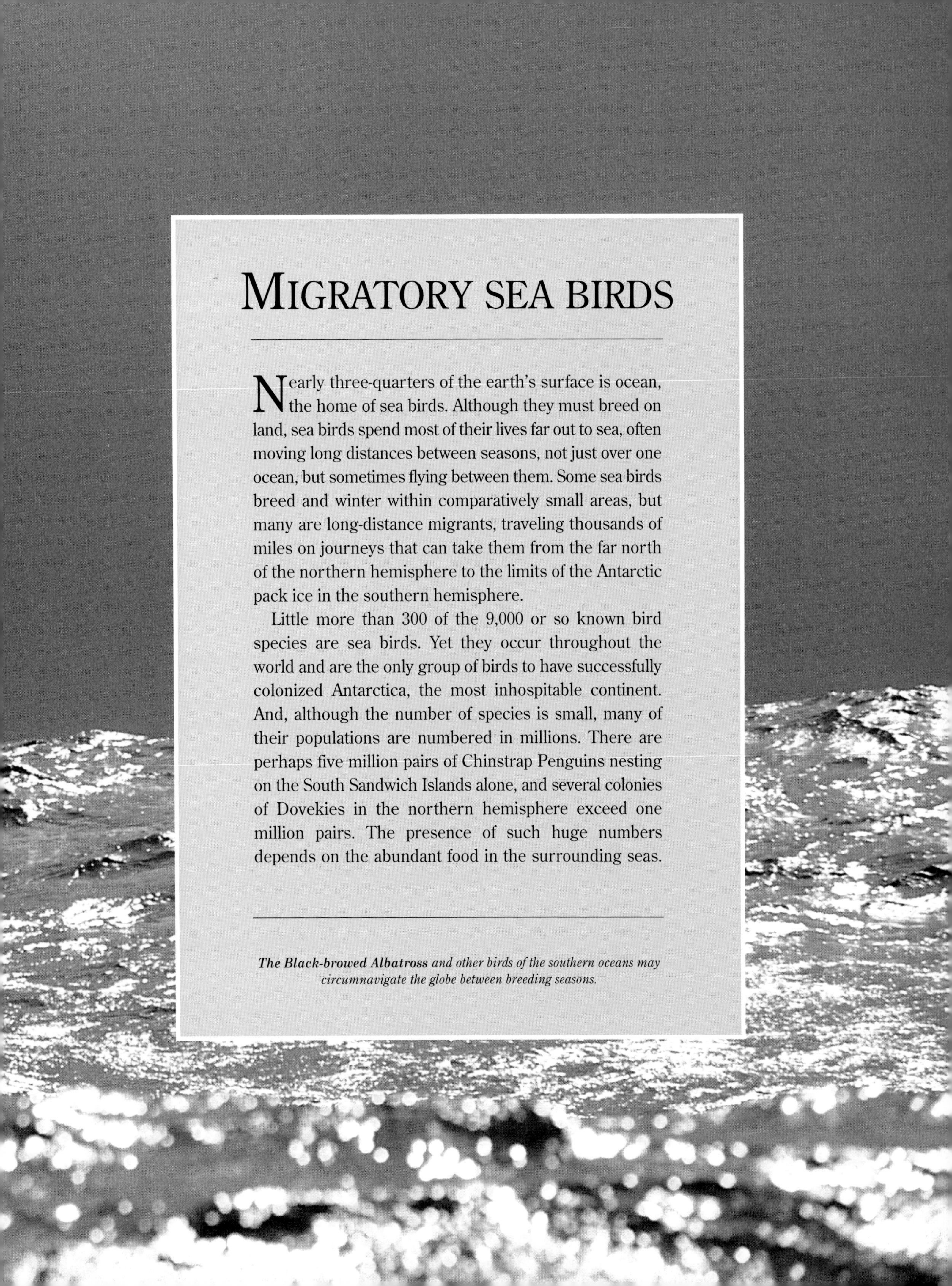

# MIGRATORY SEA BIRDS

Nearly three-quarters of the earth's surface is ocean, the home of sea birds. Although they must breed on land, sea birds spend most of their lives far out to sea, often moving long distances between seasons, not just over one ocean, but sometimes flying between them. Some sea birds breed and winter within comparatively small areas, but many are long-distance migrants, traveling thousands of miles on journeys that can take them from the far north of the northern hemisphere to the limits of the Antarctic pack ice in the southern hemisphere.

Little more than 300 of the 9,000 or so known bird species are sea birds. Yet they occur throughout the world and are the only group of birds to have successfully colonized Antarctica, the most inhospitable continent. And, although the number of species is small, many of their populations are numbered in millions. There are perhaps five million pairs of Chinstrap Penguins nesting on the South Sandwich Islands alone, and several colonies of Dovekies in the northern hemisphere exceed one million pairs. The presence of such huge numbers depends on the abundant food in the surrounding seas.

*The Black-browed Albatross and other birds of the southern oceans may circumnavigate the globe between breeding seasons.*

# Patterns of migration

*Food for sea birds accumulates where warm and cool ocean currents meet.*

The sea is not a uniform habitat. There are immense variations between different parts, particularly in the amount of plankton and numbers of fish that live there. Sea birds feed either from the surface of the sea or in the top 100–170 feet (30–50 m) and must find areas where this thin layer contains plenty of food. This they do either where the water is comparatively shallow, such as close to coasts, or where the meeting of cold and warm currents produces turbulence in the form of upwellings of cold water. The highest density of plankton – the smallest, most primitive life form in the oceans – occurs in these regions, attracting squid and fish and, in turn, seals, whales, and birds.

By far the most important area of upwellings for all sea birds, and one which explains the enormous numbers of birds that breed in Antarctica, lies close to the Antarctic pack ice in an area known as the Antarctic Divergence. Here, a warm current that has flowed south from the Atlantic, Pacific, and Indian oceans rises to the surface, bringing with it abundant nutrients. These stimulate huge "blooms," or growths, of phytoplankton, minute plants which flourish in the continuous daylight of the Antarctic summer. They are fed on by animal plankton which in turn feed the krill, swarms of small shrimplike organisms whose numbers can exceed 30,000 in a cubic yard of water. Krill can sustain all the larger marine life of the region, from fish to whales, and every sort of sea bird, whether they feed directly on the krill or on the abundant fish species higher in the food chain.

Plankton flourishes in cold water. The warm waters of the current are cooled by contact with the pack ice and flow north again, carrying the plankton in their stream. The cold water sits on top of the warm because it is mixed with substantial quantities of fresh water (from the summer meltwaters of the ice cap and from glaciers), which is lighter than salt water. It is not until this northward flowing cool water has traveled several hundred miles that it sinks below much warmer surface water in a region known as the Antarctic Convergence. There is thus a broad band of cold water around Antarctica that is rich in food and home not only to the millions of sea birds breeding in the region, but also to many sea birds which breed in the northern hemisphere and migrate here for the northern winter.

The same conditions of nutrient-rich water and abundant plankton and fish also occur elsewhere. Major currents

flow north from Antarctica along the coasts of South America – the Peru Current in the west and the Falkland in the east – and Africa, where the Benguela Current travels up the western side of the continent. Equally, cold currents flow south from the Arctic Ocean. They include the Oya Shio in the Pacific and the Labrador Current in the Atlantic.

In contrast to these deep ocean currents, surface currents are greatly influenced by prevailing winds. The best-known

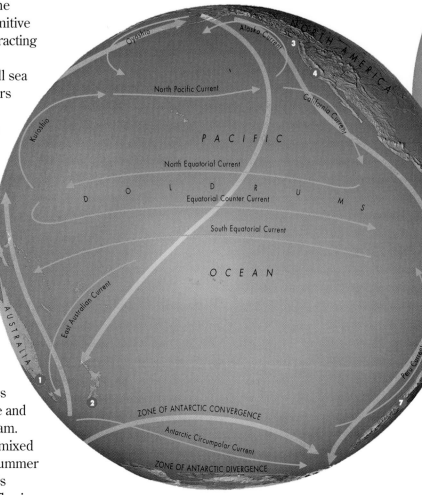

*The central regions of the major oceans – the Pacific, Atlantic, and Indian – all lie in tropical or subtropical latitudes where temperatures are more or less constantly warm. Here there is little plankton growth and comparatively low densities of fish, with* *the result that these areas tend to be less attractive to sea birds than areas of turbulence. This, combined with the presence of the rich coastal currents, channels much sea bird migration (which is often considered – wrongly – to be on a* *broad front, across the widest stretches of sea) into comparatively narrow bands, which follow quite closely the coasts of the continents.*
*Sea birds moving south from the North Atlantic, for example, tend to stay close to the western coasts of Europe and Africa,*

*Many sea bird species* roam vast distances from their breeding colonies, traveling the oceans in search of nutrient-rich waters where food is plentiful. Several species cross the equator on migration.

*With a breeding population estimated at hundreds of millions,* **Wilson's Storm-Petrel** *is probably the world's most numerous sea bird. Small in size and weighing only 1⅛ ounce (32 g), it travels from Antarctica as far north as Labrador.*

**Sabine's Gulls** *are long-distance migrants. Those breeding in the marshy tundra and islets of Arctic Alaska and Siberia winter off the coasts of Peru and Colombia; Canadian and Greenland breeders migrate to southern Africa.*

wind-assisted current is the Gulf Stream, which flows from the region of Florida, northwestward along the East Coast of North America before heading across the Atlantic toward northern Europe. Its major effect, for sea birds, is to produce an interaction between its own warm water and the colder water flowing south from the Arctic. The upwellings that result are vital to the survival of the many sea birds that nest around the coasts of Greenland, Iceland, and Svalbard.

## HOT SPOTS

Sea bird colonies abound in areas where the cold waters of ocean currents meet warmer water to produce upwellings rich in food. These regions are also visited extensively by migrant sea birds. Since many of these areas are in the open ocean, cruise ships can provide an ideal platform for watchers. And, because sea birds take their food from shallow waters, many stretches of coastline are prime sites.

1. Coast around Melbourne, Victoria
2. Invercargill/ Stewart Island, New Zealand
3. Vancouver Is., British Columbia
4. Monterey, California
5. Florida Keys
6. Coast around Lima, Peru
7. Coast around Valparaiso, Chile
8. Talan Island, Russia
9. Cape Cod, Massachusetts
10. Bonaventure/ Gaspe Is., New Brunswick
11. St. Ives, England
12. Falkland Islands

*where the Benguela Current offers ample feeding opportunities. Some, however do make the relatively short ocean crossing from western Africa to northeastern South America before continuing down the coast to Cape Horn and beyond.*

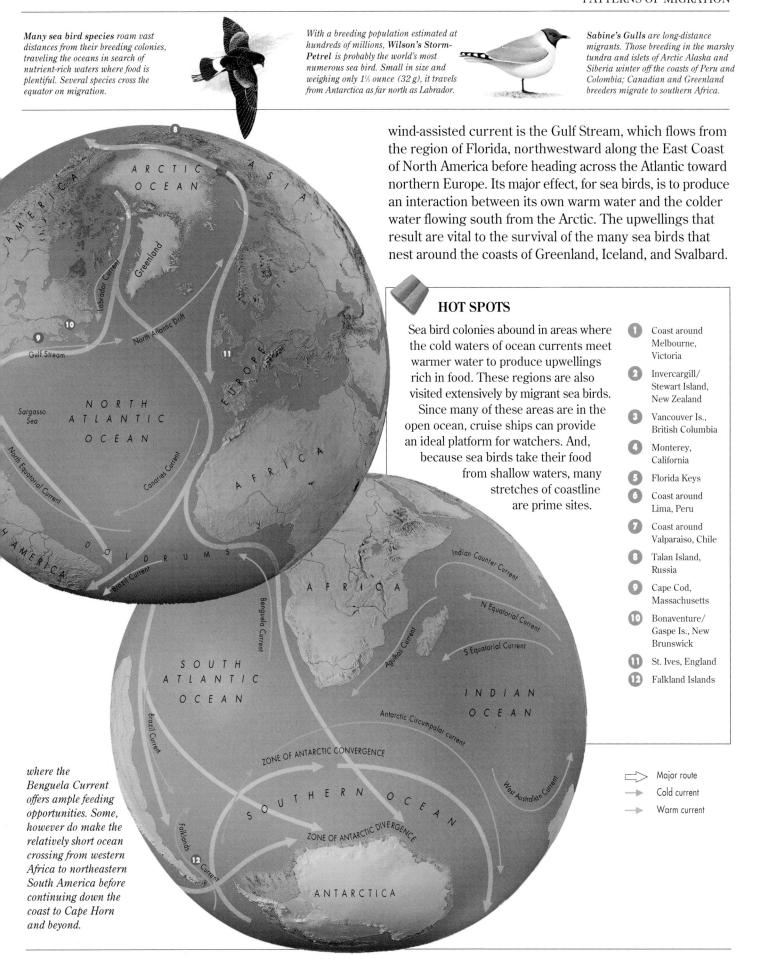

⇨ Major route
→ Cold current
→ Warm current

# Penguins

*Fasting males incubate their eggs in freezing blizzards as females feed at sea.*

All species of penguins are confined to the southern hemisphere, although the Galápagos Penguin nests close to the equator and has wandered across it as far north as Panama. The majority of species, however, occur well to the south, with several nesting in Antarctica. Here, they are extremely numerous – colonies of hundreds of thousands are not uncommon.

The species that nest in the warmer waters around South America and southern Africa are largely sedentary, wandering only short distances out to sea when they are not ashore breeding. Those nesting on oceanic islands farther south tend to move north during the winter, following the fish that make up their diet. The Antarctic species, which need open water in which to feed, must stay beyond the northern limits of the pack ice.

Little is known about penguin movements, other than in the breeding season, because the birds are difficult to follow while at sea. The appearance of juveniles long distances from the nearest colony suggests that these birds wander widely, in particular immediately after they leave the colony. Young King and Little penguins can move more than 600 miles (1,000 km), while juvenile Jackass Penguins, which breed on the coasts of South Africa, may reach the equator on the continent's Atlantic seaboard.

In the breeding season, many Antarctic species make long, regular trips between nests and feeding grounds. King Penguins are the champions. Small young, which require frequent feeding, are guarded by one parent while the other may travel up to 250 miles (400 km) for food. Once the young are old enough to be left by both parents in a nursery, the feeding trips may double in length.

The Emperor Penguin is unique among Antarctic birds in that it breeds in winter. This is probably so that when the chick is ready to leave the colony, at about five months old, food is plentiful and conditions are favorable for its survival. As soon as she has laid the single egg, the female passes it to the male, who places it on top of his feet and lowers a pouch of skin over the top. The female then leaves the colony to feed, returning when the egg is ready to hatch.

The male incubates the egg for up to 65 days, keeping it at a temperature of 88°F (31°C); around him temperatures may fall to −76°F (−60°C) and winds blow at 125 mph (200 km/h). To conserve heat, the males huddle in dense packs, taking turns to shuffle into and out of the center of the group, where the temperature is several degrees higher than on the fringes.

Adélie Penguin

*Although Adélie Penguins rarely travel more than 30 miles (50 km) from their colonies to find food, they are capable of navigating over longer distances if necessary. Birds taken from the Antarctic coast and released inland on featureless snow fields headed north, the direction that would inevitably bring them to the sea and thus to food and safety. That these movements were confined to periods when the birds could see the sun proved that they were navigating with its aid.*

**Magellanic Penguins** breed on the Falkland Islands and along the coasts of Argentina and Chile. They nest in colonies of up to 200,000 pairs, laying their eggs in burrows or shaded depressions which offer protection against both predators and extreme heat. These birds, insulated to cope with cold, wet conditions, often find it difficult to keep cool.

During the nesting season, adults obtain small fish and squid from the shallow waters close to the colony. At the end of the season, the birds move away, following northward-flowing ocean currents up the coast. In the east, they may travel 600 miles (1,000 km), to southern Brazil.

Chilean breeders move with the Peru Current, which supports vast stocks of small fish. Groups of penguins may work together or cooperate with sea lions and other predators to concentrate the fish, making them easier to catch.

Magellanic Penguin

**Adélie Penguin**
*Pygoscelis adeliae*
**Weight** 8 lb 13oz–14 lb 5 oz/4–6.5 kg
**Journey length** 600–2,175 miles/
1,000–3,500 km

**Magellanic Penguin**
*Spheniscus magellanicus*
**Weight** 10–15 lb 7 oz/4.5–7 kg
**Journey length** 60–600 miles/
100–1,000 km

**Emperor Penguin**
*Aptenodytes forsteri*
**Weight** 42–101 lb/19–46 kg
**Journey length** 600–1,500 miles/
1,000–2,500 km

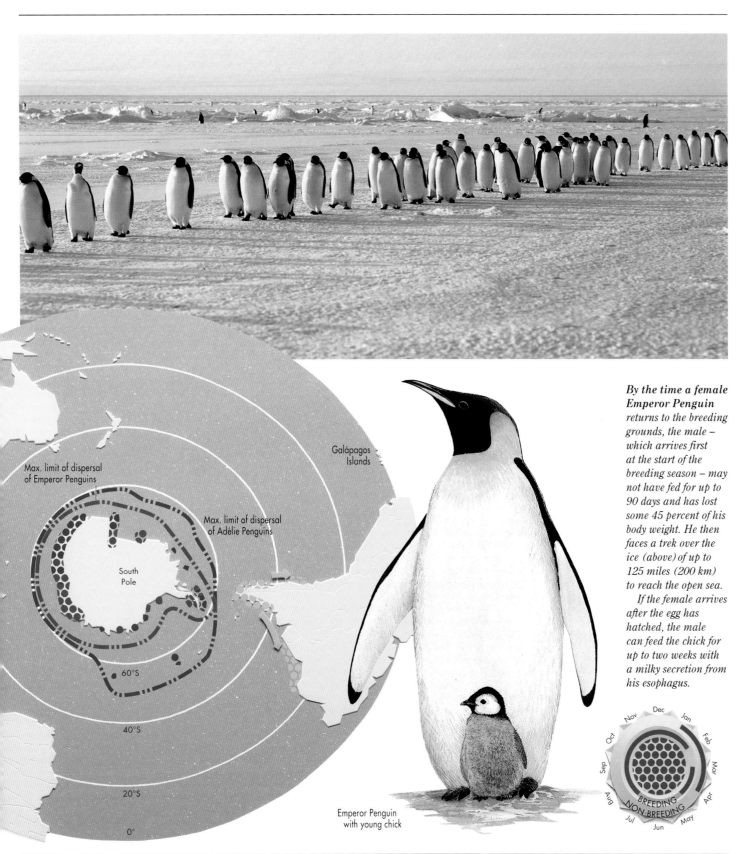

Emperor Penguin
with young chick

*By the time a female Emperor Penguin* returns to the breeding grounds, the male – which arrives first at the start of the breeding season – may not have fed for up to 90 days and has lost some 45 percent of his body weight. He then faces a trek over the ice (above) of up to 125 miles (200 km) to reach the open sea.

If the female arrives after the egg has hatched, the male can feed the chick for up to two weeks with a milky secretion from his esophagus.

157

# Albatross

*These solitary travelers return to the same island and the same mate each year.*

The largest species of albatross have the longest wingspans of any flying birds, exceeding 11 feet (3.5 m) in the Wandering Albatross. All are consummate fliers, gliding on outstretched wings in and out of the wave troughs, where they find enough uplift from the wind to maintain their soaring flight for days at a time.

Because they rely almost entirely on soaring – indeed they find flapping flight extremely tiring – albatross live only in areas of near-constant wind. In calm conditions they are forced to settle on the sea and wait for the wind to pick up again. The southern oceans, where the winds blow almost continuously in the "roaring forties" and "furious

*Albatross* rarely reach the North Atlantic. Once there, a bird is unlikely to be able to cross the doldrums – an area of notorious calm north of the equator – and is probably trapped for the rest of its life.

In 1967, a Black-browed Albatross was seen in the Firth of Forth, Scotland. It was there in 1968 and 1969. Then, in 1972, what was almost certainly the same bird appeared in the Shetland Islands. It returned most years for the breeding season, and was there again in summer 1994. For several years it built a nest, without finding a mate to share it.

Black-browed Albatross

*The Wandering Albatross takes almost a full year to complete its breeding cycle, so nests only every second year. The single egg is incubated for 11 weeks. Once it has hatched, the chick is brooded by one of its parents for the first four weeks, then left while the adults travel to find food. Since they return only every few days,*

*the chick grows slowly and is nine months old before it is ready to leave the nest.*

*Young Wandering Albatross take time to reach maturity and do not make a first breeding attempt until they are at least nine years old. This slow rate of reproduction is high enough to maintain numbers of this long-lived species. There are authentic records of birds aged 40 years or more.*

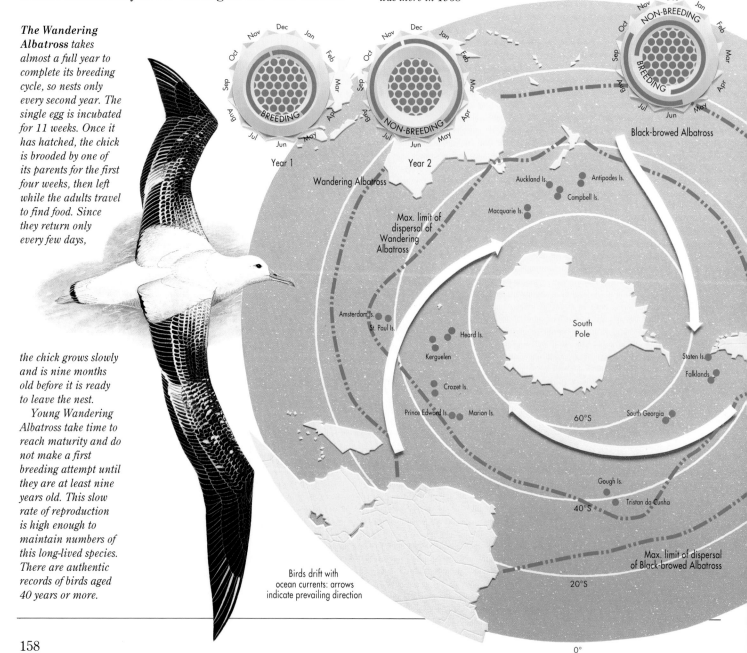

Year 1
Year 2

Wandering Albatross

Max. limit of dispersal of Wandering Albatross

Black-browed Albatross

Auckland Is.
Antipodes Is.
Campbell Is.
Macquarie Is.

Amsterdam Is.
St. Paul Is.

Heard Is.

South Pole

Staten Is.

Kerguelen

Falklands

Crozet Is.

Prince Edward Is.
Marion Is.
60°S
South Georgia

Gough Is.

40°S
Tristan da Cunha

Max. limit of dispersal of Black-browed Albatross

20°S

Birds drift with ocean currents: arrows indicate prevailing direction

0°

**Wandering Albatross**
*Diomedea exulans*
**Wingspan** 8 ft 2 in–11 ft 6 in/2.5–3.5 m
**Weight** 13 lb 12 oz–25 lb/6.25–11.3 kg
**Journey length** 3,000–12,500 miles/
5,000–20,000 km

**Black-browed Albatross**
*Diomedea melanoptris*
**Wingspan** 7 ft 6 in–8 ft 6 in/2.3–2.6 m
**Weight** 6 lb 10 oz–11 lb/3–5 kg
**Journey length** 3,000–9,300 miles/
5,000–15,000 km

**Waved Albatross**
*Diomedea irrorata*
**Wingspan** 7 ft 10 in/2.4 m
**Weight** 46 lb/21 kg
**Journey length** 950 miles/
1,500 km

Galápagos
Islands

*Albatross pair for life,* but separate at the end of the breeding season and do not meet again until they return to the nest site, one or – in the case of the larger species such as the Wandering and Royal albatrosses – two years later.

They reestablish and reinforce the pair bond by performing an elaborate series of displays at the nest site. These include clattering their bills together, posturing with outstretched wings and dancing, all accompanied by a variety of loud calls.

Colonies of breeding albatross vary considerably in size, from perhaps a few dozen pairs to, in Laysan and Black-browed albatross, among others, more than 100,000 pairs.

Waved Albatross

**The Waved Albatross** is the only species confined to the tropics. About 12,000 breeding pairs nest on Española in the Galápagos, and a colony of 50 pairs was discovered on La Plata, off the Ecuador coast, in 1974.

*Waved Albatross* are unusual in not building a nest but laying their egg on the bare ground. During incubation, the adult may shuffle around, moving the egg up to 130 feet (40 m) from where it was laid.

fifties," are home to 10 of the 14 albatross species. Nesting on remote oceanic islands, these birds make extraordinary journeys searching for food: some may regularly travel right around the globe in these latitudes. The other four species inhabit the central and northern Pacific, also nesting on small islands. They disperse across the Pacific, but do not leave it on longer journeys.

The main food of most albatross is squid, which live in deep water during the day but move to the surface in great schools at night. Where there is a concentration of food, many albatross of different species may gather in flocks, but normally they are solitary, constantly on the move searching for food. Humans have also helped in this respect: generations ago, albatross followed whaling ships for the debris thrown overboard; today they feed on the galley waste from ocean-going cruise ships.

Humans equally pose one of the major threats to albatross – the birds become hooked on long fishing lines and trapped in near-invisible monofilament nets.

# Shearwaters and petrels

*Ten-week-old shearwater chicks undertake 6,000-mile migrations.*

A group of about 90 species of highly specialized sea birds which spend by far the greater part of their lives at sea, the shearwaters and petrels come in to land solely to breed. Since many of the smaller species are vulnerable to predators when they are breeding, they nest in burrows which they visit only at night.

All of these birds have a well-developed sense of smell which is used in two ways. First, it enables them to locate sources of food – largely the floating carcasses of dead fish and marine mammals, and the offal and other waste products jettisoned overboard from fishing vessels – over great distances in the wide expanses of the oceans, even at night. Second, it helps in pinpointing the nesting burrow, which the incoming birds have to find among a colony of

thousands of pairs and in darkness. These birds are well known for the persistent, musky odor which clings to their plumage, and it is thought that this may be distinctive enough to allow an individual to recognize its own nest site.

Greater Shearwaters breed in the South Atlantic, on the Falkland Islands and on islands in the Tristan da Cunha group, where there are between six and nine million pairs. Outside the breeding season, Greater Shearwaters move around the Atlantic Ocean in a giant loop. They leave the colonies in March and April, heading northwest across the equator to the rich fishing waters off eastern North America, which they reach in May. They spend the whole summer here, then gradually move east across the North

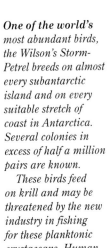

*One of the world's* most abundant birds, the Wilson's Storm-Petrel breeds on almost every subantarctic island and on every suitable stretch of coast in Antarctica. Several colonies in excess of half a million pairs are known.

These birds feed on krill and may be threatened by the new industry in fishing for these planktonic crustaceans. Human intervention has also been of benefit to storm-petrels, however. The virtual elimination of great whales from the southern oceans has removed a major competitor.

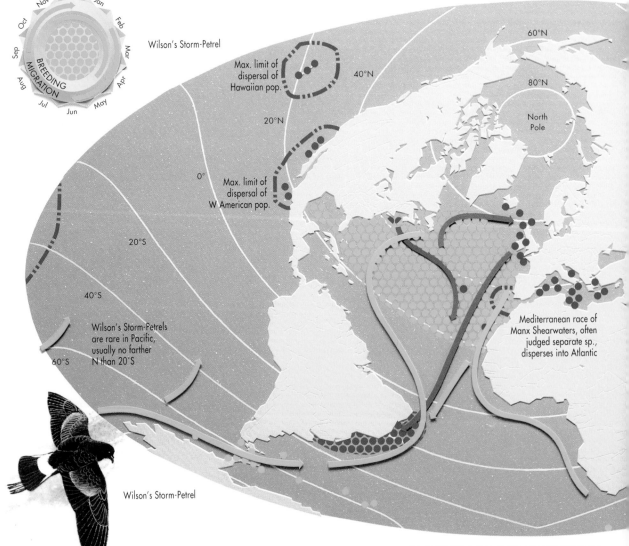

Wilson's Storm-Petrel

Max. limit of dispersal of Hawaiian pop.

Max. limit of dispersal of W American pop.

Wilson's Storm-Petrels are rare in Pacific, usually no farther N than 20°S

Mediterranean race of Manx Shearwaters, often judged separate sp., disperses into Atlantic

Wilson's Storm-Petrel

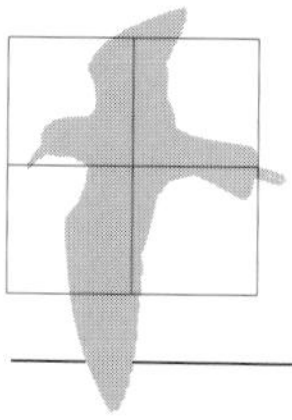

**Wilson's Storm-Petrel**
*Oceanites oceanicus*
**Wingspan** 15–17 in/38–42 cm
**Weight** 1¼–1½ oz/34–45 g
**Journey length** 3,000–9,300 miles/
5,000–15,000 km

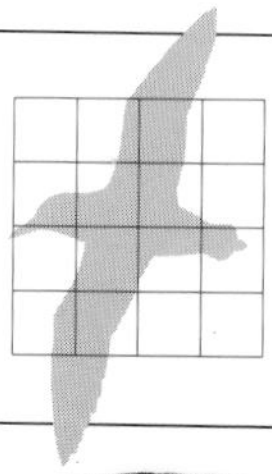

**Manx Shearwater**
*Puffinus puffinus*
**Wingspan** 30–35 in/76–89 cm
**Weight** 12 oz–1 lb 4 oz/350–575 g
**Journey length** 5,300–7,800 miles/
8,500–12,500 km

**Short-tailed Shearwater**
*Puffinus tenuirostris*
**Wingspan** 3 ft–3 ft 3 in/95–100 cm
**Weight** 1 lb 1 oz–1 lb 12 oz/480–800 g
**Journey length** 6,800–8,500 miles/
11,000–13,500 km

*Manx Shearwaters
breed on islands in the
North Atlantic. The
major colonies are
off the west coasts
of Britain, Ireland,
and France, with
the largest, 150,000
pairs – half the world
population – on Rhum,
off western Scotland.*

*Manx Shearwater
chicks fledge at 10
weeks and set off
immediately on
migration, crossing
the equator to winter*

*off the coasts of Brazil
and Argentina. One
chick, banded shortly
before it fledged on
Skokholm Island,
Wales, was found off
Brazil only 17 days
later, having traveled
almost 6,000 miles
(10,000 km).*

Atlantic. They are abundant off the European
continental shelf in July and August, by which
time they are heading due south again.
Some birds are back at their breeding
colonies by the end of August; others
make a wide, looping sweep in the
South Atlantic, completing a figure-eight before arriving
back at the breeding grounds in mid-September.

Storm-petrels may seem too small and fragile to survive
in the stormy oceans where they live, but they are well
adapted to their marine existence, feeding on the wing by
fluttering close to the sea's surface and scooping up krill
or plankton. They also patter with their feet on the water,
which may have the effect of attracting their prey.

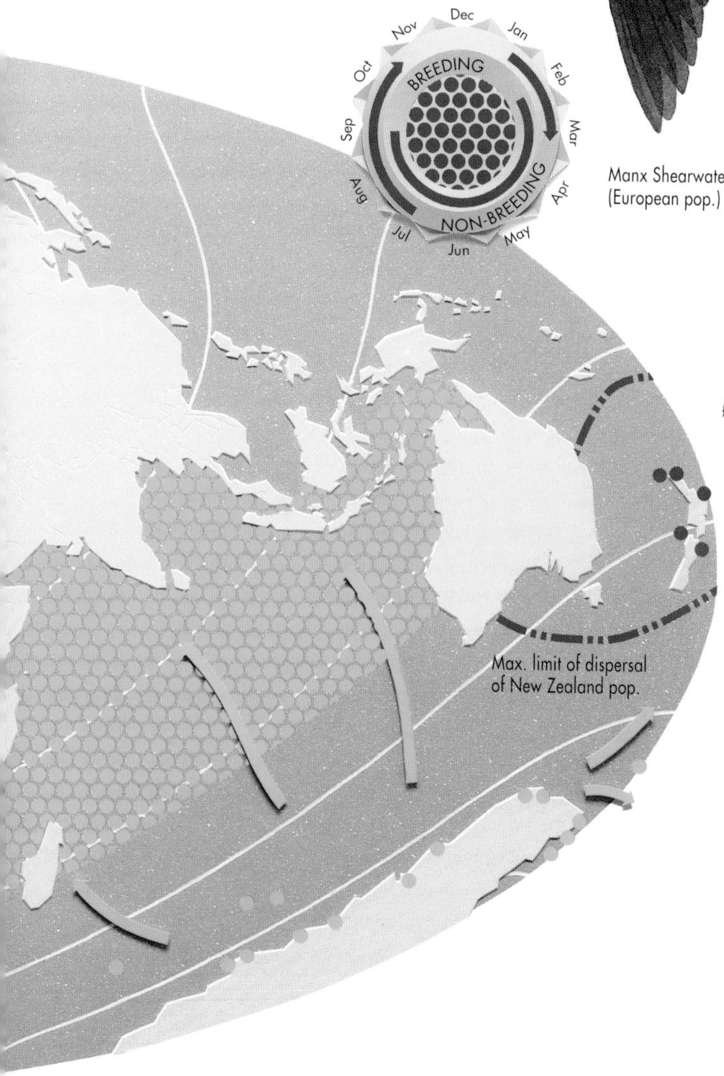

Manx Shearwater
(European pop.)

Max. limit of dispersal
of New Zealand pop.

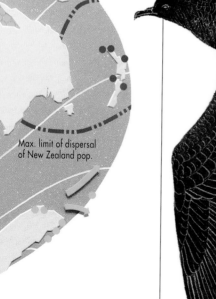

Short-tailed
Shearwater

## A RICH RESOURCE

Human exploitation of
birds has often been
responsible for their near
extinction, but where
matters are regulated and
monitored, populations
can survive a harvest of
eggs or young.

Short-tailed Shearwaters
breed on islands off the
coasts of Australia
and Tasmania.
There are
perhaps 23
million birds worldwide,
half of which nest in
Tasmania. Here, about
600,000 so-called mutton
bird chicks are culled
annually. The population
is monitored to make
sure that it withstands
this level of harvest.

Nothing is wasted:
the feathers are used in
upholstery and the down
to fill sleeping bags; the
meat is eaten; the fat
is added to cattle feed;
and the oil is used by the
pharmaceutical industry.

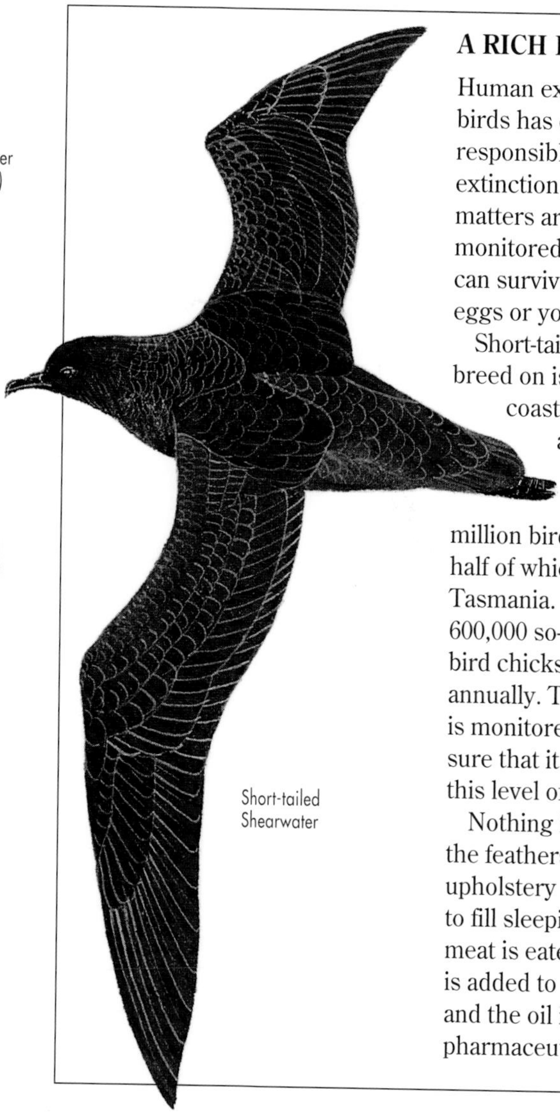

# Skuas, jaegers, gulls, and auks

*One group of migrants survives by pirating food from other species.*

Long-tailed Jaeger

Gulls and skuas/jaegers are closely related; indeed, the six species of skuas and jaegers clearly evolved from gulls. All skuas and jaegers are great travelers. The four species breeding in the northern hemisphere, Great, Arctic, Long-tailed, and Pomarine, all nest in northerly latitudes. Of these, the great majority of Arctic and Long-tailed jaegers – and at least some of the other two species – winter in the oceans of the southern hemisphere. The South Polar Skua – one of the two species nesting in the southern hemisphere – is known regularly to visit the North Atlantic during the southern winter. A South Polar Skua, banded as a chick on an island in Antarctica at 65°S, was shot six months later in western Greenland at 65°N, a distance of more than 9,300 miles (15,000 km), one of the longest journeys ever recorded for a banded bird.

The gulls are among the most widespread and successful sea birds. There are some 45 species, which occur in both

*Like other skuas, the Long-tailed Jaeger is a predator and a pirate, pursuing other birds until they disgorge or drop the food they are carrying.*

*In the breeding season, jaegers may nest close to colonies of other sea birds and wait for the adults bringing food to their chicks. Once a jaeger has begun to chase its* target, few birds are able to get away.

*Migrant jaegers harry victims from above, forcing them down toward the sea. Slowed by the weight of food in its beak or crop, the victim usually drops it. The jaeger then swoops down to take the food for itself.*

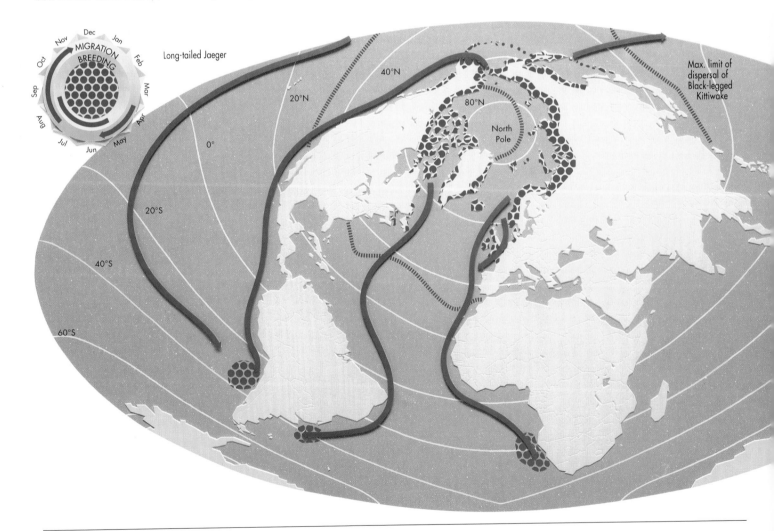

**Long-tailed Jaeger**
*Stercorarius longicaudus*
**Wingspan** 3 ft 5 in–3 ft 10 in/1.05–1.17 m
**Weight** 9–13 oz/250–360 g
**Journey length** 5,000–9,000 miles/
8,000–14,400 km

**Black-legged Kittiwake**
*Rissa tridactyla*
**Wingspan** 3 ft 1 in–3 ft 11 in/95–120 cm
**Weight** 11 oz–1 lb 3 oz/300–535 g
**Journey length** 300–3,000 miles/
500–5,000 km

**Ivory Gull**
*Pogophila eburnea*
**Wingspan** 3 ft 6 in–3 ft 11 in/1.08–1.2 m
**Weight** 1 lb 2 oz–1 lb 9 oz/500–700 g
**Journey length** 125–1,250 miles/
200–2,000 km

hemispheres, although they are more common in the north. These are gregarious birds, breeding in colonies on coastal and some inland marshes and feeding throughout the year in large flocks. Colonies may be tens of thousands strong, particularly if there is a major source of food nearby. Following an elaborate courtship ritual of display and calling, gulls pair for life. A pair usually returns to the same nest site each year, often the colony where one, but not both, of the birds was hatched.

Outside the breeding season most gulls undertake migratory or dispersive movements, or both, sometimes wintering well out to sea. Some are long-distance travelers, although others of the same species may, in a different part of the range, be fairly sedentary. Black-headed Gulls breeding in Japan, for example, migrate south almost to the equator and winter on the islands of Indonesia. Those that breed in Britain, by contrast, simply disperse over comparatively short distances, usually westward to avoid cold weather. The most traveled reach only as far as Spain.

All of the 22 species of auks are confined to the northern hemisphere, where they breed on the coasts, mainly on cliff ledges or in burrows, and winter at sea. Many species extend into the high Arctic, where they are among the most common birds, nesting in huge colonies and feeding on the fish and plankton which abound in the northern seas.

Auks are not good fliers. Although – unlike penguins – they have retained their powers of flight, their short, stubby wings are better suited to underwater swimming. Parents and chicks setting off from the breeding areas on a southerly migration toward the wintering grounds normally start by swimming. The Thick-billed Murres that breed in Svalbard winter off southern Greenland some 1,900 miles (3,000 km) away, and probably cover much of that distance in the water.

Black-legged Kittiwake

*The Black-legged Kittiwake (below) breeds on the coasts of the North Atlantic, into the Arctic. Outside the breeding season its movements are more dispersive than truly migratory.*

*Many adults stay within 250–300 miles (400–500 km) of their colony, but the juveniles gradually move farther and farther away from their birthplace in their first two or three winters, reaching their maximum distance (up to 2,175 miles/ 3,500 km) after three years. They return to the colony to breed when four or five years old.*

*Ivory Gulls (above) are among the world's most northerly breeding birds, nesting in small colonies on Franz Josef Land, Svalbard,* *Greenland, and the islands of Arctic Canada. Some nests are on cliff ledges, others have been found on "nunataks," rocky peaks projecting from* *inland ice sheets. One colony made its home on a floating "ice island" some 1,600 sq feet (150 m²) in area, carved from a glacier. The island was about* *25 miles (40 km) from the nearest land, and the 75 to 100 pairs of Ivory Gulls were nesting among the rocks and stones that littered its surface.*

# Terns

*Arctic Terns are the world's migratory champions, circumnavigating the globe every year.*

Of all birds, the Arctic Tern performs the longest known regular migration. These birds breed in the northern hemisphere, from temperate latitudes to the most northerly land in the world: the tip of Greenland, all the islands of Arctic Canada and Siberia, and Svalbard. They winter on the edge of the Antarctic pack ice. A straight-line distance from the Arctic to the Antarctic is about 9,300 miles (15,000 km). Few birds, however, travel in straight lines, and the Arctic Tern is no exception.

Terns nesting in the Arctic areas of eastern Canada and Greenland head southeast toward Europe to join the European, Svalbard, and Russian Arctic breeders. They all then head south down the coast of Iberia and western Africa. Some split off around Cape Verde and make their way down the South American coast, but the majority stay off the coast of Africa. Once past the Cape of Good Hope, they continue to head south for Antarctica, but are gradually pushed eastward by the prevailing winds until they are in the southern Indian Ocean.

As the pack ice retreats during the southern summer, the terns follow it southward, since its boundary usually marks an area of good feeding. By continuing south, the birds enter a zone of westerly winds and, when it is time to head back north, are thus south of the Atlantic Ocean again. They follow more or less the same route back up the coast of Africa. Once across the equator, they fan out, with the birds from Canada taking a more northwesterly route, while European breeders hug the coast.

Arctic Terns feed mainly on small fish. One of their most important prey species in northern waters is the sand eel,

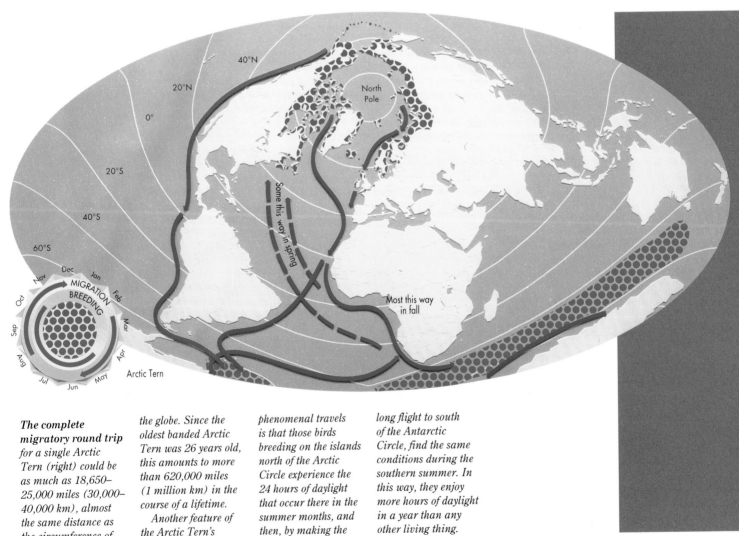

**The complete migratory round trip** *for a single Arctic Tern (right) could be as much as 18,650– 25,000 miles (30,000– 40,000 km), almost the same distance as the circumference of* *the globe. Since the oldest banded Arctic Tern was 26 years old, this amounts to more than 620,000 miles (1 million km) in the course of a lifetime.*

*Another feature of the Arctic Tern's* *phenomenal travels is that those birds breeding on the islands north of the Arctic Circle experience the 24 hours of daylight that occur there in the summer months, and then, by making the* *long flight to south of the Antarctic Circle, find the same conditions during the southern summer. In this way, they enjoy more hours of daylight in a year than any other living thing.*

**Arctic Tern**
*Sterna paraisaea*
**Wingspan** 29–33 in/75–85 cm
**Weight** 3–4 oz/80–120 g
**Journey length** 9,300–12,500 miles/ 15,000–20,000 km

a preference that has posed problems for some Arctic Terns, notably those breeding in Shetland, Scotland. Here, there were about 40,000 pairs in 1980, but after a series of complete breeding failures, numbers had halved by 1990. This has been linked to their inability to catch sand eels, which have been commercially fished with no limits on numbers taken.

The Shetland sand eel fishery was closed by government order in March 1991, ostensibly to conserve stocks for future fishing. It is nevertheless hoped that as sand eel stocks recover, the terns – and many other sea bird species that have suffered food shortages in this area – will benefit. Early indications were that this was working.

These birds are colonial nesters. In the high Arctic, colonies are generally small, consisting of a few to perhaps 100 pairs, but farther south, colonies are much larger, with some holding as many as 10,000 pairs. Nests are usually placed only 10–13 feet (3–4 m) apart. The clutch of two or three eggs is laid in a shallow scrape in the sand or pebbles, and newly hatched chicks are covered in a camouflaging gray and buff down which makes them difficult to see when they are crouched on the ground.

Arctic Terns are extremely aggressive in defense of their nests and make strenuous and concerted efforts to drive any intruder away from the area of the colony. Foxes intending predation and humans wanting to count the number of nests receive the same treatment. The adult birds from all over the colony rise up and make repeated swoops at the head, often striking with the bill, which is capable of drawing blood from an unprotected scalp.

# ALMOST MIGRATIONS

Conventional migrations are regular, taking place at the same time each year, and fixed in distance and direction. Others are less predictable. In some falls few, if any, birds leave the breeding area, while in others the whole population may shift thousands of miles. Such movements are known as irruptions, since they are most noticeable in the areas to which the birds move en masse. Here they "irrupt," often in spectacular numbers.

Irruptive species breed largely in the north and divide into three broad categories: the raptors and owls, the seed and berry eaters, and the birds of the steppes, such as Pallas's Sandgrouse. All have one thing in common, a relatively restricted diet which is itself subject to wide fluctuations in abundance. Thus, irruptive raptors and owls feed on voles and lemmings, which have a four- to five-year cycle of scarcity and abundance. Similarly, most irrupting seed and berry eaters feed on trees such as spruce, pine, and birch, which after a heavy crop may rest the following year. Sandgrouse take a variety of seeds, but live in areas subject to droughts which prevent the plants from flowering and seeding.

*Reliant on voles and lemmings to feed themselves and their young, Rough-legged Hawks are forced south when rodent populations crash.*

# Irruptions

*Failures of prey species and of seed or berry crops force reluctant migrants south.*

The most commonly irruptive birds of prey include the Northern Goshawk and Rough-legged Hawk. Among the owls, the Snowy, Short-eared, and Horned irrupt most frequently. All five species breed in the forests and tundra of the far north, the Horned Owl in North America only, the other species in both North America and Eurasia. They are equally irruptive in both continents.

These species feed on prey that have marked cycles of abundance. The reason why prey species show such strong cyclical fluctuations in numbers is uncertain, but may be due to variations in the climate combined with the availability of their own food supply, largely seeds and plants. Whatever the cause, the effect on predators of changes in their prey populations is marked.

The Northern Goshawk and Horned Owl eat mainly grouse and hares. In North America, the snowshoe hare, which has an approximately 10-year cycle of abundance, is the preferred target. In Eurasia, the principal food is grouse, which peaks and troughs about every four years. Thus, in North America, the Northern Goshawk and Horned Owl irrupt every 10 years, while in Eurasia the Goshawks move every four years.

Rough-legged Hawks and Snowy and Short-eared owls all feed on small rodents, mainly voles and lemmings, which also fluctuate in approximately four-year cycles. In years when voles and lemmings abound, hawks and owls breed very successfully, rearing large broods of young. Since food is plentiful, many of these birds survive the winter in the same area, so bird numbers are higher than usual in the following spring. Once the crash in vole and lemming numbers begins, the predators, having reached a high level of population themselves, either have to move or risk starvation. It is at this point that the predators migrate to find alternative food supplies.

Pallas's Sandgrouse breed in central Asia, Russia, Mongolia, and northern China, and normally make short-distance movements to the south. At infrequent intervals, large numbers move west into Europe, reaching as far as Britain and Ireland. The weather seems to play the major part in stimulating such

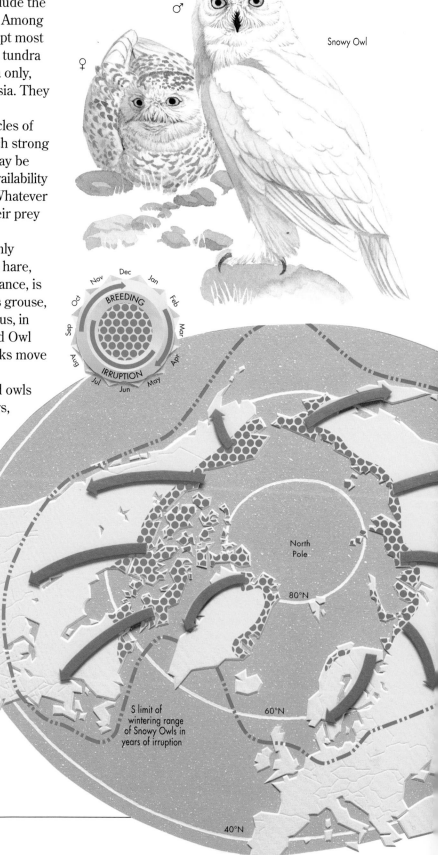

Snowy Owl

♂

♀

Nov Dec Jan
Oct Feb
Sep BREEDING Mar
Aug Apr
Jul IRRUPTION May
Jun

North Pole

80°N

60°N

S limit of wintering range of Snowy Owls in years of irruption

40°N

**Snowy Owl**
*Nyctea scandiaca*
**Wingspan** 4 ft 8 in–5 ft 5 in/1.42–1.66 m
**Weight** 2 lb 10 oz–6 lb 8 oz/1.2–2.95 kg
**Journey length** 300–3,000 miles/
500–5,000 km

**Rough-legged Hawk**
*Buteo lagopus*
**Wingspan** 3 ft 11 in–4 ft 11 in/1.2–1.5 m
**Weight** 1 lb 5 oz–3 lb 11 oz/600 g–1.66 kg
**Journey length** 300–2,800 miles/
500–4,500 km

**Red Crossbill**
*Loxia curvirostra*
**Wingspan** 10–11 in/25–28 cm
**Weight** 1¼–1½ oz/38–42 g
**Journey length** 300–2,175 miles/
500–3,500 km

*When lemming numbers are high, Snowy Owls breed well and rear large broods of young. When prey numbers are low, the owls may not be able to breed at all and leave northern areas early on much longer migrations than usual. They head south and stop only when they find a source of food. In "normal" years, Snowy Owls stay in Canada and northern Europe, but in years of irruption, North American breeders may travel to the Gulf States, while Eurasian birds may reach the Mediterranean.*

*Birds that wander long distances from the breeding grounds are probably unable to return the following spring.*

North American race
*sancti-johannis*

Rough-legged
Hawk

Eurasian race
*lagopus*

movements: drought probably results in a poor seed crop, then exceptional cold in the following spring means that nest sites remain snow-covered, forcing the birds to move away.

More numerous than irruptive predators are seed and berry eaters. Several species of finches breeding in the northern forests make unusually long mass movements when the seed crop of certain trees fails. Fruiting and seeding trees do not seem to have regular cycles of success and failure, but it is common for a productive year to be followed by one in which the trees appear to rest.

Good years enable northerly breeding tits, finches, and thrushes to survive through that fall and winter, so there is a large breeding population the following spring. These birds, and the young that they rear, then find there are few berries and seeds to eat that fall and are forced to migrate.

*Rough-legged Hawks breed in the Arctic tundra of North America and Eurasia. The extent of their migration is dictated by food stocks. When lemmings and voles are plentiful, the birds winter in the northern U.S. and northern Europe. In irruptive years, they may reach Florida and the Gulf coast, western Europe, northern Africa, and the Middle East.*

*These birds are doubly adapted to fluctuating food supplies in that they can also shift breeding areas, often breeding hundreds of miles south, east or west of their normal range when small mammals are scarce.*

*When northern-latitude trees fail to produce a seed crop, all of the birds that rely on the crop are forced to irrupt. Thus, in any autumn, if one species is irrupting, the chances are that several others will be doing so too.*

*The graph shows this synchrony by illustrating the numbers of four species of finches found during the annual Christmas count in Chesapeake Bay, Maryland, over 10 winters. Although numbers of individuals vary from bird to bird and year to year, they peak and trough in the same years for all species.*

Red
Crossbill

Evening
Grosbeak

Pine Siskin

Purple Finch

Evening Grosbeak

Red Crossbill

Number
of birds
counted
120
60
60
30
200
100
20
10

1962   '63   '64   '65   '66   '67   '68   '69   '70   '71

# Catalog of migrants

This list follows the order of the chapters in the book. Within each section, birds are listed according to the systematic order.

**Abbreviations**
**N** North/northern
**S** South/southern
**E** East/eastern
**W** West/western
**Wn** Wingspan
**Wt** Weight
C America = Central America
NZ = New Zealand
US = United States

## NORTH AMERICAN MIGRANTS

WESTERN GREBE
*Aechmophorus occidentalis*
**Wn** 38–42 in **Wt** 2 lb 3 oz–3 lb 12 oz
**Breeds** W-central N America S to Mexico, Apr to Sep
**Winters** Coasts of California & Mexico, Oct to Mar
**Journey length** 1,100–2,500 miles

EARED GREBE
*Podiceps nigricollis*
**Wn** 22–23 in **Wt** 9–14 oz
**Breeds** W-central US & S Canada; also Eurasia, May to Sep
**Winters** California, Gulf of Mexico S to Guatemala, Oct to Apr
**Journey length** 300–3,000 miles

DOUBLE-CRESTED CORMORANT
*Phalacrocorax auritus*
**Wn** 49–54 in **Wt** 3 lb 8 oz–4 lb 10 oz
**Breeds** Central & N US, S & E Canada, Apr to Oct **Winters** W & S coasts US, Mexico & Cuba, Nov to Mar
**Journey length** 300–3,400 miles

AMERICAN BITTERN
*Botaurus lentiginosus*
**Wn** 41–49 in **Wt** 13 oz–1 lb 4 oz
**Breeds** US & S Canada, Apr to Oct
**Winters** S US, Mexico & C America S to Panama, Nov to Mar
**Journey length** 500–4,200 miles

LEAST BITTERN *Ixobrychus exilis*
**Wn** 15–23 in **Wt** 4–6 oz
**Breeds** SE Canada, E & W US, C America, N S America, Mar to Oct
**Winters** Mexico to N S America, Nov to Feb
**Journey length** 600–2,500 miles

WOOD DUCK *Aix sponsa*
**Wn** 26–29 in **Wt** 1 lb 2 oz–1 lb 15 oz
**Breeds** Central & S US, Feb to Aug
**Winters** S US, Mexico & Cuba, Sep to Jan
**Journey length** 125–1,250 miles

AMERICAN BLACK DUCK *Anas rubripes*
**Wn** 33–37 in **Wt** 2 lb 9 oz–3 lb
**Breeds** NE US & E Canada, Mar to Sep
**Winters** SE US, Oct to Feb
**Journey length** 185–2,175 miles

CANVASBACK *Aythya valisneria*
**Wn** 32–36 in **Wt** 1 lb 14 oz–3 lb 8 oz
**Breeds** NW US & W Canada, May to Sep
**Winters** S US & Mexico, Oct to Apr
**Journey length** 300–3,400 miles

LESSER SCAUP *Aythya affinis*
**Wn** 27–31 in **Wt** 1 lb 12 oz–1 lb 14 oz
**Breeds** W US & W Canada, May to Sep
**Winters** S US, Mexico & C America S to Panama, Oct to Apr
**Journey length** 600–5,600 miles

BUFFLEHEAD *Bucephala albeola*
**Wn** 21–24 in **Wt** 12–16 oz
**Breeds** Alaska, W & S Canada, Apr to Aug
**Winters** E & W coasts of N America, inland S US & N Mexico, Sep to Mar
**Journey length** 300–3,400 miles

NORTH AMERICAN RUDDY DUCK
*Oxyura jamaicensis*
**Wn** 20–24 in **Wt** 14 oz–1 lb 10 oz
**Breeds** N & W US, SW Canada; also Eurasia, Mar to Sep **Winters** S & SE US, Mexico, Oct to Feb
**Journey length** 600–2,500 miles

BLACK VULTURE *Coragyps atratus*
**Wn** 55–59 in **Wt** 3 lb 5 oz–5 lb 8 oz
**Breeds** S & SE US, Mar to Sep
**Winters** S & SE US, C & S America, Oct to Feb
**Journey length** 60–600 miles

BALD EAGLE *Haliaeetus leucocephalus*
**Wn** 70–90 in **Wt** 6 lb 10 oz–15 lb 7 oz
**Breeds** N US & Canada, Mar to Sep
**Winters** Alaska & Newfoundland S to S US, Oct to Feb
**Journey length** 60–2,800 miles

NORTHERN HARRIER *Circus cyaneus*
**Wn** 39–47 in **Wt** 11 oz–1 lb 9 oz
**Breeds** Central US N to N Canada; also Eurasia, Apr to Aug
**Winters** S US S to W Indies & Colombia, Sep to Mar
**Journey length** 300–3,000 miles

SHARP-SHINNED HAWK *Accipiter striatus*
**Wn** 20–28 in **Wt** 4–13 oz
**Breeds** N US, Alaska, S & NW Canada, sedentary in W Indies & S America, Apr to Sep
**Winters** S US & Mexico, Oct to Mar
**Journey length** 60–3,000 miles

COOPER'S HAWK *Accipiter cooperii*
**Wn** 29–37 in **Wt** 7 oz–1 lb 2 oz
**Breeds** S Canada, US & N Mexico, Apr to Sep
**Winters** US, C America & W Indies, Oct to Mar
**Journey length** 0–1,250 miles

BROAD-WINGED HAWK *Buteo platypterus*
**Wn** 31–36 in **Wt** 7 oz–1 lb 3 oz
**Breeds** S Canada & E US, Apr to Sep
**Winters** S Florida to Brazil, Bolivia & Peru, Oct to Mar
**Journey length** 1,000–8,700 miles

RED-TAILED HAWK *Buteo jamaicensis*
**Wn** 47–53 in **Wt** 1 lb 2 oz–2 lb 10 oz
**Breeds** S Canada & US S to Panama & W Indies, Mar to Sep
**Winters** US, except extreme N, S to Panama & W Indies, Oct to Feb
**Journey length** 0–1,850 miles

FERRUGINOUS HAWK *Buteo regalis*
**Wn** 51–55 in **Wt** 2 lb–3 lb 15 oz
**Breeds** W Canada & NW US, Mar to Sep **Winters** SW US & N Mexico, Oct to Feb
**Journey length** 125–2,500 miles

PRAIRIE FALCON *Falco mexicanus*
**Wn** 35–43 in **Wt** 1 lb 5 oz–2 lb 14 oz
**Breeds** SW Canada & W US, Apr to Sep
**Winters** W US to Mexico, Oct to Mar
**Journey length** 0–1,250 miles

PEREGRINE FALCON *Falco peregrinus*
**Wn** 35–43 in **Wt** 1 lb 5 oz–2 lb 14 oz
**Breeds** Alaska, N Canada & W-central US; also Eurasia, May to Sep
**Winters** E coast of US, coasts of Mexico & W Indies, Oct to Apr
**Journey length** 1,250–3,750 miles

SORA RAIL *Porzana carolina*
**Wn** 13–15 in **Wt** 2–4 oz
**Breeds** S Canada, N & central US, Apr to Sep
**Winters** S US, C America & S America S to N Peru & Guyana, Oct to Mar
**Journey length** 1,850–4,350 miles

AMERICAN AVOCET
*Recurvirostra americana*
**Wn** 30–33 in **Wt** 10 oz–1 lb 1 oz
**Breeds** S Canada, W & extreme E US, May to Sep
**Winters** S US to Guatemala, Oct to Apr
**Journey length** 300–2,800 miles

SEMIPALMATED PLOVER
*Charadrius semipalmatus*
**Wn** 16–20 in **Wt** 1–2 oz
**Breeds** Alaska & N Canada S to Newfoundland, May to Aug
**Winters** E & W coasts S US to S S America, Oct to Mar
**Journey length** 4,000–8,000 miles

MOUNTAIN PLOVER
*Charadrius montanus*
**Wn** 19–23 in **Wt** 2–3 oz
**Breeds** Montana to New Mexico, Apr to Aug **Winters** S California & N Mexico, Sep to Mar
**Journey length** 370–1,500 miles

AMERICAN GOLDEN PLOVER
*Pluvialis dominica*
**Wn** 23–28 in **Wt** 4–7 oz
**Breeds** Alaska & Arctic Canada, May to Aug
**Winters** Bolivia & S Brazil to central Argentina, Oct to Mar
**Journey length** 5,900–8,200 miles

MARBLED GODWIT *Limosa fedoa*
**Wn** 29–33 in **Wt** 9 oz–1 lb 5 oz
**Breeds** Central S Canada & central N US, Apr to Aug
**Winters** E & W coasts of US S to Chile, Oct to Mar
**Journey length** 900–5,600 miles

LONG-BILLED CURLEW
*Numenius americanus*
**Wn** 31–39 in **Wt** 1 lb 9 oz–3 lb 1 oz
**Breeds** SW Canada & NW US, Apr to Sep
**Winters** California & Gulf S to Guatemala, Oct to Mar
**Journey length** 300–3,400 miles

UPLAND SANDPIPER
*Bartramia longicauda*
**Wn** 25–26 in **Wt** 4–6 oz
**Breeds** Alaska, W & S Canada, central & N US, May to Sep
**Winters** Brazil, Paraguay, Uruguay & Argentina, Oct to Apr
**Journey length** 5,900–7,500 miles

GREATER YELLOWLEGS
*Tringa melanoleuca*
**Wn** 27–29 in **Wt** 4–8 oz
**Breeds** S Alaska & Canada from British Columbia to Newfoundland, Apr to Aug
**Winters** S coasts of US S to S S America, Oct to Mar
**Journey length** 1,500–8,000 miles

LESSER YELLOWLEGS *Tringa flavipes*
**Wn** 23–25 in **Wt** 2–4 oz
**Breeds** E Alaska & Canada E to Hudson Bay, May to Aug
**Winters** S US, W Indies & S America, Oct to Apr
**Journey length** 1,500–9,300 miles

SOLITARY SANDPIPER *Tringa solitaria*
**Wn** 21–23 in **Wt** 1–2 oz
**Breeds** Alaska & S Canada, May to Aug
**Winters** S US & W Indies S to Peru, N Argentina & Uruguay, Sep to Apr
**Journey length** 2,175–6,800 miles

SPOTTED SANDPIPER *Actitis macularia*
**Wn** 14–15 in **Wt** 1–2 oz
**Breeds** Canada & US S to California & S Carolina, May to Sep
**Winters** Extreme S US, W Indies, C & S America S to Peru, Bolivia & Brazil, Oct to Mar
**Journey length** 600–6,800 miles

WILSON'S PHALAROPE *Phalaropus tricolor*
**Wn** 15–16 in **Wt** 1–3 oz
**Breeds** W Canada, W & central US, May to Aug
**Winters** S America from Bolivia & Peru to Chile & Argentina, Sep to Apr
**Journey length** 4,475–8,000 miles

SHORT-BILLED DOWITCHER
*Limnodromus griseus*
**Wn** 17–20 in **Wt** 3–5 oz
**Breeds** S Alaska, N-central & E Canada, May to Aug
**Winters** S US, C America, W Indies & S America S to Peru & Brazil, Sep to Mar
**Journey length** 1,500–5,300 miles

SURFBIRD *Aphriza virgata*
**Wn** 19–21 in **Wt** 3–5 oz
**Breeds** Alaska & NW Canada, May to Aug
**Winters** W coast of N & S America; Galápagos, Sep to Apr
**Journey length** 300–8,700 miles

BONAPARTE'S GULL *Larus philadelphia*
**Wn** 35–39 in **Wt** 6–7 oz
**Breeds** Alaska & W Canada, May to Oct
**Winters** Coastal US S to Mexico & W Indies, Oct to Mar
**Journey length** 300–3,400 miles

RING-BILLED GULL *Larus delawarensis*
**Wn** 47–61 in **Wt** 1 lb 2 oz–1 lb 10 oz
**Breeds** Central & E Canada, central N US, Mar to Aug
**Winters** N US S to Mexico, Sep to Mar
**Journey length** 60–2,500 miles

MEW GULL *Larus canus*
**Wn** 43–51 in **Wt** 11 oz–1 lb 3 oz
**Breeds** NW N America & N Eurasia; resident in W Europe, May to Sep
**Winters** Pacific coasts of N America, W Europe, N & Baltic seas & E Asia, Oct to Apr
**Journey length** 300–4,350 miles

HERRING GULL *Larus argentatus*
**Wn** 54–61 in **Wt** 1 lb 9 oz–3 lb 1 oz
**Breeds** Alaska, Canada & NE US; also Eurasia, Mar to Oct
**Winters** NE & NW US S to Mexico, Oct to Mar
**Journey length** 60–2,500 miles

FORSTER'S TERN *Sterna forsteri*
**Wn** 28–32 in **Wt** 3–5 oz
**Breeds** S-central Canada, N US, May to Sep **Winters** S US S to Guatemala, Sep to Apr
**Journey length** 125–2,800 miles

LEAST TERN *Sterna antillarum*
**Wn** 18–21 in **Wt** 1–2 oz
**Breeds** S US S to C America & W Indies, May to Sep
**Winters** Coasts of N, C & N S America & W Indies, Sep to Apr
**Journey length** 60–1,850 miles

BLACK-BILLED CUCKOO
*Coccyzus erythropthalmus*
**Wn** 14–16 in **Wt** 1–2 oz
**Breeds** S Canada & US, except extreme W & S, May to Oct
**Winters** NW S America to Peru, Sep to Apr
**Journey length** 2,175–4,700 miles

YELLOW-BILLED CUCKOO
*Coccyzus americanus*
**Wn** 15–18 in **Wt** 1–3 oz
**Breeds** SE Canada & US, except NW, S to central Mexico & W Indies, May to Sep
**Winters** S America from Venezuela & Colombia to Argentina, Sep to Apr
**Journey length** 1,250–5,000 miles

LONG-EARED OWL *Asio otus*
**Wn** 35–39 in **Wt** 7–15 oz
**Breeds** S Canada & US except extreme S, Mar to Aug
**Winters** US S to N Mexico, Sep to Feb
**Journey length** 0–3,000 miles

FLAMMULATED OWL *Otus flammeolus*
**Wn** 13–15 in **Wt** 2–3 oz
**Breeds** W US S to Mexico, Apr to Sep
**Winters** Mexico to Guatemala, Sep to Mar
**Journey length** 300–3,000 miles

BURROWING OWL *Athene cunicularia*
**Wn** 20–24 in **Wt** 5–8 oz
**Breeds** S-central Canada, W & central US, Mexico, C & S America, Apr to Oct
**Winters** SW US, Mexico, C & S America, Oct to Apr
**Journey length** 0–1,250 miles

CHUCK WILL'S WIDOW
*Caprimulgus carolinensis*
**Wn** 26–27 in **Wt** 2–2¼ oz
**Breeds** S-central & E US, Apr to Sep
**Winters** Extreme SE US, W Indies, N S America, Sep to Mar
**Journey length** 300–2,500 miles

VAUX'S SWIFT *Chaetura vauxi*
**Wn** 13–15 in **Wt** ½–1 oz
**Breeds** S Alaska, SW Canada & W US, May to Sep
**Winters** Venezuela & Colombia, Oct to Apr
**Journey length** 600–4,350 miles

BROAD-TAILED HUMMINGBIRD
*Selasphorus platycercus*
**Wn** 5–6 in **Wt** 1/14 oz
**Breeds** W & SW US, N Mexico, Apr to Aug
**Winters** Mexico to Guatemala, Sep to Mar
**Journey length** 125–2,800 miles

RUFOUS HUMMINGBIRD
*Selasphorus rufus*
**Wn** 5–6 in **Wt** 1/15 oz
**Breeds** Alaska, SW Canada & NW US, Apr to Aug
**Winters** Mexico, Sep to Mar
**Journey length** 300–3,750 miles

BELTED KINGFISHER *Megaceryle alcyon*
**Wn** 18–20 in **Wt** 4–7 oz
**Breeds** Alaska, central & S Canada & US, Apr to Sep
**Winters** S US, Mexico & C America S to Panama, Sep to Apr
**Journey length** 0–4,700 miles

EASTERN KINGBIRD *Tyrannus tyrannus*
**Wn** 11–12 in **Wt** 1½ oz
**Breeds** S Canada & US except SW, Apr to Sep
**Winters** S America S to N Argentina, Oct to Mar
**Journey length** 1,850–6,800 miles

GRAY KINGBIRD *Tyrannus dominicensis*
**Wn** 11–12 in **Wt** 1⅔–1¾ oz
**Breeds** S Florida & W Indies, Mar to Sep
**Winters** W Indies to N S America, Oct to Feb
**Journey length** 125–1,500 miles

WESTERN KINGBIRD *Tyrannus verticalis*
**Wn** 11–12 in **Wt** 1⅔–1¾ oz
**Breeds** SW Canada, W US & N Mexico, Apr to Sep

**Winters** Central Mexico S to Nicaragua, Oct to Mar
**Journey length** 1,100–3,400 miles

**Great Crested Flycatcher**
*Myiarchus crinitus*
**Wn** 10–11 in **Wt** 1½ oz
**Breeds** S & E Canada, E & central US, Apr to Oct
**Winters** Extreme S Florida S to Mexico & N S America, Oct to Mar
**Journey length** 155–3,400 miles

**Olive-sided Flycatcher**
*Contopus borealis*
**Wn** 9–11 in **Wt** 1–1½ oz
**Breeds** S Alaska, W & S Canada, N & W US, Apr to Sep
**Winters** C & S America S to Peru, Sep to Mar
**Journey length** 1,850–5,600 miles

**Eastern Wood-Pewee** *Contopus virens*
**Wn** 9–10 in **Wt** 1½ oz
**Breeds** S & E Canada & E US, Apr to Sep
**Winters** Costa Rica, Colombia & Venezuela S to Peru & W Brazil, Oct to Mar
**Journey length** 1,250–4,475 miles

**Western Wood-Pewee**
*Contopus sordidulus*
**Wn** 9–10 in **Wt** 1–1½ oz
**Breeds** S Alaska, W Canada, W US & N Mexico, Apr to Sep
**Winters** Panama & Venezuela S to Bolivia, Oct to Mar
**Journey length** 1,100–4,700 miles

**Eastern Phoebe** *Sayornis phoebe*
**Wn** 9–11 in **Wt** 1 oz
**Breeds** Central & S Canada, central & E US, Apr to Oct
**Winters** S & SE US S to S Mexico, Oct to Apr
**Journey length** 0–3,400 miles

**Gray Flycatcher** *Empidonax wrightii*
**Wn** 9–10 in **Wt** ½ oz
**Breeds** W US, Apr to Sep
**Winters** SW US & Mexico, Oct to Mar
**Journey length** 185–1,850 miles

**Dusky Flycatcher**
*Empidonax oberholseri*
**Wn** 8–9 in **Wt** ½ oz
**Breeds** W Canada & W US, Apr to Sep
**Winters** SW US & Mexico, Oct to Mar
**Journey length** 185–2,175 miles

**Hammond's Flycatcher**
*Empidonax hammondii*
**Wn** 8–9 in **Wt** ½ oz
**Breeds** S Alaska, W Canada & W US, May to Sep
**Winters** SW US & Mexico S to Nicaragua, Oct to Apr
**Journey length** 300–4,000 miles

**Least Flycatcher** *Empidonax minimus*
**Wn** 7–8 in **Wt** ½ oz
**Breeds** S Canada & N US, May to Sep
**Winters** Mexico to Panama, Oct to Apr
**Journey length** 1,250–4,475 miles

**Acadian Flycatcher**
*Empidonax virescens*
**Wn** 8–9 in **Wt** ½ oz
**Breeds** S Ontario & E US, May to Sep
**Winters** Costa Rica to Ecuador & Venezuela, Oct to Apr
**Journey length** 1,100–3,400 miles

**Willow Flycatcher** *Empidonax traillii*
**Wn** 8–9 in **Wt** ½ oz
**Breeds** SW Canada, N & central US, May to Sep
**Winters** S America S to Argentina, Oct to Apr
**Journey length** 2,175–6,000 miles

**Alder Flycatcher**
*Empidonax alnorum*
**Wn** 8–9 in **Wt** ½ oz
**Breeds** Alaska, W & S Canada, NE US, May to Sep **Winters** C America S to Panama, Oct to Apr
**Journey length** 2,800–4,700 miles

**Yellow-bellied Flycatcher**
*Empidonax flaviventris*
**Wn** 7–9 in **Wt** ½ oz
**Breeds** S Canada, NE US, May to Sep
**Winters** E Mexico S to E Panama, Oct to Apr
**Journey length** 2,800–4,700 miles

**Western Flycatcher**
*Empidonax difficilis*
**Wn** 7–9 in **Wt** ½ oz
**Breeds** British Columbia & W US, Apr to Oct
**Winters** N Mexico to Honduras, Oct to Apr
**Journey length** 300–4,350 miles

**Violet-green Swallow**
*Tachycineta thalassina*
**Wn** 10–11 in **Wt** ½ oz
**Breeds** Alaska, W Canada, W US & Mexico, Apr to Oct
**Winters** Mexico & C America S to Panama, Oct to Mar
**Journey length** 600–5,600 miles

**Purple Martin** *Progne subis*
**Wn** 13–15 in **Wt** ¾–1 oz
**Breeds** S Canada, US & Mexico, Apr to Oct
**Winters** W Indies, S America S to Brazil, Nov to Mar
**Journey length** 600–5,900 miles

**Cliff Swallow** *Hirundo pyrrhonota*
**Wn** 12–13 in **Wt** ¾–1 oz
**Breeds** Alaska, Canada, US & N Mexico, Apr to Oct
**Winters** S America S to Argentina, Nov to Mar
**Journey length** 1,250–6,800 miles

**House Wren** *Troglodytes aedon*
**Wn** 5–7 in **Wt** ¼–½ oz
**Breeds** S Canada, US & N Mexico, Mar to Oct
**Winters** S US & Mexico, Oct to Mar
**Journey length** 60–1,500 miles

**Winter Wren** *Troglodytes troglodytes*
**Wn** 5–6 in **Wt** ⅓–⅔ oz
**Breeds** S Alaska, S Canada & N US; also Eurasia, Mar to Sep
**Winters** S US, Oct to Feb
**Journey length** 125–1,850 miles

**Marsh Wren** *Cistothorus palustris*
**Wn** 5–8 in **Wt** ½ oz
**Breeds** S Canada & N US, Apr to Oct
**Winters** S US & Mexico, Oct to Mar
**Journey length** 185–2,500 miles

**Sedge Wren** *Cistothorus platensis*
**Wn** 5–7 in **Wt** ¼–½ oz
**Breeds** S & SE Canada, NE US, Apr to Oct
**Winters** SE US & Mexico, Oct to Mar
**Journey length** 600–2,500 miles

**Ruby-crowned Kinglet**
*Regulus calendula*
**Wn** 5–6 in **Wt** ¼ oz
**Breeds** Alaska, S Canada & W US, Apr to Oct
**Winters** S & E US, Mexico & Guatemala, Oct to Mar
**Journey length** 185–5,900 miles

**Blue-gray Gnatcatcher**
*Polioptila caerulea*
**Wn** 5–7 in **Wt** ¼ oz
**Breeds** S US, Mexico & Cuba, Mar to Oct
**Winters** S Mexico S to Honduras, Nov to Feb
**Journey length** 60–1,250 miles

**Eastern Bluebird** *Sialia sialis*
**Wn** 9–12 in **Wt** 1–1¼ oz
**Breeds** SE Canada, E US & C America S to Nicaragua, Mar to Oct
**Winters** SE US S to Nicaragua, Oct to Mar
**Journey length** 0–2,500 miles

**Western Bluebird** *Sialia mexicana*
**Wn** 9–12 in **Wt** 1–1¼ oz
**Breeds** SW Canada, W US & Mexico, Mar to Oct
**Winters** SW US & Mexico, Oct to Mar
**Journey length** 0–2,800 miles

**Mountain Bluebird**
*Sialia currucoides*
**Wn** 10–12 in **Wt** 1–1¼ oz
**Breeds** SW Canada, W US, Apr to Oct
**Winters** SW US, N Mexico, Oct to Mar
**Journey length** 0–3,000 miles

**Wood Thrush** *Hylocichla mustelina*
**Wn** 11–13 in **Wt** 1½–2½ oz
**Breeds** SE Canada & E US, Mar to Sep
**Winters** Mexico to Panama, Oct to Mar
**Journey length** 600–3,750 miles

**Veery** *Catharus fuscescens*
**Wn** 11–12 in **Wt** ¾–1½ oz
**Breeds** S Canada & N US, May to Sep
**Winters** N S America, Oct to Apr
**Journey length** 2,500–5,000 miles

**Swainson's Thrush** *Catharus ustulatus*
**Wn** 10–11 in **Wt** ¾–1½ oz
**Breeds** Alaska, W & S Canada, W US, May to Oct
**Winters** Mexico to Argentina, Oct to Apr
**Journey length** 1,500–6,800 miles

**Hermit Thrush** *Catharus guttatus*
**Wn** 9–11 in **Wt** 1 oz
**Breeds** S Alaska, S Canada, NE & W US, Apr to Oct
**Winters** S US & C America S to El Salvador, Oct to Mar
**Journey length** 125–5,000 miles

**Northern Shrike** *Lanius excubitor*
**Wn** 11–13 in **Wt** 1¾–3 oz
**Breeds** Alaska & N Canada; also Eurasia, May to Sep
**Winters** S Canada & N US, Oct to Apr
**Journey length** 300–3,400 miles

**Gray Catbird** *Dumetella carolinensis*
**Wn** 9–10 in **Wt** 1–2 oz
**Breeds** S Canada, US except SW, Apr to Sep
**Winters** SE US, W Indies & C America S to Panama, Oct to Mar
**Journey length** 185–4,000 miles

**Sage Thrasher** *Oreoscoptes montanus*
**Wn** 9–10 in **Wt** 1½–2½ oz
**Breeds** W US, Apr to Oct
**Winters** SW US, N Mexico, Oct to Mar
**Journey length** 85–2,500 miles

**Brown Thrasher** *Toxostoma rufum*
**Wn** 11–12 in **Wt** 1¾–2¾ oz
**Breeds** S Canada, central & E US, Apr to Oct
**Winters** E & S US, Oct to Mar
**Journey length** 0–1,500 miles

**Sprague's Pipit** *Anthus spragueii*
**Wn** 11–12 in **Wt** ¾ oz
**Breeds** Prairies of S Canada & N US, Apr to Sep
**Winters** Central-S US & Mexico, Oct to Apr
**Journey length** 1,250–3,000 miles

**Cedar Waxwing** *Bombycilla cedrorum*
**Wn** 10–12 in **Wt** 1¼–2 oz
**Breeds** S Canada & N US, Apr to Oct
**Winters** S US, Mexico & C America S to Panama, Nov to Mar
**Journey length** 0–3,400 miles

**Black-capped Vireo** *Vireo atricapillus*
**Wn** 6–9 in **Wt** ¼–½ oz
**Breeds** Oklahoma, Texas & NE Mexico, Mar to Aug
**Winters** Central Mexico, Sep to Feb
**Journey** 435–1,250 miles

**Yellow-throated Vireo**
*Vireo flavifrons*
**Wn** 7–9 in **Wt** ½–¾ oz
**Breeds** SE Canada & E US, Apr to Oct
**Winters** SE US, Mexico, W Indies, C America & N S America, Nov to Mar
**Journey length** 300–4,000 miles

**Bell's Vireo** *Vireo bellii*
**Wn** 7–9 in **Wt** ½ oz
**Breeds** Central & W US, N Mexico, Mar to Sep
**Winters** Mexico & C America S to Nicaragua, Oct to Feb
**Journey length** 185–2,500 miles

**Gray Vireo** *Vireo vicinior*
**Wn** 7–9 in **Wt** ½–¾ oz
**Breeds** SW US & N Mexico, Mar to Sep
**Winters** W Mexico, Oct to Feb
**Journey length** 155–1,400 miles

**Solitary Vireo** *Vireo solitarius*
**Wn** 7–9 in **Wt** ½–¾ oz
**Breeds** S Canada, NE & W US, Mexico, Guatemala & El Salvador, Apr to Oct
**Winters** Extreme S US, Mexico, C America & W Indies, Oct to Mar
**Journey length** 600–4,700 miles

**Black-whiskered Vireo** *Vireo altiloquus*
**Wn** 8–10 in **Wt** ¾–1 oz
**Breeds** Coastal Florida & W Indies, May to Sep
**Winters** S America S to Brazil & Peru, Oct to Apr
**Journey length** 1,250–2,800 miles

**Warbling Vireo** *Vireo gilvus*
**Wn** 7–9 in **Wt** ½–¾ oz
**Breeds** SW Canada, US & N Mexico, Apr to Oct
**Winters** N Mexico, C America & S America S to Bolivia, Nov to Mar
**Journey length** 300–5,600 miles

**Philadelphia Vireo** *Vireo philadelphicus*
**Wn** 7–9 in **Wt** ½–¾ oz
**Breeds** S Canada, May to Sep
**Winters** Guatemala S to Panama & NW Colombia, Oct to Apr
**Journey length** 2,175–4,700 miles

**Prothonotary Warbler**
*Protonotaria citrea*
**Wn** 7–9 in **Wt** ½–¾ oz
**Breeds** E US, Apr to Sep
**Winters** W Indies & N S America, Oct to Mar
**Journey length** 900–3,000 miles

**Blue-winged Warbler**
*Vermivora pinus*
**Wn** 7–9 in **Wt** ¼–½ oz
**Breeds** E & NE US, Apr to Sep
**Winters** Mexico to Panama, Oct to Mar
**Journey length** 1,100–2,500 miles

**Golden-winged Warbler**
*Vermivora chrysoptera*
**Wn** 7–9 in **Wt** ¼–½ oz
**Breeds** SE Canada & NW US, Apr to Sep
**Winters** Guatemala to Colombia & Venezuela, Oct to Mar
**Journey length** 1,500–3,400 miles

**Tennessee Warbler**
*Vermivora peregrina*
**Wn** 7–9 in **Wt** ¼–½ oz
**Breeds** S Canada & N US, May to Sep
**Winters** Central Mexico to Venezuela & W Indies, Oct to Apr
**Journey length** 1,850–3,000 miles

**Orange-crowned Warbler**
*Vermivora celata*
**Wn** 7–9 in **Wt** ½–¾ oz
**Breeds** Alaska, S Canada & W US, Apr to Sep
**Winters** Extreme S US, Mexico & Guatemala, Oct to Mar
**Journey length** 600–5,300 miles

**Nashville Warbler**
*Vermivora ruficapilla*
**Wn** 7–9 in **Wt** ¼–½ oz
**Breeds** SE Canada, NE & NW US, Apr to Sep
**Winters** Mexico & Guatemala, Oct to Mar
**Journey length** 300–3,000 miles

**Virginia's Warbler** *Vermivora virgineae*
**Wn** 6–8 in **Wt** ¼–½ oz
**Breeds** Mountains of W US, May to Sep
**Winters** Mexico, Oct to Apr
**Journey length** 1,250–2,175 miles

**Northern Parula** *Parula americana*
**Wn** 6–8 in **Wt** ¼–½ oz
**Breeds** SE Canada & E US, Apr to Sep
**Winters** Florida, W Indies & Mexico S to Nicaragua, Oct to Mar
**Journey length** 300–3,000 miles

**Black-and-white Warbler**
*Mniotilta varia*
**Wn** 6–8 in **Wt** ½ oz
**Breeds** S Canada & E US, Apr to Sep
**Winters** SE US, Mexico, C America, W Indies & N S America, Oct to Mar
**Journey length** 300–4,700 miles

**Black-throated Blue Warbler**
*Dendroica caerulescens*
**Wn** 6–8 in **Wt** ½ oz
**Breeds** SE Canada & NE US, May to Sep
**Winters** W Indies, C America & N S America, Oct to Apr
**Journey length** 1,500–4,000 miles

**Cerulean Warbler** *Dendroica cerulea*
**Wn** 6–7 in **Wt** ¼–½ oz
**Breeds** SE Canada & E US, Apr to Sep
**Winters** S America from Colombia & Venezuela to Bolivia, Oct to Mar
**Journey length** 2,175–4,350 miles

**Blackburnian Warbler**
*Dendroica fusca*
**Wn** 6–7 in **Wt** ½ oz
**Breeds** S & E Canada & NE US, May to Sep
**Winters** Costa Rica, Panama & S America S to Peru, Oct to Apr
**Journey length** 1,500–4,700 miles

**Chestnut-sided Warbler**
*Dendroica pensylvanica*
**Wn** 6–8 in **Wt** ¼–½ oz
**Breeds** SE Canada & NE US, May to Sep
**Winters** Guatemala to Colombia, Oct to Apr
**Journey length** 1,850–4,000 miles

**Cape May Warbler** *Dendroica tigrina*
**Wn** 6–8 in **Wt** ¼–½ oz
**Breeds** S Canada & NE US, May to Sep
**Winters** W Indies, Oct to Apr
**Journey length** 1,500–2,500 miles

**Magnolia Warbler**
*Dendroica magnolia*
**Wn** 6–8 in **Wt** ¼–½ oz
**Breeds** S Canada & NE US, May to Sep
**Winters** W Indies, C America & N S America, Oct to Apr
**Journey length** 1,500–4,000 miles

**Yellow-rumped Warbler**
*Dendroica coronata*
**Wn** 7–9 in **Wt** ½ oz
**Breeds** Alaska, Canada & W US, Apr to Sep
**Winters** S US, Mexico, C America, W Indies & N S America, Oct to Mar
**Journey length** 300–6,000 miles

**Black-throated Gray Warbler**
*Dendroica nigrescens*
**Wn** 6–8 in **Wt** ½ oz
**Breeds** W Canada, W US & NW Mexico, Apr to Sep
**Winters** Mexico & Guatemala, Oct to Mar
**Journey length** 155–3,750 miles

**Townsend's Warbler**
*Dendroica townsendi*
**Wn** 6–8 in **Wt** ¼–½ oz
**Breeds** S Alaska, W Canada & NW US, Apr to Sep
**Winters** W California, Mexico & C America S to Nicaragua, Oct to Mar
**Journey length** 125–4,000 miles

**Hermit Warbler**
*Dendroica occidentalis*
**Wn** 7–9 in **Wt** ½ oz
**Breeds** N California & Oregon, May to Sep
**Winters** SW California, Mexico & C America S to Nicaragua, Oct to Apr
**Journey length** 185–3,400 miles

**Black-throated Green Warbler**
*Dendroica virens*
**Wn** 6–8 in **Wt** ¼–½ oz

**Breeds** E & S Canada & NE US, Apr to Sep
**Winters** Mexico & W Indies, Oct to Mar
**Journey length** 1,100–2,800 miles

**GOLDEN-CHEEKED WARBLER**
*Dendroica chrysoparia*
**Wn** 7–9 in **Wt** ½ oz
**Breeds** Texas, Apr to Sep
**Winters** Mexico S to Nicaragua, Oct to Mar
**Journey length** 900–1,500 miles

**GRACE'S WARBLER** *Dendroica graciae*
**Wn** 6–8 in **Wt** ¼–½ oz
**Breeds** SW US & N Mexico, Apr to Sep
**Winters** Mexico S to Nicaragua, Oct to Mar
**Journey length** 155–1,250 miles

**PRAIRIE WARBLER** *Dendroica discolor*
**Wn** 6–7 in **Wt** ¼–½ oz
**Breeds** SE Canada & E US, Apr to Oct
**Winters** Florida, W Indies & C America S to Nicaragua, Oct to Mar
**Journey length** 470–2,500 miles

**BAY-BREASTED WARBLER**
*Dendroica castanea*
**Wn** 7–9 in **Wt** ½ oz
**Breeds** S Canada & NE US, May to Sep
**Winters** Panama to Colombia & Venezuela, Oct to Apr
**Journey length** 2,175–3,400 miles

**PINE WARBLER** *Dendroica pinus*
**Wn** 7–9 in **Wt** ½ oz
**Breeds** SE Canada & E US, Apr to Oct
**Winters** SE US, Mexico & W Indies, Oct to Mar
**Journey length** 0–2,500 miles

**PALM WARBLER** *Dendroica palmarum*
**Wn** 7–9 in **Wt** ½ oz
**Breeds** S Canada & NE US, May to Sep
**Winters** SE US, Mexico S to Honduras & W Indies, Oct to Apr
**Journey length** 600–3,000 miles

**MOURNING WARBLER**
*Oporornis philadelphia*
**Wn** 6–8 in **Wt** ½ oz
**Breeds** S Canada & NE US, May to Sep
**Winters** S C America & N S America, Oct to Apr
**Journey length** 1,500–4,350 miles

**MACGILLIVRAY'S WARBLER**
*Oporornis tolmiei*
**Wn** 6–8 in **Wt** ¼–½ oz
**Breeds** W Canada & W US, Apr to Sep
**Winters** Mexico to Panama, Oct to Mar
**Journey length** 1,250–5,000 miles

**CONNECTICUT WARBLER** *Oporornis agilis*
**Wn** 6–9 in **Wt** ½ oz
**Breeds** S Canada & N US, May to Sep
**Winters** C & S America S to Brazil, Oct to Apr
**Journey length** 2,500–5,600 miles

**KENTUCKY WARBLER** *Oporornis formosus*
**Wn** 6–8 in **Wt** ¼–½ oz
**Breeds** E US, Apr to Oct
**Winters** C & N S America, Nov to Mar
**Journey length** 1,250–5,000 miles

**WILSON'S WARBLER** *Wilsonia pusilla*
**Wn** 5–7 in **Wt** ¼–½ oz
**Breeds** Alaska, Canada & W US, May to Sep
**Winters** Mexico to Panama, Oct to Apr
**Journey length** 2,500–5,600 miles/

**HOODED WARBLER** *Wilsonia citrina*
**Wn** 6–8 in **Wt** ½ oz
**Breeds** SE Canada & E US, Apr to Sep
**Winters** Mexico to Panama, Oct to Mar
**Journey length** 2,500–4,350 miles

**OVENBIRD** *Seiurus aurocapillus*
**Wn** 9–10 in **Wt** ½–¾ oz
**Breeds** S Canada, central & E US, Apr to Oct
**Winters** Florida, Mexico to N S America & W Indies, Nov to Mar
**Journey length** 600–4,350 miles

**NORTHERN WATERTHRUSH**
*Seiurus noveboracensis*
**Wn** 9–10 in **Wt** ½–¾ oz
**Breeds** Alaska, Canada & N US, May to Oct
**Winters** Florida, Mexico & W Indies S to Peru, Nov to Apr
**Journey length** 1,850–6,000 miles

**AMERICAN REDSTART** *Setophaga ruticilla*
**Wn** 6–8 in **Wt** ½ oz
**Breeds** S Canada, central & N US, Apr to Sep
**Winters** S Mexico S to Ecuador & W Indies, Oct to Mar
**Journey length** 1,500–4,700 miles

**ROSE-BREASTED GROSBEAK**
*Pheucticus ludovicianus*
**Wn** 9–12 in **Wt** 1¼–2 oz
**Breeds** S Canada & NE US, May to Oct
**Winters** C America & N S America, Nov to Apr
**Journey length** 2,500–5,000 miles

**INDIGO BUNTING** *Passerina cyanea*
**Wn** 6–9 in **Wt** ½–¾ oz
**Breeds** Central & E US, Apr to Sep
**Winters** Mexico to Panama & W Indies, Oct to Mar
**Journey length** 470–3,750 miles

**LAZULI BUNTING** *Passerina amoena*
**Wn** 6–9 in **Wt** ½–¾ oz
**Breeds** SW Canada & W US, Apr to Oct
**Winters** Mexico, Nov to Mar
**Journey length** 600–3,400 miles

**PAINTED BUNTING** *Passerina ciris*
**Wn** 6–9 in **Wt** ½–¾ oz
**Breeds** S & SE US & N Mexico, Mar to Sep
**Winters** Mexico to Panama & Cuba, Oct to Feb
**Journey length** 300–3,000 miles

**GREEN-TAILED TOWHEE**
*Pipilo chlorurus*
**Wn** 10–12 in **Wt** 1–1¼ oz
**Breeds** W US, Apr to Sep
**Winters** SW US & Mexico, Oct to Mar
**Journey length** 300–3,000 miles

**BAIRD'S SPARROW** *Ammodramus bairdii*
**Wn** 6–9 in **Wt** ½–¾ oz
**Breeds** Prairies of S Canada & N US, May to Sep
**Winters** N Mexico, Oct to Apr
**Journey length** 1,500–2,500 miles

**AMERICAN TREE SPARROW**
*Spizella arborea*
**Wn** 8–9 in **Wt** ¾–1 oz
**Breeds** Alaska & N Canada, May to Sep
**Winters** US, Oct to Apr
**Journey length** 1,500–3,750 miles

**MCCOWN'S LONGSPUR**
*Calcarius mccownii*
**Wn** 6–9 in **Wt** ½–¾ oz
**Breeds** Prairies of S Canada & N US, Apr to Oct
**Winters** Texas, Arizona & N Mexico, Nov to Mar
**Journey length** 600–2,800 miles

**DICKCISSEL** *Spiza americana*
**Wn** 8–9 in **Wt** ½–¾ oz
**Breeds** S Canada, central & E US, Apr to Sep
**Winters** S Mexico S to N S America, Oct to Mar
**Journey length** 900–4,700 miles

**RUSTY BLACKBIRD**
*Euphagus carolinus*
**Wn** 12–14 in **Wt** 2–3 oz
**Breeds** Alaska, Canada & NE US, May to Oct
**Winters** E & SE US, Nov to Apr
**Journey length** 300–4,000 miles

**SUMMER TANAGER**
*Piranga rubra*
**Wn** 11–13 in **Wt** 2–2½ oz
**Breeds** S US & N Mexico, Mar to Sep
**Winters** S Mexico, W Indies & S to Brazil, Oct to Feb
**Journey length** 600–4,350 miles

**EVENING GROSBEAK**
*Coccothraustes vespertinus*
**Wn** 11–14 in **Wt** 1¾–3 oz
**Breeds** S Canada, N & W US, Mar to Oct
**Winters** Breeding range plus S & E US, Nov to Feb
**Journey length** 0–1,250 miles

## EURASIAN MIGRANTS

**RED-NECKED GREBE** *Podiceps grisegena*
**Wn** 30–33 in **Wt** 14 oz–2 lb 2 oz
**Breeds** N Europe, Asia & N America, Apr to Sep
**Winters** Coasts of N America, E Asia & NW Europe, Oct to Mar
**Journey length** 155–2,500 miles

**HOODED GREBE** *Podiceps auritus*
**Wn** 23–25 in **Wt** 11 oz–1 lb 1 oz
**Breeds** N Europe, Asia & N America, Apr to Sep
**Winters** Coasts of N America, E Asia & NW Europe, Oct to Mar
**Journey length** 155–3,000 miles

**WHITE PELICAN** *Pelecanus onocrotalus*
**Wn** 106–141 in **Wt** 20 lb–24 lb 4 oz
**Breeds** Scattered waters from Greece to Mongolia; resident in Africa & India, Apr to Sep
**Winters** Red Sea S to E Africa, Oct to Mar
**Journey length** 900–4,000 miles

**LITTLE BITTERN** *Ixobrychus minutus*
**Wn** 20–22 in **Wt** 4–6 oz
**Breeds** Central & S Europe, SW Asia; resident in Africa, India & Australia, Apr to Sep
**Winters** E Africa S to S Africa, Oct to Mar
**Journey length** 1,500–6,800 miles

**SQUACCO HERON** *Ardeola ralloides*
**Wn** 31–36 in **Wt** 7–13 oz
**Breeds** S Europe & SW Asia; resident in Africa, Apr to Sep
**Winters** W, E & S Africa, Nov to Mar
**Journey length** 2,500–5,300 miles

**LITTLE EGRET** *Egretta garzetta*
**Wn** 34–37 in **Wt** 14 oz–1 lb 6 oz
**Breeds** S Europe, N Africa, SW Asia; resident in S Africa, India, SE Asia & Australasia, Mar to Sep
**Winters** N, W & E Africa, Oct to Mar
**Journey length** 300–4,000 miles

**PURPLE HERON** *Ardea purpurea*
**Wn** 47–59 in **Wt** 1 lb 3 oz–2 lb 11 oz
**Breeds** S Europe, SW Asia & China; resident in E Africa, India, SE Asia, Apr to Sep
**Winters** W & E Africa, SE Asia, Oct to Mar
**Journey length** 1,850–4,350 miles

**GLOSSY IBIS** *Plegadis falcinellus*
**Wn** 31–37 in **Wt** 1 lb 3 oz–1 lb 11 oz
**Breeds** SE & SW Europe; resident in E & S Africa, India & Australia, Apr to Sep
**Winters** W & E Africa, Oct to Mar
**Journey length** 2,175–2,800 miles

**HERMIT IBIS** *Geronticus eremita*
**Wn** 49–53 in **Wt** 2 lb 9 oz–3 lb 3 oz
**Breeds** Morocco & Turkey, Feb to Aug
**Winters** Morocco, Mauritania & NE Africa, Sep to Jan
**Journey length** 300–1,850 miles

**SPOONBILL** *Platalea leucorodia*
**Wn** 45–51 in **Wt** 2 lb 14 oz–3 lb 12 oz
**Breeds** W & S Europe, central & S Asia; resident in India, Apr to Sep
**Winters** N & NE Africa, SE China, Oct to Mar
**Journey length** 155–2,175 miles

**BEAN GOOSE** *Anser fabalis*
**Wn** 55–68 in **Wt** 4 lb 7 oz–8 lb 15 oz
**Breeds** N Europe & Asia, May to Sep
**Winters** W Europe, Japan & China, Oct to Apr
**Journey length** 600–2,800 miles

**EURASIAN WIGEON** *Anas penelope*
**Wn** 29–33 in **Wt** 14 oz–2 lb 6 oz
**Breeds** N Europe & Asia, May to Sep
**Winters** W Europe, NE Africa, India, Japan & SE Asia, Oct to Apr
**Journey length** 300–4,700 miles

**NORTHERN PINTAIL** *Anas acuta*
**Wn** 31–37 in **Wt** 1 lb 3 oz–2 lb 14 oz
**Breeds** N Europe, Asia & N N America, May to Sep
**Winters** Europe, S Asia, W & E Africa, N & C America, Oct to Apr
**Journey length** 300–5,600 miles

**GARGANEY** *Anas querquedula*
**Wn** 23–24 in **Wt** 9 oz–1 lb 5 oz
**Breeds** W & central Europe & Asia, May to Sep
**Winters** W & E Africa, India & SE Asia, Oct to Mar
**Journey length** 2,175–4,350 miles

**NORTHERN SHOVELER** *Anas clypeata*
**Wn** 27–33 in **Wt** 12 oz–2 lb 3 oz
**Breeds** W & N Europe, N Asia, Apr to Sep
**Winters** Europe, E Africa, India, SE Asia & Japan, Oct to Mar
**Journey length** 60–4,700 miles

**RED-CRESTED POCHARD** *Netta rufina*
**Wn** 33–34 in **Wt** 1 lb 13 oz–3 lb 2 oz
**Breeds** S Europe, SW & central Asia, Apr to Sep
**Winters** Mediterranean countries, Indian subcontinent, Oct to Mar
**Journey length** 60–2,175 miles

**FERRUGINOUS DUCK** *Aythya nyroca*
**Wn** 24–26 in **Wt** 1 lb–1 lb 10 oz
**Breeds** Central & S Europe, SW Asia, Mar to Sep
**Winters** Mediterranean countries, NE Africa, N Pakistan & India, Oct to Mar
**Journey length** 60–2,800 miles

**TUFTED DUCK** *Aythya fuligula*
**Wn** 26–28 in **Wt** 14 oz–2 lb 4 oz
**Breeds** N Europe & Asia, Apr to Sep
**Winters** W & S Europe, S Asia & Japan, Oct to Mar
**Journey length** 60–4,000 miles

**HARLEQUIN DUCK**
*Histrionicus histrionicus*
**Wn** 24–27 in **Wt** 1 lb 2 oz–1 lb 10 oz
**Breeds** NW & NE N America, Iceland, Greenland & NE Asia, May to Sep
**Winters** Coastal areas of breeding range, Oct to Apr
**Journey length** 30–1,250 miles

**COMMON GOLDENEYE**
*Bucephala clangula*
**Wn** 25–31 in **Wt** 1 lb 2 oz–2 lb 12 oz
**Breeds** N Europe, Asia & N America, May to Sep
**Winters** W & S Europe, SE Asia & US, Oct to Apr
**Journey length** 300–1,850 miles

**COMMON MERGANSER** *Mergus merganser*
**Wn** 32–38 in **Wt** 2 lb–4 lb 12 oz
**Breeds** N Europe, Asia & N America; resident in S-central Asia, Apr to Sep
**Winters** W Europe, E Asia & US, Oct to Apr
**Journey length** 60–1,850 miles

**BLACK KITE** *Milvus migrans*
**Wn** 62–70 in **Wt** 1 lb 6 oz–2 lb 1 oz
**Breeds** Eurasia except extreme N, resident in Indian subcontinent, SE Asia, Africa & Australasia, Apr to Sep
**Winters** Africa, India, SE Asia, Oct to Mar
**Journey length** 600–2,800 miles

**EGYPTIAN VULTURE**
*Neophron percnopterus*
**Wn** 61–70 in **Wt** 3 lb 8 oz–4 lb 13 oz
**Breeds** S Europe, N Africa & SW Asia; resident in W & E Africa & Indian subcontinent, Apr to Sep
**Winters** W & E Africa, Arabian peninsula & Indian subcontinent, Oct to Mar
**Journey length** 600–1,850 miles

**SHORT-TOED EAGLE** *Circaetus gallicus*
**Wn** 72–76 in **Wt** 2 lb 15 oz–5 lb 2 oz
**Breeds** Central & S Europe, SW Asia; resident in Indian subcontinent, Oct to Mar
**Winters** N tropics of Africa & Indian subcontinent, Mar to Oct
**Journey length** 600–3,750 miles

**PALLID HARRIER** *Circus macrourus*
**Wn** 37–47 in **Wt** 8 oz–1 lb 5 oz
**Breeds** Central-E Europe & central-W Asia, Apr to Oct
**Winters** Tropical Africa S to Cape, Indian subcontinent, Oct to Apr
**Journey length** 2,175–7,000 miles

**MONTAGU'S HARRIER** *Circus pygargus*
**Wn** 41–47 in **Wt** 8 oz–1 lb
**Breeds** S & central Europe & central-W Asia, Apr to Sep
**Winters** Tropical Africa S to Cape, Indian subcontinent, Oct to Mar
**Journey length** 2,175–7,150 miles

**LEVANT SPARROWHAWK** *Accipiter brevipes*
**Wn** 25–29 in **Wt** 5–10 oz
**Breeds** SE & central-E Europe, Apr to Aug
**Winters** NE Africa, Sep to Apr
**Journey length** 900–3,000 miles

**LESSER SPOTTED EAGLE**
*Aquila pomarina*
**Wn** 52–62 in **Wt** 2 lb 6 oz–4 lb 12 oz
**Breeds** E & SE Europe; resident in Indian subcontinent, Apr to Oct
**Winters** E & SE Africa, Oct to Mar
**Journey length** 1,850–6,400 miles

**SPOTTED EAGLE** *Aquila clanga*
**Wn** 61–71 in **Wt** 3 lb–7 lb 1 oz
**Breeds** E Europe & forests of Russia, Mongolia & N China, Apr to Sep
**Winters** SE Europe, Indian subcontinent & SE Asia, Oct to Mar
**Journey length** 600–4,350 miles

**BOOTED EAGLE** *Hieraaetus pennatus*
**Wn** 39–47 in **Wt** 1 lb 2 oz–2 lb 12 oz
**Breeds** S Europe, SW & central Asia, Apr to Oct
**Winters** Tropical Africa S to Cape & Indian subcontinent, Oct to Mar
**Journey length** 2,175–6,800 miles

**NORTHERN HOBBY** *Falco subbuteo*
**Wn** 32–36 in **Wt** 5–12 oz
**Breeds** Eurasia except extreme N & S, Apr to Sep
**Winters** S Africa, Indian subcontinent & SE Asia, Oct to Mar
**Journey length** 600–7,150 miles

**SOOTY FALCON** *Falco concolor*
**Wn** 33–43 in **Wt** 11–16 oz
**Breeds** NE Africa & Arabia, May to Oct
**Winters** Madagascar & Mozambique, Nov to May
**Journey length** 1,500–4,000 miles

**SPOTTED CRAKE** *Porzana porzana*
**Wn** 14–16 in **Wt** 2–5 oz
**Breeds** W Europe except extreme N, S & W Asia, Apr to Aug
**Winters** E & SE Africa & Indian subcontinent, Sep to Mar
**Journey length** 1,850–7,000 miles

**LITTLE CRAKE** *Porzana parva*
**Wn** 13–15 in **Wt** 1–3 oz
**Breeds** S and central Europe, central-W Asia, Apr to Sep **Winters** E Africa & Pakistan, Oct to Mar
**Journey length** 1,250–4,475 miles

**BAILLION'S CRAKE** *Porzana pusilla*
**Wn** 12–14 in **Wt** 1–2 oz
**Breeds** S & central Europe, middle latitudes of Asia; resident in S Africa & Australasia, Apr to Oct
**Winters** E Africa, Indian subcontinent & SE Asia, Oct to Apr
**Journey length** 600–4,700 miles

**MANCHURIAN CRANE** *Grus japonensis*
**Wn** 90–98 in **Wt** 13 lb 4 oz–19 lb 13 oz
**Breeds** E Russia & NE China; resident in Japan, Apr to Oct

**Winters** Korea & N China, Nov to Mar
**Journey length** 600–1,250 miles

**Collared Pratincole**
*Glareola pratincola*
**Wn** 23–25 in **Wt** 2–3 oz
**Breeds** S Europe & SW Asia; resident in Africa, Apr to Sep
**Winters** Sub-Saharan Africa, Oct to Mar
**Journey length** 900–3,750 miles

**Black-winged Pratincole**
*Glareola nordmanni*
**Wn** 23–26 in **Wt** 3–4 oz
**Breeds** Central-E Europe & W Asia, Apr to Sep
**Winters** W & S Africa, Oct to Apr
**Journey length** 1,750–6,000 miles

**Little Ringed Plover**
*Charadrius dubius*
**Wn** 16–18 in **Wt** 1–1¾ oz
**Breeds** Eurasia except extreme N; resident in Indian subcontinent & SE Asia, Mar to Sep
**Winters** Tropical Africa, Indian subcontinent, SE Asia & Australasia, Sep to Mar
**Journey length** 600–5,300 miles

**Mongolian Plover**
*Charadrius mongolus*
**Wn** 17–22 in **Wt** 1½–2½ oz
**Breeds** E Siberia, W China, Himalayas, May to Sep
**Winters** Coasts of E Africa, Arabia, Indian subcontinent & Australasia, Oct to Apr
**Journey length** 1,250–8,000 miles

**Greater Sand Plover**
*Charadrius leschenaultii*
**Wn** 20–23 in **Wt** 3–4 oz
**Breeds** SE Europe & central Asia, Apr to Aug
**Winters** Coasts of E Africa, Arabia, Indian subcontinent & Australasia, Aug to Apr
**Journey length** 900–6,000 miles

**Caspian Plover** *Charadrius asiaticus*
**Wn** 21–24 in **Wt** 2–3 oz
**Breeds** SW Asia, Apr to Sep
**Winters** E & S Africa, Oct to Mar
**Journey length** 1,500–6,700 miles

**Sociable Plover** *Chettusia gregaria*
**Wn** 27–29 in **Wt** 6–9 oz
**Breeds** Central-E Europe & W Asia, Apr to Oct
**Winters** NE Africa, Iraq & Pakistan, Oct to Apr
**Journey length** 1,250–3,400 miles

**Jack Snipe** *Lymnocryptes minimus*
**Wn** 14–16 in **Wt** 1¼–3¼ oz
**Breeds** N Eurasia, Mar to Oct
**Winters** W & S Europe, N & tropical Africa, Middle East & Indian subcontinent to Vietnam, Oct to Mar
**Journey length** 300–5,000 miles

**Great Snipe** *Gallinago media*
**Wn** 18–19 in **Wt** 5–9 oz
**Breeds** N Europe & NW Russia, Apr to Oct
**Winters** Tropical & S Africa, Oct to Mar
**Journey length** 2,175–8,200 miles

**Pintail Snipe** *Gallinago stenura*
**Wn** 17–18 in **Wt** 3–5 oz
**Breeds** N & central Asia, May to Sep
**Winters** Indian subcontinent, SE Asia & Indonesia, Sep to Apr
**Journey length** 1,500–6,000 miles

**Black-tailed Godwit** *Limosa limosa*
**Wn** 27–32 in **Wt** 6 oz–1 lb 2 oz
**Breeds** Temperate Europe, W & E Asia, Mar to Aug
**Winters** Mediterranean, tropical Africa, Indian subcontinent, SE Asia & Australasia, Sep to Mar
**Journey length** 900–7,800 miles

**Whimbrel** *Numenius phaeopus*
**Wn** 29–35 in **Wt** 10 oz–1 lb 5 oz
**Breeds** N Eurasia, Alaska & central-N Canada, Apr to Oct
**Winters** Coasts of Africa, Arabia, Australasia, N, C & S America, Oct to Apr
**Journey length** 1,500–9,300 miles

**Spotted Redshank** *Tringa erythropus*
**Wn** 24–26 in **Wt** 4–7 oz
**Breeds** N Eurasia, May to Aug
**Winters** Mediterranean, tropical Africa, Indian subcontinent & SE Asia, Sep to Apr
**Journey length** 1,250–5,300 miles

**Marsh Sandpiper** *Tringa stagnatilis*
**Wn** 21–23 in **Wt** 2–4 oz
**Breeds** Central-E Europe, W & central Asia, Apr to Sep
**Winters** Tropical & S Africa, Arabia, Indian subcontinent & Australasia, Oct to Mar
**Journey length** 1,850–7,500 miles

**Greenshank** *Tringa nebularia*
**Wn** 26–27 in **Wt** 5–10 oz
**Breeds** N Eurasia, Apr to Oct
**Winters** Tropical & S Africa, Arabia, Indian subcontinent, SE Asia & Australasia, Oct to Apr
**Journey length** 1,500–7,500 miles

**Green Sandpiper** *Tringa ochropus*
**Wn** 22–24 in **Wt** 2–4 oz
**Breeds** N Eurasia, Apr to Aug
**Winters** W & S Europe, tropical Africa, Middle East, Indian subcontinent & SE Asia, Sep to Mar
**Journey length** 300–5,600 miles

**Wood Sandpiper** *Tringa glareola*
**Wn** 22–22 in **Wt** 1¾–3½ oz
**Breeds** N Eurasia, Apr to Aug
**Winters** Tropical & S Africa, Indian subcontinent, SE Asia & Australasia, Sep to Apr
**Journey length** 1,500–8,000 miles

**Terek Sandpiper** *Xenus cinereus*
**Wn** 22–23 in **Wt** 2–4 oz
**Breeds** NE Europe & N Asia, May to Aug
**Winters** Coasts of Africa, Arabia, Indian subcontinent, SE Asia & Australasia, Sep to Apr
**Journey length** 1,850–8,000 miles

**Common Sandpiper** *Actitis hypoleucos*
**Wn** 14–16 in **Wt** 1¼–2½ oz
**Breeds** Eurasia except S, Apr to Aug
**Winters** Tropical & S Africa, Indian subcontinent, SE Asia & Australasia, Sep to Apr
**Journey length** 300–8,000 miles

**Great Black-headed Gull**
*Larus ichthyaetus*
**Wn** 58–66 in **Wt** 2 lb 2 oz–4 lb 7 oz
**Breeds** Central-E Europe & central Asia, Apr to Oct
**Winters** Caspian Sea, Red Sea, Gulf & coasts of Indian subcontinent, Oct to Apr
**Journey length** 155–3,750 miles

**Mediterranean Gull**
*Larus melanocephalus*
**Wn** 36–39 in **Wt** 9–14 oz
**Breeds** S & W Europe, Apr to Sep
**Winters** Coasts of W Europe, Black & Mediterranean seas, Sep to Apr
**Journey length** 155–1,850 miles

**Common Black-headed Gull**
*Larus ridibundus*
**Wn** 39–43 in **Wt** 6–12 oz
**Breeds** Eurasia; resident in W Europe, Apr to Sep
**Winters** Coasts & offshore E N America, Europe, N Africa, Middle East & E Asia, Oct to Mar
**Journey length** 300–4,700 miles

**Little Gull** *Larus minutus*
**Wn** 29–31 in **Wt** 3–5 oz
**Breeds** N-central Europe & N-central Asia, Apr to Oct
**Winters** Coasts of Europe & Caspian Sea, Oct to Apr
**Journey length** 300–2,175 miles

**Gull-billed Tern**
*Gelochelidon nilotica*
**Wn** 39–45 in **Wt** 7–10 oz
**Breeds** S Europe, S & central Asia, E & W coasts of N America, Apr to Sep
**Winters** W & S Europe, tropical Africa, Arabia, S Asia, Australasia, C & S America, Oct to Mar
**Journey length** 300–6,000 miles

**Sandwich Tern** *Sterna sandvicensis*
**Wn** 37–41 in **Wt** 8–10 oz
**Breeds** NW Europe, Mediterranean, Black & Caspian seas; also SE US, W Indies & S America, Apr to Oct
**Winters** Coasts of W & S Europe, Black & Caspian seas, Arabia, W & S Africa; Gulf of Mexico & S America, Oct to Apr
**Journey length** 300–6,800 miles

**Common Tern** *Sterna hirundo*
**Wn** 30–38 in **Wt** 4–6 oz
**Breeds** Eurasia except extreme N & S, Canada & E US, Apr to Sep
**Winters** Coasts & offshore Eurasia, Africa, Australasia, N & S America, Sep to Mar
**Journey length** 600–8,000 miles

**White-cheeked Tern** *Sterna repressa*
**Wn** 29–32 in **Wt** 4–5 oz
**Breeds** Red Sea, Gulf, E Africa & W India, Apr to Oct
**Winters** Coastal areas to S of breeding range, Oct to Apr
**Journey length** 300–1,250 miles

**Whiskered Tern** *Chlidonias hybridus*
**Wn** 29–30 in **Wt** 3–4 oz
**Breeds** S Europe, SW & SE Asia; resident in SE Africa, India & Australia, May to Oct
**Winters** Tropical Africa, Indian subcontinent & Indonesia, Oct to Apr
**Journey length** 1,850–5,000 miles

**White-winged Black Tern**
*Chlidonias leucopterus*
**Wn** 24–26 in **Wt** 2–3 oz
**Breeds** Central-E Europe, W & E Asia, May to Sep
**Winters** Tropical & S Africa, SE Asia & Australasia, Oct to Apr
**Journey length** 2,175–5,600 miles

**Stock Dove** *Columba oenas*
**Wn** 24–27 in **Wt** 9–13 oz
**Breeds** Europe except extreme N, SW Asia; resident in W Europe & parts of SW Asia, Mar to Oct
**Winters** W & S Europe, SW Asia, Mar to Oct
**Journey length** 60–2,500 miles

**Yellow-eyed Stock Dove**
*Columba eversmanni*
**Wn** 23–24 in **Wt** 6–8 oz
**Breeds** Iran & Afghanistan N to Kazakhstan, Apr to Oct
**Winters** NW India & Pakistan, Oct to Apr
**Journey length** 300–1,250 miles

**Wood Pigeon** *Columba palumbus*
**Wn** 29–31 in **Wt** 11 oz–1 lb 6 oz
**Breeds** Europe, N Africa & W Asia; resident in W Europe & N Africa, Apr to Oct **Winters** W & S Europe & SW Asia, Oct to Apr
**Journey length** 60–2,175 miles

**Rufous Turtle Dove**
*Streptopelia orientalis*
**Wn** 20–23 in **Wt** 6–10 oz
**Breeds** E & S Asia; resident in S of breeding range, May to Oct
**Winters** India, Burma, Japan & China, Oct to Apr
**Journey length** 300–2,500 miles

**Great Spotted Cuckoo**
*Clamator glandarius*
**Wn** 22–24 in **Wt** 5–7 oz
**Breeds** S Europe, S Africa; resident in tropical Africa, May to Sep
**Winters** Tropical Africa, Oct to Apr
**Journey length** 1,850–2,800 miles

**Oriental Cuckoo** *Cuculus saturatus*
**Wn** 20–22 in **Wt** 3–5 oz
**Breeds** Asia except central & SW; resident in Indonesia, May to Aug
**Winters** SE Asia, Indonesia & Australia, Sep to Apr
**Journey length** 300–7,150 miles

**European Nightjar**
*Caprimulgus europaeus*
**Wn** 22–25 in **Wt** 2–4 oz
**Breeds** Europe & W Asia, Apr to Sep
**Winters** E & S Africa, Oct to Apr
**Journey length** 1,850–7,500 miles

**Red-necked Nightjar**
*Caprimulgus ruficollis*
**Wn** 25–26 in **Wt** 2–4 oz
**Breeds** Iberia & NW Africa, Apr to Oct
**Winters** W Africa, Oct to Mar
**Journey length** 1,100–2,000 miles

**Egyptian Nightjar**
*Caprimulgus aegyptius*
**Wn** 22–26 in **Wt** 2–3 oz
**Breeds** NW & NE Africa, Kazakhstan, Turkmenistan & Iraq, Mar to Oct
**Winters** Tropical W & E Africa, Oct to Mar
**Journey length** 900–3,400 miles

**Pallid Swift** *Apus pallidus*
**Wn** 16–18 in **Wt** 1–1¾ oz
**Breeds** S Europe, N Africa & Gulf, Mar to Oct
**Winters** Tropical Africa, Oct to Feb
**Journey length** 1,100–3,400 miles

**Alpine Swift** *Apus melba*
**Wn** 21–23 in **Wt** 3–4 oz
**Breeds** S Europe, N Africa, Middle East & SW Asia; resident in India & E & S Africa, Apr to Oct
**Winters** E & S Africa, Oct to Apr
**Journey length** 600–5,600 miles

**Blue-cheeked Bee-eater**
*Merops superciliosus*
**Wn** 18–19 in **Wt** 1½–2 oz
**Breeds** N Africa, Middle East, SW Asia & Pakistan; scattered resident in tropical & S Africa, May to Sep
**Winters** W Africa, SE Africa & Pakistan, Oct to Apr
**Journey length** 600–2,500 miles

**Short-toed Lark**
*Calandrella brachydactyla*
**Wn** 9–11 in **Wt** ½–1 oz
**Breeds** S Europe, N Africa, Middle East & SW Asia, Mar to Sep
**Winters** Tropical Africa, SW Asia, Oct to Mar
**Journey length** 300–2,800 miles

**Red-rumped Swallow** *Hirundo daurica*
**Wn** 12–13 in **Wt** ¾–1 oz
**Breeds** S Europe, N Africa, S Asia; resident in Indian subcontinent & Africa, Apr to Sep
**Winters** Tropical Africa, Indian subcontinent & Burma, Sep to Apr
**Journey length** 600–3,000 miles

**House Martin** *Delichon urbica*
**Wn** 10–11 in **Wt** ½–¾ oz
**Breeds** Eurasia & N Africa, Apr to Oct
**Winters** Sub-Saharan Africa, India, SE Asia & Philippines, Oct to Apr
**Journey length** 900–8,000 miles

**Blyth's Pipit** *Anthus godlewskii*
**Wn** 11–12 in **Wt** ¾–1 oz
**Breeds** Central Asia & Mongolia S to Tibet, May to Aug
**Winters** India & Sri Lanka, Sep to Apr
**Journey length** 900–3,000 miles

**Tawny Pipit** *Anthus campestris*
**Wn** 9–11 in **Wt** ½–1 oz
**Breeds** S & central Europe, N Africa, W & central Asia, Apr to Sep
**Winters** Tropical Africa, Arabia & Indian subcontinent, Sep to Mar
**Journey length** 900–4,475 miles

**Olive-tree Pipit** *Anthus hodgsoni*
**Wn** 9–10 in **Wt** ½–1 oz
**Breeds** N & E Asia, May to Sep
**Winters** Indian subcontinent, SE Asia & Philippines, Oct to Apr
**Journey length** 300–5,600 miles

**Tree Pipit** *Anthus trivialis*
**Wn** 9–10 in **Wt** ½–1 oz
**Breeds** Europe, W & central Asia, May to Sep
**Winters** Tropical & S Africa & Indian subcontinent, Oct to Apr
**Journey length** 600–6,500 miles

**Pechora Pipit** *Anthus gustavi*
**Wn** 9–10 in **Wt** ½–1 oz
**Breeds** N Asia, Jun to Sep
**Winters** Philippines & Indonesia, Oct to Apr
**Journey length** 5,000–5,600 miles

**Meadow Pipit** *Anthus pratensis*
**Wn** 8–9 in **Wt** ½–¾ oz
**Breeds** W, N & central Europe, Iceland, Apr to Oct
**Winters** S & W Europe, N Africa & SW Asia, Oct to Apr
**Journey length** 60–3,000 miles

**Citrine Wagtail** *Motacilla citreola*
**Wn** 9–10 in **Wt** ½–¾ oz
**Breeds** Central Europe & Asia except extreme E, May to Sep
**Winters** Indian subcontinent & SE Asia, Oct to Apr
**Journey length** 300–4,700 miles

**Gray Wagtail** *Motacilla cinerea*
**Wn** 9–10 in **Wt** ½–1 oz
**Breeds** Europe except N & E, Asia; resident in W Europe, Apr to Oct
**Winters** W & S Europe, E Africa, Indian subcontinent, SE Asia & Australasia, Oct to Apr
**Journey length** 0–5,300 miles

**White Wagtail** *Motacilla alba*
**Wn** 9–11 in **Wt** ½–1 oz
**Breeds** Eurasia; resident in W & S Europe & S Asia, Apr to Oct
**Winters** N & tropical Africa, Arabia, Indian subcontinent & SW Asia, Oct to Apr
**Journey length** 0–5,600 miles

**Siberian Accentor** *Prunella montanella*
**Wn** 8–9 in **Wt** ½–¾ oz
**Breeds** N Asia, May to Sep
**Winters** N China, Oct to Apr
**Journey length** 1,850–2,500 miles

**Rufous Bush Robin**
*Cercotrichas galactotes*
**Wn** 8–10 in **Wt** ¾ oz
**Breeds** SW & SE Europe, SW Asia & N Africa; resident in tropical Africa, Apr to Sep
**Winters** Tropical W & E Africa, Sep to Apr
**Journey length** 600–3,400 miles

**Thrush Nightingale**
*Luscinia luscinia*
**Wn** 9–10 in **Wt** ¾–1 oz
**Breeds** Central Europe, W Asia, Apr to Sep
**Winters** E & SE Africa, Oct to Mar
**Journey length** 2,500–6,500 miles

**Siberian Rubythroat** *Luscinia calliope*
**Wn** 9–10 in **Wt** ½–1 oz
**Breeds** N & E Asia, May to Aug
**Winters** SE Asia & Philippines, Sep to Apr
**Journey length** 900–5,000 miles

**Siberian Blue Robin** *Luscinia cyane*
**Wn** 7–8 in **Wt** ½ oz
**Breeds** S Siberia S & E to Korea & Japan, May to Aug
**Winters** SE Asia & Philippines, Sep to Apr
**Journey length** 1,250–3,400 miles

**Red-flanked Bluetail**
*Tarsiger cyanurus*
**Wn** 8–9 in **Wt** ½ oz
**Breeds** E Asia & Himalayas, May to Sep
**Winters** S China & SE Asia, Oct to Apr
**Journey length** 600–3,400 miles

**White-throated Robin**
*Irania gutturalis*
**Wn** 10–11 in **Wt** ½–1 oz
**Breeds** Turkey & SW Asia, May to Sep
**Winters** Kenya & Tanzania, Oct to Apr
**Journey length** 1,250–3,400 miles

**Whinchat** *Saxicola rubetra*
**Wn** 8–9 in **Wt** ½–¾ oz
**Breeds** Europe & extreme W Asia, Apr to Sep
**Winters** Tropical & E Africa, Oct to Mar
**Journey length** 1,850–6,000 miles

**Common Stonechat** *Saxicola torquata*
**Wn** 7–8 in **Wt** ½–¾ oz
**Breeds** Eurasia; resident in W Europe, S & E Africa, Apr to Oct
**Winters** N & E Africa, Middle East, Indian subcontinent & SE Asia, Oct to Apr
**Journey length** 0–5,300 miles

**Isabelline Wheatear**
*Oenanthe isabellina*
**Wn** 10–12 in **Wt** ¾–1¼ oz
**Breeds** SE Europe & S Asia, Apr to Sep
**Winters** Tropical & E Africa, Arabia & Pakistan, Oct to Apr
**Journey length** 300–3,000 miles

**Pied Wheatear** *Oenanthe pleschanka*
**Wn** 9–11 in **Wt** ½–1 oz
**Breeds** E Europe & W & central Asia, Apr to Sep
**Winters** E Africa, Oct to Apr
**Journey length** 1,850–5,600 miles

**Black-eared Wheatear**
*Oenanthe hispanica*
**Wn** 9–10 in **Wt** ½–¾ oz
**Breeds** S Europe & N Africa, Apr to Sep
**Winters** Tropical Africa, Sep to Mar
**Journey length** 600–2,175 miles

**Red-tailed Wheatear**
*Oenanthe xanthoprymna*
**Wn** 10–12 in **Wt** ¾–1 oz
**Breeds** E Turkey, Turkmenistan & Uzbekistan, Apr to Oct
**Winters** NE Africa, Arabia & Pakistan, Oct to Mar
**Journey length** 300–1,850 miles

**White's Thrush** *Zoothera dauma*
**Wn** 17–18 in **Wt** 4–7 oz
**Breeds** NE Asia; partly resident in Himalayas & Indonesia, May to Oct
**Winters** N India to S China & Philippines, Oct to Apr
**Journey length** 300–4,000 miles

**Song Thrush** *Turdus philomelos*
**Wn** 12–14 in **Wt** 2½–4 oz
**Breeds** Europe & NW Asia; resident in W & S Europe, Apr to Oct
**Winters** W & S Europe, N Africa & Middle East, Oct to Mar
**Journey length** 0–4,000 miles

**Mistle Thrush** *Turdus viscivorus*
**Wn** 16–18 in **Wt** 3½–6 oz
**Breeds** Europe & W Asia; resident in W & S Europe, Apr to Oct
**Winters** W & S Europe, N Africa & SW Asia, Oct to Mar
**Journey length** 0–3,000 miles

**Pallas' Grasshopper Warbler**
*Locustella certhiola*
**Wn** 6–7 in **Wt** ½–¾ oz
**Breeds** E & central Asia, Jun to Sep
**Winters** India & Sri Lanka to Indochina & Indonesia, Oct to Apr
**Journey length** 2,175–3,750 miles

**Lanceolated Warbler**
*Locustella lanceolata*
**Wn** 5–7 in **Wt** ½ oz
**Breeds** N Asia, Jun to Sep
**Winters** Indochina & Indonesia, Oct to Apr
**Journey length** 1,850–5,600 miles

**Grasshopper Warbler**
*Locustella naevia*
**Wn** 5–7 in **Wt** ½ oz
**Breeds** Europe & W Asia, Apr to Sep
**Winters** W Africa & Indian subcontinent, Oct to Mar
**Journey length** 1,850–4,000 miles

**River Warbler** *Locustella fluviatilis*
**Wn** 7–8 in **Wt** ½–¾ oz
**Breeds** E Europe & NW Asia, May to Aug
**Winters** SE Africa, Oct to Apr
**Journey length** 3,750–5,900 miles

**Savi's Warbler** *Locustella luscinioides*
**Wn** 7–8 in **Wt** ½–¾ oz
**Breeds** Central Europe & W Asia, Apr to Sep
**Winters** Tropical Africa, Oct to Mar
**Journey length** 2,500–3,700 miles

**Aquatic Warbler**
*Acrocephalus paludicola*
**Wn** 6–7 in **Wt** ½ oz
**Breeds** Central & E Europe, Apr to Aug
**Winters** W Africa, Sep to Mar
**Journey length** 3,000–4,700 miles

**Sedge Warbler**
*Acrocephalus schoenobaenus*
**Wn** 6–8 in **Wt** ¼–¾ oz
**Breeds** Europe except extreme S, NW Asia, Apr to Sep
**Winters** Tropical & S Africa, Oct to Mar
**Journey length** 2,500–7,150 miles

**Paddyfield Warbler**
*Acrocephalus agricola*
**Wn** 5–7 in **Wt** ¼–½ oz
**Breeds** E Europe, W & central Asia, May to Sep
**Winters** Indian subcontinent, Sep to Apr
**Journey length** 600–4,000 miles

**Blyth's Reed Warbler**
*Acrocephalus dumetorum*
**Wn** 6–7 in **Wt** ¼–½ oz
**Breeds** E Europe, W & central Asia, May to Aug
**Winters** Indian subcontinent, Sep to Apr
**Journey length** 900–4,000 miles

**Marsh Warbler** *Acrocephalus palustris*
**Wn** 7–8 in **Wt** ¼–½ oz
**Breeds** Europe except extreme W & N, May to Sep
**Winters** E & S Africa, Oct to Apr
**Journey length** 3,000–6,500 miles

**Great Reed Warbler**
*Acrocephalus arundinaceus*
**Wn** 9–11 in **Wt** ¾–1½ oz
**Breeds** Eurasia except extreme N, Apr to Sep
**Winters** Tropical & S Africa, Indochina & Indonesia, Oct to Mar
**Journey length** 1,500–6,500 miles

**Thick-billed Warbler**
*Acrocephalus aedon*
**Wn** 8–9 in **Wt** ¾–1 oz
**Breeds** S Siberia E to N China, May to Aug
**Winters** S China, Indochina, India & Burma, Sep to Apr
**Journey length** 1,850–3,750 miles

**Booted Warbler** *Hippolais caligata*
**Wn** 7–8 in **Wt** ¼–½ oz
**Breeds** E Europe & W Asia, May to Sep
**Winters** Indian subcontinent, Oct to Apr
**Journey length** 600–4,350 miles

**Upcher's Warbler** *Hippolais languida*
**Wn** 7–9 in **Wt** ½–¾ oz
**Breeds** Turkmenistan, Uzbekistan & Iran, Apr to Sep
**Winters** E Africa, Oct to Mar
**Journey length** 1,500–3,400 miles

**Olive-tree Warbler**
*Hippolais olivetorum*
**Wn** 9–10 in **Wt** ½–¾ oz
**Breeds** Greece & Balkans, May to Aug
**Winters** SE Africa, Oct to Mar
**Journey length** 3,000–4,350 miles

**Icterine Warbler**
*Hippolais icterina*
**Wn** 7–9 in **Wt** ½ oz
**Breeds** Europe except SW, extreme W Asia, May to Aug
**Winters** S Africa, Oct to Apr
**Journey length** 3,000–7,500 miles

**Melodious Warbler**
*Hippolais polyglotta*
**Wn** 6–7 in **Wt** ¼–½ oz
**Breeds** SW Europe & NW Africa, May to Aug
**Winters** W Africa, Sep to Apr
**Journey length** 1,500–3,400 miles

**Subalpine Warbler** *Sylvia cantillans*
**Wn** 5–7 in **Wt** ¼–½ oz
**Breeds** SW & S Europe & NW Africa, Apr to Sep
**Winters** Tropical Africa, Oct to Mar
**Journey length** 1,500–2,500 miles

**Menetries' Warbler** *Sylvia mystacea*
**Wn** 5–7 in **Wt** ¼–½ oz
**Breeds** SW Asia, Mar to Oct
**Winters** E Africa & Arabia, Oct to Mar
**Journey length** 600–2,800 miles

**Rüppell's Warbler** *Sylvia rueppelli*
**Wn** 7–8 in **Wt** ¼–½ oz
**Breeds** Greece & Turkey, Apr to Sep
**Winters** Tropical E Africa, Oct to Mar
**Journey length** 1,500–2,175 miles

**Desert Warbler** *Sylvia nana*
**Wn** 5–7 in **Wt** ¼–½ oz
**Breeds** S Asia; resident in W Sahara, Apr to Oct
**Winters** NE Africa, Arabia to Pakistan, Oct to Mar
**Journey length** 300–2,500 miles

**Orphean Warbler** *Sylvia hortensis*
**Wn** 7–9 in **Wt** ½–1 oz
**Breeds** S Europe, N Africa & Iran, Apr to Sep
**Winters** Tropical Africa, Arabia & Indian subcontinent, Oct to Mar
**Journey length** 900–2,800 miles

**Barred Warbler** *Sylvia nisoria*
**Wn** 9–10 in **Wt** ¾–1 oz
**Breeds** Central & E Europe, W Asia, May to Sep
**Winters** E Africa, Nov to Apr
**Journey length** 1,850–4,700 miles

**Lesser Whitethroat** *Sylvia curruca*
**Wn** 6–8 in **Wt** ¼–½ oz
**Breeds** Eurasia except extreme E, May to Aug
**Winters** Tropical Africa, Arabia & Indian subcontinent, Sep to Mar
**Journey length** 600–4,000 miles

**Garden Warbler** *Sylvia borin*
**Wn** 7–9 in **Wt** ½–1¼ oz
**Breeds** Europe & NW Asia, Apr to Sep
**Winters** Tropical & S Africa, Oct to Mar
**Journey length** 2,500–6,800 miles

**Blackcap** *Sylvia atricapilla*
**Wn** 7–9 in **Wt** ½–1 oz
**Breeds** Europe & N Africa; resident in SW Europe & N Africa, Apr to Oct
**Winters** SW Europe, N, W & E Africa, Nov to Mar
**Journey length** 0–5,900 miles

**Green Warbler** *Phylloscopus nitidus*
**Wn** 6–7 in **Wt** ⅕–⅖ oz
**Breeds** Turkey, Georgia, Iran & Turkestan, May to Oct
**Winters** S India, Oct to Apr
**Journey length** 2,500–3,000 miles

**Greenish Warbler**
*Phylloscopus trochiloides*
**Wn** 5–8 in **Wt** ⅕–⅖ oz
**Breeds** E Europe, W & S Asia, Apr to Sep
**Winters** India & SE Asia, Oct to Mar
**Journey length** 600–4,700 miles

**Pallas' Leaf Warbler**
*Phylloscopus proregulus*
**Wn** 4–6 in **Wt** ⅕–⅖ oz
**Breeds** E & S Asia, Apr to Sep
**Winters** S China, India & Indochina, Oct to Mar
**Journey length** 600–3,400 miles

**Yellow-browed Warbler**
*Phylloscopus inornatus*
**Wn** 5–7 in **Wt** ⅕–⅖ oz
**Breeds** Asia except SE & SW, May to Sep
**Winters** Arabia, Indian subcontinent, SE Asia & Indochina, Oct to Apr
**Journey length** 600–5,600 miles

**Radde's Bush Warbler**
*Phylloscopus schwarzi*
**Wn** 6–8 in **Wt** ¼–½ oz
**Breeds** Central-E Asia, May to Sep
**Winters** Burma & Indochina, Oct to Apr
**Journey length** 1,250–2,500 miles

**Dusky Warbler** *Phylloscopus fuscatus*
**Wn** 5–7 in **Wt** ¼–½ oz
**Breeds** E Asia, May to Sep
**Winters** N India E to S China & Indochina, Oct to Apr
**Journey length** 900–3,000 miles

**Bonelli's Warbler** *Phylloscopus bonelli*
**Wn** 6–7 in **Wt** ⅕–⅖ oz
**Breeds** S Europe & N Africa, Apr to Aug
**Winters** Tropical Africa, Sep to Mar
**Journey length** 1,500–3,000 miles

**Chiffchaff** *Phylloscopus collybita*
**Wn** 5–8 in **Wt** ⅕–⅖ oz
**Breeds** Europe & N Asia except extreme E; resident in SW Europe, Mar to Sep **Winters** SW Europe, N & tropical Africa, Arabia & Indian subcontinent, Sep to Mar
**Journey length** 0–5,600 miles

**Red-breasted Flycatcher**
*Ficedula parva*
**Wn** 7–8 in **Wt** ¼–½ oz
**Breeds** NE Europe & N Asia, Apr to Sep
**Winters** Indian subcontinent E to S China, Oct to Mar
**Journey length** 1,850–5,000 miles

**Semi-collared Flycatcher**
*Ficedula semitorquata*
**Wn** 9 in **Wt** ½ oz
**Breeds** SE Europe, Georgia & Turkmenistan, May to Sep
**Winters** E Africa, Oct to Mar
**Journey length** 3,000–3,750 miles

**Collared Flycatcher**
*Ficedula albicollis*
**Wn** 8–9 in **Wt** ¼–½ oz
**Breeds** E Europe, Apr to Aug
**Winters** SE Africa, Oct to Mar
**Journey length** 3,000–6,000 miles

**Golden Oriole** *Oriolus oriolus*
**Wn** 17–18 in **Wt** 1¾–3 oz
**Breeds** Europe & W & S Asia, Apr to Aug **Winters** S Africa & Indian subcontinent, Sep to Mar
**Journey length** 600–6,800 miles

**Lesser Gray Shrike** *Lanius minor*
**Wn** 12–13 in **Wt** 1½–2 oz
**Breeds** E Europe & W Asia, Apr to Sep
**Winters** S Africa, Oct to Mar
**Journey length** 4,000–6,500 miles

**Woodchat Shrike** *Lanius senator*
**Wn** 10–11 in **Wt** 1–1¾ oz
**Breeds** S Europe & N Africa, Apr to Sep **Winters** Tropical & SE Africa, Oct to Mar
**Journey length** 1,500–4,000 miles

**Masked Shrike** *Lanius nubicus*
**Wn** 9–10 in **Wt** ½–¾ oz
**Breeds** Greece, Turkey & Middle East, Oct to Mar **Winters** Tropical & E Africa, Nov to Feb
**Journey length** 1,500–2,800 miles

## WINTER VISITORS FROM THE FAR NORTH

**Red-throated Loon** *Gavia stellata*
**Wn** 41–45 in **Wt** 2 lb 3 oz–4 lb 3 oz
**Breeds** Circumpolar Arctic & subarctic, May to Sep
**Winters** Coastal waters of N America & Eurasia, Oct to Apr
**Journey length** 155–4,700 miles

**Arctic Loon** *Gavia arctica*
**Wn** 43–51 in **Wt** 2 lb 14 oz–7 lb 8 oz
**Breeds** Circumpolar Arctic & subarctic, also N forested areas with lakes, Apr to Sep
**Winters** Pacific coasts of N America & Asia & coasts of Europe, Oct to Apr
**Journey length** 155–4,000 miles

**Common Loon** *Gavia immer*
**Wn** 50–57 in **Wt** 6 lb 3 oz–9 lb 15 oz
**Breeds** Arctic & subarctic N America, Greenland & Iceland, May to Sep
**Winters** Coasts of N America & W Europe, Oct to Apr
**Journey length** 60–4,000 miles

**Yellow-billed Loon** *Gavia adamsii*
**Wn** 53–59 in **Wt** 9 lb 6 oz–14 lb 2 oz
**Breeds** Circumpolar Arctic except Greenland, May to Sep
**Winters** N Pacific coasts of N America & Asia & coast of Norway, Oct to Apr
**Journey length** 300–3,400 miles

**Pink-footed Goose**
*Anser brachyrhynchus*
**Wn** 53–66 in **Wt** 3 lb 15 oz–7 lb 6 oz
**Breeds** Iceland, E Greenland & Svalbard, May to Sep
**Winters** NW Europe, Sep to Apr
**Journey length** 500–2,500 miles

**Greater White-fronted Goose**
*Anser albifrons*
**Wn** 51–64 in **Wt** 3 lb 2 oz–7 lb 6 oz
**Breeds** Circumpolar Arctic, May to Sep
**Winters** W US, NW & S Europe, Far East, Oct to Apr
**Journey length** 1,500–3,400 miles

**Lesser White-fronted Goose**
*Anser erythropus*
**Wn** 47–53 in **Wt** 2 lb 14 oz–5 lb 8 oz
**Breeds** Arctic Eurasia, May to Sep
**Winters** S Europe, SW Asia, China, Oct to Apr
**Journey length** 1,850–3,750 miles

**Ross's Goose** *Anser rossii*
**Wn** 47–53 in **Wt** 2 lb 10 oz–3 lb 15 oz
**Breeds** Arctic Canada, May to Sep
**Winters** W US, Oct to Apr
**Journey length** 2,300–2,900 miles

**Greater Scaup** *Aythya marila*
**Wn** 28–33 in **Wt** 1 lb 10 oz–3 lb
**Breeds** Circumpolar Arctic, May to Sep
**Winters** Coasts of N America & Eurasia, Oct to Apr
**Journey length** 300–4,000 miles

**King Eider** *Somateria spectabilis*
**Wn** 33–40 in **Wt** 2 lb 11 oz–4 lb 7 oz
**Breeds** Circumpolar Arctic, Jun to Sep
**Winters** Coasts of E US, Alaska, E Siberia & Norway, Oct to May
**Journey length** 600–3,400 miles

**Spectacled Eider** *Somateria fischeri*
**Wn** 33–36 in **Wt** 3 lb 1 oz–4 lb 1 oz
**Breeds** Coasts of NE Siberia & N Alaska, Jun to Sep
**Winters** Bering Sea, Oct to May
**Journey length** 185–500 miles

**Steller's Eider** *Polysticta stelleri*
**Wn** 27–29 in **Wt** 1 lb 2 oz–2 lb 3 oz
**Breeds** Coasts of E Siberia & Alaska, Jun to Sep
**Winters** Coasts of S Alaska & NE Asia, Oct to May
**Journey length** 300–900 miles

**Black Scoter** *Melanitta nigra*
**Wn** 31–35 in **Wt** 1 lb 9 oz–3 lb 3 oz
**Breeds** Arctic Eurasia & Alaska, May to Sep
**Winters** Coasts of N America, Eurasia & NW Africa, Oct to Apr
**Journey length** 300–4,350 miles

**White-winged Scoter** *Melanitta fusca*
**Wn** 35–38 in **Wt** 3 lb–4 lb 6 oz
**Breeds** Circumpolar Arctic & subarctic, May to Sep
**Winters** Coasts of N America & Eurasia, Oct to Apr
**Journey length** 125–3,000 miles

**Surf Scoter** *Melanitta perspicillata*
**Wn** 30–36 in **Wt** 1 lb 7 oz–2 lb 8 oz
**Breeds** Arctic N America, May to Sep
**Winters** Coasts of N America, Oct to Apr
**Journey length** 300–2,800 miles

**Gyr Falcon** *Falco rusticolus*
**Wn** 51–62 in **Wt** 1 lb 12 oz–4 lb 10 oz
**Breeds** Circumpolar Arctic, May to Sep
**Winters** N Canada & Eurasia, Oct to Apr
**Journey length** 300–1,500 miles

**Eurasian Dotterel**
*Charadrius morinellus*
**Wn** 22–25 in **Wt** 3–4 oz
**Breeds** Arctic Eurasia, also mountain tops farther S, May to Oct
**Winters** N Africa & Middle East, Nov to Apr
**Journey length** 1,850–5,600 miles

**European Golden Plover**
*Pluvialis apricaria*
**Wn** 26–29 in **Wt** 5–10 oz
**Breeds** Arctic & subarctic Europe & W Asia, Apr to Sep
**Winters** W & S Europe & N Africa, Oct to Mar
**Journey length** 300–4,000 miles

**Black-bellied Plover**
*Pluvialis squatarola*
**Wn** 27–32 in **Wt** 6–12 oz
**Breeds** Circumpolar Arctic, May to Sep
**Winters** Coasts of S N America, S America, S Africa, Arabia, Indian subcontinent, SE Asia & Australasia, Oct to Apr
**Journey length** 1,500–8,700 miles

**Great Knot** *Calidris tenuirostris*
**Wn** 24–25 in **Wt** 5–7 oz
**Breeds** NE Siberia, May to Sep
**Winters** Pakistan to S China, S to Australia, Oct to Apr
**Journey length** 3,000–8,700 miles

**Sanderling** *Calidris alba*
**Wn** 15–17 in **Wt** 1–2½ oz
**Breeds** Arctic Canada, Greenland & NW Siberia, May to Aug
**Winters** Coasts of N & S America, Africa, Arabia, Indian subcontinent, SE Asia & Australasia, Sep to Apr
**Journey length** 1,500–9,600 miles

**Semipalmated Sandpiper**
*Calidris pusilla*
**Wn** 13–14 in **Wt** ¾–1½ oz
**Breeds** Arctic N America, Jun to Sep
**Winters** Coasts of C & S America S to Peru & Uruguay, Oct to May
**Journey length** 4,350–7,150 miles

**Western Sandpiper** *Calidris mauri*
**Wn** 13–14 in **Wt** ½–1¼ oz
**Breeds** NE Siberia & Alaska, May to Sep
**Winters** S US, W Indies, C America & S America S to Peru, Oct to Apr
**Journey length** 4,700–6,800 miles

**Rufous-necked Stint**
*Calidris ruficollis*
**Wn** 13–14 in **Wt** ¾–1½ oz
**Breeds** NE Siberia, Jun to Sep
**Winters** S China S to Australia & NZ, Oct to Apr
**Journey length** 3,000–8,700 miles

**Little Stint** *Calidris minuta*
**Wn** 13–14 in **Wt** ½–1½ oz
**Breeds** Arctic Eurasia except NE Siberia, Jun to Aug
**Winters** S Europe, tropical & S Africa, Arabia & Indian subcontinent, Sep to Apr
**Journey length** 2,175–8,400 miles

**Temminck's Stint**
*Calidris temminckii*
**Wn** 13–14 in **Wt** ½–1¼ oz
**Breeds** Arctic Eurasia, May to Aug
**Winters** S Europe, tropical Africa, SE Asia & Indian subcontinent, Sep to Apr
**Journey length** 1,250–5,300 miles

**Least Sandpiper** *Calidris minutilla*
**Wn** 12–13 in **Wt** ¾–1¼ oz
**Breeds** Alaska & N Canada, May to Aug
**Winters** Coasts of S US, C America, W Indies & N S America, Sep to Apr
**Journey length** 1,500–5,300 miles

**White-rumped Sandpiper**
*Calidris fuscicollis*
**Wn** 15–17 in **Wt** ¾–1½ oz
**Breeds** Arctic Canada & Alaska, Jun to Aug
**Winters** S America from equator to Tierra del Fuego, Sep to Apr
**Journey length** 5,300–9,300 miles

**Baird's Sandpiper** *Calidris bairdii*
**Wn** 15–18 in **Wt** 1–1½ oz
**Breeds** NE Siberia, Alaska, Arctic Canada & NW Greenland, Jun to Aug
**Winters** S America, Sep to Apr
**Journey length** 5,000–9,600 miles

**Pectoral Sandpiper**
*Calidris melanotos*
**Wn** 16–19 in **Wt** 1½–3¾ oz
**Breeds** NE Siberia, Alaska, Arctic Canada, May to Aug
**Winters** S America, Australia & NZ, Sep to Apr
**Journey length** 5,600–9,600 miles

**Sharp-tailed Sandpiper**
*Calidris acuminata*
**Wn** 16–18 in **Wt** 1½–4 oz
**Breeds** N Siberia, May to Aug
**Winters** Pacific islands S of equator S to Australia & NZ, Sep to Apr
**Journey length** 5,600–9,000 miles

**Curlew Sandpiper** *Calidris ferruginea*
**Wn** 16–18 in **Wt** 1¼–3½ oz
**Breeds** N Siberia, Jun to Aug
**Winters** Tropical & S Africa, coasts of Indian subcontinent, SE Asia & Australasia, Sep to May
**Journey length** 3,750–9,000 miles

**Rock Sandpiper** *Calidris ptilocnemis*
**Wn** 16–18 in **Wt** 2–4 oz
**Breeds** Alaska, May to Sep
**Winters** W coasts of Canada & US, Oct to Apr
**Journey length** 300–1,850 miles

**Purple Sandpiper** *Calidris maritima*
**Wn** 16–18 in **Wt** 2–4 oz
**Breeds** Arctic Europe, NW Siberia, Iceland, Greenland & NE Canada, May to Aug
**Winters** Coasts of NW Europe, Iceland & E US, Sep to Apr
**Journey length** 125–3,750 miles

**Stilt Sandpiper**
*Micropalama himantopus*
**Wn** 16–18 in **Wt** 1½–2¼ oz
**Breeds** Arctic & subarctic N America, May to Aug
**Winters** Central S America, Sep to Apr
**Journey length** 5,300–6,800 miles

**Buff-breasted Sandpiper**
*Tryngites subruficollis*
**Wn** 16–18 in **Wt** 1¾–3¼ oz
**Breeds** Alaska & NW Arctic Canada, May to Aug
**Winters** Central Argentina & Paraguay, Sep to Apr
**Journey length** 5,600–6,800 miles

**Long-billed Dowitcher**
*Limnodromus scolopaceus*
**Wn** 18–20 in **Wt** 3¼–5 oz
**Breeds** NE Siberia & Alaska, May to Sep **Winters** S US S to Guatemala, Oct to Apr
**Journey length** 3,000–5,000 miles

**Bar-tailed Godwit** *Limosa lapponica*
**Wn** 27–31 in **Wt** 7 oz–1 lb
**Breeds** Arctic Eurasia & NW Alaska, May to Sep
**Winters** Coasts of W Europe, Africa, Madagascar, Arabia, Indian subcontinent, SE Asia & Australasia, Oct to Apr
**Journey length** 1,250–9,000 miles

**Hudsonian Godwit** *Limosa haemastica*
**Wn** 25–29 in **Wt** 6–14 oz
**Breeds** Alaska, NE Arctic Canada & Hudson Bay, May to Sep
**Winters** S America, Oct to Apr
**Journey length** 5,600–9,300 miles

**Bristle-thighed Curlew**
*Numenius tahitiensis*
**Wn** 28–32 in **Wt** 7–16 oz
**Breeds** W Alaska, Jun to Sep
**Winters** Pacific islands, Oct to Apr
**Journey length** 5,600–6,000 miles

**Wandering Tattler**
*Heteroscelus incanus*
**Wn** 16–20 in **Wt** 3–5 oz
**Breeds** Alaska & NW Canada, May to Aug
**Winters** Mexico, S America & Australasia, Sep to Apr
**Journey length** 2,500–9,300 miles

**Ruddy Turnstone**
*Arenaria interpres*
**Wn** 19–22 in **Wt** 3–7 oz
**Breeds** NW Europe & circumpolar Arctic, May to Aug
**Winters** Coasts of N & S America, Europe, Africa, Arabia, Indian subcontinent, SE Asia & Australasia, Sep to Apr
**Journey length** 300–9,300 miles

**Black Turnstone**
*Arenaria melanocephala*
**Wn** 18–21 in **Wt** 2–6 oz
**Breeds** Alaska, May to Sep
**Winters** W coasts of Canada, US & Mexico, Oct to Apr
**Journey length** 600–3,750 miles

**Surfbird** *Aphriza virgata*
**Wn** 21–23 in **Wt** 3–6 oz
**Breeds** Alaska, May to Sep
**Winters** W coasts US, C & S America, Oct to Apr
**Journey length** 1,250–9,300 miles

**Red-necked Phalarope**
*Phalaropus lobatus*
**Wn** 12–16 in **Wt** 1–1¾ oz
**Breeds** Circumpolar Arctic, May to Aug
**Winters** Offshore from W S America, Arabian peninsula & Indonesia, Sep to Apr
**Journey length** 3,000–6,500 miles

**Red Phalarope** *Phalaropus fulicarius*
**Wn** 15–17 in **Wt** 1¼–2¾ oz
**Breeds** Circumpolar Arctic, May to Aug
**Winters** Offshore W S America, W & SW Africa, Sep to Apr
**Journey length** 2,500–9,300 miles

**Pomarine Jaeger**
*Stercorarius pomarinus*
**Wn** 49–54 in **Wt** 1 lb 3 oz–2 lb
**Breeds** Circumpolar Arctic, May to Sep
**Winters** Offshore in N & W S Atlantic, W, S & E N Pacific and Indian oceans, Oct to Apr
**Journey length** 600–9,300 miles

**Parasitic Jaeger**
*Stercorarius parasiticus*
**Wn** 43–49 in **Wt** 11 oz–1 lb 7 oz
**Breeds** Circumpolar Arctic & subarctic, May to Sep
**Winters** Offshore in N & S Atlantic, W, S & E N Pacific and Indian oceans, Oct to Apr
**Journey length** 600–10,000 miles

**Sabine's Gull** *Larus sabini*
**Wn** 35–39 in **Wt** 5–8 oz
**Breeds** Arctic Canada, Alaska, N & E Siberia, Jun to Aug
**Winters** Offshore E coasts of Atlantic & Pacific, Sep to May
**Journey length** 1,250–8,700 miles

**Iceland Gull** *Larus glaucoides*
**Wn** 55–59 in **Wt** 1 lb 10 oz–1 lb 14 oz
**Breeds** Greenland & Baffin Island, May to Aug
**Winters** N Atlantic, Sep to Apr
**Journey length** 600–1,850 miles

**Glaucous Gull** *Larus hyperboreus*
**Wn** 59–64 in **Wt** 2 lb 6 oz–4 lb
**Breeds** Circumpolar Arctic, Apr to Oct
**Winters** N Atlantic & N Pacific, Nov to Mar
**Journey length** 300–1,850 miles

**Thayer's Gull** *Larus thayeri*
**Wn** 55–59 in **Wt** 1 lb 10 oz–2 lb
**Breeds** Central Arctic Canada, May to Aug
**Winters** Coasts of SW Canada & W US, Sep to Apr
**Journey length** 1,500–3,000 miles

**Glaucous-winged Gull**
*Larus glaucescens*
**Wn** 55–59 in **Wt** 2 lb–3 lb 8 oz
**Breeds** Alaska & NW Canada, Apr to Aug
**Winters** Coasts of W US & NW Mexico, Sep to Apr
**Journey length** 300–2,800 miles

**Ross's Gull** *Rhodostethia rosea*
**Wn** 35–39 in **Wt** 4–9 oz
**Breeds** NE Siberia, Jun to Aug
**Winters** N Pacific, Sep to May
**Journey length** 1,500–3,000 miles

**Aleutian Tern** *Sterna aleutica*
**Wn** 29–31 in **Wt** 3½–4 oz
**Breeds** E Siberia & W Alaska, May to Sep
**Winters** N Pacific, Oct to Apr
**Journey length** 600–1,850 miles

**Thick-billed Murre** *Uria lomvia*
**Wn** 25–28 in **Wt** 1 lb 10 oz–2 lb 11 oz
**Breeds** Cirumpolar Arctic coasts & islands, May to Aug
**Winters** N Pacific & N Atlantic, Sep to Apr
**Journey length** 900–1,850 miles

**Black Guillemot** *Cepphus grylle*
**Wn** 20–22 in **Wt** 10 oz–1 lb 2 oz
**Breeds** Arctic & N coasts & islands, Apr to Aug
**Winters** N Atlantic & Arctic oceans, Sep to Mar
**Journey length** 125–1,500 miles

**Dovekie** *Alle alle*
**Wn** 15–18 in **Wt** 4–6 oz
**Breeds** Greenland, Iceland, Svalbard & islands N of Siberia, May to Aug
**Winters** N Atlantic, Sep to Apr
**Journey length** 300–3,000 miles

**Crested Auklet** *Aethia cristatella*
**Wn** 15–18 in **Wt** 7–10 oz
**Breeds** NE Siberia & Alaska, Apr to Aug
**Winters** Bering Sea & N Pacific, Sep to Mar
**Journey length** 300–1,250 miles

**Horned Lark** *Eremophila alpestris*
**Wn** 11–13 in **Wt** 1–1¾ oz
**Breeds** Circumpolar Arctic; resident in US, SE Europe & central Asia, May to Sep
**Winters** Coasts of NW Europe & N America, Oct to Apr
**Journey length** 600–3,000 miles

**Red-throated Pipit**
*Anthus cervinus*
**Wn** 9–10 in **Wt** ½–¾ oz
**Breeds** Arctic Eurasia, May to Sep
**Winters** Tropical & E Africa, SE Asia & Indonesia, Oct to Apr
**Journey length** 3,750–5,900 miles

**Siberian Thrush** *Zoothera sibirica*
**Wn** 13–14 in **Wt** 2–2¾ oz
**Breeds** Arctic & N Siberia, May to Sep
**Winters** India, SE Asia & Indonesia, Oct to Apr
**Journey length** 2,500–4,700 miles

**Varied Thrush** *Ixoreus naevius*
**Wn** 14–15 in **Wt** 2¼–3 oz
**Breeds** Alaska & NW Canada; resident in S of range, Apr to Sep
**Winters** British Columbia, W US & NW Mexico, Nov to Mar
**Journey length** 0–3,750 miles

**Gray-cheeked Thrush**
*Catharus minimus*
**Wn** 11–12 in **Wt** ¾–1½ oz
**Breeds** Alaska & N Canada, Jun to Sep
**Winters** N S America, Oct to Apr
**Journey length** 3,000–6,000 miles

**Arctic Warbler** *Phylloscopus borealis*
**Wn** 6–8 in **Wt** ¼–½ oz
**Breeds** Arctic & subarctic Eurasia, Jun to Aug
**Winters** SE Asia & Indonesia, Sep to Apr
**Journey length** 1,500–5,900 miles

**Hoary Redpoll** *Acanthis hornemanni*
**Wn** 6–8 in **Wt** ½–¾ oz
**Breeds** Circumpolar Arctic, Apr to Sep
**Winters** N America & N Eurasia, Oct to Apr
**Journey length** 300–1,250 miles

**Harris' Sparrow** *Zonotrichia querula*
**Wn** 7–10 in **Wt** ½–1 oz
**Breeds** Central Arctic Canada, May to Aug
**Winters** Mississippi valley, Sep to Apr
**Journey length** 1,850–2,800 miles

**Smith's Longspur** *Calcarius pictus*
**Wn** 6–9 in **Wt** ½–1 oz
**Breeds** Arctic Canada, May to Aug
**Winters** Mississippi valley, Sep to Apr
**Journey length** 1,850–2,800 miles

## SOUTH AMERICAN MIGRANTS

**Great Grebe** *Podiceps major*
**Wn** 39–42 in **Wt** 3 lb 5 oz–3 lb 12 oz
**Breeds** NW Peru, Paraguay & SE Brazil S to Patagonia & S Chile, Oct to Mar, though can breed year-round
**Winters** Coastal waters of S America, Apr to Sep
**Journey length** 125–900 miles

**Black-faced Ibis** *Theristicus melanopis*
**Wn** 39–43 in **Wt** 2 lb 7 oz–3 lb 1 oz
**Breeds** S Chile & S Argentina; resident in Ecuador, Peru & NW Bolivia, Sep to Mar
**Winters** N Argentina, Apr to Sep
**Journey length** 300–2,175 miles

**Black-necked Swan**
*Cygnus melanocorypha*
**Wn** 55–66 in **Wt** 7 lb 11 oz–14 lb 12 oz
**Breeds** Tierra del Fuego N to central Chile, where sedentary, Jul to Jan/Feb
**Winters** Argentina & Chile, except S, Paraguay & S Brazil, Feb to Jul
**Journey length** 125–2,175 miles

**Red Shoveler** *Anas platalea*
**Wn** 27–33 in **Wt** 1 lb 2 oz–1 lb 5 oz
**Breeds** Tierra del Fuego N to central Chile & N Argentina, where sedentary, Sep to Feb
**Winters** Central Argentina & central Chile N to S Brazil & S Peru, Feb to Aug
**Journey length** 300–3,000 miles

**Argentine Blue-billed Duck**
*Oxyura vittata*
**Wn** 21–24 in **Wt** 1 lb 4 oz–1 lb 6 oz
**Breeds** Chile & Argentina N to SE Brazil, where sedentary, Oct to Feb
**Winters** Central Chile & central Argentina N to Paraguay & central Brazil, Mar to Sep
**Journey length** 125–2,175 miles

**Plumbeous Kite** *Ictinia plumbea*
**Wn** 33–37 in **Wt** 7–10 oz
**Breeds** N Argentina & Paraguay N to central Mexico, Oct to Apr in S, Mar to Sep in N
**Winters** Argentinian breeders to Brazil, Apr to Sep; Mexican & C American breeders to N S America, Sep to Mar
**Journey length** 300–2,500 miles

**Long-winged Harrier** *Circus buffoni*
**Wn** 45–51 in **Wt** 14 oz–1 lb 7 oz
**Breeds** Argentina, except S, Bolivia & Chile; resident in Colombia & Trinidad, Oct to Mar

**Winters** N S America, Mar to Sep
**Journey length** 300–3,000 miles

**Least Seedsnipe**
*Thinocorus rumicivorus*
**Wn** 14–15 in **Wt** 2–3 oz
**Breeds** Argentina & Chile N to Ecuador; resident in N of range, Oct to Feb **Winters** N Chile & Bolivia to Colombia, Mar to Sep
**Journey length** 300–3,750 miles

**Rufous-chested Dotterel**
*Onaradrius modestus*
**Wn** 22–25 in **Wt** 3–4 oz
**Breeds** Tierra del Fuego & S Chile, Oct to Feb
**Winters** Argentina, Chile, Uruguay & E Brazil, Mar to Sep
**Journey length** 125–2,000 miles

**Green-backed Firecrown**
*Sephanoides sephanoides*
**Wn** 5–6 in **Wt** 1/15 oz
**Breeds** Tierra del Fuego N to central Chile & W Argentina, Oct to Feb
**Winters** E Argentina, Mar to Sep
**Journey length** 125–300 miles

**Striped Cuckoo** *Tapera naevia*
**Wn** 19–21 in **Wt** 2 oz
**Breeds** S Mexico S to N Argentina & SE Brazil, Mar to Jun in N; Oct to Jan in S
**Winters** S breeders move N, Mar to Sep
**Journey length** 300–900 miles

**Fork-tailed Flycatcher**
*Tyrannus savana*
**Wn** 9–11 in **Wt** 1 oz
**Breeds** Central Argentina & Uruguay N to SE Mexico; sedentary around equator, Oct to Jan in S, Mar to Jun in N
**Winters** N pops. to N S America, Jul to Feb; S pops. to N Argentina & Brazil, Feb to Sep
**Journey length** 300–1,250 miles

**Large Elaenia** *Elaenia spectabilis*
**Wn** 10–11 in **Wt** 1 oz
**Breeds** S Brazil & N Argentina, Oct to Jan
**Winters** Amazonia, Feb to Sep
**Journey length** 300–1,500 miles

**Brown-chested Martin** *Progne tapera*
**Wn** 13–15 in **Wt** 3/4–1 oz
**Breeds** N Argentina & S Brazil N to N Colombia & Guyana, also SW Ecuador & W Peru; sedentary in N, Oct to Feb
**Winters** Bolivia & S Brazil N to central Panama, Mar to Sep
**Journey length** 300–1,500 miles

## AFRICAN MIGRANTS

**Dwarf Bittern** *Ixobrychus sturmii*
**Wn** 17–19 in **Wt** 3–4 oz
**Breeds** Tropics S from Senegal, Nigeria, Chad & S Sudan, Jun to Sep
**Winters** S from breeding range to E Cape Province & Transvaal, Nov to Apr
**Journey length** 300–3,000 miles

**Malagasy Pond Heron** *Ardeola idae*
**Wn** 31–35 in **Wt** 8 oz
**Breeds** Madagascar & Aldabra, Nov to May
**Winters** Central & E Africa, May to Oct
**Journey length** 600–1,850 miles

**Abdim's Stork** *Ciconia abdimii*
**Wn** 43–51 in **Wt** 2 lb 10 oz–3 lb 1 oz
**Breeds** Tropics from Senegal to Ethiopia & extreme SW Arabia, Apr to Sep
**Winters** E & S Africa, Nov to Mar
**Journey length** 600–4,350 miles

**Southern Pochard**
*Aythya erythrophthalma*
**Wn** 29–33 in **Wt** 1 lb 3 oz–2 lb 3 oz
**Breeds** Ethiopia S to Cape Province; mainly sedentary, S breeders disperse N in dry season, timing variable
**Winters** S birds move N to Kenya & Uganda, Sep to Mar
**Journey length** 1,250–3,000 miles

**African Scissor-tailed Kite**
*Chelictinia riocourii*
**Wn** 25–29 in **Wt** 6–7 oz
**Breeds** Tropics from Senegal to Ethiopia, Somalia & N Kenya, Mar to Aug
**Winters** Gambia & N Nigeria in W, central Kenya in E, Oct to Feb
**Journey length** 125–900 miles

**Wahlberg's Eagle** *Aquila wahlbergi*
**Wn** 49–55 in **Wt** 15 oz–1 lb 14 oz
**Breeds** Savanna S from Gambia, Niger, Chad & Eritrea to N Cape Province, Sep/Oct to Mar/Apr
**Winters** Mainly N, but some sedentary, May to Aug
**Journey length** 60–600 miles

**Madagascar Pratincole**
*Glareola ocularis*
**Wn** 23–26 in **Wt** 3–4 oz
**Breeds** E Madagascar, Sep to Mar
**Winters** Coasts of E Africa from N Mozambique N to S Somalia, Apr to Sep
**Journey length** 500–1,100 miles

**Brown-chested Plover**
*Vanellus superciliosus*
**Wn** 23–25 in **Wt** 3½–4 oz
**Breeds** Ghana E to Central African Republic, Jan to May
**Winters** Zaïre, Tanzania & Uganda, Jun to Dec
**Journey length** 600–2,500 miles

**Damara Tern** *Sterna balaenarum*
**Wn** 19–20 in **Wt** 1–1½ oz
**Breeds** W coast of Africa from Angola to S Africa, Nov to May
**Winters** N Gulf of Guinea, Jul to Oct
**Journey length** 1,250–2,800 miles

**Jacobin Cuckoo**
*Clamator jacobinus*
**Wn** 17–19 in **Wt** 2–3 oz
**Breeds** Sub-Saharan Africa from Senegal to Red Sea, S to Cape Province; other races Indian subcontinent, Oct to Mar in S, May to Jul in N
**Winters** N movement of N breeders to Ethiopia, Sudan & Chad, Oct to Apr; N movement of S breeders up to & perhaps N of equator, Apr to Sep
**Journey length** 600–2,175 miles

**African Cuckoo** *Cuculus gularis*
**Wn** 21–23 in **Wt** 3–5 oz
**Breeds** Senegal to Ethiopia & S to S Africa, Oct to Mar in S, Apr to Jul in N
**Winters** N of breeding range, timing variable but generally May to Sep in S, Sep to Mar in N
**Journey length** 300–1,250 miles

**African Emerald Cuckoo**
*Chrysococcyx cupreus*
**Wn** 13–15 in **Wt** 1¼–1½ oz
**Breeds** Sub-Saharan Africa from Gambia, Sudan & Ethiopia S to S Africa; timing variable to occur with that of weavers; Oct to Mar in S, May to Jul in N
**Winters** N of breeding range, Apr to Sep in S, Aug to Apr in N
**Journey length** 300–600 miles

**Didric Cuckoo** *Chrysococcyx caprius*
**Wn** 12–13 in **Wt** ½–1½ oz
**Breeds** Tropics from Senegal to Ethiopia & S to S Africa, timing variable, Sep to Apr in S, Jun to Sep in N
**Winters** S breeders move N perhaps as far as equator, May to Aug; N breeders move N, Oct to May; some resident in equatorial region, where timing variable
**Journey length** 300–1,850 miles

**Pennant-winged Nightjar**
*Macrodipteryx vexillarius*
**Wn** 25–26 in **Wt** 2–3 oz
**Breeds** Tropics S of equator to S Tanzania, Zambia & Angola, Sep to Jan/Feb
**Winters** S Sudan W to Nigeria, Feb/Mar to Sep
**Journey length** 1,250–2,500 miles

**White-rumped Swift** *Apus caffer*
**Wn** 13–14 in **Wt** 3/4–1 oz
**Breeds** Tropical W & E Africa S to S Africa, Sep to Mar; small numbers Spain & Morocco, Mar to Jun
**Winters** S breeders to equator, Apr to Aug; W African breeders may be resident, may disperse N, Nov to Jan
**Journey length** 300–2,500 miles

**Gray-headed Kingfisher**
*Halcyon leucocephala*
**Wn** 12–13 in **Wt** 1¼–1¾ oz
**Breeds** Senegal to Ethiopia & N Somalia S to N Zaïre, Kenya & Tanzania; resident in Cape Verde Islands, Mar to May in N, Dec to Mar in S
**Winters** Central Nigerian breeders to S Nigeria Nov to Feb before breeding, to Sudan & Niger after, May to Oct
**Journey length** 600–1,500 miles

**Blue-cheeked Bee-eater**
*Merops superciliosus*
**Wn** 18–19 in **Wt** 1¼–2 oz
**Breeds** Tropical W Africa, E, NW & S Africa; also SW Asia & India; Mar to Jul in W, May to Sep in N, Oct to Mar in S
**Winters** S African breeders N to Zaïre & E Africa, May to Sep; W African breeders resident; N African breeders to W Africa E to Nigeria, Oct to Apr
**Journey length** 300–5,000 miles

**Red-breasted Swallow**
*Hirundo semirufa*
**Wn** 12–13 in **Wt** ½–¾ oz
**Breeds** Tropics from Senegal to Ethiopia S to S Africa, Apr to Jul in N, Nov to Feb in S
**Winters** Some N movement though more sedentary in N, Aug to Feb in N; Mar to Aug in S
**Journey length** 300–900 miles

**African Reed Warbler**
*Acrocephalus baeticatus*
**Wn** 6–7 in **Wt** ¼–½ oz
**Breeds** Tropics from Senegal to Somalia S to Angola, Mozambique & Zambia, Apr to Jul in N, Nov to Feb in S
**Winters** N; S breeders travel farther, Aug to Feb in N, Mar to Aug in S
**Journey length** 300–1,250 miles

**Amethyst Starling**
*Cinnyricinclus leucogaster*
**Wn** 9–10 in **Wt** 1–1¼ oz
**Breeds** Tropics from Senegal to Somalia & S to Namibia & Botswana; also SW Arabia, Mar to Jul in N, Oct to Feb in S
**Winters** Toward equator; some sedentary or nomadic, Aug to Feb in N, Mar to Aug in S
**Journey length** 300–900 miles

## AUSTRALASIAN MIGRANTS

**Cattle Egret** *Bubulcus ibis*
**Wn** 34–37 in **Wt** 12–14 oz
**Breeds** S & E Asia to Australia & NZ; also Africa, S Europe, S, C & S N America, Sep to Feb
**Winters** Australian breeders winter SE Australia, Tasmania & NZ; some from NW Australia winter in SW, Mar to Aug
**Journey length** 300–2,800 miles

**Gray Falcon** *Falco hypoleucos*
**Wn** 37–39 in **Wt** 1 lb–1 lb 9 oz
**Breeds** Inland Australia to coast in W; Jul to Dec, Nov to Mar in W
**Winters** N Australia & New Guinea, Jan to Jun
**Journey length** 300–1,250 miles

**Australian Hobby**
*Falco longipennis*
**Wn** 32–36 in **Wt** 5–11 oz
**Breeds** Australia except central desert, Sep to Mar
**Winters** E Indonesia & New Guinea, Apr to Aug
**Journey length** 500–900 miles

**South Island Pied Oystercatcher**
*Haematopus finschi*
**Wn** 31–33 in **Wt** 1 lb–1 lb 3 oz
**Breeds** Central & E parts of S Island, NZ, Sep to Feb
**Winters** N & E coasts of S Island, coasts of N Island & Stewart Island, NZ, Feb to Aug
**Journey length** 60–750 miles

**Wrybill** *Anarhynchus frontalis*
**Wn** 20–22 in **Wt** 2–2½ oz
**Breeds** Central S Island, NZ, Jul to Dec
**Winters** N N Island, NZ, Dec to Jul
**Journey length** 500–870 miles

**Australian Pratincole**
*Stiltia isabella*
**Wn** 21–23 in **Wt** 2¼–2¾ oz
**Breeds** E, inland & N Australia; probably resident in N, timing variable, May to Dec
**Winters** N Australia N to New Guinea, Java, Borneo & Sulawesi, Dec to Jun
**Journey length** 300–2,175 miles

**Double-banded Plover**
*Charadrius bicinctus*
**Wn** 17–21 in **Wt** 2–3 oz
**Breeds** N, S and Chatham Islands, NZ; sedentary on Auckland Islands, Sep to Feb
**Winters** N N Island, NZ, & SE & E Australia, Mar to Aug
**Journey length** 300–1,500 miles

**Orange-bellied Parrot**
*Neophema chrysogaster*
**Wn** 11–13 in **Wt** 1¾–2 oz
**Breeds** Tasmania, Nov to Mar
**Winters** Coastal SE Australia, Victoria & Tasmania, Apr to Oct
**Journey length** 155–470 miles

**Cockatiel** *Nymphicus hollandicus*
**Wn** 14–17 in **Wt** 2–3 oz
**Breeds** Australia, except coasts, timing variable, Aug to Mar
**Winters** N, Apr to Aug
**Journey length** 300–600 miles

**Channel-billed Cuckoo**
*Scythrops novaehollandiae*
**Wn** 51–62 in **Wt** 1 lb 5 oz–1 lb 12 oz
**Breeds** N tropical Australia S to New S Wales & N S Australia, Oct to Jan
**Winters** N Australia & New Guinea to Sulawesi, Feb/Mar to Sep
**Journey length** 300–2,175 miles

**Long-tailed Cuckoo**
*Urodynamis taitensis*
**Wn** 17–20 in **Wt** 2–2¼ oz
**Breeds** NZ, Sep to Feb
**Winters** Samoa, Tonga, Fiji, Mar to Aug
**Journey length** 1,500–2,175 miles

**White-throated Nightjar**
*Eurostopodus mystacalis*
**Wn** 24–25 in **Wt** 2–2½ oz
**Breeds** E Australia, Queensland to Victoria, Oct to Jan
**Winters** N Australia & New Guinea, Feb to Sep
**Journey length** 300–900 miles

**Buff-breasted Paradise Kingfisher**
*Tanysiptera sylvia*
**Wn** 7–9 in **Wt** ¾ oz
**Breeds** N Queensland; resident in New Guinea, Nov to Jan
**Winters** New Guinea, Feb to Oct
**Journey length** 300–900 miles

**Dollarbird** *Eurystomus orientalis*
**Wn** 21–23 in **Wt** 4–5 oz
**Breeds** E India to Japan, China, Philippines, S to Australia & NZ, Apr to Aug in N, Oct to Jan in S
**Winters** N breeders S to Malaysia, Borneo & Sumatra, Sep to Mar; S breeders N to New Guinea & E Indonesia, Feb to Sep
**Journey length** 600–1,850 miles

**Red-breasted Pitta**
*Pitta erythrogaster*
**Wn** 15–17 in **Wt** 2–3 oz
**Breeds** NE Queensland, Oct to Jan
**Winters** New Guinea, Indonesia & Philippines, Feb to Sep
**Journey length** 600–2,500 miles

**Tree Martin** *Hirundo nigricans*
**Wn** 10–11 in **Wt** ½–¾ oz
**Breeds** S Australia, Aug to Jan
**Winters** N Australia N to New Caledonia, New Guinea & Indonesia, Feb to Jul
**Journey length** 600–3,000 miles

**Common Cicadabird**
*Coracina tenvirostris*
**Wn** 12–14 in **Wt** 1½–1¾ oz
**Breeds** E & SE Australia, Oct to Jan
**Winters** N & E Australia, Feb to Sep
**Journey length** 300–1,250 miles

**White-winged Triller**
*Lalage sueurii*
**Wn** 10–11 in **Wt** 1–1¼ oz
**Breeds** Throughout Australia except central desert, Sep to Jan/Feb
**Winters** New Guinea & Indonesia, Feb/Mar to Aug
**Journey length** 600–2,175 miles

**Flame Robin** *Petroica phoenicea*
**Wn** 8–9 in **Wt** ½ oz
**Breeds** E Australia from SE Queensland S to Victoria & Tasmania, Sep to Jan
**Winters** At lower altitudes & W into drier regions, Feb to Aug
**Journey length** 60–300 miles

**Australian Reed Warbler**
*Acrocephalus australis*
**Wn** 8–9 in **Wt** ¾–1 oz
**Breeds** S Australia, except drier areas, & Tasmania, Sep to Jan
**Winters** N & NE Australia, Feb to Aug
**Journey length** 300–900 miles

**Rufous Songlark**
*Cinclorhamphus mathewsi*
**Wn** 7–9 in **Wt** ¾–1 oz
**Breeds** Throughout Australia except extreme N; resident in N of range, Aug to Feb
**Winters** N & NE Australia, Mar to Jul
**Journey length** 300–900 miles

**White-throated Gerygone**
*Gerygone olivacea*
**Wn** 6–8 in **Wt** ¼–½ oz
**Breeds** N, E & SE Australia, Aug to Jan
**Winters** N Australia & New Guinea, Feb to Jul/Aug
**Journey length** 125–900 miles

**Black-faced Monarch**
*Monarcha melanopsis*
**Wn** 9–11 in **Wt** 1–1¼ oz
**Breeds** E Australia from NE Queensland to Victoria; probably resident in N, Nov to Jan
**Winters** N Australia & New Guinea, Feb to Oct
**Journey length** 300–1,250 miles

**Satin Flycatcher**
*Myiagra cyanoleuca*
**Wn** 9–11 in **Wt** 1–1¼ oz
**Breeds** E & SE Australia & Tasmania; probably resident in N, Nov to Jan
**Winters** E Australia, Feb to Oct
**Journey length** 125–1,100 miles

**Rufous Fantail** *Rhipidura rufifrons*
**Wn** 8–9 in **Wt** ½–¾ oz
**Breeds** New Guinea, Pacific & Indonesian islands, N, E & SE Australia & Tasmania; resident in N, Nov to Jan
**Winters** New Guinea, Pacific & Indonesian islands, N & E Australia, Feb to Oct
**Journey length** 300–900 miles

**Yellow-faced Honeyeater**
*Meliphaga chrysops*
**Wn** 7–8 in **Wt** ½ oz
**Breeds** E & SE Australia & Tasmania; resident in N of range, Jul to Jan
**Winters** E Australia, Feb to Jun
**Journey length** 125–900 miles

**Eastern Spinebill**
*Acanthorhynchus tenuirostris*
**Wn** 6–7 in **Wt** ½ oz
**Breeds** E, SE Australia & Tasmania; resident in N of range, Aug to Jan
**Winters** E Australia, Feb to Jul
**Journey length** 125–900 miles

## MIGRATORY SEA BIRDS

**King Penguin**
*Aptenodytes patagonicus*
**Wt** 19 lb 13 oz–33 lb 1 oz
**Breeds** Falklands, S Georgia, islands in S Ocean, Sep/Nov to Sep/Oct; breeds twice every 3 years
**Winters** At sea, Sep to Sep
**Journey length** 250–600 miles

**Gentoo Penguin** *Pygoscelis papua*
**Wt** 4 lb 7 oz–6 lb 10 oz
**Breeds** Antarctic Peninsula & islands in S Ocean; sedentary around latter, Jun/Nov (varies with colony) to Apr
**Winters** At sea, Apr to Jun/Nov
**Journey length** 300–1,500 miles

**Little Penguin** *Eudyptula minor*
**Wt** 2 lb–2 lb 7 oz
**Breeds** S Australia, NZ & neighboring islands; timing variable, breeding recorded in all months
**Winters** At sea: mainly sedentary, timing variable
**Journey length** 0–155 miles

**Galapagos Penguin**
*Spheniscus mendiculus*
**Wt** 2 lb 3 oz–3 lb 5 oz
**Breeds** Galápagos Islands, year-round
**Winters** Seas around breeding area, year-round
**Journey length** 0–60 miles

**Royal Albatross**
*Diomedea epomophora*
**Wn** 120–138 in **Wt** 19 lb 13 oz–21 lb
**Breeds** NZ, Campbell, Auckland & Chatham islands, Oct every other year
**Winters** S Pacific between Australia & S America; also in S Atlantic & off S Africa, perhaps circumpolar year-round
**Journey length** 3,750–9,300 miles

**Buller's Albatross** *Diomedea bulleri*
**Wn** 80–83 in **Wt** 5 lb 5 oz–6 lb 13 oz
**Breeds** Islands off NZ, Oct/Jan to Jul/Oct
**Winters** S Pacific as far as W coast of S America, Jul to Oct/Jan
**Journey length** 600–7,500 miles

**Black-footed Albatross**
*Diomedea nigripes*
**Wn** 75–83 in **Wt** 6 lb 10 oz–7 lb 15 oz
**Breeds** Hawaiian Islands & islands off SE Japan, Nov to Jul
**Winters** N Pacific, Jul to Nov
**Journey length** 600–6,000 miles

**Laysan Albatross**
*Diomedea immutabilis*
**Wn** 76–79 in **Wt** 5 lb 1 oz–6 lb 3 oz
**Breeds** Hawaiian Islands & islands off SE Japan & W Mexico, Nov to Jul
**Winters** N Pacific, Jul to Nov
**Journey length** 600–4,350 miles

**Shy Albatross** *Diomedea cauta*
**Wn** 86–100 in **Wt** 7 lb 8 oz–9 lb 11 oz
**Breeds** Islands off NZ, Tasmania & Crozet Island, Sep to Jul
**Winters** At sea between S Africa, Australia & W S America, Jul to Sep
**Journey length** 1,250–7,500 miles

**Yellow-nosed Albatross**
*Diomedea chlororhynchus*
**Wn** 78–100 in **Wt** 5 lb 8 oz–6 lb 7 oz
**Breeds** Tristan da Cunha, Gough Island & islands in S Ocean, Aug/Sep to Jul
**Winters** At sea between E S America, S Africa & Australia, Jul to Aug/Sep
**Journey length** 600–7,500 miles

**Gray-headed Albatross**
*Diomedea chrysostoma*
**Wn** 70–86 in **Wt** 6 lb 10 oz–8 lb 4 oz
**Breeds** Circumpolar on islands in S Ocean, Oct to Aug every other year
**Winters** Circumpolar at sea, Aug to Oct in year following breeding
**Journey length** 1,250–9,300 miles

**Sooty Albatross**
*Phoebetria fusca*
**Wn** 78–80 in **Wt** 5 lb 5 oz–5 lb 15 oz
**Breeds** Islands in S Atlantic & Indian oceans, Jul/Aug to May/Jun every other year
**Winters** At sea between E S America, S Africa & Australia, May/Jun to Jul/Aug in year following breeding
**Journey length** 1,250–7,500 miles

**Light-mantled Sooty Albatross**
*Phoebetria palpebrata*
**Wn** 72–85 in **Wt** 6 lb 3 oz–6 lb 13 oz
**Breeds** Circumpolar on islands in S Ocean, Sep/Oct to Jul every other year
**Winters** Circumpolar at sea, Jul to Sep in year following breeding
**Journey length** 1,250–9,300 miles

**Northern Giant Petrel**
*Macronectes halli*
**Wn** 70–78 in **Wt** 8 lb 6 oz–11 lb
**Breeds** Circumpolar on islands in S Ocean, Aug to Mar/Apr
**Winters** Circumpolar at sea, Mar/Apr to Aug
**Journey length** 600–9,300 miles

**Southern Fulmar**
*Fulmarus glacialoides*
**Wn** 44–47 in **Wt** 1 lb 10 oz–1 lb 14 oz
**Breeds** Antarctica & adjacent islands, Nov to Mar
**Winters** Circumpolar at sea around N & S Australian & S American coasts, Mar to Nov
**Journey length** 600–3,400 miles

**Antarctic Petrel**
*Thalassoica antarctica*
**Wn** 39–40 in **Wt** 1 lb 2 oz–1 lb 11 oz
**Breeds** Antarctica, Nov to Jun
**Winters** S Ocean N to Antarctic Convergence, Jul to Oct
**Journey length** 600–1,500 miles

**Cape Petrel** *Daption capense*
**Wn** 31–35 in **Wt** 12 oz–1 lb 1 oz
**Breeds** Antarctic & subantarctic islands & islands off NZ, Nov to Mar
**Winters** Circumpolar at sea as far N as equator in Pacific, Mar to Nov
**Journey length** 600–5,000 miles

**Great-winged Petrel**
*Pterodroma macroptera*
**Wn** 37–39 in **Wt** 1 lb–1 lb 10 oz
**Breeds** Subantarctic islands, SE Australia & N Island, NZ, Apr to Sep
**Winters** S Ocean N to subtropics of Atlantic, Indian & Pacific oceans, Oct to Mar
**Journey length** 600–2,800 miles

**White-headed Petrel**
*Pterodroma lessonii*
**Wn** 42–43 in **Wt** 1 lb 4 oz–1 lb 13 oz
**Breeds** Islands off NZ & in S Indian Ocean, Oct to Mar
**Winters** Circumpolar at sea, Mar to Oct
**Journey length** 600–6,000 miles

**Black-capped Petrel**
*Pterodroma hasitata*
**Wn** 35–39 in **Wt** 14 oz–1 lb 5 oz
**Breeds** W Indies, Dec to Jun
**Winters** Tropical & subtropical Caribbean & Atlantic, Jul to Nov
**Journey length** 600–1,500 miles

**Atlantic Petrel** *Pterodroma incerta*
**Wn** 40–41 in **Wt** 1 lb 2 oz–1 lb 9 oz
**Breeds** Tristan da Cunha & Gough Islands, Mar to Oct
**Winters** S Atlantic between S Africa & S America, Oct to Mar
**Journey length** 600–2,800 miles

**Mottled Petrel**
*Pterodroma inexpectata*
**Wn** 29–32 in **Wt** 9–16 oz
**Breeds** S Island, Stewart & Snares islands, NZ, Oct to Mar
**Winters** Bering Sea & Gulf of Alaska, Apr to Aug
**Journey length** 3,000–8,000 miles

**Solander's Petrel**
*Pterodroma solandri*
**Wn** 37–41 in **Wt** 1 lb–1 lb 3 oz
**Breeds** Lord Howe & Philip islands off E Australia, Mar to Aug
**Winters** NW Pacific, Sep to Feb
**Journey length** 3,000–5,600 miles

**Kerguelen Petrel**
*Pterodroma brevirostris*
**Wn** 31–32 in **Wt** 12–13 oz
**Breeds** Tristan da Cunha & islands in S Indian Ocean, Aug to Mar
**Winters** Circumpolar at sea, Mar to Jul
**Journey length** 3,000–7,500 miles

**Kermadec Petrel**
*Pterodroma neglecta*
**Wn** 35–37 in **Wt** 1 lb 2 oz
**Breeds** Islands in S Pacific, year-round depending on locality
**Winters** S Pacific & S N Pacific, year-round
**Journey length** 1,250–3,750 miles

**Juan Fernandez Petrel**
*Pterodroma (externa) externa*
**Wn** 37–38 in **Wt** 1 lb–1 lb 3 oz
**Breeds** Juan Fernandez Islands, Oct to Jun **Winters** N into S & central N Pacific, Jun to Oct
**Journey length** 2,500–4,700 miles

**White-necked Petrel**
*Pterodroma (externa) cervicalis*
**Wn** 37–41 in **Wt** 13 oz–1 lb 3 oz
**Breeds** Kermadec Islands N of NZ, Oct to Mar
**Winters** NW Pacific N to Japan, Mar to Sep
**Journey length** 3,000–5,300 miles

**Cook's Petrel** *Pterodroma cookii*
**Wn** 25–25 in **Wt** 6–7 oz
**Breeds** Islands off NZ, Oct to Mar
**Winters** N Pacific N to Aleutian Islands, Mar to Oct
**Journey length** 3,000–6,500 miles

**Mas a Tierra Petrel**
*Pterodroma (cooki) defilippiana*
**Wn** 25–26 in **Wt** 6–7 oz
**Breeds** Juan Fernandez Islands, Jul to Feb **Winters** W Pacific N to W C America, Mar to Jun
**Journey length** 1,250–2,500 miles

**Black-winged Petrel**
*Pterodroma nigripennis*
**Wn** 24–27 in **Wt** 5–7 oz
**Breeds** Islands off NZ & E Australia, Nov to Apr
**Winters** W Pacific N to Hawaiian Islands, Apr to Oct
**Journey length** 2,800–5,900 miles

**Stejneger's Petrel**
*Pterodroma longirostris*
**Wn** 20–25 in **Wt** 5–6 oz
**Breeds** Juan Fernandez Islands, Nov to Apr **Winters** S N Pacific N to Japan & perhaps California, Jun to Nov
**Journey length** 4,350–6,000 miles

**Blue Petrel** *Halobaena caerulea*
**Wn** 22–27 in **Wt** 6–8 oz
**Breeds** Subantarctic islands, Sep to Mar
**Winters** S Ocean N to subtropical waters off S America, Apr to Aug
**Journey length** 1,850–5,600 miles

**Salvin's Prion** *Pachyptila salvini*
**Wn** 22 in **Wt** 6 oz
**Breeds** Amsterdam, St. Paul, Crozet & Prince Edward islands, S Indian Ocean, Oct to Mar
**Winters** S Ocean N to S Africa & Australia, Mar to Sep
**Journey length** 600–4,350 miles

**Antarctic Prion** *Pachyptila desolata*
**Wn** 22–25 in **Wt** 5–6 oz
**Breeds** Subantarctic & S Indian Ocean islands & islands off NZ, Nov to Apr
**Winters** S Ocean N to subtropical waters off S America & S Africa, Apr to Oct
**Journey length** 600–3,400 miles

**Slender-billed Prion**
*Pachyptila belcheri*
**Wn** 21–22 in **Wt** 5 oz
**Breeds** Falkland, Crozet & Kerguelen islands, Oct to Apr **Winters** S Ocean, N to 15°S off S America & to S Africa & Australia, Apr to Sep
**Journey length** 1,500–4,700 miles

**Black Petrel** *Procellaria parkinsoni*
**Wn** 43–47 in **Wt** 1 lb 8 oz–1 lb 9 oz
**Breeds** Islands off Japan, Korea & E China, Mar to Oct; islands off N Island, NZ, Nov to May
**Winters** N breeders W Pacific S to N & E Australia, Oct to Feb; S breeders W coasts of C & S America, Jun to Oct
**Journey length** 3,750–6,800 miles

**Bulwer's Petrel** *Bulweria bulwerii*
**Wn** 26–28 in **Wt** 3–5 oz
**Breeds** Islands in E N Atlantic & in N Pacific from E China to Hawaii, Apr to Sep
**Winters** Subtropical & tropical Atlantic, Pacific & Indian oceans, Oct to Mar
**Journey length** 3,000–5,000 miles

**Gray Petrel** *Procellaria cinerea*
**Wn** 45–51 in **Wt** 2 lb–2 lb 11 oz
**Breeds** Islands in S Atlantic, S Indian Ocean & off NZ, Feb to Jul
**Winters** S Ocean N to equator in E Pacific, Aug to Jan
**Journey length** 1,500–5,600 miles

**White-chinned Petrel**
*Procellaria aequinoctialis*
**Wn** 52–57 in **Wt** 2 lb 4 oz–3 lb 2 oz
**Breeds** S Ocean islands, Oct to Apr
**Winters** S Ocean N to equator in E Pacific, May to Sep
**Journey length** 1,500–5,600 miles

**Streaked Shearwater**
*Calonectris leucomelas*
**Wn** 47–48 in **Wt** 1 lb–1 lb 3 oz
**Breeds** Islands of Japan S to E China & Korea, Mar to Sep
**Winters** W Pacific S to N & E Australia, Oct to Feb
**Journey length** 3,750–5,300 miles

**Cory's Shearwater**
*Calonectris diomedea*
**Wn** 39–49 in **Wt** 1 lb 4 oz–2 lb 2 oz
**Breeds** Mediterranean islands, Berlengas, Azores, Canary & Cape Verde islands, Apr to Oct
**Winters** Atlantic W to Gulf of Mexico, S Atlantic coasts of S America & Africa & S Indian Ocean, Nov to Mar
**Journey length** 2,500–6,000 miles

**Pink-footed Shearwater**
*Puffinus creatopus*
**Wn** 42–43 in **Wt** 1 lb 9 oz–1 lb 12 oz
**Breeds** Juan Fernandez Islands & islands off W S America, Nov to Apr
**Winters** E N Pacific N to Alaska, Apr to Oct
**Journey length** 3,750–6,800 miles

**Flesh-footed Shearwater**
*Puffinus carneipes*
**Wn** 38–42 in **Wt** 1 lb 4 oz–1 lb 11 oz
**Breeds** Islands in S Indian Ocean & off Australia & NZ, Sep to Mar
**Winters** Indian Ocean & W N Pacific N to Bering Sea, Mar to Sep
**Journey length** 3,750–8,800 miles

**Greater Shearwater** *Puffinus gravis*
**Wn** 39–46 in **Wt** 1 lb 9 oz–2 lb 2 oz
**Breeds** Tristan da Cunha group, Gough Island & Falklands, Oct to Apr
**Winters** N Atlantic N to Greenland, Iceland & Norway, May to Oct
**Journey length** 4,350–9,000 miles

**Buller's Shearwater** *Puffinus bulleri*
**Wn** 37–38 in **Wt** 12–15 oz
**Breeds** Islands off N Island, NZ, Oct to Apr **Winters** N Pacific N to Bering Sea, Apr to Sep
**Journey length** 4,350–8,700 miles

**Sooty Shearwater** *Puffinus griseus*
**Wn** 37–42 in **Wt** 1 lb 7 oz–2 lb 2 oz
**Breeds** S Chile & Falkland Islands, islands off S Australia & NZ, Oct to Apr/May
**Winters** N Pacific & N Atlantic N to subarctic waters, May to Sep
**Journey length** 6,000–8,400 miles

**Hutton's Shearwater** *Puffinus huttoni*
**Wn** 28–35 in **Wt** 12–13 oz
**Breeds** S Island, NZ, Sep to Apr
**Winters** Coasts of E, S & W Australia, May to Aug
**Journey length** 1,500–4,700 miles

**Fluttering Shearwater**
*Puffinus gavia*
**Wn** 29–30 in **Wt** 8–15 oz
**Breeds** Islands off N Island, NZ, Sep to Jan
**Winters** Seas off SE Australia, Feb to Aug
**Journey length** 1,850–2,500 miles

**Black-bellied Storm-Petrel**
*Fregetta tropica*
**Wn** 17–18 in **Wt** 2–2¼ oz
**Breeds** Circumpolar S Ocean islands, Nov to Apr
**Winters** S Ocean N to Indian Ocean & to equator in Atlantic & Pacific, May to Oct
**Journey length** 3,000–5,300 miles

**Swinhoe's Storm-Petrel**
*Oceanodroma monorhis*
**Wn** 17–18 in **Wt** 1¼–1½ oz
**Breeds** Japan, China & Korea, Apr to Sep
**Winters** N Indian Ocean & Arabian Sea, Oct to Mar
**Journey length** 5,000–8,000 miles

**Leach's Storm-Petrel**
*Oceanodroma leucorhoa*
**Wn** 17–18 in **Wt** 1¼–1½ oz
**Breeds** Islands in N Pacific S to Mexico & in N N Atlantic, May to Sep
**Winters** Equatorial Pacific Ocean & S Atlantic, Oct to Apr
**Journey length** 3,000–5,600 miles

**Black Storm-Petrel**
*Oceanodroma melania*
**Wn** 18–20 in **Wt** 1½–1¾ oz
**Breeds** Islands in Gulf of California, May to Sep
**Winters** E Pacific S to N S America, Oct to Apr
**Journey length** 600–2,800 miles

**Matsudaira's Storm-Petrel**
*Oceanodroma matsudairae*
**Wn** 21–22 in **Wt** 2 oz
**Breeds** Kazan-retto (Volcano Islands) SE of Japan, Jan to Jun
**Winters** Indian Ocean, Jul to Dec
**Journey length** 4,350–6,000 miles

**South Polar Skua**
*Catharacta maccormickii*
**Wn** 51–55 in **Wt** 2 lb 10 oz–3 lb 8 oz
**Breeds** Antarctica, Oct to Apr
**Winters** N Pacific & E Atlantic, May to Sep
**Journey length** 3,000–9,300 miles

**White-cheeked Tern** *Sterna repressa*
**Wn** 22–25 in **Wt** 4–5 oz
**Breeds** NZ & neighboring islands, Sep to Jan
**Winters** S & E Australia, Feb to Aug
**Journey length** 600–1,500 miles

**Cayenne Tern** *Sterna eurygnatha*
**Wn** 37–39 in **Wt** 7–10 oz
**Breeds** Coasts of Venezuela S to N Brazil, Mar to Sep
**Winters** Coasts of S America S to Argentina, Oct to Feb
**Journey length** 1,250–3,750 miles

# CATALOG
# OF SPECIES

There are about 9,300 bird species recorded worldwide. This wonderfully varied class of animals includes birds that live in habitats from the polar ice caps to the tropical rain forest. It encompasses birds that fly, that swim or that are confined to the ground. This comprehensive catalog of nearly 1,000 species describes birds from every family of living birds to represent the astonishing diversity of bird life on this planet. The scientific classification of bird species – as with that all of living things – helps us to understand their origins, evolution and relationship to other species. For this reason the information in this section is presented according to order, family and genus. This means that similar birds can be compared with their near relatives. The text describes the physical characteristics of each featured species as well as giving information about its habitat, diet, and breeding habits. Both common and Latin names are used. Where relevant, threats to the survival of the species are outlined.

*A colony of white ibis (Eudocimus albus) congregate in trees in Florida USA. These sociable birds build nests from twigs and sticks.*

# OSTRICH, RHEAS, CASSOWARIES, EMU, KIWIS, TINAMOUS

♂ race *massaicus* "Masai Ostrich"

OSTRICH

♂

race *molybdophanes* "Somali Ostrich"

juv

race *massaicus* ♀ with eggs and chick

♀

♂ turning eggs

EMU

GREATER RHEA

DWARF CASSOWARY

chick

DOUBLE-WATTLED CASSOWARY

ANDEAN TINAMOU

GREAT TINAMOU

LITTLE TINAMOU

BROWN KIWI

LITTLE SPOTTED KIWI

THICKET TINAMOU

eggs

ELEGANT CRESTED TINAMOU

# OSTRICH, RHEAS, CASSOWARIES, EMU, KIWIS, TINAMOUS

## FAMILY STRUTHIONIDAE
### Ostrich
There is only one species in this family.

### 1/ OSTRICH
*Struthio camelus*
RANGE: **Africa: formerly widespread throughout and into Middle East; now fragmented, with main populations in W and E Africa and South Africa**
HABITAT: **dry savanna**
SIZE: **$78\frac{3}{4}$–$98\frac{1}{2}$ in (200–250 cm) high to top of head**

Both the numbers and range of the world's largest and heaviest bird have been reduced dramatically in the last 100 years by hunting and habitat destruction. Today the Ostrich survives chiefly in the protected game parks of East Africa. There are 4 races: of the 2 illustrated here, the Masai Ostrich *S. c. massaicus* occurs in southern Kenya and Tanzania, while the Somali Ostrich *S. c. molybdophanes* occurs mainly in the Horn of Africa.

Adapted to survive in dry and seasonal conditions, the Ostrich can withstand a 25 percent loss in body weight through dehydration. With its strong legs and toes, it can run swiftly over open terrain, compensating for its inability to fly.

The taller male chooses a breeding site and 3 or more females may mate with him, each laying her clutch of 2–11 creamy white eggs in a communal nest that is a mere scrape on the ground. In all, 10–40 or more (record is 78) eggs are laid but no more than 19–25 can be incubated. Incubation takes 42 days, the dominant female sitting on the eggs during the daytime and the male taking his turn at night. Chicks leave the nest soon after hatching.

## FAMILY RHEIDAE
### Rheas
Large flightless birds. Powerful legs. Plumage gray or brown, with some white. Sexes similar. Nest in scrapes on ground. Eggs 10–50, golden-yellow, fading to off-white in Greater Rhea, green in Lesser Rhea. Incubation 35–40 days, chicks leave nest soon after hatching. 2 species.

### 2/ GREATER RHEA
*Rhea americana*
RANGE: **S Brazil to Patagonia**
HABITAT: **grassland**
SIZE: **$51\frac{1}{4}$ in (130 cm) high to top of head**

The range of this, the largest bird in the Americas, has contracted enormously in recent years because of hunting and the spread of agriculture. Its stronghold is the Argentinian pampas, where flocks of more than 100 birds may still be found during the dry winters.

During the spring, the males become solitary and much more aggressive, fighting to win harems of 2–15 females. Each successful male constructs a nest scrape, about 3 ft (1 m) in diameter, in which the females lay their eggs. The male assumes sole responsibility for incubation, taking just an hour's feeding and watering break each midday. All the eggs in the clutch tend to hatch on the same day, and the male continues to cover his brood for warmth during the cold nights.

## FAMILY DROMAIIDAE
### Emu
There is only one species in this family.

### 3/ EMU
*Dromaius novaehollandiae*
RANGE: **Australia**
HABITAT: **open and semiarid bush**
SIZE: **71 in (180 cm ) high to top of head**

Second only to the Ostrich in size, the Emu is unique among all birds in the form of its feathering, with 2 quills of equal size sprouting from each growing point. Though it feeds on coarse grasses, it prefers succulent plants and also eats fruit, flowers, seeds and insects. It is a nomadic species, some individuals ranging as far as 620 mls (1,000 km) in a single year as they follow the pattern of rainfall. Males feed intensively in the fall, building up large reserves of body fat for the breeding season. Each mates with 1–3 females, and a total of 8–20 blue-green eggs are laid in the nest depression. The male incubates these for 56 days. Chicks leave the nest when 2–7 days old, but the male must care for them for up to 18 months before they are fully independent.

The Emu is the only large flightless species that has maintained much of its former range. It may even have become more numerous with the spread of farmland—it learned to exploit grain crops to such effect that the Australian army was enlisted to shoot the birds in the "Emu Wars" of 1932. Despite the slaughter of many birds, the Emus won.

## FAMILY CASUARIIDAE
### Cassowaries
Large, flightless. Powerful legs. Plumage black. Blue and red skin on head and neck. Prominent horny "casque" on the top of the head, which may help clear the way through dense vegetation. Sexes similar. Nest on ground. Eggs 4–8, pale to dark green. Incubation 50 days, chicks leave nest soon after hatching. 3 species.

### 4/ DOUBLE-WATTLED CASSOWARY
*Casuarius casuarius*
RANGE: **New Guinea, N Australia**
HABITAT: **moist forest**
SIZE: **63 in (160 cm) high to top of head**

Formerly common and widespread in New Guinea, the Double-wattled Cassowary is now rare due to hunting pressure and the destruction of its forest habitat. It is solitary for much of the year, wandering large territories in search of fallen fruit, insects and small vertebrates on the forest floor. It makes contact with other individuals only when breeding.

Courtship is initiated by the male, as he circles the considerably larger and brighter female, uttering booming notes from his inflated throat pouch. After laying her eggs, the female departs. In the next few weeks she will wander through the territories of several successive males, mating with each one and laying batches of eggs in each of their nests. The males incubate the eggs and care for the young alone.

### 5/ DWARF CASSOWARY
*Casuarius bennetti*
RANGE: **New Guinea, New Britain**
HABITAT: **forest up to 10,000 ft (3,000 m)**
SIZE: **$43\frac{1}{4}$ in (110 cm) high to top of head**

The Dwarf Cassowary, or Moruk, is widely regarded as the world's most dangerous bird. Prior to nesting, the females may become exceedingly aggressive, attacking any nearby creature by slashing with a lethally sharp, enlarged claw, 4 in (10 cm) in length. Such attacks have been known to cause fatal injuries among the New Guinea highlanders.

This species ranges higher than the other cassowaries, reaching bushy mountainous terrain, where it can pluck fruit from shrubs and heathy plants. The horny head casque may be used to turn over leaf litter to reveal food.

## FAMILY APTERYGIDAE
### Kiwis

Flightless ground-dwellers. Long, downcurved bill, rounded body. Acute sense of smell; nostrils at tip of long bill rather than at base as in other birds. Plumage brown or gray, hairlike. Sexes similar, though females larger. Nest on ground. Eggs 1–2, white. Incubation 65–85 days, chicks leave nest within 7 days of hatching. 3 species.

## 6/ BROWN KIWI
### Apteryx australis
RANGE: **New Zealand**
HABITAT: **native forest, pine plantations**
SIZE: **27½ in (70 cm)**

The Brown Kiwi is widespread in New Zealand, although it has disappeared due to human settlement and forest destruction in many parts of its range. Flightless and nocturnal, it spends most of its time in dense undergrowth. It has no visible wings or tail but it has strong, stout legs for running. Its plumage of coarse body feathers gives the bird a shabby appearance but protects it when moving through dense, thorny thickets.

Kiwis were once thought to subsist primarily on earthworms. Recent studies of their stomach contents have shown that they have a much more catholic diet including beetles, cicadas, grubs, spiders, pond-life and fallen berries. They can detect items of food under several inches of soil, using the nostrils at the tip of the long bill.

## 7/ LITTLE SPOTTED KIWI
### Apteryx owenii       ?
RANGE: **South Island of New Zealand**
HABITAT: **dry, open forest, woodland, meadows**
SIZE: **19¾ in (50 cm)**

This, the smallest of the kiwis, is the most furtive and shy of the 3 species, although it was the most familiar to the early aboriginal settlers of New Zealand. It has suffered since that time, partly because the Maoris slaughtered thousands of the birds to make ceremonial feather cloaks, but also because they were killed for their meat. After the arrival of European settlers, the introduction of cats, rats and pigs accelerated their decline, causing them to disappear entirely from North Island.

Relative to its body size, the Little Spotted Kiwi lays the largest egg of any bird. The egg is 4–5 times heavier than those of other, similar-sized birds, and the female requires a 24-day laying cycle to produce it. The yolk makes up over 60 percent of the weight of the egg (twice as much as in a normal egg), and the young take a lengthy 70 days to hatch. The chicks can feed themselves within a week of hatching.

## FAMILY TINAMIDAE
### Tinamous

Plump body, short tail. Flight clumsy. Plumage mainly brown or gray with bars, streaks and spots. Coloration bolder in females. Ground-nesters. Eggs 1–12, glossy, variable in color, including green, yellow, blue and nearly black. Incubation by male for 16–20 days, chicks leave nest soon after hatching. 46 species.

## 8/ GREAT TINAMOU
### Tinamus major
RANGE: **SE Mexico to E Bolivia and Brazil**
HABITAT: **tropical and subtropical rain forest**
SIZE: **17¾ in (45 cm)**

The Great Tinamou dwells deep in the rain forests of Central and South America, preferring areas where there is a distinct layer of understory vegetation beneath the forest canopy. It is heard much more often than it is seen, uttering a long trill that rises and then declines in pitch. Like all tinamous, it spends most of its time on the ground but, if disturbed, it will burst from the floor with a loud roar of wings and fly a short distance through the forest.

In Brazil it nests during May and June, the male clearing a slight depression in the forest floor, where the female lays her glossy violet eggs. It is likely that the female lays more than one clutch, each with a different male, but detailed information on their breeding habits is lacking. Many tinamous have highly prized flesh, and this species is avidly hunted both by indigenous forest people and by settlers. The birds are also threatened by the exploitation and destruction of their habitat.

## 9/ LITTLE TINAMOU
### Crypturellus soui
RANGE: **S Mexico to E Bolivia and SC Brazil**
HABITAT: **scrubby forest edge, secondary forest, overgrown clearings**
SIZE: **9½ in (24 cm)**

The classification of this widespread species is extremely complicated, involving at least 14 races with no clear division from one form to the next. It may be quite common in some areas, although its timidity and small size cause it to be easily overlooked. Only its tremulous whistled call – one of the most haunting sounds of the American tropical forests – yields any clue as to its presence.

The Little Tinamou nests in June and July, laying 2 eggs the color of terracotta clay. These are incubated by the male alone. Outside the breeding season, the birds often gather in small foraging parties. Unlike many species (though like the Thicket Tinamou), its flesh is not highly regarded, and hunting seems to impose few risks on its future.

## 10/ THICKET TINAMOU
### Crypturellus cinnamomeus
RANGE: **Mexico, Costa Rica, Colombia, Venezuela**
HABITAT: **semiarid regions in scrubby woodland and forest edge**
SIZE: **12 in (30 cm)**

Though the Thicket Tinamou can fly nimbly with a rapid, quail-like flutter, it prefers to hide rather than escape from danger, remaining absolutely motionless on the forest floor. It often occurs in areas where people have disturbed the natural vegetation, and it feeds on small insects, berries and other items of vegetation that it finds on the ground. The bird's song consists of a mournful and pure trio of fluty whistles, the second higher in pitch than the others. It is a frequent sound during the early morning and the late evening.

The Thicket Tinamou is a solitary bird for much of the year, keeping within a small home range. The breeding season is from March to July, when the females each lay 3–7 lustrous purple eggs. The newly hatched young are soon able to find their own food and become independent after approximately 20 days, when they are still only half-grown.

## 11/ ANDEAN TINAMOU
### Nothoprocta pentlandii
RANGE: **Andes from S Ecuador to N Chile and N Argentina**
HABITAT: **puna meadows above 10,000 ft (3,000 m)**
SIZE: **11 in (28 cm)**

There are some 7 races of this small tinamou along the spine of the Andes Mountains. They are typical inhabitants of the short-grass meadows of the puna zone, habitats that can become mercilessly cold at night. In the southern part of the species' range in Chile, the birds frequently enter the terraced alfalfa fields of the Aymara Indians.

The Andean Tinamou's mellow whistles are easy to hear but, with its cryptic coloration, alert senses and rather shy disposition, it is extremely difficult to spot. When disturbed, it will fly off strongly with intermittent wing beats, rather like a partridge or grouse, and if pressed will fly distances of several hundred yards. The male incubates the glossy, chocolate-colored eggs alone and cares for the young after hatching.

## 12/ ELEGANT CRESTED TINAMOU
### Eudromia elegans
RANGE: **Argentina, Paraguay, Bolivia, N Chile**
HABITAT: **arid and semiarid steppe, scrub and woodland**
SIZE: **15¾ in (40 cm)**

Named for its long, forward-curving black crest, this species is widespread across southern South America. It occupies a variety of open habitats up to about 11,500 ft (3,500 m) in altitude. Unusually among the tinamous, it has only 3 toes on each foot, lacking the short, backward-pointing fourth toe. This adaptation may allow it to run more efficiently across the open terrain.

Elegant Crested Tinamous are fairly gregarious. Up to 100 adults may gather in a single flock, although smaller groups are the norm. Like many other tinamous, they are fond of "dustbathing," rubbing their feathers vigorously in the dry earth. This may help keep their plumage in good condition, including ridding it of parasites.

The classification of the genus *Eudromia* is still under debate but there appear to be 2 distinct, although closely related, species. The second species is the more northerly Quebracho Crested Tinamou *E. formosa*.

fully grown chick

KING PENGUIN

GENTOO PENGUIN

juv

young chick

EMPEROR PENGUIN

juv

FJORDLAND
CRESTED PENGUIN

well-grown chick

ADÉLIE PENGUIN

CHINSTRAP PENGUIN

ROCKHOPPER
PENGUIN

ROYAL PENGUIN

MACARONI PENGUIN

YELLOW-EYED PENGUIN

LITTLE PENGUIN

juv

juv

JACKASS PENGUIN

HUMBOLDT PENGUIN

chick in
nesting burrow

MAGELLANIC PENGUIN

juv

GALAPAGOS PENGUIN

# PENGUINS

## FAMILY SPHENISCIDAE
### Penguins
Medium to large flightless marine birds; wings modified to form flat paddles. Plumage blue-black or blue-gray above, white below. Sexes similar. Eggs 1–2, whitish. Incubation 33–62 days. Chicks remain with parents, or in nurseries without them, for up to 10 weeks, or over 13 months in King Penguin. 18 species.

## 1/ KING PENGUIN
*Aptenodytes patagonicus*
RANGE: **subantarctic, Falkland Islands**
HABITAT: **oceanic; breeds on coasts**
SIZE: **37½ in (95 cm)**

The King Penguin has a most unusual breeding cycle, for each pair raises only 2 chicks every 3 years. In the first year the single egg is laid in November (early summer in the Southern Hemisphere) and incubated by both parents alternately until it hatches after 55 days. By June the chick has reached 80 percent of its adult weight. The parents virtually stop feeding it in winter and it has to survive until spring on very little food, banded together with other chicks in nurseries to resist the cold. Regular feeding starts again in September and the chick fledges 2–3 months later, ready to spend the summer hunting at sea.

Meanwhile, the parent birds have to molt, and cannot lay again until February (late summer). By winter the chicks are still very small and many die during the next few months. Those that survive fledge the following January. Parents following this timetable cannot breed again until the following summer. In some colonies it seems that most adults breed only once every 2 years.

## 2/ EMPEROR PENGUIN
*Aptenodytes forsteri*
RANGE: **Antarctic**
HABITAT: **oceanic; breeds on pack ice**
SIZE: **45¼ in (115 cm)**

Standing some 110 cm (43 in) high to the top of its head, the Emperor is the largest of the penguins. It also has the most southerly distribution, for it breeds around the Antarctic coasts in huge colonies on the sea ice that surrounds the continent in winter. It is rarely seen north of the ice.

Each pair produces an egg in May or June (early winter). The female then goes to sea to feed, leaving the male to incubate the egg on his feet beneath a fold of skin for some 60 days, during which time temperatures plummet to as low as −75°F (−60°C). His body warmth is vital to the unhatched chick, so the male cannot leave the egg for a moment and cannot feed. During his 110-day fast, which begins during courtship, the male loses 45 percent of his initial body weight. He survives the intense winter cold and blizzards by huddling together with the other brooding males.

The female returns at about the time of hatching and feeds the chick, freeing the male to make a long journey across the ice to feed in open water. Later, the chicks gather into nurseries, freeing both parents to go to sea to gather food. The chicks make their way to the sea in midsummer before it becomes frozen over.

## 3/ GENTOO PENGUIN
*Pygoscelis papua*
RANGE: **Antarctic, subantarctic, S South America**
HABITAT: **oceanic; breeds on coasts**
SIZE: **31¾ in (81 cm)**

Gentoo Penguins found in the northern parts of their range tend to be more sedentary, often remaining at their colonies throughout the year, while those that breed on the Antarctic continent disappear from the land for the winter.

The breeding colonies are small and are often sited on headlands or behind beaches. Breeding starts as the snow clears in spring: the 2 eggs are laid in a saucer of vegetation and pebbles and are incubated by both parents. About a month after hatching, the chicks gather into nurseries, while the parents make short daily trips to gather food. Krill is a very important part of the diet, and breeding fails in years when the krill do not appear close to the shore.

## 4/ ADÉLIE PENGUIN
*Pygoscelis adeliae*
RANGE: **Antarctic**
HABITAT: **oceanic; breeds on rocky coasts**
SIZE: **28 in (71 cm)**

The most southerly of the penguins, apart from the Emperor, the Adélie nests in large colonies on islands and headlands around much of the Antarctic coast. Suitable breeding sites are limited by the availability of ground that becomes bare of snow in summer, near water that becomes free of ice; the breeding adults must have ready access to open water to provide food for their chicks. Experienced breeders return to the same sites year after year and usually to the same mates. The Antarctic summer is very short, so they have little time to breed. The eggs are laid in late November (midsummer) and incubated first by the male and then by the female for a total of 35 days. After 3–4 weeks in the nest, the dark, woolly chicks band together in nurseries while the adults gather food. In another 4 weeks the chicks are fledged, going to sea in February (late summer) when they are only three-fourths of the adult weight.

## 5/ CHINSTRAP PENGUIN
*Pygoscelis antarctica*
RANGE: **Antarctic**
HABITAT: **oceanic; breeds on rocky coasts**
SIZE: **26¾ in (68 cm)**

The most numerous penguin, with several million in the South American sector of the Antarctic alone, the population of the Chinstrap, or Bearded, Penguin seems to be increasing because of the extra food made available by the great reduction in numbers of krill-eating whales as a result of the whaling industry.

Chinstraps are the most aggressive of Antarctic penguins and, where they breed alongside Gentoos or Adélies, male Chinstraps may attack their larger neighbors and oust them from their nests. Generally, though, they prefer better drained sites, often nesting on sloping, rocky ground that the other 2 species avoid. They lay later than the others and, unusually, the female takes the first shift of incubation, so she must fast for up to 30 days as well as expending energy in producing the 2 eggs.

## 6/ FJORDLAND CRESTED PENGUIN
*Eudyptes pachyrhynchus*
RANGE: **New Zealand, on SW of South Island (Fjordland) and Stewart Island**
HABITAT: **rocky shores; breeds in coastal forest or small caves**
SIZE: **28 in (71 cm)**

Also known as the Victoria Penguin, the Fjordland Crested Penguin is a relatively rare species, with a population in the region of 5,000 birds. It feeds on squid, krill and fish.

It usually nests in small groups, beneath rocky overhangs or in dense vegetation, and defends its territory with harsh cries. As with other crested penguins, the female lays 2 eggs, but the second egg is considerably larger than the first. Both eggs hatch, but only one chick is reared – usually from the second egg. The smaller first egg appears to be an insurance against the second being infertile; when both hatch, the larger chick monopolizes the food supply and the other starves and dies.

## 7/ ROCKHOPPER PENGUIN
*Eudyptes chrysocome*
RANGE: subantarctic islands, S South
America
HABITAT: oceanic; breeds on island cliffs
SIZE: $21\frac{1}{2}$ in (55 cm)

The Rockhopper is the smallest of the polar penguins, and one of the most quarrelsome. It is named for its skill at scaling steep rock faces to reach its clifftop nest sites. Instead of waddling along like most penguins, it hops from boulder to boulder with its feet together, head thrust forward and flippers held back. The birds generally come ashore at a particular landing place, move onto special drying areas to dry and preen their feathers, then ascend to the colony along customary, well-worn paths. Rockhopper Penguins in the northern part of the range lay their eggs earlier than those in the south, the timing being related to the ocean temperature.

## 8/ ROYAL PENGUIN
*Eudyptes schlegeli*
RANGE: Macquarie Island, S of New
Zealand
HABITAT: oceanic; breeds on coasts
SIZE: 30 in (76 cm)

The Royal Penguin may be only a race or a color phase of the Macaroni Penguin; it differs from that species in its larger size, stouter bill and the gray and white sides to its face, chin and throat. Royal Penguins are generally thought to be restricted to Macquarie Island, but birds with features characteristic of the species have been seen with Macaroni Penguins at other southern ocean island breeding colonies. Intermediates between Royal and Macaroni Penguins have turned up at Macquarie Island and at Marion Island, in the southern Indian Ocean. Although well known by early explorers and sealers, the Royal Penguin was not described scientifically until 1876.

As with other species of penguin, Royal Penguins were killed for the oil that could be gained by boiling their bodies. Between 1894 and 1914 some 150,000 birds were taken every season, although this does not seem to have had major long-term effects on the population. Today, there is probably a total population of over 1 million on Macquarie Island, and the largest single colony contains up to half a million birds and covers more than 15 acres (6 hectares) of coastal terraces.

## 9/ MACARONI PENGUIN
*Eudyptes chrysolophus*
RANGE: subantarctic, South America
HABITAT: oceanic; breeds on coasts
SIZE: $27\frac{1}{2}$ in (70 cm)

The Macaroni Penguin is typical of the crested penguins, with long, slender yellow plumes flowing back on each side of its head and a large, deeply sculptured bill. It moves on land by hopping, a remarkably efficient technique that enables it to climb rapidly from sea level up to its nesting colonies, which are usually located on steep terrain such as scree slopes and glacial moraines. These colonies can be immense: one on South Georgia numbers some 5 million pairs.

Like the Rockhopper Penguin, the Macaroni

Penguin is unusual in that, although 2 eggs are laid, the first is much smaller than the second and either fails to hatch or produces a weak chick that soon dies. The 36-day incubation is carried out in 2 long shifts, 1 by each parent, during which each loses up to 30 percent of its body weight. After breeding, the parents spend 2 weeks fattening up on krill caught on long offshore foraging trips before molting.

## 10/ YELLOW-EYED PENGUIN
*Megadyptes antipodes*                     [?]
RANGE: New Zealand, on SE South Island,
Stewart, Auckland and Campbell islands
HABITAT: inshore waters; breeds in scrub
or low forest
SIZE: 30 in (76 cm)

This large penguin with its bright yellow eye is one of the rarest of all penguins, partly because agricultural land reclamation has destroyed its breeding habitat in several areas. However, the population may also be limited as a result of the birds' unusual nesting habits, for the pairs breed in isolation.

Yellow-eyed Penguins feed mainly on fish and squid, coming ashore every night to roost on sandy beaches. Each bird is a resident of a particular area and they form strong, long-lasting pair-bonds.

## 11/ LITTLE PENGUIN
*Eudyptula minor*
RANGE: New Zealand, Chatham Island, S
Australia, Tasmania
HABITAT: inshore; roosts and breeds on
coast
SIZE: $15\frac{3}{4}$ in (40 cm)

The Little Penguin (also called the Little Blue, or Fairy, Penguin) is the smallest of the penguins. It lives on cool temperate coasts, feeding mainly on fish in shallow inshore waters. The bird spends each night ashore, favoring rocky beaches.

Little Penguins are monogamous and they generally return to the same mate each year. They will also return to the same nest site – in a cave, burrow, or beneath vegetation, often some distance inland. The pair may breed in isolation or as part of a colony, but among individual populations breeding times are well synchronized. Two broods can be raised in a season.

## 12/ JACKASS PENGUIN
*Spheniscus demersus*                     [S]
RANGE: coasts of S Africa
HABITAT: cool coastal oceans; breeds on
coast
SIZE: $27\frac{1}{2}$ in (70 cm)

There were once a million or more Jackass Penguins, but the population has dropped to 150,000 in the last 20 years. The birds were badly affected by the oil pollution that first hit their breeding and feeding areas in 1967, when the Suez Canal was closed and oil tankers were diverted around southern Africa. Today they are under threat from increased commercial fishing for the pilchards that once made up half their diet.

Although it feeds in the cool Benguela Current,

the Jackass Penguin breeds on dry land under the hot African sun. It avoids overheating by nesting in burrows or under rocks, and by being active on land only at night.

## 13/ HUMBOLDT PENGUIN
*Spheniscus humboldti*                     [?]
RANGE: coastal Peru and Chile to 40° S
HABITAT: shores, offshore islands and
offshore waters
SIZE: $26\frac{3}{4}$ in (68 cm)

Penguins are all cold-adapted birds but some species occur in tropical areas where the water is cooled by cold currents sweeping up from Antarctica. The Humboldt, or Peruvian, Penguin is one of these, occurring on coasts washed by the cold Humboldt Current. It feeds largely on fish such as anchovies, cooperating to herd them into compact shoals which can be preyed on at will.

At one time the Humboldt Penguin nested in burrows excavated in deep guano (accumulated, dried bird droppings) on offshore islands, but since the removal of much of the guano they have nested in caves on the shoreline. They nest at any time of year and new eggs, hatchlings and large chicks may appear side by side in a cave.

## 14/ MAGELLANIC PENGUIN
*Spheniscus magellanicus*
RANGE: S coast of South America from
Chile to Brazil
HABITAT: coasts and offshore islands
SIZE: $27\frac{1}{2}$ in (70 cm)

Magellanic Penguins are noisy birds when ashore, producing a loud, staccato braying which is answered by neighboring birds, building up until the whole colony is in uproar. They use their feet to dig holes in grassy slopes or beneath forest trees, often high above the water. The holes are big enough to accommodate both adults, which retire to them at night.

The adult penguins prey mainly on fish and cuttlefish, returning to their burrows and feeding their brood by regurgitation. Groups of older chicks often leave the burrows and congregate on the beach, where they are more conveniently fed by their parents. At the end of the breeding season they migrate to more northerly waters.

## 15/ GALAPAGOS PENGUIN
*Spheniscus mendiculus*
RANGE: Galapagos Islands
HABITAT: coasts and offshore waters
SIZE: $19\frac{1}{2}$ in (50 cm)

Like the Humboldt Penguin, the Galapagos Penguin owes its distribution to the cold Humboldt Current, which flows up the west coast of South America to the Galapagos island group, a volcanic archipelago astride the Equator.

It feeds on small fish, often in the company of boobies, terns and shearwaters. Between sorties, the birds rest on sandy shores and rocky beaches. The birds generally nest in small groups on sheltered coasts and, since soft soil for burrowing is rare on the islands, the 2 eggs are generally laid in caves or holes in the volcanic rock.

# LOONS, GREBES

non-breeding

RED-THROATED LOON

ARCTIC LOON

non-breeding

race *viridigularis*

COMMON LOON

non-breeding

non-breeding

YELLOW-BILLED LOON

LITTLE GREBE

non-breeding

PIED-BILLED GREBE

non-breeding

ATITLAN GREBE

non-breeding

SHORT-WINGED GREBE

non-breeding

GREAT CRESTED GREBE

non-breeding

HOARY-HEADED GREBE

non-breeding

HORNED GREBE

CLARK'S GREBE

HOODED GREBE

WESTERN GREBE

# LOONS, GREBES

## FAMILY GAVIIDAE
### Divers

Large diving waterbirds. Breeding plumage white below, variable above but always with vertical white stripes on neck; winter plumage grayish, paler above than below. Sexes similar. Nest in mound of vegetation. Eggs usually 2, dark brown to olive, spotted or blotched in black. Incubation 24–29 days. Chicks leave nest within 1 day of hatching but are brooded on parents' backs or under a wing for warmth and protection. 4 species.

## 1/ RED-THROATED LOON
*Gavia stellata*

RANGE: circumpolar Arctic S to temperate latitudes
HABITAT: breeds on freshwater lakes and pools; winters mainly on coastal waters
SIZE: $20\frac{3}{4}$–27 in (53–69 cm)

The Red-throated Loon is a slender, graceful bird, with a slightly upturned bill and a rusty-red throat patch. Unlike other members of its family, which require a long run across the water to become airborne, the Red-throated Loon can take off easily from small bodies of water. This allows it to nest beside pools only 33 ft (10 m) across in its breeding grounds on the Arctic tundra and on temperate moorland. Such pools seldom contain enough fish and the birds fly several miles to larger lakes or to the ocean to obtain food for their young.

The female usually lays 2 eggs and they are incubated by both parents for about 28 days. After hatching, competition between the young for the food brought by the parents frequently leads to the death of the weaker chick.

## 2/ ARCTIC LOON
*Gavia arctica*

RANGE: circumpolar Arctic and N temperate latitudes; winters to S
HABITAT: breeds on large, deep lakes; winters on coastal waters
SIZE: $22\frac{3}{4}$–$28\frac{3}{4}$ in (58–73 cm)

In its handsome breeding plumage, the Arctic Loon has a glossy black throat patch that shimmers with color in strong sunlight. In the Siberian race *G. a. viridigularis,* the throat patch has a green sheen, while the northern European race *G. a. arctica,* which is illustrated, and the race *G. a. pacifica* from North America and coastal northeast Siberia, both have a purple gloss to the throat. However, some ornithologists consider the latter to be a separate species entirely, named the Pacific Loon, *G. pacifica.*

Arctic Loons prefer to breed alongside large lakes, where they find most of their food, though they will fly up to 7 mls (10 km) to other waters if necessary. When feeding, they dive for about 45 seconds, probably reaching depths of 10–20 ft (3–6 m). They occasionally use their wings under water to assist their webbed feet.

The nest is a low mound of aquatic vegetation next to the water. The normal clutch is 2 and incubation lasts for about 28 days. Fledging takes another 12–13 weeks, by which time the young birds are beginning to catch their own fish.

## 3/ COMMON LOON
*Gavia immer*

RANGE: N North America, Greenland and Iceland; winters to S
HABITAT: breeds on large, deep lakes; winters on coastal waters
SIZE: 27–$35\frac{3}{4}$ in (69–91 cm)

With its greater size, thick neck and strong spear-shaped bill, the Common Loon is a much heavier bird than the Red-throated and Arctic loons. In the breeding season, its upperparts are patterned all over with bold white barring, and 2 white necklaces mark its black head and neck. Its calls, used to advertise and defend the breeding territory, are among the loudest of any bird and consist of a variety of yodeling, howling and wailing cries that can carry for long distances across the water. At their most intense, these sound like manic laughter.

It has been suggested that "loon," came originally from the old Norse name *lomr. Lomr* may mean to moan, in which case it refers to the birds' wailing calls, but some sources suggest it means lame or clumsy and refers to the birds' awkward gait on land. A loon's feet are set far back on its body, so it usually humps itself along on its breast and belly. It builds its nest close to the water's edge so that it has the minimum distance to move on land.

## 4/ YELLOW-BILLED LOON
*Gavia adamsii*

RANGE: circumpolar high Arctic
HABITAT: breeds beside freshwater pools and rivers; winters on coastal waters
SIZE: 30–$35\frac{3}{4}$ in (76–91 cm)

The Yellow-billed Loon is the largest of the 4 species. It is very similar in plumage at all times of the year to the Common Loon, though in summer the white pattern on the upperparts is more bold and the slightly upturned bill is a conspicuous pale cream.

The Yellow-billed Loon's habit of nesting at the edge of running water is unique among the divers and appears to occur only in the Russian part of the bird's range; such behavior has not been

recorded in North America. It is essential that the river is not subject to dramatic fluctuations in level, which could either flood the nest or leave it stranded so far from the water that the parents would have great difficulty shuffling across land to reach their young.

## FAMILY PODICIPEDIDAE
### Grebes

Medium to large diving waterbirds. Usually brown or gray underparts, whitish beneath; head, throat and neck often brightly colored in breeding season. Sexes similar. Nest on floating decaying vegetation. Eggs 2–6, white or cream. Incubation 20–30 days. Chicks leave nest soon after hatching but are brooded on parents' backs or go to a nursery nest for warmth and protection. 20 species.

## 5/ LITTLE GREBE
*Tachybaptus ruficollis*

RANGE: S Eurasia, Africa and Indonesia; northerly breeders migrate S for winter
HABITAT: shallow fresh water; winter habitat includes sheltered estuaries and coastal waters
SIZE: $9\frac{3}{4}$–$11\frac{1}{2}$ in (25–29 cm)

The Little Grebe is a dumpy, short-necked waterbird lacking any kind of a tail and with a short, slightly upturned bill. During the breeding season, this species becomes much more vocal than most other grebes, uttering a distinctive and penetrating trill. A bird attempting to chase a rival from its territory will call vigorously, rush low over the water at its opponent and indulge in violent splashing and diving. During courtship, both sexes will often trill together in duet. The birds' nest is a floating platform of waterweed anchored to vegetation or sometimes to a bush growing in the water. The 4–6 eggs are incubated by both sexes for about 20 days.

## 6/ PIED-BILLED GREBE
*Podilymbus podiceps*

RANGE: **S South America N to S Canada**
HABITAT: **shallow standing or slow-moving fresh water**
SIZE: **12¼–15 in (31–38 cm)**

The short, stocky body of the Pied-billed Grebe contrasts markedly with the bird's large head and prominent bill. The bill is not unlike a chicken's, nearly half as deep as it is long. It is whitish in color with a black band at the midpoint, making it the most conspicuous feature on this otherwise rather dull dark gray-brown bird.

Many Pied-billed Grebes are sedentary, spending summer and winter on the same stretch of water. They sometimes form loose flocks in winter but break up into breeding pairs and establish territories in the spring. In the northern parts of the range, the lakes and pools freeze over in winter. Birds that breed there either migrate south to find suitable winter quarters or move to brackish, ice-free lagoons on the coast.

## 7/ ATITLAN GREBE
*Podilymbus gigas*   X

RANGE: **confined to Lake Atitlan, Guatemala**
HABITAT: **reedy margins of a large lake**
SIZE: **18¾ in (48 cm)**

The Atitlan Grebe is a close relative of the Pied-billed Grebe, though it is half as large again in size. Its wings are very short and the bird is practically flightless. The species' home, Lake Atitlan, lies at an altitude of over 6,000 ft (nearly 2,000 m) in the Guatemalan highlands.

Since it is confined to this single body of water, the Atitlan Grebe is vulnerable to any adverse changes that may occur in the lake. It has probably never been very numerous, but its numbers dropped dramatically after the introduction into the lake of alien fish that competed for food with the grebes and preyed on their chicks. In 1965 there were only 80 grebes left. Later the population started to recover, but subsequent destruction of the reedbeds around the lake, pollution and a drop in water level prompted numbers to fall again. Since the 1970s, the population has steadily declined and the bird is now apparently extinct.

## 8/ SHORT-WINGED GREBE
*Rollandia micropterum*

RANGE: **confined to Lakes Titicaca, Umayo and Poopo in Peru and Bolivia**
HABITAT: **large mountain lakes**
SIZE: **11 in (28 cm)**

Like other grebes of Central and South American lakes, the Short-winged Grebe is incapable of flight. It lives on a series of lakes 10,000 ft (over 3,000 m) high in the central Andes. At such altitudes the nights are bitterly cold. Like a number of other small grebes, it therefore indulges in "sun-basking" to offset the loss of heat from its body.

Early in the morning, and again in the late afternoon, Short-winged Grebes rest on the water, with their backs to the sun. They raise their wings slightly and lift the feathers on their backs and sides to allow the sunshine to penetrate to the skin. By soaking up warmth in this way, they reduce the amount of energy they need from their food just to keep warm.

## 9/ HOARY-HEADED GREBE
*Podiceps poliocephalus*

RANGE: **W and SE Australia and New Zealand**
HABITAT: **large open waters, including swamps, lakes and estuaries**
SIZE: **9¾–11½ in (25–29 cm)**

The Hoary-headed Grebe takes its name from the fine white streaking running from front to back across its brown forehead and cheeks. It is a short, stubby bird, lacking all but a rudimentary tail. Unlike most other grebes, the species is highly colonial when breeding. Colonies can consist of several hundred pairs with each nest only 3 ft (1 m) apart from the next. This species also differs from most other grebes in that it rarely calls. With no territory to defend, there is little need for loud cries or trills.

Hoary-headed Grebes site their nests in vegetation in shallow water. As with other Australian waterbirds, nesting takes place when floods appear after heavy rain; the timing of breeding can therefore differ from one year to the next.

## 10/ GREAT CRESTED GREBE
*Podiceps cristatus*

RANGE: **temperate Eurasia, E and South Africa, Australia and New Zealand**
HABITAT: **shallow, standing or slow-moving fresh water with emergent vegetation; moves to estuaries and coastal lagoons in winter**
SIZE: **18–20 in (46–51 cm)**

The Great Crested Grebe is renowned for its elaborate courtship rituals. Both sexes have a double black head crest and chestnut and black tippets (ear ruffs) and, during courtship, they erect these feathers, which gives their heads a markedly triangular outline. The pair indulge in a "weed-dance," during which pieces of waterweed are held in the bill as the 2 birds come together, breast to breast, and rear up out of the water, swinging their heads from side to side. The dance is both elegant and stately.

Like other grebes, the Great Crested Grebe feeds on fish, insects, crustaceans and mollusks. When the young hatch, the parents feed them small fish and also a supply of small feathers. Adults, too, will regularly swallow feathers molted from their belly and flanks. It is believed that the feathers bind material together in the gut, helping the birds regurgitate waste pellets. Regular regurgitation probably helps to clear the gut of harmful parasites.

## 11/ HORNED GREBE
*Podiceps auritus*

RANGE: **circumpolar N North America and Eurasia**
HABITAT: **breeds on both small and large waters; winters on large lakes and sheltered coasts**
SIZE: **12¼–15 in (31–38 cm)**

The courtship behavior of the Horned Grebe, like that of the Great Crested Grebe, is dramatic and elaborate. To enhance their appearance, the birds erect the golden-chestnut crests running back and upward from each eye and the black tippets, or ear ruffs, under their eyes.

In one ritual, however, the display feathers are smoothed down as one bird rears up out of the water and bends its head and neck downward. As it does so, it bears a striking resemblance to a penguin and this particular display has been called the "ghostly penguin dance."

Horned Grebes gather a pile of aquatic vegetation for their nest. Sometimes they anchor the pile to plants in the water, but often it rests on a small rock at or just below the water level.

## 12/ HOODED GREBE
*Podiceps gallardoi*   R

RANGE: **S Patagonia**
HABITAT: **large freshwater lakes**
SIZE: **14 in (36 cm)**

The Hooded Grebe was recognized as a new species only in 1974 and was at first believed to be confined to a single lake in Santa Cruz province, southwest Argentina. Subsequent investigations have revealed that it is widely, but thinly, distributed over a considerable area, inhabiting a number of large, basaltic lakes scattered throughout the region. The population of Hooded Grebes is quite small, though not as tiny as was once thought. Two estimates made in 1986 put the number at 3,000–5,000 individuals.

## 13/ WESTERN GREBE, CLARK'S GREBE
*Aechmophorus occidentalis, A. clarkii*

RANGE: **W North America, from S Canada to Mexico**
HABITAT: **breeds on freshwater lakes; winters mainly on the ocean**
SIZE: **22–29 in (56–74 cm)**

Until recently, Clark's Grebe (also known as the Mexican Grebe) was considered a race of the Western Grebe but it is now regarded as a separate species. The birds share the same general range and habitat, although Clark's Grebe is much less common to the north. Hybrids between the 2 species are occasionally reported.

Western Grebes perform a series of elaborate courtship rituals. During their "rushing" ceremony, for example, male and female rise up out of the water together. Holding themselves erect, with only their legs under the surface, they rush along side by side for about 22–33 yd (20–30 m) before sinking back into the water.

Western Grebes are fairly gregarious, with several birds breeding on the same water. Flocks of many hundreds or even thousands gather at migration stopovers and in the wintering areas.

# ALBATROSSES, SHEARWATERS AND PETRELS, STORM-PETRELS, DIVING-PETRELS

juv

adult + egg at nest

WAVED ALBATROSS

adult feeding
chick at nest

BLACK-BROWED ALBATROSS

WANDERING ALBATROSS

juv

white phase

SOOTY ALBATROSS

imm

SOUTHERN GIANT PETREL

at nest

NORTHERN FULMAR

PINTADO PETREL

BROAD-BILLED PRION

CAHOW
at nest burrow

SHORT-TAILED SHEARWATER

MANX SHEARWATER

CORY'S SHEARWATER

race *mauretanicus*
"Balearic Shearwater"

LEACH'S STORM-PETREL

WILSON'S STORM-PETREL

COMMON DIVING-PETREL

LITTLE SHEARWATER

# ALBATROSSES, SHEARWATERS AND PETRELS, STORM-PETRELS, DIVING-PETRELS

## FAMILY DIOMEDEIDAE
**Albatrosses**

Large, open ocean birds. Long, narrow wings and long, hooked bill. White with dark upperparts, wing tips, brow or tail; 2 species all dark. Sexes similar. Nest usually on pile of soil and vegetation. 1 egg, white. Incubation 65–79 days, chicks remain in nest 4–12 months. 14 species.

## 1/ WANDERING ALBATROSS
*Diomedea exulans*

RANGE: **S oceans, N of 60° S; breeds on several islands across S oceans**
HABITAT: **oceanic**
SIZE: **42–53 in (107–135 cm)**

Together with the Royal Albatross *D. epomophora* and the Amsterdam Island Albatross *D. amsterdamensis*, this species is one of the "great albatrosses." These 3 are the largest of all seabirds and have the greatest wingspans of any bird species, with a spread of 8–11 ft (2.5–3.3 m). The birds spend most of their time out over the open ocean, soaring with the help of the thermal currents, sometimes covering up to 300 mls (500 km) a day. It lands on the ocean only in calm weather or to feed on squid, fish and food refuse from ships. It comes to land on subantarctic islands only to nest and rear its young.

Wandering Albatrosses are slow-breeding but long-lived, with an average lifespan of 30 years. Although capable of breeding when 3–4 years old, they do not start doing so until they are 7–8. Since incubation takes 11 weeks, and fledging 40 weeks, breeding is possible only in alternate years.

## 2/ WAVED ALBATROSS
*Diomedea irrorata*

RANGE: **SE Pacific Ocean; breeds on Hood Island, (Galapagos) and Isla de la Plata (W of Ecuador)**
HABITAT: **waters of Humboldt Current**
SIZE: **33–37 in (84–94 cm)**

This exclusively tropical albatross numbers some 6,000–12,000 individuals. It feeds on fish, squid and other invertebrates. Its long, narrow wings make it an efficient glider but give it poor braking power and a high stalling speed. This makes land arrivals and departures difficult, especially on its nesting islands which are strewn with boulders and cacti. Successful breeding is preceded by an elaborate courtship dance called the "ecstatic ritual." Calls noted during courtship include *ha-ha-ha* noises and a drawn out *whoo-oo*.

## 3/ BLACK-BROWED ALBATROSS
*Diomedea melanophris*

RANGE: **S oceans, from 65° to 10° S; breeds on several islands across S oceans**
HABITAT: **oceanic**
SIZE: **32½–36½ in (83–93 cm)**

One of the most numerous of the albatrosses, this species nests alongside the similar Gray-headed Albatross *D. chrysostoma*, often gathering in great colonies. The nest is a barrel-shaped pile of mud and grass, about 24 in (60 cm) high. The male arrives at the colony a week before the female, who stays for 1 day for mating, goes to sea for

another 10 days and finally returns 2 days before laying. The species' main food is krill, which may explain why it can nest every year, while the Gray-headed Albatross, which feeds on nutritionally poor squid, breeds only in alternate years.

## 4/ SOOTY ALBATROSS
*Phoebetria fusca*

RANGE: **Atlantic and Indian oceans; breeds on several islands in this region**
HABITAT: **oceanic**
SIZE: **33–35 in (84–89 cm)**

The Sooty Albatross and its close relative, the Light-mantled Sooty Albatross *P. palpebrata*, differ from other members of their family in their proportionally longer, narrower wings and tapering tail and more solitary nesting habits. Their flight is graceful and agile and their displays include synchronized flights up and down in front of the colony by courting and established pairs. They breed on cliffs or at sites inland where there is sufficient slope in front of the nests to enable them to take off easily. They start breeding when they are 11–13 years old, after a 3–4 year courtship, and young are reared only in alternate years.

## FAMILY PROCELLARIIDAE
**Shearwaters and petrels**

Small, medium or large short-tailed, slender-winged, open ocean birds. Plumage usually black, gray or brown, with white. Sexes similar. Nest in burrows or crevices; sometimes on ledges or open ground. Eggs 1, white. Incubation 43–60 days, chicks remain in nest 2–5 months. 72 species.

## 5/ SOUTHERN GIANT PETREL
*Macronectes giganteus*

RANGE: **S oceans, N to 10° S; breeds on various islands and on Antarctic coasts**
HABITAT: **oceanic**
SIZE: **33¾–39 in (86–99 cm)**

Popularly called Stinkers because of their rank smell and their habit of feeding on carrion, the 2 species of giant petrel (the other is the Northern

Giant Petrel *M. halli*) were separated only recently on the basis of slight physical but marked ecological differences. The largest of the petrels, these birds rival some of the albatrosses in size. They are agile on land and feed on land as well as at sea. They use their massive bills to rip into the flesh of dead animals such as seals and whales.

The nest is a low saucer of pebbles or soil and vegetation. Both sitting adults and nestlings defend themselves with the common petrel habit of spitting oil. The white phase of this species is spread through the breeding population, accounting for 15 percent of birds in places.

## 6/ NORTHERN FULMAR
*Fulmarus glacialis*

RANGE: **North Pacific and Atlantic oceans**
HABITAT: **oceanic; breeds on coasts**
SIZE: **17¾–19½ in (45–50 cm)**

The Northern Fulmar has grown in numbers over the last 100 years, either because of the increased quantities of offal discarded first by whalers and now by fishing boats, or through changes in ocean water temperatures. St Kilda once had the only colony in the British Isles, but colonies are now found on all cliff coasts and the total British and Irish population is now over 350,000 pairs.

The nests are sited on sea cliffs but sometimes farther inland on cliffs, walls and buildings. The birds visit the sites for most of the year, performing soaring displays and uttering cackling calls. Of the 2 plumage forms, the pale phase is the more numerous in the Arctic, the dark phase at lower latitudes, although the detailed picture is complex and a range of intermediates also occurs.

## 7/ PINTADO PETREL
*Daption capense*

RANGE: **S oceans and W coast of South America; breeds on islands in S oceans**
HABITAT: **oceanic**
SIZE: **15¾–16 in (38–40 cm)**

A regular follower of ships, this petrel, also known as the Cape Petrel or Cape Pigeon, gathers in large flocks where surface currents cause a concentration of krill and other crustaceans. Pintado Petrels breed in colonies on cliff faces, making pebble nests on open ledges. The males clear snow from the ledges and guard the sites, while the females spend 2–3 weeks feeding at sea, returning 1 day before laying.

## 8/ CAHOW
*Pterodroma cahow*                                    E

RANGE: **nonbreeding range unknown; breeds on 5 small islets off E Bermuda**
HABITAT: **open seas; breeds on rocky islets**
SIZE: **16 in (41 cm)**

Before the arrival of settlers, hundreds of thousands of Cahows may have bred in Bermuda. Hunters, domestic animals and accompanying rats soon forced the birds from the mainland onto rocky islets. Even there, they declined through competition for nest sites with tropicbirds, predation by rats and poisoning by DDT. Their numbers are now extremely low. The Cahow takes its name from its eerie mating call, heard in late autumn. The birds used to dig burrows on their former nesting grounds, but now lay their single egg in a rocky burrow formed by water erosion. An alternative name is Bermuda Petrel.

## 9/ BROAD-BILLED PRION
*Pachyptila vittata*

RANGE: **S oceans; breeds on various islands in S oceans, also on coasts of South Island (New Zealand)**
HABITAT: **oceanic**
SIZE: **9¾–11¾ in (25–30 cm)**

The shape of the bill, with its wide base, gives the Broad-billed Prion an almost froglike appearance. The edges of the bill are fringed with comblike plates that act as filters in the same manner as the baleen plates of whales. The bird scoops a mouthful of water and squeezes it back out through the plates, leaving the prey behind. Pinhead-sized crustaceans called copepods provide most of its food. The Broad-billed Prion breeds in colonies in summer. It usually visits its nest at night, to avoid predation by marauding skuas.

## 10/ CORY'S SHEARWATER
*Calonectris diomedea*

RANGE: **breeds Mediterranean and Atlantic islands; winters E coast North America, S to Uruguay and into W Indian Ocean**
HABITAT: **warm seas**
SIZE: **18–20¾ in (46–53 cm)**

Cory's Shearwaters take most of their food from the water's surface, eating fish, squid and other crustaceans. They sometimes gather in such huge concentrations on the ocean that they have been mistaken for land.

The birds breed on uninhabited islands, where their colonies are so dense that the nest-burrows are almost touching. The incubation period for the single egg is about 54 days, and the young fledge 14 weeks later. Young and, latterly, adults and eggs have been cropped for food on the Selvagens and other island groups, and they have even been "farmed" by the provision of artificial burrows.

## 11/ SHORT-TAILED SHEARWATER
*Puffinus tenuirostris*

RANGE: **breeds S Australia, Tasmania; migrates to N Pacific after breeding**
HABITAT: **coasts and offshore waters in breeding season; open ocean otherwise**
SIZE: **16–17 in (41–43 cm)**

This species lives in flocks, diving from the ocean surface or from the air 3 ft or more beneath the waves to catch krill and sometimes small squid and fish. At times, the ocean may become churned white with plunging birds. They nest in burrows under tussocks in vast colonies. The chicks are deserted by the parents in late April or early May (or at 13 weeks old) and swim out to sea.

This species is known in Australia as the Muttonbird because of its tasty flesh. Some fat nestlings are still killed, for their meat and for their oily stomach contents which are used in pharmaceuticals. The harvest is strictly controlled and poses no threat to the species' survival.

## 12/ MANX SHEARWATER
*Puffinus puffinus*

RANGE: **breeds N Atlantic and Mediterranean islands; migrates S as far as South America after breeding**
HABITAT: **offshore oceans above continental shelf**
SIZE: **11¾–15 in (30–38 cm)**

The contrast between the dark upperparts and light underparts of the Manx Shearwater is much less distinct in the browner Balearic Shearwater *P. p. mauretanicus*, a race which breeds in the western Mediterranean.

Manx Shearwaters nest in colonies, usually on isolated islands. They arrive at the colonies as early as February and choose mainly the darkest nights to visit their burrows as a defence against attacks from Great Black-backed Gulls *Larus marinus*. The pairs call to one another with a variety of loud, raucous screams and howls. The chicks fledge at 70 days, but are deserted by their parents 1–2 weeks earlier.

## 13/ LITTLE SHEARWATER
*Puffinus assimilis*

RANGE: **N and S Atlantic, S Pacific and Indian oceans; breeds on Atlantic islands and the Antipodes Islands**
HABITAT: **coastal waters**
SIZE: **9¾–11¾ in (25–30 cm)**

Unlike most shearwaters, Little Shearwaters do not gather in large groups on the ocean but are solitary. These birds occupy the nest area for up to 4 months before the eggs are laid, defending the site against other shearwaters. This is probably because they nest in crevices, which are in short supply, instead of digging their own burrows.

## FAMILY HYDROBATIDAE
### Storm-petrels

Small, open ocean birds. Plumage black, or black and brown with white rump feathers. Sexes similar. Nest in crevices and burrows. Eggs 1, white, may be speckled. Incubation 40–50 days, chicks remain in nest 2–2½ months. 20 species.

## 14/ WILSON'S STORM-PETREL
*Oceanites oceanicus*

RANGE: **breeds from Tierra del Fuego and the Falkland Islands to the coasts of Antarctica; migrates to N Indian Ocean and N Atlantic Ocean after breeding season**
HABITAT: **oceanic**
SIZE: **6–7½ in (15–19 cm)**

Arguably the most abundant seabird in the world, Wilson's Storm-Petrel regularly gathers in large flocks to feed and follows in the wake of ships. This small bird's diet consists largely of crustaceans, which it catches by plucking them from the surface, pattering its feet on the water to "anchor" itself against the breeze. The egg, laid in a burrow, is one-quarter of the adult's weight. At its peak, the nestling reaches twice the adult weight; it fledges at 1½ times the adult weight.

## 15/ LEACH'S STORM-PETREL
*Oceanodroma leucorhoa*

RANGE: **breeds from Japan NE to Alaska, then S to Mexico; winters S to C Pacific and S Atlantic**
HABITAT: **oceanic**
SIZE: **7½–8½ in (19–22 cm)**

This species feeds mainly on crustaceans, fish and squid, although it also follows whales and seals to feed on their feces. Generally solitary at sea, it breeds in colonies under banks and boulders. The concentration of birds flying around over the colony may become so dense that midair collisions take place. The bird excavates nest-burrows up to 6 ft (1.8 m) long, digging with its bill and feet. The birds return to their burrow at night and there is some evidence that they locate their individual tunnels by smell.

## FAMILY PELECANOIDIDAE
### Diving-petrels

Compact, small to medium, short-necked, auklike birds. Plumage black above, white below. Sexes similar. Nest in burrows. Eggs 1, white. Incubation 45–53 days, chicks remain in nest 1½–2 months. 4 species.

## 16/ COMMON DIVING-PETREL
*Pelecanoides urinatrix*

RANGE: **breeds on many S ocean islands, coasts of S Australia, Tasmania, New Zealand**
HABITAT: **oceanic**
SIZE: **7¾–9¾ in (20–25 cm)**

The diving-petrels of the southern oceans are, in some respects, the ecological counterpart of the smaller species of northern auks. Their wings are small, which gives them a whirring, auklike flight, and they use them to "fly" underwater. Diving-petrels are best known for their habit of flying into one side of a steep wave and out of the other.

The Common, or Subantarctic, Diving-Petrel is known in New Zealand by the Maori name of "Kuaka," which describes its call. It is especially vocal at night, when it moves to and from its nest burrows under the cover of darkness to avoid attacks by skuas.

# TROPICBIRDS, PELICANS, GANNETS AND BOOBIES

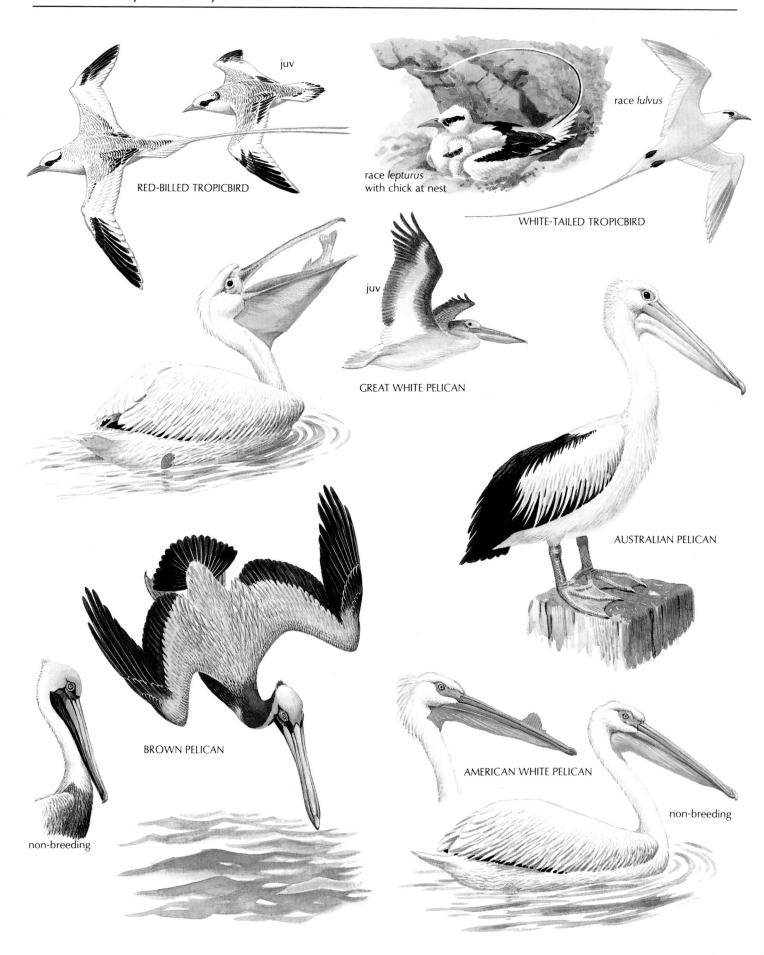

juv

RED-BILLED TROPICBIRD

race *lepturus*
with chick at nest

race *fulvus*

WHITE-TAILED TROPICBIRD

juv

GREAT WHITE PELICAN

AUSTRALIAN PELICAN

BROWN PELICAN

non-breeding

AMERICAN WHITE PELICAN

non-breeding

white phase

juv

white phase
Galapagos form

NORTHERN GANNET

brown phase

MASKED BOOBY

white-tailed
brown phase

RED-FOOTED BOOBY

juv

white-tailed and
white-headed brown phase

BROWN BOOBY

♂

race *brewsteri*

race *plotus*

juv

♂

♀ with chick at nest

PERUVIAN BOOBY

ABBOTT'S BOOBY

# TROPICBIRDS, PELICANS, GANNETS AND BOOBIES

## FAMILY PHAETHONTIDAE
### Tropicbirds

Elegant, highly aerial seabirds with 2 elongated central tail feathers, longer in the male; juveniles lack these. Plumage white, marked with black and sometimes tinged pink or gold. Bills stout and curved, serrated on the cutting edge to hold prey. Legs very short. Nest in holes or on bare ground. Eggs 1, blotched red-brown. Incubation 40–46 days. Chicks left alone at nest while parents forage; leave nest at 11–15 weeks. 3 species.

### 1/ RED-BILLED TROPICBIRD
*Phaethon aethereus*

RANGE: **tropical Atlantic, E Pacific, NW Indian oceans**
HABITAT: **open sea; breeds on islands**
SIZE: **$35\frac{1}{2}$–$39\frac{1}{2}$ in (90–100 cm)**

These attractive seabirds wander far over the tropical oceans, singly or in pairs. Although they dive into the ocean to catch fish and squid, they spend most of their time in flight and seldom land on the surface. Their narrow tail streamers are the same length as their bodies. These may help to stabilize the birds both underwater and when they are twisting through the air in pursuit of flying fish. Courtship takes place mainly in the air, with several birds screaming shrilly as they fly close together with rapid wing beats and make long glides with downward-curving streamers. Adults often bear scars on their heads and necks from fierce fights over mates and nest sites.

Breeding colonies on islands contain hundreds of pairs, the birds usually nesting on rock ledges or in crevices. They may lay in any month of the year. The single chick is fed on average twice every 3 days until it flies off alone 12–13 weeks after hatching.

### 2/ WHITE-TAILED TROPICBIRD
*Phaethon lepturus*

RANGE: **all tropical and subtropical oceans**
HABITAT: **open sea; breeds on islands**
SIZE: **28–$31\frac{1}{2}$ in (71–80 cm)**

The White-tailed Tropicbird has 13–16 in (33–40 cm) long tail streamers. It competes for nest sites with the larger Red-billed and Red-tailed Tropicbirds. Such competition may have forced the golden race *P. l. fulvus*, which breeds only on Christmas Island, to nest in tree holes in the dense jungle. Elsewhere, the species nests in crevices, beneath rocky overhangs or on the bare ground – as is the case with the other race illustrated, *P. l. lepturus*, which breeds on several islands in the Indian Ocean.

Both parents incubate the single egg, which hatches after about 40 days. The chick is ready to fly some 11 weeks later. White-tailed Tropicbirds do not have an annual breeding cycle. Instead, the average interval between successful egg-laying is about 40 weeks.

## FAMILY PELECANIDAE
### Pelicans

Large waterbirds, with long, straight bills and extensible throat pouches. Plumage usually gray or white. Sexes similar. Nest on the ground or in trees. Eggs 1–4, white. Chicks remain in nest for about 5 weeks (tree-nesting species) or 3 weeks (ground-nesters); chicks of ground-nesters then collect in nurseries, or "pods." Incubation 28–31 days. 7 species.

### 3/ GREAT WHITE PELICAN
*Pelecanus onocrotalus*

RANGE: **S Europe, Africa, Asia**
HABITAT: **lakes and inland seas**
SIZE: **55–69 in (140–175 cm)**

This large white pelican is intensely gregarious, roosting and resting in great flocks. It normally fishes in groups, forming a circle of birds which swim forward, periodically jerking their wings open and plunging their bills toward the center of the circle. In this way they "herd" schools of fish and scoop them up in their huge throat pouches. This pelican's daily food intake of about $2\frac{1}{2}$ lb (1.2 kg) may comprise either a few large fish or hundreds of small ones.

Adult birds develop a crest, a yellow patch on the foreneck and a pinkish bloom to the plumage during the breeding season. The males display in groups to attract receptive females. Mated pairs display further and the female selects a nest site. Breeding colonies of up to 30,000 pairs may occur, sometimes far from water.

### 4/ AUSTRALIAN PELICAN
*Pelecanus conspicillatus*

RANGE: **Australia and Tasmania**
HABITAT: **shallow marine and inland waters**
SIZE: **59–71 in (150–180 cm)**

The Australian Pelican is a highly sociable bird, feeding, roosting and nesting in large flocks. Adults have a short gray crest and a yellowish or pinkish throat pouch, which becomes scarlet during courtship. Males display communally,

with rituals that include swinging the head and clapping the mandibles of the bill together. After they have paired up, a male and female parade to the nest site.

They breed on small islands, often making their nests in bushes, and may lay their eggs at any time of the year. Two weeks after hatching, the young may climb into the adult's pouch to feed on regurgitated food. Pelicans feed predominantly on fish but also catch crustaceans and other aquatic animals.

### 5/ AMERICAN WHITE PELICAN
*Pelecanus erythrorhynchos*

RANGE: **North America**
HABITAT: **freshwater lakes and shallow coastal waters**
SIZE: **50–70 in (127–178 cm)**

The American White Pelican occurs in flocks at all times. The birds arrive in their breeding colonies, which are often far from their feeding areas, in April or May. By this time the males have developed a horny knob on the upper mandible which they lose after the breeding season. Courtship is communal, and after a male and female have paired up the female leads the male away in a ritual parade.

The birds build a nest of stones, sticks and weeds on the ground, which may form a substantial mound. They avoid perching on trees at all times of the year, preferring to rest on the ground, often on islands and sand-spits; they roost near the water's edge.

## 6/ BROWN PELICAN
*Pelecanus occidentalis*

RANGE: **Pacific and Atlantic coasts of North and South America; Galapagos Islands**
HABITAT: **shallow coastal waters and islands**
SIZE: **$43\frac{1}{4}$–54 in (110–137 cm)**

Unlike the other pelicans, this species feeds by diving for fish, making spectacular plunges into the water from heights of 10–33 ft (3–10 m) above the surface. As it enters the water, it opens its bill and traps the prey in its expanded pouch.

Brown Pelicans nest in colonies on the ground or in trees. The male occupies a potential nest site from which he displays, leaving the spot only for brief flights until he attracts a mate. Mating takes place on the site and the male then collects branches and other nesting material to present ritually to his partner. The sexes share in incubation of the 2–3 eggs for 30 days. During the first week after hatching, the adults provide the young with well-digested fish which they regurgitate into the nest. The young finally fly from the nest after 11–12 weeks.

Brown Pelicans have a variety of calls, including grunts and "pops" in the adults and screams and groans uttered by the chicks.

## FAMILY SULIDAE
## Gannets and boobies

Plunge-diving seabirds, with torpedo-shaped bodies. Long, stout bills with serrated cutting edges and closed nostrils. Long, pointed wings and short legs. Plumage white below, variable above. Feet and facial skin often brightly colored and variable between sexes. Nest on ground, on cliffs or in trees. Eggs 1–4, whitish. Incubation 42–55 days, chicks remain at or near nest for 14–22 weeks. 9 species.

## 7/ NORTHERN GANNET
*Sula bassana*

RANGE: **E and W coasts of North Atlantic**
HABITAT: **marine offshore**
SIZE: **$35\frac{1}{2}$ in (90 cm)**

This conspicuous white bird is renowned for its spectacular plunging dives from heights of up to 100 ft (30 m), with its wings half-folded and its body dropping vertically into the water. Shoals of mackerel and herring attract great flocks which appear to be in a feeding frenzy as they alternately rise and plummet into the ocean.

Northern Gannets nest in huge colonies, of which there are about 37 in the world, containing a total of more than 200,000 pairs. The birds remain largely faithful to their mate and their nest site, and indulge in complex displays concerned with pair-bonding and with site ownership. Their colonies are intensely active and noisy. Because the peak food supply is both seasonal and dependable, egg-laying takes place on a consistently similar date every year. With an assured food supply, the single chick has a high chance of survival, but large numbers of the white-spotted brown juveniles die on migration to the south of their breeding range, before they reach maturity.

## 8/ PERUVIAN BOOBY
*Sula variegata*

RANGE: **coastal Peru and N Chile**
HABITAT: **offshore waters**
SIZE: **29 in (74 cm)**

One of the 3 abundant seabirds of the famous guano islands of Peru (together with the Guanay Cormorant and the Chilean Pelican), the Peruvian Booby relies on the shoals of anchovettas in the cold Humboldt Current to sustain its immense local concentrations. The population is numbered in millions and the mass diving of huge flocks of these birds is an unforgettable experience. Guano consists of the rocklike dried droppings of the birds, built up over many years to depths of up to 300 ft (90 m).

Overexploitation of the anchovetta stocks by fishing fleets has led to a catastrophic decline in the numbers of Peruvian seabirds. In some years, the natural oceanographic phenomenon El Niño brings warm water into the fishing grounds, which also causes severe reductions in food supply and results in colossal seabird mortality. Formerly, the birds could rapidly recover their numbers after the event but since overfishing, the rate of recovery has been much slower.

## 9/ ABBOTT'S BOOBY
*Sula abbotti*                              E

RANGE: **E Indian Ocean**
HABITAT: **open sea**
SIZE: **31 in (79 cm)**

Abbott's Booby is a beautiful and highly unusual member of its family; it is also the most scarce. The species nests only on Christmas Island, beneath the rain forest canopy, and there are fewer than 2,000 pairs. About 30 percent of the rain forest, including significant sections of the bird's habitat, has been destroyed by phosphate mining operations. Today, most of the island is a national park.

The survival of the species is hampered by a low rate of breeding. After an extremely prolonged growing period of 22 weeks in the nest, the single offspring is fed for another 33 weeks in the nesting tree. This means that it is confined to the island during the monsoon (from November to March), when it is at risk from high winds and starvation. The long breeding cycle prevents the birds from nesting every year and most pairs lay at 2-year intervals. Breeding rates are further reduced by the adults' habit of taking "rest" years. The juvenile birds that are reared are unique among the gannets and boobies in that their plumage closely resembles that of the adult males.

## 10/ MASKED BOOBY
*Sula dactylatra*

RANGE: **all tropical oceans**
HABITAT: **open sea**
SIZE: **30–33 in (76–84 cm)**

Also known as the Blue-faced Booby, this mainly dazzling white booby fishes over the open ocean and tends to nest on arid islands. Despite the low density and patchy distribution of prey far out at sea, its breeding colonies may contain thousands of pairs.

Breeding Masked Boobies have a number of ritual displays and their pair-bonding behavior includes the symbolic building of a nest, using mere fragments of no structural value. The usual clutch is 2 eggs, although the first-hatched chick invariably kills its sibling early in life. This prevents competition for the often scarce food. The laying of a second egg is an insurance policy against breeding failure. Should the first egg fail to hatch, or the oldest chick quickly perish, the second chick will take its place.

## 11/ RED-FOOTED BOOBY
*Sula sula*

RANGE: **all tropical oceans**
HABITAT: **open sea**
SIZE: **28–31 in (71–79 cm)**

The Red-footed Booby is probably the most numerous member of its family. There are several color phases across its huge range, but all have conspicuous red feet. Unlike most other members of the family, the species nests in trees. This habit may have partly protected it from human disturbance, helping to account for its comparative abundance today.

In their relatively nonseasonal environment, the birds breed opportunistically, waiting until there is an ample food supply. However, it is common for the supply to fail at a later stage, causing heavy mortality among the young. The surviving juveniles disperse widely and may travel thousands of miles from their birthplace. They can be distinguished from the adults by their blackish-brown bills, purplish facial skin and yellowish legs.

## 12/ BROWN BOOBY
*Sula leucogaster*

RANGE: **all tropical oceans**
HABITAT: **open sea**
SIZE: **$29\frac{1}{2}$–$31\frac{1}{2}$ in (75–80 cm)**

The Brown Booby breeds mainly on islands, often on cliffs or steep slopes. On well-vegetated slopes, the birds will perch freely in trees. They frequently share the islands with Red-footed or Masked Boobies, but avoid competition by hunting farther inshore, specializing in low, slanting dives to catch fish and squid. The birds spend much time in the air and perform some of their courtship rituals in flight.

The breeding colonies tend to be smaller and more scattered than those of the Red-footed and Masked Boobies. As with the Masked Booby, older chicks kill their siblings. On many islands the birds breed annually, but on Ascension Island in the Atlantic they tend to breed at less than yearly intervals, triggered by favorable changes in the food supply. Of the two races illustrated, *S. l. plotus* breeds in and around the Indian Ocean, Australia and some Pacific islands, while *S. l. brewsteri* nests in the eastern Pacific and along the western coast of Mexico.

# CORMORANTS, ANHINGAS, FRIGATEBIRDS

race *carbo*

race *lucidus*
"White-breasted Cormorant"

race *sinensis*

juv

GREAT CORMORANT

DOUBLE-CRESTED
CORMORANT

SHAG

non-breeding

non-breeding

race *hypoleucos*

CAPE CORMORANT

non-breeding

PIED CORMORANT

feeding chicks
at nest

juv

RED-LEGGED CORMORANT

GUANAY CORMORANT

race *varius*

race *albiventor*
"Falkland Islands Shag"

non-breeding

race *atriceps*
"Blue-eyed
Cormorant"

IMPERIAL SHAG

ANHINGA

♂

♀

PYGMY CORMORANT

non-breeding

FLIGHTLESS CORMORANT

juv

GREAT FRIGATEBIRD

♂

♂

chick at nest

CHRISTMAS ISLAND FRIGATEBIRD

# CORMORANTS, ANHINGAS, FRIGATEBIRDS

## FAMILY PHALACROCORACIDAE
### Cormorants
Medium to large fish-eaters; dive underwater. Long neck and long, laterally flattened, hooked bill, large feet set far back on body. Plumage dark, white head and underparts in some species. Sexes similar. Nest on cliffs, on ground or in trees. Eggs 1–6, pale blue. Incubation 22–26 days, chicks remain in nest for about 28 days. 32 species.

### 1/ DOUBLE-CRESTED CORMORANT
*Phalacrocorax auritus*

RANGE: **North America**
HABITAT: **marine and inland waters**
SIZE: **29–36 in (74–91 cm)**

This medium-sized, gregarious cormorant breeds in colonies containing up to 3,000 pairs, both on the coast and inland close to dependable supplies of food. The male's courtship display includes dances in the water, during which he presents the female with nesting material, and ritualized displays on the nest site. The birds lose the double crest on the crown after pairing. The crests of eastern races such as *P. a. auritus* are dark, while those of western races such as *P. a. albociliatus* are mainly white.

Young birds are fed by their parents about 6 times per day, a rate typical of inshore birds. After about a month the young leave the individual nest sites and start to wander around the colony in groups. At 5–6 weeks they start to fly.

### 2/ GREAT CORMORANT
*Phalacrocorax carbo*

RANGE: **N Atlantic, Africa, Eurasia, Australasia**
HABITAT: **coastal and fresh water**
SIZE: **$31\frac{1}{2}$–$39\frac{1}{2}$ in (80–100 cm)**

There are several races of the Great Cormorant, showing varying amounts of white in the plumage. They include *P. c. carbo*, which breeds around the North Atlantic, *P. c. sinensis*, which breeds from southern Europe to central Asia, and *P. c. lucidus* of sub-Saharan Africa.

In some places, this species is persecuted because of its appetite for fish. Its daily intake of food averages 14–25 oz (400–700 g), equivalent to some 15 percent of its body weight. The birds catch their prey during underwater dives that may last for over a minute.

The breeding colonies may number up to 2,000 pairs, although they are usually smaller and often fragmented. They may be located on the coast or inland, on cliffs, slopes or in trees. The courtship display includes wing-flicking, covering and uncovering the conspicuous white flank patch, and a throwing back of the head.

### 3/ CAPE CORMORANT
*Phalacrocorax capensis*

RANGE: **South Africa, Namibia**
HABITAT: **coasts**
SIZE: **$24$–$25\frac{1}{4}$ in (61–64 cm)**

The Cape Cormorant is abundant in southwestern Africa, with more than 1 million birds benefiting from the nutrient-rich Benguela Current that

flows past the coast. It is a highly gregarious species and can be seen feeding with other types of bird, often well offshore. Valued for its guano (rocklike, dried droppings used as a fertilizer), it is encouraged to roost and nest on artificial "guano platforms."

In its huge breeding colonies, which may contain 100,000 birds, the nests are placed on cliffs, on the ground or in bushes. The female usually lays 2–3 eggs and breeding is timed to coincide with periods when pilchards are especially abundant. Like the Guanay Cormorants of Peru, however, the birds may desert their breeding colonies en masse if food suddenly becomes scarce. Outside the breeding season, the Cape Cormorant disperses widely along the coast.

### 4/ SHAG
*Phalacrocorax aristotelis*

RANGE: **coastal W and S Europe and N Africa**
HABITAT: **marine coasts**
SIZE: **$25\frac{1}{2}$–$31\frac{1}{2}$ in (65–80 cm)**

The adult Shag is an attractive bird with blackish-green plumage, green eyes and a long, wispy, forward-curving crest in the breeding season. Although usually a quiet bird like other cormorants, it has a sonorous grunting call, often accompanied by throat-clicking. It prefers clear, cold oceans, avoiding estuaries and inland waters, and will travel up to 7 mls (11 km) from its colony in order to feed.

Typically, Shag colonies are neither large nor dense, although some reach a total of more than 1,000 pairs. After breeding, the birds tend to disperse along the coast, but northern populations, such as those from northern Norway, may migrate more than 600 mls (1,000 km) south. There is evidence that some breeding colonies have their own specific wintering areas.

### 5/ GUANAY CORMORANT
*Phalacrocorax bougainvillei*

RANGE: **coastal Peru and Chile**
HABITAT: **marine coasts**
SIZE: **30 in (76 cm)**

Once called the most valuable fowl in the world because of its guano (accumulated dried droppings used as a fertilizer), the Guanay Cormorant used to breed in colonies of hundreds of thousands, or even millions per island, on islands off Peru. The birds still breed at densities of about 3 nests per yard and when the 2–3 young are present with their parents, the huddle is exceedingly dense.

As a denizen of the cold Humboldt Current, the bird relies on the abundant shoals of anchovettas to sustain its numbers. Overfishing has caused a dramatic decline in the numbers of these cormorants. In the past, the population regularly suffered from a loss of food with the periodic incursion of warm water into the region (a phenomenon called El Niño).

However, mass mortality was quickly followed by an exponential increase in the surviving population once the cold up-welling current returned. Now, the stock of anchovettas has been so reduced by the fishermen that the birds can no longer make good their numbers following the periodic crashes.

### 6/ PIED CORMORANT
*Phalacrocorax varius*

RANGE: **Australia and New Zealand**
HABITAT: **coasts; also estuaries and inland waters**
SIZE: **26–33 in (66–84 cm)**

This striking cormorant, although patchily distributed, sometimes congregates in groups of many thousands. It nests in colonies on islands, either on the ground or in low shrubs and trees, sometimes using the same trees as other species. Although eggs may be laid in autumn and spring, individual birds probably nest once a year.

Throwing back the head is a typical part of the courtship ritual in cormorants, and in the Pied Cormorant the display is greatly enhanced by the bird's bright facial pattern. Of the two races illustrated, *P.v. hypoleucos* breeds along the coast of Western Australia and locally inland, while *P.v. varius* occurs in New Zealand. Adults of the latter race have yellow rather than orange facial skin.

## 7/ RED-LEGGED CORMORANT
*Phalacrocorax gaimardi*

RANGE: **SW South America**
HABITAT: **marine coasts**
SIZE: **28–30 in (71–76 cm)**

This strikingly handsome bird is unusual among the cormorants for its relatively solitary habits, unexpectedly chirpy voice and its restricted distribution on the Pacific coast of South America. It occurs on almost all of the Peruvian guano islands, but often sparsely, nesting alone or in small groups in cavities on ocean cliffs. Only occasionally do the birds cluster densely enough to be termed colonial.

Similarly, when foraging, the Red-legged Cormorant often flies singly for long distances and hunts alone or in pairs, although feeding groups sometimes occur. The birds build large nests which include items such as the cases of tube-dwelling worms and fronds of gelatinous seaweed that glue the structure to the rock.

## 8/ IMPERIAL SHAG
*Phalacrocorax atriceps*

RANGE: **S South America, subantarctic islands, Antarctic peninsula**
HABITAT: **marine coasts**
SIZE: **$28\frac{1}{4}$ in (72 cm)**

Several races of the Imperial Shag are recognized with a distribution that stretches across the southern latitudes. They have varying amounts of white in their plumage and differently colored caruncles (swollen outgrowths at the base of the upper mandible of the bill), but all have distinctive blue rings around the eyes throughout the year and a forward-curving, wispy crest in the breeding season. Two races are illustrated: the Falkland Islands Shag or King Cormorant *P.a. albiventor* and the Blue-eyed Cormorant *P.a. atriceps* of mainland South America.

The Falkland Islands Shag is an isolated race and the only cormorant that occurs on these South Atlantic islands. It forms huge colonies on flattish rocks and may also nest among penguins and albatrosses. The Blue-eyed Cormorant, by contrast, is widespread along the coast of southern Chile and Argentina.

## 9/ PYGMY CORMORANT
*Phalacrocorax pygmeus*                    ?

RANGE: **Eurasia**
HABITAT: **inland waters**
SIZE: **$17\frac{3}{4}$–$21\frac{3}{4}$ in (45–55 cm)**

The smallest of the cormorants, the Pygmy Cormorant differs from most members of its family in its preference for densely vegetated lowland freshwater habitats in warm latitudes. It nests in trees or among reeds, most colonies numbering tens or hundreds of birds. Where it nests in waterside trees, it often shares the branches with herons, egrets and ibises. Young

birds leave the nest before they can fly; they fledge after about 10 weeks.

Outside the breeding season, many Pygmy Cormorants migrate south, and it is in the wintering areas that larger flocks of the birds may gather. At this time of the year they may also visit brackish and saltwater habitats.

## 10/ FLIGHTLESS CORMORANT
*Nannopterum harrisi*                    R

RANGE: **Galapagos Islands**
HABITAT: **marine, close to breeding islands**
SIZE: **35 in (89 cm)**

The Flightless Cormorant occurs only on the islands of Fernandina and Isabela in the Galapagos archipelago, where it numbers about 800 pairs. It is highly sedentary and, as its name suggests, it is unable to fly, having only vestigial wings. It feeds by diving into the ocean from the shore; octopuses form a large part of its diet.

In its relatively seasonless tropical environment, the Flightless Cormorant can breed at any time of the year, although the peak nesting period is from March to September. A single bird may breed several times in 12 months. Although it may readily shift nest site and change its mate for successive breeding attempts, it frequently retains both. A bird taking over from its mate at the nest will ritually present its partner with seaweed as a way of maintaining the pair-bond.

## FAMILY ANHINGIDAE
### Anhingas
Large, freshwater fish-eaters. Extremely long, slender neck. Small head and long, thin, dagger-shaped bill with serrated cutting edges. Very long tail with corrugated outer feathers. Plumage black, brown, gray and white. Females paler than males. Nest in trees or reeds near water. Eggs 2–6, pale green. Incubation 26–30 days, chicks leave nest after about 5 weeks. 4 species.

## 11/ ANHINGA
*Anhinga anhinga*

RANGE: **SE USA to N South America**
HABITAT: **inland and brackish waters; can occur on coasts**
SIZE: **34 in (86 cm)**

The Anhinga, like the other members of its family, is much more slender than the cormorants, with an elongated neck and a thin, straight bill. Often it swims with only the head and neck above the surface, the neck held in a sinuous S-shape resembling the curve of a snake. Indeed, Snake Bird is an alternative name for this species. It occurs in rivers, lakes and lagoons, where it hunts for fish by stealth, spearing them underwater with its sharp bill. Like other darters, it has a hinge mechanism in its neck, enabling it to snap its head forward suddenly to seize prey.

Darters have large, broad wings which are excellent for soaring, and in level flight they alternate flaps with glides. Their courtship ritual includes an aerial display, in which they plane down to the nesting area from great heights. They are gregarious birds at all times, sometimes breeding in groups of several hundred, along with cormorants and herons.

## FAMILY FREGATIDAE
### Frigatebirds
Large aerial seabirds. Long wings, deeply forked tail. Long, hooked bill. Breeding males black with varying amounts of white beneath and with a scarlet throat pouch. Females and immatures mostly dark brown with white on underparts. Nest in trees or on ground. Eggs 1, white. Incubation 44–55 days, chicks remain in nest for 5–6 months. Young fed for up to 1 year. 5 species.

## 12/ CHRISTMAS ISLAND FRIGATEBIRD
*Fregata andrewsi*                    V

RANGE: **Christmas Island and surrounding oceans**
HABITAT: **oceanic**
SIZE: **35–40 in (89–102 cm)**

This species breeds only on Christmas Island in the eastern Indian Ocean, where fewer than 1,000 pairs remain. The frigatebirds have suffered from years of human persecution, but they are now fully protected in their island home. Ironically, the Christmas Island Frigatebird occasionally causes the death of another rare endemic bird, Abbott's Booby *Sula abbotti*, by hounding it for fish and forcing it to crash down into the jungle canopy.

Like other frigatebirds, the males display in small groups to passing females by presenting their inflated scarlet throat pouch, trembling their outspread wings and producing a distinctive warbling call. If a female is attracted by a male's courtship display, she descends alongside him. After mating, the pair build a flimsy nest of twigs on the display site.

## 13/ GREAT FRIGATEBIRD
*Fregata minor*

RANGE: **tropical and subtropical Indian and Pacific oceans, and off Brazil**
HABITAT: **open sea**
SIZE: **$34$–$39\frac{1}{2}$ in (86–100 cm)**

With a maximum wingspan of over 6 ft (2 m), but weighing a mere $2\frac{1}{2}$ lb (1.2 kg), the frigatebirds have a far greater wing area than any seabirds of comparable weight. They spend most of their lives in the air and seldom land on the water. Instead they feed on the wing by snatching surface prey. Some individuals, particularly younger adults, practice "piracy", harrying other seabirds until they drop their meals. Although they lack waterproof plumage and cannot swim, the frigatebirds range hundreds of miles from dry land.

The Great Frigatebird is probably the most numerous of the frigatebirds. Thousands of pairs may gather in breeding colonies in trees and bushes on oceanic islands, often in company with Lesser Frigatebirds.

The breeding cycle of the Great Frigatebird is one of the longest in the seabird world, with the single young requiring 6 months to fledge and at least another 6 months of support from its parents. Adults can therefore breed only once in 2 years. The breeding rate is further reduced by the adults' habit of taking "rest" years and by the heavy loss of eggs and young through interference from nonbreeding males that attack nesters and steal nest material.

BLACK-CROWNED NIGHT HERON

juv

AMERICAN BITTERN

WHITE-CRESTED
TIGER HERON

LITTLE BITTERN

♂

BOAT-BILLED
HERON

SQUACCO HERON

juv

CATTLE EGRET

race *rogersi*

race *virescens*

race *sundevalli*

winter

GREEN-BACKED HERON

LITTLE EGRET

winter

BLACK HERON

juv

PURPLE HERON

winter

GREAT EGRET

GRAY HERON

juv

GOLIATH HERON

white phase
"Great White
Heron"

GREAT BLUE HERON

# HERONS AND BITTERNS

## FAMILY ARDEIDAE
### Herons and bitterns

Small to large. Long-legged, most with long neck and powerful, stabbing bill. Some males larger or more colorful than females. Nest in trees, bushes, reedbeds. Eggs 1–7, variable. Incubation 14–30 days, chicks remain in nest 28–55 days. 60 species.

## 1/ GRAY HERON
*Ardea cinerea*

RANGE: **widespread in Eurasia and Africa**
HABITAT: **shallow freshwaters of all types; also coasts, especially in winter**
SIZE: $35\frac{1}{2}$–$38\frac{1}{2}$ in (90–98 cm)

This species haunts a variety of waterside habitats, where it catches fish, frogs and small mammals in its long, daggerlike bill. It breeds farther north than any other heron, and some populations suffer high rates of mortality in severe weather. However, the birds have a marked capacity for recovering their numbers after such losses.

Gray Herons usually build their nests in tall trees up to 80 ft (25 m) above the ground. Colony size is variable, with about 200 being the maximum in most areas, although concentrations of over 1,000 breeding birds have been recorded. A pair readily lays another clutch of eggs if their first is destroyed; they can repeat this 2–3 times.

## 2/ GREAT BLUE HERON
*Ardea herodias*

RANGE: **S Canada to Central America, Caribbean, Galapagos Islands; winters S USA to N South America**
HABITAT: **river edges, marshes, swamps, mudflats**
SIZE: **40–50 in (102–127 cm)**

This species is the largest of the North American herons. Although most populations have blue-gray plumage, a white color phase – the Great White Heron – occurs in marine habitats in southern Florida and Cuba.

Great Blue Herons forage largely in water, walking slowly or standing and waiting for prey to draw near. Occasionally they hunt more actively, running, hopping and flicking their wings. They feed mostly on fish, aquatic invertebrates, frogs and small mammals. Breeding adults have plumes on their backs and perform elaborate courtship displays which include feather-fluffing, stereotyped postures, twig-shaking and display flights. They nest in colonies, usually in remote areas, with nests in trees up to 130 ft (40 m) above the ground.

## 3/ GOLIATH HERON
*Ardea goliath*

RANGE: **S and E Africa, Madagascar, S Iraq**
HABITAT: **coastal and inland wetlands with extensive shallows**
SIZE: **53–59 in (135–150 cm)**

The largest of the heron family, this huge bird can wade through much deeper water than related species. Although it eats some amphibians, it feeds chiefly on fish, including specimens up to

$4\frac{1}{2}$–$6\frac{1}{2}$ lb (2–3 kg) in weight. It typically occurs alone or as a single pair.

The Goliath Heron nests on the ground in reeds or on a low bush standing in the water. The nest itself is built from reed stems or twigs and is up to 3 ft (1 m) across. The 2–3 pale blue eggs are incubated by both parents for about 4 weeks, and the young take another 6 weeks to fledge.

## 4/ PURPLE HERON
*Ardea purpurea*

RANGE: **S Eurasia, Africa**
HABITAT: **freshwater wetlands with extensive emergent vegetation**
SIZE: $30\frac{3}{4}$–$35\frac{1}{2}$ in (78–90 cm)

The Purple Heron has longer toes than other, similar-sized species. These enable the bird to walk over floating vegetation without sinking and to stride over thick bushes without having to grasp individual twigs. The large feet are clearly visible in flight and form a useful clue to identification.

Most Purple Herons nest in small colonies of up to 20 pairs in dense stands of reeds or rushes growing in shallow water. Occasionally, they choose low trees. The nest is a platform of reeds or twigs and extra platforms are often constructed nearby. These are used by the nonincubating bird and, later, by the developing young.

## 5/ GREAT EGRET
*Egretta alba*

RANGE: **worldwide, especially widespread in S hemisphere**
HABITAT: **freshwater wetlands of all kinds; also coasts in winter**
SIZE: $33\frac{1}{2}$–40 in (85–102 cm)

This extremely widespread heron suffered greatly in the late 19th century from the demands of the millinery trade. It is estimated that over 200,000 of these birds were killed for their plumage in a single year. The Royal Society for the Protection of Birds (RSPB) in Britain and the Audubon Society in America were originally formed in response to the outcry caused by the carnage of

this bird and other birds for their plumage. Today, land drainage and habitat destruction are the chief threats to the bird's wellbeing.

Great Egrets breed in low trees or reedbeds, usually in small colonies. Each male establishes a small territory around his chosen nest site and begins the construction of the nest, building a platform of twigs or reeds on which he displays to the female. Both sexes then finish the nest ready for laying, although some building work will continue until the young have fledged.

## 6/ BLACK HERON
*Egretta ardesiaca*

RANGE: **sub-Saharan Africa and Madagascar**
HABITAT: **shallow freshwater wetlands and coastal swamps**
SIZE: $17\frac{1}{4}$–$18\frac{1}{2}$ in (44–47 cm)

The uniform, dark, slate-gray plumage of the Black Heron is common to both sexes. This is a widespread bird occurring in shallow waters across much of tropical Africa. Its nests are normally found scattered throughout large colonies of other herons and egrets.

The Black Heron is renowned for its special hunting posture. Moving slowly across shallow water, it lowers its head and long neck and half raises its wings, bringing them forward until the edges meet over the top of its head. It is as if a small, black umbrella is drifting across the water's surface. The function of this odd behavior may be to shade the water from the sun, in this way greatly increasing the heron's chances of spotting the movement of fish or other prey beneath the surface.

## 7/ LITTLE EGRET
*Egretta garzetta*

RANGE: **S Eurasia, Africa and Australasia**
HABITAT: **shallow fresh and brackish water, also estuaries and coasts**
SIZE: **$21\frac{3}{4}$–$25\frac{1}{2}$ in (55–65 cm)**

A century ago, this species was nearly exterminated from parts of its range to satisfy the hat trade, eager for the 10 in (25 cm) long plumes which form part of the bird's breeding plumage. These feathers are silky in appearance and soft to the touch. However, changing fashions and active campaigning by bodies such as the RSPB and Audubon Society have removed this threat.

Little Egret colonies can contain many hundreds or even thousands of pairs. They are remarkably agile when climbing over thin twigs and build their nests in trees. The young leave the nest before fledging to perch on nearby branches.

## 8/ CATTLE EGRET
*Bubulcus ibis*

RANGE: **S Eurasia, Africa, Australasia, S USA and northern S America**
HABITAT: **freshwater wetlands, farmland and open country**
SIZE: **19–21 in (48–53 cm)**

The Cattle Egret has an enormous range that spans 6 continents. In the past 50 years, it has successfully colonized North and South America, Australia and New Zealand. In Australia, there have also been deliberate introductions of this beneficial species.

Cattle Egrets commonly feed around grazing cattle and wild game herds, which flush prey such as grasshoppers, beetles and lizards from cover as they move. The birds' food includes many invertebrates that are serious parasites of cattle, such as ticks and blood-sucking flies.

During the breeding season, Cattle Egrets sport long, buff feathers on their heads, backs and chests, and their bills and legs assume a bright pinkish-red color. They nest in dense colonies, often in company with other species. The nests can be virtually touching, with as many as 100 in a single tree.

## 9/ SQUACCO HERON
*Ardeola ralloides*

RANGE: **S Europe, SW Asia, Africa**
HABITAT: **freshwater marshes, swamps and lakes**
SIZE: **$17\frac{1}{4}$–$18\frac{1}{2}$ in (44–47 cm)**

As a result of its overall buff plumage and retiring habits, the Squacco Heron is a difficult species to spot among marsh vegetation. As it takes flight, however, there is a startling change in appearance, with the white wings, rump and tail becoming clearly visible.

Like many herons and egrets, the Squacco Heron gains an elegant crest and ornamental back plumes for the breeding season. In addition, its bill and legs, which are yellowish-green in winter, change to blue and pink respectively. Breeding takes place in mixed colonies with related species, the nests being built in low trees, bushes or reeds. Each clutch contains 3–6 eggs laid on a platform of twigs or reeds.

## 10/ GREEN-BACKED HERON
*Butorides striatus*

RANGE: **worldwide tropics and subtropics**
HABITAT: **freshwater and coastal wetlands**
SIZE: **$15\frac{3}{4}$–19 in (40–48 cm)**

The Green-backed, or Striated, Heron shows great differences in plumage across its vast geographical range, with races that include *B. s. sundevalli* of the Galapagos Islands, *B. s. rogersi* of northwest Australia and the American race *B. s. virescens*. It is usually a secretive species, feeding mainly at night and creeping among dense marsh vegetation. However, it sometimes feeds by day at urban ponds, stalking around the edges or perching on jetties and boats.

Colonial breeding is rare and restricted to small, loose groups. Most nests are solitary and placed in low bushes or trees, often overhanging water. The nest itself is built of twigs, but is so flimsy that the 2–4 eggs may be visible from below.

## 11/ BLACK-CROWNED NIGHT HERON
*Nycticorax nycticorax*

RANGE: **worldwide except N temperate regions and Australia**
HABITAT: **salt, brackish and freshwater wetlands**
SIZE: **$22\frac{3}{4}$–$25\frac{1}{2}$ in (58–65 cm)**

The Black-crowned Night Heron is an extremely widespread species. It lives up to its name in being active mainly in the evening and through the night, hunting for frogs and toads, small fish and crustaceans.

Breeding takes place in colonies in trees, with up to 30 nests crowded into a single tree. Although they sometimes nest with other heron species, Black-crowned Night Herons are usually segregated in their own part of the colony. Each nest is an untidy platform of twigs, initiated by the male and completed by the female while the male continues to supply the twigs. When feeding their young, the birds hunt more frequently during the daytime.

## 12/ BOAT-BILLED HERON
*Cochlearius cochlearius*

RANGE: **Mexico S to Bolivia, N Argentina**
HABITAT: **edges of lakes and rivers, mangroves and other wooded swamps**
SIZE: **$17\frac{3}{4}$–$19\frac{3}{4}$ in (45–50 cm)**

Perhaps the most bizarre of the herons in appearance, this species features a wide, flattened bill and a prominent black crest. The sexes have similar plumage, but juvenile birds are buffy below, and their crests are not as pronounced as those of the adults.

Generally, Boat-billed Herons are sedentary and gregarious in habit. They roost during the day in mangroves or other shady trees and emerge to feed at night, standing crouched and waiting for prey, or walking slowly through the shallows. Occasionally they feed more actively, darting around and sometimes using their broad bills as scoops with which to capture stationary prey. They eat mainly fish, shrimp and other aquatic invertebrates, and often utter froglike croaks when feeding.

## 13/ WHITE-CRESTED TIGER HERON
*Tigriornis leucolophus*

RANGE: **tropical W Africa**
HABITAT: **riverine forest**
SIZE: **$23\frac{1}{2}$–$31\frac{1}{2}$ in (60–80 cm)**

Little is known about this highly secretive bird. It lives in dense tropical forests, apparently breeds in solitary pairs, and feeds mainly at night. The "Tiger" part of its common name comes from the pronounced bars or stripes on its plumage. The alternative name of tiger bittern has been used for this and several related species because of their bitternlike booming call and their adoption of an upright posture typical of the bitterns.

The few nests that have been found were placed in trees beside rivers. The timing of egg-laying is probably related to rainfall patterns and changes in water level. The normal clutch appears to consist of 1–2 whitish, red-blotched eggs.

## 14/ LITTLE BITTERN
*Ixobrychus minutus*

RANGE: **parts of Europe, W Asia, sub-Saharan Africa, Australia; European population winters in tropical Africa**
HABITAT: **freshwater marshes, peat bogs, disused clay pits and similar habitats, with dense vegetation and tall reeds**
SIZE: **$10\frac{1}{2}$–14 in (27–36 cm)**

This shy, tiny bittern is generally reluctant to fly and is not easily flushed from cover. If startled, it will often "freeze," beak pointing skyward, the delicately streaked plumage of its breast camouflaging it against the reeds among which it lives. When it does take to the air, it reveals a surprisingly bold pattern of greenish-black head, back, tail and flight feathers contrasting sharply with the creamy-buff neck and wing patches.

Little Bitterns are active chiefly at dusk or at night. They stalk their prey by walking slowly in a crouched position among the reeds. Sometimes they simply stand and wait for their food to come to them. They eat mostly small fish, frogs, insects, spiders and shrimp.

## 15/ AMERICAN BITTERN
*Botaurus lentiginosus*

RANGE: **C Canada to C USA; winters S USA, Caribbean, Mexico, Central America**
HABITAT: **fresh and saltwater marshes, swamps and bogs**
SIZE: **$25\frac{1}{4}$ in (64 cm)**

The American Bittern is a stocky brown heron with a black and brown wing pattern in flight. Juvenile birds have more streaking on the back and breast, but closely resemble adults. Like other bitterns, these birds often point their bills to the sky when threatened and even sway back and forth like reeds in the wind.

The male American Bittern's 3-syllable pumping or booming call probably serves to advertise territory as well as to attract females. The nest is a platform woven of plant material on a mound of vegetation or on the ground among cats'-tails or other emergent plants. The population of this species is declining all over its range because of marsh drainage and other habitat changes.

# WHALE-HEADED STORK, HAMMERKOP, STORKS, SPOONBILLS AND IBISES, FLAMINGOS

WHITE STORK

BLACK STORK

at nest

juv

WOOD STORK

WHALE-HEADED STORK

MARABOU STORK

juv

AFRICAN OPEN-BILL STORK

HAMMERKOP

SACRED IBIS

HERMIT IBIS

winter

GLOSSY IBIS

juv

SCARLET IBIS

ROSEATE SPOONBILL

juv

race *roseus*

juv

WHITE SPOONBILL

ANDEAN FLAMINGO

GREATER FLAMINGO

feeding chick on nest

# WHALE-HEADED STORK, HAMMERKOP, STORKS, SPOONBILLS AND IBISES, FLAMINGOS

## FAMILY SCOPIDAE
**Hammerkop**
There is only one species in this family.

### 1/ HAMMERKOP
*Scopus umbretta*
RANGE: **S and C Africa, Madagascar**
HABITAT: **shallow fresh water**
SIZE: **$19\frac{1}{2}$ in (50 cm)**

The erected crest on the back of this bird's head mirrors the stout beak and produces the distinctive, hammerhead shape from which the species takes its name. Hammerkops feed on frogs, fish and invertebrates and build huge, domed nests which are among the most extraordinary constructions in the bird world. Up to 6 ft (2 m) high and across and weighing 55–110 lb (25–50 kg), it is made of sticks, reeds, grass and dead plant stems placed in a tree fork, on a cliff or on the ground. The actual nest chamber lies inside and the entrance hole is reduced in size with mud. Finally the nest itself is lined with waterweed and dry grass. The whole structure may take 6 weeks to build.

The 3–7 whitish eggs are incubated for about 30 days. The young make their first flight at about 7 weeks but may return nightly for up to a month thereafter to roost in the nest.

## FAMILY BALAENICIPITIDAE
**Whale-headed Stork**
There is only one species in this family.

### 2/ WHALE-HEADED STORK
*Balaeniceps rex*      S
RANGE: **Sudan, Uganda, Zaire to Zambia**
HABITAT: **swamps**
SIZE: **$39\frac{1}{4}$–$47\frac{1}{4}$ in (100–120 cm)**

This species takes its name (and its alternative name of Shoebill) from its huge, clog-shaped bill which it carries pointing downward, even resting it on its neck. Its eyes are also exceptionally large and set forward, giving it binocular vision.

The large bill is probably an adaptation for catching and holding the large, slippery lungfish which form one of its main sources of food. It also eats young crocodiles, turtles and smaller fish. Like other storks, this species claps the mandibles of its bill together in display and threat, producing in this case a loud, hollow sound. The Whale-headed Stork usually nests on floating vegetation, laying a clutch of 1–3 white eggs, which are incubated for about 30 days. The young leave the nest when 13–14 weeks old, returning to roost there for a week or so.

## FAMILY CICONIIDAE
**Storks**
Large, long-legged and long-necked wading birds; long, heavy bill. Plumage mainly black, gray and white. Sexes similar. Nest in trees, on cliffs or (White Stork) buildings. Eggs 3–5 (1 in Saddle-bill Stork), white. Incubation 30–50 days. Nestling period 7–18 weeks. 19 species.

### 3/ WOOD STORK
*Mycteria americana*
RANGE: **SE USA, Mexico, Central America, W South America to N Argentina**
HABITAT: **ponds, marshes, swamps, lagoons**
SIZE: **$33\frac{3}{4}$–40 in (86–102 cm)**

Wood Storks are gregarious birds and sometimes flocks of 100 or more soar high above the ground on thermals, flying with their heads and necks extended. Wood Storks feed mostly on fish, but also take reptiles, frogs and aquatic invertebrates. They forage in water up to their bellies, moving their open bill from side to side. When it encounters prey, the bird snaps it shut. They nest colonially, with up to 25 nests per tree, placed up to 100 ft (30 m) above the ground.

### 4/ AFRICAN OPEN-BILL STORK
*Anastomus lamelligerus*
RANGE: **sub-Saharan Africa, Madagascar**
HABITAT: **swamps, marshes, flooded areas and margins of large rivers**
SIZE: **$35\frac{1}{2}$ in (90 cm)**

When this species closes its bill, only the tips of the mandibles meet. Behind them, the 2 halves of the bill curve away from each other to leave a wide gap – hence the common name. This is an adaptation for dealing with the bird's principal food, large water snails: by inserting the tip of its bill into the snail, the stork can snip through the muscle and withdraw the snail from its shell. As well as wading through shallows seeking snails, African Open-bill Storks have been seen riding on the backs of Hippopotamuses.

### 5/ BLACK STORK
*Ciconia nigra*
RANGE: **temperate and S Eurasia, S Africa**
HABITAT: **forest swamps; also open, drier country**
SIZE: **$37\frac{1}{2}$–$39\frac{1}{4}$ in (95–100 cm)**

There is an interesting dichotomy in the habitat and nest sites of the Black Stork. Some, perhaps the majority, inhabit wet places, particularly well-wooded areas with plentiful streams and pools in extensive clearings. Here, the birds breed in large trees, building nests of sticks reinforced with earth and grass.

The other habitat type is much drier, more open country, where the birds nest on cliff ledges or even in caves, at altitudes of up to 6,500 ft (2,000 m). In both cases, however, the birds shun contact with people, in contrast to their close relative, the White Stork.

### 6/ WHITE STORK
*Ciconia ciconia*      ?
RANGE: **temperate and S Europe, N Africa, S and E Asia; winters in Africa, India and S Asia**
HABITAT: **open, moist lowlands and wetlands, generally close to human habitation**
SIZE: **$39\frac{1}{4}$–$45\frac{1}{4}$ in (100–115 cm)**

The natural nest sites of the White Stork are trees and cliff ledges, but a great many pairs, certainly the majority in Europe, nest on buildings. Despite much human affection for the species, its population has declined in many areas because of the drainage of marshy feeding areas and the use of pesticides on farmland where many also feed.

The main display of the White Stork involves bill-clappering, in which the mandibles are clapped rapidly together. This persists as a form of greeting between the pair throughout the nesting period.

### 7/ MARABOU STORK
*Leptoptilos crumeniferus*
RANGE: **tropical and subtropical Africa**
HABITAT: **large wetlands and open country**
SIZE: **59 in (150 cm)**

An adult Marabou Stork has a large throat pouch that hangs down in front of its neck. The pouch contains a system of air sacs that can be inflated and deflated through a connection with the nostrils. The pouch certainly is not a food-storing crop, as has sometimes been assumed, but it seems likely that it has a role in courtship display.

Marabou Storks obtain much of their food from scavenging and they are often attracted to lion kills and human rubbish tips. They are also regular intruders at flamingo colonies, where they prey on both eggs and chicks.

## FAMILY THRESKIORNITHIDAE
### Spoonbills and ibises

Large, long-legged. Bills thin, downcurved (ibises) or long, spatulate (spoonbills). Plumage mainly black, brown or white, but also red and pink. Sexes similar. Nest of sticks in trees, reeds or on cliffs. Eggs 2–5, white or blue. Incubation about 21 days, nestling period 14–21 days; young return to be fed until 5–11 weeks old. 31 species.

### 8/ SACRED IBIS
*Threskiornis aethiopica*

RANGE: sub-Saharan Africa, Madagascar, Iraq
HABITAT: inland and coastal shallow wetlands
SIZE: $25\frac{1}{2}$–$29\frac{1}{2}$ in (65–75 cm)

This species is now extinct in Egypt where it was venerated in ancient times. It is depicted in many murals and in hieroglyphics and mummified specimens are common in burial places; over 1.5 million birds were found in one group of tombs.

When the Sacred Ibis flies, bare patches of skin under the wings and at the sides of the breast show as scarlet, contrasting with the black and white body and wings. The black head and neck are naked, lacking feathers, but they do not become so until the bird is about 2 years old. Until then they are feathered white, mottled with black.

### 9/ HERMIT IBIS
*Geronticus eremita*                    E

RANGE: NW Africa and Turkey
HABITAT: mountainous and semiarid deserts; also upland wetlands, farmland
SIZE: 28–31 in (71–79 cm)

Sadly, this is a seriously threatened species that now breeds only in Morocco and Turkey, although it formerly bred in southern Europe and in the Middle East. The reasons for the decline are unclear, but the bird seems unable to adapt to changes in food supply and, perhaps, climate. Dry seasons are known to cause considerable mortality among the young. The few remaining colonies of the Hermit Ibis (also known as the Northern Bald Ibis or Waldrapp) are on cliffs in steep valleys. Here, nests of twigs, grass and straw are built, often decorated with bits of paper.

### 10/ SCARLET IBIS
*Eudocimus ruber*

RANGE: Venezuela, Colombia, coastal Guianas and Brazil; Trinidad
HABITAT: coastal swamps, mangroves, lagoons, estuaries, mudflats
SIZE: 24 in (61 cm)

This species is gregarious, foraging and roosting communally, often with several heron and egret species. A sunset flight of Scarlet Ibises to their roost in a mangrove thicket is a magnificent sight. Their range overlaps in several places with the White Ibis *E. albus* and hybridization occurs.

Scarlet Ibises feed mainly on crabs, mollusks and other invertebrates, probing for them on mudflats with their curved bills. They will also take fish, frogs and insects. They breed colonially, constructing nests of twigs and sticks.

### 11/ GLOSSY IBIS
*Plegadis falcinellus*

RANGE: widespread but scattered in Central America, Africa, S Eurasia and Australasia
HABITAT: shallow freshwater and coastal wetlands
SIZE: 22–26 in (56–66 cm)

The overall dark chestnut and black plumage of this bird has a purple and green iridescence that gives the species its name. Glossy Ibises breed in colonies, sometimes of thousands of pairs, almost always in association with herons and egrets. However, they are clearly less tolerant of disturbance than these other species and have declined in many areas. Outside the breeding season, flocks of Glossy Ibises feed in shallow wetlands and open fields. They roost communally, often sharing waterside trees with herons.

### 12/ WHITE SPOONBILL
*Platalea leucorodia*

RANGE: temperate and S Eurasia, India, tropical W and NE Africa
HABITAT: shallow fresh, brackish and saltwater wetlands
SIZE: 31–35 in (79–89 cm)

This bird feeds with the mandibles of its bill held slightly open and the spoon-shaped tip immersed in shallow water. As the bird swings its head from side to side, the bill makes scything movements below the surface in search of shrimp and other aquatic life. Feeding usually takes place with small groups of birds wading in lines, which may increase efficiency if one bird is able to catch prey disturbed by the next one.

White Spoonbills are sensitive to disturbance, and this, as well as the drainage and pollution of their marshland habitats, has caused the population to decline in many areas.

### 13/ ROSEATE SPOONBILL
*Ajaia ajaja*

RANGE: SE USA, Central America, Colombia, Ecuador, E Peru, Bolivia, N Argentina
HABITAT: marshes, lagoons, mangroves, mudflats
SIZE: $31\frac{3}{4}$ in (81 cm)

These spectacular pink and white spoonbills are gregarious birds, often seen foraging or flying in small flocks. They sweep their bills through shallow water to catch small fish, crustaceans and other aquatic invertebrates, and also eat some plant material. In the USA, they were persecuted by plume-hunters for the millinery trade. Although they suffer locally from habitat destruction, their numbers and range in south-central USA have recently increased.

Roseate Spoonbills nest in small colonies, often with a variety of heron species. They are monogamous and have elaborate courtship behavior that includes the presentation of twigs, flight displays and bill-clapping. Their nests of sticks and twigs are constructed in bushes, trees or reeds or, occasionally, on the ground.

## FAMILY PHOENICOPTERIDAE
### Flamingos

Large, very long-legged and long-necked wading birds. Plumage red, pink and white. Sexes similar. Nest a mound of mud. Eggs 1–2, white. Incubation about 28 days, nestling period 5–8 days; chicks dependent on adults for food for another 4 weeks. 5 species.

### 14/ GREATER FLAMINGO
*Phoenicopterus ruber*

RANGE: S Europe, SW Asia, E, W and N Africa, West Indies, Central America, Galapagos Islands
HABITAT: saline or alkaline lakes, lagoons and deltas
SIZE: $49\frac{1}{4}$–57 in (125–145 cm)

The extraordinary slender build and the curious bill of a flamingo are both adaptations for feeding. Small shrimp and other crustaceans are sifted from the bottom mud by a pumping action of the tongue which forces mud and water through the comblike lamellae on either side of the bill. The head is held upside down at the end of the very long neck and swung to and fro as the bird walks slowly forward. The great length of the legs and the neck allows the birds to feed in much deeper water than other species, so avoiding competition.

There are 2 races of the Greater Flamingo. *P. r. ruber* breeds on the Caribbean Islands and surrounding mainland coasts, with an outpost in the Galapagos Islands. It has much redder plumage than the other race and its bill is orange-pink and black with a yellowish base. The second race *P. r. roseus*, with paler plumage and a pink and black bill, is restricted to the Old World.

### 15/ ANDEAN FLAMINGO
*Phoenicoparrus andinus*                    ?

RANGE: Andes of Peru, Bolivia, Chile, Argentina above 8,000 ft (2,500 m)
HABITAT: salt lakes
SIZE: 40 in (102 cm)

Andean Flamingos are spectacular in flight. Like other flamingos, they fly with their neck extended and their legs trailing behind, uttering gooselike "honking" calls. Their numbers have declined recently and they may now be the scarcest flamingos, probably with fewer than 50,000 birds.

As with other flamingos, both sexes constantly repair their mud nest mound while incubating the single egg. The downy white chicks have straight bills at first and are fed liquid secretions from the adults' crops until their bills are fully developed. This avian "milk" contains fat, protein, some carbohydrates and blood cells. It is also rich in red pigment, obtained by the birds from their food, which gives flamingos' feathers their pink and red coloring. Mobile young gather into a common flock, or nursery, guarded by the adults in turn.

CRESTED SCREAMER

WHITE-FACED WHISTLING DUCK

GRAYLAG GOOSE

race *rubrirostris*

race *anser*

race *flavirostris*

race *albifrons*
juv

race *albifrons*

WHITE-FRONTED GOOSE

juv

BLACK SWAN

FRECKLED DUCK

♂

♂ winter

♀

♂

juv

race *bewickii*
"Bewick's Swan"

race *columbianus*
"Whistling Swan"

race *bewickii*
"Bewick's Sw
variations in
patte

MUTE SWAN

TUNDRA SWAN

MAGELLAN GOOSE

race *picta*
"Lesser Magellan Goose"
white phase

race *picta*
♂ barred phase

race *leucoptera*
"Greater Magellan Goose"
♀

MAGPIE GOOSE ♀ feeding chick

race *atlanticus*
"Greater Snow Goose"
snow phase

race *caerulescens*
"Lesser Snow Goose"
blue phase

SNOW GOOSE

HAWAIIAN GOOSE

RED-BREASTED GOOSE

race *minima*

race *canadensis*

EGYPTIAN GOOSE

CANADA GOOSE

213

# SCREAMERS, SWANS, GEESE AND RELATIVES

## FAMILY ANHIMIDAE
### Screamers
Large, gooselike waterbirds. Long, partially webbed toes and short, hooked bill. Mainly black, gray and brown. Sexes similar. Nest on ground close to water. Eggs 2–7, whitish. Incubation 40–45 days, chicks leave nest and feed themselves soon after hatching. 3 species.

## 1/ CRESTED SCREAMER
*Chauna torquata*

RANGE: S Brazil, Uruguay and N Argentina
HABITAT: **marshes in open grassland and woodland**
SIZE: $33\frac{1}{2}$–$37\frac{1}{2}$ in (85–95 cm)

Screamers take their name from their loud, far-carrying calls, though these are more a harsh honking than a true scream. They can be heard up to nearly 2 mls (3 km) away.

The Crested Screamer has a short, downcurved bill, long, thick legs and only a trace of webbing between the long toes. Two sharp, bony spurs project from the bend of each wing. The spurs are used in fighting, either between rival screamers or to drive off enemies, including hunting dogs and other predators. Screamers often fly to great heights, sailing in wide circles until almost out of sight.

The large nest, a mound of vegetation, is built close to shallow water. When they hatch, the young already have a covering of down feathers and they leave the nest within a few hours. They fledge when about 60–75 days old.

## FAMILY ANATIDAE
### Swans, geese and ducks
Medium to large waterbirds. Most thickset, with webbed feet and flattened bills. Plumage variable, often bright. Sexes different in many species. Nests usually platform of vegetation; some hole-nesters. Eggs 4–14, pale, unmarked. Incubation 18–39 days, young leave nest and (except Magpie Goose) feed themselves soon after hatching. 147 species.

## 2/ MAGPIE GOOSE
*Anseranas semipalmata*

RANGE: N Australia and S New Guinea
HABITAT: **overgrown swamps and lagoons and adjacent farmland**
SIZE: $29\frac{1}{2}$–$33\frac{1}{2}$ in (75–85 cm)

With its long neck, long legs and bold pied plumage, the Magpie Goose is one of the most distinctive of all wildfowl. It has only partial webbing between the toes and the male has a pronounced dome to the top of the head.

The natural food of the Magpie Goose includes aquatic plants and seeds. In northern Australia the birds have damaged rice crops, both by grazing and trampling, but careful adjustment of water levels in the rice paddies has helped to reduce the problem.

The nest is a large platform of vegetation, plucked off and trampled in shallow water, before being built up into a mound. Uniquely among wildfowl, the parents feed their young bill to bill.

## 3/ WHITE-FACED WHISTLING DUCK
*Dendrocygna viduata*

RANGE: **tropical South America, sub-Saharan Africa, Madagascar and the Comoro Islands**
HABITAT: **rivers, lakes, swamps, marshes**
SIZE: $17$–$18\frac{3}{4}$ in (43–48 cm)

The White-faced Whistling Duck has the upright stance, long neck and long legs typical of the whistling ducks. It has broad wings and powerful flight and can also swim buoyantly, upending to feed on seeds and invertebrates.

A pair of White-faced Whistling Ducks will indulge in mutual preening. The 2 birds stand facing one another and nibble gently at each other's head and neck feathers. This may have a useful function in ridding these relatively inaccessible areas of parasites, but it is likely that such intimate actions help to reinforce the pair bond. The birds usually nest in tall vegetation, but occasionally choose the fork of a low tree.

## 4/ MUTE SWAN
*Cygnus olor*

RANGE: **temperate Eurasia; introduced to parts of North America, South Africa and Australia**
HABITAT: **lowland freshwater lakes and marshes; coastal lagoons and estuaries**
SIZE: $49\frac{1}{4}$–$61$ in (125–155 cm)

The Mute Swan is a familiar sight in town parks in Britain where it has long been protected. Much wilder populations occur in continental Europe and Asia, forming flocks on lakes and estuaries. The species is misnamed, since it utters a variety of snoring, snorting and hissing calls and its wings produce a loud throbbing sound in flight.

Males (called cobs) have larger knobs on their bills than females (pens), especially in the breeding season. A pair of Mute Swans will vigorously defend a territory around the mound of vegetation that forms their nest. However, the birds breed colonially in a few places and there the strong territorial instinct is reduced so much that their nests are only about 3 ft (1 m) apart.

## 5/ BLACK SWAN
*Cygnus atratus*

RANGE: **Australia; introduced into New Zealand**
HABITAT: **large freshwater and brackish marshes and lagoons; also estuaries and coastal bays**
SIZE: $45\frac{1}{4}$–$55$ in (115–140 cm)

The Black Swan is a highly gregarious species, occurring in enormous flocks, up to 50,000 strong. It breeds in colonies of hundreds of pairs, the nests placed just beyond pecking distance from one another. Like many Australian waterbirds, the Black Swan can delay breeding in times of drought but can quickly take advantage of sudden rains and flood conditions. Long-distance movements have also been recorded in response to such extremes of climate.

The nest is typically a pile of vegetation, up to 3 ft (1 m) across at the base, built in shallow water. The 5–6 pale green eggs are incubated for up to 40 days by both parents. In most other wildfowl, the female carries out the incubation alone.

## 6/ TUNDRA SWAN
*Cygnus columbianus*

RANGE: **breeds Arctic North America and USSR; winters S to temperate latitudes**
HABITAT: **breeds on marshy tundra; winters on freshwater marshes and estuaries**
SIZE: $47\frac{1}{4}$–$59$ in (120–150 cm)

Three races of the all-white Tundra Swan are recognized: these include the Whistling Swan *C. c. columbianus* of North America and the Bewick's Swan *C. c. bewickii* of Eurasia, both illustrated. The amount of yellow on the bill of the Bewick's Swan is extremely variable and can in fact be used to identify individual birds.

Most swans return each winter to the same locality and there is great faithfulness between pairs. The birds build their nest on marshy ground and lay a clutch of 3–5 eggs. The young swans migrate with their parents and they spend their first winter together as a family.

## 7/ WHITE-FRONTED GOOSE
*Anser albifrons*

RANGE: circumpolar Arctic; winters S to
temperate latitudes
HABITAT: breeds in tundra; winters on
open marshes and on agricultural land
SIZE: 26–33¾ in (66–86 cm)

White-fronted Geese have a high-pitched, laugh-ing call and are actually named "laughing geese" in more than one European language. They are gregarious birds, occurring in winter flocks of many tens of thousands. When nesting, however, they scatter widely across the tundra. There are 4 or 5 races, distinguished by bill color and plumage: those illustrated are *A. a. albifrons*, breeding in Arctic Siberia, and *A. a. flavirostris*, breeding in western Greenland.

The nest is a shallow hollow, lined with down from the female's breast. The down both insulates and helps to conceal the 4–7 eggs. The goslings quickly learn to peck at grass and other surround-ing vegetation. This, together with the under-ground parts of marsh plants and several different agricultural crops, provides most of their food.

## 8/ GRAYLAG GOOSE
*Anser anser*

RANGE: mainly temperate latitudes of
Eurasia
HABITAT: freshwater marshes and open
water; often winters on farmland
SIZE: 29½–35½ in (75–90 cm)

The Graylag Goose once bred widely throughout western Europe, but the drainage of marshes and deliberate persecution caused a dramatic reduc-tion in its breeding range. However, it is now expanding again and some wintering flocks con-tain tens of thousands of geese. There are 2 races: *A. a. anser* breeds in Europe, while the pink-billed *A. a. rubrirostris* breeds in Asia. They overlap in eastern Europe and western USSR.

Large winter flocks on farmland may damage crops and pasture. The bill of the Graylag Goose is adapted for probing in marshy ground and pulling up roots; it is also ideal for grazing and for slicing pieces off turnips and potatoes.

## 9/ SNOW GOOSE
*Anser caerulescens*

RANGE: Arctic North America; winters on
both seaboards and S to Gulf of Mexico
HABITAT: breeds on Arctic tundra; winters
on freshwater and salt marshes farmland
SIZE: 25½–33 in (65–84 cm)

There are few more magnificent sights than a flock of tens of thousands of Snow Geese. Glisten-ing white, the birds descend like snowflakes, their black wing tips seeming to flicker as they turn before landing. The 2 races, the Greater and the Lesser, are distinguished mainly by size. While the adult Greater Snow Goose is always white, the Lesser Snow Goose shows both the white "snow" phase and a dark gray "blue" phase.

Snow Geese nest in colonies of many thousands of pairs on the Arctic tundra. In winter, they journey south, some flying non-stop for 2,000 mls (3,500 km) or more to reach the Gulf of Mexico, where harvested rice fields provide ample food.

## 10/ HAWAIIAN GOOSE
*Branta sandvicensis*  V

RANGE: confined to the Hawaiian Islands
HABITAT: sparsely vegetated slopes of
volcanoes
SIZE: 22–28 in (56–71 cm)

By 1952, extensive hunting and introduced pred-ators had reduced the once numerous population of the Hawaiian Goose, estimated at 25,000 birds at the end of the 19th century, to as few as 30 individuals. Since then, captive breeding in both Hawaii and England has enabled well over 1,000 birds to be released back into the wild. By 1976, the total population in the wild was around 750.

The Hawaiian Goose has only partial webbing on its feet, reflecting its largely terrestrial habits. In its home on the Hawaiian Islands, there is little standing water. The nest is a simple scrape in the ground, usually in the shelter of a rock or a clump of vegetation.

## 11/ CANADA GOOSE
*Branta canadensis*

RANGE: Arctic and temperate North
America; introduced into Europe and New
Zealand
HABITAT: lowland wetlands
SIZE: 21½–43¼ in (55–110 cm)

The Canada Goose has been divided into 10–12 races, based on distribution, size and coloring. The smallest races (such as *B. c. minima* from west Alaska) breed in the Arctic; the larger races (such as *B. c. canadensis* from eastern Canada) breed farther south. In recent decades, the large birds have successfully moved into town parks and many are tame. Introduced birds in Britain (of the race *B. c. canadensis*) have colonized gravel workings and are now common throughout the lowland parts of the country.

The bird's nest is usually placed on the ground, often sheltered by vegetation, but tree and even cliff-ledge nest sites have been reported, and rafts and other artificial platforms are readily adopted.

## 12/ RED-BREASTED GOOSE
*Branta ruficollis*

RANGE: breeds in the Siberian Arctic;
winters close to the Black, Caspian and
Aral seas
HABITAT: breeds on tundra; winters on
open farmland close to major wetlands
SIZE: 20¾–21½ in (53–55 cm)

A remarkable association exists between this scarce, strikingly plumaged goose and various birds of prey. Red-breasted Geese nest on the Arctic tundra, concentrating in small groups of up to 5 pairs around the nests of Peregrines, Rough-legged Hawks and, sometimes, large gulls. In defending their own nests against predators, these aggressive birds keep intruders, such as gulls and Arctic Foxes, away from the nests of the surrounding geese.

The geese may site their nests within 33 ft (10 m) of birds of prey, apparently without risk of attack from their "protectors." The nest is usually placed on a steep bank or on the top of a low cliff. The total world population is probably fewer than 25,000 individuals.

## 13/ FRECKLED DUCK
*Stictonetta naevosa*  ?

RANGE: Australia
HABITAT: open freshwater and brackish
lakes and swamps
SIZE: 19½–21½ in (50–55 cm)

This duck takes its name from the fine, buff or whitish speckles on its plumage. Like many Australian waterfowl, it is highly responsive to the vagaries of the climate. Prolonged drought in the areas where it is most numerous, in the southwest and southeast of the country, sends birds wandering over great distances. Where they find water, pairs quickly settle down to breed and rear young. Later, if conditions permit, there will be a return to their normal distribution until the next drought again disperses the birds. Freckled Ducks always place their nests close to water, often supported by the twigs or branches of flooded bushes.

## 14/ MAGELLAN GOOSE
*Chloephaga picta*

RANGE: S South America and the Falkland
Islands
HABITAT: grassland and marshes
SIZE: 23½–25½ in (60–65 cm)

As grazing birds, Magellan Geese have come into conflict with sheep farmers in South America. Bounties have been offered for both birds and eggs, but although large numbers are killed and eggs are systematically removed, the species is not under serious threat. Its habitats are extensive and the human population is sparse. Although pressure on the birds is severe in some areas, in others the geese are unmolested.

The white and gray male has a whistling call used in display, to which the rufous and gray-brown female responds with a lower cackling. The illustration shows the 2 races of the Magellan Goose: the Lesser *C. p. picta*, with its white and barred phases, and the Greater *C. p. leucoptera*.

## 15/ EGYPTIAN GOOSE
*Alopochen aegyptiacus*

RANGE: Nile valley and sub-Saharan Africa
HABITAT: tropical and subtropical
wetlands
SIZE: 24¾–28¾ in (63–73 cm)

A large, upright bird, the Egyptian Goose has 2 color phases, one gray-brown on the upperparts, the other red-brown. The species is remarkable for the great variety of nest sites that it uses. Some birds nest on the ground, like most other geese and sheldgeese, often choosing the shelter of bushes or clumps of grass. Other pairs prefer to nest off the ground, using ledges on cliffs or old buildings. Some select the abandoned nests of other birds, often high in the crowns of trees.

A typical clutch consists of 5–8 eggs, which are incubated by the female for about 28 days. The downy young that hatch out on ledges or in trees face a perilous tumble to the ground as they leave the nest. The parents do not assist the chicks, but call to them from below until they pluck up courage to step into space.

WOOD DUCK
♂
♀

race crecca
♀
GREEN-WINGED TEAL
race carolinensis
♂
race crecca
♂

MUSCOVY DUCK
♂

COMB DUCK    race melanotos
race melanotos
♀
♂

MALLARD
♂
♀

race chlorotis
♂
NEW ZEALAND TEAL
race chlorotis
♀

race armata
"Chilean Torrent
Duck" ♂

TORRENT
DUCK

race armata
♀

NORTHERN SHOVELER
♀
♂

AMERICAN WIGEON

AFRICAN PYGMY GOOSE

AMERICAN BLACK DUCK

NORTHERN PINTAIL

NORTHERN SHELDUCK

juv

race *gambensis*
♀

SPUR-WINGED GOOSE

MAGELLANIC FLIGHTLESS
STEAMER DUCK

juv

# SHELDUCKS, STEAMER DUCKS, PERCHING DUCKS AND DABBLING DUCKS

## 1/ NORTHERN SHELDUCK
*Tadorna tadorna*

RANGE: **temperate Eurasia; winters S to N Africa, India, China and Japan**
HABITAT: **estuaries, shallow seas**
SIZE: **23–26 in (58–67 cm)**

These large, gooselike birds feed with a scything action of the bill through soft mud and sand, picking up mollusks, crustaceans and other invertebrates. In early spring, they gather in groups in which the males court the females with melodious whistling calls, rearing up and throwing back their heads. Arguments with neighbors often develop into furious aerial chases.

Most Northern Shelducks nest in holes, either underground or in hollow trees. They will also nest under buildings and in straw stacks. The young of several broods often combine into large "nurseries," under the care of just a few of the parents. The rest of the adults depart for their molting grounds. Much of the population of northwestern Europe, numbering some 100,000 birds, migrates to molt in the Waddenzee on the north German coast.

## 2/ MAGELLANIC FLIGHTLESS STEAMER DUCK
*Tachyeres pteneres*

RANGE: **extreme S South America**
HABITAT: **marine, especially rocky or gravelly coasts with offshore kelp beds**
SIZE: **24–33 in (61–84 cm)**

The heavy, bulky build of the Magellanic Flightless Steamer Duck is enhanced by the large head and strong bill. It is incapable of flight, though it can escape predators by furiously threshing and paddling over the water with its stubby wings. It is this action, once described as "steaming," that earned these ducks their name. The males, in particular, also use their wings to strike one another in combat. The blows are reinforced by large bony knobs on the carpal joints at the bends of the wings.

Magellanic Flightless Steamer Ducks feed exclusively on marine invertebrates, especially mussels and crabs. They dive for their food among forests of kelp fronds and also dabble in gravel under shallow water.

The nest is usually among grass tussocks near water, but is occasionally in a deserted penguin burrow. Although generally sited close to water, nests of this species have been found up to half a mile (1 km) inland.

## 3/ SPUR-WINGED GOOSE
*Plectropterus gambensis*

RANGE: **most of sub-Saharan Africa**
HABITAT: **fresh waters in open grassland**
SIZE: **29½–39 in (75–100 cm)**

With its long legs and neck, this large goose appears rather ungainly. It uses its long bill for grazing on waterside vegetation or for pulling up aquatic plants, and it also feeds on floating seeds.

Spur-winged Geese have a hidden weapon, a spur 1 in (2.5 cm) long on the carpal joint at the bend of each wing. It is used in disputes when competing birds strike each other with opened wings. The nest is usually a mound of vegetation

built among tall plants and up to 14 eggs are laid. The goslings develop their wing spurs when only a few weeks old. There are 2 races: *P. g. gambensis*, which occurs over most of the species' range, and *P. g. niger* found south of 15°S, which has the white on the underparts restricted to the center of the chest and lower belly.

## 4/ MUSCOVY DUCK
*Cairina moschata*

RANGE: **Central and South America**
HABITAT: **freshwater marshes and pools in wooded areas; brackish coastal lagoons**
SIZE: **26–33 in (66–84 cm)**

The Muscovy Duck has been widely introduced outside its native lands as a domestic fowl. Unlike the glossy greenish-black wild birds, the domestic birds may be green-black, gray or white or a mixture of colors. The knob at the base of a domestic male's bill is red and surrounded by bare red skin. Muscovy Ducks are omnivorous, feeding on the leaves and seeds of marsh plants, as well as small reptiles, fish, crabs and insects.

In the wild, these shy birds roost in small groups in trees, safe from ground predators. The only time they leave the shelter of the forest is when the savannas are flooded. Both wild and domestic Muscovy Ducks prefer to nest in holes in trees, and they take readily to nest-boxes.

## 5/ COMB DUCK
*Sarkidiornis melanotos*

RANGE: **sub-Saharan Africa, India, Southeast Asia and tropical South America**
HABITAT: **rivers, swamps, lakes**
SIZE: **22–30 in (56–76 cm)**

This bird takes its name from the fleshy blackish knob at the base of the male's bill: this knob has a crenellated edge rather like a comb. Comb Ducks are highly mobile, with flocks of 50 or more birds moving to take advantage of flooded conditions in different areas.

Outside the breeding season, flocks of Comb Ducks often consist entirely of males or of females. During the breeding season, each male may have 2 mates and several nesting "pairs" can form small breeding colonies. The nest is usually in a hole in a tree, in an old wall or on the ground, well concealed in tall vegetation.

## 6/ AFRICAN PYGMY GOOSE
*Nettapus auritus*

RANGE: **sub-Saharan Africa, Madagascar**
HABITAT: **freshwater pools, large lakes; less often coastal lagoons and estuaries**
SIZE: **12–13 in (30–33 cm)**

The drake African Pygmy Goose is among the most attractive of the smaller wildfowl. Although the bird is really a duck, the rounded head and short, stubby bill are gooselike, hence the name.

African Pygmy Geese spend much of their time perching in trees, on branches overhanging the water, usually in pairs or small groups but sometimes in groups of up to 200 birds. They peck seeds and small leaves from the surface, dive to reach underwater plants, or pluck seeds, leaves and buds from emergent vegetation. They are especially fond of water lily seeds. The bird's nest is usually placed in a hole, normally in a tree, cliff or termite mound, but frequently in the thatched roof of a hut.

## 7/ WOOD DUCK
*Aix sponsa*

RANGE: **North America: E population breeds S Canada to Florida, W population breeds British Columbia to California; winters in S of breeding range**
HABITAT: **fresh waters in wooded areas; more open flooded areas in winter**
SIZE: **17–20 in (43–51 cm)**

The remarkable coloration of the male Wood Duck greatly contrasts with the mottled gray-brown of the female. It was the drake's superb plumage which nearly led to the species' extinction. In the 19th century the feathers were in great demand for ornament and for fishing flies.

However, because protection measures were taken in time, and since the Wood Duck's habit of nesting in tree holes meant that it took readily to nest-boxes, it was possible to restore the species to many areas of eastern North America in which tree clearance and drainage, as well as shooting, had led to its serious decline.

## 8/ TORRENT DUCK
*Merganetta armata*
RANGE: **Andes**
HABITAT: **fast-flowing streams**
SIZE: **17–18 in (43–46 cm)**

The Torrent Duck is perfectly adapted to life in fast-flowing water. It has a streamlined shape, powerful legs, a broad, stiff tail used for steering, and sharp claws to enable it to cling to slippery rocks. It feeds by making frequent underwater forays from its perch on a boulder. It forages for caddis fly and other larvae on the river bottom, catches small fish, and picks various food items from the surface. Although few nests have been found, they are always near water in a crevice or hollow of some kind, between rocks or under overhangs. The ducklings are able to tackle the most turbulent water as soon as they hatch.

Several races have been described, separated geographically along the 5,000-ml (8,000-km) length of the Andes. The one illustrated is the Chilean Torrent Duck *M.a. armata* of central Chile and western Argentina.

## 9/ AMERICAN WIGEON
*Anas americana*
RANGE: **breeds N and C North America; winters S to Gulf of Mexico**
HABITAT: **freshwater marshes, ponds; winters on marshes, coastal lagoons**
SIZE: **18–22 in (45–56 cm)**

American Wigeons are highly gregarious in winter, occurring in flocks of many tens of thousands. In summer the breeding pairs disperse, spreading throughout the pothole country of the North American prairies and northward into the wooded muskeg of Canada and Alaska.

Although classed as a dabbling duck, the American Wigeon obtains only some of its plant food by dabbling in shallow water. More often, tightly packed flocks of birds graze on marshes and pastures. The nest is a shallow cup of grasses in concealing vegetation near water.

## 10/ GREEN-WINGED TEAL
*Anas crecca*
RANGE: **breeds North America, N Eurasia; winters S USA, Central America, Caribbean, temperate Eurasia, tropical Asia**
HABITAT: **freshwater pools, marshes; in winter also on estuaries, coastal lagoons**
SIZE: **13–15 in (34–38 cm)**

This abundant small duck has 2 distinct races, the European *A.c. crecca*, with a horizontal white flank stripe, and the North American *A.c. carolinensis*, with a vertical white chest stripe. These are male characteristics; females are indistinguishable.

Green-winged Teals can launch themselves almost vertically into the air when disturbed,

"springing" off the water, whence comes an old collective noun for a group of these agile and beautiful little ducks – a "spring" of teal. Once in flight, dense flocks will wheel and turn in perfect unison. The male has a characteristic, far-carrying, liquid *preep preep* call. The diet consists of small invertebrates and some seeds, most of which the birds find by dabbling in the shallows.

## 11/ NEW ZEALAND TEAL
*Anas aucklandica*                        V
RANGE: **isolated sites in New Zealand**
HABITAT: **freshwater swamps and streams among trees; estuaries and ocean bays**
SIZE: **14–18 in (34–46 cm)**

The entire population of these secretive, night-time feeding birds may now number fewer than 2,000. Estimates suggest that there are about 1,000 of the race *A. a. chlorotis*, once widespread throughout New Zealand, but now found only in small isolated populations in areas relatively free of predators, notably on Great Barrier Island. Some 500 of the race *A. a. aucklandica* survive on several islands near Auckland Island, and about 30 of the race *A. a. nesiotis* remain on Dent Island, an islet off Campbell Island.

Habitat destruction and introduced predators seem to have been the main causes of the bird's severe decline. However, captive breeding programs are proving successful and several hundred birds have been released back into the wild in recent years.

Both of the island races are flightless: presumably, flightlessness was an adaptation to life on small islands where there were originally no ground predators. When cats were introduced, they soon took their toll of this easy prey.

## 12/ MALLARD
*Anas platyrhynchos*
RANGE: **N hemisphere, N of the tropics; introduced to Australia and New Zealand**
HABITAT: **wide range of fresh and coastal waters**
SIZE: **20–25½ in (50–65 cm)**

The success of the Mallard, ancestor of most domestic ducks, reflects its supreme adaptability. It can become completely tame in urban areas, relying on human handouts for food, although it is as wild as any wildfowl in other habitats.

Mallards feed by dabbling in shallows, or upending to reach greater depths. They are omnivorous, eating both invertebrates and plant matter. Natural nest sites are in thick vegetation close to water, but in towns the birds use holes in trees and buildings and even window ledges.

## 13/ AMERICAN BLACK DUCK
*Anas rubripes*
RANGE: **NE North America; winters S to Gulf of Mexico**
HABITAT: **freshwater marshes in woods; winters on estuaries, coastal marshes**
SIZE: **21–24 in (53–61 cm)**

American Black Ducks feed on plants and invertebrates and nest in dense vegetation close to water. As with some other close relatives of the Mallard,

but unlike nearly all other northern hemisphere dabbling ducks, the male lacks any bright nuptial plumage. The species may now be under threat because females are more attracted by brightly colored male Mallards than by their own kind. Since the recent expansion of the Mallard's range in eastern North America, hybridization has become more common and widespread. Habitat degradation and overhunting pose further threats to the bird's population.

## 14/ NORTHERN PINTAIL
*Anas acuta*
RANGE: **Eurasia and North America; winters S to Panama, C Africa, India, Philippines**
HABITAT: **open marshes; winters on estuaries and coastal lagoons**
SIZE: **male 25–29 in (63–74 cm) including 4 in (10 cm) central tail feathers; female 17–25 in (43–63 cm)**

The handsome drake Northern Pintail has long tail streamers which he cocks out of the water as he swims. This species is strongly attracted to fall stubblefields; a single site may hold more than 500,000 birds. In some parts of North America, wheat and corn is grown specially for them. It is left unharvested in the fall to attract the vast hordes and keep them from damaging more vulnerable crops.

Apart from pecking at grain, Northern Pintails feed mainly in the water. They upend, using their long necks to reach deeper than other ducks sharing their range. They scour the bottom of pools and marshes for plant roots and leaves, as well as aquatic invertebrates.

## 15/ NORTHERN SHOVELER
*Anas clypeata*
RANGE: **Eurasia and North America S of the Arctic Circle; winters S to the subtropics**
HABITAT: **freshwater pools and marshes; also on estuaries and coastal lagoons in winter**
SIZE: **17–20 in (44–52 cm)**

This bird's distinctive bill acts as a superb filter for food. As the duck swims along with the front half of the bill submerged, it creates a stream of water that flows in at the bill's tip. Rapid tongue action aids the flow and directs it out at each side, any particles being strained from the water by intermeshing projections on the upper and lower mandibles.

Groups of Northern Shovelers often circle slowly as they feed. Their combined paddling action brings food items – tiny seeds and floating animals – to the surface in deep water. Northern Shovelers will also dabble in shallows, selecting larger food items. Here, however, they come into competition with other ducks, something their sieving method normally avoids.

# DIVING DUCKS, SEA DUCKS, SAWBILLS AND STIFFTAILS

♀
♂
♀ variant

TUFTED DUCK

♂
♀
imm ♂

COMMON EIDER

♂
♀

RED-CRESTED POCHARD

♂
♀

CANVASBACK

race *nigra* ♂

race *nigra* ♀

race *americana* ♂

HARLEQUIN DUCK
♂
♀

BLACK SCOTER

WHITE-BACKED DUCK

MARBLED TEAL

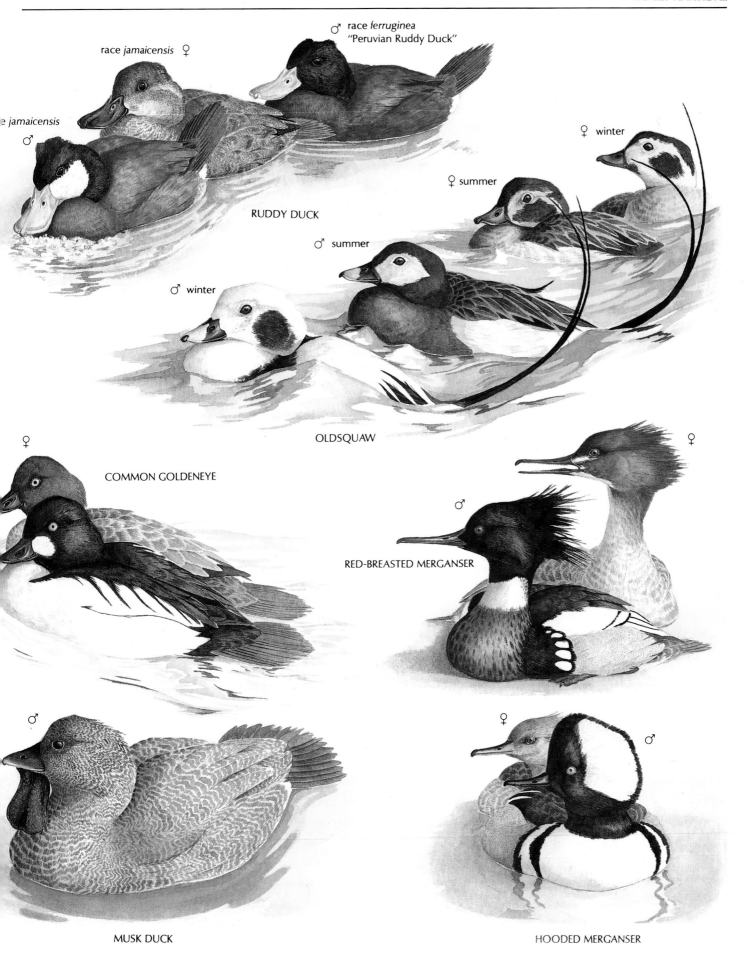

race *jamaicensis* ♀

♂ race *ferruginea*
"Peruvian Ruddy Duck"

*jamaicensis*
♂

♀ winter

♀ summer

♂ summer

♂ winter

RUDDY DUCK

OLDSQUAW

♀

COMMON GOLDENEYE

♀

♂

RED-BREASTED MERGANSER

♂

♀

♂

MUSK DUCK

HOODED MERGANSER

# DIVING DUCKS, SEA DUCKS, SAWBILLS AND STIFFTAILS

## 1/ MARBLED TEAL
*Marmaronetta angustirostris*   [?]
RANGE: **Mediterranean region E to Pakistan and NW India**
HABITAT: **shallow freshwater and brackish lakes, lagoons and marshes**
SIZE: **15¼–16½ in (39–42 cm)**

The Marbled Teal takes its name from the whitish blotches that liberally mark its sandy-gray plumage. Although it resembles the teals, which are dabbling ducks, this species is now generally regarded as more closely related to the pochards, or diving ducks, and is increasingly known as the Marbled Duck. In particular, its courtship displays and other behavior patterns are more similar to the diving ducks.

Breeding usually takes place in small colonies, sometimes with the nests no more than 3 ft (1 m) apart. The normal nest site is on the ground, concealed under low bushes or in thick vegetation close to the water. However, in southern Spain nests have been found concealed in the roofs of grass- and reed-thatched huts. The birds do not excavate holes in the thatch but make use of natural cavities.

Populations of this duck have declined over most of its range as shallow wetlands have been drained. However, there have been recent increases in numbers reported from Spain and North Africa.

## 2/ RED-CRESTED POCHARD
*Netta rufina*
RANGE: **E Europe and SC Asia**
HABITAT: **freshwater lakes, rivers, deltas and coastal lagoons**
SIZE: **20¾–22½ in (53–57 cm)**

Red-crested Pochards have been spreading slowly north in Europe in the last 50 years. Their principal range is in the Mediterranean basin, but there are small pockets of breeding birds farther north in France, the Netherlands and Denmark. Birds from these countries began to appear regularly in eastern England in the 1950s and 1960s, but the picture has become confused since then by escapes from captivity. This colorful species is popular with waterfowl keepers.

The birds lay a clutch of up to 10 pale green or olive eggs in a well-concealed nest of aquatic vegetation, often built on a base of twigs. The female incubates alone, while the male moves away and joins other males for the annual molt.

## 3/ CANVASBACK
*Aythya valisineria*
RANGE: **S Canada to Mexico**
HABITAT: **breeds on prairie marshes; winters on lakes, lagoons and estuaries**
SIZE: **18¾–24 in (48–61 cm)**

The Canvasback is the largest of the pochards, or diving ducks. Both male and female have a relatively long sloping forehead, high, peaked crown, long bill and long neck giving them a distinctive silhouette. The Canvasback is one of the typical breeding species of the prairie pothole country of southern Canada and northern USA – a vast area of rolling farmland with numerous small ponds (potholes) and marshes.

The ducks feed mainly on aquatic vegetation, diving to depths of 30 ft (9 m). Often, they are closely followed by American Coots and American Wigeons. As soon as the Canvasbacks surface with a beakful of food, the other birds give chase and try to steal it.

## 4/ TUFTED DUCK
*Aythya fuligula*
RANGE: **Eurasia**
HABITAT: **lakes and ponds, sometimes in towns; winters on larger waters, estuaries, lagoons**
SIZE: **15¾–18½ in (40–47 cm)**

Tufted Ducks are gregarious birds that gather in large winter flocks and breed in loose colonies, with their nests only a few yards apart. They have successfully moved into towns and cities, colonizing park lakes and relying on people for scraps of food.

Tufted Ducks are expert divers, able to reach depths of 16–20 ft (5–6 m) and remain underwater for 20–30 seconds. Their natural diet includes a wide variety of small mollusks and other aquatic invertebrates. The birds' nests are rarely far from water, concealed in tussocks of grass or under bushes. There the females incubate the clutches of 7–12 eggs for about 24 days.

## 5/ COMMON EIDER
*Somateria mollissima*
RANGE: **Arctic and N temperate Eurasia and North America**
HABITAT: **coastal waters, estuaries**
SIZE: **19½–28 in (50–71 cm)**

The down feathers that the female Common Eider plucks from her breast to line the nest have long been valued by people for their insulating properties. In Iceland and Norway, breeding colonies of Common Eiders have been protected in order to maximize the production of eider down. Artificial nesting sites, the control of predators and freedom from disturbance have enabled colonies of up to 10,000 pairs to become established and to be maintained over many years. The down is care-

fully collected and cleaned, and then sold to manufacturers of sleeping bags and quilts. Pure eider down is still considered superior to any man-made substitute and commands a high price.

With heat loss delayed by the insulating feathers around the nest, the female Common Eider incubates her clutch of 4–6 olive-green eggs for 28 days. After hatching, the young from several broods may come together to form a "nursery."

## 6/ HARLEQUIN DUCK
*Histrionicus histrionicus*
RANGE: **Iceland, Greenland, Labrador, NW North America, NE Siberia and Japan**
HABITAT: **fast-flowing rivers and streams and inshore coastal waters**
SIZE: **13¼–17¾ in (34–45 cm)**

The strikingly marked Harlequin Duck is most at home in fast-flowing water, in which it is an expert swimmer. It can maneuver upstream with great skill, using eddies and slack water close to the bank, and sometimes rushes over the surface of the water, half-flying, half-swimming. Swimming with the current, it can shoot rapids and pass through turbulent water without difficulty. When on the ocean, which it mainly frequents in winter, it seems to spend most of the time just where the surf is breaking most vigorously.

In flight, the Harlequin Duck passes fast and low over the water, precisely following each bend in a stream. Its nest, like that of most other ducks, is well concealed in vegetation, often overhanging a river bank.

## 7/ OLDSQUAW
*Clangula hyemalis*
RANGE: **Arctic Eurasia and North America; winters S to cool temperate regions**
HABITAT: **breeds on tundra pools and by the coast; winters in ocean bays**
SIZE: **14–18½ in (36–47 cm)**

Oldsquaw have no fewer than 4 plumage changes during the course of a year: both sexes have distinct summer, fall, winter and eclipse plumages, the last one after breeding. They are sea ducks, spending nearly all their time on salt water, although some birds breed beside fresh water. The courtship display of the male includes a far-carrying yodeling call that is wonderfully evocative of wild places.

This duck is among the most accomplished divers of all wildfowl. It can remain underwater for as long as a minute and reach depths of 180 ft (55 m), a feat proven by individuals becoming entangled in fishing nets. It pursues and catches fish during dives, while in shallower water it plucks mollusks and crustaceans from the bottom.

## 8/ BLACK SCOTER
*Melanitta nigra*

RANGE: Arctic and N temperate Eurasia and North America; winters to the S
HABITAT: breeds on freshwater lakes and marshes; winters in ocean bays and estuaries
SIZE: $17\frac{3}{4}$–$21\frac{1}{4}$ in (44–54 cm)

The only relief from the all-black plumage of the male Black Scoter is a patch of yellow on the bill. In the Eurasian race *M. n. nigra* the yellow covers only a small area halfway along the upper mandible, but in the North American race *M. n. americana* the yellow covers most of the upper mandible and a prominent knob at the base of the bill. The latter is sometimes regarded as a separate species.

During courtship, rival males rush at each other, seemingly skating over the surface, with their heads outstretched, before coming to an abrupt halt in a flurry of spray. The females, too, will indulge in short rushes, usually at males they are rejecting. Another display given by the male involves raising the head and tail out of the water and producing a surprisingly pure and musical whistle. On a still day the sound can carry for many hundreds of yards.

Black Scoters nest beside large lakes as well as tiny moorland pools. If possible, they take their young to the ocean soon after hatching.

## 9/ COMMON GOLDENEYE
*Bucephala clangula*

RANGE: N Eurasia and North America; winters to S
HABITAT: breeds on lakes and pools in forests; winters on lakes, estuaries, ocean bays
SIZE: $16\frac{1}{2}$–$19\frac{1}{2}$ in (42–50 cm)

The Common Goldeneye's head is distinctively rounded and its steep forehead and short bill help in identification at long range. The bird's natural breeding site is a cavity in a tree or a dead stump. Inside the nest-hole, the only lining materials for the 8–12 eggs are a few chips of rotten wood and down feathers plucked from the female's breast.

With forest clearance, tree holes have become rarer and the Common Goldeneye has declined in many areas. However, the species takes readily to nest-boxes and programs involving several hundreds or even thousands of boxes are in operation. A nest-box program played a vital role in persuading the species to colonize Scotland in recent years.

## 10/ HOODED MERGANSER
*Mergus cucullatus*

RANGE: 2 populations. W population breeds S Alaska to NW USA; winters S Alaska to California. E population breeds S Canada, N and C USA; winters Florida, N Mexico
HABITAT: breeds and winters by rivers and lakes in forests; also winters on estuaries, coasts
SIZE: $16\frac{1}{2}$–$19\frac{1}{2}$ in (42–50 cm)

The male Hooded Merganser has a pronounced black and white crest on his head. When raised, the crest forms a quarter-circle of white outlined in black, greatly enlarging the appearance of the head. The bird's bill is long and thin and is used for grasping fish.

The Hooded Merganser places its nest in a hole in a tree up to 52 ft (16 m) above the ground. Here the female lays and incubates 6–12 white eggs. It was once thought that the female brought the newly hatched young down to the ground in her bill. In fact, it has since been discovered that all she does is to call encouragingly from the base of the tree and wait for the young to tumble down to her. Being so light and covered in soft down, they rarely come to much harm.

## 11/ RED-BREASTED MERGANSER
*Mergus serrator*

RANGE: N Eurasia and North America; winters S to Mediterranean, E China, Gulf of Mexico
HABITAT: breeds by rivers, estuaries and coasts; winters on estuaries and coastal bays
SIZE: $20\frac{1}{2}$–$22\frac{3}{4}$ in (52–58 cm)

The Red-breasted Merganser is just as much at home on the ocean as it is on fresh water. It is a long-necked, long-bodied duck, whose bill is also long and thin with a hooked tip. Serrations along the sides of the mandibles help the bird grasp fish.

The Red-breasted Merganser's appetite for fish has brought it into conflict with fishing interests, particularly on rivers with trout and salmon. The true effect of the bird on fish stocks is mostly rather slight but, as is often the case with wild predators, the bird is accused of causing more damage than it actually carries out. In some places it is ruthlessly hunted.

## 12/ RUDDY DUCK
*Oxyura jamaicensis*

RANGE: North and South America; introduced into Britain
HABITAT: breeds and winters on well-vegetated lakes; also winters on coastal lagoons and bays
SIZE: $13\frac{3}{4}$–17 in (35–43 cm)

The male Ruddy Duck has white cheeks, a black cap and a remarkable large blue bill, which gives every appearance of having just been painted. The tail consists of short stiff feathers that can be held up at a jaunty angle or kept flat along the water, contributing to the bird's dumpy appearance. The race *O. j. jamaicensis* occurs in the West Indies, while *O. j. ferruginea*, the Peruvian Ruddy Duck, is found in Peru and Bolivia.

The male Ruddy Duck's display has been compared to the movements of a toy boat. He rushes over the water, paddling furiously, with his tail and lower body submerged, chest lifted out of the water, shoulders hunched, head down and bill pressed down onto his raised chest. In another sequence, the male beats his bill rapidly on his chest before jerking his head forward and calling. Although the male does not help the female with incubation of the eggs, he often stays close by and then accompanies his mate and his growing brood.

## 13/ MUSK DUCK
*Biziura lobata*

RANGE: S Australia and Tasmania
HABITAT: breeds by freshwater and brackish lakes and marshes; winters on lakes, estuaries and coastal bays
SIZE: male $24$–$28\frac{3}{4}$ in (61–73 cm); female $18\frac{1}{2}$–$23\frac{1}{2}$ in (47–60 cm)

Both sexes of the Musk Duck have dark oily-looking plumage, but the male alone has a flat lobe of skin hanging down below the lower mandible. The male is also nearly one-third larger than the female – an unusual size difference in any kind of bird.

The male Musk Duck has a particularly vigorous display, throwing his head back over his body, fanning his tail back till it almost meets his head, and splashing noisily with both feet together. At the same time, he utters a loud grunt followed immediately by a piercing whistle.

The male is strongly territorial, defending an area of fresh water against other males and attempting to attract several females to his territory. The bird's nest is concealed in vegetation at the water's edge or occasionally in a hollow of a tree stump or root.

## 14/ WHITE-BACKED DUCK
*Thalassornis leuconotos*

RANGE: sub-Saharan Africa
HABITAT: freshwater lakes, pools and marshes
SIZE: 15–$15\frac{3}{4}$ in (38–40 cm)

The White-backed Duck is a stubby bird, with no more than a rudimentary tail. Its overall shape, with its low sloping back and long neck, gives the bird more the appearance of a grebe than a duck. The race, *T. l. insularis* that occurs on Madagascar is a little smaller and darker than the more widespread African race.

The White-backed Duck lives exclusively in freshwater habitats, particularly those with plenty of emergent vegetation. It is perfectly adapted to an aquatic life, being an accomplished diver, and comes onto dry land only to breed. Its feet are placed so far to the rear of its body that it can barely walk. It either builds its nest right on the edge of the water or uses the old, floating nests of coots and grebes. The 4–6 eggs are large for the size of the bird and are a glossy brown, quite unlike those of any other wildfowl.

# NEW WORLD VULTURES, OSPREY, KITES, HONEY BUZZARDS AND FISH EAGLES

♂ ANDEAN CONDOR

♂

KING VULTURE

TURKEY VULTURE

CRESTED BAZA
race *subcristata*

dark phase

pale phase

WESTERN HONEY
BUZZARD

AMERICAN SWALLOW-TAILED KITE

OSPREY
race *carolinensis*

♂

BRAHMINY KITE

juv

juv

BALD EAGLE

juv

SNAIL KITE
♂

♀

BLACK KITE
race *migrans*

WHITE-TAILED SEA EAGLE

juv

BAT HAWK
race *alcinus*

juv

AFRICAN FISH EAGLE

# NEW WORLD VULTURES, OSPREY, KITES, HONEY BUZZARDS AND FISH EAGLES

## FAMILY CATHARTIDAE
### New World vultures
Large carrion-feeders. Broad wings, powerful bill. Plumage mostly brownish black. Naked head or face. Sexes alike. Nest in hollows in trees or rocks. Eggs 1–2, white, cream, pale green, some blotched brown. Incubation 32–41 days; 54–58 days in King Vulture and condors. Chicks remain in nest 10–25 weeks. 7 species.

## 1/ TURKEY VULTURE
*Cathartes aura*

RANGE: **S Canada to Tierra del Fuego, Caribbean, Falkland Islands**
HABITAT: **variable, including desert, grassland, farmland, forest**
SIZE: **$25\frac{1}{2}$–$31\frac{1}{2}$ in (65–80 cm)**

The Turkey Vulture, or "buzzard" as it is popularly known, is a common and conspicuous bird over large parts of its range. A carrion-feeder and general scavenger, it is adaptable enough to thrive in an extraordinarily wide range of habitats and climatic zones, from the cold deserts of Patagonia to the tropical forests of Amazonia. Most populations are more or less resident in one area, but those of western USA are migratory, wintering in South America.

Turkey Vultures are easy to recognize in gliding flight by the distinctive raised angle of their wings and by their habit of continually tilting from one side to the other as they fly.

## 2/ KING VULTURE
*Sarcorhamphus papa*

RANGE: **C Mexico to N Argentina; Trinidad**
HABITAT: **tropical forest**
SIZE: **30 in (76 cm)**

With its striking plumage and the ornate pattern of bare skin and wattles on its head, the King Vulture is one of the most colorful of all the birds of prey. The immature birds are almost all black at first but become increasingly white as they grow older.

Although they are quite common, King Vultures are often difficult to spot when flying high over the dense forest they usually frequent. Unlike the other New World vultures, they seldom occur in groups. Their strong bills enable them to tackle a wide variety of carrion, and they can locate animal remains even in dense cover using their well-developed sense of smell. They often take advantage of dying fish stranded on river banks.

## 3/ ANDEAN CONDOR
*Vultur gryphus*

RANGE: **Andes, from W Venezuela to Tierra del Fuego**
HABITAT: **high mountains; down to the coast in Peru and S Chile**
SIZE: **$43\frac{1}{4}$ in (110 cm)**

With a weight of up to 25 lb (12 kg) and a wingspan of over 10 ft (3 m), this immense high-mountain vulture is the largest of all the world's birds of prey. Soaring majestically for hours on outstretched wings, it can withstand most of the buffeting winds that howl around the Andean summits and rake the tip of South America.

Although Andean Condors have become scarce in many parts of their range, in others they remain fairly numerous and groups of them may gather at large carcasses. They feed extensively on carrion, sometimes also attacking and killing sickly or dying animals. They are regular visitors to the vast seabird colonies along the Peruvian coast where they prey heavily on eggs.

## FAMILY PANDIONIDAE
### Osprey
There is only one species in this family.

## 4/ OSPREY
*Pandion haliaetus*

RANGE: **breeds North America, Eurasia (mainly migrants), NE Africa, Australia; winter visitor and nonbreeding migrant elsewhere**
HABITAT: **coasts, rivers, lakes, wetlands**
SIZE: **$21\frac{3}{4}$–$23\frac{3}{4}$ in (55–58 cm)**

The Osprey has an almost worldwide distribution. Several races are recognized, differing slightly in size and in the plumage on the breast. The one illustrated is the North American race *P. h. carolinensis*, with a pale breast band (especially females) and a dark crown. The sexes sometimes differ in darkness of breast and crown, and females are larger than males, as in most birds of prey. Many Ospreys are coastal birds, but others breed around inland lakes and rivers.

They feed almost exclusively on fish, soaring or circling up to 100 ft (30 m) above the water and often hovering briefly. When they catch sight of prey near the surface, they make a spectacular headlong plunge, throwing their feet forward at the last moment. The soles of the feet have sharp spines that help the birds grasp slippery fish.

The large nest is built on a cliff, in a tree or even on the ground in some habitats. Incubation of the 2–4 red-blotched creamy-white eggs takes about 38 days. Ospreys suffered decades of poisoning in the USA from the pesticide DDT, but the population is now recovering its numbers.

## FAMILY ACCIPITRIDAE/1
### Honey buzzards and kites
Medium to large birds of prey. Plumage highly variable, but usually darker above than below. Sexes similar. Nest of sticks in tree, often mixed with rubbish (kites). Eggs white, spotted reddish, 1–3 (honey buzzards); 2–7 (kites). Incubation 30–35 days (honey buzzards); 28–38 days (kites). Chicks remain in nest 40–45 days (honey buzzards); 25–60 days (kites). 32 species.

## 5/ CRESTED BAZA
*Aviceda subcristata*

RANGE: **N and E Australia, New Guinea, Moluccas, Bismarck Archipelago, Solomon Islands**
HABITAT: **forest and woodland, particularly rain forest edge; also clearings and gardens**
SIZE: **$13\frac{3}{4}$–18 in (35–46 cm)**

The Crested, or Pacific, Baza is a medium-sized attractively plumaged bird of prey, with a short crest that can be raised or lowered. Its prominent eyes, barred plumage and short legs combine to give it a pigeonlike or cuckoolike appearance. The northeastern and eastern Australian race *A. s. subcristata* is illustrated; there is a total of 15 other races, which tend to be darker in the east and paler in the west.

The bird hunts either from a perch in the tree canopy or by flying slowly over the treetops. When it spots prey such as large insects and tree frogs, it may snatch them with a fast dive or reach them by hovering into the foliage, clambering among the branches or even hanging from twigs with beating wings. Occasionally, lizards and small birds provide prey; the Crested Baza is also partial to fruit such as figs.

Breeding birds perform undulating display flights, climbing with deep, labored flaps and then diving while uttering a reedy 2-note whistle. The fragile nest is built high in the tree canopy, and the 2–3 (rarely up to 5) eggs are incubated by both sexes.

## 6/ WESTERN HONEY BUZZARD
*Pernis apivorus*

RANGE: **Europe E to Central Asia; winters sub-Saharan Africa**
HABITAT: **mature woodland**
SIZE: **$20\frac{1}{2}$–$23\frac{1}{2}$ in (52–60 cm)**

The underparts of the Western Honey Buzzard vary greatly in color, from almost white to almost black, with various intermediate forms. All forms, however, have a characteristic pattern of bars on the underside of the wings and tail. Other distinctive features are the small, cuckoolike head, the long, rather narrow tail and the flat angle of the wings when the bird is gliding.

This species is a highly specialized feeder, relying almost entirely on bees, wasps and hornets. It eats the larvae, the pupae and even the nests, as well as the adult insects, carefully breaking off the stings before swallowing them. Birds from the northern part of the range migrate to Africa for the winter.

## 7/ AMERICAN SWALLOW-TAILED KITE
*Elanoides forficatus*

RANGE: **SE USA, Mexico S to N Argentina**
HABITAT: **woodland and forest**
SIZE: **$23\frac{1}{2}$ in (60 cm)**

With its distinctive black and white plumage and long, deeply forked tail, this beautiful bird is unlikely to be mistaken for any other species. Few birds of prey can match the sheer gracefulness of its flight.

The American Swallow-tailed Kite feeds entirely on the wing, capturing aerial insects and eating them as it flies along. It will also pluck small lizards and snakes from trees and bushes and snatch eggs and nestlings of small birds, eating all of these morsels without landing on the ground. It can even swoop down to the surface of water and take a drink in flight, rather like a giant swallow.

## 8/ BAT HAWK
*Machaerhamphus alcinus*

RANGE: **Southeast Asia, tropical Africa**
HABITAT: **forested and well-wooded country; also towns with plentiful trees**
SIZE: **$18\frac{1}{2}$ in (47 cm)**

Although the Bat Hawk resembles a large falcon in general shape, its leisurely flight action is more like that of a kite. When hunting, however, it breaks into a fast pursuit with rapid wing beats.

It is largely inactive during the day, hunting over open areas or around the mouths of bat caves at dusk. As well as catching and eating small bats in flight, it also preys on swallows and swiftlets. Immature birds are browner than the adults above and show more white plumage below. The largest and darkest of the 3 races is the one illustrated: *M.a. alcinus* from Malaysia, Sumatra and Borneo. A wholly dark adult form of the Bat Hawk occurs in tropical Africa.

## 9/ SNAIL KITE
*Rostrhamus sociabilis*

RANGE: **Florida, Cuba, E Mexico S to Argentina**
HABITAT: **freshwater marshes with open water**
SIZE: **17 in (43 cm)**

The Snail Kite has large, fairly broad wings in relation to its smallish body. Although it is not particularly graceful in the air, it is perfectly equipped for slow, flapping flight as it quarters marshland vegetation in search of its principal prey – aquatic apple snails of the genus *Pomacea*.

When it locates a snail, this bird swoops down to the water, snatches the shell with one foot and takes it to a perch, where it uses its long, finely hook-tipped bill to extract the flesh from within. The Florida population of this species, known as the Everglade Kite, came close to extinction but its numbers have increased dramatically due to legal protection and habitat management.

## 10/ BLACK KITE
*Milvus migrans*

RANGE: **S Europe, much of Africa and Asia, Australia**
HABITAT: **open or semiopen lowlands, often wetlands; human settlements**
SIZE: **$21\frac{3}{4}$–$23\frac{1}{2}$ in (55–60 cm)**

This widespread and common bird is poorly named, for its plumage is really dark brown. Birds from the western part of the range, such as *M. m. migrans* of most of Europe, the Middle East and northwest Africa, tend to have pale heads. The eastern races are darker with whitish patches at the base of the outer wing feathers. African races are distinctive for their all-yellow bills.

The versatile Black Kite can kill small prey on the ground and snatch fish from the surface of water, but it also feeds widely on carrion. It is a bold scavenger and thief, entering villages to steal food and visiting refuse tips in and around towns.

## 11/ BRAHMINY KITE
*Haliastur indus*

RANGE: **S and Southeast Asia, N Australia**
HABITAT: **coastal and inland waters**
SIZE: **19 in (48 cm)**

The distinctive Brahminy Kite hunts rather like a harrier. It quarters at low altitude before dropping down to take live prey such as frogs, small reptiles and insects from the ground and fish from the water. It also feeds on carrion and is a common scavenger around human habitations and harbors in some regions, including India.

The nest is a pile of sticks lined with leaves, usually placed in a tree or among mangroves. The female lays and incubates up to 4 eggs, the male providing her with food while she is on the nest.

## FAMILY ACCIPITRIDAE/2
### Sea and fish eagles

Large birds of prey. Broad wings, soaring flight. Massive bill. Plumage usually brown and white. Sexes similar. Nest of sticks on cliff or in tree. Eggs 1–2, white. Incubation 40–45 days, chicks remain in nest for about 10 weeks. 10 species.

## 12/ AFRICAN FISH EAGLE
*Haliaeetus vocifer*

RANGE: **sub-Saharan Africa**
HABITAT: **coastal and inland waters**
SIZE: **29–33 in (74–84 cm)**

With its unique combination of white, chestnut and black plumage, this handsome fish eagle is unmistakable. It usually occurs close to water and is common over much of its range. It is a wonderfully agile flier, and although it can lift fish straight from the surface while still in flight, it usually makes a spectacular plunge into the water with its feet stretched forward.

The African Fish Eagle spends much of its time perching in an upright pose on a favorite lookout post. It is a vocal bird, both on its perch and while in flight. Its far-carrying, almost gull-like call is one of the best-known wild sounds of Africa.

## 13/ BALD EAGLE
*Haliaeetus leucocephalus*

RANGE: **North America**
HABITAT: **usually near lakes, rivers, coasts**
SIZE: **31–37 in (79–94 cm)**

This, the national bird of the USA, is common today only in Alaska and parts of the northwestern states. Persecution and pesticide contamination have caused it to become a rarity in much of eastern USA, although long-term recovery programs have helped to bring about a gradual increase in its population.

Versatile predators, Bald Eagles catch a variety of live prey including birds, small mammals and, especially, fish. Groups of them congregate at salmon spawning grounds in Alaska where the mass of exhausted fish provide rich pickings. Bald Eagles also scavenge widely and will rob other birds, such as Ospreys, of their catches. Pairs remain faithful and maintain their bond each year with spectacular aerial displays in which the 2 birds lock talons and tumble downward through the air.

## 14/ WHITE-TAILED SEA EAGLE
*Haliaeetus albicilla*

RANGE: **W Greenland, Iceland, N, C and SE Europe (recently reintroduced to Britain, to Rhum in the Inner Hebrides), N Asia**
HABITAT: **coasts, lakes, rivers, wetlands**
SIZE: **$27\frac{1}{2}$–$35\frac{1}{2}$ in (70–90 cm)**

White-tailed Sea Eagles are more bulky and have heavier bills than most other eagles likely to be seen in the same northerly areas. Their immense, broad wings give them a vulturelike appearance in flight.

Magnificent soarers, White-tailed Sea Eagles can also perform deft aerial maneuvers if the occasion demands. They are skilled hunters of waterfowl, seabirds and small mammals, and expertly snatch fish from the surface of water with their talons, usually after a shallow diving approach. They will rob birds, and perhaps even otters, of their prey and readily feed on carrion. The huge nest of sticks may be built in the top of a tree, on a crag or on the ground on a small island if it is free of terrestrial predators.

# OLD WORLD VULTURES, SNAKE EAGLES, HARRIER-HAWKS AND HARRIERS

RÜPPELL'S GRIFFON

LAMMERGEIER

LAPPET-FACED VULTURE

race *melanotis*

EUROPEAN BLACK VULTURE

CRESTED SERPENT-EAGLE

juv

juv

PALM-NUT VULTURE

EGYPTIAN VULTURE

MARSH HARRIER

race *aeruginosus*

♂ ♀

race *cyaneus*

HEN HARRIER

♀

♂

AFRICAN
HARRIER-HAWK

race
*caerulescens*

CRANE HAWK

♂ ♀

PIED
HARRIER

dark phase

pale phase

SHORT-TOED EAGLE

♀

BATELEUR

juv

229

# OLD WORLD VULTURES, SNAKE EAGLES, HARRIER-HAWKS AND HARRIERS

## FAMILY ACCIPITRIDAE/3
### Old World vultures

Large, soaring birds. Carrion-feeders. Broad wings. Bare head or face. Plumage variable, mainly dark. Sexes similar. Nest of sticks, in trees or on cliff ledges. Eggs 1–2, white or pale brown, sometimes with darker markings. Incubation 42–60 days, chicks remain in nest for 10–18 weeks. 15 species.

## 1/ EUROPEAN BLACK VULTURE
*Aegypius monachus* [?]

RANGE: S Europe, Turkey E to China
HABITAT: **mainly open country, including mountains**
SIZE: $39\frac{1}{2}$–$43\frac{1}{4}$ in (100–110 cm)

Weighing up to 25 lb (12 kg) and with a wingspan of over 9 ft (2.75 m) on large individuals, this is the biggest of all the Old World vultures. Although its plumage is in fact dark sooty-brown, it appears black from a distance. Even at long range, the pale feet are conspicuous in flying birds. Immatures are slightly paler in plumage.

The European Black, or Cinereous, Vulture is almost extinct over most of its range in Europe, but some 400 pairs still survive in the sierras of south-central Spain. A powerful bird, it is generally, but not always, able to dominate griffon vultures at carcasses. Unlike them, it readily descends into vegetation cover to feed on carrion. Each pair returns annually to the same treetop nest, adding new material to the already huge platform of sticks.

## 2/ LAPPET-FACED VULTURE
*Aegypius tracheliotus*

RANGE: **sub-Saharan Africa, Middle East, S Arabia**
HABITAT: **arid open country, extending into mountains and semidesert**
SIZE: $39\frac{1}{2}$–$41\frac{1}{4}$ in (100–105 cm)

A massive, dark bird, this is the most powerful of the African vultures. It usually dominates and often robs other species at carcasses, where it is often the last to arrive. It can break easily through flesh with its huge beak and, since there are no feathers on its neck, it can probe deep inside a carcass without fouling its plumage with blood.

The Lappet-faced Vulture is normally a solitary bird but may occur in small groups at times. However, each pair usually nests alone, building a flat structure of sticks, up to 10 ft (3 m) wide and 3 ft (1 m) deep, at the top of a thorny tree. A single egg is laid in a depression in the middle of the nest lined with dry grass. Both sexes take turns to incubate the egg over a 7-week period.

## 3/ RÜPPELL'S GRIFFON
*Gyps rueppellii*

RANGE: **Senegal to N Nigeria, Sudan, W Ethiopia, Uganda, Kenya, N Tanzania**
HABITAT: **wild, open country, in both mountains and lowlands**
SIZE: 35–37 in (89–94 cm)

The basically dark adult plumage of Rüppell's Griffon is patterned with extensive pale scalloping, especially on the underparts. The underwing

pattern is very distinctive – a bold white bar near the inner leading edge and 2 rows of white spots across the entire wing.

Rüppell's Griffon is a powerful species usually capable of dominating all but the larger Lappet-faced Vulture when feeding on carrion. It is the central African representative of the small group of griffon vultures. All are large, gregarious birds and superb long-distance foragers which gather in dense flocks at carcasses.

## 4/ EGYPTIAN VULTURE
*Neophron percnopterus*

RANGE: **N, C and E Africa, S Europe, Middle East, SW Asia, India**
HABITAT: **open country; cliffs and crags preferred for breeding**
SIZE: 21–26 in (53–66 cm)

This largely whitish bird is widespread over Africa and the warm, drier regions of Europe and Asia. It feeds largely on carrion but, being small and weak-billed, it generally waits its turn at a carcass to pick up minor scraps left behind by larger vultures. Otherwise, it is a versatile scavenger on all sorts of food. In some parts of Africa, Egyptian Vultures are among the few true tool-users in the bird world. They have been seen picking up stones in their bills and hurling them onto Ostrich eggs to break open the thick shells.

Egyptian Vultures prefer to breed in rocky terrain, where they build their nests on crags and in caves. Their aerial display flights involve dives and swoops, with the birds rolling over and presenting their talons to each other in midair.

## 5/ LAMMERGEIER
*Gypaetus barbatus*

RANGE: **Africa, S Europe E to C Asia**
HABITAT: **mainly mountains and high plateaus**
SIZE: $39\frac{1}{2}$–$45\frac{1}{4}$ in (100–115 cm)

This huge, distinctively colored bird is scarce over most of its range and particularly favors wild, remote, mountain regions. The prominent bristles that extend from its black mask have

earned it the alternative name of Bearded Vulture. Young Lammergeiers are generally brownish, with more uniform plumage than their parents.

Lammergeiers are quite unlike other large vultures in shape. In flight, their long, narrow wings and longish tails make them look almost like gigantic falcons. Their seemingly effortless gliding ability is unequaled, and they spend most of the day on the wing. At carcasses, they specialize in feeding on tough hide and bones. These birds are well known for their habit of dropping bones from a height on to rocky sites, or "ossuaries," smashing them open so that the marrow is accessible. The same sites are used for many years in succession.

## 6/ PALM-NUT VULTURE
*Gypohierax angolensis*

RANGE: **tropical Africa**
HABITAT: **mainly woodland and cultivated land; also mangroves, harbors**
SIZE: 22–$24\frac{1}{2}$ in (56–62 cm)

Although it starts life with the dark brown coloration common to many Old World vultures, this curious bird becomes increasingly mottled during the immature stage until it eventually takes on the striking white adult plumage.

Its diet is also remarkable. Although it feeds to some extent on crabs, small fish, amphibians and various invertebrates, it is largely vegetarian – a most unusual feature for a bird of prey. Its principal food is the husk of the oil palm fruit, and it tends to be rare in places where oil palms are not found. The Palm-nut Vulture remains in the same area for much of the year. It often lives close to water.

## FAMILY ACCIPITRIDAE/4
### Snake eagles

Large, mainly specialist feeders on reptiles. Short, powerful toes. Plumage usually gray or brown. Sexes similar. Nest small, built of sticks, in tree. Eggs 1, usually white. Incubation 35–55 days, chick leaves nest at 10–15 weeks. 12 species.

## 7/ SHORT-TOED EAGLE
*Circaetus gallicus*

RANGE: **S and E Europe, NW Africa, Middle East, SW Asia, India**
HABITAT: **mixed open country, including mountains**
SIZE: **24½–26½ in (62–67 cm)**

Short-toed Eagles show marked variation in plumage. Basically brown above and white below, they usually, but by no means always, have dark heads and the underparts and underwings have a variable amount of dark speckles and bars.

Short-toed Eagles are accomplished fliers, often foraging at low altitude and frequently hovering. Their short, powerful toes are adapted for dealing with their main prey, the snakes and lizards that they find on open hillsides and other suitable terrain. In parts of southern Europe, the birds follow the plow to snatch prey disturbed from the ground. Large snakes are torn apart and eaten on the ground, but the birds will take off with small snakes and swallow them whole.

## 8/ BATELEUR
*Terathopius ecaudatus*

RANGE: **sub-Saharan Africa, SW Arabia**
HABITAT: **savanna, open woodland, plains, semidesert**
SIZE: **22–24 in (56–61 cm)**

Long-winged, almost tail-less and colorful, the Bateleur is quite unlike any other bird of prey. The bird's common name is French for "tightrope-walker," an apt allusion to its fast, gliding flight in which it continually tilts from side to side. It is often on the wing for most of the day. During the breeding season it performs spectacular courtship flights, with fast pursuits, dives and even the occasional 360-degree lateral roll.

Bateleurs are typical birds of the African savanna. They take a wide range of animal prey, including small mammals, snakes, lizards and some invertebrates, but many are primarily hunters of birds. They also feed readily on carrion and are bold and aggressive pirates of other predators and scavengers.

## 9/ CRESTED SERPENT-EAGLE
*Spilornis cheela*

RANGE: **India, China, Southeast Asia, Indonesia, Philippines**
HABITAT: **mainly forest or woodland; some races in open savanna**
SIZE: **11–21 in (28–53 cm)**

With over 20 geographical races, many of them island forms, this is an extremely variable species both in terms of size and, to a lesser extent, plumage. Most races have dark brown plumage in the adult with a prominent blackish crest or "hood." The race illustrated, *S.c. melanotis*, is from the southern part of the Indian peninsula.

Except when they are soaring above the canopy, Crested Serpent-Eagles can be very difficult to spot in their forest habitat. They hunt largely in tree cover, usually watching from a perch and swooping to the ground to catch reptiles such as tree snakes. They also eat dead snakes. This species also preys occasionally on small mammals and birds.

## FAMILY ACCIPITRIDAE/5
**Harrier-hawks and the Crane Hawk**

Medium-sized, long-legged, long-tailed birds of prey. Plumage mainly gray. Sexes similar. Nest of twigs, in tree or rock crevice. Eggs 1–3, white. Incubation 35–40 days (?), chicks remain in nest about 7 weeks (?). 3 species.

## 10/ AFRICAN HARRIER-HAWK
*Polyboroides typus*

RANGE: **sub-Saharan Africa**
HABITAT: **forest, woodland, savanna, bush, cultivated land**
SIZE: **24–26¾ in (61–68 cm)**

The African Harrier-Hawk, or Gymnogene, does much of its hunting in bushes and trees rather than in flight. The small size of its head and its slender, double-jointed legs enable it to search for prey in all kinds of holes, hollows and crevices. It feeds on a range of small prey including insects and other invertebrates, mammals, birds and eggs. It frequently raids the nests of colonial weavers. The fruit of the oil palm is a favored food in West Africa.

The nest of twigs lined with green leaves is built in the tree canopy or low down in a rock crevice under cover. Both sexes share in incubating the 1–2 eggs and in feeding the young, although the female takes the major role. The immature birds are mainly brown, paler on the belly with barred tails.

## 11/ CRANE HAWK
*Geranospiza caerulescens*

RANGE: **Mexico S to Argentina**
HABITAT: **tropical lowlands, usually with trees, often near water**
SIZE: **16–20 in (41–51 cm)**

There is considerable variation among the 6 races of this bird, ranging from the black race *G.c. nigra* found in most of Mexico to others in South America, such as *G.c. caerulescens* of eastern Ecuador and Colombia to the Guianas and northern Brazil, which are pale gray above and usually finely barred darker gray below. All, though, show the characteristically banded black and whitish tails. Immatures are generally more yellow-brown below.

Whether this bird is closely related to the 2 species of harrier-hawk is unclear, but it, too, forages slowly and methodically, searching in a variety of holes and cavities for a broadly similar range of prey. It also has extremely flexible leg joints. It usually occurs near water and often inhabits forested swamps, or woodland with pools and streams.

## FAMILY ACCIPITRIDAE/6
**Harriers**

Slender, long-winged, long-legged birds of prey. Plumage usually grayish or black and white in males, brownish in females. Nest on ground or in bush. Eggs 3–6, occasionally up to 8 or more, usually plain white. Incubation 28–31 days, chicks leave nest after 36–60 days. 10 species.

## 12/ HEN HARRIER
*Circus cyaneus*

RANGE: **North and South America, N Europe, N Asia; migrates to S**
HABITAT: **largely open country, dry or wet**
SIZE: **17¼–20½ in (44–52 cm)**

Like the Marsh Harrier, this is a widespread species. Whereas the lower underparts of the male in the European race *C.c. cyaneus* are plain whitish, those of the American race *C.c. hudsonius* are marked with reddish-brown spots. Immatures, like the females, are browner, streaked dark below, and show a white rump above a clearly barred tail.

In many areas, the fortunes of Hen Harriers are closely tied to the population cycles of small mammals such as voles. They hunt for these with a low, quartering flight, during which the wings show the characteristic *V* posture common to all harriers. Although they usually roost singly on the ground, Hen Harriers sometimes congregate on winter nights in groups of about 10.

## 13/ PIED HARRIER
*Circus melanoleucos*

RANGE: **E Siberia S to Mongolia, N Korea, N Burma; winters to the S**
HABITAT: **open country, including steppe and wetlands**
SIZE: **18–20 in (46–51 cm)**

The handsome male Pied Harrier is unmistakable. The females, however, are rather similar to those of Pallid and Montagu's Harriers, but they are much paler and only sparsely streaked below. The immature birds are brown above and dark chestnut below.

Pied Harriers are frequent visitors to rice paddies in their winter quarters, where they feed largely on frogs. In the breeding season they are, like other harriers, birds of open country, including steppe, bogs with scattered birches and lowland meadows. Here, they feed mainly on small mammals and birds but also catch frogs, lizards and some invertebrates.

## 14/ MARSH HARRIER
*Circus aeruginosus*

RANGE: **W Europe E across Asia, Madagascar, Borneo, Australia**
HABITAT: **usually lowland wetlands, especially with reedbeds**
SIZE: **19–22¾ in (48–58 cm)**

The sexes show markedly different plumage among the harriers, and this species is no exception. A widespread bird, it also shows marked variation across its geographical range. The race *C.a. aeruginosus*, illustrated, is from Europe, Israel, and Central Asia. Immatures are dark brownish in color.

The Marsh Harrier generally nests in thick marsh vegetation, but it forages widely over nearby lowland habitats. The prey ranges from small mammals and birds to amphibians, small fish and large invertebrates. Carrion is sometimes eaten. When the female is incubating and tending the young, the male hunts for them both, calling his mate off the nest when he returns with food and dropping it for her to catch in midair.

# GOSHAWKS, SPARROWHAWKS AND BUTEONINES

juv

GABAR GOSHAWK

pale phase

dark phase

♀

DARK CHANTING-GOSHAWK

NORTHERN GOSHAWK

♀

♀

NORTHERN
SPARROWHAWK

white phase
"White Goshawk"

gray phase
"Gray Goshawk"

♂

♂

♂

BESRA SPARROWHAWK

juv

SHARP-SHINNED HAWK

race *novaehollandiae*

VARIABLE GOSHAWK

COOPER'S HAWK

juv

LIZARD BUZZARD

SLATE-COLORED HAWK

GRASSHOPPER
BUZZARD-EAGLE

juv

COMMON BLACK HAWK

SAVANNA HAWK

CROWNED SOLITARY EAGLE

# GOSHAWKS, SPARROWHAWKS AND BUTEONINES

## FAMILY ACCIPITRIDAE/7
### Goshawks, sparrowhawks and relatives

Small to large birds of prey, many feeding mainly or entirely on birds. Broad wings and long tails. Plumage mainly gray, brown or blackish, often barred below. Sexes may differ in size (females larger) and plumage. Nest very varied, usually of sticks in tree. Eggs usually 1–6, white often blotched brown. Incubation 28–50 days, chicks remain in nest 25–110 days. 53 species.

## 1/ DARK CHANTING-GOSHAWK
### Melierax metabates
RANGE: sub-Saharan Africa, SW Morocco, SW Arabia
HABITAT: open woodland, bush, savanna
SIZE: 16–19 in (41–48 cm)

The Dark Chanting-Goshawk is a medium-sized, rather long-legged hawk, likely to be confused only with the slightly larger Pale Chanting-Goshawk M. canorus. The 2 species are largely separated geographically and by habitat. They take their name from the males' tuneful, whistling "chants," delivered from the tops of trees early in the breeding season.

Dark Chanting-Goshawks keep a lookout for prey from the tops of bushes, trees, termite mounds or similar vantage points, swooping down swiftly to seize lizards, small mammals, small birds and insects. They will also pursue flying birds and regularly forage on the ground.

## 2/ GABAR GOSHAWK
### Micronisus gabar
RANGE: sub-Saharan Africa, SW Arabia
HABITAT: woodland and scrub
SIZE: 11–14 in (28–36 cm)

Gabar Goshawks resemble true sparrowhawks in general appearance, although some all-black, melanistic forms occur. Immature birds have browner upperparts than the adults and streaked plumage on the throat and breast.

Gabar Goshawks are bold and active hunters, both chasing birds in the air and seizing them, as well as lizards, on the ground. At the start of the breeding season, the males perch high in trees, uttering piping display calls, and a pair will often display by chasing each other in and out of the trees. The female generally builds the nest, lining the center with soil, matted spiders' webs and even pieces of rag. She also incubates the eggs and brings most of the food to the young.

## 3/ LIZARD BUZZARD
### Kaupifalco monogrammicus
RANGE: sub-Saharan Africa
HABITAT: savanna and bush
SIZE: 13¾–15 in (35–38 cm)

Lizard Buzzards are smallish, long-legged but rather heavily built hawks found in the tropical grasslands and wooded savanna of Africa. Although they resemble the adults, the immature birds are somewhat duller and browner in their overall plumage.

Unlike most birds of prey, this species catches much of its prey in tall grass or other dense

ground vegetation. It hunts from a series of perches either in cover or on exposed branches. Large insects, lizards and small snakes form the bulk of its food, along with frogs and small rodents. Although it eats some of its larger victims on the ground, it carries most of its prey back to the perch.

## 4/ VARIABLE GOSHAWK
### Accipiter novaehollandiae
RANGE: coastal N and E Australia, Tasmania, New Guinea, E Indonesia, Solomon Islands
HABITAT: forest and forest edge, riverine forest
SIZE: 13–21¾ in (33–55 cm)

This striking bird has some 20 races. Plumage and size vary greatly, as the species' name suggests. The Australian and Tasmanian birds of the race A. n. novaehollandiae are larger, and may be gray above and white beneath, or all white. Birds of the race A. n. leucosomus from New Guinea and nearby islands may be gray above and rufous beneath, dark gray and chestnut, or all white. Many of the other island races are small and brightly colored.

The Variable Goshawk feeds on birds, reptiles and mammals up to the size of rabbits, as well as some insects and carrion. It searches for most of its prey from a concealed perch, even the white forms remaining remarkably inconspicuous in the forest canopy. The birds often attack after a stealthy glide and display great agility when pursuing prey through the trees.

## 5/ BESRA SPARROWHAWK
### Accipiter virgatus
RANGE: W Himalayas E to S China, Southeast Asia, Indonesia, Philippines
HABITAT: evergreen forest or other well-timbered areas
SIZE: 11–14 in (28–36 cm)

The barring on the underparts of the Besra Sparrowhawk is obscured to varying degrees by a chestnut coloration, which is most heavy on the

race of A. v. vanbemmeli from Sumatra. The race illustrated, with pale underparts and strong barrings, is A. v. besra, found in India south of Bombay and on Sri Lanka and the Andaman Islands. Immature Besra Sparrowhawks are generally browner above than the adults.

This species is common over much of the forested country from southern Asia to Indonesia. Like most sparrowhawks, it is a fast and agile bird-catcher, taking prey both on the wing and from the ground. It also eats some large insects and lizards. Courtship involves chasing and soaring displays during which the birds frequently call. The nest of sticks is placed in a tree and is often built on top of an old crow's nest or even a squirrel's drey.

## 6/ NORTHERN SPARROWHAWK
### Accipiter nisus
RANGE: Europe and NW Africa E to Bering Sea and Himalayas
HABITAT: chiefly woodland or forest
SIZE: 11–15 in (28–38 cm)

Widespread over much of Eurasia, Northern Sparrowhawks are almost entirely hunters of birds, with small mammals usually forming less than 3 percent of their diet. Although they sometimes pursue and fly down prey in the open, they more often hunt in cover, systematically moving from one perch to the next and taking prey in a short, swift attack. They are supremely agile in the air, able to twist and turn rapidly around obstacles and maneuver to surprise their victims. Bird prey varies considerably in size, from Great Tits Parus major to Common Pheasants Phasianus colchicus, with females generally taking larger species than the males.

Both sexes build the nest, usually close to the tree trunk, some 20–50 ft (6–15 m) above the ground. The 4–5 eggs are laid at intervals of 2 or more days and are incubated solely by the female. The European race A. n. nisus is illustrated; there are 5 other races, of which A. n. wolterstorffi from Corsica and Sardinia is the most distinct, being smaller and much darker. Some northerly populations migrate south for the winter to Africa and parts of southern Asia.

## 7/ SHARP-SHINNED HAWK
*Accipiter striatus*

RANGE: **North, Central and South America, Caribbean**
HABITAT: **woods, forests and other well-timbered areas**
SIZE: **$9\frac{3}{4}$–13 in (25–33 cm)**

This species shows considerable geographical variation across its range. In North America, males are slate-gray above and closely barred rufous below, while the large females are brown above and barred brown below. The race *A. s. velox*, found over much of the species' North American range, is typical of this type. In stark contrast, the race *A. s. chionogaster*, found in Guatemala, Honduras, El Salvador and Nicaragua, is very dark above and white below. There is also some size variation. Races from the West Indies, for instance, are all rather small.

In its general behavior, the Sharp-shinned Hawk is similar to most small members of the genus *Accipter*. It is principally a bird-catcher, surprising its prey with a sudden dash from cover. Populations that breed in northern North America spend the winter from central USA south to Costa Rica.

## 8/ COOPER'S HAWK
*Accipiter cooperii*

RANGE: **S Canada S to NW Mexico**
HABITAT: **woodland, riverside belts of trees**
SIZE: **14–20 in (36–51 cm)**

Cooper's Hawk is midway in size between the Sharp-shinned Hawk and Northern Goshawk. Principally a woodland bird, it rarely strays from cover except when hunting. It is an active bird-catcher, using both pursuit and snatch-and-grab tactics. It snatches mammals such as squirrels and chipmunks during sallies from a lookout perch and skilfully pursues bats emerging from their roosts. The female is much larger than the male and can tackle prey up to the size of the Ruffed Grouse *Bonasa umbellus*.

The male builds the nest using sticks that he breaks from trees in flight, grasping them with his talons as he passes. The nest is usually placed at least 33 ft (10 m) up in the branches of a conifer.

## 9/ NORTHERN GOSHAWK
*Accipiter gentilis*

RANGE: **circumpolar N**
HABITAT: **temperate and boreal woods and forests**
SIZE: **19–26 in (48–66 cm)**

The Northern Goshawk occurs across Eurasia and North America, with considerable geographical variation. Siberian races are much paler than the race *A. g. gentilis* of Europe, southwest Asia and Morocco, while North American birds (of 3 races) have noticeably dark crowns and a prominent white stripe above the eye. Juveniles are brown above, with pronounced dark drop-shaped markings below. There is a marked size difference between the sexes, with females up to 50 percent heavier than the males.

Northern Goshawks are powerful, fast-moving hunters, with females fully capable of subduing full-grown cock pheasants or hares. They prey on a wide variety of bird and mammal species, depending on which are available in each locality. Some reports suggest that the birds store items of prey that are too large to consume in one meal.

## FAMILY ACCIPITRIDAE/8
**Buzzards and other buteonines, harpy eagles**

Large birds of prey, feeding mainly on mammals and reptiles caught on the ground. Long, broad wings adapted for soaring. Females usually only slightly larger than males. Sexes usually similar in plumage: brown, rufous, black and white in various combinations. Nest usually of sticks in tree. Eggs 1–4, white or cream, often with brown or reddish markings. Incubation 21–60 days, nestling period 45–100 days. 55 species.

## 10/ GRASSHOPPER BUZZARD-EAGLE
*Butastur rufipennis*

RANGE: **W, C and E Africa**
HABITAT: **mainly savanna, bush and semidesert**
SIZE: **$15\frac{3}{4}$–17 in (40–43 cm)**

Kestrel-like at rest, and reminiscent of a harrier in flight, the Grasshopper Buzzard-Eagle is nevertheless a distinctive bird when seen at close range. It is primarily insectivorous, catching large numbers of grasshoppers and mantises, although it also takes some small birds, mammals and snakes. It is well known for its habit of hunting around grass fires and over burnt ground to take advantage of fleeing and exposed prey.

The Grasshopper Buzzard-Eagle is migratory, moving from its drier breeding grounds, where it spends the rainy season, to more wooded habitats in the dry season. It usually nests in a low tree, building a deep structure of sticks and lining it with leaves.

## 11/ SLATE-COLORED HAWK
*Leucopternis schistacea*

RANGE: **Amazonia, S Venezuela, E Colombia, Ecuador, Peru and Bolivia**
HABITAT: **forests**
SIZE: **17–18 in (43–46 cm)**

The hawks in the Central and South American genus *Leucopternis* are small to medium birds of prey. They are similar to buzzards, except that their wings are short and rounded – a typical adaptation for hunting and maneuvering in forests. Immature birds show much irregular white barring on both the lower underparts and leg feathers.

The Slate-colored Hawk usually occurs along forest streams, flooded stretches and swamps. It hunts from a series of perches, waiting quietly for prey to appear below and dropping down to seize its victims at the water's edge. Its prey includes frogs and snakes. Little else is known of this bird's behavior.

## 12/ COMMON BLACK HAWK
*Buteogallus anthracinus*

RANGE: **S USA to coastal South America, Caribbean**
HABITAT: **coastal lowlands, including wetlands; inland streams**
SIZE: **18–$22\frac{3}{4}$ in (46–58 cm)**

This distinctly broad-winged, short-tailed bird is most common in low-lying coastal savanna, although it also occurs along wooded streams farther inland. It tends to be a rather sluggish hunter, using low, concealed perches or foraging on the wing at low altitude. It does little soaring, except during the breeding season.

Coastal populations feed extensively on crabs but also take other shore invertebrates and stranded fish. To expose the flesh of a crab, the bird hooks its bill under the front of the shell and tears it off backward. Other prey includes insects, frogs, snakes and small rodents, but rarely birds.

## 13/ SAVANNA HAWK
*Buteogallus meridionalis*

RANGE: **E Panama to C Argentina**
HABITAT: **open grassland, including wet areas**
SIZE: **20–24 in (51–61 cm)**

Adult Savanna Hawks are strikingly rufous birds, especially in flight, when they also show dark wing edges and a broad white band and white tip to the otherwise black tail. Immatures are a duller, darker brown above and buffish-white below, with thickly streaked dark sides to the breast.

Rather long-legged birds, Savanna Hawks spend much of their time sitting in a characteristically upright pose on exposed perches. They hunt from these, preying on insects, amphibians, snakes, fish, small mammals and small birds. Occasionally, the hawks drop onto prey from flight, and groups of them may be attracted to grass fires or may follow the plow to snatch creatures disturbed from hiding.

## 14/ CROWNED SOLITARY EAGLE
*Harpyhaliaetus coronatus*                    ?

RANGE: **E Bolivia to N Patagonia**
HABITAT: **sparse woodland and savanna**
SIZE: **29–32 in (74–81 cm)**

This South American species is a large, robust bird of prey with longish legs and a short tail that gives it a distinctive silhouette in flight. Immatures are browner above than the adults and buffish-white with dark streaking on their underparts. Crowned Solitary Eagles occur mainly in dry, open country with scattered trees.

Described as ponderous and rather sluggish, and frequently as very tame, the Crowned Solitary Eagle perches freely on fenceposts, utility poles and bare trees. It hunts either from its perch or by sailing low over the ground, catching small to medium-sized mammals and birds and, probably, also snakes.

# BUTEOS AND OTHER BUTEONINES, HARPY EAGLES

BLACK-COLLARED HAWK

juv

HARRIS' HAWK

GRAY HAWK

juv

race *lineatus*

RED-SHOULDERED HAWK

ZONE-TAILED HAWK

pale phase

dark phase
juv

HAWAIIAN HAWK

race *kriderii*
"Krider's Hawk"

pale phase

dark phase

light phase

race *sancti-johannis*
dark phase

EURASIAN BUZZARD

RED-TAILED HAWK

race *borealis*

race *lagopus*
typical

ROUGH-LEGGED HAWK

LONG-LEGGED
BUZZARD

typical

typical

race *augur*
"Augur Buzzard"

typical

race *rufofuscus*

JACKAL BUZZARD

dark phase

typical

GUIANA CRESTED EAGLE

NEW GUINEA HARPY EAGLE

juv

AMERICAN
HARPY EAGLE

PHILIPPINE EAGLE

# BUTEOS AND OTHER BUTEONINES, HARPY EAGLES

## 1/ BLACK-COLLARED HAWK
*Busarellus nigricollis*

RANGE: **Mexico S to Argentina**
HABITAT: **tropical lowlands, open or semi-open country near water**
SIZE: **19–20 in (48–51 cm)**

At rest, this is a bulky but rather small-headed hawk; in flight, it shows its broad, blunt wings and very short tail. Immature birds are duller than the distinctive adults, with dark streaking. Its principal food is fish, which it snatches either from the surface in swooping flight or by plunging into shallow water, usually from a low perch. Small spines on the undersides of its feet help the bird grasp and hold its prey. An alternative common name for this species is Fishing Buzzard.

Common in some parts of its extensive range, the Black-collared Hawk breeds around swamps and marshes or occasionally in plantations. Its nest is a large platform of sticks, sometimes decorated with leaves, placed up to 50 ft (15 m) high in a mangrove or other tree.

## 2/ HARRIS' HAWK
*Parabuteo unicinctus*

RANGE: **SW USA, Central and South America**
HABITAT: **lowlands, with or without scattered trees, semideserts**
SIZE: **19–22 in (48–56 cm)**

Harris' Hawk is primarily a bird of dry, open habitats. It is an accomplished hunter, taking a wide variety of small to medium-sized birds, including ducks, as well as small rodents, other mammals up to the size of full-grown rabbits, and lizards. It hunts by gliding at low levels or by swooping suddenly onto prey from a low perch. It sometimes perches on the ground.

The nest is a relatively neat structure of twigs, sticks and roots, lined with grass, leaves and pieces of bark. This is usually built up to 33 ft (10 m) from the ground in a tree or cactus. The 2–4 eggs are incubated for some 30 days and the young leave the nest after about 6 weeks.

## 3/ GRAY HAWK
*Buteo nitidus*

RANGE: **SW USA, Central and South America**
HABITAT: **tropical and subtropical woodland and forest**
SIZE: **15–17 in (38–43 cm)**

Despite its common name, the Gray Hawk is a small member of the genus *Buteo*. It is typically broad-winged, but fast-moving and agile when hunting. A woodland bird, its short wings and long tail allow it to steer skilfully around trees in pursuit of prey. It takes some birds, but over most of its range it preys mainly on lizards, snatching them by gliding down from a lookout perch.

The usual call of the Gray Hawk is a high-pitched *cree-ee-ee*, but it also utters flutelike cries in flight, apparently during courtship. The bird's nest is often well hidden by foliage, and placed 33–40 ft (10–12 m) up in a large tree. Populations of this species from southwestern USA and northern Mexico are migratory.

## 4/ RED-SHOULDERED HAWK
*Buteo lineatus*

RANGE: **North America, S to C Mexico**
HABITAT: **mixed or deciduous woodland and nearby open country**
SIZE: **16–20 in (41–51 cm)**

This widespread, handsomely proportioned buteo often occurs in damp woodland. A generally secretive bird, it keeps to cover for most of the time, although it is sometimes seen around open areas in winter. It takes a wide variety of prey, including birds, small mammals, lizards, snakes, frogs and toads. Its flight is active, with rapid wing beats followed by periods of gliding. It often calls while in the air.

There are 5 races of the Red-shouldered Hawk. The races *B.l. texanus* and *B.l. elegans* from southwestern USA and Mexico are much darker and more rufous below than those of the eastern race *B.l. lineatus*. Two isolated races, *B.l. alleni*, and *B.l. extimus* in Florida are typically much paler on the head and underparts, often showing little or no rufous barring below.

## 5/ ZONE-TAILED HAWK
*Buteo albonotatus*

RANGE: **SW USA, Central and South America**
HABITAT: **wooded and semiopen country**
SIZE: **18–21 in (46–53 cm)**

The Zone-tailed Hawk is a slim, rather rakish buteo that takes its name from the gray bands on its tail. The sexes are similar in plumage, although, as in many birds of prey, females are noticeably larger and immatures show copious white spotting below.

These birds are found in a variety of semiopen landscapes, usually with at least some trees, and in broken ground on the middle and lower slopes of mountains. In some parts of their range, especially in tropical America, they occur in more wooded country. They usually hunt for prey in flight, sometimes flying with Turkey Vultures *Cathartes aura*, which have a similar silhouette. It has been suggested that this resemblance allows them to approach closer to prey that would not

normally flee from a nonpredatory passing vulture. Their victims include rodents, lizards, amphibians and birds, which they catch with a rapid swoop. Zone-tailed Hawks are courageous defenders of nests and will swoop at, or even strike, people who come too close.

## 6/ HAWAIIAN HAWK
*Buteo solitarius*  $\boxed{R}$

RANGE: **island of Hawaii; has also wandered to Maui and Oahu**
HABITAT: **varied; especially in light woodland and edges of fields, generally from 2,000–5,000 ft (600–1,500 m), but usually with trees**
SIZE: **16–18 in (41–46 cm)**

One of Hawaii's many endemic breeding birds, the Hawaiian Hawk is among the smallest of the buteos. Rats are its main prey, but these were introduced to the islands by settlers. Previously the Hawaiian Hawk must have eaten mainly large insects and birds. It is an adaptable species and usually occurs alone or in pairs.

There are 2 color phases in this species. In the light phase, adults are basically dark brown above, with somewhat paler heads, and whitish below with rusty markings. Immatures are generally paler, except on the wings. Dark phase adult birds are blackish-brown below, but with some pale feathering on the throat. The immature birds are similar but with irregularly mottled and barred underparts.

## 7/ RED-TAILED HAWK
*Buteo jamaicensis*

RANGE: **North and Central America, Caribbean**
HABITAT: **extremely varied, but usually with some tree cover**
SIZE: **20–24¾ in (51–63 cm)**

This large, handsome buteo is widespread throughout its range and tolerant of a great variety of habitats, from woodland to prairies and alpine meadows. Highly versatile in its hunting methods, the Red-tailed Hawk catches a wide range of prey, including mammals, birds, reptiles and insects. Although it often swoops from a high perch or utility pole, it can also quarter the ground in flight before stopping, and hover in one spot by flapping against a moderate wind.

There are about 14 races of the Red-tailed Hawk, varying considerably in plumage and, to a certain extent, in size. Most, such as *B.j. borealis* of eastern North America, are basically dark brown above and pale below, show some degree of dark marking across the belly and have chestnut tails. Some of the birds in Alaska and Canada are uniformly dark above and below, with a dusky tail. The distinctive Krider's Hawk *B.j. kriderii* occurs mainly in the Great Plains region.

## 8/ EURASIAN BUZZARD
*Buteo buteo*

RANGE: **Europe E across Asia to the Bering Sea**
HABITAT: **varied, but usually with some tree cover**
SIZE: **20–22½ in (51–57 cm)**

The Eurasian Buzzard is a fairly thickset, medium to large hawk, with broad wings and a rather short, but ample, tail. It shows more variation in plumage than any other European bird of prey. Pale forms are present in many populations and very frequent in some, resulting in a bewildering range of plumage. Many of these have white heads, underparts and underwings. The Steppe Buzzard *B. b. vulpinus*, from the north and east of the range, is characterized by dark red to gray-brown underparts and an orange-gray tail.

The Eurasian Buzzard spends much of its time in the air, soaring over open terrain and woodland edges, with its wings raised in a shallow *V*. Rodents and other small mammals form the bulk of its prey, and it frequently feeds on carrion during the winter. It often calls in flight, uttering a far-carrying, plaintive cry. In many places, this is one of the most common birds of prey, although it has declined dramatically in parts.

## 9/ ROUGH-LEGGED HAWK
*Buteo lagopus*

RANGE: **N Europe E across Asia, North America**
HABITAT: **mainly Arctic or subarctic open terrain**
SIZE: **20–24 in (51–61 cm)**

The Rough-legged Hawk is slightly larger than the Eurasian Buzzard, but is noticeably bulkier, with longer wings and a longer tail. Like the Eurasian Buzzard, it is variable in plumage, with several races across its circumpolar range. The 2 races illustrated, *B. l. lagopus* of northern Europe and northwestern USSR and *B. l. sancti-johannis* of North America, both occur in pale and dark phases and a wide range of intermediates.

This species often hovers when hunting. Its numbers are closely governed by the abundance of small rodents, its main prey. In its Arctic breeding grounds in Scandinavia, lemmings are its principal source of food, and their population cycles markedly affect the bird's breeding success. Like northerly Eurasian Buzzards, Rough-legged Hawks are highly migratory, wintering far to the south of their breeding range.

## 10/ LONG-LEGGED BUZZARD
*Buteo rufinus*

RANGE: **C and SE Europe E to C Asia, N Africa**
HABITAT: **mainly lowland, open country, often arid or semiarid**
SIZE: **20–26 in (51–66 cm)**

This species is similar to the Rough-legged Hawk in general outline, and almost suggests a small eagle in flight. Its plumage is very variable, with both dark and pale phases and intermediates. At close quarters, juvenile birds show pale margins to the feathers on their dark upperparts and are less uniform in appearance than the adults.

Long-legged Buzzards are birds of dry steppe, semidesert and mountainous habitats, reaching altitudes of 13,000 ft (4,000 m). Lizards and small mammals provide the bulk of their prey. Populations from the northern part of the range migrate south for the winter, occurring in a belt from northern Africa east to northern India.

## 11/ JACKAL BUZZARD
*Buteo rufofuscus*

RANGE: **E and S Africa**
HABITAT: **varied; mainly hilly country**
SIZE: **18–21 in (46–53 cm)**

This is a very common and widespread bird in Africa, with 2 principal races, differing in the color of their underparts. The Jackal Buzzard *B.r. rufofuscus* occurs in southern Africa, while the Augur Buzzard *B.r. augur* ranges from Zimbabwe to the Ethiopian highlands. The species takes its name from its high-pitched, yelping call.

Jackal Buzzards fly with markedly raised wings and a rocking, side-to-side action. They hunt both on the wing and from perches, swooping to seize rodents, lizards, snakes, birds and insects. Often seen perching on telegraph poles and fenceposts, these birds frequently fly down to feed on carrion by the roadside, even darting between speeding cars. They breed either on cliffs or in trees, using their large stick nests for several years in succession.

## 12/ GUIANA CRESTED EAGLE
*Morphnus guianensis*    R

RANGE: **Honduras S to N Argentina**
HABITAT: **tropical lowland forest**
SIZE: **31–35 in (79–89 cm)**

This very large, handsome bird of prey occurs in 2 forms, the less common dark phase having once been regarded as a separate species. The broad, rounded wings and long tail equip the bird for maneuvering around forest trees in pursuit of prey. Although it may regularly soar above the forest canopy, it spends most of its time perched in tall trees. It preys on small monkeys, opossums, birds and reptiles.

The Guiana Crested Eagle is uncommon throughout its range, and, like most lowland rain forest birds, it faces the threat of deforestation. Although it is known to build a bulky nest high in the tallest forest trees, there are few details of its breeding habits.

## 13/ AMERICAN HARPY EAGLE
*Harpia harpyja*    R

RANGE: **S Mexico S to N Argentina**
HABITAT: **lowland tropical forest**
SIZE: **36–43¼ in (91–110 cm)**

A huge forest eagle, this species has immense feet and talons that make it one of the most powerful birds of prey in the world. A mighty predator, it can tackle large monkeys, sloths and porcupines, as well as eat some birds and reptiles.

The American Harpy Eagle picks most of its prey from the trees, plunging through the canopy and maneuvering with great skill between the branches. Its nest is composed of thick sticks and is about 5 ft (1.5 m) across. It is often built in the crown of a giant silk-cotton tree up to 165 ft (50 m) from the ground.

## 14/ NEW GUINEA HARPY EAGLE
*Harpyopsis novaeguineae*    ?

RANGE: **New Guinea**
HABITAT: **rain forest and gallery forest; visits clearings and gardens**
SIZE: **29½–35½ in (75–90 cm)**

The New Guinea Harpy Eagle is a very large eagle, with an erectile crest, a facial ruff, short wings, a long tail and bare legs. With a naturally low population density and probably also a low reproductive rate, it is threatened by hunting for its wing and tail feathers by New Guinea highlanders, equipped today with firearms, which has exterminated it in some areas. It is also threatened by habitat destruction.

This enigmatic species hunts in the style of a goshawk, perching inconspicuously inside the forest and changing perches by flying through or below the canopy. It feeds on mammals up to the size of wallabies and piglets, as well as on birds and reptiles. It may locate its prey by sound, dropping from its perch into the undergrowth, the erected ruff of feathers on its face possibly helping it to concentrate the sound as the facial disks of owls do. It is agile on the ground, where it will pursue prey on foot. Pairs of these birds advertise their presence and maintain contact by dueting with loud, resonant calls at dawn and dusk.

## 15/ PHILIPPINE EAGLE
*Pithecophaga jefferyi*    E

RANGE: **Philippines**
HABITAT: **rain forest**
SIZE: **34–40 in (86–102 cm)**

Now restricted to a few patches of forest on some of the Philippine islands, this magnificent eagle is one of the rarest and most endangered birds of prey in the world, with an estimated population of only 200 birds. It is threatened with extinction principally by severe losses of its forest habitat.

The Philippine Eagle is a huge, powerful and distinctive bird, short-winged and long-tailed, with a remarkably deep, laterally compressed bill. Sometimes known as the Monkey-eating Eagle, it is a fearsome hunter both of monkeys and flying lemurs (colugos). It is also big enough to tackle small deer and large birds such as hornbills. It hunts either from a perch in the trees, or by gliding low over the canopy, watching for any movement below.

INDIAN BLACK EAGLE

juv

race *heliaca*

juv

race *adalberti*

IMPERIAL EAGLE

GREATER SPOTTED EAGLE

juv

GOLDEN EAGLE

WEDGE-TAILED
EAGLE

juv

VERREAUX'S EAGLE

dark phase

pale phase

BLACK-AND-WHITE
HAWK-EAGLE

BOOTED EAGLE

race *limnaetus* dark phase

CHANGEABLE HAWK-EAGLE

race *cirrhatus*

LONG-CRESTED EAGLE

juv

ORNATE HAWK-EAGLE

juv

CROWNED EAGLE

juv

BLACK-AND-CHESTNUT EAGLE

MARTIAL EAGLE

241

# BOOTED EAGLES

## FAMILY ACCIPITRIDAE/9
### Booted eagles
Large birds of prey with feathered legs. Feed mainly on live prey. Sexes similar in plumage, females usually larger. Plumage usually brown, some forest-dwelling species with black and white, a few also with chestnut, one all black. Large stick nest usually in trees or on cliff ledges; sometimes use abandoned nest of another bird of prey. Eggs usually 1–2, white with brown or reddish markings. Incubation 40–50 days, nestling period 50–120 days. 31 species.

## 1/ INDIAN BLACK EAGLE
*Ictinaetus malayensis*
RANGE: **India, Sri Lanka, Burma, Malaysia SE to Sulawesi, Moluccas**
HABITAT: **mainly hill forests**
SIZE: **27–31¾ in (69–81 cm)**

The Indian Black Eagle has a relatively light-weight body and very long wings with long primary feathers which it spreads wide like outstretched fingers: these features enable this unusual eagle to fly remarkably slowly over or through the forest canopy in its search for prey.

Although it takes a wide range of prey, including lizards, small mammals and birds, it is best known for its habit of snatching up eggs or nestlings, sometimes tearing the whole nest from among the branches and carrying it off to devour the contents at leisure. Its highly specialized feet, with the outer toe and talon very short but the others equipped with very long, straight talons, doubtless help it to achieve this.

The Indian Black Eagle also occurs in more open terrain, quartering the ground like a giant harrier. It may seize small mammals on the ground and can put on a surprising burst of speed when it snatches bats and swiftlets from around the mouths of caves.

## 2/ GREATER SPOTTED EAGLE
*Aquila clanga*
RANGE: **breeds extreme E Europe E across N Asia; some birds resident, others winter in S of range, many winter as far S as NE Africa, Middle East, N India and China**
HABITAT: **mainly woodland or forest, usually near water or wetlands**
SIZE: **26–29 in (66–74 cm)**

This thickset eagle's wings usually appear remarkably broad and blunt-ended in flight. Apart from a whitish crescent across the rump, adults are dark brown, although an uncommon pale phase is light buffish-brown. The prominent white spots on the juveniles give the species its name. Juvenile pale phase birds are strikingly pale sandy-buff with blackish flight feathers.

The Greater Spotted Eagle scavenges widely, readily visiting carrion, but also hunts a wide variety of live prey, including small mammals, birds, reptiles, amphibians and insects. Bird prey includes waterbirds, from young herons snatched from their nests to ducks and coots; in dealing with the latter, the eagle may separate one bird from a flock and then repeatedly stoop at it, forcing it to dive until it becomes exhausted and can easily be seized when at the surface.

## 3/ IMPERIAL EAGLE
*Aquila heliaca*  [?]
RANGE: **breeds E Europe to C Asia, Spain; some populations migratory, especially in C Asia (winter S to N India)**
HABITAT: **mainly lowland areas, usually with trees**
SIZE: **31–33 in (79–84 cm)**

This imposing eagle is only slightly smaller than the Golden Eagle; its crown and neck feathers are even more striking, being yellowish-white rather than gold. Although it is still widespread in parts of central Asia, numbers of European birds have decreased greatly.

The Spanish race of this bird, *A. h. adalberti*, is geographically isolated from its much more widespread eastern European and Asian counterpart *A. h. heliaca*. It differs principally in having a much more extensive area of white plumage on the leading edge of the wings, and is often regarded as a separate species. The Spanish Imperial Eagle is now an extremely rare and endangered bird.

## 4/ GOLDEN EAGLE
*Aquila chrysaetos*
RANGE: **Europe, N Asia, North America, parts of N Africa and Middle East**
HABITAT: **mountains, plains, sea coasts**
SIZE: **30–39 in (76–99 cm)**

A consummate flier, even in the strongest winds, this is generally regarded as the most impressive of the *Aquila* eagles. Contrary to popular belief, it is not normally a spectacular hunter, relying instead on patient quartering at low altitude and a sudden rush-and-pounce attack. Medium-sized mammals and birds usually form its main prey, but it will also feed on carrion.

Although it is the most widespread and numerous large eagle in the northern hemisphere, the Golden Eagle has declined in numbers in some parts of its range. This is as a result of human disturbance and habitat modification as well as direct persecution, including poisoning and shooting, because of the bird's allegedly serious depredations of game and lambs.

Golden Eagles usually build their nest of branches on cliffs or crags, or in trees. Most pairs have several nests, which they use roughly in rotation. If it is re-used over many successive seasons a nest can grow to a huge size: up to 6 ft (2 m) high and up to 5 ft (1.5 m) across.

## 5/ WEDGE-TAILED EAGLE
*Aquila audax*
RANGE: **Australia, Tasmania, S New Guinea**
HABITAT: **varied, but avoids intensively settled and cultivated areas**
SIZE: **33¾–41 in (86–104 cm)**

This is a huge, dark eagle with a long, wedge-shaped tail. Young birds are brown with a pale nape and shoulders, and gradually darken until they are almost black in their seventh year. The small Tasmanian population is threatened by habitat destruction and direct persecution.

Wedge-tailed Eagles search for food by soaring, quartering the ground or by sitting on a high perch. They take live mammals, birds and reptiles up to the size of a young kangaroo or ibis. Their main prey in pastoral areas consists of rabbits and hares, although they sometimes kill lambs and young goats. Juvenile eagles often eat carrion, gathering like vultures at animals killed on roads. Pairs perform soaring and undulating or rolling and foot-clasping displays. The huge stick nest is built in a substantial tree fork or, occasionally, on a cliff ledge and the 1–2 (rarely 3) eggs are incubated mainly by the female.

## 6/ VERREAUX'S EAGLE
*Aquila verreauxii*
RANGE: **sub-Saharan Africa, Sinai, S Arabia**
HABITAT: **rocky mountains, cliffs and gorges; also dry savanna**
SIZE: **31¾–37¾ in (81–96 cm)**

Also widely known as the Black Eagle, this is the African counterpart of the Golden Eagle. It has a marked preference for medium-sized mammals, and in many parts of its range it feeds chiefly on hyraxes. Its narrow wing bases and broad primary feathers give this elegant, well-proportioned eagle a unique outline in flight.

Verreaux's Eagle is a superb flier, and it indulges in spectacular display flights, alternating breathtakingly steep dives with great upward swoops, often followed by a roll or a somersault. Males perform a remarkable pendulum-like series of gyrations. Although 2 eggs are usually laid and hatched, it is extremely rare for more than 1 chick to survive: the older chick kills its weaker, younger sibling. This "Cain and Abel" rivalry is found in other birds of prey, but is virtually invariable in this species.

## 7/ BOOTED EAGLE
*Hieraaetus pennatus*

RANGE: **breeds NW Africa, SW Europe, SE Europe E into Asia; most European birds winter in Africa S of Sahara, most Asian birds in India**
HABITAT: **forest and woodland and adjacent open country, especially in hilly and upland areas**
SIZE: **18–20¾ in (46–53 cm)**

This eagle is a dashing hunter. It feeds on a variety of birds and small mammals, perching high in a tree or soaring above the forest canopy to spot its prey, then diving or stooping after it from heights of 330–800 ft (100–250 m) or more.

The Booted Eagle takes its common name from its heavily feathered legs. It occurs in a pale phase and a dark phase. Pale phase birds outnumber dark phase birds in most of Europe by about 7 to 3, but in Asia the proportions seem more equal. Pale phase juveniles have much gingery smudging and streaking on the underparts, while those of the dark phase are similar to the adults.

## 8/ BLACK-AND-WHITE HAWK-EAGLE
*Spizastur melanoleucus*

RANGE: **Central and South America**
HABITAT: **forests, adjacent open country**
SIZE: **20¾–24 in (53–61 cm)**

The prey of the Black-and-white Hawk-Eagle is believed to consist largely of small to medium-sized mammals and birds. In some parts of the bird's range in South America, it occurs along rivers, perhaps because these often provide the only open spaces in forests. In such habitats, it is known to take birds up to the size of cormorants and mergansers.

Although it is such a conspicuous bird, it is rarely seen and seems to be a relatively scarce and local species. Immatures are rather similar to the adults, but with whitish edges to the wing coverts.

## 9/ LONG-CRESTED EAGLE
*Spizaetus occipitalis*

RANGE: **sub-Saharan Africa**
HABITAT: **woodland, cultivated land, open country with trees**
SIZE: **20–22 in (51–56 cm)**

The Long-crested Eagle preys mainly on small rodents, catching them by dropping down from a prominent perch. Over much of Africa, this bird is well known through its habit of hunting from fenceposts, utility poles and roadside trees. It hunts chiefly in the early morning and toward evening and often rests in the shade of a large tree during the heat of midday.

They are noisy birds, especially at the onset of the breeding season, uttering loud, high-pitched screaming cries and a harsh *kik-kik-kik-kik-kik-kee-eh* call, both from perches and on the wing. Immatures are similar to the adults, but are rather browner and show white tips to the neck and upper wing covert feathers.

## 10/ CHANGEABLE HAWK-EAGLE
*Spizaetus cirrhatus*

RANGE: **India, Sri Lanka, Southeast Asia**
HABITAT: **savanna, open country, forests in some areas**
SIZE: **22–31¾ in (56–81 cm)**

Different races of this species vary considerably in plumage and size, and while most have a prominent crest (hence the alternative name for the species, Crested Eagle) some have only a vestigial crest, and others are completely crestless. Generally, adults are like the race *S. c. cirrhatus*, from India south of the Ganges Plain and West Bangladesh. The almost crestless race, *S. c. limnaetus*, from the Himalayas to the Philippines, Borneo and Java, is unusual in having a dark phase as well as the normal form.

This eagle hunts mainly from a perch and seizes most of its prey – mainly small mammals and lizards, along with a few birds – on the ground. It builds its large nest of sticks lined with leaves high in a big tree.

## 11/ ORNATE HAWK-EAGLE
*Spizaetus ornatus*

RANGE: **Central and South America; Trinidad and Tobago**
HABITAT: **tropical forest and adjacent open country**
SIZE: **24–26 in (61–66 cm)**

Like most forest birds of prey, the Ornate Hawk-Eagle carries out most of its hunting from a perch. Its prey includes a variety of small mammals and birds up to the size of chachalacas, the smaller herons, quails and parrots. These birds are most easily seen when soaring, wheeling in leisurely circles, usually fairly low above the forest canopy, holding their wings horizontal but angled slightly forward. During the breeding season, pairs take part in aerial displays, soaring together. The male may perform aerial loops and undulating displays. At this time, these handsome birds are very noisy, calling with high-pitched screams and whistling notes.

## 12/ CROWNED EAGLE
*Spizaetus coronatus*

RANGE: **sub-Saharan Africa**
HABITAT: **mainly forests, sometimes hillsides and more open areas**
SIZE: **31¾–35¾ in (81–91 cm)**

Named for its short crest, this large, powerful and impressive eagle is a formidable predator, feeding almost entirely on mammals. In dense forest, monkeys are the main prey. Here, its short, broad wings and long tail give the Crowned Eagle great maneuverability in flight. In more open areas, it takes such animals as small antelopes, hyraxes, mongooses and rats, and occasionally even domestic cats. Females are larger than males and usually have more heavily barred underparts and a shorter crest.

In contrast to many eagles, a pair of Crowned Eagles usually builds only one nest, which may be used over a long period of time. It is constructed from sticks, with a lining of green branches, and sited high in a forest tree, at a height of 40–150 ft (12–45 m). Just before mating, the male displays to his mate by running around her with wings raised to show off their striking, rich chestnut linings. Usually, both parents share the duties of incubation and care of the young.

## 13/ BLACK-AND-CHESTNUT EAGLE
*Spizaetus isidori*

RANGE: **Andes from Venezuela to Argentina**
HABITAT: **mainly mountain forest, usually at 5,300–9,200 ft (1,600–2,800 m)**
SIZE: **24¾–29 in (63–74 cm)**

This thickset, rather powerful bird is sometimes known as Isidor's Eagle. It probably carries out most of its hunting by soaring around the treetops and swooping down on its prey. It takes many medium-sized tree-dwelling mammals, such as monkeys, sloths and squirrels, and also quite large birds such as guans and curassows. Some prey is caught on the ground.

The Black-and-chestnut Eagle builds a large nest, which may measure more than 3 ft (1 m) deep and 6 ft (2 m) or more across. This is constructed almost entirely from live branches, which the bird collects by plunging down and breaking off the branch with its momentum as it passes it.

Like so many eagles, this species is sparsely distributed, even in the most suitable habitats, and is threatened by deforestation.

## 14/ MARTIAL EAGLE
*Polemaetus bellicosus*

RANGE: **sub-Saharan Africa**
HABITAT: **mainly savanna; also some cultivated areas**
SIZE: **31¾–37¾ in (81–96 cm)**

This is the largest and most powerful African eagle. It also spends much more time on the wing than most other species, except for the Bateleur, and often soars at great heights. Hunting both from perches and on the wing, it kills a wide range of birds, small to medium-sized mammals and lizards. The birds can spot prey from a considerable distance and usually attack it by a long, slanting stoop at high speed.

The female is usually more heavily spotted than the male and is larger; a large female may have a wingspan of 8½ ft (2.6 m). Immatures are paler above than the adults and have clear white plumage from the throat to the under tail coverts.

Breeding success is variable, with some pairs rearing only 1 young bird in 3 years. The birds are vulnerable to persecution, chiefly by farmers who often unfairly accuse them of taking livestock.

# SECRETARY BIRD, CARACARAS AND FALCONS

YELLOW-HEADED CARACARA

SECRETARY BIRD

CRESTED CARACARA

LAUGHING FALCON

AFRICAN PYGMY FALCON

BARRED FOREST-FALCON

race *ruficollis* red phase

COLLARED FALCONET

race *guerilla*

race *sparverius*

race *sparveroides* red-chested phase

AMERICAN KESTREL

MAURITIUS KESTREL

AUSTRALIAN KESTREL

♀ ♂

EURASIAN KESTREL

♀ ♂

dark phase

pale phase

ELEONORA'S FALCON

♂

NORTHERN HOBBY

APLOMADO FALCON

pale phase

dark phase

gray phase

juv

GYR FALCON

♂

PEREGRINE FALCON

# SECRETARY BIRD, CARACARAS AND FALCONS

## FAMILY SAGITTARIIDAE
### Secretary Bird
There is only one species in this family.

### 1/ SECRETARY BIRD
*Sagittarius serpentarius*
RANGE: **sub-Saharan Africa**
HABITAT: **open savanna and grassland**
SIZE: **$49\frac{1}{4}$–59 in (125–150 cm)**

The Secretary Bird takes its name from the fancied resemblance of its distinctively ornamented head to an old-fashioned clerk or secretary, with a quill pen stuck behind his ear.

Secretary Birds forage for prey on the ground, striding along with a deliberate, measured tread, and are famous for their ability to immobilize and kill snakes. They also feed widely on other reptiles, as well as small mammals, the eggs and young of ground-nesting birds and large insects.

During courtship displays, the birds soar high above the ground, their long legs and tail projecting behind them, and utter weird groaning calls. The nest is a great flat platform of sticks up to 8 ft (2.4 m) across. The 2–4 greenish-white eggs are incubated by the female for about 45 days. The young leave the nest at 10–11 weeks.

## FAMILY FALCONIDAE/1
### Caracaras
Large birds with naked faces and deep, powerful bills. Mainly omnivorous carrion-eaters, with long legs and flat claws. Plumage mainly dark, some white or pale below or on head, some finely barred. Sexes alike. Nest of sticks usually in trees or on cliffs. Eggs 2–3, whitish, buff or pinkish, marked red-brown. Incubation about 32 days, nestling period about 42 days. 9 species.

### 2/ CRESTED CARACARA
*Polyborus plancus*
RANGE: **Florida and SW USA, Central and South America**
HABITAT: **open or semiopen country**
SIZE: **20–24 in (51–61 cm)**

The Crested Caracara is capable of killing a wide variety of prey, including small mammals, young or disabled birds, fish, frogs, insects and other invertebrates, as well as being a scavenger and carrion-eater. Unlike the vultures with which they often associate at a carcass, Crested Caracaras do not soar, but have a direct, purposeful flight with noisy wing beats. They patrol highways early in the morning in search of animals killed during the night, often finding them before the vultures, which depend on warm thermal air currents later in the day for soaring.

### 3/ YELLOW-HEADED CARACARA
*Milvago chimachima*
RANGE: **Panama S to N Argentina**
HABITAT: **savanna, scrub, semiopen country**
SIZE: **$15\frac{1}{4}$–18 in (39–46 cm)**

This caracara is a fairly small, lightly built species, but, like its larger and more robust relatives, it is a scavenger and carrion-eater,

as well as a predator of various insects and assorted small birds and mammals. It is particularly well known for its habit of perching on livestock to feed on the ticks on their skin.

Yellow-headed Caracaras spend much of their time in small groups, and often perch high in trees. They have a buoyant flight with even wing beats and occasional sweeping glides. They build large stick nests, usually in a tree.

## FAMILY FALCONIDAE/2
### Falcons
Small to medium birds of prey, compact, most with long, pointed wings. Typically highly aerial, many catching prey in midair. Toothed and notched bills for killing prey with bite to the neck. Sexes usually similar in plumage (except most kestrels); females larger. Plumage varied, but most darker above than below; many with brown, chestnut and blue-gray. No nest; use scrape on cliff ledge or in tree cavity, or take over old nests of other birds. Eggs 2–6, usually buff, heavily speckled with red-brown. Incubation 28–36 days, nestling period 25–49 days. 48 species.

### 4/ LAUGHING FALCON
*Herpetotheres cachinnans*
RANGE: **Central and South America**
HABITAT: **tropical lowlands, in both semi-open and wooded country**
SIZE: **17–20 in (43–51 cm)**

This unique bird takes its name from its cackling alarm call. More frequently heard, however, especially at dawn and dusk, is a distinctive, 2-note call, typically *gua-co*, with the first note higher, repeated continuously. The Laughing Falcon likes to perch on an exposed branch in the topmost layer of the forest, where it can watch for prey – chiefly snakes – without being seen. Once it sights a snake, the bird drops on it like a stone and seizes the reptile just behind the head with its bill. It usually kills it swiftly with a powerful bite that may sever the snake's head. It then carries its prey to a perch – in its bill if it is a small snake and in its feet if it is a large one. It swallows small snakes whole, but has to tear larger ones to pieces.

### 5/ BARRED FOREST-FALCON
*Micrastur ruficollis*
RANGE: **Central and South America**
HABITAT: **tropical and subtropical forest**
SIZE: **$12\frac{1}{4}$–15 in (31–38 cm)**

The forest-falcons form a distinctive group of long-tailed birds with short, rounded wings, adapted for hunting birds in woodland. The Barred Forest-Falcon forages on the wing or sallies out from a perch to catch prey. It eats a variety of small birds, as well as some lizards and small rodents. It takes advantage of birds following army ants in search of food, dashing out from cover to snatch them by surprise.

This species shows considerable variation in plumage across its wide range. The races illustrated are *M. r. guerilla* from Mexico to Nicaragua and *M. r. ruficollis* from Brazil and Paraguay.

### 6/ AFRICAN PYGMY FALCON
*Polihierax semitorquatus*
RANGE: **E and S Africa**
HABITAT: **arid thornbush and scrub**
SIZE: **$7\frac{1}{2}$–$9\frac{1}{2}$ in (19–24 cm)**

This tiny African falcon is almost shrikelike, with its habit of sitting on exposed perches and diving swiftly on to its prey. It eats small lizards, small birds and small rodents, seized on the ground, as well as many large insects, which are often caught in midair. This is usually a solitary species, found in pairs or groups of up to 4 birds, which generally remain in the same area day after day and year after year. It uses the abandoned nests of other birds, especially weavers and starlings, for roosting, sheltering from rainstorms and nesting.

### 7/ COLLARED FALCONET
*Microhierax caerulescens*
RANGE: **India SE to Malaysia**
HABITAT: **forests with open clearings**
SIZE: **$5\frac{1}{2}$–$7\frac{1}{2}$ in (14–19 cm)**

This tiny falcon uses exposed perches for hunting. Insects are its main prey, and it frequently catches them in flight by darting out from the perch and returning to eat them on its perch. It may also take a few small birds. The Collared Falconet is often known as the Red-legged Falconet, but this is an inappropriate name, as the bird has only some chestnut feathering on its black legs.

## 8/ AMERICAN KESTREL
*Falco sparverius*

RANGE: **breeds SE Alaska and Canada S to extreme S South America; N birds winter S to Panama**
HABITAT: **open country: mountain meadows, grassland, deserts, open woodland, agricultural land and urban areas**
SIZE: **9–12¼ in (23–31 cm)**

The American Kestrel feeds on insects and other invertebrates and on small snakes, lizards, birds and small mammals, including bats, catching its prey either by swooping down on it from a perch or after hovering overhead.

One of the brightest-plumaged of all the kestrels, the American Kestrel is unusual in that, even as juveniles, the sexes have distinct plumages. There is considerable geographical variation in size and in plumage, particularly in that of the male. The 2 races illustrated are *F. s. sparverius*, from much of North America, and the red-chested phase of *F. s. sparveroides* from Cuba and the Isle of Pines.

## 9/ EURASIAN KESTREL
*Falco tinnunculus*

RANGE: **breeds most of Europe, Africa, Asia; N and E birds winter from Britain S to S Africa and N India S to Sri Lanka**
HABITAT: **diverse, from moors to tropical savanna and urban areas; avoids tundra, dense forest, deserts**
SIZE: **12¼–13¾ in (31–35 cm)**

The Eurasian Kestrel is one of the world's most abundant birds of prey, with a very wide distribution and the ability to adapt well to a range of artificial habitats.

Although it is a competent bird-catcher, and feeds widely on insects and other invertebrates, the Eurasian Kestrel is best-known as a hunter of small mammals. It frequently hovers for prolonged periods on fast-beating wings as it scans the ground. When prey is spotted, the bird descends in a series of swoops and hoverings, before finally dropping to snatch it in its feet. It also hunts from a high perch and will sometimes snatch birds in midair. Most of the 10 or 11 races are similar to the race illustrated, *F. t. tinnunculus* from Europe, northwest Africa and Asia South to Arabia, Tibet and extreme southeastern USSR.

## 10/ MAURITIUS KESTREL
*Falco punctatus*  [E]

RANGE: **SW corner of Mauritius**
HABITAT: **a few areas of dense evergreen forest in rugged gorges and escarpments**
SIZE: **11–13 in (28–33 cm)**

Although it never seems to have been very abundant, the Mauritius Kestrel was once widespread in the dense forest that used to clothe much

of the island of Mauritius. Today, it is restricted to the few areas of forest that remain. By 1974 only 6 individuals were believed to be left. The numbers improved slightly in the 1980s and have been supplemented by a captive breeding and release program. But total numbers are probably still below 50, making this one of the most endangered birds in the world.

Its rather short, rounded wings do not equip the Mauritius Kestrel well for hovering, but give it great maneuverability in the forest canopy. Lizards, especially iridescent green tree geckos, small birds and large insects, seem to be its major food.

## 11/ AUSTRALIAN KESTREL
*Falco cenchroides*

RANGE: **Australia, Tasmania, New Guinea**
HABITAT: **open and lightly wooded country, farmland, urban areas**
SIZE: **11¾–13¾ in (30–35 cm)**

Like some of its relatives, this kestrel, which is also known as the Nankeen Kestrel, has adapted well to artificial landscapes. It hunts in the usual kestrel fashion, including hovering, and preys mainly on large insects, small mammals and reptiles. Mouse and locust plagues may attract large concentrations of these birds.

Courting Australian Kestrels perform aerial maneuvers in mock aggression, and the male may ritually feed the female before mating. No nest is built. Instead, the 3–7 eggs are laid in a tree hollow or sometimes on a cliff ledge or city building or in the old stick nests of other birds.

## 12/ NORTHERN HOBBY
*Falco subbuteo*

RANGE: **breeds Europe, NW Africa, Asia; winters in E and S Africa S to Cape Province, and S to N India and S China**
HABITAT: **mainly semiopen country with some tree cover**
SIZE: **12¼–14 in (31–36 cm)**

The Northern Hobby is a long-winged, aerial hunter, swift and extremely agile in the air. It feeds mainly on flying insects, such as dragonflies, and on birds, and is even capable of catching fast-flying, agile swifts and swallows, although it probably takes far more immatures than adults. It often eats insects on the wing, holding them in its feet, but usually takes birds back to a perch to deal with. It often hunts in the evening, taking birds flocking together at roosts and sometimes bats.

## 13/ ELEONORA'S FALCON
*Falco eleonorae*

RANGE: **breeds Canary Islands, Morocco and Mediterranean islands; winters chiefly in Madagascar**
HABITAT: **breeds on sea cliffs and adjacent rocky tablelands; outside breeding season in wider range of habitats**
SIZE: **14–15¾ in (36–40 cm)**

Named after a medieval Sardinian princess, this large, rakish falcon has even longer wings than the Northern Hobby. It occurs in 2 main color phases, a pale phase and a dark phase. Eleonora's Falcon breeds in colonies, usually of 5–20 birds,

but sometimes up to 200, timing the rearing of its young to coincide with a superabundant food supply – the millions of small birds crossing the Mediterranean on their autumn migration. In winter it feeds mainly on flying insects.

## 14/ APLOMADO FALCON
*Falco femoralis*

RANGE: **breeds Mexico to extreme S South America; birds from extreme N and S winter to S and N respectively**
HABITAT: **open or lightly wooded country**
SIZE: **14½–17¾ in (37–45 cm)**

This falcon feeds mainly on birds and insects taken in flight. It is sufficiently swift and agile to catch such fast-flying birds as pigeons and parrots. Until the beginning of the 20th century, the Aplomado Falcon bred regularly in southwestern USA, but it became increasingly rare and was last known to nest in Texas and New Mexico in the 1950s, although single birds have been seen occasionally since then. The reasons for this decline are unknown, but a significant factor may have been the development of the species' habitat for agriculture. It is now scarce in northern Mexico, where the use of pesticides poses a serious threat.

## 15/ GYR FALCON
*Falco rusticolus*

RANGE: **Greenland, Iceland and Arctic Europe, Asia and North America**
HABITAT: **sea cliffs, uplands, other open country**
SIZE: **20–22¾ in (51–58 cm)**

This is the largest and most powerful of the falcons, fully capable of taking prey the size of grouse and ducks, or sometimes even larger, more formidable birds, including buzzards and owls. The Gyr Falcon will also catch small rodents and occasionally kills mammals as large as hares. It generally catches its prey after a long, level chase low over the ground, in which it demonstrates its speed and stamina.

## 16/ PEREGRINE FALCON
*Falco peregrinus*  [V]

RANGE: **almost cosmopolitan; absent from Sahara, C Asia, most of South America**
HABITAT: **mountains, uplands, sea cliffs**
SIZE: **14–18¾ in (36–48 cm)**

To many, the Peregrine Falcon is the ultimate predatory bird – a robustly built, fast-flying falcon which typically kills its prey in a spectacular diving stoop, often from a great height. Most of the prey comprises medium-sized birds, almost all of which are caught or killed on the wing. Pigeons and doves are the preferred prey wherever they occur in the bird's range.

Long persecuted by egg-collectors, gamekeepers and pigeon fanciers, the Peregrine Falcon faced a new threat from the effects of pesticides in the 1950s and 1960s and many populations in Europe and North America declined alarmingly. More recently, there has been a recovery in some areas including Britain, but in parts of Europe numbers are still low.

# MEGAPODES, GUANS AND CURASSOWS, TURKEYS, GROUSE, NEW WORLD QUAILS

chick emerging from nest mound

AUSTRALIAN BRUSH-TURKEY

MALLEE FOWL

CRESTED GUAN

PLAIN CHACHALACA
♀
♂

red phase
♀

dark phase
♀

NOCTURNAL CURASSOW

GREAT CURASSOW
♂

SPRUCE GROUSE

race *scoticus*
"Red Grouse"

♂

♂ summer

♂ winter

WILLOW PTARMIGAN

♀ summer

♀

♂

♀

WILD TURKEY

WESTERN CAPERCAILLIE

gray phase

♀

GREATER PRAIRIE CHICKEN

RUFFED GROUSE

♂

race *virginianus*

♀

gray phase

♂

♂

♀

race *ridgwayi*
"Masked Bobwhite"

♂

CALIFORNIA QUAIL

MONTEZUMA QUAIL

NORTHERN BOBWHITE

## FAMILY MEGAPODIIDAE
### Megapodes

Large, robust ground birds with sturdy legs. Sexes similar. Eggs white to brown with chalky covering. Clutch size for individual female known only for Mallee Fowl (5–33 eggs, usually 15–24) and Orange-footed Scrub Fowl *Megapodius reinwardt* (3–13 eggs). Eggs laid in mounds of decaying vegetation or sand which provide heat for incubation (about 50 days for Australian Brush-Turkey and Mallee Fowl). Young independent upon hatching. 19 species.

### 1/ AUSTRALIAN BRUSH-TURKEY
*Alectura lathami*

RANGE: **coastal and subcoastal E Australia from Cape York to mid-New South Wales**
HABITAT: **rain forest, thick scrub, well-vegetated urban areas**
SIZE: **$27\frac{1}{2}$ in (70 cm)**

The powerful legs and feet of the Australian Brush-Turkey are typical of the ground-feeding megapodes. It uses its feet to rake up a variety of animal and vegetable foods from the forest floor, including insects and other invertebrates, fruits and seeds. Powerful runners, Australian Brush-Turkeys fly only to escape danger or to roost in trees at night.

Like most megapodes, it lays its eggs in a mound which acts as an incubator. Built of leaf litter and soil raked together by the male, the mound heats up as the organic matter decays. The male maintains the correct temperature of about 33°C (91.4°F) by adding material or opening up the mound to ventilate it and advertises his handiwork with loud booming calls. These can attract several females, which between them lay a total of 18–24 eggs in separate hollows excavated by the male. When the young hatch they dig their way out of the mound and immediately run off to live a solitary and independent life. They can fly within hours of leaving the nest mound.

### 2/ MALLEE FOWL
*Leipoa ocellata*   [V]

RANGE: **inland S Australia, extending to coast in some areas**
HABITAT: **eucalyptus scrub and woodland (mallee)**
SIZE: **$23\frac{1}{2}$ in (60 cm)**

The Mallee Fowl is a denizen of the low, multi-stemmed eucalyptus woodland known as mallee. Most of this unique habitat has been cleared for cereal cultivation and the few nature reserves may be too small to maintain viable populations of the species. The Mallee Fowl feeds by using its large feet to rake through leaf litter in search of seeds, buds, insects and other small animals.

In late winter and spring, the male and female build the nest mound, using moist leaf litter and sand, with an egg chamber of wet, rotting litter. The male maintains a constant temperature of 91.4°F (33°C) in the mound by testing it with the sensitive inside of his bill. When he has assessed the temperature, he opens or closes the mound to release or retain the heat produced by fermentation or, later in the season, to expose or protect it from the fierce sun. The female lays her eggs from spring to fall.

## FAMILY CRACIDAE
### Guans and curassows

Large, often tree-dwelling forest birds with blunt wings and long, broad tails. Plumage generally dark with white patches; many species with crests or casques. Males often larger. Nests of twigs and rotting foliage, low in trees or on ground. Eggs 2–4, white or cream. Incubation 22–34 days. Chicks leave nest at 1 day old; in some species can fly at 3–4 days, but are cared for by females or both parents for some time. 45 species.

### 3/ PLAIN CHACHALACA
*Ortalis vetula*

RANGE: **S Texas to W Nicaragua and NW Costa Rica; introduced to islands off Georgia**
HABITAT: **lowland semiarid scrub forest, thickets, forests**
SIZE: **18 in (46 cm)**

The Plain Chachalaca is generally a shy bird in the wild and is usually located by its call – a raucous repetition of its name which is taken up by others in a harsh, rhythmic chorus, most often during the twilight of dawn and dusk. Like other members of its family, it walks along branches to feed on berries, buds and tender young leaves. In the breeding season – from early March to September in Texas – the pinkish-gray bare skin on each side of the male's chin turns bright red.

### 4/ CRESTED GUAN
*Penelope purpurascens*

RANGE: **Mexico to W Ecuador and N Venezuela**
HABITAT: **humid forest, scrub, hilly areas up to 3,300 ft (1,000 m)**
SIZE: **$35\frac{3}{4}$ in (91 cm)**

This bird has disappeared from many areas as a result of forest clearance and uncontrolled hunting and now has a rather patchy distribution. Most active at dawn and dusk, they are often seen in pairs, walking or running along branches to feed on wild figs, berries and succulent foliage. Although primarily tree-dwelling, they sometimes descend to the ground to eat fallen fruit. In the dry season the males perform a display in which they fly slowly with wings beating rapidly to produce a loud drumming rattle.

### 5/ NOCTURNAL CURASSOW
*Nothocrax urumutum*

RANGE: **NW South America to E Peru**
HABITAT: **forests**
SIZE: **26 in (66 cm)**

As its name suggests, this species is most active at night. It sings on both moonlit and dark nights from high in the forest with a soft dovelike cooing, followed by a pause and a guttural hoot. Its odd specific name, *urumutum*, is derived from a Brazilian Indian name based on its song.

The Nocturnal Curassow is a secretive bird, and is said to spend the day concealed in a tree cavity or a hole in the ground. It will descend to the forest floor to feed on ripe fallen fruit, but always retreats to the trees for safety. The 2 white eggs are laid in a large nest of sticks, built in a tree and usually well concealed by vegetation.

### 6/ GREAT CURASSOW
*Crax rubra*

RANGE: **Mexico to W Ecuador and W Colombia**
HABITAT: **humid to semiarid, undisturbed mature forest; also scrub**
SIZE: **38 in (97 cm)**

The Great Curassow is sensitive to disturbance, and is one of the first birds to disappear when a forest is exploited by man. It is also hunted throughout its range; its populations have become increasingly fragmented and it is now rare.

It normally feeds on the forest floor on a variety of leaves and fruit, but retires to the upper canopy for cover. Usually seen in pairs, it forages in small family groups after breeding. The song of the male is a long, low, booming sound with a ventriloquial quality. The female is variable in color, the red phase and dark phase being most common; there is also a rare barred phase.

## FAMILY MELEAGRIDIDAE
### Turkeys
Large ground birds with strong legs and bare skin on head and neck. Plumage dark with metallic highlights; males brighter and usually much bigger than females. Ground-nesters. Eggs 8–15, cream speckled brown. Incubation 28 days. Chicks usually leave nest after 1 night, but are cared for by female for first 2 weeks. 2 species.

### 7/ WILD TURKEY
*Meleagris gallopavo*
RANGE: USA, Mexico
HABITAT: forests, clearings, brushland
SIZE: male 48 in (122 cm); female $33\frac{3}{4}$ in (86 cm)

Wild Turkeys are opportunists with broad tastes; they will eat seeds, nuts, berries, green foliage and small animals, such as grasshoppers and other invertebrates and even lizards and salamanders. The birds generally forage on the ground, although they are strong fliers over short distances and roost in trees at night.

The polygamous males attract hens during the breeding season by elaborate displays, strutting and gobbling with fanned tails and swollen wattles. The hens incubate the eggs and tend their broods alone.

## FAMILY TETRAONIDAE
### Grouse
Medium to large, plump birds with short, rounded wings. Males generally larger, with darker, ornamented plumage. Females cryptic. Ground-nesters. Eggs 5–12, white to brown with dark blotches. Incubation 21–27 days. Chicks leave nest within a few hours of hatching; many can fly short distances within 5–8 days. 17 species.

### 8/ SPRUCE GROUSE
*Dendragapus canadensis*
RANGE: W Alaska to E Canada and N USA
HABITAT: boggy areas in conifer forest with carpets of moss
SIZE: 15–17 in (38–43 cm)

The Spruce Grouse is a typical forest grouse, feeding on the buds, twigs and needles of coniferous trees during the winter but switching to berries and other fruits in summer.

Although solitary and largely silent for much of the year, the male displays energetically and noisily in the mating season. Inflating the red skin above his eyes and uttering low-pitched hoots, he struts and whirrs his wings in a forest clearing to attract a female.

### 9/ WILLOW PTARMIGAN
*Lagopus lagopus*
RANGE: N hemisphere at latitudes above 50° N
HABITAT: treeless tundra, moors, heaths, Arctic willow bogs
SIZE: $14\frac{1}{2}$–$16\frac{1}{2}$ in (37–42 cm)

Populations of the Willow Ptarmigan undergo regular 3–10 year cycles, depending on locality. The increases may be related to nutrient cycles

in the soil that affect the birds' food plants. Although the chicks are fed on insects as well as plant food, adults often feed mainly on the catkins, twigs and buds of willow and birch, and the shoots and berries of bilberries and other plants. Birds of the British and Irish race *L. l. scoticus*, known as the Red Grouse, live largely on the young shoots of heather. Red Grouse, formerly considered a separate species, do not molt into white plumage like other races.

### 10/ WESTERN CAPERCAILLIE
*Tetrao urogallus*
RANGE: N Europe, including Scotland
HABITAT: mature conifer forest
SIZE: male $34\frac{1}{4}$ in (87 cm); female $23\frac{1}{2}$ in (60 cm)

This magnificent, turkeylike bird is the biggest of the grouse and the species most intimately associated with forests. It feeds largely on pine seeds and pine needles in winter, but switches in summer to a diet of leaves, stems and berries of bilberries, cranberries and bog whortleberries, together with other sedges and plants. The chicks are fed on insects at first.

In spring, the males gather together at traditional sites, or "courts," in forest clearings, to perform a dramatic courtship ritual. With tail fanned out and throat feathers puffed up, a male challenges rival males with a song consisting of a series of clicking notes, rather like water dripping into a bucket, which accelerate until they run together into a soft drum-roll sound and end in a noise like the popping of a cork from a wine bottle.

### 11/ RUFFED GROUSE
*Bonasa umbellus*
RANGE: Alaska, Canada, N USA
HABITAT: deciduous and conifer forest, abandoned farmland
SIZE: 17 in (43 cm)

This highly prized gamebird, which occurs in distinct gray and red phases, is notable for its courtship display. The monogamous male lays claim to a thick stand of aspens and attracts a mate by beating his wings to produce a hollow, accelerating drumming. At the same time, he raises his head crest, extends his neck ruff and fans his tail to its full extent. After mating, the female usually selects a nest site among male aspen trees where she can feed on the catkins during incubation of her 11–12 eggs.

### 12/ GREATER PRAIRIE CHICKEN
*Tympanuchus cupido*
RANGE: SC Canada to Gulf of Mexico
HABITAT: grassland
SIZE: 17–$18\frac{3}{4}$ in (43–48 cm)

Once common on the American prairies, this large grouse has become increasingly rare as its habitat has dwindled. It feeds on leaves, buds, fruits and seeds, as well as on insects such as grasshoppers in summer. In spring the males gather at traditional "booming grounds" – communal courtship arenas – where they inflate their orange neck pouches and perform spectacular stamping dances, accompanied by loud booming cries.

## FAMILY PHASIANIDAE/1
### New World quails
Small to medium, rounded birds, with strong serrated bills. Plumage brighter than on Old World quails, males with distinctive markings. Ground-nesters. Eggs 6–16, white, sometimes marked. Incubation 18–23 days. Chicks leave nest within a few hours in some species and can fly when only 1 week old. 31 species.

### 13/ CALIFORNIA QUAIL
*Lophortyx californica*
RANGE: British Columbia S to Baja California
HABITAT: brush and grassland, irrigated and fallow arable land
SIZE: $9\frac{1}{2}$–11 in (24–28 cm)

The California Quail is an attractive, very gregarious bird which forms winter flocks, or coveys, of 200–300 birds. These usually forage together on foot for seeds, especially those of vetches and other legumes. The birds rarely fly unless alarmed but, unlike other quails, they roost in dense trees or shrubs rather than on the ground.

California Quails nest among low herbage, carefully concealing their eggs in shallow scrapes lined with dead leaves and grasses.

### 14/ NORTHERN BOBWHITE
*Colinus virginianus*
RANGE: E USA to SW USA and Mexico
HABITAT: open pine forests, clearings
SIZE: $7\frac{3}{4}$–11 in (20–28 cm)

Named in imitation of its cheerful mating call, this is a social species which forms flocks, or coveys, of 15–30 birds in fall. The birds feed together on the seeds and fruits of grasses, shrubs and crops such as sorghum and soybeans. Each covey roosts on the ground in a tight bunch with heads pointing out, and explodes into the air if flushed.

The race *C. v. virginianus* occurs in central and eastern USA. The Masked Bobwhite *C. v. ridgwayi* is a distinctive southern race, with a small, endangered population, which has been reintroduced from Mexico to its former range in southeastern Arizona.

### 15/ MONTEZUMA QUAIL
*Cyrtonyx montezumae*
RANGE: S Arizona, New Mexico, Texas, N Mexico
HABITAT: open, grassy, pine, juniper and oak woodland
SIZE: 7 in (18 cm)

The handsome Montezuma Quail is a bird of the mountainous, arid southwest of America and is able to tolerate long periods without rain. Its stout legs are well adapted for digging up moisture-rich bulbs and the tubers of nut grasses; it also eats a variety of seeds and insects.

Its call is a gentle whistle. The birds usually nest in the late summer rainy season. After the chicks are fledged, they form flocks, or coveys, of 8–10 birds which feed on the ground and hide in the grass if disturbed.

251

# PARTRIDGES AND OLD WORLD QUAILS

♂

HIMALAYAN SNOWCOCK

♂ SEE-SEE PARTRIDGE

♀

race
castaneiventer

ROCK PARTRIDGE

race cranchii

race
melanogaster

RED-NECKED FRANCOLIN

♂

"Montana" phase
♂

GRAY PARTRIDGE

INDIAN GRAY FRANCOLIN

♂

♂

MADAGASCAR PARTRIDGE

♀

LONG-BILLED WOOD PARTRIDGE

♀

♂

♀

♂

COMMON HILL-PARTRIDGE

STONE PARTRIDGE

CRESTED WOOD-PARTRIDGE

♀

♂

♀

♂

ASIAN BLUE QUAIL

♂

CEYLON SPURFOWL

COMMON QUAIL

# PARTRIDGES AND OLD WORLD QUAILS

## FAMILY PHASIANIDAE/2
### Partridges and francolins
Stout, rounded, medium-sized gamebirds, with short, powerful wings and strong legs. Sexes distinct, with males brighter. Mostly ground-feeding seed-eaters. Nest usually open scrape on ground. Eggs usually 2–19, whitish to dark olive. Incubation 16–25 days, chicks leave nest soon after hatching. 98 species.

## 1/ SEE-SEE PARTRIDGE
*Ammoperdix griseogularis*
RANGE: S USSR, Iran to NW India
HABITAT: arid foothills and semidesert
SIZE: $9\frac{1}{2}$ in (24 cm)

The See-see Partridge is typical of the rough, broken, treeless terrain found on the rocky hillsides of central and southern Asia. It forages in flocks of up to 20 individuals, picking through the rocks and vegetation for seeds and other morsels.

Single birds are very rarely seen except during the mating season, when each male establishes and defends his own breeding territory. The mating system is basically monogamous, but several females may lay their eggs in the same nest, which is usually sited in a sheltered position near a tuft of grass.

## 2/ HIMALAYAN SNOWCOCK
*Tetraogallus himalayensis*
RANGE: E Afghanistan E to W Nepal, NW China
HABITAT: high-altitude mountain slopes
SIZE: 20–22 in (51–56 cm)

Found high up on some of the highest mountains in the world, the large Himalayan Snowcock is well adapted to its harsh environment. Its predominantly gray and white plumage blends in with the landscape of gray rock and snow, and its broad diet includes the seeds, leaves, shoots and roots of a variety of plants, particularly sedges. It often has to cover a lot of ground to find enough to eat and may range over an area of up to 250 acres (1 square kilometer) each day.

In autumn and winter it often associates in larger flocks of 15–20 birds, but in the breeding season the flocks break up as the males court the females with loud 5-note whistles. The nests, which are simple hollows lined with dry grass and feathers, are often made in caves.

## 3/ ROCK PARTRIDGE
*Alectoris graeca*
RANGE: European Alps, SE Yugoslavia, Greece, Bulgaria
HABITAT: rocky heaths, pastures, grassland
SIZE: $13\frac{1}{2}$–15 in (34–38 cm)

The Rock Partridge is a common sight in the grasslands and among the vineyards of the eastern Mediterranean area, where flocks of up to 100 birds may work their way between the vines in search of seeds, fruits and shoots. Like many partridges, it has a variable diet, for although it is essentially vegetarian in adulthood, the breeding females and chicks eat quantities of insects, spiders and other small animals.

Rock Partridges are monogamous and often pair for life. As with other partridges in the genus *Alectoris*, the female may lay 2 clutches of up to 14 eggs each season, incubating 1 clutch herself while the male incubates the other.

## 4/ RED-NECKED FRANCOLIN
*Francolinus afer*
RANGE: C and S Africa
HABITAT: forest clearings with brushwood
SIZE: $11\frac{3}{4}$–16 in (30–41 cm)

The francolins are a group of fairly large, powerful gamebirds distinguished by the patches of bare skin on their heads or necks. The Red-necked Francolin is a very variable species with as many as 18 races, found throughout much of Africa south of the Equator. The races illustrated are *F. a. cranchii* from northern Angola, northern Zambia and western Tanzania; *F. a. melanogaster* from Mozambique and eastern Tanzania; and *F. a. castaneiventer* from southern and eastern Cape Province to northern Transvaal.

It often feeds in mixed groups with other francolins, searching for food among the low vegetation of forest edges and clearings. Much of its diet consists of tubers, bulbs, shoots, berries, roots and seeds, but it will also eat insects and other invertebrates.

The mated pairs tend to remain within their breeding territories throughout the year, suggesting that the pairs mate for life. The clutch of 3–9 eggs is laid in a scrape under a shrub and incubated by the female alone. As with many gamebirds, the chicks develop fast and are able to fly 10 days after hatching.

## 5/ INDIAN GRAY FRANCOLIN
*Francolinus pondicerianus*
RANGE: E Iran, India, Sri Lanka
HABITAT: dry plains, thorny scrub
SIZE: 13 in (33 cm)

Its ability to tolerate dry conditions has made the Indian Gray Francolin one of the most common resident gamebirds in southern Asia. Recognized by its distinctive yellow throat markings, it lives in grasslands and semiarid thorny scrub, often near crops or villages. The birds usually occur in small family groups, roosting together in small trees or shrubs. They feed on weed seeds and cultivated grain, as well as large numbers of insects during the summer.

The breeding season in India is prolonged and nests containing eggs have been recorded in every month of the year. The brood of 6–9 chicks is generally reared by both parents.

## 6/ GRAY PARTRIDGE
*Perdix perdix*
RANGE: W and C Europe
HABITAT: open country, farmland
SIZE: $11\frac{3}{4}$ in (30 cm)

Originally a bird of open grassland and steppe, the Gray Partridge has adapted well to farmland. It is a common sight in arable fields in many parts of Europe, although in some areas, such as Britain, it has been badly hit by the widespread use of farm pesticides, which destroy the insects that form the main food supply for the chicks during the first 2 weeks after hatching. Herbicides have also had a serious effect, since these kill the "weeds" that the insects live on.

Outside the breeding season the birds associate in family flocks, or coveys, but in late winter the breeding adults form monogamous pairs. Each male defends a territory which, on farmland, includes a hedgerow to provide cover for the nest. The female lays the largest clutch of any bird, up to 25 eggs, or even more, and an average of 19 in some areas.

The "Montana" variety, illustrated along with a more typical adult male, has far more chestnut on its breast and belly.

## 7/ LONG-BILLED WOOD PARTRIDGE
*Rhizothera longirostris*
RANGE: **Malaysia, Sumatra, W Borneo**
HABITAT: **dry forest, especially bamboo**
SIZE: **14 in (36 cm)**

This large tropical partridge lives at altitudes of up to 4,000 ft (1,200 m) in dense upland forest, particularly in areas of thick bamboo. This preference for remote, inaccessible country, coupled with its extreme wariness, means that it is rarely seen – although it will occasionally give away its location by calling loudly at night.

In Malaya the local people are said to catch the birds by luring them into traps with imitations of their calls, which suggests that they are territorial. Apart from this, little is known about their breeding behavior. Only one nest has been found, located in a bamboo thicket; in captivity the female lays 2–5 eggs, incubating them for 18–19 days.

## 8/ MADAGASCAR PARTRIDGE
*Margaroperdix madagarensis*
RANGE: **Madagascar**
HABITAT: **secondary scrub and grassland**
SIZE: **12 in (30 cm)**

Many partridges breed as monogamous pairs, and the males and females are similar in appearance. The male Madagascar Partridge, by contrast, is much brighter than the female, indicating an emphasis on courtship that is typical of polygamous species, in which the male courts and mates with many females. The birds nest from March to June and a large clutch of up to 20 eggs has been reported.

The Madagascar Partridge is a medium-sized grassland bird that lives in heathy, mountainous areas. It often forages on cultivated ground, particularly where it is overrun with weeds and secondary scrub. It also occurs in rice fields, where it probably eats rice grain as well as weed seeds and insects.

## 9/ COMMON HILL-PARTRIDGE
*Arborophila torqueola*
RANGE: **N and E India, S Tibet**
HABITAT: **evergreen forest and scrub**
SIZE: **10 in (25 cm)**

The Common Hill-Partridge is a denizen of thick undergrowth in the upland forests of India and south China. It is usually found at altitudes of 5,000–9,000 ft (1,500–2,700 m), in pairs or groups of up to 10 birds.

The male has a distinctive black throat pattern that is echoed in reduced form in the plumage of the female. The birds pair off in April to July throughout most of their range, laying 4–5 eggs in a scrape beneath a bush or near the base of a tree.

## 10/ CRESTED WOOD-PARTRIDGE
*Rollulus roulroul*
RANGE: **S Burma, Thailand, Malaysia, Sumatra and Borneo**
HABITAT: **tropical forest**
SIZE: **10 in (25 cm)**

Partridges in general are open country birds, but the wood-partridges of Southeast Asia are found in thick tropical rain forest, where they are rarely seen and difficult to study. The Crested Wood-Partridge is the most spectacular of these species, with richly colored plumage and, in the male, a red, brushlike crest. It feeds on seeds, fruit, insects and small mollusks and appears to eat more animal material than most partridges.

Its nesting habits are also atypical. Instead of the usual scrape, it builds a large domed nest with a small entrance and, in one case, a captive female was seen to lead her brood back to the nest each evening and close the entrance with twigs – a routine that continued until the chicks were 25 days old.

## 11/ STONE PARTRIDGE
*Ptilopachus petrosus*
RANGE: **Africa, Senegal to Kenya**
HABITAT: **rocky hills**
SIZE: **10 in (25 cm)**

This bantamlike African species is well adapted to the arid conditions of areas such as the sub-Saharan Sahel region, where pairs or small family groups can be seen combing the sandy landscape for seeds, insects and some green plants. For preference, however, it frequents areas of dense vegetation among boulder-strewn rocky hills.

The breeding period is very variable, owing to the erratic nature of the food supply in the arid habitat. The birds form monogamous pairs which appear to be permanent, but outside the breeding period the family groups may gather together to feed in larger flocks.

## 12/ CEYLON SPURFOWL
*Galloperdix bicalcarata*
RANGE: **Sri Lanka**
HABITAT: **moist upland forest to 5,000 ft (1,500 m)**
SIZE: **13–14 in (33–36 cm)**

The Ceylon Spurfowl lives in the dense tropical forests that mantle the foothills and mountains of Sri Lanka, feeding on a variety of seeds, tubers and berries. The birds prefer jungle-covered hillsides with river valleys, where they establish well-defined breeding territories which they defend vigorously against intruders. Because of this, they are easily caught by the local people, who use captive decoy birds to lure them to traps.

The breeding adults may form permanent pairbonds. They lay a clutch of 2 eggs during the monsoon period from November to March.

As with other members of the family, the young forage with their parents in small family groups, or coveys, and rapidly learn to find their own food.

## FAMILY PHASIANIDAE/3
### Old World quails
Small, compact, like miniature partridges. Ground birds of open grassland and swamp. Adults seed-eaters, chicks eat insects. Mainly monogamous, but males often brighter. Some breed on migration. Nest a scrape on the ground. Eggs 4–15, white to olive. Incubation 14–22 days, chicks leave nest soon after hatching. 9 species.

## 13/ COMMON QUAIL
*Coturnix coturnix*
RANGE: **Eurasia**
HABITAT: **open grassland**
SIZE: **7 in (18 cm)**

The Common Quail is rarely seen in the wild, but is well known from its distinctive, loud, ventriloquial, trisyllabic call, often rendered as *wet-my-lips*. It usually forages close to the ground beneath the cover of vegetation, and will run when it is alarmed rather than take flight. Despite this, it will fly long distances to reach its breeding grounds; those that breed in Europe migrate from Africa each year. The males arrive first and call to attract the females when they appear. The normal clutch is 7–12 eggs and the chicks are cared for by the female alone.

In Europe the Common Quail has adapted well to agricultural landscapes, particularly cereal crops, but, like the Gray Partridge, its breeding success is limited by the lack of insect food for its chicks in areas where pesticides and herbicides are in common use.

## 14/ ASIAN BLUE QUAIL
*Coturnix chinensis*
RANGE: **W India, Southeast Asia, Philippines, Indonesia, New Guinea, NE Australia**
HABITAT: **open grassland**
SIZE: **5½ in (14 cm)**

One of the smallest of all gamebirds, this boldly marked quail is found over a wide range throughout much of eastern Asia and Australasia. It favors dense grassland, swamp edge and cultivated ground, where it feeds mainly on grass seeds and some insects. It generally forages in family coveys of 6–7 individuals.

In many areas it is nomadic, moving into an area to breed after rainfall. The 4–7 eggs are incubated by the female alone for about 16 days – the shortest incubation period of any gamebird.

# PHEASANTS, GUINEAFOWL

BLOOD PHEASANT

BLYTH'S TRAGOPAN

HIMALAYAN
MONAL PHEASANT

RED JUNGLEFOWL

race *nycthemera*

SILVER PHEASANT

CHEER PHEASANT

typical hybrid

race *colchicus*

melanistic hybrid

typical hybrid

COMMON PHEASANT

LADY AMHERST'S PHEASANT

♂

GREAT ARGUS PHEASANT

♀

COMMON PEAFOWL

♀

♂

CONGO PEAFOWL

HELMETED GUINEAFOWL

VULTURINE GUINEAFOWL

# PHEASANTS, GUINEAFOWL

## FAMILY PHASIANIDAE/4
### Pheasants

Medium to large, often colorful, long-tailed birds. Sexes distinct, with males often spectacular in polygamous species. Generally vegetarian ground-feeders found in tropical and subtropical forest. Nest usually a scrape on ground. Eggs 2–12, whitish to olive. Incubation 18–28 days, chicks leave nest soon after hatching. 48 species.

## 1/ BLOOD PHEASANT
*Ithaginis cruentus*

RANGE: **Himalayas, Nepal, Tibet, China, Burma**
HABITAT: **high-altitude coniferous forest**
SIZE: **$17\frac{3}{4}$ in (45 cm)**

Like all pheasants, the Blood Pheasant is at risk from habitat destruction and human exploitation for food, but it is less vulnerable than most because of its preference for remote places. There is extensive geographical variation in the plumage, with 2 main types; the illustration shows the type found in races in the north of the species' range.

This is a gregarious bird and flocks of 10–30 individuals may be seen working their way through the forest, feeding on fir and juniper sprouts, berries, mosses and bamboo shoots. Blood Pheasants also eat insects during the breeding season in April and May.

## 2/ BLYTH'S TRAGOPAN
*Tragopan blythii*    R

RANGE: **Assam, Burma, Tibet**
HABITAT: **densely wooded valleys at high altitude**
SIZE: **$24\frac{3}{4}$–$27\frac{1}{4}$ in (63–69 cm)**

This is one of 5 species of tragopan which live in the forests of Asia. The males all have striking plumage which plays an important part in courtship. They are unusual among pheasants because they nest in trees, often using old nests built by other species.

Blyth's Tragopan has a preference for the thick undergrowth of dense evergreen mountain forest. It feeds mainly on seeds, berries and buds, although it will also take insects and other small animals. In hard winters when food is scarce it tends to move down to lower altitudes, but not as much as other mountain-dwelling pheasants. At night it roosts in trees, which are often some distance from the feeding areas.

## 3/ HIMALAYAN MONAL PHEASANT
*Lophophorus impejanus*

RANGE: **E Afghanistan, NW Pakistan, S Tibet, Burma**
HABITAT: **open mixed forest on rocky slopes**
SIZE: **$22$–$25\frac{1}{4}$ in (56–64 cm)**

The glorious iridescent metallic plumage of the male Himalayan Monal Pheasant is one of the most spectacular sights of the Asian forests, particularly during courtship when the bird indulges in dramatic display flights over the cliffs and crags of its mountain home. The female is dull

by comparison, to provide camouflage while she incubates her clutch of 4–5 eggs.

For much of the year these birds prefer to live in oak and mixed forest, feeding on ground-living insects and tubers, but in autumn they often move up into the mountain grasslands above the tree line to forage for insect larvae. They will dig through the snow with their bills to reach food, excavating holes up to 12 in (30 cm) deep. Like other pheasants, they are threatened by hunting throughout their range.

## 4/ RED JUNGLEFOWL
*Gallus gallus*

RANGE: **Southeast Asia**
HABITAT: **forests and open country**
SIZE: **male $23\frac{1}{2}$–$31\frac{1}{2}$ in (60–80 cm); female 17–18 in (43–46 cm)**

This bird, the wild ancestor of the domestic fowl, is an opportunist feeder which is at home in a variety of habitats. Normally found in forest with fairly dense undergrowth, frequently with bamboo, it often emerges into clearings and scrubland at the forest edge, where flocks of up to 50 birds forage for a variety of foods, including grain, seeds and insects.

The birds appear to feed in the same area throughout the year. They breed in the dry season from March to May, the polygamous males courting several females with displays of their superb plumage. The 5–6 eggs are laid in a hollow scraped in the ground near a bush.

## 5/ SILVER PHEASANT
*Lophura nycthemera*

RANGE: **S China, E Burma, Indochina, Hainan**
HABITAT: **broad areas of grassland bordered by forest**
SIZE: **male $35\frac{1}{2}$–50 in (90–127 cm); female $21\frac{3}{4}$–$26\frac{3}{4}$ in (55–68 cm)**

The Silver Pheasant is essentially a grassland bird and rarely penetrates into dense forest. Like the Red Junglefowl, it has a broad diet, feeding on a wide range of animal and vegetable matter

including beetles, flower petals, grass and leaves. Its plumage is variable throughout its range and there are about 14 races. The one shown, *L. n. nycthemera* from South China and northeast Vietnam, is the largest and whitest.

Like most grassland pheasants, it has a polygamous mating system, with dominant males courting many females and defending their territory with loud whistling calls.

## 6/ CHEER PHEASANT
*Catreus wallichii*    E

RANGE: **Himalayas**
HABITAT: **steep, grassy hillsides**
SIZE: **male $35\frac{1}{2}$–$46\frac{1}{2}$ in (90–118 cm); female 24–30 in (61–76 cm)**

Many of the pheasants of Asia are threatened with extinction as a result of habitat destruction and hunting, and the Cheer Pheasant is no exception. It is now extinct in many areas of Pakistan but attempts are being made to reintroduce it, using birds bred in captivity.

In the wild the Cheer Pheasant has a preference for grass-covered hillsides with scattered trees and will often forage around human settlements. The adults are largely vegetarian, but the young appear to feed on insects during the first 2 weeks after hatching.

Cheer Pheasants are territorial but the territories are quite small, with up to 6 breeding pairs occupying 250 acres (1 square kilometer). The 9–10 eggs are laid in a nest built on the ground, usually in the lee of a large boulder.

## 7/ COMMON PHEASANT
*Phasianus colchicus*

RANGE: **Asia; introduced to Europe, Australia and North America**
HABITAT: **lowland farmland, woodland, upland scrub**
SIZE: **male $29\frac{1}{2}$–$35\frac{1}{2}$ in (75–90 cm); female $20\frac{1}{2}$–$25\frac{1}{4}$ in (52–64 cm)**

Introduced to many areas of the world for shooting, the Common Pheasant is the most widely distributed of all the gamebirds. The well-camouflaged females can be hard to spot, but the colorful males are a frequent and conspicuous sight on open farmland. In Europe there are now a variety of races, including *P. c. torquatus*, from eastern China, and *P. c. colchicus*, from Transcaucasia and the eastern and southeastern Black Sea region, plus a bewildering variety of typical and dark (melanistic) forms. The melanistic form and some others result partly from interbreeding with the Green Pheasant *Phasianus versicolor*, from Japan.

In its native range (chiefly in India, Southeast Asia and China) the Common Pheasant lives on open forest-grassland. It is an opportunist feeder, taking a variety of seeds, grain, fruit, insects and other small animals, and this is one reason why it has adapted so well to other habitats such as agricultural land.

The male is polygamous, gathering a harem of females on his display territory and defending them against rival males. In autumn the birds are gregarious, but in winter the sexes tend to segregate. Common Pheasants roost in trees at night.

## 8/ LADY AMHERST'S PHEASANT
*Chrysolophus amherstiae* [?]

RANGE: **China, NE Burma; introduced to Britain**
HABITAT: **high bamboo-covered mountain slopes**
SIZE: **male $45\frac{1}{4}$–59 in (115–150 cm); female $22\frac{3}{4}$–$26\frac{3}{4}$ in (58–68 cm)**

One of the most spectacular of the true pheasants, this is also one of the most elusive: a secretive bird which rarely emerges from the thorny thickets and bamboo scrub of its remote mountain habitat. Even those introduced to Britain are not often seen, for the wild population breeds in dense woodland with thick undergrowth, and little is known about its breeding biology.

Bamboo shoots form an important part of its diet in its native range, but it will also eat small animals, including spiders, earwigs and beetles. Lady Amherst's Pheasants have even been seen feeding in shallow flowing water, turning over stones in search of aquatic animals.

## 9/ GREAT ARGUS PHEASANT
*Argusianus argus*

RANGE: **Borneo, Sumatra, Malaya and Thailand**
HABITAT: **lowland and hill forest**
SIZE: **male up to 80 in (203 cm); female up to 30 in (76 cm)**

Male pheasants of polygamous species are generally much more ornate than the females. The Great Argus Pheasant of Southeast Asia is an extreme example of this rule, for the adult male has very large secondary wing feathers, decorated with golden eyespots, which he uses to dazzling effect in courtship.

Each male clears a display site in the forest a considerable distance from that of his nearest rival. Having attracted a female with loud calls, he dances before her. At the climax of the dance he spreads his wing feathers in 2 great, glittering fans and if the female is sufficiently impressed, she will consent to mating. She then leaves to lay her eggs and rear the chicks alone, while the male courts other females. The normal clutch consists of only 2 eggs.

Birds of both sexes tend to be solitary by habit. They eat a wide range of foods, including fallen fruits, ants, slugs and snails.

## 10/ COMMON PEAFOWL
*Pavo cristatus*

RANGE: **Sri Lanka, India, Pakistan, Himalayas; introduced worldwide**
HABITAT: **forests and semiopen country with streams**
SIZE: **male $78\frac{3}{4}$–90 in (200–229 cm); female 34 in (86 cm)**

The dramatic display of the male Common Peafowl (often known as the Peacock) is a familiar sight in parks and gardens throughout the world, where it has been widely introduced as an ornamental bird.

In its native Asia it favors deciduous forests flanking hillside streams, with thick undergrowth and thorny creepers. It will also forage over farmland, particularly among dense, tall crops such as sugar cane. It has a broad diet, which includes grain, berries, green crops, insects, small reptiles and mammals.

The long train of the male consists of greatly elongated upper tail coverts, which can be thrown up and spread out into a spectacular fan by raising the tail beneath. Thus glorified, the male will back slowly toward a potential mate before swiveling around to dazzle her with the full radiance of his display. Compliant females are gathered into a harem and jealously guarded.

## 11/ CONGO PEAFOWL
*Afropavo congensis* [S]

RANGE: **Congo and associated river systems**
HABITAT: **tropical rain forest**
SIZE: **$22\frac{3}{4}$–28 in (58–71 cm)**

The 49 species of pheasant are all natives of Asia, with one exception – the Congo Peafowl. This exquisite bird is a denizen of the dense tropical rain forests of central Africa, which effectively concealed it from western scientists until its "discovery" in 1936.

Although it resembles the Common Peafowl in build and diet – eating a wide variety of fruits and insects, including termites which it digs from their mounds – the Congo Peafowl has a quite different breeding system. Both sexes have superb iridescent plumage, and they are believed to form monogamous pairs. In captivity the hen bird lays 3 eggs which are incubated by both parents. An undisputed nest has never been found in the wild, but it is possible that the birds nest in trees.

## FAMILY NUMIDIDAE
### Guineafowl

Large ground-feeding birds with strong bills and long legs. Plumage typically black, spotted with white; sexes similar. Gregarious, roost in trees. Nest simple scrape on the ground. Eggs 6–22, cream to light brown. Incubation 23–30 days, chicks leave the nest 1–2 days after hatching. 6 species.

## 12/ HELMETED GUINEAFOWL
*Numida meleagris*

RANGE: **E Chad to Ethiopia, E to Rift Valley, S to borders of N Zaire, N Kenya and Uganda**
HABITAT: **open grassland**
SIZE: **21–$22\frac{3}{4}$ in (53–58 cm)**

Distinguished by the conspicuous horny casque on top of its naked, richly pigmented head, the Helmeted Guineafowl has been domesticated all over the world as a food species. In the wild it is a common resident throughout its range.

Outside the breeding season, Helmeted Guineafowl may forage in flocks consisting of several hundred birds, searching for bulbs, tubers, berries, insects and snails on savanna, farmland and scrub edge. Working together in a large flock may help the birds to locate scattered food resources, as well as providing some form of defence against predators, but during the breeding season the flock splits up into monogamous pairs. The clutch, consisting of 6–19 eggs, is laid in a scrape on the ground and is incubated by the female alone.

## 13/ VULTURINE GUINEAFOWL
*Acryllium vulturinum*

RANGE: **sub-Saharan Africa**
HABITAT: **edges of evergreen forest**
SIZE: **$19\frac{3}{4}$ in (50 cm)**

The largest and most impressive of the guineafowl, this species has a distinctive red eye and a flamboyant hackle of elongated, iridescent feathers striped in black, white and blue. Locally common throughout its range, it lives in matted thickets and tangled scrub at the margins of lowland forest, forming flocks of 20–30 birds which often follow troops of monkeys to feast on fallen fruit.

The flocks break up in the breeding season, as with other guineafowl, and the breeding adults form pairs. The clutch of 4–6 eggs is laid in a scrape on the ground, and incubated by the female for 24–30 days.

# MESITES, BUTTONQUAILS, PLAINS-WANDERER, CRANES, LIMPKIN, TRUMPETERS

♀

PLAINS-WANDERER

♀

race *sylvatica*
LITTLE BUTTONQUAIL

♀
QUAIL PLOVER

GRAY-WINGED
TRUMPETER

BLACK CROWNED
CRANE

race *pavonina*

juv

LIMPKIN

WHITE-BREASTED MESITE

race *tabida*
"Greater Sandhill Crane"

rust-stained

juv

juv

SANDHILL CRANE

DEMOISELLE CRANE

SARUS CRANE

race *antigone*

juv

BROLGA

juv

WHOOPING CRANE

juv

juv

SIBERIAN WHITE CRANE

juv

chick

COMMON CRANE

# MESITES, BUTTONQUAILS, PLAINS-WANDERER, CRANES, LIMPKIN, TRUMPETERS

## FAMILY MESITORNITHIDAE
### Mesites
Medium-sized ground-dwellers. Seldom fly. Plumage brown or gray above, paler or spotted below. Sexes alike or different. Twig nests in bushes. Eggs 1–3, whitish, with brown spots. Incubation unknown, chicks leave nest soon after hatching. 3 species.

### 1/ WHITE-BREASTED MESITE
*Mesitornis variegata*  R
RANGE: **3 tiny areas in W Madagascar**
HABITAT: **undisturbed dry forest**
SIZE: **9¾ in (25 cm)**

All 3 species of mesite are found only in Madagascar and all are endangered. This thrush-sized bird scratches about for insects among the dead leaves that carpet the forest floor. It has been seen only in 3 isolated pockets of remote forest; in 1986 it was rediscovered in one of these, in the Ankara nature reserve, having last been seen there in 1931. The main threat to this species is tree-felling, but if feral rats, cats or dogs become established in its last refuge, it will be even more at risk.

## FAMILY TURNICIDAE
### Buttonquails
Small to medium ground-dwelling quail-like birds, with only 3 toes. Plumage buff with brown, gray and cream markings; females brighter. Nest in ground hollow. Eggs 3–7, pale gray to buff, heavily marked with chestnut, gray or other colors. Incubation 12–14 days, chicks leave nest almost immediately after hatching. 15 species.

### 2/ LITTLE BUTTONQUAIL
*Turnix sylvatica*
RANGE: **S Spain, Africa, S and Southeast Asia, Indonesia, Philippines**
HABITAT: **dry grassland, scrub; sometimes crops**
SIZE: **5–6 in (13–15 cm)**

Buttonquails are similar in general appearance to quails (pp. 114–17), although they are not related to them. They have the peculiar habit of slinking low on the ground and rocking backward and forward on their feet.

Shy and secretive, the Little Buttonquail keeps to the undergrowth, where it feeds on grass seeds and some insects. The larger female advertises with a low, cooing call, dominates courtship and mates with several males in succession. Each male must incubate his clutch – for a period of 13 days – and rear the chicks alone.

### 3/ QUAIL PLOVER
*Ortyxelos meiffrenii*
RANGE: **a narrow band S of Sahara**
HABITAT: **very dry, sandy bush**
SIZE: **6 in (15 cm)**

Restricted to arid areas, the Quail Plover inhabits regions with enough rough, dry grasses to make it very difficult to see as it skulks secretively on the ground. If it is flushed from its hiding place, it takes to the air with a strange, jerky, butterfly-like flight, resembling the flight of a bush-lark –

hence its alternative common name of Lark Quail. When it flies, it reveals a distinctive black and white pattern on its wings.

The common names of this odd little bird, which is classified in a different genus from the rest of the buttonquails, reflect its puzzling appearance: it looks like a cross between a small, dumpy plover, a typical buttonquail and a lark. When it runs it looks rather like a miniature courser.

The Quail Plover has a very patchy distribution, although it is locally quite common, especially where the grass *Cenchurus catharticus* grows. Its nest is a shallow scrape lined with grass and often edged with small pebbles. The male incubates the 2 eggs alone.

## FAMILY PEDIONOMIDAE
### Plains-wanderer
There is only one species in this family.

### 4/ PLAINS-WANDERER
*Pedionomus torquatus*  ?
RANGE: **inland SE Australia**
HABITAT: **sparse native grassland**
SIZE: **6–6¾ in (15–17 cm)**

The Plains-wanderer feeds during the day (not by night as was once believed), foraging for seeds and some insects. It walks furtively through the grass, sometimes stopping to bob its head like a wader or to stand on tiptoe and crane its neck to check for any trouble. When danger threatens, it prefers to freeze in a squatting position rather than take to the air.

The nest is a grass-lined scrape made under a clump of grass. The female, dominant in courtship, calls with a mournful booming and may mate with several males. The clutch of 2–5 yellowish eggs with gray markings is incubated mainly by the male for about 23 days. The chicks soon leave the nest and are reared by the male.

The Plains-wanderer has declined in numbers, due to conversion of much of its habitat to cropland and dense pasture. It is a sedentary bird, abandoning an area only when forced to do so by fire, cultivation or overgrazing.

## FAMILY GRUIDAE
### Cranes
Large, long-legged, long-necked birds. Plumage mainly white or gray, with colored plumes or bare skin. Males usually larger. Platform nest of vegetation on ground or in shallow water. Eggs 1–3 (up to 4 in Gray Crowned Crane), white or various colors. Incubation 28–36 days. Chicks leave nest soon after hatching; remain with parents until fledged at 2–4 months. 15 species.

### 5/ COMMON CRANE
*Grus grus*
RANGE: **N temperate Eurasia; winters S to N Africa, India and Southeast Asia**
HABITAT: **breeds in open forest swamps and moorland bogs; winters in shallow wetlands**
SIZE: **43¼–47¼ in (110–120 cm)**

Like the other members of the crane family, the Common Crane is famous for its dancing display. This is performed not only during courtship, but also by small groups of birds. The birds walk around in circles, bowing, bobbing, pirouetting and stopping, bending to pick up small objects and toss them over their heads. These rituals are interspersed with graceful jumps high into the air.

The species' main call is a loud trumpeting, which is uttered by courting pairs as they stand facing each other with outspread wings, necks stretched and bills pointing skyward. It is also heard from the V-formations of migrating flocks.

### 6/ SANDHILL CRANE
*Grus canadensis*
RANGE: **breeds NE Siberia, Alaska, Canada, N USA; winters S USA to C Mexico; small resident populations in Florida and Mississippi, Cuba**
HABITAT: **tundra, marshes, grassland, fields**
SIZE: **42 in (107 cm)**

Sandhill Cranes may congregate at migration stopovers or on the wintering grounds in flocks of hundreds, creating an extraordinary din with their grating, rattling, trumpetlike calls. They are ground-gleaners, foraging for a wide variety of plants, aquatic invertebrates, insects, worms, frogs and small mammals.

There are 5 races, varying in size. The race illustrated, the Greater Sandhill Crane *G. c. tabida*, breeds from southwest British Columbia to northern California and Nevada. The rusty-brown color of adults in some areas is due to their habit of probing with their bills into mud and soil containing reddish iron oxide. When they preen, they transfer the stain to their plumage.

## 7/ WHOOPING CRANE
*Grus americana*　　　　　　　　　　E

RANGE: **breeds C Canada; winters coastal Texas**
HABITAT: **breeds on muskeg and prairie pools; prairie and stubble fields on migration; winters on coastal marshes**
SIZE: **51 in (130 cm)**

In flight, adult Whooping Cranes show black outer flight feathers that contrast with their otherwise white plumage. Like all cranes, they fly with their heads and necks extended. With a total population of fewer than 200 individuals, it is one of the world's most endangered birds. Attempts are being made to start new populations by using Sandhill Cranes as foster parents.

Whooping Cranes are opportunist feeders, taking a wide variety of plant and animal food from dry land and shallow water. The courtship ceremony involves elaborate dances, and the bird's most common call is a whooping or trumpeting *ker-loo*.

## 8/ SARUS CRANE
*Grus antigone*

RANGE: **India, Southeast Asia, N Australia**
HABITAT: **cultivated plains, marshes, river banks**
SIZE: **47¼–55 in (120–140 cm)**

One of the larger members of its family, the Sarus Crane has recently extended its range to Australia, a jump of nearly 3,000 mls (5,000 km) from its range in Southeast Asia. It was first identified there in 1964 in northeast Queensland. Over the next 10 years, it was reported from more than 30 localities and it now seems to be well established and more than holding its own in competition with the smaller, native Brolga.

## 9/ BROLGA
*Grus rubicundus*

RANGE: **N and E Australia S to Victoria**
HABITAT: **shallow, open swampland and wet grassland**
SIZE: **37½–49¼ in (95–125 cm)**

The Brolga is a large, gray crane native to damp habitats in parts of Australia. It has declined in abundance in the southeastern section of its range because of the drainage of shallow wetlands. It feeds mainly on tubers, which it digs up from the mud with its bill, but will also eat grain, insects, mollusks and small vertebrates.

Brolgas perform elaborate dancing displays, bowing and stretching, advancing and retiring,

with much wing-flapping and trumpeting. They also leap high and plane down again, and hurl pieces of grass or twigs. Elements of their display have been incorporated into Aboriginal dances.

## 10/ SIBERIAN WHITE CRANE
*Grus leucogeranus*　　　　　　　E

RANGE: **breeds in 2 areas in N Siberia; winters around Caspian Sea, India and perhaps China**
HABITAT: **breeds on marshy tundra and forest tundra; winters in shallow freshwater wetlands**
SIZE: **47¼–55 in (120–140 cm)**

Formerly more widespread and fairly common, this is now one of the rarest cranes, probably numbering no more than a few hundred breeding individuals. It seems to be intolerant of disturbance and unable to adapt to change.

The principal known wintering site of the Siberian White Crane is at the Bharatpur nature reserve in northern India. Here, a mere 30–40 birds arrive each autumn, having run the gauntlet of a long migration, hunters and the Himalayas.

In a truly international conservation initiative, Siberian White Crane eggs are taken from nests in the Siberian tundra and flown to the International Crane Foundation in the USA. The chicks are reared by hand, to produce eggs when they are 6 or more years old. These eggs are then flown back to the USSR, where they are placed in the nests of Common Cranes. The aim of this captive breeding program is to establish a viable population in European Russia.

## 11/ DEMOISELLE CRANE
*Anthropoides virgo*

RANGE: **breeds SE Europe and C Asia; winters NE Africa, India E to Burma**
HABITAT: **breeds on marshes and drier steppes; winters on open wetlands and agricultural land**
SIZE: **35½–39½ in (90–100 cm)**

On migration, large numbers of these cranes regularly cross high mountain ranges, including the Himalayas. At one pass, over 60,000 were counted in a 12-day period in autumn, most flying at altitudes of 16,500–26,000 ft (5,000–8,000 m).

Wintering flocks of Demoiselle Cranes can number many thousands and may cause damage to arable crops before the harvest. After the harvest, the birds clean up the spilt grain and take many invertebrates from the ground.

## 12/ BLACK CROWNED CRANE
*Balearica pavonina*

RANGE: **Africa, from Senegal to C Ethiopia, N Uganda and NW Kenya**
HABITAT: **open swamps, marshes, grassland**
SIZE: **43¼–51 in (110–130 cm)**

This crane is a widespread and familiar bird in some parts of its range and is well regarded by local people. A closely related species, the Gray Crowned Crane *B. regulorum*, sometimes regarded as merely a race of this species, occurs in southern Africa.

A pair or small group of Crowned Cranes begin their display by bowing several times toward one another. Then, spreading their wings, they proceed to hop and prance, jumping 3–6 ft (1–2 m) into the air and landing gently on dangling feet.

## FAMILY ARAMIDAE
Limpkin
There is only one species in this family.

## 13/ LIMPKIN
*Aramus guarauna*

RANGE: **SE USA, Antilles, S Mexico E of Andes to N Argentina**
HABITAT: **marshes, open or wooded swamps, mangroves**
SIZE: **23–28 in (58–71 cm)**

The Limpkin is a long-legged wading bird which flies with its neck and head extended. It is largely terrestrial, has rounded wings and makes only short, low flights. The call, often given at night, consists of a variety of shrieks and screams, or melancholy wails and cries. Limpkins walk with an undulating tread so that they appear to be limping – hence their common name.

Limpkins probe and grasp with their laterally compressed bill, which is well adapted for removing freshwater snails from their shells. The birds also feed on mussels, and occasionally on seeds, small reptiles and frogs, insects, worms and crayfish. Although usually solitary, they sometimes hunt in small groups. The nest is a woven mat of reeds and sticks built in or under shrubs and trees near water. The normal clutch contains 6–7 brown-spotted buff eggs, which are incubated for about 20 days. The chicks leave the nest the day they hatch but remain with their parents.

## FAMILY PSOPHIIDAE
Trumpeters
Ground-dwellers. Thickset body, small head. Weak, rounded wings. Plumage mainly black. Sexes alike. Nest in tree holes or palms. Eggs 6–10, white or green. Incubation period unknown, chicks leave nest soon after hatching. 3 species.

## 14/ GRAY-WINGED TRUMPETER
*Psophia crepitans*

RANGE: **Guianas, E Venezuela to W Ecuador, N Peru, Brazil N of the Amazon**
HABITAT: **tropical rain forest**
SIZE: **18–21 in (46–53 cm)**

This bird is sometimes known as the Common Trumpeter. A gregarious species, it feeds on the rain forest floor and roosts in flocks of up to 20 individuals. It is largely terrestrial and a poor flier, although it roosts in trees up to 33 ft (10 m) above the ground. Like the other members of the family, it is a noisy bird, uttering a variety of booming and trumpeting calls – hence the common name for this group of birds.

Trumpeters eat mainly fallen fruits, nuts and insects, and have been known to follow along beneath foraging arboreal animals, pecking at the debris dropped to the ground. Their courtship displays are noisy affairs, often conducted by groups; birds strut, dance and even somersault.

GIANT WOOD RAIL

WATER RAIL

OKINAWA RAIL

race *crepitans*

CLAPPER RAIL

race *levipes*

INACCESSIBLE ISLAND RAIL

WEKA

race *australis*
"South Island Weka"

race *greyi*
"North Island Weka"

ZAPATA RAIL

race *murivagans*

♀

♂

BLACK RAIL

YELLOW RAIL

race *jamaicensis*

CORN CRAKE

SORA

juv

NEW GUINEA FLIGHTLESS RAIL

WATER COCK

♂

♀

race *chloropus*

mutual retreat display

COMMON MOORHEN

race *porphyrio*

race *melanotus*

PURPLE SWAMPHEN

# RAILS, CRAKES, GALLINULES

## FAMILY RALLIDAE
### Rails

Small to medium ground-dwelling birds with long legs and short, rounded wings. Uniform in structure, but family splits naturally into 3 groups: the rails; the crakes and gallinules; and the more aquatic coots. Mostly drab brown, reddish-brown or gray, with pale spots or flashes in some species; some more brightly colored. Sexes generally similar. Nest on ground or in bushes. Eggs 2–16, whitish, yellowish or brownish, often with reddish, gray, brown or black spots or blotches. Incubation 20–30 days. Chicks leave nest soon after hatching to be cared for by both parents; independent in up to 8 weeks. 124 species.

## 1/ GIANT WOOD RAIL
*Eulabeornis ypecaha*
RANGE: **Brazil, Paraguay, Uruguay, Argentina**
HABITAT: **wet river valleys with good cover**
SIZE: **21 in (53 cm)**

Like most rails, this species is a secretive, cautious bird. It usually stays well concealed, but if there is no obvious danger it will display an engaging curiosity. It feeds alone during the day, using its long bill to probe the soft soil and plant debris for small animals; but at night the birds often gather in small groups just before roosting and join in a chorus of loud wails and screams.

These rails appear to breed in isolated pairs, nesting about 3 ft (1 m) above the ground in the branches of shrubs or small trees. The 5 or so glossy eggs vary in color between different nests from a clear white to pastel yellow or even pink.

## 2/ OKINAWA RAIL
*Rallus okinawae*　　　　　　　　　　?
RANGE: **N Okinawa Island, S Japan**
HABITAT: **dense upland evergreen forest, near swampy or grassy areas**
SIZE: **11 in (28 cm)**

Short-winged and effectively flightless, the Okinawa Rail is typical of many species of rail that have evolved on islands. With no native predators to escape from, flight was unnecessary, so the birds abandoned it as a waste of energy.

Although this particular rail had been seen alive a few times over the previous 3 years, it was not described scientifically until 1981, when a roadside carcass was found and examined. The Okinawa Rail's population of some 500 birds is threatened by deforestation. It is closely related to the more widespread Barred Rail *R. torquatus* found on islands in the west Pacific. Like the Barred Rail, it roosts in trees, eats large insects and other invertebrates, and lays 4 eggs.

## 3/ WATER RAIL
*Rallus aquaticus*
RANGE: **Eurasia, from Iceland to Japan; N Africa**
HABITAT: **marshes, swamps, wet meadows**
SIZE: **11 in (28 cm)**

With its very narrow body, the Water Rail has the ideal build for slipping noiselessly, in a rather rat-like fashion, through the reed stems of its habitat.

Although one of the most widespread and common rails, it is a shy, skulking bird, particularly in summer, but when the marshes freeze in winter it often emerges to forage across open ground.

The Water Rail will tackle a wide variety of prey, from insects to amphibians and nestling birds, and may leap up to 3 ft (1 m) to snatch a dragonfly from its perch above the water. Like almost all rails, it can swim well when necessary. Although rarely seen during the breeding season, it is often heard then and at other times as it utters a wide range of loud, blood-curdling groans and piglike grunts and squeals, a process known as "sharming." The nest is well hidden, often in a tussock of rushes, and the 5 or more highly mobile chicks, covered in black down, are soon able to race around the marsh after their parents.

## 4/ CLAPPER RAIL
*Rallus longirostris*
RANGE: **S Canada to N Peru; Caribbean islands**
HABITAT: **brackish estuaries and salt marsh, especially with glasswort plants**
SIZE: **12½–18 in (32–46 cm)**

The species takes its common name from the loud clattering, cackling calls that sound like an old-fashioned clapper or rattle. These birds characteristically respond to thunder with a chorus of vocal response. Once a common sight on salt marshes throughout much of America, the Clapper Rail has suffered badly from habitat loss and hunting over the last 50 years. Even without these pressures, it leads a precarious existence, nesting among salt marsh grasses where it is liable to lose whole clutches of eggs to a single high spring tide. When the eggs do survive to hatch, however, the downy, black chicks, like the adults, can swim well and even submerge by grasping underwater plants with their feet when threatened.

Clapper Rails feed mainly on crabs and smaller crustaceans, supplemented by seeds and tubers. In severe winters the northern birds move south, but most are resident.

## 5/ INACCESSIBLE ISLAND RAIL
*Atlantisia rogersi*　　　　　　　　R
RANGE: **Inaccessible Island (S Atlantic)**
HABITAT: **tussock grass**
SIZE: **5 in (12.5 cm)**

This rail, which weighs a mere 1⅕ oz (34.7 g) is the world's smallest flightless bird. Discovered as late as 1923, it lives rather like a small mammal, constructing runs and burrows through the roots of windy and exposed tussock grass meadows. Almost 2,000 mls (3,200 km) from land both to east and west, Inaccessible Island is uninhabited and very small, with a total area of only 4½ sq mls (12 sq km). There are an estimated 4,000 Inaccessible Island Rails but, like almost all flightless rails, they would be easy meat for ground predators and their continued survival will be at risk should cats, rats or other predators be introduced to the island.

## 6/ WEKA
*Gallirallus australis*
RANGE: **New Zealand**
HABITAT: **scrubland, forest edge**
SIZE: **21 in (53 cm)**

Wekas are very large, flightless rails with powerful bills and feet. They are inquisitive and omnivorous birds, with a diet that includes grass, seeds, fruit, mice, birds, eggs, beetles and snails. They frequently raid garbage pails and even enter fowl runs to eat the chicks. They can be voracious predators of other ground-dwelling birds and have upset the natural population balance on some of the islands to which they have been introduced. Conversely, Wekas kill many rats.

There are 4 races, distinguished by details of plumage and slight differences in size. The North Island race *G. a. greyi*, with grayer underparts, was once more widespread, but is now found only in the Gisborne district in the west, where it thrives in both rural and urban habitats; it has also been reintroduced to other parts of North Island, sometimes with success. The pale-colored Buff Weka *G. a. hectori* was once found in the east of South Island, but was extinct there by the early 1920s. Fortunately, it had been introduced to Chatham Island in 1905 and the population there is thriving. The race *G.a. australis*, which is quite common in parts of the western side of South Island, has a streaked red-brown and black breast; there is also a dark phase in the southwest. The Stewart Island race *G.g. scotti* also has a dark phase.

## 7/ ZAPATA RAIL
*Cyanolimnas cerverai*                                       R

RANGE: **Cuba**
HABITAT: **dense, scrubby marshland**
SIZE: **11¾ in (30 cm)**

This little-known rail inhabits only one part of its Caribbean island home – the Zapata Swamp, southeast of Havana. It is a noisy bird with a loud, croaking alarm note, making it surprisingly easy to locate among the thick marshland plants.

It often has a trusting and inquisitive nature and, owing to its unusually short wings, is a poor flier. This makes it vulnerable to attack, but so far the remoteness of its swampland habitat has guaranteed its survival. It is distributed over a larger area of the Zapata Swamp than was previously thought and should be in no immediate danger, unless there is a severe drought, fire or some other such catastrophe.

## 8/ YELLOW RAIL
*Coturnicops noveboracensis*

RANGE: **E Canada to Mexico; also Siberia, China, Japan**
HABITAT: **hay meadows and tussock grass near fresh running water**
SIZE: **7 in (18 cm)**

With its short bill and compact form, this bird is more of a crake than the rail its name suggests. It is one of the few members of its family to occur in both the Old and New Worlds. In North America it is most familiar as a winter migrant, and many birds are shot as they fly south.

In summer it has very precise habitat requirements, which include plenty of clear running water and a good supply of snails. It finds both of these in remote, sheltered hay meadows, where it often gives itself away by a call that sounds like stones being clacked together.

The nest is superbly concealed in the grass. The nestlings are very mobile by 2 days after hatching and are able to haul themselves through the vegetation, using the well-developed claw on each wing. They are fed by the parents at first, but gradually become independent when they are about 3 weeks old.

## 9/ BLACK RAIL
*Laterallus jamaicensis*

RANGE: **S North America, Caribbean, Central and South America to N Chile**
HABITAT: **marshes, among reeds and sedges**
SIZE: **6¾ in (17 cm)**

Timid and unpredictable, this tiny bird is extremely hard to follow. At the slightest alarm it will leave its feeding area or nest and vanish noiselessly into the dense vegetation. If it has to flee, it never attempts a long run across open

ground, but darts like lightning from one tussock to the next.

There are 4 races, 2 of which are illustrated: *L.j. murivagans* from coastal Peru and *L.j. jamaicensis* of central and eastern USA, Cuba and Jamaica. The Black Rail's semiroofed nest of fine grasses might be mistaken for that of a finch in the absence of the 4–7 pale cream eggs with reddish spots, which are typical of the rails.

## 10/ CORN CRAKE
*Crex crex*                                       ?

RANGE: **Europe, W Asia, N Africa; winters in sub-Saharan Africa**
HABITAT: **coarse grassland, hay meadows**
SIZE: **9¾ in (25 cm)**

The Corn Crake has suffered a dramatic decline over the last century – probably as a result of changing agricultural techniques and the increased use of pesticides.

The males are very vocal just before the eggs are laid, pointing their heads up and producing a sound like a splinter drawn across a comb. Advertising their ownership of territory to the females and challenging rival males, they utter their craking call both day and night. Once incubation is underway, however, they fall silent.

In flight, they can be recognized by their rich chestnut wing patches. Although their flight appears weak, fluttering and brief, with dangling legs, they can fly fast and strongly when they migrate by night, traveling long distances to their winter quarters as far away as South Africa.

## 11/ SORA
*Porzana carolina*

RANGE: **Canada to Venezuela and Peru, including Caribbean islands**
HABITAT: **freshwater marshes, also wet meadows in prairie regions; winters by salt and brackish waters**
SIZE: **9 in (23 cm)**

Many thousands of these birds fell to the shotguns of American hunters each year as they migrated to their coastal wintering grounds; now the birds face a threat from the destruction of their breeding marshes. Although they are still among the most abundant and widespread of American rails, the days are gone when dense flocks of Soras were to be found huddled on salt marshes, islands and even seagoing vessels.

In its summer haunts the Sora is a shy bird, rarely seen, and usually detected by its call: a loud, staccato *cuck* accompanied by sneezing and whinnying sounds. It lays a large clutch – usually 8–12 eggs – which is incubated by both sexes.

## 12/ NEW GUINEA FLIGHTLESS RAIL
*Amaurornis ineptus*

RANGE: **N and S New Guinea**
HABITAT: **mangrove swamps, bamboo thickets at edges of rivers**
SIZE: **14–15 in (36–38 cm)**

This little-known flightless rail is so large, powerful and stout-limbed that it resembles a miniature cassowary (pp. 42–45). It has a heavy, hatchet-

like bill and strong feet with which it can defend itself against most predators, including the dogs introduced to New Guinea. It also uses its powerful bill to dispatch and devour rats. A wary bird, the New Guinea Flightless Rail can run swiftly and may also take to the branches of shrubs or trees to escape danger. It roosts in trees, usually more than 24 in (60 cm) above the ground. Like many other rails, it has a harsh voice, uttering an *aaah-aaah* call rather like the squealing of a pig.

## 13/ WATER COCK
*Gallicrex cinerea*

RANGE: **India to Japan, Philippines, Sulawesi (Celebes)**
HABITAT: **reedy swamps, paddy fields, sugar cane, brackish marshes**
SIZE: **17 in (43 cm)**

Sometimes known by its Hindi name, Kora, this largely vegetarian species is a twilight feeder, which eats shoots, tubers and seeds, as well as the odd insect. In the breeding season the males can be aggressively territorial, but during the rest of the year it is a cautious, retiring bird, scuttling for cover at the first hint of danger.

During the breeding season, the male can be distinguished from his mate by his almost black plumage and a vivid, blood-red frontal shield. In winter he loses this head ornamentation and becomes brown and gray like the female. The pair builds a cootlike nest of aquatic vegetation and raises 2 broods of 3–6 chicks each year.

## 14/ COMMON MOORHEN
*Gallinula chloropus*

RANGE: **throughout temperate and tropical Eurasia, Africa, North and South America; but not Australasia**
HABITAT: **small ponds, rivers, wet marshes**
SIZE: **13¾ in (35 cm)**

Possibly the most abundant species of rail in the world, the Common Moorhen is an unlikely candidate for success, for it is a poor flier and a barely adequate swimmer, preferring to search for food on foot with a delicate, high-stepping gait. Males are highly territorial and will fight with their large feet; many are badly injured in the process. The chicks become independent very quickly and often help their parents feed a second brood.

## 15/ PURPLE SWAMPHEN
*Porphyrio porphyrio*

RANGE: **Europe, Africa, S Asia, Southeast Asia to Australasia**
HABITAT: **reedbeds, scrubby marsh margins, tussock swamps**
SIZE: **17¾ in (45 cm)**

The Purple Swamphen has earned itself a bad reputation in some areas owing to its habit of feeding on the tender shoots of cultivated rice. Largely vegetarian, it may become extremely numerous where food is plentiful; scores of birds can often be seen in the early morning, when they climb the marsh vegetation to sunbathe as the first rays of dawn penetrate the mist. Usually, a single pair seems to do all the nesting; occasionally, a second female may lay in the nest.

# GALLINULES AND COOTS, FINFOOTS, KAGU, SUNBITTERN, SERIEMAS, BUSTARDS

TAKAHE

GIANT COOT

aggressive encounter

EURASIAN COOT

SUNGREBE

KAGU

display

SUNBITTERN

RED-LEGGED SERIEMA

courtship display

LITTLE BUSTARD

GREAT BUSTARD

♂ courtship display

chicks

race *undulata*

race *macqueenii*

HOUBARA BUSTARD

AUSTRALIAN BUSTARD

♂ race *ruficrista*

♀ race *vigorsii*

CRESTED BUSTARD

VIGORS' BUSTARD

BENGAL FLORICAN

# GALLINULES AND COOTS, FINFOOTS, KAGU, SUNBITTERN, SERIEMAS, BUSTARDS

## 1/ TAKAHE
*Porphyrio mantelli*    E

RANGE: **New Zealand, now restricted to Murchison and Kepler ranges in SW South Island; introduced to Mana Island**
HABITAT: **mountain tussock grassland and (rarely) adjacent woodland**
SIZE: **$24\frac{3}{4}$ in (63 cm)**

Like many other flightless island birds, this large rail has suffered a catastrophic decline in the face of competition and predation by introduced animals. It was first described scientifically in 1849. Its numbers dwindled rapidly until, by 1900, it was believed to be extinct.

In 1948 it was rediscovered living in remote alpine and subalpine tussock grassland in southwest South Island. Here it feeds on the seed heads and tender bases of the grasses. Today it has to compete for the grass with introduced deer and generally loses the contest.

Takahes mate for life, nesting on the ground among tussocks. Introduced predators, such as stoats, take a heavy toll of the eggs and young, and the breeding success rate is low. Captive breeding, conservation and predator control have helped to preserve the species, but the Takahe remains endangered.

## 2/ GIANT COOT
*Fulica gigantea*

RANGE: **Peru, Chile, Bolivia and Argentina**
HABITAT: **mountain lakes, usually above 11,500 ft (3,500 m) in puna**
SIZE: **$23\frac{1}{2}$ in (60 cm)**

Life at high altitudes is especially harsh in winter, but instead of migrating to lower altitudes, the Giant Coots congregate in small flocks around the widely scattered volcanic springs of the region. There they find pools that are kept clear of ice by the warm water and enough food to see them through until spring. This bird builds a large floating nest, up to 10 ft (3 m) in diameter, anchored to emergent weed in shallow water.

## 3/ EURASIAN COOT
*Fulica atra*

RANGE: **widespread through Europe, Asia, Japan and Australasia**
HABITAT: **large ponds, lakes and marshes, usually at low altitude**
SIZE: **17 in (43 cm)**

The most widespread and common of all the coots, the species is a bold and familiar bird in Europe. It feeds mainly on aquatic plants, but it also eats aquatic insects.

During the spring breeding season both sexes are extremely territorial, and the slightest violation of a boundary by another coot will provoke a tremendous show of strength as the intruder is attacked with both claws and bill.

In winter coots become very sociable, flocking together in hundreds or even thousands on food-rich lakes and rivers. Juvenile birds are much paler than the adults, with lighter, duller legs, a grayish bill and brown eyes, and lack the adults' white frontal shield.

## FAMILY HELIORNITHIDAE
### Finfoots

Medium to large, elongated, grebelike, aquatic birds. Long head and neck, broadly lobed toes and long, graduated, stiff tail. Plumage brown and gray with white markings. Females smaller. Nest a shallowly indented platform of twigs lined with leaves, on low branches or flood debris. Eggs 2–4, cream, with reddish-brown or purple markings. Incubation 11 days (Sungrebe); naked helpless chicks are carried from nest by parent even before their eyes have opened (Sungrebe). 3 species.

## 4/ SUNGREBE
*Heliornis fulica*

RANGE: **Mexico to Bolivia and Argentina**
HABITAT: **heavily forested lowland streams, freshwater ponds and lagoons**
SIZE: **$11–11\frac{3}{4}$ in (28–30 cm)**

Named for their cootlike lobed feet, the finfoots appear to be close relatives of the rails, although superficially they resemble grebes. The Sungrebe, or American Finfoot, frequents the slower backwaters of large streams where it rarely emerges from the shade of bankside vegetation. It eats mollusks, insects and other small animals, as well as some seeds. It often swims half submerged.

The nest is built in a bush over water. When the 2 chicks hatch, they are removed and carried by the male, both on the water and in the air, clamped tightly into pouches beneath each wing.

## FAMILY RHYNOCHETIDAE
### Kagu

There is only one species in this family.

## 5/ KAGU
*Rhynochetos jubatus*    E

RANGE: **New Caledonia**
HABITAT: **dense forest**
SIZE: **$23\frac{1}{2}$ in (60 cm)**

One of the most endangered birds in the world, the Kagu is another example of a ground-dwelling island bird that has been virtually wiped out by introduced predators and habitat loss. Effectively flightless, it feeds on the ground, stalking over the forest floor with a curiously upright stance and probing in the soil with its large bill for grubs, worms and snails.

Both sexes have the flamboyant crest, and during courtship they dance around each other with wings spread to display the black, red and white bars on the slate-gray plumage. They nest on the ground, both parents taking turns to incubate the single cream or yellowish egg with red-brown and gray blotches for 36 days. The young bird becomes independent some 14 weeks after hatching.

## FAMILY EURYPYGIDAE

There is only one species in this family.

## 6/ SUNBITTERN
*Eurypyga helias*

RANGE: **S Mexico to Bolivia and C Brazil**
HABITAT: **forested streams, rivers, lakes**
SIZE: **18 in (46 cm)**

This bird forages with slow, sedate steps and occasionally wades through shallow water, but will fly across deeper pools. It feeds mainly on insects, spiders, small crustaceans, frogs and small fish, seizing them from the mud and rocks, from beneath the water or among damp litter on the forest floor, with heronlike jabs of its long, straight bill.

Although the Sunbittern spends most of its time in the shade, it is sometimes found in sunny clearings, when its spectacular display is seen to best advantage. The bird lowers its neck, spreads its wings and raises and fans its tail, suddenly revealing the striking areas of orange-chestnut surrounded by pale orange-buff on its primary wing feathers. These resemble a sunset – hence the bird's common name.

The Sunbittern lays its 2 whitish or buff dark-blotched eggs in a bulky, globular nest of stems and leaves in a tree some 10–20 ft (3–6 m) above the ground. Both sexes incubate the eggs for about 27 days; the nestling period is some 21 days.

## FAMILY CARIAMIDAE
### Seriemas

Large, terrestrial birds with long necks, long legs and elongated bodies. Plumage gray-brown and white, with black and white on wings and black or black and white at end of tail. Nest of sticks in bush or low tree. Eggs 2, whitish to buff with brown, gray or purple markings. Incubation 25–26 days; chicks, though covered in down on hatching, remain in nest until they are well grown. 2 species.

### 7/ RED-LEGGED SERIEMA
*Cariama cristata*

RANGE: C and E Brazil S through Paraguay to N Argentina
HABITAT: mixed grassland and open scrub
SIZE: $27\frac{1}{2}$ in (70 cm)

The Red-legged, or Crested, Seriema rarely flies, usually escaping danger by running rapidly with its head lowered. It spends all its time on the ground except for roosting and nesting low in trees and bushes. It has an omnivorous diet, which regularly includes small snakes.

Seriemas are hunted for their meat and are shy and wary of humans. Red-legged Seriemas are often taken from the nest and reared among domestic chickens where they make excellent "watchdogs," warning farmers of approaching predators or other intruders with their noisy yelping or screaming calls.

## FAMILY OTIDIDAE
### Bustards

Medium to large terrestrial birds with long legs, long necks and sturdy tapering bodies. Feet with 3 toes. Sexes usually differ in size and/or plumage. Plumage cryptic combinations of brown, buff, chestnut, gray, black and white. Nest a bare scrape in the ground. Eggs 1–6, olive, olive-brown, reddish. Incubation 20–25 days. Chicks leave nest soon after hatching, fledge at about 5 weeks. 22 species.

### 8/ LITTLE BUSTARD
*Tetrax tetrax* [?]

RANGE: S Europe, NW Africa E to C Asia
HABITAT: open areas with tall grasses, open scrubland, farmland
SIZE: $15\frac{3}{4}$–$17\frac{3}{4}$ in (40–45 cm)

Short, stocky birds, these are among the lightweights of the bustard family, weighing less than $2\frac{1}{4}$ lb (1 kg). Outside the breeding season, the male's striking slate-gray chin and throat and black and white neck pattern are replaced by buff feathers with dark markings.

Little Bustards are gregarious birds, forming flocks of up to a thousand or more outside the breeding season at favored feeding grounds, including fields of crops. The displays of breeding males, both to advertise ownership of their territories to nearby males and to attract females, are comical to watch. They include surprisingly loud foot stamps, nasal *prrt* calls and a hissing sound produced by the short, seventh primary feather when the bird flaps its wings and leaps 3–6 ft (1–2 m) vertically into the air, revealing his white breast and underwings.

### 9/ HOUBARA BUSTARD
*Chlamydotis undulata* [?]

RANGE: breeds Canary Islands, N Africa, Middle East, SW and C Asia; Asian breeders winter S to Arabia, Pakistan, Iran and NW India
HABITAT: semidesert, arid plains and steppes
SIZE: $21\frac{1}{2}$–$25\frac{1}{2}$ in (55–65 cm)

Outside the breeding season, the Houbara Bustard lives in small flocks of 4–10 birds, occasionally more, which feed and roost together. It is omnivorous, feeding on fruit, seeds, shoots, leaves and flowers as well as large insects, spiders, centipedes, small lizards and snakes.

The greatest threat to the Houbara Bustard is from excessive hunting, particularly in its winter quarters. As with other bustards, habitat destruction is also playing a part in its decline. The North African race *C. u. undulata* and the larger, paler race *C. u. macqueenii* from Egypt east to Central Asia are illustrated.

### 10/ AUSTRALIAN BUSTARD
*Choriotis australis*

RANGE: N and inland Australia
HABITAT: open woodland, grassland and shrub steppe
SIZE: $31\frac{1}{2}$–$47\frac{1}{4}$ in (80–120 cm)

This species was once quite common, but has declined greatly since the European settlement of Australia, due to heavy hunting, agriculture and the depredations of introduced mammals.

The male Australian Bustard displays by inflating his neck with air, so that the long neck feathers spread out into a great fan or apron, drooping his wings and raising his tail. He struts about in this posture with his head thrown back, uttering loud booming and roaring noises. He mates with any females attracted to his small display mound.

### 11/ GREAT BUSTARD
*Otis tarda* [?]

RANGE: Morocco, Iberia, parts of N and C Europe, Turkey, parts of S USSR
HABITAT: extensive gently undulating grassy plains and steppes, lightly wooded areas, farmland
SIZE: $29\frac{1}{2}$–$41\frac{1}{4}$ in (75–105 cm)

This imposing bird is the world's heaviest flying bird: a particularly large male can weigh as much as 40 lb (18 kg). Females are much lighter, at up to 11 lb (5 kg). Great Bustards are sociable outside the breeding season, forming large flocks that move around in search of seasonally available plant and invertebrate food. Many flocks contain only one sex, especially immature males.

At the onset of the breeding season, mature males leave the flock and make their way to the traditional display grounds. Several males display together, each raising and spreading his tail so that it lies flat along his back, retracting his neck and inflating his throat pouch with air. This exposes the white neck and undertail feathers. At the same time, the bird twists his partially opened wings to reveal white "rosettes" of feathers on either side of his body.

### 12/ CRESTED BUSTARD
*Eupodotis ruficrista*

RANGE: just S of Sahara, from N Senegal locally to W and E Sudan; E Africa, from Ethiopia to EC Tanzania; S Africa S to N South Africa
HABITAT: arid or semiarid savanna
SIZE: $19\frac{1}{2}$ in (50 cm)

This small, rather stocky bustard is found in 3 widely separated areas of Africa. Two of its 3 races, the small, scarce northern race *E. r. savilei* and the eastern race *E. r. gindiana* are sometimes regarded as separate species, Savile's Bustard and the Buff-crested Bustard. The southern race *E. r. ruficrista* is illustrated.

The Crested Bustard is usually encountered singly or in pairs. A secretive bird, it often avoids detection by hiding motionless in thick cover. Males perform dramatic "rocket flights," in which they call with increasing volume, then run forward and fly up vertically to about 100 ft (30 m), throw themselves upside-down, puff out their breast feathers and then drop vertically, flapping their wings to halt their fall at the last moment, then gliding down to land.

### 13/ VIGORS' BUSTARD
*Eupodotis vigorsii*

RANGE: W South Africa, S Namibia
HABITAT: dry, open, stony Karoo, semidesert and desert edge with scattered shrubs and short grass
SIZE: $22$–$23\frac{1}{2}$ in (56–60 cm)

Also known as the Black-throated Bustard or Karoo Korhaan, Vigors' Bustard is very variable in plumage, particularly in the redness of the upperparts, grayness of the underparts and overall intensity of color.

Vigors' Bustard lives in groups of up to 8 individuals, and each group defends a small territory of a few hundred yards radius for a month or more during the breeding season. It is a noisy bird, especially in the morning and sometimes at night, its calls carrying long distances. Pairs perform croaking duets, the female replying with a *kok* note to the male's *squark*.

### 14/ BENGAL FLORICAN
*Houbaropsis bengalensis* [?]

RANGE: NE India, Nepal, Kampuchea, S Vietnam
HABITAT: plains with tall grasses interspersed with scattered shrubs
SIZE: $26$–$26\frac{3}{4}$ in (66–68 cm)

All bustards are threatened by habitat destruction and hunting, but none more than the Bengal Florican, which is rare, patchily distributed and seriously at risk. There are probably only a few hundred birds left in India and Nepal, and the tiny populations in Indochina are unknown.

Unusually for a bustard, the female is slightly larger than the male and differs greatly in her plumage from the striking black and white male. The sexes remain more or less separate apart from the brief mating period. Males perform courtship displays in which they leap 25–30 ft (8–10 m) into the air, emitting a strange, deep humming sound and uttering loud croaks.

# SHOREBIRDS: JACANAS, OYSTERCATCHERS, STILTS AND AVOCETS, THICK-KNEES AND OTHERS

non-breeding

PHEASANT-TAILED JACANA

CRAB PLOVER

race *jacana* juv

race *hypomelaena*

WATTLED JACANA

race *jacana*

PALEARCTIC OYSTERCATCHER

♂

♀

GREATER PAINTED-SNIPE

AMERICAN BLACK OYSTERCATCHER

# FAMILIES JACANIDAE, ROSTRATULIDAE, DROMADIDAE, HAEMATOPODIDAE, IBIDORHYNCHIDAE, RECURVIROSTRIDAE, BURHINIDAE

IBISBILL

PIED AVOCET

RED-NECKED AVOCET

chick

race *mexicanus*
"Black-necked Stilt"

race *knudseni*
"Hawaiian Stilt"

race *himantopus*

juv

race *himantopus*

BLACK-WINGED STILT

STONE-CURLEW

CAPE DIKKOP

BANDED STILT

BEACH THICK-KNEE

# SHOREBIRDS: JACANAS, OYSTERCATCHERS, STILTS AND AVOCETS, THICK-KNEES AND OTHERS

## FAMILY JACANIDAE
### Jacanas

Medium, long-legged waterbirds. Extremely elongated toes and claws for walking on floating vegetation. Plumage mostly brown, with black and white on head. Females larger. Nest on floating leaves or platforms. Eggs 4, heavily marked and shiny. Incubation 22–24 days. Chicks leave nest soon after hatching, but depend on male for protection for some time. 8 species.

### 1/ PHEASANT-TAILED JACANA
*Hydrophasianus chirurgus*

RANGE: **India to S China, Southeast Asia, Indonesia; N population winters in S Asia**
HABITAT: **well-vegetated fresh water**
SIZE: **$12\frac{1}{4}$ in (31 cm); up to $22\frac{3}{4}$ in (58 cm) in breeding plumage**

The striking Pheasant-tailed Jacana's long, drooping tail, present only in the breeding season, is unique among the Charadriiformes. Each female mates with 7–10 males in a season and it is the males' responsibility to incubate the eggs. If disturbed, a male may remove the eggs to a safer spot by pressing each one between his throat and breast and walking backward over the vegetation. The young can run, swim and dive as soon as they leave the nest. When danger threatens, they may submerge themselves almost completely beneath a floating leaf at a command from their father.

### 2/ WATTLED JACANA
*Jacana jacana*

RANGE: **Panama S to C Argentina; Trinidad**
HABITAT: **tropical freshwater ponds, marshes, streams with emergent vegetation**
SIZE: **8–9 in (20–23 cm)**

The Wattled Jacana runs across the surface of floating leaves, searching for snails and other invertebrates and pecking pieces of vegetation. It also frequents damp pastures. Its flight is straight, swift and close to the water and is interspersed with periods of gliding. The race *J. j. jacana* is found over most of the species' South American range, and the dark race *J. j. hypomelaena* occurs from western Panama to northern Colombia.

Females mate with more than one male in each season and compete vigorously with one another for the opportunity to mate. Since the males incubate and care for the young, one female may even destroy the eggs of a successful rival in order to gain access to a male. Studies in Panama showed that each female's territory overlapped with the territories of up to 3 males.

## FAMILY ROSTRATULIDAE
### Painted-snipes

Small, dumpy wading birds. Broad, rounded wings. Plumage brown and chestnut, marked with black, buff, white and yellow. Sexes differ. Nest on ground among vegetation. Eggs 2–4, white or yellowish, blotched black and purple. Incubation 20–22 days. Chicks leave nest soon after hatching, but depend on male for protection for some time. 2 species.

### 3/ GREATER PAINTED-SNIPE
*Rostratula benghalensis*

RANGE: **Africa, Asia and Australia**
HABITAT: **well-vegetated freshwater wetlands, including marshes, paddy fields**
SIZE: **$6\frac{1}{2}$–9 in (17–23 cm)**

When feeding out in the open, this wading bird will freeze motionless if danger threatens, holding its position until the threat has passed. The female is both larger and more brightly colored than the male. She calls, a soft *koht-koht-koht*, at dusk and at night, often while in flight.

Males and females face each other in the courtship display, spreading their wings outward and forward until the tips are in front of their heads, at the same time fanning their tails. Each female may lay several clutches, each incubated by different males. The nest is a mound of waterweeds among vegetation in shallow water.

## FAMILY DROMADIDAE
### Crab Plover

There is only one species in this family.

### 4/ CRAB PLOVER
*Dromas ardeola*

RANGE: **coasts of Indian Ocean; breeds Gulf of Oman, Gulf of Aden and Red Sea**
HABITAT: **sandy beaches and coastal dunes**
SIZE: **15–16 in (38–41 cm)**

In its typical pose, with the head hunched between the shoulders, the body of the Crab Plover appears gull-like, but the bird's long legs clearly indicate that it is a wader. It uses its thick bill to capture and crack open the shells of crabs. Both sexes have the same bold black and white plumage.

The birds breed in dense colonies. Unlike other members of the Order Charadriiformes, this species excavates nesting tunnels up to 5 ft (1.5 m) long, and the sandy ground of a breeding colony becomes honeycombed with holes. A single, large, pure white egg is laid in a chamber at the end of each tunnel. The chick remains in the nest tunnel after hatching and is fed by the parents which bring live crabs from the shore.

## FAMILY HAEMATOPODIDAE
### Oystercatchers

Large, thickset waders. Long, stout bill. Plumage black or black and white, with orange-red bill and pink legs. Sexes similar. Nest in scrapes, sometimes colonially. Eggs 3–4, brown or gray, spotted and streaked. Incubation 24–29 days. Chicks leave nest soon after hatching, but are fed by parents for at least 6 weeks. 11 species.

### 5/ PALEARCTIC OYSTERCATCHER
*Haematopus ostralegus*

RANGE: **breeds Eurasia; winters S to Africa and Indian Ocean**
HABITAT: **breeds on coasts and near inland fresh waters; winters only on coasts**
SIZE: **$15\frac{3}{4}$–18 in (40–46 cm)**

Like that of other oystercatchers, the stout orange bill of the Palearctic Oystercatcher is triangular in cross-section and reinforced so that it does not bend easily. Birds that feed mainly on cockles and mussels have a bladelike tip suited to hammering open the shells and severing the muscle within. Those that feed on invertebrates in sand and mud have finer, more pointed bills for probing.

Territories are advertised and boundaries disputed by noisy displays involving loud, piping calls, which take place among groups of these birds all year round. The nest is a mere scrape on the ground, sometimes decorated with stones or pieces of shell. Outside the breeding season the adults develop a white neck collar, making them similar to an immature bird in its first winter.

### 6/ AMERICAN BLACK OYSTERCATCHER
*Haematopus bachmani*

RANGE: **Pacific coast of North America, from Alaska to Baja California**
HABITAT: **rocky coasts and islands, occasionally sandy beaches**
SIZE: **15 in (38 cm)**

Oystercatchers have loud, piercing calls which can be heard above the sound of crashing surf, facilitating communication between individuals.

**FAMILIES JACANIDAE, ROSTRATULIDAE, DROMADIDAE, HAEMATOPODIDAE, IBIDORHYNCHIDAE, RECURVIROSTRIDAE, BURHINIDAE**

They are noisy birds, frequently calling at night. The downy, highly mobile chicks follow their parents, which first present food to them and then train them to find and procure food for themselves. Opening mollusks and crab shells is a very difficult task; it can be accomplished in less than a minute by an experienced bird but many months are required to master the technique. Young birds are able to fly in about 35 days but associate with their parents for up to a year, learning feeding techniques.

## FAMILY IBIDORHYNCHIDAE
### Ibisbill

There is only one species in this family.

## 7/ IBISBILL
*Ibidorhyncha struthersii*

RANGE: **Central S Asia**
HABITAT: **stony, upland river valleys**
SIZE: **15–16 in (38–41 cm)**

This rare, little-known species takes its name from its distinctive, downcurved red bill which superficially resembles that of an ibis. The bold plumage is common to both sexes. It haunts remote mountain regions, where it uses its bill to probe among stones of riverbeds and rake through gravel to find small fish and invertebrates.

During courtship, the rear of the black cap is raised in display to form a slight crest. Aerial displays are used to defend breeding territories. The nest is a shallow scrape on a patch of shingle containing up to 4 pale, spotted eggs. The incubation period is thought to be about 30 days.

## FAMILY RECURVIROSTRIDAE
### Stilts and avocets

Large, long-legged, long-billed waders. Plumage mostly black and white. Sexes similar. Nest in scrapes. Eggs 3–4, buff-brown, dark markings. Incubation 22–26 days. Chicks leave nest soon after hatching, but depend on parents for protection often until well after fledging. 7 species.

## 8/ BLACK-WINGED STILT
*Himantopus himantopus*

RANGE: **worldwide in tropics, subtropics and warm temperate latitudes**
HABITAT: **coastal and inland wetlands**
SIZE: **13¾–15¾ in (35–40 cm)**

The extraordinarily long, bright pink legs of this slender shorebird extend 7 in (18 cm) beyond the tail when the bird takes to the wing. The length of the legs allows the Black-winged Stilt to feed in deeper water than other shorebirds, but when feeding on dry terrain, it has to bend its legs awkwardly so that its bill can reach the ground.

The birds breed in loose colonies in marshy ground or on the bare mud of salt pans. When incubating the eggs, the adults have problems with their long legs. In the sitting posture, each folded leg projects behind in a prominent *V* shape. The race *H. h. himantopus* is from Eurasia, India and Africa; the race *H. h. knudseni* is restricted to Hawaii, where it is rare and endangered; and the race *H. h. mexicanus* occurs from North America south to northern South America.

## 9/ BANDED STILT
*Cladorhynchus leucocephalus*

RANGE: **S Australia**
HABITAT: **inland salt lakes, estuaries and lagoons**
SIZE: **15–16 in (38–41 cm)**

The Banded Stilt eats brine shrimp and other crustaceans, wading, and sometimes swimming, to probe and peck in the water. It feeds in flocks, the members of the group sometimes converging to herd their prey.

Although it can occur in flocks of several thousand, the Banded Stilt has seldom been found breeding. It nests erratically in huge, massed colonies, where occasional heavy rains fill desert salt pans. The eggs are laid in a scrape on flat nesting islands left by the receding water. The downy chicks may swim several miles to shore, in groups with adults.

## 10/ PIED AVOCET
*Recurvirostra avosetta*

RANGE: **breeds W and C Eurasia; winters mainly in Africa and the Middle East**
HABITAT: **saline or brackish wetlands, coastal and inland**
SIZE: **16½–17¾ in (42–45 cm)**

The delicately pointed, upturned bill of the Pied Avocet is a highly specialized feeding tool. It is held slightly open just below the surface of shallow water or very soft mud and swept from side to side as the bird walks slowly forward. Small invertebrates and larger worms are located by touch. The species can also upend in deeper water and sweep its bill to and fro through the mud on the bottom. Pied Avocets nest on muddy islets, forming dense colonies usually containing some 10–200 pairs. Each pair defends the few yards around the nest against rivals, but all the pairs cooperate in driving away intruders.

## 11/ RED-NECKED AVOCET
*Recurvirostra novaehollandiae*

RANGE: **S and inland Australia**
HABITAT: **lagoons, lakes, marshes, estuaries**
SIZE: **15¾–17¾ in (40–45 cm)**

The Red-necked Avocet haunts shallow waters inland and on the coast. It is a sociable species, feeding and roosting in flocks and nesting in loose colonies. They feed on small crustaceans, aquatic insects, worms, mollusks and some seeds. Like Pied Avocets, they forage by sweeping their upturned bills from side to side through shallow water or mud and sometimes stir the water up with their bills to reveal more food. Their partially webbed feet enable them to swim.

## FAMILY BURHINIDAE
### Thick-knees (stone-curlews)

Large, thickset, terrestrial birds. Stout bill, large eyes. Plumage mainly brown. Sexes alike. Nests on ground. Eggs 2–3, white to brownish-gray, spotted and blotched. Incubation 25–27 days. Chicks can stand and walk by 2 days old and leave nest soon after, but fed by parents for first few days. 9 species.

## 12/ STONE-CURLEW
*Burhinus oedicnemus*

RANGE: **W and S Europe, SW Asia, N Africa, Middle East, Indian subcontinent**
HABITAT: **open farmland, heaths, semi-desert**
SIZE: **15¾–17¼ in (40–44 cm)**

The Stone-Curlew lives mainly in dry, open terrain. It can run swiftly across the ground, and is partly nocturnal in habits. In spring, each pair establishes a territory that may be many acres in extent. They indulge in circling display flights and call frequently at dusk, often continuing through the night. The far-carrying call is similar to a call of the curlew, hence the species' name.

The nest is a shallow scrape on the ground, almost always placed to give a good all-around view. Some pairs decorate their nests with small stones and even pellets of rabbit dung. The incubating bird is well camouflaged and slips quietly away in times of danger, long before an intruder has approached the nest.

## 13/ CAPE DIKKOP
*Burhinus capensis*

RANGE: **sub-Saharan Africa**
HABITAT: **open or scrub country**
SIZE: **17 in (43 cm)**

Unlike other thick-knees, the Cape, or Spotted, Dikkop is not particularly shy and will nest close to towns and villages. It has even been found in large suburban gardens. It is most active at dusk and during the night, resting in the shade of bushes, such as acacias, during the heat of the day. Its nest is a bare scrape.

This species often appears along roads at night, on the lookout for snails and other invertebrates on the open ground. Unfortunately, this habit makes it a frequent casualty of speeding traffic.

## 14/ BEACH THICK-KNEE
*Esacus magnirostris*

RANGE: **coasts of N Australia, New Guinea, New Caledonia, Solomon Islands, Philippines, Indonesia, Andaman Islands**
HABITAT: **sandy beaches and inshore reefs**
SIZE: **20¾–22¾ in (53–58 cm)**

Also known as the Beach Stone-Curlew, this species is a plain-colored, large and heavily built thick-knee that wails mournfully at night. It is almost exclusively a ground-dweller, running to escape danger, and only taking to the air when hard pressed.

The Beach Thick-knee feeds on crabs and other hard-shelled marine animals by seizing them as it walks along the tideline with its characteristic dawdling gait. It uses its heavy bill to crack and smash them open. Feeding takes place mostly at night; the bird rests during the day by squatting on its long legs. Its nest is a scrape in shingle or sand just above the high water mark, placed among beach debris or, on occasion, under a sheltering bush.

# SHOREBIRDS: COURSERS AND PRATINCOLES, PLOVERS, MAGELLANIC PLOVER

EGYPTIAN PLOVER

non-breeding

NORTHERN LAPWING

♂

CREAM-COLORED
COURSER

SOUTHERN LAPWING

AUSTRALIAN PRATINCOLE

COMMON PRATINCOLE

BLACKSMITH PLOVER

AMERICAN GOLDEN PLOVER

non-breeding

♂

KILLDEER
♂

non-breeding

race *alexandrinus*

♂

BLACK-BELLIED PLOVER

♂

SNOWY PLOVER

♂

WRYBILL

non-breeding

♀

RINGED PLOVER
♂

EURASIAN DOTTEREL

MAGELLANIC PLOVER

# SHOREBIRDS: COURSERS AND PRATINCOLES, PLOVERS, MAGELLANIC PLOVER

## FAMILY GLAREOLIDAE
### Coursers and pratincoles
Small, long-legged (coursers) or long-winged and short-legged (pratincoles) birds. Plumage mainly brown, buff, white. Bolder markings on head and breast. Sexes alike. Nest in scrapes. Eggs 2–4, buff or brown, variably marked. Incubation 17–31 days. Chicks leave nest soon after hatching; fed by parents for first few days. 17 species.

## 1/ EGYPTIAN PLOVER
*Pluvianus aegyptius*
RANGE: W, C and NE Africa
HABITAT: river valleys and marshes
SIZE: $7\frac{1}{2}$–$8\frac{1}{4}$ in (19–21 cm)

The Egyptian Plover's breeding habits are unique among shorebirds. The adults bury their 2–3 eggs under a thin layer of sand, about $\frac{1}{8}$ in (3 mm) thick. Warmed by the sun, the sand helps to incubate the clutch. Should the weather become cooler, the parents incubate the eggs by sitting on them in the normal way, and they also do so at night. Conversely, if the daytime temperature becomes very high, the male or female will cool the eggs by shading them with its body or by wetting the sand with water carried in its belly feathers.

The young hatch in the sand and quickly leave the "nest" area. Until the chicks are about 3 weeks old, they crouch whenever danger threatens and the adults quickly cover them with sand.

## 2/ CREAM-COLORED COURSER
*Cursorius cursor*
RANGE: N and E Africa, Middle East to W Pakistan; N African birds winter just S of Sahara, Middle Eastern birds in Arabia, SW Asian birds in NW India
HABITAT: open arid plains with sparse vegetation; margins of cultivated land
SIZE: $8\frac{1}{4}$–$9\frac{1}{2}$ in (21–24 cm)

The pale sandy-brown plumage of this species provides perfect camouflage in its desert habitat. It is much more conspicuous in flight, however, when it reveals the striking black and white pattern on the underside of its wings.

The Cream-colored Courser feeds by running about vigorously and grabbing beetles, grasshoppers and other invertebrates in its bill and also by digging for concealed prey with its bill. When disturbed, it will run swiftly, stopping at intervals to rise onto tiptoe and stretch its neck to check for danger. Northern (especially northeastern) populations are the most migratory, whereas island races are year-round residents.

## 3/ AUSTRALIAN PRATINCOLE
*Stiltia isabella*
RANGE: breeds N and inland Australia; most populations winter N to extreme N Australia, New Guinea and other Papuan islands, Indonesia
HABITAT: bare, open plains, fields, edges of lagoons
SIZE: $7\frac{3}{4}$–9 in (20–23 cm)

The graceful Australian Pratincole feeds both in the air and by running about on the ground, snapping up insects in its wide gape. It needs to

drink frequently at its hot, dry breeding grounds and can tolerate brackish water by excreting excess salt through special nasal glands.

They breed in loose colonies on stony plains, usually near water. The courtship display involves both male and female running, head down, toward or parallel to one another; they also pump their heads up and down, touch heads with their bills pointing to the ground, and half open their upwardly pointing wings. The clutch of 2 eggs is laid on the bare ground and incubated by both sexes. The incubating bird remains in the hot sunshine, raising its feathers and panting to lose heat. Soon after hatching, the chicks are led to the shade of vegetation or burrows.

## 4/ COMMON PRATINCOLE
*Glareola pratincola*
RANGE: S Eurasia, N Africa; winters S Africa
HABITAT: flood plains, deltas, steppes
SIZE: $9\frac{1}{4}$–$10\frac{1}{2}$ in (23.5–26.5 cm)

As with other pratincoles, the long-winged, fork-tailed appearance of the Common, or Collared, Pratincole in flight is reminiscent of a tern or even a large swallow. Large flocks gather to feed on flying ants and other insects and will follow swarms of locusts over long distances in Africa.

Common Pratincoles have rather ternlike breeding habits. Large colonies nest on bare or sparsely vegetated ground, the 2–3 eggs in each clutch laid in a slight scrape. When a predatory bird appears over the colony, all the adults in the area will fly up and mob it, giving harsh *kirrik* calls until the intruder moves away.

## FAMILY CHARADRIIDAE
### Plovers
Small to medium, short-billed waders. Plumage mainly black, brown and white. Sexes similar, or males slightly larger. Ground-nesters. Eggs 2–4, cryptically patterned in most species. Incubation 18–38 days, chicks leave nest and can feed themselves soon after hatching. 65 species.

## 5/ NORTHERN LAPWING
*Vanellus vanellus*
RANGE: breeds temperate Eurasia; most populations migrate S in winter to Mediterranean, India, China
HABITAT: breeds on open ground, including farmland, freshwater marshes, saltmarshes; also visits estuarine mud flats
SIZE: 11–$12\frac{1}{4}$ in (28–31 cm)

The Northern Lapwing is a common and familiar bird over much of Europe. Its broad, rounded wings produce a distinctive creaking sound during the wheeling, rolling and tumbling display flight. The sounds are accompanied by a characteristic plaintive cry, from which the bird takes its alternative English name, Peewit.

The female carries out most of the incubation of the 4 eggs. The young are perfectly camouflaged, and crouch down the instant they hear their parents' alarm calls. Modern intensive farming and land drainage have drastically reduced the Northern Lapwing's habitat in many areas and the species is also vulnerable to severe winters.

## 6/ SOUTHERN LAPWING
*Vanellus chilensis*
RANGE: South America, mainly E of Andes
HABITAT: savanna, wet grassland, farmland
SIZE: $14\frac{1}{2}$–15 in (37–38 cm)

This plover readily adapts to feeding on cultivated land, taking earthworms, grubs and insects. The slightest intrusion, day or night, causes it to utter its loud, strident alarm calls. For this reason, it is often regarded as a semidomesticated "watchdog" at farmsteads and suburban homes. It is a gregarious bird, found in small flocks at any time of the year.

When approached, an incubating bird will slip away some distance from the nest before taking flight. It will then make sweeping passes at the intruder while emitting loud cries of protest.

## 7/ BLACKSMITH PLOVER
*Anitibyx armatus*

RANGE: **Kenya to South Africa**
HABITAT: **margins of fresh and saline wetlands and adjacent open ground**
SIZE: **11–12¼ in (28–31 cm)**

The bold plumage of the adult Blacksmith Plover becomes even more striking when the bird takes flight, enhanced by the contrast between the black and gray upperwings and the black and white underwings. The bird's nest is no more than a shallow depression in the ground, often merely the hoofprint of a grazing mammal. This species takes its name from its harsh and metallic call – a *chink-chink* just like the sound of a blacksmith's hammer striking the anvil.

## 8/ AMERICAN GOLDEN PLOVER
*Pluvialis dominica*

RANGE: **breeds Arctic North America; winters C South America**
HABITAT: **breeds on tundra; otherwise coastal mud flats, inland marshes and grassland**
SIZE: **9½–11 in (24–28 cm)**

There is a striking difference in this bird between the breeding and nonbreeding plumage. However, the upperparts of adult and immature have a golden hue all year. The speckling on the back camouflages the incubating bird. This species undertakes a long seasonal migration apparently accomplished nonstop by many birds. Eastern Canadian breeders take the shortest "Great Circle" route over the western Atlantic, but other populations take inland routes across the USA.

## 9/ BLACK-BELLIED PLOVER
*Pluvialis squatarola*

RANGE: **breeds circumpolar Arctic; winters worldwide on coasts to S**
HABITAT: **breeds on lowland tundra; winters on coastal mud flats and lagoons**
SIZE: **10½–11¾ in (27–30 cm)**

Although the black axilliary feathers, or "armpits," of this bird are seen only in flight, they form a unique and distinctive field character. They are especially useful in winter when the overall gray plumage of the standing bird lacks any obvious distinguishing marks. The Black-bellied Plover is highly migratory, reaching the southern shores of Australia and South Africa from its breeding grounds in the high Arctic. Adults share incubation of the 4 eggs, but the male takes more responsibility for rearing the chicks.

## 10/ RINGED PLOVER
*Charadrius hiaticula*

RANGE: **breeds Arctic E Canada and Eurasia; winters Europe and Africa**
HABITAT: **breeds on shingle beaches and tundra; winters along coasts and some inland wetlands**
SIZE: **7–7¾ in (18–20 cm)**

The white collar and broad black breast band of the adult Ringed Plover gives the species its name. The breast band is blacker and deeper in the adult male than in the female. This species' wistful *too-li* call is used by the off-duty bird to call its mate from the nest when danger threatens. Later, when the chicks have hatched, Ringed Plovers are experts at the broken-wing display, in which they pretend to be injured. They flutter with drooped wings and spread tail while calling loudly and plaintively, in an effort to distract a potential predator away from the vulnerable young in the nest.

## 11/ KILLDEER
*Charadrius vociferus*

RANGE: **breeds S Canada to SC Mexico, West Indies, coastal Peru and extreme N Chile; winters N South America**
HABITAT: **open expanses near wet areas, ponds, rivers**
SIZE: **8¼–9¾ in (21–25 cm)**

This plover takes its name from its *killdee-killdee* calls. Widespread through the Americas, it is a rare visitor to Europe and Hawaii.

Killdeers make their nest scrapes in an area with short, sparse vegetation or none at all. Bits of grass, pebbles and other loose material end up in the scrape as a result of a ritual ceremony in which the birds slowly walk away from the nest while tossing the material over their shoulders. The birds often nest on gravel roads where their eggs are crushed by cars. They may also nest on flat gravel rooftops, although the chicks are sometimes trapped by parapets or perish when they leap to the ground. However, they often survive leaps from buildings 3–4 stories high.

## 12/ SNOWY PLOVER
*Charadrius alexandrinus*

RANGE: **temperate and S Eurasia and North America, South America, Africa**
HABITAT: **coastal and inland brackish or saline wetlands**
SIZE: **6–6¾ in (15–17.5 cm)**

The worldwide range of this bird is belied by its British name, Kentish Plover, which merely relates to the place where it was first discovered in England in 1787. The species formerly bred in small numbers in the county of Kent, but it died out there early this century through egg collecting and habitat destruction. The Eurasian and North African race *C. a. alexandrinus* is illustrated.

The 3–4 eggs are laid in a shallow scrape in the sand. Their buff color with fine black marks acts as excellent camouflage. The young, too, are cryptically patterned. When their parents give the alarm call, they flatten themselves to the ground and become indistinguishable from small irregularities in the surface of the sand.

## 13/ WRYBILL
*Anarhynchus frontalis*

RANGE: **New Zealand**
HABITAT: **breeds along shallow, stony rivers; winters on estuaries, in harbors**
SIZE: **7¾ in (20 cm)**

This small plover is unique in that the tip of its bill bends to the right. It feeds by walking in clockwise circles, probing over mud and under pebbles. The bird's winter migration from South Island to North Island takes place in January and it returns to its southern breeding grounds in August. Its total world population numbers some 4,000–5,000 birds.

Wrybills nest in small scrapes among pebbles and near water. Sadly, spring floods now often wipe out breeding populations. Introduced plant species have colonized many braided rivers, stabilizing sand and pebble banks and influencing flow patterns, possibly forcing the birds to breed in less favorable locations.

## 14/ EURASIAN DOTTEREL
*Eudromias morinellus*

RANGE: **breeds Arctic and mountainous Eurasia; winters N Africa and Middle East**
HABITAT: **breeds on tundra and mountain plateaus; winters on open, often stony ground**
SIZE: **7¾–8½ in (20–22 cm)**

Although the bright white eye stripes and white chest band of this bird are very distinctive, they act to break up its outline when it is nesting among the short tundra or mountain vegetation of its breeding grounds.

The male Eurasian Dotterel is solely responsible for incubation and the rearing of young. Each female often lays 2 or more clutches of 3 eggs for different males. The birds are extremely tame, allowing people to approach them closely at all times of the year. There are many recorded cases of incubating males being touched while on the nest, or even returning to sit on eggs or young held on the ground in a person's hand.

## FAMILY PLUVIANELLIDAE
**Magellanic Plover**

There is only one species in this family.

## 15/ MAGELLANIC PLOVER
*Pluvianellus socialis*

RANGE: **breeds Tierra del Fuego N through S Patagonia; winters N on the coast of Argentina**
HABITAT: **shores of lakes, ponds, lagoons; winters by river mouths and bays**
SIZE: **7¾ in (20 cm)**

This enigmatic shorebird's entire population may number fewer than 1,000 individuals. Few ornithologists have seen it, and it may be more closely related to turnstones (pp. 142–45) or sheathbills (pp. 146–49) than to plovers. It forages by pecking, turning stones and digging.

Magellanic Plovers nest near shallow fresh or brackish water where each pair defends a strip of shoreline about 1,000–1,500 ft (300–500 m) long. The nest scrape, which is lined with gravel, is usually placed in an area of shingle, small rocks or gravel mixed with sand. The sexes share incubation of the 2 dark-streaked grayish eggs. Usually, only a single chick survives. Uniquely among shorebirds, it is fed partly by regurgitation from the parents' bills; they continue to feed it for at least 12 days after it has fledged at about 28 days.

# SHOREBIRDS: SANDPIPERS AND SNIPES

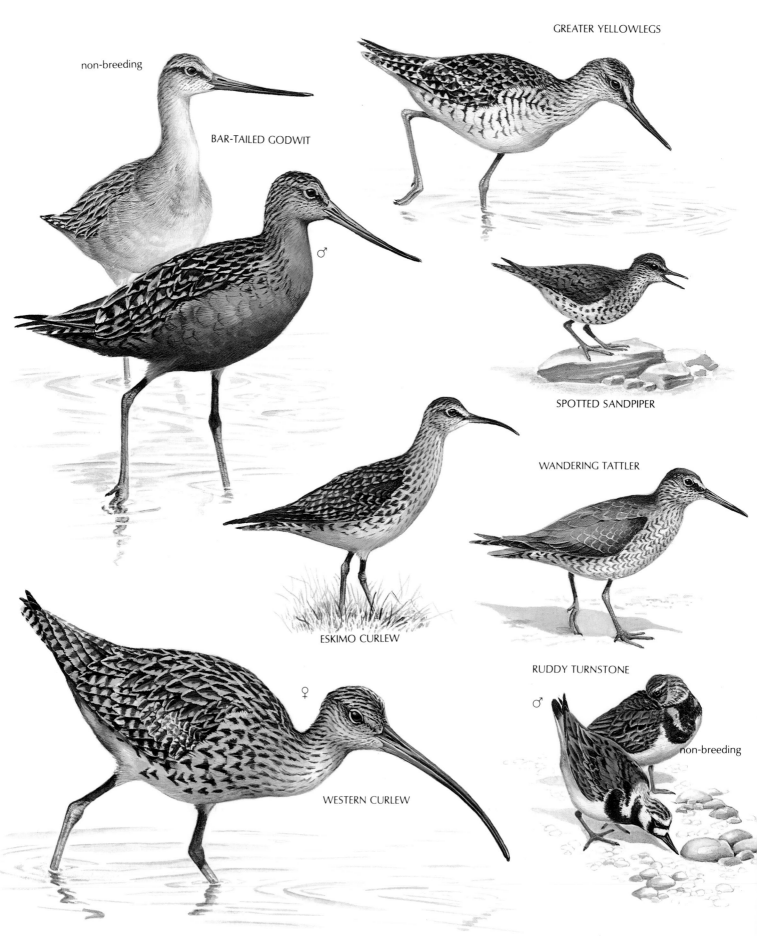

GREATER YELLOWLEGS

non-breeding

BAR-TAILED GODWIT

♂

SPOTTED SANDPIPER

WANDERING TATTLER

ESKIMO CURLEW

RUDDY TURNSTONE

♀

♂

non-breeding

WESTERN CURLEW

RED-NECKED PHALAROPE

♂

non-breeding

♀

non-breeding

RED KNOT

♂

non-breeding

DUNLIN

chick

SPOON-BILLED
SANDPIPER

EURASIAN WOODCOCK

♂

variants

♂

COMMON SNIPE

♀

SHORT-BILLED DOWITCHER

RUFF

281

# SHOREBIRDS: SANDPIPERS AND SNIPES

## FAMILY SCOLOPACIDAE
### Sandpipers and snipes
Small to large, mainly long-billed, often long-legged shorebirds. Plumage patterned brown, black and white, some with reddish breeding plumage. Sexes similar. Ground-nesters. Eggs 2–4, buff or green, variably marked. Incubation period 18–30 days. Chicks leave nest within 1 day of hatching and may travel up to $1\frac{1}{4}$ mls (2 km) to feeding areas; cared for by parents until they fledge. 86 species.

## 1/ BAR-TAILED GODWIT
*Limosa lapponica*

RANGE: **breeds Eurasian Arctic; winters S to S Africa and Australasia**
HABITAT: **breeds on marshy and scrubby tundra; winters on estuaries**
SIZE: **$14\frac{1}{2}$–16 in (37–41 cm)**

The rich mahogany-chestnut summer plumage of this species provides good camouflage for nesting birds against the colored mosses and low scrub of the Arctic tundra. The thin, slightly upturned bill is approximately 20 percent longer in the female than in the male. In a typical flock feeding along the edge of the tide, the females wade and probe in deeper water than the males.

The nest is usually placed on a drier raised hummock above the damp ground. Both sexes incubate the 4 eggs and rear the young, the off-duty bird often perching, incongruously, on top of a bush or low tree.

## 2/ ESKIMO CURLEW
*Numenius borealis*  [E]

RANGE: **formerly bred (still breeds?) NW Territories, Canada and Alaska; wintered (still winters?) mainly from S Brazil to C Argentina**
HABITAT: **Arctic tundra in breeding season; prairies and coastal grassland on migration; pampas grassland in winter**
SIZE: **$11\frac{1}{2}$–$13\frac{1}{4}$ in (29–34 cm)**

This diminutive curlew is one of the world's rarest birds, with a total population of perhaps fewer than 20 individuals. Once it was an abundant species: until the end of the last century, the Eskimo Curlew was seen in huge flocks on migration, when it was shot by the thousands during its long journey across southern Labrador, Nova Scotia, New England and the Mississippi valley en route to its South American winter quarters.

This relentless, wholesale slaughter by hunters, especially between 1850 and 1890, was the main reason for its catastrophic decline, but the large-scale conversion of grasslands for agriculture has almost certainly contributed to its demise. Adverse climatic changes may also have played a part.

Although no breeding or wintering sites are currently known, it is still seen occasionally in tiny numbers on migration: there were at least 4 reliable reports of the species in 1987. Today, it is fully protected by law in Canada and the United States, but, sadly, this protection may have come too late.

## 3/ WESTERN CURLEW
*Numenius arquata*

RANGE: **breeds temperate and N Eurasia; winters S to Africa, India, Southeast Asia**
HABITAT: **breeds on open vegetated land; winters mainly on coastal wetlands**
SIZE: **$19\frac{1}{2}$–$23\frac{1}{2}$ in (50–60 cm)**

The distinctive, long, decurved bill of the Western Curlew is perfectly adapted for the bird's main feeding technique of probing deeply into soft mud. The movement of invertebrate prey is detected by the sensitive tips of the mandibles. Food items are also picked from the surface, including mollusks, worms and, while inland, even berries.

During courtship, the male Western Curlew indulges in a shallow, gliding flight accompanied by a rich, bubbling and trilling song, which can also be heard outside the breeding season. It is one of the most evocative spring sounds of upland moorland areas. The nest is a shallow hollow among grass tussocks, lined with grass stems.

## 4/ GREATER YELLOWLEGS
*Tringa melanoleuca*

RANGE: **breeds N North America, non-breeders S along coasts; winters SW Canada to extreme S South America; vagrant elsewhere**
HABITAT: **breeds on tundra; otherwise coastal mudflats and marshes, shores of inland lakes**
SIZE: **14 in (36 cm)**

The Greater Yellowlegs is usually seen alone or in small flocks. It nests in muskeg country, along the tundra-forest edge and on the high tundra of North America, migrating south for the winter to warmer regions. It feeds mainly in shallow waters, wading in to sweep its bill with a sideways motion or dash about after visible prey. Its diet consists largely of small fish, insects and their larvae, snails, worms and tadpoles.

This species sometimes associates with the Lesser Yellowlegs *T. flavipes*, especially during migration. When it does, its greater size and its longer, stouter bill make it easy to distinguish.

## 5/ SPOTTED SANDPIPER
*Actitis macularia*

RANGE: **breeds North America; winters S from Mexico to S Brazil**
HABITAT: **open and wooded areas, usually near water**
SIZE: **$7\frac{1}{2}$ in (19 cm)**

The Spotted Sandpiper occupies varied habitats from sea level to the tree line. Tipping up its tail at nearly every step, it teeters along the water margins, stalking diverse aquatic and terrestrial insects. Its main call is a clear, whistled *peet-weet*, and it utters a repetitious *weet* during the breeding season. Its curious, jerky flight, with short glides on down-bowed wings alternating with groups of shallow, flickering wing beats, is shared only by its close relative in the Old World, the Common Sandpiper *A. hypoleucos*. Like a number of other American shorebirds, including the Greater and Lesser Yellowlegs, the Spotted Sandpiper is a rare wanderer to Europe; in 1975, a pair nested in Scotland, but deserted their 4 eggs.

Certain females of this species may be polyandrous, mating with 2 or more males. Females may or may not help with incubation.

## 6/ WANDERING TATTLER
*Heteroscelus incanus*

RANGE: **breeds Alaska; winters from Pacific coast of Central America to Australia**
HABITAT: **breeds by mountain streams; winters on rocky coasts and reefs**
SIZE: **$10\frac{1}{4}$–$11\frac{1}{2}$ in (26–29 cm)**

This species is well named for its extraordinary transoceanic migration. From a restricted breeding area in Alaska, it flies to wintering grounds scattered over numerous Pacific islands as far west as the Great Barrier Reef in Australia.

The nest is placed on bare shingle beside a mountain stream and is sometimes just a bare scrape among the stones. In other cases, it is lined with rootlets, grass and small twigs. Little is known about the bird's breeding details, as few nests have been found. It seems likely that both parents incubate the 4 eggs and rear the young.

## 7/ RUDDY TURNSTONE
*Arenaria interpres*

RANGE: breeds circumpolar Arctic, and N temperate region in Scandinavia; winters S worldwide to C Argentina, South Africa and Australia
HABITAT: breeds on tundra and coastal plains; winters on coasts
SIZE: $8\frac{1}{4}$–$10\frac{1}{4}$ in (21–26 cm)

Flocks of these birds walk busily over heaps of seaweed on the shore, flicking pieces with the bill, quickly grabbing any morsel of food that appears. Invertebrates and their larvae make up the main part of their diet, but the birds also feed on other items, including dead animals and human waste. Males are duller than females. During the breeding season, each pair defends a small territory around the nest site. Both adults share in incubating the 3–4 eggs and in rearing the young.

## 8/ RED-NECKED PHALAROPE
*Phalaropus lobatus*

RANGE: breeds circumpolar Arctic and N temperate regions; winters in the tropics
HABITAT: breeds on freshwater marshes, including uplands; marine in winter
SIZE: 7–$7\frac{1}{2}$ in (18–19 cm)

Like the other 2 species of phalarope, Red-necked Phalaropes are adapted for swimming, rather than merely wading, with lobed toes to propel them through water. They feed daintily while swimming, spinning around to stir up the water and picking small creatures from the surface.

As with the other phalaropes, the female Red-necked Phalarope is more brightly colored than the male and takes the dominant role in courtship. After she has laid her clutch of 4 eggs in a shallow cup among moss, the male carries out all the incubation and rearing of the young – hence the adaptive significance of his duller plumage, since it is an advantage for him to be better camouflaged than the female. A proportion of females lay more clutches for other males, but still take no part in tending the young.

## 9/ EURASIAN WOODCOCK
*Scolopax rusticola*

RANGE: breeds temperate Eurasia; many winter S to Mediterranean, India and Southeast Asia
HABITAT: broad-leaved or coniferous woodland; feeds more in the open in winter
SIZE: 13–$13\frac{3}{4}$ in (33–35 cm)

This shorebird is unusual in that it inhabits woodland, where its cryptic coloration provides excellent camouflage. During the breeding season the male performs "roding" flights at dusk and dawn, flying very slowly with irregular, flickering wing beats just above the tops of the trees and seeking females on the ground. As he does so, he utters several very quiet, deep, grunting notes followed by a thin, wheezy, high-pitched *tsiwick*.

After mating, the male Eurasian Woodcock may stay with the female until the clutch is laid, but he then leaves the incubation and rearing of the chicks entirely to her. The female can fly short distances carrying her chicks between her legs.

## 10/ COMMON SNIPE
*Gallinago gallinago*

RANGE: breeds N temperate North America and Eurasia; many winter widely to S
HABITAT: freshwater and coastal wetlands
SIZE: $9\frac{3}{4}$–$10\frac{1}{2}$ in (25–27 cm)

The Common Snipe pushes its long, straight bill vertically into water and soft mud in search of invertebrates. The rhythmic upward and downward pumping action of its bill as it feeds is reminiscent of a sewing machine at work.

When displaying over the breeding territory, the male Common Snipe circles high in the air and then dives groundward. As he does so, he holds out his outer tail feathers at a sharp angle to the rest of his tail. The air rushing past makes them vibrate and give out a bleating sound, often known as "winnowing." Other species of snipe make a similar noise with their tails. The nest is a scrape, often placed near a grassy tussock.

## 11/ SHORT-BILLED DOWITCHER
*Limnodromus griseus*

RANGE: breeds N North America; winters North America S to Brazil
HABITAT: breeds muskeg, ponds, marshes; winters chiefly on coastal mudflats
SIZE: $10\frac{1}{2}$–$12\frac{1}{4}$ in (27–31 cm)

The Short-billed Dowitcher is a medium-sized, short-legged, dumpy shorebird, showing a white wedge-shaped patch from the tail to the middle of the back in flight. In winter plumage it is difficult to distinguish this bird from its close relative, the Long-billed Dowitcher *L. scolopaceus*. The 2 species often occur together on migration.

However, whereas Long-billed Dowitchers generally prefer freshwater pools on migration and in their wintering quarters, Short-billed Dowitchers favor saltwater and brackish habitats outside the breeding season. Here they feed in mud and shallow water, often in large flocks. They often submerge their heads entirely in water as they probe for aquatic insects, other marine life and plant food.

## 12/ RED KNOT
*Calidris canutus*

RANGE: breeds Arctic Canada and Siberia; winters South America, S Africa and Australia
HABITAT: breeds on tundra; winters on estuaries and beaches
SIZE: 9–$9\frac{3}{4}$ in (23–25 cm)

The Red Knot undergoes a marked change in plumage through the year, from its rich chestnut-orange breeding dress to the pale gray of winter. Flocks that form in fall and winter can be tens of thousands strong and will perform rapid aerial maneuvers in which the entire flock twists and turns with great synchrony. At a distance, the flock can give the appearance of a writhing mass of smoke.

Although the rather duller, white-bellied female helps with incubation, she departs soon after, leaving the male to rear the brood. This means that more invertebrate food is available for the chicks than if a second adult were present.

## 13/ DUNLIN
*Calidris alpina*

RANGE: circumpolar Arctic and N temperate regions; winters S to subtropics
HABITAT: breeds on tundra, moorland, marshes; winters on estuaries or inland wetlands
SIZE: $6\frac{1}{4}$–$8\frac{1}{2}$ in (16–22 cm)

The Dunlin is the most common small shorebird of the Northern Hemisphere. It may occur in passage and winter flocks of tens of thousands in favored estuaries, but also appears in tiny groups in small coastal creeks. Extensive banding has shown that wintering birds return year after year not just to the same estuary, but to the same part of the estuary, with almost no mixing between flocks only a few miles apart. This species is very variable in size, birds of southern and western races being far smaller than those of some of the east Siberian and New World races.

Dunlins nest in shallow depressions among short vegetation. Both sexes share in the incubation of the 4 eggs, but the female leaves soon after the young have hatched.

## 14/ SPOON-BILLED SANDPIPER
*Eurynorhynchus pygmeus*                    ?

RANGE: breeds NE Siberia; winters coasts of SE India to Burma, coastal SE China
HABITAT: breeds on coastal marshy tundra; winters on muddy coasts and brackish lagoons
SIZE: $5\frac{1}{2}$–$6\frac{1}{4}$ in (14–16 cm)

The spoon-shaped bill of this species is an adaptation for feeding. The bird forages in soft mud or shallow water, sweeping its bill from side to side as it walks. The broadened bill tip is already obvious in the newly hatched young.

The Spoon-billed Sandpiper's total population is small, with a best estimate of no more than 2,800 pairs; the true figure may well be considerably lower. However, accurate censuses are extremely difficult to carry out. The male apparently carries out most of the incubation of the 4 eggs as well as rearing the young.

## 15/ RUFF
*Philomachus pugnax*

RANGE: breeds N Eurasia; winters Mediterranean, S Africa, India and Australia
HABITAT: lowland freshwater wetlands, marshes and wet pastures
SIZE: $7\frac{3}{4}$–$12\frac{1}{2}$ in (20–32 cm)

In the breeding season, the male Ruff develops remarkable plumes, variable in both color and pattern, around his head and neck. Groups of rival males form "leks" at which they display to one another and advertise to visiting females. Some hold small territories within the lek, while others move from one position to another.

Each female may mate with one or more males, before moving away up to 1,600 ft (500 m) from the lek area. There she makes a shallow scrape, lays a clutch of 4 eggs, incubates them and rears the young. The males, in all their finery, take no part in nesting.

WHITE-BELLIED SEEDSNIPE

SNOWY SHEATHBILL

GREAT SKUA

non-breeding

LONG-TAILED JAEGER

IVORY GULL

juv

typical

non-breeding

GRAY GULL

race *argenteus*
non-breeding

non-breeding

MEW GULL

race *michahellis*

race *argenteus*

HERRING GULL

non-breeding

FRANKLIN'S GULL

GREAT BLACK-BACKED GULL

first winter

race *scopulinus*
"Red-billed Gull"

race *hartlaubii*
"Hartlaub's Gull"

juv

non-breeding

ROSS'S GULL

BLACK-LEGGED KITTIWAKE

SILVER GULL

first winter

non-breeding

juv

non-breeding

SABINE'S GULL

SWALLOW-TAILED GULL

285

# SEEDSNIPES, SHEATHBILLS, SKUAS AND JAEGERS, GULLS

## FAMILY THINOCORIDAE
### Seedsnipes
Small, dumpy partridgelike. Plumage cryptic, males more strongly marked. Nest in scrapes. Eggs 4, buff or cream, speckled and blotched. Incubation 25 days, nestling period 49–55 days. 4 species.

## 1/ WHITE-BELLIED SEEDSNIPE
*Attagis malouinus*
RANGE: Tierra del Fuego N to S Chile and Argentina
HABITAT: sparsely vegetated hillsides above the treeline
SIZE: 10–11½ in (26–29 cm)

The bright white underparts and underwings of the White-bellied Seedsnipe contrast markedly with its patterned pale brown upperparts, particularly when the bird is in flight. Apart from its main diet of seeds, it also consumes green leaves and cactus buds. Succulent plant parts appear to be the only source of water for the bird, since it has never been seen to drink.

The female lays her eggs in a scrape on the ground lined with pieces of vegetation. She carries out incubation while the male acts as a lookout, perching near the nest and warning of approaching danger. The young are led away from the nest by both parents within a few hours of hatching.

## FAMILY CHIONIDIDAE
### Sheathbills
White, pigeonlike with horny bill sheath. Sexes alike. Crevice-nesters. Eggs 2 (sometimes 3 or 4), white or grayish, blotched. Incubation 28–32 days, nestling period 50–60 days. 2 species.

## 2/ SNOWY SHEATHBILL
*Chionis alba*
RANGE: breeds Antarctic peninsula and islands N to South Georgia; winters N to Patagonia and the Falkland Islands
HABITAT: marine coasts
SIZE: 15¾ in (40 cm)

The pure white Snowy Sheathbill is a versatile scavenger that haunts seabird colonies, especially those of penguins, and visits the garbage tips of Antarctic scientific bases. It feeds on carcasses, feces and offal of every description and also snatches eggs and chicks from the breeding penguins. Outside the breeding season, its diet consists of intertidal beach animals and algae.

The nest is placed in a rock crevice or under a boulder. Both parents take turns to incubate the 2–4 eggs, but it is rare for more than 2 young to be reared. The young take up to 9 weeks to fledge.

## FAMILY STERCORARIIDAE
### Skuas and jaegers
Large seabirds, some with elongated central tail feathers. Plumage all brown, or brown above, creamy white below. Sexes alike. Nest in scrapes. Eggs usually 2, olive, brown blotches. Incubation 23–30 days, nestling period 24–55 days. 7 species.

## 3/ GREAT SKUA
*Catharacta skua*
RANGE: temperate and Arctic North Atlantic
HABITAT: breeds on open ground, usually near the coast; winters at sea, though probably within 30 mls (50 km) of the coast
SIZE: 20–26 in (51–66 cm)

Great Skuas obtain much of their food by chasing other seabirds and forcing them to disgorge whatever they are carrying. In the case of the Gannet, which is significantly larger than the Great Skua, the attacker seizes hold of a wing tip or the bird's tail and forces it down onto the ocean. It continues to hold on fast until the Gannet disgorges.

Breeding takes place in loose colonies, each pair vigorously defending its own territory. Encroaching animals, or humans, are repeatedly dive-bombed and struck on the head until they retreat. The nest is a shallow scrape on the ground.

## 4/ LONG-TAILED JAEGER
*Stercorarius longicaudus*
RANGE: breeds circumpolar high Arctic; winters in S hemisphere
HABITAT: breeds on Arctic tundra and marshes; winters at sea
SIZE: 19½–22¾ in (50–58 cm)

The Long-tailed Jaeger is the most slender and elegant member of its family, with a central pair of tail feathers that extend about 7 in (18 cm) beyond the remainder. During the breeding season, this species concentrates on hunting lemmings, rather than parasitizing other seabirds. The breeding performance of the jaegers is closely linked to the abundance of lemmings. In years when lemmings are scarce, the jaegers may not breed at all, or will fail to rear any young, but they breed very successfully in good lemming years.

The nest is a shallow, lined scrape on the ground, and both parents incubate the 2 eggs. When food is short, the first chick to hatch may kill the second chick so that it does not have to share the limited food supply.

## FAMILY LARIDAE
### Gulls
Heavy-bodied, long-winged seabirds. Plumage mainly white, gray and black in adults, brown markings in juveniles. Sexes similar. Nest sites variable. Eggs usually 2–3, greenish or brownish, mottled. Incubation 21–35 days, nestling period 21–49 days. 47 species.

## 5/ IVORY GULL
*Pagophila eburnea*
RANGE: high Arctic islands and coasts
HABITAT: breeds on cliffs; winters among or on the edge of pack-ice
SIZE: 15¾–18 in (40–46 cm)

The Ivory Gull is a dumpy, almost pigeon-shaped, all-white bird. When it walks, its short legs give it a rolling gait. It obtains much of its food by scavenging among the channels in pack-ice, following Polar Bears and picking up the remnants of their meals, as well as their feces.

The Ivory Gull nests on cliff ledges on remote Arctic islands in colonies varying in size from a handful to several hundred pairs. It also breeds on nunataks, rocky peaks projecting from the icecaps of Greenland and Spitsbergen.

## 6/ GRAY GULL
*Larus modestus*
RANGE: breeds N Chile; winters Chile, Peru and Ecuador
HABITAT: breeds on coastal deserts, coasts
SIZE: 18 in (46 cm)

This abundant gull of the Pacific coast of South America is remarkable for breeding in the barren deserts that extend 50 mls (80 km) inland from the coast of northern Chile. The birds nest in loose colonies of several thousand pairs on the dry, boulder-strewn ground. Cooling onshore breezes prevent temperatures rising too high but, even so, the incubating birds stand over the clutch of 1–2 eggs to shade them from the heat of the day. The desert provides no food, but the Gray Gulls find all they need to eat on the coast, by foraging along the tideline or following trawlers.

## 7/ MEW GULL
*Larus canus*

RANGE: temperate and N Eurasia and NW North America
HABITAT: breeds in marshes and wet scrubland; winters on the shores of oceans and large lakes
SIZE: 15¾–18 in (40–46 cm)

Mew Gulls nest in colonies, sometimes on the ground, but often in the tops of bushes or scrub. In parts of Norway the birds are encouraged to nest in open boxes on poles because their eggs provide food for the local inhabitants. The usual clutch contains 3 eggs, which are incubated by both parents for about 3 weeks. The young take another 4–5 weeks to fledge.

In winter, the birds gather in large roosts on estuarine mudflats or large fresh waters. They may feed along the shore or fly well inland to forage for invertebrates in pastures, returning to the roosting site in the evening.

## 8/ HERRING GULL
*Larus argentatus*

RANGE: circumpolar N, temperate and Mediterranean
HABITAT: varied; coastal and inland, including urban areas
SIZE: 22–26 in (56–66 cm)

The Herring Gull is one of the most successful of all seabirds, having adapted in recent decades to living on human refuse and nesting on roofs in many areas. It is now commonplace in towns, some well inland, and strenuous efforts have been made to prevent the gulls from nesting on, and fouling, important buildings.

The Herring Gull's nest is an untidy gathering of vegetation and scraps of garbage. Soon after they have hatched in the nest, the young peck instinctively at the prominent red spot on the lower mandible of their parents' bills. The action induces an adult bird to regurgitate the food in its crop. The race *L. a. argenteus* breeds in northwest Europe, while the yellow-legged *L. a. michahellis* breeds in the Mediterranean region, though it is expanding northward.

## 9/ GREAT BLACK-BACKED GULL
*Larus marinus*

RANGE: coastal NE North America, SW Greenland and NW Europe
HABITAT: coasts, locally inland waters and moors
SIZE: 28–31 in (71–79 cm)

The Great Black-backed Gull takes its name from its large size and black back and wings. It is a highly predatory gull, especially in the breeding season when it may live almost exclusively on seabirds and, if they are available, rabbits. At other times of the year, it often obtains food by scavenging at garbage tips, around fishing ports and along the shore.

Breeding may take place in loose colonies or the birds may build solitary nests, usually on a rock promontory or on a ridge with a good view all around. The nest is a bulky pile of vegetation.

## 10/ FRANKLIN'S GULL
*Larus pipixcan*

RANGE: breeds on North American prairies; winters on coasts of Central and South America
HABITAT: breeds in freshwater marshes; winters on coasts
SIZE: 13–15 in (33–38 cm)

The soft gray upperparts and white underparts of this gull have earned it the local name of Prairie Dove. Within its restricted breeding range, the species is abundant, nesting in colonies of several thousand pairs in marshes or beside lakes. The birds feed on surrounding farmland, eating a variety of agricultural pests such as wireworms and cutworms.

The nests are built of vegetation close to or in shallow water. The females lay 3 eggs and the young hatch with either a gray or a brown downy coat, although these two color phases do not persist in the adult plumage.

## 11/ SILVER GULL
*Larus novaehollandiae*

RANGE: S Africa, Australia, New Zealand
HABITAT: coasts, inland lakes and rivers
SIZE: 15–17 in (38–43 cm)

There are several races of the Silver Gull, including *L. n. novaehollandiae* of southern Australia and Tasmania, *L. n. forsteri* of northern Australia and New Caledonia, the Red-billed Gull *L. n. scopulinus* of New Zealand, and Hartlaub's Gull *L. n. hartlaubii* of southern Africa. All are common and adaptable birds, which have successfully exploited urban habitats. They often feed around harbors and garbage tips, and forage widely over farmland.

The Red-billed Gull breeds in huge colonies numbering as many as 100,000 birds. Some of the largest colonies occur on offshore islands. At least one breeding site, however, is located well inland, in an area of thermal springs.

## 12/ ROSS'S GULL
*Rhodostethia rosea*

RANGE: Arctic Siberia, Canada and Greenland
HABITAT: breeds on Arctic tundra and scrub; winters at sea
SIZE: 11¾–12½ in (30–32 cm)

Perhaps the most beautiful of all the gulls, Ross's Gull in its breeding plumage has white underparts suffused with pink. For a long time the breeding grounds of this small gull were quite unknown, though they were obviously in northern latitudes. They were finally discovered in northern Siberia in 1905, where the birds were found nesting among low scrub in river valleys. More recently, breeding has been confirmed in northern Canada and in Greenland. The birds build a nest of vegetation that may stand 8 in (20 cm) above the damp, swampy ground.

## 13/ BLACK-LEGGED KITTIWAKE
*Rissa tridactyla*

RANGE: circumpolar Arctic and temperate coasts
HABITAT: coastal and open sea
SIZE: 15¼–18 in (39–46 cm)

This widespread species is often known simply as the Kittiwake: the other species, the Red-legged Kittiwake, is restricted to the Bering Sea region of the North Pacific. Kittiwakes traditionally nest in large colonies on narrow cliff ledges, building a nest of seaweed, lined with grass. As the seaweed dries, it cements itself to the rock. In recent years, ledges on buildings have proved attractive to Black-legged Kittiwakes, and there are now many nesting colonies around harbors and fishing ports.

The 2–3 eggs are incubated by both parents for about 27 days. The young, when they hatch, have strong claws on their toes, enabling them to cling to their precarious home.

## 14/ SWALLOW-TAILED GULL
*Creagrus furcatus*

RANGE: breeds Galapagos Islands and Colombia; winters off NW South America
HABITAT: breeds on coasts; winters on open sea
SIZE: 21½–23½ in (55–60 cm)

With its dark gray head, boldly patterned wings and deeply forked tail, the Swallow-tailed Gull has a particularly striking appearance. Its eyes are much larger than those of most gulls and are more forward-facing, giving the bird binocular vision. These are adaptions that help the birds find food at night. Swallow-tailed Gulls range several hundred miles from their breeding grounds out over the ocean and take squid and other sea creatures that come to the surface after dark.

The bird's nest is a cup of small stones among rocks in which it lays a single egg. The incubation period is 34 days and the young chick is then brooded and guarded by one parent throughout the day.

## 15/ SABINE'S GULL
*Xema sabini*

RANGE: circumpolar Arctic
HABITAT: breeds Arctic coasts and islands; winters on the open sea
SIZE: 13–14 in (33–36 cm)

Small invertebrates form the principal food for the elegant Sabine's Gull and the bird uses various methods to pursue its prey. These include pecking daintily along the water's edge, running over mud like a shorebird, swimming and spinning around on the water like a phalarope, and diving into the ocean from above.

Presumably as a defense against predators, parents lead their young away from the nest as soon as they hatch. The adults also perform a distraction display if danger threatens their chicks. Both these types of behavior are more typical of shorebirds than of gulls.

BLACK TERN

non-breeding

CASPIAN TERN

ARCTIC TERN

ROYAL TERN

SOOTY TERN

COMMON NODDY

WHITE TERN

juv

juv

INCA TERN

bridled form

BLACK SKIMMER

COMMON MURRE

non-breeding

non-breeding

DOVEKIE

BLACK GUILLEMOT

ATLANTIC PUFFIN

non-breeding

chick

ANCIENT MURRELET

MARBLED MURRELET

# TERNS, SKIMMERS, AUKS

## FAMILY STERNIDAE
### Terns

Slender seabirds, with long, pointed wings and forked tails. Plumage mainly white, gray, brown and black. Sexes alike. Nest sites variable. Eggs 1–3, cream, greenish or brownish, blotched. Incubation 13–30 days, chicks leave nest soon after hatching but remain near parents. 41 species.

## 1/ BLACK TERN
*Chlidonias nigra*

RANGE: **breeds central S Eurasia and North America; winters in tropics mainly N of Equator**
HABITAT: **breeds on marshes and pools; winters on coasts**
SIZE: **$8\frac{1}{2}$–$9\frac{1}{2}$ in (22–24 cm)**

The Black Tern feeds mainly on aquatic insects and their larvae and obtains almost all its prey in flight. Instead of hovering above the water and then diving into it, like many other species of tern, the Black Tern and the other "marsh terns" of the genus *Chlidonias* hover and then swoop down to peck from the water's surface in mid-flight. Black Terns also hawk for insects in midair and even follow the plow on farmland, darting down to snatch small worms and other invertebrates exposed on the soil.

The bird's nest is composed of aquatic vegetation and is often floating, anchored to growing plants. The usual clutch is 3 eggs. The young leave the nest when they are a few days old and hide in nearby vegetation.

## 2/ CASPIAN TERN
*Hydroprogne caspia*

RANGE: **worldwide, but breeding range is fragmentary**
HABITAT: **breeds on coastal and inland marshes; winters on coasts**
SIZE: **$18\frac{3}{4}$–$23\frac{1}{4}$ in (48–59 cm)**

The Caspian Tern is the largest of the terns, with an orange-red, daggerlike bill. It breeds in large colonies or in solitary pairs, its nests merely scrapes in the ground, sometimes with a little vegetation.

The Caspian Tern's range is remarkable in covering all 5 continents, but the breeding areas are hundreds of miles apart. This is probably because the species requires remote coastal and marshland nesting sites with rich feeding areas close by. Such places are naturally scarce and some potential sites may have become unsuitable due to human activity.

## 3/ ARCTIC TERN
*Sterna paradisaea*

RANGE: **breeds circumpolar Arctic and sub-Arctic; winters S to Antarctic Ocean**
HABITAT: **breeds on coasts; winters at sea**
SIZE: **13–15 in (33–38 cm)**

The annual migration of the Arctic Tern is probably the longest of any bird. From their breeding grounds in the Arctic, the birds fly south to winter in the oceans just north of the Antarctic pack-ice, a round trip of more than 20,000 mls (32,000 km) every year. Because they breed in the

northern summer and visit the Antarctic Ocean during the southern summer, they experience more daylight hours in the course of a year than any other living animal.

Arctic Terns breed in colonies on shingle beaches and among rocks. Like some other terns, they vigorously defend their nests against predators, or even approaching humans, by dive-bombing and actually striking the intruders around the head with their beaks.

## 4/ SOOTY TERN
*Sterna fuscata*

RANGE: **tropical and subtropical latitudes**
HABITAT: **breeds on coasts and islands; winters on the open sea**
SIZE: **17–$17\frac{3}{4}$ in (43–45 cm)**

The Sooty Tern is mainly black above and white beneath, with a long, forked tail. It takes its alternative name, Wideawake Tern, from its loud, repeated call of *ker-wacky-wack*, and perhaps also from its nocturnal feeding habits. The bird hardly ever seems to land on the water, but obtains its food by swooping down and pecking from the surface. It seems likely that it actually sleeps on the wing.

Nesting takes place in enormous colonies, numbering tens or even hundreds of thousands of birds. However, egg-collecting by humans has been a serious problem in some areas, and variations in food supply can also cause significant fluctuations in breeding success.

## 5/ ROYAL TERN
*Thalasseus maximus*

RANGE: **breeds on coasts of Central America and W Africa; winters on coasts to S**
HABITAT: **coastal and marine**
SIZE: **18–$20\frac{3}{4}$ in (46–53 cm)**

In the past, Royal Terns were commonly observed on the west coast of Africa but it was thought that they were migrants from the American breeding range. Then a large colony was discovered about 30 years ago in Mauritania, and smaller ones

subsequently in Senegal and Gambia. It is still not known whether the species undergoes any transatlantic migration or whether the colonies are entirely separate.

Colonies are often large, with up to several thousand pairs. The young are looked after by their parents for an unusually long time. Adults have been observed still feeding chicks that are 5 months old.

## 6/ INCA TERN
*Larosterna inca*

RANGE: **Ecuador to Chile**
HABITAT: **coastal and marine**
SIZE: **$15\frac{3}{4}$–$16\frac{1}{2}$ in (40–42 cm)**

The dapper blue-gray plumage of the Inca Tern is adorned with an extraordinary white moustachial plume that extends back below the eye and then curls around and down toward the breast. This is a gregarious species, roosting in flocks of many thousands on sandy beaches, along with flocks of gulls.

Inca Terns are graceful flyers, often hovering over the water before dipping down with rapid movements to snatch a food item from the surface. They also follow feeding whales and seals to seize scraps of food.

## 7/ COMMON NODDY
*Anous stolidus*

RANGE: **equatorial**
HABITAT: **breeds on cliffs and wooded islands; winters on the open sea**
SIZE: **$15\frac{3}{4}$–$17\frac{3}{4}$ in (40–45 cm)**

The Common Noddy's pale lavender-gray forehead and crown give the bird a white-capped appearance when seen in the distance. The name "noddy" refers to the bird's habit of bowing and nodding its head during courtship. The pair indulge in prolonged displays, with the male ritually presenting food to his mate.

The Common Noddy's choice of nest site varies greatly over its wide range. In many places colonies nest in the open on the ground, others use broad cliff ledges, while some build nests of twigs and plant stems in the branches of trees and scrub. The female lays only 1 egg and the combined incubation and fledging periods total over 11 weeks.

## 8/ WHITE TERN
*Gygis alba*
RANGE: equatorial
HABITAT: open sea; nests on wooded islands
SIZE: 11–13 in (28–33 cm)

The White Tern has pure white plumage, large black eyes and a slightly upturned black bill. In flight, the wings appear almost translucent against the sky and this, together with its buoyant and graceful flight, has led to the species also being called the Fairy Tern (although there is another species, *Sterna nereis*, in Australia, New Zealand and New Caledonia that is more properly known by this name).

Unlike most terns, with their colonial habits, this species is a solitary breeder. It does not build a nest, but lays its single egg on a tiny cliff ledge, or on a horizontal tree branch supported by a small fork or even just a knot or slight unevenness on the branch. There is often barely room for the incubating bird. The chick hatches after about 5 weeks, complete with strong feet and claws with which it clings to its tiny nest site.

## FAMILY RYNCHOPIDAE
### Skimmers
Medium waterbirds. Extended, flattened lower bill. Black or brown, white or pale gray underparts. Sexes similar. Nest in scrapes. Eggs 2–5, white-beige, blotched. Incubation 22–24 days, nestling period 25–30 days. 3 species.

## 9/ BLACK SKIMMER
*Rynchops niger*
RANGE: S North America, Caribbean and South America
HABITAT: coastal and riverine marshes
SIZE: 15¾–19½ in (40–50 cm)

Like the 2 other species of skimmer, the Black Skimmer has an extraordinary bill in which the lower mandible is flattened and is a third as long again as the rounded upper mandible. When feeding, the bird flies close to the surface of the water, with only the tip of the lower mandible submerged. As soon as this encounters prey, such as small fish and shrimp, the bird throws its head downward and snaps its bill shut.

Much feeding takes place at dawn and dusk, and also by moonlight. Uniquely among birds, skimmers have vertical pupils in their eyes that can be closed to slits in bright sunshine, or opened to full circles in poor light.

## FAMILY ALCIDAE
### Auks
Small to medium short-tailed, short-necked marine divers. Flightless following annual molt. Dark brown or black, underparts white. Sexes similar. Nest ashore on ledges or in crevices. Eggs 1–2, variable. Incubation 29–42 days, nestling period 2–50 days. 22 species.

## 10/ DOVEKIE
*Alle alle*
RANGE: North Atlantic and adjacent Arctic
HABITAT: breeds on coastal scree and in rock crevices; otherwise on open sea
SIZE: 7¾–9¾ in (20–25 cm)

The Dovekie is a small, stubby seabird, with little or no neck and short wings. Its principal food is plankton, small crustaceans and other marine animals. During the breeding season it brings food back to the nest in its crop, which, when full, produces a distinct bulge in the throat.

Breeding colonies may contain several million pairs of Dovekies, their nests placed deep among the fallen rocks of coastal scree. Colonies are constantly patrolled by the species' main predators, Glaucous Gulls, which wait their chance to snatch unwary birds as they enter or leave their nest-holes.

## 11/ COMMON MURRE
*Uria aalge*
RANGE: circumpolar Eurasia and North America
HABITAT: open sea; breeds on coastal cliffs
SIZE: 15¾–17 in (40–43 cm)

On land, the upright stance of the Common Murre, combined with its dark head and upperparts and white underparts, give the bird the appearance of a small penguin. The bridled form is a genetic variation that occurs only in the North Atlantic, more often in northern populations.

Common Murres breed in large colonies on narrow cliff ledges. Each pair's single egg is markedly pointed so that it will roll in a circle if pushed and not fall off the ledge. The chicks leave the nest site when they are only about 3 weeks old. Their wing covert feathers grow first, giving them just enough power to half-glide, half-fly from the ledge down to the water. The chicks then swim away out to sea, usually with the male parents. This early departure from the ledges means that the parents can take their young to the food supply instead of continuing to bring the food to them from as far as 50 mls (80 km) away.

## 12/ BLACK GUILLEMOT
*Cepphus grylle*
RANGE: North Atlantic and adjacent Arctic
HABITAT: breeds on coasts; winters mainly in coastal waters
SIZE: 11¾–14 in (30–36 cm)

In contrast to its pale, mottled winter plumage, the breeding dress of the Black Guillemot is a bold jet-black, except for a broad white patch on the upper side of the wing and white on the inner half of the underwing. The bird also has bright red legs and feet that show up distinctly in clear water and on land. It utters a loud and melodious whistling call, both in flight and on the water, and as it calls, it reveals the bright red lining of its mouth. During courtship, one bird circles closely around its mate, producing a softer version of the whistle at frequent intervals.

Black Guillemots breed alone or in small colonies of up to 100 pairs. They may nest under boulders, in rock crevices or in caves, laying their eggs on the bare earth or rock.

## 13/ MARBLED MURRELET
*Brachyramphus marmoratus*
RANGE: N Pacific, S to Japan and California
HABITAT: inshore marine; breeds in woodland and tundra near the coast
SIZE: 9½–9¾ in (24–25 cm)

The Marbled Murrelet takes its name from the pale edgings to its feathers that give the bird a mottled appearance, especially in the breeding season. Although it is an abundant species, with hundreds of thousands occurring off the coasts of Alaska, its breeding habits are virtually unknown. Only a few solitary nests have ever been found. Two of these were several miles inland in forested areas, placed in the fork of a large branch and in a tree hollow about 100 ft (30 m) above the ground. Two other nests were in hollows in the open tundra of small subarctic islands.

## 14/ ANCIENT MURRELET
*Synthliboramphus antiquus*
RANGE: N Pacific and Bering Sea, S to Japan and Mexico
HABITAT: coastal and open sea; breeds on coasts
SIZE: 9½–10½ in (24–27 cm)

Large breeding colonies of Ancient Murrelets, containing up to 40,000 pairs, occur in coastal forests. The birds make their nests in burrows up to 3 ft (1 m) deep among rocks, grass or even tree roots. The eggs are incubated by both parents. The incubating bird calls from the burrow to help its mate find the correct nest entrance within the colony. The young leave the nest within 2–3 days of hatching and scramble down the slopes and cliffs from the nest site to join their parents on the open ocean.

This species' curious name comes from the fine, hairlike white feathers on its head that develop during the breeding season, resembling the white hairs of an old person.

## 15/ ATLANTIC PUFFIN
*Fratercula arctica*
RANGE: N Atlantic and adjacent Arctic
HABITAT: open sea; breeds on coasts
SIZE: 11–11¾ in (28–30 cm)

The most distinctive feature of the Atlantic Puffin is its large red, yellow and gray-blue bill, shaped rather like the bill of a parrot. The coloring of this extraordinary appendage is particularly bright during the breeding season and helps to attract mates.

The depth of the bill, and especially its sharp edges, enable the bird to catch and hold fish. A dozen or more can be held at one time and, as each fish is caught, it is held between the tongue and the upper mandible, freeing the lower mandible for more catches. Atlantic Puffins also use their beaks to excavate nesting burrows, which can be several yards long, in grassy clifftops.

# SANDGROUSE, DOVES AND PIGEONS

BLACK-BELLIED SANDGROUSE

PALLAS' SANDGROUSE

♂

♀

chicks

FERAL PIGEON
checkered type

FERAL PIGEON
red type

WOOD PIGEON

ROCK DOVE

SNOW PIGEON

LAUREL PIGEON

race *rufescens*

race *turtur*

TURTLE DOVE

LARGE BROWN CUCKOO-DOVE

NAMAQUA DOVE

FLOCK BRONZEWING

SPINIFEX PIGEON

juv

MOURNING DOVE

DIAMOND DOVE

GALAPAGOS DOVE

# SANDGROUSE, DOVES AND PIGEONS

## FAMILY PTEROCLIDIDAE
### Sandgrouse
Dumpy, medium, seed-eating ground birds. Usually long-tailed. Cryptic plumage. Sexes differ. Nest in scrape on ground. Eggs 3 (rarely 2), dull pinkish, greenish or cream with brown or olive spots or blotches. Incubation 21–31 days, chicks leave nest soon after hatching. 16 species.

## 1/ PALLAS' SANDGROUSE
*Syrrhaptes paradoxus*
RANGE: **SW USSR to China and Mongolia**
HABITAT: **arid open plains and valleys**
SIZE: **11¾–16 in (30–41 cm)**

Uniquely in its family, Pallas' Sandgrouse has a lengthened tip to the longest wing feather. Like most sandgrouse, and as an adaptation to its arid habitat, the male has highly absorbent belly feathers which enable him to store water after immersing his underparts in a water hole and carry it back to his chicks. They drink it eagerly as he stands erect, allowing the water to run down a central groove in his belly feathers.

In the last century and early in this one, thousands of these birds would, from time to time, spread west across Europe. These events occurred mainly in the spring and early summer, probably triggered by unseasonal cold weather and food shortages. After such irregular irruptions, breeding often took place far to the west of the normal range, even in Britain. The last large irruption took place in 1908, although there have been a few smaller ones since then, involving only a few birds. It is not clear why these dramatic movements have apparently ceased, but it is probably due to a contraction in the range of the species in western Siberia since the early 1900s.

## 2/ BLACK-BELLIED SANDGROUSE
*Pterocles orientalis*
RANGE: **S to SE Europe, N Africa, SW Asia**
HABITAT: **flat and upland plains, saltflats**
SIZE: **13–13¾ in (33–35 cm)**

As with other sandgrouse and all birds of arid areas, water plays a vital role in the daily regime of the Black-bellied Sandgrouse. Flocks of up to 50 birds forage during the day for tiny seeds. They roost in the open, then just before dawn fly to the nearest source of fresh water, natural or artificial. In regions with little water, flocks may come from a wide area until several hundred or even thousand may have gathered. Much jostling and squabbling takes place as each bird drinks its fill, before finally departing for another day's feeding.

In flight, flocks of Black-bellied Sandgrouse utter a soft gurgling or bubbling call, helping to keep the birds in contact with one another.

## FAMILY COLUMBIDAE
### Doves and pigeons
Small to large, dumpy, mainly tree-dwelling birds. Plumage variable. Sexes usually similar. Simple twig nest; a few nest on the ground or in holes. Both sexes produce a curdlike substance, "pigeon's milk," from their crop to feed the young. It resembles mammalian milk in composition. Eggs 1–2, white. Incubation 13–28 days, nestling period 12–36 days. 300 species.

## 3/ ROCK DOVE & FERAL PIGEON
*Columba livia*
RANGE: **native to S Eurasia and N Africa; domesticated worldwide**
HABITAT: **cliffs and gorges, close to open country; domestic form mainly urban**
SIZE: **12¼–13½ in (31–34 cm)**

The wild Rock Dove is a bird of cliffs and rocky terrain, but its feral descendants thrive in towns and cities throughout the world. Originally, wild-caught Rock Doves were reared for food and, later, for producing fancy breeds and racing pigeons. Escapes, which still continue, soon led to feral populations gathering in urban areas, using building ledges for nest sites and gleaning scraps of food from the streets and surrounding fields. These Feral Pigeons vary greatly in plumage. While some are similar to Rock Doves in coloration, others are rusty red or checkered.

The remarkable homing ability exploited in racing pigeons is at odds with the almost entirely sedentary habits of both wild and feral birds. In the wild, movements of more than a few miles are rare, yet racing pigeons can find their way home from distances of hundreds or even thousands of miles without difficulty.

## 4/ SNOW PIGEON
*Columba leuconota*
RANGE: **Himalayas, NW Burma, W China and SW Turkestan**
HABITAT: **mountainous areas with high rainfall, above 6,500–10,000 ft (2,000–3,000 m)**
SIZE: **12¼–13½ in (31–34 cm)**

As well as having white plumage, the Snow Pigeon lives up to its name by inhabiting areas close to or even above the snow line. It nests in cliff caves, sometimes forming small colonies.

Outside the breeding season, Snow Pigeons roost on cliff ledges well up the mountainsides, flying down into the nearby valleys for food as soon as the sun rises high enough. Birds foraging for seeds in a field still partly covered by melting snow are quite difficult to see, as the patterned plumage provides effective camouflage.

## 5/ WOOD PIGEON
*Columba palumbus*
RANGE: **Europe, N Africa, SW Asia, Iran and India; also Azores**
HABITAT: **woodland and adjacent farmland**
SIZE: **15¾–16½ in (40–42 cm)**

Wood Pigeons are serious pests of agricultural crops in some areas, with flocks sometimes numbering thousands or even tens of thousands. These birds frequently raid fields planted with cereals, brassicas (cabbages, kale and brussels sprouts), clover and peas.

The distinctive display flight of the male Wood Pigeon (also rarely performed by the female) consists of a towering flight with several slow wing beats toward the top, when the wings produce 2–3 very loud claps. These sounds may come either from direct contact between the wings or by a whip-crack effect of the feather tips. The bird then glides downward and flies up again to repeat the process.

## 6/ LAUREL PIGEON
*Columba junoniae*　　　　Ⓡ
RANGE: **Canary Islands (Las Palmas, Gomera and Tenerife)**
HABITAT: **mountainous, scrub-covered slopes and adjacent cultivated areas**
SIZE: **14½–15 in (37–38 cm)**

Hunting and habitat destruction have contributed to the scarcity of this species, restricted as it is to just one group of islands. Laurels form part of the scrub vegetation in which it lives, hence its name.

The natural food of the Laurel Pigeon is chiefly fruit, berries and seeds obtained from trees in mountainous areas. Much feeding also takes place on harvested flax and cereal crops farther down the slopes. The Laurel Pigeon can run quickly, rather like a partridge. At other times, it walks with a long, swinging gait, accompanied by bowing of the head and raising of the tail.

## 7/ TURTLE DOVE
*Streptopelia turtur*

RANGE: **Europe, N Africa, SW Asia; winters in Africa S of the Sahara but N of the Equator**
HABITAT: **open woodland and cultivated land with trees in sheltered lowlands**
SIZE: **$10\frac{1}{4}$–11 in (26–28 cm)**

The soft, purring *turr-turr* call, from which the Turtle Dove takes its name, is a familiar sound of summer days in Europe. The notes are repeated several times as a territorial advertisement song lasting about 15 seconds. Another call, given in moments of excitement and, perhaps, anger, is a short, explosive popping sound just like the pulling of a cork from a bottle.

Although it is protected through most of its European breeding range, the Turtle Dove is shot and netted in huge numbers for sport and for food while on migration, particularly in countries bordering the Mediterranean. The 2 races illustrated are *S. t. turtur* of Europe, the Canary Islands and Asia Minor and *S. t. rufescens* of Egypt and northern Sudan.

## 8/ LARGE BROWN CUCKOO-DOVE
*Macropygia amboinensis*

RANGE: **E coast of Australia, New Guinea, Indonesia, Philippines**
HABITAT: **rain forest shrubbery and forest edge**
SIZE: **$11\frac{3}{4}$–$17\frac{3}{4}$ in (30–45 cm)**

This bird spends much of its time in the tops of trees or shrubs, making short flights from one perch to another on its rounded wings. Its penetrating, high-pitched *coo* carries well through the dense rain forest vegetation.

Large Brown Cuckoo-Doves feed on a variety of fruits from the forest canopy and understory and are particularly fond of introduced weeds and shrubs on the forest edge. They are agile climbers and can reach berries on thin branches. Sometimes, the birds will pick grit from the ground to aid digestion. Their nest is a platform of twigs and vines built in a low fork, in a vine tangle or on the top of a tree fern. The single white egg is incubated by both sexes.

## 9/ NAMAQUA DOVE
*Oena capensis*

RANGE: **sub-Saharan Africa, Arabia, S Israel**
HABITAT: **open semidesert and arid scrub**
SIZE: **$10\frac{1}{4}$–11 in (26–28 cm)**

Almost half the total length of this small dove is taken up by its extraordinarily long, diamond-shaped tail. Each time the bird lands, the tail is raised and fanned. The male also fans his tail during his courtship display while he indulges in a hovering, butterflylike flight, descending close to the female.

Although they are brightly patterned, Namaqua Doves are difficult to see on the ground, as they blend perfectly with the background of dry soil and stones. The birds walk with a peculiar mincing gait, often appearing rather hunchbacked, as they peck here and there for tiny seeds and the occasional insect.

## 10/ FLOCK BRONZEWING
*Phaps histrionica*

RANGE: **inland N Australia**
HABITAT: **native grassland**
SIZE: **$10\frac{1}{2}$–$11\frac{1}{2}$ in (27–29 cm)**

The Flock Bronzewing, or Flock Pigeon, has long wings that enable it to cover great distances in its search for food and water in a dry environment. Once observed in immense flocks, it has declined severely through the overgrazing of its habitat by domestic livestock.

Flock Bronzewings feed on the ground, foraging for the seeds of grass and other plants. They also pick up the undigested seeds from cattle dung. They rest and feed in the blazing sun and must fly to water holes twice daily, in the morning and evening, to replenish their water reserves. During the breeding period, courting males bow and partly open their wings to show the bronze panels. The loosely colonial nests are grass-lined scrapes under tussocks or bushes. Both sexes incubate the eggs, the male sitting by day and the female by night.

## 11/ SPINIFEX PIGEON
*Petrophassa plumifera*

RANGE: **inland N Australia**
HABITAT: **hummock grassland in arid, rocky terrain**
SIZE: **$7\frac{1}{2}$–9 in (19–23 cm)**

Small flocks of this desert-dwelling bird scurry along the ground, often for long distances, or make short, low flights with bursts of flapping followed by glides. At night, they huddle together to roost on the ground. They feed on the seeds of grasses and other plants of the dry interior of Australia and drink frequently.

Male Spinifex Pigeons perform bowing displays in courtship and rivals fight by chasing, circling and buffeting each other with their wings. The birds may breed throughout the year but do so mostly in spring or after rain has fallen.

## 12/ DIAMOND DOVE
*Geopelia cuneata*

RANGE: **northern and inland Australia; usually absent from coastal E and S**
HABITAT: **dry woodland and scrub**
SIZE: **$7\frac{1}{2}$–$8\frac{3}{4}$ in (19–22 cm)**

The tiny Diamond Dove is widespread across the drier parts of Australia and is seen in the extreme east and south only after irregular coastward movements during dry periods. It feeds on the ground, eating the small seeds of grasses, herbs and other plants, as well as some green vegetation and insects. It walks along slowly when feeding but can also scurry with its tail held clear of the ground. In arid regions, it must drink daily, in the morning and in the afternoon; it wanders nomadically in search of food and water.

In courtship, the male performs a bowing display with his tail raised and fanned. The frail nest of twigs or grass stems is built in a low tree fork and the 2 white eggs are incubated by both male and female.

## 13/ MOURNING DOVE
*Zenaida macroura*

RANGE: **SE Alaska, S Canada to C Panama, Caribbean**
HABITAT: **farms, open woods, towns, gardens**
SIZE: **$11\frac{3}{4}$ in (30 cm)**

This long-tailed sandy dove shows white outer tail feathers in flight. The sexes appear similar but juvenile birds have heavy spotting on their wings. Outside the breeding season, Mourning Doves are generally found in flocks and they roost communally. They are mostly ground feeders, taking a variety of grain and seeds and, occasionally, small invertebrates. The advertising call is a series of 3–4 mournful coos, from which the birds take their common name.

Mourning Doves are widely hunted gamebirds, but their populations remain large. They produce 2 or 3 broods each season and have benefited from the conversion of forests to farmland. In the deep South, for example Mississippi, they begin nesting in February and continue until the end of October, sometimes having as many as 6 nesting attempts in a season.

They are monogamous and have elaborate courtship displays, with the male strutting before the female or chasing her, while puffing his feathers and cooing. The males also perform display flights, with periods of noisy flapping and gliding. They are solitary nesters, building a flimsy platform in shrubs or trees at heights of up to 50 ft (15 m).

## 14/ GALAPAGOS DOVE
*Zenaida galapagoensis*

RANGE: **Galapagos Islands**
HABITAT: **dry, rocky, low-lying areas with some scrub or cactus**
SIZE: **8 in (20 cm)**

Like many Galapagos birds, this dove is very tame. It spends much of its time on the ground, and is an accomplished walker and runner. Although it occasionally eats cactus pulp, it feeds mostly on seeds. It sometimes scratches for food, flicking dirt toward its body. Although usually silent, its occasional calls consist of long, rolling cooing notes.

The male's courtship display includes strutting, tail-spreading, bowing, wing-drooping and feather-puffing. The male and female also run around each other. The simple nest is made of grass and often placed on the ground under a sheltering rock. The birds have also been known to use an old nest of the Galapagos Mockingbird *Nesomimus trifasciatus* for a foundation. Like many other doves, the Galapagos Dove may perform distraction displays to lure intruders away from its nest.

# DOVES AND PIGEONS

COMMON GROUND-DOVE

♂

♀

INCA DOVE

RUDDY QUAIL DOVE

♀

♂

WHITE-TIPPED DOVE

BLUE CROWNED PIGEON

juv

NICOBAR PIGEON

VICTORIA CROWNED PIGEON

PHEASANT PIGEON

TOOTH-BILLED PIGEON

juv

AFRICAN GREEN PIGEON

GREEN IMPERIAL PIGEON

race *magnificus*

race *puella*

WOMPOO FRUIT-DOVE

MADAGASCAR BLUE PIGEON

juv

TOP-KNOT PIGEON

LUZON BLEEDING HEART

NEW ZEALAND PIGEON

# DOVES AND PIGEONS

## 1/ COMMON GROUND-DOVE
*Columbina passerina*
RANGE: **S USA and Caribbean to Ecuador and Brazil; Bahamas**
HABITAT: **open country, roadsides, farms, grassland**
SIZE: **6½ in (16.5 cm)**

Common Ground-Doves are tiny birds, little larger than sparrows. They usually occur in pairs, although they will often gather in flocks in winter. Largely terrestrial, they forage on the ground, bobbing their heads as they walk. Small seeds and berries make up the bulk of their diet, along with the occasional insect. Their usual call is a soft, cooing whistle. When they do fly, their bright chestnut primary wing feathers are apparent. The female is generally duller than the male.

Courtship displays are elaborate, with the male strutting about before the female or chasing her, cooing as he does so and puffing his feathers out. The birds nest mostly on the ground, but will also use bushes, palm fronds, vines and low shrubs. The flimsy cup is made from grasses and plant fibers. The pair sometimes re-use the nest for a second brood and occasionally use the old nest of another species as a platform for their own.

## 2/ INCA DOVE
*Scardafella inca*
RANGE: **locally from SW USA to N Costa Rica**
HABITAT: **towns, open areas, farms, riverside scrub, cactus, mesquite**
SIZE: **8 in (20 cm)**

This tiny dove reveals the rich chestnut color of its primary wing feathers when it takes flight. Its usual call is a series of 2-note coos, but it also utters a variety of soft or throaty display, threat and alarm calls. Inca Doves form flocks in winter and roost communally. On cold nights, they are known to huddle together in groups, with some birds on top of the others forming "pyramids." They are largely terrestrial feeders, foraging mainly for seeds and cultivated grain. As with all pigeons, the young are fed on crop "milk" – a liquid food secreted in the esophagus of the adults.

Inca Doves are monogamous, with an elaborate courtship display in which the male struts, head-bobs, fans his tail and utters cooing notes. They nest in bushes or shady trees, 3–23 ft (1–7 m) above the ground.

## 3/ WHITE-TIPPED DOVE
*Leptotila verreauxi*
RANGE: **S Texas and Mexico S to W Peru, C Argentina and Uruguay; Trinidad and Tobago, Aruba**
HABITAT: **arid to semiarid environments; open woodland, plantations**
SIZE: **11 in (28 cm)**

This solitary, terrestrial dove, also known as the White-fronted Dove, feeds mostly on seeds it finds on the ground, but it also eats some insects. Although often hidden among trees, shrubs or other cover, it emerges into the open to feed. If disturbed, it will frequently fly up to perch in a tree. Its voice has been likened to the sound

produced when a person blows across the top of a narrow-mouthed bottle. White-tipped Doves build a flimsy platform nest of small twigs, in which they lay a clutch of 2 white eggs. Over much of this bird's extensive range, nesting occurs in all months of the year, but breeding is seasonal in some localities.

## 4/ RUDDY QUAIL DOVE
*Geotrygon montana*
RANGE: **Mexico, Central America S to Bolivia and Brazil; Caribbean**
HABITAT: **humid lowland forest**
SIZE: **9 in (23 cm)**

This dove is especially adapted for life in the shadows of tropical forests. Although it appears as a beautifully colored bird in good light, the colors blend into the shadows of the forest floor, allowing the Ruddy Quail Dove to remain undetected from only a few yards away. Its diet includes seeds and small fruit found on the forest floor. The repetitive call is a deep, booming *coo*.

The flimsy twig nest is lined with leaves and placed on a stump, a low branch, or a tangle of vegetation less than 6 ft (2 m) above the forest floor. The parents share the incubation duties, with the incoming parent often bringing a leaf to add to the nest.

## 5/ NICOBAR PIGEON
*Caloenas nicobarica*
RANGE: **Nicobar and Andaman islands, E through Indonesia and the Philippines to New Guinea and the Solomon Islands**
HABITAT: **forested islands**
SIZE: **13 in (33 cm)**

The Nicobar Pigeon is a ground pigeon, with a knob on its bill, a cape of long, hacklelike plumes and a white tail. It occurs only on small islands over its extensive range. This is perhaps because competitors or predators exclude the species from breeding on large islands and continental areas. It has declined markedly in abundance through heavy hunting pressure and clearance of habitat.

The Nicobar Pigeon forages alone on the

ground for fallen fruits, seeds and nuts. It can even eat hard nuts that humans can open only with a hammer. This is made possible by the bird's muscular gizzard. Nicobar Pigeons commute in large flocks between their foraging and breeding islands.

## 6/ LUZON BLEEDING HEART
*Gallicolumba luzonica*
RANGE: **Luzon and Polillo islands (Philippines)**
HABITAT: **forests**
SIZE: **11–12 in (28–30 cm)**

Of all the 5 species of bleeding heart dove, this bird most lives up to its name. The bright red oval patch on its breast forms a groove between surrounding pink "blood-stained" feathers and has misled many people into believing the bird is seriously injured. It is an important element in the bird's courtship displays.

Although it lives exclusively in forests, the Luzon Bleeding Heart obtains all its food on the ground, where it forages for fallen seeds and berries. Unusually for a bird in the pigeon family, it also takes some grubs and other invertebrates. When danger threatens, it usually flies only a short distance before it lands and scuttles off into thick vegetation.

## 7/ PHEASANT PIGEON
*Otidiphaps nobilis*
RANGE: **New Guinea and offshore islands, Aru Islands**
HABITAT: **foothill and mountain rain forest**
SIZE: **18 in (46 cm)**

The Pheasant Pigeon is a large, fowl-like, ground-dwelling pigeon. In many respects, it resembles a megapode (pp. 110–13) rather than other pigeons. It keeps to the undergrowth, walking with its bantamlike tail pumping up and down, but it can run fast and will fly heavily and noisily to escape danger. It feeds on fallen fruits, berries, seeds, insects and mollusks.

In courtship, the male performs a bowing display with his tail raised and gives a loud, growling call. The female responds by preening his head. The nest of sticks is placed in a tree, in the undergrowth or on the ground between the buttressed roots of a tree. The male supplies the material for the nest and the female works it into a platform. Both parents incubate the single white egg and rear the young.

## 8/ VICTORIA CROWNED PIGEON
*Goura victoria* [?]
RANGE: N New Guinea, Biak and Yapen islands
HABITAT: lowland rain forest
SIZE: 26 in (66 cm)

There are 3 species of crowned pigeon in New Guinea: the Victoria Crowned Pigeon, the Blue Crowned Pigeon *G. cristata* and the Maroon-breasted Crowned Pigeon *G. scheepmakeri*. They are the world's largest pigeons, but have sadly declined in abundance as a result of heavy hunting pressure.

Victoria Crowned Pigeons forage on the ground in small flocks, searching for fallen fruit, berries and seeds. If disturbed, they fly off noisily to perch on a tree branch. A male defends his territory by opening one wing, ready to strike buffeting blows on any intruder, while fanning and tilting his tail. In courtship he performs a bowing display, nodding his lowered head and fanning his tail up and down while giving a booming call. Male and female then preen each other.

## 9/ TOOTH-BILLED PIGEON
*Didunculus strigirostris* [V]
RANGE: Upolu and Savaii islands (Samoa)
HABITAT: wooded mountainsides at altitudes of 1,000–4,500 ft (300–1,400 m)
SIZE: 13 in (33 cm)

The massive hooked bill of this pigeon is reminiscent of the bill of that symbol of extinction the Dodo *Raphus cucullatus*, which was a distant relative. It is itself now vulnerable, having significantly declined since its discovery in 1845, through persecution by people and also through the introduction of cats, rats and, especially, pigs to its island homes. Its total world population is estimated at between 5,000 and 7,000 individuals.

Formerly believed to be strictly a ground feeder, the Tooth-billed Pigeon has recently been found to feed frequently on fruits in trees. It can fly strongly and roosts in trees. It probably also breeds in trees, although no nest has been found.

## 10/ AFRICAN GREEN PIGEON
*Treron calva*
RANGE: sub-Saharan Africa
HABITAT: forests, riverine woods, savanna
SIZE: 11 in (28 cm)

The overall dark olive-green plumage of this small pigeon provides perfect camouflage in its typical forest habitat. A feeding flock moving through the foliage will freeze on the approach of danger and become almost impossible to spot until it starts to move again. This is an agile species, capable of climbing through foliage and clinging to twigs in its search for fruit and seeds. It can even hang upside-down while feeding.

There are some 18 races of this species. Plumage color varies from darker green in more forested areas to a paler, yellowish green in drier regions. The race illustrated, *T. c. calva*, occurs in Guinea, northern Angola and western Congo.

## 11/ WOMPOO FRUIT-DOVE
*Ptilinopus magnificus*
RANGE: E coast of Australia, from Cape York to N New South Wales, lowland New Guinea
HABITAT: rain forest
SIZE: 13¾–17¾ in (35–45 cm)

Despite its striking and beautiful coloration (it is also known as the Magnificent Fruit-Dove), this pigeon is difficult to locate in the forest canopy, unless it calls with the deep double coo that gives it its common name. It has declined in abundance in the south of its range through habitat destruction, and has also suffered from heavy hunting.

Wompoo Fruit-Doves feed in the canopy, eating a variety of fruits. They clamber about in the foliage and often reveal their presence by the sound of falling fruit. They make seasonal movements in search of food, mostly keeping to rain forest canopy. Their frail stick nests are built on leafy branches and they lay a single white egg.

No other pigeons – indeed, few birds – show such a great difference in size between races as this species. The race *P. m. puella* from New Guinea is one of the smallest – scarcely larger than a Turtle Dove *Streptopelia turtur* – while the race *P. m. magnificus* from southeastern Australia is the size of a Wood Pigeon *Columba palumbus*.

## 12/ MADAGASCAR BLUE PIGEON
*Alectroenas madagascariensis*
RANGE: Madagascar
HABITAT: evergreen forest
SIZE: 10¼ in (26 cm)

Parties of up to 12 or more of these pigeons move through the forests of Madagascar, keeping mainly to the treetops and feeding exclusively on fruit. They would be extremely difficult to see at all, if it were not for their habit of perching on dead trees projecting above the level of the forest canopy or, occasionally, on the forest edge. These birds are thought to undertake migratory movements within Madagascar, possibly related to dry and wet seasons, but the details are not clear.

Few, if any, nests of this species have been found. However, judging by the spread of dates when adults in breeding condition and juvenile birds have been collected, the breeding season is a prolonged one, lasting at least from July to March.

## 13/ GREEN IMPERIAL PIGEON
*Ducula aenea*
RANGE: India, Southeast Asia, Philippines, Indonesia, New Guinea
HABITAT: evergreen forest, mangrove swamps; also more open country with scattered woods
SIZE: 17–18 in (43–46 cm)

The principal food of this large, handsome pigeon is soft fruits, often those varieties containing hard stones. This species does not have the muscular

gizzard for grinding up hard objects and the long gut of most members of its family. Instead, it has a relatively soft stomach and short, wide gut, through which the fruit stones pass intact. The seed within is able to germinate and form new trees in the course of time.

Flocks of Green Imperial Pigeons forage through forest trees, searching for any that are in fruit. They return each night to communal roosts. If the day's food tree is not exhausted, they will return to it the next day until they have eaten the entire crop.

## 14/ TOP-KNOT PIGEON
*Lopholaimus antarcticus*
RANGE: E coast of Australia
HABITAT: rain forest
SIZE: 16½–17¾ in (42–45 cm)

The Top-knot Pigeon is named for the remarkable double crest it sports on its head. It feeds on a variety of rain forest fruits, including those of palms, and has taken readily to the introduced Camphor Laurel planted in towns and farmland. This large pigeon feeds only in the tree canopy, where it scrambles about among the foliage. Although still seen in large flocks, it has declined in abundance through habitat destruction. Its flocks fly strongly and purposefully on long, pointed wings, either above the canopy or over open country. They are nomadic birds, making long seasonal movements in search of food.

In the breeding season, the male Top-knot Pigeon performs a unique bowing display, quite unlike that of other pigeons. He erects his crest and presses his bill on his breast, his body held erect. Then he makes a deep bow, uttering a squeak at its lowest point before raising his body again. The nest is a platform of sticks built high in the outer branches of a tree, and the single white egg is incubated by both sexes.

## 15/ NEW ZEALAND PIGEON
*Hemiphaga novaeseelandiae*
RANGE: New Zealand
HABITAT: forests; also woodland patches in farmland
SIZE: 20 in (51 cm)

This is a large, colorful pigeon, with back and neck plumage that may appear gray, bronze-purple or green, depending on the light. It is a heavy bird that lands noisily in trees and crashes about while feeding. It eats a range of fruits, flowers and green vegetation, including leaves and grass. It tends to perch quietly when people approach, often allowing them to come within 3–6 ft (1–2 m).

In spring, the New Zealand Pigeon regularly performs a flight display, involving loops and stalls. Breeding takes place predominantly in summer. The nest is an open bowl of interlacing twigs, placed in the forest canopy or at a branching point well off the ground. The large Chatham Island race *H. n. chathamensis* of this species is currently endangered, with a population of no more than about 50 birds.

# KEA, KAKAPO, VULTURINE PARROT, COCKATOOS, LORIES AND LORIKEETS

KEA

KAKAPO

GALAH

♂

SULFUR-CRESTED
COCKATOO

♂

race *weberi*

RED LORY

race *moluccanus*

race *somu*

race *rubritorquis*

race *haematodus*

race *lory*

RAINBOW LORIKEET

BLACK-CAPPED LORY

VULTURINE PARROT

♀ RED-TAILED
BLACK COCKATOO

♂

PALM COCKATOO

BUFF-FACED
PYGMY PARROT

♂

race *insignis*
"Rajah Lory"

♂ ♀

BLACK LORY

COCKATIEL

race *atra*

COLLARED LORY

PURPLE-CROWNED LORIKEET

# KEA, KAKAPO, VULTURINE PARROT, COCKATOOS, LORIES AND LORIKEETS

## FAMILY PSITTACIDAE
## Parrots

Small to large fruit, seed and nectar-eaters. Tree, shrub and ground-dwellers. Distinctive, down-curved, hooked bills. Contains several distinct subgroups, including the lories and lorikeets, which feed on pollen and nectar using brush-tipped tongues; the cockatoos, with their movable crests and narrow, stubby tongues; and the typical parrots and parakeets, which have broad, fleshy tongues with spoon-shaped tips. Plumage very variable: mostly greenish, but some brilliantly colored. Sexes generally similar. Nest typically in tree cavities. Eggs 1–8, white. Incubation 17–35 days, nestling period 21–70 days. 340 species.

## 1/ KEA
### Nestor notabilis
RANGE: **South Island (New Zealand)**
HABITAT: **mountain forest and ridges often above snow line; coastal forest in winter**
SIZE: **18 in (46 cm)**

Of the 6 parrot species native to New Zealand, the Kea, its close relative the Kaka *N. meridionalis*, and the Kakapo are all very unusual. The Kea uses its elongated upper bill (longer in the male) to tear into carrion, fruit, leaves and insects. It has been accused of killing sheep, and many Keas have been shot, but the accusations are probably unfounded, and it is now protected by law.

The Kea's name reflects its call, which is unforgettable when heard echoing among the mist-veiled mountain tops. The male is polygamous and will often breed with several females at the same time. The nests are built on the ground, on rock ledges or in hollow logs.

## 2/ KAKAPO
### Strigops habroptilus      E
RANGE: **New Zealand, originally widespread, now reduced to 2 introduced populations on Little Barrier Island and Codfish Island**
HABITAT: **forest and scrub; may depend on fruiting yellow-wood trees for breeding**
SIZE: **24¾ in (63 cm)**

The Kakapo is quite unlike other parrots, for it is a nocturnal, ground-dwelling bird that is the only parrot to have become completely flightless. It is the heaviest of all parrots. The Kakapo evolved at a time when there were no ground predators to attack it or devour its eggs; the introduction of stoats, rats and other predators by European settlers proved disastrous, and it has now virtually disappeared from the mainland. The last breeding population on Stewart Island declined dramatically in recent years, and in the mid-1980s nearly all the remaining birds were transferred to predator-free Codfish Island.

Another unique feature of the Kakapo is its mating system. Normally solitary, the males gather at traditional mating grounds, or "leks," in late summer and advertise for mates with loud booming calls which may be heard over ½ ml (1 km) away. The females visit the leks and mate with the males of their choice. The nest is built in a burrow or among dense vegetation, and the female incubates and rears the 1–2 chicks alone.

## 3/ VULTURINE PARROT
### Gypopsitta vulturina
RANGE: **NE Brazil**
HABITAT: **dry and periodically flooded forest**
SIZE: **9 in (23 cm)**

This odd-looking parrot owes its name to its distinctive bare forehead. It is possible that, as in vultures, this enables the bird to feed without matting its head plumage – except that in the parrot's case the food is fruit pulp and not bloody carcasses. There is another parrot sometimes called the Vulturine Parrot, but better known as Pesquet's Parrot *Psittrichas fulgidus*, from New Guinea, that also feeds on soft fruit and has a similarly bare forehead.

The Vulturine Parrot is an inconspicuous bird, normally seen feeding quietly on fruits, seeds and berries in the upper forest canopy. The details of its way of life and nesting habits are still unknown and may remain so, for it is rapidly declining as its native forests fall to the chainsaw.

## 4/ PALM COCKATOO
### Probosciger aterrimus
RANGE: **New Guinea, including some smaller islands, NE Australia**
HABITAT: **edges of rain forest bordering on savanna, in lowlands up to 2,500 ft (750 m)**
SIZE: **19½–24¾ in (50–63 cm)**

This magnificent bird with its splendid crest is the largest of all cockatoos and the largest Australian parrot. It is also notable for its dramatic displays, given as pairs establish their territories before the beginning of the breeding season, which ranges from August to February. The male – slightly larger than the female – grips a stick with his foot and pounds a tree trunk to produce a loud drumming. As with all parrots, the bird's feet have 2 forward-pointing and 2 backward-pointing toes, which give it a strong, dexterous grip.

The nest is built in a steeply sloping tree cavity, usually in open woodland on the edge of the rain forest, and the female incubates the single egg alone. The pair may use the same cavity for several years in succession. Outside the breeding season the birds often forage in small groups.

Although not yet endangered, the Palm Cockatoo is threatened by the illegal cage-bird trade, by hunting and by destruction of its habitat.

## 5/ RED-TAILED BLACK COCKATOO
### Calyptorhynchus magnificus
RANGE: **N and W Australia, with isolated inland populations**
HABITAT: **scrub, open woods, river forest**
SIZE: **19½–24 in (50–61 cm)**

Like the 2 other species of black cockatoo, this species is a seed-eater. A feeding group of Red-tailed Black Cockatoos will often make themselves obvious by audibly snapping their bills as they split nuts to eat the seeds and scatter the husks on the ground beneath the trees. In savanna they forage in large nomadic flocks of up to 100 birds, but in forested country they tend to be less gregarious, often occurring in pairs or small family groups. In some parts of their range, the species has declined since forestry work has resulted in a scarcity of nest-hollows. The distinctive helmetlike crest of both sexes is raised when they are landing and when they are alarmed or excited.

## 6/ GALAH
### Eolophus roseicapillus
RANGE: **most of Australia**
HABITAT: **eucalyptus woodland, watercourse vegetation and grassland**
SIZE: **13¾ in (35 cm)**

This is the most common cockatoo – indeed, one of the most common of all parrots – in Australia. It is one of the few species to have benefited from the European settlement, having increased its range and numbers in response to forest clearance, crop planting and the provision of water points. It is considered a pest by cereal growers, for it takes grain as well as grass seeds, fruits, green shoots and insects. The Galah is sometimes known as the Roseate Cockatoo.

The nest is usually in a vertical tree hollow, though holes in cliffs are sometimes used. The pairs bond for life and defend the nest-hollow against intruders. Both male and female share the incubation and feeding of the 2–6 young. The newly fledged birds gather into treetop nurseries of up to 100 birds, which eagerly await the return of their parents with food. After 6–8 weeks, the young are left to fend for themselves while their parents go away to molt. Young Galahs spend their first 2 or 3 years among large wandering flocks of nonbreeding birds.

## 7/ SULFUR-CRESTED COCKATOO
*Cacatua galerita*
RANGE: **Melanesia, New Guinea, N and E Australia**
HABITAT: **lowland forest, savanna and partly cleared land up to 5,000 ft (1,500 m)**
SIZE: **15–19½ in (38–50 cm)**

Common throughout most of its range, this handsome, noisy parrot often associates in large flocks outside the breeding season, descending on grasses, shrubs and trees to feed on seeds, fruits, palm hearts and insects. It can even be seen in urban areas. It is an occasional pest in crops and is sometimes shot for this reason. Sulfur-crested Cockatoos also suffer as a result of hunting in New Guinea. While the flock is feeding on the ground, a few birds stand sentinel in nearby trees and warn of danger with loud, raucous cries. At dusk the flock returns to a habitual roost.

During the breeding season the flocks break up. Breeding pairs nest in vertical cavities in eucalyptus trees, usually near water, and both parents incubate the 2–3 eggs.

## 8/ COCKATIEL
*Nymphicus hollandicus*
RANGE: **Australia, throughout interior**
HABITAT: **open scrub, woods, near water**
SIZE: **12½ in (32 cm)**

This slender cockatoo, which is sometimes called the Quarrion, usually forages for fruits and seeds in pairs or small groups, but occasionally these groups gather into great flocks that can cause extensive damage to crops, especially sunflower, sorghum and millet. Northern birds are nomadic, but in the south they are seasonal migrants.

Both sexes are crested, but the male's facial markings are brighter. They usually breed after rainfall, at any time of year. The 5 eggs are laid on a bed of wood-dust in any suitable tree cavity close to water and are incubated by both birds.

## 9/ BUFF-FACED PYGMY PARROT
*Micropsitta pusio*
RANGE: **N and E New Guinea lowlands and offshore islands, Bismarck Archipelago**
HABITAT: **lowland forest, regrowth and remnant trees**
SIZE: **3 in (8 cm)**

One of 6 very similar pygmy parrots found on New Guinea and neighboring islands, the Buff-faced Pygmy Parrot is a tiny bird, with short, stiff, spiny tail feathers like those of woodpeckers

(pp. 214–21). The stiffened feathers are used for the same purpose – to support the parrot as it forages for food on tree trunks.

It is exceptional among birds in feeding on lichen and fungi, but it will also eat fruits, seeds and insects, picking them out of the bark as it works its way smoothly and acrobatically over the trunk and branches. The birds travel in groups and roost together in holes made in the nests of tree-dwelling termites. The nest-holes, too, are excavated in termites' nests that are still occupied by the insects.

## 10/ BLACK LORY
*Chalcopsitta atra*
RANGE: **W New Guinea and adjacent islands**
HABITAT: **forest edge, groups of trees in savanna, coastal plantations**
SIZE: **11¾ in (30 cm)**

The Black Lory is a medium-sized parrot with a long, rounded tail. The northwestern race *C. a. atra*, which is all black except for a purple rump, is typical of western races, whereas the eastern race *C. a. insignis*, which is sometimes known as the Rajah Lory, has red markings on the face, under the wings and on the belly.

Large flocks of Black Lories have been seen foraging along the forest edges and descending upon coconut palms and flowering trees in clearings, calling with shrill screeches that sound as if they are made by much smaller birds. Details of their lifestyle are obscure

## 11/ RED LORY
*Eos bornea*
RANGE: **Moluccas**
HABITAT: **coastal and mountain forest up to 4,000 ft (1,250 m), mangroves**
SIZE: **12¼ in (31 cm)**

On moonlit nights, flocks of 20 or more Red Lories will often fly to and fro over the coastal forests of Seram, screeching loudly. At rich feeding sites, such as flowering *Eugenia* trees, many more will gather to feast on the nectar, mopping it up with the brush-tipped tongues typical of lories and lorikeets. They also eat pollen and small insects.

These birds appear to nest in cavities high up in mature trees. From the successful breeding of a pair of Red Lories in captivity, 2 eggs were produced, and the young birds left the nest at 7 and 9 weeks after hatching. They had still not acquired the adult plumage at 7 months.

## 12/ RAINBOW LORIKEET
*Trichoglossus haematodus*
RANGE: **SW Pacific including Indonesia, New Guinea, N and E Australia**
HABITAT: **rain forest, eucalyptus forest and coconut groves up to 6,500 ft (2,000 m)**
SIZE: **11–12½ in (28–32 cm)**

This is one of the most widespread, spectacular and variable of the lories, with 21 races scattered over the southwest Pacific. The illustration shows *T. h. weberi* of Flores Island, *T. h. haematodus* of the southern Moluccas and western New Guinea, *T. h. moluccanus* of eastern Australia and Tas-

mania and *T. h. rubritorquis* of northern Australia.

Rainbow Lorikeets normally feed in the upper canopy in screeching, chattering flocks of 5–20 birds, eating fruits, insects, pollen and nectar; they are important pollinators of coconut flowers. They spend the night in great communal roosts, sometimes with several thousand birds.

## 13/ BLACK-CAPPED LORY
*Lorius lory*
RANGE: **lowland New Guinea and offshore islands**
HABITAT: **undisturbed rain forest, swamp forest**
SIZE: **11 in (28 cm)**

This stocky, rather shy bird has a ringing, melodious cry, quite unlike the usual screeching of parrots. It is usually seen in pairs or small groups flying just above the treetops, but larger flocks gather at flowering or fruiting trees where they feed on nectar, pollen, flowers, fruit and insects.

During the courtship display, the perching male faces his mate in an upright posture with his wings open and head turned to one side, and bobs his body up and down. The 1–2 white eggs are incubated by the female – though the male roosts in the nest at night – and take 24 days to hatch.

There are 7 races, including *L. l. lory*, from northwestern New Guinea and nearby islands, and *L. l. somu*, from southern New Guinea.

## 14/ COLLARED LORY
*Phigys solitarius*
RANGE: **Fiji Islands**
HABITAT: **rain forest, disturbed forest, plantations, coconut palms, urban trees**
SIZE: **8 in (20 cm)**

Feeding flocks of these small lories often congregate around coconut palms, landing on the fronds and working their way down to the nectar-rich flowers in short, fluttering leaps, displacing other birds, such as honeyeaters, which may already be feeding. The nest is sometimes made in a rotting coconut still on the tree, but usually the birds make use of a cavity in a tree trunk or stump. The 2 young are fed by both parents for about 8 weeks.

## 15/ PURPLE-CROWNED LORIKEET
*Glossopsitta porphyrocephala*
RANGE: **SW and S Australia (not Tasmania)**
HABITAT: **dry open woods, mallee scrub**
SIZE: **6¼ in (16 cm)**

Small nomadic flocks of Purple-crowned Lorikeets are a common sight in dry eucalyptus woodland from December to August, outside the breeding season. The flocks visit flowering and fruiting trees to feed on fruits; they also harvest pollen and nectar from the blossoms, using comb-like fringes on their tongues. Rich food sources will attract many flocks which feed together, but they split up again to move on.

The nests of Purple-crowned Lorikeets are usually in unlined hollows in eucalyptus trees, with knot-hole entrances, often in loose colonies. Both birds may roost in the hollow, but only the female incubates the 2–3 eggs.

JOSEPHINE'S LORY

WHISKERED LORIKEET

race marshalli

race coxeni

DOUBLE-EYED FIG PARROT

ECLECTUS PARROT

AUSTRALIAN
KING PARROT

imm

BUDGERIGAR

SWIFT PARROT

RED-CHEEKED
PARROT
♀

♂

imm

imm

race *platenae*

♂

race *discurus*

♀

BLUE-CROWNED RACKET-TAILED PARROT

RED-FRONTED PARAKEET

CRIMSON ROSELLA

VASA PARROT

GRAY PARROT

NIGHT PARROT

# LORIES AND LORIKEETS, PARROTS AND PARAKEETS

## 1/ JOSEPHINE'S LORY
*Charmosyna josefinae*
RANGE: W and C New Guinea
HABITAT: mountain forest, at
2,500–6,500 ft (800–2,000 m)
SIZE: 9½ in (24 cm)

This slender, long-tailed parrot is quiet and unobtrusive in its habits and easily overlooked as it forages through the forest canopy in the mountains of New Guinea. It flies in pairs or small groups, sometimes with Fairy Lorikeets *C. pulchella*, landing to gather pollen and nectar from tree blossom, or climbing slowly through the tendrils of a clinging vine to feed at the large white flowers. Occasionally it gives a soft squeaking call, but most of the time it searches in silence.

## 2/ WHISKERED LORIKEET
*Oreopsittacus arfaki*
RANGE: W, C and NE New Guinea
HABITAT: mountain forest, at
6,500–12,300 ft (2,000–3,750 m)
SIZE: 6 in (15 cm)

Rarely seen beyond the mist forests of the New Guinea mountains, this slim, active bird, which is also known as the Plum-faced Lorikeet, often forages in small, mixed flocks in the company of flowerpeckers, honeyeaters and other lorikeets. Gathering in flowering trees, the birds search busily among the foliage for nectar, pollen, fruits and flowers, clambering out onto the thin outer twigs and often hanging upside-down to reach tempting blossoms.

In display the male struts back and forth along a branch, calling excitedly, then bobs and thrusts his head toward the female. Details of the nest and eggs are unknown.

## 3/ DOUBLE-EYED FIG PARROT
*Opopsitta diophthalma*
RANGE: New Guinea, W Papuan islands and NE Australia
HABITAT: subtropical and tropical rain forest up to 5,300 ft (1,600 m)
SIZE: 6 in (15 cm)

A rain of chewed debris drifting down from a fig tree will often betray a party of Double-eyed Fig Parrots feeding high in the canopy. True to their name, these small green parrots feed mainly on the seeds of figs, although they also eat other fruits, as well as nectar and insects. They feed quietly, but the parties often call noisily when moving between the trees, or home to their communal roosts at night.

The males are more colorful than the females and their head color varies among the 8 races. Of these, *O. d. coxeni* from southeast Queensland and northeast New South Wales is now threatened as a result of habitat loss. Other races include *O. d. marshalli* from the Cape York Peninsula in northern Queensland.

Both sexes prepare the nest, excavating a short tunnel in soft timber, usually near the rain forest edge. There are 2 eggs.

## 4/ RED-CHEEKED PARROT
*Geoffroyus geoffroyi*
RANGE: Lesser Sundas, Moluccas, New Guinea, NE Australia
HABITAT: wide range of lowland forest, including secondary forest, rain forest, mangroves, savanna, up to 2,500 ft (800 m)
SIZE: 7¾–9¾ in (20–25 cm)

Red-cheeked Parrots are more often heard than seen as they feed on fruits, seeds, nectar and flower buds in the upper forest canopy. They usually forage in pairs or groups of up to 30, but sometimes gather in great feeding aggregations around rich food sources such as concentrations of fruiting trees. After feeding all day, the big flock splits up into smaller groups which spend the night in communal roosts.

Both the male, with his brightly coloured face and bill, and the duller female are involved in drilling the nest-hole in a dead tree at the forest edge, but the female incubates the 2–4 eggs alone.

## 5/ BLUE-CROWNED RACKET-TAILED PARROT
*Prioniturus discurus*
RANGE: Philippines, Jolo Island (Sulus)
HABITAT: forests, clearings, banana groves
SIZE: 10½ in (27 cm)

The 9 species of racket-tailed parrot owe their name to their curious, elongated central tail feathers, which extend into bare shafts with disk-shaped "rackets" on the ends. These appear on both sexes as they mature, but those of the female are shorter than the male's.

The Blue-crowned Racket-tailed Parrot is widely distributed through the Philippines, with 5 races showing color variations. The most distinctive are the widespread race *P. d. discurus*, which is largely green with a blue crown, and *P. d. platenae* found on Palawan and its adjacent islands, which has a completely blue head and blue-green underparts.

These birds are most commonly seen in undisturbed forest, flying high above the canopy in small, noisy flocks. Uttering shrill screeches, the whole flock will descend to strip a fruiting tree, and in newly cleared land near forest they can cause considerable damage in banana plantations as they feed on the green maturing fruit. They often forage in the company of cockatoos, Bald Starlings *Sarcops calvus* and pigeons, eating fruits, nuts and seeds. Their breeding behavior has not been studied, but they appear to nest colonially in tall dead trees.

## 6/ ECLECTUS PARROT
*Eclectus roratus*
RANGE: Lesser Sundas, Solomon Islands, New Guinea, NE Australia
HABITAT: lowland rain forest and dense savanna up to 3,300 ft (1,000 m)
SIZE: 15–17¾ in (38–45 cm)

Plumage differences between the sexes are not unusual among parrots, but few differ so dramatically as the male and female Eclectus Parrot. Both are glossy, brilliant birds, but whereas the male is bright green with blue and red patches, the female is crimson with a blue belly. When they are feeding among the green foliage, this makes her more conspicuous than her mate, something which is unique among parrots.

Calling loudly, pairs or small parties travel widely through the upper canopy in search of fruits, nuts, nectar and leaf buds. In the evening they engage in display flights before gathering in large groups of up to 80 birds to roost for the night. The nest is built in a large vertical hollow in a rain forest tree near a stream. It is possible that the birds breed communally, with other adults helping the pair rear their brood of 2 chicks.

## 7/ AUSTRALIAN KING PARROT
*Alisterus scapularis*

RANGE: **E Australia except Tasmania**
HABITAT: **dense forest; visits open woodland and parkland outside breeding season**
SIZE: **17 in (43 cm)**

Although vividly colored, the Australian King Parrot is a subdued bird compared to other parrots. It tends to feed quietly and unobtrusively in the forest canopy, taking tree seeds – especially those of eucalyptus and acacias – as well as fruits, nuts and nectar. When the family groups disperse after breeding, the immature birds often gather into large flocks and cause severe damage to orchard crops.

Males and females are dramatically different in appearance, the males having brilliant scarlet plumage, whereas females are largely green. They breed in dense forest, frequently nesting in trees with very deep cavities; the entrance may be over 33 ft (10 m) up the tree, but the 3–6 eggs are often laid close to ground level.

## 8/ CRIMSON ROSELLA
*Platycercus elegans*

RANGE: **E Australia except Tasmania**
HABITAT: **eucalyptus forest, woods and gardens up to 6,000 ft (1,900 m); in N restricted to mountain forests above 1,500 ft (450 m)**
SIZE: **14 in (36 cm)**

There are 2 very closely related rosellas – the Yellow Rosella *P. flaveolus* and the Adelaide Rosella *P. adelaidae* – which are considered by some ornithologists to belong to the same species as the Crimson Rosella. However, their coloration is so different that they are frequently classified as separate species. The Crimson Rosella is the most striking, both sexes having the same rich red and blue plumage; in immature birds much of the red is replaced by green.

The adults occur in pairs or small groups and stay in the same area throughout the year, but the immature birds are nomadic, wandering in flocks of up to 30. They feed mainly on the seeds of grasses, shrubs and trees such as eucalyptus and acacias, but will also eat fruits, nectar and insects. They nest in tree cavities.

## 9/ RED-FRONTED PARAKEET
*Cyanoramphus novaezelandiae*

RANGE: **New Zealand, New Caledonia**
HABITAT: **mature forest, tall scrub on treeless islands**
SIZE: **9¾–11 in (25–28 cm)**

Once widespread in New Zealand and nearby islands, this long-tailed parrot has declined to the point where 2 island races are now extinct and another is likely to follow them. Fortunately it breeds well in captivity, and captive-bred birds have been released at various island and mainland sites. This species is also known as the Red-crowned Parakeet.

It eats a variety of fruits, seeds, flowers, leaves and buds, working its way through the lower and middle branches of trees and often coming down to ground level to feed on any fallen items as well as grass shoots. The pair breeds in a cavity such as a rock crevice, a tree hole, a burrow or a hole at the base of a grass tussock. The female alone incubates the eggs, but the male helps feed the 5–9 young.

## 10/ SWIFT PARROT
*Lathamus discolor*

RANGE: **breeds Tasmania; winters SE Australia**
HABITAT: **eucalyptus woodland, parkland**
SIZE: **9¾ in (25 cm)**

The Swift Parrot is named for its fast, direct flight, a valuable asset to a bird which migrates long distances each year. It breeds only in Tasmania and the adjacent islands, crossing the 125 ml (200 km) Bass Strait in March to spend the southern winter on the Australian mainland.

It usually forages in small parties, which gather into large flocks for migration and to take advantage of particularly rich food sources. The birds feed in the canopy on nectar, pollen, fruit, seeds and insects.

In Tasmania the pairs often breed in loose colonies, each nesting in an unlined tree cavity high above the ground. As with most parrots, the female alone incubates the 3–5 eggs.

## 11/ BUDGERIGAR
*Melopsittacus undulatus*

RANGE: **throughout inland Australia**
HABITAT: **tussock grassland, arid and semiarid scrub and woodland close to water**
SIZE: **6½ in (17 cm)**

This small parrot is best known as a solitary cage bird, but in the wild it is a gregarious, wide-ranging nomad which often travels in large flocks. The flocks occur throughout the year in the Australian heartland, but their size varies with the food supply; in years of relatively high rainfall and abundant food the Budgerigar is one of the most numerous of all Australian parrots. Wild birds are always green.

Budgerigars are agile, swift-flying birds, and the flocks rarely stay in one place for long. They feed mainly in the early morning and late afternoon, avoiding the hottest part of the day, and spend much of their time collecting seeds from ground vegetation including grasses and weeds.

They breed at any time of year when food is abundant, usually after rains. The pairs nest in colonies, using small tree cavities such as eucalyptus knot-holes, and may raise several broods each season.

## 12/ NIGHT PARROT
*Geopsittacus occidentalis*    Ⅰ

RANGE: **arid and semiarid regions of central Australia**
HABITAT: **low succulent vegetation bordering salt lakes; tussock grasses when in seed**
SIZE: **9 in (23 cm)**

For many years the Night Parrot was thought to be extinct, but recent sightings show that it still exists, albeit in very reduced numbers. Its decline has probably been accelerated by overgrazing of its habitat by sheep and rabbits and by its vulnerability, as a ground-nester, to predators such as foxes and cats.

Rarely seen, it remains a mystery in many respects. It may be nocturnal, as its name implies, but there is little evidence for this. It spends most of its time on the ground, feeding singly or in pairs on the seeds of grasses and shrubs.

The 2–4 eggs are laid on a rough stick platform placed under spinifex tussocks or low shrubs and reached by a tunnel through the foliage.

## 13/ VASA PARROT
*Coracopsis vasa*

RANGE: **Madagascar, Comoro Islands**
HABITAT: **forest and savanna below 3,300 ft (1,000 m)**
SIZE: **19½ in (50 cm)**

These noisy, conspicuous parrots are usually seen in small flocks, although larger groups may gather at favorite feeding or roosting sites. They feed on fruits, nuts, berries and seeds up in the treetops and are fond of resting on the branches of dead trees. Their flight, often high above the forest canopy, is distinctive and rather crowlike, with slow, flapping wing beats. Little is known of the species' breeding habits, although it is thought that the breeding season lasts from at least October to December, and the birds nest in sites such as the hollow limbs of trees.

Like its only close relative, the Black Parrot *C. nigra* of Madagascar, the Comoro Islands and Praslin Island in the Seychelles, the Vasa Parrot is hunted for food; habitat destruction is an even greater threat to these birds.

## 14/ GRAY PARROT
*Psittacus erithacus*

RANGE: **C Africa, Sierra Leone E to Kenya and NW Tanzania**
HABITAT: **lowland forest, wooded savanna, mangroves**
SIZE: **13 in (33 cm)**

In eastern Gabon vast flocks of over 5,000 Gray Parrots gather at traditional roosting sites each night, perching on the fronds of oil palms. Elsewhere the roosts are smaller, but it is common to find more than 100 birds in a single tree. In the morning they leave in small groups, often following regular routes, to feed in the rain forest or feast on palm nuts in plantations. On their return in the evening, they call with loud, rhythmic whistles and raucous shrieks before settling down.

They breed in loose colonies, each pair occupying its own tree. The 2–4 eggs are laid in a cavity and incubated by the female, but the chicks are fed by both birds.

The Gray Parrot is renowned the world over as a cage bird and has remarkable powers of vocal mimicry. There is evidence of a reduction in numbers due to trapping near towns, but in many places this is an abundant species, with regular roosts of 5,000–10,000 birds occurring in 2 places in Gabon.

# PARROTS AND PARAKEETS, MACAWS, HANGING PARROTS

PEACH-FACED LOVEBIRD

♂

HYACINTH MACAW

ROSE-RINGED PARAKEET

race *luchsi*

SUN CONURE

MONK PARAKEET

race *monachus*

♀

race *ochrocephala*

race *tresmariae*

♂

YELLOW-CROWNED AMAZON

SPECTACLED PARROTLET

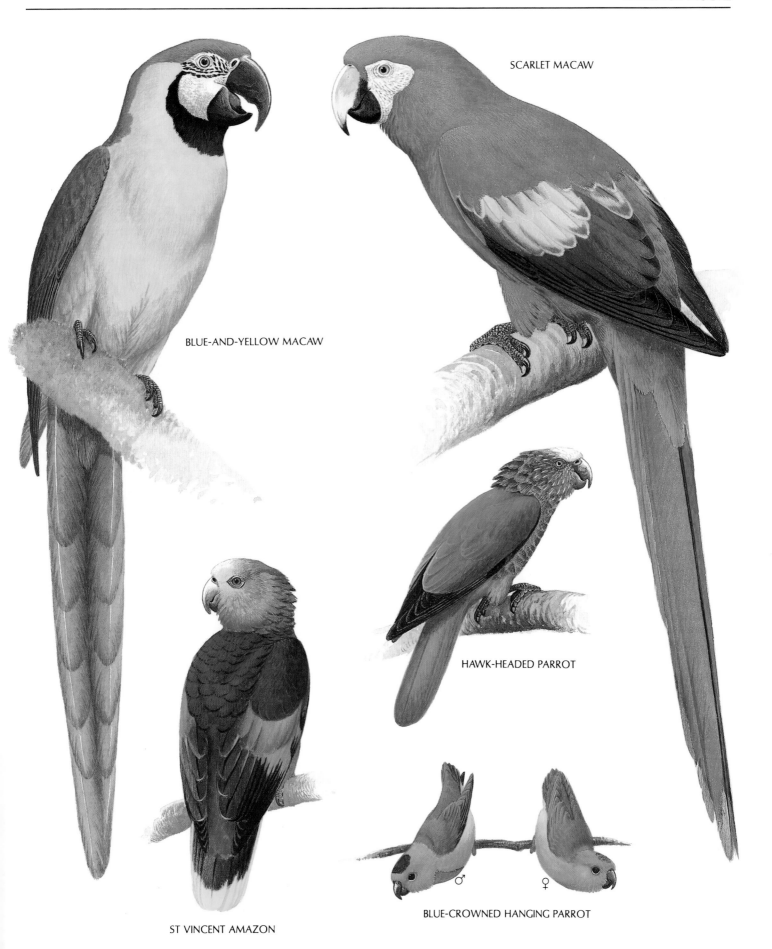

SCARLET MACAW

BLUE-AND-YELLOW MACAW

HAWK-HEADED PARROT

♂ ♀

ST VINCENT AMAZON

BLUE-CROWNED HANGING PARROT

# PARROTS AND PARAKEETS, MACAWS, HANGING PARROTS

## 1/ PEACH-FACED LOVEBIRD
*Agapornis roseicollis*
RANGE: SW Angola, Namibia (not NE), N
Cape Province
HABITAT: dry wooded steppe, usually in
belts of trees along watercourses
SIZE: 6 in (15 cm)

Abundant ripening seeds in the dry steppe of
southwest Africa may attract flocks of up to 200
Peach-faced Lovebirds. Small, noisy and agile,
they climb through the vegetation using their bills
for support, gathering the seeds of trees and
grasses, as well as grain crops and sunflowers.

As with other lovebirds, pairs of Peach-faced
Lovebirds preen each other attentively – hence
their name – and nest in colonies, either in rock
crevices, under eaves, or by moving into the
many-chambered nests of communal weaver
birds. The male feeds his mate as she broods the
eggs and young.

## 2/ BLUE-CROWNED HANGING PARROT
*Loriculus galgulus*
RANGE: Malaya, Singapore, Sumatra,
Borneo and some adjacent islands
HABITAT: light woodland in lowlands,
plantations, orchards, gardens
SIZE: 4¾ in (12 cm)

Like the other 10 species of hanging parrot, the
Blue-crowned Hanging Parrot takes its name
from its extraordinary habit of roosting at night or
resting during the day by hanging upside-down
from a branch. The bird holds its feet together and
arches its body so far back that its head may be
behind its feet.

These little parrots are most commonly seen
flying above the treetops on fast-whirring wings,
or feeding in flowering shrubs and trees. Their
diet consists of nectar, flowers, fruits, seeds and
possibly also small insects. When feeding on
sticky food such as nectar, the birds constantly
brush their fine, pointed bills on leaves and twigs.

When they climb, Blue-crowned Hanging Parrots take extremely long strides, turning the
whole body as they stretch each leg forward. They
may also hold their tails stiffly against a branch as
a prop, like woodpeckers, and grasp twigs with
their bills.

Blue-crowned Hanging Parrots nest between
January and July, choosing a hollow in a dead or
living tree. This is lined with a very thick layer of
leaves, which are carried to the nest-hole by the
female in her rump feathers. Like some other
hanging parrots, this species is very popular as a
cage bird in its native range.

## 3/ ROSE-RINGED PARAKEET
*Psittacula krameri*
RANGE: C Africa E to Uganda, India, Sri
Lanka; introduced to Middle and Far
East, North America, England,
Netherlands, Belgium, West Germany
HABITAT: woodland, farmland
SIZE: 16 in (41 cm)

Bold, gregarious opportunists, Rose-ringed Parakeets will often associate in flocks of a thousand
or more to feast on crops of grain or ripening fruit.
They will even invade grainstores, ripping open
the sacks with their hooked bills and squabbling
over the spoils.

During the breeding season the flocks split up;
each pair nests in a tree cavity after an elaborate
courtship ritual in which the female twitters and
rolls her eyes at the strutting male, rubs bills with
him and accepts gifts of food.

## 4/ HYACINTH MACAW
*Anodorhynchus hyacinthinus*  [?]
RANGE: C Brazil, E Bolivia, NE Paraguay
HABITAT: dry forest along watercourses,
wet forest edges, among palms
SIZE: 37½–39½ in (95–100 cm)

Easily recognized by its cobalt-blue plumage and
gray-black bill, the Hyacinth Macaw is the largest
of all the parrots. It feeds mainly on palm fruits
and nuts, and small flocks of 3–6 birds are often
sighted foraging among palm trees in swampy
places, or on the edge of the forest. When disturbed, these majestic macaws screech loudly,
circle overhead with their long tails streaming,
then settle in the tops of tall trees.

Little is known about the breeding habits of the
Hyacinth Macaw in the wild, although pairs have
been seen nesting in the hollow trunks of palms
and large deciduous trees. These birds laid
clutches of 2–3 eggs, and the young flew from the
nest some 4 months after egg-laying.

Like many parrots, the Hyacinth Macaw is
endangered by hunting and trapping for the pet
trade, and only 2,500–5,000 remain in the wild,
mostly in Brazil.

## 5/ BLUE-AND-YELLOW MACAW
*Ara ararauna*
RANGE: E Panama to N Bolivia and SE
Brazil
HABITAT: forests along watercourses and
swampy regions up to 1,500 ft (500 m)
SIZE: 86 cm (34 in)

Although the large Blue-and-yellow Macaw is
threatened by habitat destruction and large-scale
trapping for the cage-bird trade, it is still common
in the more remote parts of its range and can often
be seen flying over the treetops in pairs, screeching raucously.

It feeds on a variety of leaves, seeds, fruits and
nuts. In Manu National Park, Peru, Blue-and-
yellow Macaws have been seen eating at least 20
species of plant, many containing substances that
are distasteful or toxic to humans, but apparently
not to them. These macaws, and others, are often
attracted to mineral licks where they eat clay, and
this may help detoxify the noxious compounds in
their diet.

Blue-and-yellow Macaws nest in tree cavities
and usually lay a clutch of 2 white eggs.

## 6/ SCARLET MACAW
*Ara macao*
RANGE: S Mexico, Central America to N
Bolivia and C Brazil
HABITAT: lowland forest, to 1,300 ft
(400 m)
SIZE: 33½ in (85 cm)

Probably the best known of all the New World
parrots, these spectacular macaws are generally
seen in pairs, family groups or flocks of up to 20
birds. At sunrise they fly from their communal
roosting sites to scattered feeding grounds in the
forest, where they eat a variety of leaves, fruits
and seeds taken from high in the trees. They are
noisy in flight, uttering loud metallic screeches,
but they always feed in silence. At dusk they
return to their roosts, flying wing tip to wing tip
through the thickening twilight.

They nest in cavities in large trees, and the
availability of sites appears to limit the number of
breeding pairs in any population. The chicks

fledge at 3 months, but remain with their parents for some time thereafter.

Scarlet Macaws are adaptable birds which thrive in a variety of habitats, and they are more widely distributed than any other macaw species. Despite this, they are now under threat and several local populations have become extinct through deforestation and trapping.

## 7/ SUN CONURE
*Aratinga solstitialis*

RANGE: **NE South America**
HABITAT: **savanna**
SIZE: **11¾ in (30 cm)**

A series of shrill, 2-note screeches will often draw attention to this brilliantly colored, gregarious parrot, which frequently gathers in large noisy flocks to feed on blossoms, fruits, seeds and nuts in the treetops.

It uses cavities in palm trees as nesting sites, but the details of its breeding behavior in the wild are still unknown. In captivity the female alone incubates the clutch of 4 eggs for a month and the young fledge some 8 weeks after they have hatched.

The Sun Conure is very similar to the Jandaya Conure *A. jandaya* and the Golden-capped Conure *A. auricapilla*; indeed, some ornithologists consider them all to be races of the same species.

## 8/ MONK PARAKEET
*Myiopsitta monachus*

RANGE: **C Bolivia, Paraguay and S Brazil to C Argentina; introduced to USA, Puerto Rico**
HABITAT: **open woods, savanna, arid acacia scrub, cultivated land**
SIZE: **11½ in (29 cm)**

This common parrot is an extremely social bird, gathering in well-organized flocks of 100 or more to feed on seeds, fruits, flowers and insects while sentinels keep watch for predators from nearby vantage points. On farmland the Monk Parakeet can become a pest, frequently raiding citrus orchards and cereal crops.

Uniquely among parrots, it builds a bulky nest of dry, often thorny twigs in the upper branches of a tree. Some pairs nest in isolation, but others build their nests alongside or on top of existing nests to form a massive structure with up to 20 separate compartments. They use the nests throughout the year for roosting as well as breeding, each pair incubating a clutch of 5–8 eggs on a bed of twigs. Birds that have escaped from captivity have nested in the wild in several areas of North America.

Primarily a lowland species, the Monk Parakeet is abundant throughout most of its range. Four races are usually recognized, of which 2 are similar to *M. m. monachus* from southern Brazil, Uruguay and northeastern Argentina. The fourth race is the distinctive *M. m. luchsi*, known only from one area of central Bolivia.

## 9/ SPECTACLED PARROTLET
*Forpus conspicillatus*

RANGE: **E Panama, Colombia, W Venezuela**
HABITAT: **open woods, forest edges and clearings, savanna**
SIZE: **4¾ in (12 cm)**

Most South American parrots are being badly hit by deforestation, but the little Spectacled Parrotlet prefers open country and is actually increasing its range as the forests come down. Small flocks are often to be seen over clear-felled areas, busily foraging among the scrub and undergrowth for leaf buds, fruits, berries, and the seeds of grasses and herbaceous plants. As they feed, they keep up a constant chatter and twitter of soft, finchlike calls, quite unlike the raucous screeches of larger parrots. The flight of the Spectacled Parrotlet is swift but erratic.

Males are brighter than females, with blue markings on the wing, rump, lower back, and behind the eye. Immatures resemble females. The clutch of 4 white eggs is laid in a cavity in a tree or fencepost, or sometimes even in a termite nest.

## 10/ YELLOW-CROWNED AMAZON
*Amazona ochrocephala*

RANGE: **C Mexico, Trinidad, S to Amazon basin and E Peru; introduced to S California and S Florida**
HABITAT: **deciduous and humid lowland forest, open woods, savanna, pine ridges**
SIZE: **13¾ in (35 cm)**

The Yellow-crowned Amazon has suffered badly in some localities from deforestation and, because of its high reputation as a mimic of human speech, from the activities of the trappers who supply the pet trade. Despite this reputation, it does not seem to mimic other birds or animals in the wild, confining itself to a variety of metallic shrieks, whistling contacts, and repeated, screeching *kurr-owk* squawks.

It is a very variable species, with 9 races, including *A. o. ochrocephala* of western Colombia, northern Brazil and Trinidad and *A. o. tresmariae*, found on the Tres Marias Islands off western Mexico. The race *A. o. oratrix*, from Mexico, has an entirely yellow head; it is in great demand as a cage bird and is now regarded as rare and in need of immediate protection. Like the race *A. o. auropalliata* from the Pacific slope of Central America, it is often regarded as a separate species.

Yellow-crowned Amazons are opportunist feeders which gather in small groups in the treetops to forage for a wide variety of seeds, berries, fruits and flowers. At dusk they return to their habitual roosts, flying with characteristic shallow wing beats below body level, rather like those of a duck.

## 11/ ST VINCENT AMAZON
*Amazona guildingii*     E

RANGE: **St Vincent (Lesser Antilles)**
HABITAT: **humid forest at 1,150–2,000 ft (350–600 m)**
SIZE: **15¾–18 in (40–46 cm)**

This large, picturesque, and colorful amazon parrot is found only in the forests of the island of St Vincent, where it has suffered badly from habitat loss due to agricultural development, and from hunting. Once in imminent danger of extinction, it has been saved – for the present – by protective legislation and captive breeding initiated in 1988, and the population now numbers some 450–500 individuals.

The adult plumage is variable and virtually no 2 birds are exactly alike, but there are 2 basic color phases: the yellow-brown phase, illustrated, and the green phase, which has the upper parts mainly dusky green, the base of the primaries green, and the underwing coverts and undersides of the flight feathers green.

Noisy and gregarious, these parrots often forage in flocks of up to 20, gathering fruits, seeds, and flowers from the upper canopy. The flocks break up into pairs at the onset of the dry season in January or February, but the number of breeding pairs in any area is limited by the number of suitable nest-holes in large, mature trees. The 2 eggs are incubated by the female alone. Juveniles leave the nest as duller versions of the adults and do not progress from green juveniles to yellow-brown adults as has sometimes been suggested.

## 12/ HAWK-HEADED PARROT
*Deroptyus accipitrinus*

RANGE: **South America N of the Amazon, W to SE Colombia and NE Peru**
HABITAT: **mixed forest and savanna**
SIZE: **13¾ in (35 cm)**

This handsome parrot, which is sometimes known as the Red-fan Parrot, has long red and blue feathers on its nape which can be raised to form a ruff, giving it a uniquely hawklike appearance. This bird is also distinctive in flight, for it normally flies low through the forest, skimming the treetops, giving a few shallow flaps followed by a short glide, with its wings held angled slightly downward, its rounded gray-black tail feathers spread and its head raised. It sometimes calls with a variety of chattering notes and soft whistles.

Hawk-headed Parrots have been seen in pairs and in small flocks of up to 10 birds, which spend much of the day feeding or resting in the treetops. Their diet consists of the fruits, seeds and nuts of various palms and other plants.

The Hawk-headed Parrot nests in old woodpecker holes in trees, but little else is known about its breeding behavior. Like many parrots, it is under threat from deforestation and is declining in numbers in the southern part of its range.

# TURACOS, CUCKOOS, HOATZIN

GREAT BLUE TURACO

GRAY
GO-AWAY BIRD

VIOLET TURACO

juv

race *corythaix*
"Knysna Turaco"

PRINCE RUSPOLI'S TURACO

GREEN TURACO

GREAT SPOTTED CUCKOO

imm

♀

♂

EURASIAN CUCKOO

YELLOW-BILLED CUCKOO

young being fed by Dunnock

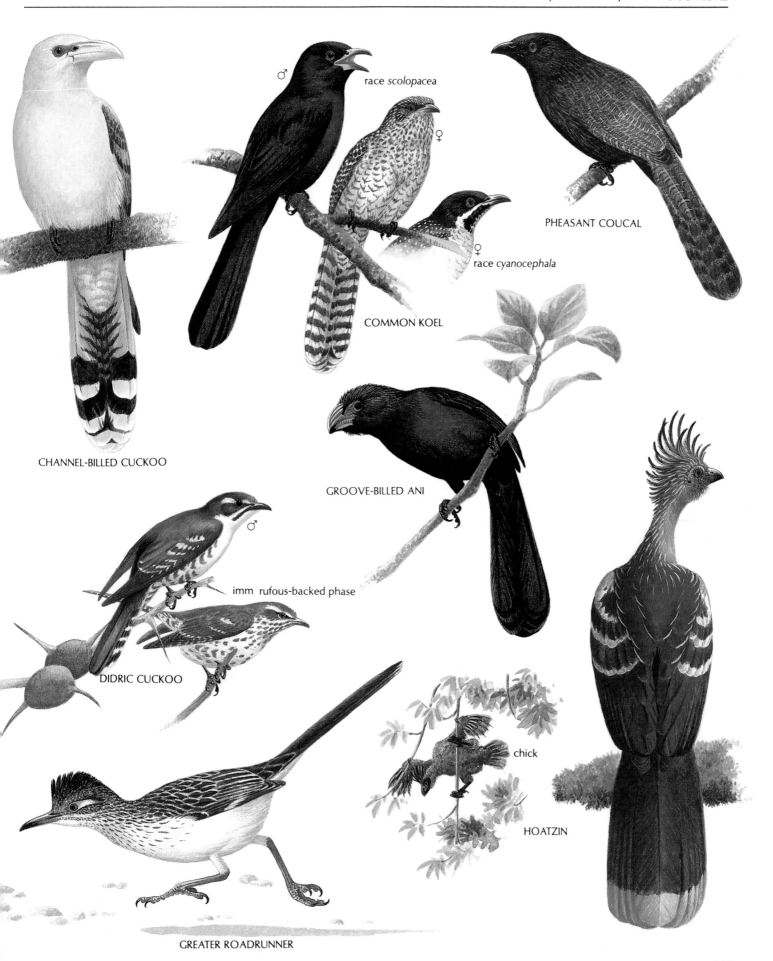

♂ race *scolopacea*

♀

♀ race *cyanocephala*

PHEASANT COUCAL

COMMON KOEL

CHANNEL-BILLED CUCKOO

GROOVE-BILLED ANI

♂

imm rufous-backed phase

DIDRIC CUCKOO

chick

HOATZIN

GREATER ROADRUNNER

313

# TURACOS, CUCKOOS, HOATZIN

## FAMILY MUSOPHAGIDAE
### Turacos

Medium to large woodland birds. Plumage gray, green, blue or purple, with silky, hairlike feathers on head and breast of most species and unique green and red pigments in plumage of *Musophaga* and *Tauraco* species. Sexes alike. Nests in trees, usually flimsy platform of twigs. Eggs 2, whitish. Incubation 21–24 days. Silky nestlings use tiny claws on wing joints to scramble to edge of nest at 10–12 days; at about 4 weeks, leave nest for good, several days before they can fly. 20 species.

### 1/ GREAT BLUE TURACO
*Corythaeola cristata*

RANGE: W Africa from Guinea to Nigeria, Congo Basin to Kenya and Tanzania
HABITAT: lowland rain forest, patches of forest in savanna, mountain forest
SIZE: $29\frac{1}{2}$ in (75 cm)

This beautiful bird is by far the largest of the turacos: its alternative name is the Giant Turaco. It is adept at running along branches but is a poor flier. Most flights are merely glides from tall trees, and they often end abruptly in low vegetation; the bird then climbs quickly back to the treetops.

Great Blue Turacos usually move around in small parties, several of which may congregate at large fruit-bearing trees near the borders of their territories. The birds start feeding soon after dawn and continue to feed for much of the day, except when it is very hot. At dusk each party flies noisily toward a traditional roosting tree. The nest is built in a tall tree.

### 2/ GRAY GO-AWAY BIRD
*Corythaixoides concolor*

RANGE: S Africa, N to Angola and Zaire
HABITAT: dry, open woodland, parks, gardens
SIZE: 19 in (48 cm)

A loud, nasal, descending *g'wa-ay g'wa-ay* is often the first indication that this bird is about. It is also known as the Gray Lourie. A sociable species, it travels in parties of up to 20 birds, hopping busily about the trees. It is a greedy, untidy feeder, dropping many fruits, pods and flowers of the figs and acacias that make up much of its diet. It sometimes eats crops of vegetables in gardens.

A clutch of 3, or rarely 4, eggs is laid in a loose nest of sticks, usually built in a thorny acacia tree.

### 3/ VIOLET TURACO
*Musophaga violacea*

RANGE: W Africa, Senegal to Cameroon
HABITAT: tall forest, riverside forest
SIZE: 17 in (43 cm)

The Violet Turaco, or Violet Plantain-eater, prefers to stay well out of sight in the dense canopy of tall trees, where it searches for fruits, especially figs, by running along branches or bounding from bough to bough. If disturbed, it will keep still but when approached too closely it flies away with powerful flaps and long glides, which show off its crimson wings. The red in the plumage of this and other turacos is produced by a copper-based pigment called turacin. The Violet Turaco's

main call is a long series of deep, gargling *cou-cou-vhou* notes that run into each other, producing a pulsing roar when, as is nearly always the case, 2 birds call in a slightly asynchronous duet.

### 4/ GREEN TURACO
*Tauraco persa*

RANGE: patchy from Senegal E to Zaire, Tanzania and S to South Africa
HABITAT: evergreen forest, forested savanna, abandoned cultivation, gardens
SIZE: $16\frac{1}{2}$ in (42 cm)

There are several races of this widespread turaco. The race illustrated is the typical South African race *T. p. corythaix*, known as the Knysna Turaco or Knysna Lourie. Two northern races have rounded, plain green crests, while others have pointed crests tipped with white or blue. The brilliant green plumage in this and other *Tauraco* species is not due to iridescence, as in other birds, but to a unique green pigment, turacoverdin, which contains copper.

Green Turacos feed in groups in the treetops, gorging themselves on fruit. If one begins to call, the rest will follow, producing a chorus of growling, guttural cries. In the nesting season the birds pair off and become very territorial. The male courts his mate by displaying his wings and feeding her with regurgitated food.

### 5/ PRINCE RUSPOLI'S TURACO
*Tauraco ruspolii*    R

RANGE: 2 locations in Ethiopia
HABITAT: juniper forest with dense undergrowth, scrub, acacia
SIZE: 16 in (41 cm)

This elusive turaco has been found only within 2 small areas in Ethiopia – one 45 by 20 mls (70 by 30 km) and the other a mere 10 mls (25 km) square. It has typical cackling, growling and gobbling calls, but very little is known about its way of life. As it is secretive and difficult to find, its population is hard to estimate, and it may be at risk both from loss of habitat and from competition with the White-cheeked Turaco *T. leucotis*.

## FAMILY OPISTHOCOMIDAE
### Hoatzin

There is only one species in this family.

### 6/ HOATZIN
*Opisthocomus hoazin*

RANGE: Amazon and Orinoco river basins and rivers of the Guianas, from Guyana and Brazil to Ecuador and Bolivia
HABITAT: flooded and riverside forest
SIZE: $23\frac{3}{4}$ in (60 cm)

This odd bird is a poor flier which usually glides from tree to tree, clumsily flapping up to reach its goal and clambering through the foliage, using its large but weak wings for support. The adults gather in groups of 10–50 to loaf in the trees and feed on the leaves of arum and other marsh plants, communicating with harsh croaking calls.

They are cooperative breeders, and 2–6 adults may help build the nest and care for the eggs and young. They lay 2–3 yellow-buff eggs, dappled with blue or brown spots. The Hoatzin is the only tree-dwelling bird in which the chicks habitually leave the nest soon after hatching. The nestlings have 2 hooked claws on the first and second digits at the bend of each wing, which they use to grip twigs as they explore around the nest. These claws reminded ornithologists of the 3-clawed wings of the earliest known bird, *Archaeopteryx* (p. 16), and it was suggested that the Hoatzin was a "living fossil." Today it is sometimes classified with the gamebirds (pp. 110–21) but is probably most closely related to the cuckoos.

## FAMILY CUCULIDAE
### Cuckoos and coucals

Medium to large, mainly scrub and woodland birds. Size and weight unusually variable in both sexes. Plumage generally browns, grays, often with barred or streaked underparts and spots or flashes in open tail. Eggs 10–15 per season in parasitic species (more if losses high), variable in color to mimic hosts' eggs; 2–5, usually bluish or whitish, in nonparasitic species. Incubation period 11–16 days, nestling period 16–24 days. 138 species.

## 7/ GREAT SPOTTED CUCKOO
*Clamator glandarius*

RANGE: **breeds SW Europe to Asia Minor, Africa; N populations winter in N Africa and S of Sahara, S populations winter in C Africa**
HABITAT: **open woods, bushy heath, scrub**
SIZE: **15¾ in (40 cm)**

The generic name of this bird, *Clamator* from the Latin for a noisy speaker, gives a clue to one of its most prominent characteristics – a rasping, chattering call, with a gobbling quality, often given from a hidden perch. The Great Spotted Cuckoo is often seen hopping about on the ground or in bushes, searching for caterpillars. It is fond of the large, hairy kinds, although it may remove most of the hairs before swallowing the insects.

This cuckoo lays its eggs in the nests of various species of crow. Unlike that of the Eurasian Cuckoo, the nestling does not throw the eggs or chicks of its foster parent out of the nest, but usually successfully competes for food with the chicks or smothers them.

## 8/ EURASIAN CUCKOO
*Cuculus canorus*

RANGE: **breeds Europe, Asia S to Nepal, China, Japan; winters in Africa**
HABITAT: **farmland with hedgerows, woods, heaths and moors**
SIZE: **13 in (33 cm)**

The monotonous but attractive 2-note call of the male Eurasian Cuckoo is a welcome symbol of spring in many parts of its breeding range. Most females resemble the males, but in addition to the common gray phase, females also have a rare rufous phase. Juvenile birds also show a similar variation, with the rufous phase more common than in the female.

The Eurasian Cuckoo lays its eggs in the nests of other birds: over 100 host species have been recorded in Europe. The female cuckoo finds the nests of host birds when fresh eggs have been laid; an egg is removed from each and a cuckoo's egg laid in its place, often closely resembling the existing eggs. When the chick hatches after 12 days, it throws the other eggs and chicks out of the nest to monopolize the food brought by its foster parents. After 17 days it leaves, eventually flying south for the winter – 1 or 2 months after the adult cuckoos have departed.

## 9/ DIDRIC CUCKOO
*Chrysococcyx caprius*

RANGE: **sub-Saharan Africa**
HABITAT: **savanna woodland, farmland, plantations**
SIZE: **7–8 in (18–20 cm)**

Although present all year near the Equator, this small, colorful cuckoo is a migrant in both the north and south of its range. Males are brighter than females and are fond of high, open perches from which they can pounce on their insect prey.

The eggs are laid in the nests of a variety of birds, including bishops, weavers and sparrows, or occasionally wagtails and flycatchers. The female sometimes removes one of the host's eggs immediately, and when the cuckoo chick hatches,

it usually ejects any remaining eggs and nestlings, and is reared alone. It is fledged at about 21 days. Immature birds have 2 color phases: a rufous-backed phase and a green-backed phase.

## 10/ COMMON KOEL
*Eudynamys scolopacea*

RANGE: **N and E Australia, India, Southeast Asia to New Guinea and Solomon Islands**
HABITAT: **forests with fruiting trees**
SIZE: **15½–18 in (39–46 cm)**

In the breeding season this cuckoo can often be heard calling – the male uttering loud, shrill whistles and the characteristic *ko-el* call, while the female responds with short, piercing whistles.

Like most cuckoos, they lay their eggs in the nests of other birds: in India, the hosts are crows, while in Australia they include large honeyeaters and orioles. The chick takes all the food and either starves out or ejects the other nestlings. The adults forage for fruits in the forest canopy and often visit gardens to steal cultivated fruits.

There are 15 or more races of the Common Koel, including the race *E. s. scolopacea* from India, Sri Lanka and the Nicobar Islands and *E. s. cyanocephala* from eastern Australia, which is sometimes considered to be a separate species.

## 11/ CHANNEL-BILLED CUCKOO
*Scythrops novaehollandiae*

RANGE: **breeds N and E Australia; winters New Guinea to Sulawesi (Celebes)**
HABITAT: **open forest, swamp woodland**
SIZE: **23–25½ in (58–65 cm)**

With its heavy curved bill, this bulky bird looks more like a toucan than a cuckoo. It usually feeds singly or in small groups in the tops of large trees, eating ripe figs and other fruits, as well as large insects. It is most active at dawn and dusk, but it also feeds at night, when it can be located by its raucous, repetitive cries.

It generally lays its eggs in the nests of crows and butcherbirds such as the Pied Currawong *Strepera graculina*, often laying 2 or more eggs in one nest. When the young hatch they do not throw out the other nestlings but simply take most of their food.

## 12/ YELLOW-BILLED CUCKOO
*Coccyzus americanus*

RANGE: **S Canada, USA S to Central America; winters in South America**
HABITAT: **open woods, streamside thickets**
SIZE: **12¼ in (31 cm)**

The handsome Yellow-billed Cuckoo is usually seen as it makes a dash across a forest clearing or flies swiftly from tree to tree. It is surprisingly agile among the trees as it forages for fruit and insects; it has a taste for hairy tent caterpillars and when these are abundant the Yellow-billed Cuckoos are often not far behind.

Unlike Old World cuckoos, these birds build their own nests: small flimsy affairs placed in bushes or trees. They rarely lay their eggs in the nests of other species, but a female will sometimes lay in the nest of another Yellow-billed Cuckoo.

## 13/ GROOVE-BILLED ANI
*Crotophaga sulcirostris*

RANGE: **SW USA to N South America**
HABITAT: **open brushy areas, pastures, orchards, secondary woodland, thickets**
SIZE: **13½ in (34 cm)**

This rather unkempt-looking bird, with its large, parrotlike bill and floppy tail, is usually seen in small, loose flocks, foraging for grasshoppers and other insects in the wake of grazing cattle (or, in the tropics, in the wake of army ants).

It is a sociable bird, roosting in groups of 30–40. It also breeds communally, with up to 4 pairs building a bulky cup nest in a thorn bush or tree. All the birds share the duties of incubation and feeding the chicks, and young birds of previous broods may help to feed later broods.

## 14/ GREATER ROADRUNNER
*Geococcyx californianus*

RANGE: **W USA, E to Louisiana, S to S Mexico**
HABITAT: **semidesert, chaparral, grassland, farmland, occasionally moist woodland**
SIZE: **20–24 in (51–61 cm)**

This slender, ground-dwelling bird has earned a place in popular mythology, partly on account of its athleticism – it can run at 12 mls (20 km) per hour or more – and partly because it occasionally kills and eats small rattlesnakes. Normally it takes less challenging prey, including gophers, mice, lizards, scorpions, tarantulas and centipedes, as well as large insects and various fruits.

The Great Roadrunner has evolved unusual ways of surviving in its hostile environment. On cold desert nights, it allows its body temperature to fall slightly, saving energy, and becomes slightly torpid. When day breaks, the bird warms itself up by exposing patches of dark skin on its back to the heat of the sun. Roadrunners live in permanent pairs, staying in their breeding territory throughout the year. The compact cup nest is built in a low tree or shrub, or on a clump of cactus, and the young are tended by both parents.

## 15/ PHEASANT COUCAL
*Centropus phasianinus*

RANGE: **N and E Australia, New Guinea, Timor**
HABITAT: **tall, dense ground cover including long grass, swamp vegetation and cane fields**
SIZE: **19¾–27½ in (50–70 cm)**

Coucals are giant, ungainly ground cuckoos, with long tails, which spend much of their time stalking through dense undergrowth in search of small animals such as insects, crabs, frogs, lizards, mice and nestlings.

The mottled and barred brown plumage of the Pheasant Coucal makes it difficult to see in thick cover, but it often gives itself away by rapid hooting calls. It flies heavily on short, rounded wings. The females are larger than the males.

The nest is a platform of sticks, usually sited on trampled ground or in a low bush and hooded by pieces of surrounding vegetation pulled over it. Both adults incubate the 2–5 eggs.

# BARN AND BAY OWLS, TYPICAL OWLS

COMMON
BARN-OWL

race *alba*

EASTERN SCREECH OWL

rufous phase

gray phase

brown
individual

BAY OWL

CRESTED OWL

EURASIAN
SCOPS OWL

gray individual

PEL'S FISHING OWL

juv

SPECTACLED OWL

GREAT HORNED OWL

juv

race *pallescens*

race *virginianus*

BROWN FISH
OWL

NORTHERN
HAWK OWL

SNOWY OWL

♂

♀

race *bubo*

NORTHERN EAGLE OWL

# BARN AND BAY OWLS, TYPICAL OWLS

## FAMILY TYTONIDAE
### Barn and bay owls
Medium, nocturnal predators. Soft, dense plumage, heart-shaped facial disk, relatively small eyes and long, slender, feathered legs and feathered toes. Large ears, sense of hearing exceptional. Sexes alike in plumage but females mostly slightly larger than males. Orange-buff to blackish-brown upperparts, white, rufous or blackish-brown underparts. Nest in barns, holes in trees or among rocks, or on ground (Grass Owl *Tyto capensis*). Eggs usually 2–6 (sometimes up to 11), white. Incubation 27–34 days, nestling period 49–56 days. 14 species.

### 1/ COMMON BARN-OWL
*Tyto alba*

RANGE: **Americas, Europe, Africa, Arabia, India, Southeast Asia, Australia**
HABITAT: **mainly open or semiopen lowlands, including farmland**
SIZE: **13–13¾ in (33–35 cm)**

In many areas, these beautiful birds nest in barns, outbuildings, ruins and the like, but in others they prefer holes in trees. Common Barn-Owls hunt mostly on the wing, low down, with a characteristic light, buoyant action, frequent changes of direction and, sometimes, periods of hovering. They can locate and capture their prey solely by using their phenomenal sense of hearing. Small rodents are normally the main prey, and cyclic fluctuations in their numbers partly govern the numbers and breeding success of the owls.

Most Common Barn-Owls, such as the race *T. a. alba* from Britain, France, southern Europe and Tenerife and Gran Canaria in the Canary Islands, are strikingly white below and pale sandy-gold and gray above. By contrast, other races, such as *T. a. guttata* from central and eastern Europe, have a dark buffish breast.

### 2/ BAY OWL
*Phodilus badius*

RANGE: **N India, Southeast Asia**
HABITAT: **mainly tropical forest**
SIZE: **9–13 in (23–33 cm)**

Although this is apparently a fairly common and widespread species, relatively little is known about its ecology. Its short wings and long tail are typical of an owl which hunts in thick cover, and it is known to prey on small mammals, birds, lizards, amphibians and insects. The fact that hunting birds have often been seen around water also suggests that they may eat fish. Typical nesting and roosting sites of this species are in holes or crevices in trees. This was the only known bay owl until 1951 when the Congo, or Itombwe, Bay Owl was first described: it is still known only from a single specimen.

## FAMILY STRIGIDAE
### Typical owls
Small to large predators, great majority wholly or partly nocturnal. Soft, dense plumage. Large head with saucer-shaped facial disk and very large eyes and ears, with exceptional night vision and very senstive hearing. Feathered legs and toes (except fishing owls and fish owls). Sexes generally alike

in plumage, but females usually larger. Usually cryptically patterned brown or gray. Nest mainly in holes or in abandoned nests of other species; a few nest on ground or in burrows. Eggs 1–14, (usually 2–7), white. Incubation 15–35 days, nestling period 24–52 days; young may leave nest before they can fly, 15–35 days after hatching. 160 species.

### 3/ EURASIAN SCOPS OWL
*Otus scops*

RANGE: **breeds S Europe, N Africa, E to SW Siberia; N populations and some S ones, winter in tropical Africa**
HABITAT: **open woodland, parks, orchards, gardens, roadside trees, town squares**
SIZE: **7½–7¾ in (19–20 cm)**

This small, superbly camouflaged owl (which may be either gray-brown or red-brown in basic color) is particularly hard to detect at its daytime roost. Indeed, it is far more often heard than seen, its song – a monotonously repeated single, plaintive, whistling, note – being one of the most characteristic sounds of the Mediterranean night. The Scops Owl is unusual among European owls in being largely a true summer migrant. Large insects such a crickets, cicadas, cockchafers and moths are its main prey, with moths frequently taken in flight and often attracting the owls to hunt around streetlights.

### 4/ EASTERN SCREECH OWL
*Otus asio*

RANGE: **E North America from extreme S Quebec and Ontario to E Montana and C Texas and from S Canada to the tip of Florida and NE Mexico**
HABITAT: **open forest, riverside woodland, orchards and other cultivated land, parks and gardens with large trees**
SIZE: **7½–9 in (19–23 cm)**

There are 2 color phases of this small owl: a rust-red rufous phase and a gray phase. The ear tufts are conspicuous when erect, but may be held against the head where they are nearly invisible.

Like many nocturnal owls, Eastern Screech Owls are more often heard than seen. Their primary song is a tremulous, descending whinny. They also utter a quickly repeated, monotonous *who-who-who* all on one pitch. Twitters and barks are given in agitation and in response to predators around the nest. A very close relative (formerly regarded as belonging to the same species), the Western Screech Owl *O. kennicottii*, found to the west of the Rockies, is very similar in appearance but can be distinguished by its different songs – a series of short whistles accelerating in tempo and a brief trill followed by a longer one.

This species has a varied diet, eating large invertebrates, fish, amphibians, reptiles, birds and mammals. Small mammals and birds and large insects form their chief prey, but these owls sometimes kill birds larger than themselves.

### 5/ CRESTED OWL
*Lophostrix cristata*

RANGE: **S Mexico to Bolivia, E Ecuador, Amazonian Brazil E of Andes**
HABITAT: **forest, tall, second growth and patches of woodland bordering streams and rivers, chiefly in tropical lowlands**
SIZE: **15–15¾ in (38–40 cm)**

These distinctive owls are sometimes considered to form a link between the small *Otus* owls and the large *Bubo* owls, and recent evidence also suggests a relationship with the spectacled owls *Pulsatrix* of Central and South America. The Crested Owl is somewhat rare and local in distribution over its large range, but its perceived rarity could be due to its strictly nocturnal habits. During the day it roosts in thick cover, usually only 10–30 ft (3–9 m) up, and often near a stream. Although the sexes are alike, this owl has 2 color phases, one uniform dark brown, the other pale buff. Its diet is known to include large cockroaches, beetles, caterpillars and other insects, but may also incorporate other small animals.

The voice of this enigmatic owl has only recently been recorded. Its calls are brief, beginning with 3–4 low stuttering notes followed by a deep-throated growl that has a somewhat resonant quality.

## 6/ SPECTACLED OWL
*Pulsatrix perspicillata*
RANGE: **S Mexico to NW Argentina and S Brazil**
HABITAT: **lowland forest, savanna, plantations**
SIZE: **17–18 in (43–46 cm)**

As with some other species of owl, the Spectacled Owl shows some evidence of 2 color phases: one dark on the upperparts, one lighter. Birds from Central America tend to be darker than those from South America. As with most owls, females are, on average, larger than males. The Spectacled Owl has a voice that includes a gruff *bu-hu-hu*, a descending whistled call and a series of 6–8 low resonant hoots with a slight popping quality – sometimes likened to the resonant tapping of a woodpecker. At times 2 of these birds will duet, each calling with a slightly different tone.

During the day, the Spectacled Owl usually perches hidden just below the forest canopy, but on rare occasions it has been seen hunting on overcast or foggy days. Its diet includes a diversity of small mammals (including rodents and bats), birds, lizards, land crabs and large insects.

The 2 eggs are laid in tree hollows and cavities. The chicks leave the nest before they can fly well and are tended by their parents for some time. In contrast to their parents, the young are white with brown wings and have brown spectacles.

## 7/ GREAT HORNED OWL
*Bubo virginianus*
RANGE: **North America, except tundra regions of Alaska and Canada, S to Tierra del Fuego**
HABITAT: **lowlands to tree line in deciduous or coniferous boreal, temperate and tropical forests, prairies, deserts, farmland and occasionally suburban areas**
SIZE: **17–20¾ in (43–53 cm)**

Because of its large size and huge range, this is one of the most commonly observed owls. The Great Horned Owl is closely related to its Eurasian counterpart, the Northern Eagle Owl. Like that species, it has been separated into many races, which vary both in size and color.

The largest races are found at high latitudes and altitudes and the smallest in tropical lowland forests and deserts. The birds in humid forests are darkest, while those from deserts or areas with snow for much of the year are much paler. There are also orange-breasted and white-breasted color phases. The race *B. v. virginianus* is a dark form from eastern North America, while the race *B. v. pallescens* is a pale desert race from Arizona and northwestern Mexico. The song of the Great Horned Owl consists of a series of booming hoots, and it has a range of calls including barks, growls and screams.

Great Horned Owls lay their eggs in a variety of sites, often taking over abandoned stick nests of hawks, crows and magpies. They also nest in large cavities in trees and cliffs. Occasionally they will nest in open farm buildings and other man-made structures or even on the ground. The usual clutch is 2–3 white eggs. The female is responsible for the incubation, which requires about 32 days. The young leave the nest when they are

about 5–6 weeks old but do not fly well until they are 9–10 weeks old.

Great Horned Owls prey predominantly upon small mammals and birds but have a very wide diet that includes invertebrates, fish, amphibians, reptiles, mammals and birds. Their prey ranges in size from large insects to jack rabbits, skunks and grouse.

## 8/ NORTHERN EAGLE OWL
*Bubo bubo*
RANGE: **N Africa, Eurasia (not British Isles)**
HABITAT: **mainly wild, broken country, often in hills with tree cover, but not dense forests; also desert edge**
SIZE: **23½–29½ in (60–75 cm)**

Northern Eagle Owls are very large, powerful nocturnal predators, able to take mammals up to the size of young Roe Deer and birds as big as cock Capercaillies *Tetrao urogallus*. It is also known to prey on other owls and on raptors as large as buzzards. Mostly, though, they feed on a wide variety of very much smaller prey. The male's song is a deep double hoot, perfectly described in the species' German name *Uhu*, and audible over half a mile (1 km) or more away in still conditions. The largest, darkest and most heavily streaked Northern Eagle Owls tend to be those from northern populations such as the race *B. b. bubo* from Europe to France, Greece and northern Ukraine, while the smallest and palest are the desert forms from north Africa and the Middle East.

## 9/ BROWN FISH OWL
*Bubo zeylonensis*
RANGE: **Middle East (rare); India and Southeast Asia**
HABITAT: **forest and woodland along streams and lakes**
SIZE: **21¼–22½ in (54–57 cm)**

This is the most widespread of the 4 Asian fish owls. They are all large birds, specially adapted to their way of life in having bare legs and feet, with many tiny, sharp spines on the soles of their toes which enable them to grasp wet and slippery prey. The Brown Fish Owl's feet are bare because feathers would soon become soiled with fish scales and slime and are not needed for protection against the bites of prey, as may be their function in other owls. One fish owl, Blakiston's Fish Owl *B. blakistoni* does have feathered legs, doubtless to protect it from the extreme cold it experiences in the rivers of eastern Siberia, northeastern China and northern Japan in winter.

Although the Brown Fish Owl is fairly well known, much of its ecology has never been studied. The birds are known to hunt from trees overhanging the water, from rocks or by wading in the shallows, but have also been seen flying over the surface and taking fish from the water. Fish and freshwater crabs dominate their diet, plus some reptiles, amphibians, insects, small mammals and birds.

Brown Fish Owls lay their 1–2 eggs on a ledge or cleft in a cliff, in a tree hole or in the deserted nest of a bird of prey; in India, they have been known to use abandoned buildings.

## 10/ PEL'S FISHING OWL
*Scotopelia peli*
RANGE: **sub-Saharan Africa, excluding SW**
HABITAT: **forested river banks, wetlands**
SIZE: **20–24 in (51–61 cm)**

This is the most widely distributed and best known of the 3 African fishing owls, as well as the largest. Its calls, usually heard soon after dark and before dawn, are a series of resounding hoots, repeated at 10-second intervals for several minutes at a time and audible up to 2 mls (3 km) away. It occasionally catches frogs, crabs and mussels but its main food is fish weighing 3½–9 oz (100–250 g). The bird makes a shallow dive from a low perch above the water, catching the fish in its feet. Sandbanks are also used as fishing places. Its legs and feet are unfeathered, as are those of the other fishing owls.

## 11/ SNOWY OWL
*Nyctea scandiaca*
RANGE: **circumpolar Arctic**
HABITAT: **mainly on tundra; also in other wild habitats, from coastal islands to moorland**
SIZE: **20¾–26 in (53–66 cm)**

The Snowy Owl has a rounded head with a curiously catlike expression. There is a particularly great difference in size between the sexes, females being up to 20 percent larger than males. Also unusual is the marked difference in plumage between the almost all-white male and the strongly barred and chevroned female.

This species is a sufficiently large and versatile predator to be able to take a wide range of small to medium-sized bird and mammal prey, but over much of its breeding range it feeds largely on lemmings. Its distribution, numbers and breeding performances are closely tied to the regular population cycles of lemmings, so it is a nomadic and opportunist bird. Many wander far south in winter, and numbers can be large and reach "invasion" proportions when food shortages follow a bumper breeding year. Although most hunting is done at dawn and dusk, Snowy Owls also hunt in broad daylight.

## 12/ NORTHERN HAWK OWL
*Surnia ulula*
RANGE: **N Eurasia, North America, mainly subarctic**
HABITAT: **boreal and mountain forest with easy access to clearings and forest edge**
SIZE: **14–15¼ in (36–39 cm)**

This distinctive species is one of a relatively small number of owls which are habitually active during the daytime. Superficially, it resembles a small hawk, with its short, rounded wings and long tail, and its occasional aerial hunting forays, when it dashes through the trees in pursuit of a bird, can be reminiscent of the Sparrowhawk *Accipter nisus*. Mainly, though, it hunts from a prominent perch. In summer, the prey consists almost entirely of small voles, plus some other mammals and small birds, but in winter the Northern Hawk Owl may take a greater proportion of birds. Like other northern owls, its numbers can vary dramatically in relation to the availability of its prey.

# TYPICAL OWLS

NORTHERN PYGMY OWL

gray phase

rufous phase

PEARL-SPOTTED OWLET

PAPUAN HAWK-OWL

race *ocellata*

ELF OWL
young in nest-hole

race *leucopsis*

BOOBOOK OWL

LITTLE OWL

race *vidalii*

race *lilith*

race *hypugaea*

juv at nest-burrow entrance

BURROWING OWL

race *sylvatica*
rufous phase

chick

race *aluco*
gray phase

GREAT GRAY OWL

EURASIAN TAWNY OWL

LONG-EARED OWL

race *otus*
cryptic posture

race *nebulosa*

AFRICAN WOOD OWL

NORTHERN
SAW-WHET OWL

SHORT-EARED OWL

juv

JAMAICAN OWL

# TYPICAL OWLS

## 1/ AFRICAN WOOD OWL
*Strix woodfordi*
RANGE: **sub-Saharan Africa, except extreme S**
HABITAT: **forests, plantations**
SIZE: **11¾–13¾ in (30–35 cm)**

The African Wood Owl is a big-headed, cryptically colored, highly nocturnal wood owl. It generally hunts from a low perch, taking most of its prey from the ground, but also picks insects off vegetation while in flight and is surprisingly agile at hawking for flying insects. Insects of many kinds form its main prey, but a few frogs, small snakes, birds and small mammals are also eaten.

This species was, until recently, placed in the genus *Ciccaba*, along with 4 species found in Central and South America. Although these species are similar in appearance to the African Wood Owl and share features such as the relatively simple structure of their inner ears, many ornithologists now believe that the similarities are due to convergent evolution in similar habitats, rather than to a true relationship, and classify the African Wood Owl in the genus *Strix*, along with Eurasian wood owls such as the Eurasian Tawny Owl and Great Gray Owl.

## 2/ EURASIAN TAWNY OWL
*Strix aluco*
RANGE: **Europe, N Africa, parts of W Asia, China, Korea, Taiwan**
HABITAT: **chiefly woodland or areas with some trees, including urban areas**
SIZE: **14½–15¼ in (37–39 cm)**

Seldom seen, due to its strictly nocturnal habits, the Eurasian Tawny Owl is nevertheless better known than other European owls through its familiar song – a long, quavering hooting, used to proclaim territorial ownership, advertise its presence to a mate, and during courtship. The male's hoot is slightly lower pitched and more clearly phrased than that of the female; sometimes they perform a duet to strengthen the pair-bond. More often, however, the female replies with a *kewick* call, a variant of which is used by both sexes as a contact call. This combination is popularly represented as *tu-whit, to-woo* and wrongly ascribed to a single bird.

The Eurasian Tawny Owl is primarily a hole-nester, most often in trees and, like other owls, has a breeding regime in which the female remains with the young until they are well grown, while the male hunts for the whole family. The birds feed mainly on small mammals, but they are very adaptable and will readily switch to other prey, such as small birds. It is this versatility which lies behind their wide distribution and their ability to colonize villages, towns and large cities.

Between 10 and 15 races of the Eurasian Tawny Owl are recognized, with distinct reddish-brown and gray color phases in most regions. The reddish-brown phase is more common in the race *S. a. sylvatica* of western Europe (and predominates in Britain), and the gray phase is more common in the northern and eastern European race *S. a. aluco*.

## 3/ GREAT GRAY OWL
*Strix nebulosa*
RANGE: **N Europe, N America, N Asia**
HABITAT: **dense, mature boreal forest**
SIZE: **25½–27½ in (65–70 cm)**

Despite its size – it has a wingspan of over 5 ft (1.5 m) – this magnificent northern forest owl feeds largely on voles. It is often active in daylight and is also capable of finding and capturing its prey in deep snow, apparently by hearing alone. In northern Europe, most Great Gray Owls breed in the old nests of other birds of prey, but some nest on tree stumps and broken-off trunks or on the ground, while a few use artificially built nests and nest-boxes. This is one of a number of owls which is exceptionally bold in defense of its nest: it will launch determined attacks on and even strike humans, occasionally causing injuries.

There are 2 races: *S. n. nebulosa* of North America and *S. n. lapponica* of Eurasia. The North American race has more barred and mottled underparts, with fewer streaks.

## 4/ PEARL-SPOTTED OWLET
*Glaucidium perlatum*
RANGE: **sub-Saharan Africa**
HABITAT: **woodland and savanna**
SIZE: **6½–7 in (17–18 cm)**

As it is often active by day, the Pearl-spotted Owlet is often the most readily seen owl in woodland and savanna in Africa. Prominent "false eyes" on the rear of its head are a useful identification feature. It shows a decided preference for open bush-type savanna and shuns areas where the ground cover is other than sparse.

A vigorous and active hunter, this little owl operates from a perch, striking in a rapid dive and taking insects, small reptiles and small mammals. It also chases and catches flying insects and bats, and some birds. The Pearl-spotted Owlet is the most diurnal of the African owls, regularly hunting during the day, especially during the breeding season, although it also hunts at night. It usually nests in the abandoned tree hole of a barbet or woodpecker, but sometimes chooses a natural hole or an artificial nest-box.

## 5/ NORTHERN PYGMY OWL
*Glaucidium gnoma*
RANGE: **W North America (N to Alaska, E to Rocky Mountains) S to Guatemala**
HABITAT: **dense woodland in mountains and foothills**
SIZE: **6½ in (17 cm)**

Small, earless owls with long tails and shrikelike flight, this species and the Ferruginous Pygmy Owl *G. brasilianum*, from the extreme southwestern USA, look much alike, but occupy different habitats. Both these species and many of their relatives have a pair of prominent, white-edged black patches at the back of their heads; these markings, which resemble eyes, may help the owls to survive by confusing predators and prey.

The tiny Northern Pygmy Owl is strong and ferocious out of all proportion to its size. It sometimes takes prey much larger than itself. It feeds on mice, large insects, ground squirrels, gophers, chipmunks and small birds. It is active during the daytime, hunting mainly in the early morning and late afternoon.

This species nests in natural cavities or old woodpecker excavations in trees, mostly in coniferous woods. There are 2 color phases, a gray one and reddish-brown one.

## 6/ ELF OWL
*Micrathene whitneyi*
RANGE: **SW USA S to Baja California and N Mexico; winters in Mexico**
HABITAT: **deserts, riparian areas, mountain oak and mixed pine and oak forests**
SIZE: **5¼–5¾ in (13.5–14.5 cm)**

The Elf Owl is the world's smallest owl. Within its range, its short tail and less robust shape distinguish it from other Lilliputian, "earless" owls, the Northern Pygmy Owl and the Ferruginous Pygmy Owl.

Unlike the pygmy owls, the Elf Owl is strictly nocturnal. Hiding in daylight – often in plain sight, but motionless – it becomes active as night falls, using its feet to catch prey, often hovering over the ground and above trees and flowers, or darting after insects from a perch, much like a flycatcher. Its diet consists mainly of sphinx moths, grasshoppers, beetles, crickets and scorpions. It sometimes hawks for insects around campfires and streetlamps. Noisy chirps and puppylike yips, often in a series, are its most common calls.

The Elf Owl uses holes excavated by woodpeckers as roosting and nesting cavities. It has to dispute ownership of the holes with the woodpeckers or, when appropriating those abandoned by them, with other hole-nesting birds, from other owls to flycatchers and Cactus Wrens.

## 7/ LITTLE OWL
*Athene noctua*
RANGE: Europe, N Africa, Middle East, Asia
HABITAT: varied open or semi-open areas
SIZE: $8\frac{1}{4}$–9 in (21–23 cm)

The Little Owl shows considerable variation in color, ranging from extremes such as the dark, strongly marked race *A. n. vidalii* from western Europe, to the very pale desert races, such as the Middle Eastern race *A. n. lilith*.

This is a relatively easily seen owl, as it is quite active during the day and also often roosts in open and rather obvious situations, frequently in traditional sites. It is much more terrestrial than most owls, often foraging on foot and also sometimes nesting in holes in the ground, including rabbit burrows. Like the Burrowing Owl, the Little Owl has the comical-looking habit of bobbing its head up and down when agitated. Although hunting may commence before dusk, it is mainly done after dark. A wide variety of small mammals and birds, reptiles, amphibians and invertebrates from insects to earthworms, are eaten, the last predominating in most areas.

## 8/ BURROWING OWL
*Athene cunicularia*
RANGE: extreme SW Canada, W USA, Florida, Central America and South America (except the Amazon Basin)
HABITAT: grassland, deserts, farmlands with low-growing or sparse vegetation, airports, golf courses
SIZE: 7–$9\frac{3}{4}$ in (18–25 cm)

The Burrowing Owl is often active in daylight. This, coupled with its open land habitat, make it more visible than most owls. It can easily be distinguished from other small owls in its range by its long, sparsely feathered legs.

Burrowing Owls feed largely on insects and small mammals. They lay their eggs in a burrow in the ground, often one excavated by a small mammal. Where there are no burrowing animals, they excavate their own burrows in sandy soil, using their bills as well as their long legs.

The owls spend much of their time perched at the entrance to their burrows or on a hummock or fencepost, blinking in the sunlight and bobbing their bodies up and down dramatically when disturbed. They have a mellow *toot tooo* territorial song and adults utter a harsh rattle if a predator approaches the nest. The young make a sound like a rattlesnake when cornered.

## 9/ NORTHERN SAW-WHET OWL
*Aegolius acadicus*
RANGE: E and C North America from Nova Scotia S to N Midwest USA; W North America from S Alaska to S California; also extends S in E and W mountain ranges, in W as far as S Mexico
HABITAT: coniferous, deciduous and mixed deciduous and coniferous forests and woods, riverside thickets
SIZE: $6\frac{1}{2}$–$7\frac{1}{2}$ in (17–19 cm)

This relatively tame little owl is a smaller version of the more widespread Tengmalm's, or Boreal, Owl of northern Europe, Siberia, Alaska and Canada. The 2 species overlap in a 125 ml (200 km) wide zone in southern Canada and the northern Midwest USA, and it is still not completely understood how they can coexist.

The odd name refers to the bird's song, which resembles the sound of a saw-blade being sharpened. Northern Saw-whet Owls also utter a variety of whistles, single notes and rasping sounds. They eat mainly mice and voles, supplemented with the occasional small bird, and lay their eggs in abandoned woodpecker holes.

## 10/ PAPUAN HAWK-OWL
*Uroglaux dimorpha*
RANGE: sparsely distributed throughout New Guinea; Yapen Island
HABITAT: lowland rain forest, rarely reaching as high as 5,000 ft (1,500 m)
SIZE: $11\frac{3}{4}$–13 in (30–33 cm)

As its name suggests, the Papuan Hawk-Owl is more hawklike than other owls, with a slim build, small head and a very long tail for an owl, which accounts for half its total length. Although they share the same rather hawklike appearance, the southern hawk-owls of the genera *Uroglaux* and *Ninox* are very different in other ways and are not closely related.

The Papuan Hawk-Owl is a rare and little-known species, whose calls and nesting habits still remain to be discovered. It feeds on insects, rodents and birds up to the size of pigeons.

## 11/ BOOBOOK OWL
*Ninox novaeseelandiae*
RANGE: Australia, Tasmania, Lesser Sundas, Moluccas, S New Guinea, Norfolk Island, New Zealand
HABITAT: forest, woodland, scrub, urban trees
SIZE: $9\frac{3}{4}$–$13\frac{3}{4}$ in (25–35 cm)

This common small brown owl's familiar double hoot, from which it takes its name, is reminiscent of the call of the European Cuckoo *Cuculus canorus*. Some of the 14 or so races have been regarded as separate species. There are 4 Australian races, including the pale rufous or sandy-brown *N. n. ocellata* from northern, inland and much of western Australia and the darker, heavily spotted *N. n. leucopsis* from Tasmania.

Boobook Owls feed mainly on insects, sometimes caught around town lights, and also on small mammals, birds and geckos. By day they roost in thick foliage or sometimes in tree hollows, caves or buildings.

## 12/ LONG-EARED OWL
*Asio otus*
RANGE: breeds Europe, parts of N Africa, N Asia, N America; birds from extreme N migrate S, some beyond breeding range in America and Far East
HABITAT: woods, forests, copses, shelterbelts, mature scrub
SIZE: $13\frac{3}{4}$–$14\frac{1}{2}$ in (35–37 cm)

Like the Short-eared Owl, the Long-eared Owl is a long-winged bird which hunts over open country, specializing largely in taking small mammal prey, such as voles, and fluctuating widely in numbers and distribution in response to a cyclic food supply. Long-eared Owls nest in dense woods, plantations, stands of trees and tall, thick scrub, almost always using the old nests of birds such as crows or raptors, or sometimes squirrel's dreys.

Long-eared Owls are strictly nocturnal. Like Scops Owls and Screech Owls, they often adopt an extraordinary elongated, cryptic posture when perched in trees during the daytime and look exactly like broken branches. Compared with the Eurasian race *A. o. otus*, most North American Long-eared Owls of the race *A. o. wilsonianus* are more barred than streaked below, have a more golden-red facial disk and yellow rather than orange-red eyes.

## 13/ SHORT-EARED OWL
*Asio flammeus*
RANGE: N Europe, N Asia, North and South America; N populations migrate E, W or S, some far to S of breeding range
HABITAT: moors, heath, grassland, marshes and other open habitats
SIZE: $14\frac{1}{2}$–$15\frac{1}{4}$ in (37–39 cm)

In contrast to the Long-eared Owl, this species nests on the ground in open country, including the edges of wetlands, coastal dunes and small islands. Both species are partial migrants, with Short-eared Owls commonly frequenting coastal marshes and even farmland in winter.

Often hunting by day (especially in winter), Short-eared Owls can be very conspicuous and easily seen – unlike most owls. The male's song is a series of low, muted hoots, often uttered during aerial display flights. Like the Long-eared Owl, this species displays in flight by clapping its wing tips rapidly beneath its body; the sound thus produced carries a surprisingly far.

## 14/ JAMAICAN OWL
*Pseudoscops grammicus*
RANGE: Jamaica
HABITAT: woodland, parklike areas
SIZE: $11\frac{3}{4}$–14 in (30–36 cm)

As with some of the other "unique" owls that are placed in a genus of their own, this one's affinities are uncertain. Whatever its ancestry, its population is limited since it is found only on the island of Jamaica. Very little is known of its biology. This strictly nocturnal owl hunts in both open country and woodland. The voice of the Jamaican Owl is a guttural growl, sometimes interpreted as a *wow*, and an occasional high-pitched, tremulous *whoooo*. It nests in a tree cavity or in a protected fork between branches hidden by vegetation.

# OILBIRD, FROGMOUTHS, POTOOS, OWLET-NIGHTJARS, NIGHTHAWKS AND NIGHTJARS, SWIFTS

OILBIRD

nestling

race *brachyurus* ♂

race *phalaenoides* ♂

dark brown phase

TAWNY FROGMOUTH

COMMON POTOO

gray phase

AUSTRALIAN OWLET-NIGHTJAR

gray phase

race *sennetti* ♂

rufous phase
roost hole

COMMON NIGHTHAWK

race *minor* ♀

COMMON POORWILL ♀

♂

# FAMILIES STEATORNITHIDAE, PODARGIDAE, NYCTIBIIDAE, AEGOTHELIDAE, CAPRIMULGIDAE, APODIDAE

WHIP-POOR-WILL

♂

♀

EUROPEAN NIGHTJAR

♂

courtship display flight

♂

STANDARD-WINGED NIGHTJAR

SCISSOR-TAILED NIGHTJAR

♂

♀

courtship display flight

nest site

BLACK SWIFT

EDIBLE-NEST SWIFTLET

BROWN SPINETAILED SWIFT

CHIMNEY SWIFT

nest

WHITE-THROATED SWIFT

# OILBIRD, FROGMOUTHS, POTOOS, OWLET-NIGHTJARS, NIGHTHAWKS AND NIGHTJARS, SWIFTS

## FAMILY STEATORNITHIDAE
### Oilbird
There is only one species in this family.

### 1/ OILBIRD
*Steatornis caripensis*
RANGE: **Panama to N South America, Trinidad**
HABITAT: **humid forest, caves**
SIZE: **19 in (48 cm)**

Flocks of these large, social birds feed together at night, often traveling long distances from the caves where they roost and nest colonially to find the oily fruits of laurels, palms and incense trees. Many of these fruits are aromatic and it is likely that the Oilbirds find them using their excellent sense of smell. They do not settle on the trees, but gather the fruit in flight with their long hooked bills and store it in their stomachs, digesting it during the day when they are back in the caves.

In the pitch darkness of the cave they find their way by echolocation. The 2–4 white eggs are incubated in a nest of regurgitated fruit, seeds and the birds' own droppings by both parents for 32–35 days. The chicks remain in the nest for 90–120 days. Fed on a similar diet to the parents they put on a lot of fat and in the late nestling period may weigh half as much again as an adult. Local people sometimes kill them for their oil. The birds are now widely protected by law.

## FAMILY PODARGIDAE
### Frogmouths
Medium to large with short, rounded wings and cryptic plumage. Flat bills with huge gape. Nocturnal, mainly insect-eaters; large eyes. Sexes usually similar. Nest built of twigs or down, spiders' webs and lichens in tree. Eggs 1–3, white. Incubation 30 days, nestling period 30 days. 13 species.

### 2/ TAWNY FROGMOUTH
*Podargus strigoides*
RANGE: **Australia and Tasmania**
HABITAT: **open forest, rain forest edge, urban trees**
SIZE: **13¾–21 in (35–53 cm)**

A master of camouflage, the Tawny Frogmouth roosts by day on the branch of a tree, where its cryptic, mottled gray plumage looks like bark.

It varies geographically in size and color; the northern race *P. s. phalaenoides*, for example, is smaller and paler than the southern race *P. s. brachyurus*. Females of some races have an uncommon rufous phase. The Tawny Frogmouth feeds at night on small ground animals such as beetles, centipedes, frogs and mice, which it catches by planing down from a perch.

## FAMILY NYCTIBIIDAE
### Potoos
Medium to large with soft, cryptic plumage. Nocturnal insect-eaters; small bills with huge gape; very large eyes. Sexes alike. Eggs 1–2, white, spotted, laid in small depression on tree stump or branch with no nest. Incubation at least 33 days, nestling period 44–50 days. 5 species.

### 3/ COMMON POTOO
*Nyctibius griseus*
RANGE: **W Mexico to Uruguay, West Indies**
HABITAT: **lowland tropical forest, forest edge, open woods along streams, mangroves**
SIZE: **14–16 in (36–41 cm)**

Named for its melancholy 2-note call, the Common Potoo feeds by night, flying up from a favored perch to capture in its large mouth insects on the wing. By day it normally perches motionless on a branch, stiffening to resemble a snag of splintered wood if it is alarmed. Its intricately patterned cryptic plumage varies from grayish to dark brown. It nests in a tree, usually laying a single egg which is placed in an unlined depression in a tree branch.

## FAMILY AEGOTHELIDAE
### Owlet-nightjars
Small, dumpy, with large-eyed, owl-like faces and strong legs. Also known as owlet-frogmouths. Bill with huge gape. Insect-eaters. Plumage cryptic gray, brown, rufous, black and white; sexes similar. Nest in a tree or rock cavity. Eggs 2–5, white. Incubation and nestling period unknown for most species. 8 species.

### 4/ AUSTRALIAN OWLET-NIGHTJAR
*Aegotheles cristatus*
RANGE: **Australia, Tasmania, S New Guinea**
HABITAT: **open forest and woodland**
SIZE: **8¼–9¾ in (21–25 cm)**

The Australian Owlet-Nightjar is a delicate, mottled gray or rufous bird, with short wings, large eyes, very soft plumage and a mothlike flight. The race *A. c. cristatus* from southern Australia is gray-bellied, whereas *A. c. leucogaster* from northern Australia has a white belly.

It feeds by night, hunting for insects on the wing, pouncing from a perch or chasing them on the ground. By day it roosts alone in a crevice or hole, but will sometimes sun itself at the entrance and often utters its churring call in daylight.

Both male and female build the nest — a bed of fresh acacia and eucalyptus leaves at the base of a tree hollow or cliff crevice. They also probably share the incubation of the 2–5 (usually 3) eggs for about 26 days. Both sexes feed the young, which leave the nest on fledging at about 20–30 days, but they stay with their parents for several months thereafter.

## FAMILY CAPRIMULGIDAE
### Nighthawks and nightjars
Short-legged, long-tailed, hawklike insect-eaters, with large eyes and small bills with huge gape. Cryptic gray, brown, rufous and black plumage, often with white patches on head, wings and tail, most prominent in males. Active mainly at twilight. Nest a shallow scrape on ground. Eggs 1–2, white or pale brown, usually blotched, cryptic. Incubation 16–20 days, nestling period 16–20 days. 82 species.

### 5/ COMMON NIGHTHAWK
*Chordeiles minor*
RANGE: **breeds in North America (except extreme N) and West Indies; winters in South America S to Argentina**
HABITAT: **open fields, gravelly areas, grassland, savanna, semidesert, towns**
SIZE: **9½ in (24 cm)**

The white patches on the sharply pointed wings of the Common Nighthawk are often its most conspicuous feature as it swoops and wheels through the twilight in pursuit of flying insects. It will eat moths, flies, grasshoppers, beetles, mosquitoes and ants; indeed, one bird was found to have the remains of 2,175 ants in its stomach.

The male performs a dramatic courtship ritual, swooping down with booming wings onto a perch near a potential mate, then displaying on the ground. The bird's color varies from dark brown in the eastern North American race *C. m. minor* to paler grayish brown in the Great Plains race *C. m. sennetti*: these color differences are subtle in adults but striking in juveniles.

## 6/ COMMON POORWILL
*Phalaenoptilus nuttallii*

RANGE: breeds in W USA and Mexico; winters S to C Mexico
HABITAT: arid and semiarid country, prairie, scrub woodland, pine forest
SIZE: 8 in (20 cm)

The smallest of the North American nightjars, the Common Poorwill is usually seen as it flies up from roadsides at night. In flight it resembles a large moth. The male has bolder white tips to his tail than the female. The name "poorwill" is derived from its simple 2-note whistle.

It usually catches its insect prey by aerial pursuit, flying up to take moths, grasshoppers and beetles, but it will also snap up insects from the ground. In desert areas during winter the Common Poorwill becomes torpid and enters a state resembling hibernation. This is most unusual among birds.

## 7/ WHIP-POOR-WILL
*Caprimulgus vociferus*

RANGE: breeds in E USA and S Canada, also SW USA and Mexico; winters from Mexico through Central America to Panama
HABITAT: deciduous, mountain and mixed pine-oak forests and woods
SIZE: 9¾ in (25 cm)

The Whip-poor-will takes its name from its distinctive call, which may be repeated 100 times or more without interruption. Like all nightjars, it feeds at night and by twilight, pursuing insects on the wing. The hunting bird flies close to the ground, its wide mouth gaping to scoop up prey.

Whip-poor-wills tend to synchronize their breeding with the full moon, presumably to make hunting easier when they are feeding the young. The eggs are laid directly on the ground, after a courtship in which both birds display on the ground, strutting with their differently patterned tails spread while the male purrs to his mate and she "chuckles" in return.

## 8/ EUROPEAN NIGHTJAR
*Caprimulgus europaeus*

RANGE: breeds in Europe, E to C Asia and N to S Scandinavia; winters in Africa
HABITAT: scrub, heathland, recently felled woodland
SIZE: 11 in (28 cm)

This bird, like other members of its family, is usually located by its song — a persistent, monotonous churring, accompanied by wing claps during the male's evening display flights in the breeding season. He has white spots on his wings and tail which are prominent during various displays.

The tiny bill of the nightjar gives little indication of the huge gape, which is fringed with stiff bristles to improve its efficiency as a snare. The bird always hunts on the wing, wheeling and darting through the gloom as it chases moths and other night-flying insects.

By day it rests, perched horizontally along a branch or on the ground, relying on its superb camouflage for concealment.

## 9/ STANDARD-WINGED NIGHTJAR
*Macrodipteryx longipennis*

RANGE: tropical Africa
HABITAT: open forest
SIZE: 11 in (28 cm)

The Standard-winged Nightjar is named for the flaglike "standards" of the male's wings: these are the second primary flight feathers which become elongated to 18–21 in (45–53 cm) in the breeding season. The male uses them in his courtship display. He circles slowly around a potential mate, with his wings vibrating rapidly and the standards blowing up over his back. The effect is spectacular, but the standards must hamper flight and make the male more vulnerable to predators. Once they have done their job, they usually break off, allowing the bird to fly normally again.

## 10/ SCISSOR-TAILED NIGHTJAR
*Hydropsalis brasiliana*

RANGE: E Peru, Brazil S of Amazon, Paraguay, Uruguay, N and C Argentina
HABITAT: lowland forest, dry woods, clearings
SIZE: male 20 in (51 cm); female 11¾ in (30 cm)

Like the Standard-winged Nightjar, this species has elongated feathers, in this case the central and outermost feathers of the tail. Both sexes have them, but they are much longer in the male. They are probably important in the bird's courtship display, but little is known about its breeding behavior. The Scissor-tailed Nightjar hunts by night, capturing its prey by aerial pursuit. It usually flies close to the ground, mouth open, ensnaring large moths and smaller insects.

## FAMILY APODIDAE
### Swifts

Small to medium, long-winged, highly aerial insect-eaters; short beaks with huge gape; very short legs and strong feet for clinging to vertical surfaces. Generally dull brown or black with white markings, sexes alike. Nest a cup of saliva-cemented material attached to a crevice, or on a branch or leaf. Eggs 1–6, white. Incubation 17–28 days, nestling period 34–72 days. 92 species.

## 11/ BLACK SWIFT
*Nephoecetes niger*

RANGE: W North America from Alaska to California and Central America S to Costa Rica, West Indies; winters in tropical America
HABITAT: mountains
SIZE: 7 in (18 cm)

This is the largest and rarest North American breeding swift. Like all swifts, it hawks for insects on the wing. In bad weather the insects tend to fly low, so the swift hunts near the ground. In good weather the hunting is better high above the ground, and the swift will often ascend so high that it fades from sight.

It nests on cliffs and in canyons and often chooses a site behind a waterfall, so that it has to fly in and out through the cascading water. This provides excellent defense against predators.

## 12/ EDIBLE-NEST SWIFTLET
*Aerodramus fuciphagus*

RANGE: Malaysia, Indonesia
HABITAT: tropical forest with caves, limestone areas, sandstone sea cliffs
SIZE: 4 in (10 cm)

All swifts use dried saliva to cement their nesting materials together, but the cave swiftlets use more than most. The nests of this species are cups of almost pure saliva and are collected in great quantities for use in Chinese bird's-nest soup.

The birds breed in vast colonies in the high recesses of large caves. The adults use echolocation to navigate in the dark and so find their way to the nest.

## 13/ BROWN SPINETAILED SWIFT
*Hirundapus gigantea*

RANGE: India, Southeast Asia, Indonesia
HABITAT: forested valleys, grassy hilltops
SIZE: 8¼ in (21 cm)

Despite its heavy-bodied appearance, this bird is a spectacularly fast and acrobatic performer in the air. It uses its speed and agility to catch flying insects such as bees, wasps, flies and beetles and, like many other swifts, it spends much of its life on the wing. A courting pair will even mate in flight, falling down through the air as they press their bodies together. The nest is built in a rock crevice or hollow tree. It is made of leaves, feathers and other material gathered in flight and is glued together with saliva.

## 14/ CHIMNEY SWIFT
*Chaetura pelagica*

RANGE: breeds E USA and S Canada; winters in Central and NE South America
HABITAT: open and wooded areas, often in towns
SIZE: 5 in (13 cm)

This small, dark swift is an extremely gregarious bird which nests and roosts in huge colonies, sometimes numbering several thousand birds, which may overlap like shingles on a roof. Originally the nest sites and roosting sites were hollow trees, but today the colonies take over air shafts or large chimneys.

The nest is made of thin twigs which the bird snatches in its feet while in flight. There is some evidence of cooperative breeding, with "helpers" assisting the pair with rearing the young.

## 15/ WHITE-THROATED SWIFT
*Aeronautes saxatilis*

RANGE: N Central America and W USA
HABITAT: mountains and ocean cliffs
SIZE: 6¾ in (17 cm)

This is a common and conspicuous bird in areas where there are plenty of suitable nest sites, such as crevices in cliffs. Their penetrating, screaming calls are freely uttered as the birds wheel over the crags and cliffs. This species is only a summer visitor to much of its range in the USA. It often breeds high in the mountains, and has been recorded nesting at 13,000 ft (4,000 m). The clutch size is large for a swift, with as many as 6 eggs.

# SWIFTS, TREE SWIFTS, HUMMINGBIRDS

nest

LESSER SWALLOW-
TAILED SWIFT

nest

AFRICAN
PALM SWIFT

EURASIAN SWIFT

ALPINE SWIFT

♀  ♂

CRESTED TREE SWIFT

nest

REDDISH
HERMIT

WHITE-TIPPED SICKLEBILL

LONG-TAILED HERMIT

♂

VIOLET SABREWING

♀

♀
at nest

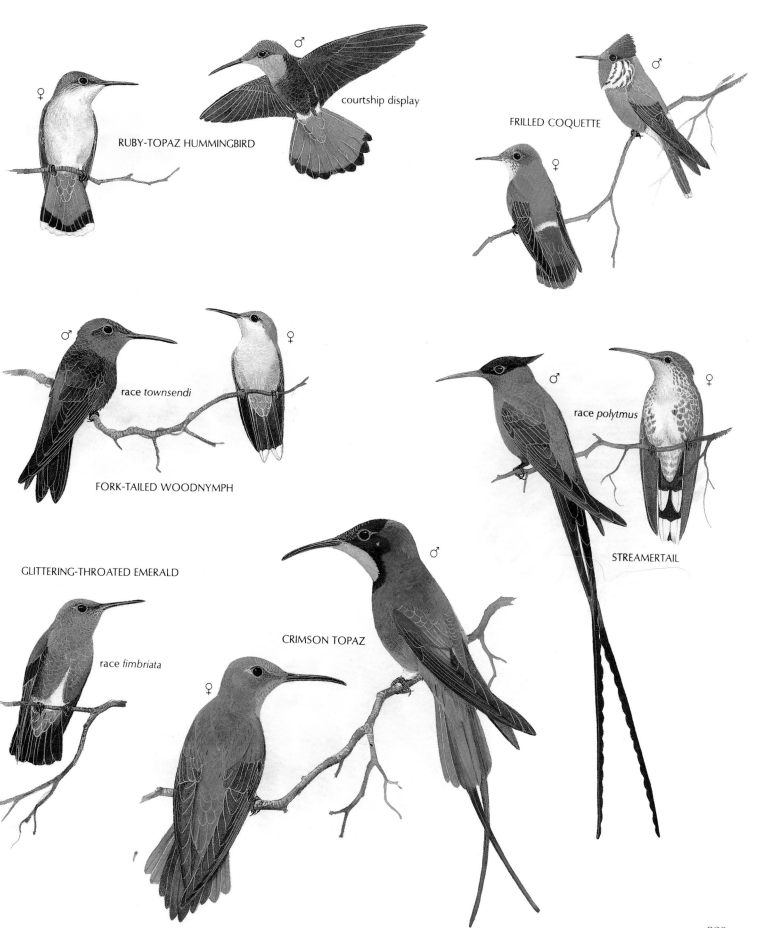

♀
RUBY-TOPAZ HUMMINGBIRD

♂
courtship display

FRILLED COQUETTE
♀
♂

♂
race *townsendi*
♀
FORK-TAILED WOODNYMPH

♂
race *polytmus*
♀
STREAMERTAIL

GLITTERING-THROATED EMERALD
race *fimbriata*
♀

CRIMSON TOPAZ
♂

# SWIFTS, TREE SWIFTS, HUMMINGBIRDS

## 1/ LESSER SWALLOW-TAILED SWIFT
*Panyptila cayennensis*

RANGE: **S Mexico to Peru and Brazil**
HABITAT: **aerial, over many types of terrain**
SIZE: **5 in (13 cm)**

With its deeply forked tail, this is the most swallowlike of all the true swifts, although in the air it usually holds its tail closed in a single point. Its flight is fast and agile, if slightly erratic, as it coasts and then accelerates with rapid wing beats. It is normally seen alone or in pairs, flying very high, but it sometimes joins other swifts as they wheel through the sky hawking for flying insects.

The nest is a large, conical tube of felted plant down and feathers, gummed together with saliva and attached to a tree trunk, wall or rock face. The nest is used for roosting as well as breeding.

## 2/ AFRICAN PALM SWIFT
*Cypsiurus parvus*

RANGE: **sub-Saharan Africa, except much of Ethiopia, Somalia and S Africa**
HABITAT: **aerial, near palms**
SIZE: **6 in (15 cm)**

This slender, pale brown swift is always found in association with palms and may gather in huge flocks at favorite trees. Even in the middle of urban areas it may be very common indeed. It usually forages in groups at treetop height, circling and jinking on its long, narrow wings and occasionally spreading its deeply forked tail as it banks into a steep turn.

Its nest is little more than a pad of feathers and plant down, glued to the vertical underside of a palm frond with saliva. The 2 eggs are also glued to the nest, and the parents incubate them by turns, clinging vertically to the nest. The nestlings have long curved claws, enabling them to cling on tightly as the palm fronds are whipped about violently during windy weather.

## 3/ ALPINE SWIFT
*Tachymarptis melba*

RANGE: **Mediterranean and S Asia to India, also S and E Africa; N birds winter in Africa S to South Africa and in India**
HABITAT: **aerial over hilly country**
SIZE: **8¾ in (22 cm)**

More than twice the size of the Eurasian Swift, this powerful swift may even resemble a small falcon in silhouettte. It is usually seen hunting high over the rocky terrain which, at one time, provided its only nest sites, on cliffs. Today it often nests and roosts in tall buildings, and this has enabled it to expand northward, over less rugged terrain. The birds build the nest from straw and feathers gathered in flight. Most clutches contain 3 eggs. A Swiss study has shown that the adults return to the same site year after year and have a high survival rate – 2 lived to 19 years.

Alpine Swifts are monogamous, retaining the same mate for several years, but they breed in colonies of up to 170 pairs. They rarely fly in bad weather, preferring to roost in the colony; at such times nonbreeding adults will roost in the open nearby, clustering together for warmth.

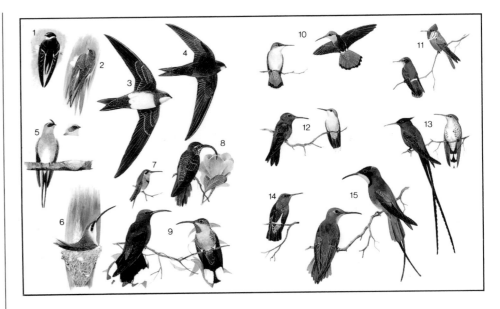

## 4/ EURASIAN SWIFT
*Apus apus*

RANGE: **most of Europe, parts of N Africa and C Asia and E almost to Pacific; winters in tropical Africa**
HABITAT: **aerial; breeds in buildings and rock crevices**
SIZE: **5½ in (14 cm)**

No land bird is more aerial than the Eurasian Swift. It feeds, drinks, sleeps and mates on the wing, returning to earth only to lay its eggs and feed its chicks. A young bird may spend up to 4 years in the air, from the moment it leaves the nest to the day it returns to the colony to rear its own family. Not surprisingly, it is a superb flier: wheeling, climbing and diving as it scoops flying insects from the air, or engages in excited chases, uttering its characteristic shrill, screaming calls.

These swifts nest in colonies, mostly in roof spaces. The adults feed their young on insects carried back in their throat pouches. When insects are scarce during cold or adverse weather, the young will survive for several days without food by becoming torpid, so reducing energy loss.

## FAMILY HEMIPROCNIDAE
### Tree swifts
Medium swifts with crests and long, forked tails. Able to perch (unlike true swifts). Plumage brighter than true swifts, males with chestnut cheeks. Nest a tiny basket of plant fragments glued to side of a branch with saliva. Eggs 1, white. Incubation and nestling period unknown. 3 species.

## 5/ CRESTED TREE SWIFT
*Hemiprocne longipennis*

RANGE: **India, Southeast Asia**
HABITAT: **open woods, clearings, gardens**
SIZE: **6 in (15 cm)**

True swifts spend nearly all their time in the air, but the Crested Tree Swift is well able to perch and often lands on treetops to rest and preen, sitting bolt upright with its crest raised. Refreshed, it swoops away in graceful arcs to gather insects on the wing, or dive down to a forest pool to scoop up a billful of water. It is most active at dawn and dusk and can often be seen hunting in loose flocks. The Latin names for the genus and family mean "half-swallow": indeed, these birds have evolved several swallowlike characteristics, including their shape and plumage and the habit of hawking for insects from a perch.

Unlike true swifts, these birds breed as isolated pairs and vigorously defend their territories. The single egg fills the tiny nest like an acorn in its cup. The nest is a fragile basket made of bark and leaf fragments glued together with saliva and similarly cemented to the side of a branch. Both parents take turns to incubate the egg, their weight supported by the branch.

## FAMILY TROCHILIDAE
### Hummingbirds
Small, slender-billed nectar-eaters. Agile in the air, can hover and fly backward. Brilliant, often iridescent plumage; males often brighter, some with ornate tail feathers. Eggs 1–2, white. Cup nest, usually on horizontal twig. Incubation 14–23 days, nestling period 18–38 days. 334 species.

## 6/ LONG-TAILED HERMIT
*Phaethornis superciliosus*

RANGE: **E Mexico to Bolivia and C Brazil**
HABITAT: **lowland forest understory and tall secondary growth**
SIZE: **6 in (15 cm)**

Hermits are so-called because they keep to the dark understory of tropical forests, especially along streams and edges where they forage along regular routes. The very long, downcurved bill of the Long-tailed Hermit equips it for extracting nectar from large flowers such as heliconias and passion flowers, but it also gleans insects and spiders from leaves and cobwebs.

The males form singing assemblies, or "leks," and compete with each other to attract mates. The best singers usually mate with all the available females. The nest is a deep cup of plant fibers and spiders' silk attached beneath the drooping tip of a large leaf or palm frond.

## 7/ REDDISH HERMIT
*Phaethornis ruber*
RANGE: **Colombia and Venezuela to N Bolivia and S Brazil**
HABITAT: **humid forest undergrowth, forest edge, secondary woodland, scrub**
SIZE: **3½ in (9 cm)**

Like other hermits, this small hummingbird prefers to fly along a circuit of food sources instead of establishing a feeding territory, picking insects from beneath large leaves between visits to nectar-bearing flowers. It has an insectlike, weaving flight that generates an audible humming – a common characteristic of hummingbirds and the origin of their name.

For courtship, the males sing competitively in a group, called a lek. Their shrill, repetitive calls attract females, which mate with the males of their choice, then leave to build cone-shaped nests on palm-frond tips close to the ground.

## 8/ WHITE-TIPPED SICKLEBILL
*Eutoxeres aquila*
RANGE: **Costa Rica to W Ecuador and NE Peru**
HABITAT: **forest understory, forest edge, secondary growth**
SIZE: **5 in (13 cm)**

This highly specialized hummingbird has a strongly downcurved bill for probing the curved blooms of plants such as certain heliconias. It prefers to feed at hanging bunches of flowers, clinging to them with its powerful feet as it sips the nectar. In the process it becomes well dusted with pollen and unwittingly carries it to other heliconia flowers to bring about cross-pollination.

Many tropical plants rely on hummingbirds as pollinators. In this case, the precise fit of the bird's bill in the flower suggests that both have evolved together, providing the plant with a reliable pollinator and the White-tipped Sicklebill with an exclusive source of nectar.

## 9/ VIOLET SABREWING
*Campylopterus hemileucurus*
RANGE: **S Mexico to W Panama**
HABITAT: **mountain forest, in understory and at edges, especially near streams**
SIZE: **6 in (15 cm)**

This large, elegant hummingbird is named for the glittering violet plumage of the male and the thickened and flattened shafts of the outer 2 primary feathers. The female is mainly gray and, unusually for a hummingbird, smaller.

Less aggressive than other hummingbirds of its size, the Violet Sabrewing rarely maintains feeding territories. It often takes nectar from banana flowers and is common in banana plantations. It can often be located while feeding by its explosive twittering.

During the 6-month breeding season, the males associate in leks to sing for mates, each perching on a sapling and calling with evenly spaced, piercing notes. The female builds the cup-shaped nest alone.

## 10/ RUBY-TOPAZ HUMMINGBIRD
*Chrysolampis mosquitus*
RANGE: **Trinidad and Tobago, N and C South America**
HABITAT: **arid open country, gardens, lowlands up to 5,750 ft (1,750 m)**
SIZE: **3½ in (9 cm)**

Common in the lowlands of Trinidad and Tobago during much of the year, the striking Ruby-topaz Hummingbird was collected by the thousands during the last century when many species of hummingbird were sold as ornaments for the parlor and for dressing ladies' hats. The females escaped this fate, having relatively drab greenish-gray plumage.

The glittering male courts his mate alone, putting on a spectacularly beautiful display in which he circles rapidly around her with widely fanned tail and raised crown feathers. He is very aggressive at this time and will even attack birds of prey. The nest is a tiny lichen-covered cup lined with plant down.

## 11/ FRILLED COQUETTE
*Lophornis magnifica*
RANGE: **E and C Brazil**
HABITAT: **forest, scrub, parkland**
SIZE: **2¾ in (7 cm)**

All the hummingbirds of the genus *Lophornis* are adorned with crests, but the male Frilled Coquette is one of the most spectacular. His fanlike ruffs of white feathers tipped with iridescent green form a dramatic contrast with the rich chestnut crown feathers, and in flight he looks more like a butterfly than a bird, as he hovers to feed from a flower.

During courtship the male and female hover together, dancing up and down in the air. After mating, the female builds a simple cup-shaped nest in low vegetation, fastening it down by working the fibers of the bottom and one side around the supporting twig.

## 12/ FORK-TAILED WOODNYMPH
*Thalurania furcata*
RANGE: **NW and C South America from W Ecuador to E Bolivia and Paraguay**
HABITAT: **humid forest and forest edge in lowlands and foothills**
SIZE: **male 4 in (10 cm); female 3 in (8 cm)**

Although solitary by nature, the Fork-tailed Woodnymph is a bold, inquisitive bird that shows very little fear of man. It will often approach passers-by and hover in front of them in a blur of wings before returning to its feeding routine. There are some 23 races; the race *T.f. townsendi* (illustrated) occurs from eastern Guatemala to southwestern Honduras.

Unusually for a hummingbird, the female is considerably smaller than her mate. Being so small has its drawbacks: small hummingbirds need to absorb a great deal of energy to maintain their body heat and may have to eat up to half their body weight in food every day. At night hummingbirds often become torpid, regaining their normal temperature when the sun raises the air temperature the following day.

## 13/ STREAMERTAIL
*Trochilus polytmus*
RANGE: **Jamaica**
HABITAT: **semiarid lowlands to high mountains, including man-made habitats**
SIZE: **9¾ in (25 cm)**

Many hummingbirds are threatened by the destruction of their native forests, but the Streamertail thrives in open country, and its numbers have actually increased as the Jamaican forests have been felled. Known locally as the Doctor Bird, it is a common sight throughout the island and a frequent visitor to suburban flower gardens.

The male is the most spectacular of all Jamaican hummingbirds. He has glittering green plumage with two 6 in (15 cm) long, black tail feathers. During the mating display he will fly before a perched female in short pendulums, chirping rhythmically, or perch near her and wave his fluttering streamers from side to side.

The race *T.p. polytmus*, from most of Jamaica, has a red bill tipped with black in the male; dull red-brown with a black tip in the female. The other race, *T.p. scitulus*, is restricted to the extreme eastern part of the island and has an entirely black bill.

## 14/ GLITTERING-THROATED EMERALD
*Amazilia fimbriata*
RANGE: **N South America, E of Andes to S Bolivia and S Brazil**
HABITAT: **shrubby secondary growth, forest edge, up to 1,650 ft (500 m)**
SIZE: **3 in (8 cm)**

This tiny hummingbird feeds mainly on nectar, taking it from blossoms in low shrubbery or at midheight in the forest. It often perches on bare, exposed twigs, calling with a soft tapping note like 2 small pebbles being struck together. Like many other hummingbirds, it will defend its feeding territory vigorously against intruders.

It nearly always nests low down, often less than 3 ft (1 m) from the ground, attaching its nest to a fork in a bush or the tip of a low tree branch. In Surinam it seems to nest at any time of year, but elsewhere its breeding may be more seasonal.

The race illustrated is *A.f. fimbriata*, from French Guiana, southern Venezuela and eastern Brazil.

## 15/ CRIMSON TOPAZ
*Topaza pella*
RANGE: **Guianas, SE Venezuela, NE Brazil, E Ecuador**
HABITAT: **rain forest**
SIZE: **male 8 in (20 cm); female 7 in (18 cm)**

The Crimson Topaz is a relatively large hummingbird, but over a third of the male's length is accounted for by 2 long, slender, inward-curving tail feathers. They are the finishing touch to a plumage which is quite breathtaking in its beauty.

With their relatively short bills, these birds are less specialized than long-billed hummingbirds and will take nectar from a wide variety of flowers, as well as catching insects. Their calls have been described as a chicklike *peep peep*.

# HUMMINGBIRDS

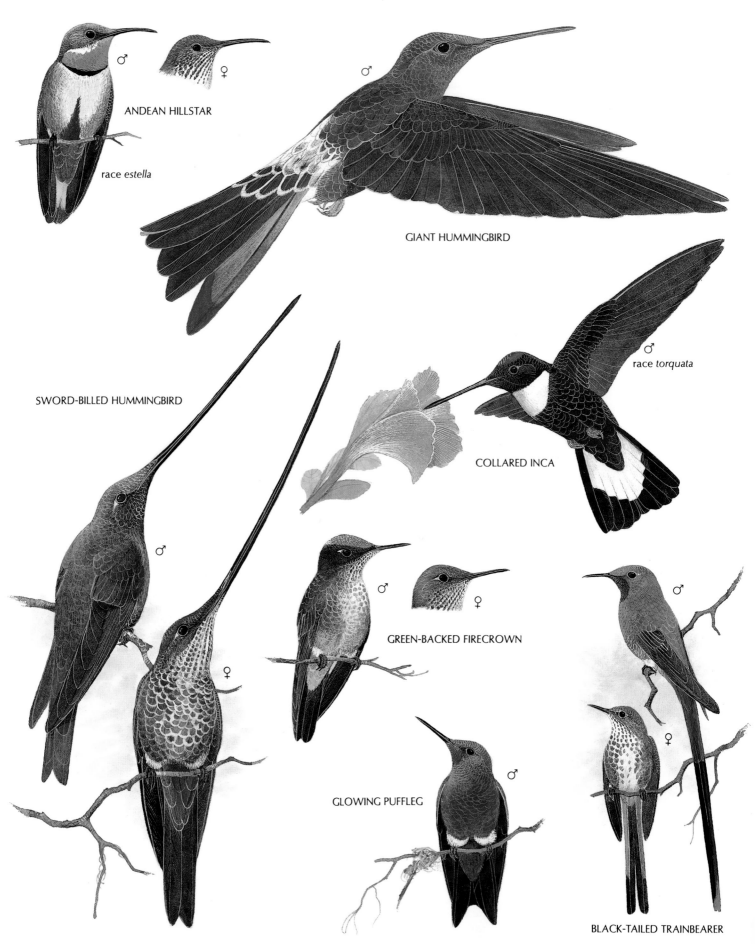

ANDEAN HILLSTAR

race *estella*

GIANT HUMMINGBIRD

SWORD-BILLED HUMMINGBIRD

COLLARED INCA

race *torquata*

GREEN-BACKED FIRECROWN

GLOWING PUFFLEG

BLACK-TAILED TRAINBEARER

RED-TAILED COMET

BEARDED HELMETCREST

race *guerinii*

LONG-TAILED SYLPH

MARVELOUS SPATULETAIL

RUBY-THROATED HUMMINGBIRD

feeding chicks

BEE HUMMINGBIRD

at nest

AMETHYST WOODSTAR

CALLIOPE HUMMINGBIRD

# HUMMINGBIRDS

## 1/ ANDEAN HILLSTAR
*Oreotrochilus estella*

RANGE: **Andes from Ecuador to Argentina, Chile and N Peru**
HABITAT: **rocky gorges, grassy low scrubby growth with grasses, high plateaus**
SIZE: **5 in (13 cm)**

The Andean Hillstar lives in the harsh climate and sparse vegetation above 13,000 ft (4,000 m). The race *O. e. estella* is from southern Peru to northern Chile and northwestern Argentina; the males of some other races, isolated on high mountains, such as *O. e. chimborazo* from Mount Chimborazo, Ecuador, have a different pattern of colors on the head. Like some other hummingbirds, the Andean Hillstar can become torpid to cope with periods of extreme stress in its tough environment.

This species uses its disproportionately large feet to perch rather than hover when it is feeding on nectar. Females feed in abundant gorges containing high concentrations of blooms close to nest sites, whereas males tend to feed in open areas where the flowers are more dispersed. Courtship thus brings the male into the female's territory, which is the reverse of the situation in most hummingbirds.

Nests are well protected from the weather as a result of their hammocklike structure and thick insulation of mosses, lichens and plant down. The 2 white eggs are incubated for 20 days. The young fledge in 22–38 days and often continue to use the nest as a roost.

## 2/ GIANT HUMMINGBIRD
*Patagona gigas*

RANGE: **Andes from Ecuador to Chile and Argentina**
HABITAT: **mountain scrub and river bank forest, cultivated land**
SIZE: **7½–7¾ in (19–20 cm)**

This is the largest of all hummingbirds. In flight, it resembles a large swift with a long bill. Its long, pointed wings occasionally perform a flap-sail flight pattern, and its wing beats are noticeably slower than those of other hummingbirds when hovering before flowers to glean food.

When incubating the 2 eggs, the adult birds seem to overflow the tiny nest, which is constructed of mosses and lichens on top of a large branch. Young birds are fed regurgitated nectar and insects.

## 3/ COLLARED INCA
*Coeligena torquata*

RANGE: **NW Venezuela to N Bolivia**
HABITAT: **wet, humid mountain forest, shrubby forest edge**
SIZE: **6 in (15 cm)**

One of the more common hummingbirds in its preferred habitat, the Collared Inca feeds low at forest shrubbery and forest edges. It hovers for long periods at pendant flowers on shrubs and vines, and also takes flying insects that have been stirred up by mixed flocks of forest birds. The race *C. t. torquata* from Colombia and eastern Ecuador is illustrated; other races have differently

colored plumage on their crowns, lower back and underparts.

These silent birds dart about actively, following their chosen circuits, or "trap-lines," of flowers rather than defending a feeding territory. The breeding season is variable; it is generally in spring and summer, although a nest has been found in November.

## 4/ SWORD-BILLED HUMMINGBIRD
*Ensifera ensifera*

RANGE: **Venezuela to N Bolivia**
HABITAT: **humid mountain forest, forest edge, shrubby hillside**
SIZE: **9¾ in (25 cm)**

Seldom seen at ground level, the Sword-billed Hummingbird habitually stays in the middle and upper levels of trees. Its uniquely long bill, which is nearly the length of its body, enables it to reach nectar deep inside the longest flower corollas. It particularly favors *Datura* and *Passiflora* flowers, which it finds along regular routes through the forest, and also hawks the occasional insect in midair.

When it is perched, the Sword-billed Hummingbird holds its bill upward, presumably because its neck and body would otherwise be unable to bear the strain. The call of this unusual species is a low, guttural *trrr*. Breeding begins in early spring. The mossy cup nest is built among the roots of epiphytic plants, such as bromeliads, growing on trees high above the ground.

## 5/ GREEN-BACKED FIRECROWN
*Sephanoides sephanoides*

RANGE: **breeds Chile and W Argentina; winters to E Argentina**
HABITAT: **scrub and gardens**
SIZE: **4¼ in (11 cm)**

This common hummingbird is known to feed on the nectar of *Escallonia serrata* and the waxy-white flowers of *Pernettya mucronata*. It also searches old yucca heads for insects and seizes tiny flying insects. The male Green-backed Firecrown has a twittering song and a high-pitched

*tsee*, often followed by a metallic rattling call.

The flight of this species is rather slow for a hummingbird, and at intervals the bird may fold its wings and drop down 12 in (30 cm) or so before beating its wings again.

## 6/ GLOWING PUFFLEG
*Eriocnemis vestitus*

RANGE: **NW Venezuela to E Ecuador and N Peru**
HABITAT: **high mountain forest edge, scrub**
SIZE: **3½ in (9 cm)**

In good light this bird's brilliant colors, particularly its upper tail coverts, really do glow, while its spectacular white leg muffs make it look as though each leg is wrapped in fresh cotton. All pufflegs have these leg muffs, which vary in color between the different species.

The Glowing Puffleg is both solitary and pugnacious, chasing potential competitors from the flowering shrubs at which it hovers or briefly clings to sip nectar.

## 7/ BLACK-TAILED TRAINBEARER
*Lesbia victoriae*

RANGE: **Colombia and Ecuador S to S Peru**
HABITAT: **grassy slopes and shrubby areas, upper subtropical and temperate zones of the Andes**
SIZE: **male up to 9¾ in (25 cm), female up to 5½ in (14 cm)**

This species favors the drier highlands and is replaced by the Green-tailed Trainbearer *L. nuna* at lower elevations. The Black-tailed Trainbearer sips nectar from the flowers of tall shrubs and trees at all levels. The male's song is a rattling trill that descends at the end; it changes to simple, high-pitched chip notes while he is foraging.

The deeply forked tail is much longer in the male than in the female, measuring up to over half his total length. During courtship displays he spreads his magnificent tail wide as he chases and dives near his potential mate, producing a sound like the ripping of a piece of cloth. The nest is a wide, open cup.

## 8/ RED-TAILED COMET
*Sappho sparganura*

RANGE: Andes of Bolivia, Chile and W Argentina
HABITAT: high Andean scrub, brush and plateau
SIZE: 7¾ in (20 cm)

All comet hummingbirds have long, iridescent red tails tipped with velvety black, although the different species vary in the shades of red.

The Red-tailed Comet is often seen feeding at flowering bushes with other hummingbirds. A red-flowered plant, *Psitacanthus cuneifolius*, parasitic on the creosote bush, is a particular favorite of this species. In between feeding bouts, the bird perches to conserve energy in sunny sheltered areas, but may give chase after giving *chit-it* calls if another male appears. In flight both sexes fan their forked tails, and at rest they nervously bob their tails up and down.

The nest is woven out of plant fibers and moss, often lined with hair, and is sited in a sheltered spot on a wall, tree or rock ledge.

## 9/ BEARDED HELMETCREST
*Oxypogon guerinii*

RANGE: NW Venezuela, N and C Colombia
HABITAT: bushy or grassy slopes above 10,000 ft (3,000 m)
SIZE: 4¼ in (11 cm)

The female Bearded Helmetcrest lacks the unique crest and white beard of the male, but both are well camouflaged to blend into their open environment. The race shown, *O. g. guerinii*, is found in eastern Colombia and has a white beard with a black central stripe and glittering green borders in the male.

Bearded Helmetcrests forage at low flowering shrubs by hovering or clinging briefly to sip nectar from the blossoms or capture visiting insects. Outside the main flowering season, the Bearded Helmetcrest is often found between scrub and open grasslands, sometimes walking across the matted grass or making short, hovering leaps in search of insects.

The deep, thick, cup nests, which are attached to rocky cliffs, steep banks or branches of the shrub *Espeletia*, have been spotted in July and September, and a young fledgling was once found in December.

## 10/ LONG-TAILED SYLPH
*Aglaiocercus kingi*

RANGE: Venezuela, Colombia, Ecuador, Peru and Bolivia
HABITAT: from 3,000–10,000 ft (900–3,000 m) in tropical and subtropical humid forest and scrub, gardens, plantations
SIZE: male 7 in (18 cm); female 4 in (10 cm)

The Long-tailed Sylph feeds at almost any level in forest edge and open areas. It forages by "trap-lining" – making a regular circuit of flowers within a territory – and sometimes joins other hummingbirds in the forest canopy. It also takes nectar or insects while hovering or briefly perching, and will dart out to capture tiny insects. It can reach speeds of 30–47 mph (50–75 km/h).

The domed moss and plant fiber nest with a side entrance is fastened to a leafy twig. Nesting occurs between February and October.

## 11/ MARVELOUS SPATULETAIL
*Loddigesia mirabilis* [?]

RANGE: N Peru
HABITAT: subtropical forest and scrub
SIZE: male 11½ in (29 cm); female 4 in (10 cm)

The Marvelous Spatuletail has only 4 fully developed tail feathers, compared with the 10 typical of other hummingbirds. Particularly marvelous are the 2 outermost tail feathers of the male, each of which has a long, bare shaft ending in a broad spatule, or racket, and curve inward to cross over one another.

During his courtship display the male frames his iridescent throat plumage with his decorative tail feathers, flying back and forth in front of his prospective mate.

Little is known about this very localized species, recorded only from the Chachapoyas region of Peru, east of the Rio Utcubamba between 7,500 and 8,500 ft (2,300 and 2,600 m).

## 12/ RUBY-THROATED HUMMINGBIRD
*Archilochus colubris*

RANGE: breeds E North America; winters coastal SE USA to NW Costa Rica
HABITAT: woodland and swamp
SIZE: 3½ in (9 cm)

These tiny migratory birds generally reach wintering grounds in south Mexico and Central America after achieving the remarkable feat of crossing the Gulf of Mexico. Males leave their breeding territories immediately after the nesting season, and females follow soon after the young have fledged. The young migrate alone.

Male Ruby-throated Hummingbirds defend nectar resources as breeding territories with highly stylized pendulum displays; females defend the nest area. Outside the breeding season, both sexes defend nectar sources vigorously. Red tubular flowers are a favored food source; tiny flying insects and small spiders are also eaten.

Antisocial at all times, these birds do not form a pair-bond. The female builds the tiny nest of spiders' webs and plant down, often near water, where she incubates the 2 white eggs and rears the young alone.

## 13/ AMETHYST WOODSTAR
*Calliphlox amethystina*

RANGE: South America E of Andes to S Peru, N Bolivia, Paraguay, NE Argentina
HABITAT: tropical forest, scrub, savanna, grassland
SIZE: 2¼–3 in (6–8 cm)

The Amethyst Woodstar is one of the smallest of all hummingbirds, and females are smaller than males. It is found in almost any habitat within its range except rain forest, but populations can be quite local.

This is a solitary species, which makes its rounds of flowering shrubs and small trees in

search of nectar and tiny insects. It forages well into the canopy and often perches high. Its hovering wings, beating at up to 80 times per second, make a distinctive insectlike buzz. The male arcs back and forth like a pendulum when displaying to the female. The nest is a tiny cup of plant fiber and down, which generally straddles a small branch.

## 14/ BEE HUMMINGBIRD
*Calypte helenae* [?]

RANGE: Cuba and Isle of Pines
HABITAT: forest and forest edge, gardens; occasionally in fairly open country
SIZE: 2¼ in (6 cm)

The Bee Hummingbird is the smallest bird in the world, the male being slightly smaller than the female. Its body measures only ½ in (1.25 cm), the bill and tail making up the total length. It weighs no more than 1/15 oz (2 g) – even some large beetles weigh 20 times as much.

Uncommon and local in distribution, the Bee Hummingbird can be found in many areas from the coast to the mountain. It feeds from near ground level into the canopy of open forest on any plant which blooms and produces nectar.

When feeding from flowers, the Bee Hummingbird holds its body horizontal, unlike the common hummingbird of Cuba, the Cuban Emerald *Chlorostilbon ricordii* and many other hummingbirds, which feed vertically. Its tiny wings beat 50–80 times a second as it hovers.

It is sometimes hard to distinguish these tiny birds from insects, and their voices are also insectlike. When at rest, the Bee Hummingbird perches on small, exposed branches high off the ground. Its eggs, too, are minuscule, varying from ¼ in (6.35 mm) to less than ½ in (11.4 mm) long.

## 15/ CALLIOPE HUMMINGBIRD
*Stellula calliope*

RANGE: breeds W North America; winters SW Mexico
HABITAT: mountain meadows, edges of coniferous forest
SIZE: 3 in (8 cm)

The Calliope Hummingbird is the smallest bird breeding in the North American continent north of Mexico. Juveniles resemble females, lacking the male's magenta-striped gorget and possessing cinnamon underparts.

Northward migration in early spring usually follows the Pacific coast, since snow on high mountains restricts the availability of nectar and insect foods. Southward migration in late summer follows mountain ridges, and late wildflowers are the main food source during this time.

Male birds form territories around favored food plants and repel interlopers with wide *U*-shaped aggressive displays, using the sun's brilliant reflection from the metallic purple feathers on their chins for added effect.

Female territories center on the tiny plant down and spiders' web nest, typically built in a tree near the edge of the forest. The 2 eggs hatch after 15 days' incubation, and the chicks fledge after 20 days' care, exclusively by the female. Once the young are able to feed themselves, she chases them away from her own food source.

race *striatus*

SPECKLED MOUSEBIRD

RESPLENDENT
QUETZAL

♀

♂

♀

♂

LESSER PIED
KINGFISHER

♀

GREEN KINGFISHER

♂

STORK-BILLED KINGFISHER

SHOVEL-BILLED KINGFISHER

♂

race *novaeguineae*

LAUGHING KOOKABURRA

♂

♀

BAR-TAILED
TROGON ♀

♂

♂

ORANGE-BREASTED
TROGON

♀

BELTED KINGFISHER

COLLARED TROGON

♀

race *ispida*

♂

♂

AFRICAN PYGMY
KINGFISHER

race *hispidoides*
in nest–burrow

RIVER KINGFISHER

race *doris*

♂

nest in termite colony

SACRED KINGFISHER

COMMON PARADISE KINGFISHER

race *galatea*

BLUE-BREASTED KINGFISHER

# MOUSEBIRDS, TROGONS, KINGFISHERS

## FAMILY COLIIDAE
### Mousebirds

Small, gregarious birds. Long, spikily pointed tails. Short, rounded wings. Outer toes very mobile. Soft plumage brown or gray, with loose crest. Some have bright red or blue face or neck markings. Sexes similar. Untidy cup nest in bushes. Eggs 1–8, whitish or speckled. Incubation 11–14 days, nestling period about 17 days. 6 species.

## 1/ SPECKLED MOUSEBIRD
*Colius striatus*

RANGE: **C, E and S Africa**
HABITAT: **woodland, scrub, gardens, hedges**
SIZE: **11¾–14 in (30–36 cm)**

Mousebirds take their name from their striking, rodentlike appearance as they creep and scramble through vegetation. Members of family groups follow each other with alternate whirring and gliding flight, their extremely long tails, up to 8½ in (22 cm) long, projecting stiffly behind them. They often perch in clusters and more than 20 birds may roost together in a tight bunch. There are some 17 races: *C. s. striatus* from southwestern South Africa is illustrated.

Speckled Mousebirds use their robust, arched, hooked bills to feed on all kinds of vegetable matter. Flocks of them can cause much damage in gardens and orchards.

## FAMILY TROGONIDAE
### Trogons

Medium forest birds. Bill wide, hooked, with stiff bristles around gape. Feet small and weak. Tail long, often square-ended and broad. Plumage soft, dense and colorful; males with upperparts often brilliant metallic green, breast and belly bright red, pink, orange or yellow. Sexes fairly similar, but females duller. Unlined nest in cavity. Eggs 2–4, buffish or whitish. Incubation (known only for few American species) 17–19 days, nestling periods about 17–18 days. 39 species.

## 2/ RESPLENDENT QUETZAL
*Pharomachrus mocinno*                    [V]

RANGE: **S Mexico to W Panama**
HABITAT: **humid cloud forest, usually at 4,000–10,000 ft (1,200–3,000 m)**
SIZE: **13¾–15 in (35–38 cm)**

The male Resplendent Quetzal's middle wing coverts are very long and the upper tail coverts form a train of filmy streamers, up to 3 ft (1 m) long. These undulate and flutter during normal flight, as well as in aerial courtship displays. Where areas of undisturbed cloud forest still exist, Resplendent Quetzals can still be fairly common, but their numbers have decreased due to the destruction of forest. The birds have also suffered from persistent trapping for the cage-bird trade, despite legal protection.

Resplendent Quetzals are mainly fruit-eaters, although they will also take some invertebrates, and even small vertebrates, when feeding their young. They generally keep to the canopy, where their green upperparts provide surprisingly effective camouflage in the leafy shade.

## 3/ COLLARED TROGON
*Trogon collaris*

RANGE: **tropical Mexico S to W Ecuador, N Bolivia and E Brazil; Trinidad**
HABITAT: **humid and wet forest and forest edges; also riverine forest in Amazonia**
SIZE: **9¾ in (25 cm)**

The most widespread of the New World trogons, this species is typical of the family both in color and pattern. Collared Trogons are usually solitary or travel in pairs. They often sit motionless for extended periods, but will sally out from perches to snatch insects or pluck hanging fruit.

Collared Trogons nest in unlined cavities, usually enlarging existing holes in rotting wood or breaking into arboreal termite nests. Both sexes share the incubation and care of the young.

## 4/ BAR-TAILED TROGON
*Apaloderma vittatum*

RANGE: **mountains of C Africa, from Nigeria to Mozambique**
HABITAT: **forest**
SIZE: **11 in (28 cm)**

Usually found alone or in pairs, the Bar-tailed Trogon is a somewhat sluggish African bird. It often sits for long periods on a favorite perch in the midlevels of the forest and is inconspicuous there until it swoops out after a flying insect. Although silent for much of the time, the Bar-tailed Trogon has a characteristic sharp *wup* note that it repeats with increasing volume about 12 times. It is a sedentary, territorial species, but the size of individual territories varies considerably.

## 5/ ORANGE-BREASTED TROGON
*Harpactes oreskios*

RANGE: **Burma to Vietnam, Java, Borneo**
HABITAT: **evergreen forest, bamboo; also sparse woodland**
SIZE: **11¾ in (30 cm)**

The plumage of the male Orange-breasted Trogon is not as resplendent as that of many other species but it is, perhaps, more subtly beautiful. This species sometimes takes insects from the ground; it also flutters to snatch prey from twigs and can catch winged insects in flight. Across its range, this species is less confined to wet evergreen forest than most other Southeast Asian trogons.

## FAMILY ALCEDINIDAE
### Kingfishers

Small to medium, long-billed, large-headed. Plumage variable, bright. Sexes alike or differ. Nest in holes they excavate in earth banks, rotting trees or termite mounds, or in existing holes in trees. Eggs usually 2–3 in tropics, up to 10 at higher latitudes, white. Incubation 17–27 days, nestling period 22–37 days. 92 species.

## 6/ BELTED KINGFISHER
*Megaceryle alcyon*

RANGE: **breeds through most of North America; winters in ice-free areas S to West Indies and N Colombia**
HABITAT: **streams, rivers, ponds, marshes**
SIZE: **11¾ in (30 cm)**

This solitary kingfisher prefers clear waters with overhanging trees, wires or other perches. It usually hovers and dives for fish, but will also prey on insects, crayfish, frogs, snakes and even the occasional mouse. A loud, dry, rattling call often announces the presence of this bird.

The breeding distribution of the Belted Kingfisher seems to be limited only by the availability of foraging sites and earth banks in which it can excavate its nest chamber. This lies at the end of an upward-sloping tunnel 3–16 ft (1–5 m) long.

## 7/ LESSER PIED KINGFISHER
*Ceryle rudis*

RANGE: **Africa, Middle East, S Asia**
HABITAT: **lakes, broad rivers, estuaries**
SIZE: **9¾ in (25 cm)**

By hovering rather than perching as it watches for fish, the Lesser Pied Kingfisher can hunt over broad stretches of water. It is the only kingfisher species that regularly fishes far offshore.

Studies of breeding colonies in Uganda show that the Lesser Pied Kingfisher leads a complex social life. As in many tropical birds, the breeding pair receive help with the nesting chores from up to 4 full-grown, nonbreeding adults. Sometimes these are the offspring from the previous year, but often the helpers are quite unrelated. The system allows a colony to raise the greatest number of young under the prevailing conditions.

## 8/ GREEN KINGFISHER
*Chloroceryle americana*

RANGE: **extreme S USA S to W Peru, C Argentina, and Uruguay; Trinidad, Tobago**
HABITAT: **streams bordered by shrubby habitat or forest, some mountain streams**
SIZE: **7½ in (19 cm)**

Generally solitary, the Green Kingfisher would easily go unnoticed as it watches for prey were it not for its characteristic habit of frequently raising its head and bobbing its tail. More than one Green Kingfisher may be seen in a suitable site, but they jealously guard their favorite hunting perches and are rarely seen together. Clarity of the water is important for hunting success. This species dives mainly for small fish, 1–2 in (3–5 cm) in length. Its flight is straight and low over the water, the white on the wings and sides of the tail flashing conspicuously as it passes.

This species utters a low, but distinctive *choot* or *chew* call and a descending series of *tew-tew-tew* notes. Its alarm call is a soft, ticking rattle.

## 9/ RIVER KINGFISHER
*Alcedo atthis*

RANGE: **breeds Europe, NW Africa, Asia, Indonesia to Solomon Islands; winters in S of range**
HABITAT: **clear, slow-moving streams and small rivers, canals, ditches, reeds, marshes; coasts in winter**
SIZE: **6¼ in (16 cm)**

This bird and the Belted Kingfisher are the most northerly breeding species of kingfisher. Along with the European race *A. a. ispida*, the illustration shows *A. a. hispidoides*, which ranges from northern Sulawesi to the Bismarck Archipelago off Papua New Guinea.

The River Kingfisher is aggressively territorial, defending a ½–3 ml (1–5 km) stretch of stream in winter, even from its mate. In spring it will drive away both rivals and small songbirds. It excavates its burrow in the bank of a stream, river or gravel pit, usually above water; most nest-burrows are 18–36 in (45–90 cm) long. It rarely feeds away from water and is an expert fisher.

## 10/ AFRICAN PYGMY KINGFISHER
*Ceyx picta*

RANGE: **tropical Africa**
HABITAT: **grassy glades near forest edge, streams, lakeshores, dry woodland**
SIZE: **4¾ in (12 cm)**

This bird is one of the world's smallest kingfishers. Although it takes some of its prey from water, it feeds mainly on dry land, where it catches insects, millipedes, spiders and, occasionally, even small frogs. At higher latitudes, from Senegal to Eritrea and from Zambia to Natal, this species is a breeding visitor, arriving for the summer rainy season. It migrates at night, and many birds are killed when, attracted by the light, they collide with windows and buildings.

## 11/ LAUGHING KOOKABURRA
*Dacelo novaeguineae*

RANGE: **E and SE Australia; introduced to Tasmania and SW Australia**
HABITAT: **open forest, urban trees**
SIZE: **15¾–17¾ in (40–45 cm)**

This giant kingfisher has a loud, rollocking, territorial call that sounds like maniacal human laughter. It also utters softer chuckles. There are just 2 races: *D. n. novaeguineae*, is the widespread and well-known bird of the eastern half of Australia, while the other, smaller race *D. n. minor* is confined to the Cape York Peninsula.

Laughing Kookaburras feed by pouncing on a variety of terrestrial invertebrates, reptiles, small mammals, birds and nestlings. They can even devour snakes up to 3 ft (1 m) in length. Although they are not closely associated with water, they will sometimes catch fish with plunging dives and, on occasion, raid suburban goldfish ponds. They live in family groups that defend the same territories year round.

## 12/ SHOVEL-BILLED KINGFISHER
*Clytoceyx rex*

RANGE: **mainland New Guinea**
HABITAT: **forest**
SIZE: **12½ in (32 cm)**

The forests of New Guinea have the greatest diversity of kingfishers in the world. This large, brown bird is one of the more unusual species, with a massive, stubby bill that is often caked in mud. The tail, which is brown in females and blue in males, is often cocked when the bird is perched.

The Shovel-billed Kingfisher is often seen on the ground, foraging on exposed mud banks. It digs for insects, snails, earthworms and small vertebrates and forages in mangroves for crabs.

## 13/ STORK-BILLED KINGFISHER
*Halcyon capensis*

RANGE: **Southeast Asia, E Pakistan, India, Nepal, Sri Lanka**
HABITAT: **rivers and streams in wooded lowlands, paddy fields; sometimes at wooded lakes or on the coast, especially among mangroves**
SIZE: **13–14 in (33–36 cm)**

This is one of 3 species of stork-bill in Southeast Asia. They are among the biggest of the world's many kingfisher species, exceeded in size only by the kookaburras, the Shovel-billed Kingfisher and 3 giant *Megaceryle* species.

All species of stork-bill are vocal, but shy, birds. They are rather sluggish in habit, hunting from a branch overhanging water and plunging down vertically for fish, frogs, crustaceans, insects and small land vertebrates such as lizards and nestling birds.

## 14/ BLUE-BREASTED KINGFISHER
*Halcyon malimbica*

RANGE: **tropical W Africa**
HABITAT: **rain forest, gallery forest, mangroves**
SIZE: **9¾ in (25 cm)**

This large kingfisher is the forest-dwelling counterpart of the better-known Woodland Kingfisher *H. senegalensis* of Africa's savanna woodlands. The latter has a loud, trilling "laughing" song lasting about 3 seconds. The Blue-breasted Kingfisher has a similar song, but it is greatly slowed down, with 7–10 long, plaintive whistles. It is usually unseen as it sings, perched in the dark undergrowth.

The breeding site of this species is an unlined cavity that the birds excavate in the nest of a termite colony. This is usually located in a tree some 33 ft (10 m) above the forest floor.

## 15/ SACRED KINGFISHER
*Halcyon sancta*

RANGE: **Australia, Tasmania, Indonesia, New Guinea, Solomon Islands, some SW Pacific islands, New Zealand**
HABITAT: **open forest and woodland**
SIZE: **7½–9 in (19–23 cm)**

This kingfisher is a land-dweller that often occurs far from water. Although its population is widely distributed, most of its 6 or so races are very similar in plumage. However, the color of the bird's breast can vary considerably from season to season. The female is similar to the male, but with a duller, greener crown, back, wings and tail and usually with paler underparts.

Sacred Kingfishers feed on a variety of ground-dwelling insects and small reptiles, catching their prey by pouncing from perches. Those living near water also catch small fish and crustaceans. This is a migrant bird in southern Australia, arriving to breed in spring and wintering on the Indonesian islands to the north. The nest is a hole excavated in a rotting tree or termite nest. The birds open up an initial cavity by flying at the nest site and striking it with their bills.

## 16/ COMMON PARADISE KINGFISHER
*Tanysiptera galatea*

RANGE: **New Guinea, offshore islands, Moluccas**
HABITAT: **lowland rain forest, swamp forest, gallery forest, patches of scrub, plantations**
SIZE: **13–17 in (33–43 cm)**

The Common Paradise Kingfisher perches inconspicuously, low in the forest understory, slowly pumping its tail, which is two-thirds the length of its body. It feeds on insects, worms and lizards, which it catches with a pounce to the ground or a sallying flight to nearby foliage. Adults are highly sedentary, maintaining small territories that they strongly defend. The 3–5 white eggs are laid in a tunnel, excavated by both sexes in a termite nest. The races illustrated are *T. g. galatea* of northwest New Guinea, the western Papuan islands and Morotai, and *T. g. doris* of the northern Moluccas.

# TODIES, MOTMOTS, BEE-EATERS, ROLLERS AND GROUND-ROLLERS, CUCKOO-ROLLER, HOOPOE, WOOD-HOOPOES, HORNBILLS

juv

CUBAN TODY

race *nubicus*
"Northern Carmine
Bee-eater"

CARMINE BEE-EATER

BLUE-CROWNED MOTMOT

juv

EUROPEAN BEE-EATER

AUSTRALIAN BEE-EATER

juv

juv

juv

EUROPEAN ROLLER

EASTERN BROAD-
BILLED ROLLER

♂

SCALY GROUND-ROLLER

CUCKOO-ROLLER

race *epops*

HOOPOE

# FAMILIES TODIDAE, MOMOTIDAE, MEROPIDAE, CORACIIDAE, LEPTOSOMATIDAE, UPUPIDAE, PHOENICULIDAE, BUCEROTIDAE

♀ ♂

GREEN WOOD-HOOPOE

EASTERN YELLOW-BILLED HORNBILL

race *bicornis*

GREAT INDIAN HORNBILL

race *coronatus*

MALABAR PIED HORNBILL

♀

♂

SOUTHERN GROUND HORNBILL

341

# TODIES, MOTMOTS, BEE-EATERS, ROLLERS AND GROUND-ROLLERS, CUCKOO-ROLLER, HOOPOE, WOOD-HOOPOES, HORNBILLS

## FAMILY TODIDAE
### Todies

Small, large-headed, long-billed. Plumage mainly bright green above, throat red, underparts white or with pastel tints. Sexes alike. Nest in excavated earthen burrows. Eggs 2–5, white. Incubation 21–22 days, nestling period 19–20 days. 5 species.

### 1/ CUBAN TODY
*Todus multicolor*

RANGE: **Cuba and Isle of Pines**
HABITAT: **bushy ravines, thickets on mountain slopes, grazed open woodland**
SIZE: **$4\frac{1}{4}$ in (11 cm)**

This tody feeds mainly on flying insects, darting out from a favorite perch to capture them with an audible snap of its bill. Occasionally, it will prey on small lizards. Sedentary, and occurring either alone or in pairs, this species defends its territory against other todies. The call of the Cuban Tody is a rapid, staccato rattle. A whirring sound made by the wings is most often heard during the breeding season. As a group, todies are renowned for their voracious appetites and for the rapid rate at which they feed their young.

## FAMILY MOMOTIDAE
### Motmots

Small to medium, heavy-billed. Long, usually racket-tipped tail. Plumage usually brown or rufous, with blues and greens, boldly marked face and crown. Sexes similar. Nest in crevices or burrows. Eggs 3–4, white. Incubation 15–22 days, nestling period 24–38 days. 9 species.

### 2/ BLUE-CROWNED MOTMOT
*Momotus momota*

RANGE: **E Mexico to NW Peru, NW Argentina and SE Brazil; Trinidad, Tobago**
HABITAT: **rain forest, deciduous forest, coffee and cocoa plantations, semiopen habitats**
SIZE: **16 in (41 cm)**

Alone or in pairs, this motmot perches with an upright stance, swinging its racket-tipped tail from side to side like a pendulum. The racket shape results from the preening of segments of the inherently weak vane from the long central tail feathers. This species' diet includes insects and spiders, as well as some fruit. Prey items are characteristically held in the serrated bill and thrashed against a branch before they are swallowed. The call of the Blue-crowned Motmot is a fairly loud double note of low frequency, sometimes uttered in a long sequence *hudu ... hudu, du, du, du.*

## FAMILY MEROPIDAE
### Bee-eaters

Small, large-headed, graceful birds. Long, slightly downcurved bills. Central tail feathers usually long. Plumage mainly green with rufous, buff, yellow, red, carmine, blue or black. Sexes similar. Nest in burrows. Eggs 2–4 in tropics, up to 10 in Eurasia, white. Incubation 18–22 days, nestling period 22–31 days. 23 species.

### 3/ AUSTRALIAN BEE-EATER
*Merops ornatus*

RANGE: **Australia, New Guinea, Lesser Sundas**
HABITAT: **light woodland, scrub, grassland, sandy pasture, arable land**
SIZE: **$8\frac{1}{4}$–11 in (21–28 cm)**

Also known as the Rainbow Bird, this is the only bee-eater that occurs in Australia. Its winter range extends across the islands to the north, and some birds migrate up to 2,500 mls (4,000 km).

Australian Bee-eaters feed on a variety of large insects, catching their prey in flight. They are gregarious birds throughout the year, and groups of 30–40 may breed cooperatively.

### 4/ EUROPEAN BEE-EATER
*Merops apiaster*

RANGE: **breeds NW Africa, Europe, SW Asia, S Africa; winters W and SE Africa**
HABITAT: **warm, wooded and cultivated lowland**
SIZE: **$9\frac{3}{4}$–$10\frac{1}{2}$ in (25–27 cm)**

Banding has shown that some individuals migrate 10,000 mls (16,000 km) between their summer and winter quarters. In Europe, their principal food is bumblebees, but the birds feed largely on honeybees and dragonflies in Africa. Thousands of European Bee-eaters are killed each year by beekeepers. Migrants crossing the Red Sea also run the gauntlet of attacks by Sooty Falcons, but on the whole the species is not endangered.

### 5/ CARMINE BEE-EATER
*Merops nubicus*

RANGE: **breeds N and S tropics of Africa; winters nearer the Equator**
HABITAT: **open bushy savanna, river plains, open pastures, tilled fields with trees or hedges, marshes, mangroves**
SIZE: **14–$15\frac{1}{4}$ in (36–39 cm)**

Carmine Bee-eaters are gregarious birds, nesting in colonies of 100–1,000 pairs, and, in some cases, 10,000 pairs. Their tail streamers measure up to 5 in (12 cm). Northern birds such as *M. n. nubicus* have blue-green throats, while their southern counterparts *M. n. nubicoides* have vivid pink throats. These 2 populations breed 1,250 mls (2,000 km) apart, at opposite times of the year, and are sometimes regarded as separate species.

Carmine Bee-eaters hunt on the wing, flying far to find swarms of locusts, bees, ants and cicadas. They are strongly attracted to bush fires, where they can readily catch fleeing grasshoppers. They also hunt by riding on the backs of ostriches, bustards, storks, cranes, antelopes, camels, goats and cattle, snatching prey that the animals disturb from the grass.

## FAMILY CORACIIDAE
### Rollers and ground-rollers

Medium, stout birds. Short-necked, large-headed. Plumage mainly blue and rufous, with lilac, olive and brilliant azure. Sexes similar. Nest in holes. Eggs 2–6, white. Incubation 17–19 days, nestling period 25–30 days. 12 species.

### 6/ EUROPEAN ROLLER
*Coracias garrulus*

RANGE: **breeds Mediterranean, E Europe to W Siberia; winters tropical Africa**
HABITAT: **open forest, especially with clearings and patches of heathland; also parks, well-wooded farmland**
SIZE: **$11\frac{3}{4}$–$12\frac{1}{2}$ in (30–32 cm)**

During this century, European Rollers have dwindled in number in northwestern parts of their range because of changes in land management. But in eastern Europe and Asia they remain common as breeding birds, and in parts of Africa they winter in abundance.

European Rollers feed principally on insects, although they have also been known to eat snails and frogs. They normally hunt from a low perch, swooping down to seize their prey on the ground or, sometimes, catching insects in midair. Rollers take their name from their aerobatic, rolling display flights, and this species is no exception, rocking from side to side as it dives steeply down and even performing aerial somersaults.

## 7/ EASTERN BROAD-BILLED ROLLER
*Eurystomus orientalis*
RANGE: N and E Australia, New Guinea, Southeast Asia, India, China
HABITAT: woodland
SIZE: 11½ in (29 cm)

This species is often known as the Dollarbird in the Far East and Australia, owing to the large, coinlike, whitish mark on each wing, which is conspicuous when the bird takes flight.

Eastern Broad-billed Rollers sally out from treetop perches to catch large beetles and other flying insects, often with aerobatic maneuvers. If they cannot swallow their victims in flight, they will take them back to the perch and batter their bodies against the wood to soften them. Usually seen alone or in pairs, these birds have a harsh, chattering call.

## 8/ SCALY GROUND-ROLLER
*Brachypteracias squamigera*            R
RANGE: NE and C Madagascar
HABITAT: deep rain forest with scant undergrowth
SIZE: 11¾ in (30 cm)

This species dwells in the shade of the forest floor, where it feeds mainly on insects and small lizards. It is a rather heavy, slow bird that moves only a few steps between lengthy pauses or uses its short, rounded wings to make whirring flights to low perches. This bird is perhaps less rare than was once thought, for its silent and secretive habits make it extremely difficult to locate. However, its habitat continues to disappear, and the loss is threatening the population of this and many other forest animals.

## FAMILY LEPTOSOMATIDAE
### Cuckoo-Roller
There is only one species in this family.

## 9/ CUCKOO-ROLLER
*Leptosomus discolor*
RANGE: Madagascar and Comoro Islands
HABITAT: forest and scrub
SIZE: 16½ in (42 cm)

Pairs of these birds are relatively common in savanna with scattered tall trees from sea level up to 6,500 ft (2,000 m). But the birds cannot survive in newly cleared areas which are gradually eroding their natural range. They are usually seen in the high canopy, flying slowly from tree to tree or feeding from the highest branches. They take locusts, stick insects, beetles and larvae, along with larger prey such as chameleons. The male Cuckoo-Roller has an undulating display flight. Distinctive calls may be given from a conspicuous perch, and pairs keep in close contact with soft, bubbling calls. Nesting takes place in a tree hole, where the 2 cream-buff eggs are laid in an unlined chamber.

## FAMILY UPUPIDAE
### Hoopoe
There is only one species in this family.

## 10/ HOOPOE
*Upupa epops*
RANGE: Europe, Asia, Africa, Madagascar; N birds winter in the tropics
HABITAT: woodland, savanna, parks, lawns, orchards, farmland
SIZE: 11 in (28 cm)

The Hoopoe's striking plumage, its mobile crest, its far-carrying *hoo-poo-poo* call, and its association with human settlement make it a familiar bird. Daytime migrants are so conspicuous that, despite pungent, defensive secretions, they are a favorite prey of Eleonora's and Sooty Falcons. The nest is a thinly lined cavity in a tree or wall or in the ground. The eggs vary in color from gray to pale yellow or olive and become heavily stained in the nest. The clutch size varies from 2–9, and incubation takes 15–16 days. The nestling period lasts about 4 weeks.

## FAMILY PHOENICULIDAE
### Wood-hoopoes
Long-tailed, short-legged. Long, downcurved bill. Plumage black, glossy blue or green; white spots in the wings and tail. Sexes similar. Nest in tree holes. Eggs 2–5, pale blue. Incubation 16–18 days, nestling period 27–30 days. 8 species.

## 11/ GREEN WOOD-HOOPOE
*Phoeniculus purpureus*
RANGE: sub-Saharan Africa
HABITAT: woodland, thorn bushes
SIZE: 15–16 in (38–41 cm)

This is the most widespread and best known of Africa's 8 species of wood-hoopoe. It feeds by gleaning caterpillars, insect eggs and grubs, spiders and other food items from tree trunks, branches and foliage.

Green Wood-Hoopoes are noisy, gregarious birds that indulge in remarkable social territorial displays. Several times each hour, they will cackle loudly, rock back and forth in an exaggerated manner, preen and pass pieces of bark from one to another. Each breeding pair is helped at the tree-hole nest by up to 10 birds.

## FAMILY BUCEROTIDAE
### Hornbills
Medium to large. Long bill, often with large casque. Long tail, broad wings. Plumage black, white, brown or gray. Bill, facial skin, eyes and feet often brightly colored. Sexes alike or differ. Nest in holes in trees or rocks, entrance usually sealed. Eggs 1–7, white. Incubation 25–40 days, nestling period 45–86 days. 48 species.

## 12/ EASTERN YELLOW-BILLED HORNBILL
*Tockus flavirostris*
RANGE: NE Africa
HABITAT: dry woodland savanna
SIZE: 19½–23½ in (50–60 cm)

This hornbill has a rare mutual association with the dwarf mongoose, in which each helps the other locate food and watch for predators. It displays in pairs, holding its wings fanned and head bowed, and uttering hoarse clucking calls.

The eggs are laid in a natural tree hole, the entrance to which is then reduced to a narrow, vertical slit by the female, using mud and droppings. Safely enclosed within the hole, she incubates the eggs and receives insects and fruit through the slit from the male. Feeding continues in this way until the chicks are half-grown. The female then breaks free, and the chicks reseal the nest until they have fledged.

## 13/ MALABAR PIED HORNBILL
*Anthracoceros coronatus*
RANGE: India
HABITAT: monsoon forest
SIZE: 29½–31½ in (75–80 cm)

This occurs in small flocks that move about together to feed on fruit and small creatures gleaned from foliage. The race *A. c. coronatus* is found in southern India and Sri Lanka.

Flocks of Malabar Pied Hornbills congregate at regular roost sites within which mated pairs remain close together throughout the year. In summer, they move off to nest alone. The eggs are incubated by the female in a natural tree hole. The male carries fruit to his incarcerated mate, storing them in his crop and regurgitating them one at a time through the narrow slit in the nest wall.

## 14/ GREAT INDIAN HORNBILL
*Buceros bicornis*
RANGE: India E to Thailand, S to Sumatra
HABITAT: tropical rain forest
SIZE: 39¼–47¼ in (100–120 cm)

This large hornbill lives high in the forest canopy, feeding mainly on fruit, such as figs, and some small animals. In flight, its "whooshing" wing beats can be heard over half a mile (1 km) away. Its loud, honking calls are also obvious. The race *B. b. bicornis* occurs in western India and from the Himalayas to Indochina and Malaysia.

Great Indian Hornbills nest in tree cavities, both sexes helping to seal the entrance. After the nesting cycle of 4–5 months, the families may form into small flocks that range widely in search of food. Much of the rain forest habitat in western India and mainland Asia has been felled, making this spectacular bird a vulnerable species.

## 15/ SOUTHERN GROUND HORNBILL
*Bucorvus cafer*
RANGE: Africa S of the Equator
HABITAT: open savanna and grassland
SIZE: 35½–51 in (90–130 cm)

This, the largest of the hornbills, differs from most other species in being carnivorous and largely terrestrial and in not sealing the entrance to its nest. Groups of up to 11 birds occupy territories of about 40 square miles (100 square kilometers) and proclaim their presence at dawn with booming calls. They catch small animals while patrolling their territories on foot.

Only the dominant pair breeds, but the other group members help in territorial defense, in lining the nest with dry leaves, and in feeding the breeding female and single chick.

# JACAMARS, PUFFBIRDS, BARBETS

PARADISE JACAMAR

GREAT JACAMAR

♂

race
*hyperrhynchus*

WHITE-NECKED PUFFBIRD

♀

RED-HEADED BARBET

TOUCAN BARBET

♂

race *leucolaima*

YELLOW-RUMPED TINKERBIRD

race *jacksoni*

DOUBLE-TOOTHED BARBET

COLLARED PUFFBIRD

RUSTY-BREASTED NUNLET

race *morphoeus*

WHITE-FRONTED NUNBIRD

race *davisoni*

BLUE-THROATED BARBET

SWALLOW-WINGED
PUFFBIRD

♀

race *woodwardi*

GREEN BARBET

♂

RED-AND-YELLOW BARBET

race *erythrocephalus*

race *olivacea*

# JACAMARS, PUFFBIRDS, BARBETS

## FAMILY GALBULIDAE
### Jacamars

Small to medium, with long, pointed bills. Plumage iridescent golden-green and purple above and mainly chestnut and white below, or dark chestnut, brown or blackish, often with white on the underparts. Sexes differ slightly. Nest in burrows. Eggs 2–4, white. Incubation 20–23 days, nestling period 19–26 days (Rufous-tailed Jacamar *Galbula ruficauda*). 17 species.

### 1/ PARADISE JACAMAR
*Galbula dea*

RANGE: S Venezuela and Guianas S to N Bolivia
HABITAT: humid tropical forest and forest edge, savanna, margins of watercourses
SIZE: 11¾ in (30 cm)

This striking jacamar has central tail feathers up to 7 in (18 cm) in length, making the tail longer than the bird's body. Its sleek, black, iridescent plumage flashes copper, bronze and blue as the bird darts about in the sunlight after insects. The sexes have similar plumage. This species excavates nest cavities in termite mounds in trees. The song is a series of peeping notes.

Paradise Jacamars are usually seen alone, in pairs or in small groups. It perches quietly, its head moving from side to side as it scans the surroundings before sallying out in pursuit of its insect prey. Typically, a bird begins its attack with a dive from its perch, followed by a twisting pursuit, with sudden changes in direction. When successful, the bird returns with an undulating flight and bangs the prey, held in its bill, against the perch before eating it. It often accompanies mixed-species flocks.

### 2/ GREAT JACAMAR
*Jacamerops aurea*

RANGE: Costa Rica S through N South America to N Bolivia
HABITAT: humid tropical forest, secondary growth woodland, edges of water
SIZE: 11¾ in (30 cm)

This is the largest of the jacamar species. The heavy bill is nearly 2 in (5 cm) long. Immatures are similar to adults, but less iridescent.

Great Jacamars are usually solitary or found in pairs. Compared with smaller jacamars, they may appear sluggish in habit as they perch quietly on exposed limbs, usually just under the canopy or lower down. They catch most of their prey, including butterflies, beetles and dragonflies, with a sallying flight, but they will also dart forward to glean insects, spiders, lizards and other small vertebrates from vegetation. Their vocalizations include loud whistles and a variety of soft call notes. Pairs nest in termite mounds in trees, up to 50 ft (15 m) from the ground.

## FAMILY BUCCONIDAE
### Puffbirds

Small to medium. Large-headed, stout. Plumage black, brown, reddish-brown and white. Sexes differ slightly. Nest in burrows. Eggs 2–3 (occasionally 4), white. Incubation unknown. Nestling period 20–30 days. 32 species.

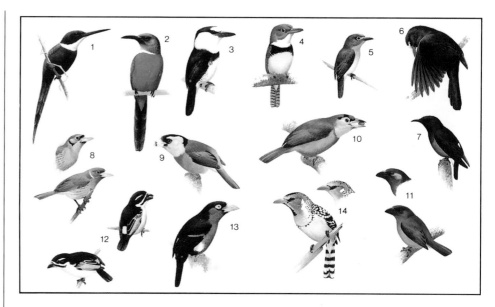

### 3/ WHITE-NECKED PUFFBIRD
*Notharchus macrorhynchos*

RANGE: S Mexico to N South America, N Bolivia, SE Brazil, Paraguay, N Argentina
HABITAT: humid tropical forest, open secondary growth, savanna
SIZE: 9¾ in (25 cm)

Both sexes share the contrasting black and white plumage, but immature birds have buff-gray on the forehead and underparts. The bill is heavy and hooked and this, together with the puffed-up feathers of the head, gives the bird a large-headed appearance. The race illustrated, *N. m. hyperrhynchus*, occurs in Mexico.

White-necked Puffbirds often sit quietly on their perches for extended periods. They feed by sallying out and hawking large insects in flight, or by taking them from foliage. Occasionally, these birds will drop down from the canopy and forage around army ant swarms. They also take lizards and small vertebrates. This species is usually quiet, but occasional calls include a series of weak twitters or purring notes. Both sexes help to excavate the nesting cavity in arboreal termite mounds.

### 4/ COLLARED PUFFBIRD
*Bucco capensis*

RANGE: N South America S to N Peru
HABITAT: humid tropical forest
SIZE: 7¾ in (20 cm)

This little-known puffbird has the large-headed appearance typical of its family. Its bill is stout and well adapted for dealing with large insects. Its song is a series of *ca-will* notes, rather like that of the nightjar called the Common Poorwill *Phalaenoptilus nuttallii*. There are few details of its nesting habits, but presumably it nests in the same way as other puffbirds.

Collared Puffbirds sit quietly on their perches from the middle layers of the forest up to the subcanopy, where they are easy to overlook. They are largely insectivorous, catching flying prey on the wing or gleaning insects from foliage, but they probably eat some small vertebrates as well. They are usually found alone or in pairs, but they sometimes accompany mixed-species flocks.

### 5/ RUSTY-BREASTED NUNLET
*Nonnula rubecula*

RANGE: S Venezuela, N Peru, N Brazil S to Paraguay and N Argentina
HABITAT: humid tropical forest; especially seasonally flooded forest
SIZE: 6 in (15 cm)

This small, inconspicuous member of the puffbird family is sleeker in appearance than most puffbirds. Like most of them, it typically sits quietly on a perch and sallies out to capture flying insect prey, or gleans insects and other items from vines or other vegetation. It may also take small lizards. Its perches are often in the midlevel to understory layers, where it sits upright and often allows people to approach closely.

Rusty-breasted Nunlets are generally quiet, unlike their noisy relatives, the nunbirds. Very little is known of their breeding biology, but they probably nest in burrows they dig in the ground or in termite nests, like other puffbirds.

### 6/ WHITE-FRONTED NUNBIRD
*Monasa morphoeus*

RANGE: Central America, W Venezuela S to N Bolivia, Amazonian Brazil
HABITAT: humid tropical forest, river edges, swamps, secondary growth forest
SIZE: 11¾ in (30 cm)

These birds change perches frequently, much more than most other members of the puffbird family. They fly directly, with rapid wing beats followed by short glides. They sit quietly on each perch and sally out to catch flying insects or glean prey from foliage on the ground. Sometimes groups of up to 6 birds will join mixed-species flocks. The race illustrated is *M. m. morphoeus* from southern and eastern Brazil.

White-fronted Nunbirds are more vocal than other puffbirds, uttering a wide variety of rolling, churring and whistling notes. Groups of 10 or more may sing in chorus. A few nesting records suggest that this species excavates a downward-sloping burrow, about 3 ft (1 m) long, in the ground. The eggs are laid in a chamber at the end. Up to 6 adults may help with the nesting duties.

## 7/ SWALLOW-WINGED PUFFBIRD
*Chelidoptera tenebrosa*

RANGE: N South America E of the Andes S to N Bolivia and S Brazil
HABITAT: forest edge, savanna, scrub
SIZE: 6 in (15 cm)

This puffbird is common along waterways from sea level up to at least 3,300 ft (1,000 m). It occurs alone, in pairs or in small groups of 3–6. While other puffbirds forage within the forest, this species forages above it. It sallies from its perch in fast pursuit of flying insects, returning at a more leisurely pace with its prey.

The voice of the Swallow-winged Puffbird consists of weakly whistled *pi-pu* and *pit-wit-wit* calls. This species nests in sandy banks along streams and road cuttings, excavating a 3–6 ft (1–2 m) burrow that angles downward. It lays 2 eggs on bare dirt or pieces of grass. These hatch into naked, slaty black chicks which begin coming to the burrow entrance when their growing feathers are still surrounded by sheaths, but they quickly retreat when disturbed.

## FAMILY CAPITONIDAE
### Barbets
Small to medium, plump, large-headed arboreal birds. Stout, often notched bills. Facial bristles. Plumage colorful, with green, blue, red, yellow and black. Sexes usually similar. Nest in tree holes. Eggs 2–4, white. Incubation 12–19 days, nestling period 20–35 days. 81 species.

## 8/ RED-HEADED BARBET
*Eubucco bourcierii*

RANGE: Costa Rica, Panama, Colombia, Ecuador, W Venezuela, N Peru
HABITAT: humid mountain forest
SIZE: 6 in (15 cm)

The Red-headed Barbet usually lives at altitudes of 4,000–8,000 ft (1,200–2,400 m), but on the western slopes of the Andes in Colombia it may be found at 1,300 ft (400 m). Often just one or a pair of these birds will accompany a mixed flock of forest species. As well as feeding on fruit and, occasionally, some small vertebrates, they spend much of their time foraging around clusters of dead leaves in search of invertebrates. Despite their small size, they are rather sluggish and heavy in their movements, often pausing to tug at a berry or probe into bark and foliage. They are often heard tearing into dried leaves well before they are seen.

Although usually silent, they are known to give low, cicadalike rattling calls and squirrel-like sputters and chatters. The males have been heard singing with a prolonged, toadlike trill.

## 9/ TOUCAN BARBET
*Semnornis ramphastinus* [V]

RANGE: W Colombia, W Ecuador
HABITAT: humid mountain forest and forest edge at, 3,300–8,000 ft (1,000–2,400 m)
SIZE: 7¾ in (20 cm)

This is the largest and most heavily built of the American barbets. It usually forages singly or in pairs, although it will also follow mixed-species flocks. It hops actively along branches, often cocking its tail and turning to and fro in sudden about-face movements. At other times, it sits quietly for lengthy spells. It eats mainly fruit and invertebrates, but it will occasionally take small vertebrates such as lizards.

The song of the Toucan Barbet is a rhythmic series of loud, resonant, almost honking notes that may continue for several minutes. A pair will duet, either in synchrony or out of time. If disturbed, this bird will snap its bill loudly. The Toucan Barbet is popular as a cage bird: this, and the loss of its forest habitat, has caused a marked decline in its numbers.

## 10/ BLUE-THROATED BARBET
*Megalaima asiatica*

RANGE: N India, Southeast Asia
HABITAT: light mixed forest, gardens
SIZE: 9 in (23 cm)

The Blue-throated Barbet is common from the Himalayan foothills down to low level plains. It prefers groves of fig trees around villages and wooded slopes, where it searches for fruit. It also eats large insects, which it strikes against a branch before swallowing. The race illustrated is *M. a. davisoni*, which ranges from southern Burma to southern China and northern Indochina.

It is a noisy species, which often calls together with other barbets, making a confusion of sounds. Pairs may call in such rapid succession that their duets sound as if they are coming from a single bird. The nest-hole is excavated in a tree branch, and the cavity may be used for several years, although a fresh entrance is often cut each season.

## 11/ GREEN BARBET
*Cryptolybia olivacea*

RANGE: E Kenya, Tanzania, Malawi, S Africa
HABITAT: mountain forest to coastal woods
SIZE: 7¾ in (20 cm)

The Green Barbet has a very scattered distribution, being found in just a few isolated areas. It often occurs in groups or in mixed-species flocks, foraging for fruit, including figs, as well as termites and beetles, and is active, restless and sociable. Roosting holes excavated in trees may accommodate 4–5 birds, and other adults may help breeding pairs excavate nest-holes.

Its song is a series of up to 29 notes, with both male and female singing together, either at the same tempo or with one at twice the speed of the other. Up to 5 races of this bird are recognized; these include *C. o. olivacea*, which is found in eastern Kenya and Tanzania, and *C. o. woodwardi* of northern Natal province.

## 12/ YELLOW-RUMPED TINKERBIRD
*Pogoniulus bilineatus*

RANGE: sub-Saharan Africa
HABITAT: evergreen forest thickets
SIZE: 4 in (10 cm)

This widespread species, which is also known as the Golden-rumped Tinkerbird, has 10 races across tropical Africa. These include *P. b. jacksoni* of east Africa and *P. b. leucolaima*, which ranges from Senegal to southern Sudan and south to northern Angola. It prefers dense forest and riverside trees, where it eats a wide variety of berries and seeds. It usually pauses to feed between fluttery flights through tangled vines and dense foliage, but will cross open spaces to isolated trees with plentiful fruit.

The Yellow-rumped Tinkerbird's song consists of groups of 3–5 notes given in a series lasting several minutes. The tiny bird fluffs its throat, droops its wings and flicks its tail at each note, constantly looking from side to side as it sings. A solitary, aggressive species, it uses its songs and attacks on intruders to maintain a well-defined territory around its nest-hole.

## 13/ DOUBLE-TOOTHED BARBET
*Lybius bidentatus*

RANGE: W Africa E to Ethiopia and Kenya; S as far as N Angola
HABITAT: clearings, forest edge, parkland
SIZE: 9 in (23 cm)

Despite its bright coloration, this bird is less conspicuous than might be expected, preferring to keep to the shade of trees and bushes. A frequent, short, sharp note may be the best clue to its whereabouts. It feeds by darting out to catch flying termites or by clambering about to reach figs, fruit and nuts. The Double-toothed Barbet is named for the 2 prominent sharp projections on the upper mandible of its bill.

When several Double-toothed Barbets gather together, they flick and droop their tails and call a variety of low, grating sounds. Their song is a prolonged, buzzing trill. The nesting territories of this species are large, and the pair may fly long distances to reach fruiting trees.

## 14/ RED-AND-YELLOW BARBET
*Trachyphonus erythrocephalus*

RANGE: E Ethiopia, Kenya, N Tanzania
HABITAT: woods, bushy areas, grassland with scattered trees
SIZE: 9 in (23 cm)

This is a ground-loving barbet, often found under bushes or foraging around termite mounds and banks of bare earth. It even clears dead insects from the fronts of parked cars. It is tame and bold, readily entering houses in search of food. There are 3 races: the one shown is *T. e. erythrocephalus*, from southern Kenya and northern Tanzania, which has more red on the head than the others.

The Red-and-yellow Barbet is aggressive to any smaller birds, and fights between rivals are frequent. Nevertheless, it is a gregarious species and up to 10 may feed together or gather to mob a snake or some other predator. They will also roost together in a group of holes dug in a bank. Nesting territories are defended, but up to 4 adult and 5 younger birds may attend each nest as communal helpers. The dominant pair often duet, producing a babbling medley, which sounds rather like *red 'n' yellow, red 'n' yellow*, from the top of a bush.

♂

imm

INDIAN HONEYGUIDE

race *prasinus*

RED-NECKED ARACARI

BLACK-THROATED
HONEYGUIDE

EMERALD TOUCANET

race *bitorquatus*

♀

♂

GOLDEN-COLLARED
TOUCANET

PLATE-BILLED MOUNTAIN
TOUCAN

BLACK-BILLED MOUNTAIN TOUCAN

GROOVE-BILLED TOUCANET

GREEN ARACARI

♂

♀

♂ GUIANAN TOUCANET

♀

KEEL-BILLED TOUCAN

TOCO TOUCAN

## FAMILY INDICATORIDAE
### Honeyguides

Small, gray-green birds with white tail markings. Sexes generally similar. Wax is a unique feature of their diet and 2 species guide mammal "helpers" to bee hives. Like cuckoos, most species rely on other species to raise their broods. Eggs 2–8, whitish, thick-shelled. Incubation 12–14 days, nestling period up to 30 days. 17 species.

### 1/ BLACK-THROATED HONEYGUIDE
*Indicator indicator*

RANGE: **Senegal to Ethiopia, and S to South Africa**
HABITAT: **woodland, open country with scattered trees, rarely dense forest**
SIZE: **8 in (20 cm)**

Honeyguides are often very difficult to see, for they tend to be solitary, inconspicuous birds that perch quietly in the forest, occasionally fluttering up to catch a fly on the wing or foraging in mixed-species flocks, and the Black-throated, or Greater, Honeyguide is no exception. The female of this species is browner and paler than the male.

When it locates a nest of bees, however, the Black-throated Honeyguide becomes very demonstrative, flicking its tail and chattering noisily to attract the attention of a human or a Honey Badger, or Ratel, and guide it to the hive. It falls silent while its "helper" breaks open the nest to get at the honey, then feeds on the bee grubs and wax, which it probably digests with the aid of bacteria in its gut. Other mammals that are possibly used as helpers are baboons, genets and mongooses. The Scaly-throated Honeyguide *I. variegatus* may also occasionally use helpers.

The male Black-throated Honeyguide advertises his readiness to mate by calling repeatedly from a favorite perch; he may use the same one for several years running. The eggs are laid among those of hole-nesting birds such as barbets, bee-eaters and woodpeckers, one to each nest. The naked, blind hatchling attacks the host's young with the hook on its bill, killing them so as to monopolize the food supply.

### 2/ INDIAN HONEYGUIDE
*Indicator xanthonotus*

RANGE: **Himalayas, from Pakistan to N Burma**
HABITAT: **forests, especially near cliffs and rock faces**
SIZE: **6 in (15 cm)**

This olive-brown, sparrow-sized bird is also known as the Yellow-rumped Honeyguide – a reference to the only bright feature of its plumage. This can make the bird quite conspicuous when it is perching with wings drooped, but usually it is hard to locate and observe, being a quiet denizen of thick woodland. As a result, many details of its behavior remain a mystery. The female is slightly smaller and duller than the male.

A study carried out in Nepal revealed that the males defend territories which are centered on the nests of giant honeybees. Wax is an important component of the species' diet, but it is not known whether the Indian Honeyguide guides mammals to hives. The nesting habits of this species are

also uncertain, although it is possible that, like the African honeyguides, it parasitizes other birds. The males are polygamous, each mating with up to 18 females.

## FAMILY RAMPHASTIDAE
### Toucans

Medium, with very large, lightweight, brightly colored bills, strengthened by thin, bony, internal struts. Plumage black with red, yellow and white, olive and blue, or mainly green. Males and females generally alike but male's bill longer. Diet chiefly fruit and insects. Restricted to tropical American forests. Nest in tree holes usually with no lining except wood chips and a bed of regurgitated seeds. Eggs 2–4, white. Incubation 15–16 days, nestling period 43–51 days. 35 species.

### 3/ EMERALD TOUCANET
*Aulacorhynchus prasinus*

RANGE: **C Mexico through SE Peru to NW Venezuela**
HABITAT: **highland forest, highland and lowland forest edge, clearings**
SIZE: **11¾–13 in (30–33 cm)**

The brilliant green plumage of the Emerald Toucanet can make these birds very hard to see when they are sitting quietly among the foliage, but they are a glorious sight when they are feeding in the open. They usually forage in pairs or small flocks of 5–10 birds, seeking a wide range of food, including fruit, insects and the occasional lizard, as well as eggs and nestlings.

They are active, excitable birds, often cocking their tails and stretching their necks. They are also noisy, calling to each other with a variety of loud croaks, barks and rattles. The penetrating "song" of the Emerald Toucanet is said to resemble the sound of a crosscut saw.

The race *A. p. prasinus* is just one of many races and occurs in southeast Mexico; other races have the base of the lower mandible colored dark red instead of black.

### 4/ GROOVE-BILLED TOUCANET
*Aulacorhynchus sulcatus*

RANGE: **N Colombia, N Venezuela**
HABITAT: **humid forest, forest edge, secondary woodland**
SIZE: **14 in (36 cm)**

Similar to the Emerald Toucanet in both appearance and habits, the Groove-billed Toucanet is usually found at lower elevations, although it rarely descends into the warm lowlands. The 2 species occur together throughout the range of the Groove-billed Toucanet, especially at elevations of 5,000–6,500 ft (1,600–2,000 m).

Pairs or small flocks of these birds forage together in noisy, energetic fashion, feeding on fruit, insects or nestling birds anywhere from the high forest canopy to the smaller trees of the understory. Like the Emerald Toucanet, the Groove-billed Toucanet lays its eggs in a tree cavity, often in a hole that has been excavated by a woodpecker.

### 5/ GREEN ARACARI
*Pteroglossus viridis*

RANGE: **Colombia, N Bolivia, Venezuela, Guianas, Brazil**
HABITAT: **lowland rain forest**
SIZE: **11¾ in (30 cm)**

The aracaris are generally smaller and more lightly built than toucans and typically have red rumps and green wings and backs. There are 9 species found in Central America and Amazonia, but it is unusual to find more than 2 species in any one area. In some, the female differs slightly from the male: in the Green Aracari, the female's head and throat are chestnut, whereas the male's head and throat are black.

The Green Aracari is a lowland species, and rarely occurs higher than 2,000 ft (600 m), but it often ventures out of the forest interior to feed among the scattered trees and scrub of the forest edge. The birds forage through the canopy in small groups, actively seeking fruiting trees. They straggle through the foliage in single file, often leaping from branch to branch instead of flying, calling to one another with loud rattling cries. The birds lay their eggs in a tree cavity excavated by a woodpecker. These cavities are also used for roosting, and several birds may squeeze into the same hole each night.

## 6/ RED-NECKED ARACARI
*Pteroglossus bitorquatus*
RANGE: **lower Amazonia S of Amazon in Brazil**
HABITAT: **rain forest, forest edge, scrub**
SIZE: **15 in (38 cm)**

Also known as the Double-collared Aracari, this species is distinguished by its bright yellow breast band. It is very similar to the Ivory-billed Aracari *P. flavirostris*, however, this species does not have a breast band. The Amazon River separates the ranges of these 2 species, with the Ivory-billed Aracari to the north and the Red-necked Aracari to the south; the 2 have probably evolved from the same ancestor. There are 3 races, distinguished by the color of head, throat and bill: the one illustrated is *P. b. bitorquatus* from northeast Brazil.

Like other toucans, the Red-necked Aracari is an opportunist feeder. Loose bands consisting of 2–5 birds move through the forest in search of fruiting trees, picking up a variety of small animals, eggs and nestlings on the way. At night they roost in tree holes.

## 7/ GOLDEN-COLLARED TOUCANET
*Selenidera reinwardtii*
RANGE: **NW South America E of the Andes**
HABITAT: **lowland rain forest, forest edge**
SIZE: **13 in (33 cm)**

The toucanets of the genus *Aulacorhynchus* are upland birds but the 6 species in the genus *Selenidera* are restricted to lowland forests.

The Golden-collared Toucanet is generally uncommon throughout its range; it usually feeds in the rain forest interior. It rarely travels in flocks, preferring to forage alone or in pairs, high in the trees. Unusually for toucans, the sexes differ markedly in appearance.

Its normal call is a low, guttural, froglike croak, although one race is said to utter barking growls. Like other toucans, the Golden-collared Toucanet feeds mainly on berries and other fruits, generally swallowing them whole and disgorging the seeds and stones elsewhere at a later stage. In this way, toucans help to disperse the seeds of fruit-bearing plants throughout the forest.

## 8/ GUIANAN TOUCANET
*Selenidera culik*
RANGE: **NE Amazonia, Guianas and N Brazil S to lower reaches of Amazon**
HABITAT: **lowland rain forest, forest edge**
SIZE: **13¾ in (35 cm)**

The Guianan Toucanet has a longer bill than the other lowland toucanets and a shorter tail and wings. In other respects, however, it is typical of the genus *Selenidera*, with distinct sexual differences and conspicuous yellow tufts behind each eye, which may play an important role in the birds' courtship display.

Its behavior is also typical, since it is usually seen alone, in pairs or in small groups, searching for berries and small insects among the foliage at any level of the forest. The elusive nature of the Guianan Toucanet and its preference for remote habitats make it difficult to study and little is known about the nesting behavior of this or any other *Selenidera* species.

## 9/ PLATE-BILLED MOUNTAIN TOUCAN
*Andigena laminirostris*
RANGE: **NW South America, from SW Colombia through W Ecuador**
HABITAT: **humid and wet mountain forest and forest edge**
SIZE: **20 in (51 cm)**

This is one of 4 species of mountain toucan found in the forests of the Andes. It is unique in having an additional yellow plate on each side of its upper mandible. The function of this light, horny structure, if any, is not known.

The Plate-billed Mountain Toucan lives in humid mountain forests, from the subtropical zone at 1,000 ft (300 m) to the mid-altitude temperate zone at about 10,500 ft (3,200 m), but is generally uncommon throughout its range. It usually occurs in small groups, which join with other species in large feeding flocks that work their way through the forest. It has the typical broad diet of the toucans, taking insects and other small animals as well as fruit.

## 10/ BLACK-BILLED MOUNTAIN TOUCAN
*Andigena nigrirostris*
RANGE: **N South America, Colombia to NE Ecuador**
HABITAT: **mountain forest, cloud forest, forest edge, open areas with scattered trees**
SIZE: **20 in (51 cm)**

This is the most northerly of the mountain toucans and is considered to be comparatively common. However, this may be because it is a rather conspicuous bird, easily seen and recorded as it moves about the forest in search of fruit and animal prey. It is most often seen in wet mountain forest between 6,500 ft (2,000 m) and 10,000 ft (3,000 m). Above this altitude it becomes much less common and is replaced by the very similar Gray-breasted Mountain Toucan *A. hypoglauca*.

It normally associates in pairs or small groups, communicating with other birds with nasal yelping calls and hollow rattlings of its great black bill. Mountain toucans nest in tree cavities, like other toucans, but their nesting behavior has not been closely studied.

## 11/ KEEL-BILLED TOUCAN
*Ramphastos sulfuratus*
RANGE: **tropical Mexico to N Colombia and NW Venezuela**
HABITAT: **tropical lowland forest, forest edge, open areas with scattered trees, plantations**
SIZE: **17¾–22 in (45–56 cm)**

The 8 species of the genus *Ramphastos* are the largest and best known of the toucans. The Keel-billed Toucan is one of the most colorful of the group, with its bright yellow breast and multi-hued bill. Young birds are much duller than adults, and their bills continue to grow for some weeks after they fledge.

Normally seen in pairs or small flocks of 6–12 birds, Keel-billed Toucans feed on a wide variety of plant material, including catkins, berries and other fruits. A feeding bird will reach out and pluck a fruit with the tip of its long bill, then toss its head back to swallow its prize with a gulp. It also dines on insects and spiders, as well as occasional snakes, lizards, eggs and nestlings.

The Keel-billed Toucan has a distinctive, strongly undulating flight pattern, with intensive bursts of flapping alternating with short glides. Its voice is a series of mechanical clicks, like that of a tree frog, and it may also produce a harsh, dry rattle, like castanets.

## 12/ TOCO TOUCAN
*Ramphastos toco*
RANGE: **E South America, Guianas through Brazil to N Argentina**
HABITAT: **open woodland, river forest, forest edge, plantations, palm groves; avoids continuous lowland forest**
SIZE: **24 in (61 cm)**

The most familiar of all the toucans, the Toco Toucan is also the largest, with a massive bill which may be up to 7½ in (19 cm) long. Like that of other toucans, the bill is composed of lightweight horny material, braced internally by a system of struts, so it is not as heavy as it looks.

Toco Toucans are unusual in that they avoid dense rain forest, preferring more open habitats. They are often seen around human dwellings and are relatively common throughout their range. They generally forage in loose flocks, flying from site to site with the undulating flap-glide flight pattern characteristic of their genus, and communicating with toadlike croaks.

Like all toucans, the Toco Toucan nests in a tree cavity, favoring holes that are barely wide enough to permit entry and often using the same hole for several years in succession. The nest is lined with chips of wood and often covered with an accumulation of regurgitated seeds.

NORTHERN WRYNECK

GUIANAN PICULET

♀

♂

RUFOUS PICULET

♀

♂

GROUND WOODPECKER

race *ruber*

juv

RED-BREASTED SAPSUCKER

race *lepidus*

NUBIAN WOODPECKER

♂

CARDINAL WOODPECKER

♀

race *hemprichii*

WHITE WOODPECKER

♂

ACORN WOODPECKER

♂ race *flavigula*

♀

acorns wedged
in tree holes

♂

race *formicivorus*

RED-HEADED WOODPECKER

juv

race *numidus* ♂

race *pinetorum* ♀

GREAT SPOTTED WOODPECKER

juv

♂

race *septentrionalis* ♂

race *sanctorum* ♂

HAIRY WOODPECKER

# WOODPECKERS

## FAMILY PICIDAE
### Woodpeckers

Small to large, with stout, straight, pointed to chisel-tipped bills and strong, slender necks, and stiff tails used for support when climbing (except in wrynecks, subfamily Jynginae, and piculets, subfamily Picumninae). Most species (not wrynecks) habitually communicate by drumming with bills on trees. Most solitary, great majority tree-dwellers. Wrynecks blotched and peppered pattern of browns, sexes alike. Piculets brownish with red, orange or yellow marks and 3 white stripes on tail, females with white spots on black crown. Typical woodpeckers (subfamily Picinae) often black and white, some red, brown or green; usually with red or yellow on head, sexes differ in almost all species (females often lack colors on head). Nest an unlined, excavated cavity typically in tree, sometimes in termite nest, rarely in ground. Eggs 2–14, white. Incubation 11–21 days, nestling period 18–35 days. 199 species.

## 1/ NORTHERN WRYNECK
*Jynx torquilla*

RANGE: **breeds Eurasia to N Africa; winters C Africa and S Asia**
HABITAT: **open forest, parkland**
SIZE: **6¼–6½ in (16–17 cm)**

When disturbed at its nest, the Northern Wryneck twists and writhes its neck into strange positions – hence its common name. These contortions resemble the movements of a snake and, when combined with snakelike hissing sounds, serve as an effective deterrent to small predators.

Northern Wrynecks feed predominantly on ants and other insects, taken from the ground or gleaned from vegetation on which they climb like other woodpeckers. However, they do not use their tail as a brace – it is soft-feathered, quite unlike the stiff prop of typical woodpeckers. Communication rarely includes the drumming characteristic of the piculets and true woodpeckers: instead, a repeated nasal *kwee*, a rattling call and brief *tuck* notes are heard. Tree-hole nest sites are usually usurped from other species, the birds often evicting the eggs and young of the legitimate occupiers in the process.

With their cryptic, nightjarlike plumage, these are unusual birds, classified in a subfamily of their own. They have only one close relative, the very similar Rufous-necked Wryneck *J. ruficollis* from southern Africa.

## 2/ GUIANAN PICULET
*Picumnus minutissimus*

RANGE: **Guianas**
HABITAT: **lowland forest edge, savanna, coffee plantations**
SIZE: **3½ in (9 cm)**

There are 27 species of piculet, which are, like the wrynecks, classified in a separate subfamily from the true woodpeckers. These tiny birds are all bewilderingly similar in appearance and all, like the wrynecks, lack the stiffened, proplike tail feathers of the true woodpeckers. The Guianan Piculet, which is also known as the Arrowhead Piculet, forages in pairs for small insects on twigs and branches of small trees and shrubs.

The nest cavity is excavated by male and female in soft wood, and both birds roost there during the breeding season. Nests are defended fiercely: a female feeding young has been seen to attack and chase off various species of bird that approached the nest site too closely.

## 3/ RUFOUS PICULET
*Sasia abnormis*

RANGE: **Burma, Thailand S through Malaya to Sumatra, Borneo, W Java and other Indonesian islands**
HABITAT: **lowland forest, dense second growth, bamboo thickets, river bank vegetation**
SIZE: **3½ in (9 cm)**

This restless little bird creeps and hops rapidly over the surfaces of low saplings, branches, vines, grasses and bamboo in search of food. It often forages among the vegetation in pairs or family groups for ants, their eggs, and the larvae of other insects. It also searches among the leaf litter of the woodland floor and investigates crevices for food. It is fond of habitats near water, and its toes have prominent ridges on their undersides that probably help it cling to smooth, wet branches. Unlike most members of the family, the Rufous Piculet has only 3 toes, not 4. The nest is a tiny hole about 1 in (2.5 cm) across, drilled in a decaying hollow bamboo or an old tree.

## 4/ WHITE WOODPECKER
*Melanerpes candidus*

RANGE: **S Surinam and Brazil to E Bolivia, Paraguay, W Uruguay, N Argentina**
HABITAT: **open woods, palm groves, savanna, chaco woodland**
SIZE: **10½ in (27 cm)**

The sociable White Woodpecker is often seen in small flocks. Its flight pattern is less undulating than that of other woodpeckers, and it will travel long distances to reach favored foraging sites. An omnivorous bird, the White Woodpecker eats some insects, but feeds mainly on plant matter. Its habit of eating oranges and other commercially grown fruit, which it may devour regularly in

small flocks, has made it an unpopular species with orchard owners. The White Woodpecker also eats honey and grain.

During the breeding season, these woodpeckers indulge in communal bobbing and bowing displays. They nest in branch stubs, where the female typically lays 3–4 eggs, which are probably incubated by both parents.

## 5/ RED-HEADED WOODPECKER
*Melanerpes erythrocephalus*

RANGE: **E USA and S Canada**
HABITAT: **open woods, parks, scattered trees**
SIZE: **7½ in (19 cm)**

Both male and female of this handsome species have the completely red head that the juveniles lack until the spring following their year of hatching. They are highly aggressive birds whose red heads may help them when they are usurping nest-holes from other species of woodpecker (typically the Red-bellied Woodpecker *M. carolinus*); the striking head pattern seems to scare off the other birds.

Unusually for woodpeckers, the species catches flying insects in midair and swoops down to capture grasshoppers and other insects from the ground, rather than gleaning them from tree surfaces. The latter habit often exposes them to traffic dangers and many are killed on the roads.

In winter, migrant Red-headed Woodpeckers congregate in oak woodlands, where they feed on acorns. Nest sites, typically in isolated trees, but sometimes in utility poles or even in buildings, are often usurped from other species. If excavating a cavity themselves, the birds begin at a preexisting crack in soft wood. Clutches generally consist of 3–5 eggs, and the young are fed on insects and fruit by both parents.

## 6/ ACORN WOODPECKER
*Melanerpes formicivorus*

RANGE: **NW Oregon S to Baja California, SW USA S to W Panama and N Colombia**
HABITAT: **oak savanna, parkland, mixed pine and oak woods**
SIZE: **8 in (20 cm)**

The Acorn Woodpecker's presence is easily detected by its characteristic food larders. Tree surfaces, utility poles, fenceposts and the sides of buildings are excavated and acorns firmly wedged in for future use. Its diet includes other nuts, insects and fruits, which are also stored. The 2 races illustrated are *M.f. formicivorus* from southwestern USA and northwestern Mexico and the isolated race *M.f. flavigula* from Colombia. Acorn Woodpeckers live in groups of 3–12 birds, which defend a communal territory of 10–15 acres (4–6 hectares) that comprises the group larder, foraging and nest sites.

## 7/ RED-BREASTED SAPSUCKER
*Sphyrapicus ruber*

RANGE: **NW North America**
HABITAT: **coastal evergreen and some mountain coniferous forest, aspen and pine forest**
SIZE: **7½ in (19 cm)**

The male and female Red-breasted Sapsucker, unlike those of other sapsuckers, are indistinguishable in appearance. The race *S.r. ruber* from southeast Alaska to west Oregon is illustrated; the only other race, *S.r. daggetti*, found in northern coastal California and the mountains of central and southern California, is smaller, with a paler head, longer white "moustache" stripe, paler belly and more prominent white markings on the back. Unlike the related Yellow-bellied Sapsucker *S. varius* which migrates long distances, the Red-breasted Sapsucker is sedentary.

Sapsuckers excavate tiny holes in trees with a high sugar concentration, from which they can extract sugary sap. Exploratory holes are in horizontal rows, and when a good supply of sweet sap is found, vertical rows and even grid-shaped patterns are excavated. Insects, taken either from places where they are attracted to sap exuding from the tree or in midair, complete their diet.

The nest cavities generally have small entrance holes to deter competitors and are situated in trees with heart rot fungus. Clutches typically consist of 4–7 eggs, and the young are fed insects.

## 8/ NUBIAN WOODPECKER
*Campethera nubica*

RANGE: **EC Africa**
HABITAT: **savanna**
SIZE: **7 in (18 cm)**

The Nubian Woodpecker's unforgettably loud, far-reaching series of metallic calls increases in tempo and ends with a squeaky trill. When one bird begins to call, its mate very often joins in as a duet, and their outburst may elicit vocal responses from neighboring pairs.

Nubian Woodpeckers glean insects mainly from the surface of trees, but also take some from within the bark. In addition, they sometimes drop to the ground to search for insect food. In Kenya, they have been reported as tapping the fruits of the baobab tree in order to induce ants to emerge, after which they snapped them up with the long, sticky tongue typical of woodpeckers.

Nests are either natural cavities or excavated holes in rotted wood. Nesting occurs before and during the main rains. Of a clutch of 2–5 eggs no more than 2 young fledge and they seem to acquire adult plumage rapidly.

## 9/ GROUND WOODPECKER
*Geocolaptes olivaceus*

RANGE: **South Africa**
HABITAT: **upland grassland in rocky country**
SIZE: **11 in (28 cm)**

This unusual woodpecker has completely forsaken the trees. It forages alone or in small groups on the ground, pecking and probing to retrieve ants, their larvae and pupae, and hopping among rocks to probe crevices. On the rare occasions when it does take to the air, it flies heavily and for short distances, its red rump feathers showing conspicuously.

Ground Woodpeckers can be quite vocal, uttering a burst of up to 5 far-carrying *ree-chick, ree-chick* notes, both in territorial defense and as a location call for pair members. Other calls are a triple *tchew-kee* at the nest and harsh *peer* notes uttered in alarm. These woodpeckers mob terrestrial predators and hide from aerial ones. They drink regularly, and their distribution may be linked to the availability of water.

Breeding takes place from August to January. Nests, excavated primarily by the male, are sited at the end of a long tunnel in a dirt bank beside a stream or road cutting. A total of 4–5 eggs is laid and incubated, and the fledged young often remain with their parents for some time to forage as a family group.

## 10/ CARDINAL WOODPECKER
*Dendropicos fuscescens*

RANGE: **sub-Saharan Africa**
HABITAT: **open forest, forest clearings and edges, savanna, brush**
SIZE: **5–6 in (13–15 cm)**

Also known as the Little Woodpecker, this is the most common woodpecker in sub-Saharan Africa. There are some 9 races, including the distinctive *D.f. lepidus* from parts of west and central Africa and *D.f. hemprichii* from Ethiopia, Somalia, and north and east Kenya.

The Cardinal Woodpecker probes and taps tree crevices to reveal subsurface insects; it also gleans moths, spiders and other insects from tree surfaces. It can excavate or snap off small twigs to reach beetle larvae inside, and also takes fruit in season. Foraging birds move rapidly over the branches and twigs of trees and bushes, often hanging upside-down, wings beating to maintain their position, as they investigate every nook and cranny. They call occasionally to maintain contact with their mate or other members of a family group. They may also join foraging parties of other bird species.

A sharp and tinny rattling call is used for territorial defense. Both sexes may also drum softly, ending with a sharp call.

## 11/ GREAT SPOTTED WOODPECKER
*Picoides major*

RANGE: **N Eurasia to Middle East and N Africa**
HABITAT: **deciduous and coniferous forest from Arctic taiga to Mediterranean scrub**
SIZE: **8½–9 in (22–23 cm)**

The Great Spotted Woodpecker is widely distributed and, like its New World equivalent, the Hairy Woodpecker, shows considerable geographical variation. North African populations, such as the race *P.m. numidus* from northern Algeria and Tunisia, have a distinctive red and black checkered gorget extending right across the breast. Races found in northern Iran, the Caucasus and adjacent parts of southern USSR are smoky-breasted in contrast to the white of more northern populations, including the race *P.m. pinetorum* from Europe.

Most Great Spotted Woodpeckers are sedentary, but some northern populations may migrate south in winter to find food. Populations have declined as forests have been cleared, although the species is very adaptable and lives in all types of woodland, including parks and large gardens. Reforestation in Scotland has, in turn, led to the increase of the population there.

Although rather secretive at times, these birds often betray their presence with a loud *tchick* call, and on warm spring days the woods echo with the sound of their courtship and territorial drumming.

Their diet varies seasonally to include an abundance of insects in summer and vegetable material, including seeds, in winter. The birds use branches or stumps of trees as anvils to break open seeds in winter, and can wedge pine cones into crevices in order to peck out the kernels with their bills. Occasionally during the breeding season, Great Spotted Woodpeckers hack their way into nest-boxes or natural cavities and kill and eat the chicks of other hole-nesting birds, especially tits.

## 12/ HAIRY WOODPECKER
*Picoides villosus*

RANGE: **Alaska and Canada, S to Central America, W Panama and Bahamas**
HABITAT: **coniferous and deciduous forest**
SIZE: **7–9½ in (18–24 cm)**

The Hairy Woodpecker is, in many respects, a New World counterpart of the Great Spotted Woodpecker. It is one of the most widely distributed and geographically variable of all woodpeckers. For instance, the race *P.v. septentrionalis*, from Alaska, Canada and parts of the central and western USA, has striking black and white plumage and may weigh up to 5 oz (135 g), whereas the race *P.v. sanctorum*, from southern Mexico and Central America, has black, white and chocolate-brown coloring and is much smaller, weighing only about 1½ oz (38 g). Northern populations may migrate south for food in winter, but most birds are sedentary.

Hairy Woodpeckers forage on trunks and major limbs of trees for surface and subsurface insects, berries, and seeds. Their calls include a loud *peek* location call and a rattling call.

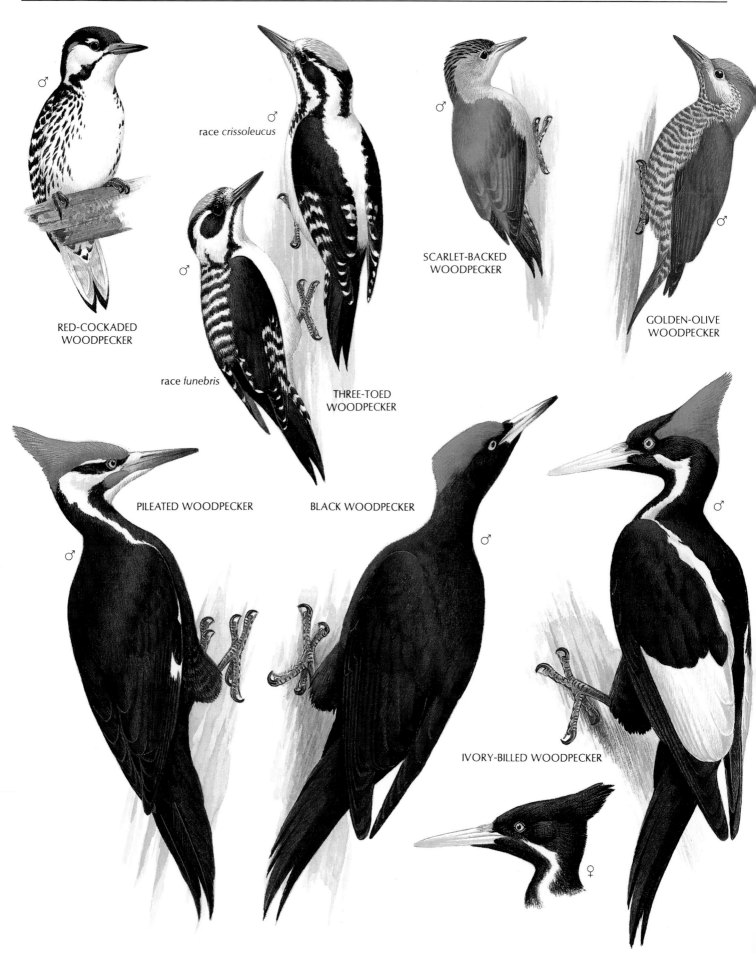

♂

race *crissoleucus*

♂

RED-COCKADED
WOODPECKER

♂

race *funebris*

THREE-TOED
WOODPECKER

SCARLET-BACKED
WOODPECKER

♂

GOLDEN-OLIVE
WOODPECKER

♂

PILEATED WOODPECKER

BLACK WOODPECKER

♂

♂

IVORY-BILLED WOODPECKER

♀

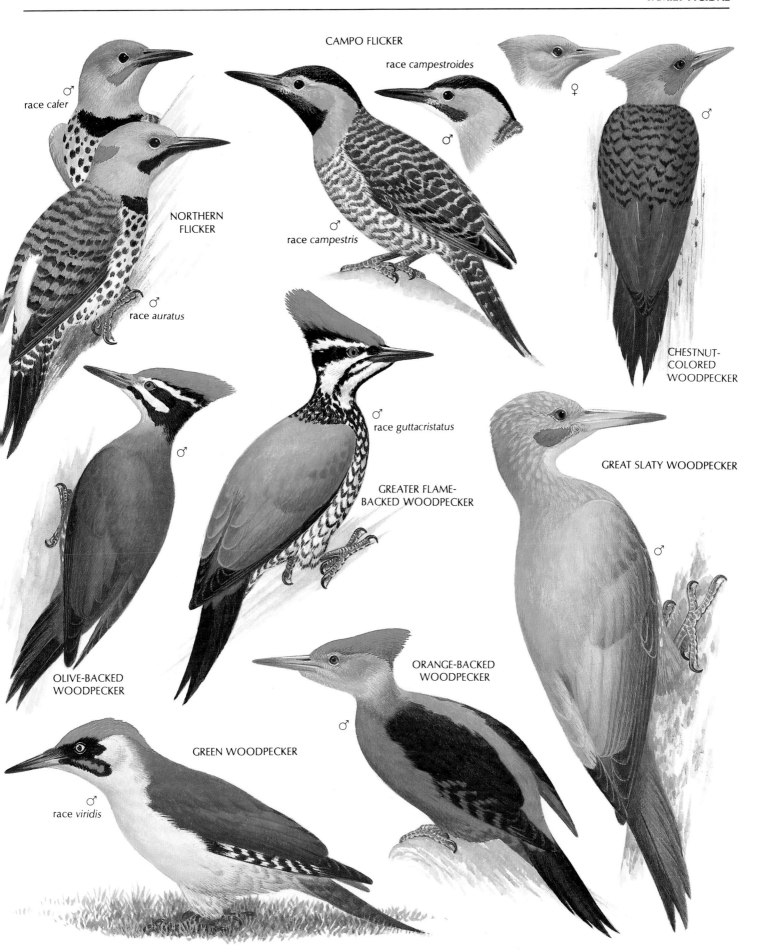

race *cafer* ♂

NORTHERN
FLICKER

race *auratus* ♂

CAMPO FLICKER

race *campestroides*

♀

race *campestris* ♂

♂

CHESTNUT-
COLORED
WOODPECKER

race *guttacristatus* ♂

GREATER FLAME-
BACKED WOODPECKER

GREAT SLATY WOODPECKER

♂

♂

OLIVE-BACKED
WOODPECKER

ORANGE-BACKED
WOODPECKER

♂

GREEN WOODPECKER

race *viridis* ♂

357

# WOODPECKERS

## 1/ RED-COCKADED WOODPECKER
*Picoides borealis* ⊻
RANGE: **SE USA**
HABITAT: **mature open pine forest**
SIZE: **7 in (18 cm)**

This species has declined dramatically, largely because of human control of natural forest fires and the clear-cutting of forests in their early stages. Fire is an integral part of this bird's ecosystem, perpetuating pines while excluding hardwood trees, thus keeping the forests open. The bird's population is now fragmented, and the species is regarded as being at risk.

Red-cockaded Woodpeckers live in social groups called "clans." Each of these comprises one breeding pair, their fledglings, and male offspring from previous years (young females disperse in their first winter). The clans forage over home ranges that average about 200 acres (80 hectares) in size. This species nests and roosts in holes in the trunks of living pines. Even with the weakening effect of heart rot fungus, excavation may take several months. Small holes drilled above and below each cavity provide a continuous flow of gum that repels climbing rat snakes.

## 2/ THREE-TOED WOODPECKER
*Picoides tridactylus*
RANGE: **N North America S to N USA,
N Eurasia S to S Scandinavia, S Siberia,
W China, N Japan; isolated mountain
populations farther S**
HABITAT: **damp, dense coniferous forest**
SIZE: **8½ in (22 cm)**

Like its close relative, the Black-backed Woodpecker *P. arcticus*, this species is unusual in having only 3 toes on each foot, heavily barred flanks and yellow rather than red on the crown of the male. Its range is closely linked to the distribution of spruce trees and the bark beetles that infest them, although it will use other conifers and other food resources. These are 8 races: the 2 that are illustrated are *P. t. crissoleucus* of northern Siberia, which is a relatively white race, and *P. t. funebris* of southwest China and Tibet, which is the blackest of all the races.

The Three-toed Woodpecker carefully scours each tree on which it forages. It gleans insects from bark surfaces, scales bark from trees to obtain prey from beneath, and will also excavate insects from soft wood.

## 3/ SCARLET-BACKED WOODPECKER
*Veniliornis callonotus*
RANGE: **SW Colombia, W Ecuador, NW
Peru**
HABITAT: **arid scrub, dry forest**
SIZE: **5½ in (14 cm)**

Within its limited range, this stunning species shows considerable geographical variation in the amount of barring on the breast. Females lack the red tips on the black crown feathers, but are otherwise very similar to males. The Scarlet-backed Woodpecker occurs at elevations of up to 3,300 ft (1,000 m). Little else is known of its ecology or habits. Nesting appears to take place between May and October.

## 4/ GOLDEN-OLIVE WOODPECKER
*Piculus rubiginosus*
RANGE: **Mexico to Argentina; Trinidad,
Tobago**
HABITAT: **forest, forest edge, secondary
growth**
SIZE: **7½–9 in (19–23 cm)**

This woodpecker is widely distributed and fairly common in some areas. In more northerly parts of its range, it occurs in pine-oak and oak forest; to the south it is found in oak and tropical deciduous forest and, at times, in tropical evergreen forest. There are about 20 races; *P. r. aeruginosus* is from northeastern Mexico.

A rather quiet, secretive bird, the Golden-olive Woodpecker feeds on tree-dwelling invertebrates, blackberries and other fruits. Its foraging includes much peering and poking into bark crevices and the excavation of sub-surface insects. Occasionally, it will feed on the ground. In Colombia, it is reported to join mixed-species foraging flocks.

## 5/ NORTHERN FLICKER
*Colaptes auratus*
RANGE: **North America S to Nicaragua**
HABITAT: **open forest, savanna, open areas
with widely scattered trees**
SIZE: **10–14 in (25.5–36 cm)**

Until recently, the Red-shafted Flicker (*C. a. cafer* and similar races) of western North America, the Yellow-shafted Flicker (*C. a. auratus* and the similar *C. a. luteus*) of eastern North America, and the Gilded Flicker (*C. a. chrysoides* and similar races) of southwestern USA and northern Mexico were considered to be separate species. Well-documented hybridization among these and other different forms has led to their present designation as a single species.

Although they occasionally take food from trees, Northern Flickers are perfectly at home on the ground, where they have become specialists in feeding on ants. They have a variety of calls, and both sexes produce the characteristic woodpecker drumming sound with their bills. In the absence of suitable trees for drumming, they often drum on buildings, television antennas and other

artificial structures. Although they can excavate nest-holes in soft wood or cacti, they frequently use natural cavities or renovate old nests.

## 6/ CAMPO FLICKER
*Colaptes campestris*
RANGE: **Surinam and lower Amazon Basin
to E Bolivia, S Brazil, Paraguay, Uruguay,
Argentina**
HABITAT: **grassland, savanna, forest edge**
SIZE: **11¾ in (30 cm)**

This species is an ant specialist and is not known to take other foods – it seems to be the most specialized of the flickers. Most food is taken from the ground, where the bird hops about in uneven terrain or walks on level turf. It often forages in small groups, sometimes in company with the Green-barred Flicker *C. melanochloros*. Foraging groups seem especially attracted to areas that have been recently burned. There are 2 races, often regarded as separate species: the northern *C. c. campestris* and the southern *C. c. campestroides*, often known as the Field Flicker.

Perhaps as a reflection of the scarcity of suitable nest sites, 2 or more pairs of Camp Flickers sometimes nest in close proximity. Nonbreeding adults may help out at some nests and, after fledging, family groups may remain together for some time.

## 7/ CHESTNUT-COLORED WOODPECKER
*Celeus castaneus*
RANGE: **Mexico to Panama**
HABITAT: **dense, tropical evergreen forest
and secondary growth**
SIZE: **9–9¾ in (23–25 cm)**

This is a fairly common woodpecker in many areas, but one that is difficult to see because of its dark plumage and shaded habitat. It is often easy to locate, however, because of its constant tapping as it forages on large branches and tree trunks in the middle to upper layers of the forest. The Chestnut-colored Woodpecker is often seen in pairs and may feed cooperatively to some extent.

This species is considered a pest in some cocoa plantations where it damages the fruit.

The call note of the Chestnut-colored Woodpecker is a low *kwar* or *keeyark*. This is sometimes followed by a lower, weaker *heh-heh-heh*. Other calls include a sharp, double squeak and a *howp* similar to that of a trogon.

## 8/ PILEATED WOODPECKER
*Dryocopus pileatus*

RANGE: S Canada, E and NW USA
HABITAT: forest, especially moist forest
SIZE: 15–18¾ in (38–48 cm)

Unlike some other large species, the Pileated Woodpecker still thrives in many areas, partly because ants and termites, some of its staple prey, are always abundant. It forages for insects both in wood on the ground and in trees, and it also feeds readily on fruit in season. The female has a less extensive red cap than the male, the front of her crown being black, and she lacks the red on her "moustache" stripe.

The call of the Pileated Woodpecker is a loud series of *kuk-kuk-kuk* notes. The bird carefully selects a drumming surface that will resonate very loudly across the forest.

## 9/ BLACK WOODPECKER
*Dryocopus martius*

RANGE: Eurasia except for SW China
HABITAT: northern to warm-temperate hardwood and coniferous forest
SIZE: 17¾ in (45 cm)

The Black Woodpecker, like its New World counterpart, the Pileated Woodpecker, has a large home range, estimated at 375–7,500 acres (150–3,000 hectares), depending on the quality of the habitat. Because of its large size, the boundaries are not clearly defined and several birds may have overlapping ranges.

This is a solitary species that is normally seen in pairs only during the breeding season. At other times, the sexes maintain separate territories or at least feed alone. The Black Woodpecker feeds primarily on ants, termites and the larvae of wood-boring beetles, but may occasionally eat the eggs and nestlings of other birds. It also eats some fruit in season.

## 10/ IVORY-BILLED WOODPECKER
*Campephilus principalis*    E

RANGE: mountains of E Cuba (possibly also SE USA)
HABITAT: extensive, remote, mature forest
SIZE: 19½ in (50 cm)

This is the third largest woodpecker in the world, exceeded in size only by the closely related, and possibly extinct, Imperial Woodpecker *C. imperialis* of Mexico and the Great Slaty Woodpecker. It is one of the world's rarest birds. It is intimately associated with virgin forests, and its demise is tied to the loss of the forests and direct persecution by people. The felling of mature forests also cut back the bird's principal food supply of large beetle larvae. Since the early 1940s, records of Ivory-billed Woodpeckers in the USA have been treated with scepticism, but a slim hope remains

that some birds might have survived in remote forests in Louisiana, Mississippi or Florida.

The Cuban population of this bird declined at about the same time as the US population, but in recent years a few birds have been discovered in rugged, forested terrain in the island's eastern mountains. The Cuban government has set the area aside as a reserve.

## 11/ GREEN WOODPECKER
*Picus viridis*

RANGE: W Eurasia from S Scandinavia, Europe to mountains of N Africa, Turkey, Iran, W Russia
HABITAT: deciduous and mixed forest edge, secondary growth, parklike habitats
SIZE: 11¾ in (30 cm)

This bird spends much of its time foraging on the gound for ants and grubs. When it finds an anthill, the Green Woodpecker tears into it with a vigorous twisting of the head and probing of the beak. It also gleans insects and spiders from tree surfaces, consumes fruits and seeds, and sometimes raids beehives. The female has an all-black "moustache," while juveniles have only a faint one and barred underparts. There are several races, including *P. v. viridis* of Europe and *P. v. vaillantii* of north Africa, which has strongly barred underparts and less red on the head in the female, whose "moustache" resembles that of the male.

The Green Woodpecker tends to be solitary outside the breeding season. Both sexes have similar calls, including a far-carrying laughing cry and a series of *kwit-up* notes with variations. This species rarely drums.

## 12/ OLIVE-BACKED WOODPECKER
*Dinopium rafflesii*

RANGE: Southeast Asia from Tenasserim through Malay Peninsula to Sumatra, Borneo
HABITAT: dense lowland forest
SIZE: 11 in (28 cm)

This species is sometimes known as the Olive-backed Three-toed Woodpecker, a name which reveals both plumage and structural characteristics. It forages alone or in pairs in the forest understory by gleaning and probing for surface and sub-surface insects and spiders. Occasionally, it drops to the ground to investigate fallen logs.

The calls of the Olive-backed Woodpecker include a rapid, descending series of *kwee* notes. A slow tapping is used in communications between pair members at the nest site, but no drumming has been recorded.

## 13/ GREATER FLAME-BACKED WOODPECKER
*Chrysocolaptes lucidus*

RANGE: S Asia from India to SW China, Greater Sundas and the Philippines
HABITAT: forest, forest edge, mangroves
SIZE: 13 in (33 cm)

This species is sometimes known as the Crimson-backed Woodpecker or Greater Golden-backed Woodpecker. Most of its food consists of insects.

It will tap along a branch to locate prey, and then dig into the wood to reach them. It has also been seen catching termites on the ground and even seizing winged termites in the air.

The Greater Flame-backed Woodpecker engages in distinctive and frequent bouts of drumming prior to nesting, often producing long, loud, rapid bursts that decrease in intensity. Vocalizations include a *keek* call note and a laughing series of *kow* notes that have been described as "harsh, loud, prolonged ... incessant and strident, such as might be made by a giant cicada." Many races have been described, most of them isolated geographically from one another. The race illustrated is *C. l. guttacristatus*, which ranges from northwest India to northern Vietnam.

## 14/ ORANGE-BACKED WOODPECKER
*Reinwardtipicus validus*

RANGE: S Burma, S Thailand, Malaysia, Sumatra, Java, Borneo
HABITAT: lowland forest, secondary growth, partially cleared areas with large trees
SIZE: 11¾ in (30 cm)

This is a noisy woodpecker which taps loudly, calls frequently and forages from near ground level to the forest canopy. It forages by tapping to locate sub-surface insects and excavating to remove them. Occasionally, it scales bark from trees to reveal prey beneath. Its vocalizations all seem to be based on a metallic *pit* note. These notes are given singly, as a double note, or as a series of up to 9 notes. The Orange-backed Woodpecker excavates its nests in dead trees. The young remain with the parents and are fed large insect larvae for some time after fledging. They will also follow adults to excavations, where they retrieve food for themselves.

## 15/ GREAT SLATY WOODPECKER
*Mulleripicus pulverulentus*

RANGE: N India to SW China, Thailand, Vietnam, Malaysia, Indonesia
HABITAT: lowland forest and swamp forest
SIZE: 20 in (51 cm)

Although a bird of the virgin forest, the Great Slaty Woodpecker will also live in partially cleared areas with large trees if there is undisturbed forest nearby. It is found in pairs or family groups that travel together to scattered feeding sites. These birds seem to use much of the range of foraging techniques used by other woodpeckers – gleaning, peering and poking, excavating and chasing insects on or near the ground. Their primary food seems to be ants, although they will also take termites and beetle larvae.

The loudest, most distinctive call of the Great Slaty Woodpecker is a braying cackle. Other vocalizations include a *dit* note, a rattling series of *dit*s and a flight call, rendered as *dwot*. Both sexes share in the nesting duties, and the young may remain with them for long periods, perhaps until the beginning of the next breeding season.

# BROADBILLS, WOODCREEPERS, OVENBIRDS

LESSER GREEN BROADBILL

♂

AFRICAN BROADBILL

COMMON MINER

WEDGE-BILLED
WOODCREEPER

LONG-BILLED
WOODCREEPER

RED-BILLED SCYTHEBILL

race *nigrirostris*

BARRED WOODCREEPER

race
*radiolatus*

PALE-BREASTED SPINETAIL

DES MURS' WIRETAIL

STREAK-BACKED
CANASTERO

SCALE-THROATED EARTHCREEPER

FIREWOOD-GATHERER

nest

BUFF-FRONTED
FOLIAGE-GLEANER

RUFOUS HORNERO

nest

PLAIN XENOPS

# BROADBILLS, WOODCREEPERS, OVENBIRDS

## FAMILY EURYLAIMIDAE
### Broadbills
Small to medium, stout birds, with large eyes and broad heads. Bill flattened with wide gape. Plumage loose, often colorful, especially in Asian species. Sexes differ in about half the species. Nest oval or purse-shaped, suspended. Eggs 2–8, white or pinkish, sometimes speckled. Incubation and nestling periods unknown. 14 species.

### 1/ AFRICAN BROADBILL
*Smithornis capensis*

RANGE: **Africa, from Ivory Coast and Kenya S to Natal and Angola**
HABITAT: **forest, secondary woodland, thickets**
SIZE: **5 in (13 cm)**

A dumpy, somewhat lethargic denizen of dense bush, the African Broadbill is a solitary, inconspicuous bird, which usually hunts from a perch low down among dimly lit vegetation. It feeds on flying insects, catching them in midair after short pursuit flights that may briefly show off its white rump patch.

It is heard more often than seen, particularly during the brief but remarkable display flight when, with wings vibrating rapidly, the bird flies in a tight circle around its perch. The vibration of its wings generates a distinctive rattling trill which can be heard from several yards away. The performance is often repeated over and over again, but since it usually occurs in a small clear space amid dense foliage, it is rarely seen.

### 2/ LESSER GREEN BROADBILL
*Calyptomena viridis*

RANGE: **Lower Burma and peninsular Thailand to Sumatra and Borneo**
HABITAT: **forest and secondary woodland, up to 5,500 ft (1,700 m) in Borneo**
SIZE: **8 in (20 cm)**

Although the bill of this Asian broadbill is higher and more arched than those of other species, it is almost concealed by the elongated feathers that surround it, giving the bird's head a rounded, almost froglike appearance.

The male looks as though he should be conspicuous, with his shining grass-green plumage, but he blends in well with the rich greens of the tropical forest and can be surprisingly hard to see. These birds move rather deliberately, although they are often livelier and noisier when foraging in small groups, calling with low whistles or the bubbling notes characteristic of the family.

The female is often larger than her mate and her plumage is a duller green. She lays 2 eggs in a pear-shaped nest, woven from plant fiber and suspended from low twigs just above the ground.

## FAMILY DENDROCOLAPTIDAE
### Woodcreepers
Medium, slender, insect-eating tree-climbers, with stiff, spiny tails. Bills very variable, from short and stout to long, thin and downcurved. Plumage brown to rufous, often streaked. Sexes alike. Nest built in tree cavities. Eggs 2–3, white or greenish-white. Incubation 15–20 days, nestling period unknown. 52 species.

### 3/ WEDGE-BILLED WOODCREEPER
*Glyphorhynchus spirurus*

RANGE: **S Mexico to N Bolivia, Amazonia**
HABITAT: **humid tropical forest, secondary woodland**
SIZE: **5½ in (14 cm)**

The cryptic coloration of the Wedge-billed Woodcreeper makes it hard to see when it clings motionless to a tree trunk. It hunts by hitching its way up trees and along branches, using its stiffened tail feathers as a prop in much the same way as a woodpecker. As it climbs, it taps at the bark with its short, slightly upturned bill, searching for small insects and spiders. Widespread and common, it is usually seen singly or in pairs, and it often occurs in mixed-species flocks.

### 4/ LONG-BILLED WOODCREEPER
*Nasica longirostris*

RANGE: **Venezuela to N Bolivia, Amazonia**
HABITAT: **humid tropical forest, seasonally flooded forest, swamps**
SIZE: **14 in (36 cm)**

The bill of this distinctive woodcreeper is ideally suited for probing the layered foliage of bromeliads and similar plants that grow on tropical forest trees. These plants often harbor a rich variety of insects, spiders and other small animals. The bird also searches for prey in the bark like its shorter-billed relatives. It is an agile climber which usually hunts alone or in pairs, communicating with eerie whistles.

### 5/ BARRED WOODCREEPER
*Dendrocolaptes certhia*

RANGE: **Mexico to N Bolivia, Amazonia**
HABITAT: **humid tropical forest, secondary woodland**
SIZE: **11 in (28 cm)**

The strongly built Barred Woodcreeper is noted for its habit of following columns of army ants as they swarm over the forest floor. It ignores the ants themselves, preying instead on the insects that try to escape them; woodcreepers have been seen flying back and forth from tree trunks, snatching the escapees from the ground or hawking them in midair. At other times it forages for prey much like other woodcreepers, working its way up one tree, then flying down to the foot of another to repeat the process.

The bill of the Costa Rican race *D. c. nigrirostris* is mainly black, whereas that of the upper Amazonian race *D. c. radiolatus* is red. More than 10 other races have been recognized, with a subtle variety of bill colors and plumage details: some Mexican populations have ivory-colored bills.

### 6/ RED-BILLED SCYTHEBILL
*Campylorhamphus trochilirostris*

RANGE: **Panama, through N South America to Bolivia, Paraguay, N Argentina**
HABITAT: **humid tropical forest, swamps**
SIZE: **11¾ in (30 cm)**

The spectacular downcurved red bill of this quite unmistakable woodcreeper is a superb adaptation for penetrating the convoluted foliage of tree ferns, bromeliads and other epiphytes (plants that grow on trees) in search of prey. This impressive bird feeds on spiders, insects and even the small frogs that live in the pools of water within the plants. It can also insert its long bill into the smallest bark crevice to pick out an insect that would be safe from almost any other bird. Like other woodcreepers and woodpeckers (pp. 214–21), Red-billed Scythebills use their stiffened tail feathers to support themselves on vertical tree trunks while clinging on with their strong feet.

## FAMILY FURNARIIDAE
### Ovenbirds
Medium, active, often ground-dwelling, extraordinarily diverse in form and habits. Plumage drab, sexes similar. True ovenbirds build domed mud nests; others build stick nests or use cavities. Eggs 2–5, white to blue. Incubation about 15 days, nestling period 13–18 days (known for only 6 species). 227 species.

## 7/ COMMON MINER
*Geositta cunicularia*

RANGE: S South America, from Peru and Brazil to Tierra del Fuego
HABITAT: arid sandy plains, dunes, grassland, from coasts to mountaintops
SIZE: $6\frac{3}{4}$–$7\frac{1}{2}$ in (17–19 cm)

The Common Miner takes its name from the long nest-burrow which it excavates in a slope, earth bank, cutting or sand dune. Up to 10 ft (3 m) long, the burrow ends in a roomy chamber which serves as a nest-hole during the breeding season and a roosting site for the rest of the year.

The birds forage for insects and seeds on the ground, running rapidly for short distances, then abruptly stopping to utter loud call-notes and peer about, frequently flicking up their tails and wing tips. After eating an insect, a Common Miner will often clean its bill by wiping both sides on a rock.

## 8/ SCALE-THROATED EARTHCREEPER
*Upucerthia dumetaria*

RANGE: S South America
HABITAT: arid slopes and thorny brush
SIZE: $9\frac{3}{4}$ in (25 cm)

The earthcreepers are all large, brown, ground-dwelling birds with downcurved bills. Normally silent and inconspicuous, the Scale-throated Earthcreeper often lives in arid terrain, where it searches for insects among the stones and boulders, or plunges its long bill into clumps of bunchgrass. If alarmed, it tends to run and hide rather than fly away; when it does fly, it rarely goes far.

The pair digs a nest-burrow up to 5 ft (1.5 m) deep in a sloping hillside or earth bank, lining the nest chamber with grasses and roots.

## 9/ RUFOUS HORNERO
*Furnarius rufus*

RANGE: E South America from Brazil to Argentina
HABITAT: groves of trees, open country
SIZE: 8 in (20 cm)

The word *hornero* is Spanish for "baker" – a reference to the bird's remarkable nest, which is made of mud reinforced with straw and shaped like a traditional baker's oven. Often built on top of a broad fencepost, or even on a house, the nest is a complex structure with a low entrance hole and a spiral, ascending passageway leading to the nesting chamber. It may take months to complete and is very durable, yet the birds build a new one each year. Abandoned nests are often adopted by other birds.

Rufous Horneros forage on the ground, using their strong, sharp bills to dig out earthworms and insect larvae. They move with a characteristic, high-stepping, deliberate gait, and the pairs will often sing together with loud ringing calls.

## 10/ DES MURS' WIRETAIL
*Sylviorthorhynchus desmursii*

RANGE: Chile and Argentina
HABITAT: humid forest, in thick understory, especially bamboo thickets
SIZE: $9\frac{1}{2}$ in (24 cm)

A secretive, little-known denizen of dense forest, Des Murs' Wiretail, also known as Des Murs' Spinetail, is remarkable for its strange tail feathers. There are only 6 of them: the short outer pair is hidden among the tail coverts and the middle and inner pairs are very long – up to 3 times the length of the bird's body – but reduced to little more than fringed shafts. These often appear very worn, suggesting that they are used for some sort of abrasive purpose or for display.

Although they often show little fear of humans, Des Murs' Wiretails rarely emerge from the thick foliage where they find their food. However, they often reveal their presence by their persistent calls. They nest close to the ground amid dry vegetation, building a globular nest of plant fiber.

## 11/ PALE-BREASTED SPINETAIL
*Synallaxis albescens*

RANGE: SW Costa Rica to Argentina, E of Andes; Trinidad, Margarita Island
HABITAT: forest edge, plantations, mangroves, thickets, reedbeds, savanna, arid areas
SIZE: $6\frac{1}{4}$ in (16 cm)

The Pale-breasted Spinetail is usually seen foraging alone or with its mate, giving harsh chattering calls and bobbing its tail rapidly up and down as it picks its way over the ground in search of insect prey.

This bird has many races over its great range, but plumage differences are slight. Its choice of habitat is equally wide, ranging from sea level to at least 7,000 ft (2,100 m). It nests in trees or bushes, building a coarse, globe-shaped nest of small twigs with a narrow, tubular side entrance. Southern populations migrate northward outside the breeding season.

## 12/ STREAK-BACKED CANASTERO
*Thripophaga wyatti*

RANGE: NW Venezuela, NE Colombia, Ecuador to S Peru
HABITAT: mountain grassland with scattered bushes from the tree line to the snow line in the Andes
SIZE: 6 in (15 cm)

Although widespread and locally common, the Streak-backed Canastero has a patchy distribution on the open, rocky terrain just below the snow line on the Andes. It is occasionally found below the tree line in open terrain. The Streak-backed Canastero feeds on insects, hopping or running over the ground and frequently raising or flicking up its slightly cocked tail as it probes among the stones and grasses for its prey. When startled, it dives into thick vegetation.

In Spanish the word *canastero* means "basket maker," and refers to the large, domed basketlike nests of small twigs and grass built by this and the other 21 species of canastero.

## 13/ FIREWOOD-GATHERER
*Anumbius annumbi*

RANGE: Brazil, Uruguay, Paraguay, Argentina
HABITAT: open scrub and weedy areas
SIZE: $8\frac{1}{4}$ in (21 cm)

The nests of this common bird look like great piles of sticks ready for the fire, and are often built on conspicuous sites such as isolated trees or utility poles. The birds favor thorny twigs, lining them with wool and soft grass, and each nest may last for several years. The nests often incorporate brightly colored rags, bones, pieces of metal and other debris into the main structure of their remarkable nests, and may add snakeskin, crab shells, snail shells and fragments of bark to the lining of the neatly arched tunnel leading to the main section.

The Firewood-Gatherer generally hunts on the ground, searching out insects and other small animals among clumps of grass or weeds. Its call is a rapid *chick-chick-chee*, sung with such gusto that the bird's whole body shakes during the performance.

## 14/ BUFF-FRONTED FOLIAGE-GLEANER
*Philydor rufus*

RANGE: Costa Rica S to N Argentina
HABITAT: humid and wet mountain forest
SIZE: $7\frac{1}{2}$ in (19 cm)

Sometimes foraging completely alone, but often as single birds in mixed flocks with other species, this bird lives up to its name by gleaning insects and spiders from tangled masses of vines growing up the trunks of forest trees, or by hopping rapidly along horizontal branches to search for prey among the foliage near their tips. The Buff-fronted Foliage-gleaner frequently twists its body and sweeps its tail when looking for insects, perhaps to dislodge or frighten them from their hiding places. Its curious calls have been described as froglike croaks and a snorting *churr*. It nests in a burrow excavated in an earth bank.

## 15/ PLAIN XENOPS
*Xenops minutus*

RANGE: SE Mexico to W Ecuador, and E of Andes S to N Argentina, Paraguay, S Brazil
HABITAT: humid forest and forest edge
SIZE: $4\frac{3}{4}$ in (12 cm)

There are several *Xenops* species and all but one have a distinctive white crescent on the cheek like that of the Plain Xenops. They also share a characteristic foraging habit, hopping and sidling along branches, peering from side to side in search of insects, spiders and other small creatures. Sometimes they hitch their way up tree trunks in the manner of woodcreepers, stopping to pry into small rotten twigs.

The Plain Xenops nests in a rotten stump, either excavating a cavity itself or taking over a hole dug by one of the small woodpeckers known as piculets. It roosts alone in a similar hole, usually choosing an old woodpecker nest.

BARRED ANTSHRIKE

race *intermedius*

BLUISH-SLATE ANTSHRIKE

BERTONI'S ANTWREN

WHITE-FLANKED ANTWREN

GRAY ANTBIRD

race *cinerascens*

race *naevia*

CHESTNUT-TAILED ANTBIRD

SILVERED ANTBIRD

♂

WHITE-PLUMED ANTBIRD

♂ race *crissalis*

BLACK-FACED ANT-THRUSH

SCALED ANTPITTA

race *guatimalensis*

♂

SLATE-CROWNED ANTPITTA

♂

RUFOUS GNATEATER

BLACK-THROATED
HUET-HUET

♂

juv

♂

SLATY BRISTLEFRONT

♀

UNICOLORED TAPACULO

# ANTBIRDS AND GNATEATERS, TAPACULOS

## FAMILY FORMICARIIDAE
### Antbirds and gnateaters

Small to medium, generally long-legged birds forming a very diverse family, including antshrikes, antvireos, antwrens, ant-thrushes and antpittas, as well as species simply called antbirds. Many (including gnateaters, sometimes classified in separate family) short-necked, round-bodied, almost tailless. Wings rounded for short flights in dense vegetation. Sexes usually differ. Males often dark gray or black, often with white spots and bars, sometimes with reddish-brown; females often brown. Gnateaters have pale brown upperparts, even paler below, with patterned heads, usually with tuft of long, silvery-white plumes behind each eye in males of most species and females of some. Most species suspend cup nests in forks of branches; some nest on top of fallen tree trunks or inside hollow stubs of palms; a few on the ground. Eggs 2, usually white or creamy (some pale blue or brown) with many dark (especially brown) markings. Incubation 14–16 days, nestling period 9–12 days. 246 species.

## 1/ BARRED ANTSHRIKE
*Thamnophilus doliatus*
RANGE: **Mexico to extreme N Argentina**
HABITAT: **lowland thickets and tangles**
SIZE: **5½–6¾ in (14–17 cm)**

This species is typically found in semiopen areas, such as dry forests or bushy savannas, but it is widespread where it has few competitors. In the heart of Amazonia where antbirds abound, however, it is confined to shrubby growth on river banks and islands.

The Barred Antshrike searches for insects primarily in the dim light of often impenetrable thickets. More often heard than seen, members of a pair keep in touch through a large repertoire of songs and calls. The song is a rolling rattle that ends in an emphatic nasal note. As it sings, the Barred Antshrike stretches its neck, raises its striking crest and vibrates its slightly fanned tail. The amount of black barring on the underparts of the male varies between races.

## 2/ BLUISH-SLATE ANTSHRIKE
*Thamnomanes schistogynus*
RANGE: **SW Amazonia**
HABITAT: **lowland forest**
SIZE: **5½ in (14 cm)**

In the permanent mixed-species flocks that sweep through the forest understory, this species serves as a sentinel guarding against hawks and other predators. As the advancing flock disturbs insects from their hiding places, the Bluish-slate Antshrike sallies out to capture them in the air or on foliage. Sometimes it gives false alarm calls to freeze its flock mates, which gives it an advantage in capturing fleeing insects. Occasionally the Bluish-slate Antshrike chases a small bird and forces it to disgorge an insect it has captured but not yet consumed. To construct its nest, the bird piles a huge ball of large dead leaves on a horizontal branch, which makes it appear like aerial leaf litter.

## 3/ WHITE-FLANKED ANTWREN
*Myrmotherula axillaris*
RANGE: **Central America to SE Brazil**
HABITAT: **humid lowland forest**
SIZE: **4 in (10 cm)**

White-flanked Antwrens are tiny dynamos that often flick their wings to flash white underneath. They almost always travel through the forest together with birds of one or more other species in mixed-species flocks.

White-flanked Antwrens are moderately specialized in foraging behavior, primarily finding insects on living leaves about 6–65 ft (2–20 m) off the ground. They typically move rapidly through branches, but also search by traveling up and down through the vines that encircle the tree trunks. In addition to simply picking insects off leaves, these antwrens are sometimes more acrobatic in their search for food, stretching, leaning, hanging and hovering to obtain prey.

## 4/ BERTONI'S ANTWREN
*Drymophila rubricollis*
RANGE: **SW Brazil, adjacent Paraguay and Argentina**
HABITAT: **bamboo thickets**
SIZE: **5½ in (14 cm)**

Bertoni's Antwren is associated with bamboo, an extremely important element in the South American landscape. Hopping and fluttering among the highly flexible bamboo stalks, this sprightly little bird uses its long tail to help it retain its balance. From its precarious perches, this bird reaches out in all directions to capture small insects, often knocking over dead leaves caught up in the bamboo in search of hidden prey. Pairs occupy a small territory within which they forage by themselves or temporarily associate with mixed flocks. Bertoni's Antwren has only recently been re-established as a species, distinct from the closely related Ferruginous Antwren *D. ferruginea*.

## 5/ GRAY ANTBIRD
*Cercomacra cinerascens*
RANGE: **Amazonia**
HABITAT: **forest**
SIZE: **6 in (15 cm)**

The Gray Antbird haunts the twisted masses of vines and lianas that are often found from mid-heights to the crowns of tall trees. It is very difficult to see, but it may be located by listening for its harsh, repeated *cruick-shank* song. This active forager often contorts its long tail up, down, or sideways as it stretches to pick off prey. In display, the long tail wags back and forth while the head moves in the opposite direction, giving the bird the grotesque shape of the letter *Z*.

Several races have been described: *C. c. cinerascens* from upper Amazonia has a small white patch between the "shoulders" and narrow white edges to its greater wing coverts.

## 6/ SILVERED ANTBIRD
*Sclateria naevia*
RANGE: **Amazonia**
HABITAT: **near water in wooded areas**
SIZE: **5½–6 in (14–15 cm)**

This bird is especially abundant where streams cut their way through areas of swampy forest. It works through the overhanging vegetation close to the water, picking insect prey from the surface of the water, from floating leaves and from twigs and branches. Less often, the Silvered Antbird hops on damp leaf litter or tree roots or through grass near the water's edge, but only if dense cover is nearby. Its distinctive song begins with a single emphatic note and continues with a long, rapidly delivered staccato series of notes that rises slightly and then softly trails off.

There are several races, including *S. n. naevia* of northeastern Venezuela, the Guianas and northern Brazil, which has gray and white scalloped underparts in the male and heavily brown-mottled white underparts in the female, and *S. n. argentata* of upper Amazonia, with only a few gray edges to the feathers of the male's underparts and the sides of the neck and body bright chestnut in the female.

## 7/ CHESTNUT-TAILED ANTBIRD
*Myrmeciza hemimelaena*
RANGE: **Amazonia, mostly S of River Amazon**
HABITAT: **forest undergrowth**
SIZE: **4¾ in (12 cm)**

The Chestnut-tailed Antbird is found close to the forest floor, perching on branches, vertical stems and logs. It moves quickly through the undergrowth and picks prey off leaves, plant stems, or tops of fallen logs. It only occasionally jumps down to the leaf litter to capture insects or to use the ground as a perch from which to sally to the undersides of overhead leaves. The male utters a short series of loud, clear whistles that accelerate and fall in pitch; the female answers with a slower, more evenly paced, downward series.

## 8/ WHITE-PLUMED ANTBIRD
*Pithys albifrons*
RANGE: **Amazonia, mostly N of River Amazon**
HABITAT: **forest undergrowth**
SIZE: **4¼ in (11 cm)**

The White-plumed Antbird feeds almost entirely by snapping up cockroaches, katydids and other insects fleeing formidable columns of army ants. To catch escaping insects, the White-plumed Antbird and other ant-following birds perch in the midst of the column of ants near the ground where the ants are thickest. The White-plumed Antbird moves from one vertical perch to another, apparently to avoid competitors as well as the ants. Competition is fierce for the best perches, and this small species is often relegated to the less desirable fringes of the ant swarm.

## 9/ BLACK-FACED ANT-THRUSH
*Formicarius analis*
RANGE: **S Mexico to Amazonia**
HABITAT: **forest and woodland floor**
SIZE: **6¾–7½ in (17–19 cm)**

Pairs of Black-faced Ant-Thrushes forage apart but within easy calling distance of each other. Normally they strut about on the leaf litter, their tails cocked and their heads and tails bobbing slightly. They pick prey mostly off the ground, sometimes flicking leaves aside with their bills.

When it sings, the Black-faced Ant-Thrush stretches its head way up, dropping its tail slightly. The short song is distinctive but variable. There are many races, including *F. a. crissalis* from southeastern Venezuela, the Guianas and northern Brazil, which is typical of most, and *F. a. connectens* from eastern Colombia, which lacks the cinnamon color on the sides of the neck.

## 10/ SCALED ANTPITTA
*Grallaria guatimalensis*
RANGE: **Mexico to Peru and Trinidad**
HABITAT: **mountains on damp ground near or in forest understory**
SIZE: **6¼–7½ in (16–19 cm)**

Very shy and difficult to see, the Scaled Antpitta travels alone, taking springing hops across the ground, searching for beetles and other insects, as well as other invertebrates, such as millipedes. In response to tape recordings of its song, the Scaled Antpitta hops up on a fallen log or tree stump or, if startled, flies rapidly for a short distance. Platform nests of Scaled Antpittas have been found mostly on top of fallen logs, but also inside lush plants growing against tree trunks and within the tangled branches of shrubs.

There are several races, including *G. g. guatimalensis*, found from southern Mexico to northern Nicaragua, and *G. g. regulus* from western Colombia, Ecuador and Peru, which differs from the rest in having a distinct white center line on its throat and a white crescent-shaped bar on its lower throat, bordered below by a black band.

## 11/ SLATE-CROWNED ANTPITTA
*Grallaricula nana*
RANGE: **Andes and mountains of Colombia and Venezuela**
HABITAT: **thickets and understory**
SIZE: **4¼ in (11 cm)**

Extremely secretive birds, Slate-crowned Antpittas flick their wings constantly as they jump and scurry about on fallen logs and on branches very close to the ground. To capture small insects, they glean them from the branches and logs or make very short aerial sallies to foliage and stems, less often to the forest floor. Only occasionally do they move along the ground, rapidly attacking prey on the leaf litter. Upon hearing the songs of rivals, Slate-crowned Antpittas crouch down, puff out their feathers until they resemble fuzzy balls, and quietly stare out with their oversized eyes to locate the intruders.

## 12/ RUFOUS GNATEATER
*Conopophaga lineata*
RANGE: **E and S Brazil, adjacent Paraguay and Argentina**
HABITAT: **forest understory**
SIZE: **5 in (13 cm)**

Gnateaters are extraordinarily shy of humans. Of the 8 species, the Rufous Gnateater is perhaps the most abundant and most easily observed. The characteristic white tuft of feathers behind the eye is normally folded into a thin line or obscured entirely. Females differ from males only in having this tuft of feathers gray rather than white.

Rufous Gnateaters move rapidly through stems, twigs and fallen limbs usually less than 3 ft (1 m) from the ground. From these low perches they obtain small insects by making short sallying flights, chiefly onto the ground, but also to nearby foliage and especially overhead leaves. Mostly solitary except while breeding, gnateaters deliver a peculiar call that sounds like a soft sneeze and that may serve to maintain territorial space between individuals.

## FAMILY RHINOCRYPTIDAE
**Tapaculos**

Small to medium ground-dwellers, with short, rounded wings, often with very large, strong feet. Large movable flap covering nostril. Typically gray or brown, marked with black or rufous; long tail often held upright. Sexes mostly similar. Nest of grass, twigs and moss placed in earthen tunnels, rock crevices, hollow trees, thick plants and detritus on ground, or (as domed structure) in bushes. Eggs 2–3, typically white. Incubation and nestling periods unknown. 30 species.

## 13/ BLACK-THROATED HUET-HUET
*Pteroptochos tarnii*
RANGE: **S Chile and adjacent Argentina**
HABITAT: **forest floor**
SIZE: **9½ in (24 cm)**

Tapaculos of the genus *Pteroptochos* are the largest and strongest-legged of the family. The Black-throated Huet-huet (named for the sound of its call) lives in thickets and heavy undergrowth in wooded areas, primarily in the densest forests, but occasionally in deforested areas. It is a solitary bird, except when it forms breeding pairs during the season.

The Black-throated Huet-huet hunts for insects, especially beetles and their larvae, by moving rapidly across the ground or over mats of bamboo, and by exploring rotting fallen trees. It uncovers its prey by turning leaves and debris over with its bill. When pursued, it usually runs away but occasionally flies short distances before hiding in low trees.

## 14/ SLATY BRISTLEFRONT
*Merulaxis ater*
RANGE: **SE Brazil**
HABITAT: **forest thickets**
SIZE: **7½ in (19 cm)**

The Slaty Bristlefront lives on mountain slopes in tangled vegetation often containing bamboo, epiphytes or large vine-covered boulders. It works up and down steep banks, knocking over deposits of large dead leaves and creeping over and under boulders to search for insects. It walks with its body held horizontally and does not cock up its tail quite as much as other tapaculos.

When the Slaty Bristlefront pauses to sing, it lifts its body diagonally and points its bill skyward. The long, vibrant song consists of rapidly delivered clear metallic notes that fall in pitch and volume, ending with a faster series of soft guttural notes. The call is ringing and metallic.

## 15/ UNICOLORED TAPACULO
*Scytalopus unicolor*
RANGE: **Andes S to N Bolivia**
HABITAT: **mountain forest thickets and undergrowth**
SIZE: **5 in (13 cm)**

The Unicolored Tapaculo inhabits high-altitude, humid and wet forest containing low tangles of vegetation, which in Peru often includes bamboo. Seeking insect prey, it hops on the ground or through fallen moss-covered limbs or bushy vegetation, often holding its tail upright. Members of this genus are very difficult to observe. At times these birds simply vanish underground, scurrying under piles of fallen leaves like rodents. Many a frustrated observer has stood "toe to bill" with a *Scytalopus* at his feet, singing but hidden under thick plants or tangles of roots.

KINGLET CALYPTURA

LOVELY COTINGA

SNOWY COTINGA

BARRED FRUITEATER

SCREAMING PIHA

AMAZONIAN UMBRELLABIRD

THREE-WATTLED BELLBIRD

♀

♂

♂

♀

courtship display

♂

♂

GUIANAN COCK OF THE ROCK

♂

♂

WHITE-BEARDED MANAKIN

THRUSHLIKE MANAKIN

LONG-TAILED MANAKIN

RED-CAPPED MANAKIN

race *chrysopterus*

♂

♀

♂

courtship display

GOLDEN-WINGED MANAKIN

## FAMILY COTINGIDAE
### Cotingas

Small to large forest birds. Plumage variable. Males often brightly colored and ornamented, females duller. Nest usually in trees. Eggs 1–3, usually buff or olive, spotted and blotched with dark brown and gray. Incubation 19–28 days, nestling period 21–44 days. 65 species.

### 1/ BARRED FRUITEATER
*Pipreola arcuata*

RANGE: **E and W slopes of the Andes, from W Venezuela and N Colombia to C Bolivia**
HABITAT: **cloud forest, generally above 6,500 ft (2,000 m)**
SIZE: **8½ in (22 cm)**

Fruiteaters forage singly or in pairs in the middle and upper layers of humid cloud forests, feeding on a variety of small fruits and small amounts of insect prey. Like other cotingas, they pluck fruit and snatch insects by sallying out in short flights from a perch. As they are quite heavy-bodied birds, they take fruit from a perched position or in a clumsy hover.

The Barred Fruiteater is the largest member of its genus and tends to occur at the highest altitudes, usually from 6,500 ft (2,000 m) up to the tree line at some 10,000–11,500 ft (3,000–3,500 m). Its song is an extremely high, thin, almost hissing *se-e-e-e-e-e-a-a-a-a*.

### 2/ KINGLET CALYPTURA
*Calyptura cristata*                    Ⅰ

RANGE: **near Rio de Janeiro, Brazil**
HABITAT: **virgin forest, dense secondary growth**
SIZE: **3 in (7.5 cm)**

This is by far the smallest of the cotingas and, although externally similar to a manakin, aspects of its anatomy clearly show it to be a true cotinga. It has a very restricted range and no ornithologist has seen it this century.

Descriptions of foraging behavior indicate a diminutive opportunist, peering and poking into crevices for arthropods and snatching a ripe berry here and there. Its voice was reported to be loud for such a small bird and was described as brief, raucous and disagreeable.

### 3/ SCREAMING PIHA
*Lipaugus vociferans*

RANGE: **Amazonian South America, S Venezuela, Guianas, SE coastal Brazil**
HABITAT: **lowland forest**
SIZE: **9¾–11 in (25–28 cm)**

The Screaming Piha lives among the trees, feeding primarily on fruit, as well as some insects and other arthropods. It is inconspicuous and often difficult to see, but the explosive, whistled song of the male is one of the characteristic sounds of the South American rain forest.

Male Screaming Pihas occupy large territories which they defend by their loud voices. These territories may be arranged in groups, with several birds adjacent to one another. The territorial call begins with a series of 3–5 accelerating, increasingly loud whistled *weeoo* notes, and

finishes with a piercing pair of *weeet weeoo* notes, dropping in pitch at the end. The males call frequently through the day, spending only a fraction of their time feeding.

### 4/ LOVELY COTINGA
*Cotinga amabilis*

RANGE: **S Mexico to N Costa Rica**
HABITAT: **tropical forest**
SIZE: **7¾ in (20 cm)**

The Lovely Cotinga is one of the most striking of all Central American birds. The northernmost of the 7 species in the genus *Cotinga* occurs alone or in mixed-species flocks high in the forest canopy. Here, it feeds mostly on fruit. Like many Central American forest birds, it moves to higher ground to nest, dispersing to lower altitudes at other times. As with the males of the other *Cotinga* species, the intense blue of the male Lovely Cotinga's plumage results from the effect of light hitting the feathers, and is not a pigment as in cotingas of other genera.

The Lovely Cotinga has a strong, undulating flight. As they beat the air, the outer wing feathers of the male produce a rattling, tinkling sound, and this noise features in his courtship display flights above the canopy. The female uses strands of vegetation and fungus to construct the flimsy, shallow, cup nest. This is usually placed at least 100 ft (30 m) high in a large tree. As with some other cotingas, the female may destroy the nest after the young fledge, possibly to reduce the chance of a predator discovering the nest site, which may be used year after year.

### 5/ SNOWY COTINGA
*Carpodectes nitidus*

RANGE: **Caribbean slopes of Honduras, Nicaragua, Costa Rica, W Panama**
HABITAT: **evergreen tropical forest**
SIZE: **7½–8¼ in (19–21 cm)**

The Snowy Cotinga is a rather tame bird, sometimes allowing people to approach close by. Much of the time it lives in the tree canopy, but it also frequents the forest edge and clearings that have

scattered trees. Its white color and pigeonlike flight have earned it the local name of *Paloma del espiritu santo* or "Dove of the holy spirit."

The Snowy Cotinga is primarily a fruit-eater but very little is known of its ecology. The few existing reports indicate that it may feed in flocks of 15 or more birds and that it may also take insects and spiders from the foliage.

### 6/ AMAZONIAN UMBRELLABIRD
*Cephalopterus ornatus*

RANGE: **Amazonian South America, S Venezuela**
HABITAT: **open clearings, river edge or islands in lowland rain forest**
SIZE: **20 in (51 cm)**

This is the largest of all cotingas and one of the largest passerines. The 3 species of umbrellabird take their name from their fluffy, platformlike crests. The Amazonian Umbrellabird is entirely black, with a stout, crowlike bill and a long, feathered wattle hanging from its throat. The female is slightly smaller than the male and her crest and wattle are less well developed.

The most widespread of the umbrellabirds, the Amazonian Umbrellabird tends to haunt open patches in the rain forest and travelers occasionally glimpse it crossing over large rivers, with a deeply undulating flight, some 150 ft (50 m) above the water. The male's advertisement call is a long, booming *boooo* note, which he utters in an elaborate display, leaning forward and down with his crest spread and throat-wattle dangling.

### 7/ THREE-WATTLED BELLBIRD
*Procnias tricarunculata*

RANGE: **Honduras to W Panama**
HABITAT: **breeds in forests above 5,000 ft (1,500 m); migrates to lower tropical forests**
SIZE: **male 11¾ in (30 cm); female 9¾ in (25 cm)**

This is one of 4 species of bellbird, renowned for their extremely loud, explosive calls, the striking differences in plumage between the sexes, and the variety of bizarre wattles that adorn the heads of the males. In the Three-wattled Bellbird, one of the wattles hangs from the base of the upper mandible, while the other 2 hang from the edges of the bird's mouth. Bellbirds are difficult to observe because they restrict their activities to the crowns of large, fruiting trees. The huge gape of their bills allows them to eat large fruits whole and regurgitate the seeds later.

Male Three-wattled Bellbirds take no part in nesting, and try to mate with several females in each season. They defend large territories with their calls, which are some of the loudest sounds uttered by any bird. Each call consists of a deafening, explosive *bock* note, sounding more like a hammer hitting an anvil than the bell from which the bellbirds take their common name. This is followed by a sharp, ringing squeak. The female Three-wattled Bellbird builds the shallow cup nest of thin twigs, and must tend the single young in the nest for more than 30 days until it fledges – one of the longest nestling periods of any passerine.

## 8/ GUIANAN COCK OF THE ROCK
*Rupicola rupicola*
RANGE: S Venezuela, Guianas, N Brazil, E Colombia
HABITAT: lowland tropical forest with rocky outcrops and boulders
SIZE: 12½ in (32 cm)

The brilliant-orange male Guianan Cock of the Rock and the equally handsome, blood-red or orange-red male Andean Cock of the Rock *R. peruviana* are among the most brightly colored of all tropical American birds. They are also remarkable for their group displays at traditional sites called "leks." Here, each male owns an area, or "court," of his own.

At a Guianan Cock of the Rock lek, 5–25 males occupy courts that may be adjacent or up to 33 ft (10 m) apart; each court is 3–6 ft (1–2 m) in diameter. Here they compete for the attention of the drabber, visiting females. The males are highly aggressive toward one another and perform ritualized threat displays, such as perching on vertical branches with the feathers of their wing and tail coverts fluffed up. They often utter a raucous *ka-rhaaow* call when flying into the lek and a variety of squawking and cawing notes during their aggressive encounters. They also make a low, whistling sound with their wings.

When a female visits the lek, the males fly down to the bare dirt patch in the center of each display court and "freeze" in a crouching posture. The female chooses a partner but is often interrupted by a neighboring, competing male as she tries to mate with her chosen male. She alone builds the nest, a large cup of mud and vegetation attached to a sheer rock face, cave or crevice. The same nest site may be used year after year.

## FAMILY PIPRIDAE
### Manakins
Small, forest birds. Large head, short bill. Males brightly colored, usually with much black. Females olive-green. Cup nest, low in cover. Eggs 2, whitish or buff, with brown markings. Incubation 17–21 days, nestling period 13–15 days. 51 species.

## 9/ THRUSHLIKE MANAKIN
*Schiffornis turdinus*
RANGE: S Mexico to W Ecuador, Amazonia, Venezuela, Guianas
HABITAT: tropical forest
SIZE: 6½ in (17 cm)

The male Thrushlike Manakin has drab, brownish plumage, like the female. This is a marked contrast to that of most other males in its family, which are much brighter than the females, and there is now some uncertainty over the classification of this and the other 2 species of *Schiffornis*.

The song of the Thrushlike Manakin is a pure, syncopated, whistled series of 3–4 phrases, showing distinct variations across the bird's range.

As with the true manakins, the male may mate with several females, but he does not perform elaborate displays. Instead, he relies on persistent singing to defend his territory. The female alone builds the large cup nest composed of leaves, moss and twigs, placing it inconspicuously near the trunk or in the fork of a tree. The nestlings are notable for their long, copious black down.

## 10/ WHITE-BEARDED MANAKIN
*Manacus manacus*
RANGE: tropical South America, NE Argentina; Trinidad
HABITAT: secondary growth woodland, riverside forest, forest edge
SIZE: 4 in (10 cm)

The White-bearded Manakin is one of the best-known species in the family, haunting a variety of wooded, lowland habitats, usually below 3,300 ft (1,000 m). The attractive white, black and gray plumage of the male contrasts with the dull olive-green of the female.

This is one of the few species of manakin that displays in a concentrated "lek" of small, adjacent courts. Each male creates his own display court, clearing leaves and vegetation from a patch of forest floor about 3 ft (1 m) wide. A large lek may host more than 50 males, and is usually first detected from many yards away by the birds' bright calls and the firecrackerlike snaps made by the males' specialized wing feathers. The display behavior includes a number of ritualized postures, movements and wing noises performed on the bare display court and on vertical and horizontal perches near the ground. Females visit one or more leks, choose a mate, and perform all the nesting duties alone.

## 11/ GOLDEN-WINGED MANAKIN
*Masius chrysopterus*
RANGE: Andes from W Venezuela to Ecuador, E Andes in N Peru
HABITAT: humid cloud forest, from 4,000–7,500 ft (1,200–2,300 m); down to 2,000 ft (600 m) in W Colombia and Ecuador
SIZE: 4 in (10 cm)

The Golden-winged Manakin was until recently almost completely unknown in the wild. The male's combination of velvety-black and canary-yellow plumage, recumbent crest and black horns is unique in the family. The waxy, barbless feathers behind the crown vary in color accord-

ing to race. The race *M. c. chrysopterus* of the eastern slopes of the Andes is illustrated.

The Golden-winged Manakin feeds on a variety of small fruits. It may forage alone or in mixed flocks of tanagers and other fruit-eating birds. The males defend large territories with froglike *nurrt* calls. Their complex displays include flying down on to a mossy fallen log, rebounding, and turning right around in midair. On the log, they adopt motionless, chin-down postures, with the tail pointed up, and side-to-side bowing displays, with the body plumage fluffed and the tail cocked at an angle.

## 12/ LONG-TAILED MANAKIN
*Chiroxiphea linearis*
RANGE: W Central America, from S Mexico to N Costa Rica
HABITAT: dry woodland, open secondary growth
SIZE: male 7¾–8½ in (20–22 cm); female 4¼ in (11 cm)

The male of this species is remarkable for the extremely elongated, wirelike, central tail feathers that are 4–5 in (10–12 cm) long and extend well beyond the rest of his tail. The females are dull olive-green, with only slightly elongated central tail feathers. As in most other manakins, immature males are similar in plumage to the females, but molt gradually over 3–4 years into the brilliant, full adult male regalia.

Male Long-tailed Manakins exhibit extraordinary courtship behavior, in which pairs or trios perform cooperative displays. In the main "cartwheel" display, the birds hop along a thin horizontal branch, each male, in turn, leaping up and fluttering over his companion or companions, when he reaches a special jumping off spot. The males within each group establish a dominance hierarchy, and if a visiting female remains at the display site to mate, the subordinate males fly off to leave her with the dominant male.

## 13/ RED-CAPPED MANAKIN
*Pipra mentalis*
RANGE: S Mexico to W Colombia and W Ecuador
HABITAT: lowland tropical forest and secondary growth woodland
SIZE: 4 in (10 cm)

The male Red-capped Manakin defends a territory in the trees, advertising his presence with short *psit* calls and a longer, whistled *ptsweee* repeated frequently throughout the day. He can also produce a mechanical *snap* noise with his wing feathers in flight. The center of display activity is a main horizontal perch at least 13 ft (4 m) above the forest floor. The male performs flight displays to this perch from positions 16–32 ft (5–10 m) away, giving an excited, accelerating series of calls as he lands.

On the main perch, the male performs a variety of rituals, including the "backward slide," in which he lowers his foreparts, spreads his wings slightly, stretches his legs, exposing the yellow thighs, and slides backward along the perch with a series of extremely rapid steps. As in other manakins, the olive-green female carries out all the parental duties.

# TYRANT FLYCATCHERS

WHITE MONJITA

WHITE-FRONTED GROUND TYRANT

EASTERN PHOEBE

♂ ♀

race nanus

race pica

PIED WATER TYRANT

VERMILION FLYCATCHER

race mexicanus

SCISSOR-TAILED FLYCATCHER

EASTERN KINGBIRD

juv

BOAT-BILLED FLYCATCHER

GREAT KISKADEE

GREAT CRESTED FLYCATCHER

ROSE-THROATED BECARD

♂
race *albiventris*

♀

♀

♂

MASKED TITYRA

ACADIAN FLYCATCHER

WHITE-THROATED SPADEBILL

♂
race *coronatus*

ROYAL FLYCATCHER

# TYRANT FLYCATCHERS

## FAMILY TYRANNIDAE
### Tyrant flycatchers

Small to medium perching birds. Plumage generally dull olive above, yellowish or whitish below; some species with black, gray, brown, chestnut and white, some with red, orange, yellow or white crown stripes, many with crests (large and bright in 1 species). Sexes generally similar. Nests very variable, from woven cups in trees to globular nests with side entrances, hanging nests and excavated cavities. Eggs 2–8, whitish, sometimes mottled brown. Incubation 14–20 days, nestling period 14–23 days. 397 species.

## 1/ WHITE-THROATED SPADEBILL
*Platyrinchus mystaceus*

RANGE: **S Mexico to Argentina and Bolivia; Trinidad and Tobago**
HABITAT: **humid forest undergrowth, forest edge, second growth, open brush**
SIZE: **4 in (10 cm)**

This tiny, inconspicuous, stub-tailed flycatcher is usually found alone or in pairs, foraging somewhat nonchalantly for insects among the branches of the forest understory. It will perch silently for long periods, occasionally flitting its wings nervously, but when it spies an insect creeping along the underside of a nearby leaf it makes a quick dash and scoops it up with its broad, shovel-shaped bill. When it does call, it utters a short sharp *squeep*, and has a thin, high, buzzing song. The male usually has a concealed yellow crown stripe, which is much smaller or entirely lacking in the female.

In Mexico this species is found close to sea level, but in Bolivia it is most common at altitudes of 3,000–6,500 ft (900–2,000 m). It nests in trees, building a compact, cup nest of plant fibers.

## 2/ ROYAL FLYCATCHER
*Pnychorhynchus coronatus*

RANGE: **S Mexico to Guianas, Bolivia, Brazil**
HABITAT: **shaded lower levels of humid forest edge, often near streams**
SIZE: **6½ in (16.5 cm)**

The Royal Flycatcher is a rather nondescript-looking bird, but very occasionally, when aroused, it has been seen to erect its crest to form a spectacular fan. In males the crest feathers are vermilion tipped with blue, but in females the vermilion is replaced by orange in some races and yellow in others. Normally, the closed crest projecting backward, and its long broad bill give this species a hammer-headed appearance.

The birds are usually seen alone or in pairs in shady lowland forest, where they perch on low branches and sally out in pursuit of flying insects. Their broad bills make efficient insect-traps, and the long bristles on either side may help to catch prey and protect their eyes.

The nest is an elongated, loose, baglike structure up to 6 ft (1.8 m) long, attached to a slender branch or vine above a shaded stream.

## 3/ ACADIAN FLYCATCHER
*Empidonax virescens*

RANGE: **breeds USA from Great Lakes region S to E Texas, Gulf coast and C Florida; winters in Central and South America**
HABITAT: **moist, mature woodland**
SIZE: **5½–6½ in (14–16.5 cm)**

The flycatchers of the genus *Empidonax* are all very alike, being small, erect tail-flickers with similar habits, but their songs are distinctive. The song of the Acadian Flycatcher is particularly memorable, since the explosive *peet-sa*, with the accent on the first syllable, sounds like a demand for pizza.

Typically found in wet woodland, the Acadian Flycatcher hunts beneath the canopy of tall trees, darting after flying insects and catching them on the wing. Its nest is a frail, saucer-shaped basket suspended from horizontal forked twigs and lined with grasses, plant down, spiders' webs and, in the South, Spanish moss. From below, the nest is well camouflaged with long streamers.

## 4/ EASTERN PHOEBE
*Sayornis phoebe*

RANGE: **breeds N and E North America; winters SE and SC USA to Mexico**
HABITAT: **woods, farms, usually near water**
SIZE: **7 in (18 cm)**

Named for its pleasantly raspy *fee-bee* song, delivered incessantly during the breeding season, the Eastern Phoebe is a familiar sight on farmland and wooded roadsides throughout much of North America. It hunts in typical flycatcher fashion, sallying after insects from an exposed perch, and wagging its tail from side to side in a distinctive manner as it lands. When prospecting above a quiet pond surface for flies, it may hover briefly or flutter in pursuit like a butterfly, its bill clicking as it snaps up a meal.

An opportunist nester, it often uses man-made structures as breeding sites, favoring niches protected from the weather such as the rafters of farm outbuildings, porches and bridge supports.

## 5/ VERMILION FLYCATCHER
*Pyrocephalus rubinus*

RANGE: **breeds SW USA to S Argentina; a few birds wander to California and Gulf coast in winter**
HABITAT: **semiarid woodland near streams, ponds and rivers**
SIZE: **5½–6½ in (14–16.5 cm)**

Sallying out from a favored perch over a shallow pond or stream bed, a male Vermilion Flycatcher is a spectacular sight, with his brilliant plumage unique among tyrant flycatchers. By comparison, the female is undistinguished, with only a wash of salmon on her lower belly. Of the 12 or so races that have been described, those illustrated are *P. r. mexicanus*, found from southwestern USA to Mexico, and the race *P. r. nanus*, which occurs only in the Galapagos Islands, apart from San Cristobal (Chatham) Island. The Galapagos race has been isolated long enough to have developed distinct plumage – paler, duller red in males and plain yellowish underparts in females, rather than the streaked, creamy pink ones of mainland females. It has shorter wings and tail, longer legs and a different song.

As befits his dazzling coloration, the male is bold and aggressive in defense of the nest. He also puts on a fine courtship display, rising vertically in the air on vibrating wings with crest erect and tail lifted, singing his soft, tinkling song ecstatically, then hovering and slowly fluttering down to the female.

## 6/ WHITE-FRONTED GROUND TYRANT
*Muscisaxicola albifrons*

RANGE: **Peru to NW Bolivia and N Chile**
HABITAT: **rocky hillsides with bushes, at 13,000–16,500 ft (4,000–5,000 m)**
SIZE: **9 in (23 cm)**

The ground tyrants are long-legged mountain birds that hunt on the ground, rather like pipits. This is the largest and also the one found at the highest altitudes. The rocks and scattered bushes of its open habitat provide commanding perches for spotting its invertebrate prey, and when it does so it makes a quick flight or a dash across the ground to snatch it.

Most ground tyrants build open cup nests in crevices between rocks on the ground, but the details for this species are unknown.

## 7/ WHITE MONJITA
*Xolmis irupero*
RANGE: **E Brazil, Uruguay, Paraguay, E Bolivia, N Argentina**
HABITAT: **open country, brush, savanna**
SIZE: **6½ in (17 cm)**

This relatively quiet, strikingly white and black flycatcher usually hunts from a perch. It will sit patiently on an exposed branch or fencepost, watching the ground intently. When the White Monjita spies an insect it flies down in graceful fashion to seize its meal. If a suitable perch is not available, it may hover briefly to search for prey. Its normal flight is swift and undulating, but the birds never seem to go far. White Monjitas nest in tree cavities and the abandoned nests of ovenbirds. They are often parasitized by the Shiny Cowbird *Molothrus bonariensis*.

## 8/ PIED WATER TYRANT
*Fluvicola pica*
RANGE: **Panama, N and C South America E of the Andes; Trinidad**
HABITAT: **river banks, ponds and marshes**
SIZE: **4¾–5½ in (12–14 cm)**

Often seen in pairs around freshwater marshes and ponds in lowlands, these attractive and relatively tame flycatchers feed by gleaning insects from foliage on or near the ground, or over the water. While waiting for their next meal they frequently flick their tails downward, sometimes giving a distinctive nasal, buzzing *zhreeo* call.

In Trinidad they nest throughout the year, weaving a ball of dried grasses and leaves at the end of a small branch or in a bush, often over water, and lining the nest with feathers.

There are 2 races: *F.p. pica* is from Colombia, Venezuela, the Guianas, northern Brazil and Trinidad, while the southern race *F.p. albiventer*, sometimes considered a separate species, is from southern Brazil, eastern Bolivia, Paraguay, Uruguay and northern Argentina.

## 9/ GREAT CRESTED FLYCATCHER
*Myiarchus crinitus*
RANGE: **breeds E North America from SC and E Canada to Texas and Gulf coast; winters S Florida to Mexico and South America**
HABITAT: **open woods, woodland edge**
SIZE: **7–8 in (18–20 cm)**

This noisy flycatcher is a familiar bird in settled areas, where its annual return to breed in specially provided nest-boxes is often eagerly awaited. If there are no nest-boxes, the birds will occupy deserted woodpecker holes, hollow posts and a variety of other cavities, natural and artificial, provided they are near open areas where they can pursue flying insects.

Great Crested Flycatchers and some other cavity-nesting flycatchers are well known for

their habit of using cast snakeskins as nesting material. It was once thought that these somehow repelled marauding snakes on the prowl for eggs and nestlings, but the presence of various plastics in many nests suggests that the birds simply have a preference for such materials.

## 10/ GREAT KISKADEE
*Pitangus sulphuratus*
RANGE: **S Texas to Argentina**
HABITAT: **semiopen areas, streamside thickets, woodland edge, orchards**
SIZE: **9–9¾ in (23–25 cm)**

One of the biggest and brightest of the tyrant flycatchers, the Great Kiskadee is a bold, noisy and aggressive opportunist. It dives for small fish or tadpoles from a perch, kingfisher-style, but after 3–4 such dives it has to dry out in the sun. At other times it will launch itself into the air to capture beetles, wasps and other flying insects, and may even forage for berries and seeds when insects are scarce. Its wide diet also includes the occasional small mammal, frog or lizard.

This bird is named for its bawling *kis-ka-dee* calls, usually heard in the morning or evening. It builds a bulky, domed nest of straw and weed stems, sometimes incorporating the smaller nest of another flycatcher in its own.

## 11/ BOAT-BILLED FLYCATCHER
*Megarhynchus pitangua*
RANGE: **C Mexico to NW Peru, S Brazil and N Argentina**
HABITAT: **savanna, forest edge, clearings, plantations, usually near water**
SIZE: **9 in (23 cm)**

The massive, powerful bill of this large tyrant flycatcher reflects its varied diet which includes not only insects, but also berries, catkins and even the occasional frog or other small vertebrate. It can be found along almost any forest edge, but is most common along river banks where it often makes itself evident by its quarrelsome behavior and habit of mobbing passing hawks.

The nest is an open stick cup built high above the ground near the end of a bough. The female incubates the eggs alone, but the male stands guard in her absence.

## 12/ SCISSOR-TAILED FLYCATCHER
*Tyrannus forficata*
RANGE: **breeds SW USA, uncommonly E to Mississippi; wanders N to Canada on migration; winters extreme S USA to Mexico and Central America**
HABITAT: **open country with scattered trees and brush**
SIZE: **11¾–15 in (30–38 cm)**

Spectacular behavior, delicate beauty and an exquisite forked tail place the scissor-tailed flycatcher in a class by itself. The courtship "sky dance" is famous, involving vertical and zigzag dives, tumbles and somersaults with the long tail feathers streaming and flicking like satin ribbons, all accented by rolling cackles that sound appropriately like applause.

In the true flycatcher manner it hunts from a perch, darting out after flying insects or dropping to the ground for grasshoppers or crickets. Between forays it will sit quietly on a fencepost, bare branch or treetop, sometimes for hours.

## 13/ EASTERN KINGBIRD
*Tyrannus tyrannus*
RANGE: **breeds S Canada through USA to the Gulf coast; winters in Central and South America**
HABITAT: **open areas, woodland edge, streamsides, orchards**
SIZE: **8¼–9 in (21–23 cm)**

Celebrated for its dauntless defence of its breeding territory, the male Eastern Kingbird will attack anything that enters its airspace. Its main targets are larger birds, such as crows and hawks, which are chased relentlessly and rained with blows. At times this species will even land on its flying victim to knock it about more effectively. Its noisy, blustering calls typify its temperament.

Outside the breeding season it often forages in small, loose flocks. It feeds mainly on flying insects taken on the wing, but will also pluck berries from bushes while hovering. At dusk it retreats to a communal roost which may number hundreds or even thousands of birds.

## 14/ ROSE-THROATED BECARD
*Pachyramphus aglaiae*
RANGE: **S Texas and S Arizona to Costa Rica**
HABITAT: **open woodland and dry scrub**
SIZE: **6 in (15 cm)**

Traditionally classified with the cotingas, the becards are now considered to be tyrant flycatchers. This species is the northernmost representative of the genus. Pairs are often seen perched conspicuously on the tops of trees on the edges of open areas, where they feed on insects, spiders and fruits seized during short flights.

The nest is a large, globular structure of sticks and other assorted vegetation, suspended from a branch some 20–70 ft (6–20 m) above a clearing. The clutch size of 5–6 eggs is large for a tropical bird and may be related to the protection provided by the walled hanging nest.

## 15/ MASKED TITYRA
*Tityra semifasciata*
RANGE: **S Mexico to W Ecuador, Guianas and Amazonia**
HABITAT: **clearings in moist tropical forest, open woodland and second growth**
SIZE: **8 in (20 cm)**

Tityras are common birds of the forest edge throughout the American tropics. The Masked Tityra is the most wide-ranging species: a strong flier with a stout bill, it is frequently seen perched conspicuously in the top of a tree near a clearing and often draws attention to itself with noisy croaks and low grunts. The birds form monogamous pairs which stay together throughout the year and nest in cavities, sometimes driving off woodpeckers from choice sites. The female incubates the eggs, but both parents feed the young.

# TYRANT FLYCATCHERS, SHARPBILL, PLANTCUTTERS, PITTAS, NEW ZEALAND WRENS, ASITIES, LYREBIRDS, SCRUB-BIRDS

SHORT-TAILED
PYGMY TYRANT

race *rubrigastra*

race *wetmorei*

MANY-COLORED
RUSH TYRANT

COMMON TODY FLYCATCHER

TORRENT TYRANNULET

SLENDER-FOOTED
TYRANNULET

race *frater*

SHARPBILL

♂ courtship display

♂

RUFOUS SCRUB-BIRD

SUPERB LYREBIRD

♀

**FAMILIES TYRANNIDAE, OXYRUNCIDAE, PHYTOTOMIDAE, PITTIDAE, XENICIDAE, PHILEPITTIDAE, MENURIDAE, ATRICHORNITHIDAE**

race granatina

GARNET PITTA

race ussheri

RUFOUS-TAILED
PLANTCUTTER

♀    ♂

GURNEY'S PITTA

♂

AFRICAN PITTA

race chloris

WATTLED FALSE SUNBIRD

RAINBOW PITTA

♂

♀

RIFLEMAN

# TYRANT FLYCATCHERS, SHARPBILL, PLANTCUTTERS, PITTAS, NEW ZEALAND WRENS, ASITIES, LYREBIRDS, SCRUB-BIRDS

## 1/ SLENDER-FOOTED TYRANNULET
*Zimmerius gracilipes*

RANGE: Guianas, S Venezuela, E Colombia, S to N Bolivia and E Brazil
HABITAT: forest, savanna, secondary growth
SIZE: $4\frac{1}{2}$ in (11.5 cm)

The Slender-footed Tyrannulet spends most of its time high in the outer canopy of tall trees, where its olive-green and yellow plumage and diminutive size make it very difficult to see against the foliage. Here it flutters about, gleaning insects from the leaves. Its diet also includes some berries. It often occurs singly or in pairs, but also joins mixed-species flocks. The Slender-footed Tyrannulet's call is a sharp, unmelodious *what*.

## 2/ TORRENT TYRANNULET
*Serpophaga cinerea*

RANGE: Costa Rica, W Panama, NW Venezuela, Colombia, N Bolivia
HABITAT: rocky streams in foothills and mountains
SIZE: 4 in (10 cm)

The Torrent Tyrannulet typically perches on a rock in midstream or on a bare branch hanging over water, where it nervously flicks its tail up and down as it watches for prey. Flying insects are caught after short pursuits and, at times, other insect food is picked from gravel bars. It usually occurs in pairs. The call note is a soft *tsip*, which is often repeated in a twittering manner, and which has a tonal quality that allows it to be heard above the sound of rushing water.

## 3/ MANY-COLORED RUSH TYRANT
*Tachuris rubrigastra*

RANGE: parts of Peru, Bolivia, Paraguay, S Brazil, Uruguay, E Argentina
HABITAT: tall cats'-tails and rushes of coastal and freshwater marshes
SIZE: $4\frac{1}{4}$ in (11 cm)

The Many-colored Rush Tyrant is local in distribution, scattered in small populations where suitably extensive habitat exists. Many seemingly suitable sites have not been colonized. It sometimes shows up in other habitats when on migration. This species has relatively long legs, which it uses to clamber about the stems of cats'-tails and rushes to glean insects in a wrenlike fashion. It also makes short sallying flights into the air to catch flying insects.

## 4/ SHORT-TAILED PYGMY TYRANT
*Myiornis ecaudatus*

RANGE: Costa Rica S to N Bolivia, Amazonian Brazil, Guianas, Trinidad
HABITAT: humid forest and forest edge
SIZE: $2\frac{3}{4}$ in (7 cm)

This elusive species of open wet and humid tropical forest is a tiny, virtually tailless bird that is the smallest of all the tyrant flycatchers. From its perch it flies up to snatch prey from foliage or

out to capture flying insects. It perches quietly for long periods and is easily overlooked. The voice of the Short-tailed Pygmy Tyrant befits its size – a repeated high-pitched *eek*, which sounds remarkably like a tree frog or a cricket.

## 5/ COMMON TODY FLYCATCHER
*Todirostrum cinereum*

RANGE: S Mexico to NW Peru, Bolivia, SE Brazil
HABITAT: bushy areas, secondary growth, thickets, gardens, overgrown clearings
SIZE: $3\frac{1}{2}$–4 in (9–10 cm)

This tiny flycatcher is a common bird, regularly seen in pairs. It forages by moving quickly among leaves to snatch insects, cocking its tail slightly and jerking it from side to side as it flutters and hops within the foliage. Its foraging actions are often more reminiscent of those of wrens than of other tyrant flycatchers. Sometimes it also sallies out after prey. The calls of this species include low, but sharp, chipping notes and a musical trill which members of a pair use to keep in contact with each other.

## FAMILY OXYRUNCIDAE
### Sharpbill

There is only one species in this family.

## 6/ SHARPBILL
*Oxyruncus cristatus*

RANGE: Costa Rica, Panama, SE Venezuela, Guyana, Surinam, E Peru, E and SE Brazil, Paraguay
HABITAT: rain and cloud forest from 1,300–6,000 ft (400–1,800 m), forest edge, secondary growth
SIZE: 6 in (15 cm)

The Sharpbill is a stocky bird which, true to its name, has a sharply pointed, conical bill. It moves rapidly through the forest canopy, alone or in mixed flocks. It gleans insects and spiders from the foliage at the tips of branches or from the bark of large limbs, and also eats ripe berries. To reach

its food, it often hangs upside-down like a tit. Its song is a rough, slightly descending trill.

The long crest of brightly colored, silky feathers on the bird's crown is usually concealed. This crest is crimson or scarlet in most races, including *O. c. frater* of Costa Rica and western Panama, but orange in the race *O. c. hypoglaucus* from Guyana and southeastern Venezuela.

The one nest that has been found was a shallow cup of loosely interwoven leaf stalks and a few dried leaves, with a thin coating of liverworts and spiders' webs. This was secured, with a dried salivalike substance, to a high branch.

## FAMILY PHYTOTOMIDAE
### Plantcutters

Small, long-tailed birds. Conical beak with serrated edges. Plumage streaked gray-brown above, rufous below in male; gray-brown above, pale ocher below in female. Nest in bushes and trees. Eggs 2–4, greenish-blue with dark spots. Incubation and nestling periods unknown. 3 species.

## 7/ RUFOUS-TAILED PLANTCUTTER
*Phytotoma rara*

RANGE: C and SC Chile, extreme W Argentina
HABITAT: open country with scattered bushes and thorn trees, wooded rivers, gardens, orchards
SIZE: $7\frac{1}{2}$–8 in (19–20 cm)

Although the 3 species of plantcutter are traditionally placed in a family of their own, recent data on their biochemistry and natural history suggest that they might be better incorporated in the cotinga family (pp. 230–33). As their name suggests, they use their thick, serrated bills for cutting or chewing off pieces of leaves, buds and fruits. Because of this behavior, the birds are sometimes regarded as pests. This species is also known as the Chilean Plantcutter.

During the breeding season, these birds remain in pairs, but at other times they may occur in groups of up to 6 individuals. The males sing with a rasping, metallic wheeze.

## FAMILY PITTIDAE
### Pittas
Small, very short-tailed, thrushlike birds of the forest floor. Plumage colorful. Sexes similar or different. Nest large, oval or domed, in fallen branches or bushes. Eggs 2–7 (usually 3–5), glossy white or pale buff, with reddish or purplish speckles or spots and fine lilac or gray markings. Incubation and nestling periods uncertain, probably 15–17 days and 14–21 days. 29 species.

### 8/ GARNET PITTA
*Pitta granatina*
RANGE: **peninsular Burma, Sumatra, Borneo**
HABITAT: **swampy forest**
SIZE: **6 in (15 cm)**

The bright colors of the Garnet Pitta conceal rather than draw attention to it in the contrasted shade of the forest floor. The race *P.g. ussheri* occupies northern Borneo, while *P.g. granatina* occurs in the south of the island.

The Garnet Pitta eats fruit, seeds and insects, foraging for them on the ground among leaf litter. It makes a prolonged whistling call that increases in volume and rises in pitch before stopping abruptly. The status of this rare bird is unclear, but it is certainly declining with the felling of its forest habitat.

### 9/ GURNEY'S PITTA
*Pitta gurneyi*   E
RANGE: **peninsular Thailand and Burma**
HABITAT: **lowland forest**
SIZE: **8¼ in (21 cm)**

This colorful pitta was once described as not uncommon in the forests of Thailand, but so much of its habitat has been destroyed that it has become one of the world's most endangered birds. Indeed, it had not been seen for 34 years until its rediscovery in 1986. Even then, a nest was raided by bird trappers for the cage-bird trade. Gurney's Pitta is most noisy in the morning and evening, uttering a sharp double note accompanied by flapping wings and a jerk of the tail.

### 10/ AFRICAN PITTA
*Pitta angolensis*
RANGE: **W Africa from Sierra Leone to Cameroon, then S to N Angola; also Uganda, E Zaire, Tanzania, E Zimbabwe and Mozambique; nonbreeders sometimes seen S as far as Cape Province**
HABITAT: **thick evergreen forest**
SIZE: **8 in (20 cm)**

This bird is the only pitta that occurs in Africa. It prefers dense undergrowth, hopping along beneath the vegetation in search of slugs and insects, especially termites. It will scratch through the cover of leaf litter to the surface of anthills, flitting its tail up and down continually as it does so. If alarmed, the African Pitta utters a short, soft call and usually runs away rapidly, though it may sometimes fly into a tree to crouch out of sight behind a branch. It also has a threat display in which it crouches with feathers fluffed out, wings spread and bill pointing skyward.

### 11/ RAINBOW PITTA
*Pitta iris*
RANGE: **N Australia**
HABITAT: **thick bush, monsoon forest**
SIZE: **7 in (18 cm)**

Dense monsoon forest, mangrove swamps and bamboo thickets provide a home for this pitta. Uncommon and sedentary, it searches the forest floor for insects. It rarely flies, keeping to the ground, where it is well concealed and difficult to locate despite its bright coloration. A loud, clear, whistling call (often rendered as *want a whip*) may give it away. The call is often given from a tree in which the bird roosts.

## FAMILY XENICIDAE
### New Zealand wrens
Small, stocky birds, endemic to New Zealand. Poor fliers. Plumage greenish and whitish with some yellow. Females are generally duller than males. Nest in holes. Eggs 2–5, white. Incubation 19–21 days, nestling period 23–25 days (Rifleman); unknown for other 2 species. 3 species.

### 12/ RIFLEMAN
*Acanthisitta chloris*
RANGE: **New Zealand**
HABITAT: **forest, ranging from mature stands to secondary growth scrubland**
SIZE: **3 in (8 cm)**

The Rifleman has 3 races on North, South and Stewart islands, of which the southern race *A. c. chloris* is illustrated. It feeds by spiraling up tree trunks and probing for insects under the bark; its slightly upturned bill is well adapted for this task. It also gleans prey from foliage in the canopy. It remains in family groups for much of the year and is nonmigratory. Breeding takes place from October to January, with some nesting pairs assisted by unmated males.

## FAMILY PHILEPITTIDAE
### Asities
Plump tree-dwellers, endemic to Madagascar. Plumage black with yellow fringe to feathers in male, greenish in females; or metallic blue and yellow in males, dark green and yellowish in females. Partial breeding details known only for Velvet Asity *Philepitta castanea*: nest pear-shaped, suspended from branch and woven on to it at top, with projecting roof near side entrance at top. Eggs 3, white. 4 species.

### 13/ WATTLED FALSE SUNBIRD
*Neodrepanis coruscans*
RANGE: **Madagascar**
HABITAT: **thick forest**
SIZE: **4 in (10 cm)**

Locally common in the past in eastern Madagascar, the Wattled False Sunbird is threatened by habitat destruction. It occupies areas from sea level up to 6,000 ft (1,800 m), becoming increasingly common with higher altitude. In the forest, it may be found anywhere from the ground cover and leaf litter, through the middle layers to the high canopy. It also survives in undergrowth and in saplings in degraded forest, showing a degree of adaptability that may help it to survive in its rapidly changing environment.

The Wattled False Sunbird is solitary or found in small family groups, moving quietly through the foliage with soft, hissing contact calls. It visits long, showy flowers to feed, but, unlike the true sunbirds, its chief food is insects. The female lacks the blue wattle around the eye of the male and is duller and greener above.

## FAMILY MENURIDAE
### Lyrebirds
Large, long-legged, strong feet. Plumage brown above, buffish or gray-brown below. Males have very long, lyre-shaped tails. Nest bulky, domed. Eggs, usually 1, light gray to purplish-brown, with darker spots or streaks. Incubation about 50 days, nestling period about 47 days. 2 species.

### 14/ SUPERB LYREBIRD
*Menura novaehollandiae*
RANGE: **SE Australia, introduced to Tasmania**
HABITAT: **eucalyptus and rain forest**
SIZE: **male 31½–38½ in (80–98 cm); female 29–33 in (74–84 cm)**

The Superb Lyrebird is one of the largest and most remarkable of the passerines, renowned for the male's 20–24 in (50–60 cm) long lyre-shaped tail. It feeds mostly on the ground, scratching for insects and other large invertebrates.

From midwinter, male Superb Lyrebirds scratch up display mounds and sing. The song contains rich and powerful elements, along with a great variety of mimicked sounds from other birds. On still days, the song can be heard from some distance. When a female is present, the male's song becomes more frantic and he raises and vibrates his tail over his head and back. A successful male may mate with several females.

## FAMILY ATRICHORNITHIDAE
### Scrub-birds
Small, sturdy. Long tail, long legs, small wings. Plumage brown above, white and rufous-brown below. Males have black markings on breast. Nest domed. Eggs 1–2, buffish, brown blotches. Incubation 36–38 days, nestling period 21–28 days (Western Scrub-bird *A. clamosus* only). 2 species.

### 15/ RUFOUS SCRUB-BIRD
*Atrichornis rufescens*   R
RANGE: **CE Australia**
HABITAT: **forest margins**
SIZE: **6½–7 in (16.5–18 cm)**

The Rufous Scrub-bird is restricted to 5 upland regions in northeastern New South Wales and extreme southeastern Queensland. It inhabits cool temperate rain forest where this adjoins eucalyptus forest, or subtropical rain forest where the canopy is fairly open. Both sites are moist and have dense ground cover. Rufous Scrub-birds can be extremely difficult to spot; usually they are detected only by the male's loud chipping song. Most of these birds are now in protected areas and their populations are being closely monitored.

dark phase

light phase

CLAPPER LARK

♂

♀

BLACK-CROWNED FINCH LARK

SINGING BUSH LARK

♂ fall

fall ♀

spring ♂

BLACK LARK

LESSER SHORT-TOED LARK

CRESTED LARK

HOOPOE LARK

♂

SKY LARK

HORNED LARK

WHITE-EYED
RIVER MARTIN

TREE SWALLOW

juv

WHITE-BANDED SWALLOW

♀

♂

PURPLE MARTIN

BANK SWALLOW

WHITE-BACKED SWALLOW

381

# LARKS, SWALLOWS AND MARTINS

## FAMILY ALAUDIDAE
### Larks

Small ground dwellers, with elongated hind claws. Plumage mainly brown, cryptic, some with black and white markings; males of one species black. Sexes in most species similar. Nest on ground. Eggs 2–6, speckled, in most species. Incubation 10–16 days, nestling period about 10 days. 81 species.

## 1/ SINGING BUSH LARK
### Mirafra javanica
RANGE: parts of Africa, Arabia, India, Malaysia, Indonesia, Australia
HABITAT: grassland, including crops
SIZE: 5–5½ in (12.5–14 cm)

This species has more than 20 races spread across its vast range. Its shade of plumage is variable, even within one race, the overall coloration generally matching that of the native habitat. The palest birds tend to occur in areas of bleached sand. It has been suggested that the fresh, darker plumage attained by many birds after the molt is timed to coincide with the rainy season, when the ground is darkest.

Singing Bush Larks feed on the ground, searching for invertebrates and seeds. They have a varied, melodious song, often with mimetic components, which is usually uttered in flight. Their nests are partly domed structures built under grassy tussocks.

## 2/ CLAPPER LARK
### Mirafra apiata
RANGE: S Africa
HABITAT: grassland of the highveld and dry Karoo
SIZE: 6 in (15 cm)

This solitary, medium-sized lark is easy to overlook as it forages across the ground for insects and seeds. It becomes conspicuous only when calling and displaying. It often imitates the calls of other birds, from plovers to waxbills, and performs a distinctive display flight consisting of a steep climb, a loud rattling of the wings and a downward dive. The descent is accompanied by a clear, whistling call. The Clapper Lark may repeat this display every 15–30 seconds.

Breeding takes place from October to February, timed to coincide with the ripening of seeds after the rainy period. The domed nest of fine grass and rootlets has a side entrance and is usually concealed at the base of a clump of vegetation.

## 3/ BLACK-CROWNED FINCH LARK
### Eremopterix nigriceps
RANGE: Cape Verde islands, S Sahara, E Africa, S Arabia, W Pakistan, NW India
HABITAT: grassy semidesert
SIZE: 4 in (10.5 cm)

These tiny larks are gregarious outside the breeding season and may form mixed foraging flocks in areas where several species occur. They feed on seeds and insects, taking them either from the ground or directly from low vegetation. They walk and run quickly across their dry, open habitat and typically crouch low against the ground when they stop, although they will also stand more erect on occasion.

The Black-crowned Finch Lark makes a cup nest in bare ground and is one of several desert species that may build a windbreak of pebbles to protect the site.

## 4/ HOOPOE LARK
### Alaemon alaudipes
RANGE: N Africa, Sahara, Arabia E to Iran, Afghanistan
HABITAT: deserts
SIZE: 7¾ in (20 cm)

Seemingly well camouflaged on the ground, this lark is striking in flight when it reveals its black and white patterned wings. This wing pattern coloration and the long, downcurved bill are features shared by the much larger and completely unrelated Hoopoe Upupa epops (pp. 202–5) and give the bird its name. The Hoopoe Lark walks and runs across the ground, stopping suddenly to dig for food with its bill. Insect larvae provide much of its food, but it will also catch adult insects, snails and even small lizards. It breaks through to a snail's flesh by dropping or hammering the shell against a stone.

The Hoopoe Lark is not a sociable bird, although loose flocks may gather at garbage dumps. In the hottest areas, it avoids nesting on the baking surface, placing its nest several inches off the ground in vegetation.

## 5/ BLACK LARK
### Melanocorypha yeltoniensis
RANGE: S USSR, C Asia
HABITAT: steppe grassland
SIZE: 7½ in (19 cm)

The male of this thickset lark has unmistakable plumage – all black in the breeding season, but scalloped with the pale buff fringes of new feathers in the fall. The Black Lark's bill is small and conical, and the bird uses it to feed on seeds through most of the year. It remains on the bleak steppes through the winter, often digging through several inches of snow to reach its food.

It also catches a variety of invertebrates when these become available later in the year.

The song of the Black Lark consists of short phrases uttered from a perch. The nest is a shallow depression in the ground, sheltered by a tussock of plants.

## 6/ LESSER SHORT-TOED LARK
### Calandrella rufescens
RANGE: Canary Islands, N Africa E through Middle East, C Asia to N China
HABITAT: open grassland, semidesert, dry cultivated fields
SIZE: 5 in (13 cm)

The Lesser Short-toed Lark varies markedly in the color of its plumage, depending on the background color of its local habitat. The best distinguishing characteristic of this species is its prritt call, often uttered as a contact note. A close relative, the Short-toed Lark C. cinerea, overlaps with this species in range, and even in mixed flocks it is difficult to tell the 2 birds apart. The marginally larger Short-toed Lark, however, has a distinctly different 2-syllable call.

The Lesser Short-toed Lark feeds largely on insects through the winter. Gregarious outside the breeding season, it becomes territorial when nesting. Northern populations tend to migrate south for the winter.

## 7/ CRESTED LARK
### Galerida cristata
RANGE: N Africa, Europe, Middle East E to India, N China, Korea
HABITAT: open wasteland, arable fields, grassland, semidesert
SIZE: 7½ in (19 cm)

This species is remarkably similar to its close relative the Thekla Lark G. theklae and is best distinguished by its distinctive whee, whee, whee, whee-ooo call. In addition, the Crested Lark tends to breed at lower altitudes.

The Crested Lark spends most of its time on or near the ground, often perching on rocks and low vegetation. It has adapted to many artificial environments; indeed, it has been suggested that the species is steadily shifting its emphasis from steppe and semidesert habitats into areas where cultivation, deforestation and settlement have created open terrain.

## 8/ SKY LARK
*Alauda arvensis*

RANGE: **Europe, extreme N Africa, Middle East, NC and E Asia, Japan; introduced to Vancouver Island (Canada), Hawaii, Australia and New Zealand**
HABITAT: **open areas, arable fields**
SIZE: **7 in (18 cm)**

The Sky Lark is one of the best known species, renowned for its varied, prolonged song which is almost exclusively given in flight as the bird rapidly climbs, hovers and gradually descends.

This species has adapted well to cultivation and is now one of the most typical farmland birds in Europe. It feeds on the ground, taking seeds, grain and insects both from the surface and from low vegetation. The more northerly populations migrate southward for the winter.

## 9/ HORNED LARK
*Eremophila alpestris*

RANGE: **breeds high Arctic and mountains of Eurasia, SW and C Asia, Atlas Mts, most of North America; N races winter S of breeding range; isolated nonmigratory population in Andes**
HABITAT: **breeds Arctic, steppe and mountain plains in Old World, diverse habitats in North America; winters on beaches, coastal dunes, salt marshes and low-lying arable land**
SIZE: **6 in (15 cm)**

In Eurasia, the Horned Lark's distribution is discontinuous and widely separated by types of habitat in which different species of lark predominate. In North America, however, this species occurs in a variety of open habitats, including prairies, pastures, cultivated fields and deserts. There, the absence of competition from other lark species enables it to live much more widely. No fewer than 41 races have been described from its vast range, of which the northeastern North American race *E. a. alpestris* is shown here.

Northern populations of the Horned Lark tend to be highly migratory, wintering in flocks when they feed mainly on seeds. During the breeding season, the birds appear to be largely insectivorous. They feed on the ground and are almost constantly on the move as they forage.

## FAMILY HIRUNDINIDAE
### Swallows and martins

Small, streamlined, highly aerial birds, with wide gapes. Long, pointed wings. Tail usually forked. Plumage chiefly metallic blue-black, greenish black or brown above, pale or chestnut below. Sexes similar. Mud nests, holes or burrows. Eggs 1–8, white, some spotted red-brown. Incubation 13–16 days, nestling period 16–24 days (24–28 days in New World martins). 81 species.

## 10/ WHITE-EYED RIVER MARTIN
*Pseudochelidon sirintarae*                          [I]

RANGE: **C Thailand**
HABITAT: **river marshes in winter; summer habitat unknown**
SIZE: **6 in (15 cm)**

This species was discovered as recently as 1968, roosting in winter on the 62,000 acre (25,000 hectare) Lake Boraphet in Nakhon Sawan Province, central Thailand. In 1968, 10 birds were found, followed by 2 more in 1972. All that is known about the ecology of these birds is that they roost with thousands of swallows of other species.

The only other existing species in the genus *Pseudochelidon* is the African River Martin *P. eurystomina*, which occurs in Gabon and along the lower Congo and Ubangi rivers. Both these birds are unlike all other members of the family and probably diverged from the rest of the swallows and martins early in their evolution.

## 11/ TREE SWALLOW
*Tachycineta bicolor*

RANGE: **breeds C Alaska and Canada to CE USA; winters S USA, Caribbean, Central America**
HABITAT: **open areas near water, especially flooded areas with dead trees**
SIZE: **5–6 in (12.5–15 cm)**

During migration, this species forms huge flocks that often roost in the low vegetation of coastal marshes. Although it relies primarily on a diet of flying insects, in extreme cold it has been observed feeding on bayberries.

The Tree Swallow nests in ready-made holes, choosing old woodpecker cavities, crevices and nest-boxes in which to build its cup-shaped nest of dried grasses or pine needles. This is then lined with white feathers. The competition for feathers is keen and adults have been known to pluck feathers from the backs of domestic ducks. The usual clutch contains 4–6 white eggs and extra bird may occasionally assist the parents in caring for the brood.

## 12/ PURPLE MARTIN
*Progne subis*

RANGE: **breeds North America; winters in Amazon Basin, and sometimes as far N as Florida**
HABITAT: **open areas, often near water**
SIZE: **7 in (18 cm)**

This species has become intimately associated with human settlement in eastern North America. The Indians of southeastern USA provided calabash gourds for Purple Martins to use as nest sites. In return, the birds mobbed crows and other animals that fed on the Indians' crops or on meat hung out to dry. Early European settlers continued the tradition of providing homes for the birds. In western North America, the birds still nest in natural sites, usually dead trees with woodpecker holes.

Both parents feed the young which fledge within about 4 weeks of hatching. Young birds can catch flying insects within 5 days of fledging and are quickly independent of their parents.

## 13/ WHITE-BANDED SWALLOW
*Atticora fasciata*

RANGE: **S Venezuela, Guianas, Amazonian Brazil, NW Bolivia**
HABITAT: **rivers and small clearings, forest edge**
SIZE: **6 in (15 cm)**

Locally common along clear streams and less so along large, muddy rivers, this swallow seems to prefer areas with rocky, fast-flowing water fringed with forest. It usually occurs in small groups, and is both conspicuous and easily identified on the wing, although its deeply forked tail is often held closed in a point.

The White-banded Swallow flies somewhat erratically and close to vegetation and rocks as it pursues flying insects. At rest, it often perches on large rocks or other debris in the water. A whole group of birds may perch unnoticed until they suddenly take to the air.

## 14/ WHITE-BACKED SWALLOW
*Cheramoeca leucosterna*

RANGE: **S, E and W Australia**
HABITAT: **dry and sandy areas, forest edge**
SIZE: **6 in (15 cm)**

This somewhat nomadic swallow has recently expanded its range southward toward the coast. Usually seen in pairs or small groups, it favors areas near fresh water. Like others of its family, it feeds on flying insects, but its flight is more fluttering than that of many swallow species.

The White-backed Swallow is relatively quiet, but has a twittering song and gives a single *chip* or *chek* note in flight. It roosts and nests in holes about 30 in (75 cm) or more deep, excavated in sandy river banks, road cuttings and sand dunes. In cold weather, several roosting birds may use a single tunnel, and if the cold lasts for a prolonged period, the birds are able to enter a state of torpor to conserve energy.

## 15/ BANK SWALLOW
*Riparia riparia*

RANGE: **breeds North America and Eurasia; winters South America, Africa, Mediterranean, Near East, N India, E China, Southeast Asia**
HABITAT: **open and semi-open areas near water**
SIZE: **12–14 cm (5–5½ in)**

Also known as the Sand Martin outside of North America, this species is well known for its habit of excavating burrows in river banks. Other nest sites include cliffs formed by cuttings, gravel pits, and sawdust and coal dust piles. It typically digs its own burrow using its beak and feet, but it may also renovate old tunnels. The burrows are 1–4 ft (30–120 cm) long and are usually clustered near the top of a bank. Bank Swallows are highly gregarious and nest areas often contain several hundred pairs. The tunnels are so closely packed that they occasionally intersect one another.

Following the breeding season, Bank Swallows migrate south, often in company with other swallows. Together, they can form huge flocks, some containing 250,000 birds.

# SWALLOWS AND MARTINS, WAGTAILS AND PIPITS, CUCKOO SHRIKES

BLUE SWALLOW

race *rustica*

race *erythrogaster*

BARN SWALLOW

HOUSE MARTIN

FANTEE SAW-WING

FOREST WAGTAIL

race *yarrellii* juv

race *yarrellii* ♂

race *alba*
"White Wagtail"

PIED WAGTAIL

race *flava*
"Blue-headed Wagtail"

race *feldegg*
"Black-headed Wagtail"

race *leucocephala*
"White-headed Wagtail"

race *flavissima*
♂

GOLDEN PIPIT

race *flavissima*
"Yellow Wagtail"
♀

YELLOW WAGTAIL

WATER PIPIT

ROCK PIPIT

BUFF-BELLIED PIPIT

♂

CAPE LONGCLAW

♂

WHITE-WINGED TRILLER

eclipse plumage ♂

RICHARD'S PIPIT

♂

♀

LONG-TAILED MINIVET

BLUE CUCKOO-SHRIKE

BLACK-FACED CUCKOO-SHRIKE

# SWALLOWS AND MARTINS, WAGTAILS AND PIPITS, CUCKOO SHRIKES

## 1/ BARN SWALLOW
*Hirundo rustica*

RANGE: **breeds Europe and Asia, N Africa, North America; winters in S hemisphere**
HABITAT: **open areas, often near water**
SIZE: **7 in (18 cm)**

Although almost cosmopolitan, this species has only 6 races, including the widespread *H.r. rustica*, which breeds over much of Eurasia and north Africa, and *H.r. erythrogaster* of North America.

The Barn Swallow has benefited greatly from the destruction of forest habitats, the construction of buildings and bridges, and the provision of utility wires and fences. Over much of its nesting range, it attaches its mud nest to the rough walls of barns and other human structures and depends on wires for use as perches. Barn Swallows prey on small flying insects that they catch mainly during low flights over water or moist vegetation.

## 2/ BLUE SWALLOW
*Hirundo atrocaerulea*

RANGE: **parts of E and S Africa**
HABITAT: **mountain grassland near streams**
SIZE: **7¾ in (20 cm)**

The Blue Swallow is the only member of its family that is listed in the African *Red Data Book*. Its population is regarded as vulnerable in Zimbabwe and endangered in South Africa because of widespread disturbance to its upland habitat. This species is unusual on several counts. It is migratory, but keeps within the tropics, breeding in the southern part of its range and wintering in Uganda. It shows marked sexual differences, in that the male has a long, forked tail while the female's tail is short. Lastly, it nests alone rather than in groups or colonies.

## 3/ HOUSE MARTIN
*Delichon urbica*

RANGE: **breeds Europe, Asia (except far N, S), N Africa, irregularly S Africa; winters sub-Saharan Africa, Southeast Asia**
HABITAT: **open areas particularly near water and human habitations**
SIZE: **5 in (13 cm)**

House Martins are familiar birds in many areas, having adapted well to human settlement. They feed primarily on flying insects, especially flies and aphids. Outside the nesting season they feed and roost in very large flocks. They have a soft, twittering song, and their calls include shrill, high-pitched contact and alarm calls.

House Martins are often colonial, and their nests are sometimes so close that they are attached to one another. Their original breeding sites include sheltered cliffs, both inland and on the coast, and rock outcrops, but in many parts of their range, particularly in Europe, they have forsaken these sites for man-made ones, under the eaves of buildings, under bridges and in culverts.

## 4/ FANTEE SAW-WING
*Psalidoprocne obscura*

RANGE: **Sierra Leone to Cameroon**
HABITAT: **savanna, forest edge, grassland, flooded areas**
SIZE: **6½ in (17 cm)**

This species occurs in a variety of open habitats, usually in small groups. It flies low, snatching flying insects such as small beetles. The name saw-wing (or rough-wing) used for this and the other 8 *Psalidoprocne* species of Africa and for the 2 American *Stelgidopteryx* species, refers to the series of barbs on the outer web of the outer primary wing feathers of the male. Their function is unknown, but they may produce the noise made by the bird's wings during courtship. Fantee Saw-wings excavate horizontal nest-burrows in road cuttings and earth banks.

## FAMILY MOTACILLIDAE
**Wagtails and pipits**

Small, largely terrestrial, rather slender, long-tailed, long-toed birds. Plumage of wagtails either black and white or with gray, brown, bluish or greenish upperparts and whitish, yellowish or yellow underparts; Golden Pipit and longclaws mostly streaked brown above with yellow or reddish underparts; pipits mostly brown, streaked, paler below. Sexes differ slightly, alike in most pipits. Nest on ground; wagtails also nest in crevices in rocks and walls. Eggs 2–7, white, gray or brown, typically speckled brown. Incubation 12–20 days, nestling period 12–18 days. 58 species.

## 5/ FOREST WAGTAIL
*Dendronanthus indicus*

RANGE: **breeds Manchuria, Korea, SE USSR; winters Southeast Asia, Indonesia**
HABITAT: **open areas in moist, often evergreen forest**
SIZE: **6 in (15 cm)**

This species belongs to a separate genus from most wagtails, and its tail-wagging action is unique in that the whole body sways from side to side, rather than up and down as in *Motacilla* species. The Forest Wagtail also differs from most members of its family in its preference for trees rather than open country and often occurs along wooded streams. Although most of its food is obtained at ground level, it will also run along branches to snatch insects.

## 6/ YELLOW WAGTAIL
*Motacilla flava*

RANGE: **breeds Europe E across Asia to coastal Alaska; winters Africa, S Asia**
HABITAT: **marshes, lowland grassland, some arable crops**
SIZE: **6½ in (17 cm)**

Some 18 races of this bird have been described, in which the head pattern of the breeding male varies. The race *M.f. flavissima* of northwest Europe, Spain and north Africa has the most yellow head and is the race that best deserves the name Yellow Wagtail. Other races include: *M.f. leucocephala* of Mongolia, central Asia and northwest India; *M.f. flava* of northern Europe and southern Africa; and *M.f. feldegg* of southeast Europe, Asia Minor, Iraq and Iran. Females are generally indistinguishable racially.

The Yellow Wagtail occurs in flocks that run gracefully through the ground vegetation foraging for invertebrates.

## 7/ PIED WAGTAIL
*Motacilla alba*

RANGE: **breeds most of Eurasia, except tropics; N birds winter S to Africa N of Equator, Arabia, India and Southeast Asia**
HABITAT: **open ground, often near water**
SIZE: **7 in (18 cm)**

This striking bird habitually bobs its tail. Its plumage varies across its extensive range. The wholly black-backed adult Pied Wagtail *M.a. yarrellii* of the British Isles, Spain and Morocco differs markedly from the gray-backed White Wagtail *M.a. alba* of the rest of Europe, north and east Africa, Iran, Arabia and Russia.

The Pied Wagtail is fond of water and often paddles into shallows and puddles as it searches for aquatic insects. It is also common in open ground away from water, and regularly occurs around farmyards, parks and buildings. It often uses communal roosts outside the breeding season. In some areas, these include artificially heated structures, such as power station cooling towers and heated greenhouses.

## 8/ GOLDEN PIPIT
*Tmetothylacus tenellus*

RANGE: **Horn of Africa S to Tanzania**
HABITAT: **dry open country**
SIZE: **5$\frac{1}{2}$ in (14 cm)**

The male Golden Pipit is a striking bird showing characteristics of both the wagtails and the pipits. A sedentary bird, this species is often very local in occurrence, even where apparently suitable habitat is extensive. It occurs in small flocks or family groups. The Golden Pipit performs its simple song during parachutelike glides from the tops of bushes to the ground, with its wings held in a *V* above its back.

## 9/ CAPE LONGCLAW
*Macronyx capensis*

RANGE: **South Africa, C Zimbabwe**
HABITAT: **open damp grassland**
SIZE: **7$\frac{1}{2}$ in (19 cm)**

This is a robustly built bird, generally seen doggedly foraging in small parties through short grassland. It quickly chases or pounces on any food item that is startled from cover and will often beat large insects on the ground before swallowing them. From time to time, it stands on a clump or mound to scan its surroundings.

The Cape Longclaw utters whistling and piping calls as well as a catlike *meeoo* of alarm. It frequently calls when perched on a fence or mound, as well as during its fluttering display flight, when it rises some 33 ft (10 m) into the air.

## 10/ RICHARD'S PIPIT
*Anthus novaeseelandiae*

RANGE: **sub-Saharan Africa, much of C, E and S Asia, New Guinea, Australia, New Zealand; N populations migrate to S of breeding range**
HABITAT: **open country**
SIZE: **7 in (18 cm)**

This large pipit has an upright stance and a long tail that it habitually wags up and down. It exhibits considerable variation in plumage, with the upperparts of many races quite darkly marked. The race illustrated is *A. n. novaeseelandiae* of South Island, New Zealand.

Richard's Pipit, sometimes called the New Zealand Pipit, hunts for invertebrates on the ground and will sometimes pursue insects in the air. It gives chirruping and trilling calls and sings in flight. The nest is placed in a slight depression on the ground. Its populations in warmer areas have a longer breeding season and may lay several small clutches.

## 11/ BUFF-BELLIED PIPIT
*Anthus rubescens*

RANGE: **breeds NE Siberia, N North America, W Greenland; winters S to Southeast Asia and Central America**
HABITAT: **breeds on mountains and tundra; winters on beaches, fields**
SIZE: **6$\frac{1}{2}$ in (17 cm)**

The Buff-bellied Pipit nests on the tundra in the north of its range but is a mountain bird farther south. It is both widespread and common in North America and is sometimes known as the American Pipit. Where this species' range meets that of the Water Pipit in Siberia, the 2 birds show differing habitat preferences. The Water Pipit tends to breed on open ground, while the Buff-bellied Pipit prefers more rocky areas.

## 12/ WATER PIPIT
*Anthus spinoletta*

RANGE: **S European mountains E across Asia to Lake Baikal; C and E Asian races winter S to Southeast Asia and Japan**
HABITAT: **breeds in mountains; winters in open country at lower elevations**
SIZE: **6$\frac{1}{2}$ in (17 cm)**

Formerly considered races of the same species, the Water Pipit, Rock Pipit and Buff-bellied Pipit have recently been separated on the basis of detailed studies. They are largely separate in geographical range and in habitat preferences.

The Water Pipit breeds above the tree line in high mountain areas, usually siting its nest close to rushing streams. In some regions it occurs close to glaciers and even nests above the snow line. In winter, however, it is driven by harsh conditions down to lower altitudes, to such habitats as flooded or damp meadows, watercress beds and other damp, arable land, and even to estuaries and coastal mudflats.

## 13/ ROCK PIPIT
*Anthus petrosus*

RANGE: **breeds NW France, British Isles, Scandinavia, Faroe Islands; some N populations winter in NW and S Europe**
HABITAT: **seashore**
SIZE: **6$\frac{1}{2}$ in (17 cm)**

The Rock Pipit gains most of its food by foraging among beach debris, searching for invertebrates such as insects and their larvae, mollusks and small crustaceans. In some regions, resident Rock Pipits defend feeding territories all year.

The birds nest either on sea cliffs or in a bank or under dense vegetation close to the shore. Seaweed is often incorporated into the cup nest. The normal clutch size is 4–5, but up to 9 eggs have been recorded in one nest.

## FAMILY CAMPEPHAGIDAE
### Cuckoo-shrikes

Small to medium, tree-dwellers. Most species grayish, black or pied, but one group with bright reds and yellows. Sexes differ in most species. Nest a shallow cup. Eggs 2–5, white or greenish, sometimes spotted. Incubation 14–23 days, nestling period 12–25 days. 70 species.

## 14/ BLACK-FACED CUCKOO-SHRIKE
*Coracina novaehollandiae*

RANGE: **breeds India, Southeast Asia, New Guinea, Australia; many SE Australian and Tasmanian birds winter in N Australia and New Guinea**
HABITAT: **woodland and forests**
SIZE: **13 in (33 cm)**

Black-faced Cuckoo-Shrikes have an undulating flight and when they land they shuffle their wings in a distinctive manner. The birds feed on larvae, beetles and other large insects that they snatch from leaves after scanning the foliage from below. The rather metallic voice of this bird includes a rolling *churrrink* contact call and a higher, trilling *chereer-chereer-chereer*, often given in display.

## 15/ BLUE CUCKOO-SHRIKE
*Coracina azurea*

RANGE: **Sierra Leone to Zaire**
HABITAT: **primary and secondary forest**
SIZE: **8$\frac{1}{2}$ in (22 cm)**

The Blue Cuckoo-Shrike is an unobtrusive bird that frequents the tops of tall trees. Although often solitary, it may be seen in small parties that hunt diligently through the foliage for beetles, grasshoppers and caterpillars. The calls of the Blue Cuckoo-Shrike range from grating noises to more pleasant musical notes.

## 16/ WHITE-WINGED TRILLER
*Lalage sueurii*

RANGE: **Sulawesi, Lesser Sundas, Java, SE New Guinea, Australia**
HABITAT: **open woodland and shrubland**
SIZE: **7 in (18 cm)**

Outside the breeding season, the male resembles the grayish-brown and buff female. An alternative name for the trillers is "caterpillar-eaters," and, indeed, they do take many larvae, which they glean or snatch from foliage. Nectar and fruit are also sometimes eaten.

White-winged Trillers are migrants, arriving as late as November in southern Australia. Males sing their vigorous trilling songs from the treetops, often pursuing one another.

## 17/ LONG-TAILED MINIVET
*Pericrocotus ethologus*

RANGE: **breeds E Afghanistan through Himalayas to Southeast Asia and China, N to Manchuria**
HABITAT: **open forest, sparsely wooded hills, mainly 3,300–8,000 ft (1,000–2,500 m)**
SIZE: **7 in (18 cm)**

A flock of these lively scarlet and black birds flying over the treetops against a snowy Himalayan backdrop is an unforgettable sight. Highly gregarious, Long-tailed Minivets are always on the move, hovering and fluttering in search of insects, buds and fruit. Individuals in a group keep in contact with sweet, twittering calls. This species is migratory in some areas, and many birds move to lower altitudes in winter.

CRESTED FINCHBILL

STRIATED GREEN BULBUL

race *monticola*

RED-WHISKERED BULBUL

SPOTTED GREENBUL

YELLOW-THROATED LEAFLOVE

race *flavicollis*

BEARDED GREENBUL

race *chloronotus*

race *barbatus*

LONG-BILLED BULBUL

CHESTNUT-EARED BULBUL

HONEYGUIDE GREENBUL

GARDEN BULBUL

race *barbatus*

race *leucogenys*

race *tricolor*

race *leucotis*

WHITE-CHEEKED BULBUL

race *flavostriatus*

race *notata*

YELLOW-STREAKED
GREENBUL

race *sinensis*

BLACK BULBUL

race
ucothorax

GREEN-TAILED BRISTLE-BILL

race *eximia*

WESTERN NICATOR

race *psaroides*

BLACK-COLLARED BULBUL

## FAMILY PYCNONOTIDAE
**Bulbuls**

Medium to small, drab, gregarious birds of trees and scrub. Often hooded or with pale eye ring. Short, slightly curved bills, stout legs. Generally melodious voices. Sexes similar. Nest cup-shaped, in tree. Eggs 2–5, purplish-pink. Incubation 12–14 days, nestling period 14–18 days. 124 species.

## 1/ CRESTED FINCHBILL
*Spizixos canifrons*

RANGE: **Assam, W Burma**
HABITAT: **forest, clearings, mountain scrub to 8,000 ft (2,500 m)**
SIZE: **8 in (20 cm)**

Most bulbuls have slender, medium-length bills, but the aptly named finchbills have short, stout bills which are like those of finches and used for the same purpose: cracking seeds. Adult Crested Finchbills have yellowish bills which look white in the field and are very distinctive.

Crested Finchbills are gregarious birds which often forage in flocks of 50 or more among bamboo, low, cut scrub and abandoned cultivation. Sometimes one will move to a high perch and use it as a base for catching flies on the wing, but they feed mainly on berries and seeds.

The 2-note alarm call is musical but strident, increasing to 5 syllables when the bird is really excited, with a rich, fluty quality typical of bulbuls.

## 2/ STRIATED GREEN BULBUL
*Pycnonotus striatus*

RANGE: **E Himalayas, W Burma**
HABITAT: **evergreen forest, rhododendron forest, bushes, to 10,000 ft (3,000 m)**
SIZE: **8 in (20 cm)**

This bulbul is a resident of hill forests but moves down to lower levels in winter. It prefers jungle and bushy forest that is not too dense or too high; flocks of up to 15 birds straggle loosely from bush to bush in search of fruit, each bird giving almost continuous sharp *tyiwut* calls. They will also join in a communal, full-throated but disjointed warbling song whenever they pause in their lively passage through the trees.

## 3/ RED-WHISKERED BULBUL
*Pycnonotus jocosus*

RANGE: **China, Assam, Nepal, India**
HABITAT: **open humid jungle, gardens**
SIZE: **8 in (20 cm)**

There are 6 races of this widespread and common species, each distinguished by the pattern of white on the tail feathers, the dark collar, the length of crest and bill, and the color of the back. The race shown is *P.j. monticola* of China and Assam, which has white tail tips and the darkest back.

Red-whiskered Bulbuls are familiar in gardens, even in the noisiest cities, where they live in pairs or gather in loose flocks. Each pair tends to remain in its territory all year, eating fruits and buds (often doing damage in gardens) or dropping to the ground to feed on ants. Their calls are typically noisy, full-throated and cheerful.

## 4/ WHITE-CHEEKED BULBUL
*Pycnonotus leucogenys*

RANGE: **Himalayas, NW India to S Iran**
HABITAT: **scrub jungle, bushy hillsides, villages**
SIZE: **8 in (20 cm)**

Sprightly and active, the White-cheeked Bulbul is common up to 7,000 ft (2,100 m) in the dry Himalayas, but in wetter east Nepal it occurs only in the lower, drier valleys.

It likes bushes of wild raspberry, berberis and roses, and small parties are often seen bustling noisily along hedgerows from village to village. In Kashmir it is a fearless, familiar bird, often entering houses to steal scraps from tables. It is a jaunty bird which perches on bush tops, bowing and flicking its wings and tail and keeping up a constant stream of calls.

The Himalayan race *P.l. leucogenys* is a long-crested form; *P.l. leucotis* is a crestless race with a much wider range farther west.

## 5/ GARDEN BULBUL
*Pycnonotus barbatus*

RANGE: **N Africa S to Tanzania**
HABITAT: **open forest, gardens, town parks**
SIZE: **7 in (18 cm)**

All over its large range the Garden, or Common, Bulbul announces its presence with the high, rich, fluty or bubbling calls typical of its family. It is an adaptable species which will thrive almost anywhere where there are fruits, buds and berries, although it does not like dense forest. In some areas, such as Egypt, it has extended its range to take advantage of the increase in irrigated orchards. It is often seen near houses and other buildings and can be very tame, but in more remote areas can be very inconspicuous.

The northern race *P. b. barbatus* is white under the tail but the southern race *P. b. tricolor* has a splash of yellow in the same place.

## 6/ HONEYGUIDE GREENBUL
*Baeopogon indicator*

RANGE: **W Africa from Sierra Leone to the Congo**
HABITAT: **forest clearings and secondary growth**
SIZE: **8 in (20 cm)**

This is a rather large, heavily built bulbul with conspicuous white outer tail feathers like those of a honeyguide (pp. 210–13). It also behaves a little like a honeyguide, keeping to the tops of tall trees, but its calls are quite distinctive, and its fluty, jumbled song resembles that of a thrush.

The Honeyguide Greenbul is a little-known species; its breeding behavior has not been studied in detail, although nests have been found placed far out on slender branches near the tops of forest trees.

## 7/ SPOTTED GREENBUL
*Ixonotus guttatus*

RANGE: **Ghana and Gabon to C Zaire**
HABITAT: **primary and secondary tropical forest**
SIZE: **6 in (15 cm)**

Easily recognized by the amount of white in its plumage, this is a common and fairly conspicuous bird. It lives in loose groups which draw attention to themselves by repeated cheerful calls and restless behavior in the treetops. Like some other bulbuls, it will often raise one wing over its back while it perches.

The nest of the Spotted Greenbul is built in a low tree beneath the high canopy of the forest and is a typical bulbul construction of thin rootlets and leaf stalks woven into the form of a shallow cup.

## 8/ YELLOW-THROATED LEAFLOVE
*Chlorocichla flavicollis*
RANGE: **W Africa from Senegal to Cameroon, Central African Republic and the Congo**
HABITAT: **forest edge and thorny thickets**
SIZE: **7 in (18 cm)**

The Yellow-throated Leaflove is a bird of the dense thickets where the savanna blends into the forest and is rarely seen among the tall forest trees. In some areas it is common, living in pairs or small parties which, although hidden by the dense foliage, are easily located by their loud, throaty, bubbling calls.

Some races, such as *C. f. flavicollis*, have the yellow throat referred to in the name, but others, such as *C. f. soror* of the Central African Republic, Congo and Sudan, are white-throated and duller.

## 9/ YELLOW-STREAKED GREENBUL
*Phyllastrephus flavostriatus*
RANGE: **Nigeria and Cameroon E and S to South Africa**
HABITAT: **mountain forest**
SIZE: **8 in (20 cm)**

This large bulbul is quite easily identified by its plumage and its liking for thick forests high in the mountains, where it keeps to trees and thick bush, often in the highest branches.

It creeps about close to the main trunks or in clustered creepers, searching for insects in the bundles of dead leaves that collect among the stems. Although rather sluggish, it will twist and stretch, or even hang upside-down, as it searches for food. This bird also has a habit of raising one wing over its back, lowering it and then raising the other.

Several races are distinguished on the basis of the color of the underparts and grayness of the head. The race shown is *P. f. flavostriatus* from eastern South Africa.

## 10/ GREEN-TAILED BRISTLE-BILL
*Bleda eximia*
RANGE: **W Africa, from Sierra Leone to Central African Republic and the Congo**
HABITAT: **tall tropical forest**
SIZE: **8 in (20 cm)**

Although this bulbul is always found among tall trees, it spends most of its time on or near the ground, often in the mixed-bird flocks that are so characteristic of African woodlands. It is frequently seen picking ants out of the huge columns of these insects that march across the leaf litter beneath the canopy.

It has a loud, explosive call, but its song is mellow, varied and thrushlike. The western race *B. e. notata* has a conspicuous yellow spot on its face, absent in the eastern race *B. e. eximia*.

## 11/ WESTERN NICATOR
*Nicator chloris*
RANGE: **Senegal to Gabon and the Congo, Zaire and Uganda**
HABITAT: **thick forest**
SIZE: **8¾ in (22 cm)**

In the color plate this looks like a conspicuous bird, but in the forest it can be very hard to see, for it rarely emerges from the dense foliage of tall trees. The Western Nicator lives in the tops of smaller trees or among the lower canopy of forest giants, and often the only clues to its presence are its harsh, wheezy or whistling calls and its beautiful, full-throated song.

The only time it comes close to the ground is when nesting, for it builds its frail, flat nest in a fork 3–6 ft (1–2 m) from the forest floor.

This species closely resembles some of the shrikes and was formerly classified with them in the family Laniidae (pp. 254–57).

## 12/ BEARDED GREENBUL
*Criniger barbatus*
RANGE: **Sierra Leone to Gabon and Central African Republic**
HABITAT: **rain forest**
SIZE: **8 in (20 cm)**

The most remarkable feature of the Bearded Greenbul is its beautiful, arresting whistle; it also sometimes utters a loud, throaty babbling. It is a gregarious bird which often joins mixed-species flocks roaming through the lower levels of the rain forest canopy.

The eastern race *C. b. chloronotus* has distinctive white throat feathers, whereas the race *C. b. barbatus*, found from Sierra Leone to Togo, has a yellow throat.

The nest, built on top of a shrub, is made of dead leaves, pieces of rotten wood and plant fiber, and is decorated with a few green sprays.

## 13/ LONG-BILLED BULBUL
*Setornis criniger*
RANGE: **Borneo, Sumatra, Bangka Islands**
HABITAT: **lowland primary forest**
SIZE: **7 in (18 cm)**

Although the striking Long-billed Bulbul is a common resident of the lowlands of Borneo, very little is recorded about its behavior or breeding biology.

Its white-tipped outer tail feathers help identify it in the dense woodland it prefers. Its varied diet is typical of bulbuls and includes dragonfly nymphs, beetles and other insects, and a wide range of fruits and berries.

## 14/ CHESTNUT-EARED BULBUL
*Hypsipetes amaurotis*
RANGE: **Japan, Taiwan, S China**
HABITAT: **forested slopes, gardens, parks**
SIZE: **10½ in (27 cm)**

Sociable and noisy, the Chestnut-eared Bulbul visits bird feeders in Japanese gardens and is a familiar sight in parks and wooded areas in towns. The birds that breed in the north move south in winter, often roaming in sizable flocks that communicate with continual loud, fluty, rhythmic calls. In summer this species is very common in forests on lower mountain slopes.

For a bulbul it is a slim, long-tailed and slender-billed bird, with none of the stubby appearance of many of its African relatives. The race *H. a. amaurotis* is the Japanese form; *H. a. nagamichii* is the race found on Taiwan.

## 15/ BLACK BULBUL
*Hypsipetes madagascariensis*
RANGE: **SW India, Nepal E to Vietnam, Thailand, China**
HABITAT: **oak, pine, rhododendron forest**
SIZE: **9 in (23 cm)**

Several races have been described within the large range of the Black Bulbul. *H. m. sinensis* from southwest China, Thailand and Laos is a dark one, whereas *H. m. psaroides*, found along the Himalayas, is paler; the race *H. m. leucothorax* of western China and northern Vietnam has a white head.

The Black Bulbul is a summer visitor to the higher parts of its range, up to 10,000 ft (3,000 m) in the Himalayas, but elsewhere it is mainly resident. Common and very noisy, the birds may gather in boisterous bands of 100 or more individuals which stay a little while in one tree, fly up to catch insects or strip the twigs of berries, then swiftly stream out to the next.

The song is a series of clipped, single notes interspersed with a ringing bell-like tone, but other calls have been compared to a squealing pig and a creaky gate.

## 16/ BLACK-COLLARED BULBUL
*Neolestes torquatus*
RANGE: **Gabon, Congo, Zaire, Angola**
HABITAT: **grassy woodland, savanna**
SIZE: **6 in (15 cm)**

In many respects the small Black-collared Bulbul is an unusual member of its family. Indeed, its bright pigmentation, upright stance and arched bill misled early birdwatchers into the belief that it was a shrike. It keeps to more open areas than most bulbuls and has a unique display flight, ascending to 100 ft (30 m) or more and hovering in one spot for 2–3 minutes, emitting a continuous stream of twittering calls.

Despite all this, its feeding habits are typical of a bulbul, for it moves around in small parties and feeds on fruit.

# LEAFBIRDS, FAIRY BLUEBIRDS, SHRIKES, BORNEAN BRISTLEHEAD

race *tiphia*

♂

COMMON IORA

♀

race *multicolor*

race *multicolor*

♂

race *multicolor*

♂

race *frontalis*

♂

race *aurifrons*

GOLDEN-FRONTED LEAFBIRD

♀

♂

BLUE-BACKED FAIRY BLUEBIRD

courtship display

PUFFBACK

♂

BRUBRU SHRIKE

race *ludovicianus*

juv

♂

BLACK-HEADED TCHAGRA

♂

courtship display

LOGGERHEAD SHRIKE

FIERY-BREASTED BUSH-SHRIKE

COMMON GONOLEK

♂

♂

FISCAL SHRIKE

race *collaris*

♂

♀

YELLOW-BILLED SHRIKE

♀

race *subcoronatus*

RED-BACKED SHRIKE

BORNEAN BRISTLEHEAD

race *tricolor*

♂

♂

race *erythronotus*

LONG-TAILED SHRIKE

FOUR-COLORED BUSH-SHRIKE

# LEAFBIRDS, FAIRY BLUEBIRDS, SHRIKES, BORNEAN BRISTLEHEAD

## FAMILY CHLOROPSEIDAE
### Leafbirds

Small to medium tree-dwellers. Plumage mostly green and yellow, males with black on face. Sexes differ. Cup-shaped nest. Eggs 2–3, pinkish or white with brown blotches. Incubation about 14 days, nestling period unknown. 12 species.

### 1/ COMMON IORA
*Aegithina tiphia*

RANGE: **India, Sri Lanka to Southeast Asia, Java, Borneo**
HABITAT: **forest, groves, cultivated land**
SIZE: **5½ in (14 cm)**

A small, active, insect-eating bird, the Common Iora is remarkable for its display. The courting male fluffs out his rump and his long white flank feathers and jumps into the air, gliding down again to his perch like a feathered ball. Often to be seen in pairs, the birds call constantly with a variety of sweet, sometimes mournful, whistles.

This species molts twice yearly; the male in his nonbreeding plumage resembles the duller female, except for his black tail. Of the races illustrated, *A. t. tiphia* ranges from the Himalayas to Burma, while *A. t. multicolor* occurs in southern India and Sri Lanka.

### 2/ GOLDEN-FRONTED LEAFBIRD
*Chloropsis aurifrons*

RANGE: **Sri Lanka, India, Himalayas to Southeast Asia, Sumatra**
HABITAT: **forest, open woodland, scrub**
SIZE: **7½ in (19 cm)**

There are several races of this widely distributed bird, differing both in size and in the color of the chin and throat. They include the blue-throated *C. a. aurifrons* of Bangladesh and India, and the black-throated *C. a. frontalis* of central and southern India. The blue shoulder patches, which are found in all races, are often concealed when the bird is at rest.

A great mimic, this leafbird is often to be seen foraging with almost titlike agility in flowering or fruiting trees; it is partial to both figs and mistletoe. As it spends much time exploring blossoms for nectar and insects, it is an important pollinator. It is a resident bird in most of its range, although it moves to lower zones in the Himalayas in winter.

## FAMILY IRENIDAE
### Fairy bluebirds

Medium-sized tree-dwellers. Very long upper and under tail coverts. Plumage brilliant blue and black. Females duller, greener. Eyes intensely red. Nest a twig platform in a tree fork. Eggs 2–3, glossy olive with brown blotching. Incubation and nestling period unknown. 2 species.

### 3/ BLUE-BACKED FAIRY BLUEBIRD
*Irena puella*

RANGE: **W India, Nepal to Southeast Asia, Philippines**
HABITAT: **heavy deciduous or evergreen forest**
SIZE: **10½ in (27 cm)**

A fruiting fig tree is a magnet for Blue-backed Fairy Bluebirds and their bustling activity, and incessant sharp, liquid calls add great charm to the forest scene. They are always on the move in the forest, usually working their way through the canopy or the middle layers of vegetation, and seldom descend to the ground.

When moving through the heavy shade of the foliage small groups of the birds can look dull black, until a shaft of sunlight suddenly illuminates the sapphire mantles of the males. In some races the upper tail coverts almost conceal the tail.

## FAMILY LANIIDAE
### Shrikes

Small to medium. Sharply hooked bill. Plumage variable, often bright. Sexes usually similar. Nest in trees and shrubs. Eggs 2–7, variable, streaked or blotched. Incubation 12–18 days, nestling period 12–20 days. 69 species.

### 4/ BRUBRU SHRIKE
*Nilaus afer*

RANGE: **tropical Africa**
HABITAT: **savanna woodland; occasionally forest edge**
SIZE: **6 in (15 cm)**

This bird is usually heard before it is seen. It takes its name from the male's repeated *bruuu-bruuu* call with which he proclaims his territory and keeps in close contact with the female. Like some other shrikes, when a pair are close together they often engage in "duetting," with the female answering the male's calls.

The Brubru Shrike occurs mainly in the tree canopy, where it gleans insects from the foliage, but it occasionally catches food on the wing.

### 5/ PUFFBACK
*Dryoscopus gambensis*

RANGE: **W, C and E Africa**
HABITAT: **savanna woodland; also thickets, forest clearings, mangroves and gardens**
SIZE: **7 in (18 cm)**

The species' name reflects the male's ability to fluff up the long, gray-white feathers of the lower back. During the courtship display, these feathers resemble a ball-shaped powder puff. This bird occurs singly or in pairs and spends most of its time in the tree canopy, rarely descending to ground level. It feeds mainly on insects but occasionally catches small lizards.

The Puffback is a vocal bird, with a wide variety of calls, including a chattering alarm note. In the breeding season, the male sings a melodious and warbling song and the female often joins in the singing during territorial disputes.

### 6/ BLACK-HEADED TCHAGRA
*Tchagra senegala*

RANGE: **sub-Saharan Africa, NW Africa, SW Arabia**
HABITAT: **open savanna woodland with bushes and long grass, margins of cultivated land**
SIZE: **8¾ in (22 cm)**

The Black-headed Tchagra feeds much like a thrush, hopping, running and creeping through the ground cover. It will also search for food among foliage and catches some of its prey in flight. Insects and their larvae make up the bulk of its diet but it also feeds on tadpoles, along with the occasional adult tree frog, and it often eats soft fruits.

Although this bird is secretive, its song-flight is conspicuous. Males defend territories throughout the year, singing a series of plaintive whistled notes from an exposed perch. During the courtship song-flights, they ascend noisily into the air and whistle as they glide back down to cover. Duetting is well developed, the female adding a drawn-out trill to the male's song; she often joins him in his song-flight.

## 7/ COMMON GONOLEK
*Laniarius barbarus*

RANGE: **W Africa**
HABITAT: **thorny acacia, dense shrub and woodland in savannas; also mangroves and riverside thickets**
SIZE: **8¾ in (22 cm)**

A shy bird, the Common Gonolek is more often heard than seen. It hops nimbly through thickets and makes brief flights from cover to cover, using rapid, shallow wing beats followed by long glides. It preys on insects and other invertebrates, usually catching its food on the ground, but also foraging over tree trunks and branches and among foliage.

The male has a variety of calls, the most common being a repeated *whee-u* note. A pair will duet regularly, although the clicking notes contributed by the female are uttered so quickly that the performance sounds as if it is coming solely from the male. The birds are highly sensitive to disturbance and will readily abandon, or even destroy, their nests.

## 8/ FOUR-COLORED BUSH-SHRIKE
*Telophorus quadricolor*

RANGE: **coastal regions of E and S Africa**
HABITAT: **dense tangled bush; also forest edge**
SIZE: **8 in (20.5 cm)**

Although their plumage is bright, these birds are difficult to observe in the wild. Usually it is the male's bell-like whistle that reveals their presence. The female shares the multihued appearance of the male but her tail is a lighter green, her throat is more orange-yellow and there are no red tinges on her underparts. An alternative name is Gorgeous Bush-Shrike.

The flimsy, shallow nest is placed in the fork of a shrub about 3 ft (1 m) above the ground. It is built from twigs, grass and rootlets and is lined with leaf stalks. The female bird carries out most of the incubation.

## 9/ FIERY-BREASTED BUSH-SHRIKE
*Malaconotus cruentus*

RANGE: **W and C Africa**
HABITAT: **lowland rain forest**
SIZE: **10 in (25 cm)**

This beautiful bush-shrike usually occurs in pairs, although sometimes in groups of up to 6, in the tangled foliage of the rain forest canopy and middle layer. It searches among the leaves for beetles, grasshoppers, caterpillars and other invertebrates. Seeds and the remains of frogs have also been found in its stomach.

The large shallow cup nest of vine stems, leaf stalks and small twigs lined with black rootlets is loosely bound to branches. The 3 eggs are pinkish-white, spotted and blotched with maroon and pale purple. Like many other rain forest creatures, the Fiery-breasted Bush-Shrike is threatened by habitat destruction.

## 10/ YELLOW-BILLED SHRIKE
*Corvinella corvina*

RANGE: **W and C Africa, E to W Kenya**
HABITAT: **savanna woodland, suburban gardens**
SIZE: **12 in (30 cm)**

Although its plumage is fairly drab, this shrike is conspicuous because of its noisy habits, its large size and its tapering, 7 in (18 cm) long tail. An alternative name is Western Long-tailed Shrike. The sexes differ in the central flank feathers that are exposed when the birds preen or display. These are rufous in the male but cinnamon or maroon in the female.

This is a noisy, gregarious species, occurring in groups of some 6–15 birds. All the members of a group help to defend the communal territory as well as feed the incubating female, the nestlings and the dependent juveniles. They catch insects, spiders, slugs and lizards, either by swooping from a perch or by pouncing on them after quartering a feeding site from the air.

## 11/ RED-BACKED SHRIKE
*Lanius collurio*

RANGE: **Europe, W Siberia, W Asia; winters mainly E and S Africa**
HABITAT: **breeds in bushes, thickets and hedgerows; winters in savanna woodland**
SIZE: **6¾ in (17 cm)**

The Red-backed Shrike usually hunts by swooping from a perch to catch insects and small vertebrates such as frogs, birds and bats. Like many other northern shrikes, it has the habit of impaling its prey on thorns or barbed wire fences and keeping "larders" of stored food.

The species is widespread across western Eurasia, where it prefers to breed in lightly wooded areas with a rich undergrowth of thorn bushes. It winters in Africa, taking a southward route several hundred miles to the west of its return journey. Individual birds faithfully return to the same breeding and wintering areas. Both sexes build a deep cup nest, usually placed low in a thorn bush and lined with rootlets and wool.

## 12/ LONG-TAILED SHRIKE
*Lanius schach*

RANGE: **Iran and C Asia to China, Southeast Asia, Philippines, Indonesia, New Guinea**
HABITAT: **open country, scrub, farmland**
SIZE: **10 in (25 cm)**

This species, which is named for its long tail, shows marked variation in plumage across its vast geographical range. The Rufous-backed Shrike *L. s. erythronotus* of central Asia and western India has a gray head, for instance, while the Black-headed Shrike *L. s. tricolor* of the Himalayas, Burma and northern Indochina has a black head.

Only the northerly populations migrate to lower latitudes after the breeding season; other populations are sedentary. The birds eat a wide variety of insects and small vertebrates, impaling and storing some in "larders." Their calls are harsh and discordant but the subdued song is melodious, with many mimicked components.

## 13/ LOGGERHEAD SHRIKE
*Lanius ludovicianus*

RANGE: **S Canada to Mexico and Florida**
HABITAT: **open country with thickets, hedgerows and farmland**
SIZE: **8¼–9 in (21–23 cm)**

The Loggerhead Shrike occurs over much of North America, with the more northerly populations retreating southward in winter. It prefers open, thinly wooded country, where it feeds largely on insects, often impaling its prey on thorns. Habitat destruction and pesticides have caused its numbers to decline steadily.

The northern populations tend to lay more eggs than their southern counterparts. Studies of breeding birds in northern Colorado and Florida revealed average clutch sizes of 6.39 and 4.33 respectively. The southern races, including *L. l. ludovicianus* of southeastern USA, also tend to have lighter plumage.

## 14/ FISCAL SHRIKE
*Lanius collaris*

RANGE: **sub-Saharan Africa**
HABITAT: **open woodland savanna; also parks and forest clearings**
SIZE: **8¾ in (22 cm)**

This widespread shrike has several races. Some, such as *L. c. subcoronatus* of southwest Africa, have a white eyebrow, while others, such as *L. c. collaris* of southern Africa, lack this. In all but one race, the females differ from the males in having chestnut flanks.

It is an aggressive, solitary species that readily attacks and kills other birds. Its "larders" of impaled prey may include grasshoppers, beetles, moths, butterflies, frogs and lizards. It maintains its territorial boundaries with both visual and vocal displays, although its song of tuneful whistles and mimicked sounds is reserved for courtship and nest displays. Both sexes build the deep cup nest of grass and twigs, often in the fork of a thorn tree up to 20 ft (6 m) above the ground.

## FAMILY PITYRIASIDIDAE
**Bornean Bristlehead**
There is only one species in this family.

## 15/ BORNEAN BRISTLEHEAD
*Pityriasis gymnocephala*

RANGE: **Borneo**
HABITAT: **lowland forest**
SIZE: **10 in (25 cm)**

This rare, rain forest bird takes its name from the short, bristlelike feathers that cover the top and sides of its head. The female shares the heavy build, massive hooked beak and general coloration of the male but differs in having red spots on the flanks.

The Bornean Bristlehead spends most of its time in the forest canopy, where it hunts for a variety of insects and their larvae. It is a sociable bird and often forms mixed foraging parties with other species. It utters both a harsh, crowlike call and a high-pitched whining, sometimes in chorus with others in the group. Little is known of its nesting habits.

# HELMET SHRIKES, VANGA SHRIKES, WAXWINGS, PALMCHAT, DIPPERS, WRENS

HELMET BIRD

CORAL-BILLED NUTHATCH

♂

LONG-CRESTED
HELMET SHRIKE

BOHEMIAN
WAXWING

juv

GRAY HYPOCOLIUS

juv

♂

PHAINOPEPLA

♀

PALMCHAT

juv

NORTH AMERICAN DIPPER

WHITE-THROATED DIPPER

race *gularis*

SEDGE WREN

race *zetlandicus*

WINTER WREN

BICOLORED WREN

ROCK WREN

race *indigenus*

FLUTIST WREN

ZAPATA WREN

BLACK-CAPPED DONACOBIUS

# HELMET SHRIKES, VANGA SHRIKES, WAXWINGS, PALMCHAT, DIPPERS, WRENS

## FAMILY PRIONOPIDAE
### Helmet shrikes

Medium, highly sociable, tree-dwelling insect-eaters. Rather titlike when feeding. Sexes alike. Plumage in various combinations of black, brown and white, with patches of yellow, gray or chestnut in some species. Many with brightly colored bills and irises; *Prionops* species with colored eye wattles. Neat, compact nest built in forks or on horizontal boughs of trees high above ground. Eggs 2–6, white, pale blue, olive-green, or other colors, blotched or spotted with chestnut, brown or violet-brown. Incubation and nestling periods unknown. 9 species.

### 1/ LONG-CRESTED HELMET SHRIKE
*Prionops plumata*

RANGE: sub-Saharan Africa, except arid areas and S South Africa and Namibia
HABITAT: open deciduous woodland, orchard bush and cultivated areas with scattered trees
SIZE: 8¼ in (21 cm)

The conspicuous and gregarious Long-crested Helmet Shrike, like the other members of its family, invariably occurs in groups of up to 10 or more: these are smaller in this species in the breeding season (averaging 7 birds) than at other times. The group members chatter noisily as they leapfrog along the same foraging route in their territory each day. A wide range of loud, rolling, ringing calls is used to maintain contact and structure, and duetting probably reinforces the pair-bond. This species is also known as the Straight-crested Helmet Shrike, White Helmet Shrike or Common Helmet Shrike.

## FAMILY VANGIDAE
### Vanga shrikes

Small to medium, tree-dwelling, chiefly insect-eaters. Huge variations in bill shape and color of plumage. Sexes differ in some species. Many metallic black above, white beneath; some also with gray and chestnut; 2 species mainly blue. Breeding details known for only 8 species. Nest of twigs in trees. Eggs 3–4, white, cream, pink, greenish-blue, heavily blotched with gray or brown. Incubation and nestling periods unknown. 13 species.

### 2/ HELMET BIRD
*Euryceros prevostii*

RANGE: NE Madagascar
HABITAT: primary, dense evergreen forest from sea level to 6,000 ft (1,800 m)
SIZE: 10½–12¼ in (27–31 cm)

Its large, heavy bill distinguishes the Helmet Bird from all other members of the family. It is also known as the Helmeted Vanga.
  Communal groups of 5–10 birds are usually found in mixed feeding flocks in the middle layer of the forest, moving quickly through the foliage to glean insects from small branches. The Helmet Bird has also been known to eat frogs and small reptiles. Although this odd species is difficult to observe, its tremulous, prolonged whistle is easy to identify, particularly at dusk.

### 3/ CORAL-BILLED NUTHATCH
*Hypositta corallirostris*

RANGE: E Madagascar
HABITAT: evergreen forest from sea level to 6,000 ft (1,800 m)
SIZE: 5–6 in (13–15 cm)

Like its much bigger and very different-looking relative the Helmet Bird, this small vanga is usually found in mixed feeding flocks in the middle layer of the forest. Although it does not climb head downward as true nuthatches do (pp. 302–5), it clings with its feet to the upper parts of tree trunks to gather its insect food. The female and juvenile differ from the male in having dark slate-gray underparts and dark brown crowns. Although examination of female specimens has shown that the species breeds in August and September, little else is known of its reproductive habits.

## FAMILY BOMBYCILLIDAE
### Waxwings

Small to medium, rather starlinglike. Tree-dwelling, usually gregarious. Feed largely on insects in summer and fruits in winter. Plumage soft, dense and silky, mainly brown, pinkish, gray and black, sometimes with red and yellow. Sexes alike except in Phainopepla. Usually nomadic, strongly territorial. Nest chiefly of twigs, in trees. Eggs 2–7, blue or greenish-white. Incubation 12–16 days, nestling period 16–25 days. 8 species.

### 4/ BOHEMIAN WAXWING
*Bombycilla garrulus*

RANGE: breeds N Eurasia and North America; irregular winter migrant to temperate areas S to 35°N
HABITAT: breeds in dense coniferous or mixed forest; occasionally found in town parks and gardens in winter
SIZE: 8 in (20 cm)

The beautiful pinkish-buff plumage of the Bohemian Waxwing is offset by yellow tips to the tail feathers, and waxlike red blobs at the tips of the secondary wing feathers, from which the common name of this species is derived. During their courtship display, the male presents the female with a berry or ant pupa, which the birds then pass back and forth from beak to beak but never swallow.

### 5/ PHAINOPEPLA
*Phainopepla nitens*

RANGE: breeds SW USA, S to Baja California and C Mexico; winters in S
HABITAT: brushland, river banks and chaparral in wetter areas
SIZE: 8 in (20 cm)

The flight of this species is buoyant and fluttery, but direct and often very high. Its call note is a querulous whistled *warp*, and its brief warbling song is seldom heard. The Phainopepla is particularly fond of mistletoe berries and also takes winged insects in flycatcherlike style. The male builds the well-concealed, cuplike tree nest. The first, early spring nesting is usually followed by a second nesting in a cooler, wetter habitat.

### 6/ GRAY HYPOCOLIUS
*Hypocolius ampelinus*

RANGE: breeds SW Asia and Middle East; occasional migrant to Himalayan foothills, N India and Pakistan
HABITAT: fields, scrub and gardens in semiarid climates
SIZE: 8½ in (22 cm)

These sociable birds communicate with squeaking calls. Outside the breeding season, small groups of them feed together on fruits, berries and the occasional insect. Both male and female build the bulky and untidy nest, generally well concealed among the leaves of a palm tree. If disturbed, the birds desert the nest and reputedly return and destroy it before building another.

## FAMILY DULIDAE
### Palmchat

There is only one species in this family.

## 7/ PALMCHAT
*Dulus dominicus*

RANGE: **Hispaniola, Gonave (West Indies)**
HABITAT: **open woodland, palms, pines**
SIZE: **7 in (18 cm)**

The Palmchat is sometimes included in the waxwing family, but its plumage is much coarser and it has a heavier bill. Palmchats are sociable birds which live in large communal nests woven around the trunk and base of the fronds of a royal palm tree. Some nests have housed as many as 30 pairs, each with a separate entrance burrow in the side of the mass leading into its own compartment.

Palmchats characteristically perch very close together and are often noisy and aggressive, a whole group suddenly making raucous calls, then falling silent. They spend almost all their time in trees, where they feed on berries and flowers.

## FAMILY CINCLIDAE
### Dippers

Small, plump, short-tailed, with long, strong legs and feet. Sexes similar. Unique among passerines in being adapted to swim, dive and walk under water. Movable membrane over nostrils, closed when head submerged. Characteristically bob their whole bodies up and down (hence name). Soft, long, dense plumage; chiefly black, brown or gray, in some species with white cap, back or "bib." Nest large, globe-shaped, built over running water. Eggs 4–5, white. Incubation 12–18 days, nestling period 19–24 days. 5

## 8/ WHITE-THROATED DIPPER
*Cinclus cinclus*

RANGE: **Europe and C Asia**
HABITAT: **fast-flowing upland streams**
SIZE: **7–8¼ in (18–21 cm)**

The White-throated Dipper has a rich diet of insect larvae, fish fry and fish eggs, freshwater shrimp and mollusks. Male and female both build the dome-shaped nest of moss, grass and leaves, with an entrance directly over running water. The birds generally roost communally during the winter. The race illustrated is *C. c. gularis*, from western and northern Britain. By contrast, the race *C. c. cinclus*, from northern Europe, has a black belly, while the race *C. c. leucogaster* of central Asia has a white belly.

## 9/ NORTH AMERICAN DIPPER
*Cinclus mexicanus*

RANGE: **Alaska to S Mexico**
HABITAT: **fast-flowing upland streams from 2,000 ft (600 m) up to the tree line**
SIZE: **7–8¼ in (18–21 cm)**

The North American Dipper is territorial in the summer, and to a variable extent during the winter, unless frozen streams force it to move to lower altitudes. Like other dippers, it has a well-developed, whitish nictitating membrane which protects its eyes from spray and when it is submerged. A dipper uses this membrane, which appears dramatically white against its dark head plumage, in a blinking action to signal alarm, excitement or aggression, combining it with the bobbing, or "dipping," of its body.

## FAMILY TROGLODYTIDAE
### Wrens

Small, agile insect-eaters, with short wings and plump bodies; many species with cocked-up tails. Plumage generally brown, chestnut, gray or black, often barred or streaked, some species with white cap, back or "bib." Sexes similar. Nest in cavities, roofed, with side entrance, some with access tunnel. Eggs 2–10, white or white with reddish speckles. Incubation 12–20 days, nestling period 12–18 days. 69 species.

## 10/ BLACK-CAPPED DONACOBIUS
*Donacobius atricapillus*

RANGE: **E Panama to Bolivia, N Argentina**
HABITAT: **marsh vegetation, swampy river bank scrub, wet meadows**
SIZE: **9 in (23 cm)**

The Black-capped Donacobius is the largest of all species of wren. When disturbed from cover, this species typically flies to an open perch on marsh grasses where it scolds. During displays, pair members perch together and each bobs its head and wags its tail. Orange patches of skin on the neck are often exposed, and the pair calls antiphonally.

## 11/ BICOLORED WREN
*Campylorhynchus griseus*

RANGE: **Colombia, Venezuela, N Brazil, Guyana**
HABITAT: **semiarid to arid savanna, cactus scrub, open woods, some habitats near human habitations**
SIZE: **8½ in (22 cm)**

This large, bold and conspicuous wren is usually found on or close to the ground, poking and peering into crevices in search of insects and their eggs. Its song is less guttural and scratchy than those of its close relatives, though the Giant Wren *C. chiapensis* of southeastern Mexico has similar characteristics of song, plumage and behavior, and is sometimes considered to be merely a race of the Bicolored Wren.

## 12/ ROCK WREN
*Salpinctes obsoletus*

RANGE: **breeds W Canada and NW USA to Costa Rica; winters in N breeding areas**
HABITAT: **arid and semiarid rocky barrens**
SIZE: **6 in (15 cm)**

The Rock Wren is distinguished from other wrens by its cinnamon rump and the buff tips of its outer tail feathers. It survives in a harsh rock-strewn environment, with little or no vegetation, by eating a variety of small insects and worms.

Its harsh and gritty song is reminiscent of that of the Northern Mockingbird *Mimus polyglottos* or the Brown Thrasher *Toxostoma rufum*.

Both male and female build a cup nest of any available materials beneath overhanging rocks or in a rock crevice. Often they construct a path of rock chips, and occasionally small bones and other objects, leading to the entrance.

## 13/ SEDGE WREN
*Cistothorus platensis*

RANGE: **breeds S Canada to E and C USA, C Mexico S to W Panama; winters in SE USA, E Mexico**
HABITAT: **wet, grassy meadows, drier bogs and marshes dominated by sedges**
SIZE: **4¼ in (11 cm)**

The Sedge Wren is slightly smaller than its relative the Marsh Wren *C. palustris*, but its song is quite distinct – a weak, staccato, chattering trill, often delivered at night. Its call note, a robust *chip*, is often doubled. As with other wrens, the male constructs dummy nests, from which the female selects one for egg laying.

## 14/ ZAPATA WREN
*Ferminia cerverai*     R

RANGE: **Zapata Swamp (Cuba)**
HABITAT: **sawgrass and woody hummocks in drier parts of the swamp**
SIZE: **6¼ in (16 cm)**

The Zapata Wren is the only wren native to the Greater Antilles. Almost flightless, this species was only discovered in 1926, and by 1974 it had become extremely rare. Any draining of the swamp could further jeopardize this wren and 2 other Zapata Swamp endemics, the Zapata Rail *Cyanolimnas cerverai* and the Zapata Sparrow *Torreornis inexpectata*.

## 15/ WINTER WREN
*Troglodytes troglodytes*

RANGE: **breeds C and S Canada, Alaska, coastal W USA, parts of E USA, Europe, Asia E to Japan, N Africa; N populations winter to S**
HABITAT: **woodland, gardens, cultivated land, moors, heaths, rocky islands**
SIZE: **3 in (8 cm)**

The tiny, cock-tailed Winter Wren, the only wren that occurs in the Old World, is equally at home in a damp, broad-leaved wood, in the gorse and bracken of an upland moor, or on the cliffs of a windswept Atlantic or Pacific island.

There are nearly 40 races, including *T. t. indigenus* of the British mainland, *T. t. zetlandicus* of the Shetland Islands and *T. t. helleri* of Kodiak Island, off Alaska. Races are paler in hot, desert regions, darker in wetter places.

## 16/ FLUTIST WREN
*Microcerculus ustulatus*

RANGE: **S Venezuela, Guyana, N Brazil**
HABITAT: **humid mountain forest**
SIZE: **4¾ in (12 cm)**

As its name suggests, the song of this wren has a flutelike character. It can start with 3–4 single notes and end with a long ascending whistle, or consist of a descending series of high-pitched whistles and may last up to 30 seconds.

The Flutist Wren lives in dense and humid cloud forest at altitudes of 2,800–7,000 ft (850–2,100 m). It spends much of its time alone foraging for insects on the ground and in the forest understory.

# MOCKINGBIRDS, ACCENTORS, THRUSHES

GRAY CATBIRD

NORTHERN MOCKINGBIRD

juv

BROWN THRASHER

ALPINE ACCENTOR

juv

BROWN TREMBLER

juv

DUNNOCK

BLUE SHORTWING

race *cruralis* ♀

♂

RUFOUS SCRUB-ROBIN

NIGHTINGALE

juv

EUROPEAN ROBIN

juv

♂ race *svecica*

BLUETHROAT

race *cyanecula* ♂

juv

RED-CAPPED ROBIN-CHAT

# MOCKINGBIRDS, ACCENTORS, THRUSHES

## FAMILY MIMIDAE
### Mockingbirds

Small to medium, long-tailed birds. Plumage usually brown or gray above and paler but marked below; brighter in some. Sexes similar. Cup nest. Eggs 2–5, whitish to greenish-blue, often with dark markings. Incubation 12–13 days, nestling period 12–13 days. 30 species.

## 1/ GRAY CATBIRD
*Dumetella carolinensis*

RANGE: **breeds S Canada, USA; winters Central America, West Indies**
HABITAT: **dense vegetation in woodland edge; readily adapts to human settlements**
SIZE: **7¾ in (20 cm)**

The Gray Catbird often forages on the ground and has a habit of flinging leaves about during its search for food. Its diet includes a variety of fruits and invertebrates. Since it can survive on fruit alone, it can winter occasionally in some northern areas. This bird is well known for the catlike cries that give it its name and is a versatile mimic.

A nocturnal migrant, the Gray Catbird often arrives in the southern USA in spring in large waves. Nesting activities begin soon after arrival. The female builds a low, well-concealed nest in dense thickets, bushes, small trees or tangles of vines. The male provides some help by bringing materials such as twigs, strips of bark, leaves, grasses and even paper and string. Usually 2 broods are raised in one season, the nestlings of the first brood being fed mostly with insects, while those of the second receive much fruit. Gray Catbirds are aggressive in defense of their nests and young.

## 2/ NORTHERN MOCKINGBIRD
*Mimus polyglottos*

RANGE: **S Canada, USA, Mexico, Caribbean islands; introduced to Bermuda, Hawaiian islands**
HABITAT: **open areas in cities, suburbs, countryside, deserts**
SIZE: **9–11 in (23–28 cm)**

Despite its rather drab gray and white plumage, the Northern Mockingbird is a familiar and popular species, chosen as the state bird for 5 states of the USA. It is an accomplished mimic, usually repeating learned phrases in each song. It is sometimes called the American Nightingale because of its habit of singing on moonlit nights. Its diet includes fruit, berries and invertebrates, and good sources of food are often vigorously defended against all competing species.

This bird's habit of wing flashing – pausing as it runs along the ground and deliberately raising and partially opening its wings – is a common but, as yet, poorly explained form of behavior. Some ornithologists believe it may be a way of startling potential prey out of hiding.

Breeding begins as early as mid-February. The nests are open cups composed of sticks and lined with fine grasses, rootlets, leaves and plant down. Pieces of string, cotton, plastic and hair are often incorporated into the nest, which is usually well concealed in a bush or the lower branches of a tree, often near human dwellings.

## 3/ BROWN THRASHER
*Toxostoma rufum*

RANGE: **E USA and S Canada to the foothills of the Rocky Mountains**
HABITAT: **woodland, forest edge, hedgerows, scrubland, pastures, gardens**
SIZE: **9¾ in (25 cm)**

This well-known species is most commonly observed skulking along the ground in search of food, or singing on an exposed perch. It typically forages by poking through leaves and other ground cover with its bill, occasionally pausing to pick up leaves and toss them aside. It feeds mostly on insects, but also eats other invertebrates and some small vertebrates. Fruits and acorns also contribute to its diet, especially in winter.

Breeding begins as early as March in the southern part of the range and continues through July. The male sings from the top of a tree or tall shrub, head held high and long tail drooping. His song is a series of rapid, short, musical phrases, usually uttered in pairs; it resembles the song of the Northern Mockingbird, but is wilder. The nest is a bulky cup of sticks, lined with dead leaves, grasses and fine rootlets. It is often placed in thorny bushes to provide added protection.

## 4/ BROWN TREMBLER
*Cinclocerthia ruficauda*

RANGE: **Lesser Antilles**
HABITAT: **rain forest; also secondary forest**
SIZE: **9–9¾ in (23–25 cm)**

This uncommon species – named for its strange and unexplained habit of violently shaking – has been driven from much of its former range by a combination of human predation, habitat destruction and the introduction of predators. The Brown Trembler feeds on seeds, fruit, large invertebrates and small vertebrates such as frogs and lizards.

It moves about chiefly by hopping on the ground and through vegetation and by making short, direct flights. It has also been observed flapping upward in trees, hanging upside-down and clinging vertically like a woodpecker. It nests in tree cavities, hollow tree-fern stumps and, less commonly, at the bases of palm fronds.

## FAMILY PRUNELLIDAE
### Accentors

Small. Plumage streaked rufous or brownish-gray above, grayish with rufous-brown markings below. Sexes similar. Nest on ground, in low vegetation or in rock crevices. Eggs 3–6, pale bluish-green to blue. Incubation 11–15 days, nestling period 12–14 days. 12 species.

## 5/ ALPINE ACCENTOR
*Prunella collaris*

RANGE: **from Iberia and NW Africa E through S and E Asia to Japan**
HABITAT: **breeds in rocky areas and alpine meadows from about 5,000 ft (1,500 m) to at least 16,500 ft (3,300 m); usually winters lower down**
SIZE: **7 in (18 cm)**

The accentors have the distinction of being the only family of birds that is almost entirely restricted to the Palearctic region. The Alpine Accentor has a huge range within this region, but it normally occurs only at high altitudes, where it is well adapted to survive the harsh conditions.

The Alpine Accentor is a larger and stouter bird than any other accentor, with quite colorful plumage. It has rippling, larklike calls, and a larklike song, uttered from the ground, from a perch or often in a brief, larklike song-flight.

Alpine Accentors regularly breed as high as 16,500 ft (5,000 m) in central Asia, and in the Himalayas they have been seen even at an altitude of almost 26,250 ft (8,000 m) on Mount Everest. In winter, they usually move down to the lower slopes in family parties and small flocks, although they usually stay above 5,000 ft (1,500 m). They sometimes peck at crumbs in ski resorts and also visit bird tables. Isolation on various mountain ranges has resulted in the evolution of some 9 different races distinguished by generally slight details of plumage.

## 6/ DUNNOCK
*Prunella modularis*

RANGE: **Europe S to C Spain and Italy and E to the Urals, Lebanon, Turkey, N Iran, Caucasus**
HABITAT: **scrub, heathland, mixed woodland, young coniferous forest, farmland hedgerows, parks, gardens, vacant urban land, scrubby coastal cliffs and dunes**
SIZE: **5$\frac{1}{2}$ in (14 cm)**

This generally unobtrusive little bird spends much of its time in cover among shrubs and hedgerows, but also forages on the open ground for its food with a curious, shuffling, jerky, rather mouselike gait; it can also hop. In winter it feeds mainly on seeds and in summer eats chiefly insects and their larvae.

At one time it was known in the British Isles as the Hedge Sparrow, from the superficial similarity of its plumage to that of a female House Sparrow. Because of its typical accentor appearance, the name Hedge Accentor is perhaps the most satisfactory, but the bird is generally known in Britain by its old English name Dunnock, from its gray-brown, or dun, coloration.

The Dunnock has interesting breeding habits. The birds establish 3 different types of territory: those held by a solitary male, those held by a conventional male-female pair, and larger territories held by a male-female pair plus an additional male. The extra male in the last type of territory sometimes mates with the female, helps the other male defend the territory and helps feed the young. The situation is further complicated by the regular occurrence of associations between 1 male and 2 or even 3 females, and between 2 or 3 males and 2 to 4 females.

## FAMILY TURDIDAE
**Thrushes**

Small to medium. Plumage variable, some mostly brown or gray, others brightly colored. Sexes alike or dissimilar. Nest sites variable. Eggs 1–10, pale, often speckled. Incubation 12–15 days, nestling period 12–15 days. 329 species.

## 7/ BLUE SHORTWING
*Brachypteryx montana*

RANGE: **E Nepal to W and S China, Taiwan, Philippines, Borneo, Sumatra, Java**
HABITAT: **upland forest thickets of rhododendron and oak**
SIZE: **6 in (15 cm)**

The 6 species of shortwing are insectivorous, wrenlike birds, with short tails and rounded wings. They breed mainly in Southeast Asia and the islands of Indonesia. The Blue, or White-browed, Shortwing is typical of the group in its preference for dense undergrowth in evergreen forests. In the mountain forests of northern Burma it ranges as high as 8,500 ft (2,600 m).

There are some 13 races, differing mainly in plumage details. In some, such as the race *B. m. cruralis* from the Himalayas, northern Burma and western China, the female is brown, while in others, such as *B. m. poliogyna* from north and central Luzon and Mindoro in the Philippines, she

is similar to the male but with a chestnut-brown head and neck. In some races, some males have the brown female plumage.

The female lays 3 white eggs inside a domed nest, built against clumps of moss on a tree trunk or on a rock. The side entrance runs parallel with the face of the trunk or rock and is hidden from view. Nevertheless, the nest is sometimes parasitized by the Small Cuckoo *Cuculus poliocephalus*, which lays its own eggs inside.

## 8/ RUFOUS SCRUB-ROBIN
*Erythropygia galactotes*

RANGE: **Mediterranean, SW Asia E to Pakistan, C Asia**
HABITAT: **open grassland, scrub, stony country, oases, parks, gardens**
SIZE: **6 in (15 cm)**

The Rufous Scrub-Robin is intermediate in form between the thrushes and the warblers. It stands high off the ground on its long pinkish-gray legs and it can cock its long rufous tail up over its back to create a *U* shape. Although it is sometimes rather skulking by nature, it is not a particularly shy bird. The male's song is rich and flutelike and is often uttered during the display flight.

The diet of this species includes worms, ants and beetles, as well as fruit. The nest is a loose structure of grasses and twigs placed in a shrub about 6 ft (2 m) above the ground. Its lining of wool and plant down sometimes includes fragments of snake skin. Populations of this bird that breed in sub-Saharan Africa are sedentary, while those of North Africa and Eurasia winter in the south of their range.

## 9/ EUROPEAN ROBIN
*Erithacus rubecula*

RANGE: **Europe and N Africa E to W Siberia and N Iran**
HABITAT: **woodland and forest; also gardens, parks in Britain**
SIZE: **5$\frac{1}{2}$ in (14 cm)**

The European Robin has an upright, bold stance on the ground, regularly flicking its wings and tail. It is commonly seen as it flits from one low perch to another, and the red breast figures prominently in the bird's display. Continental European races are shy, but in Britain, where this species is the national bird, many can be seen around human habitations. Most populations are resident, and their songs can be heard for much of the year. The European Robin is larely monogamous, and both sexes defend winter territories. Although they are very aggressive birds, they rarely make physical contact during fights. When they do, one may peck the other to death.

Invertebrates form the basic diet of European Robins, although the birds will eat seeds and fruit during cold, winter weather. Nesting takes place in hollows in banks, holes in trees and walls, and in an extraordinary variety of artificial items including discarded cans, kettles and even unmade beds. The nest is a cup of moss, feathers and sometimes plastic strips, built on a base of leaves.

## 10/ NIGHTINGALE
*Luscinia megarhynchos*

RANGE: **NW Africa, Eurasia S to Caucasus, E to Altai range; winters Nigeria E to Kenya, Tanzania**
HABITAT: **woodland, dense hedges, thickets near water, shrubland**
SIZE: **6$\frac{1}{2}$ in (16.5 cm)**

The somberly colored Nightingale has declined in numbers in Britain, France and some other parts of Europe. The Nightingale is richly praised for its fine song, which consists of deep, plaintive notes, trills and slurred *jug-jugs*. It sings both at night and in the daytime.

This species forages on the ground and in the dense vegetation under the shrub layer, searching for insects such as ants and beetles. In late summer it will also eat berries and soft fruits. The nest is well hidden among nettles or ivy in a dark spot usually on or close to the ground. The typical clutch contains 4–5 olive-green eggs.

## 11/ BLUETHROAT
*Luscinia svecica*

RANGE: **Eurasia, W Alaska**
HABITAT: **wooded tundra, alpine meadows, dry, stony slopes, shrubby wetlands**
SIZE: **5$\frac{1}{2}$ in (14 cm)**

There are some 10 races of this delightful little bird across its vast range. In some, such as *L. s. svecica* of the northernmost latitudes, the center of the blue throat patch is red, while in others, such as *L. s. cyanecula* of Spain, central Europe and parts of western USSR, the center spot is white.

The Bluethroat flies close to the ground with a flitting action, followed by a flat glide or swoop into low cover. It has a more upright stance on the ground than the European Robin, but, like that species, frequently flicks its tail. The song is more tinkling than that of the Nightingale. It may be uttered in the air or from a perch and often dominates the sounds of the Arctic tundra.

The Bluethroat's diet consists largely of insects, sometimes caught in the air, but usually found by turning over leaf litter. The cup-shaped nest is built on the ground in thick vegetation, in a clump of grass, under a shrub, or sometimes in a hollow in a bank.

## 12/ RED-CAPPED ROBIN-CHAT
*Cossypha natalensis*

RANGE: **South Africa N to Somalia, SW Ethiopia, W to Cameroon**
HABITAT: **dense evergreen forest and undergrowth**
SIZE: **7$\frac{3}{4}$ in (20 cm)**

The genus *Cossypha* contains some of the most distinctively marked of the so-called African robins. Although its plumage is striking, the Red-capped, or Natal, Robin-Chat is a shy bird and could be overlooked were it not for its loud, warbling songs which often mimic other birds.

Nowhere very common, this species has extended its choice of habitat to include deciduous as well as evergreen forests. Its diet consists mostly of insects and fruit. Both sexes build the nest, placing it among branches, creepers or mossy boulders.

FIRE-CRESTED ALETHE

WHITE-THROATED ROBIN

♂

♀

♀

♂

COMMON REDSTART

ASIAN
MAGPIE-ROBIN

PHILIPPINE WATER REDSTART

HODGSON'S GRANDALA

♀

juv

♂

EASTERN BLUEBIRD

404

WHITE-CROWNED FORKTAIL

♂ GREEN COCHOA

♂ STONECHAT

race *hibernans*

♀

ARNOT'S CHAT

♂ ♀

♂ ROCK THRUSH

♀

DESERT WHEATEAR

race *homochroa* ♂

## 1/ FIRE-CRESTED ALETHE
*Alethe castanea*
RANGE: C Africa
HABITAT: tropical forest
SIZE: 6¼–6¾ in (16–17 cm)

One of 6 species of alethe or forest-robin, this bird is somewhat thrushlike, with long legs. It is active and pugnacious, erecting its tawny orange crest and spreading its tail when excited or threatened.

Fire-crested Alethes search for insects in the shaded undergrowth of tropical forests. They often associate with parties of safari ants that march across the ground. The advancing ants disturb insects in their path, which the birds wait to snap up.

This species' nest is a cup of moss and roots placed on a tree stump or on a heap of leaf litter on the forest floor. The clutch consists of 2–3 pinkish eggs blotched with lilac or maroon.

## 2/ ASIAN MAGPIE-ROBIN
*Copsychus saularis*
RANGE: India, S China, Southeast Asia, Indonesia, Philippines
HABITAT: up to 6,500 ft (2,000 m) in scrub, around cultivation, gardens; also coastal mangroves
SIZE: 8 in (20 cm)

The magpie-robins occur in Africa and tropical Asia. They are sometimes known as shamas and tend to range in color from bluish to black. They are fine singers, and the Asian Magpie-Robin is no exception. Its loud, varied and melodious song is interspersed with some discordant notes and imitations of other birds' calls. It often cocks its tail while perching.

Asian Magpie-Robins are regularly seen hunting for insects in gardens in Borneo, and they are common in many towns in Peninsular Malaysia. They nest in holes, often in buildings and under the eaves of houses. The clutch consists of 3–6 eggs which are pale blue-green, blotched and mottled with reddish brown. They are incubated by both parents for 12–13 days.

## 3/ WHITE-THROATED ROBIN
*Irania gutturalis*
RANGE: Turkey to Afghanistan; winters S through Arabia and Iran to Kenya, Tanzania, Zimbabwe
HABITAT: stony slopes with shrubs, oak steppes up to 9,500 ft (2,850 m); dense scrub along dry riverbeds in winter
SIZE: 6¾ in (17.5 cm)

The male White-throated Robin is easy to recognize in his breeding range but may be confused with the robin-chats in his winter quarters. This species resembles a Nightingale *Luscinia megarhynchos* in its gait, moving across the ground with hops and drooping wings. In flight it reveals its long wings and tail. It often perches on weed stems, as well as bushes and stones. The male has a loud, fluid and melodious song.

White-throated Robins are monogamous. The female builds the nest in the lower part of a shrub or tree some 6–50 in (15–125 cm) above the ground. The nest has a base of dry twigs, bark or leaves and is lined with wool, hair, feathers or

even pieces of rag. The 4–5 greenish-blue eggs are spotted with yellow or brown spots. The young hatch after 13 days.

## 4/ COMMON REDSTART
*Phoenicurus phoenicurus*
RANGE: Europe, Asia S to Iran and E to Lake Baikal; winters S to Arabia and W and E Africa
HABITAT: forests with clearings, heaths, moors with scattered trees, parks, orchards; winters on savanna and woodland
SIZE: 5½ in (14 cm)

The Common Redstart is a small, elegant chat with rather long wings and an orange-chestnut tail that it characteristically quivers up and down. Its diet consists mainly of insects, and the male's aerial flycatching technique, as well as his prominent display flight, demand open spaces in its woodland habitat. The female feeds mainly on the ground. Both sexes supplement their diet with small snails, berries and fruit.

Common Redstarts often site their nests in tree holes, including those abandoned by woodpeckers. They may use cavities in stone walls in hilly country and will even nest in holes in the ground. The female lays and incubates 5–7 pale blue eggs, sometimes producing 2 broods in a single season.

## 5/ PHILIPPINE WATER REDSTART
*Rhyacornis bicolor*                    [?]
RANGE: Luzon Island (Philippines)
HABITAT: mountain streams
SIZE: 5½ in (14 cm)

The Philippine Water Redstart lives along clear mountain streams and rivers. It often occurs in rocky gorges and other inaccessible terrain. It feeds mainly on insects which it gleans from boulders among the torrents, but little else is known of its lifestyle.

The breeding habits of this bird are probably similar to those of its close relative, the Plumbeous Water Redstart *Phoenicurus fuliginosus*, which is found in the mountains of central, east and Southeast Asia. This species nests in stream banks and lays eggs of a whitish hue thickly speckled with brown marks.

## 6/ HODGSON'S GRANDALA
*Grandala coelicolor*
RANGE: Himalayas, mountains of SE Tibet and W China
HABITAT: boulder-strewn alpine meadows, rocky slopes, scree and cliffs above scrub zone
SIZE: 8¾ in (22 cm)

Hodgson's Grandala is a bird of the high mountains of Asia, foraging in scrub and on the open slopes up to 14,800 ft (4,500 m) above sea level. It feeds on insects, especially caterpillars and other larvae, as well as on seeds and berries. Occasionally, it turns to cultivated fruit. The only member of its genus, it is a short-legged, long-winged bird. When perched, it looks rather like a rock thrush, but in flight it more closely resembles a starling. It spends much of the time in the air and usually occurs in flocks.

The nest is a cup of dry grass, covered with moss and lined with feathers. It is built on a rock ledge, often on a vertical cliff. The clutch contains 2 greenish-white eggs with brown markings.

## 7/ EASTERN BLUEBIRD
*Sialia sialis*

RANGE: E North America and Central
America
HABITAT: **open woodland, roadsides,
farms, orchards, gardens, parks**
SIZE: $5\frac{1}{2}$–$7\frac{1}{2}$ in (14–19 cm)

Eastern Bluebirds often form flocks in autumn and winter and several birds may roost together in the same cavity during winter. Typically they have a hunched appearance when perching. They often fly down from their perch to catch insects on the ground. In colder months, berries become an important part of their diet. Nesting usually takes place in natural tree cavities and old woodpecker holes. Although the eggs of this species are typically blue, some individual females lay clutches of white eggs. Multiple broods are common, with 2 chicks often produced in a single season in northern areas, and up to 4 in southeastern USA.

In many areas, the Eastern Bluebird has declined in numbers because of competition for nest sites with other birds. The provision of nest-boxes by conservation organizations and concerned individuals has helped the species, however, and it has consequently made something of a comeback in recent years.

## 8/ WHITE-CROWNED FORKTAIL
*Enicurus leschenaulti*

RANGE: **Himalayas, S to Malaysia,
Indochina, Sumatra, Java and Borneo**
HABITAT: **rocky streams, forest rivers,
swamps**
SIZE: **8–11 in (20–28 cm)**

This is the largest and darkest of the 7 species of forktail, all of which have black and white plumage. It lives close to mountain torrents, where it forages for insects on the surface of the water or along rocky banks. Its penetrating alarm call is a high-pitched screech.

The White-crowned Forktail nests in crevices in vertical banks covered with ferns or in hollows in trees or rocks, where the nest is often soaking wet. It is built of green moss mixed with rootlets, fibers and dead leaves. Both sexes incubate the 3–4 cream or rich buff eggs which are densely marked with brick-red or brownish speckles.

## 9/ GREEN COCHOA
*Cochoa viridis* [?]

RANGE: **Himalayas and mountains of N
Southeast Asia**
HABITAT: **undergrowth, often near streams
in dense evergreen forest**
SIZE: **11–$11\frac{3}{4}$ in (28–30 cm)**

One of 3 species of cochoa, this bird haunts forested mountain slopes, usually 3,300–5,000 ft (1,000–1,500 m) above sea level. It is a shy and retiring species and lives singly or in pairs. It searches through the undergrowth for insects and other invertebrates and berries.

The nest is a shallow cup of green moss, leaves and fibers built in a tree. A white, threadlike fungus is typically present and this seems to be a characteristic feature of the nests of this genus. The clutch varies from 2–4; the eggs are sea-green with reddish-brown blotches.

## 10/ STONECHAT
*Saxicola torquata*

RANGE: **much of Eurasia and Africa**
HABITAT: **grassland, heaths, plantations,
coastal gorse**
SIZE: **5 in (12.5 cm)**

There are some 24 races of this widespread bird, including *S. t. hibernans* of the British Isles, western France and the west coast of the Iberian peninsula. The western races are residents or partial migrants, while the eastern ones are migratory, spending their winters in northeast Africa, Arabia, India and Southeast Asia. The species has declined in parts of western Europe after suffering hard winters and habitat changes.

The Stonechat uses low, exposed perches to spot its invertebrate prey, which it usually catches after a glide or hop to the ground. In spring the perch is usually about 3 ft (1 m) above the ground, but in summer, when the vegetation is taller, the preferred height is about 5 ft (1.6 m). The birds may also feed on small fish, lizards, seeds and berries and sometimes take fast-flying insects, such as flies, butterflies and moths, in flight or by hovering in front of foliage.

Stonechats are largely monogamous, each pair building its nest either on or very near the ground. The structure is a loose cup of unwoven grass stems or leaves with a lining of wool or hair. The female lays 4–6 pale bluish eggs with reddish-brown marks.

## 11/ ARNOT'S CHAT
*Myrmecocichla arnoti*

RANGE: **C, E and S Africa**
HABITAT: **open woodland, margins of
cultivated land**
SIZE: **7 in (18 cm)**

Sometimes known as the White-headed Black Chat, this species is now only locally common because of destruction of its forest habitat. It is a conspicuous, thickset bird, rather like a thrush, and has a loud, whistled song, which first rises then falls in pitch. This is often combined with mimicry of other bird calls. In addition, its wings make a noise when it flies. It forages at low level for spiders and insects, particularly ants, which are gathered from the gnarled trunks of trees and from the ground.

Arnot's Chat is fairly easy to observe and is generally seen in pairs or family parties. The nest is made of coarse plant material and sited in a hole or a hollow. The clutch contains 2–4 bluish or greenish eggs which are speckled with rufous or mauve markings.

## 12/ DESERT WHEATEAR
*Oenanthe deserti*

RANGE: **N Africa, Middle East, C Asia,
Mongolia**
HABITAT: **heaths, coasts, dunes, rocky
mountain passes; N and high-altitude S
breeders move to lower altitudes or
migrate S in winter**
SIZE: **$5\frac{1}{2}$–6 in (14–15 cm)**

One of a score of wheatear species, this bird occurs in a variety of dry, open habitats where there are sandy or stony soils. Most of its populations are migratory, although some are only partial migrants. The illustration shows the north African race *O. d. homochroa*, which has been seen in Britain as a rare vagrant.

The Desert Wheatear perches freely on low shrubs, mounds and stones from which it can watch the ground for ants, beetles and their larvae, spiders, worms and small lizards. Seeds may also form part of the diet.

In the breeding season, the male Desert Wheatear performs a song-flight up to 25–30 ft (8–10 m) into the air and utters a few mournful notes. The female builds a rather bulky nest of grass and dead leaves among stones, in a hole in the ground or in a rabbit burrow. The 4–5 pale blue eggs with reddish-brown spots are incubated by the female for 13–14 days.

## 13/ ROCK THRUSH
*Monticola saxatilis*

RANGE: **breeds NW Africa, S and C Europe
E to Lake Baikal and China; winters in W
Africa**
HABITAT: **rocky, shrubby terrain,
vineyards; savanna, stony gullies,
gardens in winter**
SIZE: **$7\frac{1}{4}$ in (18.5 cm)**

This bird of rocky terrain has a rather long body and looks more like a short-tailed chat than a thrush. It is essentially a ground bird, although it may also perch on trees, buildings and overhead wires. The Rock Thrush is shy and solitary on its breeding grounds, shooting behind boulders or plummeting down crags when disturbed.

The male has a far-carrying, mellow, piping or warbling song. He begins singing from a perch, then climbs steeply into the air with slow, powerful wing beats. His song reaches a peak at the top of his ascent, then he soars, flutters his wings quickly and mimics song phrases of other birds before parachuting silently down to earth.

The large insects on which the Rock Thrush feeds are obtained by swooping from a perch down to the ground or, more rarely, during flight. Many kinds of berries are also eaten. The nest site is a horizontal crack in the rock face, crag or ruin, or under a boulder. The female builds the nest from grass and moss and incubates 4–5 pale blue eggs with some speckles at the broader end.

BLUE WHISTLING THRUSH

VARIED THRUSH

♂

♀

RUFOUS-THROATED
SOLITAIRE

WHITE'S THRUSH

race *dauma*

ORANGE-BILLED
NIGHTINGALE-THRUSH

HERMIT THRUSH

WOOD THRUSH

♂

♀

BLACKBIRD

ISLAND THRUSH

race *layardi*

race *papuensis*

race *niveiceps*

juv

FIELDFARE

RED-LEGGED THRUSH

juv

CLAY-COLORED
ROBIN

AMERICAN ROBIN

AUSTRAL THRUSH

## 1/ RUFOUS-THROATED SOLITAIRE
*Myadestes genibarbis*
RANGE: **West Indies**
HABITAT: **mountain forest**
SIZE: **7½ in (19 cm)**

The Rufous-throated Solitaire is a tropical forest bird, with a diet consisting mainly of fruit but also including insects and other invertebrates. It obtains much of its food from a perched position, although it will occasionally hover and regularly darts out from a prominent perch to catch flying beetles and moths on the wing. Its song is a series of flutelike, whistling notes.

The cup nest consists primarily of moss and other plant material. It is built in the side of a bank, in a tree cavity, in the fork of a branch or in the heart of a tree fern or bromeliad. Each pair usually rears 2 chicks, which emerge from the egg with a covering of blackish natal down. Both parents take part in feeding the young.

## 2/ BLUE WHISTLING THRUSH
*Myiophoneus caeruleus*
RANGE: **C Asia, India, W China, Southeast Asia, Java, Sumatra**
HABITAT: **edges of mountain and forest streams; also limestone rock faces**
SIZE: **11¾–12½ in (30–32 cm)**

Sometimes known as the Whistling Schoolboy, this dark blue songbird with glistening blue spots is one of about 6 semiaquatic species within the thrush family. Its rich songs can be heard ringing out over the roar of tumbling waters as it forages on and around the wet rocks, damp moss and water surface for insects, snails and crustaceans.

Male and female Blue Whistling Thrushes look alike and each pair generally lives alone. Both adults share nest-building, incubation and the care of the young. The nest is a mossy cup often placed on a ledge in a small cave. The female lays 3–5 gray-green eggs with brown spots.

## 3/ WHITE'S THRUSH
*Zoothera dauma*
RANGE: **E Europe E to China and Japan, Southeast Asia, Indonesia, New Guinea, E and S Australia; N populations migrate S**
HABITAT: **woodland and forest**
SIZE: **10¼–11 in (26–28 cm)**

Usually shy and secretive, this large thrush feeds on the forest floor, turning over the dead leaves with its bill in its search for earthworms, snails and insects. It suddenly opens its wings and tail to panic insects into movement, and apparently also raises itself up on its toes and vibrates its whole body rapidly for several seconds to bring worms to the surface.

White's Thrush is usually solitary outside the breeding season, but birds from migratory populations may form small flocks when traveling.

There is much regional variation in the song: indeed, the analysis of their songs using sonagraphs formed part of the evidence that led to the recent separation of 2 Australian races into full species – the Bassian Thrush *Z. lunulata* and the Russet-tailed Ground Thrush *Z. heinei*. Races living in Siberia, Manchuria and Japan have a

haunting, melancholy song, consisting of repeated loud, fluting whistles, which may continue for hours on end, while those found in southern Asia, including *Z. d. dauma* of the Himalayas, southwest China and parts of Burma and Southeast Asia, have a typically thrushlike song.

## 4/ VARIED THRUSH
*Ixoreus naevius*
RANGE: **W coast of North America, from NC Alaska S to N California**
HABITAT: **moist coniferous forest**
SIZE: **7¾–9¾ in (20–25 cm)**

The Varied Thrush often forages on the ground, taking a variety of insects, snails, earthworms, seeds and fruit. In winter it migrates from the mountains to the valleys in search of food. The song is a long, vibrating whistle, followed by a pause and then a series of rapidly trilled notes all at different pitches.

The nesting season begins in late April. The female builds a bulky cup nest of twigs, moss and mud, lined with fine grasses, on the horizontal branch of a small tree. The clutch of 2–5 pale blue eggs with a few brown speckles is incubated solely by the female for about 14 days, but both sexes feed the nestlings. Juvenile Varied Thrushes resemble the females, but they have an incomplete breast band and speckling on the breast.

## 5/ ORANGE-BILLED NIGHTINGALE-THRUSH
*Catharus aurantiirostris*
RANGE: **Mexico, Central America, Venezuela, Colombia**
HABITAT: **low rain forest and cloud forest, forest edge, dense thickets, coffee plantations**
SIZE: **6½ in (17 cm)**

The Orange-billed Nightingale-Thrush is a shy, secretive bird that forages for invertebrates on the ground, near the ground in dense thickets or at low levels in trees. It has a poor voice compared with most other nightingale-thrushes; its simple song consisting of short, jumbled

warbles with a rather squeaky tone. Although it often sings uninterrupted for long periods, it usually does so from a concealed perch where it is difficult to observe. This bird also has a nasal *waa-a-a-a* call.

The bulky cup nest of moss and grass is generally built low in a thicket or shrub, and the average clutch consists of 2 pale blue eggs with brown spots. This species is parasitized by the Bronze Cowbird *Molothrus aeneus*.

## 6/ HERMIT THRUSH
*Catharus guttatus*
RANGE: **North and Central America**
HABITAT: **coniferous, deciduous or mixed woodland, forest edge, thickets**
SIZE: **6–7¾ in (15–20 cm)**

The Hermit Thrush has one of the most beautiful of all bird songs. The song has a clear, flutelike introductory note followed by a series of rising and falling phrases of different pitches. This bird has a habit of slowly raising and dropping its tail several times a minute while perched; this is usually accompanied by a low *chuck* call.

Hermit Thrushes forage mainly on the ground for insects, spiders, snails, earthworms and also salamanders. In winter, fruits and seeds make up an important part of their diet. The nest is a cup of twigs, dried grass, moss and, sometimes, mud, constructed by the female. In the eastern part of the bird's range, the nest is commonly built on the ground in a natural depression. In the west, it is usually placed in a low tree.

## 7/ WOOD THRUSH
*Hylocichla mustelina*
RANGE: **E North and Central America, from S Canada to Panama**
HABITAT: **woodland, wooded slopes, parks, often near streams**
SIZE: **7½–8½ in (19–22 cm)**

The Wood Thrush is a migratory species which winters in the south of its range. It has a rapid *pit-pit-pit* alarm call and, in addition, raises its head feathers when alarmed. This bird generally forages at ground level but also catches insect food among tree foliage.

Male Wood Thrushes first appear in the southern USA in March or April. They then move north and begin singing when they arrive in their nesting territories. The song consists of loud, flute-like phrases with 3–5 notes, each differing in pitch and ending with a soft, guttural trill. The female builds a bulky cup nest of dead leaves, moss and rootlets, the lack of grass distinguishing it from the nest of an American Robin. Often, a piece of white paper or cloth is included in the base.

## 8/ BLACKBIRD
*Turdus merula*

RANGE: **breeds NW Africa, Europe E to India, S China; N and some E populations winter S to Egypt, SW Asia, Southeast Asia; introduced to Australia, New Zealand**
HABITAT: **diverse, including forest, farmland, moors, scrub, gardens, parks, inner city**
SIZE: **9½–9¾ in (24–25 cm)**

The Blackbird is a familiar species throughout western Europe, where its melodious, fluty song is a common sound over a wide range of habitats. From its original woodland haunts, the bird has spread into gardens and even into the centers of towns and cities. Today, gardens harbor the densest populations, followed by parks and farmland. Densities are lowest deep in woodland, where the birds are often much shyer.

Blackbirds prise earthworms from the soil all year round and, by avidly turning over leaf litter, they catch a variety of insects and other invertebrates. They have a mixed diet, and at certain times of the year the fruits of hawthorn, holly, elder and yew provide an important source of food. Their nest is a substantial cup of grasses or roots, cemented together with wet leaves or mud. The usual clutch contains 3–5 pale greenish eggs with red-brown speckles.

## 9/ ISLAND THRUSH
*Turdus poliocephalus*

RANGE: **Christmas Island, Taiwan, Indonesia through Melanesia to Samoa and Fiji**
HABITAT: **dense rain forest and clearings**
SIZE: **9½–9¾ in (24–25 cm)**

In size, habits and call-notes, the Island Thrush resembles the Blackbird and the American Robin. There are about 50 races of this species reflecting its wide geographical range. Many are restricted to single islands or groups of islands, including *T.p. niveiceps* of Taiwan and *T.p. layardi* of Viti Levu Island, in Fiji, and *T.p. papuensis* of southeastern New Guinea.

The altitude at which Island Thrushes live differs from one island to another. In New Guinea, the birds occur above the tree line from 7,500 ft–13,500 ft (2,300 m–4,100 m). In Viti Levu, they range from sea level over 3,300 ft (1,000 m) up to the tops of the highest mountains. Island Thrushes are also found on low coral islands. They are basically ground-feeding birds, with a diet that includes worms and snails. They build their nests on rocky ledges.

## 10/ FIELDFARE
*Turdus pilaris*

RANGE: **breeds N Eurasia E to C Siberia, Greenland; winters widely in Europe, SW Asia**
HABITAT: **subarctic scrub, light coniferous and birch woodland, parks, gardens, towns; winters in open country, woodland edges, fields**
SIZE: **10¼ in (26 cm)**

This is a gregarious, noisy species of thrush that has colonized parts of western Europe, including parts of the British Isles, in recent years. It is essentially a migratory species that breeds in northern latitudes and usually only winters in the southern part of its range.

The Fieldfare eats many kinds of invertebrates, as well as plant food such as seeds and fruit. Fruit is especially important in autumn and winter, and the bird is a specialist feeder on apples and haws. The nest is a bulky cup of grass reinforced with roots and mud, usually placed in the fork of a tree. The typical clutch consists of 5–6 pale blue eggs with brown markings. When defending their young, the adults will readily and accurately "bomb" predators with their droppings.

## 11/ RED-LEGGED THRUSH
*Turdus plumbeus*

RANGE: **West Indies**
HABITAT: **forest areas in mountains and lowlands, gardens, city lawns**
SIZE: **9¾–11 in (25–28 cm)**

This striking bird is the most widespread of the West Indian thrushes. Its plumage varies among the islands, the chin and throat ranging from white to black, and the belly from reddish yellow to gray and white. Its song is rather weak and melancholy and, when disturbed, the bird utters a loud *wet-wet* call, sometimes repeatedly.

The Red-legged Thrush frequents a variety of habitats. In some areas it is shy and difficult to observe, while in others it is quite bold and easy to watch. It commonly forages on the ground, making loud, rustling sounds as it searches under dead leaves for insects. It has an omnivorous diet, including insects, reptiles and fruit. The cup nest is built in a bush, in the fork of a branch or among the fronds of a palm.

## 12/ AUSTRAL THRUSH
*Turdus falcklandii*

RANGE: **Chile, Argentina, Falkland Islands, Juan Fernandez Islands**
HABITAT: **farmland with some trees, groves of willows, forest borders**
SIZE: **9¾–10½ in (25–27 cm)**

The Austral Thrush frequently feeds on the ground, hopping about on grassy areas and cocking its head from side to side to look for earthworm burrows. It takes insects and other arthropods from the ground or from plant debris and also feeds on fruit. The territorial song, which is made up of repeated whistled phrases such as *tee-yoo*, *churr* and *tee*, is delivered from a conspicuous perch. This species also utters an alarm call *kreep* in rapid succession.

The nesting season of the Austral Thrush runs

from September to January, with each pair producing up to 3 broods per season. The bulky nest of grasses often has a base of mud. The female carries out the incubation, but both adults are active in feeding the nestlings.

## 13/ CLAY-COLORED ROBIN
*Turdus grayi*

RANGE: **SE Mexico, Central America, coastal Colombia**
HABITAT: **open woodland, woodland edge and clearings, usually near streams**
SIZE: **9–9½ in (23–24 cm)**

The Clay-colored Robin is one of the best known tropical American songsters, with a musical, caroling song. A generalist in feeding habits, it spends much of its time on the ground searching for insects, earthworms, slugs and lizards. Fruit also forms part of its diet, and it has been known to come to feeding stations for bananas. Although somewhat secretive and solitary, it often lives close to human settlements.

The nesting season usually lasts from March to June, but it varies from region to region. In central Panama, for example, the birds nest mainly during the dry season from December to April. They build a bulky cup nest of mud, moss, twigs, leaves and other plant materials, the structure placed low in a small bush or in dense cover in a tree. Incubation of the 2–4 eggs takes 12–13 days, with the young hatching at different times.

## 14/ AMERICAN ROBIN
*Turdus migratorius*

RANGE: **North America**
HABITAT: **forest borders, woodland, parks, lawns, suburbs**
SIZE: **9–11 in (23–28 cm)**

Like the much smaller European Robin, this species is also known colloquially as the Robin Redbreast. It is the largest of the North American thrushes and is a very common and well-known bird. It is a habitat generalist, occurring in almost any environment with cover, from city suburbs to western mountainsides 12,000 ft (3,600 m) high.

American Robins usually feed on grassy ground, cocking their heads to search for earthworm burrows. Experiments have shown that the birds locate earthworms by sight rather than sound, as was previously believed. Their diet also includes insects, snails and much fruit, especially in winter.

In the southern portion of its range, the American Robin has both resident and migratory populations. Migration northward begins in February, with the males leaving first. The females arrive in the north in April, by which time the males have started singing. The song is a musical caroling of short rising and falling phrases, sometimes described as *cheerily cheer-up cheerio*. Both male and female build the bulky cup nest of protruding twigs, grass and mud. This is placed in any sheltered location, from the ground to the treetops. The birds may also nest on buildings and fences. Each year, 2, or sometimes 3, broods may be raised. The male will care for the young of the first brood while the female incubates the second clutch.

# LOGRUNNERS, BABBLERS

EASTERN WHIPBIRD

♀

race *pulcher*

♂

MID-MOUNTAIN RAIL-BABBLER

♂

race *castanonota*

PALE-BREASTED THRUSH-BABBLER

race *albicollis*

WHISKERED YUHINA

race *temporalis*

GRAY-CROWNED BABBLER

race *flavicollis*

LARGE WREN-BABBLER

race *rubeculus*

WREN-TIT

race *fasciata*

WHITE-NECKED TREE-BABBLER

race *leucolophus*

RED-BILLED LEIOTHRIX

WHITE-CRESTED LAUGHING-THRUSH

race *bicolor*

race *strigula*

CHESTNUT-TAILED MINLA

race *malayana*

CHESTNUT-HEADED FULVETTA

race *caudatus*

COMMON BABBLER

young in nest

WHITE-NECKED ROCKFOWL

413

## FAMILY ORTHONYCHIDAE
**Logrunners**

Small to medium, secretive birds. Plumage mainly brown, black or white; some brighter, with blue, chestnut and olive-green. Sexes alike or different. Cup or domed nest, usually in dense shrubs. Eggs 1–3, white or pale blue. Incubation 17–21 days, nestling period 12–14 days. 19 species.

### 1/ EASTERN WHIPBIRD
*Psophodes olivaceus*

RANGE: E coast of Australia from N Queensland to Victoria
HABITAT: thick shrubbery in wet forest, dense heath
SIZE: $9\frac{3}{4}$–$11\frac{3}{4}$ in (25–30 cm)

The Eastern Whipbird is a secretive species. It takes its name from the contact call uttered while pairs forage out of sight of each other in thick cover. The male gives a long whistle ending in a sharp whip-crack, and this is answered by 2 or 3 chirrups from the female.

Eastern Whipbirds make low, short flights on their short wings, with their long tails fanned. Usually, however, they bounce along the ground and through shrubs, sometimes raising their short crests. They feed on insects and larvae by raking through leaf litter with their bills and feet and by probing into crevices and low shrubbery. The nest is a cup of twigs built in the thick foliage of the understory layer. The young leave the nest before they can fly and are guarded by the adults while they hide in the undergrowth.

### 2/ MID-MOUNTAIN RAIL-BABBLER
*Ptilorrhoa castanonota*

RANGE: New Guinea, Batanta Island, Yapen Island
HABITAT: lower mountain forest
SIZE: 9 in (23 cm)

The 3 species of rail-babbler replace each other altitudinally in New Guinea. This species, which is also known as the Chestnut-backed Jewel-Babbler, is as handsome as its relatives and, like them, has several races that differ in plumage details. Those illustrated are *P. c. pulcher* of southeastern New Guinea and *P. c. castanonota* from the Vogelkop region of New Guinea.

The Mid-mountain Rail-Babbler has a beautiful song of clear, bell-like whistles, uttered from the ground or from a fallen log. Pairs or small groups of this species often occur together, walking on the ground and foraging in the leaf litter or probing in the earth on the forest floor.

## FAMILY TIMALIIDAE
**Babblers**

Small to medium, thrushlike. Plumage diverse: many species brown and gray; many dense forest species brighter, with red, blue, yellow. Sexes similar, except in some colorful groups. Nest open or domed, usually in bushes or trees. Eggs 2–7, various colors. Incubation 13–16 days, nestling period 13–16 days (except for rockfowls: incubation 24 days, nestling period 26 days). 256 species.

### 3/ PALE-BREASTED THRUSH-BABBLER
*Illadopsis rufipennis*

RANGE: W Africa E to Kenya and Tanzania
HABITAT: forests
SIZE: $5\frac{1}{2}$ in (14 cm)

There are few groups of birds that conceal themselves more effectively or are more drab in plumage than this African babbler and its close relatives. A sedentary species of thick forest, the Pale-breasted Thrush-Babbler spends its life either on or close to the forest floor. It is quite possible to spend weeks in a forest where these birds are comparatively common without ever catching a glimpse of one.

There is some evidence that this species is most active at dawn and dusk, when it seems to forage more widely for insects and small mollusks. In the fading light, it can sometimes be seen on paths and in clearings. The call is thought to be a series of ascending whistled notes, since this sound is commonly heard when these birds are about. The breeding habits are apparently unknown.

### 4/ GRAY-CROWNED BABBLER
*Pomatostomus temporalis*

RANGE: N and E Australia
HABITAT: open woodland
SIZE: $9\frac{3}{4}$ in (25 cm)

The Gray-crowned Babbler is a perky, excitable bird with a slender, downcurved bill. It lives in family groups of up to 12 individuals, which defend communal territories. Each group usually consists of a pair or trio and their offspring from previous years. These all forage together, bounding along the ground or along branches, and making short, weak, fluttering and gliding flights. They feed on invertebrates and lizards by probing into leaf litter, soil, foliage and bark crevices, or by turning over rocks, sticks and cowpats.

Each group builds many nests, some of which are used only for roosting: these are bulky, globular stick nests, with a side entrance. The normal clutch consists of 2–3 pale brown, finely pencilled eggs. These are incubated by the female. More than one female may lay in the nest. The whole group cooperates to feed the sitting female and young. The 2 races of this species shown here are *P. t. temporalis* of southern Queensland and eastern New South Wales and *P. t. rubeculus* of northern and northwestern Australia.

### 5/ LARGE WREN-BABBLER
*Napothera macrodactyla*

RANGE: Malay Peninsula, Java, Sumatra
HABITAT: forests
SIZE: $7\frac{1}{2}$ in (19 cm)

The Large Wren-Babbler is a dumpy, short-tailed bird of dense forest undergrowth. It occurs in lowland rather than hill forest, and must therefore be under greater threat from logging operations than some of its highland relatives.

This bird's song is a series of repeated whistles. However, it is often very difficult to catch sight of the singing bird among the rotting debris and sun-dappled obscurity of the forest floor. The habits of this species are not well known, although nesting has been recorded in West Java in March and September. The nest is a large, cup-shaped construction sited in a thicket, and the female lays a clutch of 2 buff-colored eggs, speckled with red.

### 6/ WHITE-NECKED TREE-BABBLER
*Stachyris leucotis*

RANGE: S Thailand to Sumatra, Borneo
HABITAT: forests
SIZE: 6 in (15 cm)

The White-necked Tree-Babbler haunts tall, mature forest in the lowlands and foothills of its range. A sedentary bird, it keeps close to ground level and is one of a number of species with such habits about which extremely little is known. It is, however, not uncommon, particularly in the southern part of its range.

This species has a rather heavy bill and strong feet, and appears to feed on beetles and caterpillars. One nest found in dense scrub consisted of a compact cup of grass, roots and fibers and held 3 white eggs.

## 7/ WREN-TIT
*Chamaea fasciata*
RANGE: **USA from W Oregon S to N Baja California**
HABITAT: **chaparral, coniferous brushland**
SIZE: **6 in (15 cm)**

The Wren-Tit, the only American member of the babbler family, is more closely related to the thrushes than to the wrens and titmice, for which it is named. At first sight, it may act and look like a wren, but its pale eyes, streaked breast and long, unbarred tail help to distinguish it. The plumage varies in color, from reddish-brown in northern races to grayish-brown in southern races such as *C. f. fasciata*.

The Wren-Tit dwells secretively in dense chaparral and low tangles, which it seldom leaves except to make short, weak, tail-pumping flights from bush to bush. There it gleans food from the bark surfaces of shrubs, taking ants, wasps, beetles, caterpillars, bugs, flies and spiders. It also eats various berries and is an irregular visitor to bird feeders, where it will eat breadcrumbs.

The voice of the Wren-Tit is its signature, likely to be heard before the bird is seen. The male sings year round. His loud song begins with a series of accelerating staccato notes and runs together in a descending trill at the end *pit-pit-pit-r-r-r*. The female sings a similar, but trill-less version.

Wren-Tits mate for the life of either member of the pair. The nest is placed low in a tree or shrub. Both sexes construct the compact cup of fibers, bark and grasses, bound with spiders' webs and ornamented by small lichens. Male and female alike incubate the 3–5, pale greenish-blue eggs and tend the young, which leave the nest when they are 15–16 days old.

## 8/ COMMON BABBLER
*Turdoides caudatus*
RANGE: **S Iraq and Indian peninsula E to Bangladesh**
HABITAT: **dry scrub and bushes in open country**
SIZE: **9 in (23 cm)**

A gregarious, untidy-looking babbler, this species scuttles and hops below the bushes or along a hedgerow in an almost ratlike manner, jerking its long tail spasmodically. It is a reluctant flier and, when forced into the air, it will flap and glide rather feebly to the next patch of cover. It forages for insects, grain and berries and, when the bushes are in flower, it supplements its diet with nectar. There are 4 races: the one illustrated is *T. c. caudatus* from India and part of west Pakistan, which is darker and browner than the others.

The Common Babbler is a noisy bird, especially when alarmed. Flocks constantly utter musical whistling calls to keep in contact as they move through the undergrowth. The communal habits of this bird extend to cooperative breeding, with nonbreeding birds in the flock helping with the care of the young. The nest is a small, deep cup with noticeably thick walls. The typical clutch consists of 3–5 turquoise eggs.

## 9/ WHITE-CRESTED LAUGHING-THRUSH
*Garrulax leucolophus*
RANGE: **Himalayas through Southeast Asia to Sumatra**
HABITAT: **undergrowth, scrub and bamboo thickets**
SIZE: **11 in (28 cm)**

As a flock of these gregarious birds forages through the grass and bushes, or in low foliage, there is a constant, subdued chuckling and chirruping. Every now and then, these sounds erupt into bursts of wild, cackling laughter, from which the birds take their name.

White-crested Laughing-Thrushes are active, strong-footed birds that typically bounce over the ground or follow one another in short glides over gulleys or ravines. They are primarily birds of the foothills, where they have sedentary habits. Those birds that nest at higher altitudes tend to move down to the lower slopes in winter. The illustration shows 2 races, *G. l. leucolophus* of the Himalayas and *G. l. bicolor* of Sumatra.

## 10/ RED-BILLED LEIOTHRIX
*Leiothrix lutea*
RANGE: **Himalayas, Burma, S China**
HABITAT: **undergrowth in forests**
SIZE: **5 in (13 cm)**

A loud, melodious, warbling song, combined with attractive plumage, have long made this a favorite cage bird, especially in China. In the wild, the song is often uttered from the cover of dense undergrowth in a shady ravine, where the bird's bright colors are difficult to detect.

Outside the breeding season, the Red-billed Leiothrix often occurs in small parties that forage through bamboo, grass or scrub. They frequently feed in company with other small babblers, keeping in touch with a constant, low, piping note. This species is resident throughout its range but, like many other birds of the Himalayas, it tends to move to lower altitudes in winter. It becomes scarcer toward the western limits of its range.

## 11/ CHESTNUT-TAILED MINLA
*Minla strigula*
RANGE: **Himalayas and Southeast Asia**
HABITAT: **deciduous or evergreen forest and rhododendron groves**
SIZE: **6¼ in (16 cm)**

This is a common and colorful little babbler, often seen in company with other species as it searches through the foliage. It is a bird of the middle story of the forest, where it moves quite acrobatically among the small twigs. Small parties of Chestnut-tailed Minlas keep up a constant chirruping as the flock moves onward, bird after bird flitting across clearings or from one treetop to the next. Insects provide the bulk of its food, but it also eats seeds and berries.

The Chestnut-tailed Minla, which is sometimes known as the Bar-throated Siva, is resident throughout its range. Of the 2 races illustrated, *M. s. strigula* occurs in the eastern Himalayas and *M. s. malayana* occurs in Malaysia. The latter is one of the most common small birds on top of the highest peaks in the Malay Peninsula.

## 12/ CHESTNUT-HEADED FULVETTA
*Alcippe castaneceps*
RANGE: **Himalayas and Southeast Asia**
HABITAT: **thick undergrowth and scrub, forest edge and clearings**
SIZE: **4 in (10 cm)**

This tiny, titlike babbler is a bird of high altitudes, ranging up to 13,000 ft (4,000 m) above sea level. Although it often occurs in groups of up to 30 of its own species, it also joins mixed-species flocks to forage through hill forest. It builds a deep nest in low bamboo, rhododendron or juniper bushes.

Chestnut-headed Fulvettas are active, noisy birds. Every twig or branch, patch of moss or clump of fern is searched carefully as the birds swing on the slender stems or flutter upside-down. They will also launch briefly into the air after a passing insect. The contact note is a repeated cheeping, and the birds also have a rising, 3-note song.

## 13/ WHISKERED YUHINA
*Yuhina flavicollis*
RANGE: **Himalayas E to Burma and Laos**
HABITAT: **secondary forest and scrub, clearings and forest edge**
SIZE: **5 in (13 cm)**

The erect crest (common to several closely related species) gives this familiar babbler a perky appearance as it swings through the twigs, or clings briefly to a tree trunk, like a tit, while inspecting the bark for insects or grubs. Its diet also includes many varieties of berry and seed. It is a gregarious species, often associating with other birds in mixed foraging parties, and is highly vocal, keeping up a continual "chipping" note.

The Whiskered Yuhina ascends the mountains to somewhat lower altitudes than some other Himalayan babblers. It is widely distributed in the foothills in winter. Of the 2 races illustrated, *Y. f. flavicollis* occurs in the eastern and *Y. f. albicollis* in the western Himalayas.

## 14/ WHITE-NECKED ROCKFOWL
*Picathartes gymnocephalus* [V]
RANGE: **W Africa from Guinea and Sierra Leone to Togo**
HABITAT: **rock outcrops with caves in primary forest**
SIZE: **15¾ in (40 cm)**

The 2 species of rockfowl are mysterious birds of strange appearance and uncertain relationships. The function of the brightly colored bare skin on the rockfowls' heads is also unknown, since the birds spend much of their time in the darkness of caves and in the dim light of dense forest. They are ground-dwellers that move with long, springy hops as they search for insects, frogs or crustaceans. They forage among moss-covered rocks, often near forest streams.

The rockfowls' dependence on caves for nesting is unusual among birds. They construct mud nests on the smooth cave ceilings, possibly using existing wasps' nests as foundations. The White-necked Rockfowl is a sociable bird and breeds colonially. The alarm note is a repeated guttural call; it also utters a curious, low, muffled groan.

415

# PARROTBILLS, OLD WORLD WARBLERS

♂

♂

BEARDED REEDLING

♀

VINOUS-THROATED PARROTBILL

race *webbianus*

race *bulomachus*

HALF-COLLARED GNATWREN

♂

BLUE-GRAY GNATCATCHER

♀

race *cetti*

CETTI'S WARBLER

race *albiventris*

AFRICAN SEDGE-WARBLER

GRASSHOPPER WARBLER

race *australis*

race *stentoreus*

CLAMOROUS REED-WARBLER

SEDGE WARBLER

SEYCHELLES BRUSH-WARBLER

first winter

ICTERINE WARBLER

BARRED WARBLER

first winter

## FAMILY PARADOXORNITHIDAE
### Parrotbills
Small to medium, titlike, mostly brown and gray. Plumage soft and loose. Most species with strongly arched bills. Sexes alike except in Bearded Reedling. Nest compact, cup-shaped, in bamboo, grass or reed. Eggs 2–7, whitish or blue with reddish speckling. Incubation 12–13 days, nestling period 9–12 days. 19 species.

## 1/ BEARDED REEDLING
*Panurus biarmicus*
RANGE: W Europe, Turkey, Iran across Asia to E Manchuria
HABITAT: reedbeds
SIZE: 6 in (15 cm)

A metallic, pinging call and a glimpse of a tawny, long-tailed bird like a tiny pheasant whirring over the reedbeds on rounded wings is becoming an increasingly familiar experience throughout western Europe.

Although they are basically sedentary birds, confined to a restricted habitat, Bearded Reedlings tend to flock together in the fall and will undertake mass movements away from their breeding quarters. Over the last 30 years or so these movements have become annual events and the species has colonized many sites beyond its previous range.

Delightfully active and acrobatic, the Bearded Reedling is adept at straddling 2 reeds with its feet turned outward to grip each stem. In summer it feeds mainly on insects such as mayflies, but in winter it will eat seeds, particularly those of the common reed *Phragmites*. Pairs often roost together on reed stems, the male distinguished by his blue-gray head and jaunty black moustaches.

## 2/ VINOUS-THROATED PARROTBILL
*Paradoxornis webbianus*
RANGE: Manchuria, S through China and Korea to Burma
HABITAT: bamboo groves, scrub, tea plantations and reedbeds
SIZE: 4¾ in (12 cm)

This is an abundant bird in parts of China. Outside the breeding season they often move through the undergrowth in large flocks in search of seeds and insects, keeping in touch with one another with a constant sharp, chirruping call.

The plumage varies with race: *P.w. webbianus* of parts of coastal eastern China has a chestnut crown and nape, whereas *P.w. bulomachus* of Taiwan has a rufous-pink crown and nape. All races have a strong bill which is used for tearing bamboo and reed stems to expose the insects within. The bills of some other members of the family are even more powerful, but the name "parrotbill" somewhat overemphasizes their massiveness and, strictly speaking, applies to only a couple of species.

## FAMILY SYLVIIDAE
### Old World warblers and relatives
Small, tree-dwelling or grassland birds. Plumage generally unobtrusive, although some tropical species brighter. Sexes usually similar, although males often brighter. Nests open, domed or purse-shaped in shrubs or on ground. Eggs usually 2–7, pale with fine speckles. Incubation 10–17 days, nestling period 9–20 days (40 days in some). 376 species.

## 3/ HALF-COLLARED GNATWREN
*Microbates cinereiventris*
RANGE: Central and South America from Nicaragua to Colombia, Ecuador and Peru
HABITAT: lowland forest
SIZE: 4½ in (11.5 cm)

This slender, dainty little bird is one of a dozen or so gnatwrens and gnatcatchers found in the Americas. Classified in a subfamily of their own (the Polioptilinae), they are the only New World members of this family. They are very like the Old World warblers and are probably descended from warblers that found their way to the New World. Gnatwrens are predominantly brown birds, with long bills and wrenlike cocked tails. They are found in the lower levels of woodland and forest, in contrast to gnatcatchers, all but one of which live higher in the tree canopy.

The Half-collared, or Tawny-faced, Gnatwren is a lively bird with an engaging habit of bobbing or wagging its tail. It forages actively for insects, either making excursions from a perch down to the ground or flitting among the foliage. It will often hover to pick its prey off a twig or leaf.

Its nest is a tight cup of plant down, leaves or petals bound with spiders' webs and covered in lichen or moss. There are 2–3 whitish eggs with dark spots.

## 4/ BLUE-GRAY GNATCATCHER
*Polioptila caerulea*
RANGE: North America from S Canada to Guatemala and Cuba; winters S of South Carolina along Atlantic coast, and S of S Mississippi and S Texas
HABITAT: forest, timbered swamps, thorny chaparral, wooded areas of towns
SIZE: 4½–5 in (11.5–13 cm)

The Blue-Gray Gnatcatcher is typical of the gnatcatcher group: bluish-gray, slender, with a long tail, which it often cocks like a wren, and a long, thin, pointed bill. It is a tiny, restless bird, often pugnacious, which forages among the leaves and twigs of trees for insects. It will sometimes catch these on the wing, or pick them off leaves while hovering like a kinglet (pp. 282–85). Its song is a wheezy whisper.

The nest is usually placed in a tree fork or on a branch. It is a beautifully constructed cup made of plant down, bound together with spider and insect silk and covered with pieces of lichen. Both adults build the nest, and they also share the incubation of the 4–5 tiny, pale blue, brown-spotted eggs.

## 5/ CETTI'S WARBLER
*Cettia cetti*
RANGE: Mediterranean E to Iran and Turkestan; currently spreading N
HABITAT: swamps, scrub alongside reedbeds, dense bushes and hedges with brambles and tamarisks, edges of cornfields
SIZE: 5½ in (14 cm)

In 1900 Cetti's Warbler was largely confined to Mediterranean climates, but in recent years it has been advancing north and has been recorded as far north as Sweden. One of 11 species in its genus, it is a small, plumpish bird with a short, graduated tail; the males are heavier and longer-winged than the females. The central Asian race *C.c. albiventris* is larger and does not molt in spring like the western race *C.c. cetti*, and as a result is much paler.

Skulking and secretive, Cetti's Warbler spends most of its time in dense cover, but it occasionally shows itself on top of a bush or hedge. The position of the male is often given away by his brief, explosive song.

Males play little part in breeding and may mate with 2 or more females. The female builds the nest – usually among dense vegetation such as an overgrown hedge, a reedbed or bramble thicket – and incubates the 3–5 brick-red eggs alone.

## 6/ AFRICAN SEDGE-WARBLER
*Bradypterus baboecalus*
RANGE: **S Africa (except dry W) N to Chad and Ethiopia**
HABITAT: **reedbeds, swamps, sewage works**
SIZE: **6–7½ in (15–19 cm)**

The tropical and subtropical marshes and scrublands of Africa and Asia are home to 11 species of *Bradypterus* bush warbler.

The African Sedge-Warbler is one of the most common of these birds in some areas of Africa, particularly around lagoons and in swamps. If its accustomed haunts are badly affected by drought in the dry season, it will migrate to find areas where water is still plentiful.

Shy by nature, it rarely emerges from among the sedges and rushes where it forages close to the ground for insects, but it can be located by its call, a series of sharp, staccato notes. It builds a rather bulky nest of strips of sedge, lined with rootlets, and lays a clutch of 2–4 eggs.

## 7/ GRASSHOPPER WARBLER
*Locustella naevia*
RANGE: **Europe S to N Spain and Balkans, Baltic and W USSR, C Asia E to Tian Shan; winters NW Africa, Iran, India, Afghanistan**
HABITAT: **marshes, wet meadows with shrubs, moist woods, osiers, rough grassland, heaths, dunes, conifer plantations**
SIZE: **5 in (12.5 cm)**

Visually undistinguished, the Grasshopper Warbler is renowned for its extraordinary song: a vibrant, high-pitched mechanical trill, resembling the whirr of an angler's reel, formed from double or triple notes produced at a rate of up to 1,400 triplets a minute.

Tracking the source of the song can be difficult, for the bird is able to "throw its voice" like a ventriloquist and it only rarely emerges from cover to sing in the open. Although a restless, agile species, it is very retiring: it generally forages for its insect prey deep within the foliage and, when disturbed, it often prefers to creep away through the grass rather than take flight.

The nest is as hard to find as the bird itself, for it is usually well hidden in low vegetation, with a concealed entrance.

## 8/ SEDGE WARBLER
*Acrocephalus schoenobaenus*
RANGE: **Europe (except Spain, Portugal and some Mediterranean coasts) E to Siberia and SE to Iran; winters Africa S of Sahara and E of Nigeria**
HABITAT: **osiers, marsh ditches, lakes, sewage works, gravel pits, conifer plantations, cereal and rape fields**
SIZE: **5 in (12.5 cm)**

The reed warblers of the genus *Acrocephalus* are essentially marsh-dwelling birds that occur in many parts of the Old World. The Sedge Warbler is one of the best known, for although it tends to keep to dense cover like most of its family, the male can be quite conspicuous early in the breeding season. It often advertises its presence with a stuttering call that is interspersed with mimicry of other species.

Sedge Warblers feed mainly on slow-moving insects which they pick out of low vegetation; in Africa they take many lake flies. They nest in hedges, among osiers, reeds or coarse grass, or even among standing crops of beans, rape or cereals, binding the cup-shaped nest securely to the stems.

## 9/ CLAMOROUS REED-WARBLER
*Acrocephalus stentoreus*
RANGE: **NE Africa, across S Asia to Australia**
HABITAT: **swampy vegetation, especially reedbeds**
SIZE: **6¼ in (16 cm)**

Like other reed warblers, the Clamorous Reed-Warbler is a denizen of thick reedbeds, but it will often venture into other swampy habitats; during droughts it will move into scrubland and even into gardens. The birds in southern Australia appear to leave in the fall, although their destination is not known. There are numerous races, including the southeast Australian and Tasmanian race *A. s. australis* and the Middle Eastern race *A. s. stentoreus*.

The bird owes its name to its loud, varied song, which has harsh scratchy notes interspersed with melodious phrases. It feeds on insects gleaned from vegetation and, sometimes, by flycatching.

The nest is skilfully woven from reed sheaths and decayed water plants and is attached to several reed stems.

## 10/ SEYCHELLES BRUSH-WARBLER
*Bebrornis sechellensis*    R
RANGE: **Cousin and Aride islands, Seychelles**
HABITAT: **dense scrub and swamp**
SIZE: **5 in (13 cm)**

There are 2 species of warbler in the genus *Bebrornis*: one on the island of Rodriguez and this species which occurs in very small numbers on Cousin Island. With a population of only 30 individuals in 1968, it faced extinction but was saved by the International Council for Bird Preservation (ICBP). As a result of habitat conservation and translocation of birds to Aride Island from their original home on Cousin Island,

numbers were increased to over 450 by 1987.

A distinctive warbler with a weak and fluttering flight, its favored haunts are the dense bushy growth alongside old coconut plantations, mangroves and coastal scrub. It pursues flying insects and forages for caterpillars among the branches of small trees and bushes.

The nest is an oval cup of grass and coconut fiber lined with fine material such as cotton and wood shavings; it is built among bamboos, mangroves and other shrubs up to 16 ft (5 m) above ground level.

## 11/ ICTERINE WARBLER
*Hippolais icterina*
RANGE: **N and E Europe S to Alps, Asia Minor and Caucasus, Asia E to Altai Mountains; winters E and tropical Africa**
HABITAT: **open broad-leaved woods, parks, riversides, farmland, orchards and large gardens**
SIZE: **5 in (13 cm)**

The tree warblers of the genus *Hippolais* are relatively large, heavily built birds with prominent legs and feet and a habit of flicking their tails. The Icterine Warbler is one of the more striking members of the group, with bright yellow underparts and a powerful mimetic song. In fall its plumage is duller.

It is a lively, active warbler, more conspicuous than many as it moves about the tree canopy in search of insects and their larvae. In fall it will also take fruits, especially berries.

The nest of the Icterine Warbler is a fine example of tree architecture. Built in the fork of a tree, it is made of stems or grasses held together with wool and spiders' silk; some nests incorporate bark, paper or even rags. The 4–5 eggs are variable in size.

## 12/ BARRED WARBLER
*Sylvia nisoria*
RANGE: **C and E Europe, Asia E to Tian Shan**
HABITAT: **thorny scrub, wet fields with trees, broad-leaved woods, parks, peat bogs; winters on thorn savanna**
SIZE: **6 in (15 cm)**

The Barred Warbler is a stout little bird with distinctive barred underparts and staring yellowish-white irises to its eyes. When excited it raises its crown feathers to form a small crest.

This is one of a genus of 17 or 18 species of active insect-eating warblers. It is shy and secretive with a preference for thick cover, where it searches through the foliage for ants, young locusts, beetles and a variety of bugs. When startled, it utters a harsh chattering alarm note, but its song is rich and melodious, resembling that of the Nightingale.

In Europe the Barred Warbler often builds its nest close to that of a Red-backed Shrike, down near the ground, possibly gaining protection from other predators in this way.

# OLD WORLD WARBLERS

race *atricapilla*

♀

♂

BLACKCAP

♂

race *heineken*

♂ melanistic form

♂ CYPRUS WARBLER

♀

♂ DARTFORD WARBLER

♀

WILLOW WARBLER

race *chloronotus*

race *proregulus*

YELLOW-BREASTED
FLYCATCHER-WARBLER

PALLAS'S LEAF-WARBLER

RUBY-CROWNED KINGLET

♀

♂

♂

GOLDCREST

♀

♂

♀

SEVERTZOV'S TIT-WARBLER

♂

race *saharae*

non-breeding

TINK-TINK CISTICOLA

race *buryi*

♂

STREAKED SCRUB-WARBLER

song-flight

♂

KAROO PRINIA

ZITTING CISTICOLA

421

# OLD WORLD WARBLERS

## 1/ BLACKCAP
*Sylvia atricapilla*

RANGE: Eurasia E to River Irtysh in Siberia and N Iran, NW Africa and Atlantic islands; winters Mediterranean and Africa S to Tanzania
HABITAT: broad-leaved and conifer woods, overgrown hedges, scrub with tall trees
SIZE: $5\frac{1}{2}$ in (14 cm)

This active, lively bird is often easy to observe in the trees as it combs the foliage for insects. The glossy black cap of the male and the reddish-brown cap of the female are distinctive. The male has a wavy or rippling song full of rich, pure notes; he is also an accomplished mimic.

Before the females arrive on the breeding grounds, the male often builds several rudimentary "cock's nests" of dry grass or roots, each slung between 2 twigs, up to 10 ft (3 m) from the ground. The female may reject them all and build one of her own – sometimes with the male's help – or she may accept one of his, finishing it off with a lining of down or wool. Both adults incubate the 4–6 eggs, which vary greatly in color and markings.

The race *S. a. heineken* found on Madeira and the Canary Islands is darker than the European race *S. a. atricapilla*. An even darker (melanistic) variety of *S. a. heineken* was once numerous, but now seems to be rarer.

## 2/ CYPRUS WARBLER
*Sylvia melanothorax*

RANGE: Cyprus, but may wander to nearby coasts of E Mediterranean
HABITAT: hill scrub and orange groves up to 6,500 ft (2,000 m)
SIZE: $5\frac{1}{4}$ in (13.5 cm)

Very similar to the Sardinian Warbler, and sometimes regarded as the same species, the Cyprus Warbler is usually heard rather than seen as it forages for food among the hillside orange groves or maquis scrub of its native island. It is distinguished from its close relative by its strongly barred underparts.

When glimpsed, it is a restless bird which tends to hold its tail up at right angles to its body. It usually keeps to cover, betraying its presence with a harsh single-note alarm call. On Cyprus its caution is well merited, since many are trapped each year (along with other warblers) to be pickled in jars and exported as a gastronomic delicacy.

The nest – a cup of leaves and grass with a hair lining and 3–5 eggs – is built in scrub.

## 3/ DARTFORD WARBLER
*Sylvia undata*

RANGE: S England, W France, S Europe E to Italy and Sicily, N Africa E to Tunisia
HABITAT: in N, lowland heath with dense heather or gorse; in S, spiny maquis
SIZE: 5 in (12.5 cm)

In the north of its range this small, dark warbler suffers badly in cold winters for, despite its susceptibility to harsh weather, it does not migrate to warmer latitudes. It has also been a victim of habitat loss as the heathlands have been exploited for farming, forestry, housing and

mineral extraction. Its declining habitat is also vulnerable to human disturbance and fire.

Dartford Warblers are generally skulking, furtive birds that keep to the bushes, but on sunny mornings the males will propel themselves some 7 ft (2 m) into the air in dancing song-flights. They feed almost exclusively on insects in summer but often eat small fruits during winter.

The nest is built of grass and moss with wool, down and spiders' cocoons, near the ground in a cistus, heather or gorse bush.

## 4/ WILLOW WARBLER
*Phylloscopus trochilus*

RANGE: Scandinavia and NW Europe to E Siberia and Alaska; winters tropical and S Africa
HABITAT: open woods, scrub, conifer plantations, moorland with shrubs, hedges
SIZE: 4 in (10.5 cm)

The Willow Warbler is one of about 45 species of leaf warbler in the genus *Phylloscopus*: all small, slender, graceful birds with basically green, yellow or brown plumage. It is almost identical to the Chiffchaff *P. collybita* in appearance but its song is completely different: a descending series of liquid, silvery notes, in contrast to the chiffchaff's 2-note repetition of its name.

It is an adaptable bird which will thrive in any type of open woodland, and its song is a common sound in many regions. It feeds on insects taken on the wing or picked off the foliage with delicate precision. In winter, when the insect supply fails in the north, it flies south to Africa.

The nest is a domed structure with a side entrance, built on or near the ground by the female. If disturbed on the nest, she may feign injury, fluttering along the ground to lure the intruder away from the eggs or nestlings.

## 5/ PALLAS'S LEAF-WARBLER
*Phylloscopus proregulus*

RANGE: Himalayas, mountains from Altai to Sakhalin; vagrants often reported to W; winters N India and S China
HABITAT: pine or birch forest; winters in light woodland, mixed forest or scrub
SIZE: $3\frac{1}{2}$ in (9 cm)

This is a diminutive leaf warbler with a distinctive yellow crown stripe, double wing bar and rump. The western Chinese race *P. p. chloronotus* has a duller, ocher crown stripe and wing bar compared with other races, such as *P. p. proregulus* of central and northeast Asia.

It is a vivacious, highly active bird which often feeds by hovering among the leaves. It will also hawk after flying insects in the manner of a flycatcher. In its wintering grounds it spends most of its time in the forest canopy.

Its nest is domed, with a hair or feather lining, and is built on the branch of a moss-covered tree.

## 6/ YELLOW-BREASTED FLYCATCHER-WARBLER
*Seicercus montis*

RANGE: Malaysia, Sumatra to Borneo, Palawan and Timor, usually above 6,500 ft (2,000 m)
HABITAT: mountain forest
SIZE: 4 in (10 cm)

There are several species of flycatcher-warbler in the genus *Seicercus* found from the Himalayas to Southeast Asia. The Yellow-breasted Flycatcher-Warbler is one of these; it is generally seen in mountain gullies and among the scrub and undergrowth in forest clearings – either alone, in pairs or in small parties. The male has an attractive trilling song.

Like all the flycatcher-warblers, it builds a dome-shaped nest, locating it in a crevice beneath an overhanging bank. It lays only 2 white eggs.

## 7/ RUBY-CROWNED KINGLET
*Regulus calendula*

RANGE: North America, from NW Alaska S to Arizona, also E Canada to Nova Scotia; winters S to N Mexico
HABITAT: mixed woods, spruce bogs, fir woods
SIZE: $3\frac{3}{4}$–$4\frac{1}{2}$ in (9.5–11.5 cm)

Similar to the Goldcrest of Eurasia, this tiny, short-tailed American species is an active, nervous bird which habitually flits its wings with sudden, jerking movements. This is a useful recognition point, since the characteristic scarlet patch on the crown is often concealed.

It hunts assiduously for insects among the twigs and leaves and may also dart after any that fly past. It will also feed on fruits and seeds. In contrast with that of the other Kinglets, such as the Goldcrest, the song of the male Ruby-crowned Kinglet is surprisingly rich.

The nest is a distinctive cup-shaped construction of plant down, slung beneath a pine branch and covered in lichens and lined with feathers.

## 8/ GOLDCREST
*Regulus regulus*

RANGE: discontinuous, from Azores and NW Europe and Scandinavia to E Asia
HABITAT: conifer woods to 14,700 ft (4,500 m), also some broad-leaved woods
SIZE: $3\frac{1}{2}$ in (9 cm)

This attractive little bird gets its name from its black-bordered erectile crest, which is orange in the male and yellow in the female.

Small groups of Goldcrests can often be seen flying from tree to tree in coniferous forest, drawing attention to themselves by their soft but extremely shrill, high-pitched *zee* calls. They feed mainly on small insects, which they obtain by diligent searching of the foliage or by hovering at the ends of branches, but they have also been seen sipping tree sap.

Goldcrests suffer badly in cold weather but after a succession of mild winters they may increase their numbers tenfold. They may lay up to 13 eggs, incubating them for the unusually long period (for passerines) of 14–17 days.

## 9/ SEVERTZOV'S TIT-WARBLER
*Leptopoecile sophiae*

RANGE: Pakistan, NW India, Nepal, Sikkim and China, from Tian Shan to Sichuan
HABITAT: rhododendron and juniper scrub above the tree line
SIZE: $4\frac{1}{4}$ in (11 cm)

Very like the Goldcrest in appearance, and often considered to be a close relation, Severtzov's Tit-Warbler is restricted to mountain habitats where it feeds on insects gathered in the scrub belt from 8,000–13,000 ft (2,500–4,000 m). The true relationships of these 2 species remain a matter of controversy. Indeed, at one time both they and the Goldcrest and its relatives were considered to be atypical members of the tit family Paridae.

A lively bird, it is difficult to observe, since it spends much of its time in dense undergrowth, hopping and flitting about restlessly. Occasion-

ally it will perch on the top of a bush with its tail cocked, uttering loud, high-pitched calls, but soon flies down to the base of the nest bush to disappear from view again.

Its habits are not well known but it appears to migrate up and down the mountains with the seasons. Its nest is an oval dome of leaves with an entrance at the top, built some 6 ft (2 m) above the ground among dense rhododendron foliage. Outside the breeding season, it may live in small flocks sometimes with other small insect-eating birds.

## 10/ STREAKED SCRUB-WARBLER
*Scotocerca inquieta*

RANGE: N Africa from Morocco to Red Sea, Iran and Afghanistan
HABITAT: rocky desert and semidesert with sparse bushes, dry hillsides, wadis
SIZE: 4 in (10 cm)

This pale, excitable, nervous bird belongs to a somewhat amorphous group of birds known as the bush warblers, which includes the genera *Cisticola, Cettia* and *Prinia*.

In the eastern part of its range the Streaked Scrub-Warbler can be found in hills up to 9,800 ft (3,000 m) but it comes down to lower slopes for the winter. It feeds on insects, small snails and seeds, tending to stay in cover but rushing about like a frenzied mouse when upset by an intruder. It may hop about on the ground or among low vegetation with its long tail cocked up and waving up and down or from side to side. During spring and summer, the Streaked Scrub-Warbler is usually encountered in family groups.

There are several distinct races, including the pale *S. i. saharae*, found in southeast Morocco and Algeria, and the dark *S. i. buryi* of southern Arabia.

## 11/ TINK-TINK CISTICOLA
*Cisticola textrix*

RANGE: Zaire, S Angola, Zambia and South Africa in S and on highveld N to Transvaal
HABITAT: short grassland with bare patches between tufts; flat marshland in the Cape
SIZE: $3\frac{1}{2}$–4 in (9–10 cm)

The cisticolas are a large group of small, shy, brownish birds, many with dark streaks in their plumage. In general they fall into 3 categories: birds of grassland, savanna or swamp.

The Tink-tink Cisticola is a grassland species: a tiny, short-tailed, solitary bird which feeds on the ground on insects, especially grasshoppers. The nest is a ball of dry grass, built within or under a grass tussock. The normal clutch is of 4 eggs, which are pale pink, greenish or turquoise with brown spots.

Although normally inconspicuous, the male has a rattling song produced during a display flight that often takes the bird high in the air, well beyond the range of human vision. The Tink-tink Cisticola is also known as the Pinc-pinc, or Cloud, Cisticola.

## 12/ ZITTING CISTICOLA
*Cisticola juncidis*

RANGE: discontinuous around Mediterranean, W France, sub-Saharan Africa, India, Sri Lanka, Southeast Asia, Indonesia, N Australia
HABITAT: grassland, marshy savanna, paddy fields, brush in open areas
SIZE: 4 in (10 cm)

This is a diminutive brown bird which, when perched, frequently cocks its tail in a jaunty fashion. This short, rounded tail gives it its alternative name of Fan-tailed Warbler. It is restless and shy and best known for its song – a series of high, rasping *dzeep* notes separated by very short intervals uttered by the male during a jerky, high, aerial song-flight. He may climb to a height of 115 ft (35 m) or more and circle around over a wide area of territory, several hundred yards in breadth. Sometimes, however, a male will sing from a fence or other perch instead of or prior to making a song-flight.

Although essentially a lowland bird, the Zitting Cisticola can be found at altitudes of up to 4,400 ft (1,330 m) in Southeast Asia. It spends most of its time in the grass, foraging for adult and larval insects, particularly bush crickets, and rarely flies unless disturbed.

The nest is a delicate pear-shaped construction with the entrance at the top, made from spiders' webs woven around the living stems of grasses and club-rushes and lined with plant down. Many males are polygamous and build several "cock's nests" to attract breeding females.

## 13/ KAROO PRINIA
*Prinia maculosa*

RANGE: S Namibia, S and E South Africa
HABITAT: Karoo veld, valleys and mountain slopes, farmland and coastal scrub
SIZE: 5–6 in (13–15 cm)

There are about 26 species of prinia in Africa and Asia. Sometimes known as wren-warblers, they are generally short-billed birds with long tails; some are similar to the cisticolas. They favor grasslands and scrubby habitats and some prefer to remain on the ground or among low vegetation instead of taking to the wing. They are commonly found in small groups outside the breeding season.

The Karoo Prinia is common in some parts of southern Africa and is able to tolerate very dry conditions. It can be hard to spot as it hunts for insects through the bushes and tall grasses, but when alarmed it may perch on top of a tall plant, flicking its wings and uttering its harsh chirping calls. If approached closely, it often dives into thick vegetation and hides, but it can become quite tame in gardens.

The small pear-shaped nest is intricately woven into twigs or plant stems and is so well disguised that it is extremely difficult to find. The female lays 3–5 bright blue eggs, with dark reddish-brown spots.

# OLD WORLD WARBLERS

ASHY PRINIA

winter

BLACK-COLLARED APALIS

♂

LONG-TAILED TAILORBIRD

at nest ♂

race *brachyura*
"Green-backed
Camaroptera"

BLEATING CAMAROPTERA

race *brevicaudata*
"Gray-backed
Camaroptera"

MOUSTACHED GRASS-WARBLER ♂

race *brachyura*

YELLOW-BELLIED
EREMOMELA

SOUTHERN TIT-WARBLER

race *carnapi*

NORTHERN CROMBEC

LITTLE MARSHBIRD

GRAY LONGBILL

race *punctatus*

FERNBIRD

BROWN SONGLARK

♂

♀

SPINIFEXBIRD

race *badiceps*

FIJI WARBLER

race *ruficapilla*

GREEN HYLIA

## 1/ ASHY PRINIA
*Prinia socialis*
RANGE: **Indian subcontinent and W Burma**
HABITAT: **scrub, grassland, grain fields, open forest, reedbeds, stream banks, mangroves**
SIZE: **5 in (12.5 cm)**

This long-tailed bird is a common sight in the scrublands of southern Asia, where it can be found on hills up to 4,000 ft (1,200 m). Its range of habitats is typical of the tropical prinias.

It is a very nervous bird and, when seen, it is usually hopping restlessly through the foliage cocking its tail. It feeds on insects gleaned from low vegetation and also takes nectar from flowers.

In the northern race *P. s. stewarti*, there is a marked difference between summer and winter plumages, and the tail is longer in winter.

The purselike nest is built in a bush and the 3–5 eggs are incubated by both adults for 12 days.

## 2/ BLACK-COLLARED APALIS
*Apalis pulchra*
RANGE: **Africa, from Cameroon to Sudan and Kenya**
HABITAT: **undergrowth in highland forest**
SIZE: **5 in (12.5 cm)**

The *Apalis* warblers are mainly forest-dwellers of slender build with long, thin, graduated tails and gray, green or brown plumage.

The Black-collared Apalis is a noisy, lively resident of mountain and upland forests in central Africa. In areas where it is common, it can often be seen sidling up and down plant stems with its tail cocked up and wagging from side to side. It feeds mainly on insects picked out of the ground vegetation. The male has a brief, warbling song.

This species occasionally adopts the nests of other birds but, if it has to, it will build a purse-shaped nest of its own, using moss and lichens with a lining of soft feathers.

## 3/ MOUSTACHED GRASS-WARBLER
*Melocichla mentalis*
RANGE: **From W Africa to Ethiopia in the N, down to Angola and across to Zambezi River in the S**
HABITAT: **edges of mountain evergreen forest with coarse grass and scattered trees, marshy land along streams**
SIZE: **7–8 in (18–20 cm)**

This is a stoutly built species which looks more like a bulbul (pp. 250–53) than a warbler. Only the male sports the black cheek stripe that gives the species its name.

Its alarm note is a rasping call, but the male has an attractive, thrushlike song and will sometimes sing or sunbathe on top of a tuft of grass. In general, though, it is a solitary, stealthy species which often skulks behind vegetation. It feeds mainly on insects, especially grasshoppers and beetles. It lays 2 pinkish-white eggs, marbled with red, in a bowl-shaped nest built in a tussock.

## 4/ LONG-TAILED TAILORBIRD
*Orthotomus sutorius*
RANGE: **Indian subcontinent, Southeast Asia to Java, S China; up to 5,250 ft (1,600 m) in Southeast Asia**
HABITAT: **thickets, scrub, bamboo, gardens**
SIZE: **4¾ in (12 cm); breeding male 6 in (15.5 cm)**

Widespread and familiar throughout southern Asia, the Long-tailed Tailorbird is often seen hopping about in bushes and around verandas in search of insects and spiders. It has a habit of carrying its tail high over its back and jerking it up and down. The tail is usually longest in the breeding male.

Its name is derived from its astonishing nest-building technique. Taking 1 or 2 large leaves on a low bush or branch, it uses its bill as a needle to perforate the edges and sew them together using individual stitches of cottony plant material or the silk from spiders' webs or insect cocoons. The nest itself, made of soft plant fibers, is formed inside this pocket. The 2–3 eggs are incubated by both of the parents.

## 5/ BLEATING CAMAROPTERA
*Camaroptera brachyura*
RANGE: **sub-Saharan Africa**
HABITAT: **woodland thickets, forest edge, riverine bush, parks, gardens**
SIZE: **5 in (12.5 cm)**

Of the half dozen or so camaropteras found in Africa, this is the most common. There are 2 groups: a green-backed group of races, including *C. b. brachyura*, which occurs mostly down the eastern edge of Africa, from Kenya south to South Africa, and a gray-backed group, *C. b. brevicaudata*, which is widespread elsewhere. This is often regarded as a separate species, the Gray-backed Camaroptera *C. brevicaudata*. The green-backed birds prefer moist evergreen forests, whereas the gray-backed ones favor dry thorn-veld and open broad-leaved woodlands.

Skulking by habit, these birds are not always easy to see as they forage among the vegetation, but their alarm call is quite distinctive, like the bleating of a lamb. Another equally curious call sounds like stones being tapped together.

Its soft, downy nest is made within a frame formed from the broad leaves of a single twig or spray, with more leaves added to make a roof.

## 6/ YELLOW-BELLIED EREMOMELA
*Eremomela icteropygialis*
RANGE: **Africa from Sudan, Ethiopia and Somalia S through Kenya and Tanzania to Zimbabwe and Transvaal**
HABITAT: **woodland, bushveld, scrub**
SIZE: **4–4¼ in (10–11 cm)**

This pert, short-tailed warbler is common in many parts of its range, although in dry areas it tends to be nomadic. It is usually seen in pairs or family parties, busily seeking insects among the twigs and branches of trees, especially acacias.

Its nest is a thin-walled cup of dry grass, bound together with spiders' silk and sited in a bush. The hen bird usually lays a clutch of 2–3 white, chocolate-spotted eggs.

## 7/ NORTHERN CROMBEC
*Sylvietta brachyura*
RANGE: **widespread across the S Sahel zone from Senegal in the W to Somalia in the E; thence through Uganda and Kenya to Tanzania**
HABITAT: **acacia woodland, dry scrub, coastal bush**
SIZE: **3½ in (9 cm)**

The Northern Crombec is a plump little warbler with an extremely short tail. Its habit of running along branches and climbing through the foliage of thorn trees in search of insects has earned it the alternative name Nuthatch Warbler.

Usually seen in pairs, they are common birds in many parts of Africa. The Northern Crombec is one of 9 species of crombec, all African. There are about 6 races. In contrast to the others, such as *S. b. brachyura* of Senegal to Ethiopia, *S. b. carnapi* of Cameroon and Central African Republic has distinctive chestnut underparts.

ORDER PASSERIFORMES

FAMILY SYLVIIDAE

## 8/ SOUTHERN TIT-WARBLER
*Parisoma subcaeruleum*
RANGE: S Africa N to Angola and S Zambia
HABITAT: thornveld, semiarid scrub, dry
hillsides, savanna thickets, riverine bush
SIZE: $5\frac{1}{2}$–$6\frac{1}{4}$ in (14–16 cm)

This is one of 5 warblers in the genus *Parisoma*,
all found in Africa and Arabia. As its name
suggests, the Southern Tit-Warbler is a titlike
bird, commonly seen alone or in pairs hopping
restlessly through the foliage in search of insects,
spiders and fruit, or taking short, low flights from
tree to tree. The male has a piping, bubbling song
which often includes mimicry of other species.

The nest is a thin-walled cup of grass, roots and
spiders' webs built in a tree. The 2–3 white eggs
are adorned with greenish-brown spots.

## 9/ GRAY LONGBILL
*Macrosphenus concolor*
RANGE: W and C Africa from Sierra Leone
to Uganda
HABITAT: undergrowth, vines and
creepers, canopy of dense forest
SIZE: 5 in (13 cm)

Variously known as longbills or bush-creepers,
the 5 species of *Macrosphenus* are all found only
in Africa. The Gray Longbill is typical of the
genus: a secretive bird, with a long, thin, hook-
tipped bill and loose-feathered flanks, which
frequents dense vegetation and feeds largely on
insects.

They are a poorly studied group, and the facts
about their breeding are hazy; an undisputed
Gray Longbill nest has yet to be described, so the
size, color and number of eggs are not known.

## 10/ LITTLE MARSHBIRD
*Megalurus gramineus*
RANGE: E and SW Australia, Tasmania
HABITAT: grassy swamps and marshes
SIZE: 5 in (13 cm)

The Little Marshbird, or Little Grassbird, is an
inconspicuous, furtive denizen of swamp vegetation, where it feeds on a variety of small insects
and spiders gleaned from the foliage. It rarely
flies, but when it does, it flutters its wings continuously, moving slowly and keeping low down,
with its tail trailing downward. This elusive little
bird is best detected by its trisyllabic song, with
the first syllable short and the second and third
much longer. Sometimes, it misses out the first
short syllable.

It is usually associated with coastal marshland,
but in wet years it is often found far inland,
suggesting that it is an opportunistic, nomadic
species – despite its weak flight.

A pair of Little Marshbirds will often breed in
an old Reed Warbler nest but, if they have to, they
will build a deep, cup-shaped nest using grasses
and other plant material. There are 3–5 eggs.

## 11/ FERNBIRD
*Megalurus punctatus*
RANGE: New Zealand
HABITAT: reed mace swamps, marshy
scrub with ferns, bracken
SIZE: 7 in (18 cm)

Once widespread and common throughout New
Zealand, the Fernbird has been badly hit by
habitat loss as more and more swamps and ferny
areas have been reclaimed for agriculture. As a
result, the population has become fragmented.
The race illustrated, *M. p. punctatus*, occurs on the
main (North and South) islands; other races,
differing in plumage, occur on small offshore
islands.

The Fernbird usually feeds on or near the
ground. It is reluctant to take flight and will travel
only short distances on the wing, flying clumsily
with its tail hanging down. It has a mechanical
2-note call, consisting of a low note followed by a
clicking one. As they travel through the dense
vegetation, pairs maintain contact by calling to
one another, the male uttering one note and the
female the other. Occasionally, males may sing a
simple warbling song.

Both adults build the nest: a deep cup of neatly
woven dry rushes and grasses hidden deep
among swamp plants.

## 12/ BROWN SONGLARK
*Cinclorhamphus cruralis*
RANGE: C and S Australia (not Tasmania)
HABITAT: grasslands and saltbush plains
SIZE: male $9\frac{1}{2}$ in (24 cm); female $7\frac{1}{2}$ in
(19 cm)

The Brown Songlark takes its name from the
male's loud, jangling, somewhat discordant song,
which it utters in a song-flight that involves
quivering wings and dangling legs. As he descends, with his wings held aloft, the male makes
a clucking sound. If he lands on a perch rather
than on the ground, he may carry on singing with
his tail cocked like that of a wren.

Brown Songlarks live in open country and are
among the most common birds on arable farmland. They feed on the ground, taking seeds and
insects, although the male frequently perches on a
post or telephone wire. They are migratory in the
southern part of their range.

The male weighs twice as much as the female.
This disparity suggests that the male is polygamous, because the males of species that have more
than one mate face greater competition in acquir-
ing mates than do those of monogamous species.
Evolution favors larger, stronger males, which
have more chance of ousting rivals.

## 13/ SPINIFEXBIRD
*Eremiornis carteri*
RANGE: N and W inland Australia
HABITAT: arid grassland and semidesert
with spinifex grass
SIZE: $5\frac{1}{2}$ in (14 cm)

The aptly named Spinifexbird is a secretive
species that rarely flies, spending most of its time
hidden in dense thickets of spinifex grass (*Triodia*
spp.), an abundant plant in the dry Australian
grasslands. It feeds on beetles and a range of other
insects, as well as seeds. If danger threatens, it
may climb to the top of a clump of spinifex to gain
a good view of its surroundings. When forced to
fly, the Spinifexbird flutters along, low over the
ground, its tail trailing behind it and pumping up
and down.

It has a high-pitched call that appears to vary
between individuals. The male's song is a high-
pitched, whistling warble. Each pair nests near
the ground in a clump of spinifex, laying only 2
eggs which are pinkish white, speckled with lilac
and reddish-brown.

## 14/ FIJI WARBLER
*Cettia ruficapilla*
RANGE: Fiji
HABITAT: mountain forests and scrub
SIZE: 5–$6\frac{1}{4}$ in (13–16 cm)

This drab, long-legged warbler is a shy bird that
hops and flits through dense undergrowth in an
apparently ceaseless search for food, combing the
branches of tree ferns and other plants for insects
and their larvae, spiders, harvestmen and mites.

Now often placed with warblers such as Cetti's
Warbler (pp. 278–81) in the genus *Cettia*, it is also
sometimes classified in the genus *Vitia*. It is
confined to the 4 larger islands in the Fiji group;
on Taveuni it is restricted to wet forest but
elsewhere it is common in dense scrub. Some of
the islands have distinct races: *C. r. badiceps* of
Viti Levu and *C. r. ruficapilla* of Kandavu are
examples.

Fiji Warblers build untidy, roofed nests with
side entrances and lay 2 chocolate-colored eggs.
Many pairs are parasitized by cuckoos.

## 15/ GREEN HYLIA
*Hylia prasina*
RANGE: W and C Africa from Guinea to W
Kenya, S to N Angola
HABITAT: forest undergrowth
SIZE: $4\frac{1}{2}$ in (11.5 cm)

This is a species of somewhat uncertain status
which is often placed among the sunbirds. It has a
more specialized diet than most warblers, using
its short, slightly curved bill to gather sap-
sucking scale insects and wax. Although quite
common, the Green Hylia can be elusive; when
seen, it is often feeding in a mixed party of birds
high in the canopy.

It builds a flat-domed nest at the end of a
branch, usually quite low down in a forest tree,
and lays 1–2 eggs.

427

# OLD WORLD FLYCATCHERS, MONARCH FLYCATCHERS

RUFOUS-BELLIED NILTAVA

PIED FLYCATCHER

SPOTTED FLYCATCHER

juv

JACKY WINTER

BLUE-AND-WHITE
FLYCATCHER

race *cyanomelana*

FLAME ROBIN

imm

CHIN-SPOT PUFF-BACK FLYCATCHER

BROWN-THROATED WATTLE-EYE

BLUE FLYCATCHER

AFRICAN PARADISE FLYCATCHER

chestnut phase

♂ white phase

♀

♂

imm

BLACK-FACED
MONARCH

♂ race *azurea*

♀

BLACK-NAPED
BLUE MONARCH

♂

YELLOW-BREASTED BOATBILL

♀

♂

race *sclateri*

race *sandwichensis*

ELEPAIO

429

## FAMILY MUSCICAPIDAE
### Old World flycatchers
Small to medium insect-eaters. Relatively broad, flat bills, with bristles around nostrils. Dull or brightly colored, some with ornamental wattles. Sexes often different. Nest either open cup, domed or in holes or deserted nests. Eggs 1–11, uniform green to bluish, reddish or whitish with mottling. Incubation 12–17 days, nestling period 13–19 days. 147 species.

## 1/ SPOTTED FLYCATCHER
*Muscicapa striata*

RANGE: **Eurasia N to N Russia and W Siberia, E to N Mongolia, S to NW Africa and Himalayas; winters C and S Africa, Arabia, NW India**
HABITAT: **open woods and scrub, parks, gardens; winters in acacia woods and thorn bush**
SIZE: **5½ in (14 cm)**

This rather undistinguished mouse-gray bird has a habit of sitting on a bare branch or other exposed perch, from which it makes short aerial sallies after insects, often returning to the same spot. Its flying style is erratic with many swerves and twists; it flicks its wings or tail when at rest. The Spotted Flycatcher feeds almost entirely on insects but may take berries in autumn.

The nest is placed against a wall in a creeper or shrub, on a beam or in a hole; it is a slight structure of moss, wool or hair, held together with spiders' webs. The clutch is usually 4–5 eggs (rarely 2–7). The eggs are pale blue or green with some brown spots, often around the broad end. Incubation, largely by the female, lasts 12–14 days and fledging takes 11–15 days.

## 2/ PIED FLYCATCHER
*Ficedula hypoleuca*

RANGE: **much of Europe, W Asia to River Yenisey, NW Africa; winters in tropical Africa S to Tanzania**
HABITAT: **ancient broad-leaved woodland (especially in uplands) coniferous forest, well-wooded parks, orchards, gardens**
SIZE: **5 in (13 cm)**

The Pied Flycatcher often flicks its wings and moves its tail up and down. It sallies out from a perch after insects and usually returns to a different one. Besides insects, birds will take earthworms and berries in the fall.

The strikingly black and white male sometimes mates with several females, but is often monogamous. Pied Flycatchers nest in holes in trees and walls up to a height of 23 ft (7 m) and widely use nest-boxes when these are available. The female builds a loose nest of moss, roots and strips of bark and lines it with feathers. Clutches of 1–11 eggs are known; they are pale blue in color with reddish speckles.

## 3/ BLUE-AND-WHITE FLYCATCHER
*Cyanoptila cyanomelana*

RANGE: **breeds in NE and E Asia, including Manchuria, W China and Japan; migrates through E and S China to winter in Southeast Asia, S to Greater Sundas**
HABITAT: **mountain forest and wooded regions**
SIZE: **7 in (18 cm)**

This flycatcher of the eastern Palearctic region lives in forested areas, and on migration and in its winter quarters it can be found up to heights of 6,500 ft (2,000 m).

The face, throat and breast of the Japanese race *C. c. cyanomelana* are black, while those of the race *C. c. cumatilis* are greenish-blue. The upperparts of *C. c. cumatilis* are greenish-blue with a shining blue crown. Immature males have an olive-brown head, back and breast, with a whitish throat patch and bluish wings and tail.

The nest, constructed from lichens, moss and roots, is sited in hollows in low bluffs, on cliff ledges or in holes in buildings. There are 4–5 white or pale brown eggs with pale markings at the large ends.

## 4/ RUFOUS-BELLIED NILTAVA
*Niltava sundara*

RANGE: **Himalayas to W China, Burma**
HABITAT: **forest undergrowth and scrub**
SIZE: **7 in (18 cm)**

There are 24 species of niltava. The male Rufous-bellied Niltava is distinguished from the males of his relatives by the (not always visible) shining blue neck patch and by the black throat (with only a hint of blue), with its straight lower edge. The female's distinctive feature is the white gorget on her lower throat. Immatures have brown upperparts with rusty buff spots, and buff-brown underparts with blackish scales.

In the Himalayas, the Rufous-bellied Niltava can be found breeding from 6,000–7,500 ft (1,800–2,300 m). It haunts low scrub and undergrowth, where it searches for insects such as ants and beetles. Birds have been seen on migration in northern Laos and Thailand, but more specific details are not known.

Nests are built close to the ground, usually in holes in banks, roadside cuttings, dead tree stumps or in rock crevices. The nest is lined with moss and rootlets.

## 5/ JACKY WINTER
*Microeca leucophaea*

RANGE: **most of Australia, except the deserts, Tasmania and extreme NE; also S New Guinea**
HABITAT: **open forest, woodland and eucalyptus scrub**
SIZE: **5 in (13 cm)**

The Jacky Winter, or Australian Brown Flycatcher, is a dull gray-brown bird with white eyebrows and outer tail feathers. The sexes are similar; the juvenile is spotted brown and white.

Although a dull bird, the Jacky Winter is readily detected due to its active foraging. Typically it sits on a low perch, often a fencepost, and darts out after flying insects or pounces on prey on the ground. It is most often found in partly cleared country or on the edge of woodland and farmland. Its song is a loud *peter peter*, also sometimes described as *jacky winter*.

On a horizontal branch it builds a very small, shallow nest, made of grass and rootlets, with bark and lichen. The breeding season is from July to December and the usual clutch is 2–3 eggs.

## 6/ FLAME ROBIN
*Petroica phoenicea*

RANGE: **SE Australia and Tasmania**
HABITAT: **breeds in upland eucalyptus forest and woodland; winters in more open habitat**
SIZE: **5½ in (14 cm)**

The male Flame Robin is a striking bird compared with the much duller female and immatures. Like most members of their genus, Flame Robins usually pounce on their prey from a low branch, rock or stump, although they will sometimes hawk for flying insects.

Flame Robins are most common in open woodland near to the tree line in the Great Dividing Range. In autumn they migrate to lower altitudes and often westward into drier, more open country. Nests may be built on branches, but are often in large cavities in trunks, roots or posts.

## FAMILY MONARCHIDAE
### Monarch flycatchers and fantail flycatchers

Small to medium (monarch flycatchers) or small (fantail flycatchers) insect-eaters. Several monarch flycatchers with long tail feathers. Plumage often metallic black or gray, or chestnut with white underparts and sexes sometimes differing (monarch flycatchers); or black, gray, yellow, rufous or white and sexes similar (fantail flycatchers). Nest cup-shaped (goblet-shaped in some fantail flycatchers). Eggs 2–5, whitish (or cream in some fantail flycatchers) with brown spots or blotches. Incubation and nestling period unknown for most fantail flycatchers, (12–14 days and 13–15 days for *Rhipidura* species); 13–17 days and 12–18 days for monarch flycatchers. 164 species.

### 7/ CHIN-SPOT PUFF-BACK FLYCATCHER
*Batis molitor*

RANGE: S Sudan, Kenya (except coast), SW Africa, Mozambique and E Cape Province
HABITAT: open acacia woodland, forests and their edges, cultivated areas, gardens
SIZE: $4\frac{1}{2}$ in (11.5 cm)

The Chin-spot Puff-back Flycatcher is a restless bird, hawking after insects like a true flycatcher and hovering in the air while searching leaves. It will also forage in lower branches like a tit. The wings produce a rattle in flight.

The bird builds a small, cup-shaped nest of fibers and lichens, lashed together with spiders' webs. It is usually well concealed in the fork of a tree. The 2 eggs are grayish or greenish white with a girdle of dark spots.

### 8/ BROWN-THROATED WATTLE-EYE
*Platysteira cyanea*

RANGE: W, C and E Africa, including Sudan, Uganda and Kenya
HABITAT: forest strips and secondary growth
SIZE: 5 in (13 cm)

The chief feature of the 10 species of wattle-eye, all of which are found only in Africa, is an ornamental wattle. This species is markedly black and white with bright scarlet eye-wattles. It occurs in pairs or noisy little flocks, and its habits are rather titlike or like those of a *Phylloscopus* warbler such as the Willow Warbler *P. trochilus* or Pallas's Leaf-Warbler *P. proregulus*. It feeds restlessly among the foliage and flicks its wings audibly in flight.

The nest is a small cup of fine grass, fiber and lichens, bound with spiders' webs and placed in the fork of a bush or tree. The normal clutch is of 2 cream or olive eggs with brown spots.

### 9/ BLUE FLYCATCHER
*Elminia longicauda*

RANGE: W Africa, E to Kenya, S to Angola
HABITAT: woodland and forest, gardens, farmland
SIZE: $5\frac{1}{2}$ in (14 cm)

Beautifully colored in pale cerulean blue and equally elegant in shape, this is one of the most attractive of African flycatchers. It is typically alert, upright and full of nervous energy, frequently fanning its rather long, graduated tail. At the same time, although always active and ready to chase some flying insect, it is very tame and confiding. It has a brief, twittering song, which is somewhat insignificant, but a little reminiscent of the songs of several of the sunbirds.

### 10/ BLACK-NAPED BLUE MONARCH
*Hypothymis azurea*

RANGE: Indonesia, Philippines, China, W to India
HABITAT: mixed primary or secondary forest, farmland, plantations, bamboo
SIZE: $6\frac{1}{4}$ in (16 cm)

Several races of this widespread species are known, including *H. a. ceylonensis*, which lacks a black bar across its throat, *H. a. styani* of mainland India, which is white below, and *H. a. tytleri* of the Andaman Islands, which is blue below. The race illustrated is *H. a. azurea* of the Philippines.

Black-naped Blue Monarchs are sociable birds. They are always active, with flicking wings and cocked, fanned tails. They catch insects in agile twisting and looping sallies from a perch. Insect prey is taken back to a perch and held under one foot as it is broken into pieces in a shrikelike manner. The species has no real song.

It lays 3–4 eggs in a nest of grass stems and bark shreds, placed in a fork of a tree or bush. The nest is often thickly plastered with white spiders' webs and spiders' egg cases and is secured to a branch by a binding of cobweb.

### 11/ AFRICAN PARADISE FLYCATCHER
*Terpsiphone viridis*

RANGE: sub-Saharan Africa
HABITAT: forest and riverside woodland with mature trees
SIZE: $15\frac{3}{4}$ in (40 cm)

In shady, mixed forest, or beside rivers and lakes where woodland glades and ornamental gardens provide relief from the dense canopy, this gorgeous bird flits out from a hidden perch to catch an insect in midair, giving a sudden flash of color and a glimpse of a long, trailing tail. Its call is a distinctive, sharp double or treble note.

Whereas the tails of males may be up to 8 in (20 cm) long, females usually have short tails. However, tail length, whether long or short, is not always a good guide to the sex of the bird.

The nest is a splendidly neat, surprisingly small construction of fibers and fine roots, bound and camouflaged with spiders' webs and lichens. It is always on a slender, open, bare twig in a shady spot, often over water, and the tail of the sitting bird trails elegantly over the side.

### 12/ ELEPAIO
*Chasiempis sandwichensis*

RANGE: Hawaiian islands
HABITAT: high-altitude native and exotic forests and volcanic areas
SIZE: $5\frac{1}{2}$ in (14 cm)

The 5 races of the Elepaio are found only on the Hawaiian islands. Three races – *C. s. sandwichensis*, *C. s. ridgwayi* and *C. s. bryani* – are confined to the island of Hawaii itself; *C. s. sclateri* occurs on the island of Kauai and *C. s. gayi* is scarce on the heavily populated island of Oahu. The surest way to identify this small flycatcher is by its behavior, stance and the plumage feathers common to all adults. All adults have 2 white wing bars, a white rump and a white-tipped tail. Hawaiian immatures are dull brown and those on Kauai and Oahu are rusty brown.

This active bird often perches with its tail cocked and is bold and curious by nature. It feeds on insects, gleaning them from foliage, picking them from trunks or hawking them in flight beneath the leaf canopy. In addition to various whistled and chattering calls, the song is a loudly whistled *chee-whee-o* or *e-le-pai-o*.

### 13/ BLACK-FACED MONARCH
*Monarcha melanopsis*

RANGE: E Australia and New Guinea
HABITAT: rain forest and wet eucalyptus forest
SIZE: 7 in (18 cm)

The black face of this lovely bird gives it its usual Australian name; an alternative name is the Pearly-winged Monarch. Females are very similar to males, whereas immatures lack the black face.

Black-faced Monarchs feed on insects and spiders in a variety of ways. They generally glean them from leaves and bark by moving along a branch and then repeating the process after hopping up to a higher branch. They work their way methodically up to a height of 25 ft (8 m) before descending to repeat the process. Black-faced Monarchs also hawk for insects in midair or pick them off the ground. They have a loud, whistling song and various harsher notes. The nest is constructed from thin twigs, adorned with green moss.

### 14/ YELLOW-BREASTED BOATBILL
*Machaerirhynchus flaviventer*

RANGE: NE Queensland, New Guinea
HABITAT: rain forest
SIZE: $4\frac{1}{4}$–$4\frac{3}{4}$ in (11–12 cm)

The most unusual feature of the Yellow-breasted Boatbill, or Yellow-breasted Flatbill Flycatcher, is the broad, flat bill with its strongly hooked tip.

Boatbills feed by flycatching, or by gleaning from foliage, apparently only taking small, soft-bodied insects. They tend to keep to the canopy of rain forest. Sometimes, they join mixed feeding flocks of other species. As they move through the forest, they constantly utter soft, wheezing trills to maintain contact with one another.

The nest, built mostly by the male, is suspended from a small fork by vine tendrils. The 2 eggs are white with small reddish-brown spots.

# FANTAIL FLYCATCHERS, FAIRY-WRENS, AUSTRALASIAN WARBLERS

race *rufifrons*

WHITE-BROWED FANTAIL

race *aureola*

RUFOUS FANTAIL

SILKTAIL

WILLIE WAGTAIL

SUPERB FAIRY-WREN

♀

♂

RUFOUS-CROWNED EMU-WREN

♀

♂

race *striatus*

STRIATED GRASSWREN

WHITE-THROATED GERYGONE

WEEBILL

RUFOUS BRISTLEBIRD

race *broadbenti*

INLAND THORNBILL

race *apicalis*

FERNWREN

race *maculatus*
"Spotted Scrubwren"
♂

♂
race *laevigaster*

race *humilis* ♂

ORIGMA

race *frontalis* ♂

WHITE-BROWED SCRUBWREN

NEW ZEALAND CREEPER

# FANTAIL FLYCATCHERS, FAIRY-WRENS, AUSTRALASIAN WARBLERS

## 1/ SILKTAIL
*Lamprolia victoriae*
RANGE: **Fiji Islands**
HABITAT: **rain forest**
SIZE: **5 in (13 cm)**

The Silktail is named for its silky-white rump and tail and for the satinlike, velvet-black plumage of the rest of its body. The white rump and tail are conspicuous in the dim forest interior as the bird flits about on its large, rounded wings. The race *L.v. victoriae* is common on the island of Taveuni, while *L.v. kleinschmidti* is rare on Vanua Levu.

The Silktail is usually found in small groups below the tree canopy or on the forest floor. It forages for insects in leaf litter, flicking its tail prominently. Silktails also pick off insects from low branches and foliage, sometimes hovering to feed, and also catch them in midair.

The Silktail's courtship displays involve bowing and raising the tail, or flicking the wings and fanning the tail. Both postures produce a dramatic flash of white. The single, pale pink, spotted egg is laid in a cup nest that is suspended from a low branch and often overhung by large leaves.

## 2/ WHITE-BROWED FANTAIL
*Rhipidura aureola*
RANGE: **Sri Lanka, India, Pakistan, Bangladesh**
HABITAT: **forests, gardens, scrub**
SIZE: **6½ in (17 cm)**

There are 3 races of this flycatcher: *R.a. burmanica* in the east, with its crown and back of similar color, *R.a. aureola* across the bulk of India, with a darker cap, and *R.a. compressirostris* in the south and Sri Lanka, with less white in the tail. Sexes are similar, but females are generally a little paler on the head than the males.

Restless, alert birds, White-browed Fantails are usually seen in ones or twos, but sometimes join mixed parties of birds roving through low bushes and undergrowth. The tail is often fanned and held up high, with the wings drooped. The species is thought to use its flicking wings and tail to disturb insects from crevices in old bark. The insects are caught in midair in graceful, swooping flights from a perch.

The song is a thin, clear whistle, rising and descending in a short phrase. A compact nest of plant fiber and grass, covered with spiders' webs, is placed on a high branch; 3 eggs are laid.

## 3/ WILLIE WAGTAIL
*Rhipidura leucophrys*
RANGE: **throughout Australia; rare in Tasmania, New Guinea, Soloman Islands, Bismarck Archipelago and Moluccas**
HABITAT: **open woodland, scrub, grassland**
SIZE: **7¾ in (20 cm)**

The Willie Wagtail, or Black-and-white Fantail, is one of the most common and popular Australian birds. This is due to its striking black and white plumage, its tameness, its pugnacity toward other birds and its conspicuous feeding habits. Willie Wagtails spend about half of their time feeding on the ground, where they dart about after flies, beetles and ants. They wag and twist their tails from side-to-side, often rocking their bodies or

flicking their wings. At other times they fly out after insects from low branches, stumps or even from a sheep's back.

During the breeding season Willie Wagtails are very aggressive, attacking potential predators up to the size of an eagle, vigorously fluttering around the intruder's back and head with persistent chattering calls. The nest is often placed on a conspicuous horizontal branch but, despite this, and perhaps because the birds are so aggressive, young from 65 percent of nests survive.

## 4/ RUFOUS FANTAIL
*Rhipidura rufifrons*
RANGE: **New Guinea, Pacific and Indonesian islands, N and E Australia**
HABITAT: **eucalyptus forests, rain forests and mangroves**
SIZE: **6–6½ in (15–16.5 cm)**

The Rufous Fantail takes its name from its frequent habit of fanning out its boldly patterned tail. The species has several races which have differing shades of rufous and varying amounts of black on the throat. *R.r. mariae* on Guam is nearly extinct, but races elsewhere are quite common. The race illustrated, *R.r. rufifrons*, is from eastern Australia.

Bright orange flashes in the forest understory signal these birds as they dart in and out of the sunlight. They hop and flit among the vegetation, capturing insects in flight, mostly within 15 ft (5 m) of the ground. They are not as aerobatic as their duller relative, the Gray Fantail *R. fuliginosa*.

## FAMILY MALURIDAE
### Fairy-wrens
Small ground- and shrub-dwellers. Short bills; long, thick legs; long, usually cocked, tails. Plumage various combinations of bright blues, purples, chestnut, black, red and white in breeding male fairy-wrens; chestnut black and white in some grasswrens; brown in most others. Sexes differ, except for grasswrens. Nest usually domed with side entrance. Eggs 2–4, whitish with red-brown speckling. Incubation 12–15 days, nestling period 10–12 days. 24 species.

## 5/ SUPERB FAIRY-WREN
*Malurus cyaneus*
RANGE: **SE Australia, including Tasmania**
HABITAT: **eucalyptus woodland and forest with patches of dense cover**
SIZE: **5 in (13 cm)**

The Superb Fairy-Wren, or Blue Wren, is one of Australia's most familiar and best-studied birds. Superb Fairy-Wrens feed on centipedes and other arthropods on the ground, usually in open grassy areas, but are rarely far from dense cover to which they retreat if danger threatens.

Although many nest as a single pair, one or more helpers may assist to rear the nestlings and fledglings. The breeding male closely guards the female during her fertile periods. He occasionally uses a bright yellow flower petal in his display to a female. Helpers are usually males, often in drab plumage early in the breeding season, and are frequently related to one or more of the breeding birds. The nest is domed with an entrance near the top. Although a pair and its helpers may attempt to raise 3 or 4 broods a season, many eggs and young are taken by predators, especially snakes.

## 6/ RUFOUS-CROWNED EMU-WREN
*Stipiturus ruficeps*
RANGE: **C Australia**
HABITAT: **grassland, desert and scrubland**
SIZE: **5½ in (14 cm)**

Emu-Wrens are tiny birds with very long, central tail feathers. Not only are these feathers nearly twice as long as the body of the bird, but they are unusual in lacking barbicels – the tiny hooks that interlock with one another to keep a feather smooth and neat. This gives them the open and loose appearance of an Emu's feathers.

Rufous-crowned Emu-Wrens are poorly known as they inhabit remote areas of desert, which are usually covered with dense hummocks of porcupine grass (*Triodia*) or other grasses and low shrubs. They are inconspicuous birds, keeping in touch with weak, high-pitched, trilling contact calls. They also have shorter, churring alarm calls and males sometimes sing a brief, warbling song. They feed among vegetation on insects.

## 7/ STRIATED GRASSWREN
*Amytornis striatus*

RANGE: **inland Australia**
HABITAT: **sandy desert and scrub**
SIZE: **$5\frac{1}{2}$–$6\frac{1}{2}$ in (14–16.5 cm)**

The Striated, or Striped, Grasswren's favorite habitat is sand plains with prickly porcupine grass (*Triodia*). There are 3 races, distinguished by plumage color. The one illustrated is *A. s. striatus*, found in grassland among mallee scrub in central New South Wales, northwestern Victoria and southeastern Australia.

Striated Grasswrens feed on the ground, usually in dense cover. They eat centipedes and other invertebrates, as well as small seeds. They seldom fly, but run through the undergrowth like mice and hop vigorously. The partly domed nest, made of porcupine grass, sometimes mixed with shredded bark, and lined with seeds, plant down and fur, is placed in a clump of porcupine grass. The male helps to feed the young.

## FAMILY ACANTHIZIDAE
### Australasian warblers

Small to medium, with fine bills, short tails and wings. Plumage usually brown, olive or yellow. Sexes similar. Nest neat, domed, often with a hood. Eggs 2–3 (occasionally 4), white, sometimes with spots, or dark brown. Incubation 15–20 days, nestling period 15–20 days. 65 species.

## 8/ RUFOUS BRISTLEBIRD
*Dasyornis broadbenti*

RANGE: **restricted to a small area of SE Australia; probably extinct in SW Australia**
HABITAT: **dense scrub and thickets**
SIZE: **$10\frac{1}{2}$ in (27 cm)**

The 3 species of bristlebird are all inconspicuous birds that are sparsely distributed and not well known. Rufous Bristlebirds feed on the ground on seeds and on insects and other arthropods. They are very shy and are more easily heard than seen. The song has a squeaky and harsh quality.

They nest from September to December, close to the ground, building an oval nest with a side entrance. The 2 eggs are white, heavily freckled with red and a purplish color. There are 3 races: the southwestern race *D. b. littoralis* is probably extinct, but the other 2, *D. b. whitei* from South Australia and *D. b. broadbenti* from South Australia and Victoria, are still moderately abundant.

## 9/ ORIGMA
*Origma solitaria*

RANGE: **C coastal New South Wales**
HABITAT: **forest and heathland with rocky outcrops**
SIZE: **$5\frac{1}{2}$ in (14 cm)**

The Origma, or Rock Warbler, is an attractive bird with a shrill, repetitive song. It is confined to the sandstone and limestone areas around Sydney, which are characterized by a diverse, though rather stunted, vegetation.

Origmas feed mostly on bare rock surfaces and may climb almost vertically like a treecreeper.

They eat insects and spiders. Their nesting behavior is unusual, as the nest is almost invariably placed in the dark, in a cave, a deep cleft in the rock or even behind a waterfall. They sometimes take advantage of human structures, nesting in mineshafts and buildings. The nest is spherical and is usually suspended by spiders' webs from the ceiling of a cave or building.

## 10/ FERNWREN
*Crateroscelis gutturalis*

RANGE: **NE Australia**
HABITAT: **mountain rain forest above 2,000 ft (650 m)**
SIZE: **$4\frac{3}{4}$–$5\frac{1}{2}$ in (12–14 cm)**

The Fernwren is a quiet, unobtrusive bird and lives almost entirely on the ground. Moving alone or in pairs, they throw leaf litter into the air when searching for small invertebrates such as snails. They may also take insects disturbed by the foraging activities of larger birds.

Most breeding occurs between August and October. The bulky, rounded nest is made of green moss, fern fibers, rootlets and dry leaves. It is well concealed on the ground among dense vegetation, often among ferns on steep-sided banks.

## 11/ WHITE-BROWED SCRUBWREN
*Sericornis frontalis*

RANGE: **W, S and E Australia, Tasmania**
HABITAT: **understory of forest, heathland**
SIZE: **$4\frac{3}{4}$ in (12 cm)**

There are 9 or more races of the White-browed Scrubwren. They fall into 4 main groups, exemplified by *S. f. laevigaster* from eastern Queensland and northeastern New South Wales, *S. f. frontalis* from southeastern Queensland and New South Wales, *S. f. humilis* from Tasmania and *S. f. maculatus* (the Spotted Scrubwren) from eastern and southern Western Australia. Some of these well-differentiated races have at times been regarded as separate species.

White-browed Scrubwrens have a musical, though rather erratic song, and a variety of harsh call-notes. They feed on the ground in dense cover or in low bushes on insects and seeds. Birds in the far northwest of the range experience very high temperatures that restrict their feeding. They are able to drink weak salt solutions and can also concentrate their urine to conserve water.

## 12/ INLAND THORNBILL
*Acanthiza apicalis*

RANGE: **S and C Australia**
HABITAT: **arid woodland and eucalyptus scrub; forests, coastal scrub, heaths in SW; also mangroves**
SIZE: **4 in (10 cm)**

This is a bird to appeal to identification specialists. Known by a variety of names, the Inland Thornbill, or Broad-tailed Thornbill, is sometimes treated as a race of the Brown Thornbill *A. pusilla*. To confuse the issue, both species have more than 5 races each. To complicate matters further, it is a small, basically grayish-brown bird with a reddish rump and a baffling array of calls including mimicry.

The Inland Thornbill carries its tail cocked and is a perky, conspicuous bird. It forages within shrubs for insects and sometimes seeds, working through one bush and then flying jerkily to the next. It also feeds at flowers, inserting its bill into the flower head. The female builds a domed nest of bark and grass and incubates alone. The male is usually nearby defending the territory.

## 13/ WEEBILL
*Smicrornis brevirostris*

RANGE: **almost throughout Australia**
HABITAT: **eucalyptus woodland and forest; acacia woodland**
SIZE: **$3$–$3\frac{1}{2}$ in (8–9 cm)**

The Weebill is the smallest Australian bird typified by a pale iris and eyebrow and a very short, stubby beak. The song is quite loud for such a tiny bird and resembles *I'm a weebill*.

Weebills glean insects from the outer foliage of eucalyptus and other trees, often hovering on the edge of the canopy. They eat large numbers of scale insects. They have a long breeding season, from July to February. The nest is round or pear shaped, with a side entrance and sometimes a tail.

## 14/ WHITE-THROATED GERYGONE
*Gerygone olivacea*

RANGE: **N and E Australia; migrates as far as SE Australia; also SE New Guinea**
HABITAT: **eucalyptus woodland**
SIZE: **$4\frac{1}{4}$ in (11 cm)**

When feeding, these birds move rapidly through the canopy, snatching small insects from the foliage. They have a lively, high-pitched song which has earned them the name of bush-canary.

The White-throated Gerygone is a summer visitor to the southern part of its range, arriving in September and leaving in April. The pendant nest hangs from a low eucalyptus branch and has a long tail and a side entrance with a small veranda. It is constructed from bark, tied together with spiders' webs, and is lined with feathers. Nests may be infested with ants or wasps, which may protect them from predators.

## 15/ NEW ZEALAND CREEPER
*Finschia novaeseelandiae*

RANGE: **South Island, Stewart Island and neighboring islands (New Zealand)**
HABITAT: **mature forest and scrubland**
SIZE: **5 in (13 cm)**

The New Zealand Creeper, or Brown Creeper, lives in family groups throughout the year, sometimes forming larger flocks in winter. Non-breeders may remain with their natal group for several years. They are easily detected by song and calls, but remain in the canopy and are difficult to see. The Maori name for the bird, Pipipi, is imitative of its calls.

The New Zealand Creeper gleans insects from small branches, twigs and leaves. It is territorial while breeding in the spring, but less so at other times of the year. Some cooperative breeding has been recorded, although the breeding female performs all nest-building and incubation.

# THICKHEADS, TRUE TITS, LONG-TAILED TITS, PENDULINE TITS

race *frontatus*
"Eastern Shrike-tit"

♀

♂

CRESTED SHRIKE-TIT

race *pectoralis*

♀

♂

GOLDEN WHISTLER

♂

race *littayei*

♂

race *torquata*

VARIABLE PITOHUI

race *pallidus*

race *aruensis*

BLACK-CAPPED CHICKADEE

race *britannicus*

CRESTED TIT

COAL TIT

race *aemodius*

SOUTHERN BLACK TIT

race *major*

GREAT TIT

CHINESE YELLOW TIT

race *cinereus*

race *sultanea*

race *gayeti*

SULTAN TIT

race *pendulinus*

BLUE TIT

race *bicolor*

race *atricristatus*

race *macronyx*

PENDULINE TIT

TUFTED TITMOUSE

race *caudatus*

race *minimus*

race *rosaceus*

BUSHTIT

VERDIN

race *melanotis*
"Black-eared Bushtit"

LONG-TAILED TIT

# THICKHEADS, TRUE TITS, LONG-TAILED TITS, PENDULINE TITS

## FAMILY PACHYCEPHALIDAE
### Thickheads and whistlers

Small to medium, robust birds with strong, often hooked bills. Mostly dull brown or gray, some brightly colored. Cup-shaped nests built in trees or crevices. Eggs 1–4, white to olive, spotted. Incubation 16–18 days, nestling period 13–16 days. 52 species.

## 1/ CRESTED SHRIKE-TIT
*Falcunculus frontatus*

RANGE: SE, SW and NW Australia
HABITAT: eucalyptus forests and woods
SIZE: 7 in (18 cm)

The Crested Shrike-Tit gains the second part of its name from the superficial resemblance of its plumage to the Great Tit and from its powerful, hooked, shrikelike beak, which, quite unlike a shrike, it uses to noisily pry and shred loose bark from eucalyptus trees in search of larvae and beetles. It also picks scale insects off twigs and rips open caterpillar cocoons and galls to prey on the animals within.

The race illustrated is the eastern *F.f. frontatus*. The male of the southwestern race *F.f. leucogaster* has a distinctive white abdomen, while the northern race *F.f. whitei* is smaller and yellower. The Crested Shrike-Tit's neat nest is made from shredded bark and spiders' webs, near the crown of a tree, and the birds nest in groups with non-breeding "helpers."

## 2/ GOLDEN WHISTLER
*Pachycephala pectoralis*

RANGE: E and S Australia, Tasmania, New Guinea, Indonesia and Pacific islands
HABITAT: rain forest, eucalyptus forest
SIZE: 6¼ in (16 cm)

The male Golden Whistler is one of the most colorful and melodious of Australian perching birds. It is also the most variable bird in the world, with at least 73 island races showing variations in plumage and bill pattern. Of the 3 races illustrated, *P.p. torquata* of Taveuni Island, for example, has a short bill, while *P.p. littayei* of the Loyalty Islands has an extra-long bill, as well as differences in plumage. The race *P.p. pectoralis*, which has a medium-length bill, occurs in New South Wales. The females of all races and males of some of the island races have dull olive plumage.

Golden Whistlers feed mainly on large insects, snatching or gleaning them from the foliage of wattles (*Acacia* spp.) or eucalyptus. Males tend to feed higher in the trees than females.

## 3/ VARIABLE PITOHUI
*Pitohui kirhocephalus*

RANGE: New Guinea, adjacent islands to W
HABITAT: lowland forest and forest edge
SIZE: 9 in (23 cm)

There are 7 species of pitohui, all restricted to the New Guinea area. The Variable Pitohui is remarkable for the striking geographic variation in its plumage: the largely black race *P.k. aruensis* of the Aru Islands and the gray-hooded race *P.k. pallidus* of the far western mainland and Waigeo and Batanta islands are extreme examples.

Small groups of Variable Pitohuis forage for insects among the bushes and trees, rarely visible but often advertising their presence with loud gurgling whistles and hoarse catlike sounds, as well as the musical fluttering of their wing beats.

## FAMILY PARIDAE
### True tits

Small, active, mostly brown or gray, some with brighter colors. Sexes similar. Hole-nesters. Eggs usually 4–12, white, red-brown spots. Incubation 13–14 days, nestling period 17–20 days. 50 species.

## 4/ BLACK-CAPPED CHICKADEE
*Parus atricapillus*

RANGE: Alaska, Canada, S to C USA
HABITAT: coniferous and broad-leaved forest
SIZE: 5 in (13 cm)

This is the most widely distributed tit in North America, and one of 6 species known as chickadees from their calls. It is a familiar garden visitor in winter, when small parties of 6 or so birds regularly descend on feeding stations, but in spring these parties split up into nesting pairs which spend the summer feeding in the forest.

The pair excavate their own nest-hole in the soft wood of a dead tree. They usually ignore any vacant holes, but will sometimes use a nest-box if it is previously stuffed with debris so that they have to dig their way in.

## 5/ COAL TIT
*Parus ater*

RANGE: Eurasia from Britain to Japan, N Africa
HABITAT: forests, mainly coniferous
SIZE: 4½ in (11.5 cm)

There are approximately 20 races of the widely distributed Coal Tit; most of them resemble *P.a. britannicus* of Great Britain, but the Himalayan race *P.a. aemodius* has a striking black crest.

In general, they favor conifer forests although some, such as those in Ireland, are found mainly in broad-leaved woodland. Outside the breeding season they often feed in mixed flocks, searching through the tree canopy for insects and seeds.

Coal Tits do not excavate their own nest-holes; they prefer to nest in vacant holes in trees, but will sometimes use abandoned rodent burrows in the ground.

## 6/ CRESTED TIT
*Parus cristatus*

RANGE: Europe and Scandinavia E to Urals
HABITAT: mature conifer forest
SIZE: 4½ in (11.5 cm)

The Crested Tit lives almost exclusively among mature conifer trees, particularly spruce and pine, and as a result it is patchily distributed throughout its range. Easily recognized by its speckled crest, it feeds mainly on insects, which it picks out of crevices in the bark with its short bill, and pine seeds.

Crested Tits make their own nest-holes, usually in rotting tree stumps. The female does most of the work, excavating a new hole each year.

## 7/ SOUTHERN BLACK TIT
*Parus niger*

RANGE: SE Africa, N to Tanzania
HABITAT: woods, woodland edge, lightly wooded country
SIZE: 6¼ in (16 cm)

Found in a wide variety of woodland, ranging from dense evergreen forest to scattered trees, the Southern Black Tit breeds in family groups consisting of 3–4 birds; the "helpers" are generally the breeding pair's male offspring from the previous year's brood. But, despite this extra food-gathering capacity, each family raises only 3–4 chicks each season.

Although this species is restricted to the east of southern Africa, it is very similar to a bird known as Carp's Tit, found in some parts of the west and currently held to be a separate species, *P. carpi*.

## 8/ GREAT TIT
*Parus major*
RANGE: **Eurasia, from Britain through USSR and S Asia to Japan**
HABITAT: **forests, mountain scrub, parks and gardens, mangroves**
SIZE: **5½ in (14 cm)**

The Great Tit is a very widespread, adaptable bird, and there are about 30 distinct races. Many of these are yellow-bellied, green-backed birds like *P. m. major* of Europe and central Asia, but several eastern races, including *P. m. cinereus* of Java and the Lesser Sunda Islands, have a gray back and a whitish belly. Green/yellow forms and gray/whitish ones occur together in the eastern USSR, but do not seem to interbreed.

Acrobatic and vocal, the Great Tit has a wide vocabulary of metallic call notes. It is a common visitor to gardens, where it readily breeds in nest-boxes as well as in such unlikely sites as drain-pipes and mailboxes.

## 9/ CHINESE YELLOW TIT
*Parus spilonotus*
RANGE: **Nepal, Burma, Thailand, S China**
HABITAT: **mountain forests**
SIZE: **5½ in (14 cm)**

This species is often confused with the Yellow-cheeked Tit *P. xanthogenys*, for both of them have striking crests and heavily streaked backs.

The Chinese Yellow Tit lives in all types of forest, ranging from subtropical jungle to mountain pinewoods. It forages for food high in the trees and rarely descends to ground level. Like others in its family, it generally uses a hole in a tree as a nest site, but it will occasionally nest in a hole in a wall or a rocky bank.

## 10/ BLUE TIT
*Parus caeruleus*
RANGE: **Europe E to Volga, Asia Minor, N Africa**
HABITAT: **woods, parks, gardens**
SIZE: **4¼ in (11 cm)**

These lively birds are popular visitors to suburban gardens in winter, giving virtuoso displays of agility as they cling to suspended coconuts or whisk tasty morsels away from beneath the bills of larger, slower birds. In their natural woodland habitat they often feed in loose mixed flocks with other tits such as the Great Tit and Coal Tit, working steadily from tree to tree.

An eager user of garden nest-boxes, the Blue Tit lays the largest clutch of any bird in the world (excluding some ducks and gamebirds, which do not feed their young). In good habitats, 11 eggs are common, while clutches of as many as 14–15 are by no means rare.

## 11/ TUFTED TITMOUSE
*Parus bicolor*
RANGE: **E North America, S to Texas and currently extending N to Ontario**
HABITAT: **broad-leaved forest, open woods**
SIZE: **6½ in (17 cm)**

Many tits owe their winter survival to bird lovers who put food out for them. The Tufted Titmouse is no exception, and it is likely that this is the reason why it is spreading farther north. Even without this help it is well equipped to gather winter food, for its stout bill enables it to hammer open nuts that would be too tough for most other tits to crack.

The race *P. b. bicolor* is from eastern, central and southeastern USA, and is typical of the species. At the other end of its range, in Texas, the bird has a longer, black crest. Once known as the Black-crested Titmouse, this is now generally thought to be a race, *P. b atricristatus*, of the Tufted Titmouse.

## 12/ SULTAN TIT
*Melanochlora sultanea*
RANGE: **E Nepal to S China and Southeast Asia**
HABITAT: **chiefly in lowland forest**
SIZE: **8½ in (22 cm)**

This giant among tits is so unlike the other members of its family that it has been classified in a genus of its own. Most races, such as *M. s. sultanea* of the eastern Himalayas, sport a flamboyant yellow crest, but an Indo-Chinese race *M. s. gayeti* has a black crest.

Sultan Tits live in many types of forests, where they usually hunt for food in the high branches with typical titlike resourcefulness and agility. They nest in holes in trees.

## FAMILY AEGITHALIDAE
**Long-tailed tits**
Small, tail often longer than body. Mostly brown, black, white or gray. Sexes similar. Tree-nesters; nest woven, domed. Eggs 6–10, white, red-brown spots. Incubation 13–14 days, nestling period about 18 days. 7 species.

## 13/ LONG-TAILED TIT
*Aegithalos caudatus*
RANGE: **continuous from Europe through C Asia to Japan**
HABITAT: **woods, woodland edge, scrub**
SIZE: **5½ in (14 cm)**

These tiny birds, whose tails are more than half their body length, lose heat easily, and on winter nights they huddle together in family groups to keep warm. When day breaks, the groups set off to forage together through the treetops, often in mixed flocks with other small birds.

In spring they pair up to build beautifully woven, domed nests of lichens, spiders' silk and feathers. If a pair loses its brood they will often help to feed the broods of relatives.

There are some 20 races. The British race *A. c. rosaceus* has a distinctive broad black stripe above the eye, in contrast to the white-headed northern race *A. c. caudatus*.

## 14/ BUSHTIT
*Psaltriparus minimus*
RANGE: **W North America, from British Columbia to Guatemala**
HABITAT: **open woods, chaparral scrub**
SIZE: **4¼ in (11 cm)**

This is the only North American long-tailed tit. At one time the Black-eared Bushtit of southern USA, Mexico and Guatemala was considered a separate species on the basis of the male's distinctive black mask, but it is now recognized as a local race, *P. m. melanotis*. *P. m. minimus* is one of several races found in western USA.

The Bushtit is a common and familiar bird which often feeds in gardens. Its finely woven nest is suspended from branches rather than attached at the bottom like that of the Long-tailed Tit.

## FAMILY REMIZIDAE
**Penduline tits**
Small, bill finely pointed. Pale gray, white or yellow; some species with bright yellow, red, one with chestnut and black. Sexes similar. Domed, woven nest built in shrubs or thickets. Eggs 3–10, usually white, spotted red. Incubation 13–14 days, nestling period 18 days. 10 species.

## 15/ PENDULINE TIT
*Remiz pendulinus*
RANGE: **S and E Europe, W Siberia, Asia Minor, C Asia, E to NW India, N China and Korea**
HABITAT: **reedbeds**
SIZE: **4¼ in (11 cm)**

The penduline tits are celebrated for their superbly made suspended purselike nests, which appear to be woven from woolly felt and have elaborate spoutlike entrances.

This species is the only penduline tit to occur outside Africa. There are several races: *R. p. pendulinus* of Europe, Asia Minor and western Siberia is the typical masked form, while *R. p. macronyx* of Iran has an all-black head. They are all restricted to reedbeds, where they feed on the seeds of reed mace (cat's-tail) and nest in marsh-edge trees such as willow and tamarisk.

## 16/ VERDIN
*Auriparus flaviceps*
RANGE: **SW USA and N Mexico**
HABITAT: **semi-desert scrub**
SIZE: **4¼ in (11 cm)**

This common desert bird is the only member of its family found in America. It lives and nests among thorny bushes and cactus plants, weaving a rather untidy nest out of thorn twigs and siting it within the protection of the plant's spines. The result is such an effective fortress against predators that the nests are frequently used for roosting outside the breeding season.

# NUTHATCHES, TREECREEPERS, FLOWERPECKERS, PARDALOTES

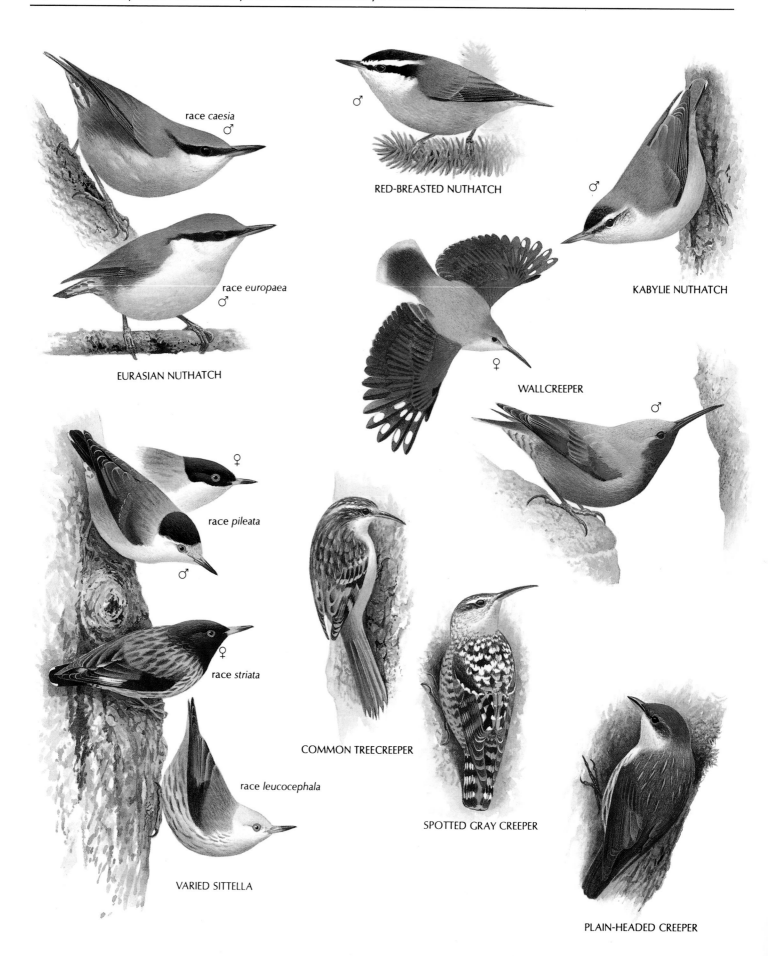

race *caesia*
♂

♂
RED-BREASTED NUTHATCH

♂
KABYLIE NUTHATCH

race *europaea*
♂

EURASIAN NUTHATCH

♀
WALLCREEPER

♀
race *pileata*
♂

♂

race *striata*
♀

COMMON TREECREEPER

race *leucocephala*

SPOTTED GRAY CREEPER

VARIED SITTELLA

PLAIN-HEADED CREEPER

# FAMILIES SITTIDAE, CERTHIIDAE, RHABDORNITHIDAE, CLIMACTERIDAE, DICAEIDAE, PARDALOTIDAE

RED-BROWED TREECREEPER

FAN-TAILED BERRYPECKER

CRIMSON-BREASTED FLOWERPECKER

MISTLETOEBIRD

race olivaceum

race montium

SCARLET-BACKED FLOWERPECKER

CRESTED BERRYPECKER

race ornatus

STRIATED PARDALOTE

race melanocephalus

## FAMILY SITTIDAE
### Nuthatches

Small, compact. Agile climbers, without stiffened tail as prop. Upperparts mostly blue-gray, underparts pale to rufous. Sexes similar. Nest in trees or rocks, mostly in holes. Eggs 4–10, white with reddish spots. Incubation 15–19 days, nestling period 23–29 days. 25 species.

### 1/ EURASIAN NUTHATCH
*Sitta europaea*

RANGE: **W Europe E to Japan and Kamchatka (USSR)**
HABITAT: **woodland with large trees**
SIZE: **4¼–5 in (11–13 cm)**

This widespread species depends on woodland trees, both for food and for the old tree holes that provide it with secure nest sites. It darts rapidly up and down trunks and branches, searching for invertebrates, seeds and nuts. It often wedges large items in crevices and hammers them vigorously with its sharp bill to break them open.

The race *S. e. europaea* from Scandinavia, eastern Europe and central Russia has very pale underparts, in contrast to races such as *S. e. caesia* of western Europe, including England and Wales. The 2 forms have met up after a long period of isolation and are intermingling.

The nest usually lies in an abandoned woodpecker hole toward the top of a tall tree and is freshly floored with flakes of pine bark and lichen. A "plaster" of dried clay and mud is used to reduce the size of the entrance hole.

### 2/ RED-BREASTED NUTHATCH
*Sitta canadensis*

RANGE: **S Canada to Mexico**
HABITAT: **coniferous forest**
SIZE: **4½–5 in (11–13 cm)**

The Red-breasted Nuthatch is closely dependent on conifers. It catches insects on their bark and hoards large quantities of their cone seeds as a food supply for the winter. Northerly birds may undertake large-scale migrations toward the south when the cone crop fails or when their population grows too large.

This species smears the rim of its tree hole with pine resin, usually the sticky "pitch" that oozes from balsam firs. The reason for this is unclear, although it may keep ants and larger creatures out of the nest. This means that the parents have to perform deft twists and turns in the air if they are to avoid becoming stuck fast themselves.

### 3/ KABYLIE NUTHATCH
*Sitta ledanti*   ℝ

RANGE: **E Algeria**
HABITAT: **mixed woodland above 5,000 ft (1,500 m)**
SIZE: **4¾ in (12 cm)**

Discovered only as recently as 1975, the Kabylie, or Algerian, Nuthatch is one of the world's rarest birds. Until recently, it was thought to live only in the Babor Forest, an area of fir, cedar and oak woodland on a single mountain in the Atlas range. In 1989, a second population was located in the Taza National Park, but the total population is

still very small (only 80–100 pairs in the Babor Forest) and the species has an uncertain future.

The Kabylie Nuthatch excavates its own nest holes in soft and rotten wood. During the summer, it feeds mainly among oak trees, where insects are most abundant, but it will also feed its nestlings on hoarded conifer seeds. In winter, seeds form its staple diet.

### 4/ WALLCREEPER
*Tichodroma muraria*

RANGE: **N Spain E to the Himalayas**
HABITAT: **rocky gorges, cliffs, mountainsides**
SIZE: **6 in (15 cm)**

There has long been debate over the classification of this species, although today it is usually placed with the nuthatches. Whatever its ancestry, the Wallcreeper must have occupied its present habitat for a long time, for it is an excellent rock climber. It uses its wings for support when climbing up sheer walls and is nimble enough to walk beneath overhangs and jump across gaps.

It is a conspicuous bird in its lonely haunts up to 8,000 ft (2,500 m) high in the Alps and up to 16,500 ft (5,000 m) in the Himalayas. It frequently flicks open its bright red wings and often spreads them to bask in the sunshine. The colorful wings and its graceful, buoyant flight, have earned it the nickname "butterfly bird." In winter the male loses his black throat and thus resembles the female.

### 5/ VARIED SITTELLA
*Neositta chrysoptera*

RANGE: **Australia**
HABITAT: **eucalyptus woodland and forest; mallee scrub in more arid areas**
SIZE: **4¼ in (11 cm)**

The feeding behavior of sittellas is very similar to that of the true nuthatches: they comb the branches of large trees, prising into the rough bark for insects. Their breeding habits, however, are distinctly different. Instead of using a hole, they build a cup-shaped nest within a tree

fork. Like many Australian birds, they live in groups all year in which birds other than the breeding pair bring food to the young.

There are 5 races of the Varied Sittella: they include *N. c. pileata* from the west and south, *N. c. striata* from the north and northeast, and *N. c. leucocephala* from the central eastern region.

## FAMILY CERTHIIDAE
### Holarctic treecreepers

Small, tree-climbing birds with stiffened tails (*Certhia*). Thin, slightly downcurved bills. Plumage mostly brown, pale underparts. Sexes alike. Cup-shaped nest. Eggs 3–9, white with red-brown spots (*Certhia*); 2–3, pale blue-green with black and lilac markings (*Salpornis*). Incubation 14–15 days, nestling period 15–16 days. 7 species.

### 6/ COMMON TREECREEPER
*Certhia familiaris*

RANGE: **W Europe to Japan**
HABITAT: **woodland, especially coniferous**
SIZE: **5 in (12.5 cm)**

The feeding behavior of the treecreepers is superficially similar to that of the nuthatches, but there are important differences. A treecreeper cannot move down a tree trunk and must use its stiff tail as support during its spiral ascent. It takes generally smaller food items, including tiny insect eggs, and is exclusively insectivorous.

The Common Treecreeper normally roosts and nests behind a loose flap of bark, and the fledglings may cling to the surrounding bark for several days after leaving the nest.

### 7/ SPOTTED GRAY CREEPER
*Salpornis spilonotus*

RANGE: **sub-Saharan Africa, India**
HABITAT: **open bush and savanna**
SIZE: **5 in (13 cm)**

This species differs in many ways from the other members of its family and belongs to a separate genus. It runs rapidly over tree bark, its progress quite unlike the jerky movements of a treecreeper.

Its tail is not stiffened and, like a nuthatch, it can run down, as well as up, trees.

The nest is a cup-shaped structure of leaves, bark and cobwebs, often straddled across the fork of a branch, but never tucked behind loose wood like the nests of other treecreepers.

## FAMILY RHABDORNITHIDAE
### Philippine creepers

Small tree-climbers. Downcurved bill. Upperparts brown, underparts white with dark streaks. Female lighter brown. Nest in tree holes. Eggs, incubation and nestling period unknown. 2 species.

## 8/ PLAIN-HEADED CREEPER
*Rhabdornis inornatus*

RANGE: **Samar Island (Philippines)**
HABITAT: **deep forests, among large trees**
SIZE: **6 in (15 cm)**

Although the Plain-headed Creeper does forage on bark, exploiting the rich supply of insect eggs and pupae, it feeds mainly in the outer canopy of the trees, gleaning insects from leaves and twigs. It is not completely dependent on insects, however, for it uses its brush-tipped tongue to take advantage of the year-round supply of flower nectar in its tropical forest home and occasionally eats small fruits. Both species in this family are confined to islands in the Philippine archipelago.

## FAMILY CLIMACTERIDAE
### Australasian treecreepers

Small tree-climbers that also feed on ground. Downcurved bill. Plumage brown, gray or blackish above, striped or rufous below. Sexes differ slightly. Nest in tree holes. Eggs 2–3, white or pinkish, brown or gray markings. Incubation 16–23 days, nestling period 25–26 days. 7 species.

## 9/ RED-BROWED TREECREEPER
*Climacteris erythrops*

RANGE: **SE Australia**
HABITAT: **tall eucalyptus forests in mountains; less often near coast**
SIZE: **$5\frac{1}{2}$–$6\frac{1}{4}$ in (14–16 cm)**

The Red-browed Treecreeper feeds largely on ants, foraging for them over the trunks and branches of smooth-barked trees, concentrating on places where the bark is peeling back. Small family groups maintain communal territories, with male birds from previous broods helping the breeding pair in nest-building and in feeding the young.

The female differs slightly from the male in that her upper breast is streaked with rufous. The immature bird has a gray rather than reddish face and few streaks on the underparts.

## FAMILY DICAEIDAE
### Flowerpeckers

Small, dumpy. Upperparts dark, glossy, underparts lighter. Sexes alike or males have bright patches. Nests open, cup-shaped, or hanging with side entrance. Eggs 1–3, white, some blotched. Incubation 12 days, nestling period about 15 days. 50 species.

## 10/ FAN-TAILED BERRYPECKER
*Melanocharis versteri*

RANGE: **New Guinea**
HABITAT: **understory shrubs and trees of upland rain forest over 4,000 ft (1,200 m)**
SIZE: **4 in (10 cm)**

The Fan-tailed Berrypecker is a common but timid and solitary bird. It feeds mainly on small fruit, taken from many different forest trees. Insects also form part of its diet, especially when it is breeding. At 4–5 in (10–12 cm) in diameter, the nest is large for the size of the bird and is constructed from stems, bark and spiders' webs placed astride a large branch. Unusually among passerines, the female is heavier than the male.

## 11/ CRIMSON-BREASTED FLOWERPECKER
*Prionochilus percussus*

RANGE: **Malay Peninsula, Sumatra, Java, Borneo, Philippines**
HABITAT: **lowland rain forest; also mangroves and overgrown plantations**
SIZE: **$3$–$3\frac{1}{2}$ in (8–9 cm)**

This is a lively, noisy bird, aggressive toward other birds even though it is one of the region's smallest species. Like many other members of its family, it spends much time among flowers, either catching spiders and insects or drinking nectar with its long, tubular tongue. However, the principal food of flowerpeckers is berries, especially those of mistletoes. These sugary fruits provide a rich source of energy for the birds. When they have passed through a flowerpecker's digestive system, the bird must remove their remains from around its vent by wiping its rear end against a branch. The wiping action deposits the seeds on the tree bark, where they can germinate.

## 12/ MISTLETOEBIRD
*Dicaeum hirundinaceum*

RANGE: **Australia, Aru Islands**
HABITAT: **varied, from dry scrub to wet forest**
SIZE: **4 in (10 cm)**

This bird has evolved an extremely close association with the 60 or so species of fruiting mistletoe in Australasia. Flowerpeckers generally have a reduced stomach, offset from the gut, but in the Mistletoebird the stomach has almost completely degenerated. The mistletoe berries pass very rapidly through the intestine, where most of the sweet flesh is stripped from the husk, but the seeds are left intact. Seeds may be defecated just 30 minutes after the berries are swallowed.

What remains of the bird's stomach is reserved for insects, food that requires a longer period of digestion. Nestlings are fed almost entirely on insects for the first week, before being weaned onto the staple diet of berries.

## 13/ SCARLET-BACKED FLOWERPECKER
*Dicaeum cruentatum*

RANGE: **India to S China, Southeast Asia, Indonesia**
HABITAT: **coastal lowland plains, open forest, scrub, gardens**
SIZE: **4 in (10 cm)**

This tiny, dumpy bird is a common inhabitant of the treetops of Southeast Asia. It is noticeable even at a distance because of its constant twittering while feeding, its frequent staccato calls and its erratic, dipping flight. It breeds from March to April, building a delicate, purse-shaped nest of cotton down and spiders' webs, suspended from a branch. The purse has a side entrance that is impossible for most predators to reach, although snakes may be able to penetrate the defences. The female incubates the eggs alone, but the male helps to feed the nestlings.

## 14/ CRESTED BERRYPECKER
*Paramythia montium*

RANGE: **C and SE New Guinea**
HABITAT: **moss forest from 6,500 ft (2,000 m) to tree line**
SIZE: **$7\frac{3}{4}$ in (20 cm)**

The Crested Berrypecker is by far the largest member of its family. Common in the high-altitude forest in its range, it is a bold and engaging species. Its strange *swish* call is rather like the sound of dry twigs being scraped lightly together. It has the bizarre habit of plucking certain large flowers and rubbing its plumage with the crushed petals. It feeds on berries and insects. The larger-crested race *P. m. olivaceum*, with less white on its head, is found in the Snow Mountains, while the race *P. m. montium* occurs in central and southeastern New Guinea.

## FAMILY PARDALOTIDAE
### Pardalotes

Small, dumpy. Plumage gray to olive. Black, white, yellow or orange markings. Females duller in some species. Nest in tree holes or in burrows. Eggs 3–5, white. Incubation 14–16 days, nestling period about 25 days. 4 species.

## 15/ STRIATED PARDALOTE
*Pardalotus striatus*

RANGE: **Australia**
HABITAT: **forest, woodland, parks with eucalyptus**
SIZE: **4 in (10 cm)**

The pardalotes are small birds that comb the foliage for insects and other food. They feed heavily on "lerps" – sugary secretions exuded by the sap-sucking larvae of psyllid scale insects – and undertake nomadic movements in search of infested trees.

The Striated Pardalote is the most widespread species, with several races. There are 2 main groups: black-crowned races, such as the cinnamon-rumped *P. s. melanocephalus* from the northeast, and stripe-crowned races, such as the southeastern race *P. s. ornatus*.

PYGMY SUNBIRD

♂

♀

SAO THOMÉ
GIANT SUNBIRD

PURPLE SUNBIRD

♀

♂

race *asiatica*

♂

eclipse

♀

♂

REGAL SUNBIRD

♀

GOLDEN-WINGED SUNBIRD

♀

♂

NORTHERN ORANGE-TUFTED SUNBIRD

♂

♂

♀

race *dabryii*

MRS GOULD'S SUNBIRD

SCARLET-CHESTED SUNBIRD

♂

♀

♂

♀

PURPLE-RUMPED SUNBIRD

♂

♀

YELLOW-BELLIED SUNBIRD

♂

♀

RED-TUFTED
MALACHITE SUNBIRD

♂

♀

SUPERB SUNBIRD

♀

YELLOW-BACKED SUNBIRD

♂

LONG-BILLED SPIDERHUNTER

## FAMILY NECTARINIIDAE
### Sunbirds

Small, males with very colorful iridescent plumage (except some forest sunbirds and all spiderhunters); slim, often long, downcurved bills. Sexes differ markedly. Nest purse-shaped, suspended from twig; made of grass, lichens and other plant materials, often bound together with spiders' webs; entrance at side, often covered by "porch;" nests of spiderhunters cup-shaped. Eggs 2–3, white, spotted or streaked. Incubation 13–15 days, nestling period 14–19 days. 120 species.

### 1/ PYGMY SUNBIRD
*Anthreptes platurus*
RANGE: **Senegal to Egypt, Ethiopia, NW Kenya**
HABITAT: **savanna, parks, gardens**
SIZE: **$6\frac{1}{4}$–7 in (16–18 cm)**

A small, short-billed sunbird typical of thorny bush, the Pygmy Sunbird is also found in wooded suburbs planted with flowering acacia and mimosa trees. Its active behavior and tameness make it easy to find and watch as it perches acrobatically on twigs to probe inside small flowers for nectar and insects, behaving rather like a cross between a small tit and a warbler. It has a thin, penetrating call.

During summer the males have long tail spikes and metallic upper plumage, but in winter they have short tails and dull plumage, like the females. This rather dull, nonbreeding eclipse plumage is a characteristic of many sunbirds.

### 2/ SAO THOMÉ GIANT SUNBIRD
*Nectarinia thomensis*
RANGE: **Sao Thomé Island (W Africa)**
HABITAT: **thick forest on W slopes**
SIZE: **9 in (23 cm)**

The largest sunbird of all, this species behaves in an unusual way for a sunbird, frequently using its strong, hooked bill to probe into the bark of trees for insects, rather like a nuthatch (pp. 302–5). Its usual call is a single cheeping note, while its song is a strident repetition of 3 notes.

Its plumage looks black from a distance, for the steely-blue feather edges show up only at close range. Apart from being slightly smaller than the male, the female is otherwise similar. The nest, which is suspended from a branch, is made of moss, dead leaves and roots, lined with dry grass.

### 3/ SCARLET-CHESTED SUNBIRD
*Nectarinia senegalensis*
RANGE: **W and E Africa from Senegal to Kenya and S to Zimbabwe**
HABITAT: **woodland, parks, riverside scrub**
SIZE: **6 in (15 cm)**

This is a large species, with marked plumage variations depending on age, sex and time of year. An adult male in his breeding condition looks intensely black, except for the magnificent, eye-catching splash of red across his breast, but out of season his eclipse plumage is like that of the dull, mottled female or juvenile.

In many areas the Scarlet-chested Sunbird is a year-round resident, but at the limits of its range it

moves short distances according to the seasons, always searching for concentrations of showy, nectar-rich flowers such as those of *Leonotis*. It is fairly common in ornamental gardens, where it is often seen feeding in small groups. Its frequent call is a descending triple note, its song a loud, but undistinguished, warbling trill.

### 4/ PURPLE-RUMPED SUNBIRD
*Nectarinia zeylonica*
RANGE: **peninsular India, Bangladesh, Sri Lanka**
HABITAT: **jungle and dry cultivated plains with deciduous trees**
SIZE: **4 in (10 cm)**

Several sunbirds have evolved long bills which enable them to drink nectar from long, tubular flowers. Purple-rumped Sunbirds, with their short bills, cannot do this; instead they use their bills to pierce large flowers neatly at the base of the petals to reach the nectar.

Males and females differ in appearance; although young males look like rather yellow females, the adult males keep their metallic plumage all year round. They are usually found in pairs, actively flitting among thick foliage and flowers, perching acrobatically to reach into the flowers or – more rarely – hovering briefly to take a fly. The pair will defend their feeding tree and nesting area vigorously if other sunbirds appear. The song is a sharp twitter or a squeaky performance given with flicking wings and tail.

### 5/ YELLOW-BELLIED SUNBIRD
*Nectarinia jugularis*
RANGE: **Southeast Asia, from Indonesia to Solomon Islands, NE Australia**
HABITAT: **coastal rain forest, mangroves and gardens**
SIZE: **$4$–$4\frac{3}{4}$ in (10–12 cm)**

The Yellow-bellied, or Olive-backed, Sunbird is the only sunbird found in Australia, where it is a common, locally nomadic species in the forests and gardens of northeast Queensland.

It is an active bird, which searches a large variety of native and exotic plants for nectar and insects. It usually clings to foliage while feeding but may hover briefly to sip nectar from a flower or pluck a spider from its web. Like most sunbirds, it is incapable of the sustained hovering practiced by hummingbirds (pp. 190–97), which are the ecological equivalents of sunbirds in the New World.

Males and females are fairly similar, but the female's underparts are yellow throughout, whereas the male has a metallic purplish-blue throat and chest. The male defends the breeding territory, but the female builds the nest: this has a dangling "tail" of loose building material.

### 6/ PURPLE SUNBIRD
*Nectarinia asiatica*
RANGE: **Iran, India, Sri Lanka, Indochina**
HABITAT: **thorny riverbeds, forest edge, scrub**
SIZE: **4 in (10 cm)**

The Purple Sunbird is a summer visitor over much of its range: in many mountainous and hilly areas it moves uphill in summer and returns to the valleys as the days shorten. It is always found around flowering trees, which it raids for nectar, and it is an important pollinator of several kinds, especially *Loranthus* species.

Single birds often catch insects on the wing like flycatchers, using their extremely agile flight and excellent eyesight; large gatherings feeding on swarming gnats have also been reported. When the male sings and displays, he opens his wings slightly to display the pectoral tufts which, as on most sunbirds, are generally hidden. Outside the breeding season, the male has a much less dramatic eclipse plumage.

There are 3 races, of which *N. a. asiatica* (illustrated) occurs throughout much of India and Sri Lanka, north to Nepal. A shorter-billed race *N. a. brevirostris*, with a less green and more purple breeding male, is found in the west towards Iran, while a long-billed, purple race *N. a. intermedia* occurs in Bangladesh and to the east.

## 7/ REGAL SUNBIRD
*Nectarinia regia*
RANGE: **W Uganda, W Tanzania**
HABITAT: **mountain forest up to 12,000 ft (3,650 m)**
SIZE: **4¼ in (11 cm)**

The Regal Sunbird exhibits the sexual differences typical of sunbirds, with splendid, metallic males and rather dowdy females. It is one of many African species of sunbird with males patterned with green, yellow, purple, blue and red, all superficially very alike. Young birds are duller and somewhat darker than the adult female.

It is often associated with the Purple-breasted Sunbird *Nectarinia purpureiventris*, with which it seeks out flowering *Symphonia* trees in the remote mountain forests of the Ruwenzori range in Uganda. Here, in dense mist, amid dripping leaves, it is more often heard than seen. Like other sunbirds, it has a rapid trilling or warbling song with little precise pattern but with plenty of energy in the performance.

## 8/ NORTHERN ORANGE-TUFTED SUNBIRD
*Nectarinia osea*
RANGE: **Syria, Israel, W and S edge of Arabian peninsula**
HABITAT: **woods, orchards, gardens**
SIZE: **4¼ in (11 cm)**

Although it prefers bushy places or groves of planted eucalyptus, acacias or mimosas, the Northern Orange-tufted Sunbird is an adaptable species that will live anywhere, from quite bare rocky wadis to well-kept gardens – as long as they provide it with tiny insects or nectar-bearing flowers. In general it is resident throughout its range, but there is some winter dispersal.

Its song is a shrill, rapid, rambling trill, quite unlike that of any other bird in its range. The males may sing as they flit about in search of food, or while perched high in a tree, hidden in dense foliage. Sharp calls uttered in flight are equally characteristic of these birds.

From July to November the mature males look like dull females, but they often have a few traces of their breeding colors on the wings or throat. This is common among sunbirds in eclipse plumage. The small orange tufts flanking the breast are visible only in display.

## 9/ RED-TUFTED MALACHITE SUNBIRD
*Nectarinia johnstoni*
RANGE: **Kenya and Uganda, S to Tanzania**
HABITAT: **alpine moorlands with giant lobelia and proteaceous flowers**
SIZE: **9¾–11¾ in (25–30 cm)**

This large sunbird is remarkable for the long tail feathers of the male which, unusually, are retained even when the bird is in its dull eclipse plumage.

The Red-tufted Malachite Sunbird has a specialized way of life, being found only on high alpine slopes with distinctive vegetation types on remote, bleak uplands such as Mount Kenya, the Aberdare Range, the Ruwenzori Mountains and Mount Kilimanjaro. There it probes the strange and eye-catching flowers of giant lobelias for nectar. It also eats many insects.

## 10/ SUPERB SUNBIRD
*Nectarinia superba*
RANGE: **Sierra Leone E to Central African Republic, S to Congo**
HABITAT: **forest edge and clearings**
SIZE: **6 in (15 cm)**

In poor light the male Superb Sunbird looks almost black, but in full sunshine his metallic plumage dazzles the eye with its breathtakingly beautiful coloration. These birds are usually found in sunny places at the edges of forests, although they also visit savanna woods and thick bush as long as there is plenty of nectar-rich blossom for them to feed from.

These stocky, fairly large sunbirds are hard to follow as they fly swiftly from tree to tree, bounding and zigzagging. Although the species has an extensive range, it is nowhere common. Moreover, the birds' chirping calls and poor, jingling song are of little help in locating them.

## 11/ GOLDEN-WINGED SUNBIRD
*Nectarinia reichenowi*
RANGE: **Uganda, Kenya, W Tanzania**
HABITAT: **highland moors, scrub, forest edge above 5,000 ft (1,500 m)**
SIZE: **9 in (23 cm)**

The Golden-winged Sunbird is a highland specialist, found on bleak moorland and mountain scrub, apparently unlikely surroundings for a nectar-feeder. But as the sun warms the landscape each day, many of the upland plants such as the orange mint *Leonotis nepetifolia* unfurl large, showy flowers that are rich in nectar, which the Golden-winged Sunbird extracts with its powerful, strongly hooked bill. Like many other sunbirds, Golden-winged Sunbirds defend patches of flowers, but when they can obtain enough nectar from flowers shared with other sunbirds they do not need to defend a feeding territory. However, they do not invest energy in defense when nectar production within a patch of flowers is low – the cost to them would outweigh the advantage.

The nonbreeding males have largely black plumage, but a male in breeding condition is a gorgeous sight. In his strange display flight, slow for a sunbird, he zigzags between bushes with wings extended and tail flashing yellow, uttering clear, liquid calls and a warbling song.

## 12/ MRS GOULD'S SUNBIRD
*Aethopyga gouldiae*
RANGE: **Indochina W to Nepal**
HABITAT: **deciduous forest**
SIZE: **4 in (10 cm)**

For such a tiny creature, this sunbird inhabits some demanding places: in Nepal it breeds at altitudes of up to 12,000 ft (3,600 m) and may remain at 9,000 ft (2,700 m) even in winter, although most descend lower.

It is a particularly active, restless sunbird, searching for nectar among the blossoms of low bushes for a while, then turning its attention to the flowers of parasitic plants in the tall forest trees.

A scarlet-breasted race *A. g. dabryii* is found in the east of the species' range. Other races are yellow-breasted, including the deep-yellow-breasted *A. g. gouldiae*, which breeds high in the mountains of Nepal.

## 13/ YELLOW-BACKED SUNBIRD
*Aethopyga siparaja*
RANGE: **Sumatra, Borneo, Malaysia, W to India**
HABITAT: **gardens, orchards, pine forest**
SIZE: **4 in (10 cm)**

The Yellow-backed, or Crimson, Sunbird is a common resident throughout its range. In the Nepal region it moves higher up the mountains in summer and descends again in winter, when it often visits gardens. Unlike many sunbirds, the male Yellow-backed Sunbird retains his bright plumage throughout the year.

It often forages alone, taking nectar from a wide variety of trees and ornamental flowers and adapting its feeding technique to suit the flower. It will pierce larger blooms such as hibiscus to reach the nectar through the base of the petals, but will drink from tubular flowers by hovering before them, rather like a hummingbird, and inserting its tubular tongue. It seems to prefer bright red flowers to any others.

## 14/ LONG-BILLED SPIDERHUNTER
*Arachnothera robusta*
RANGE: **Malaysia, Sumatra, Borneo**
HABITAT: **moist, dense forest**
SIZE: **6 in (15 cm)**

Spiderhunters are long-billed relatives of the sunbirds, found singly or in pairs and often in mixed flocks with babblers and warblers high in the forest trees. This habit, combined with their swift flight and rapid movements, makes them extremely hard to locate and watch.

When seen, they resemble large, long-billed female sunbirds. The sexes are similar, although the male has a small orange-yellow tuft on each flank. They have fast, sharp, metallic calls. They take spiders from their webs while hovering on long, whirring wings, but they also drink nectar; like some of the sunbirds they are important pollinators of several species of tree.

race *hainana*

JAPANESE WHITE-EYE

CHESTNUT-FLANKED
WHITE-EYE

race *japonica*

ORIENTAL WHITE-EYE

race *gouldii*

race *lateralis*

GRAY-BACKED WHITE-EYE

PALE WHITE-EYE

race *chlorocephala*

WOODFORD'S WHITE-EYE

AFRICAN YELLOW WHITE-EYE

RUFOUS-THROATED WHITE-EYE

TRUK WHITE-EYE

PYGMY WHITE-EYE

race *dohertyi*

CRESTED WHITE-EYE

race *subcristatus*

race *emiliae*

OLIVE BLACK-EYE

race *lugubris*

BLACK-CAPPED SPEIROPS

CINNAMON WHITE-EYE

race *melanocephalus*

# WHITE-EYES

## FAMILY ZOSTEROPIDAE
### White-eyes

Small perching birds with brush-tipped tongues, rounded wings and short legs. Plumage greenish with yellow, gray or brown underparts; most species with ring of white feathers around eye. Males sometimes brighter and bigger. Nests cup-shaped, built in trees. Eggs 2–4, whitish or pale blue. Incubation 10–12 days, nestling period 11–14 days. 85 species.

## 1/ CHESTNUT-FLANKED WHITE-EYE
*Zosterops erythropleura*
RANGE: **Manchuria, N Korea, China**
HABITAT: **forest, open woodland**
SIZE: **4¼ in (11 cm)**

Most white-eyes are rather nondescript looking birds, with cryptic greenish plumage that blends well with the leaves among which they feed. With its reddish-brown flank patches and gray, white and yellow underparts, the Chestnut-flanked White-eye has a rather more striking appearance than most species, but in other respects it is typical of this versatile group of birds.

These birds are generally seen foraging in flocks, diligently searching through the foliage for insects and their larvae and occasionally feeding on fruit. Males and females form stable pairs, often for life, and build their nests in tree forks in well-protected positions.

White-eyes, including this species, are kept as cage birds in some Asian countries because of their attractive songs, but they do not breed successfully – the young generally die.

## 2/ JAPANESE WHITE-EYE
*Zosterops japonica*
RANGE: **China, Indochina, Japan**
HABITAT: **low hill forest, parks and gardens**
SIZE: **4¼ in (11 cm)**

In the Far East the Japanese White-eye is a familiar winter visitor to gardens as it flies in to feast on seeds and soft fruit during the colder months. Small parties forage from tree to tree in the same way that winter flocks of tits move through European woods, advertising their presence with faint bell-like calls rather like those of the Spruce Siskin *Carduelis spinus* of northern Eurasia.

In summer, the Japanese White-eye uses its brush-tipped tongue to soak up nectar from large blooms, but its main diet consists of insects and spiders, which it gleans from tree foliage and picks out of bark crevices with its short, fine-pointed bill. Although these birds are regarded as pests by commercial fruit-growers, any damage they do in orchards is far outweighed by the number of insect pests they eat.

The race *Z.j. japonica* is found on Honshu Island, Japan. The distinctive *Z.j. hainana*, found on Hainan Island off southern China, is small, with brighter, more yellowish plumage.

## 3/ ORIENTAL WHITE-EYE
*Zosterops palpebrosa*
RANGE: **Afghanistan E to China, Malaysia, Indonesia**
HABITAT: **hill forest, mangroves, gardens**
SIZE: **4 in (10 cm)**

Typically small, dumpy white-eyes, with a good deal of yellow, white and green in their plumage, Oriental White-eyes live in small groups which spend much of their time in the trees, searching for weevils, ants and other insects, as well as their eggs. The parties set up a high, querulous chorus of calls as they feed, repeating the song over and over again with no variation. In forests and cultivated areas they frequently forage in mixed-species flocks with other birds.

The male and female build the nest together, weaving a delicate cup of grass and spiders' webs suspended in the fork of a tree or shrub. The pale blue eggs are incubated for 12 days and the young leave the nest 12 days after hatching, freeing the parents to produce a second brood.

## 4/ GRAY-BACKED WHITE-EYE
*Zosterops lateralis*
RANGE: **Australia, Tasmania, SW Pacific islands**
HABITAT: **practically every type of vegetation, from rain forest, mangroves, woods and heaths, to urban parks and gardens**
SIZE: **4¼–5 in (11–13 cm)**

Also known as the Gray-breasted Silvereye, the Gray-backed White-eye is a very variable species with 14 races distributed across the islands of the southwest Pacific. The races *Z. l. lateralis* of Tasmania, *Z. l. gouldii* of southwest Australia and *Z. l. chlorocephala* of the Great Barrier Reef islands illustrate the range of plumage variation. The female is usually paler than the male within a given pair, but may be brighter than other females.

Foraging Gray-backed White-eyes are constantly on the move through their habitat as they gather insects from low foliage, picking them off the leaves or snatching them as they attempt to

escape. They also eat fruit and nectar. In winter they form flocks and in Australia some populations undertake long migrations.

Between August and January both sexes defend the breeding territory and help to build the tightly woven cup nest, which is suspended 3–39 ft (1–12 m) above the ground. Both parents share the duties of incubating the 3 eggs for 14 days and feeding the young. The latter fledge when they are 12–14 days old.

## 5/ PALE WHITE-EYE
*Zosterops citrinella*
RANGE: **islands of Lesser Sundas and Torres Strait; isolated islands off N Australia**
HABITAT: **forest, monsoon scrub, mangroves, grassland with low shrubs**
SIZE: **4–4¾ in (10–12 cm)**

Although easily confused with the northern Australian race of the Gray-backed White-eye (but distinguished from the latter by its greenish yellow rather than gray back), the Pale White-eye is a distinct species restricted to remote, isolated islands in northern Australasia. Because of the relative inaccessibility of its habitat, little is known about its biology, but it is regularly seen foraging at all levels in the forest, gleaning insects from leaves and flowers and feeding on berries and nectar when these foods are available. The Pale White-eye is sometimes known as the Ashy-bellied White-eye.

The birds breed in the wet season (December to June), building a deep, cup-shaped nest of dried leaves and spiders' webs to contain the clutch of 2–4 eggs. It is probable that both the male and female brood the eggs and feed the young.

## 6/ AFRICAN YELLOW WHITE-EYE
*Zosterops senegalensis*
RANGE: **sub-Saharan Africa**
HABITAT: **open thornbush, dry woods, gardens**
SIZE: **4 in (10 cm)**

This is the typical, common white-eye of Africa. Widespread and frequently encountered in open woodland or among scattered trees, it is rarely seen in dense forest. Small parties often mix with sunbirds and other species, flitting through the canopy and down into lower bushes in a constant search for the insects that make up most of their diet. The birds maintain contact with one another by means of weak, twittering calls and piping notes as they fly from tree to tree.

The pair builds a nest of fine plant fiber decorated with lichens, either placed in a tree fork or suspended from a branch.

## 7/ WOODFORD'S WHITE-EYE
*Woodfordia superciliosa*
RANGE: **Rennell Island (Solomon Islands)**
HABITAT: **woodland, bushes**
SIZE: **5½ in (14 cm)**

Closely related to the true white-eyes of the genus *Zosterops*, this slightly larger bird has a very similar way of life, moving about in small parties that search the foliage and outer twigs of trees for small insects and seeds. It has a rather long bill for a white-eye, and its facial patch and eye ring are of bare skin, not small white or silver feathers as in most of the family. It lays its clutch of 2 eggs in a delicate nest.

Woodford's White-eye shares its tiny island with another white-eye, the Rennell Island White-eye *Zosterops rennelliana*, a smaller bird with a thin white eye ring.

## 8/ TRUK WHITE-EYE
*Rukia ruki*     E
RANGE: **Truk Islands (tropical Pacific Ocean)**
HABITAT: **dense mountain forest**
SIZE: **5½ in (14 cm)**

The tropical islands north of New Guinea have many species limited to a single island. The Truk White-eye is found at the summit of Tol Island and reputedly on some others in the group. It has always been very rare and was not seen between its discovery early this century and its rediscovery in 1975, in the 30 acres (12 hectares) of mountain forest that remain on the island. Here it keeps to the outer branches of the canopy, probing among the tangled vines and other creepers to find its insect prey.

Rather larger and more solidly built than the true white-eyes of the genus *Zosterops*, this species lacks their greenish plumage and has only a small white mark beneath its eye instead of a complete ring. It has a loud, whistled song with a musical, warbling pattern.

## 9/ RUFOUS-THROATED WHITE-EYE
*Madanga ruficollis*     ?
RANGE: **NW Buru Island (Indonesia)**
HABITAT: **forests**
SIZE: **5–5½ in (13–14 cm)**

The Rufous-throated White-eye was first described in 1923, from just 4 specimens which were collected from the mountain forests of Buru Island. It then promptly disappeared from the scientific record and has not been recorded again. It seems likely that it is now extinct.

It is (or was) a large species, not closely related to any other white-eye. Nothing is known of its habits, although the specimens described in 1923 were taken at 2,750 and 5,000 ft (840 and 1,550 m) above sea level.

## 10/ CRESTED WHITE-EYE
*Lophozosterops dohertyi*     ?
RANGE: **Sumbawa and Flores islands (Indonesia)**
HABITAT: **forests**
SIZE: **4¾ in (12 cm)**

There are 2 quite distinct races of the Crested White-eye. On Flores Island the race *L. d. subcristatus* is found in light rain forest, at altitudes of 1,000–3,500 ft (300–1,100 m); it has a pale grayish crown with a very slight crest. The race found on Sumbawa, *L. d. dohertyi*, has a darker, browner crown, with each feather sharply spotted white, and a much more obvious crest.

Their behavior is very like that of other white-eyes; sociable and energetic, yet rather unobtrusive, with a preference for feeding among the foliage and tangled creepers of the forest.

## 11/ PYGMY WHITE-EYE
*Oculocincta squamifrons*     ?
RANGE: **Borneo**
HABITAT: **damp moss forest, clearings**
SIZE: **4 in (10 cm)**

This tiny white-eye is found along the mountain chain that forms the backbone of Borneo, at altitudes of 600–4,000 ft (180–1,200 m). Basically a bird of warm, moist forest, it is often seen among secondary scrub growing in areas of felled jungle, and in clearings around villages.

It keeps low, even in mature forest, and is well known for its habit of approaching humans and cattle very closely in dense scrub – possibly to snap up the insects they disturb. Despite this, its main food appears to be berries and seeds. Its nest and eggs have never been positively identified.

## 12/ OLIVE BLACK-EYE
*Chlorocharis emiliae*
RANGE: **Borneo**
HABITAT: **low-growing mountain heath, mossy areas, rhododendron thickets**
SIZE: **4½ in (11.5 cm)**

Many isolated island white-eyes have developed distinctive plumage variations of their own, but most have retained at least part of the white eye ring characteristic of the family. The Olive Black-eye is a unique exception to the rule. There are 4 races; the race illustrated is *C. e. emiliae*, found only on Mount Kinabalu in northern Borneo.

On the high mountains of Borneo the Olive Black-eye is the commonest bird, ranging throughout the region above the tree line where conifers, rhododendrons and heathers gradually give way with increasing altitude to bare, slippery rock with stunted scrub. It nests in dense heath, building a flattened cup of dead grass and lichens, sometimes lined with bright orange moss.

Olive Black-eyes feed mainly on insects and seeds and as they forage they utter twittering, finchlike calls that may be heard all day, even into the wet, gloomy dusk when gray cloud envelops their mountain retreats.

## 13/ CINNAMON WHITE-EYE
*Hypocryptadius cinnamomeus*
RANGE: **Mindanao Island (Philippines)**
HABITAT: **mountain forest, at 3,000–6,000 ft (900–1,800 m)**
SIZE: **5 in (13 cm)**

The Cinnamon White-eye is a very local species, restricted to the mountain forests of Mount Apo on the island of Mindanao in the Philippines. Its plumage is markedly different from that of other white-eyes, and some ornithologists consider that it should be classified in a separate family.

It feeds mainly on insects, picking them off leaves and tangled vegetation with its sharp-pointed bill. Apart from this, very little is known about the Cinnamon White-eye's behavior, and its nesting habits are still a mystery.

## 14/ BLACK-CAPPED SPEIROPS
*Speirops lugubris*
RANGE: **Cameroon, Sao Thomé Island (Gulf of Guinea)**
HABITAT: **mountain forest clearings**
SIZE: **5 in (13 cm)**

In the uplands of Sao Thomé Island, the Black-capped Speirops is a common sight as it forages through the trees in small, restless feeding parties. The birds search nonstop for food, flicking their wings and flitting from tree to tree like stout, short-tailed warblers or tits and communicating with short, musical chirps.

On Sao Thomé the race *S. l. lugubris* feeds in trees, in typical white-eye fashion, but the white-throated race *S. l. melanocephalus*, found in the mountain forests of Cameroon, prefers bushy places and clearings. Little is known about the nesting behavior of either race.

# HONEYEATERS, SUGARBIRDS, AUSTRALIAN CHATS

CARDINAL HONEYEATER

MIMIC MELIPHAGA

race *chloropsis*

race *lunatus*

WHITE-NAPED
HONEYEATER

juv

race *cyanotis*

race *albipennis*

BLUE-FACED HONEYEATER

YELLOW WATTLEBIRD

imm

♂

STITCHBIRD

♀

NOISY FRIARBIRD

LONG-BEARDED
MELIDECTES

KAUAI O-O

NEW HOLLAND HONEYEATER

WESTERN SPINEBILL

♂

♀

NOISY MINER

imm

TUI

♂

♂

CRIMSON CHAT

♂

♀

♀

CAPE SUGARBIRD

453

# HONEYEATERS, SUGARBIRDS, AUSTRALIAN CHATS

## FAMILY MELIPHAGIDAE
### Honeyeaters

Small to medium mostly tree-dwelling perching birds with brushlike tongues for feeding on nectar. Plumage generally dull green or brown. Sexes typically similar, but males brighter in some species and usually larger. Nest cup-shaped, in bush or tree. Eggs 2–4, white to buff with brown spots. Incubation 13–17 days, nestling period 10–16 days. 170 species.

## 1/ CARDINAL HONEYEATER
*Myzomela cardinalis*

RANGE: **islands of Vanuatu, Samoa, Santa Cruz and Solomons**
HABITAT: **coastal scrub, secondary forest, woodland, gardens**
SIZE: **5 in (13 cm)**

In most honeyeaters the sexes are similar, but the Cardinal Honeyeater is an exception. Whereas the female is dull olive-gray with small red patches, the male has bright scarlet and black plumage. His flamboyant appearance is matched by his noisy, aggressive territorial behavior.

These dramatic-looking birds normally feed in the canopy but they venture lower down when near the forest edge, sipping nectar from flowers and gleaning insects from the foliage. They may breed at any time of year, suspending a fragile nest of plant fiber from a tree fork and laying 2–3 eggs which are incubated by both birds.

## 2/ MIMIC MELIPHAGA
*Meliphaga analoga*

RANGE: **New Guinea, Aru and Geelvink islands**
HABITAT: **rain forest, forest edge, scrub**
SIZE: **6–6½ in (15–17 cm)**

This is one of 6 very similar species which often occur together at the edges of rain forest on New Guinea and adjacent islands. It spends most of its time among the smaller trees, but often ventures out into nearby scrub or enters gardens to feed on fruit and insects and take advantage of nectar-bearing flowers. Like many honeyeaters, the Mimic Meliphaga bathes by flying into water and then returning to a perch to preen.

## 3/ WHITE-NAPED HONEYEATER
*Melithreptus lunatus*

RANGE: **E and SW Australia (not Tasmania)**
HABITAT: **eucalyptus forest and woodland**
SIZE: **5–6 in (13–15 cm)**

The White-naped Honeyeater is one of several short-beaked species with generally olive-green upper plumage and black heads. The small patch of skin, or wattle, above the eye is red in the eastern race *M. l. lunatus* and chalky white in the western *M. l. chloropsis*.

These birds forage in pairs or small groups, gleaning insects from foliage and bark and drinking nectar. Most birds are resident, but some will form flocks of 30–50 birds and migrate north for the winter.

White-naped Honeyeaters may breed as pairs or in small groups, cooperating to defend the nest

area. The nest is made of shredded bark and dry grasses bound with spiders' webs and is suspended from a fork high in the outer foliage of a tree or shrub.

## 4/ BLUE-FACED HONEYEATER
*Entomyzon cyanotis*

RANGE: **S New Guinea, N and E Australia**
HABITAT: **eucalyptus and paperbark woodland, plantations, parks, gardens; occasionally mangroves**
SIZE: **9½–11¾ in (24–30 cm)**

Well known for its pugnacious, inquisitive character, the Blue-faced Honeyeater has also earned a bad reputation as a pest of banana plantations, where it feeds on the ripe fruit. It usually forages in small groups, searching out fruit, nectar and insects in the upper foliage and branches.

Groups of 2–10 adults breed together, sharing the brooding and feeding of the 1–2 young. The nest is usually an untidy deep bowl of bark, but occasionally they will take over deserted nests of other birds. The northwestern race *E. c. albipennis* has white wing patches which are conspicuous in flight. The eastern race *E. c. cyanotis* has only a small buff patch on its wings.

## 5/ STITCHBIRD
*Notiomystis cincta*  [V]

RANGE: **Little Barrier Island (New Zealand); introduced to Hen and Kapiti islands**
HABITAT: **mature forest**
SIZE: **7–7½ in (18–19 cm)**

Once far more widespread across the northern islands of New Zealand, the Stitchbird is now reduced to three small islands off the northeast coast. Usually detected by its sharp, high-pitched call, it moves rapidly through the vegetation with its tail cocked, feeding on fruit, nectar and insects. Unlike most honeyeaters, it rarely congregates at rich feeding sites. The Stitchbird breeds in late spring and summer and, unusually for a honeyeater, nests in a hole in a tree trunk or branch, 10–60 ft (3–18 m) above the ground.

## 6/ NOISY FRIARBIRD
*Philemon corniculatus*

RANGE: **S New Guinea, E Australia**
HABITAT: **open forest, woodland and lowland savanna**
SIZE: **11¾–13¼ in (30–34 cm)**

This large honeyeater is also known as the Knobby-nosed Leatherhead because of the black, naked skin on its head and the small knob at the base of its upper mandible. It often gathers in groups at flowering trees, squabbling raucously over the spoils as it feeds on fruit and collects the nectar of banksia and eucalyptus trees. It also consumes insects, which provide valuable protein in an otherwise sugar-rich diet.

In the breeding season (July to January) the flocks break up, and the birds advertise their feeding and breeding territories with grating, discordant calls. The females incubate the 2–3 eggs alone, but both sexes feed the young.

## 7/ LONG-BEARDED MELIDECTES
*Melidectes princeps*

RANGE: **New Guinea, on E highlands of Central Range**
HABITAT: **mossy woodland, alpine scrub and grassland above tree line**
SIZE: **10½ in (27 cm)**

This species is fairly common within its confined range but, despite this, very little is known about its way of life. It seems that, like its better-known close relative the Short-bearded Melidectes *M. nouhuysi*, but unlike most other honeyeaters, the Long-bearded Melidectes spends much of its time on the ground, sifting through leaf litter to find fruit, berries, sedge seeds and insects. Its nesting behavior, too, is little known. The bulky cup-shaped nest is well concealed in an isolated shrub and on one occasion, in July, a pair of adults was seen feeding a single fledgling, suggesting, perhaps, that only one egg is laid.

After the 9 other members of the genus *Melidectes*, the closest relatives of the Long-bearded Melidectes appear to be the wattlebirds, such as the Yellow Wattlebird.

## 8/ KAUAI O-O
*Moho braccatus*  ⒠
RANGE: **island of Kauai (Hawaii)**
HABITAT: **dense rain forest**
SIZE: **7¾ in (20 cm)**

A century ago this was a common bird in forests all over its native island, but it became increasingly rare and was presumed extinct until it was rediscovered in 1960, in a small area of swamp forest. It was probably saved by its dull plumage, which made it unattractive to the Hawaiians who captured its brighter (and now extinct) relatives in great numbers.

An active, quick bird, it darts noisily from tree to tree searching for insects and spiders among the bark. Unfortunately it is now threatened by habitat destruction and introduced predators and is unlikely to survive. Indeed, it is thought that only a solitary male is still alive.

## 9/ NEW HOLLAND HONEYEATER
*Phylidonyris novaehollandiae*
RANGE: **SW and E Australia, Tasmania**
HABITAT: **heathland, mallee heath, woods and forests with shrubs**
SIZE: **6½–7½ in (17–19 cm)**

New Holland, or Yellow-winged, Honeyeaters are aggressive birds, but their aggression varies with the abundance of nectar and nesting resources. They catch insects for their protein content but rely on honeydew and nectar to supply energy. As they gather the nectar, they are dusted with pollen which is transferred to successive blossoms, and in this way they play an important role in the pollination of a wide range of Australian plants.

They may breed up to 3 times a year, depending on the availability of nectar. The males defend nest sites that are arranged in loose colonies, usually 3–6 ft (1–2 m) above the ground in shrubs. The females build the nests and incubate the 2–3 eggs, but the young are fed by both parents.

## 10/ WESTERN SPINEBILL
*Acanthorhynchus superciliosus*
RANGE: **SW corner of Australia**
HABITAT: **heathland, eucalyptus woodland with shrubs**
SIZE: **6 in (15 cm)**

The Western Spinebill is a small, active honeyeater with a long, downcurved bill. Being small, it is usually displaced from rich nectar sources by larger honeyeaters, but its very smallness enables it to forage efficiently at a wide range of less productive blooms that would not support bigger birds. It is a resourceful feeder, often hovering to sip nectar and hawking for insects.

When breeding, the male aggressively defends the nest site and engages in display flights. The nest is built by the female and she also incubates the 1–2 eggs. The nestlings are fed by both parents for 11 days.

## 11/ NOISY MINER
*Manorina melanocephala*
RANGE: **E Australia, Tasmania**
HABITAT: **open forest, woodland and partly cleared land**
SIZE: **9¾–11½ in (25–29 cm)**

Noisy Miners have a complex social system, with territorial groups of 6–30 birds gathering together into large colonies. The group members co-operate to mob predators and they will aggressively exclude most other bird species from the nesting area.

They breed communally, with as many as 12 males caring for the young of each polyandrous female. The nest, which is built by the female, is a loosely constructed bowl of twigs and grasses placed in the fork of a shrub or tree.

## 12/ YELLOW WATTLEBIRD
*Anthochaera paradoxa*
RANGE: **E Tasmania and King Island**
HABITAT: **dry eucalyptus forest and woodland, occasionally orchards and gardens**
SIZE: **17¼–18¾ in (44–48 cm)**

Named for the bright yellow wattles that hang from its cheeks, the Yellow Wattlebird is the largest of the honeyeaters and was once shot as a gamebird. Outside the breeding season it often lives in flocks of 10–12 birds; these may be sedentary or nomadic, foraging through the canopy for insects, gleaning them from the leaves, branches and bark. In addition, the birds eat nectar and fruit.

Yellow Wattlebirds breed as pairs, establishing territories in August and laying 2–3 eggs in an untidy nest built of thin twigs and grasses, placed in thick foliage.

## 13/ TUI
*Prosthemadura novaeseelandiae*
RANGE: **New Zealand**
HABITAT: **forests, suburban areas**
SIZE: **12¼ in (31 cm)**

This large, dark honeyeater is also known as the Parsonbird – a reference to the characteristic double tuft of curled white feathers at its throat, which bobs up and down during the bird's singing displays. The song is complex, involving both harsh and tuneful elements and even some notes inaudible to the human ear.

Tui often congregate in large numbers around rich food sources. They are wider-ranging than the other 2 New Zealand honeyeaters (the Stitchbird and the New Zealand Bellbird *Anthornis melanura*) and take more nectar in their diet, although some fruits and insects are also eaten.

They breed in late spring and summer, building bulky open nests of twigs in solid tree forks, well off the ground.

## FAMILY EPHTHIANURIDAE
**Australian chats**

Small, open country, perching birds with red, yellow, or black and white plumage, males brighter than females. Nest on or near ground. Eggs 3–4, white or pinkish with brown spots. Incubation 12 days, nestling period 14 days. 5 species.

## 14/ CRIMSON CHAT
*Ephthianura tricolor*
RANGE: **inland and W Australia**
HABITAT: **acacia scrub, savanna, succulent shrub-steppe, often near salt lakes**
SIZE: **4¼–4¾ in (11–12 cm)**

Closely related to the honeyeaters, the Crimson Chat is a nomad of the arid zone. After the young fledge each year, Crimson Chats gather in flocks, sometimes with several hundred birds, and move across the country picking insects off the ground and sipping nectar from flowers.

In the breeding season the males defend females and a small area around the nest, which is a well-concealed cup of fine twigs and grasses placed close to the ground in a shrub or tussock. The nests are often clumped in loose colonies and both the male and the duller female share the incubation and feeding duties.

## FAMILY PROMEROPIDAE
**Sugarbirds**

Long-billed perching birds resembling large honeyeaters. Males with greatly extended tails, sexes otherwise similar. Nest in bushes. Eggs 2, cream, buff or pinkish white, blotched, spotted and scrawled with gray, brown, chocolate or purplish-black. Incubation about 17 days, nestling period 17–21 days. 2 species.

## 15/ CAPE SUGARBIRD
*Promerops cafer*
RANGE: **S tip of South Africa**
HABITAT: **mountain slopes with protea blooms**
SIZE: **male 14½–17¼ in (37–44 cm); female 9½–11½ in (24–29 cm)**

Once considered close relatives of the Australian honeyeaters, the sugarbirds of South Africa are now often thought to be more closely related to the starlings. Nevertheless, these birds have many features in common with the honeyeaters: notably their diet.

Their chief food is insects, often caught in midair, but they also roam around in groups in search of the large flowers of protea plants, from which they drink nectar with their long bills.

In the breeding season the territorial males give loud metallic calls from bush tops and indulge in display flights, holding their extraordinarily long tails high and clapping their wings together. The tail of the male is 8½–12½ in (22–32 cm) long, whereas that of the female is only 4–6 in (11–15.5 cm) long.

# OLD WORLD BUNTINGS AND NEW WORLD SPARROWS, PLUSH-CAPPED FINCH

winter ♂

♂

race *schoeniclus*

REED BUNTING

♀

winter ♂

LAPLAND LONGSPUR

♂

SNOW BUNTING

♀

♂

race *costaricensis*

♂ winter

race *maxima*

SONG SPARROW

race *saltonis*

RUFOUS-COLLARED SPARROW

race *hyemalis*
"Slate-colored Junco"
♂

race *thurberi*
"Oregon Junco"
♂

DARK-EYED JUNCO

♂

race *caniceps*
"Gray-headed Junco"

CHIPPING SPARROW

ZAPATA SPARROW

race *inexpectata*

race *americana*
"Wing-barred Seedeater"

♂ ♀

♂ race *corvina*
"Black Seedeater"

VARIABLE SEEDEATER

♂ ♀

YELLOW-FACED GRASSQUIT

♂ ♀

LARGE GROUND FINCH

race *pallidus*

PLUSH-CAPPED FINCH

WOODPECKER FINCH

race
*erythrophthalmus*

♀

♂

race *oregonus*

♂

RUFOUS-SIDED TOWHEE

## FAMILY EMBERIZIDAE/ SUBFAMILY EMBERIZINAE
### Old World buntings and New World sparrows

Small, mainly ground-dwelling birds. Conical bills and strong feet for scratching. Chiefly seed-eaters, mostly in open habitats almost worldwide. Sexes often differ: plumage ranges from grays and dull browns in many species to yellow-red, blue-green, chestnut, black, white and black-and-white in some species. Nest cup-shaped, usually on ground or in low bush. Eggs 2–7 (usually 4–6), whitish, pale brown or pale blue, usually with reddish, brownish or blackish markings. Incubation 10–14 days, nestling period 8–15 days. 284 species.

## 1/ REED BUNTING
*Emberiza schoeniclus*

RANGE: Eurasia S to Iberia and S USSR and E to NE Asia and Manchuria; N and E populations winter S as far as N Africa, Iran and Japan
HABITAT: lowland marshes, reedbeds and, increasingly, drier habitats
SIZE: 6–6½ in (15.5–16.5 cm)

The Reed Bunting constantly flicks and half spreads its tail so that its bold white outer tail feathers serve as a conspicuous signal to others of its kind in the dense reedbeds and marshes. With the drainage of wetlands, this attractive bunting declined over much of its range, but during the past 50 years or so it has shown an increasing tendency to colonize drier habitats, such as scrubland, overgrown ditches and hedgerows.

The shape of the Reed Bunting's bill varies geographically to a striking extent, from very small, slight and pointed in races such as *E.s. parvirostris* of central Siberia, to thick and almost parrot-shaped in races such as *E.s. pyrrhuloides* of western and central Asia, western Mongolia and northwest China. The race *E.s. schoeniclus* from northwestern Europe and central Russia is one of the smaller-billed races, although its bill is stouter than that of *E.s. parvirostris*. The different sizes and shapes of the bills are related to the birds' habitat and winter diet.

## 2/ LAPLAND LONGSPUR
*Calcarius lapponicus*

RANGE: circumpolar in Arctic region; winters S to NE France and S USSR in Eurasia, and S to New Mexico and Texas in USA
HABITAT: Arctic tundra and high mountains; winters on moors, grassy fields, grain stubble and shores
SIZE: 6–6½ in (15.5–16.5 cm)

This bird prefers to breed in areas of tundra with some shrubs or dwarf trees. The male, in his handsome, bright, breeding plumage, utters a brief, tinkling, larklike song in a display flight or from a prominent perch on a rock or stunted tree. Lapland Longspurs often nest in small colonies.

Very small numbers of Lapland Longspurs established breeding sites in the late 1970s in northern Scotland, well to the south and west of the species' normal breeding range. However, by 1981 all the birds had disappeared.

In winter, Lapland Longspurs are often seen in large mixed flocks with Horned Buntings, other buntings, finches and Horned Larks *Eremophila alpestris*, keeping a low crouching position as they walk, run or hop across a windswept stubble field or bleak, deserted beach.

## 3/ SNOW BUNTING
*Plectrophenax nivalis*

RANGE: circumpolar in Arctic region; winters S to N France and S USSR in Eurasia, and S to NW California, C Kansas and Virginia in the USA
HABITAT: Arctic stony tundra and rocky shores, rock outcrops in glaciers and snowfields, and on a few high mountains; winters on sandy shores, salt marshes, in fields and on grassy moorland
SIZE: 6¼ in (16.5 cm)

The Snow Bunting is the world's northernmost breeding land bird, nesting as far north as the northern tip of Greenland. To escape the intense cold, these plump little birds sometimes burrow in the snow. Their nests are hidden deep in a crack or beneath a large stone among fragmented rocks and boulders. Breeding birds utter a brief but musical song – loud for the bird's size – both on the wing and from a rock or other low perch. Snow Buntings also have a variety of musical, rippling, twittering calls.

These birds are gregarious outside the breeding season, occurring in small flocks and larger parties of several hundred birds. At this time of year they eat mainly seeds; in the breeding season they also eat insects, buds and grasses.

## 4/ SONG SPARROW
*Melospiza melodia*

RANGE: S Alaska, C Canada S to N Mexico
HABITAT: brushy, grassy areas, often near water; also hedgerows, thickets, gardens
SIZE: 5½ in (14 cm)

This well-studied, widespread species has some resident and some migratory populations in North America. The breeding range of the species is currently expanding in southeastern USA and is just now reaching the northern portions of the Gulf Coast states. Different races of this bird show great variation in size and color. Those illustrated are the largest race, *M.m. maxima* of the Aleutian Islands, and the pale desert race *M.m. saltonis* of southwestern USA. Songs also vary among populations, so much so that researchers can identify birds by their "dialect."

During the breeding season, males sing from dawn to dusk and sometimes even into the night. Each song begins with a rhythmic introduction, which is followed by a trill, and ends with a series of irregular notes. The male is highly territorial and defends an area of slightly less than 1 acre (0.4 hectares) in prime habitat. The Song Sparrow eats mainly seeds, but insects and other invertebrates comprise up to a third of its diet.

## 5/ RUFOUS-COLLARED SPARROW
*Zonotrichia capensis*

RANGE: S Mexico S to Tierra del Fuego, Hispaniola, Netherlands Antilles
HABITAT: open and semiopen natural and disturbed habitats, including cities
SIZE: 5½–6 in (14–15 cm)

This tame and conspicuous bird is the common "sparrow" of Latin America. Most populations are resident, but the southernmost apparently migrate. Although the song of this species varies considerably over the bird's wide range, the basic pattern is easily recognizable, consisting of 1–2 slurred whistles followed by a trill. The song perches are usually exposed, and include posts, poles and the corners of buildings. There are many races, which differ chiefly in the darkness and pattern on their heads: the one illustrated, *Z.c. costaricensis*, is from Costa Rica, Panama, Venezuela and Colombia.

The nest of the Rufous-collared Sparrow is a cup of grasses and roots. This is built near the ground and may be used for successive broods. The eggs are grayish to pale greenish-blue, blotched with gray and with a concentration of rusty spots around the larger end.

## 6/ DARK-EYED JUNCO
*Junco hyemalis*

RANGE: **breeds Canada, N and C USA; N populations migrate S as far as Mexico**
HABITAT: **forests of conifers, birch, aspen; various on migration and in winter**
SIZE: **6¼ in (16 cm)**

There are 5 recognizable forms of the Dark-eyed Junco, which used to be considered separate species. Although they vary considerably in plumage, they all have white outer tail feathers, a white belly and dark eyes. The different forms interbreed freely where their ranges meet. Of those illustrated, *J. h. hyemalis* is common in the boreal forests of northern Canada and northern central USA; *J. h. thurberi* breeds in coniferous forests of the far west; and *J. h. caniceps* occurs in the southern Rockies west to eastern California.

All forms of the Dark-eyed Junco sing a musical trill, and utter a rapid twitter in flight. Although primarily seed-eaters, they take many insects during the nesting season.

## 7/ CHIPPING SPARROW
*Spizella passerina*

RANGE: **Canada S to N Nicaragua**
HABITAT: **gardens, woodland, forest edge in E; open woodland and mountains in W**
SIZE: **5–5½ in (12.5–14 cm)**

The Chipping Sparrow is a tame, confiding species, well known to people who provide bird-feeding stations. It eats large quantities of grass and weed seeds, as well as weevils, leafhoppers and other insects. On occasion, it will dart out to catch flying insects. The song is a series of "chips" which at times the bird runs together in a single-pitched, rapid trill. The Chipping Sparrow sometimes sings at night. In winter, the adult's bright chestnut crown becomes duller and streaked, its prominent white eyebrow is lost and it acquires a brown ear patch. The female carries out all the nest-building duties, although the male may accompany her while she is gathering material.

## 8/ ZAPATA SPARROW
*Torreornis inexpectata*

RANGE: **Cuba**
HABITAT: **selected open habitats with scattered trees and bushes**
SIZE: **6½ in (16.5 cm)**

This sparrow is enigmatic because its 3 different populations seem to be living in quite different environments. The western race, *T. i. inexpectata*, occurs in shrubbery near high ground in the Zapata Swamp. Another race, *T. i. sigmani*, lives in the arid scrublands of southeast Cuba, while the third, *T. i. varonai*, occurs on the island of Cayo Coco, off Cuba's north-central coast. Although these habitats differ greatly in their plant species and in the availability of water, they all consist of open terrain with a few trees and shrubs.

Although it has very short wings and seldom takes to the air, the Zapata Sparrow can fly well. The habitat of the Zapata Swamp population is now protected by the Cuban government. The population in the arid coastlands of the southeast also seems safe because the area is unsuitable for agriculture, but fire remains a serious hazard.

## 9/ VARIABLE SEEDEATER
*Sporophila americana*

RANGE: **Mexico S through Panama to parts of Colombia, Ecuador, Peru, Venezuela, Brazil and the Guianas**
HABITAT: **lowland grassy and shrubby areas, clearings, scrub, forest edge, plantations**
SIZE: **4¼–4½ in (11–11.5 cm)**

This species takes its name from the variability of its plumage among its 7 or so races. The 2 races illustrated here are *S. a. americana*, from eastern Venezuela to the lower Amazon, and *S. a. corvina*, from eastern Mexico to Panama. The birds are usually seen in small flocks in which females and immature birds predominate. As they forage, the birds cling to the stems of grasses and weeds to seize small seeds. At times, they may also feed on flowers and buds and nibble at fruit growing high in the trees.

The male Variable Seedeater's song is a fast, complex, musical twitter that it utters from an exposed perch. Both sexes also give a sweet *cheeeu* call note. Nesting seems to be timed according to the ripening of grass seeds.

## 10/ YELLOW-FACED GRASSQUIT
*Tiaris olivacea*

RANGE: **E Mexico to Colombia, Venezuela, Greater Antilles**
HABITAT: **grassy areas in clearings, pastures with scattered bushes, roadsides**
SIZE: **4 in (10 cm)**

This species is sometimes known in the cage-bird trade as the Olive Finch. Pairs and small flocks of these birds are often seen in the wild, picking small seeds from the ground or plucking them from seedheads by clinging to stems. The behavior of this species ranges from social and nonaggressive in Central America, to territorial and pugnacious in Jamaica. These differences have been attributed to the higher population density and more continuous habitat in Jamaica.

The bird's song is a thin, high-pitched, somewhat insectlike trill, which is delivered from a low perch. Its call note is a soft *tek*.

## 11/ LARGE GROUND FINCH
*Geospiza magnirostris*

RANGE: **Galapagos Islands**
HABITAT: **arid areas**
SIZE: **6½ in (16.5 cm)**

The Large Ground Finch is one of 13 species of "Darwin's finches" endemic to the Galapagos Islands. First collected by Charles Darwin, the finches provided one of the examples he used to develop his theory of evolution through natural selection. This species is the largest and also has the biggest bill, which can cope with hard seeds as well as the occasional large insect.

The bulky, dome-shaped nest with a side entrance is built of twigs, grasses and lichens and placed 3–30 ft (1–9 m) above the ground, often in a cactus. The male works on several nests and then displays to a female alongside one of them. Once the pair-bond is formed, the female either finishes one of the nests started by the male or builds a new one herself.

## 12/ WOODPECKER FINCH
*Camarhynchus pallidus*

RANGE: **Galapagos Islands (extinct on San Cristobal and Floreana)**
HABITAT: **humid highlands**
SIZE: **6 in (15 cm)**

The Woodpecker Finch is another of Darwin's finches endemic to the Galapagos Islands. When feeding, some individuals will use a cactus spine, leaf stalk or thin twig as a tool with which to extract invertebrate prey from cavities in dead branches. More commonly, the birds feed by probing their beaks into soft, decaying wood, behind bark or into crevices. They also eat some fruit. This bird has 2 types of song. A high descending whistle is usually sung near the nest, while the territorial song consists of 7–8 loud, rapid notes.

## 13/ RUFOUS-SIDED TOWHEE
*Pipilo erythrophthalmus*

RANGE: **SW Canada, USA S to Baja California**
HABITAT: **dense undergrowth, streamside thickets, open woodland forest edge**
SIZE: **8¾ in (22 cm)**

This showy, ground-dwelling bird has been split into many races, but these fall into one of 3 color forms. The eastern "red-eyed" race, *P. e. erythrophthalmus*, and the southeastern "white-eyed" races differ only in eye color; the western form, including such races as *P. e. oregonus*, differs in its white wing bars and white-spotted scapulars.

Rufous-sided Towhees enjoy a varied diet, from weed seeds and wild berries to insects. They commonly scratch through leaf litter with a raking motion and readily visit bird feeders for suet and seeds. Their stout cup nests are placed on the ground, hidden in dense undergrowth or brush, or low in dense thickets and vine tangles.

## FAMILY EMBERIZIDAE/ SUBFAMILY CATAMBLYRHYNCHINAE
Plush-capped Finch

There is only one species in this subfamily.

## 14/ PLUSH-CAPPED FINCH
*Catamblyrhynchus diadema*

RANGE: **Andes from N Venezuela to N Argentina**
HABITAT: **open woodland and shrubby slopes of Andean highlands, usually near bamboo stands**
SIZE: **5½ in (14 cm)**

The Plush-capped Finch, or Plushcap, takes its name from the stiff, golden-brown feathers at the front of its crown. Very little is known about the habits of this species, and its relationships to the buntings and tanagers are equally enigmatic. It is usually seen in isolated pairs or in mixed foraging flocks with finches, conebills and tanagers. Limited information indicates that its diet includes bamboo leaves, other vegetable matter and insects. It feeds on bamboo stalks by pressing its bill into the bases of dense leaf whorls or by gleaning insects from the stems.

# CARDINAL GROSBEAKS, TANAGERS

RED-CRESTED CARDINAL

ROSE-BREASTED GROSBEAK ♂

♀

♂ ♀

NORTHERN CARDINAL

♂

SLATE-COLORED GROSBEAK

BLUE GROSBEAK ♂

♀

♀

♂

PAINTED BUNTING

♀

♂

WHITE-WINGED SHRIKE-TANAGER

race *auricularis*

BLACK-CAPPED HEMISPINGUS

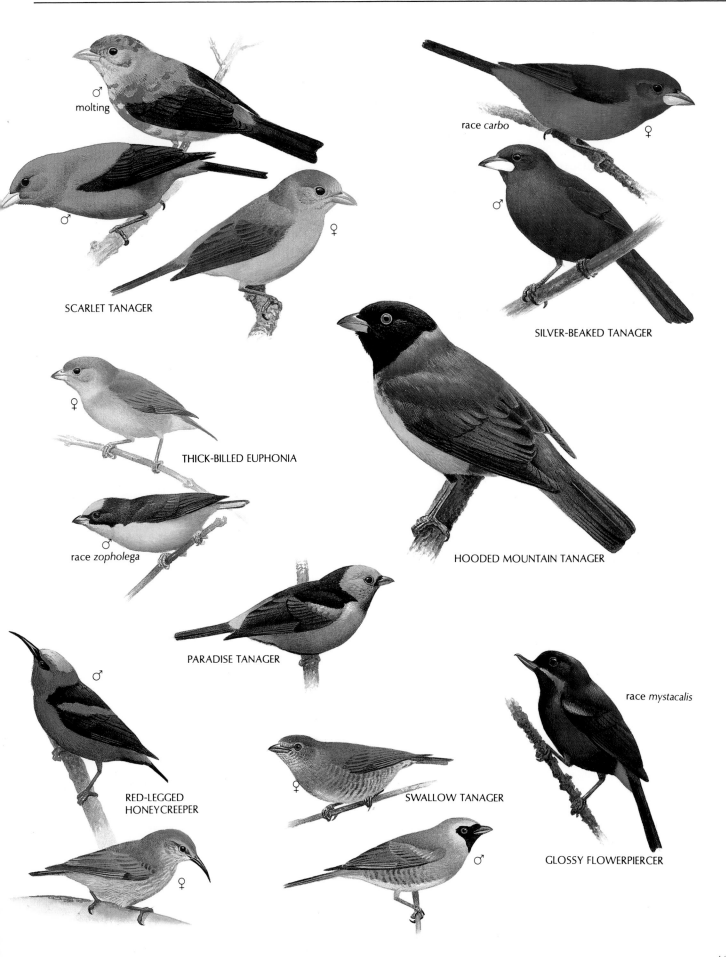

♂ molting

♂

♀

SCARLET TANAGER

race *carbo*

♀

♂

SILVER-BEAKED TANAGER

♀

THICK-BILLED EUPHONIA

race *zopholega* ♂

HOODED MOUNTAIN TANAGER

PARADISE TANAGER

♂

RED-LEGGED
HONEYCREEPER

♀

♀

SWALLOW TANAGER

♂

race *mystacalis*

GLOSSY FLOWERPIERCER

461

# CARDINAL GROSBEAKS, TANAGERS

## FAMILY EMBERIZIDAE/
## SUBFAMILY CARDINALINAE
### Cardinal grosbeaks

Small to medium birds with heavy bills. Plumage variable, often brightly colored. Sexes alike or different. Nests usually in trees and shrubs. Eggs 2–5, white, bluish, blue or greenish, unmarked or speckled or scrawled. Incubation 11–14 days, nestling period 9–15 days. 47 species.

## 1/ RED-CRESTED CARDINAL
*Paroaria coronata*

RANGE: E Bolivia, Paraguay, Uruguay, S Brazil, N Argentina; introduced to Hawaii
HABITAT: **lowland humid scrub, semiopen terrain, especially near water**
SIZE: **7½ in (19 cm)**

Red-crested Cardinals often feed on the ground in wet areas, and even walk on floating vegetation, where their large feet and long toes probably help to spread their weight. Although generally seen in pairs or small groups, they often form larger flocks outside the breeding season. Their diet includes both seeds and invertebrates.

Because of its beauty and rich, melodious song, this species has been widely trapped for the cage-bird trade, and its populations have declined in some areas. Introduced to Hawaii in 1928, it is now especially common on the island of Oahu.

## 2/ ROSE-BREASTED GROSBEAK
*Pheucticus ludovicianus*

RANGE: **SC Canada, E USA; winters S to Mexico and N South America**
HABITAT: **secondary growth woodland, trees along watercourses**
SIZE: **7¾ in (20 cm)**

This thick-billed bird has a special fondness for blossoms and buds, although it also eats beetles, grasshoppers, cankerworms, seeds and some fruit and grain. It often visits feeding stations, especially during migration. The male often delivers his liquid melodies in flight, while pursuing a female. The drabber female also sings, producing a shorter, softer tune. Mates sometimes touch bills in courtship. Both share the nesting duties, the male later caring for the fledglings while the female re-nests. The male molts into a duller, brown-tipped winter plumage before migrating.

## 3/ NORTHERN CARDINAL
*Cardinalis cardinalis*

RANGE: **SE Canada, E, C and SW USA, Mexico to Belize; introduced to Hawaii**
HABITAT: **woodland edges, swamps, thickets, suburban gardens**
SIZE: **8½ in (22 cm)**

Among the most regular and popular of birds at feeding stations, Northern Cardinals often visit in pairs or family groups to take sunflower and safflower seeds. The wild food they eat depends upon availability, but includes insects, fruit, seeds, blossoms, buds and the residues that collect in holes drilled by sapsuckers. The loud, whistling song is uttered by both males and females almost all year round. A prolonged nesting season for this species may result in up to 4 broods.

## 4/ SLATE-COLORED GROSBEAK
*Pitylus grossus*

RANGE: **C and N South America S to N Bolivia**
HABITAT: **lowland humid forest**
SIZE: **7¾ in (20 cm)**

Slate-colored Grosbeaks are often found in pairs, the females being paler than the males, with no black on their neck and breast. Typically birds of the middle to upper forest, they occasionally descend to lower levels at the forest edge. Seeds and fruit make up the bulk of their diet, and they sometimes join mixed foraging flocks with other forest birds.

The call note of this bird is a sharp, metallic *speek* or *peek*, and its song is a loud, melodious series of deliberate whistles not unlike that of the Northern Cardinal. Little is known of the nesting habits of this deep forest species.

## 5/ BLUE GROSBEAK
*Guiraca caerulea*

RANGE: **USA S to Costa Rica; winters in S part of range**
HABITAT: **fields, hedgerows, thickets, woodland edges, roadside brush**
SIZE: **6–7½ in (15–19 cm)**

The Blue Grosbeak and the Indigo Bunting *Passerina cyanea* share much the same range and habitats. The plumage of the adult males is similar, but the Indigo Bunting is a deep, rich blue almost all over, while the Blue Grosbeak is a duller blue, with 2 broad, rusty-brown wing bars. Like other "blue" birds that take their color from feather structure rather than pigmentation, the Blue Grosbeak may appear gray or black in certain lights.

This species forages for insects, seeds and fruit at ground level and in trees. The female builds a neat cup nest of woven plant matter, sometimes adding cotton, paper or even cast snakeskins. This is placed among stems or in a twig fork up to 20 ft (6 m) from the ground.

## 6/ PAINTED BUNTING
*Passerina ciris*

RANGE: **SE and S USA; winters from N Gulf Coast S to Panama, Cuba**
HABITAT: **shrubs, hedgerows, weed fields, woodland edges, moist thickets, gardens**
SIZE: **5–5½ in (12.5–14 cm)**

No other North American bird is so generously daubed in paintpot colors as the adult male Painted Bunting. Nor does any other male North American bird share the green hues of the female and immature. All are suggestive of more tropical species. Although common in suitable habitats, this bunting is often difficult to see. The greens of the females and many males, and the disruptive pattern of the males, render them inconspicuous when eating seeds in brush fields or searching for insects. During the breeding season, however, the male sings his tinkling song from an exposed perch and is easy to locate.

## FAMILY EMBERIZIDAE/
## SUBFAMILY THRAUPINAE
### Tanagers

Small to medium. Plumage variable, often bright. Sexes alike or different. Nests in most species usually open cups in trees and shrubs; Swallow Tanager nests in tunnels in banks and cliffs. Eggs usually 2, up to 4–5 in euphonias and the few North American species, blue, gray or white with lilac, brown or black markings. Incubation 12–18 days, nestling period 11–24 days. 246 species.

## 7/ BLACK-CAPPED HEMISPINGUS
*Hemispingus atropileus*

RANGE: **Andes**
HABITAT: **wet high-altitude forests and scrub**
SIZE: **5–5½ in (13–14 cm)**

When the forests are enveloped in mist clouds, small groups of these birds can be seen moving rapidly through the undergrowth, usually with other species. The Black-capped Hemispingus often feeds in bamboo, landing near the base of a diagonal stalk and then creeping upward. As it ascends, it peers into crevices and at the undersides of leaves, searching for caterpillars and other insect prey.

The Peruvian race *H.a. auricularis* has the blackish areas on the head deeper and more extensive, and the throat typically more orange-yellow than the other race *H.a. atropileus*, found from western Venezuela to Ecuador.

## 8/ WHITE-WINGED SHRIKE-TANAGER
*Lanio versicolor*
RANGE: C South America, S of the Amazon
HABITAT: lowland tropical forest
SIZE: 5–6 in (13–15 cm)

The 4 species of shrike-tanager are adept at catching flying insects in midair. While large mixed flocks of birds work their way through the middle layers of vegetation, the shrike-tanagers sit quietly upright and often sally out briefly from their perches to snap up insects that are fleeing from the marauding band of birds. In this position, they are often the first to see an approaching predator, alerting other members of the flock by uttering a loud, downward pitched *tchew* call. At times, they will give false alarms that paralyse their flock mates and improve their own chances of snapping up particularly tasty morsels.

## 9/ SCARLET TANAGER
*Piranga olivacea*
RANGE: E North America; winters mainly in N South America E of the Andes
HABITAT: forests
SIZE: 6¼ in (16 cm)

The Scarlet Tanager nests mainly in deciduous forests in eastern USA, where it eats bees, wasps, beetles, moths and their larvae, supplemented by a variety of fruits. After breeding, the male molts into olive plumage similar to that of the female. Family groups apparently break up at this time and individuals become solitary and quiet, often sitting motionless in dense foliage. This behavior continues when the birds migrate south to the tropics and is the reason that ornithologists have so little knowledge of exactly where most individuals spend the northern winter.

## 10/ SILVER-BEAKED TANAGER
*Ramphocelus carbo*
RANGE: N South America E of the Andes
HABITAT: shrubbery and low trees at forest edge and on savannas
SIZE: 6¼–6½ in (16–17 cm)

The Silver-beaked Tanager haunts the tangle of vegetation at the edges of tropical forests, where different plant species produce a succession of fruit which tanagers devour eagerly. As the same fruits are eaten by many tanager species, ecological distinctions between them relate to their insect-eating behavior. When foraging for insects, the Silver-beaked Tanager hops rapidly through the foliage, peering at leaves and darting forward to capture any prey that tries to escape.

Silver-beaked Tanagers travel and forage in small bands, rarely tolerating other species or associating with mixed flocks. Members of each group call frequently, uttering a high-pitched *tseet* and a lower-pitched alarm note *chak*. The race illustrated, *R. c. carbo* from east Peru to Surinam, is one of the palest of the 8 races.

## 11/ HOODED MOUNTAIN TANAGER
*Buthraupis montana*
RANGE: Andes
HABITAT: mountain forest, scrub near forest
SIZE: 8¼ in (21 cm)

Groups of 3–10 Hooded Mountain Tanagers are often seen flying from one feeding site to the next. After they land, they are surprisingly difficult to locate because they forage sluggishly and may remain immobile for long periods. As well as feeding on fruit, they search for insects hiding in mosses and other epiphytes or on the undersides of leaves and branches. At dawn, the mountain valleys echo to noisy choruses of *toot* and *weeck* calls, repeated individually or coupled in phrases by bands of Hooded Mountain Tanagers. Like the territorial calls of some monkeys, these outbursts may serve to advertise the presence of each group over long distances.

## 12/ THICK-BILLED EUPHONIA
*Euphonia laniirostris*
RANGE: NW South America and Central America
HABITAT: open woodland, forest edge
SIZE: 4 in (10 cm)

The 25 species of euphonia are among the smallest of the tanagers. Although their digestive systems are specially adapted to cope with mistletoe berries, the balance of diet varies greatly from one species to another. Some eat a high proportion of insect food, while the Thick-billed Euphonia relies almost entirely on fruit. It does, however, feed spiders to its nestlings.

The Thick-billed Euphonia places its domed nest in a sheltered nook or cranny, sometimes choosing the flower baskets outside human dwellings. Unlike the 4 other races, such as *E.l. zopholega* from central Peru east of the Andes, the race *E.l. melanura* has an orange-yellow, buff-tinged throat and lacks the white tail spots.

## 13/ PARADISE TANAGER
*Tangara chilensis*
RANGE: Amazonian South America
HABITAT: lowland forest, plantations nearby
SIZE: 5 in (12.5 cm)

This beautiful bird is but one of about 50 colorful species in the genus *Tangara*. Although up to 10 species may be found together, eating the same type of fruit, these birds tend to be highly specialized when foraging for insects. Paradise Tanagers are extremely gregarious birds, typically traveling through the upper layers of the forest in groups of 5–10. The groups often join up with other small birds: indeed, the Paradise Tanager is thought to be a core species around which large flocks form in the canopy layer of the Amazon forests.

## 14/ RED-LEGGED HONEYCREEPER
*Cyanerpes cyaneus*
RANGE: Central America, N South America
HABITAT: edges of forest and woodland
SIZE: 4¾ in (12 cm)

The Red-legged Honeycreeper uses its long, curved bill not only to extract nectar from flowers, but also to snatch small insects from around the undersides of branches. It picks fleshy fruit out of slowly opening seed pods before other birds can reach inside, and it can extract orange pulp from holes drilled in the fruit by woodpeckers.

Highly gregarious when not breeding, the Red-legged Honeycreeper often occurs in flocks of 5–15 individuals. Groups of up to 100 sometimes gather at groves of flowering trees.

## 15/ GLOSSY FLOWERPIERCER
*Diglossa lafresnayii*
RANGE: Andes S to Bolivia
HABITAT: stunted "elfin" forest and thickets above 8,000 ft (2,500 m)
SIZE: 5½ in (14 cm)

Flowerpiercers use their strange, upcurved bills to puncture the bases of tubular flowers so that they can extract the nectar and possibly also the small insects within. Where blooms abound, flowerpiercers are intensely competitive, not only among themselves but also with other nectar-sipping species such as hummingbirds. The Glossy Flowerpiercer is so competitive that, after breeding, males and females defend individual territories – unusual behavior for tropical tanagers.

Distinctive populations of the Glossy Flowerpiercer are separated from one another by low dips in the Andean chain and offer a fascinating portrait of evolution in progress. For example, the race illustrated, *D. l. mystacalis*, from the La Paz and Cochabanta regions of Bolivia, along with 3 other races in the same subspecies group from Bolivia and northern Peru, may already be better considered as a separate species, the Moustached Flowerpiercer. Another group of races, from western Colombia, has reddish-brown lower underparts, while another group is all black – these, too, may soon be split off as full species, known as the Chestnut-bellied Flowerpiercer and Glossy Flowerpiercer, respectively.

## 16/ SWALLOW TANAGER
*Tersina viridis*
RANGE: E Panama, South America S to N Argentina
HABITAT: open woodland, forest edge, gallery forest, secondary forest
SIZE: 5½ in (14 cm)

The Swallow Tanager uses its large bill to pluck berries as well as to catch insects in aerial pursuits. It is a sociable bird, traveling in groups of about 12, although it discourages other species from joining the flocks. When not nesting, flocks appear to move about as different fruits ripen.

At the onset of the breeding season, males and females bow to one another as part of the courtship display. Unusually for a tanager, this species places its nest in holes, choosing tunnels and cavities in earth banks, cliffs and even bridges.

463

BLACK-AND-WHITE WARBLER

BACHMAN'S WARBLER

NORTHERN PARULA

YELLOW-RUMPED WARBLER

race *coronata*
"Myrtle Warbler"

race *memorabilis*
"Audubon's Warbler"

KIRTLAND'S WARBLER

AMERICAN REDSTART

OVENBIRD

PROTHONOTARY WARBLER

464

COMMON YELLOWTHROAT

GOLDEN-FRONTED REDSTART

GOLDEN-CROWNED WARBLER

ROSE-BREASTED CHAT

race *flaveola*

juv

race *atrata*

BANANAQUIT

melanistic phase

race *amazonum*

CHESTNUT-VENTED CONEBILL

race *caboti*

465

# WOOD WARBLERS

## FAMILY PARULIDAE
**Wood warblers**

Small, slender mostly foliage-gleaning insect-eaters. Some forage on the ground. Plumage often bright, with females duller. Nest well made, in tree or on ground; 2 species nest in holes. Eggs 2–8 (usually 4–5), white to green, often blotched or splashed with brown. Incubation 10–14 days, nestling period 8–12 days. 126 species.

## 1/ BLACK-AND-WHITE WARBLER
*Mniotilta varia*

RANGE: **breeds E North America, N to Northwest Territory, W to Montana, S to C Texas; winters extreme S USA to N South America**
HABITAT: **deciduous and mixed woodland**
SIZE: **4½–5½ in (11.5–14 cm)**

With its dramatic barred plumage, the Black-and-white Warbler is often easy to see as it forages for prey on tree trunks and bare branches. It hunts using a search and snatch technique, creeping along the trunks and larger, low limbs of deciduous trees, much like nuthatches or treecreepers (pp. 302–5), and probing with its unusually long bill for insects and spiders.

It flies north in spring earlier than most wood warblers, and its thin, wiry song may be heard well into northern Canada. It builds a cup-shaped nest in a hollow or crevice, usually on the ground under an overhang or among tree roots.

## 2/ BACHMAN'S WARBLER
*Vermivora bachmanii*                    E

RANGE: **breeds SE USA; winters in Cuba**
HABITAT: **swamps, low woods**
SIZE: **4¾ in (12 cm)**

This endangered species once bred in many of the southern states of the USA, migrating to Cuba in winter via the Florida Keys and the Bahamas. By 1937 most of the breeding pairs were restricted to the I'On Swamp in South Carolina and since then no nests have been found. Adult birds were sighted in the 1970s, but since they resemble more common species such as the Hooded Warbler *Wilsonia citrina* and Wilson's Warbler *W. pusilla*, recent reports are naturally suspect.

Bachman's Warbler nests low down in thick cover, in mature hardwood forests, and the draining and cutting of its habitat may account for its decline or even extinction.

## 3/ NORTHERN PARULA
*Parula americana*

RANGE: **breeds E North America, with isolated nests in California, New Mexico, Mexico; winters Florida, West Indies, Central America**
HABITAT: **coniferous and mixed woods, swamps**
SIZE: **4½ in (11.5 cm)**

The Northern Parula is a widespread and adaptable bird, able to thrive in habitats ranging from northern spruce forests to the swamps of the southern states. Its song is a rising buzzy trill ending with an abrupt *zip* – almost identical to that of the very similar Tropical Parula *P.*

*pitiayumi* with which it is often confused. It feeds on insects, gathering them from the tree foliage.

Whenever possible, the Northern Parula builds its cup-shaped nest in a hanging tuft of tree lichen or Spanish moss, using the lichen or moss as nesting material. If neither is available it will nest in a more conventional site, such as a hanging cluster of twigs in a hemlock or spruce.

## 4/ YELLOW-RUMPED WARBLER
*Dendroica coronata*

RANGE: **breeds North America, S to C and S Mexico and Guatemala; winters S of breeding range, to Central America**
HABITAT: **coniferous and deciduous woods**
SIZE: **5–6 in (13–15 cm)**

This widespread and abundant species has 5 races. These fall into 2 groups, which were once thought to be separate species: the white-throated Myrtle Warbler, typified by *D. c. coronata* of Canada and central and eastern USA and the yellow-throated Audubon's Warbler, typified by *D. c. auduboni* of southwest Canada and western USA. The race illustrated, *D. c. memorabilis*, from southwest USA, is a particularly strongly marked form of the Audubon Warbler group.

Apart from their plumage differences, most noticeable in breeding males, their call notes are also distinct, that of Audubon's Warbler being softer than that of its eastern counterpart. Both nest in conifers and tall deciduous trees; they may interbreed where their ranges overlap.

In summer both races feed largely on insects, but in winter and during migration they take a much wider range of foods.

## 5/ KIRTLAND'S WARBLER
*Dendroica kirtlandii*                    E

RANGE: **breeds small area in C Michigan, USA; winters in the Bahamas**
HABITAT: **thickets of young jack pine**
SIZE: **6 in (15 cm)**

This large, tail-bobbing warbler is now considered endangered and is unlikely to be seen except on its nest sites in central Michigan, its

wintering grounds in the Bahamas or, during migration, somewhere between the two.

Kirtland's Warbler nests on the ground, near the base of a jack pine tree. It requires a very special habitat for breeding, one that is found only at a particular stage in the succession of vegetation: it will breed only among stands of jack pines between 8 and 22 years old. This prime habitat can be maintained only by regular forest fires or clearing. Kirtland's Warbler is particularly prone to parasitism by the Brown-headed Cowbird *Molothrus ater*, which lays its eggs in the warbler's nest.

This natural hazard has probably accelerated a decline caused largely by the erosion of its very precise habitat, and it has been reduced to fewer than 200 nesting pairs. The strict protection, habitat maintenance and control of the cowbird population are being undertaken may yet save Kirtland's Warbler. However, the mysterious loss of many young birds somewhere on their long migration between the breeding grounds and the Bahamas causes grave concern.

## 6/ AMERICAN REDSTART
*Setophaga ruticilla*

RANGE: **breeds SE Alaska, E through C Canada, S through Texas to E USA; winters extreme S USA to Brazil**
HABITAT: **deciduous and mixed woodland**
SIZE: **4¼–5¼ in (11–13.5 cm)**

Few warblers are as vividly patterned, as bold or as animated as the New World redstarts. In most of the 11 other species, placed in a different genus, *Myioborus*, the sexes are alike, but the female American Redstart is quite unlike her mate, with incandescent yellow where he has flaming orange.

The dazzling colors illuminate every flutter of wings and tail as the birds work through the foliage in search of caterpillars, or dart into the air like flycatchers to catch insects on the wing. Their songs feature shrill, sibilant, slurred notes, and they often utter sharp, staccato calls.

The female alone builds the cup nest, placing it in the fork of a tree or shrub and often decorating the lining with the gaudy feathers of brightly colored buntings or tanagers.

## 7/ OVENBIRD
*Seiurus aurocapillus*

RANGE: **breeds S Canada and E USA to Colorado and Georgia; winters SE USA to West Indies, Bahamas, Panama, N Venezuela and Colombia**
HABITAT: **forest, shrubby thickets**
SIZE: **5 in (13 cm)**

The largely brown Ovenbird might be easy to overlook were it not for its loud and unmistakable song – a clarion repetition of *teacher-teacher-teacher* that steadily increases in volume. It forages on the forest floor, poking through the leaf litter for insects, spiders and other small animals, and pausing every so often to fly to a low branch and sing.

Males are occasionally polygamous in spring, but usually the birds breed as pairs. They weave a curious domed nest out of dried grasses, pine needles, strips of bark and tiny twigs, lining it with hair. The nest is built on the ground, often at the base of a bush and sunk well into the leaf litter; it is shaped rather like a traditional bread-oven, which accounts for the bird's common name. The female alone does the incubation, often raising the young of the parasitic Brown-headed Cowbird *Molothrus ater* in place of her own.

## 8/ PROTHONOTARY WARBLER
*Protonotaria citrea*

RANGE: **breeds E USA, S Ontario; winters Mexico to N South America**
HABITAT: **moist woodland near water**
SIZE: **5½ in (14 cm)**

This golden beauty is named after the *proto-notarias* – the saffron-robed clerks who serve the Pope. It feeds mainly on insects and a few small seeds, and with its bright plumage it is particularly easy to follow as it forages low down in damp woodlands. In winter it is often found in various swamp habitats, but it also occurs in drier places. It has a loud voice, calling with a series of 7–12 short tweets, or a longer, more fluid version sung while hovering on fanned wings.

Unusually for a wood warbler, the Prothonotary Warbler is a cavity nester, usually selecting a natural tree hollow or a woodpecker hole in forest habitat near water. The nest is built mainly by the female, using small twigs, bark, moss, lichens and grasses. In southern regions, many pairs raise 2 broods a season.

## 9/ COMMON YELLOWTHROAT
*Geothlypis trichas*

RANGE: **breeds North America S to Mexico; winters Bahamas, West Indies to N South America**
HABITAT: **young second growth, weedy areas, usually near water**
SIZE: **4–5 in (10–13 cm)**

The Common Yellowthroat is widespread and often abundant on river, lake and pond edges, fresh and saltwater marshes – indeed, almost anywhere that the weeds grow rank and ground is saturated with water. It feeds on insects, spiders and their eggs, snatching them from the ground or picking them off low vegetation.

The breeding pairs nest either on or very close to the ground, and sometimes over water. Each of the 3–6 white eggs is marked with brown, gray or black spots that often coalesce to form a ring around the broad end. There may be 2 broods each season, but, as with other wood warblers, many eggs fall victim to the parasitism of the Brown-headed Cowbird *Molothrus ater*.

## 10/ GOLDEN-FRONTED REDSTART
*Myioborus ornatus*

RANGE: **Andes in extreme W Venezuela and Colombia**
HABITAT: **subtropical and temperate mountain forest at 6,000–11,200 ft (1,800–3,400 m)**
SIZE: **5½ in (14 cm)**

This species is also known as the Golden-faced Redstart, and some have suggested that it would be more appropriately named a "whitestart" because of its conspicuous white outer tail feathers.

Common in temperate forests above 8,000 ft (2,400 m), it is usually seen in groups of up to 5 or 6 birds, sometimes on their own but often with other species. It forages high in the trees, either in the topmost branches or in the dense foliage at the periphery of the tree crown, searching for insects, spiders and similar prey. Its song is high-pitched and rambling, lasting for about 15 seconds, but it often gives short *tsip* contact notes while foraging or flying from tree to tree.

## 11/ GOLDEN-CROWNED WARBLER
*Basileuterus culicivorus*

RANGE: **C Mexico to E Bolivia, Paraguay, Uruguay, N Argentina**
HABITAT: **humid forest, forest edge, scrub, clearings, deciduous woods, plantations**
SIZE: **5 in (12.5 cm)**

The various populations of this wide-ranging wood warbler occur in 3 quite distinct habitats: tropical semideciduous forest, tropical evergreen forest and upland forest. They are sometimes regarded as 3 different, but closely related species. However, the races involved vary but little in plumage, chiefly in the grayness of their upper-parts and the precise shade of their crown stripe.

Golden-crowned Warblers are usually seen in pairs or small groups, but they often join larger mixed-species flocks. They search for insects and spiders in the branches and vines of the low understory, moving quickly through the foliage or darting out to catch insects on the wing. The nest is a dome of grass placed low on a bank.

## 12/ ROSE-BREASTED CHAT
*Granatellus pelzelni*

RANGE: **S Venezuela and Guianas S through Amazonian Brazil to N Bolivia**
HABITAT: **lowland rain forest, older second growth near water**
SIZE: **5 in (13 cm)**

Often difficult to follow in the wild, the Rose-breasted Chat typically forages for insects amid tangled undergrowth, moving up into the canopy in the forest interior. It is most visible when it is feeding in scrub at the forest edge or near streams, and it will often stop to "pose" with raised, fanned tail.

Although included here with the wood warblers, the Rose-breasted Chat and its 2 close relatives, the Red-breasted Chat *G. venustus* and the Gray-throated Chat *G. sallaei*, are sometimes considered to be more closely allied to the tanagers. They are remarkable for their widely separated ranges, with one found in the Pacific lowlands of Mexico, one in Central America, and this one in South America.

## 13/ CHESTNUT-VENTED CONEBILL
*Conirostrum speciosum*

RANGE: **E of Andes from E Colombia W to the Guianas and S to N Argentina**
HABITAT: **open lowland deciduous forest, swampy forest, second growth, lake edges**
SIZE: **4–4½ in (10–11.5 cm)**

The Chestnut-vented Conebill and the 9 other conebills of the genus *Conirostrum* are sometimes considered to be aberrant wood warblers – as here – and sometimes included with the tanagers.

Whatever its affinities, this is a sociable species that forages in the treetops in pairs or small groups, often in mixed-species flocks. It frequently feeds in association with tanagers, probing blossoms for nectar, pollen and insects; at other times it gleans insects and spiders from the clustered foliage at branch tips, in typical wood warbler style. The race *C. s. amazonum* is found from the Guianas west to eastern Peru and is darker than other races.

## 14/ BANANAQUIT
*Coereba flaveola*

RANGE: **West Indies, Central and South America to N Argentina**
HABITAT: **arid to humid forest, swamp, parkland with flowering trees or shrubs**
SIZE: **4 in (10 cm)**

An active, adaptable little bird, the Bananaquit will thrive in a wide variety of habitats as long as it has some cover and a good food supply. It often feeds on nectar, using its downcurved bill to probe into small flowers or even puncture the bases of long tubular flowers to get at the nectaries. At other times it will pierce berries to suck the juice, or gather insects and spiders from the foliage.

The Bananaquit shows much geographical variation over its great range, including the many isolated Caribbean islands. Three island races are shown: *C. f. flaveola* from Jamaica; *C. f. atrata* from St. Vincent, in the melanistic phase most common in this race, as well as some others; and *C. f. caboti* from Cozumel Island and Holbox Island off the Yucatan Peninsula in southeast Mexico.

The true relationships of the Bananaquit are uncertain. Once it was classified with the honeycreepers, flowerpiercers and conebills in a family of their own, the Coerebidae. The honeycreepers and flowerpiercers are now considered to be specialized tanagers, while the conebills and Bananaquit are sometimes (as here) considered unusual members of the wood warbler family; sometimes regarded as aberrant tanagers; and sometimes placed in a reduced family Coerebidae.

race *virenticeps*

race *gujanensis*

YELLOW-THROATED VIREO

RUFOUS-BROWED PEPPERSHRIKE

GREEN SHRIKE-VIREO

RED-EYED VIREO

GRAY VIREO

COZUMEL VIREO

race *dariensis*

LESSER GREENLET

race *melanterus* ♂

race *cela* ♂

race *vitellinus* ♂

YELLOW-RUMPED CACIQUE

CRESTED OROPENDOLA

nest

race *galbula*
"Baltimore Oriole"
♂

race *bullocki*
"Bullock's Oriole"
♂

NORTHERN ORIOLE

RED-WINGED BLACKBIRD
♂

♀

♂

race *abeillei*
"Black-backed Oriole"

COMMON GRACKLE
♂

juv

BRONZED COWBIRD
♂

EASTERN
MEADOWLARK
♂

♂

♀

BOBOLINK

469

# VIREOS, AMERICAN BLACKBIRDS

## FAMILY VIREONIDAE
### Vireos
Small, with mainly green upperparts, gray or brown on back, yellow or white underparts. Sexes similar. Cuplike or baglike nest, suspended by the rim from forked branches of trees or shrubs. Eggs 2–5, white with brown spots. Incubation 11–13 days, nestling period 11–13 days. 46 species.

## 1/ RUFOUS-BROWED PEPPERSHRIKE
*Cyclarhis gujanensis*
RANGE: **Central and South America E of Andes to N C Argentina**
HABITAT: **tropical and subtropical forest edge, clearings, second growth, scrub forest, plantations**
SIZE: **6¼–6½ in (16–17 cm)**

The 2 distinctive species of peppershrike were once classified in a separate family but are now given subfamily rank within the vireo family. Both species use their heavy, strongly hooked bills to forage for insects and fruit in trees. They sit hidden, singing a monotonous litany of short but musical whistled phrases for hours, repeating one phrase for 5–10 minutes. They are weak fliers and do not migrate.

Many races of the Rufous-browed Peppershrike have been recognized. Two races are illustrated: *C. g. gujanensis* from east Colombia, south Venezuela, Guyana, Brazil, east Peru and northwestern Bolivia; and *C. g. virenticeps* from western Ecuador and northwestern Peru.

## 2/ GREEN SHRIKE-VIREO
*Vireolanius pulchellus*
RANGE: **S Mexico to W Panama**
HABITAT: **rain and cloud forest up to 5,500 ft (1,700 m)**
SIZE: **5½ in (14 cm)**

Because of its sluggish nature and ability to blend with the foliage high in the forest canopy, relatively little is known about this vireo, with its heavy, almost shrikelike beak. It usually forages alone or in pairs, taking insects by probing leaf clusters and sallying out to catch them in midair. Outside the breeding season it may join mixed flocks of other insect-eating birds to feed lower in the forest foliage. Its song of 3–4 similar syllables resembles the *peter-peter-peter* of the Tufted Titmouse *Parus bicolor*.

The race *V. p. eximius*, illustrated, found in northern Colombia and western Venezuela, is often regarded as a separate species, the Yellow-browed Shrike-Vireo.

## 3/ COZUMEL VIREO
*Vireo bairdi*
RANGE: **Cozumel Island, Mexico**
HABITAT: **open tropical forest, forest edge**
SIZE: **4¼–4¾ in (11–12 cm)**

The Cozumel Vireo is the only brown vireo; other species are green, yellow or gray above. It is a close relative of a local mainland species, the Mangrove Vireo *V. pallens*, and shares its white markings and chattering song. At least 5 song types, each of a different syllable, are recorded.

The wrenlike behavior of the Cozumel Vireo is similar to that of other scrub-foraging vireos: it takes insects and spiders from small branches and twigs, and some fruit. It is strongly territorial.

## 4/ GRAY VIREO
*Vireo vicinior*
RANGE: **breeds SW USA to NW Mexico; winters from S Arizona and W Texas to Durango and N Sinaloa**
HABITAT: **dry brushy slopes, canyons, chaparral, dwarf oak woodland, winters in desert scrub**
SIZE: **5½ in (14 cm)**

A close relative of the forest-dwelling Solitary Vireo *V. solitarius*, the Gray Vireo occupies huge breeding and winter territories. It gleans insects from foliage and, occasionally, the ground and catches flying insects in midair.

The Gray Vireo is the only vireo to sing regularly in flight; the female also sings during nesting. The 3–5 syllables are loud and non-musical, having a hoarse quality.

## 5/ YELLOW-THROATED VIREO
*Vireo flavifrons*
RANGE: **breeds S and E C Canada, USA to Gulf States; winters from S Florida, S C Mexico and Greater Antilles to Colombia and N Venezuela**
HABITAT: **mixed broad-leaved coniferous forest and woodland in summer, tropical woodland and rain forest up to 6,000 ft (1,800 m) in winter**
SIZE: **5½ in (14 cm)**

This is one of the most clean-cut and brightly patterned of all vireos; it also has a prominent yellow eye ring. The Yellow-throated Vireo forages alone or with its mate for insects and spiders and the occasional berry in treetops. Its song, a sequence of brief, 2- or 3-note phrases, separated by long pauses, resembles that of the Solitary Vireo *V. solitarius*, but sounds huskier, and is given in its winter quarters as well as on its breeding grounds, along with chattering calls.

## 6/ RED-EYED VIREO
*Vireo olivaceus*
RANGE: **breeds Canada S to the Gulf States; winters from NW South America to Amazonia**
HABITAT: **deciduous or mixed forest, river bank woodland**
SIZE: **5½ in (14 cm)**

The Red-eyed Vireo's melodious and fairly rapid song is composed of 2–3 syllables. It is highly vocal and strongly territorial in its summer breeding grounds, where it gleans treetop foliage for insects. By contrast, in its South American winter quarters the Red-eyed Vireo does not sing and eats fruit rather than insects. During the breeding season the male displays by swaying with body feathers fluffed and tail fanned, to which females may respond with a call.

## 7/ LESSER GREENLET
*Hylophilus decurtatus*
RANGE: **SE Mexico to C Panama**
HABITAT: **tropical forest and second growth below 4,300 ft (1,300 m)**
SIZE: **3½–4 in (9–10 cm)**

Greenlets are small, warblerlike insect-eaters that often join mixed-species foraging flocks high in the forest canopy. Compared to other vireos, they have more pointed bills which lack the notch at the tip of the upper mandible. The constantly repeated call of the Lesser Greenlet is similar to a single phrase of the Red-eyed Vireo's song, though higher pitched and quieter. There are 3 races of the Lesser Greenlet. The race *H. d. dariensis* from eastern Panama and northern Colombia is illustrated.

## FAMILY ICTERIDAE
### American blackbirds (American orioles)
Small to medium. Most species black (often glossy) with patches of yellow, orange or red; brown common in females and in both sexes of many grassland species. Sexes differ markedly in plumage and size in temperate, migratory species

and in polygynous species from all latitudes. Nests varied, from simple cups or domes on ground in terrestrial species to long, woven, purselike nests suspended from tree branches. Eggs very variable in color and markings, typically 4–6 in temperate species, 2–3 in tropical species. Incubation 12–15 days. Nestling periods from about 10 days in smallest species to about 10 weeks in largest ones. 96 species.

## 8/ CRESTED OROPENDOLA
*Psarocolius decumanus*

RANGE: **Panama to C South America**
HABITAT: **humid lowland and foothill forest, second growth forest, forest edge, clearings and plantations**
SIZE: **male 17–18$\frac{3}{4}$ in (43–48 cm); female 15–16 in (38–41 cm)**

Female Crested Oropendolas have the same coloration as males but are smaller. The "crest" consists of a few hairlike feathers that protrude from the crown and are generally laid flat. There are 4 races: 3 of them are similar, including *P. d. melanterus* from Panama and northern Colombia, while the other, *P. d. maculosus*, from the Amazon southward, has pale yellow feathers scattered throughout its black body plumage.

The male Crested Oropendola performs a remarkable display, in which he raises his tail and flaps his wings noisily as he leans forward so far he almost falls from his perch, the whole time uttering loud gurgling and rasping calls that accelerate to a crescendo. Its food includes fruits, seeds and a variety of invertebrates.

Gregarious at all times, the birds breed in colonies, with 7–100 nests in a single tree. Each nest is an elaborate hanging structure of woven plant fiber over 3 ft (1 m) long, suspended from the tip of a flexible tree limb. No attempt is made to conceal the nest sites, which are the focus of constant coming and going by these large, vocal and conspicuous birds.

## 9/ YELLOW-RUMPED CACIQUE
*Cacicus cela*

RANGE: **Panama to C South America**
HABITAT: **humid lowland forest, forest edge, second growth woodland, clearings, plantations; also found in villages and even in towns**
SIZE: **male 11–12$\frac{1}{2}$ in (28–32 cm); female 9$\frac{1}{2}$–10$\frac{1}{4}$ in (24–26 cm)**

The Yellow-rumped Cacique is a common bird in many parts of its range. Two of the 3 races are illustrated: *C. c. vitellinus* from Panama and northern Colombia and *C. c. cela* from northern Central America and Trinidad.

Yellow-rumped Caciques feed on berries, fruits and insects. They have a variety of calls, including loud cackles, squawks and more melodious notes. Birds of the race *C. c. cela* are frequent and excellent mimics of other birds, but those of the other 2 races seem to lack this ability.

These gregarious birds nest in conspicuous colonies, constructing hanging nests which are shorter and more oblong than those of the oropendolas, which may nest in the same tree. Cacique nests are often clumped close together, frequently near wasps' nests for protection.

## 10/ NORTHERN ORIOLE
*Icterus galbula*

RANGE: **breeds North America; winters in C and N South America**
HABITAT: **open and riverside woodland, forest edge, trees near human habitation**
SIZE: **6–6$\frac{1}{2}$ in (16–17 cm)**

Male Northern Orioles are conspicuous orange and black birds that show distinct plumage variations among races. Those illustrated are Bullock's Oriole *I. g. bullocki* from western North America to Nicaragua, the Baltimore Oriole *I. g. galbula* from eastern North America, and the Black-backed Oriole *I. g. abeillei* from south-central Mexico.

These birds weave nests of pliant plant material with top openings, where the female incubates 4–5 pale blue-gray eggs. Adults feed on insects, fruits, nectar and spring buds.

## 11/ RED-WINGED BLACKBIRD
*Agelaius phoeniceus*

RANGE: **North and Central America**
HABITAT: **marshes, watercourses, cultivated land**
SIZE: **male 7$\frac{3}{4}$–9$\frac{1}{2}$ in (20–24 cm); female 7–7$\frac{1}{2}$ in (18–19 cm)**

The Red-winged Blackbird may be the most abundant North American land bird. Males sing from exposed perches and flash their brilliant yellow-tipped "epaulettes" to defend their breeding territories. At other times, the red is often concealed when the bird perches, and only the yellow tips show.

The female builds a cup-shaped grass nest 1–10 ft (0.5–3 m) above the ground, over or near water. Breeding males roost singly in their territories; after breeding, male birds gather into large flocks, joining other American blackbirds to form flocks of 1 million or more birds. The birds illustrated are typical of most races.

## 12/ EASTERN MEADOWLARK
*Sturnella magna*

RANGE: **S and E North America to N South America**
HABITAT: **savanna, pastures, cultivated land**
SIZE: **9–9$\frac{3}{4}$ in (23–25 cm)**

This familiar American bird spends most of its time on the ground, where it walks about, frequently flicking its tail. When it does fly, it makes a series of rapid, shallow wing beats interspersed with brief glides during which its wings are held stiffly downward.

During the breeding season, the male displays his yellow breast to the female, points his bill skyward to expose his yellow throat and leaps into the air. He defends his territory by uttering his song – a sequence of clear, mellow whistling notes – from a fencepost or other prominent perch, from the ground, or in a fluttering song-flight. Typically monogamous, Eastern Meadowlarks lay 3–7 brown-spotted white eggs in a cuplike nest of woven grass and usually raise 2 broods in a season. North American birds migrate south in winter, but those from the West Indies and from Central and South America are sedentary.

## 13/ COMMON GRACKLE
*Quiscalus quiscula*

RANGE: **E USA; N populations winter S as far as Florida**
HABITAT: **open woodland, scattered trees, forest edge, areas near human habitation**
SIZE: **11–13 in (28–33 cm)**

The Common Grackle forms large, noisy roosts, often containing thousands of birds uttering loud *chuck* calls. The short, harsh, squeaky song sounds like the noise of a rusty-hinged gate. These birds nest in small colonies. The females build bulky nests of sticks and grasses 3–13 ft (1–4 m) above the ground. The nest is lined with dried grass and feathers and often with paper, string, rags and other debris.

Young birds eat insects and spiders; adults eat a wide range of animals, from earthworms and insects to fish, frogs, mice and the eggs and young of small birds. They also relish seeds and grain and large flocks of grackles can damage crops.

## 14/ BRONZED COWBIRD
*Molothrus aeneus*

RANGE: **S USA to Panama**
HABITAT: **savanna, pastures, cultivated land and human habitation in tropical and subtropical zones including arid land**
SIZE: **6$\frac{1}{2}$–8$\frac{1}{2}$ in (17–22 cm)**

This nest parasite feeds on insects and seeds, and regularly gathers in flocks of 25–30, which sometimes combine to form large groups of 500 or so birds. The male displays to the female, head thrown back and feathers ruffled, uttering a creaky whistle. After mating, the female lays one very pale bluish egg in the nest of another species, often puncturing host eggs already present. Young cowbirds, when they hatch in the host nest, are larger and more persistent than other young birds, and hence receive more food. The total number of eggs laid is unknown, but the closely related Brown-headed Cowbird·*M. ater* lays up to 40 eggs over 2 months.

## 15/ BOBOLINK
*Dolichonyx oryzivorus*

RANGE: **breeds S Canada to C USA; winters S America, mostly in N Argentina**
HABITAT: **prairies, meadows; also marshes on migration and in winter**
SIZE: **6$\frac{1}{4}$–7 in (16–18 cm)**

This bird is named for the male's loud, bubbling song, which sounds rather like *bob-o-link, bob-o-link, spink, spank, spink*, which he utters, often in a fluttering display flight over his territory, in spring and summer. The flight call, heard all year round, is also distinctive – a repeated, metallic, whistling *ink*. In his courtship display, the male erects his buff nape feathers, partly opens his wings to show off his white "shoulders," and points his bill downward. This is a polygynous species, each male mating with 2 or more females.

The Bobolink makes the longest migration of any member of its family. In summer, Bobolinks include many weed seeds and insect pests among their diet, but on their southward migration, they can be destructive to grain crops.

race *coelebs* ♂

race *spodiogenys* ♂

CHAFFINCH

race *palmae*

ISLAND CANARY ♀

♂

♂ BLUE CHAFFINCH

THICK-BILLED CANARY

♀ ORIOLE-FINCH

♂

♂

♂

♀

WESTERN GREENFINCH

RED SISKIN

AMERICAN GOLDFINCH

♀

♂

♂
race *britannica*

EURASIAN GOLDFINCH

♂ race *paropanisi*

♀ race *frontalis*

REDPOLL

HOUSE FINCH

♂

race *cabaret*

♀

ROSY FINCH

race *umbrina*
"Aleutian Rosy Finch"
♂

race *australis*
"Brown-capped
Rosy Finch"

♂

♂

race *atrata*
"Black Rosy
Finch"

♂

CAUCASIAN GREAT ROSEFINCH

## FAMILY FRINGILLIDAE/
## SUBFAMILY FRINGILLINAE
### Fringilline finches

Small, with conical bills, fairly long tails and peaked head. Sexes differ. Males brightly colored, females duller; all species with prominent shoulder patches and wing and tail markings. Nest mainly of grass, moss and other vegetation, typically in a bush or tree. Eggs 3–5, dark blue-green with purple-brown streaks and spots. Incubation 12–14 days, nestling period 11–17 days. Young fed frequently on small amounts of insects directly from parents' bills. 3 species.

## 1/ CHAFFINCH
*Fringilla coelebs*

RANGE: **Europe to W Siberia, Middle East, N Africa, Atlantic islands**
HABITAT: **woodland, gardens and open country with scattered trees**
SIZE: **6 in (15 cm)**

Over most of its range, the Chaffinch is a very common and familiar bird, often living close to human dwellings. Its simple, far-carrying song varies subtly from one area to another, forming local dialects. There are many races, those in the north, including *F.c. coelebs*, from much of the European range, tending to have brightly colored males. Races from the drier southern regions, such as *F.c. spodiogenys* of Tunisia, are paler and the sexes are more alike. There are also several races on the Atlantic islands, including 3 in the Canaries which are all heavy-billed and have slate blue on the upperparts. The latter include *F.c. palmae* of Las Palmas Island.

Chaffinches form large flocks in winter, feeding on seeds in farmland and coming into gardens to forage. In the breeding season, however, they become highly territorial. The nest is placed in a tree or a bush and is finished on the outside with moss and lichen, often making it difficult to spot.

## 2/ BLUE CHAFFINCH
*Fringilla teydea*  ℝ

RANGE: **Canary Islands**
HABITAT: **forest scrub**
SIZE: **6½ in (16.5 cm)**

Along with the Chaffinch, which is widely distributed through the archipelago, the Canary Islands have a second, much rarer species of fringilline finch, the Blue Chaffinch. It is confined to the islands of Gran Canaria, where it is declining, and Tenerife.

The 2 species occupy quite different habitats, with the Chaffinch occurring in broad-leaved forest at low altitudes and the Blue Chaffinch living at high elevations (up to the tree line) in mountain pine and pine-laurel forests. Blue Chaffinches are resident in these forests throughout the year, seldom appearing elsewhere. They are late breeders, not starting to nest until the end of May or into June. The nest is usually placed in a pine or laurel tree, often high above the ground.

## FAMILY FRINGILLIDAE/
## SUBFAMILY CARDUELINAE
### Cardueline finches

Small, with variably shaped conical bills, ranging from "tweezers" to deep, powerful bills (mandibles crossed in crossbills). Sexes differ, females duller. Very variable plumage, generally with distinctive wing and tail markings; many species streaked, particularly juveniles. Nest mainly of grass, moss and other vegetation, typically in a bush or tree. Eggs 3–5, whitish with brown spots. Incubation 12–14 days, nestling period 11–17 days. Young fed infrequently on large amounts of seeds by regurgitation (some species with special throat pouches for storing seeds). 121 species.

## 3/ ISLAND CANARY
*Serinus canaria*

RANGE: **Azores, Madeira, Canary Islands**
HABITAT: **open woodland, scrub and gardens**
SIZE: **5 in (12.5 cm)**

This close relative of the European Serin *S. serinus* was the ancestor of all domestic canaries. It was first brought into Europe in the early 16th century and was rapidly domesticated. The sexes are different in the wild form of the bird, but alike in the cage birds. The wild birds also have rather dull, streaky plumage, unlike the great majority of their domestic cousins.

Island Canaries are very common and found throughout the wooded parts of the islands on which they occur. They appear down at sea level, in gardens, vineyards, orchards and in all the cultivated areas, as well as up in the pine woods at 5,000 ft (1,500 m) or more. The male often utters his beautiful song in a showy song-flight, as he glides down from high above on quivering wings, landing on the crown of one of the tall trees in the native forests.

## 4/ THICK-BILLED CANARY
*Serinus burtoni*

RANGE: **W and E Africa**
HABITAT: **mountain forest**
SIZE: **7 in (18 cm)**

The Thick-billed Canary, or Thick-billed Seed-eater, is an unusual member of the serin group of finches, being very large with an especially heavy, robust bill. It inhabits forest edges at altitudes of 5,000–8,000 ft (1,500–2,500 m). It is notoriously difficult to locate because it remains high in the treetops and rarely calls.

Most Thick-billed Canaries occur in the mountains of Cameroon in west Africa, in the uplands on either side of Lake Victoria and in Angola. A distinct population, with white underparts streaked brown and with only a little green in the wings, occurs in the highlands of southern Tanzania. The sexes are similar in this species.

## 5/ ORIOLE-FINCH
*Linurgus olivaceus*

RANGE: **W and E Africa**
HABITAT: **upland and mountain forest**
SIZE: **5 in (13 cm)**

The striking Oriole-Finch takes its name from its similarity in color pattern to some of the orioles (pp. 354–57). It has an almost identical distribution to that of the Thick-billed Canary, being restricted to the equatorial mountain forests of Africa. Although it has been found at heights of around 9,000 ft (2,750 m), it generally lives at lower levels than the Thick-billed Canary, down to an altitude of about 1,800 ft (550 m). At these lower levels, this species is found at forest edges and in clearings.

Oriole-Finches are especially attracted to seeding nettles. Although usually rather silent birds, they utter soft, plaintive *twee* or wheezy *tzit tzit* calls from time to time and have a sweet, rather thin and high-pitched song. The nest is a shallow cup, generally placed low down, less than 3 ft (1 m) from the ground, in a bush at the forest edge.

## 6/ WESTERN GREENFINCH
*Carduelis chloris*
RANGE: **Europe, N Africa, Asia Minor, Middle East, C Asia**
HABITAT: **open woodland, bushes, gardens**
SIZE: **5¾ in (14.5 cm)**

This stocky finch is well known in gardens in winter, where it is especially fond of sunflower seeds and peanuts. An agile bird, it will readily take food from hanging dispensers. The more northerly populations migrate in winter, and, at this time, the birds turn up in many different habitats, including sea coasts.

During the breeding season, Western Green-finches take up residence in parks, gardens and along hedgerows, as well as in larger areas of open woodland. The characteristic strident, nasal calls readily draw attention to the birds, as does the butterflylike courtship display flight, which is accompanied by a pleasant, twittering song, performed by the male. They build their nests in small trees and bushes, about 7–8 ft (2–2.5 m) above the ground.

## 7/ RED SISKIN
*Carduelis cucullata*    E
RANGE: **N Colombia, N Venezuela**
HABITAT: **dry scrub**
SIZE: **4 in (10 cm)**

This striking finch formerly roamed in semi-nomadic flocks over many parts of northern South America. It was also found on Trinidad and on 2 other Caribbean islands, Gasparee and Monos, from all of which it has since disappeared. Heavy trapping for the cage-bird trade has caused it to become very rare, and it is now regarded as endangered throughout its range.

As well as being trapped as a cage bird in its own right, the Red Siskin is caught because it hybridizes easily. Canary breeders have taken advantage of its red genes for improving the plumage color of their stock of birds. Despite legal protection, the trapping persists. In 1981, there were believed to be only 600–800 birds remaining in the wild.

## 8/ AMERICAN GOLDFINCH
*Carduelis tristis*
RANGE: **S Canada, USA; N populations migrate in winter**
HABITAT: **open woodland, weedy fields, roadsides**
SIZE: **4¼ in (11 cm)**

These sparkling little finches are commonly seen in flocks feeding on the seeds of roadside thistles and other weeds. When disturbed, the flocks fly up and swirl around, twittering all the time, before settling again. Their sweet, canarylike song, usually given during a circling song-flight, has earned them the popular, if ornithologically inaccurate, name of Wild Canary.

Although the male American Goldfinch's plumage is bright and distinctive in the breeding season, it becomes duller in color, much more like that of the female, through the rest of the year. This species' nest is a neat cup in a tree or shrub.

## 9/ EURASIAN GOLDFINCH
*Carduelis carduelis*
RANGE: **N Africa, Europe, Middle East to C Asia**
HABITAT: **open broad-leaved woodland, scrub with weedy areas, gardens**
SIZE: **4¾ in (12 cm)**

Throughout much of its range, the Eurasian Goldfinch has been heavily trapped as a cage bird because of its bright, delightful plumage and lovely, liquid, twittering song. Trapping has even been blamed for the extinction of some local populations. This species has many races, divided into 2 distinct groups. Western races, such as *C. c. britannica* of the British Isles, have black on the head, while eastern races, such as *C. c. paropanisi* of central Asia, have gray. The 2 forms interbreed where they come into contact in central Asia.

Like its cousin the American Goldfinch, the Eurasian Goldfinch feeds readily on the seeds of weeds. Flocks of the birds are often seen drifting along roadsides from one patch of thistles to another. The nests are built in bushes or trees, often high up and well out on side branches.

## 10/ REDPOLL
*Acanthis flammea*
RANGE: **circumpolar in N latitudes, Britain, central Europe**
HABITAT: **birch forest, shrub tundra, young conifer plantations**
SIZE: **5½ in (14 cm)**

Since the 1950s, one race of this bird, the Lesser Redpoll *A. f. cabaret*, has increased markedly in western Europe, taking advantage of the large areas of young conifer growth established by forestry interests. Just a few decades ago, there were only isolated populations of the race in upland Britain and the Alps. Its distribution now runs continuously from Britain, northeast France, and the Low Countries to the Alps and Czechoslovakia, and up into southern Scandinavia.

Elsewhere, races of the Redpoll breed across the northern latitudes of Eurasia and North America, wintering well to the south of their breeding ranges. In North America, the numbers of the birds in most wintering areas vary on a 2-year cycle, tied to the seeding of a variety of trees. Redpolls nest in the middle levels of trees and bushes, although the most northerly race, the very pale *A. f. hornemanni*, often called the Hoary Redpoll, nests on or near the ground above the Arctic tree line. Females lack the pinkish breast and rump of the males; juveniles also lack the black throat of the adults and their red forehead, or "poll," which gives the species its name.

## 11/ ROSY FINCH
*Leucosticte arctoa*
RANGE: **C and E Siberia, NW and W North America**
HABITAT: **mountains, above the tree line; winters at lower altitudes**
SIZE: **5¾–6½ in (14.5–17 cm)**

The widespread Rosy Finch is extremely variable in size and plumage. It has many races, some nearly as large as European Starlings *Sturnus vulgaris*, others as small as House Sparrows

*Passer domesticus*. Until recently, several of the races of the Rosy Finch were regarded as separate species. The North American races include the Black Rosy Finch *L. a. atrata* of the Great Basin and the Rockies, the Brown-capped Rosy Finch *L. a. australis* of southwestern USA, and the Aleutian Rosy Finch *L. a. umbrina* of the Pribilof Islands off Alaska.

Rosy Finches live on the bare hilltops, mountain sides and high plains of remote mountains and islands. They eat mainly seeds, but often supplement their diet with insects, especially those that are blown onto snowfields. Insects rapidly become torpid in the cold and fall easy prey to the birds. In winter, most populations of this bird migrate down to adjacent valleys, lowland plains and coastal areas. Rosy Finches nest in loose colonies in rock screes and on cliffs.

## 12/ HOUSE FINCH
*Carpodacus mexicanus*
RANGE: **North and Central America, S to Mexico**
HABITAT: **towns, open woodland, scrub, deserts**
SIZE: **6 in (15 cm)**

House Finches are common in dry, open habitats in western USA. They are major pests in California, where they feed on ripening fruit and buds. Formerly common as cage birds, some were released in New York State in about 1940, where they subsequently nested in 1943. After a slow start, they increased rapidly and are now widespread in eastern North America, from Florida to Canada. The race *C. m. frontalis* (illustrated) from southwestern Canada, western USA and northwest Mexico is typical. House Finches were also introduced to Hawaii in the last century, where they are now well established and widely regarded as pests.

By contrast, one race of the bird, McGregor's House Finch *C. m. mcgregori*, formerly confined to islands off Baja California, had become very rare by the turn of the century and dwindled to extinction by 1938.

## 13/ CAUCASIAN GREAT ROSEFINCH
*Carpodacus rubicilla*
RANGE: **Caucasus and C Asia**
HABITAT: **rocky alpine meadows and rocky slopes**
SIZE: **7¾ in (20 cm)**

The Caucasian Great Rosefinch is one of several closely related and very similar *Carpodacus* finches that occur in central Asia. One of the largest species, it is a denizen of windswept and barren high mountains, at altitudes of 6,500–16,500 ft (2,000–5,000 m). In winter, flocks descend to rocky ravines and overgrown thickets in mountain valleys, but even then the birds rarely appear below 3,300 ft (1,000 m).

The colorful male Caucasian Great Rose-finches have shiny, lustrous feathers which contrast markedly with those of the drably plumaged females. The birds breed in isolated pairs or in small colonies, siting their nests in cliff crevices or between boulders.

PINE GROSBEAK

♂

♀

RED CROSSBILL

race *curvirostra*

♂

♀

NORTHERN
BULLFINCH

race *pileata*

♀

HAWFINCH

♂

EVENING GROSBEAK

♂

♀

AKIALOA

race *procerus*

♀

AKIAPOLAAU

♂

MAUI PARROTBILL

♂

♂

PALILA

AKOHEKOHE

imm

IIWI

# FINCHES

## 1/ PINE GROSBEAK
*Pinicola enucleator*
RANGE: N and W North America, N
Scandinavia E to N Siberia
HABITAT: coniferous and scrub forest
SIZE: 7¾ in (20 cm)

These large finches are often elusive and difficult
to find in their northern forest homeland. They
tend to be sparsely distributed, and their quiet,
unobtrusive habits make them easy to overlook.
Although the adult males are brightly colored,
young males are somber-toned, like the females.

Pine Grosbeaks eat mainly berries and buds,
hopping about heavily on the ground, or clambering around slowly in the treetops. While many
birds are sedentary, others leave the breeding
grounds and travel south and west in winter,
sometimes in large numbers. The magnitude of
these movements is related to the abundance of
the Pine Grosbeak's natural food; in Europe, the
size of the crop of mountain ash berries is
especially important. Few birds are seen in years
with poor crops. During winter, Pine Grosbeaks
are often seen in small flocks, when they may be
remarkably tame and approachable.

## 2/ RED CROSSBILL
*Loxia curvirostra*
RANGE: America, from Alaska S to
Guatemala, Eurasia, Algeria, Tunisia,
Balearic Islands
HABITAT: coniferous forest
SIZE: 6¼ in (16 cm)

The 4 species of crossbill and the Akepa *Loxops
coccinea*, one of the Hawaiian finches, are the only
birds in the world that have crossed bills. In the
crossbills, the beak is used to open the scales of
conifer cones, particularly those of pines, spruces
and larches, to extract the seeds that make up
almost all their diet. Their dependence on conifer
seeds often gives rise to mass migrations (or
irruptions); the birds sometimes sweep across
entire continents during years of cone crop failure.
Pines rarely suffer poor cone crops, however, and
populations that feed on these are almost
sedentary.

The race *L. c. curvirostra*, which occupies most
of the species' range in Eurasia, including parts of
the British Isles, feeds mainly on spruce; 11
isolated races are found in the Old World on
mountains and islands outside the species' main
range. These differ slightly in size and color from
*L. c. curvirostra* and have different-sized bills,
adapted for dealing with different cones. Some
populations tend to have the bill crossed to the
right and others crossed to the left. These differences may be related to clockwise and counter-
clockwise spiraling of the scales of cones.

The Scottish Crossbill *L. scoticus*, which has a
large bill for feeding on pine cones in northeast
Scotland, is generally now regarded as a distinct
species – Britain's only endemic species of bird.
There is a similar variation in bill size and diet in
the 8 New World races.

Red Crossbills can be very approachable if
feeding at low levels, but they usually forage
much higher, near the crowns of the tall forest
trees. There, they are easily overlooked if their
ringing calls are not recognized.

## 3/ NORTHERN BULLFINCH
*Pyrrhula pyrrhula*
RANGE: Europe E across Asia to Japan
HABITAT: coniferous and broad-leaved
forest, cultivated areas, gardens
SIZE: 6 in (15 cm)

The soft-plumaged and usually shy Northern
Bullfinch is often a major agricultural pest in fruit-
growing areas, where it can cause considerable
damage by eating the buds of fruit trees, especially those of pears. During the breeding season, it
carries food to the young in special pouches on the
floor of its mouth, either side of the tongue. This is
in contrast to most finches, which carry food in
their throats.

The Azores Bullfinch *P. p. murina* has much
duller plumage than its continental northern
European relative *P. p. pileata*. The sexes are alike
in the Azores Bullfinch, and both male and female
lack the white on the rump characteristic of all
other races, suggesting that it may in fact be a
separate species. It occurs in upland forest and
along the forest edge in the Azores. It is extremely
rare and believed to be endangered. At the opposite end of the species range, in the Amur region of
the extreme southeastern USSR, Manchuria and
Japan, there is a race, *P. p. griseiventris*, with a
gray breast and red face.

## 4/ HAWFINCH
*Coccothraustes coccothraustes*
RANGE: Europe, North Africa, Asia
HABITAT: broad-leaved and mixed forest,
parkland and orchards
SIZE: 7 in (18 cm)

A huge head and bill, stocky build and short tail
give the Hawfinch its distinctive, heavy appearance. The bird feeds largely on tree seeds,
such as those of hornbeam, elm and beech, which
it takes directly from the trees or forages for on the
ground. Like most finches, it takes some insects
during the summer. The young are fed partly on
insects and partly on regurgitated seeds.

However, it is the Hawfinch's ability to feed on
the kernels of thick-walled seeds, such as cherry
and olive stones, that is most well known. The

head and massive bill are specialized for cracking
these open. The skull is strengthened and modified to provide attachment for powerful muscles
that bulge out and make the bird's cheeks look
swollen. The inside of the bill contains special
pads for gripping the stones. Experiments have
revealed that the Hawfinch must be able to exert a
force equivalent to more than 100 lb (45 kg) in
order to crack open an olive stone. The bird itself
weighs only 2 oz (55 g).

Hawfinches are very shy and usually disappear
rapidly into the treetops long before they can be
clearly seen. The middle flight feathers of the
wing are curiously notched and curled at the tips,
unlike those of any other finch. The reason for this
feature is unclear, although it may have a role in
courtship. Female Hawfinches are rather duller in
plumage than the males.

## 5/ EVENING GROSBEAK
*Coccothraustes vespertinus*
RANGE: W North America, S to Mexico, E
across Canada
HABITAT: coniferous and mixed woodland
SIZE: 7¾ in (20 cm)

This large, chunky finch was originally (and
incorrectly) thought to sing only late in the day,
hence its common name. Formerly a bird primarily of the western mountains of North America,
the Evening Grosbeak has spread east across
Canada as far as Nova Scotia during this century.
This expansion of the bird's range is still continuing eastward.

During winter, the Evening Grosbeak migrates
south and east, often coming to feeding stations,
particularly if sunflower seeds are available. The
numbers occurring each winter vary enormously,
depending on the abundance of natural food. The
bird's nest is a loose, shallow cup of twigs and
roots placed in a woodland tree, sometimes up to
65 ft (20 m) above the ground.

## FAMILY FRINGILLIDAE/
## SUBFAMILY DREPANIDINAE
### Hawaiian finches

Small, beaks highly variable in shape. Endemic to Hawaiian Island group. Generally simple plumage patterns, often yellow, red or black. Sexes different, or similar with males larger. Nests in trees, bushes or grass tussocks. Eggs 2–4, white, with lines or spots. Incubation 13–14 days, nestling period 15–22 days. 20 species; over half are considered endangered and many are now extremely rare.

### 6/ PALILA
*Loxioides bailleui*    E
RANGE: **island of Hawaii**
HABITAT: **dry upper mountain forest**
SIZE: **6 in (15 cm)**

The Palila is found only in mamane and mamane/naio forest on the upper edges of the wooded zones of Mauna Kea, one of the 2 giant volcanoes on Hawaii. It now occurs only above 6,000 ft (1,800 m). Formerly it was quite common, and ranged down to lower altitudes of about 4,000 ft (1,200 m). The population is believed to number some 2,000–6,000 birds and the species is considered endangered.

Palilas are large, distinctive finches, the yellow plumage on the head being more pronounced in the males than in the females. The birds often roam about in small flocks, eating seeds, berries and insects (especially caterpillars). They hold the pods of mamane trees in their feet and crack or rip them open with their heavy bills. The call is rather bell-like, and the song is a collection of trills, whistles and warbles.

### 7/ MAUI PARROTBILL
*Pseudonestor xanthophrys*    V
RANGE: **island of Maui**
HABITAT: **upper mountain rain forest**
SIZE: **5½ in (14 cm)**

The Maui Parrotbill is confined to forests on the upper slopes of Haleakala Mountain, an extinct volcano, on the island of Maui. Usually occurring at altitudes above 5,000 ft (1,500 m), it prefers forest with thick undergrowth and an open tree canopy. This species is very rare, as indeed it was when it was first discovered by western ornithologists in the 1890s. Today only about 500 individuals remain.

The Maui Parrotbill takes its name from its distinctive, thickset beak. A stocky bird, it moves along the trunks and branches of trees and low shrubs with slow, deliberate movements, rather like a little parrot. On occasion, it may even hang upside-down. Using its strong bill, it crushes or wrenches open small branches of koas and other trees to get at the larvae of wood-boring beetles. It also eats caterpillars and other insects. Its calls include a loud *kzeet* and a thin *queet*, and its song is a series of notes descending in pitch.

### 8/ AKIALOA
*Hemignathus obscurus*    E
RANGE: **island of Kauai; extinct on Oahu, Lanai and Hawaii islands**
HABITAT: **upper mountain rain forest**
SIZE: **7½ in (19 cm)**

Of the 4 original races of the Akialoa, only one possibly still exists, the Kauai Akialoa *H. o. procerus*, which is sometimes regarded as a species in its own right. It was last seen for certain in 1967, although it had been numerous up to the 1890s. If any remain today, the population is undoubtedly very small and on the verge of extinction. Of the other races, the Lanai Akialoa *H. o. lanaiensis* has not been seen since 1894, when it probably became extinct due to habitat destruction; the Oahu Akialoa *H. o. ellisianus* was last seen in 1837; and the Hawaii Akialoa *H. o. obscurus* was last recorded in 1894–95, when it was still fairly common in the high rain forest.

The Akialoa feeds on invertebrates and nectar. It creeps up tree trunks and branches, probing in dense moss and bark in the manner of a treecreeper, searching for small insects and spiders. It also has a tubular tongue for drinking the nectar of flowers, particularly those of ohias and lobeliads. Its call is quite loud and deep and it utters a trilling song. Early descriptions referred to the song of the Kauai Akialoa as resembling that of a canary.

### 9/ AKIAPOLAAU
*Hemignathus munroi*    E
RANGE: **island of Hawaii**
HABITAT: **upper mountain forest**
SIZE: **5½ in (14 cm)**

Like most of the Hawaiian finches, the Akiapolaau is found in forests on mountain slopes, in this case from 1,500–6,500 ft (450–2,000 m). It was formerly widespread, but is now confined to small patches of forest, where perhaps as few as 1,500 birds remain.

A stocky, short-tailed bird, the Akiapolaau has an extraordinary bill that is quite unique among birds. While the lower mandible is straight and stout, the upper mandible is long, slender and sickle-shaped. As a feeding tool, the bill combines the work of a woodpecker's bill together with that of a treecreeper.

The bird feeds on the trunks and branches of tall koa and mamane trees, hammering with the lower mandible in the soft bark in search of beetle larvae, other insects and spiders. When it finds prey, it uses the thin upper mandible to winkle the creature out of hiding.

The sound of hammering on bark is often a clue to the Akiapolaau's presence. Males also utter loud *chip* and *squeet* calls while foraging. The song is a bright series of whistled notes, with a rising then falling inflection in the last 2 notes.

### 10/ IIWI
*Vestiaria coccinea*
RANGE: **islands of Kaui, Oahu, Molokai, Maui, Hawaii; extinct Lanai**
HABITAT: **mountain forest**
SIZE: **6 in (15 cm)**

The Iiwi is one of the few species of Hawaiian finch that is not at present endangered. It is fairly common in some parts of Kaui and Hawaii, although rarer on Oahu and Maui. It is almost extinct on Molokai and has already disappeared from Lanai.

The Iiwi feeds mainly on flowering trees, especially ohia and mamane trees, probing into the flowers with its long, decurved bill to drink the nectar. It is slow and deliberate in its movements and usually hides in the interior of trees, only occasionally coming into the open. It makes daily movements, often of many miles, in search of the patchily distributed but locally abundant flowering trees. As well as uttering the creaking sounds for which it is named, the Iiwi produces a variety of gurgles, humanlike whistles and reedy notes, which have been likened to a child playing a rusty harmonica.

The Iiwi is one of about 6 Hawaiian finches whose plumage was traditionally used to make colorful cloaks and other ornamentation for Hawaiian nobility. Tufts of feathers from huge numbers of birds made garments of great beauty, some of which may still be seen in museums. Although hunting for this purpose stopped long ago, it has been blamed (perhaps unjustly) for the plight of many species.

A variety of other causes has brought about the Hawaiian finches' decline. Some of the most devastating of these have been habitat destruction, the introduction of livestock, cats, rats and non-native forest birds, and the spread of bird diseases transmitted by mosquitoes.

### 11/ AKOHEKOHE
*Palmeria dolei*    V
RANGE: **island of Maui; extinct Molokai**
HABITAT: **upper mountain rain forest**
SIZE: **7 in (18 cm)**

With its spotted plumage, wing bars, reddish-orange nape and white tufted crest, the Akohekohe is unique among the otherwise simply patterned Hawaiian finches. Often known by its English name, Crested Honeycreeper, it is now very rare and confined to the higher northeastern slopes of Haleakala Mountain on Maui, from 5,800–6,500 ft (1,750–2,000 m) above sea level. It was formerly found on Molokai and once had a wider distribution on Maui. It was still locally abundant in the 1890s.

The Akohekohe is lively and active as it feeds in the tops of tall flowering trees, especially ohia-lehuas. It takes nectar as well as caterpillars and other insects. It is a noisy bird, with a variety of calls, including humanlike whistles. The sexes are similar in appearance.

# WAXBILLS, PARASITIC VIDUINE WEAVERS AND WHYDAHS, BUFFALO WEAVERS

GREEN-WINGED PYTILIA

race *melba* ♂

BLUE-CAPPED CORDON-BLEU

♀

♂

♂

GREEN MUNIA

RED-BILLED FIRE FINCH

race *rendalli* ♂

race *guttata*

ZEBRA FINCH

race *castanotis*

nest with chicks

GOULDIAN FINCH

♂ red-faced phase

juv

black-faced phase

COMMON WAXBILL

race *astrild*

BLUE-FACED PARROT-FINCH

race *sigillifera* ♂

WHITE-BACKED MUNIA

juv

race *acuticauda*

race *striata*

JAVA SPARROW

♂

♀

PIN-TAILED WHYDAH

♂

½ size in pro

PARADISE WHYDAH

♀

race *dinemelli*

WHITE-HEADED BUFFALO WEAVER

# WAXBILLS, PARASITIC VIDUINE WEAVERS AND WHYDAHS, BUFFALO WEAVERS

## FAMILY ESTRILDIDAE
### Waxbills

Small birds. Diverse plumage: some brightly colored, some dull but with striking markings. Sexes usually similar, but pronounced differences in some species. Nests of most species domed, made of grass; some species nest in holes. Nestlings of many species have distinctive patterns of spots or lines and patches of color in their mouths that may help parents identify and see their young in the darkness of the nest and stimulate them to feed them. Eggs typically 4–8, white. Incubation 10–21 days, nestling period about 16 days. 133 species.

## 1/ GREEN-WINGED PYTILIA
*Pytilia melba*

RANGE: **sub-Saharan Africa**
HABITAT: **savanna and steppe**
SIZE: **5 in (13 cm)**

Most waxbills associate in flocks, but the Green-winged Pytilia, often called the Melba Finch, nearly always lives in pairs which occupy year-round territories in thorny thickets. It feeds on the ground, on grass seeds and insects – particularly termites – which it finds in leaf litter or by breaking into termite galleries. There are several races, including *P. m. melba* from Zaire and Tanzania to Namibia and northern Cape Province.

These birds sometimes gather together at drinking sites, but the red-faced males are usually very aggressive toward each other (or indeed to any other birds with red faces or bills). During the courtship display the male and female hop round each other while the male sings, holding a grass stem or feather in his bill. The nest is built in a thorn bush or small tree, and both sexes incubate the 4–6 eggs and feed the chicks.

As with those of other African waxbills, the nests of this species are often host to parasitic viduine weavers and whydahs – in this case the Paradise Whydah and the Broad-tailed Paradise Whydah *Vidua orientalis*.

## 2/ RED-BILLED FIRE FINCH
*Lagonosticta senegalia*

RANGE: **sub-Saharan Africa**
HABITAT: **dry areas, dense brush and near cultivated land**
SIZE: **3½ in (9 cm)**

This bird is one of the most common of all African birds, possibly because it has adapted well to the new environments created by human settlement. Outside the breeding season it travels in small flocks, foraging for seeds among dense scrub and in fields under cultivation, usually near water. It feeds mainly on the ground and often frequents villages to snatch spilled grain.

Red-billed Fire Finches breed during the latter half of the rainy season, when there are plenty of ripe seeds to feed to the nestlings. In wild country the monogamous pairs nest in shrubs, particularly acacias, but in settled areas they will nest in thatched roofs or wall cavities. The nests are often parasitized by a parasitic viduine weaver, the Village Indigobird *Vidua chalybeata*.

There are 6 or more races recognized, including *L. s. rendalli* from southern Angola to southern Tanzania and northern Cape province.

## 3/ BLUE-CAPPED CORDON-BLEU
*Uraeginthus cyanocephala*

RANGE: **Somalia to Kenya and Tanzania**
HABITAT: **dry steppe and semidesert with bushes or trees, especially acacia or thorn scrub**
SIZE: **5 in (13 cm)**

The male Blue-capped Cordon-bleu, or Blue-headed Cordon-bleu, is a startling sight in the breeding season when, with plumage fluffed out, he pursues the duller female like a flying ball of blue feathers. Having caught her, he will woo her by singing and bobbing up and down before her with a carefully selected grass stem held in his bill – a display typical of the waxbill family.

Cordon-bleus are typical of the dry country in East Africa, where they forage for grass seeds and insects in pairs or small parties. They often take termites by breaching the earth tunnels that these insects build up acacia saplings. The nestlings are fed exclusively on termites and other insects.

## 4/ COMMON WAXBILL
*Estrilda astrild*

RANGE: **sub-Saharan Africa; introduced to many tropical islands**
HABITAT: **grassland and cultivated areas**
SIZE: **4 in (10 cm)**

The Common Waxbill feeds mainly on grass seeds, either plucking them from the seed heads or picking them off the ground, and will also prey on swarming termites. Highly gregarious, these birds often forage in large flocks and return to communal roosts at night. They breed in the rainy season, when insects for feeding their young are most abundant.

The nest is often highly elaborate, with a small "roosting" nest built on top of the dome-shaped breeding nest. The brood is often parasitized by the Pin-tailed Whydah. In contrast to the chicks of some parasitic cuckoos, such as the Eurasian Cuckoo *Cuculus canorus*, those of the whydah do not destroy the rightful occupants of the nest, and the adult waxbills can often be seen feeding a mixed brood. There are some 8 races, including *E. a. astrild* from much of South Africa.

## 5/ GREEN MUNIA
*Amandava formosa*

RANGE: **C India**
HABITAT: **grassland and cultivated regions**
SIZE: **4 in (10 cm)**

Locally common throughout the northern half of peninsular India, this small waxbill, which is also known as the Green Avadavat, often associates in flocks of up to 50 birds, particularly in areas with tall grass, low scrub or crops that provide good cover. Green Munias feed on the ground, probably taking seeds and small insects, although the precise details of this species' feeding habits in the wild are unknown.

Green Munias are monogamous, but they often nest close together in the breeding season, building large, round nests of grasses and leaves among thick grass or sugar cane. The 4–7 eggs are incubated by both the male and female.

## 6/ ZEBRA FINCH
*Poephila guttata*

RANGE: **Australia, Lesser Sundas**
HABITAT: **dry grassland and other open habitats with scattered trees and shrubs, near water**
SIZE: **4 in (10 cm)**

The Zebra Finch is one of the most common birds in inland Australia. As a seed-eater, it needs water daily and provision of water for livestock has allowed it to increase over the last 100 years. There are 2 races: the Australian *P. g. castanotis* and *P. g. guttata* of the Sunda Islands.

Highly gregarious, Zebra Finches live in flocks of 10–100 birds throughout the year and will even breed colonially, with several pairs nesting in the same bush. The pairs mate for life, and in arid regions they may breed at any time of year in response to rain. In southern parts of the species' range, breeding is more regular and seasonal. Its exact timing depends not only on rainfall, but also on temperature, food supply and previous breeding. They feed on grass seeds and insects, usually in the morning, then move on to a pool or stock-watering point in the afternoon to drink, bathe and preen one another.

## 7/ BLUE-FACED PARROT-FINCH
*Erythrura trichroa*
RANGE: **NE Queensland, Indonesia, Pacific islands and New Guinea**
HABITAT: **rain forest**
SIZE: **4¾ in (12 cm)**

Like the other members of its family, the Blue-faced Parrot-Finch is a seed-eater, but instead of foraging on the ground in grassland, it feeds on the seeds of trees and shrubs at all levels in the rain forest. It has a preference for the seeds of bamboo, and small nomadic parties of these birds will wander all over their range in search of seeding bamboo thickets. It sometimes emerges into open forest to feed on casuarina and grass seeds, but in general it is elusive and rarely seen.

After a prolonged and elaborate courtship involving singing, tail-twisting and hopping up and down on the part of the male and tail-twisting and the uttering of a low, trilling identity call by the female, the birds mate and build a pear-shaped nest of moss and vines. Both birds incubate the 4 white eggs, sleeping together on the nest at night. The race illustrated is *E. t. sigillifera* from Australia and New Guinea.

## 8/ GOULDIAN FINCH
*Chloebia gouldiae*
RANGE: **N Australia**
HABITAT: **grassland and open woodland**
SIZE: **5½ in (14 cm)**

This spectacularly plumaged bird occurs in 2 main color phases: most males have black faces, but about a quarter have red faces outlined with black, and there is a rare yellow phase. Its dazzling appearance has encouraged its capture for the cage-bird trade; this has contributed to a marked decline in recent years, but the seasonal burning of its grassland feeding grounds has probably been the main factor.

For much of the year it feeds on grass seeds, but instead of taking them from the ground it perches acrobatically on the seed heads, or picks out the seeds while clinging to a nearby twig. When the grasses in the Australian interior die back in the winter dry season, the finches move toward the coast, returning with the rains.

In the breeding season it feeds mainly on insects, often catching them in midair, and takes them to feed its brood of 4–8 chicks. The rudimentary nest is built in a tree hollow or termite mound. Several pairs may nest together in close association, sometimes in the same cavity.

## 9/ WHITE-BACKED MUNIA
*Lonchura striata*
RANGE: **India and Sri Lanka to Sumatra**
HABITAT: **grassland with scattered trees, cultivated land**
SIZE: **4 in (10 cm)**

This small, finchlike bird is generally found in large flocks throughout the year, foraging on the ground and amid growing vegetation for the seeds of wild grasses, particularly bamboo, as well as cultivated rice and insects. The nestlings are fed on green seeds, although according to some observers they will also take insects, like the young of many other waxbills.

The pairs breed during the rainy season, building a spherical or oval nest in a bush, tree, or sometimes among rank grass. The 3–8 eggs are brooded by both sexes, and both roost in the nest at night. There are several races, including *L. s. striata* of south India and Sri Lanka, and *L. s. acuticauda*, found from the Himalayas to Thailand. The domesticated form of this species is known as the Bengalese Finch.

## 10/ JAVA SPARROW
*Padda oryzivora*
RANGE: **Java and Bali; introduced to Africa, China, S Asia and Hawaii**
HABITAT: **scrub, grassland, bamboo thickets, mangroves, cultivated land**
SIZE: **5½ in (14 cm)**

The boldly marked Java Sparrow has become familiar well beyond its original range, owing to deliberate introductions and escapes from aviaries, for it is a popular cage bird. It feeds largely on seeds and has a strong predilection for rice. Its Latin name reflects this, *Padda* being a reference to the paddy fields and *oryzivora* meaning "rice-eating." During harvest time large flocks descend on the paddy fields to feast on the rice crop, often causing extensive damage.

Java Sparrows form monogamous pairs, breeding just after the rainy season. The nest is built among branches or in a cavity in a tree trunk, wall or roof. The juveniles begin to feed themselves soon after fledging, but are often fed by their parents for another 2–3 weeks.

## FAMILY PLOCEIDAE/SUBFAMILY VIDUINAE
**Parasitic viduine weavers and whydahs**
Small seed-eaters. Sexes differ. Plumage of males black or steel blue, with white, yellow or chestnut in whydahs; females brown and sparrowlike in many species. Male parasitic whydahs have very long tails in breeding season. Eggs 3–4, white, laid in nests of waxbills; most species restricted to a single host. Incubation about 10 days (Village Indigobird), nestling period about 20 days (Pin-tailed Whydah). 10 species.

## 11/ PIN-TAILED WHYDAH
*Vidua macroura*
RANGE: **sub-Saharan Africa**
HABITAT: **savanna, cultivated land**
SIZE: **breeding male 13 in (33 cm); non-breeding male 6 in (15 cm); female 5 in (13 cm)**

Despite his spectacular breeding plumage, with a tail almost twice the length of his body, the male Pin-tailed Whydah is surprisingly inconspicuous when searching on the ground for seeds. Pin-tailed Whydahs often forage in small, lively flocks, with one long-tailed breeding male accompanying a group of short-tailed birds, both non-breeding young males and females.

During courtship the male chases other species and flies in looping, vertical circles above his mate in a whirring, dancing display. He will sing from a favored perch for several weeks, but the song is a hissing, rather wheezy performance. The female

lays her eggs one by one in the nests of the Common Waxbill and 3 other species of waxbill, and the chicks develop alongside those of their host. The whydah chicks mimic those of the hosts with remarkable accuracy, including the number and pattern of the spots on the waxbills' palates, the colors inside their mouths and the color of the highly reflective nodules at their gapes.

## 12/ PARADISE WHYDAH
*Vidua paradisaea*
RANGE: **C Africa S to Zimbabwe**
HABITAT: **dry bush and savanna woodland**
SIZE: **breeding male 16 in (41 cm); non-breeding male 6 in (15 cm); female 5 in (13 cm)**

In breeding plumage the male Paradise Whydah is a fantastic sight, with his immensely elongated, 11 in (28 cm) black tail feathers that play an important part in the territorial and courtship display. The male flies with the 2 short, broad tail feathers held upright above the long, pointed ones, circling at a height or hovering above a female, rising and falling in jerky undulations that make the tail plumes wave up and down.

These birds are often seen in small flocks searching bare ground or grassland for seeds. The eggs are laid in the nests of Green-winged Pytilias which then rear the young whydahs with their own brood. As with the other parasitic viduine weavers and whydahs, the chicks mimic the mouth patterns of the host chicks.

## FAMILY PLOCEIDAE/SUBFAMILY BUBALORNITHINAE
**Buffalo weavers**
Medium, ground-dwelling seed- and insect-eaters of semiarid regions. Sexes alike. The 2 *Bubalornis* species are black, the 1 *Dinemellia* species is white, brown and red. Large, untidy domed nests of thorny twigs. Eggs 3–4, pale blue or grayish with olive markings. Incubation 11 days, nestling period 20–23 days. 3 species.

## 13/ WHITE-HEADED BUFFALO WEAVER
*Dinemellia dinemelli*
RANGE: **Ethiopia, Sudan S to Tanzania**
HABITAT: **dry thornbush, acacia woodland**
SIZE: **9 in (23 cm)**

When startled into flight from a dusty roadside, this large, thickset, almost parrotlike weaver shows its conspicuous red rump and tail coverts, which in combination with striking flashes of white make it unmistakable even at a brief glance. It is usually seen in pairs or small groups, often in company with Superb Starlings *Spreo superbus*, foraging on the ground beneath flat-topped acacia trees or perched low down in thorn bushes. It feeds mainly on seeds, cracking them open with its powerful bill.

These birds often breed in loose colonies, building large, ragged nests of twigs in the boughs of thorn trees which provide protection against nest-predators.

There are 2 races: the northern race *D. d. dinemelli* and the southern race *D. d. boehmi*, which has black mantle, wings and tail.

# TRUE WEAVERS AND SPARROW-WEAVERS, PASSERINE FINCHES

GOLDEN PALM WEAVER

race *albifrons*

GROSBEAK WEAVER

nest

race *collaris*

race *scutatus*

nest

RED-VENTED MALIMBE

race *philippinus*

RED-BILLED QUELEA

race *lathamii*

BAYA WEAVER

race *spilonotus*

VILLAGE WEAVER

MADAGASCAN RED FODY

♀

RED BISHOP

♂ race *orix*

♂
JACKSON'S
WIDOWBIRD

WHITE-BROWED
SPARROW-WEAVER

♂

SOCIABLE WEAVER

colonial nest

♂

STREAKED ROCK SPARROW

♀

WHITE-WINGED SNOW FINCH

race *nivalis*

♀

♂ race *domesticus*

HOUSE SPARROW

♀

♂
race *luteus*
"Sudan Golden Sparrow"

GOLDEN SPARROW

# TRUE WEAVERS AND SPARROW-WEAVERS, PASSERINE FINCHES

## FAMILY PLOCEIDAE/SUBFAMILY PLOCEINAE
### True weavers

Small, mainly tropical, mostly African, chiefly seed-eating birds. Mostly stout-billed and short-tailed (except for male widowbirds, with very long tails). Sexes often differ. Many species with bright yellow, red or glossy black plumage, especially in males; females of most *Ploceus* species with drab, sparrowlike plumage. Often breed in large colonies. Nests intricately woven, domed structures of grass, leaves and sometimes mud, suspended from branches. Eggs 2–4, white, pink, greenish or bluish with wide variety of markings. Incubation 11–17 days, nestling period 11–20 days. 105 species.

## 1/ GROSBEAK WEAVER
*Amblyospiza albifrons*

RANGE: **much of sub-Saharan Africa**
HABITAT: **swampy woodland, damp forest, reedbeds**
SIZE: **6½–7½ in (17–19 cm)**

An alternative name for this large, gregarious species is Thick-billed Weaver. The striking male reveals white patches in the wings when he flies, with a rather undulating flight. The female shares the distinctive flight, but is a much drabber bird than the male, brown above and whitish with dark streaks below. There are several races, including *A. a. albifrons*, illustrated, from the Cape Province.

The male weaves the beautifully constructed sphere-shaped nest from thin grass strips, fixing it to 2 or 3 upright grass stems. The entrance is a small hole in the side, with or without a "porch," depending on the location, and nests are often in small colonies.

## 2/ GOLDEN PALM WEAVER
*Ploceus bojeri*

RANGE: **Somalia S to Tanzania**
HABITAT: **coconut palms, coastal scrub**
SIZE: **6 in (15 cm)**

Although found locally over a wide area, this species is most common on the Kenya coast. The spectacular males are especially obvious; they are often found in small flocks, but ones and twos may also be seen in the bushes inland from the beach, or along the shoreline coconut palms, searching for fruits and berries.

Their calls are rather low pitched, sounding like a fizzing, hissing or jangling chatter. This species is very similar in appearance to the Golden Weaver *P. subaureus*, which has a similar range but is not found in Somalia and also occurs on the island of Zanzibar.

## 3/ VILLAGE WEAVER
*Ploceus cucullatus*

RANGE: **Sudan and Ethiopia S to Angola, Cape Province**
HABITAT: **forest, cultivated land, gardens**
SIZE: **6–7 in (15–18 cm)**

The males of this widespread species have a strikingly patterned plumage in the breeding season, but females and nonbreeding males have greener, streaked plumage. There are some 7 races, including *P. c. collaris* of Zaire and N Angola and *P. c. spilonotus* of South Africa, which vary according to the pattern of black on the head and the strength of coloring below.

Village Weavers, which are also called Spotted-backed Weavers, breed in noisy, lively, dense colonies, with nests made of grass strips woven into kidney-shaped balls, with or without a "spout" at the opening. The nests are slung from the tips of spreading, drooping branches, often over water. The males build the nests and display at them. Each male hangs upside-down from the base of his nest with whirring wings. He takes little interest in the eggs or chicks.

## 4/ BAYA WEAVER
*Ploceus philippinus*

RANGE: **Pakistan E to Sri Lanka, Indochina, Sumatra**
HABITAT: **scrub, cultivated land, palms, grassland**
SIZE: **5½–6 in (14–15 cm)**

The race illustrated, *P. p. philippinus*, is common all over India; there are several others, including *P. p. burmanicus* from Assam, Bangladesh, Bengal, eastern Nepal and Burma, which is more richly and darkly rufous beneath, with no yellow.

The Baya Weaver's wonderful nest is made of finely woven strips of grass, rice leaves or sugar cane, and is suspended from a drooping tree frond, telephone line or thatched roof. A male flutters noisily in excited display at the nest; once he has succeeded in attracting a female, he completes the nest lining, then, after the eggs are laid, builds another nest, and even a third or fourth, for other females.

## 5/ RED-VENTED MALIMBE
*Malimbus scutatus*

RANGE: **Sierra Leone E to Cameroon**
HABITAT: **coastal forest**
SIZE: **4¾ in (12 cm)**

Small parties of Red-Vented Malimbes may be detected by the very harsh *zee-zee-zee* or *chit-it-zeer-zeer* calls they utter constantly as they move through undergrowth, often near villages. They are chiefly insect-eaters but all feed on the husks of oil palm nuts.

The male of the race *M. s. scutopartitus* from Cameroon has a larger red breast patch than that of *M. s. scutatus* from farther west. Nests are constructed in small groups, in palm trees, each made of palm leaf ribs woven into a sphere with a very long entrance spout.

## 6/ RED-BILLED QUELEA
*Quelea quelea*

RANGE: **sub-Saharan Africa**
HABITAT: **damp woodland, swamps, cultivated land**
SIZE: **4¼–5 in (11–13 cm)**

Huge, densely packed, perfectly synchronized flocks of a million or more Red-billed Queleas move across the land like clouds of smoke, sometimes breaking the branches of trees with their combined weight. These vast swarms still devastate grain crops despite determined efforts at pest control.

Colonies contain huge numbers of spherical nests of woven green grasses, usually attached to the branches of thorn trees. There may be as many as 500 nests in a single thorn tree. The male has a sweet song, but flocks make a confused roar of chirps and wing noise.

There are several races: *Q. q. lathamii*, from southern Africa, is paler and grayer above than the West African race *Q. q. quelea*; *Q. q. aethiopica* from the northeast is more rosy below, with less or no black on the forehead of breeding males.

## 7/ MADAGASCAN RED FODY
*Foudia madagascariensis*

RANGE: **Madagascar; introduced to Mauritius, Seychelles**
HABITAT: **forest edge, savanna, cultivated land, rice paddies**
SIZE: **5 in (13 cm)**

On Madagascar this is one of the most common of birds, the red males strikingly obvious, the females browner, streaked above but unmarked below. Madagascan Red Fodies forage in groups or with mixed-bird flocks and do immense damage to the rice crop. They live in most places except the interior of the forest.

Madagascan Red Fodies have high-pitched, insectlike calls, and males sing with a very high, hissing and bubbling sound, like a tiny steam engine, displaying with wings and tail dropped and rump feathers fluffed out. These fodies live in and around villages, eating all kinds of seeds and also insects in the breeding season.

## 8/ RED BISHOP
*Euplectes orix*
RANGE: **sub-Saharan Africa**
HABITAT: **grassland**
SIZE: **4¾–5½ in (12–14 cm)**

Of all the small African grassland birds, the male Red Bishop is perhaps the most eye-catching in his breeding colors. The race *E. o. orix*, illustrated, is the southern race. A male displays to a female with his rump feathers puffed out; he will also fly with his body plumage ruffled into a vivid ball, floating or bounding above the grass with a loud purring of vibrating wings.

Males have strict territories with 3–4 females. Nests are built in loose colonies. Made of grass and attached to reeds, tall grasses or palm fronds, the nests are oval in shape, with an entrance high in one side.

## 9/ JACKSON'S WIDOWBIRD
*Euplectes jacksoni*
RANGE: **Kenya, Tanzania**
HABITAT: **highland grassland, cultivated land**
SIZE: **13¼ in (34 cm)**

The male is extraordinary and striking with his 8 in (20 cm) long tail; the female and nonbreeding male are streaky brown. Like other widowbirds, they are also often called whydahs. They are found in rather isolated areas of grassland above 5,000 ft (1,500 m) in western and central Kenya and northern Tanzania, forming flocks after breeding which move to cultivated land. Breeding males wear away special "rings" in the grass on which they display, springing into the air with heads thrown back, feet hanging and tail curved forward to touch the neck, except for 2 feathers pointing downward and outward. They have various brief, clicking and whistling songs and a softer, wheezy call note.

## FAMILY PLOCEIDAE/SUBFAMILY PLOCEPASSERINAE
**Sparrow-weavers**
Small, ground-feeding, highly gregarious, stout-billed seed- and insect-eaters. Sexes almost alike, distinguished by head and wing markings. Plumage drab, with brown upperparts and white underparts. Roofed nests, thatched with (not woven from) grass stems, mostly with 2 openings, often communal and some used for roosting. Eggs 2–5, cream, white, pinkish or pale blue, with red, brown or gray speckles, scribbles or blotches. Incubation and nestling period (Sociable Weaver) 13–14 days and 21–24 days. 8 species.

## 10/ WHITE-BROWED SPARROW-WEAVER
*Plocepasser mahali*
RANGE: **Ethiopia to South Africa**
HABITAT: **light wooded savanna and semi-desert, coming into villages**
SIZE: **6¼–7 in (16–18 cm)**

This common bird of acacia savanna is usually seen in noisy, chattering groups, either in the breeding trees or feeding on the ground on seeds and insects. The race *P. m. melanorhynchus*, from Sudan, Ethiopia, Uganda and Kenya, is illustrated. Some other races have brown markings on the breast that give the species an alternative name of Stripe-breasted Sparrow-Weaver.

White-browed Sparrow-Weavers build an untidy retort-shaped nest of dry grass at the ends of branches; there are often several nests to a tree. These nests are used for roosting by several birds; only one female in a group breeds, the remainder helping to feed the nestlings.

## 11/ SOCIABLE WEAVER
*Philetirus socius*
RANGE: **W and C southern Africa**
HABITAT: **dry acacia savanna**
SIZE: **5½ in (14 cm)**

This highly gregarious bird is most remarkable for its breeding behavior. Each colony, which may consist of anything from 6–300 birds, constructs a large communal nest in a tree or on the crosspiece of a bare utility pole. This extraordinary structure is the largest nest of any passerine. It measures up to 13 ft (4 m) deep and 25 ft (7.5 m) long and has a large roof, beneath which each individual pair has its own nest cavity. Grass stems are arranged pointing diagonally downward into the vertical entrance tunnel leading into each nest, forming a barrier against many predators. The communal nest is used by the group throughout the year, both for roosting and breeding, and may last for many years.

## FAMILY PASSERIDAE
**Passerine finches**
Small, finchlike, chiefly seed-eating, typically social birds, mainly of open country. Sexes alike or differ. Plumage mainly brown, chestnut and gray, sometimes with black and, in snow finches, white; yellow in a few species. Usually breed in large colonies. Nests typically bulky, domed structures of dried grass. Eggs 2–7, whitish, cream or pinkish with delicate brown, gray or lilac markings. Incubation 12–15 days, nestling period 15–24 days. 32 species.

## 12/ HOUSE SPARROW
*Passer domesticus*
RANGE: **throughout Eurasia excluding Far East; introduced worldwide**
HABITAT: **farmland and built-up areas**
SIZE: **5½–7 in (14–18 cm)**

The familiar House Sparrow is a seed-eater, adapted to the large seeds of grasses and cultivated grains but also feeding on invertebrates and taking a variety of scraps from bread to meat fibers. The race illustrated is *P. d. domesticus* from

much of Eurasia; other races differ in plumage details and size. The House Sparrow is an extremely successful species, nesting in holes or openly in trees in loose colonies and capable of laying as many as 7 clutches of eggs in a single year in the tropics. In places it becomes an agricultural pest.

## 13/ GOLDEN SPARROW
*Passer luteus*
RANGE: **arid zone S of Sahara, from Senegal to Arabia**
HABITAT: **arid acacia savanna**
SIZE: **4–5 in (10–13 cm)**

There are 2 races of this attractive little sparrow which are sometimes regarded as separate species: *P. l. euchlorus* from Arabia, with striking canary-yellow males, and *P. l. luteus* from Africa, in which the males have a bright chestnut back. The females of both races have a more muted brown and pale yellow plumage. This is an intensely social species, occurring in flocks of up to 1 million birds, and can be an agricultural pest. The Golden Sparrow breeds opportunistically when rains produce suitable feeding conditions, nesting in large colonies in thorn trees.

## 14/ STREAKED ROCK SPARROW
*Petronia petronia*
RANGE: **Canary Islands, Mediterranean E to China**
HABITAT: **barren open country and rocky hillsides**
SIZE: **6 in (15 cm)**

The rock sparrows and bush sparrows of the genus *Petronia* replace the sparrows of the genus *Passer* in open barren country and light woodland, respectively. The Streaked Rock Sparrow, also known as the Chestnut-shouldered Petronia, is a typical rock sparrow, a streaky brown bird resembling a female House Sparrow, but characterized by an inconspicuous yellow throat patch.

The Streaked Rock Sparrow is usually found in open country, where it nests in holes in trees or rocks, although some individuals come into the more remote villages to breed in holes in buildings. It is a sedentary bird and is relatively common, although frequently overlooked as it feeds, often in large flocks, on the ground.

## 15/ WHITE-WINGED SNOW FINCH
*Montifringilla nivalis*
RANGE: **Spain to Mongolia**
HABITAT: **high, bare mountain country above the tree line**
SIZE: **6¾ in (17.5 cm)**

The White-winged Snow Finch is one of 7 species of snow finch that all live in high mountain country. There are 4 races: the one illustrated is *M. n. nivalis* from southwest Europe.

It is one of the highest-dwelling of all birds, usually seen in small groups on rocks or on the ground near patches of melting snow. In winter it forms larger flocks that are often found near mountain huts. It builds its bulky nest in crevices or holes under rocks up to an altitude of 16,500 ft (5,000 m) or even higher.

SPLENDID GLOSSY STARLING

♂

imm

SHINING STARLING

♂

TRISTRAM'S STARLING

imm

BLACK-HEADED STARLING

♂

ROSE-COLORED STARLING

BALD STARLING

COMMON MYNAH

AMETHYST STARLING

♀

♂

SUPERB STARLING

non-breeding  ♂

WATTLED STARLING

♂

EUROPEAN STARLING

♂

juv

ROTHSCHILD'S MYNAH

GROSBEAK STARLING

HILL MYNAH

RED-BILLED OXPECKER

# STARLINGS

## FAMILY STURNIDAE
### Starlings

Small to medium, active, sociable; with long straight bills and sturdy legs. Typically dark, iridescent; some brightly colored. Sexes similar. Mostly colonial, nesting in holes. Eggs 2–7, pale blue, spotted brown. Incubation 11–18 days, nestling period 18–30 days. 108 species.

### 1/ SHINING STARLING
*Aplonis metallica*

RANGE: **Molucca Islands, Solomon Islands, New Guinea, NE Queensland**
HABITAT: **forest canopy, coastal woodlands, mangroves**
SIZE: **$8\frac{1}{4}$–$9\frac{1}{2}$ in (21–24 cm)**

Shining Starlings nest in trees, in colonies of up to 300 pairs. Each colony takes over a tree and drapes its branches with bulky, pendulous nests woven from plant stems, reminiscent of the nests of some weavers (pp. 346–49) and quite unlike the nests of other starlings. New colonies may be started by young birds which breed in immature plumage.

The Shining Starlings that breed in northern Australia migrate north after the breeding season to spend the winter (May–July) in the forests and mangrove swamps of New Guinea. There they feed alongside the resident birds, flying from tree to tree in great noisy flocks to feast on fruit, nectar and insects.

### 2/ TRISTRAM'S STARLING
*Onychognathus tristramii*

RANGE: **Israel, Jordan, Sinai Peninsula, W Arabia**
HABITAT: **rocky country, desolate ravines, spreading into towns**
SIZE: **$9\frac{3}{4}$ in (25 cm)**

In wild country, Tristram's Starling nests in rock crevices on cliffs and crags, lining the nest cavity with a sparse layer of hair, feathers, leaves and other soft material. Like many birds that are native to rocky areas, it is adapting to life on the artificial "cliffs" and "ledges" of urban areas. It is now beginning to colonize towns in Israel, where it builds its nests in tall, uninhabited buildings. Its song is sweet and wild, in keeping with its original habitat.

Tristram's Starlings feed in flocks, searching out insects and fruit in wadi beds and among low vegetation. The flocks are larger outside the breeding season and some consist entirely of newly fledged juveniles. Adult females and juveniles resemble mature males, but the head plumage is a duller gray.

### 3/ SPLENDID GLOSSY STARLING
*Lamprotornis splendidus*

RANGE: **Senegal W to Ethiopia, S to Angola and Tanzania; S populations winter N**
HABITAT: **tall woodland, secondary forest**
SIZE: **$11\frac{3}{4}$ in (30 cm)**

This large member of the glossy starling genus *Lamprotornis* is often encountered in the strips of gallery forest bordering river banks. Its wings make a distinctive swishing sound in flight, when

its back shows a humped profile. Although it is a rather shy and elusive bird, spending much of its time in the treetops, it is frequently heard uttering a variety of guttural and nasal calls, especially a *quonk quonk* and a *chak*, as well as liquid whistles. It has a wide diet, including many tree fruits. This bird breeds in holes in trees, lining its nest with dried vegetation.

### 4/ AMETHYST STARLING
*Cinnyricinclus leucogaster*

RANGE: **SW Arabia, sub-Saharan Africa, South Africa, Gabon, Congo and Zaire**
HABITAT: **rain forest, wooded savanna, woodland edge, parks, gardens**
SIZE: **$6\frac{1}{4}$–7 in (16–18 cm)**

Unusually for starlings, male and female Amethyst Starlings are quite distinct in appearance: in contrast to the gaudy violet and white male, the female, like the juvenile, has mainly brown plumage. They are also less noisy than other species, despite being highly gregarious. They nest in tree holes, lining the cavity with feathers, soft plant material and even animal dung.

In some parts of their range these starlings are year-round residents. Elsewhere they are nomadic, or even migratory, although they do not travel far. They have a taste for fruit and flocks of these birds will arrive in an area when the fruit ripens, strip the trees and then disappear. They will also take insects, often hawking for termites on the wing.

### 5/ SUPERB STARLING
*Spreo superbus*

RANGE: **SE Sudan, E to Somalia and S to Tanzania**
HABITAT: **open acacia savanna, lawns, farmland**
SIZE: **7 in (18 cm)**

This spectacular-looking starling is a common East African bird. It feeds mainly on the ground, eating a range of seeds, fruits and insects. It will devour food scraps with relish and small flocks will often gather at campsites and hotels to beg for

food, which makes it very popular with tourists.

While Superb Starlings will nest in holes like other starlings, they often build large, untidy, domed nests in low thorn bushes. Occasionally a breeding pair is assisted by one or more non-breeding birds which help to feed the chicks. Juveniles can be distinguished by their duller plumage and brown eyes.

### 6/ WATTLED STARLING
*Creatophora cinerea*

RANGE: **Ethiopia to Cape Province, Angola**
HABITAT: **open thornbush savanna**
SIZE: **$8\frac{1}{4}$ in (21 cm)**

This stocky, short-tailed bird undergoes dramatic changes in the breeding season: the male loses his head feathers, exposing bare yellow skin, and long black wattles develop on the forehead, crown and throat. The Wattled Starling has been used in medical research. Its ability to resorb its wattles has attracted the attention of cancer specialists, while the annual regrowth of its head feathers has prompted investigations by researchers attempting to find an antidote to human baldness.

Wattled Starlings feed on the ground, being particularly fond of locusts and grasshoppers. The birds are nomadic, huge flocks of them following locust swarms.

They build colonies of large, untidy domed nests in thorn trees. The eggs are pale blue, usually unmarked. This, together with the bird's habits and appearance, suggest a close affinity with the *Sturnus* starlings – indicating that this African species may have an Asian origin.

### 7/ BLACK-HEADED STARLING
*Sturnus pagodarum*

RANGE: **Afghanistan, India, Sri Lanka**
HABITAT: **woodland, scrub, farmland, gardens**
SIZE: **$8\frac{1}{2}$ in (22 cm)**

The Black-headed, or Brahminy, Starling has a varied diet. It is fond of feeding on nectar, which it extracts from flowers with its brush-tipped tongue. In the process its bill becomes dusted with pollen, which it carries to other flowers, and the bird is believed to have an important role as a pollinator of nectar-producing trees. It also eats fruit and seeds and may be an important agent in the dispersal of sandalwood (*Santalum album*) seeds. Adult birds are distinguished by their glossy black caps, crowned with elongated feathers that can be raised in a crest.

## 8/ ROSE-COLORED STARLING
*Sturnus roseus*
RANGE: **E Europe and WC Asia; migrates to India in winter**
HABITAT: **arid lowlands, steppes, hills; winters on grassland, farmland, thornbush**
SIZE: **9 in (23 cm)**

The locust-devouring habits of this bird have been appreciated for centuries. The starlings gather in large flocks wherever locusts are abundant and may settle to breed in the area. If the locusts fail to appear in subsequent years, the starlings stay away as well and may not return to breed for several seasons.

Despite this, they are not exclusively locust-eaters. They will prey on other insects and also eat fruits, seeds and nectar; occasionally a flock will cause extensive damage to a fruit crop.

Rose-colored Starlings have an unusual migration pattern: instead of flying north–south like most temperate birds, they migrate east–west. In some years, they undergo irruptions, moving in much larger numbers farther west than usual and reaching western Europe.

## 9/ EUROPEAN STARLING
*Sturnus vulgaris*
RANGE: **Europe and W Asia; introduced to North America, South Africa, S Australia, New Zealand**
HABITAT: **open woods, parks, gardens, towns**
SIZE: **8¼ in (21 cm)**

From a distance the adult has a dark, nondescript appearance, but a closer look reveals a beautiful iridescent adult plumage of blue, violet, green and bronze. The feathers have pale buff tips, giving the bird a spotted appearance, especially after the annual molt in fall. By the time the breeding season approaches, these pale tips have become worn away and the plumage is much glossier and, especially in the male, iridescent. Also, the legs change color from brown to reddish-pink and the bill changes from dark brown to yellow, with a creamy pink base in females and a steel-blue base in males.

The European Starling is an adaptable opportunist with a broad diet and a complex, variable breeding system which encompasses monogamy, polygamy, mate exchange and nest parasitism. This may account for its success as a colonist. In North America, for example, it is one of the most numerous birds, but these are all descendants of some 120 birds released in New York a century ago, which have since increased a millionfold.

## 10/ BALD STARLING
*Sarcops calvus*
RANGE: **Philippines, Sulu Islands**
HABITAT: **farmland, gardens**
SIZE: **8½ in (22 cm)**

The Bald Starling, or Coleto, has large areas of bare skin around its eyes, separated by a narrow line of short bristly feathers on the crown. This "baldness" is an extreme example of a trend found in several other Philippine and Sulawesi starlings in the genus *Basilornis*.

The Bald Starling breeds in tree holes, which are usually abandoned woodpecker nests, and feeds mainly on fruit. Its call is a metallic click, but in the Philippines, where it is kept as a cage bird, it is said to be capable of mimicking human speech.

## 11/ COMMON MYNAH
*Acridotheres tristis*
RANGE: **Afghanistan, India and Sri Lanka to Burma; currently extending its range to Malaysia and USSR; introduced to South Africa, New Zealand, Australia**
HABITAT: **farmland, parks, towns**
SIZE: **9 in (23 cm)**

The Common Mynah has learned how to profit from association with humans and as human habitation spreads, so does the range of the bird. It has a celebrated delectation for locusts and it has been introduced to many places, especially tropical islands, in the hope that it would control insect pests. Unfortunately, the bird has become a pest itself in most areas, by eating fruit.

This jaunty bird shows a conspicuous white wing patch in flight and often makes its presence felt through its loud fluty calls. Daytime flocks assemble in large communal roosts at night, and the large trees in which they sleep are the stage for a raucous musical chorus at dawn and dusk.

## 12/ HILL MYNAH
*Gracula religiosa*
RANGE: **India and Sri Lanka to Malaysia and Indonesia**
HABITAT: **mountain forests, especially in foothills**
SIZE: **11½ in (29 cm)**

Few birds can challenge the Hill Mynah's skill as a mimic and it is widely kept in captivity for its ability to learn phrases of human speech. Paradoxically, it never imitates the calls of other bird species in the wild, although it will mimic the songs of neighboring Hill Mynahs. It has a wide repertoire of calls and is generally noisy and gregarious, associating in small groups outside the breeding season.

Hill Mynahs normally feed in the trees on fruit – especially figs – as well as on nectar, insects and small lizards. They nest in tree holes, often using old woodpecker nests, and this habit has been exploited in Assam where bamboo nest-boxes are erected so that chicks can be gathered for the pet trade.

## 13/ GROSBEAK STARLING
*Scissirostrum dubium*
RANGE: **Sulawesi (Celebes)**
HABITAT: **open woodland**
SIZE: **8 in (20 cm)**

These starlings live in large flocks which forage through the treetops searching for fruit and nectar. They also form dense breeding colonies in dying trees, using their large bills to excavate pear-shaped nest-holes in the tree trunks. These wood-boring habits have given this species its alternative name of Woodpecker Starling. The protractor muscles in the skull are particularly well developed, serving as a shock absorber during the birds' tree-boring activities, as in the completely unrelated woodpeckers (pp. 214–21). There may be more than 50 nests per colony, each only 12–20 in (30–50 cm) apart; the nest trees are often so weakened by the holes that they collapse.

Grosbeak Starlings are handsome birds with red, waxy tail feathers on their rumps. They will breed in captivity and have recently attracted the interest of aviculturalists, but the trade in these birds will have to be closely controlled to ensure their survival in the wild.

## 14/ ROTHSCHILD'S MYNAH
*Leucopsar rothschildi*  E
RANGE: **NW Bali**
HABITAT: **wooded grassland, woodland**
SIZE: **8½ in (22 cm)**

With a wild population of fewer than 200 birds, Rothschild's Mynah (also known as the Bali Starling) is the rarest member of the starling family. It had a limited range when it was first recorded in 1911, occurring only on the northern coast of Bali, but since then its habitat has been cut back even more by agricultural development.

This bird's striking appearance and its ability to erect the long crest on its head have always attracted collectors and trapping for the cage-bird trade may have contributed to its decline. Much of its diet consists of large insects taken from the ground but it also eats small reptiles and fruit.

## 15/ RED-BILLED OXPECKER
*Buphagus erythrorhynchus*
RANGE: **Eritrea to South Africa**
HABITAT: **savanna with grazing mammals**
SIZE: **7–7½ in (18–19 cm)**

The oxpeckers are placed in a different subfamily from the rest of the starlings. They feed chiefly on the ticks that infest the skins of cattle and other grazing mammals such as zebras, antelopes and rhinos. They have short legs and sharp claws which enable them to cling to the hide of the moving animals while they rid them of the parasitic ticks.

There are 2 species: the Red-billed Oxpecker and the more widely distributed Yellow-billed Oxpecker, also found in west Africa. Both are sociable birds that feed in flocks and retreat to communal roosts at night. They nest in tree holes.

In recent years the adoption of chemical tick control for domestic cattle in Africa has reduced the oxpeckers' food supply and they are fewer and less widespread than before. Ways of reversing this decline are currently under investigation.

# ORIOLES AND FIGBIRDS, DRONGOS, NEW ZEALAND WATTLEBIRDS, MAGPIE-LARKS, AUSTRALIAN MUD-NESTERS, WOOD SWALLOWS, BELL MAGPIES

BLACK ORIOLE

GOLDEN ORIOLE

♀

♂

MAROON ORIOLE

♂

♀

race *rufusater*

SADDLEBACK

race *carunculatus*
imm

race *carunculatus*
"Jack-bird"

WHITE-WINGED CHOUGH

♀

HUIA

♂

PIED CURRAWONG

♀ MAGPIE-LARK

♂

**FAMILIES ORIOLIDAE, DICRURIDAE, CALLAEIDAE, GRALLINIDAE, CORCORACIDAE, ARTAMIDAE, CRACTICIDAE**

race *vielloti*
"Green Figbird"
♂

FIGBIRD

race *vielloti*
♀

race *flaviventris*
"Yellow Figbird"
♂

GREATER
RACKET-TAILED
DRONGO

HAIR-CRESTED
DRONGO

MASKED WOODSWALLOW
♂
♀

race *hypoleuca*
"White-backed Magpie"
♂

CRESTED DRONGO

race *tibicen*
"Black-backed Magpie" ♂

AUSTRALIAN MAGPIE

493

# ORIOLES AND FIGBIRDS, DRONGOS, NEW ZEALAND WATTLEBIRDS, MAGPIE-LARKS, AUSTRALIAN MUD-NESTERS, WOOD SWALLOWS, BELL MAGPIES

## FAMILY ORIOLIDAE
### Orioles and Figbird

Medium, starlinglike, tree-dwellers. Males usually black and yellow or other striking colors, females duller. Nest slung from branches high in tree, deep cup (orioles) or shallow, untidy cup (Figbird). Eggs 2–4, white, buff or pink with dark spots or blotches (orioles); usually 3, greenish, with purplish or brown markings (Figbird). Incubation and nestling periods 14–15 days for Golden Oriole; unknown for other species. 26 species.

### 1/ GOLDEN ORIOLE
*Oriolus oriolus*

RANGE: **Europe, Asia, extreme NW Africa; Asian populations resident, others winter in tropical Africa**
HABITAT: **breeds in open deciduous woodland, parks, orchards and olive groves; winters in open forest**
SIZE: **9¾ in (25 cm)**

Despite the brilliant gold and black coloration of his plumage, the secretive male Golden Oriole is surprisingly well camouflaged in the strongly dappled shadows of the woodland canopy. However, he draws attention to himself with his melodious, fluting *weela-weeoo* call.

Golden Orioles use their sharp, stout beaks to feed on insects and fruit. They spend most of their time in the trees, either alone or in pairs, only rarely descending to ground level to feed on fallen fruit. The nest is a masterpiece – an intricately woven grass hammock slung by its rim between 2 twigs. The female carries out most of the nest-building, as well as the most of the incubation and feeding of the young.

### 2/ BLACK ORIOLE
*Oriolus husii*

RANGE: **Borneo, Sulawesi (Celebes)**
HABITAT: **mountain forest**
SIZE: **8½ in (22 cm)**

The Black Oriole is a denizen of upland forests, reaching altitudes of some 3,300 ft (1,000 m). Above this limit, it appears to be replaced by its ecological counterpart, the Black-and-crimson Oriole *O. cruentus*.

Agile and active, Black Orioles move through the canopy in small bands, feeding on small fruits and insects, including foraging ants and termites. The bird's almost all-black plumage is offset by a rich chestnut patch beneath the tail which is surprisingly conspicuous when viewed from the forest floor. Because of its remote haunts, little is known of the nesting habits of this species.

### 3/ MAROON ORIOLE
*Oriolus traillii*

RANGE: **Himalayan foothills, S China, much of Southeast Asia**
HABITAT: **forests up to 10,000 ft (3,000 m)**
SIZE: **9¾ in (25 cm)**

Although the Maroon Oriole sometimes descends into low bushes or onto the forest floor, it is essentially a canopy bird, feeding on small fruits, insects and, occasionally, flower nectar. It is

often solitary but birds sometimes gather in small groups.

The Maroon Oriole has a great variety of calls, including a simple warbling song, a mewing, catlike call and a rattling laugh. It is more often heard than seen and, in poor light, the distinctive maroon plumage of the male's body often appears as dark as his blue-black head, throat and wings. However, the paler maroon tail is usually visible, especially as the bird flares its tail when it comes to land on a branch. The nest is a deep, bulky cup of woven plant fibers, bound with spiders' webs, suspended in the horizontal fork of a branch.

### 4/ FIGBIRD
*Sphecotheres viridis*

RANGE: **N and E Australia, New Guinea**
HABITAT: **rain forest, eucalyptus forest, parks, gardens**
SIZE: **11 in (28 cm)**

The plumage of the male Figbird varies across the bird's range. In the northern race *S. v. flaviventris*, the underparts are yellow, while the Green Figbird *S. v. vieilloti* from eastern Asutralia has a green belly and a gray throat. Hybridization occurs where these 2 forms meet, and birds with yellow, gray, green or white throats may be seen.

The natural habitat of the Figbird is forest, but it has become one of the most common urban birds in many parts of its range. It eats a wide variety of fruit, both wild and cultivated, as well as some insects. The shallow nest is composed of thin twigs, grass and plant tendrils, placed toward the end of a slender branch, and is often so flimsy that the eggs are visible inside against the light.

## FAMILY DICRURIDAE
### Drongos

Small to medium tree-dwellers. Short legs. Long, often forked tail. Many with crests. Plumage glossy black or gray. Sexes similar. Shallow, saucer-shaped nests in trees. Eggs 2–4, whitish, often speckled or blotched with brown. Incubation about 16 days for some species, unknown for most species. Nestling period unknown. 22 species.

### 5/ CRESTED DRONGO
*Dicrurus forficatus*

RANGE: **Madagascar and part of Comoro archipelago**
HABITAT: **forests, woods, savanna, plantations, coastal scrubland**
SIZE: **13 in (33 cm)**

The local name for this species, "Drongo," has passed into general usage in English as the name for the whole family. This is a common bird in woodland on Madagascar, preferring the canopy and middle story. It perches in a conspicuous position, ready to dash out for a passing insect or chase away an enemy, for it is an aggressive species: these are traits typical of all drongos. Like many of its relatives, this species has a long, deeply forked tail, which enables it to perform impressive aerobatics in pursuit of its insect prey.

Although rather solitary, the Crested Drongo is a vocal bird, with a wide repertoire of calls and whistles. It is a year-round resident that occurs at all altitudes from sea level to 6,000 ft (1,800 m). Its breeding season is from September to December.

### 6/ HAIR-CRESTED DRONGO
*Dicrurus hottentottus*

RANGE: **India, S China, Southeast Asia, Philippines, Indonesia**
HABITAT: **forest and secondary growth**
SIZE: **13 in (33 cm)**

The fine, curved feathers of this bird's crest are rarely visible in the wild, but the iridescence on the neck and breast gives a distinctive spangled effect. The color of these spangles is variable and is one of the characteristics that distinguishes this widespread species. A close relative, the Spangled Drongo *D. bracteatus* occurs in the Philippines, Moluccas, Australia, New Guinea, New Britain, Solomons and Lesser Sundas.

Noisy and often common birds, Hair-crested Drongos sometimes gather in parties, especially around fruiting and flowering trees, for they are nectar-feeders as well as predators of a wide range of insects. They utter an astonishing medley of musical and fluty calls, as well as some harsh and strident notes.

## 7/ GREATER RACKET-TAILED DRONGO

*Dicrurus paradiseus*

RANGE: **India, Sri Lanka, S China, Southeast Asia, Borneo**
HABITAT: **open forest, woodland edge, tea plantations**
SIZE: **13¾ in (35 cm)**

This is a spectacular drongo, with a full, curving crest and extraordinary, wirelike tail streamers, up to 13¾ in (35 cm) long, tipped with broad "rackets." In flight, the rackets give the appearance of 2 small birds or bees trailing bouncily along behind. In one of the 2 Sri Lankan races, *D. p. lophorinus*, however, the elongated tail feathers are shorter and broader without rackets, being fully vaned along their length.

The Greater Racket-tailed Drongo is primarily insectivorous, catching its prey in flight as well as taking it from the ground or among foliage. It often accompanies troupes of monkeys, feeding on the insects they disturb. It is noisy all year round, with a wide range of metallic and fluty notes and some bell-like calls. It is also a persistent and gifted mimic of other birds, squirrels and other animals.

## FAMILY CALLAEIDAE
### New Zealand wattlebirds

Medium, strong-legged. Colored, fleshy wattles. Plumage mainly black or gray. Sexes almost alike (wattles larger in males) except for Huia. Shallow, open nest among branches or in tree hollow. Eggs 2–4, whitish with purple-brown blotches and spots. Incubation 18–25 days. Nestling period known for Kokako *Callaeas cinerea*: 27–28 days. 3 species (1 probably extinct).

## 8/ SADDLEBACK

*Philesturnus carunculatus*

RANGE: **offshore islands of New Zealand**
HABITAT: **forests**
SIZE: **9¾ in (25 cm)**

This species was once widespread in New Zealand but now occurs only on about 10 offshore islands. It was reintroduced to most of these after non-native browsing and predatory mammals had been removed. The race *P. c. rufusater*, originally from North Island, has a gold band across the front of the red-brown "saddle," which the South Island race *P. c. carunculatus* lacks.

Saddlebacks have small wings and weak flight. However, their legs are strong and they run and hop through the trees rather than fly. They feed mainly on insects, probing for them under bark or tearing apart rotting wood. They also eat some fruit and nectar.

A close relative, the Huia *Heteralocha acutirostris*, is unique among birds for the remarkable difference in bill shape between the sexes. The male's straight bill is adapted for hammering open rotting wood to expose grubs, while the female's thin, curved bill is ideal for probing crevices. The Huia is almost certainly extinct, perhaps partly as a result of hunting: Maoris killed them for their tail feathers and settlers collected their skins, but habitat destruction was probably the main reason for their disappearance. The Huia was last seen alive in 1907.

## FAMILY GRALLINIDAE
### Magpie-larks

Small to medium. Plumage black and white. Sexes differ slightly. Mud nests. Eggs 3–5, white to pink, blotched red and brown. Incubation 17–18 days and nestling period 18–23 days (Magpie-Lark). 2 species.

## 9/ MAGPIE-LARK

*Grallina cyanoleuca*

RANGE: **Australia**
HABITAT: **open pasture and grassland**
SIZE: **10½ in (27 cm)**

The black and white Magpie-Lark is most abundant on farmland, where it feeds on the ground on insects, snails and other invertebrates. It also frequents the edges of lakes and ponds and has become common in towns, where it is often seen feeding alongside busy roads, seemingly oblivious to the traffic. It has a loud *pee-wee* call, which gives it one of its popular names; another is Mudlark, from its nest.

The clearance of forests and the provision of water in dry regions have probably encouraged this species. However, its population has declined in some areas, perhaps because the water has become too saline or because the snails have been poisoned in an effort to control liver flukes.

## FAMILY CORCORACIDAE
### Australian mud-nesters

Medium to large, strong-legged ground birds. Plumage sooty black with white wing patch, or gray, brown and black. Sexes alike. Mud nests. Eggs 2–5, cream or white, with brown, black and gray blotches. Incubation 18–19 days, nestling period 13–25 days. 2 species.

## 10/ WHITE-WINGED CHOUGH

*Corcorax melanorhamphos*

RANGE: **Australia**
HABITAT: **open woodland**
SIZE: **17¾ in (45 cm)**

These birds are black, with white "windows" in the center of the wings. The adults have brilliant red irises that become expanded when the birds are excited. They live in open, grassy eucalyptus woodland, feeding on the ground, turning over leaf litter and cowpats in search of large invertebrates, and sometimes eating grain.

White-winged Choughs are highly social and cooperative, living in groups of 3–12 birds. They may join even larger flocks in winter when they wander outside their breeding grounds. Several birds help to construct the mud nest, and when the young hatch, all group members help to feed them. Occasionally 2 females may lay a total of up to 10 eggs in the same nest.

## FAMILY ARTAMIDAE
### Woodswallows

Small to medium, aerial birds. Short legs, long wings. Plumage black, gray or brown, and white with chestnut in 1 species. Sexes differ in some species. Flimsy cup nest of sticks. Eggs 2–4, white or cream, spotted red-brown. Incubation 12–16 days, nestling period 16–20 days. 10 species.

## 11/ MASKED WOODSWALLOW

*Artamus personatus*

RANGE: **Australia**
HABITAT: **woodland and shrubland**
SIZE: **7½ in (19 cm)**

Woodswallows are related to bell magpies, but have taken to aerial feeding. They are long-winged, but short-tailed, and resemble bee-eaters (pp. 202–205) in their manner of feeding.

Masked Woodswallows occur throughout inland Australia. They tend to move south in spring, in some years extending well beyond their usual range. They feed mostly on aerial insects, but occasionally glean prey from the ground, taking small locusts and ants. They may even feed on the nectar from eucalyptus and mistletoes.

## FAMILY CRACTICIDAE
### Bell magpies

Medium to large, strong build. Heavy, hooked bill. Plumage gray, white and black. Sexes differ in some species. Nests in trees. Eggs 3–5, blue or green, brown blotches and streaks. Incubation 20 days, nestling period 28 days. 10 species.

## 12/ AUSTRALIAN MAGPIE

*Gymnorthina tibicen*

RANGE: **Australia, S New Guinea; introduced to New Zealand**
HABITAT: **woodland and grassland**
SIZE: **15¾ in (40 cm)**

The plumage on the back of the Australian Magpie varies according to race. For example, the race *G. t. tibicen*, often called the Black-backed Magpie, from central and northern Australia, differs markedly from the race *G. t. hypoleuca*, often called the White-backed Magpie, from southern Australia and Tasmania.

Australian Magpies eat scarab beetle larvae and other invertebrates, listening for them in the soil and then digging them up with their strong, pointed bills. These birds have a complex social organization, linked to habitat. Permanent groups, with a high breeding success, live in prime habitat with trees and grassland. More transitory groups live in poorer-quality sites, and nonbreeding flocks may occupy the areas of grassland with the fewest trees.

## 13/ PIED CURRAWONG

*Strepera graculina*

RANGE: **E Australia**
HABITAT: **forest and woodland**
SIZE: **18 in (46 cm)**

This species is primarily a tree-dweller. The name currawong comes from one of the bird's calls, but it utters a wide variety of other loud and often musical sounds. Pied Currawongs tend to inhabit forests in the breeding season, where they snatch stick insects and other large arthropods from the foliage. They are also nest-robbers, and may have a major impact on the breeding success of other birds. In winter, large numbers move into towns, where they feed on berries. Their numbers have increased with the introduction of many new berry-producing plants; by dispersing seeds, the birds have helped to spread these exotic plants.

# BOWERBIRDS, BIRDS OF PARADISE

SPOTTED CATBIRD

VOGELKOP GARDENER BOWERBIRD

♂ SATIN BOWERBIRD ♀

TRUMPET MANUCODE

♀ ♂ ♀

MAGNIFICENT RIFLEBIRD

♂ courtship display

TWELVE-WIRED BIRD OF PARADISE

KING BIRD OF PARADISE ♀

♀ ♂

♂ courtship display

SUPERB BIRD OF PARADISE

♂ race raggiana

RAGGIANA BIRD OF PARADISE

GREAT GRAY
BOWERBIRD

♀

courtship
display

♂

race *nuchalis*

♀

SICKLE-CRESTED BIRD OF PARADISE

♂

RIBBON-TAILED BIRD OF PARADISE

♂

♀

courtship display

♂

♀

KING OF SAXONY
BIRD OF PARADISE

♀

courtship display

♂

courtship display

BLUE BIRD OF PARADISE

497

# BOWERBIRDS, BIRDS OF PARADISE

## FAMILY PTILONORHYNCHIDAE
## Bowerbirds
Medium, stout with strong bills. Males of 9 species brighter than females; otherwise drab brown, gray or green. Males of most species construct ornate "bowers" to which females are attracted for mating; the females build the bulky cup-shaped nests alone. Eggs 1–2, plain white to buff or blotched at larger end. Incubation 19–24 days, nestling period 18–21 days. 18 species.

## 1/ SPOTTED CATBIRD
*Ailuroedus melanotis*
RANGE: **New Guinea, 3,000–6,000 ft (900–1,800 m); Misool and Aru islands; NE Australia**
HABITAT: **rain forest**
SIZE: **11½ in (29 cm)**

Most male bowerbirds will attempt to mate with several females each season, attracting them to their elaborate bowers by their showy plumage and ritualized courtship. By contrast, the 3 species of catbird are monogamous, the males do not build bowers and the sexes look alike.

The Spotted Catbird is typical: each pair defends a breeding territory and, although the female builds the nest, both male and female share the job of feeding the young.

Named for their catlike, wailing calls, catbirds have a broad diet, ranging from fruit and leaves to insects, small reptiles and nestlings.

## 2/ VOGELKOP GARDENER BOWERBIRD
*Amblyornis inornatus*
RANGE: **W Irian Jaya (New Guinea), 3,300–6,600 ft (1,000–2,000 m)**
HABITAT: **lower mountain rain forest**
SIZE: **10 in (25 cm)**

Among bowerbirds, the species with the least ornate plumage generally build the most impressive bowers. The male Vogelkop Gardener Bowerbird is particularly drab, but his bower is the most spectacular of all: a miniature tepee of sticks built over a mat of moss which the bird collects and decorates with colorful fruits and flowers. He then attracts potential mates – and warns off other males – by mimicking bird calls and other sounds.

The nesting biology of this species is unknown, but the females of other gardener bowerbirds build their nests and raise their young alone.

## 3/ SATIN BOWERBIRD
*Ptilonorhynchus violaceus*
RANGE: **E Australia**
HABITAT: **rain forest, rain forest edge; adjacent open vegetation in winter**
SIZE: **12 in (30 cm)**

This is probably the best known of all the bowerbirds. The male builds an "avenue" with walls of sticks placed upright in a stick mat. He sometimes daubs the walls with a paste of chewed fruit or charcoal, often applying it with a wad of plant fiber held in his bill.

As a finishing touch he adorns the mat with trinkets, showing a marked preference for blue

flowers, blue feathers, blue bottle-tops, indeed anything blue. This taste reflects his own elegant bluish-black coloration, which takes 6–7 years to develop and provides a marked contrast to the female's sober grayish-green plumage, which helps camouflage her on her nest among the vegetation.

## 4/ GREAT GRAY BOWERBIRD
*Chlamydera nuchalis*
RANGE: **N Australia and adjacent islands**
HABITAT: **riverside and open savanna woods, eucalyptus and melaleuca woods, vine thickets, well-foliaged suburbia**
SIZE: **14 in (36 cm)**

This is the largest of the bowerbirds and is generally found in drier, more open habitats than the other species. The male sports a lilac nape crest which he erects during the courtship display. Some females have similar crests, but this is unusual. The race illustrated, *C.n. nuchalis* from northeast Western Australia to northwest Queensland, has more uniform, grayer upperparts than the other race.

Like many bowerbirds, Great Gray Bowerbirds are good mimics. Males imitate bird calls and other sounds, and both sexes mimic the calls of predatory birds near their bowers and nests. They feed mainly on fruit and insects, being particularly fond of figs and grasshoppers, but they will also eat small lizards.

## FAMILY PARADISAEIDAE
## Birds of paradise
Medium, stout, strong-legged with very varied bills. Most males have spectacular plumage; females drab. Nest usually cup- or dome-shaped. Eggs 1–2, pale, spotted, blotched or smudged mainly at larger end. Incubation 17–21 days, nestling period 17–30 days. 42 species.

## 5/ SICKLE-CRESTED BIRD OF PARADISE
*Cnemophilus macgregorii*
RANGE: **C, S and E highlands of New Guinea, 8,000–11,500 ft (2,400–3,500 m)**
HABITAT: **cloud forest**
SIZE: **10 in (25 cm)**

Whereas male bowerbirds use art to attract potential mates, many birds of paradise rely on the incomparable beauty of their plumage, which is often ornamented with long, decorative tail and crest feathers. The race illustrated, *C.m. sanguineus* from Mount Hagen, has orange-red upperparts; one of the 2 others has cinnamon-yellow upperparts.

The Sickle-crested Bird of Paradise is a fruit-eating species named for its unique crest of fine filaments. The male birds probably display to passing groups of females at solitary arenas, but this has never been described. The nest, built by the female, is a bulky dome of mosses and leaves on a stick foundation and is much more elaborate than the nests of other species.

## 6/ TRUMPET MANUCODE
*Manucodia keraudrenii*
RANGE: **New Guinea and islands to E and W, 650–6,600 ft (200–2,000 m); tip of Cape York Peninsula, NE Australia**
HABITAT: **rain forest canopy**
SIZE: **11 in (28 cm)**

The 5 species of manucode breed as stable pairs instead of mating polygamously in the family tradition. Accordingly, male and female birds are very similar, with uniform metallic blue-black plumage. They share the duties of incubating the eggs and feeding the young but, unusually, they do not defend their nesting territories.

They are primarily fruit-eaters and the Trumpet Manucode, or Trumpet Bird, feeds mainly on figs. The bird is named for the loud, mournful, trumpeting call produced by the male during his courtship display, after he has chased his prospective mate through the trees.

## 7/ MAGNIFICENT RIFLEBIRD
*Ptiloris magnificus*
RANGE: **New Guinea lowlands and hills to 2,300 ft (700 m), rarely higher; tip of Cape York Peninsula, NE Australia**
HABITAT: **rain forest, forest edge**
SIZE: **13 in (33 cm)**

There are 3 species of riflebird, of which this is the most impressive. The male is promiscuous, defending a territory from a visible perch which he uses for displaying. This involves raising his rounded wings and swaying his head from side to side while emitting a powerful whistle, which is said to sound like a passing bullet – hence the species' name.

Riflebirds have strong feet which they use for climbing and for clinging to tree trunks while they probe dead wood for insects. In addition, they often use their feet to hold food on the perch while tearing it apart.

## 8/ TWELVE-WIRED BIRD OF PARADISE
*Seleucidis melanoleuca*
RANGE: **New Guinea lowlands; Salawati Island**
HABITAT: **seasonally flooded rain forest dominated by sago and pandanus palm**
SIZE: **13½ in (34 cm)**

Adult males of this long-billed, short-tailed bird are spectacularly plumaged in iridescent purple-black and sulfur-yellow, with long "wires" curving up from the flank plumes. The females are drab by comparison, as with all the birds of paradise that breed polygamously.

The males are rarely observed except during the courtship season, when they display from bare branches high in the forest. A displaying male erects the feathers of his upper breast into a large black "shield", edged with iridescent emerald green feathers; at the same time, his elongated yellow flank plumes are expanded and the 12 wires extend forward. The few nests that have been found were built in the tops of trees and each contained a single egg.

## 9/ RIBBON-TAILED BIRD OF PARADISE
*Astrapia mayeri*            [?]
RANGE: **New Guinea, W central highlands, 8,000–11,200 ft (2,400–3,400 m)**
HABITAT: **lower mountain rain forest**
SIZE: **53 in (135 cm)**

This was the last bird of paradise to be discovered by ornithologists, being initially described in 1939 on the basis of a pair of the male's long, ribbonlike central tail feathers found in a tribal headdress. Up to 39 in (1 m) long, these impressive plumes are twitched from side to side during a display which may attract several females to the male's perch high in the trees.

These birds have a broad diet, including fruits, insects, spiders, small mammals and reptiles.

## 10/ SUPERB BIRD OF PARADISE
*Lophorina superba*
RANGE: **mountains of New Guinea, 4,000–7,500 ft (1,200–2,300 m)**
HABITAT: **rain forest and forest edge**
SIZE: **10 in (25 cm)**

All the polygamous birds of paradise have intriguing courtship rituals, but few are as curious as the display of this fine-billed species. The male is equipped with highly modified breast plumage that flares into a "winged" display shield. This is mirrored behind the bird's head by a velvety cape of elongated nape feathers that fans around to meet the breast shield, giving a bizarre circular effect.

The males often display in the tops of trees but recent observations suggest that the birds also display and mate near the forest floor.

## 11/ KING OF SAXONY BIRD OF PARADISE
*Pteridophora alberti*
RANGE: **central ranges of New Guinea, 5,000–9,500 ft (1,500–2,850 m)**
HABITAT: **cloud forest**
SIZE: **8¾ in (22 cm)**

An adult male of this species presents an extraordinary appearance, having 2 head plumes up to 19¾ in (50 cm) long extending from behind his eyes. Each wirelike plume shaft is decorated along one side with small sky-blue lobes that look like little plastic flags.

During the courtship display the bird holds his plumes aloft while bounding up and down, hissing loudly. He greets a receptive female with a sweep of the plumes before mating.

## 12/ KING BIRD OF PARADISE
*Cicinnurus regius*
RANGE: **New Guinea, up to 1,000 ft (300 m), rarely to 2,800 ft (850 m)**
HABITAT: **rain forest and forest edge**
SIZE: **6¼ in (16 cm)**

Although basically a solitary species, like most of its family, the King Bird of Paradise often feeds with other bird species, gleaning insects and other small animals from foliage and bark beneath the canopy of the rain forest. It also eats fruit.

The female has inconspicuous olive-brown plumage, but males are mainly iridescent blood-red and white. This makes for a spectacular treetop display, but also renders the bird very vulnerable to attack by cruising predators. It is a risk shared by many of these flamboyant birds, but is evidently worthwhile in evolutionary terms. In one of the male's displays, he expands his breast fan and puffs up the feathers of his underparts so that he appears almost spherical. He then raises his long, wirelike tail shafts so that the green rackets at their tips are above his head, and raises and sways his head from side to side. In another display he hangs upside-down from a perch with wings spread and vibrating and his bill open, to display the bright yellow-green interior of his mouth.

## 13/ RAGGIANA BIRD OF PARADISE
*Paradisaea raggiana*
RANGE: **E New Guinea to 6,000 ft (1,800 m)**
HABITAT: **rain forest, forest edge, gardens**
SIZE: **13 in (33 cm)**

Instead of displaying alone, like most of their relatives, male Raggiana Birds of Paradise assemble in groups at traditional treetop arenas, or leks. In practice, 1 or 2 dominant males obtain nearly all the matings in any season and the other males on the lek display in vain.

When females appear at the lek, the males converge on them, calling excitedly and displaying by hopping, flapping their wings noisily and shaking their plumes. This initial frenzy is followed by a quieter but equally breathtaking display, in which each bird attempts to outdo his rivals in showing off his gaudy finery. At the height of their display, the males utter a rapid series of high-pitched nasal calls, rising and falling in pitch and intensity; during the quieter part, they give a single, ringing note. Other calls include a series of loud, raucous, bugling cries, all on one pitch, increasing in volume and slowing in tempo toward the end.

There are 5 races: the one illustrated is *P. r. raggiana* from southeast New Guinea.

## 14/ BLUE BIRD OF PARADISE
*Paradisaea rudolphi*            [?]
RANGE: **New Guinea, E central highlands, 4,300–6,000 ft (1,300–1,800 m)**
HABITAT: **rain forest, forest edge, gardens**
SIZE: **12 in (30 cm)**

One of the most glorious birds of paradise, this is also one of the most endangered as a consequence of much of its habitat having been cleared for agriculture and housing.

The male displays alone, high in the trees. Uttering low mechanical-sounding cries, including one like radio static, he swings upside down from a branch with his long tail streamers sweeping over in a graceful arc, his magnificent plumes spread in a cascade of opalescent blue. The females probably go off to nest by themselves but the details are uncertain.

BLUE JAY

SCRUB JAY

race *coerulescens*

race *californica*

AZURE-WINGED MAGPIE

SILVERY-THROATED JAY

race *chinensis*

race *margaritae*

race *glandarius*

EURASIAN JAY

GREEN MAGPIE

race *atricapillus*

race *asirensis*

race *bispecularis*

race *pica*

PANDER'S GROUND JAY

BLACK-BILLED MAGPIE

WESTERN JACKDAW

CLARK'S NUTCRACKER

RED-BILLED CHOUGH

juv

juv

PIAPIAC

race *japonensis*

JUNGLE CROW

COMMON RAVEN

PIED CROW

AMERICAN CROW

## FAMILY CORVIDAE
Crows

Medium to large, with powerful bills. Often black, but jays brightly colored. Sexes similar. Nests of twigs in trees or shrubs, some in holes. Eggs 2–8, whitish to pale green, blotched. Incubation 16–22 days, nestling period 20–45 days. 113 species.

### 1/ BLUE JAY
*Cyanocitta cristata*

RANGE: E North America, from S Canada to Mexican Gulf
HABITAT: deciduous forest, semiwoodland
SIZE: 12 in (30 cm)

Large noisy groups of food-gathering Blue Jays are a familiar sight in the gardens of North America. They hoard seeds and nuts for the winter, burying them in holes. Despite these precautions, Blue Jays in the far north normally migrate south in winter, whereas the southern birds usually stay near their nesting sites.

Although seeds and nuts make up most of its diet, the Blue Jay feeds avidly on insects – particularly the irregular outbreaks of tent moth caterpillars. It will also rob nests of eggs and chicks and take small mammals.

### 2/ SCRUB JAY
*Aphelocoma coerulescens*

RANGE: W USA and S to C Mexico; there is an isolated race in Florida
HABITAT: oak scrub in dry semidesert
SIZE: 13 in (33 cm)

Scrub Jays are communal breeders: instead of forming pairs, the birds live in year-round groups of up to a dozen individuals. Each group is based around a single breeding pair, which builds a bulky twig nest at the focus of a well-defined communal territory. The female incubates the eggs while the other birds stand guard or gather food. The young "helpers" – particularly the males – are usually earlier offspring of the breeding pair.

In contrast to western races such as *A.c. californica*, the isolated Florida race *A.c. coerulescens* has a whitish forehead.

### 3/ SILVERY-THROATED JAY
*Cyanolyca argentigula*

RANGE: Costa Rica
HABITAT: woodland, from cloud forest to oaks and firs
SIZE: 13 in (33 cm)

Of the 32 species of New World jay, 28 occur in Central America. The Silvery-throated Jay is one of these, and its similarity to many of the other species indicates that they evolved only recently from a common ancestor.

Less sociable than most jays, it is also less garrulous, having a limited repertoire of nasal clicks and squawks. Some reports suggest that it may follow columns of army ants to snap up the insects they disturb.

### 4/ EURASIAN JAY
*Garrulus glandarius*

RANGE: W Europe, across Asia to Japan and Southeast Asia
HABITAT: oakwoods, open country with oaks
SIZE: 13 in (33 cm)

The harsh screech of the Eurasian Jay is a familiar sound in European deciduous woodland. The first note is often followed by a second and a third as a family party scours the trees for insects, beech nuts and acorns.

This handsome bird has played a major part in shaping the landscape. The Eurasian Jay's habit of carrying acorns long distances (especially up-hill) and burying them has been an important factor in the dispersal of oak trees, and it is likely that the acorn has evolved to attract the Eurasian Jay. For their part, the birds rely heavily on stored acorns for winter food.

Of the many races, some have distinctive head plumage: those illustrated are *G.g. glandarius* of Europe, *G.g. atricapillus* of the Middle East and *G.g. bispecularis* of the western Himalayas.

### 5/ GREEN MAGPIE
*Cissa chinensis*

RANGE: N India to S China, Malaysia, Sumatra, Borneo
HABITAT: evergreen forest, bamboo jungle, forest clearings, gardens
SIZE: 13¾ in (35 cm)

This attractive and extremely active crow occurs in a wide variety of subtly different color phases, grading from brilliant green to a delicate blue. The 2 races illustrated are the widespread *C.c. chinensis*, and *C.c. margaritae*, found only in southern Annam (Vietnam).

The Green Magpie often feeds in mixed flocks with drongos (pp. 354–57) and laughing-thrushes (pp. 274–77), foraging for insects in the trees and on the ground. It will also scavenge for carrion, as well as eating small snakes and lizards, frogs and young birds.

### 6/ AZURE-WINGED MAGPIE
*Cyanopica cyana*

RANGE: E Asia, China, Mongolia, Korea, Japan; also S Spain and Portugal
HABITAT: open woodland, gardens, farmland
SIZE: 13 in (33 cm)

This magpie has a very odd distribution, with a virtually continuous series of races spread through eastern Asia and an isolated population in southern Spain and Portugal, some 3,000 mls (5,000 km) away. It is possible that the Iberian birds are descended from birds introduced to Spain or Portugal by early traders with the Far East, but much more likely that the species may have originally occurred throughout southern Eurasia, a range since fragmented by changes in climate (particularly glaciations) and habitat.

Azure-winged Magpies are sociable birds: they usually forage in small groups, roost together (especially in cold climates) and nest in loose colonies, each untidy nest being built in a separate tree or bush.

### 7/ BLACK-BILLED MAGPIE
*Pica pica*

RANGE: Eurasia, from W Europe to Japan; temperate North America
HABITAT: open woodland, scrub, farmland, towns
SIZE: 17¾ in (45 cm)

The Black-billed Magpie has a bad reputation for plundering the nests of other birds and it is often shot on sight on estates where there are game-birds. Elsewhere it flourishes, for it is an adaptable bird with a broad diet. It has adapted well to the man-made landscape and is now a familiar sight in suburban gardens. Most races are similar to the race *P.p. pica* of the British Isles, central and eastern Europe, although the race *P.p asirensis* of western Arabia is distinctive: very dark with less white, and a large bill.

Many pairs of Black-billed Magpies stay in their breeding territories throughout the year, but others form small winter flocks which gather at communal roosts for the night.

## 8/ PANDER'S GROUND JAY
*Podoces panderi*
RANGE: SW USSR
HABITAT: dry steppe and sandy, scrubby desert; breeds in saxaul bushes
SIZE: 13 in (33 cm)

The ground jays are a distinct group of open-country crows that normally travel by running over the ground instead of flying. Pander's Ground Jay is particularly well adapted to life in semidesert scrubland, for it can obtain all the moisture that it needs from its diet of insects and seeds.

It nests in low trees and bushes, probably using the same site each year. The 3–6 young are naked, blind and helpless when they hatch, but within 2 weeks they can run quite fast. Family parties of these birds wander widely over the plains in fall, calling to each other with loud cries and fluty whistles.

## 9/ CLARK'S NUTCRACKER
*Nucifraga columbiana*
RANGE: North America, from British Columbia to N Mexico
HABITAT: mountain conifer forest
SIZE: 13¾ in (35 cm)

Many crows hoard food for the winter but few species rely on the habit as heavily as Clark's Nutcracker. Found in some of the most inhospitable winter habitats endured by any of its family, the bird feeds almost exclusively on the seeds of conifers such as the Ponderosa Pine, extracting them with dexterous use of its powerful, slightly downcurved bill.

It may fly up to 12 mls (20 km) to gather food for its winter store, returning with up to 80 seeds carried in a pouch beneath its tongue. The hoarding sites, on steep, well-drained slopes, are often communal, but each bird makes its own cache and is able to remember its location beneath the winter snows.

## 10/ RED-BILLED CHOUGH
*Pyrrhocorax pyrrhocorax*
RANGE: W Europe, through S Asia to China
HABITAT: mountains to 11,500 ft (3,500 m), coastal cliffs, islands
SIZE: 15¾ in (40 cm)

Crows in general are opportunist feeders with broad tastes, but the Red-billed Chough is something of an expert at preying on small insects, particularly ants. It often feeds in small flocks, using its distinctive sharp, curved bill to probe for prey in very short rabbit- or sheep-cropped cliff-top or mountain turf. The erosion of this type of habitat by changes in agriculture may be one reason why Red-billed Choughs have become scarce in northwestern Europe over the past 200 years.

Red-billed Choughs are spectacular performers on the wing, with a gloriously buoyant, easy flight. In spring the courting pair takes to the air in a mutual display flight before nesting in a crevice or cave.

## 11/ PIAPIAC
*Ptilostomus afer*
RANGE: Africa, from Senegal E to Uganda, Ethiopia, Sudan
HABITAT: open country with palm trees, farmland, towns
SIZE: 15¾ in (40 cm)

This bold, resourceful crow has learned to exploit the activities of other animals for its own ends. Flocks of 10 or more will often forage and scavenge in urban areas, showing little fear of man. In grassland they run after animals such as goats and cattle to catch the creatures disturbed by their grazing. The Piapiac will even pick parasitic mites and ticks from animals' skins and is one of the few bird species tolerated in this way by elephants.

These birds are most active in the morning, and the flocks generally roost in tall trees during the hottest hours of the day. Oil-palm trees are favored, for Piapiacs are very fond of the fruit.

## 12/ WESTERN JACKDAW
*Corvus monedula*
RANGE: W Europe, excluding extreme N, to C USSR
HABITAT: woods, parks, gardens, farmland, sea cliffs, towns
SIZE: 13 in (33 cm)

The Western Jackdaw is the smallest of the *Corvus* crows in Europe and one of the most familiar. This is partly because it is a hole-nesting bird that has learned to use the cavities in church towers, chimney stacks and other parts of tall buildings as artificial substitutes for tree holes and rock crevices. It is also common on ocean and inland cliffs and quarries, where it still breeds in more natural surroundings. In such places, its agility in the air can be seen to great advantage.

Western Jackdaws enjoy a broad diet which may include anything from caterpillars to crabs. They also scavenge for refuse and rob the nests of other birds. In spring they collect soft fiber for nesting material and are often seen plucking wool from the backs of sheep.

## 13/ AMERICAN CROW
*Corvus brachyrhynchos*
RANGE: North America, from S Canada to New Mexico
HABITAT: woods, parks, farmland
SIZE: 21¾ in (55 cm)

Crows have always been regarded as pests by farmers and the American Crow is no exception. Large flocks will descend on fields of corn, sorghum or peas and inflict serious damage; the farmers retaliate by trapping and poisoning them and, as a result, the birds have become increasingly wary and difficult to control.

The American Crow's caution extends to its nesting habits. The pairs nest singly, but the male often builds a whole series of "false nests" high in the treetops, which seem designed to decoy and confuse potential predators.

## 14/ JUNGLE CROW
*Corvus macrorhynchos*
RANGE: Asia, from Afghanistan to Japan, SE to Philippines
HABITAT: woods, semicultivated land, more rarely open country
SIZE: 19 in (48 cm)

The intelligence and cunning of the Jungle Crow are well known to travelers across central Asia, for their campsites are often raided by this powerful, large-billed scavenger. There are a number of races, of which *C. m. japonensis*, found in Japan and Sakhalin Island, is the largest and thickest billed.

Strongly territorial, it will steal scraps of meat and hoard them in caches dispersed around its home range, often making use of urban drain-pipes, roofspaces and window ledges. These caches may also contain dead chicks, for the bird is a notorious nest-robber.

## 15/ PIED CROW
*Corvus albus*
RANGE: sub-Saharan Africa, Madagascar
HABITAT: open and semiopen country, forest clearings, urban areas
SIZE: 17¾ in (45 cm)

Although most of its diet consists of seeds and insects taken from the ground, the Pied Crow is most commonly seen congregating around carcasses or garbage dumps. It is a bold bird with little fear of humans or larger predators, and it is an eager mobber of African eagles and buzzards.

Its young stay in the nest a long time – they take 40 days to fledge – and the parents often fail to keep up the food supply. As a result, few pairs raise more than 3 young out of a clutch of up to 6 eggs. Many are also parasitized by Great Spotted Cuckoos. The cuckoo chicks hatch sooner, and are more vigorous and aggressive than the Pied Crow chicks, which may starve, although usually some are raised alongside the intruders.

## 16/ COMMON RAVEN
*Corvus corax*
RANGE: North America, except SE; Asia, except Southeast Asia and India; N Africa to S Sahara
HABITAT: sparsely inhabited landscapes: high mountains, sea coasts, tundra
SIZE: 25 in (64 cm)

The Common Raven is the largest, most powerful and most predatory of the crows. As big as a buzzard, it is quite capable of killing and eating a rabbit, but reports of Common Ravens attacking sheep and lambs are greatly exaggerated. Their main food is carrion, and many Common Ravens will gather around a large carcass to tear at the flesh with their heavy bills.

Like many other crows, they hoard food for the winter, but because there is usually plenty of carrion to be had, they are not greatly affected by harsh winters. If anything, they flourish, and they often nest in late winter when the mortality of local birds and mammals is at its peak.

# Index

INDEX

**GENERAL INDEX INCLUDING COMMON NAMES**

**Note: Page numbers in *italics* refer to illustrations.**

# Acknowledgments

*l* = left; *r* = right; *c* = center; *t* = top; *b* = bottom

## ARTISTS

**Norman Arlott:** pp 30, 81, 105*b*, 300-01, 304-05, 308-09, 312-13, 336-37, 344-45, 348-49, 352-53, 356-57, 388-89, 444-45, 488-89, 492-93, 496-97, 500-01.
**Dianne Breeze:** pp 121, 128, 129*b*, 131, 272-73, 276-77, 280-81.
**Hilary Burn:** pp 23*tr*, 31, 87*r*, 364-65, 416-17, 420-21, 424-25
**Chris Christoforou:** pp 95, 224-25, 228-29, 232-33.
**Richard Draper:** pp 22*b*, 24*b*, 33, 114.
**Robert Gillmor:** pp 61, 63*r*, 92, 100-01, 103*b*, 196-97, 200-01, 204-05, 208-09, 260-61, 288-89.
**Peter Hayman:** pp 37*bl*, 66-67, 68*r*, 70-71, 108, 139, 155*l*, 156-57, 158-59, 160, 161*b*, 184-85, 192-93, 264-65, 268-69, 324-25, 328-29, 332-33, 448-49.
**Gary Hincks:** pp 32.
**Aziz Khan:** pp 169*br*.
**Denys Ovenden:** pp 15, 75*t*, 76, 83, 98, 169*bl*, 180-81, 188-89, 248-49, 252-53, 256-57, 372-73, 376-77, 468-69, 472-73, 476-77, 480-81, 484-85.
**David Quinn.** pp 10, 26*br*, 36*bl*, 37*cr*, 63*l*, 77, 79, 80, 106-07, 134-35, 139*t*, 141, 149, 155*r*, 162-63, 284-85, 340-41, 436-37, 440-41, 456-57, 460-61, 464-65.
**Andrew Robinson:** pp 104, 292-93, 296-97.
**Chris Rose:** pp 36*tl*, 37*tl*, 59*l*, 68*l*, 69, 75*b*, 109, 112, 132-33, 151, 380-81, 384-85, 400-01, 404-05, 408-09, 452-53.
**David Thelwell:** pp 116, 360-61, 368-69, 392-93, 412-13.
**Owen Williams:** pp 26*tr*, 49, 57, 88, 123, 126, 143, 212-13, 216-17, 220-21.
**Ann Winterbotham:** pp 12-13, 18-19, 22*t*, 24-25, 26*bl*, 37*tc* & *tr*, 42-43, 45 & all Fact File silhouettes.
**Ken Wood:** pp 96, 169*t*, 236-37, 240-41, 244-45.
**Michael Woods:** 14, 20-21, 23*l* & *br*, 26*cr*, 36*tr* & *br*, 37*cl* & *br*, 55*l*, 59*r*, 60, 65, 78, 82, 87*l*, 89, 90-9*l*, 93, 94, 97, 103*t*, 105*t*, 110-11, 113, 115, 117, 125, 129*t*, 145, 161*t*, 168, 316-17, 320-21, 396-97, 428-29, 432-33.

## AUTHORS

**Dr Jon C. Barlow,** Curator of Ornithology, Royal Ontario Museum, Toronto, Canada.
**Robert Burton,** MA, MI Biol, natural history writer.
**Mark Cocker,** writer and conservationist.
**Dr William E. Davis, Jr.,** Chairman and Professor, Division of Science and Mathematics, Boston University, Boston, Mass., USA.
**Stephen Debus,** Research Fellow in Zoology, University of New England, Armidale, NSW, Australia.
**Jonathan Elphick,** ornithological/natural history editor, author and consultant.
**Mike Everett,** RSPB Press Officer, author.
**Dr Chris Feare,** Head of Bird Pests & Farmland Conservation Branch, ADAS Central Science Laboratories, Worplesdon, Surrey, UK.
**Dr Jim Flegg,** Deputy Director, Institute of Horticultural Research, East Malling, Kent, UK.
**Dr Hugh Ford,** Australasian Consultant.
**Clifford Frith,** author, photographer and wildlife consultant.
**Dr C. Hilary Fry,** Professor of Biology, Sultan Qaboos University, Muscat, Oman.
**Rosemarie Gnam,** ornithologist, American Museum of Natural History, New York, USA.
**Dr Llewellyn Grimes**
**Dr David Hill,** Director of Development, British Trust for Ornithology.
**Dr John Horsfall,** formerly demonstrator at the Edward Grey Institute of Field Ornithology, Oxford, UK.
**Rob Hume,** ornithological editor, author, tour leader, artist, RSPB.
**Dr George A. Hurst,** Professor of Wildlife & Fisheries, Mississippi State University, Miss., USA.
**Morton and Phyllis Isler,** research associates, Smithsonian Institution, Washington, DC, and Museum of Natural Science, Louisiana State University, Baton Rouge, La., USA.
**Dr Bette J. S. Jackson,** Associate Professor of Biology, Mary Holmes College, West Point, Miss., USA.
**Dr Jerome A. Jackson,** US Consultant.
**Dr Alan Kemp,** Head Curator, Department of Birds, Transvaal Museum, Pretoria, Republic of South Africa, Chairman IUCN/ICBP Hornbill Specialist Group.
**Dr Alan Knox,** avian taxonomist, Buckinghamshire County Museum, Halton, Buckinghamshire, UK.
**Dr John C. Kricher,** author, Professor of Biology, Wheaton College, Norton, Mass., USA.
**Dr David McFarland,** ecologist, bird artist, Queensland National Parks & Wildlife Service, Brisbane, Queensland, Australia.
**Dr Robert W. McFarlane,** ornithological consultant and author.
**Dr Ian McLean,** Senior Lecturer in Zoology, University of Canterbury, Christchurch, New Zealand.
**Dr Carl D. Marti,** Professor of Zoology, Weber State College, Ogden, Utah, USA.
**Chris Mead,** C Biol, MI Biol, author and broadcaster, Head of Bird Ringing Scheme, British Trust for Ornithology.
**Rick Morris,** natural history editor and author.
**Dr Bryan Nelson,** Hon Reader in Zoology, University of Aberdeen, Aberdeen, UK.
**Nancy L. Newfield,** ornithological consultant, author, lecturer and tour guide.
**Dr Malcolm Ogilvie,** author and wildlife consultant.
**Dr John P. O'Neill,** ornithological author and artist, Museum of Zoology, Louisiana State University, Baton Rouge, La., USA.
**Dr Christopher M. Perrins,** Consultant-in-Chief.
**Dr Richard O. Prum,** Post-doctoral Fellow, Ornithology, American Museum of Natural History, New York, USA.
**Eric Simms,** DFC, MA, MBOU, ornithologist, broadcaster, wildlife sound recordist and author.
**Dr Denis Summers-Smith,** mechanical engineer and obsessional sparrow enthusiast.
**Judith A. Toups,** ornithological consultant and author.
**Dr Juliet Vickery,** Senior Research Associate, School of Biological Sciences, University of East Anglia, Norwich, UK.
**Lori Willimont,** wildlife biologist, US Fish & Wildlife Service, Charleston, S.C, USA.
**Martin W. Woodcock,** ornithological artist and author.
**John Woodward,** natural history editor and author.

## PHOTOGRAPHS

1 William M. Smithey/Planet Earth Pictures
2-3 Jens Rydell/Bruce Coleman.4 Eugene Potapov
8-9 C.R. Knights/Ardea.
15 François Gohier/Ardea
17 R. Gorensen & J.B. Olsen/NHPA.
21 Jen & Des Bartlett/Survival Anglia.
27 Laurie Campbell/NHPA
29 F. Greenway/Bruce Coleman.
35 Nasahiro Iijima/Ardea.
38-9 Fred Bruemmer/Bruce Coleman.
41 Bomford & Borrill/Survival Anglia.
45 Michael Leach/NHPA
46 Ofer Bahat/Yossi Leshem.
47 Peter Prince.48 Hodson/Greenpeace.
48-9 Silvestris/FLPA.
50 C.H. Gomersall/RSPB.
51 Ake Lindau/Ardea.
52-3 Gunter Ziesler/Bruce Coleman.
56-7 Doug Wechsler/VIREO.
58 Jerome Jackson.
64-5 Andy Rouse/NHPA.
67 John Shaw/NHPA.
73*l* Wayn Lankinen/Aquila.73*r* Jerome Jackson
74 Jerome Jackson.
81 Stephen Krasemann/NHPA
82 D. & M. Zimmerman/VIREO.
84-5 Hellio & Van Ingen/ NHPA.89 H. Hautala/FLPA.
93 Stephen Krasemann/ FLPA.
97 Antonio Manganares/Bruce Coleman.
99 Paul Sterry/Nature Photographers.
100 Orion/Bruce Coleman.
102 George Bingham/Bruce Coleman.
109 B. Speake/Aquila.114 Dennis Avon/Ardea.
118-19 Jeff Foott Productions/Bruce Coleman.
123 David A. Ponton/Planet Earth Pictures.
124-5 Mike Read/Planet Earth Pictures.
127 Jeff Foott/Survival Anglia.
130-1 Ray Tipper
132 R. Wilmshurst/FLPA.
134 John Daniels/Ardea
136-7 M.P.L. Fogden/Bruce Coleman.
139 Peter Evans/Bruce Coleman.
140*t* M.P.L. Fogden/Bruce Coleman.
140*b* Jen & Des Bartlett/Bruce Coleman.
141 Gunter Ziesler/Bruce Coleman.
143 I.R. Beames/Ardea
144 Peter Johnson/NHPA.145 Nico Nyburgh
146*t* Nico Nyburgh.146*b* Conrad Greaves/Aquila
148*l* Dennis Avon/Ardea.
148*r* Graeme Chapman/Ardea.
149 K.W. Fink/Ardea.
150 ANT/NHPA.
150-1 C.B. & D.W. Frith/Bruce Coleman.
151*r* ANT/NHPA
152-3 Ben Osborne/Oxford Scientific Films.
157 Hans Reinhard/Bruce Coleman.
159 Rinie van Meurs/Bruce Coleman.
162-3 Norman Lightfoot/Bruce Coleman
165 Ted Levin/Oxford Scientific Films.
166-7 Hanne & Jens Eriksen/Aquila

## ILLUSTRATIONS

**Maps and calendars**
**Models** Mark Jamieson
**Tints** Cooper Dale
**Photography** Guy Ryecart
10-11, 14, 30-1, 36*bl*, 38*l*, 39, 56-7, 59, 60-1, 62-3, 65, 66-7, 68-9, 70-1, 72-3, 74-5, 76-7, 78-9, 80-1, 83, 88-9, 90-1, 92-3, 94-5, 96-7, 98-9, 100-101, 103, 104-5, 107, 108-9, 110-11, 112-13, 115, 116-17, 122-3, 124-5, 126, 128-9, 130-1, 133, 134-5, 139, 140-1, 143, 145, 146, 148-9, 150, 156-7, 158-9, 160-1, 162-3, 164, 168-9

**Relief maps**
by Oxford Cartographers
36-7, 54-5, 86-7, 120-1, 138, 142, 147, 154-5

Marshall Editions would also like to thank European Map Graphics Ltd and Hazel Hand for their assistance in compiling the maps.